Siemens NX 2019 for Engineers and Designers

Sham Tickoo
Professor
Purdue University Northwest
Hammond, Indiana, USA

Contributing Authors
Tickoo Institute of Emerging Technologies (TIET)
Gurugram, India

CADCIM Technologies
Indiana, USA

BPB PUBLICATIONS

ISBN: 978-93-89423-11-2

Limits of Liability and Disclaimer of Warranty

The information contained in this book is the best of Author's & Publisher's knowledge. We are committed to serve students with best of our knowledge and resources. We have taken utmost care and attention while editing and printing of this book but Author and Publisher should not be held responsible for errors, omissions and any other unintentional mistake that might have crept in. However, errors brought to our notice shall be gratefully acknowledged and attended to.

All trademarks referred to in the book are acknowledged as properties of their respective owners. This book is written solely for the benefit and guidance of the students.

Distributors

COMPUTER BOOK CENTRE
12, Shrungar Shopping Centre
M.G. Road
BENGALURU–560001
Ph: 25587923/25584641

DECCAN AGENCIES
4-3-329, Bank Street
HYDERABAD-500195
Ph: 24756967/24756400

MICRO MEDIA
Shop No. 5, Mahendra Chambers
150 DN Rd. Next to Capital Cinema
V.T (C.S.T.) Station
MUMBAI-400001

BPB BOOK CENTRE
376 Old Lajpat Rai Market
DELHI-110006
Ph: 23861747

INFOTECH
G-2, Sidhartha Building, 96 Nehru Place
NEW DELHI-110019
Ph: 26438245

BPB PUBLICATIONS
20, Ansari Road, Darya Ganj
New Delhi-110002
Ph: 23254990/23254991

Published by Manish Jain for BPB Publications, 20 Ansari Road, Darya Ganj
New Delhi-110002 and Printed by Repro India Pvt. Ltd, Mumbai

DEDICATION

To teachers, who make it possible to disseminate knowledge to enlighten the young and curious minds of our future generations

To students, who are dedicated to learning new technologies and making the world a better place to live in

THANKS

To employees at CADCIM Technologies and Tickoo Institute of Emerging Technologies (TIET) for their valuable help

Table of Contents

Chapter 3: Adding Geometric and Dimensional Constraints to Sketches

Chapter 4: Editing, Extruding, and Revolving Sketches

Chapter 5: Working with Datum Planes, Coordinate Systems, and Datum Axes

Chapter 6: Advanced Modeling Tools-I

Chapter 7: Advanced Modeling Tools-II

Chapter 8: Assembly Modeling-I

Chapter 9: Assembly Modeling-II

Chapter 10: Surface Modeling

Chapter 11: Advanced Surface Modeling

Chapter 12: Generating, Editing, and Dimensioning the Drawing Views

Chapter 13: Synchronous Modeling

Chapter 15: Introduction to Injection Mold Design

Chapter 16: Concepts of Geometric Dimensioning and Tolerancing

Preface

Siemens NX 2019

Siemens NX, a product of SIEMENS Corp., is one of the world's leading CAD/CAM/CAE packages. Being a solid modeling tool, it not only unites 3D parametric features with 2D tools, but also addresses every design-through-manufacturing process. Besides providing an insight into the design content, the package promotes collaboration between companies and provides them an edge over their competitors.

In addition to creating solid models and assemblies, the 2D drawing views can also be generated easily in the **Drafting** environment of NX. The drawing views that can be generated include orthographic, section, auxiliary, isometric, and detail views. The model dimensions and reference dimensions in the drawing views can also be generated. The bidirectionally associative nature of this software ensures that the modifications made in the model are reflected in the drawing views and vice-versa. In NX, you can create sketches directly in the Modeling environment.

The **Siemens NX 2019 for Engineers and Designers** textbook has been written with the intention of helping the readers effectively use the solid modeling tools in NX. After reading this textbook, you can create solid models, surface models, assemblies, sheet metal parts, and generate 2D drawing views easily in the **Drafting** environment of NX. In this edition, a chapter on basic concepts of GD&T has also been added. To make the users understand the concepts of Mold Design, a chapter on mold designing of the plastic components is available for free download. The mechanical engineering industry examples and tutorials used in this book ensure that the users can relate the knowledge of this book with the actual mechanical industry designs. The main features of this textbook are as follows:

- **Tutorial Approach**

  The author has adopted the tutorial point-of-view and the learn-by-doing approach throughout the textbook. This approach guides the users through the process of creating the models in the tutorials.

- **Real-World Projects as Tutorials**

  The author has used about 50 real-world mechanical engineering projects as tutorials in this book. This enables the readers to relate the tutorials to the models in the mechanical engineering industry. In addition, there are about 32 exercises that are also based on the real-world mechanical engineering projects.

- **Tips and Notes**

  The additional information related to various topics is provided to the users in the form of tips and notes.

- **Learning Objectives**

  The first page of every chapter summarizes the topics that are covered in that chapter.

- **Self-Evaluation Test, Review Questions, and Exercises**

  Every chapter ends with Self-Evaluation Test so that the users can assess their knowledge of the chapter. The answers to Self-Evaluation Test are given at the end of the chapter. Also, the Review Questions and Exercises are given at the end of each chapter and they can be used by the instructors as test questions and exercises.

- **Heavily Illustrated Text**

  The text in this book is heavily illustrated with about 1100 line diagrams and screen capture images.

Formatting Conventions Used in the Textbook

Please refer to the following list for the formatting conventions used in this textbook.

- Names of tools, buttons, options, groups, and toolbar, are written in boldface.

  Example: The **Extrude** tool, the **OK** button, the **Feature** group, and so on.

- Names of dialog boxes, drop-downs, drop-down lists, list boxes, areas, edit boxes, check boxes, and radio buttons are written in boldface.

  Example: The **Edge Blend** dialog box, the **Surface Drop-down** of the **Create** group, the **Tangent Edges** drop-down list of the **Shell** dialog box, the **Distance** edit box of the **Extrude** dialog box, the **Symmetric** check box in the **Pattern Feature** dialog box, the **Plain** radio button of the **Edit Background** dialog box, and so on.

- Values entered in edit boxes are written in boldface.

  Example: Enter **5** in the **Pitch Distance** edit box.

- Names and paths of the files saved are italicized.

  Example: *c03tut03.prt*, *C:\NX_2019\c03*, and so on.

- The methods of invoking a tool/option from the **Menu**, **Ribbon** are enclosed in a shaded box.

Ribbon:	Home > Standard > New
Menu:	File > New

Naming Conventions Used in the Textbook

Button

The item in a dialog box that has a 3D shape like a button is termed as **Button**. For example, **OK** button, **Cancel** button, **Apply** button, and so on.

Dialog Box

In this textbook, different terms are used for referring to the components of a dialog box. Refer to Figure 1 for the terminology used.

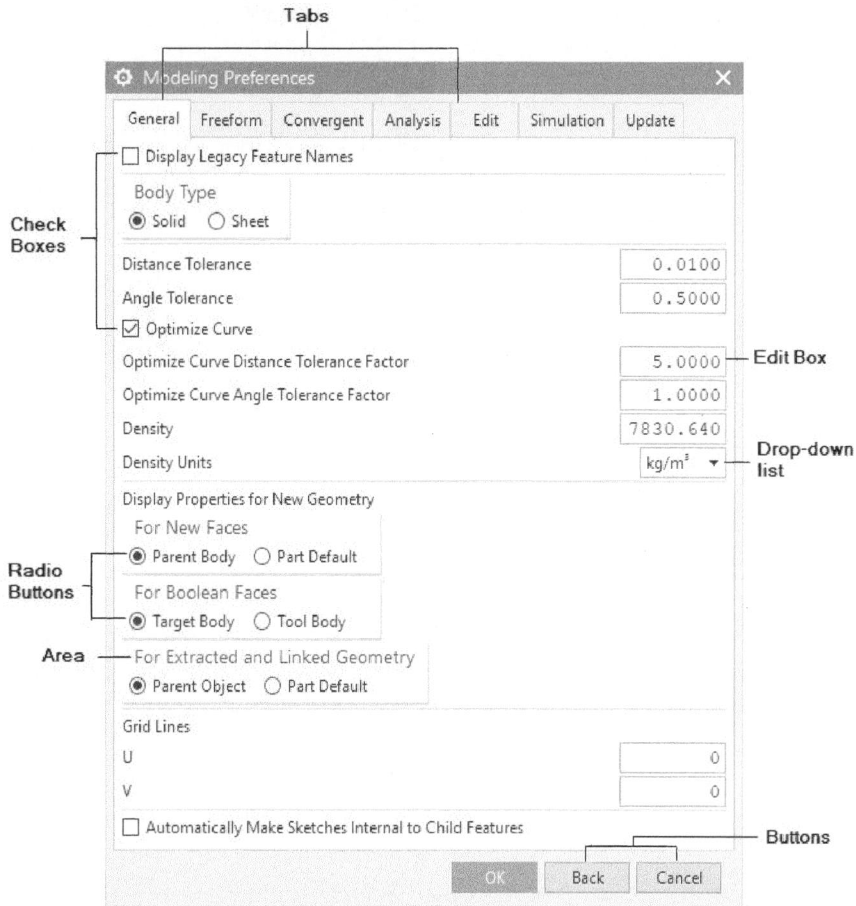

***Figure 1** The components in a dialog box*

Drop-down

A drop-down is the one in which a set of common tools are grouped together. You can identify a drop-down with a down arrow on it. These drop-downs are given a name based on the tools grouped in them. For example, the **Design Feature** drop-down, the **Blend** drop-down, and so on; refer to Figure 2.

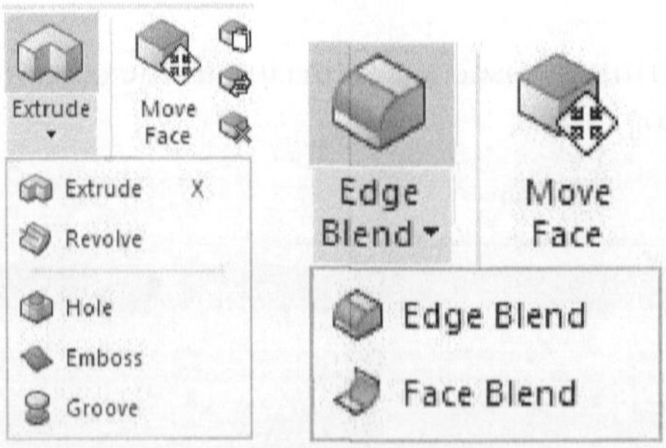

*Figure 2 The **Design Feature** drop-down and **Blend** drop-down*

Gallery

A gallery is the one in which a set of common tools are grouped together. For example, the **Detail Feature** gallery of the **More** gallery; refer to Figure 3.

*Figure 3 The **Detail Feature** gallery of the **More** gallery*

Drop-down List

A drop-down list is the one in which a set of options are grouped together. You can set various parameters using these options. You can identify a drop-down list with a down arrow on it. For example, **Boolean** drop-down list, **Layout** drop-down list, and so on; refer to Figure 4.

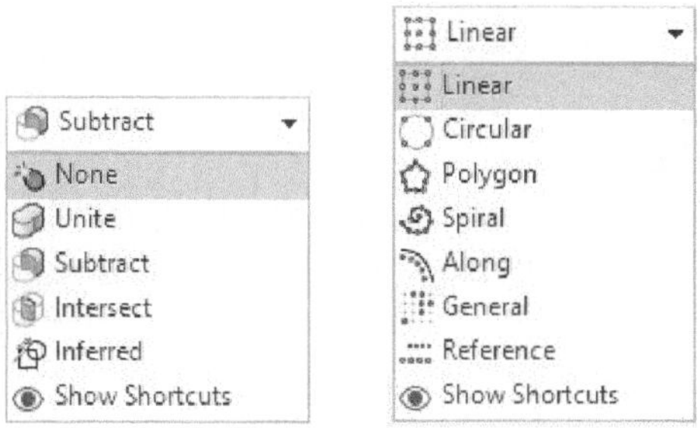

Figure 4 *The **Boolean** and **Layout** drop-down lists*

Options

Options are the items that are available in shortcut menu, drop-down list, dialog boxes, and so on. For example, choose the **Fit** option from the shortcut menu displayed on right-clicking in the drawing area; select the **Face** option from the drop-down list in the **Type** rollout; refer to Figure 5.

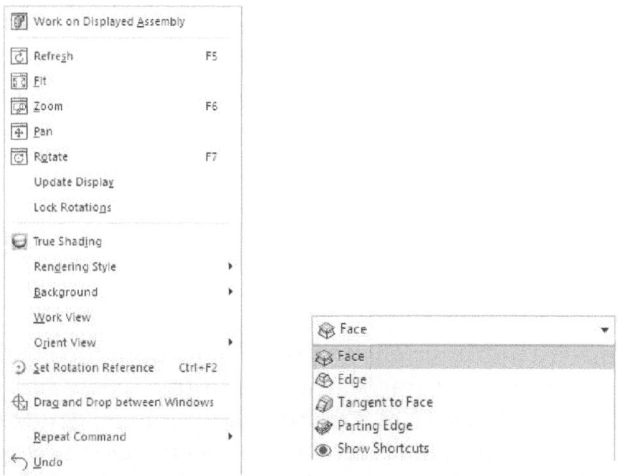

Figure 5 *Options in the shortcut menu and drop-down list in the **Type** rollout*

Symbols Used in the Textbook

Note
The author has provided additional information related to various topics in the form of notes.

Tip
The author has provided a lot of useful information to the users about the topic being discussed in the form of tips.

New
This icon indicates that the command or tool being discussed is new.

Enhanced
This icon indicates that the command or tool being discussed is enhanced.

Free Companion CD

It has been our constant endeavor to provide you the best textbooks and services at affordable price. In this endeavor, we have come out with a Free Companion CD that will facilitate the process of teaching and learning of AutoCAD 2020. If you purchase this textbook, you will get access to the files in the Companion CD.

The following resources are available in this CD:

- **Instructor Guide**
  Solutions to all review questions and exercises in the textbook are provided in this guide.

- **Part Files**
  All part files used in illustrations, examples, and exercises.

- **Input Files**
  All input files used in examples.

You can access additional learning resources by visiting ***https://allaboutcadcam.blogspot.com***.

You can get online technical support by contacting ***techsupport@cadcim.com***.

If you face any problem in accessing these files, please contact at ***sales@cadcim.com*** or the author at ***stickoo@pnw.edu*** or ***tickoo525@gmail.com***.

Stay Connected

You can now stay connected with us through Facebook and Twitter to get the latest information about our textbooks, videos, and teaching/learning resources. To stay informed of such updates, follow us on Facebook (***www.facebook.com/cadcim***) and Twitter (***@cadcimtech***). You can also subscribe to our You Tube channel (***www.youtube.com/cadcimtech***) to get the information about our latest video tutorials.

Stay Connected

You can now stay connected with us through Facebook and Twitter to get the latest information about our textbooks, videos, and teaching/learning resources. To stay informed of such updates, follow us on Facebook (***www.facebook.com/cadcim***) and Twitter ***(@cadcimtech)***. You can also subscribe to our YouTube channel (***www.youtube.com/cadcimtech***) to get the information about our latest video tutorials.

Chapter 1

Introduction to NX

Learning Objectives

After completing this chapter, you will be able to:

- *Understand different environments in NX*
- *Understand the system requirements for NX*
- *Start a new file in NX*
- *Understand the important terms and definitions used in NX*
- *Understand functions of the mouse buttons*
- *Understand the use of various hot keys*
- *Modify the color scheme in NX*

INTRODUCTION TO NX

Welcome to NX. As a new user of this software package, you will join hands with thousands of users of this high-end CAD/CAM/CAE/PLM tool. If you are already familiar with the previous releases, you can upgrade your designing skills with tremendous improvement in this latest release.

This release of NX introduces improved capabilities for convergent modeling, CAD design, drafting, tooling design, automation, design simulation, programming, data translation, validation, mold design, and much more. Active workspace in NX is built based on these items to provide seamless access to PLM capabilities right within NX.

NX, a product of SIEMENS Corp., is a completely re-engineered, next-generation family of CAD/CAM/CAE/PLM software solutions for Product Life Cycle Management. Through its exceptionally easy-to-use and state-of-the-art user interface, NX delivers innovative technologies for maximum productivity and creativity from the basic concept to the final product. NX reduces the learning curve by allowing flexibility in the use of feature-based and parametric designs.

The subject of interpretability offered by NX includes receiving legacy data from other CAD systems and even between its own product data management modules. The real benefit is that the links remain associative. As a result, any changes made to this external data are notified to you and the model can be updated quickly.

When you open an old file or start a new file in NX, you will enter the Gateway environment. It allows you to examine the geometry and drawing views that have been created. In the Gateway environment, you can invoke any environment of NX.

NX serves the basic design tasks by providing different environments. An environment is defined as a specific area, consisting of a set of tools which allows the user to perform specific design tasks in that particular area. You need to start the required environment after starting a new part file. As a result, you can invoke any environment of NX in the same working part file. The basic environments in NX are the Modeling environment, Shape Studio environment, Drafting environment, Assembly environment, and the Sheet Metal environment. These environments are discussed next.

Modeling Environment

The Modeling environment is a parametric and feature-based environment in which you can create solid models. The basic requirement for creating solid models in this environment is a sketch. You can draw the sketch directly in the Modeling environment by using the tools available in the **Direct Sketch** group of the **Home** tab. The sketch can also be drawn in the sketching environment. The sketching environment can be invoked by choosing the **Sketch** tool from the **Direct Sketch** group of the **Home** tab or by choosing the **Sketch** tool from the **Direct Sketch** group of the **Curve** tab. While drawing a sketch, various applicable constraints and dimensions are automatically applied to it. Additional constraints and dimensions can also be applied manually. After drawing the sketch, you need to convert the sketch into a feature using the tools available in the Modeling environment. You can create placed features such as fillets, chamfers, taper, and so on and can also assign materials to the models in this environment.

Shape Studio Environment

The Shape Studio environment is also a parametric and feature-based environment in which you can create surface models. The tools in this environment are similar to those in the Modeling environment. The only difference is that the tools in this environment are used to create basic and advanced surfaces. You are also provided with the surface editing tools which are used to manipulate the surfaces to obtain the required shape. This environment is useful for conceptual and industrial design.

Assembly Environment

The Assembly environment is used to assemble the components using the assembly constraints available in this environment. There are two types of assembly design approaches in NX, Bottom-up and Top-down.

In the bottom-up approach of the assembly, the previously created components are assembled together to maintain their design intent and in the top-down approach, components are created in the Assembly environment.

In the Assembly environment you can also assemble an existing assembly with the current assembly. The **Perform Analysis** tool provides the facility to check the interference and clearance between the components in an assembly.

Drafting Environment

The Drafting environment is used for the documentation of the parts or assemblies created earlier in the form of drawing views and their detailing. There are two types of drafting techniques: generative drafting and interactive drafting.

The generative drafting technique is used to automatically generate the drawing views of the parts and assemblies. The parametric dimensions added to the component in the Modeling environment during its creation can also be generated and displayed automatically in the drawing views. The generative drafting is bidirectionally associative in nature. If you modify the dimensions in the Drafting environment, the model will automatically update in the Modeling environment and vice-versa. You can also generate the Bill of Material (BOM) and balloons in the drawing views.

In interactive drafting, you need to create the drawing views by sketching them using the normal sketching tools and then adding the dimensions.

Sheet Metal Environment

The Sheet Metal application provides an environment for the design of sheet metal parts used in machinery, enclosures, brackets, and other parts normally manufactured with a brake press. The Sheet Metal application is intended mainly for designing parts with cylindrical bend regions but conical and curved bend regions are also possible. Generally, the sheet metal components are created to generate the flat pattern of a sheet, study the design of the dies and punches, study the process plan for designing, and the tools needed for manufacturing the sheet metal components.

SYSTEM REQUIREMENTS

System requirements that ensure the smooth running of NX are as follows:

- 64-bit - Windows 10 Operating System.
- 8GB of RAM is the minimum requirement but it is recommended to have 16GB or more RAM for all the applications to run smoothly.
- Java version - 1.8.0 or higher
- True Color (32-bit) or 16 million colors (24-bit)
- Screen Resolution: 1280 x 1024 or higher, widescreen format.

GETTING STARTED WITH NX

Install NX on your system and then start it by double-clicking on its shortcut icon on the desktop of your computer. After the system has loaded all the required files to start NX, the initial interface will be displayed, as shown in Figure 1-1.

Note

*When you install NX, by default its shortcut icon is not created on the desktop of your computer. So to create the shortcut icon, click **start** to display a menu. Drag **NX** icon from the **Siemens NX** folder to the desktop.*

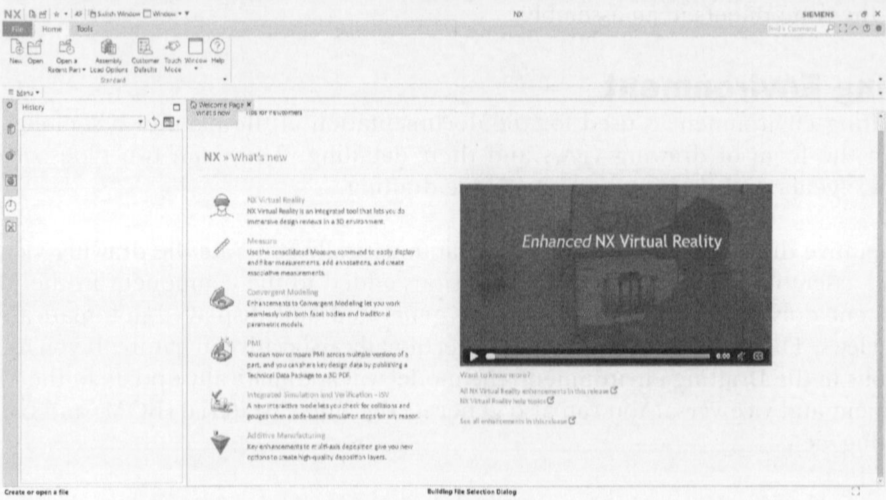

***Figure 1-1** The initial interface that appears after starting NX*

Tip

1. In this release, by default, the user interface theme is set to ***Light****. But, you can change the interface theme as per your requirement. To do so, choose* ***Menu > Preferences > User Interface*** *from the* ***Top Border Bar****; the* ***User Interface Preferences*** *dialog box will be displayed. Next, select the required option from the* ***Type*** *drop-down list available in the* ***NX Theme*** *group of the* ***Theme*** *node and choose the* ***OK*** *button.*

2. To change the ***Default Presentation of Dialog Content*** *of any dialog box, choose* ***Menu > Preferences > User interface*** *from the* ***Top Border Bar****; the* ***User Interface Preferences*** *dialog box will be displayed. Next, select the* ***Options*** *node available on the left in the dialog box; the* ***Dialog Boxes*** *group will be displayed. Now, select the* ***More*** *radio button in the* ***Default Presentation of Dialog Content*** *area and choose the* ***OK*** *button.*

Choose **File > New** from the **Ribbon**; the **New** dialog box will be displayed as shown in Figure 1-2. Make sure that **Model** template is selected in the **Templates** rollout of the dialog box. Next, enter the name of the file in the **Name** edit box and choose the **OK** button; the Modeling environment will be displayed on the screen, refer to Figure 1-3.

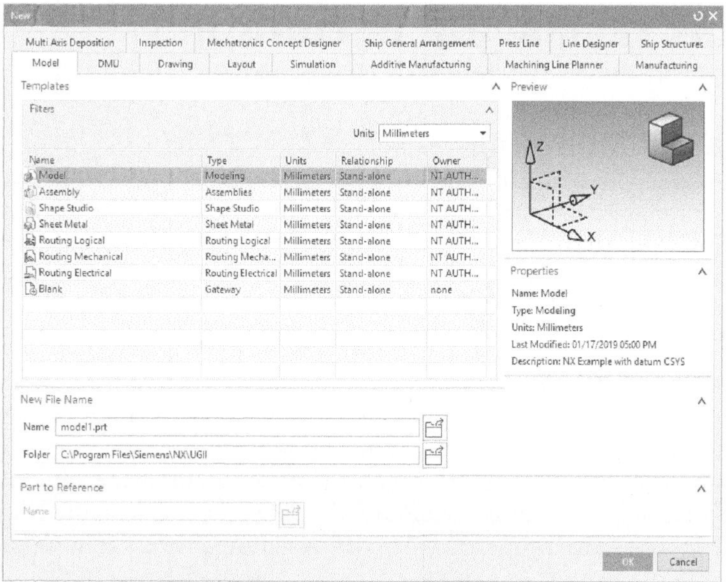

Figure 1-2 *The* ***New*** *dialog box*

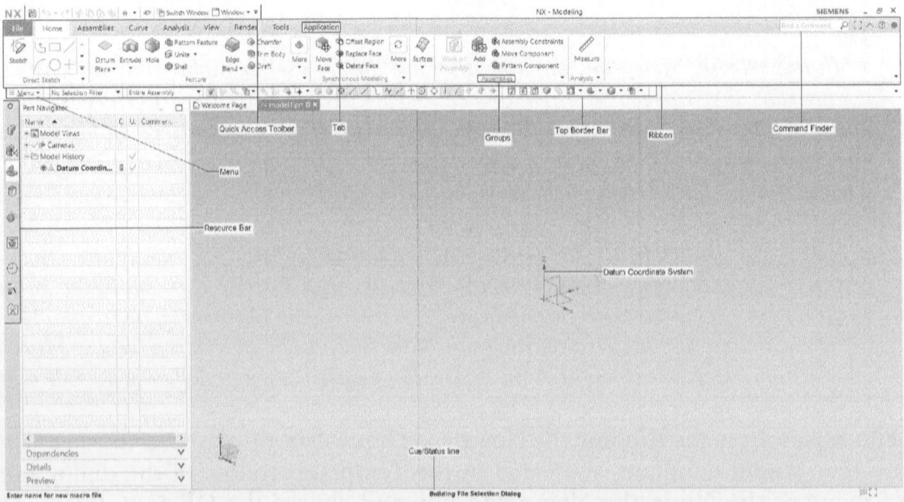

Figure 1-3 The Modeling environment displayed on screen

IMPORTANT TERMS AND DEFINITIONS

Some important terms and definitions of NX are discussed next.

Feature-based Modeling

A feature is defined as the smallest building block that can be modified individually. A model created in NX is a combination of a number of individual features and each feature is related to the other directly or indirectly. If a proper design intent is maintained while creating the model, then these features automatically adjust their values to any change in their surroundings. This provides a great flexibility to the design.

Parametric Modeling

The parametric nature of a software package is defined as its ability to use the standard properties or parameters in defining the shape and size of a geometry. The main function of this property is to derive the selected geometry to a new size or shape without considering its original dimensions. You can change or modify the shape and size of any feature at any stage of the designing process. This property makes the designing process an easy task. For example, consider the design of the body of a pipe housing, as shown in Figure 1-4.

To change the design by modifying the diameter of the holes and their number on the front, top, and bottom face, you need to select the feature and change the diameter and the number of instances in the pattern. The modified design is shown in Figure 1-5.

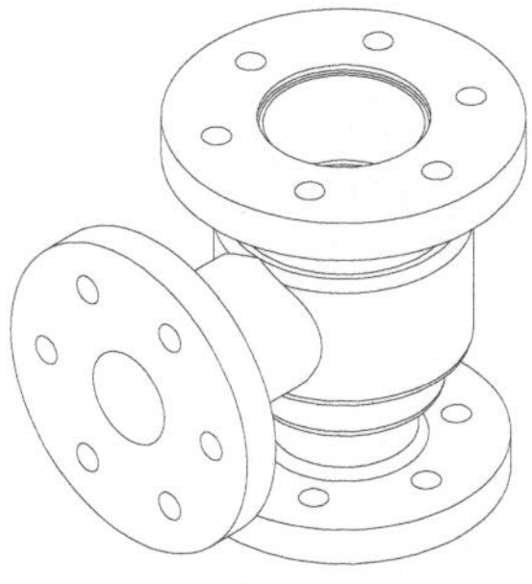

Figure 1-4 *Body of a pipe housing*

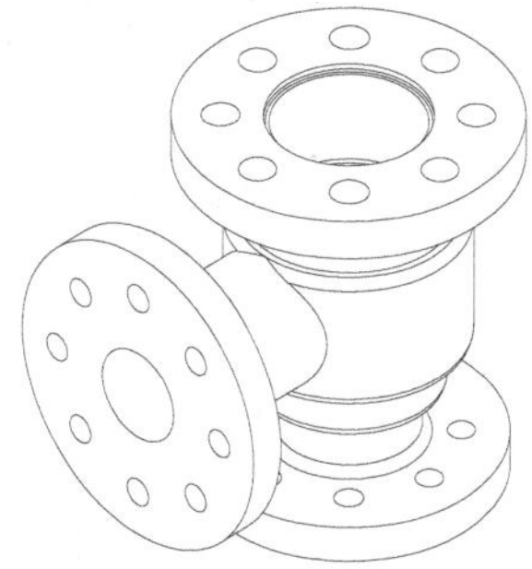

Figure 1-5 *Modified body of the pipe housing*

Bidirectional Associativity

As mentioned earlier, NX has different environments such as the Modeling environment, the Assembly environment, and the Drafting environment. The bidirectional associativity that exists between all these environments ensures that any modification made in the model in any of the environments of NX is automatically reflected in the other environments immediately. For example, if you modify the dimension of a part in the Modeling environment, the change will be reflected in the Assembly and the Drafting environments as well. Similarly, if you modify the dimensions of a part in the drawing views generated in the Drafting environment, the changes will be reflected in the Modeling and Assembly environments. Consider the drawing views of the pipe housing shown in Figure 1-6. When you modify the model in the Modeling environment, the changes will be reflected in the Drafting environment automatically. Figure 1-7 shows the drawing views of the pipe housing after increasing the diameter and the number of holes.

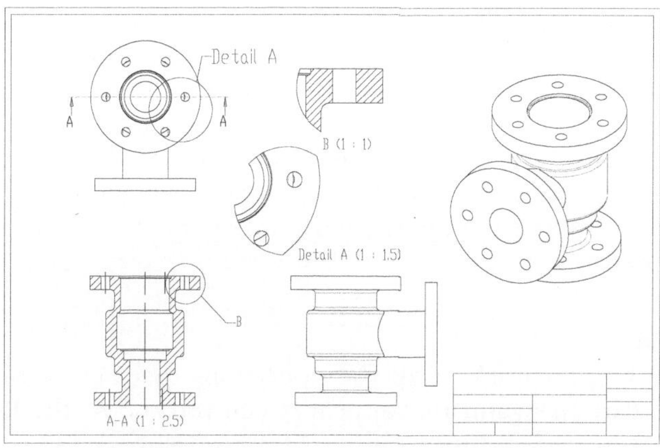

Figure 1-6 *The drawing views of a pipe housing*

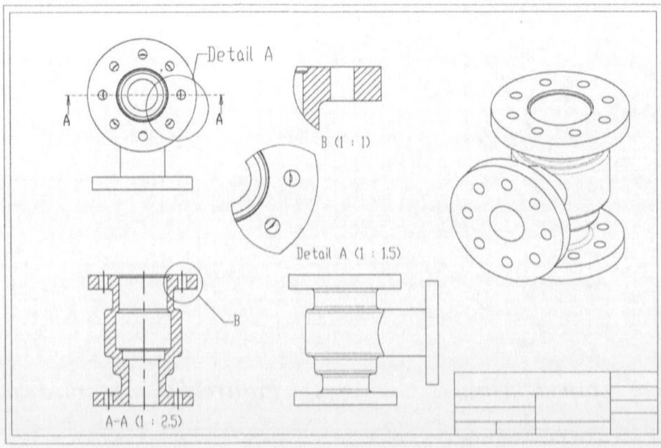

Figure 1-7 The drawing views of pipe housing after making the modifications

prt

prt is a file extension associated with all files that are created in the Modeling, Shape Studio, Assembly, Sheet Metal, and Drafting environments of NX.

Resource Bar

The **Resource Bar** combines all the navigator windows, the history palette, and the integrated web browser at one common place for a better user interface. By default, the **Resource Bar** is located on the left side of the NX window.

Roles

Roles are sets of system customized tools and toolbars used for different applications. In NX, you have different roles for different industrial applications. The **Roles** tab in the **Resource Bar** is used to activate the required role. In this book, the **Essentials** role has been used, as it contains all the required tools. To activate this role, choose the **Roles** tab from the **Resource Bar** and click on the **Content** option; a flyout will be displayed. Click on the **Essentials** icon to activate that role; the **Load Role** message box will be displayed. Next, choose the **OK** button to close the dialog box. Figure 1-8 shows the **Roles** navigator that appears when you choose the **Roles** tab in the **Resource Bar**.

Part Navigator

The **Part Navigator** keeps a track of all the operations that are carried out on the part. Figure 1-9 shows the **Part Navigator** that appears when you choose the **Part Navigator** tab in the **Resource Bar**.

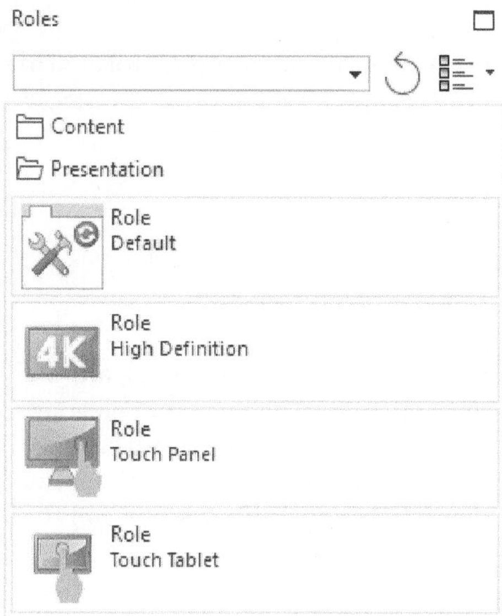

*Figure 1-8 The **Roles** navigator*

*Figure 1-9 The **Part Navigator***

Constraints

Constraints are the logical operations that are performed on an element to define its size and location with respect to the other elements or reference geometries. There are three types of constraints in NX: Geometric, Dimensional, and Assembly. The geometric and dimensional constraints available in the sketching environment are used to precisely define the size and position of the sketched elements with respect to the surroundings. The assembly constraints are available in the Assembly environment and are used to define the precise position of the components in the assembly. These constraints are discussed next.

Geometric Constraints

These are the logical operations performed on the sketched elements to define their size and position with respect to other elements. Geometric constraints are applied using two methods: automatic constraining and manual constraining. While drawing the sketch, some constraints are automatically applied to it. You will learn more about applying constraints to the sketch in later chapters of this book.

Dimensional Constraints

After creating the sketch, you need to apply different types of dimensional constraints to it. Various types of dimensions in NX are:

1. Linear Dimension
2. Radial Dimension
3. Angular Dimension
4. Perimeter Dimension

NX is a parametric software and therefore, you can modify the dimensions of a sketch at any time. You will learn more about modifying dimensions of the sketch in later chapters.

Assembly Constraints

The constraints in the Assembly environment are the logical operations performed to restrict the degrees of freedom of the component and to define its precise location and position with respect to other components of the assembly.

Solid Body

The solid body contains all the features such as extrude, pad, pocket, hole, and so on.

Sheet Body or Surfaces

Surfaces are geometric features that have zero thickness and mass. They are used to create complex shapes which are difficult to be created using the solid features. After creating the surface, you can assign a thickness to it in order to convert it into a solid body. Surfaces are created in the Modeling environment. No separate environment is required to create the surfaces. You can also invoke the Surface environment by choosing the **Shape Studio** option from the **Templates** rollout of the **New** dialog box.

Features

A feature is defined as a basic building block of a solid model. The combination of various features results in a solid body. In the Modeling environment of NX, the features are of two types:

1. Sketch-based features
2. Placed-features

The sketch-based features require a sketch for their creation and the placed-features do not require a sketch for their creation.

WCS (Work Coordinate System)

The WCS is a local coordinate system and can be repositioned to a convenient location while making a model. The XC-YC plane of the WCS is used to perform many operations. When you create a new file, by default the WCS is positioned at origin of the Datum Coordinate System, which is (0,0,0). By default, the display of WCS is turned off. To turn on the display of WCS, choose the following path; **Menu** > **Format** > **WCS** > **Display**; the WCS will be displayed in the drawing window. Note that **Display** button is a toggle button.

UNDERSTANDING THE FUNCTIONS OF THE MOUSE BUTTONS

To work in the NX environment, it is necessary that you understand the functions of the mouse buttons. The efficient use of the three buttons of the mouse along with the CTRL key can reduce the time required to complete the design task. The different combinations of the CTRL key and the mouse buttons are listed below:

1. The left mouse button is used to make a selection by simply selecting a face, surface, sketch, or an object from the geometry area or from the **Part Navigator**. For multiple selections, select the entities by dragging the left mouse button.

2. The right mouse button is used to invoke the shortcut menu which has different options such as **Zoom**, **Fit**, **Rotate**, **Pan**, and so on.

3. Press and hold the middle and the right mouse buttons to invoke the **Pan** tool. Next, drag the mouse to pan the model. You can also invoke the **Pan** tool by first pressing and holding the SHIFT key and then the middle mouse button. Figure 1-10 shows the use of a three button mouse in performing the pan functions.

4. Press and hold the middle mouse button to invoke the **Rotate** tool. Next, drag the mouse to dynamically rotate the view of the model in the geometry area and view it from different directions. Figure 1-10 shows the use of the three button mouse in performing the rotate operation.

5. Press and hold the CTRL key and then the middle mouse button to invoke the **Zoom** tool. Alternatively, press and hold the left mouse button and then the middle mouse button to invoke the **Zoom** tool. Next, drag the mouse dynamically to zoom in or out the model in the geometry area. Figure 1-10 shows the use of the three mouse buttons in performing the zoom functions.

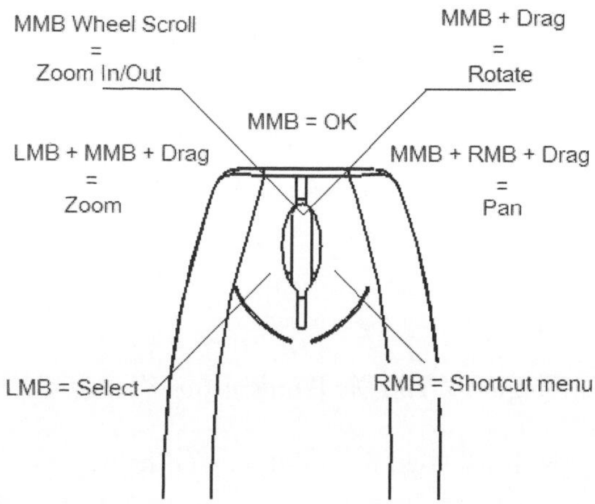

Figure 1-10 *Functions of the mouse buttons*

Various screen components of NX are discussed next.

QUICK ACCESS TOOLBAR

This toolbar is common to all the environments of NX. Figure 1-11 shows the **Quick Access** toolbar. The buttons in this toolbar are used to start a new file, open an existing file, save a file of the current document, cut and place the selection on a temporary clipboard, copy a selection, paste the content from the clipboard to a selected location, undo, redo, Touch Mode, search a tool, and invoke the help topics.

In NX, when you have a session running in which several parts are open, you can switch between the running parts using the **Switch Window** button. This button is available next to the **Touch Mode** button in the **Quick Access** toolbar, refer to Figure 1-11.

Figure 1-11 *Partial view of the **Quick Access** toolbar*

Note

1. You can use the CTRL+TAB keys to open the panel to show all files that are currently open. You can also move from item to item using the TAB key or hold the CTRL key and use the mouse wheel to scroll through them. You can also select an item to open it.

*2. The **Switch Window** button located next to the **Touch Mode** button allows you to open the panel manually. By using this button, you will be able to navigate through the displayed parts using the left and right arrowkeys on your keyboard.*

Using Multiple Windows in NX

NX allows you to use multiple windows while sketching. You can view multiple parts at once in separate tabbed windows. The **Window** drop-down list available in the **Quick Access** toolbar contains the options which allow you to view the same part or different parts in two or more separate windows. Figure 1-12 shows the **Window** drop-down list.

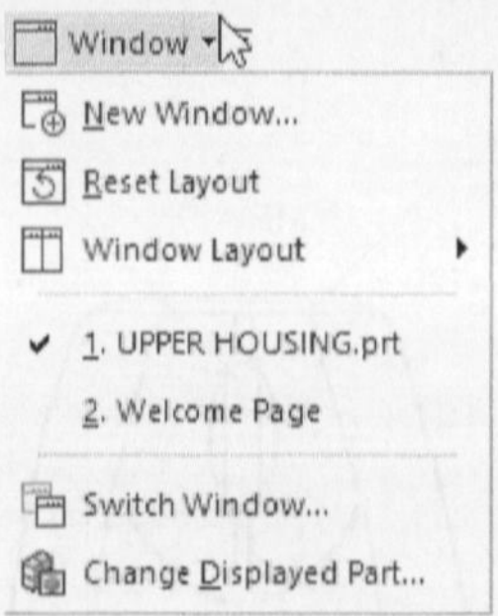

Figure 1-12 *The **Window** drop-down list*

The options available in this drop-down list are discussed next.

New Window

When you choose this option, a new file tab will be added below the **Top Border Bar**, refer to Figure 1-13. You can switch between the tabs by clicking on the respective tab. An active tab is displayed in light blue color.

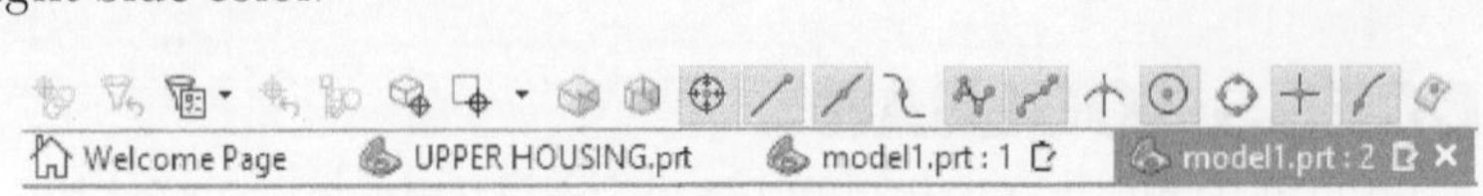

Figure 1-13 *File tab added on choosing the **New Window** option*

Window Layout

When you hover the cursor over this option, a cascading window will be displayed, refer to Figure 1-14.

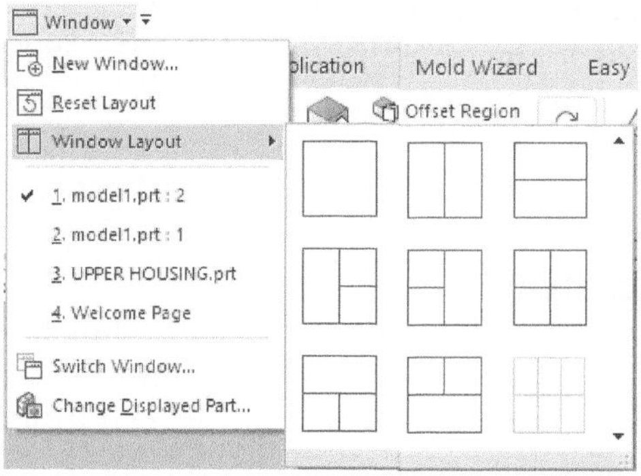

***Figure 1-14** Cascading window displaying **Window Layout** options*

You can choose the required layout option from the cascading window. Figure 1-15 shows two tabbed windows displaying the same model. These tabbed windows will appear when you choose the **2 Tabbed Groups** option (second option in the first row) from the cascading window.

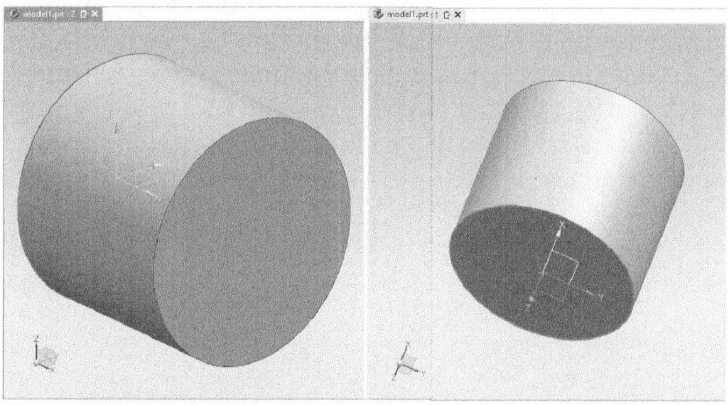

***Figure 1-15** Model displayed in two tabbed windows*

Note

*The options in the **Window Layout** cascading window will become active depending upon the number of windows that are active during a session. For instance, if you have a model or sketch open in one window and you choose the **New Window** option from the **Window** drop-down list, a new file tab will be added below the **Top Border Bar**. Now, you will notice that the first three options in the cascading window become active. Likewise, if you have three or more separate windows having three or more different models, then all the options in the cascading window will become active.*

Reset Layout

When you choose this option, all the non-active tabbed windows will close and only the active window will remain open on the screen.

RIBBON

NX offers a user-friendly design interface by providing the **Ribbon**. The **Ribbon** comprises a series of tabs. In tabs, the various tools and options are grouped together based on their functionality in different groups and galleries. The display of these tabs and their groups depends upon the environment invoked. The NX Ribbon gives you the ability to customize the interface for a truly optimized experience. NX-specific extensions such as border bars allow you to add additional commands around the perimeter of the graphics window. The different environments and some of their respective tabs and groups are discussed next.

Modeling Environment

The Modeling environment can be invoked by selecting the **Model** template from the **New** dialog box. You can also invoke the Modeling environment from any other opened environment. To do so, choose **Application > Design > Modeling** from the **Ribbon**. Some of the tabs of the Modeling environment are discussed next.

Home Tab

The **Home** tab consists of a series of groups and galleries and they are discussed next.

Direct Sketch Group

It is one of the most important groups of the **Home** tab. The tools available in this group are used to draw and edit sketches. You can apply constraints to geometric entities and assign dimension to a sketch using the tools of this group. The sketching tools available in this group are grouped together in the **Sketch Curve** gallery, refer to Figure 1-16. Note that by default, the **Sketch Curve** gallery is in collapse form. As a result, some of the tools are not visible by default. To expand this gallery, click on the lower down arrow available in front of this gallery, refer to Figure 1-17.

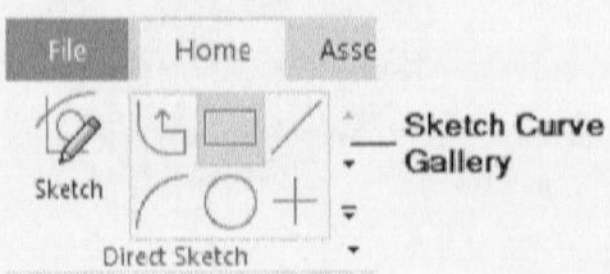

*Figure 1-16 The **Sketch Curve** Gallery of the **Direct Sketch** group*

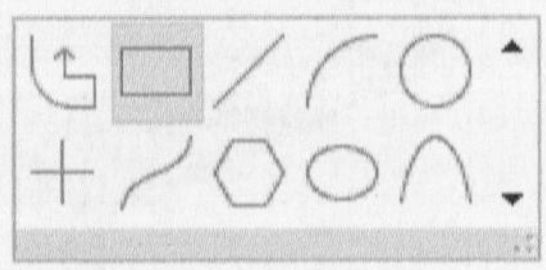

*Figure 1-17 Expanded **Sketch Curve** gallery*

Note that some of the tools such as **Fillet**, **Chamfer**, **Quick Trim**, and **Quick Extend** are still not available in the expanded **Sketch Curve** gallery. To access all the tools of the **Sketch Curve** gallery, choose the **Sketch** tool available in the **Direct Sketch** group; the **Create Sketch** dialog box will be displayed. The options available in this dialog box are discussed in later chapters. Select the required sketching plane and then choose the **OK** button. The sketching environment will become active and you will notice that the **Sketch Curve** gallery is expanded and it contains all the sketching tools including dimensioning and geometric constraints, refer to Figure 1-18.

*Figure 1-18 The expanded **Sketch Curve** gallery of the **Direct Sketch** group after invoking Sketching environment*

Feature Group

The tools in this group are shown in Figure 1-19 and are used to convert a sketch drawn in the sketching environment into a feature. This group contains sketch-based feature tools and placed-feature tools. You can create datum plane, axis, and points using the tools in this group.

*Figure 1-19 The **Feature** group*

Synchronous Modeling Group

The Synchronous modeling technology is one of the significant technologies in NX. This technology is used to modify the parts even if the modeling history is not available. The tools available in the **Synchronous Modeling** group are used to modify and improve an existing design in less time. Figure 1-20 shows the **Synchronous Modeling** group.

*Figure 1-20 The **Synchronous Modeling** group*

Curve Tab

The **Curve** tab comprises a series of groups and galleries. You can invoke the sketching environment by using the **Sketch in Task Environment** (customize to add) tool of this tab. Figure 1-21 shows the **Curve** tab.

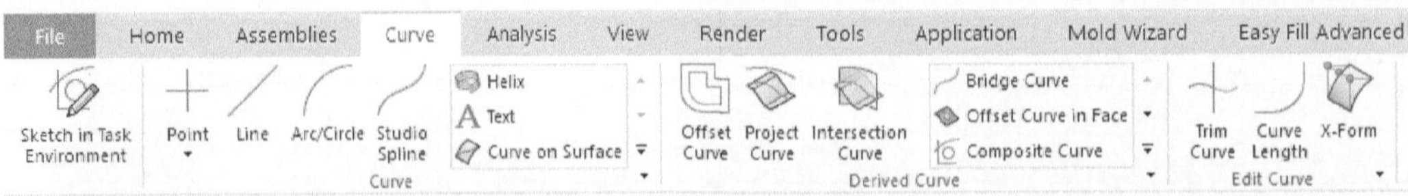

*Figure 1-21 The **Curve** tab*

Surface Tab

You can create surface designs in the Modeling environment as well as in the Shape Studio environment. The tools used to create solid bodies are also used to create surface bodies. The **Surface** group under the **Surface** tab has the tools to create the surface design. Note that this tab is not available by default. Figure 1-22 shows the **Surface** group.

*Figure 1-22 The **Surface** group*

> **Tip**
>
> *1. Some of the tabs are, by default, available in their respective environments. However, you can add more tabs to an environment. To do so, right-click on the **Ribbon**; a shortcut menu will be displayed. You will observe that the tools that are not available in the graphics window are not selected in the shortcut menu. Select any unselected option; it will become available as a tab in the **Ribbon**.*
>
> *2. By default, all tools are not available in a group. Therefore, you may need to customize the group to add those tools. To customize a group, click on the down arrow at the bottom right corner of the group; a drop-down will be displayed. Click on the tool to be added or removed from the group. Note that a tick mark available on the left of a tool indicates that it is already added to the group.*
>
> *Similarly, you can add or remove groups from the **Ribbon** by using **Ribbon Options** arrow available at the bottom right corner of the **Ribbon**.*

Some of the tabs that are available in the Modeling environment and are common to other environments of NX are discussed next.

Application Tab

Using the **Application** tab, you can invoke any other environment from the currently invoked environment. Figure 1-23 shows the **Application** tab.

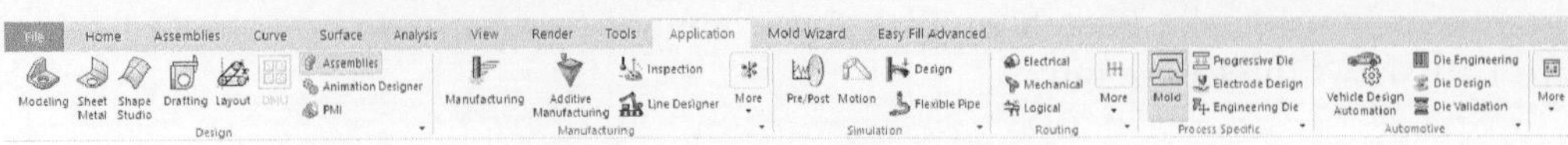

*Figure 1-23 The **Application** tab*

View Tab

The tools in the **View** tab, as shown in Figure 1-24, are used for manipulating the views of the model. The **View** tab is available in all the environments. Some of the tools in the **View** tab are not available in the **Drafting** environment.

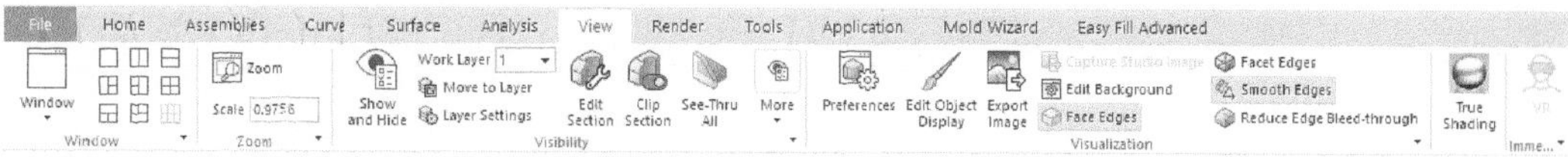

*Figure 1-24 The **View** tab*

Assembly Environment

In NX, you can invoke the assembly environment within the Modeling environment and create assemblies by using different assembly tools. The tools for assembling components are available in the **Assemblies** tab and are discussed next.

Assemblies Tab

The tools that are used to create an assembly are grouped together in the **Assemblies** tab. To add this tab to the **Ribbon**, choose **Application > Design > Assemblies** from the **Ribbon**. Note that the **Assemblies** button is a toggle button. Alternatively, choose the **Assemblies** button from the **File** menu. The tools of the **Component** group available in this tab are used to insert an existing part or assembly in the current assembly file. You can also create a new component in the assembly file using the tools in this group. Figure 1-25 shows the tools in this group.

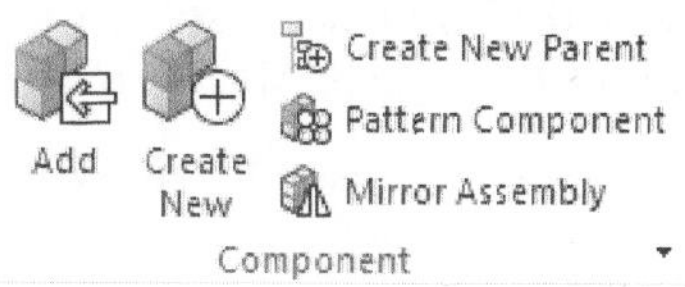

*Figure 1-25 The **Component** group*

Drafting Environment

To invoke the Drafting environment, choose **Application > Design > Drafting** from the **Ribbon**. Alternatively, this environment can be invoked by choosing the **Drafting** tool from the **File** menu. You can also invoke this environment by using the templates available in the **Drawing** tab of the **New** dialog box. The groups in the Drafting environment are discussed next.

View Group

This group is displayed in the **Home** tab after invoking the Drafting environment. The tools in the **View** group are used to insert a new sheet, create a new view, generate an orthographic view, section view, and detail view for a solid part or an assembly. Figure 1-26 shows the **View** group.

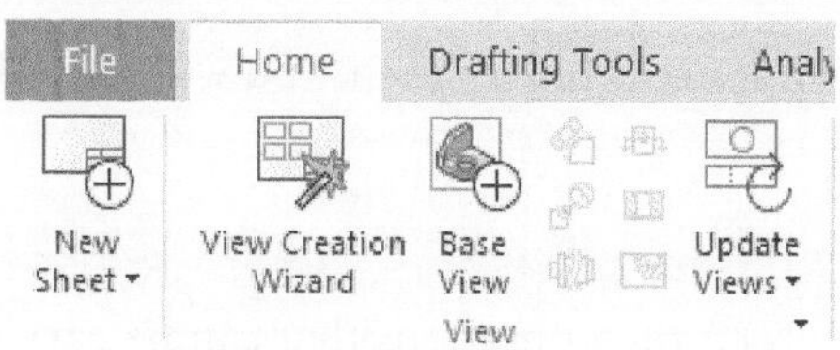

*Figure 1-26 The **View** group*

Dimension Group

The tools in the **Dimension** group are used to generate various dimensions in the drawing views. Figure 1-27 shows the **Dimension** group.

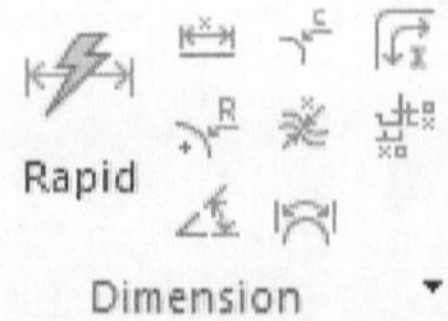

*Figure 1-27 The **Dimension** group*

Annotation Group

The tools in the **Annotation** group are used to generate the GDT parameters, annotations, symbols, and so on. Figure 1-28 shows the **Annotation** group.

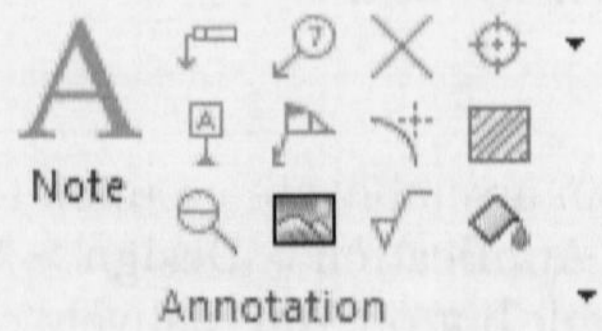

*Figure 1-28 The **Annotation** group*

Sheet Metal Environment

The tools in the Sheet Metal environment are used to create a sheet metal component. Figure 1-29 shows the groups and tools of Sheet Metal environment.

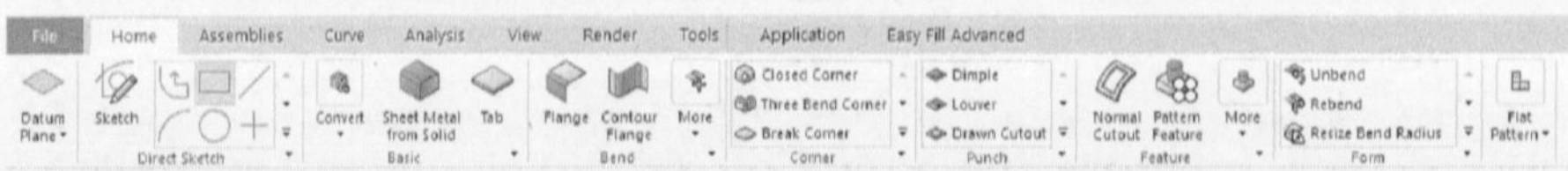

Figure 1-29 Tools in the Sheet Metal environment

STATUS BAR

The Status Bar appears at the bottom of the drawing window and comprises of two areas and buttons, as shown in Figure 1-30. These areas and buttons are discussed next.

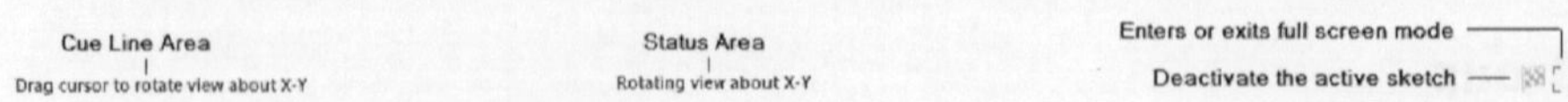

Figure 1-30 The Status Bar

Cue Line Area

The cue line area is the prompt area. In this area, you will be prompted to select the entities for completing the tool task.

Status Area

This area gives information about the operations that can be carried out.

Enters or exits full screen mode button

If you choose this button, the graphics area will be maximized and will give you a full screen display. For getting the default screen display, you need to choose this button again.

Deactivates the active sketch button

If you choose this button, the active sketch will get deactivated and you will be directed out of the sketching environment.

HOT KEYS

NX is more popularly known for its icon driven structure. However, you can still use the keys on the keyboard to invoke some tools. These keys are called hot keys. The hot keys along with their functions are listed in the table given next.

Hot Key	Function
CTRL+Z	Invokes the **Undo** tool
CTRL+Y	Invokes the **Repeat** tool
CTRL+S	Saves the current document
F5	Refreshes the **Drawing** window
F1	Invokes the NX **Help** tool
F6	Invokes the **Zoom** tool
F7	Invokes the **Rotate** tool
CTRL+M	Invokes the Modeling environment
CTRL+SHIFT+D	Invokes the Drafting environment

COLOR SCHEME

NX allows you to use various color schemes as the background screen color and also for displaying solid bodies on the screen. To change the background color scheme, choose **Menu > Preferences > Background** from the **Top Border Bar**; the **Edit Background** dialog box will be displayed.

Select the **Plain** radio button from the **Shaded Views** and **Wireframe Views** areas. Next, choose the color swatch available on the right side of the **Plain Color** option; the **Color** dialog box will be displayed. Select the **White** color swatch from the **Color** dialog box and choose the **OK** button twice to apply the new color scheme to the NX environment.

DIALOG BOXES IN NX

To create any feature, you need to follow certain steps in an order. These steps are placed in a top-down order in the dialog boxes. This layout of dialog boxes will help you throughout the feature creation operation, refer to Figure 1-31.

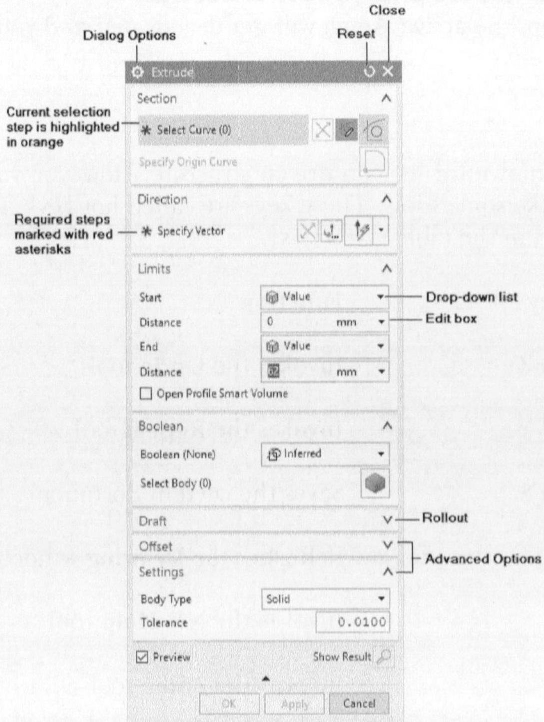

*Figure 1-31 The layout of **Extrude** dialog box*

In a dialog box, the current selection step will be highlighted in orange. The required steps are marked with red asterisks and the completed steps are marked with green check marks. The advanced options are collapsed and hidden in the rollouts. The button highlighted in green indicates next default action.

The **Reset** button is used to reset the dialog box to its initial settings. The **Hide Collapsed Groups** option from the **Dialog Options** button is used to hide all the collapsed rollouts to simplify the dialog box. To view all the collapsed rollouts, choose the **Show Collapsed Groups** option from the **Dialog Options** button, which will be available only after choosing the **Hide Collapsed Groups** option from the **Dialog Options** button. The **Close** button is used to exit the dialog box.

SELECTING OBJECTS

When no tool is invoked in the current environment, the select mode will be activated. You can ensure that the select mode is active by pressing the ESC key. In this mode, you can select a wide range of objects from different environments such as individual features, part bodies, surface bodies, planar and non-planar faces, sketched entities, sketch and assembly constraints, and so on by clicking on them. Alternatively, press and hold the left mouse button and drag a box around the objects; all objects that lie completely inside the box are selected.

DESELECTING OBJECTS

By default, the selected objects are displayed in orange color. If you want to deselect any specific object from the selection, press and hold the SHIFT key and click on it; the object will be deselected. If you want to deselect all the selected entities, press the ESC key. Alternatively, press and hold the SHIFT key and drag a box around the entities; all the entities that lie completely inside the box are deselected. Also, you can choose the **Deselect All** button from the **Selection Group** to deselect all the selected entities.

SELECTING OBJECTS USING THE QuickPick DIALOG BOX

If objects are close to each other, then it may be difficult to select the required object. In such cases, move the cursor over the object to be selected and wait for two seconds; the cursor will be changed to '+' sign with three dots. Next, press the left mouse button; the **QuickPick** dialog box will be displayed. This dialog box will list all the objects near the selected object in the drawing window. Move the cursor over the objects listed; the corresponding objects will be highlighted in the drawing window. Select the required object from the **QuickPick** dialog box; the specified object will get selected.

Self-Evaluation Test

Answer the following questions and then compare them to those given at the end of this chapter:

1. The _________ that exists between the environments of NX ensures that any modification made in the model in one environment is automatically reflected in other environments immediately.

2. The _________ is a file extension associated with all the files that are created in different environments of NX.

3. The _________ keeps a track of all the operations that are carried out on the part.

4. The _________ constraint is used to fix a selected entity in terms of its position with respect to the coordinate system of the current sketch.

5. You can invoke the _______ tool by pressing and holding the middle mouse button.

6. The _________ group is used to generate the GDT parameters, annotations, and symbols.

7. The Modeling environment of NX is a parametric and feature-based environment. (T/F)

8. You can modify an existing design quickly using the **Synchronous Modeling** tools. (T/F)

9. The generative drafting technique is used to automatically generate the drawing views of parts and assemblies. (T/F)

10. By default, the **Resource Bar** is located on the left side of the NX window. (T/F)

Answers to Self-Evaluation Test

1. bidirectional associativity, **2.** prt, **3. Part Navigator**, **4.** Fixed, **5. Rotate**, **6. Annotation**, **7.** T, **8.** T, **9.** T, **10.** T

Chapter 2

Drawing Sketches for Solid Models

Learning Objectives

After completing this chapter, you will be able to:

- *Start NX and create a new file in it*
- *Invoke different NX environments*
- *Understand the need of datum planes*
- *Create three fixed datum planes*
- *Create sketches in the Modeling environment*
- *Create sketches in the Sketch in Task Environment*
- *Use various drawing display tools*
- *Understand different selection filters*
- *Select and deselect objects*
- *Use various sketching tools*
- *Use different snap point options*
- *Delete sketched entities*
- *Exit the sketching environment*

INTRODUCTION

Most designs created in NX consist of sketch-based and placed features. A sketch is a combination of two-dimensional (2D) entities such as lines, arcs, circles, and so on. The features such as extrude, revolve, and sweep created by using 2D sketches are known as sketch-based features. The features such as fillet, chamfer, thread, and shell created without using a sketch are known as placed features. In a design, the base feature or the first feature is always a sketch-based feature. For example, the sketch shown in Figure 2-1 is used to create the solid model shown in Figure 2-2. In this model, the fillets and the chamfers are the placed features.

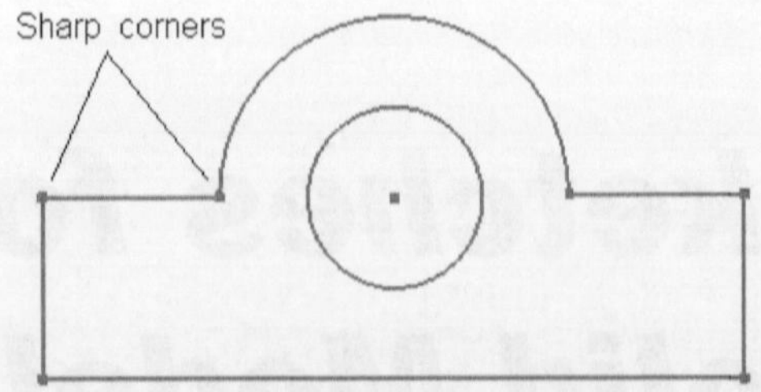

Figure 2-1 *Profile for the sketch-based feature of the solid model shown in Figure 2-2*

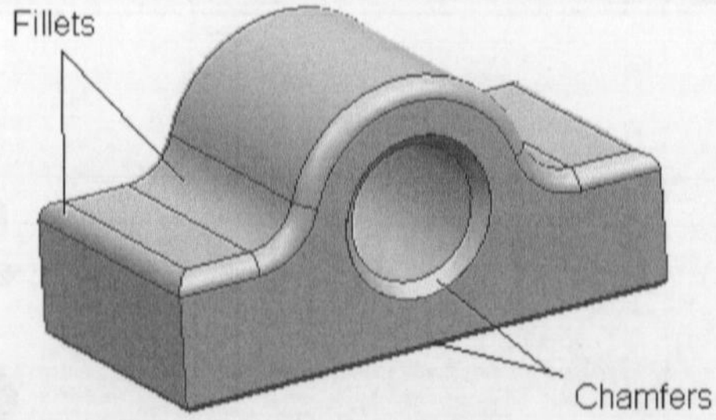

Figure 2-2 *Solid model created using the sketch-based and placed features*

As mentioned earlier, to create sketch-based features, you first need to create its sketch. In NX, you can create a sketch by using two methods: Direct sketch and Sketch in Task Environment.

In the Direct sketch method, you can create sketch, as required, directly in the Modeling environment by using the sketching tools such as **Line** and **Rectangle** of the **Direct Sketch** group. Once the sketch has been drawn, you can directly use the solid modeling tools to convert the sketch into a sketch-based feature.

In the Sketch in Task Environment method, to create the sketch, you need to invoke the sketching environment by using the **Sketch in Task Environment** tool from the **Curve** tab of the **Ribbon** (Customize to add). You will learn more about creating sketches by using these methods later in this chapter.

Unlike other solid modeling software packages where you need separate files for starting different environments, NX uses only a single type of file to start different environments. In NX, files are saved in the *.prt* format and all the environments required to complete a design can be invoked in the same *.prt* file. For example, you can draw sketches and convert them into features, assemble other parts with the current part, and generate drawing views in a single *.prt* file.

STARTING NX

You can start NX by double-clicking on its shortcut icon on the desktop of your computer. The default initial interface of NX is shown in Figure 2-3 and it displays basic information about NX. You can view more information by clicking on the topics displayed on the left of the NX screen.

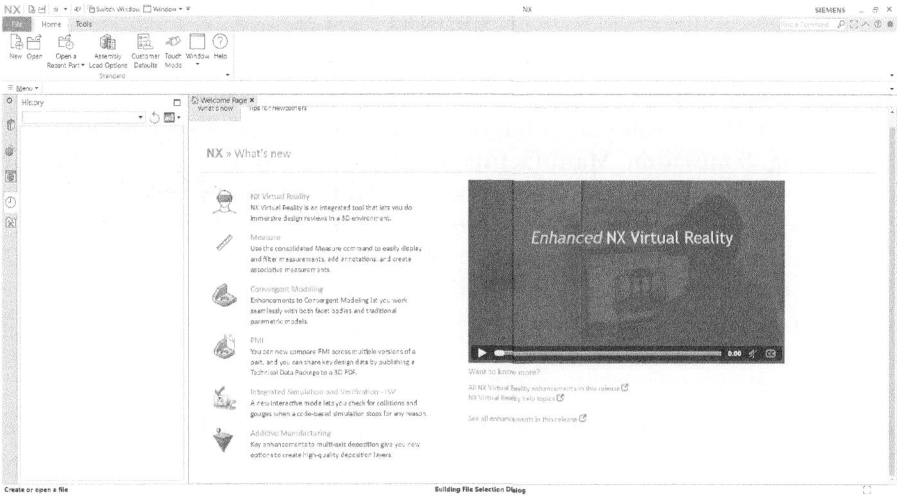

Figure 2-3 The default initial interface of NX

STARTING A NEW DOCUMENT IN NX

Ribbon:	Home > Standard > New
Menu:	File > New

New

To start a new file, choose the **New** tool from the **Standard** group of the **Home** tab in the **Ribbon** or choose **Menu > File > New** available at the left on the **Top Border Bar**; the **New** dialog box will be displayed, as shown in Figure 2-4.

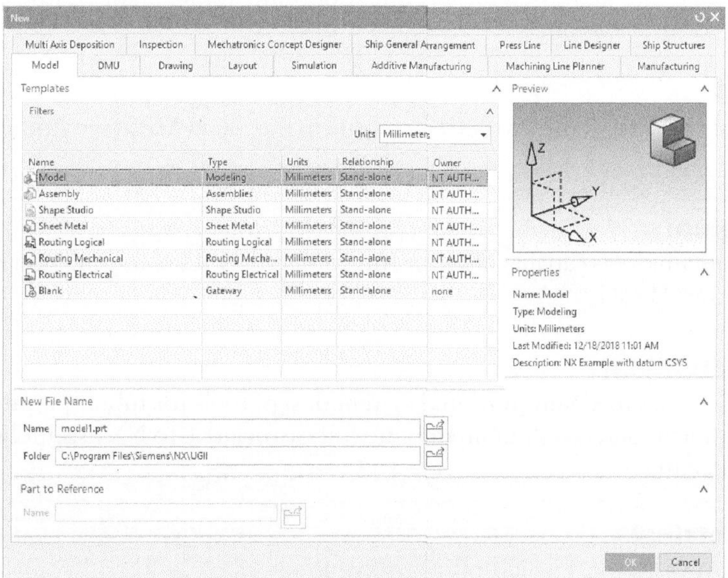

*Figure 2-4 The **New** dialog box*

The tabs and options in this dialog box are discussed next.

Templates Rollout

In the **New** dialog box, templates are grouped together under various environment types such as **Model**, **Drawing**, **Simulation**, **Manufacturing**, **Inspection**, **Machining Line Planner**, **Press Line**, **Ship General Arrangement**, **DMU**, **Layout**, **Additive Manufacturing**, **Mechatronics Concept Designer**, **Ship Structures**, and **Line Designer**. The template files related to these environments are available in their respective tabs. These files are used whenever you start a new file. These template files provide a predefined set of tools with specified environment. This saves a lot of time in setting environment and displaying tools according to your requirements.

Model Tab

By default, this tab will be chosen and the modeling templates will be displayed in the **Templates** rollout. Some of the important modeling templates are discussed next.

Model

By default, the **Model** template is selected and it is used to start a new part file in the Modeling environment for creating solid and surface models.

Assembly

The **Assembly** template is used to start a new assembly file in the Assembly environment for assembling various parts of the assembly.

Shape Studio

The **Shape Studio** template is used to start a new part file in the Shape Studio environment for creating advanced surface models.

Sheet Metal

The **Sheet Metal** template is used to start a new file in the Sheet Metal environment for creating sheet metal models.

Routing Logical

This template contains tools capable of supporting different types of routing designs, for example, piping, tubing, and HVAC.

Routing Mechanical

This template provides mechanical routed system design tools for tubing, piping, conduit, and raceways. Mechanical routed system models are fully associative to NX assemblies which in turn facilitate design changes.

Routing Electrical

This template provides tools which offer a flexible interface to logical connectivity data and rapid path creation between components.

Blank

This template is used to start a new file in the Gateway environment. The Gateway environment allows you to examine the geometry and drawing views created. You cannot modify a model in the Gateway environment. However, you can invoke any environment of NX from it.

Drawing Tab

This tab is used to specify a template for a drawing. These templates are contained in the **Templates** rollout and are used to start a new drawing file in the Drafting environment for generating the drawing views. These templates are arranged according to the sheet size (A0, A1, A2, A3, and A4) in the **Drawing** tab.

Units

This drop-down list is used to filter the templates as per the unit. The options in this drop-down list are discussed next.

Millimeters

If you select the **Millimeters** option, the templates only with the millimeters unit will be displayed in the **Templates** area.

Inches

If you select the **Inches** option, the templates only with the inches units will be displayed in the **Templates** area.

All

Select the **All** option to display all the templates (with both millimeters and inches units).

New File Name Rollout

This rollout is used to specify the name and location to save the file. The options in this rollout are discussed next.

Name

Enter the name of the new file in the **Name** text box. Alternatively, choose the button on the right side of the **Name** text box; the **Choose New File Name** dialog box will be displayed. Type the name in the **File name** edit box. Also, to specify the location to save the new file, browse the folder where you need to save the file and choose the **OK** button. However, there is a separate option to specify the location, which is discussed next.

Folder

Specify the location to save the new file in the **Folder** text box. Alternatively, choose the button on the right side of the **Folder** text box; the **Choose Directory** dialog box will be displayed. Next, browse the folder where you want to save the file and choose the **OK** button.

Note

1. It is recommended that you create a folder with the name NX in the primary drive of your computer and then create individual folder for each chapter within the NX folder. Now, you can save the part files of all the chapters in their respective folders. This will ensure a better organization of the part files created.

2. In this textbook, the **Model** *template has been used for starting a new file for illustration purpose.*

After specifying all the required options in the **New** dialog box, choose the **OK** button; the new file will open in the specified environment. Figure 2-5 shows the initial screen of the new file invoked by using the **Model** template.

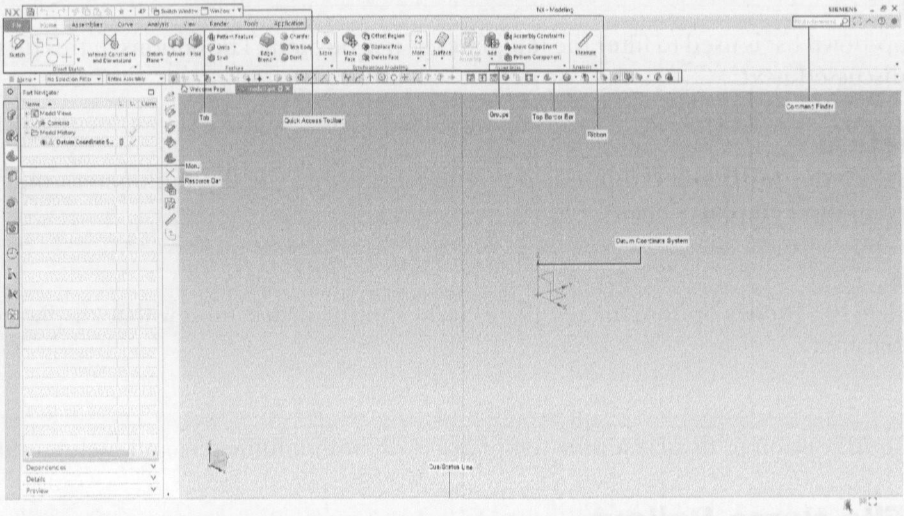

***Figure 2-5** Initial screen of the new part file*

Tip

1. To change the color of curves and dimensions, choose ***Menu > Preferences > Sketch*** *from the* ***Top Border Bar****; the* ***Sketch Preferences*** *dialog box will be displayed. Next, choose the* ***Part Settings*** *tab to change the color of curves and dimensions.*

INVOKING DIFFERENT NX ENVIRONMENTS

You can invoke different environments of NX by selecting their respective templates from the **New** dialog box. In NX, you can also switch from one environment to another. To do so, choose the **File** tab from the **Ribbon**; a menu will be displayed, refer to Figure 2-6. Next, choose the **All Applications** option from the **Start** area of the menu; a flyout will be displayed. Now, you can invoke the desired environment by selecting the required environment option from the flyout displayed.

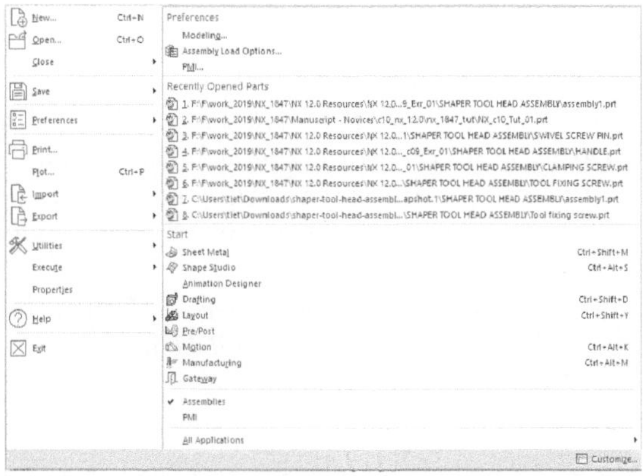

Figure 2-6 Menu showing different environments of NX

CREATING THREE FIXED DATUM PLANES (XC-YC, YC-ZC, XC-ZC)

Ribbon:	Home > Feature > Datum/Point Drop-down > Datum Plane
Menu:	Insert > Datum/Point > Datum Plane

In NX, you can create the sketch of the base feature by selecting a reference plane of the datum coordinate system as a sketching plane. Also, you can also create three fixed datum planes (YC-ZC, XC-ZC, and XC-YC) and then use one of them as the sketching plane for creating the sketch of the base feature. To create three fixed datum planes, choose **Menu > Insert > Datum/Point > Datum Plane** available at the left on the **Top Border Bar**. Alternatively, choose the **Datum Plane** tool from the **Feature** group of the **Ribbon**; the **Datum Plane** dialog box will be displayed, as shown in Figure 2-7. Next, select the **YC-ZC Plane** option from the Type drop-down list; a preview of the plane will be displayed in the drawing window. Choose the **Apply** button; the YC-ZC plane will be created. Similarly, select the **XC-ZC Plane** and **XC-YC Plane** options from the Type drop-down list to create the XC-ZC and XC-YC planes, respectively and then choose the **OK** button to exit the dialog box. Figure 2-8 shows the three fixed datum planes created.

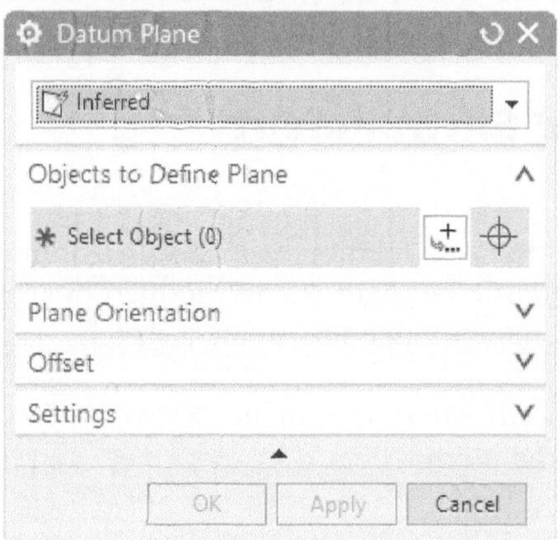

*Figure 2-7 The **Datum Plane** dialog box*

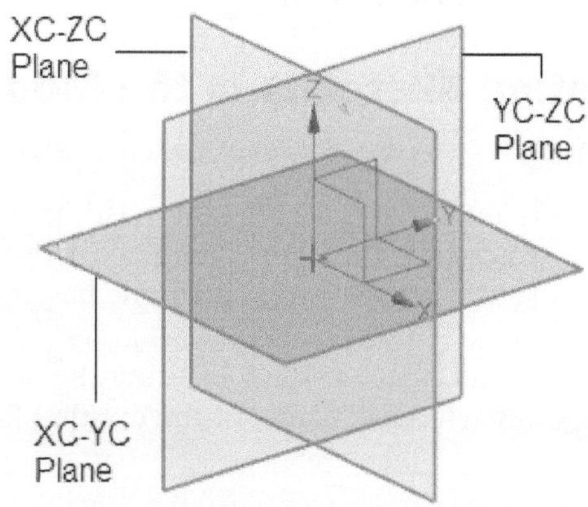

Figure 2-8 Three fixed datum planes

Tip

By default, all the tools are not available in their respective groups. Therefore, you may need to customize the groups to add those tools that are not available by default. To customize a group, click on the down arrow at the bottom right corner of the group; a drop-down with a list of tools/options will be displayed. Click on the tool to be added or removed from the group. Note that a tick mark available on left of a tool name indicates that it is already added in the group.

Similarly, you can add or remove the groups from the ***Ribbon*** *by using* ***Ribbon Options*** *arrow available at the bottom right corner of the* ***Ribbon****.*

DISPLAYING THE WCS (WORK COORDINATE SYSTEM)

Ribbon: Tools > Utilities > More Gallery *(Customize to Add)* > Display WCS

The display of WCS (Work Coordinate System) is important in selecting the planes for drawing sketches. When you start a new file, by default, the display of WCS is turned off. It is recommended to keep the display of WCS turned on while drawing sketches and creating features.

If the display of WCS is turned off, then to turn it on, choose the **Display WCS** button from the **More** gallery of the **Utilities** group of the **Tools** tab in the **Ribbon**; the WCS will be displayed at the origin of the drawing window. Note that the **Display WCS** button is a toggle button and is used to toggle the display of WCS on/off. Figure 2-9 shows the WCS with the datum coordinate system hidden for better visualization.

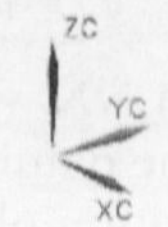

Figure 2-9 *The WCS (Work Coordinate System)*

CREATING SKETCHES

In NX, you can create the sketch of a feature by using two methods. In the first method, you can create sketch in the Modeling environment directly by invoking the sketch tools available in the **Direct Sketch** group. In the second method, you need to invoke the sketching environment by choosing the **Sketch in Task Environment** tool from the **Curve** tab of the **Ribbon**. Both these methods are discussed next.

Creating Sketches in the Modeling Environment

Ribbon: Home > Direct Sketch > Sketch

Sketch

As mentioned earlier, the base feature or the first feature in a design is always a sketch-based feature. The profiles of the sketch-based features are defined by using a sketch. Therefore, to create the base feature, first you need to create a sketch.

In NX, you can create a sketch by using the datum coordinate system plane (XC-YC, YC-ZC, or XC-ZC), any reference plane, or the existing face of the model.

To create a sketch in the Modeling environment, you can use the sketching tools available in the **Sketch Curve** gallery of the **Direct Sketch** group and create sketch directly in the modeling environment itself. However, by default, in the Modeling environment, all the sketching tools are not available. To get the full access of sketching tools in the modeling environment, choose the **Sketch** tool from the **Direct Sketch** group of the **Home** tab; the **Create Sketch** dialog box will be displayed, as shown in Figure 2-10. Also, you will be prompted to select objects to infer CSYS. The options in the various rollouts of the **Create Sketch** dialog box are discussed next.

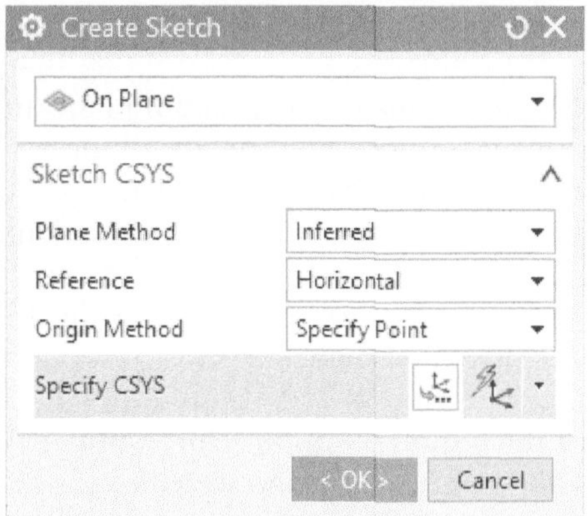

***Figure 2-10** The **Create Sketch** dialog box*

Note
*The **Direct Sketch** group will be available only when you are in the Modeling environment or Sheet Metal environment.*

Sketch Type Rollout

The options in the drop-down list of this rollout are used to specify whether you want to draw the sketch on the existing plane or on a temporary plane defined on the path.

On Plane

By default, this option is selected in the drop-down list. It is used to specify the existing plane, face, or datum coordinate system plane as the sketching plane.

On Path

Select this option from the drop-down list to specify the sketch plane on the existing path. The temporary sketch plane will be created perpendicular to the path selected as the **Normal to Path** option is selected by default in the **Orientation** drop-down list of the **Plane Orientation** rollout.

Depending upon the option selected from the drop-down list, the **Create Sketch** dialog box will be modified. The various rollouts in the modified dialog box for both the options are discussed next.

On Plane Options

By default, the rollouts related to the **On Plane** option will be displayed in the **Create Sketch** dialog box, refer to Figure 2-10. The rollouts displayed on selecting this option are discussed next.

Sketch CSYS Rollout
The options in this rollout are used to specify the sketch plane by different methods. The options in this rollout are as follows:

Plane Method: This drop down list provides two options to select the sketch plane, **Inferred** and **New Plane**.

By default, the **Inferred** option is selected in the **Plane Method** drop-down list. It allows you to select the existing planes and planar faces as the sketch planes.

The **New Plane** option is used to create a new datum plane and you can use it as a current sketch plane. As you select this option, the **Specify Plane** area is displayed in the **Sketch Plane** rollout. The options in the **Specify Plane** area are used to create a datum plane. The options to create a datum plane will be discussed in later chapters.

The options displayed in the dialog box on selecting the **Inferred** option in the **Plane Method** drop-down list are discussed next:

Reference: You can select the required option (**Horizontal** or **Vertical**) from the **Reference** drop-down list to specify the reference for the sketch.

Origin Method: The options in this drop-down list are used to specify the origin point of the sketch. This drop-down list provides two options to specify the origin point of the sketch, **Specify Point** and **Use Work Part Origin**.

The **Specify Point** option is used to select the origin point of the sketch plane. You can select a point on the sketch plane to specify it as the origin of the sketch. You can also use the **CSYS Dialog** button or the **Inferred** drop-down list available in the **Specify CSYS** area to create or locate a point.

The **Use Work Part Origin** option is used to specify the origin of the sketch plane by selecting a point location on the workpart.

When you select the **New Plane** option from the **Plane Method** drop-down list, you will be prompted to select the objects to define plane. Also, the **Specify Plane** area will be highlighted in the **Sketch Plane** rollout. You can specify the sketch plane by using the options available in this area. You can use the **Plane Dialog** button to specify the sketch plane. Also, you can reverse the direction of the specified sketch plane by using the **Reverse Direction** button available in this area. The other options displayed in the dialog box on selecting the **New Plane** option from the **Plane Method** drop-down are discussed next.

Sketch Orientation Rollout
The options in this rollout are used to specify the horizontal or vertical reference for the sketch. The sketching plane gets orientated according to the specified references. You can specify the horizontal or vertical reference using the **Reference** drop-down list of this rollout. Also, you can specify a temporary vector direction using the **Vector Dialog** button or the **Inferred Vector** drop-down list of the **Specify Vector** area. You can reverse the direction of the specified reference using the **Reverse Direction** button available in the **Specify Vector** area.

Sketch Origin Rollout

The options in this rollout are same as discussed above in the **Origin Method** drop-down list of the **Sketch CSYS** rollout.

On Path Options

Select this option from the Sketch Type drop-down list to create a sketching plane on the selected path; the rollouts related to the **On Path** option will be displayed in the **Create Sketch** dialog box, as shown in Figure 2-11. The options in these rollouts are discussed next.

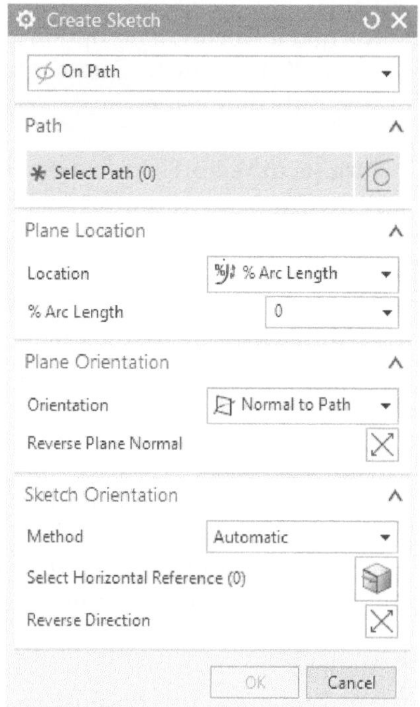

Figure 2-11 *Rollouts displayed when the* ***On Path*** *option is selected*

Path Rollout

The **Curve** button in this rollout is used to select the path. The path may be a curve or an edge of an existing solid body.

Plane Location Rollout

The options in this rollout are used to specify the location of the sketch plane along the path in terms of arc length or point. These options are discussed next.

Location

This drop-down list contains different options to specify the location of the sketch plane along the path. These options are as follows:

Arc Length: This option allows you to specify the sketch plane distance from the start point of the path. Enter the distance in the **Arc Length** edit box.

Note

The nearest endpoint of the selected path will be considered as the start point of the path.

% Arc Length: This option allows you to specify the distance of the sketch plane in terms of the percentage of arc length from the start point of path. Enter the % value in the **% Arc Length** edit box.

Through Point: This option allows you to specify the sketch plane by picking a point on the path. You can use the **Point Dialog** button or **Inferred Point** drop-down list to create or locate a point.

Plane Orientation Rollout

The options in this rollout are used to specify the direction of the sketch plane with respect to the selected path. These options are discussed next.

Orientation
This drop-down list contains different options to specify the direction of the sketch plane. These options are discussed next.

Normal to Path: This option allows you to orient the sketch plane normal to the selected path.

Normal to Vector: This option allows you to orient the sketch plane normal to the specified vector. You can use the **Vector Dialog** button or the **Inferred Vector** drop-down list to create or specify the vector.

Parallel to Vector: This option allows you to specify the sketch plane parallel to the specified vector. You can use the **Vector Dialog** button or the **Inferred Vector** drop-down list to create or specify the vector.

Through Axis: This option aligns the sketch plane so that it passes through the specified axis. Specify the axis using the **Vector Dialog** button or the **Inferred Vector** drop-down list.

Reverse Plane Normal
The **Reverse Plane Normal** button is used to reverse the direction of sketch plane.

Sketch Orientation Rollout
The options in the drop-down list of this rollout are used to specify the reference for a sketch. The sketching plane will be oriented according to the specified reference. The options in this rollout are discussed next.

Method
The options in this drop-down list are used to specify references for the orientation of a sketch. These options are discussed next.

Automatic: The **Automatic** option is selected by default in this drop-down list. As a result, the **Select Horizontal Reference** button available below this drop-down list gets activated. You can specify the horizontal reference by using this button. Specify the horizontal reference for the sketch; the sketching plane will be oriented based on the specified reference.

Note
*After selecting the **Automatic** option, if you select an existing curve as the path, the sketch will be oriented using the curve parameters and if you select an existing edge as the path, the sketch will be oriented relative to the face.*

Relative to Face: This option allows you to orient the sketch to a face which can be either inferred or explicitly selected. The path location you select determines the direction of the sketch plane.

Use Curve Parameters: This option allows you to orient the sketch using curve parameters, even if the path selected is an edge, or is part of a feature that lies on a face.

Reverse Direction
The **Reverse Direction** button in this rollout is used to reverse the direction of the specified reference.

All the options in the **Create Sketch** dialog box have already been discussed. For illustration purpose, select the **On Plane** option from the drop-down list. By default, the XC-YC plane will be selected. Next, choose the **OK** button from the **Create Sketch** dialog box; the selected reference plane will be oriented normal to the viewing direction, refer to Figure 2-12. Now, you can create a sketch by using different sketching tools.

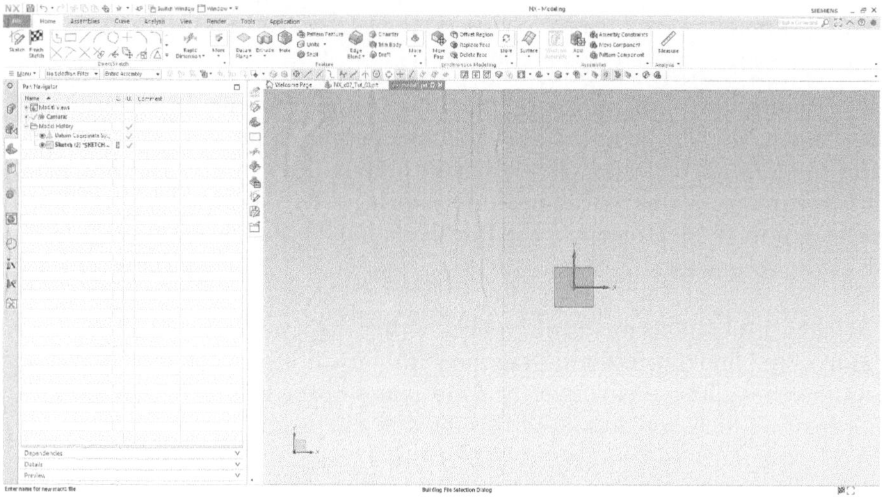

Figure 2-12 *The screen appears with XC-YC plane oriented normal to the viewing direction*

> **Tip**
>
> *If the icons of the **Ribbon** appear large, you can reduce their size. To do so, right-click on **Ribbon** to display a shortcut menu and then choose the **Customize** option; the **Customize** dialog box will be displayed. Choose the **Icons/Tooltips** tab and then select the options from the **Ribbon Bar** drop-down list available in the **Icon Sizes** area.*

Creating Sketches in the Sketching Environment

In NX, you can create a sketch in the sketching environment. You can invoke the sketching environment for creating a sketch by using the **Sketch in Task Environment** tool available in the **Curve** tab of the **Ribbon**. On choosing this tool, the **Create Sketch** dialog box will be displayed and you will be prompted to select a sketching plane. Next, select the sketching plane. The options in the **Create Sketch** dialog box are same as discussed earlier. You can specify the other required parameters in the dialog box and then choose the **OK** button; the sketching environment will be invoked. Now, you can create the sketch by using the tools that are available in the sketching environment. To finish the sketch, you need to choose the **Finish** tool from the **Sketch** group.

SKETCHING TOOLS

As discussed earlier, the tools required to draw a sketch are available in the **Sketch Curve** gallery of the **Direct Sketch** group in the **Home** tab of the Modeling environment. Also, these tools are available in the **Home** tab of the sketching environment. The sketching tools in context of the **Sketch Curve** gallery in the **Direct Sketch** group are discussed next.

Note

*In this textbook, all the sketching tools available in the **Sketch Curve** gallery of the **Direct Sketch** group are explained after invoking the sketching environment.*

Drawing Sketches Using the Profile Tool

Ribbon:	Home > Direct Sketch > Sketch Curve Gallery > Profile
Menu:	Insert > Sketch Curve > Profile

The **Profile** tool is the most commonly used tool to draw sketches in NX. This tool allows you to draw continuous lines and tangent/normal arcs. To draw continuous lines and tangent/normal arcs using this tool, choose the **Profile** tool from the **Direct Sketch** group of the **Home** tab; the **Profile** dialog box will be displayed, as shown in Figure 2-13.

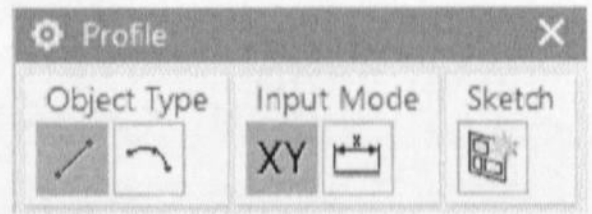

***Figure 2-13** The **Profile** dialog box*

Also, the dynamic input boxes are displayed below the cursor and you will be prompted to select the first point of the line or press and drag the left mouse button to begin the arc creation. The dynamic input boxes allow you to enter the coordinates or the length and angle of the line. The methods of creating lines and arcs using this tool are discussed next.

Note

*The **Profile** tool is also available in the **Home** tab of the Sketching environment. As a result, you can also draw continuous lines and tangent/normal arcs in the Sketching environment by using this tool.*

Drawing Lines

The option to draw straight lines is active by default when you invoke the **Profile** tool. This is because the **Line** button is chosen by default in the **Profile** dialog box. NX allows you to draw lines using two methods. These methods are discussed next.

Drawing Lines by Entering Values

In this method of drawing lines, you can enter the coordinate values or the length and angle of the line in the dynamic input boxes displayed below the cursor when you invoke the **Profile** tool. After you have entered the coordinates of the start point of the line, a rubber-band line will be displayed between the cursor and the specified point. Also, you will be prompted to select the second point of the line. On specifying the start point of the line, the mode of the dynamic input boxes will changed, refer to Figure 2-14.

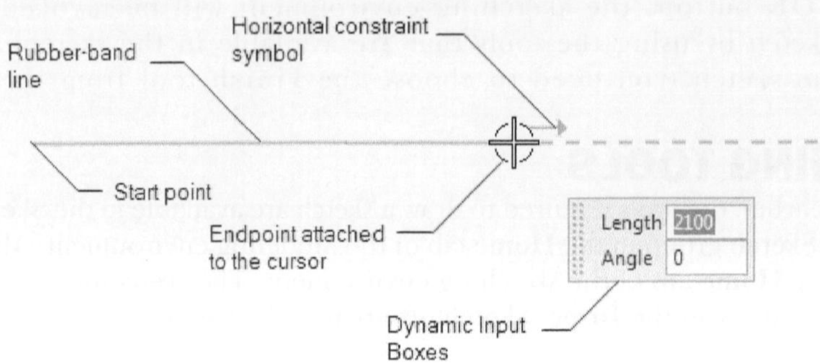

***Figure 2-14** Drawing a horizontal line*

This happens because the **Parameter Mode** button is automatically chosen in the **Profile** dialog box. As you move the cursor in the drawing window, the length and angle of the line gets modified, based on the relative position of the cursor with respect to the point specified earlier in the dynamic input boxes. You can draw a line by specifying its length and angle in these boxes.

Note

After specifying the start point of the line if you choose the ***Coordinate Mode*** *button from the* ***Profile*** *dialog box, the coordinate mode option for specifying the endpoint of the line will become active and you will be prompted to enter the X and Y coordinate values of the end point with respect to the current WCS origin.*

The line drawing process does not end after you specify the second point of the line. Instead, another rubber-band line starts with its start point at the endpoint of the last line and the endpoint attached to the cursor. You can repeat the above-mentioned process to draw a chain of continuous lines.

After drawing a line, you will notice that it is dimensioned automatically. This happens because the **Continuous Auto Dimensioning** tool is chosen by default in the **Sketch Tools** rollout of the **More** gallery of the **Direct Sketch** group in the **Home** tab. You will learn more about dimensioning and constraints in the later chapters.

Tip

You can toggle between the two dynamic input boxes by pressing the TAB key. Note that once you specify a value in one of the boxes and press the TAB key, second dynamic input box will be activated. Specify the value in the second box and then press the ENTER key or the TAB key to register the values and draw the line using these values.

Drawing Lines by Picking Points in the Drawing Window

This is the most convenient method of drawing lines and is extensively used in sketching. The parametric nature of NX ensures that irrespective of the length of the line that is drawn, you can modify it to the required values using dimensions. To draw lines using this method, invoke the **Profile** tool and pick a point in the drawing window; a rubber-band line appears. Specify the endpoint of the line by picking a point in the drawing window; another rubber-band line will appear with the start point as the endpoint of the last line and the endpoint attached to the cursor. You can continue specifying the endpoints of the lines to draw a chain of continuous lines.

While drawing a line, you will notice that some symbols are displayed along with the cursor. For example, after specifying the start point of the line, if you move the cursor in the horizontal direction, an arrow pointing toward the right will be displayed, refer to Figure 2-14. This arrow is the symbol of the **Horizontal** constraint that is applied to the line. This constraint will ensure that the line you draw is horizontal. These constraints are automatically applied to the sketch while drawing. You will learn more about the constraints in the later chapters.

Note

While drawing lines, you can disable the constraints temporarily by pressing the ALT key.

Drawing Arcs

The option to draw arcs can be activated by choosing the **Arc** button in the **Profile** dialog box. Alternatively, you can press and hold the left mouse button and drag the cursor to invoke the arc mode. Generally, the arcs that are drawn by using this tool are in continuation with lines. Therefore, the start point of the arc is taken as the endpoint of the last line. As a result, when you invoke the arc mode, you need to specify only the endpoint of the arc.

When you draw an arc in continuation with lines, you will notice that a circle with four quadrants will be displayed at the start point of the arc, as shown in Figure 2-15. This symbol is called the quadrant symbol and it helps you to define whether you need to draw a tangent arc or a normal arc. This symbol also helps you in specifying the direction of the arc.

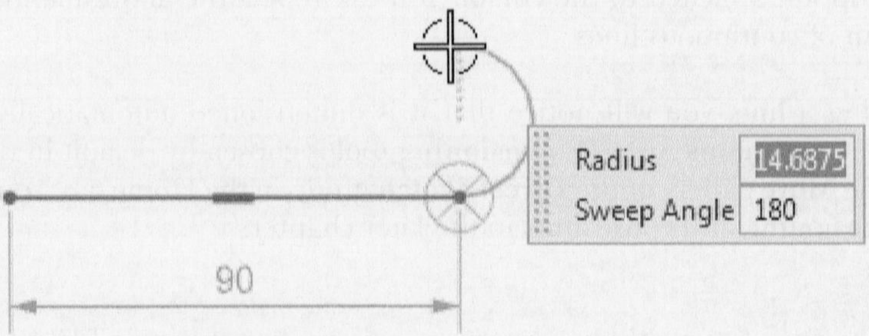

Figure 2-15 *Quadrant symbol displayed while drawing an arc using the* ***Profile*** *tool*

As evident from Figure 2-15, there are four quadrants in the quadrant symbol. The movement of the cursor in these quadrants will determine whether the arc will be tangent to the line or normal to the line. To draw a tangent arc, move the cursor to the start point of the arc and then move it in the quadrants along the line through a small distance; the tangent arc appears. Now,move the cursor to resize the arc, refer to Figure 2-15.

To draw a normal arc, move the cursor through a small distance in the quadrant normal to the line; a normal arc appears. Move the cursor to resize the arc, as shown in Figure 2-16. As you invoke the arc mode, the current dynamic input boxes change into the **Radius** and **Sweep Angle** input boxes. These boxes allow you to specify the radius and the sweep angle to draw the arc.

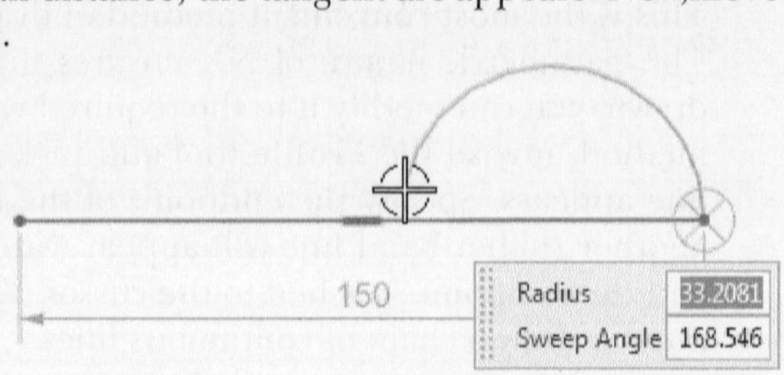

Figure 2-16 *Drawing the normal arc*

Tip

1. To restart drawing lines using the ***Profile*** *tool or to break the sequence of the continuous lines, press the ESC key once.*

2. Press the ESC key twice to exit the tool. Alternatively, right-click in the drawing area and choose the ***OK*** *option from the shortcut menu.*

Note

*If you are not drawing the arc in continuation with a line or an arc, this tool will work similar to the **Arc by 3 Points** tool which is discussed later in this chapter.*

Using Help Lines to Locate Points

You will notice that when a sketching tool is active while drawing sketches, some dotted lines are displayed from the keypoints of the existing entities. The keypoints include endpoints, midpoints, center points, and so on. These dotted lines are called the help lines. If the help lines are not displayed automatically, move the cursor to the keypoints and then move the cursor away; the help lines will be displayed. The help lines are used to locate the points with reference to the keypoints of the existing entities. Figure 2-17 shows the use of the help lines to locate the start point of a new line. You can temporarily disable the help lines by pressing the ALT key.

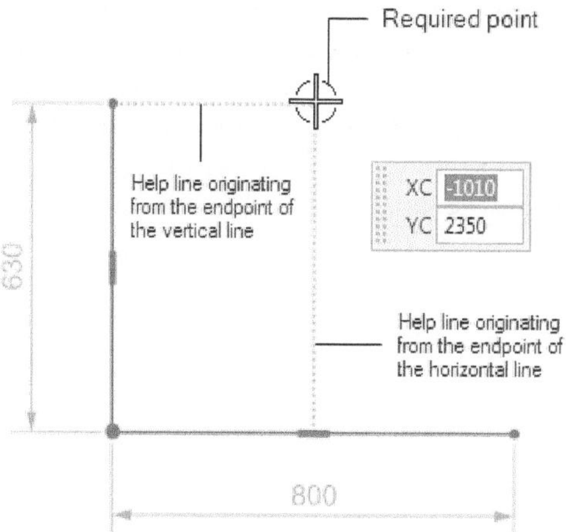

***Figure 2-17** Using the help lines to locate a point*

Drawing Individual Lines

Ribbon:	Home > Direct Sketch > Sketch Curve Gallery > Line
Menu:	Insert > Sketch Curve > Line

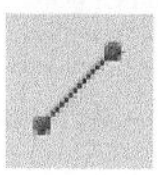

NX also allows you to draw individual lines. This can be done by using the **Line** tool. The working of this tool is similar to the working of the line mode of the **Profile** tool. The only difference is that this tool allows you to draw only one line. As a result, after you specify the endpoint of the line, no rubber-band line is displayed. Instead, you will be prompted to specify the first point of the line. You can specify the first point and the second point of the lines by picking points on the screen or by entering values in the dynamic input boxes. You can use this tool to draw as many individual lines as required.

Note

*Similar to the **Profile** tool, other sketching tools such as **Line** and **Rectangle** are also available in the Sketch in Task Environment.*

Drawing Arcs

Ribbon:	Home > Direct Sketch > Sketch Curve Gallery > Arc
Menu:	Insert > Sketch Curve > Arc

NX allows you to draw arcs using two methods. You can select a method by choosing its respective button from the **Arc** dialog box that will be displayed when you invoke the **Arc** tool. The methods of drawing arcs are discussed next.

Drawing Arcs Using Three Points

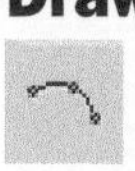

In this method, you can draw an arc by specifying its start point, endpoint, and a point on the arc. When you invoke the **Arc** tool, this method is activated by default and you will be prompted to specify the start point of the arc. You can specify the start point by clicking in the drawing window or by entering the coordinates in the dynamic input boxes. After specifying the start point of the arc, you will be prompted to specify the endpoint. You can also specify the radius of the arc by entering its value in the dynamic input box.

Note that the next prompt will depend on how you specify the endpoint. If you specify the endpoint of the arc by clicking a point in the drawing window, you will be prompted to select a point on the arc and the **Radius** dynamic input box will be displayed. However, if you specify the radius of the arc in the dynamic input box after specifying the start point, then you will be prompted to specify the endpoint of the arc. You can click anywhere in the drawing window to draw the arc. Figure 2-18 shows a three-point arc being drawn by specifying two endpoints and a point on the arc.

Tip

While drawing an arc by specifying its three points, if the start point is at the endpoint of an existing entity, the resultant arc can be drawn tangent to the selected entity. To do so, while defining the point on the arc, move the cursor such that the resulting arc is tangent to the selected entity.

Drawing an Arc by Specifying its Center Point and Endpoints

In this method, you can draw an arc by specifying its center point, start point, and endpoint. To invoke this method, choose the **Arc by Center and Endpoints** button from the **Arc** dialog box; you will be prompted to specify the center point of the arc. Specify the center point of the arc by clicking in the drawing area or by entering coordinates in the dynamic input boxes. On doing so, you will be prompted to specify the start point of the arc. After specifying the start point of the arc, you will be prompted to specify the endpoint of the arc. Note that when you specify the start point of the arc after specifying the center point, the radius of the arc will automatically be defined. Therefore, the endpoint is used only to define the arc length. Figure 2-19 shows an arc being drawn using this method.

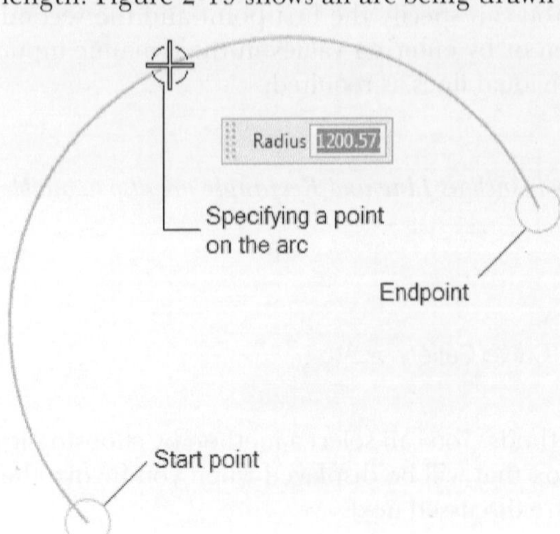

Figure 2-18 Drawing a three-point arc

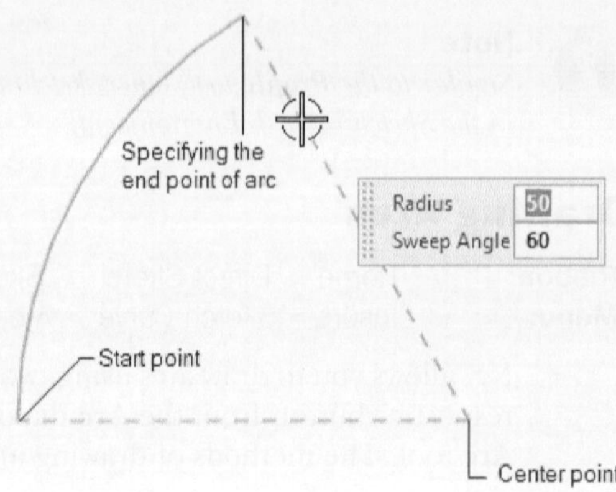

Figure 2-19 Drawing an arc by specifying its center, start, and end points

> **Tip**
> *After specifying the center point of the arc, you can also specify its radius and the sweep angle in the dynamic input boxes. In this case, you will be prompted to specify the start point and then the endpoint of the arc. The endpoint will define the direction of the arc.*

Drawing Circles

Ribbon:	Home > Direct Sketch > Sketch Curve Gallery > Circle
Menu:	Insert > Sketch Curve > Circle

In NX, you can draw circles using two methods. These methods can be activated by choosing their respective buttons from the **Circle** dialog box that are displayed when you invoke the **Circle** tool. The methods of drawing circles are discussed next.

Drawing a Circle by Specifying the Center Point and Diameter

This is the default and most widely used method of drawing circles. In this method, you need to specify the center point of a circle and a point on the circumference of the circle. The point on the circumference of the circle defines the radius or the diameter of the circle. To draw a circle using this method, choose the **Circle by Center and Diameter** button from the **Circle** dialog box; you will be prompted to specify the center point of the circle. Specify the center point of the circle in the drawing window. Next, you will be prompted to specify a point on the circle. Specify a point to define the radius. Alternatively, you can enter the value of the diameter in the dynamic input box. Figure 2-20 shows a circle being drawn by using this method.

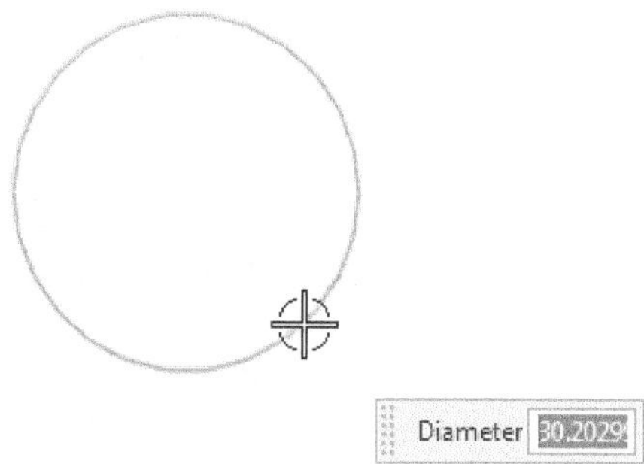

***Figure 2-20** A circle drawn using the Circle by Center and Diameter method*

> **Tip**
> *After specifying the center point of the circle, if you specify the value of diameter in the dynamic input box, the circle of the specified diameter will be created. Also, a preview of the circle of the same diameter will be attached to the cursor. Now, you can place multiple copies of the circle by specifying the center point.*

Drawing a Circle by Specifying Three Points

In this method, the circle is drawn by specifying three points on circumference. To invoke this method, choose the **Circle by 3 Points** button from the **Circle** dialog box; you will be prompted to specify the first point of the circle. This point is actually the first point on the circumference of the circle. After specifying the first point, you will be prompted to specify the second point of the circle. On specifying these two points, small reference circles will be displayed on these two points, as shown in Figure 2-21. Now, specify the third point, which is a point on the circle. You can also enter its diameter value in the **Diameter** input box. If you enter the diameter of the circle in the **Diameter** input box, you need to click in the drawing window to specify the placement point for the circle. This completes the creation of the circle.

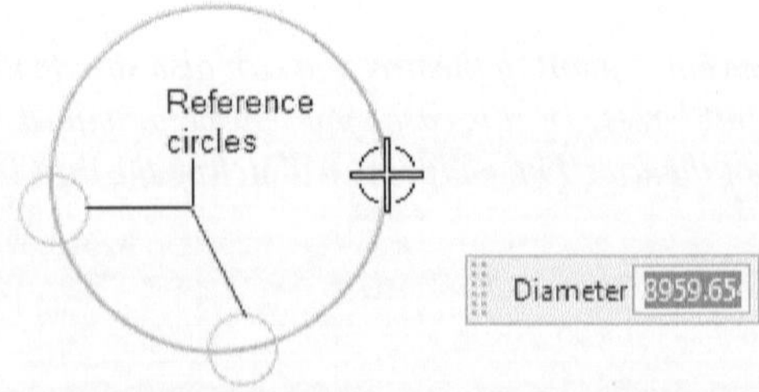

Figure 2-21 Circle drawn by using the 3 Points method

Drawing Rectangles

Ribbon:	Home > Direct Sketch > Sketch Curve Gallery > Rectangle
Menu:	Insert > Sketch Curve > Rectangle

In NX, you can draw rectangles by using three methods. These methods can be used by choosing their respective buttons from the **Rectangle** dialog box. To invoke this dialog box, choose the **Rectangle** tool from the **Direct Sketch** group. The three methods of drawing rectangles are discussed next.

Drawing Rectangles by Specifying Corners

The **By 2 Points** method is used to draw a rectangle by specifying the diagonally opposite corners of rectangle. When you invoke the **Rectangle** tool, the **By 2 Points** button is chosen by default in the **Rectangle Method** area of the **Rectangle** dialog box. Also, you will be prompted to specify the first point of the rectangle. This point will work as one of the corners of the rectangle. After specifying the first point, you will be prompted to specify the point to create the rectangle. This point will be diagonally opposite to the point that you have specified earlier. You can click anywhere on the screen to specify the second corner or enter the width and height of the rectangle in the dynamic input boxes. Figure 2-22 shows a rectangle being drawn by using the **By 2 Points** method.

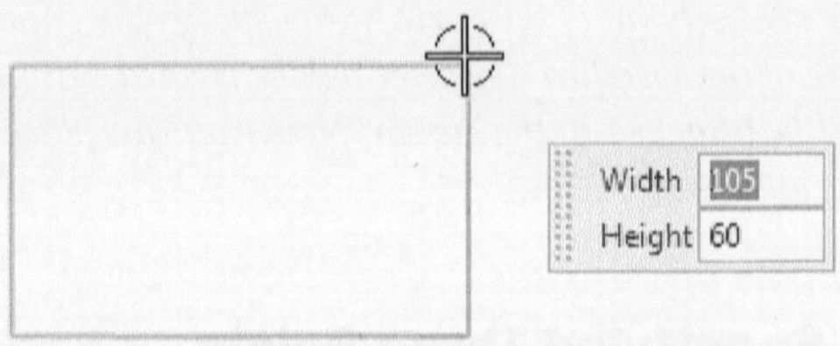

*Figure 2-22 Rectangle being drawn by using the **By 2 Points** method*

Tip

If you specify the width and height of a rectangle in the dynamic input boxes after specifying the first point, a preview of the rectangle with the specified width and height will be attached to the cursor. Now, you need to specify a point to define the direction of rectangle.

Drawing Three Points Rectangles

You can draw a three points rectangle by choosing the **By 3 Points** button from the **Rectangle** dialog box. In this method, you can draw a rectangle using three points. The first two points are used to define the length and angle of one of the sides of the rectangle and the third point is used to define the height of the rectangle. When you invoke this tool, you will be prompted to specify the first point of the rectangle. Once you specify the first point, you will be prompted to specify the second point of the rectangle. Both these corners are along the same direction. Therefore, these points define the length and orientation of the rectangle. Note that if you specify the second point at a certain angle, the resulting rectangle will also be at an angle. After specifying the second point, you will be prompted to specify a point to create the rectangle. This point is used to define the height of the rectangle. After specifying the first point, you can also specify the height, width, and the angle of the rectangle in the dynamic input boxes. Figure 2-23 shows an inclined rectangle drawn by using the **By 3 Points** method.

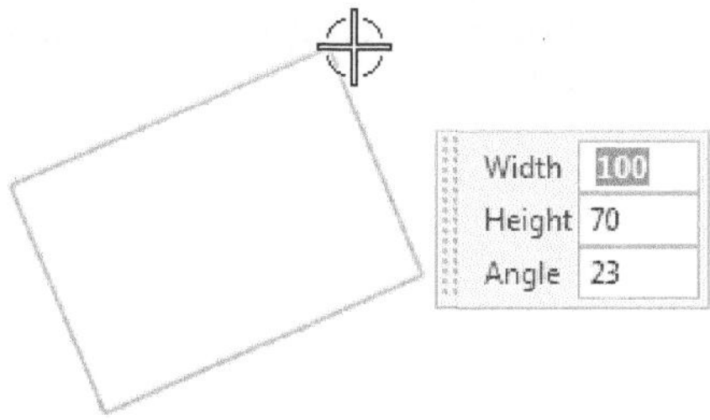

***Figure 2-23** Inclined rectangle drawn by using the **By 3 Points** method*

> **Tip**
> *After specifying the first point of a rectangle, you can toggle between the **By 2 Points** and **By 3 Points** buttons by dragging the left mouse button.*

Drawing Centerpoint Rectangles

You can draw a centerpoint rectangle by choosing the **From Center** button in the **Rectangle** dialog box. Using this method, you can draw a rectangle using three points. However, the first point is taken as the center of the rectangle in this case. When you invoke this tool, you will be prompted to specify the center point of the rectangle. Once you specify the center point, you will be prompted to specify the second point of the rectangle. Both these points are along the same direction. Therefore, these points define the width of the rectangle. Note that if you specify the second point at a certain angle, the resulting rectangle will also be created at that specified angle. After specifying the second point, you will be prompted to specify a point to create the rectangle. This point is used to define the height of the rectangle. Alternatively, you can specify the height, width, and angle of the rectangle in the dynamic input boxes which appear after you specify the first point for creating the rectangle.

Placing Points

Ribbon:	Home > Direct Sketch > Sketch Curve Gallery > Point
Menu:	Insert > Datum/Point > Point

In NX, you can place points by clicking in the drawing window. To place a point, choose the **Point** tool from the **Direct Sketch** group; the **Sketch Point** dialog box will be displayed, refer to Figure 2-24, and you will be prompted to select a point. Click in the drawing window; the point will be placed at the specified location. Also, the horizontal and vertical dimensions between the point and the origin point of the sketch will be displayed. You can edit these dimensions to change the location of the point.

> **Tip**
> *If tools to be invoked are not visible by default in the* ***Direct Sketch*** *group of the* ***Home*** *tab, you need to expand the* ***Sketch Curve*** *gallery of the* ***Direct Sketch*** *group. To expand the* ***Sketch Curve*** *gallery, click on the down arrow available at the lower right corner in the* ***Direct Sketch*** *group.*

You can also place a point by using the **Point** dialog box. To invoke this dialog box, choose the **Point Dialog** button from the **Sketch Point** dialog box; the **Point** dialog box will be displayed, refer to Figure 2-25 and you will be prompted to select the object to infer point. This dialog box contains four main rollouts, **Point Location**, **Output Coordinates**, **Offset,** and **Settings**. The options in these rollouts are discussed next.

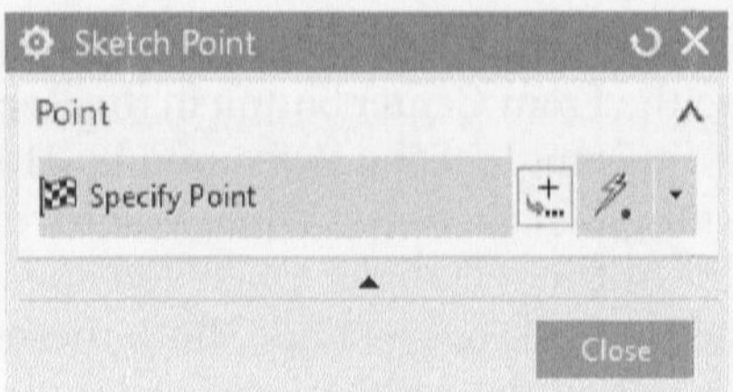

Figure 2-24 The ***Sketch Point*** *dialog box*

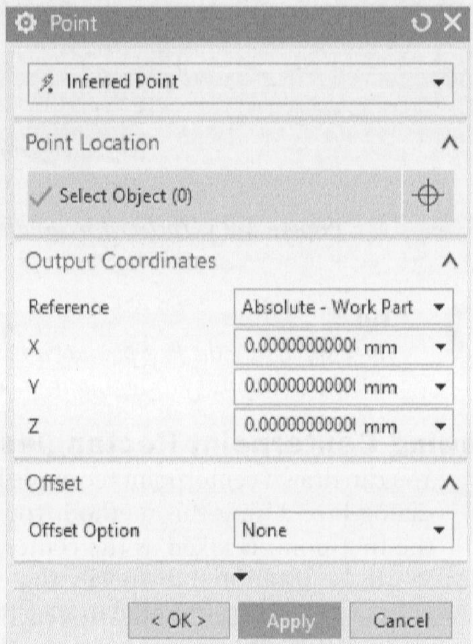

Figure 2-25 The ***Point*** *dialog box*

Type Drop-down List

Select an option from the drop-down list to specify the location for the resulting point. The options are discussed next.

Inferred Point

This option is selected by default. This option allows you to place a point in the drawing window. However, if there are some entities in the drawing window, then this option helps you to select the keypoints of the entity. For example, if there are a few lines in the drawing window, then this option helps you to select the endpoints or the midpoints of the lines.

Cursor Location

This option allows you to place a point at a location where you will click the cursor in the drawing window. If the **Cursor Location** option is selected, then the other entities in the drawing window will not be considered.

Existing Point

This option allows you to select the points that are already placed in the drawing window. As a result, you can place new point on top of the existing point.

End Point

This option allows you to place the point at the endpoint of the existing lines, arcs, or splines.

Control Point

This option allows you to place the point at the control point of the existing sketched entities. The control points include the endpoints and midpoints of lines or arcs, center points of circles, ellipses, control points of splines, and so on.

Intersection Point

This option allows you to place the point at the intersection point of the two existing sketched entities. To do so, select the **Intersection Point** option from the Type drop-down list; you will be prompted to select the first and second intersecting entities. Specify the two intersecting entities in the drawing area; a point will be placed at the intersection point of the two existing entities.

Arc/Ellipse/Sphere Center

This option allows you to place the point at the center of an existing arc, circle, ellipse, or sphere.

Angle on Arc/Ellipse

This option allows you to place the point on the circumference of the selected arc, circle, or ellipse such that the resulting point is at the specified angle with respect to X-axis. When you choose this option, the **Point** dialog box will be modified and you will be prompted to select an arc or an ellipse. Select the arc or the ellipse in the drawing; the point will be placed on the circumference of the selected entity. Next, enter the angle value for the point in the **Angle** edit box of the **Angle on Curve** rollout.

Quadrant Point

This option allows you to place the point at the quadrant of a circle, arc, or an ellipse. The point will be placed at the quadrant that is closest to the current location of the cursor.

Point on Curve/Edge

This option allows you to place the point on the selected curve or edge. The location of the point is defined in terms of its curve parameter percentage from the start point of the curve. When you select the **Point on Curve/Edge** option, the **Point** dialog box will be modified and you will be prompted to select the curve to specify the point location. Click anywhere on the curve or the edge; you will be prompted to specify the curve parameter percentage. You can specify the curve parameter by using the **Location** drop-down list in the **Location on Curve** rollout of the **Point** dialog box. You can also enter the distance of the point in the **Curve Length** edit box of the **Location on Curve** rollout.

Point on Face

This option allows you to place the point on the selected face. The location of the point is defined by specifying values in the **U Parameter** and **V Parameter** edit boxes. The **U Parameter** edit box is used to specify the horizontal position of the point whereas the **V Parameter** is used to specify the vertical position of the point. The values of these edit boxes must lie between 0.0 and 1.0. As value of the **U Parameter** edit box increases, the position of the point shifts from right to left; and if the value of the **V Parameter** edit box increases, the position of the point shifts from bottom to top. Note that this option will be available only when you invoke the **Point** dialog box by choosing **Menu > Insert > Datum/Point > Point** from the **Top Border Bar** in the Modeling environment.

Between Two Points

This option allows you to create a point between two existing points or between two keypoints of an entity. When you select this option from the Type drop-down list, the **Point** dialog box will be modified and you will be prompted to select object to infer point. Select the first point from the drawing window; you will be prompted again to select object to infer point. Select the second point; a point will be created between the two selected points. You can change the location of this point by entering the percentage value in the **%Location** edit box of the **Location Between Points** rollout.

By Expression

This option allows you to specify a point expression by using the X, Y, and Z coordinates. When you select this option from the Type drop-down list, the **Point** dialog box will be modified with new rollouts such as **Choose Expression**, **Output Coordinates**, and **Offset**. The **Choose Expression** rollout is used to display the point expression created already in the part. To create a new expression, choose the **Create Expression** button; the **Expressions** dialog box will be invoked displaying the **Visibility** and **Actions** rollouts. To create a new expression, choose the **New Expression** button from the **Actions** rollout. Next, enter the name of the point expression in the **Name** edit box and then edit the point formula as per your requirement in the **Formula** edit box. Once you have edited the values of the X, Y, and Z coordinates in the **Formula** edit box, choose the **OK** button from this dialog box; the **Point** dialog box will be displayed. The newly created point expression will be listed in the list box available in the **Choose Expression** rollout. Select the point expression from the list and then choose the **OK** button from the **Point** dialog box; a point will be created with the specified coordinates in the expression.

Point Location Rollout

This rollout is used to place a point in the drawing area and will not be available for the **Intersection Point**, **Angle on Arc/Ellipse**, **Point on Curve/Edge**, and **Point on Face** options.

Output Coordinates Rollout

This rollout is used to enter the X, Y, and Z coordinates to specify the location of the point. Also, you can specify or determine the 3D location of the points using this rollout. You can specify the point relative to the Work Coordinate System (WCS) or Absolute Coordinate System by selecting respective options from the **Reference** drop-down list in the **Output Coordinates** rollout.

Offset Rollout

This rollout is used to create a point at a specified distance from a pre-selected point. You can select an option to specify the distance of the required point from the **Offset Option** drop-down list in this rollout. The options in this drop-down list are discussed next.

Rectangular

This option allows you to create a point by specifying its X, Y, Z coordinates with respect to the pre-selected point in the **Delta X**, **Delta Y**, and **Delta Z** edit boxes, respectively.

Cylindrical

This option allows you to create a point according to the cylindrical coordinate system with respect to the pre-selected point by specifying the radius, angle, and Z direction coordinate values in the **Radius**, **Angle**, and **Delta Z** edit boxes, respectively.

Spherical

This option allows you to create a point according to the spherical coordinate system with respect to the pre-selected point by specifying the Radius, Angle 1, and Angle 2 in their respective edit boxes.

Along Vector

This option allows you to create a point along the specified vector direction at a distance specified in the **Distance** edit box.

Along Curve

This option allows you to create a point along the specified curve. The distance of the point along the arc can be specified by entering the **Arc Length** or **Percentage** value in the respective edit box.

Drawing Ellipses or Elliptical Arcs

Ribbon:	Home > Direct Sketch > Sketch Curve Gallery > Ellipse
Menu:	Insert > Sketch Curve > Ellipse

In NX, you can draw ellipses or elliptical arcs by using the **Ellipse** tool. To invoke this tool, choose **Menu > Insert > Sketch Curve > Ellipse** option from the **Top Border Bar**; the **Ellipse** dialog box will be displayed, as shown in Figure 2-26. Also, you will be prompted to select a point to specify the center point of the ellipse.

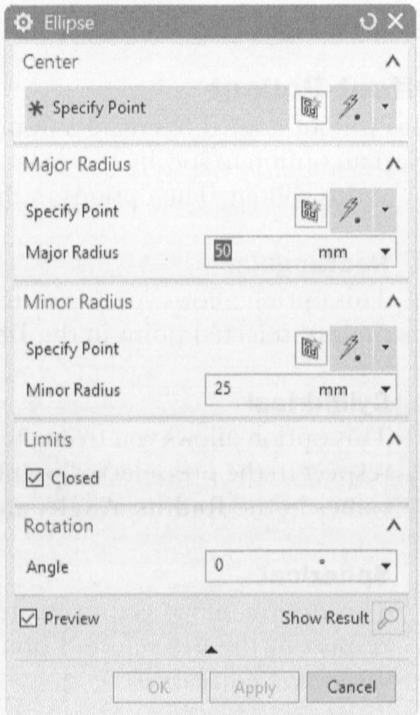

*Figure 2-26 The **Ellipse** dialog box*

Note

*By default, the **Ellipse** tool is not visible in the **Sketch Curve** gallery of the **Direct Sketch** group. You can click on the down or up arrow available on the right corner of this area to display the **Ellipse** tool and other set of sketching tools available in this gallery.*

Click anywhere on the screen. Choose the **Point Dialog** button from the **Center** rollout; the **Point** dialog box will be displayed, refer to Figure 2-25. Using the **Point** dialog box, you can define the center point of the ellipse. Alternatively, you can define the center point of the ellipse by selecting the required option from the **Inferred Point** drop-down list available in the **Center** rollout. After defining the center point by using the **Point** dialog box, choose the **OK** button from it; the **Ellipse** dialog box will be displayed again. Also, a preview of the ellipse will be displayed. Next, specify the major and the minor radii of the ellipse in the **Major Radius** and **Minor Radius** edit boxes in the **Ellipse** dialog box, respectively. If you want to draw an elliptical arc, clear the **Closed** check box in the **Limits** rollout; the **Ellipse** dialog box will be modified and the **Start Angle** and **End Angle** edit boxes for the arc will appear in it. You can specify the start and end angles in their respective edit boxes. Figure 2-27 shows the parameters related to an ellipse and Figure 2-28 shows the parameters related to an elliptical arc. If you want to retain the complement of the elliptical arc, choose the **Complement** button below the **End Angle** edit box in the **Limits** rollout; the preview of the complement of the elliptical arc will be displayed. Figure 2-29 shows an elliptical arc and Figure 2-30 shows the complement of the elliptical arc. Note that Figure 2-27 shows an inclined ellipse. To create an inclined ellipse, you need to enter rotation angle in the **Angle** edit box of the **Rotation** rollout. The specified angle value will be measured with respect to X-axis in the counterclockwise direction.

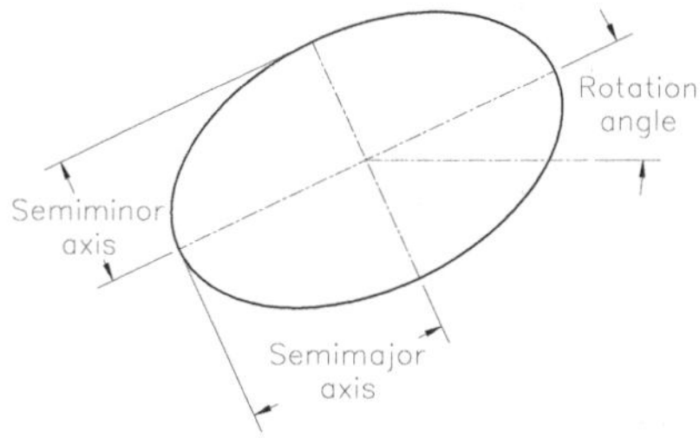

Figure 2-27 Parameters related to an ellipse

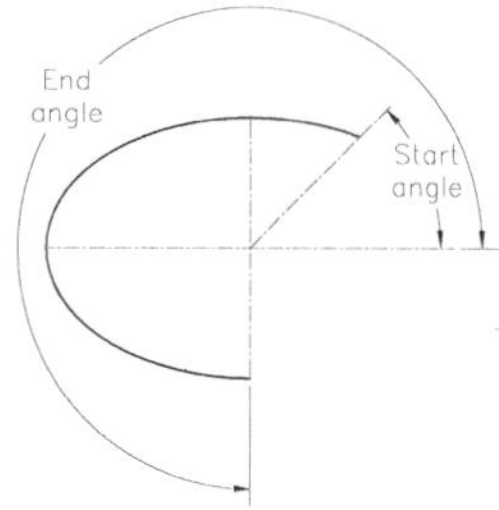

Figure 2-28 Parameters related to an elliptical arc

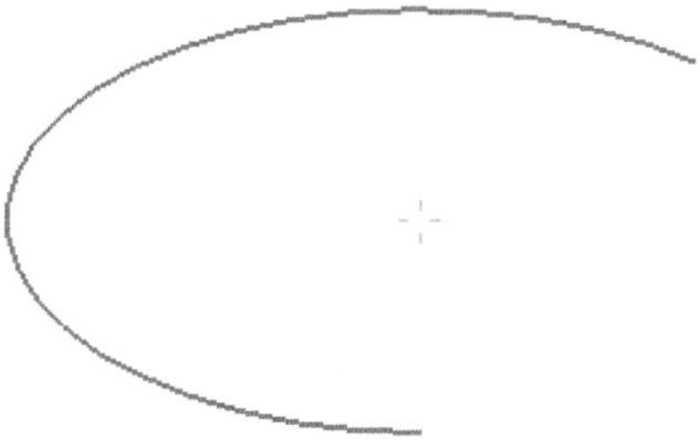

Figure 2-29 An elliptical arc

Figure 2-30 Complement of the elliptical arc shown in Figure 2-29

Drawing Conics

Ribbon:	Home > Direct Sketch > Sketch Curve Gallery > Conic
Menu:	Insert > Sketch Curve > Conic

The **Conic** tool allows you to create a conic section in the sketching environment using three points. The first two points define the endpoints of the conic and the third point defines the apex of the conic. Also, you need to specify the projective discriminant value, termed as rho value. To invoke the **Conic** tool, choose **Menu > Insert > Sketch Curve > Conic** from the **Top Border Bar**; the **Conic** dialog box will be displayed, as shown in Figure 2-31. In this dialog box, you can specify the start point and end point of the conic using the options in the **Limits** rollout. After specifying the start point and the endpoint of the conic, you need to specify the apex of the conic as the third point. Specify the apex of the conic by using the options in the **Specify Control Point** area of the **Control Point** rollout. Next, enter the Rho value in the **Value** edit box.

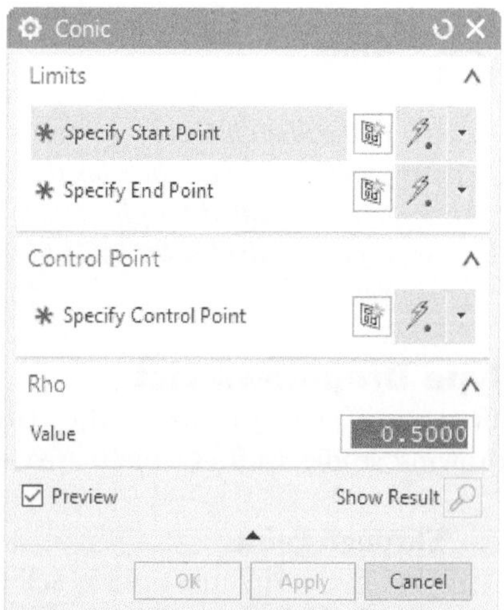

*Figure 2-31 The **Conic** dialog box*

This Rho value will define the exact shape of conics.

If 0 < Rho < 0.5, then conics of elliptical shape will be created.
If Rho = 0.5, then conics of parabolic shape will be created.

If 0.5 < Rho < 1, then conics of hyperbolic shape will be created.

Figure 2-32 shows conics with different Rho values.

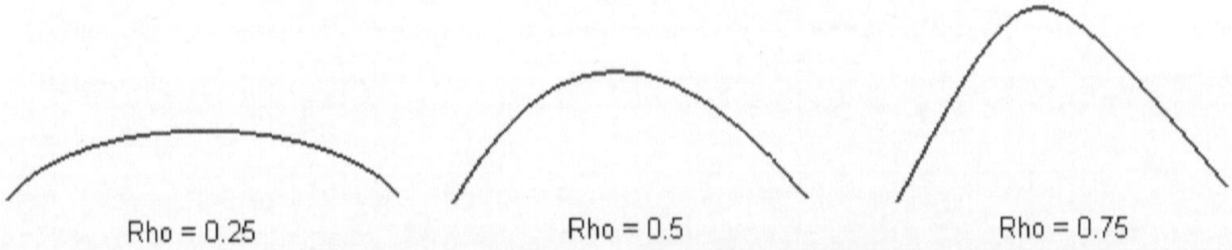

Figure 2-32 Conics with different Rho values

> **Tip**
> *Sometimes while placing points or drawing an ellipse, some red cross marks are displayed on the screen. To remove them, refresh the screen by pressing the F5 key.*

Drawing Studio Splines

Ribbon:	Home > Direct Sketch > Sketch Curve Gallery > Studio Spline
Menu:	Insert > Sketch Curve > Studio Spline

The **Studio Spline** tool allows you to create studio splines for creating free form features. When you invoke this tool, the **Studio Spline** dialog box will be displayed, as shown in Figure 2-33. The various rollouts in this dialog box are discussed next.

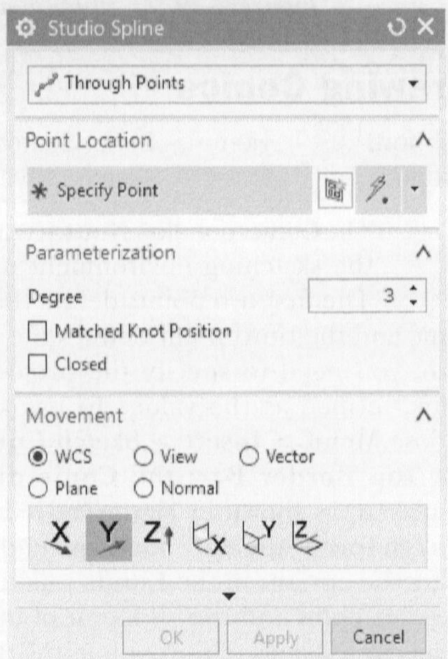

*Figure 2-33 The **Studio Spline** dialog box*

> **Note**
> *There are some tools that are not visible by default in the **Sketch Curve** gallery of the **Direct Sketch** group. You can click on the down or up arrow available on the right corner of **Direct Sketch** group to display the tools that are not visible by default.*

Type Drop-down List

There are two options in the drop-down list for drawing studio splines which are discussed next.

Through Points

This is the default option selected for drawing splines. Here, you can specify continuous points in the drawing area by clicking the left mouse button. These points will act as the defining points of the spline. While drawing a spline, you can move these points to change the shape of the spline, and then continue drawing the spline. Figure 2-34 shows a spline being drawn by using this method.

By Poles

If you select this option,, the points that you specify in the drawing window act as the poles of the spline. Figure 2-35 shows a spline being drawn by using this method. Remember that the display of poles is automatically removed when you finish drawing the spline.

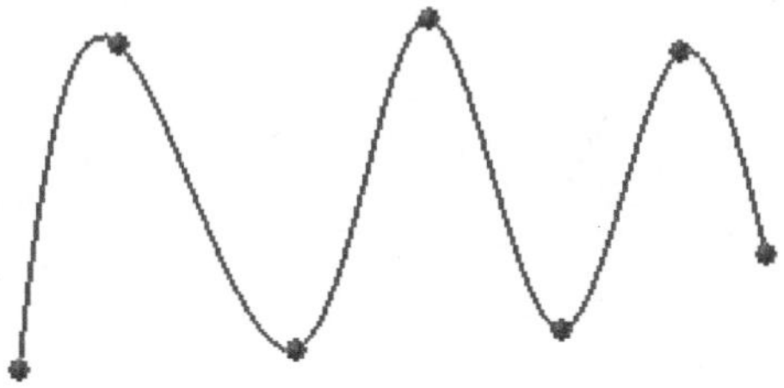

*Figure 2-34 Drawing a spline by using the **Through Points** option*

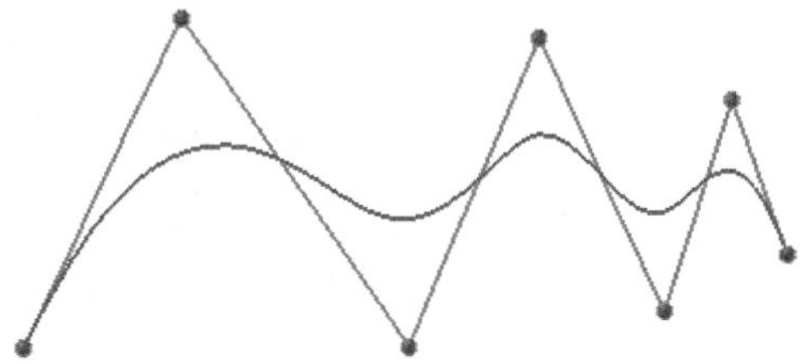

*Figure 2-35 Drawing a spline by using the **By Poles** option*

Point Location / Pole Location Rollout

The options in this rollout are used to specify the spline point or pole location. You can use the **Point Constructor** button to create or locate a point.

Parameterization Rollout

The options in this rollout are used to specify the parameters of the spline.

Degree Spinner

The **Degree** spinner is used to specify the degree of a spline. Figures 2-36 and 2-37 show splines of various degrees. Note that the degree of a spline cannot be more than the number of poles used to draw it.

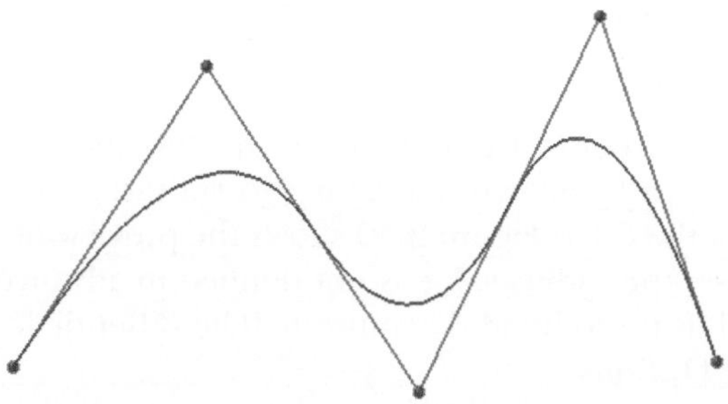

Figure 2-36 Spline of degree 2

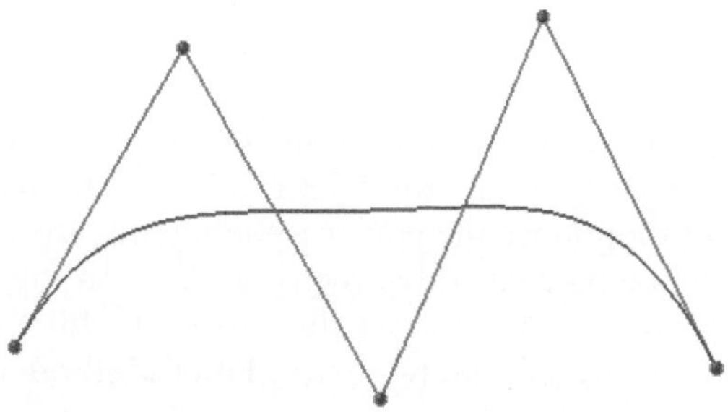

Figure 2-37 Spline of degree 4

Single Segment

This check box is available only when you select the **By Poles** option and is used to create a single segment spline. However, you can specify as many numbers of poles as you require. If you select this check box, the **Closed** check box will not be activated.

Matched Knot Position

This check box is available only when you select the **Through Points** option and is used to create a spline by matching the position of the defining points with the knots. In this case, the knots are placed only at the places where the defining points are specified. If you select this check box, the **Closed** check box will not be activated.

Closed

This check box is available for both the methods and is used to create closed splines. Figure 2-38 shows a closed spline.

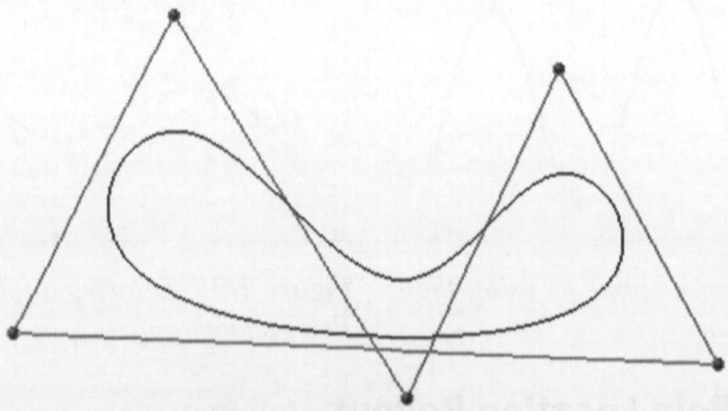

Figure 2-38 A closed spline

Filleting Sketched Entities

Ribbon:	Home > Direct Sketch > Sketch Curve Gallery > Fillet
Menu:	Insert > Sketch Curve > Fillet

Filleting is defined as the process of rounding the sharp corners of a profile to reduce the stress concentration. Fillets are created by removing the sharp corners and replacing them with round corners. In NX, you can create a fillet between any two sketched entities. You can also create a fillet using three sketched entities.

To create fillets, invoke the **Fillet** tool; the **Fillet** dialog box will be displayed, as shown in Figure 2-39. Also, you will be prompted to select or drag the cursor over curves to create a fillet.

The **Radius** dynamic input box will be displayed below the cursor. You do not need to necessarily specify the fillet radius in advance. Instead, you can select the two entities to fillet and then move the cursor to define the radius of the fillet. Figure 2-40 shows the preview of a fillet being created between two lines. In this case, the radius value is not defined in advance. As a result, as you move the cursor, the fillet radius is modified dynamically. The **Fillet** dialog box is divided into two areas, **Fillet Method** and **Options**.

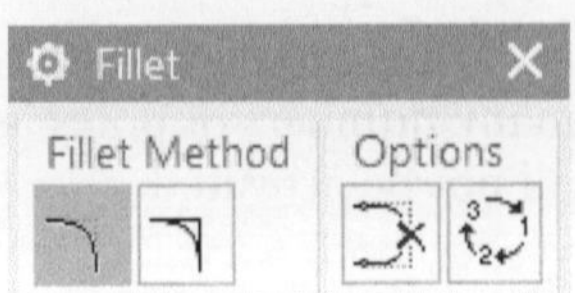

*Figure 2-39 The **Fillet** dialog box*

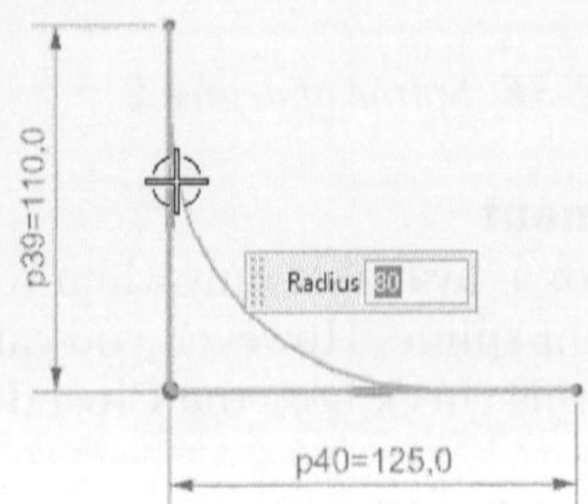

Figure 2-40 Preview of a fillet being created between two lines

Fillet Method Area

The first button in this area is the **Trim** button and is chosen by default. As a result, the sharp corner will automatically be trimmed after filleting, as shown in Figure 2-41. If you choose the **Untrim** button, the sharp corner will not be trimmed after filleting, as shown in Figure 2-42.

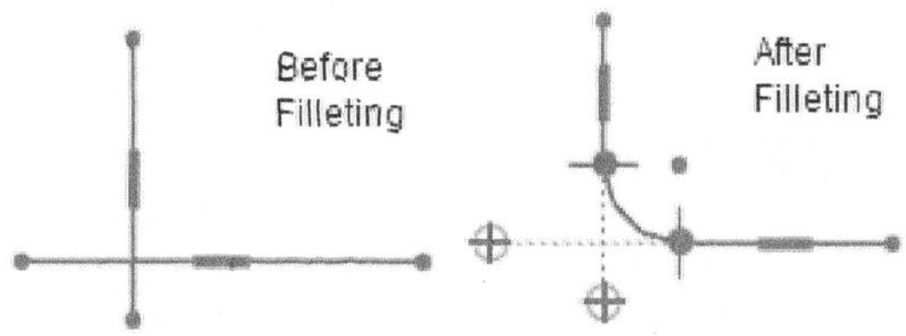

*Figure 2-41 Sharp corner before and after filleting using the **Trim** button*

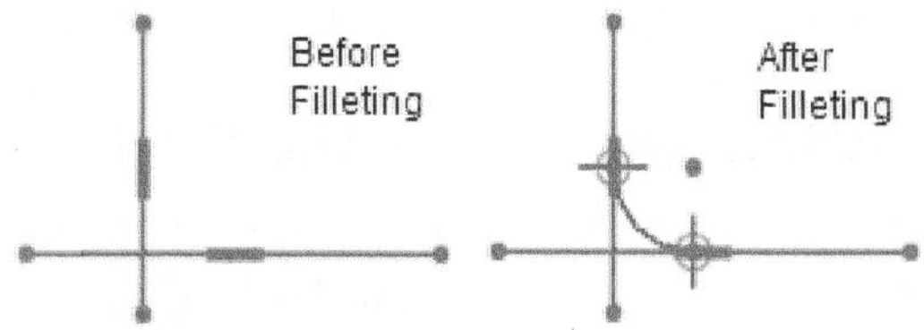

*Figure 2-42 Sharp corner before and after filleting using the **Untrim** button*

Tip

Ideally, the profiles created with the fillet may not give the desired result when used to create features. Therefore, they should be avoided in the sketch.

Options Area

The **Delete Third Curve** button in this area is useful if you are creating a fillet by using three entities. While using this option, the middle entity should be selected last. This button ensures that if the fillet is tangent to the middle entity then the middle entity is automatically deleted, as shown in Figure 2-43. If this button is deactivated, the middle entity will not be deleted, as shown in Figure 2-44. The **Create Alternate Fillet** button in this area will show all the alternative solutions for the fillet. It is recommended that this button should be turned off.

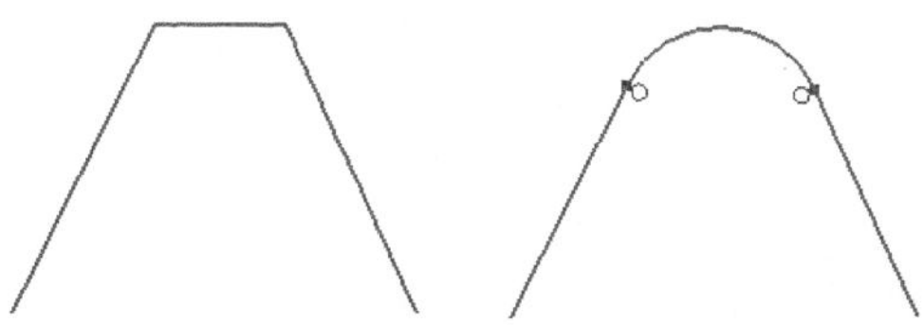

Figure 2-43 The entity before and after filleting with the third curve deleted

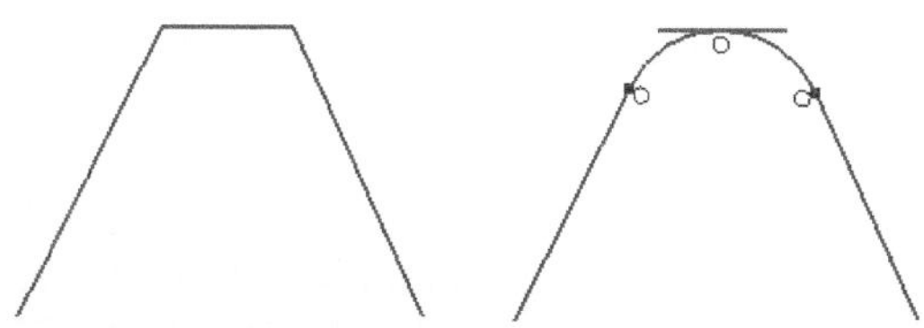

Figure 2-44 The entity before and after filleting with the third curve retained

Tip

*1. In NX, you can create fillets by simply dragging the cursor across the entities that you need to fillet. For example, if you need to create a fillet between two lines, invoke the **Fillet** tool and drag the cursor across them; the corner of these two lines will be filleted. The radius of the fillet will depend on how far you dragged the mouse from the corner.*

2. When you fillet two entities, if there is more than one solution for fillet, then the best solution will be displayed by default. If you want to view the alternate solution, press the PAGE UP key.

THE DRAWING DISPLAY TOOLS

The drawing display tools are an integral part of any solid modeling tool. These tools enable you to zoom, pan, and rotate the drawing so that you can view it clearly. The drawing display tools in NX are located in the **View** tab in the **Ribbon** and the methods of using these tools are discussed next.

Note

As most of the drawing display tools are transparent tools, you can use them at any time without exiting the other tool you are working with.

Fitting Entities in the Current Display

Ribbon:	View > Operation > Fit
Menu:	View > Operation > Fit

The **Fit** tool enables you to modify the drawing display area such that all entities in the drawing fit in the current display. You can also use the CTRL+F keys to fit the entities in the current display.

Zooming an Area

Ribbon:	View > Zoom > Zoom
Menu:	View > Operation > Zoom

The **Zoom** tool allows you to zoom into a particular area by defining a box around it. When you choose this tool, the default cursor is replaced by a magnifying glass cursor and you will be prompted to drag the cursor to indicate the zoom rectangle. Specify a point on the screen to define the first corner of the zoom area. Next, hold the left mouse button and drag the cursor. Now, release the left mouse button to specify another point to define the opposite corner of the zoom area. The area defined inside the rectangle will be zoomed and displayed on the screen.

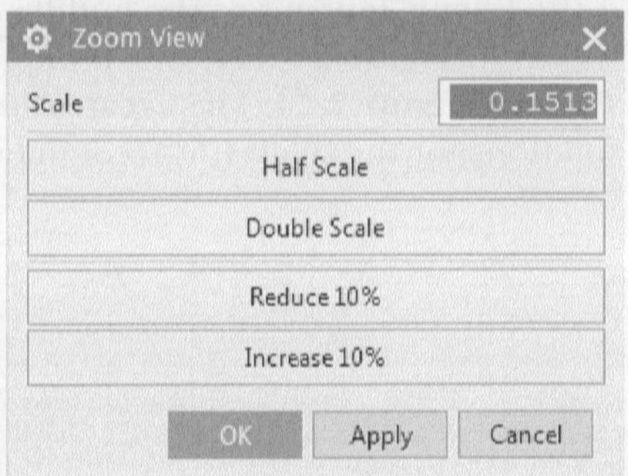

*Figure 2-45 The **Zoom View** dialog box*

You can also zoom in or out a drawing by specifying a scale value. To do so, choose **Menu > View > Operation > Zoom** from the **Top Border Bar**; the **Zoom View** dialog box will be displayed, as shown in Figure 2-45. Specify a scale value in the **Scale** edit box. In addition, you can also use the **Half Scale**, **Double Scale**, **Reduce 10%**, and **Increase 10%** buttons to zoom in or out of the drawing.

Dynamic Zooming

Ribbon:	View > Zoom > Zoom In/Out *(Customize to Add)*

The **Zoom In/Out** tool enables you to dynamically zoom in or out of the drawing. When you invoke this tool, the default cursor is changed into a magnifying glass cursor with a '+' and a '-' sign at the center of the cursor. To zoom in, press and hold the left mouse button in the drawing window and then drag the cursor upward. Similarly, to zoom out, press and hold the left mouse button and drag the cursor down.

Panning Drawings

Ribbon: View > Operation > Pan
Menu: View > Operation > Pan

The **Pan** tool allows you to dynamically pan drawings in the drawing window. When you invoke this tool, the cursor is replaced by a hand cursor and you will be prompted to drag the cursor to pan the view. Press and hold the left mouse button in the drawing window and then drag the mouse to pan the drawing.

> **Tip**
> *In NX, you can also display the Selection MiniBar and the View shortcut menu by right-clicking in the drawing area. The Selection MiniBar is a compact version of the* ***Selection Group****.*

Fitting View to Selection

Ribbon: View > Operation > Fit View to Selection *(Customize to Add)*
Menu: View > Operation > Fit View to Selection

The **Fit View to Selection** tool zooms the display such that the selected entity fits in the current display area. This tool is available only when an entity is selected in the drawing window. Note that, this tool will be active only in the sketching environment.

Restoring the Original Orientation of the Sketching Plane

Ribbon: Home > Direct Sketch > More > Sketch Tools > Orient to Sketch *(Customize to Add)*
Menu: View > Orient View to Sketch

Sometimes while using the drawing display tools, you may change the orientation of the sketching plane. The **Orient View to Sketch** tool restores the original orientation that was active when you invoked the Sketch in Task Environment. This tool is available only in the Sketch in Task Environment.

SETTING SELECTION FILTERS IN THE SKETCH IN TASK ENVIRONMENT

NX provides you with various object selection filters in the Sketch in Task Environment. These filters allow you to define the types of entities you want to select. All these filters are available in the **Selection Group** on the upper left corner in the **Top Border Bar** of the drawing window. Some of these filters are discussed next.

Type Filter

The **Type Filter** drop-down list is used to specify the type of entity to be selected as filter type. By default, the **No Selection Filter** option is selected, refer to Figure 2-46. This option allows you to select any entity from the drawing window. These entities include sketch, datums, curve, point, face, and so on. Select the required entity from the **Type Filter** drop-down list. Now, you can select only the specified entity from the drawing window.

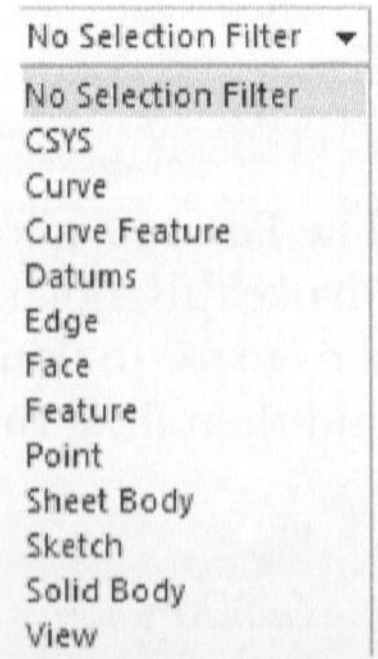

Figure 2-46 The Type Filter drop-down list

Selection Scope

This drop-down list allows you to filter the selection from the entire assembly, within the workpart and components, the workpart only, or the active sketch only. Select the required option from the **Selection Scope** drop-down list.

General Selection Filters

This flyout provides the detailed filter options. The options in the **General Selection Filters** flyout, as shown in Figure 2-47, are discussed next.

Detailed Filtering

This option is used to filter the selection using layers, type of entity, display attributes, and detailed types of entity. Select the **Detailed Filtering** option in the **General Selection Filters** flyout; the **Detailed Filtering** dialog box will be displayed. In this dialog box, you can specify layers, types of entity, details of the types of entity, and display attributes that you need to filter.

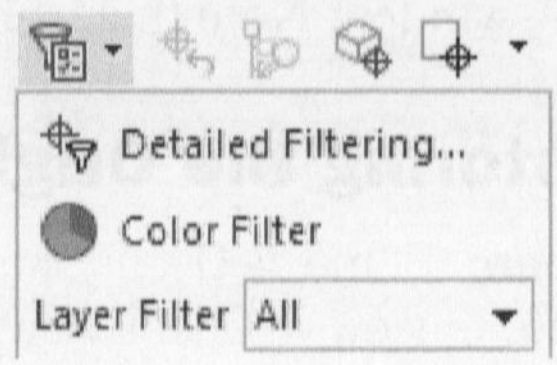

*Figure 2-47 The **General Selection Filters** flyout*

Color Filter

This option allows you to filter the selection using a specific color. Only the entities in the specified color will be selected.

Layer Filter

This drop-down list allows you to filter the selection using a specific layer. You need to select the layer from the **Layer Filter** drop-down list and the entities in this layer can only be selected. By default, the **All** option is selected, which allows to select the entities from all the layers.

Reset Filters

This tool is used to reset all the filtering options defined in the **General Selection Filters** flyout and the **Type Filter** drop-down list to their default states.

Allow Selection of Hidden Wireframe

This tool allows you to select the hidden wireframe geometries such as curves and edges.

Deselect All

When you choose this tool, all the currently selected entities are deselected.

Find in Navigator

This tool is used to highlight the selected entities in the **Part Navigator** or **Assembly Navigator** and will be activated only when you select an entity. Select the entities that you want to highlight in the **Part Navigator** or **Assembly Navigator** and choose the **Find in Navigator** tool in the **Selection Bar**. Next, choose the **Part Navigator** tab from the **Resource Bar** to view the highlighted entities. Note that, this tool will not be available in the **Sketch in Task Environment**.

SELECTING OBJECTS

After setting the selection filters, you can select objects in the drawing window of NX. When no tool is active, the select mode will be invoked. In this mode, you can select individual sketched entities from the drawing window by clicking on them. NX provides three methods for selection of multiple entities. If you want to select multiple entities at once, you can use the tools available in the **Multi-Select Gesture Drop-down** of the **Selection Group** in the **Top Border Bar**. These tools are discussed next.

Rectangle

If you choose this tool from the **Multi-Select Gesture Drop-down** of the **Selection Group** in the **Top Border Bar** and drag the cursor in the drawing window, a temporary rectangle will be created. Also, all the objects lying completely within the temporary rectangle will get selected.

Lasso

If you choose this tool from the **Multi-Select Gesture Drop-down** of the **Selection Group** in the **Top Border Bar** and drag the cursor in the drawing window, a temporary free form curve will be created. Also, all the objects lying completely within the free form curve will get selected.

Circle

If you choose this tool from the **Multi-Select Gesture Drop-down** of the **Selection Group** in the **Top Border Bar** and drag the cursor in the drawing window, a temporary circle will be created. Also, all the objects lying completely within the temporary circle will get selected.

DESELECTING OBJECTS

By default, the selected objects are displayed in orange color. If you want to deselect the individual entities from the selection, press and hold the SHIFT key and click on the particular entity you want to exclude from the selection group; the entity will be deselected. If you want to deselect all the selected entities, press the ESC key. Alternatively, press and hold the SHIFT key and drag a box around the entities; all the entities that lie completely inside the box will get deselected. Also, you can choose the **Deselect All** tool from the **Selection Group** in the **Top Border Bar** to deselect all the selected entities.

USING SNAP POINTS OPTIONS WHILE SKETCHING

While drawing a sketch, you will notice that the cursor automatically snaps to some keypoints of the sketched entities. For example, if you are specifying the center point of a circle and you move the cursor close to the endpoint of an existing line, the cursor snaps to the endpoint of the line and changes into a snap cursor. Also, the endpoint snap symbol is displayed below the cursor. This suggests that the endpoint of the line has been snapped and if you click now, the center point of the circle will coincide with the endpoint of the line.

NX allows you to control these snap settings using the snap points options in the **Selection Group** in the **Top Border Bar**, as shown in Figure 2-48. In this bar, some of the tools are chosen by default. You can choose more tools to turn on the respective snapping option.

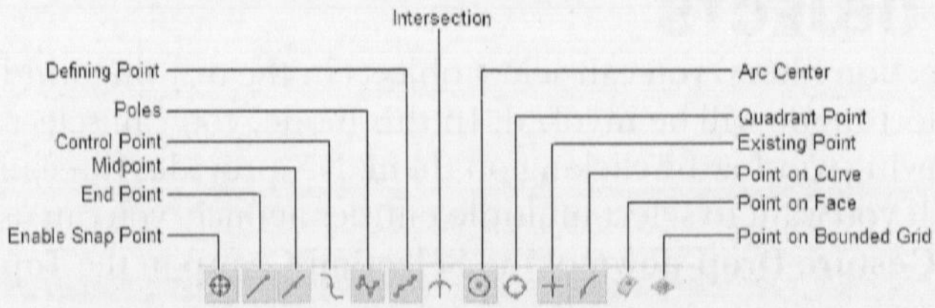

Figure 2-48 Buttons used for snap settings

DELETING SKETCHED ENTITIES

Menu:	Edit > Delete

You can delete the sketched entities by selecting them and pressing the DELETE key. You can also delete a sketched entity by choosing **Menu > Edit > Delete** tool from the **Top Border Bar**. However, if you choose this tool without selecting any sketched entity, the **Class Selection** dialog box will be displayed, as shown in Figure 2-49. You can now select the entities to be deleted and then choose the **OK** button in this dialog box. To close the dialog box, choose the **OK** or **Cancel** button.

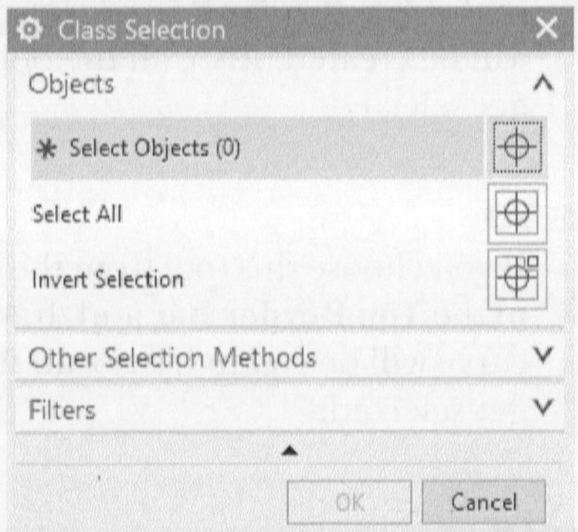

*Figure 2-49 The **Class Selection** dialog box*

EXITING THE SKETCH ENVIRONMENT

Ribbon:	Home > Direct Sketch > Finish Sketch

Finish Sketch

After drawing the sketch, you need to exit the sketching environment to convert the sketch into a feature. To exit the sketching environment, choose the **Finish Sketch** tool from the **Direct Sketch** group of the **Home** tab in the **Ribbon**. Alternatively, right-click in the drawing area and choose the **Finish Sketch** option from the shortcut menu. When you exit the sketching environment, you can convert the sketch into a solid model by using the solid modeling tools. Note that you can also invoke solid modeling tools without exiting from the sketching environment.

TUTORIALS

As mentioned in the introduction, NX is parametric in nature. Therefore, you can draw a sketch of any dimensions and then modify its size by changing the values of dimensions. However, in this chapter, you will use the dynamic input boxes to draw the sketch of exact dimensions. This will help you improve your sketching skills.

Tutorial 1

In this tutorial, you will draw a profile for the base feature of the model shown in Figure 2-50. The profile to be drawn is shown in Figure 2-51. **(Expected time: 30 min)**

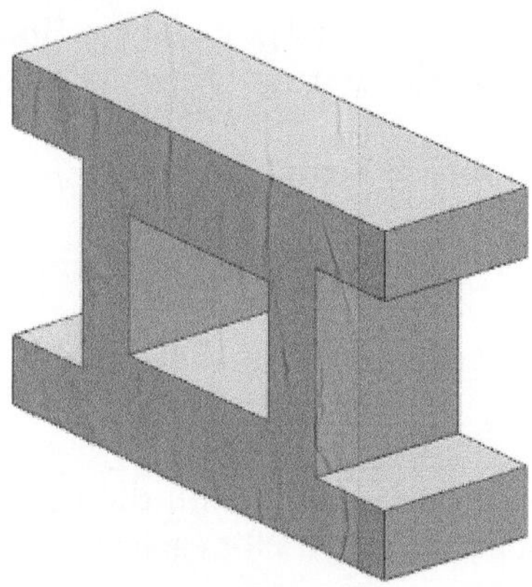

Figure 2-50 *Model for Tutorial 1*

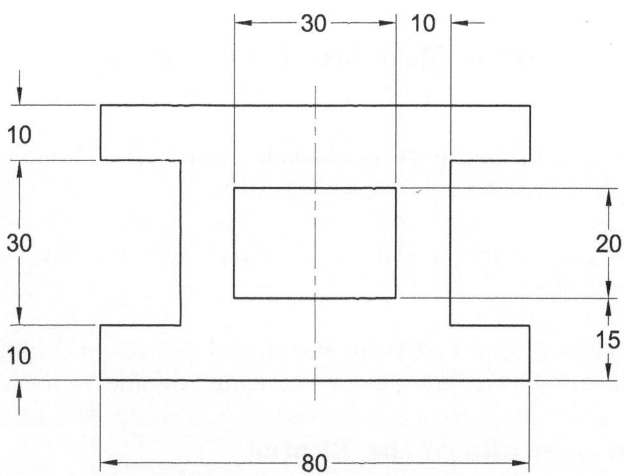

Figure 2-51 *Sketch for Tutorial 1*

The following steps are required to complete this tutorial:

a. Start a new file.
b. Select the XC-ZC plane as the sketching plane.
c. Draw the sketch of the model by using the **Profile** and **Rectangle** tools.
d. Finish the sketch and save the file.

Starting NX and Opening a New File

First, you need to start NX and then open a new file.

1. Double-click on NX shortcut icon on the desktop of your computer to start NX.

2. Choose the **New** button from the **Standard** group of the **Home** tab or choose **Menu > File > New** from the **Top Border Bar**; the **New** dialog box is displayed.

3. Select the **Model** template from the **Templates** rollout.

4. Enter **c02tut1** as the name of the document in the **Name** text box of the dialog box.

5. Choose the button on the right of the **Folder** text box; the **Choose Directory** dialog box is displayed.

   It is recommended that you create a folder with the name NX in the hard drive of your computer and then create separate folders for each chapter inside it for saving the tutorial files of this textbook.

6. In this dialog box, browse to *NX /c02* folder and then choose the **OK** button twice; a new file is started in the Modeling environment.

Drawing the Sketch in the Modeling Environment

The base sketch of this model will be created on the XC-ZC plane.

1. Choose the **Sketch** tool from the **Direct Sketch** group of the **Home** tab; the **Create Sketch** dialog box is displayed.

2. Select the XC-ZC plane from the Datum Coordinate system in the drawing window if it is not selected by default.

3. Choose the **OK** button from the **Create Sketch** dialog box; the additional sketching tools become available and the sketching plane is oriented parallel to the screen.

Drawing the Outer Profile of the Sketch

The outer profile of the sketch consists of lines and it can be drawn by using the **Profile** tool.

1. Choose the **Profile** tool from the **Sketch Curve** gallery of the **Direct Sketch** group of the **Home** tab in the **Ribbon**; the **Profile** dialog box is displayed. By default, the

Line button is active in this dialog box and the dynamic input boxes are displayed below the line cursor.

2. Move the cursor close to the origin; the coordinates of the point are displayed as **0,0** in the dynamic input boxes. Click to specify the start point of the line at this point.

   As you move the cursor on the screen, the line stretches and its length and angle values are modified dynamically in the dynamic input boxes.

3. Enter **80** in the **Length** dynamic input box and press the TAB key. Next, enter **0** in the **Angle** dynamic input box and press the ENTER key.

4. Choose the **Fit** tool from the **Operation** group of the **View** tab to fit the sketch into the drawing window.

5. Move the cursor away from the end point of the last line and then enter **10** as the length and **90** as the angle in the **Length** and **Angle** dynamic input boxes, respectively. Next, press the ENTER key.

6. Enter **15** as the length and **180** as the angle in the **Length** and **Angle** dynamic input boxes, respectively. Next, press the ENTER key.

7. Enter **30** as the length and **90** as the angle in the **Length** and **Angle** dynamic input boxes, respectively. Next, press the ENTER key.

8. Enter **15** as the length and **0** as the angle in the **Length** and **Angle** dynamic input boxes, respectively. Next, press the ENTER key.

9. Enter **10** as the length and **90** as the angle in the **Length** and **Angle** dynamic input boxes, respectively. Next, press the ENTER key.

10. Enter **80** as the length and **180** as the angle in the **Length** and **Angle** dynamic input boxes, respectively. Next, press the ENTER key.

11. Enter **10** as the length and **-90** or **270** as the angle in the **Length** and **Angle** dynamic input boxes, respectively. Next, press the ENTER key.

12. Enter **15** as the length and **0** as the angle in the **Length** and **Angle** dynamic input boxes, respectively. Next, press the ENTER key.

13. Enter **30** as the length and **-90** or **270** as the angle in the **Length** and **Angle** dynamic input boxes, respectively. Next, press the ENTER key.

14. Enter **15** as the length and **180** as the angle in the **Length** and **Angle** dynamic input boxes, respectively. Next, press the ENTER key.

15. Enter **10** as the length and **-90** or **270** as the angle in the **Length** and **Angle** dynamic input boxes, respectively. Next, press the ENTER key.

16. Press the ESC key twice to exit the **Profile** tool. The outer profile of the sketch is shown in Figure 2-52.

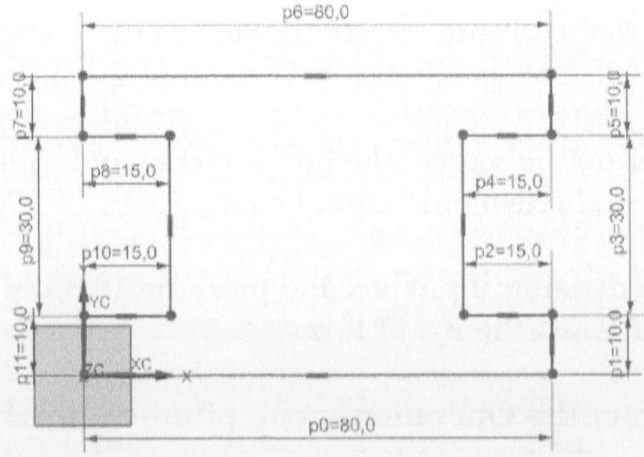

Figure 2-52 Outer profile of the sketch

Drawing the Rectangle

Next, you need to draw the inner profile which is a rectangle. You can use the **By 2 Points** option of the **Rectangle** tool to draw the rectangle.

1. Choose the **Rectangle** tool from the **Sketch Curve** gallery of the **Direct Sketch** group; the **Rectangle** dialog box is displayed and the **By 2 Points** button is chosen by default in this dialog box.

2. Enter **25** and **15** as the coordinates of the first point of the rectangle in the **XC** and **YC** dynamic input boxes, respectively. Next, press the ENTER key.

3. Enter **30** and **20** as the width and height of the rectangle in the **Width** and **Height** dynamic input boxes, respectively. Next, press the ENTER key; a preview of the rectangle is displayed. As you move the cursor in the drawing window, the preview also moves.

4. Move the cursor close to the top right corner of the drawing window and then click to draw the rectangle.

5. Press the ESC key to exit the tool. The final sketch for Tutorial 1 is shown in Figure 2-53.

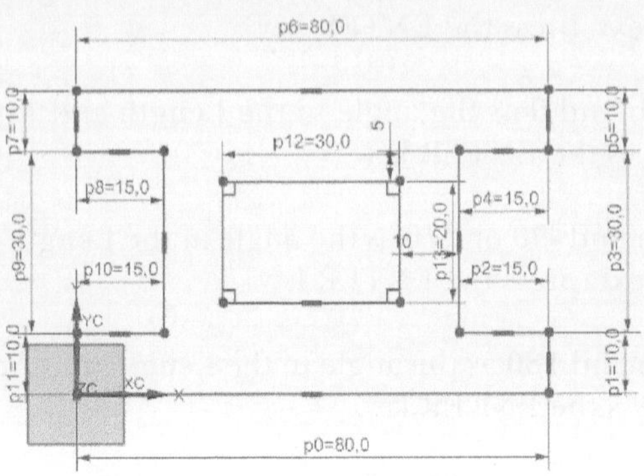

Figure 2-53 Final sketch for Tutorial 1

Finishing the Sketch and Saving the File

NX allows you to save the sketch file in the Sketch environment.

1. Choose the **Save** button from the **Quick Access** toolbar.

2. Next, choose the **Finish Sketch** tool from the **Direct Sketch** group; the Modeling environment is invoked.

3. Choose **Menu > File > Close > Selected Parts** from the **Top Border Bar**; the **Close Part** dialog box is displayed.

4. Select the name of the current file from the list area in the **Part** rollout and then choose the **OK** button to close the current file.

Tutorial 2

In this tutorial, you will draw a sketch for the model shown in Figure 2-54. The sketch to be drawn is shown in Figure 2-55. **(Expected time: 30 min)**

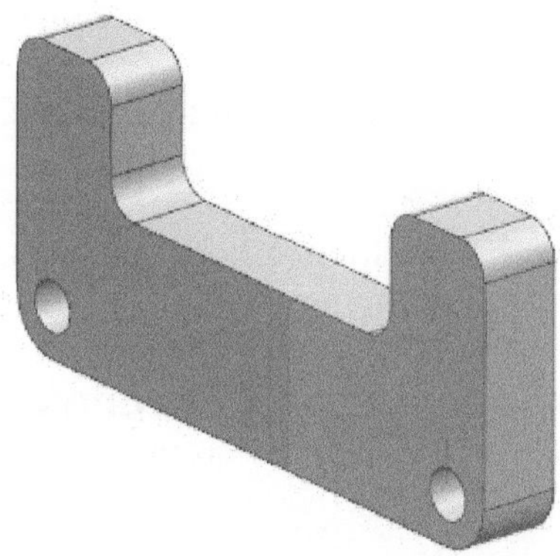

Figure 2-54 *Model for Tutorial 2*

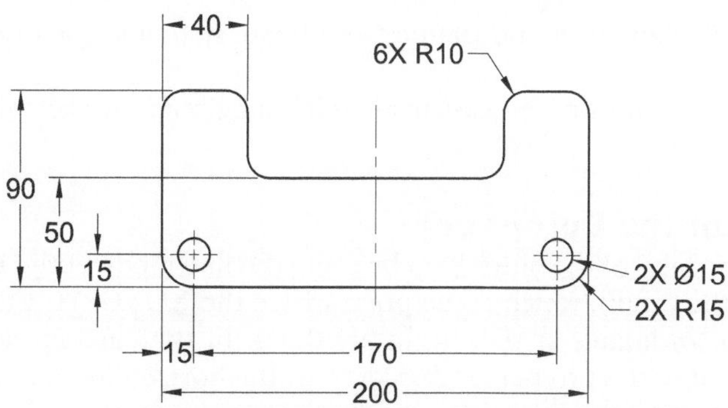

Figure 2-55 *Sketch for Tutorial 2*

The following steps are required to complete this tutorial:

a. Start a new file.
b. Draw the sketch by using the XC-ZC plane as the sketching plane.
c. Draw the outer loop of the profile by using the **Profile** tool.
d. Fillet the sharp corners of the outer loop by using the **Fillet** tool.
e. Draw circles by using the centers of fillets to complete the profile.
f. Finish the sketch and save the file.

Starting NX and Opening a New File

First, you need to start NX and then start a new file.

1. Double-click on NX shortcut icon on the desktop of your computer to start NX.

2. Choose the **New** button from the **Standard** group of the **Home** tab or choose **Menu > File > New** from the **Top Border Bar**; the **New** dialog box is displayed.

3. Select the **Model** template from the **Templates** rollout.

4. Enter **c02tut2** as the name of the document in the **Name** text box of the dialog box.

5. Choose the button on the right side of the **Folder** text box; the **Choose Directory** dialog box is displayed.

6. In this dialog box, browse to *NX/c02* folder and then choose the **OK** button twice; the new file is started in the Modeling environment.

Drawing the Sketch in the Modeling Environment

The base sketch of this model will be created on the XC-ZC plane. Therefore, you need to draw the sketch using this plane.

1. Choose the **Sketch** tool from the **Direct Sketch** group of the **Home** tab; the **Create Sketch** dialog box is displayed.

2. Select the XC-ZC plane from the Datum Coordinate system in the drawing window.

3. Choose the **OK** button from the **Create Sketch** dialog box; the sketching plane is oriented parallel to the screen.

Drawing Lines of the Outer Loop

You will draw the lines of the outer loop by using the line mode of the **Profile** tool. The line will start from the origin, which is the point where the XC-YC, YC-ZC, and ZC-XC planes intersect. The coordinates of the origin are 0,0,0. In the current view, the origin is the intersection point of the two planes displayed as the horizontal and vertical lines.

1. Choose the **Profile** tool from the **Sketch Curve** gallery of the **Direct Sketch** group of the **Home** tab in the **Ribbon** and the **Profile** dialog box is displayed. The **Line**

button is chosen by default in the dialog box and the dynamic input boxes are displayed below the line cursor.

2. Move the cursor close to the origin; the coordinates of the point are displayed as 0,0 in the dynamic input boxes. Next, click to specify the start point of the line.

   The point you specified is selected as the start point of the line and the endpoint is attached to the cursor. As you move the cursor on the screen, the line stretches and its length and angle values are modified dynamically in the dynamic input boxes. Next, you need to specify the endpoint of this line as well as the points to define the remaining lines. This can be done by using the **Length** and **Angle** dynamic input boxes.

3. Enter **200** in the **Length** dynamic input box and press the TAB key. Next, enter **0** in the **Angle** dynamic input box and press the ENTER key.

4. Choose the **Fit** tool from the **View** tab to fit the sketch into the drawing window. Since the **Profile** tool is still active, therefore you are prompted to specify the second point of the line.

5. Enter **90** in the **Length** dynamic input box and press the TAB key. Next, enter **90** in the **Angle** dynamic input box and press the ENTER key; a vertical line of 90 mm is drawn.

6. Choose the **Fit** tool again to fit the drawing into the current display.

7. Move the cursor away from the end point of the last line and then enter **40** in the **Length** dynamic input box and press the TAB key. Next, enter **-180** in the **Angle** dynamic input box and press the ENTER key; a horizontal line of 40 mm is drawn.

8. Move the cursor away from the end point of the last line and then enter **40** in the **Length** dynamic input box and press the TAB key. Next, enter **-90** in the **Angle** dynamic input box and press the ENTER key; a vertical line of 40 mm is drawn downward.

9. Move the cursor away from the end point of the last line and then enter **120** in the **Length** dynamic input box and press the TAB key. Next, enter **180** in the **Angle** dynamic input box and press the ENTER key; a horizontal line of 120 mm is drawn.

10. Move the cursor vertically upward until the horizontal help line is displayed from the top endpoint of the vertical line of 40 mm. Note that at this point, the value of the length in the **Length** dynamic input box is 40 and the value of the angle is 90. Click to specify the endpoint of this line.

11. Move the cursor horizontally toward the left and make sure that the horizontal constraint symbol is displayed. Click to specify the endpoint of the line when the vertical help line is displayed from the vertical plane. If the help line is not displayed, move the cursor once on the vertical plane and then move it back.

12. Move the cursor vertically downward to the origin. If the first line is not highlighted in yellow, move the cursor over it once and then move it back to the origin; the cursor snaps to the endpoint of the first line.

13. Click to specify the endpoint of the line when the vertical constraint symbol is displayed. Choose the **Fit** tool to fit the sketch into the drawing window.

14. Press the ESC key twice to exit the **Profile** tool. The sketch after drawing the lines is shown in Figure 2-56.

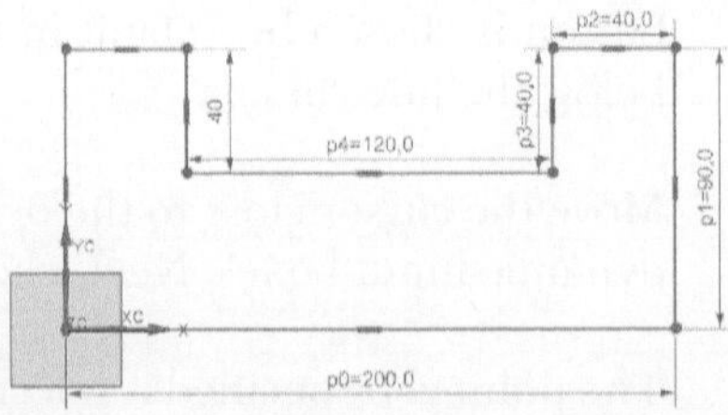

Figure 2-56 *Sketch after drawing the lines*

Filleting Sharp Corners

In this section, you need to fillet sharp corners by using the **Fillet** tool so that there are no sharp edges in the final model.

1. Choose the **Fillet** tool from the **Sketch Curve** gallery of the **Direct Sketch** group; the **Fillet** dialog box is displayed.

   In this tutorial, the lower left and lower right corners are filleted with a radius of 15 mm and the remaining corners are filleted with a radius of 10 mm.

2. Enter **15** in the **Radius** dynamic input box and press the ENTER key.

3. Move the cursor over the lower left corner of the sketch; the two lines comprising this corner are highlighted in yellow. Click to select this corner; a fillet is created at the lower left corner.

4. Similarly, move the cursor over the lower right corner and click on it when the two lines that form this corner are highlighted in yellow.

   Next, you need to modify the fillet radius value and fillet the remaining corners.

5. Enter **10** in the **Radius** dynamic input box and press the ENTER key.

6. Select the remaining corners of the sketch one by one and fillet them with a radius of 10.

7. Right-click and then choose the **OK** option from the shortcut menu to exit the **Fillet** tool. The fillets are created, refer to Figure 2-57.

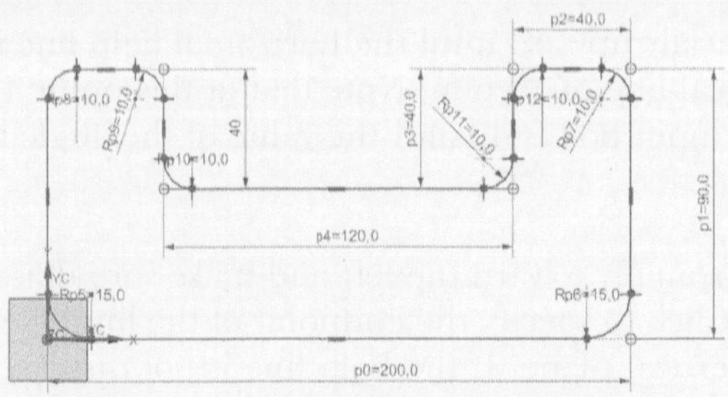

Figure 2-57 *Sketch after creating fillets*

Drawing Circles

Finally, you need to draw circles to complete the sketch. The circles will be drawn by using the **Circle** tool. Use the center points of the fillets as the center points of the circles.

1. Choose the **Circle** tool from the **Sketch Curve** gallery of the **Direct Sketch** group; the **Circle** dialog box is displayed. By default, the **Circle by Center and Diameter** button is chosen in this dialog box. Also, you are prompted to select the center of the circle.

2. Move the cursor toward the center point of the lower left fillet; the cursor snaps to the center point of the arc. Also, the center point snap symbol is displayed above the dynamic input boxes.

3. Click when the cursor snaps to the center point of the fillet to specify the center point of the circle.

4. Enter **15** in the **Diameter** dynamic input box and press the ENTER key; a circle of the specified diameter is drawn at the specified center point. Also, another circle of **15** diameter is attached to the cursor.

5. Move the cursor toward the center point of the lower right fillet; the cursor snaps to the center point of the arc and the center point snap symbol is displayed above the dynamic input box.

6. Click when the cursor snaps to the center point of the arc; the circle is drawn at the specified location.

Note

If by mistake you select an incorrect point as the center point of the circle, you can remove the unwanted circle by choosing the ***Undo*** *button from the* ***Quick Access*** *toolbar.*

7. Exit the **Circle** tool by pressing the ESC key.

This completes the sketch of the model for Tutorial 2. The final sketch for Tutorial 2 is shown in Figure 2-58.

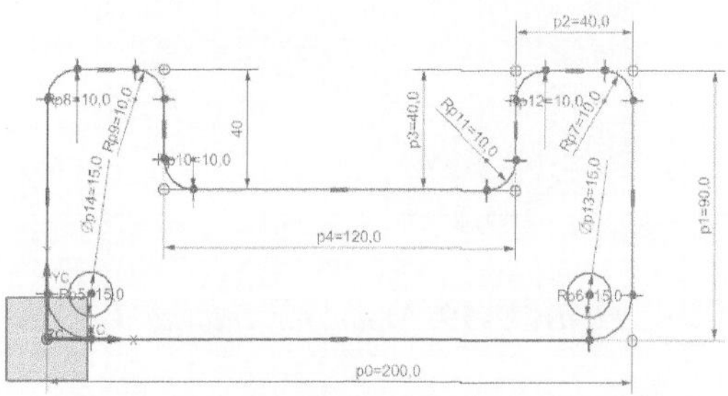

Figure 2-58 Final sketch for Tutorial 2

Finishing the Sketch and Saving the File

NX allows you to save the sketch file in the Sketch environment.

1. Choose the **Fit** tool to fit the sketch into the drawing window. 

2. Choose the **Save** button from the **Quick Access** toolbar.

3. Next, choose the **Finish Sketch** tool from the **Direct Sketch** group; the Modeling environment is invoked.

4. Choose **Menu > File > Close > Selected Parts** from the **Top Border Bar**; the **Close Part** dialog box is displayed.

5. Select the name of the current file from the list area in the **Part** rollout and then choose the **OK** button to close the current file.

Note

For better visualization, you can set the background color of the graphics window in NX as per your requirement. To set the background color, choose ***Menu > Preferences > Background*** *from the* ***Top Border Bar****; the* ***Edit Background*** *dialog box is displayed. Select the* ***Plain*** *radio button from both the* ***Shaded Views*** *and* ***Wireframe Views*** *areas. Next, choose the* ***Plain Color*** *swatch; the* ***Color*** *dialog box is displayed. From this dialog box, select the required color and choose the* ***OK*** *button twice to exit the* ***Edit Background*** *dialog box.*

Tutorial 3

In this tutorial, you will draw the profile of the model shown in Figure 2-59. The profile to be drawn is shown in Figure 2-60. **(Expected time: 30 min)**

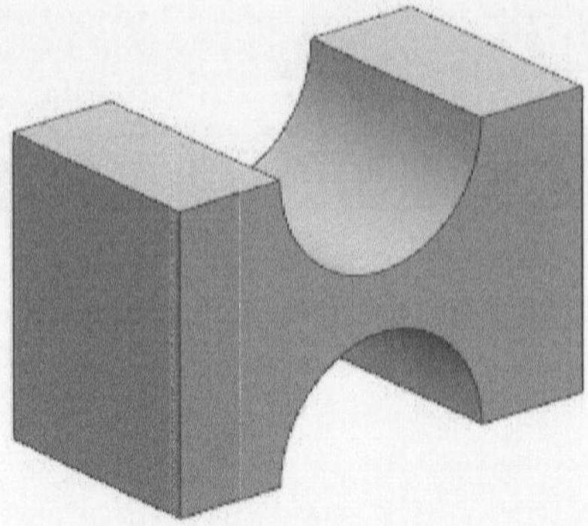

Figure 2-59 *Model for Tutorial 3*

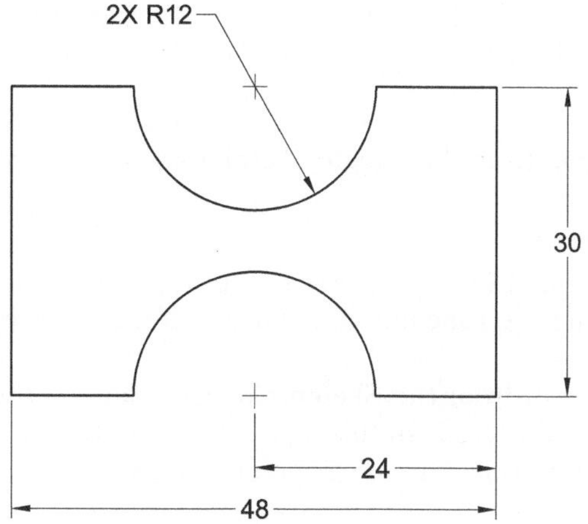

Figure 2-60 *Sketch for Tutorial 3*

The following steps are required to complete this tutorial:

a. Start a new file.
b. Select the YC-ZC plane as the sketching plane.
c. Draw the sketch of the model by using the **Profile** tool.
d. Finish the sketch and save the file.

Starting a New File

If you continue working after completing Tutorial 2, you do not need to open a new session of NX. You can start a new part file by selecting the **Model** template from the **New** dialog box.

1. Choose the **New** button from the **Standard** group of the **Home** tab or choose **Menu > File > New** from the **Top Border Bar**; the **New** dialog box is displayed.

2. Select the **Model** template from the **Templates** rollout.

3. Choose the button on the right of the **Name** text box; the **Choose New File Name** dialog box is displayed.

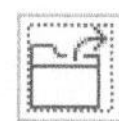

4. In this dialog box, browse to *NX/c02* and then enter **c02tut3** in the **File name** edit box. Next, choose the **OK** button twice; the new file is started in the Modeling environment.

Drawing the Sketch in the Modeling Environment

The base sketch of this model will be created on the YC-ZC plane. Therefore, you need to draw the sketch using this plane.

1. Choose the **Sketch** tool from the **Direct Sketch** group; the **Create Sketch** dialog box is displayed.

2. Select the YC-ZC plane from the drawing window. Note that the Z-axis direction of the sketching plane points toward the front side of the sketching plane and the direction of Y-axis is upward.

3. Choose the **OK** button from the **Create Sketch** dialog box to start the sketch.

Drawing the Sketch

The sketch that you need to draw consists of multiple lines and two arcs. All these entities can be drawn by using the **Line** and **Arc** options of the **Profile** tool.

1. Choose the **Profile** tool from the **Sketch Curve** gallery of the **Direct Sketch** group; the **Profile** dialog box is displayed. In this dialog box, the **Line** button is activated by default. Also, the dynamic input boxes are displayed below the line cursor.

2. Move the cursor close to the origin; the coordinates of the point are displayed as 0,0 in the dynamic input boxes. Click to specify the start point of the line at this point.

   The point you specified is selected as the start point of the line and the endpoint is attached to the cursor. As you move the cursor on the screen, the line stretches and its length and angle values are modified dynamically in the dynamic input boxes.

   Next, you need to specify the endpoint of this line. Also, you need to specify the points to define the remaining lines of the sketch. This can be done by using the **Length** and **Angle** dynamic input boxes.

3. Enter **12** in the **Length** dynamic input box and press the TAB key. Next, enter **0** in the **Angle** dynamic input box and press the ENTER key. The first line is drawn and a rubber-band line is displayed with the start point at the endpoint of the previous line and the endpoint attached to the cursor.

   Now, you need to invoke the arc mode because the next entity to be drawn is an arc.

4. Choose the **Arc** button from the **Object Type** area of the **Profile** dialog box to invoke the arc mode.

   A rubber-band arc is displayed with the start point fixed at the endpoint of the last line and the endpoint attached to the cursor. Also, the quadrant symbol is displayed at the start point of the arc.

5. Move the cursor to the start point of the arc and then move it vertically upward through a small distance. Next, move the cursor toward the right; you will notice that a normal arc starts from the endpoint of the last line.

6. Enter **12** in the **Radius** dynamic input box and press the TAB key. Next, enter **180** in the **Sweep Angle** dynamic input box and press the ENTER key.

   A preview of the resulting arc is displayed, but the arc is still not drawn. To draw the arc, you need to specify a point on the screen with the values mentioned in the dynamic input boxes.

7. Move the cursor horizontally toward the right and click when the preview of the required arc is displayed. The arc is drawn and the line mode is invoked again.

8. Enter **12** as the length and **0** as the angle in the **Length** and **Angle** dynamic input boxes, respectively, and then press the ENTER key. Choose the **Fit** tool from the **Operation** group of the **View** tab to fit the sketch into the drawing window.

9. Enter **30** as the length and **90** as the angle in the **Length** and **Angle** dynamic input boxes, respectively, and then press the ENTER key.

10. Move the cursor horizontally toward the left. Make sure that the horizontal constraint symbol is displayed. Click to specify the endpoint of the line when the vertical help line is displayed from the endpoint of the arc.

    Next, you need to draw the arc by invoking the arc mode.

11. Choose the **Arc** button from the **Profile** dialog box to invoke the arc mode; a rubber-band arc is displayed with its start point fixed at the endpoint of the last line.

12. Move the cursor to the start point of the arc and then move it vertically downward through a small distance. When the normal arc appears, move the cursor toward the left.

13. Move the cursor over the lower arc once and then move it toward the left, refer to Figure 2-61.

    A horizontal help line is displayed originating from the center of the arc being drawn. At the point where the cursor is vertically in line with the start point of the lower arc, a vertical help line appears from the start point of the lower arc, refer to Figure 2-61.

14. Click to define the endpoint of the arc when the horizontal and vertical help lines are displayed. The arc is drawn and the line mode is invoked again.

15. Enter **12** as the radius and **180** as the angle in the **Length** and **Angle** dynamic input boxes, respectively, and then press the ENTER key.

16. Move the cursor to the first line and then move it to the start point of this line; the cursor snaps to the start point of the line.

17. Click to define the endpoint of this line when the cursor snaps to the start point of the first line.

18. Press the ESC key twice to exit the **Profile** tool. The final sketch of the model is shown in Figure 2-62.

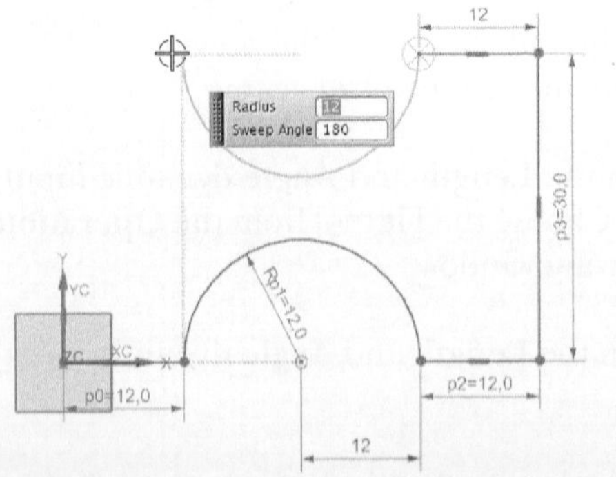

Figure 2-61 Horizontal and vertical help lines displayed to define the endpoint of the arc

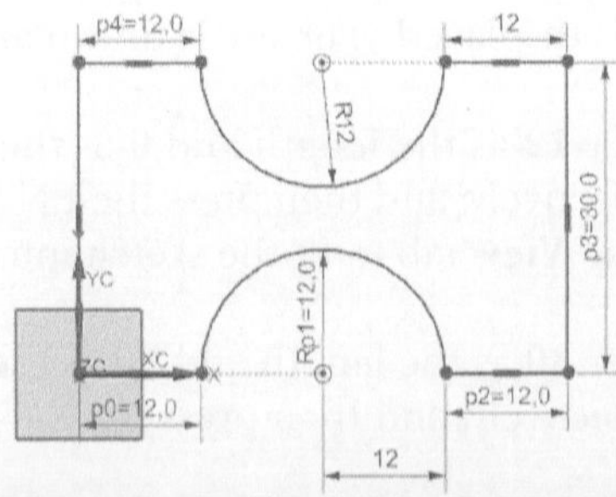

Figure 2-62 Final sketch for Tutorial 3

Finishing the Sketch and Saving the File

NX allows you to save the sketch file in the Sketch environment.

1. Choose the **Save** button from the **Quick access** toolbar or from the **File** tab to save the sketch.

2. Next, choose the **Finish Sketch** tool from the **Direct Sketch** group; the Modeling environment is invoked.

3. Choose **Menu > File > Close > Selected Parts** from the **Top Border Bar**; the **Close Part** dialog box is displayed.

4. Select the name of the current file from the list area in the **Part** rollout and then choose the **OK** button to close the current file.

Self-Evaluation Test

Answer the following questions and then compare them to those given at the end of this chapter:

1. You can restore the original orientation of the sketching plane by using the __________ tool.

2. You can invoke the arc mode within the **Profile** tool by choosing the __________ button from the **Profile** dialog box.

3. You can fillet corners in a sketch by using the __________ tool.

4. You can draw an elliptical arc by using the __________ tool.

5. If you choose the __________ button from the **Rectangle** dialog box, it will enable you to draw a centerpoint rectangle.

6. You can exit the Sketch environment by choosing the __________ tool from the **Direct Sketch** group.

7. Most of the designs created in NX consist of sketch-based features and placed features. (T/F)

8. When you invoke the Sketch environment from the **Direct Sketch** group, the **Profile** tool is invoked by default. (T/F)

9. You can use the dynamic input boxes to specify the exact values of the sketched entities. (T/F)

10. You need to choose the **Sketch in Task Environment** tool to invoke the Sketch environment. (T/F)

Review Questions

Answer the following questions:

1. Which of the following dialog boxes is displayed when you choose the **New** button from the **File** tab to start a new file?

   (a) **New Part File** (b) **New Item**
   (c) **New** (d) **Part File**

2. Which of the following tools in NX is used to create conics?

   (a) **General Conic** (b) **Conic**
   (c) **Round** (d) None

3. Which mode is automatically invoked from the **Profile** dialog box when you specify the start point of a line?

   (a) **Coordinate Mode** (b) **Angle Mode**
   (c) **Parameter Mode** (d) None

4. In NX, how many methods are used to start a new file?

   (a) 1 (b) 2
   (c) 3 (d) 5

5. Which of the following options is available in the **Studio Spline** dialog box along with the **By Poles** option to draw splines?

   (a) **No Poles** (b) **From Poles**
   (c) **From Points** (d) **Through Points**

6. The files in NX are saved with *.prt* extension. (T/F)

7. You can select entities by dragging a box around them. (T/F)

8. You can set the selection mode to select only the sketched entities. (T/F)

9. In NX, you can create fillets by simply dragging the cursor across the entities that you want to fillet. (T/F)

10. In NX, you cannot draw a rectangle from its center. (T/F)

EXERCISES

Exercise 1

Draw a sketch for the base feature of the model shown in Figure 2-63. The sketch to be drawn is shown in Figure 2-64. **(Expected time: 30 min)**

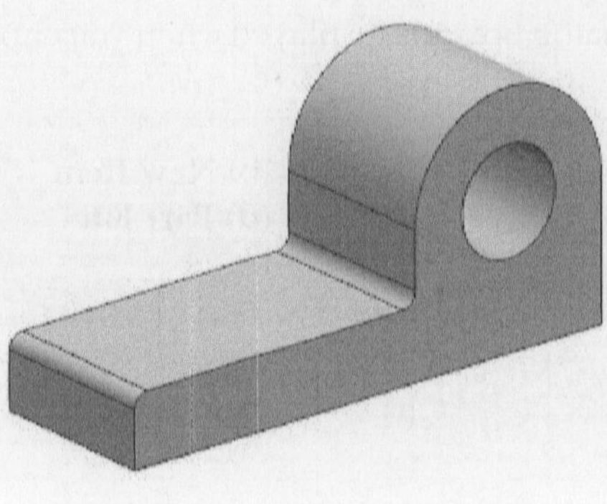

Figure 2-63 Model for Exercise 1

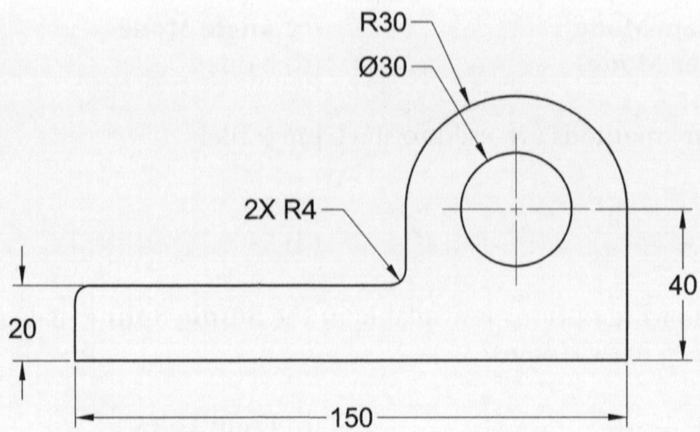

Figure 2-64 Sketch for Exercise 1

Exercise 2

Draw a sketch for the base feature of the model shown in Figure 2-65. The sketch to be drawn is shown in Figure 2-66. **(Expected time: 30 min)**

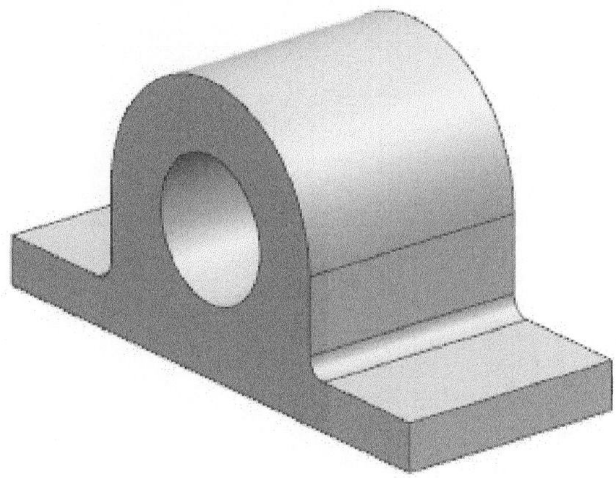

Figure 2-65 *Model for Exercise 2*

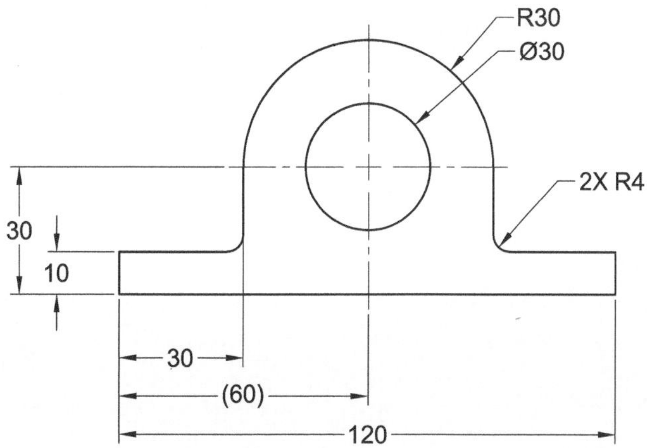

Figure 2-66 *Sketch for Exercise 2*

Answers to Self-Evaluation Test

1. Orient View to Sketch, **2.** Arc, **3.** Fillet, **4.** Ellipse, **5.** From Center, **6.** Finish Sketch, **7.** T, **8.** F, **9.** T, **10.** T

Chapter 3

Adding Geometric and Dimensional Constraints to Sketches

Learning Objectives

After completing this chapter, you will be able to:

- *Understand the concept of under-constrained, fully-constrained, and over-constrained sketches*
- *Understand different types of dimensions*
- *Measure the distance value between entities in a sketch*
- *Measure the angle between entities*
- *Understand different types of geometric constraints*
- *Configure settings for applying constraints automatically while sketching*
- *Force additional geometric constraints to sketches*
- *View and delete geometric constraints from sketches*
- *Animate a fully-constrained sketch*

CONSTRAINING SKETCHES

In the previous chapter, you learned to draw sketches. You must have noticed that the dimensions are applied automatically to the sketches when they are drawn but the dimensions are updated when you drag the sketched entities. Therefore, these dimensions do not constrain the sketch. In this chapter, you will learn to completely constrain the sketches to restrict their degrees of freedom and make them stable. The stability ensures that the size, shape, and location of the sketches do not change unexpectedly with respect to the surrounding. Therefore, it is always recommended to constrain the sketches. The geometrical constraints are applied first, some of which get automatically applied while drawing. After applying the remaining geometrical constraints, you need to add dimensional constraints using dimension tools. You will learn more about dimension tools later in this chapter.

CONCEPT OF CONSTRAINED SKETCHES

After drawing and applying the constraints, the sketch can attain any one of the following three stages:

1. Under-Constrain
2. Fully-Constrain
3. Over-Constrain

These stages are described next.

Under-Constrain

An under-constrained sketch is the one in which all the degrees of freedom of each entity are not completely defined using the geometric and dimensional constraints. The elements of the sketch that are displayed in light purple color are under-constrained. You need to apply additional constraints to them in order to constrain their degree of freedom. The under-constrained sketches tend to change their position, size, or shape unexpectedly. Therefore, it is necessary to fully define the sketched elements. Figure 3-1 shows an under-constrained sketch.

Fully-Constrain

The fully-constrained sketch is the one in which all degrees of freedom of each element are defined using the geometric and dimensional constraints. As a result, the sketch cannot change its position, shape, or size unexpectedly. These dimensions can change only if they are modified deliberately by the user. The elements of a fully-constrained sketch are displayed in dark green color. Figure 3-2 shows a fully-constrained sketch.

Over-Constrain

An over-constrained sketch is the one in which some additional constraints are applied. The over-constrained dimensions and constraints are displayed in red color. It is always recommended to delete additional constraints and make the sketch fully-constrained before exiting the sketching environment. Figure 3-3 shows an over-constrained sketch.

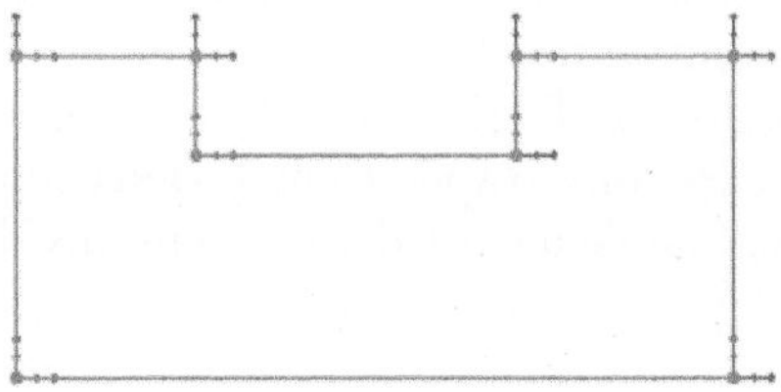

Figure 3-1 An under-constrained sketch

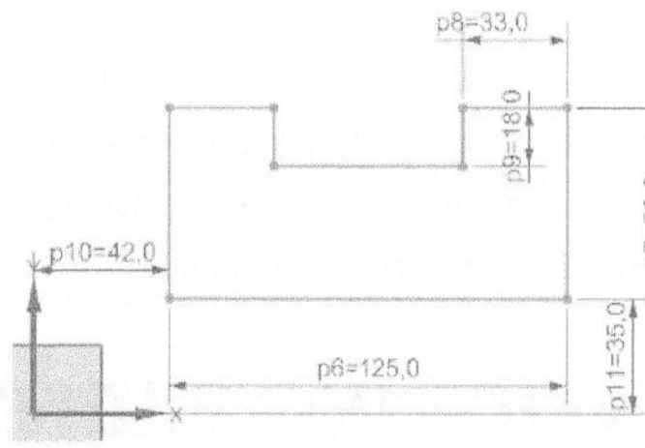

Figure 3-2 A fully-constrained sketch

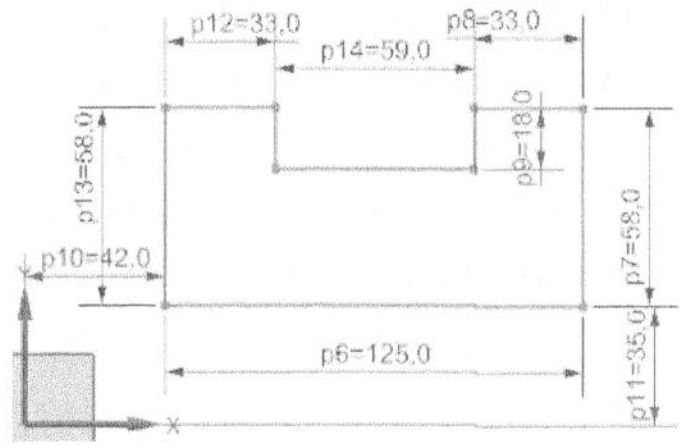

Figure 3-3 An over-constrained sketch

While applying the geometric and dimensional constraints, the status area in the Status Bar displays the number of constraints needed to fully constrain the sketch. After fully constraining the sketch, a message will be displayed in the status area of the **Status Bar** that the sketch is fully constrained.

Also, if the sketch is over-constrained, you will be informed that the sketch contains over constrained geometry. In such a case, you need to remove the unwanted constraints.

DEGREES OF FREEDOM ARROWS

Degrees of Freedom can be defined as the number of independent variables or coordinates required to ascertain the position of any system or its components. In other words, you can say, it is the number of variables that are required to determine the position of a mechanism in space. In NX, the degrees of freedom arrows are displayed on the points that are free to move (under-constrain), refer to Figure 3-4. Note that the degree of freedom arrows will be displayed only when you choose any constraining tool (geometrical or dimensional). These tools are discussed later in this chapter.

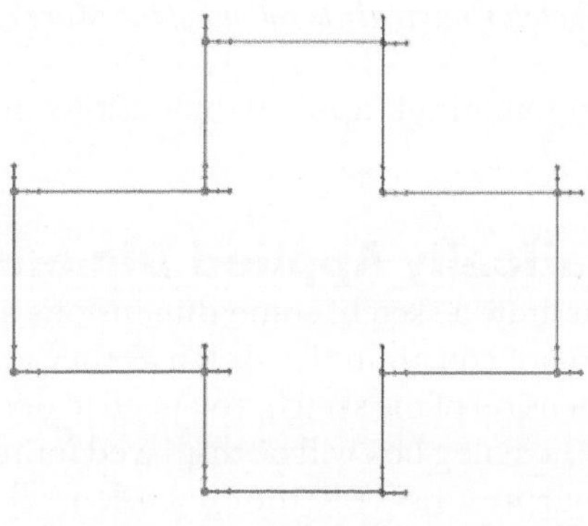

Figure 3-4 The degrees of freedom arrows displayed on points

The direction of an arrow at a particular point indicates that you need to constrain the movement along that direction. When you constrain a point, NX will remove the degree of freedom arrows. The sketch will be fully-constrained only when all the arrows disappear. The horizontal and vertical arrows indicate that the point is free to move in the X and Y directions, respectively. Various geometric and dimensional constraint tools used to fully-constrain the sketch are discussed in this chapter.

DIMENSIONING SKETCHES

After creating a sketch, you need to apply different types of dimensions (dimensional constraints) to it. The purpose of dimensioning is to control the size of the sketch and to place it with reference to some other entity. As discussed earlier, by default, sketched entities get dimensioned automatically while drawing a sketch. However, the automatically applied dimensions do not constrain the sketch. Therefore, you need to lock them to fully constrain the sketch. Also, sometimes you may need to add additional dimensions to the sketch to fully constrain it. In NX, you can apply the dimensions by using the tools grouped together in the **Dimensions Drop-down** of the **Direct Sketch** group in the **Home** tab, refer to Figure 3-5. You can also access these tools from the **Dimensions Drop-down** of the **Constraints** group in the **Home** tab of the Sketch in Task Environment. The tools available in this drop-down are listed below:

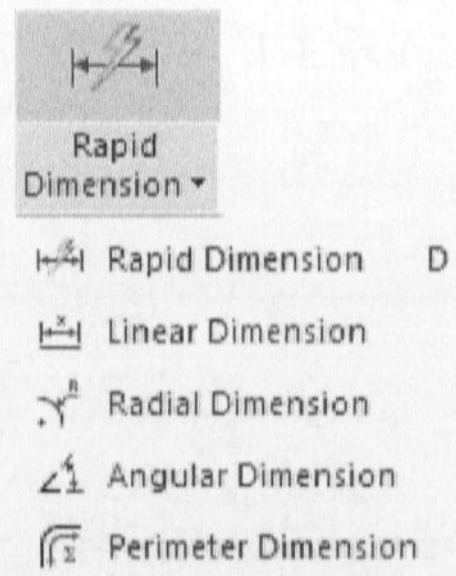

*Figure 3-5 The **Dimensions** Drop-down*

1. Rapid Dimension
2. Linear Dimension
3. Radial Dimension
4. Angular Dimension
5. Perimeter Dimension

Note

*As the **Continuous Auto Dimensioning** tool is active by default in the **More** gallery of the **Direct Sketch** group, the sketched entities will be dimensioned automatically in the sketch environment. If you do not want the sketch to be auto dimensioned, you can deactivate this tool by clicking on the **Continuous Auto Dimensioning** tool in the **Sketch Tools** rollout of the **More** gallery. Also, you can control the display of auto dimensions by using the **Display Sketch Auto Dimensions** toggle button available in the **Sketch Constraints** rollout of the **More** gallery of the **Direct Sketch** group.*

The procedure of locking the automatically applied dimensions and applying various dimensions are discussed next.

Locking the Automatically Applied Dimensions

As discussed earlier, when you draw a sketch, some dimensions are automatically applied to it. However, these dimensions do not constrain the sketch as they get modified when you drag the sketched entities. To lock a dimension of the sketch, you need to double-click on it. On doing so, an edit box will be displayed. Also, a dialog box will be displayed for respective dimension. Enter the required value in the edit box and press ENTER; the dimension will be locked and displayed in blue color. Next, choose the **Close** button from the dialog box or press ESC key to exit the dialog box.

Note

1. NX provides automatic and manual scale methods to scale sketches. When you add the first distance, radius, or diameter driving dimension, NX automatically scales the sketch to that value while maintaining the overall shape and inferred geometric constraints.

Note that the sketch is only scaled once and the next dimension you add or modify acts like any driving dimension.

2. You can dynamically edit and display the driving dimensions in a better manner to check the design intent. When you modify sketch geometry, NX moves the dimensions with the geometry. This behavior gives a neat look to the sketch by relocating the dimensions relative to the geometry.

Applying Dimensions by Using the Rapid Dimension Tool

Ribbon: Home > Direct Sketch > Dimensions Drop-down > Rapid Dimension
Menu: Insert > Sketch constraint > Dimension > Rapid

The **Rapid Dimension** tool is used to apply dimension depending upon the entity selected. For example, if you select an arc, the radial dimension will be applied. Similarly, if you select a circle, the diameter dimension will be applied and on selecting a line, linear dimension will be applied. Note that if you select an inclined line and move the cursor parallel to that line; an aligned dimension will be applied. If you move the cursor vertically upward or downward, a horizontal dimension will be applied. Similarly, if you move the cursor horizontally (right or left), a vertical dimension will be applied.

It is recommended that you use this tool to apply different type of dimensions as it saves the time required for selecting various dimensioning tools. To apply rapid dimensions, choose the **Rapid Dimension** tool from the **Dimensions Drop-down** in the **Direct Sketch** group of the **Home** tab; the **Rapid Dimension** dialog box will be displayed and you will be prompted to select the object to be dimensioned. Now the dimension will be applied based on the selection procedure adopted while selecting objects. Figure 3-6 shows the radial and linear dimensions created by using the tool.

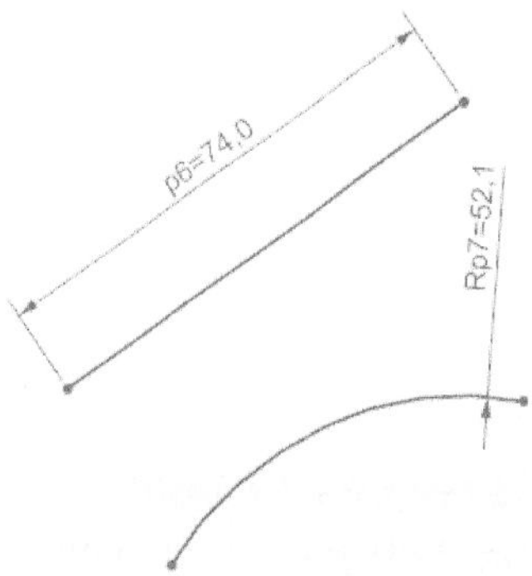

***Figure 3-6** The radial and linear dimensions created by using the **Rapid Dimension** tool*

Applying Linear Dimensions

Ribbon: Home > Direct Sketch > Dimensions Drop-down > Linear Dimension
Menu: Insert > Sketch constraint > Dimension > Linear

The **Linear Dimension** tool is used to apply horizontal, vertical, or aligned dimension to a selected line or between two points. The points can be the endpoints of line or arc, or the center points of two circles, arcs, ellipses, or parabola, or any set of points that can be identified. To apply linear dimension to a sketch, choose the **Linear Dimension** tool from the **Dimensions Drop-down** of the **Direct Sketch** group, refer to Figure 3-5; the **Linear Dimension** dialog box will be displayed, as shown in Figure 3-7.

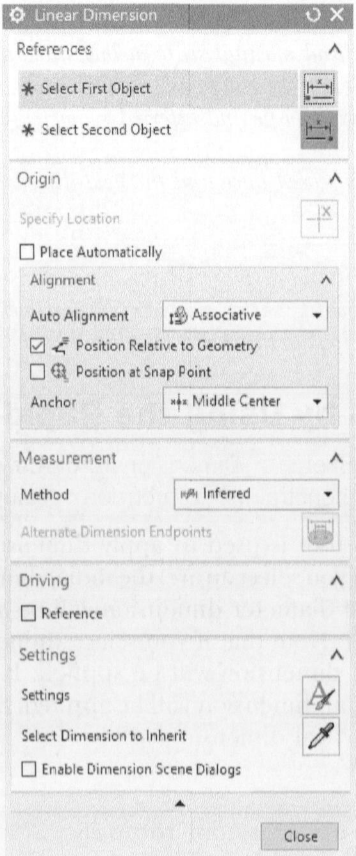

*Figure 3-7 The **Linear Dimension** dialog box*

The options in this dialog box are discussed next.

References Rollout

The options in this rollout are used to select the object to be dimensioned. Using the options in this rollout, you can select points or linear entities for applying the dimension.

Origin Rollout

This rollout is used to define the position of the dimension text. You can place the dimension at the required location. Place the dimension above or below (in case of horizontal) and left or right (in case of vertical) of the selected object by clicking on the desired place inside the drawing window. As soon as you place the dimension, an edit box will be displayed. Enter the required value in this edit box and then press ENTER. Next, press ESC to exit the dialog box. Figure 3-8 shows the horizontal, vertical, and aligned dimensions applied to a line. The **Place Automatically** check box is used to place the dimension automatically according to the object.

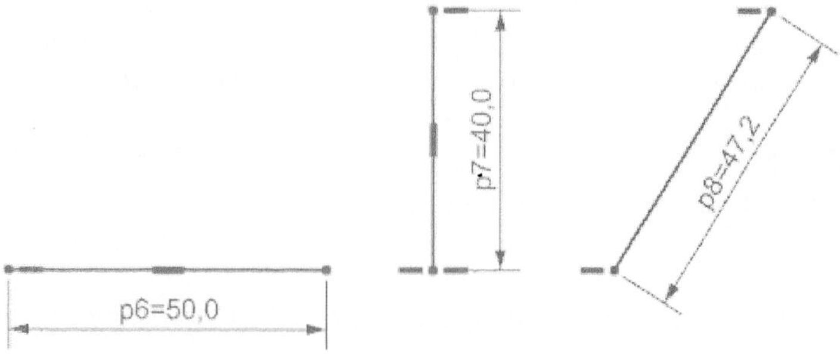

Figure 3-8 The linear dimension created for a horizontal line, vertical line, and an inclined line

Measurement Rollout

The options available in the **Method** drop-down list of this rollout are discussed next.

Inferred

The **Inferred** option is used to apply dimensions between entities based on the entities selected for dimensioning and the placement point.

Horizontal

The **Horizontal** option is used to apply horizontal dimension between entities. Note that if you select an entity that has a slant angle, only horizontal dimension can be applied.

Vertical

The **Vertical** option is used to apply vertical dimension between entities. Even if you select an entity that has a slant angle, a vertical dimension will be applied.

Point-to-Point

The **Point-to-Point** option is used to apply dimension between two points. You can select a set of points or a linear entity for applying dimension by using this option. Note that on selecting a linear entity, the dimension between its ends points will be applied, depending upon the entity selected, refer to Figure 3-8.

Perpendicular

The **Perpendicular** option is used to create the perpendicular dimension between a linear object and a point. It is mandatory that any one of the objects selected is a linear object.

Cylindrical

The **Cylindrical** option is used to apply dimension between cylindrical sections of objects.

Driving Rollout

In the **Driving** rollout, the **Reference** check box is available. This check box is used to convert the dimension into a reference dimension instead of a driving dimension.

Note

If you create a redundant dimension, NX may inform you that the sketch is over-constrained. When you convert the dimension into a reference dimension, the sketch will no longer be over-constrained.

Settings Rollout

There are two buttons in this rollout and they are discussed next.

Settings

The **Settings** button is used to change the style of the dimensions that are being applied.

Inherit Dimension Settings

This button allows you to apply the style setting of an existing dimension to the dimensions being applied.

The **Enable Dimension Scene Dialogs** check box allows you to select access handles directly on different parts of the dimension to edit dimension settings.

Note

In the figures of this chapter, some of the dimension properties such as decimal places and labels have been modified for better display of dimensions. You can modify the dimension labels only when you are in the sketching environment. As discussed, you can invoke the sketching environment by using the ***Sketch in Task Environment*** *tool. To modify the dimension label, choose* ***Curve > Sketch in Task Environment*** *from the* ***Ribbon****. If you create a sketch in the Modeling environment, then to modify the dimension labels, choose* ***Open in Sketch Task Environment*** *from the* ***Sketch Feature*** *rollout in the* ***More*** *gallery of the* ***Direct Sketch*** *group; the sketching environment will be invoked and now you can modify the dimension properties. Now, choose* ***Menu > Task > Sketch Settings*** *from the* ***Top Border Bar****; the* ***Sketch Settings*** *dialog box will be displayed. In this dialog box, select the* ***Value*** *option from the* ***Dimension Label*** *drop-down list. Next, choose the* ***OK*** *button; the dimensions labels will be modified. Alternatively, choose* ***Menu > Preferences > Sketch*** *from the* ***Top Border Bar****; the* ***Sketch Preferences*** *message box will be displayed. Next, choose* ***OK*** *from the message box; the* ***Sketch Preferences*** *dialog box will be displayed. In this dialog box, choose the* ***Sketch Settings*** *tab; the* ***Sketch Preferences*** *message box will be displayed. Choose the* ***OK*** *button. Next, in the* ***Dimension Label*** *drop-down list of the* ***Sketch Preferences*** *dialog box, select the* ***Value*** *option and then choose the* ***OK*** *button; the dimensions will be modified.*

Applying Radial Dimensions

Ribbon:	Home > Direct Sketch > Dimensions Drop-down > Radial Dimension
Menu:	Insert > Sketch Constraint > Dimension > Radial

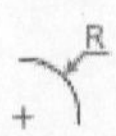

The **Radial Dimension** tool is used to apply the radial dimension to an arc or diametral dimension to a circle. To apply radial dimension, choose the **Radial Dimension** tool from the **Dimensions Drop-down** in the **Direct Sketch** group of the **Home** tab; the **Radial Dimension** dialog box will be displayed and you will be prompted to select an arc or circle to be dimensioned. Select the object to be dimensioned and then place the dimension. As soon as you place the dimension, an edit box will be displayed. Enter the required value in this edit box, and then press ENTER. Next, press ESC to exit the dialog box. You can also select the type of dimension to be applied from the **Method** drop-down list in the **Measurement** rollout. In this drop-down list, the **Radial** option is used to define the radius and the **Diametral** option is used to define the diameter dimensions. However, if you select the **Inferred** option from the drop-down list, radius dimensions will be applied to arcs and diameter dimensions will be applied to circles automatically. Figure 3-9 shows the diametral dimension applied to a circle and Figure 3-10 shows the radial dimension applied to an arc. Rest of the options in the **Radial Dimension** dialog box are the same as those discussed in the Linear Dimension.

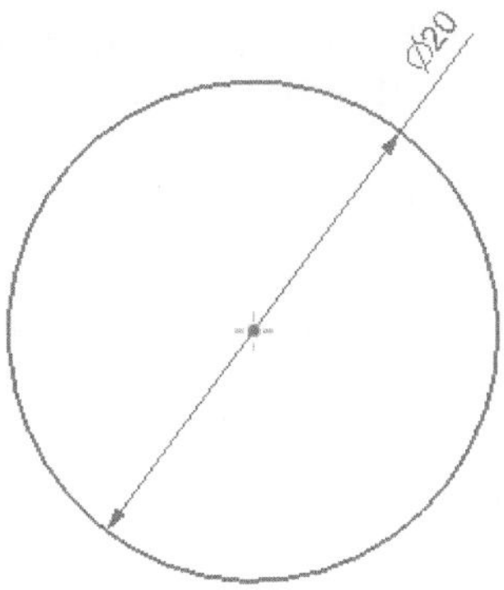

Figure 3-9 The diametral dimension applied to a circle

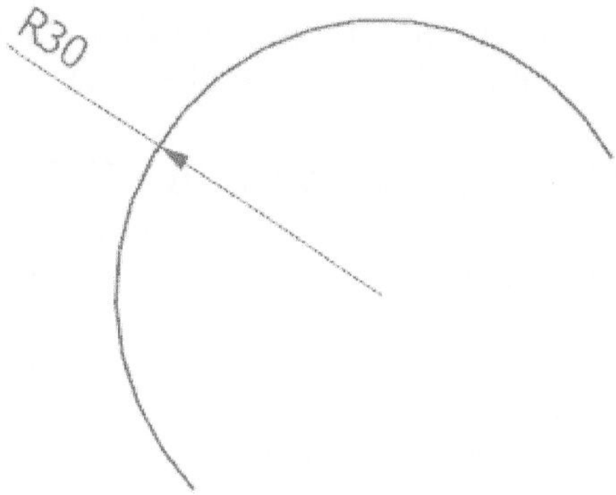

Figure 3-10 The radial dimension applied to an arc

Applying Angular Dimensions

Ribbon:	Home > Direct Sketch > Dimensions Drop-down > Angular Dimension
Menu:	Insert > Sketch Constraint > Dimension > Angular

The **Angular Dimension** tool is used to apply angular dimension between entities. Whenever an angular dimension is applied using the **Angular Dimension** tool, the angle is always measured in the counterclockwise direction. To apply angular dimension, choose the **Angular Dimension** tool from the **Dimensions Drop-down** in the **Direct Sketch** group of the **Home** tab; the **Angular Dimension** dialog box will be displayed and you will be prompted to select an object to be dimensioned. Select the entities between which the angular dimension needs to be applied and then place the dimension. Figure 3-11 shows different types of angular dimensions applied to a sketch. Rest of the options in the **Angular Dimension** dialog box are same as discussed earlier.

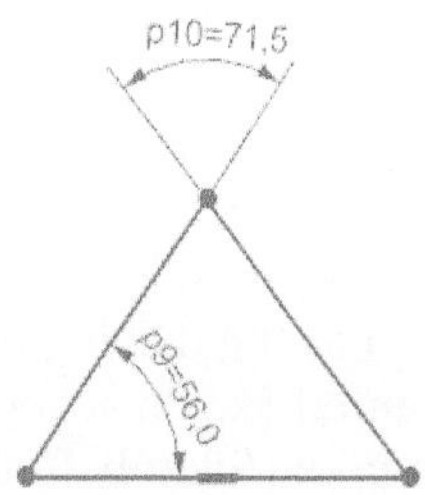

Figure 3-11 Angular dimensions applied between the entities

Applying Perimeter Dimensions

Ribbon:	Home > Direct Sketch > Dimensions Drop-down > Perimeter Dimension
Menu:	Insert > Sketch Constraint > Dimension > Perimeter

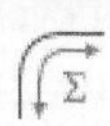

The **Perimeter Dimension** tool is used to apply the circumferential or perimeter dimension. After applying the perimeter dimension, all the dimensions of the selected objects are locked. To apply the perimeter dimension, choose the **Perimeter Dimension**

tool from the **Dimensions Drop-down** in the **Direct Sketch** group of the **Home** tab; the **Perimeter Dimension** dialog box will be displayed. Select the object and then choose the **OK** button from this dialog box; the perimeter dimension will be applied to the selected object. Note that this dimension will not be displayed in the drawing window.

You can also apply the perimeter dimension to a closed sketch. To do so, invoke the **Perimeter Dimension** dialog box and then select all the entities of the closed sketch one by one. Next, choose the **OK** button from the **Perimeter Dimension** dialog box; the dimension will be applied to the sketch. Now, if you modify the dimension of any one of the entities, the dimension of other entities will also be modified such that the total perimeter of the sketch remains the same.

Editing the Dimension Value and Other Parameters

To edit a dimension, double-click on the dimension to be edited; the respective dimension dialog box will be invoked. Also, edit boxes will be displayed in the graphics window. By using the options available in the **Driving** rollout of the dialog box, you can specify the new dimension value and control the display of expression. You can also specify the new dimension value in the edit box displayed in the graphic window. Once you have specified the new dimension value, press the ESC key to apply the change and exit the dialog box.

Animating a Fully-Constrained Sketch

Ribbon:	Home > Direct Sketch > More Gallery > Sketch Tools > Animate Dimension (Customize to add)
Menu:	Tools > Sketch Constraints > Animate Dimension

The **Animate Dimension** tool is used to animate a sketch by selecting any one of the dimensions as the driving dimension from the same sketch. Generally, this type of animation is used while creating basic mechanisms and links. When a dimension from a fully constrained sketch is animated, the whole sketch gets mechanized by the possible movements. The dimension selected from the sketch for animating is known as the driving dimension. To animate a fully constrained sketch, choose the **Animate Dimension** tool from the **Sketch Tools** gallery of the **More** gallery in the **Direct Sketch** group of the **Home** tab; the **Animate Dimension** dialog box will be displayed, as shown in Figure 3-12, and you will be prompted to select a dimension to animate. The dimensions that are applied to the sketch are listed in the list box of the same dialog box. You can select the driving dimension directly from the sketch or from the list box. After selecting the driving dimension, enter the lower limit value for the dimension inside the **Lower Limit** edit box. Similarly, enter the upper limit value for the dimension inside the **Upper Limit** edit box. The selected dimension will be animated between the lower and upper limits specified. You can also divide an animation cycle into a number of steps and then animate the design. The number of steps per cycle should be entered inside the **Steps/Cycle** edit box. To display the dimension applied during the animation,

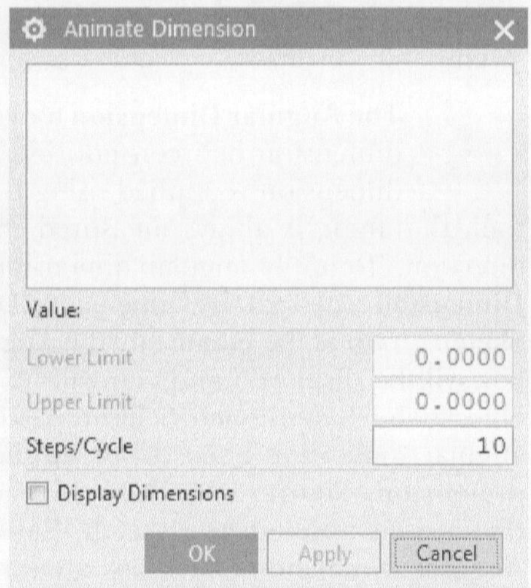

*Figure 3-12 The **Animate Dimension** dialog box*

select the **Display Dimensions** check box. For example, a fully constrained sketch from which the driving dimension is selected is shown in Figure 3-13. Figure 3-14 shows the sketch while animating. Note that at an instance, only one dimension can be selected as the driving dimension. If the sketch is not fully constrained, an undesired animation may occur.

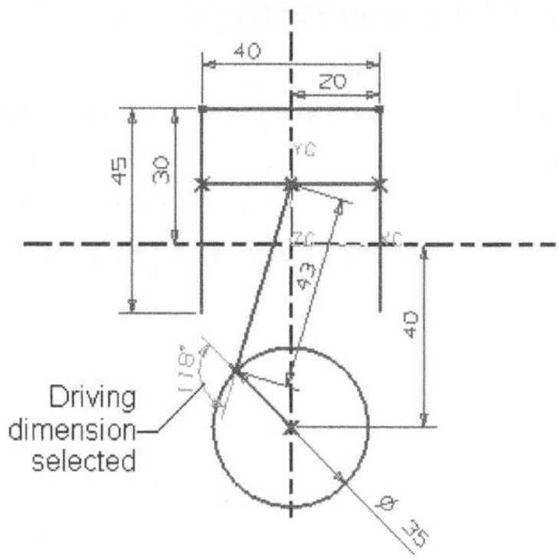

Figure 3-13 Driving dimension selected from the sketch

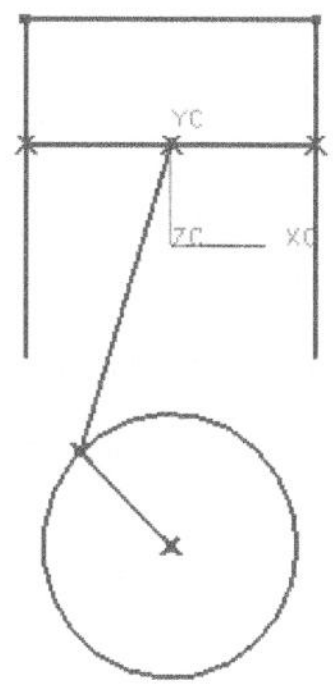

Figure 3-14 The sketch being animated

Note

You can hide and show the auto dimensions whenever you want. To do so, use the ***Display Sketch Auto Dimensions*** *toggle button available in the* ***More*** *gallery of the* ***Direct Sketch*** *group in the* ***Home*** *tab to toggle on/off the auto dimensions.*

GEOMETRIC CONSTRAINTS

Geometric constraints are the logical operations that are performed on the sketched entities to relate them to the other sketched entities using the standard properties such as collinearity, concentricity, tangency, and so on. These constraints reduce the degrees of freedom of the sketched entities and make the sketch more stable so that it does not change its shape and location unexpectedly at any stage of the design. All geometric constraints have separate symbols associated with them. These symbols can be seen on the sketched entities when the constraints are applied to them. In the sketching environment of NX, you can add various types of geometric constraints. Some of these constraints are added automatically while sketching. Additionally, you can add more constraints to the sketch manually. These are explained next.

Applying Additional Constraints Individually

Ribbon:	Home > Direct Sketch > More Gallery > Sketch Constraints > Geometric Constraints
Menu:	Insert > Sketch Constraint > Geometric Constraints

In NX, you can apply additional constraints manually by using the **Geometric Constraints** tool in the **Direct Sketch** group of the **Home** tab. To apply constraints, invoke the **Geometric Constraints** tool; the **Geometric Constraints** message box will be displayed. Select the **Don't display this message again** check box in it and then choose the **OK** button; the **Geometric Constraints** dialog box will be displayed, as shown in Figure 3-15. Select the required constraint from the **Constraint** rollout of the dialog box and then select the entities from the drawing area to apply the selected constraint.

Note

*By default, only few constraints are available in the **Constraint** rollout of the **Geometric Constraints** dialog box. You can customize constraints to add or remove the constraints from the **Constraint** rollout. Select the check boxes next to the required constraints from the **Settings** rollout; the selected constraints will be displayed in the **Constraint** rollout.*

In NX, you can also apply constraints directly without invoking the **Geometric Constraints** dialog box. To do so, select the entities from the drawing area; a contextual toolbar will be displayed with all possible constraints that can be applied to the selected entities, as shown in Figure 3-16. Select the required constraint from the contextual toolbar; the selected constraint will be applied to the selected entities.

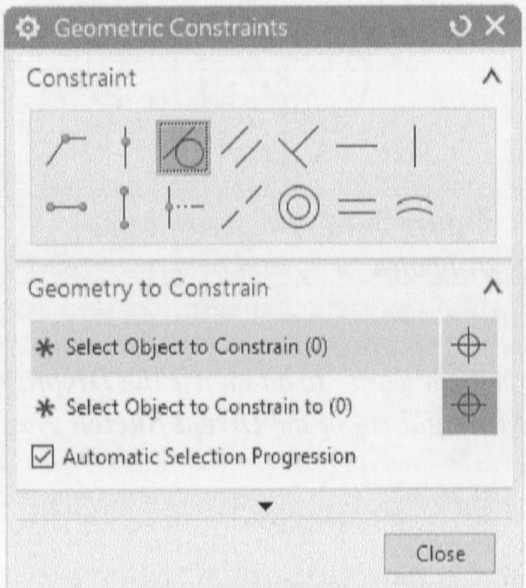

*Figure 3-15 The **Geometric Constraints** dialog box*

Figure 3-16 The contextual toolbar

Various constraints that can be applied to the sketched entities in NX are discussed next.

Fixed Constraint

The Fixed constraint is used to fix some of the characteristics of the geometry. To apply this constraint, choose the **Fixed** button *(Customize to add)* from the **Constraint** rollout of the **Geometric Constraints** dialog box. Next, select the entity to be fixed from the drawing area; the selected entity will be fixed. Alternatively, you can apply the fixed constraint using the contextual toolbar. To do so, select an entity from the drawing area; the contextual toolbar will be displayed with the possible constraints that can be applied to the selected entity. Next, choose the **Fixed** option from the contextual toolbar, refer to Figure 3-17; the selected entity will be fixed.

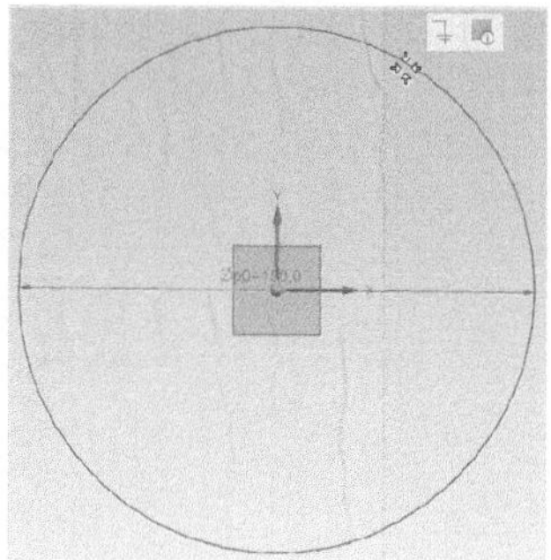

Figure 3-17 Applying the Fixed constraint to an entity

The characteristics of the geometry after applying the Fixed constraint depend on the type of geometry selected. Following are some of the examples of Fixed constraint:

1. If you apply this constraint to a point, the point will be fixed and cannot be moved.

2. If you apply this constraint to a line, its angle will be fixed; however, you can move and stretch the line.

3. If you apply this constraint to the circumference of a circular arc or an elliptical arc, the radius of the arc and the location of the center point will be fixed. However, you can change the arc-length.

Fully Fixed Constraint

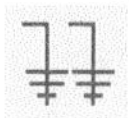

This constraint is same as the Fixed constraint with the only difference being that this constraint fixes all characteristics of a geometry. For example, if you apply this constraint to a line, the line will be fully-constrained and it cannot be moved or stretched. To apply this constraint, choose the **Fully Fixed** button *(Customize to add)* from the **Constraint** rollout and then select the entity; the selected entity will be fully fixed.

Coincident Constraint

The Coincident constraint forces two or more keypoints to share the same location. The keypoints that can be used to apply this constraint include the endpoints, center points, control points of splines, and so on. To apply this constraint, invoke the **Geometric Constraints** tool and then choose the **Coincident** button from the **Constraint** rollout. Next, select the keypoints of the sketched entities that are to be made coincident. Figure 3-18 shows the endpoints of the two lines selected to be made coincident and Figure 3-19 shows the sketch after applying the constraint.

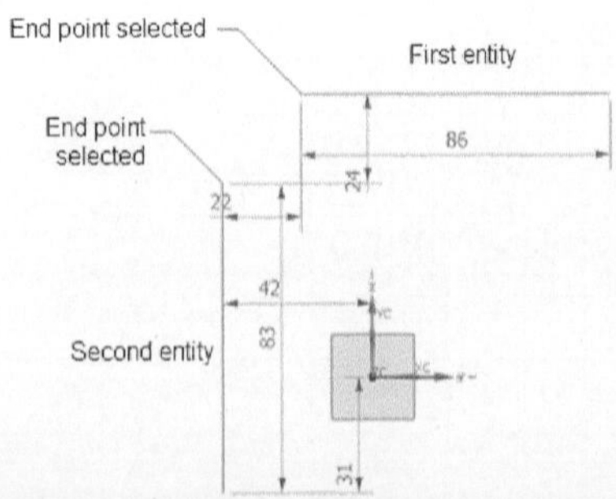

Figure 3-18 The endpoints of the first and second entities selected

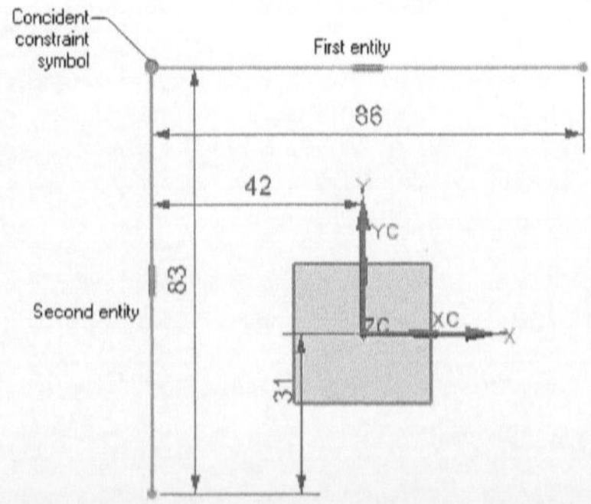

Figure 3-19 The sketch after applying the Coincident constraint

Horizontal Constraint

The Horizontal constraint forces the selected line segment to become horizontal, irrespective of its original orientation. To apply this constraint, choose the **Horizontal** button from the **Geometric Constraints** dialog box and then select the entity; the selected line segment will be forced to become horizontal.

Vertical Constraint

The Vertical constraint is similar to the Horizontal constraint with the only difference that this constraint will force the selected line to become vertical.

Point on Curve Constraint

The Point on Curve constraint is used to place selected keypoints on selected curve or line. To apply this constraint, invoke the **Geometric Constraints** tool and then choose the **Point on Curve** button from the **Constraint** rollout; you will be prompted to select the entities to be constrained. First, select a point such as the endpoint or the center point. Next, select a curve; the point will be placed on the curve. Figure 3-20 shows a sketch before applying this constraint and Figure 3-21 shows a sketch after applying this constraint.

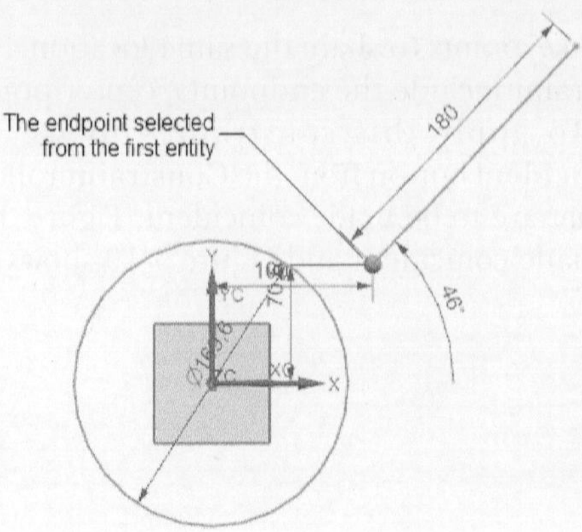

Figure 3-20 The reference elements selected from the entity to apply the Point on Curve constraint

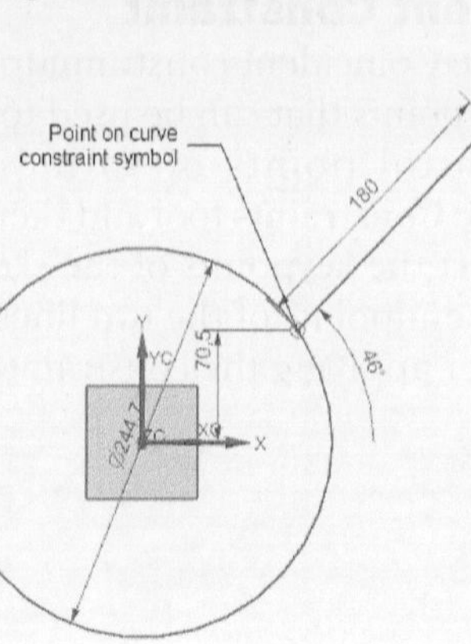

Figure 3-21 The sketch after applying the Point on Curve constraint

Midpoint Constraint

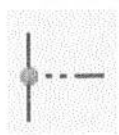

NX provides you with an extension of the Point on Curve constraint, which is the Midpoint constraint. This constraint forces the selected point to be placed in line with the midpoint of the selected line or curve. Note that this constraint is available only when the selected curve is an open entity such as a line segment or an arc. Also, it is important to note that you need to select the curve anywhere other than at its endpoints.

Parallel Constraint

The Parallel constraint forces a set of selected line segments or ellipse axes to become parallel to each other. To apply this constraint, invoke the **Geometric Constraints** tool and then choose the **Parallel** button from the **Constraint** rollout; you will be prompted to select the objects to constrain. Select the set of line segments or ellipses; the selected line segments or axes of the ellipse will become parallel to each other. Figure 3-22 shows two line segments before and after applying this constraint.

Perpendicular Constraint

The Perpendicular constraint forces a set of selected line segments or ellipse axes to become normal to each other. Figure 3-23 shows two line segments before and after applying this constraint.

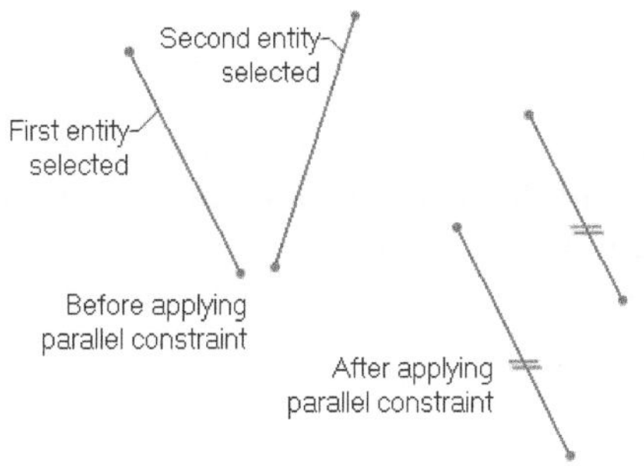

Figure 3-22 Applying the Parallel constraint

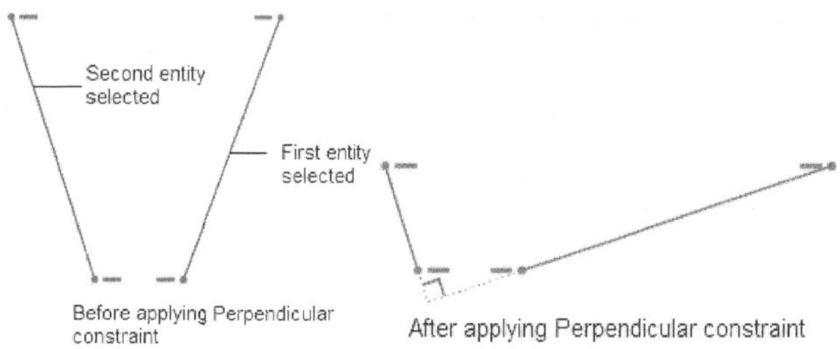

Figure 3-23 Sketch before and after applying the Perpendicular constraint

Tangent Constraint

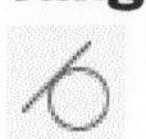

The Tangent constraint forces the selected line segment or curve to become tangent to another curve. To apply this constraint, invoke the **Geometric Constraints** tool and then choose the **Tangent** button from the **Constraint** rollout; you will be prompted to select the entities to be constrained. Select a line and a curve or select two curves; the selected line or curve will become tangent to the other selected curve. Figure 3-24 and 3-25 show the use of the Tangent constraint.

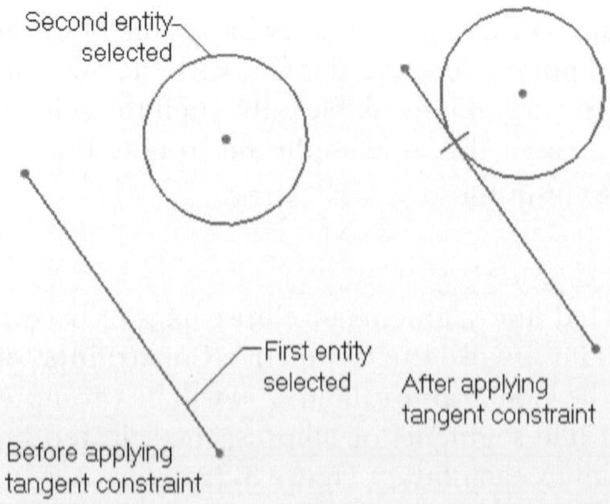

Figure 3-24 Sketch before and after applying the Tangent constraint

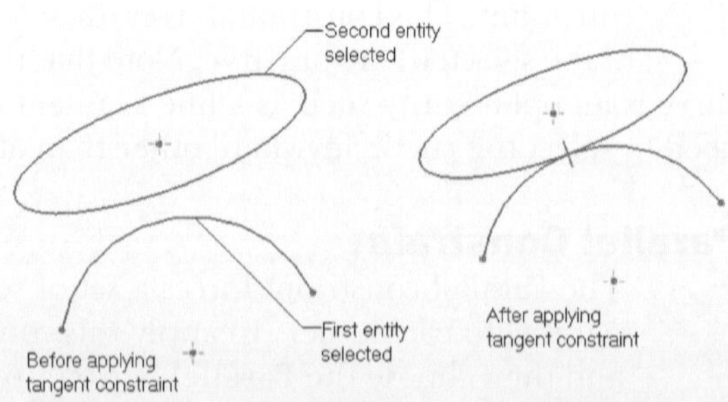

Figure 3-25 Sketch before and after applying the Tangent constraint

> **Note**
> *By default, symbols of all the constraints are displayed in the sketch. You can turn on/off the display of constraints using the* ***Display Sketch Constraints*** *tool which is discussed later in this chapter.*

Equal Length Constraint

The Equal Length constraint forces the length of the selected line segments to become equal. To apply this constraint, invoke the **Geometric Constraints** tool and then choose the **Equal Length** button from the **Constraint** rollout. Next, select the line segments that you want to make equal in length; the selected line segments will become equal in length.

Equal Radius Constraint

The Equal Radius constraint forces the selected arcs or circles to become equal in radius. To apply this constraint, invoke the **Geometric Constraints** tool and then choose the **Equal Radius** button from the **Constraint** rollout. Next, select the arcs or circles that you want to make equal in radii; the selected arcs or circles will become equal in radii.

Concentric Constraint

This constraint is used to force two curves to share the same location of the center points. The curves that can be made concentric include arcs, circles, and ellipses. The ellipses can be made concentric with a circle or an arc also. Figure 3-26 shows two circles before and after adding this constraint.

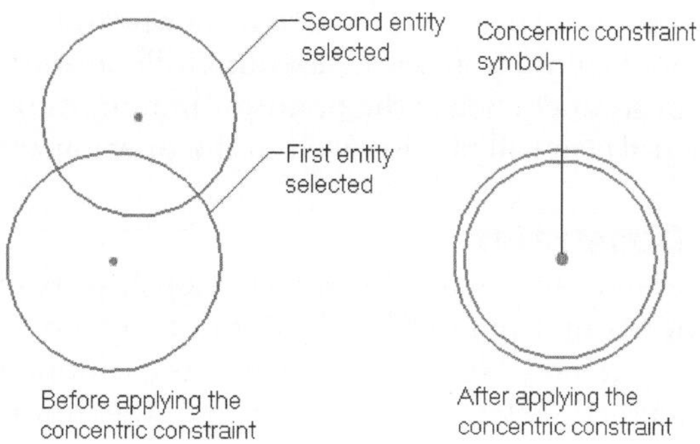

Figure 3-26 Sketch before and after applying the Concentric constraint

Collinear Constraint

This constraint forces the selected line segments to lie along the same line.

Constant Length Constraint

The Constant Length constraint makes the length of the selected line segments constant. As a result, you will not be able to modify the length of the line by using the dimension constraints or by dragging.

Constant Angle Constraint

The Constant Angle constraint makes the angle between the selected line segments constant. As a result, you will not be able to modify the angle between the lines by using the dimension constraints or by dragging.

Slope of Curve Constraint

The Slope of Curve constraint will force the slope of the spline at the selected control point to become equal to the slope of the selected line, arc, or spline segment.

Uniform Scale Constraint

The Uniform Scale constraint ensures that if you modify the distance between the endpoints of a spline, the entire spline will be scaled uniformly.

Non-Uniform Scale Constraint

The Non-Uniform Scale constraint ensures that if you modify the distance between the endpoints of a spline, it will be scaled non-uniformly and it appears to stretch.

Point On String Constraint

The Point On String constraint is used to place selected keypoints on a projected curve or line. As a result, the selected point always lies on the projected curve.

Horizontal Alignment Constraint

To apply this constraint, invoke the **Geometric Constraints** tool and then choose the **Horizontal Alignment** button from the **Constraint** rollout; you will be prompted to select the entities to be constrained. Select the points or midpoints of lines or curves you want to align; the aligned sketch will be displayed in the drawing area.

Vertical Alignment Constraint

To apply this constraint, invoke the **Geometric Constraints** tool and then choose the **Vertical Alignment** button from the **Constraint** rollout; you will be prompted to select the entities to be constrained. Next, select the points or midpoints of lines or curves you want to align; the aligned sketch will be displayed in the drawing area.

Perpendicular to String Constraint

This constraint is used to create a perpendicular constraint between a sketch curve and a recipe curve.

Tangent to String Constraint

This constraint is used to create a tangent constraint between a sketch curve and a recipe curve.

Note
The curves that are associatively projected to the sketch are called Recipe Curves.

Applying Symmetry Constraint

In NX, you can make two selected entities symmetric about a line by using the **Make Symmetric** tool. To make two entities symmetric, invoke the **Make Symmetric** tool from the **Sketch Constraints** gallery of the **More** gallery in the **Direct Sketch** group; the **Make Symmetric** dialog box will be displayed and you will be prompted to select the first object. Select the first object; you will be prompted to select the second object. Select the second object; you will be prompted to select a line or plane as the centerline. After selecting the centerline, you will notice that the selected objects have become symmetric about the centerline. Also, the selected centerline has converted into a reference element. This is because the **Make Reference** check box is selected by default in the dialog box. Next, choose the **Close** button; the **Make Symmetric** dialog box will be closed.

Applying Automatic Constraints to a Sketch

Ribbon:	Home > Direct Sketch > More Gallery > Sketch Tools > Auto Constrain (Customize to add)
Menu:	Tools > Sketch Constraints > Auto Constrain

The **Auto Constrain** tool allows you to apply the possible constraints automatically to the entire sketch. This tool is mainly used when you import geometry from another CAD system. To apply automatic constraints, choose the **Auto Constrain** tool from the **Sketch Tools** rollout of the **More** gallery in the **Direct Sketch** group; the **Auto Constrain** dialog box will be displayed, as shown in Figure 3-27. The options in this dialog box are discussed next.

Curves to Constrain Rollout

This rollout is used to select a line, a circle, or a curve to which constraints will be applied. Select the sketched entities to which the constraints are to be applied. As you select the sketched entities, the **Apply** and **OK** buttons of this dialog box will be enabled.

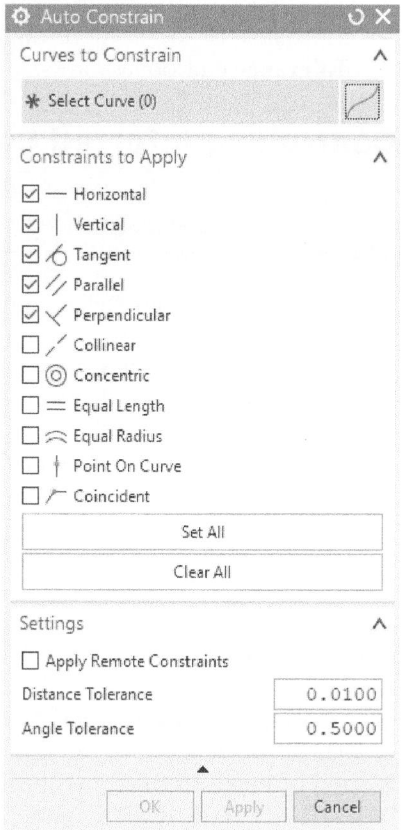

*Figure 3-27 The **Auto Constrain** dialog box*

Constraints to Apply Rollout

This rollout consists of various check boxes for major geometric constraints in NX. You can select the check boxes of the constraints that should be applied to the sketch. After selecting all the required check boxes of the constraints, choose the **Apply** button and then exit from the dialog box by choosing the **Cancel** button. After you exit the **Auto Constrain** dialog box, all possible constraints from the selected constraints will be applied to the sketch. Also, this rollout contains the options to set and clear all the geometric constraint check boxes. These options are discussed next.

Set All

If you choose this button, the check boxes for all the constraints will be selected. As a result, all the possible constraints will be automatically applied to the sketch after you exit this dialog box.

Clear All

If you choose this button, the check boxes for all the constraints will be cleared.

Settings Rollout

This rollout provides the options to set the tolerance for applying the constraints. Note that this rollout is not expanded by default. Expand this rollout to display options in it. The options in this rollout are discussed next.

Distance Tolerance

In this edit box, you can specify the maximum distance between the endpoints of two entities to be considered for applying the Coincident constraint.

Angle Tolerance

In this edit box, you can specify the angle tolerance value that will define whether the Horizontal, Vertical, Parallel, and Perpendicular constraints should be applied to the lines in the sketch after you exit the **Auto Constrain** dialog box. For example, if the deviation of lines from the X and Y axes is more than the specified value in this edit box, the Horizontal and Vertical constraints will not be applied to them.

Apply Remote Constraints

This check box is selected to apply constraints between the objects that are separated by a distance or angle more than the value entered in the **Distance Tolerance** and **Angle Tolerance** edit boxes.

Controlling Inferred Constraints Settings

Ribbon:	Home > Direct Sketch > More Gallery > Sketch Tools > Inferred Constraints and Dimensions (Customize to add)
Menu:	Tools > Sketch Constraints > Inferred Constraints and Dimensions

As mentioned earlier, some of the constraints and dimensions are automatically applied to the sketched entities while they are being sketched. These settings are controlled by the **Inferred Constraints and Dimensions** tool. When you choose this tool, the **Inferred Constraints and Dimensions** dialog box will be displayed, as shown in Figure 3-28.

This dialog box displays all the constraints that are available in NX. You can select the check box corresponding to those constraints that should be applied automatically to the sketch while the sketch is being drawn.

The **Create Dimensions for Typed Values** check box is selected by default, so the dimensions of the entities created by entering the values inside the input boxes will be displayed in the drawing area.

The **Auto Dimensioning Rules** area in the **Dimensions Inferred while Sketching** rollout displays rules for applying auto dimensions to the sketch. You can modify the order of these rules by using the **Move Up** and **Move Down** buttons.

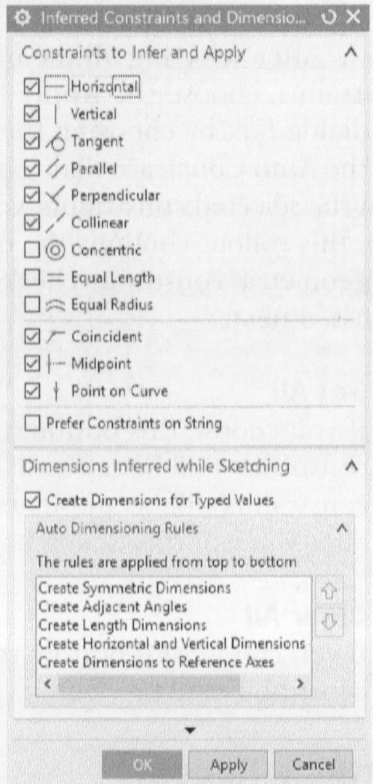

*Figure 3-28 The **Inferred Constraints and Dimensions** dialog box*

Showing All Constraints in a Sketch

Ribbon:	Home > Direct Sketch > More Gallery > Sketch Constraints > Display Sketch Constraints
Menu:	Tools > Sketch Constraints > Display Sketch Constraints

By default, all the constraints that are applied to a sketch are displayed in the sketch. You can turn on/off the display of these constraints by using the **Display Sketch Constraints** button. This is a toggle button and when you turn it off, it remains off until you turn it on. With this button turned on, you can continue working with the other sketching tools.

Sketch Relations Browser

Ribbon:	Home > Direct Sketch > More Gallery > Sketch Tools > Relations Browser
Menu:	Tools > Sketch Constraints > Sketch Relations Browser

You can use the **Relations Browser** tool to interrogate sketched objects. To do so, choose the **Relations Browser** tool from the **Sketch Tools** rollout of the **More** gallery in the **Direct Sketch** group of the Home tab; the **Sketch Realtions Browser** dialog box will be displayed, refer to Figure 3-29. In this dialog box, you can view the constraints, dimensions, and external references associated to a part of the sketch or the entire sketch. Also, it enables you to view details of the sketched objects in an active sketch and to resolve their conflicting constraints. You can also delete dimensions and constraints using this dialog box.

Using this dialog box you can view:

1. Curves and their associated constraints
2. Constraints and their associated curves
3. Dimensions and their associated curves
4. External references attached to the sketch

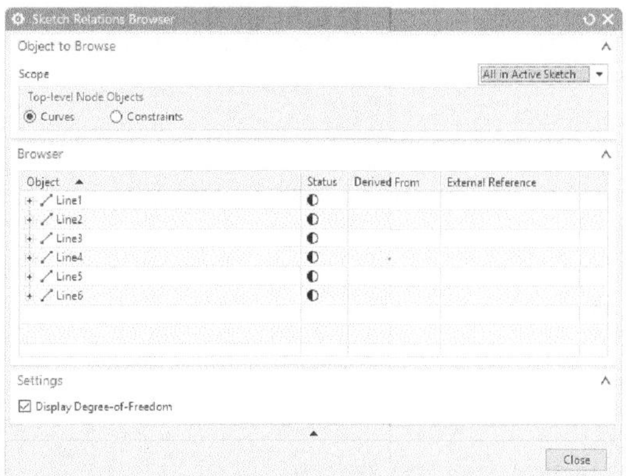

*Figure 3-29 The **Sketch Relations Browser** dialog box*

Object to Browse Rollout

The options in this rollout are discussed next:

Scope

The options available in the **Scope** drop-down list allow you to select the objects to be analyzed. These options are discussed next:

All in Active Sketch: This option is selected by default. It displays all the curves and constraints in the sketch in the **Browser** rollout.

Single Object: When you select this option from the **Scope** drop-down list, it displays the curves associated with the selected constraint, or the constraints associated with the selected curve in the **Browser** rollout. When you select an object from the drawing area, the current selection is replaced.

Multiple Objects: When this option is selected, the curves associated with the selected constraints, or the constraints associated with the selected curves are displayed in the **Browser** rollout.

Top-level Node Objects

This area of the dialog box contains two radio buttons, **Curves** and **Constraints** which are discussed next:

Curves: When you select this radio button, the curves are displayed as the top level nodes. Each curve node contains nodes of the constraints attached to it.

Constraints: When you select this radio button, the constraints are displayed as the top level nodes. Each constraint node contains nodes of the curves attached to it.

Browser Rollout

This area of the dialog box contains a table with four columns. They are discussed next:

Object

This column displays the names of the curves and constraints contained in the sketch.

Status

This column displays the constraint status of the curves. For example, overconstrained curves are indicated. Hover the cursor over the icons in this column for more information.

Derived From

This column displays the icon of the command/tool used to create relationship.

External Reference

This column displays a message when a sketch curve has a reference to an object in another file or in the same file but outside the sketch.

Settings Rollout

This area contains the **Display Degree-of-Freedom** check box which toggles the degree-of-freedom arrows on the sketch curves.

Converting a Sketch Entity or Dimension into a Reference Entity or Reference Dimension

Ribbon:	Home > Direct Sketch > More Gallery > Sketch Tools > Convert To/From Reference (Customize to add)
Menu:	Tools > Sketch Constraints > Convert To/From Reference

The **Convert To/From Reference** tool is used to convert or retain the reference property of a sketched entity or a dimension. Generally, reference elements are created for assigning the axis of revolution or for applying dimensions with reference to an entity. To convert any of these sketched entities or dimensions into a reference element, choose the **Convert To/From Reference** tool from the **Sketch Tools** rollout of the **More** gallery in the **Direct**

Sketch group; the **Convert To/From Reference** dialog box will be displayed, as shown in Figure 3-30.

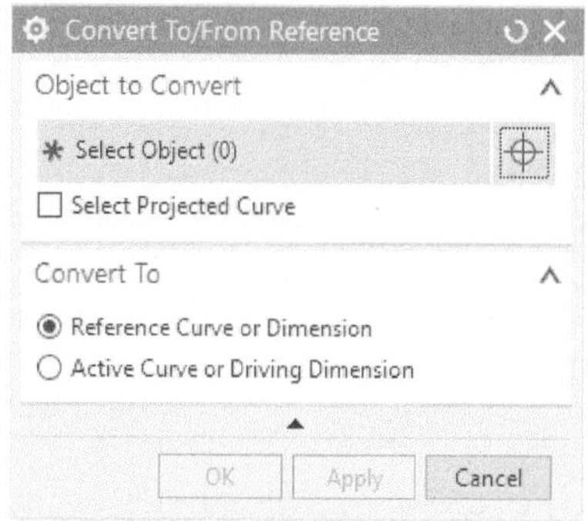

Figure 3-30 The ***Convert To/From Reference*** *dialog box*

By default, the **Reference Curve or Dimension** radio button is selected and therefore you are prompted to select the entity or dimension. Select one or more objects, or dimensions. Next, choose the **OK** button from the dialog box to convert the selected objects or dimensions into reference elements or dimensions.

To make the reference elements or dimensions active, select the **Active Curve or Driving Dimension** radio button from the dialog box and select the reference elements or dimensions. Next, choose the **OK** button.

Note

You can also convert geometric entities into reference entities and vice-versa without invoking the ***Convert To/From Reference*** *dialog box. To do so, select the entities to be converted from the drawing window and then choose the* ***Convert To/From Reference*** *tool from the* ***Sketch Tools*** *rollout of the* ***More*** *gallery in the* ***Direct Sketch*** *group. If you are working in the sketching environment invoked by using the* ***Sketch in Task environment*** *tool then you can use this tool from the* ***Constraints*** *group of the* ***Home*** *tab; the selected geometric entities will be converted into reference entities and vice-versa.*

Creating Alignment Constraints

In NX, you can control the creation of alignment constraints (horizontal or vertical). In the releases prior to NX 12.0, if an entity was placed into the sketch after snapping the existing point of the sketched entity horizontally or vertically, the respective constraint would be applied between the entities by default. NX 12 onwards, these alignment constraints will not be applied by default. However, you can control the application of these alignment constraints. To do so, choose **Menu > File > Utilities > Customer Defaults**; the **Customer Defaults** dialog box will be displayed, refer to Figure 3-31.

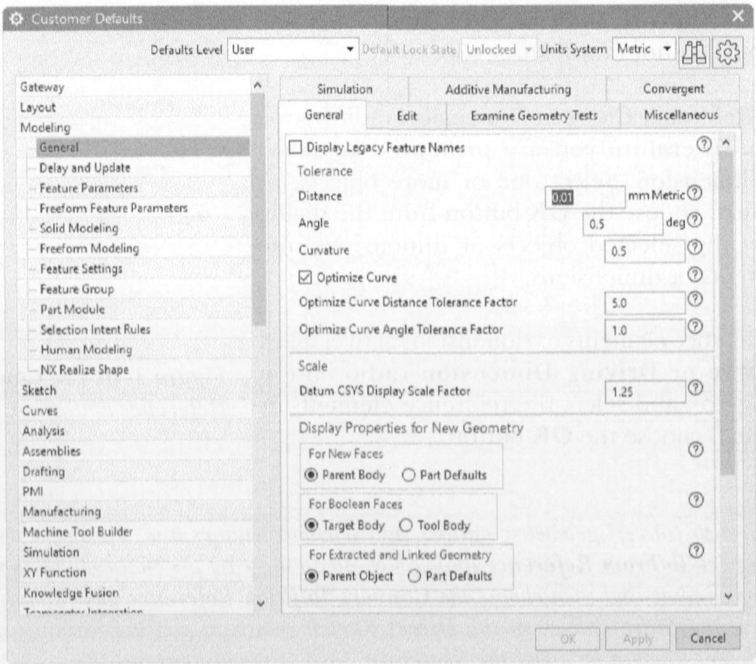

Figure 3-31 The ***Customer Defaults*** *dialog box*

In this dialog box, expand the **Sketch** node from the list box available at the left by clicking on it. Choose the **Inferred Constraints and Dimensions** sub-node; the options related it to it will be displayed on the right. Next, select the **Create Alignment Constraints** check box available under the **Constraints** tab.

After selecting this check box, the alignment constraints will be applied between entities while sketching. Figure 3-32 shows a sketch in which the right circle is placed horizontally after snapping the mid point of the left circle; the horizontal alignment constraint is applied between the centers. Notice that no alignment constraint is applied as the **Create Alignment Constraints** check box is cleared in the **Customer Defaults** dialog box, refer to Figure 3-33.

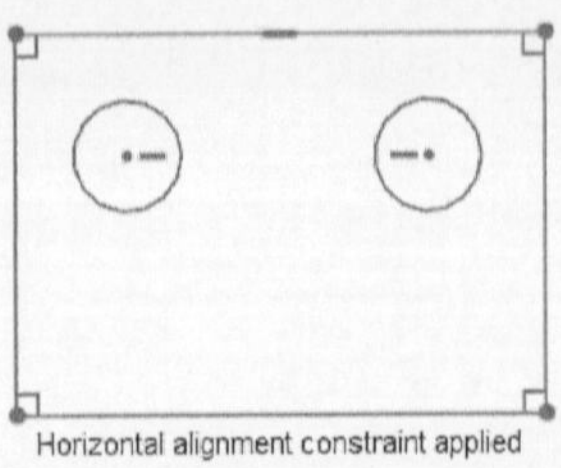

Figure 3-32 Sketch after selecting the ***Create Alignment Constraints*** *check box*

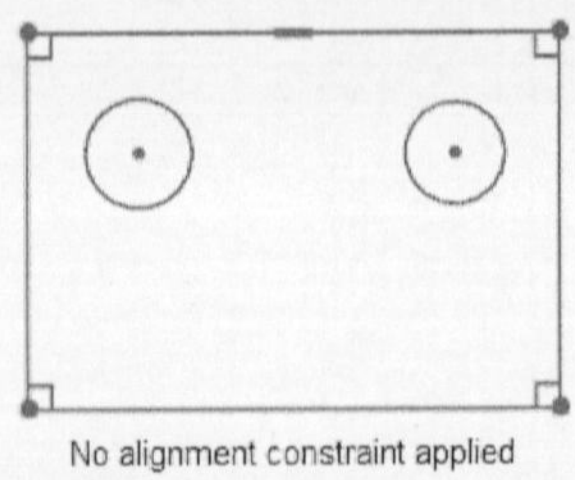

Figure 3-33 Sketch after selecting the ***Create Alignment Constraints*** *check box is cleared*

Note

To reflect the changes made in the ***Customer Defaults*** *dialog box, you need to restart the NX session.*

TUTORIALS

From this chapter onward, you will use Sketch constraints and parametric dimensions to complete the model.

Tutorial 1

In this tutorial, you will draw the profile of the model shown in Figure 3-34. The profile is shown in Figure 3-35. The profile should be symmetric about the origin. Also, you will use the parametric dimensions to complete the sketch. **(Expected time: 30 min)**

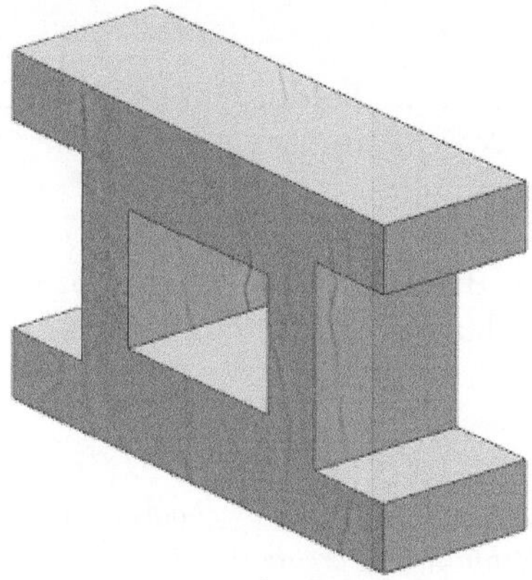

Figure 3-34 *Model for Tutorial 1*

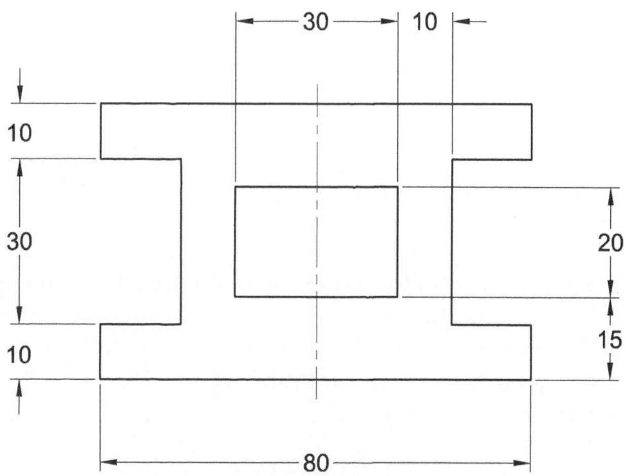

Figure 3-35 *Sketch for Tutorial 1*

The following steps are required to complete this tutorial:

a. Start a new file.
b. Draw the outer profile of the sketch using the **Profile** tool, refer to Figure 3-36.

c. Add the geometric constraints to the outer loop and modify its dimensional constraints, refer to Figure 3-37 and 3-38.
d. Draw a rectangle inside the outer loop using the **Rectangle** tool, refer to Figure 3-39.
e. Add dimensions to the rectangle to complete the sketch, refer to Figure 3-40.
f. Save the sketch and close the file.

Starting a New File and Invoking the Sketch Environment

1. Start a new file by using the **Model** template. To do so, choose the **New** button from the **File** tab of the **Ribbon**; the **New** dialog box is displayed. Next, select the **Model** template from the **Templates** rollout, and then enter **c03tut1** as the name of the document in the **Name** text box.

2. Choose the button on the right of the **Folder** text box; the **Choose Directory** dialog box is displayed. Next, browse to *C:\NX\c03* and then choose the **OK** button twice; the new file is started in the Modeling environment.

3. Choose the **Sketch** tool from the **Direct Sketch** group; the **Create Sketch** dialog box is displayed. Select the XC-ZC plane as the sketching plane and choose the **OK** button from the dialog box.

Note

You can also invoke the Sketch environment by choosing the ***Sketch in Task Environment*** *tool from the* ***Curve*** *tab of the* ***Ribbon*** *and create sketch.*

Drawing the Outer Loop and Adding Sketch Constraints

If the sketch consists of more than one closed loop, it is recommended that you first draw the outer loop and then add all the required Sketch constraints and dimensions to it. This makes it easier to draw and dimension the inner loops. Next, you need to draw the inner loop.

1. Choose the **Profile** tool from the **Direct Sketch** group of the **Home** tab; you are prompted to select the first point of the line or press and drag the left mouse button to begin with the arc creation.

2. Draw the sketch around the origin following the sequence shown in Figure 3-36. The sketch is unsymmetrical at this stage. But after adding the Sketch constraints and modifying the dimensions, it will become symmetrical. You can use the help lines to draw the sketch. For your reference, the sequence in which the lines are needed to be drawn in the sketch are indicated by numbers.

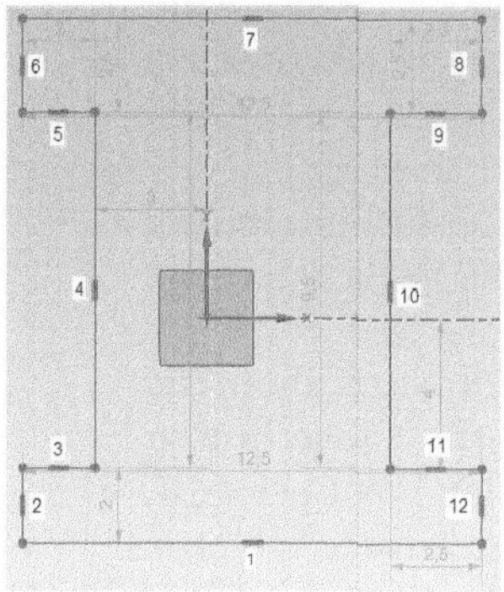

Figure 3-36 *The outer loop of the profile and the sequence in which lines have to be drawn*

Note

The dimensions shown in Figure 3-36 get automatically applied when sketch is drawn. However, those dimensions are not driving dimensions. They will change when you drag or move a sketched entity. In order to make them driving dimensions, you need to modify them. You will learn to modify these dimensions later in this tutorial.

Next, you need to apply the geometric constraints and modify dimensions. But before you do that, it is recommended that you turn on the display of constraints if not already on.

3. Choose the **Display Sketch Constraints** tool from the **Sketch Constraints** rollout of the **More** gallery in the **Direct Sketch** group to view the constraints applied to the sketch, if it is not chosen by default.

4. Choose the **Geometric Constraints** tool from the **More** gallery of the **Direct Sketch** group of the **Home** tab; the **Geometric Constraints** dialog box is displayed and you are prompted to select curves to create constraints.

5. Choose the **Equal Length** button from the **Geometric Constraints** dialog box and then select lines 1 and 7. The symbol for the equal length constraint is displayed on both the sketch members indicating that this constraint is applied between the two selected entities. Note that the **Automatic selection progression** check box should be selected in the **Geometry to Constrain** rollout to move to the succeeding points.

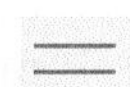

6. Similarly, apply the equal length constraint between lines 8 and 6, 6 and 2, 2 and 12, 12 and 8, 3 and 11, 9 and 5, and 10 and 4. Next, exit the dialog box.

Now, you need to make this sketch symmetric about horizontal and vertical datum axes.

7. Choose the **Make Symmetric** tool from the **Sketch Constraints** rollout of the **More** gallery in the **Direct Sketch** group; the **Make Symmetric** dialog box is displayed and you are prompted to select the first object to apply symmetry.

8. Select line 2; you are prompted to select the second object. Select line 12; you are prompted to select the centerline.

9. Select the vertical axis as the centerline; lines 2 and 12 become symmetric about vertical axis.

10. Similarly, make lines 1 and 7 symmetric about the horizontal axis. Next, choose the **Close** button from the **Make Symmetric** dialog box to close it. The sketch after applying constraints to all these entities is shown in Figure 3-37.

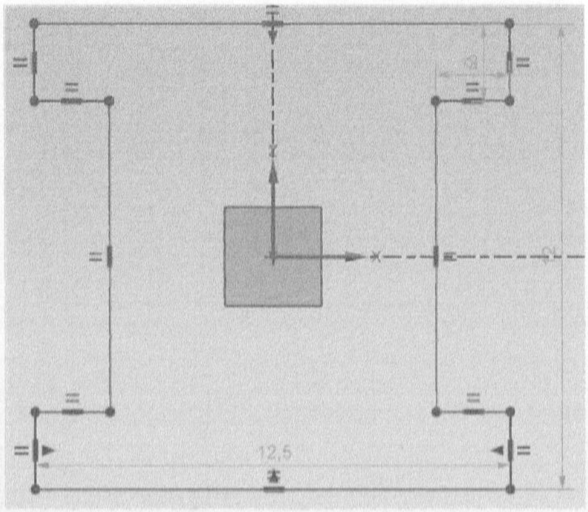

Figure 3-37 The outer profile after adding constraints

Adding Dimensions to Sketch Members

Next, you need to add dimensions to the sketch. As mentioned earlier, when you add dimensions to a sketch, the sketch gets modified accordingly.

1. Choose the **Rapid Dimension** tool from the **Direct Sketch** group of the **Home** tab; you are prompted to select an object to dimension or the dimension to edit.

2. Select line 1; the current dimension of line 1 is attached to the cursor. Now, you need to place the dimension at the required location. Click below the line 1 to place the dimension, refer to Figure 3-38. As you place the dimension, an edit box is displayed. Enter **80** in the edit box and press ENTER. Next, choose the **Fit** tool from the **Operation** group of the **View** tab.

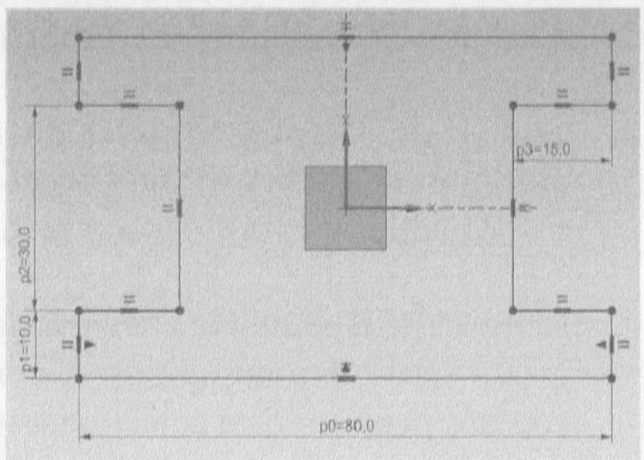

***Figure 3-38** The outer profile after adding required dimensions*

3. Select line 2 and place the dimensions on the left of the sketch. Enter **10** in the edit box displayed and press ENTER.

4. Select line 4 and place the dimension on the left of the sketch. Next, modify the dimension value to **30** and press ENTER.

5. Select line 9 and place the dimension below the line. Next, modify the dimension value to **15** and press ENTER.

   When you place the dimensions, they generally scatter all around the sketch. It is a good practice to arrange them properly.

6. Exit the **Rapid Dimension** tool by pressing the ESC key and then drag the dimensions to place them properly around the sketch, refer to Figure 3-38.

Tip

Instead of adding dimensions to a sketch, you can also modify the existing dimension. To do so, double-click on the dimension; an edit box will be displayed. Enter the required value in the edit box and press ENTER; the dimensions will be locked and displayed in blue color.

Drawing the Inner Loop and Adding Dimensions

Next, you need to draw the rectangular profile inside the outer loop.

1. Choose the **Rectangle** tool from the **Direct Sketch** group of the **Home** tab; the **Rectangle** dialog box is displayed.
2. Choose the **From Center** button from the **Rectangle** dialog box; you are prompted to specify the center of the rectangle.
3. Select origin as the center of the rectangle; you are prompted to specify the second point of the rectangle.
4. Move the cursor horizontally toward right and click to specify the second point; you are prompted to select the third point to create the rectangle.
5. Move the cursor vertically upward and click to specify the third point; the rectangle is created, refer to Figure 3-39. Press ESC to exit the tool.
6. Double-click on the horizontal dimension of the rectangle; a dynamic edit box is displayed. Modify the value of the dimension to **30** and press ENTER. Next, drag and place the dimension above the sketch.
7. Similarly, double-click on the vertical dimension of the rectangle and modify the value of the dimension to **20**. Next, press ESC. Next, place the dimension on the left of the sketch, refer to Figure 3-40.

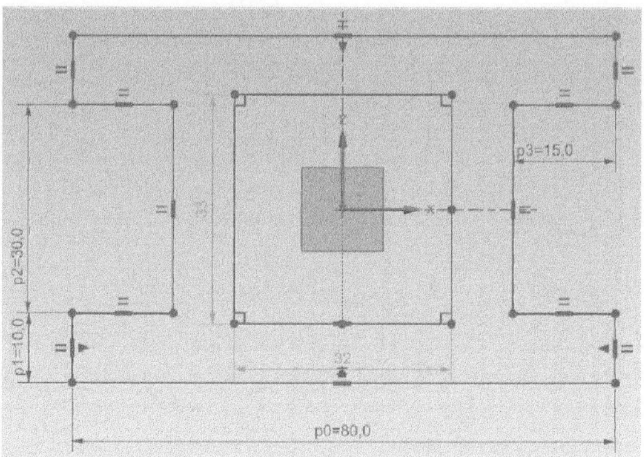

***Figure 3-39** The sketch after drawing the inner loop and turning on the display of constraints*

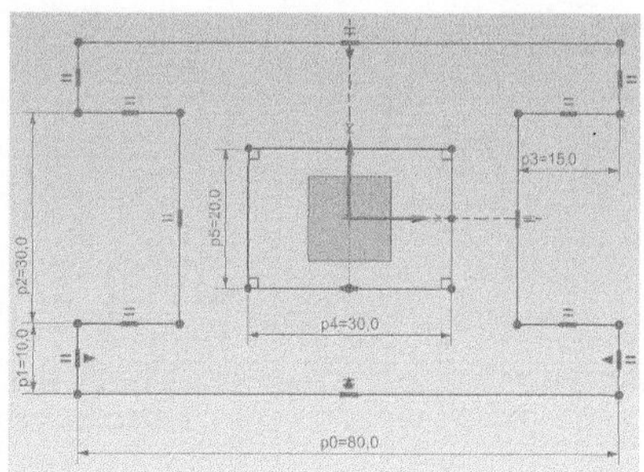

***Figure 3-40** The sketch after adding required dimensions and constraints*

Saving and Closing the File

1. Exit the sketching environment by choosing the **Finish Sketch** tool from the **Direct Sketch** group of the **Home** tab. Next, choose the **Save** button from the **Quick Access** toolbar to save the sketch. Note that the name and location of the document had already been specified when you started new file.

2. Choose **Menu > File > Close > All Parts** from the **Top Border Bar** to close the file.

Tutorial 2

In this tutorial, you will create the profile for the model shown in Figure 3-41. The profile is shown in Figure 3-42. You will use the geometric and dimensional constraints to complete this sketch. **(Expected time: 30 min)**

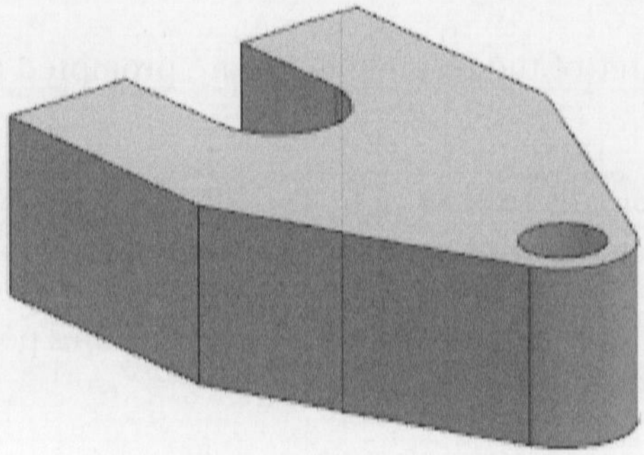

Figure 3-41 *Model for Tutorial 2*

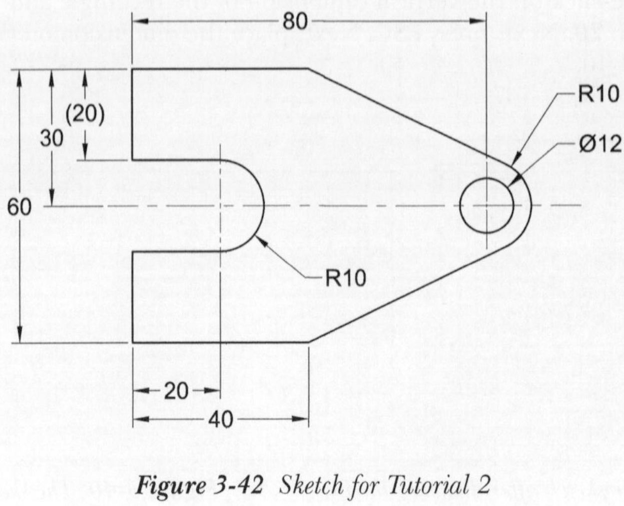

Figure 3-42 *Sketch for Tutorial 2*

The following steps are required to complete this tutorial:

a. Start a new file in NX and invoke the Sketch environment.
b. Draw the sketch using the **Profile** tool, refer to Figure 3-43.
c. Add the geometric and dimensional constraints to the sketch, refer to Figures 3-44 and 3-45.
d. Save the sketch and close the file.

Starting a New File in NX and Invoking the Sketch Environment

1. Start a new file with the name *c03tut2.prt* using the **Model** template and specify its location as *C:\NX\c03*.

2. Turn on the display of WCS by choosing the **Display WCS** tool from **Tools > Utilities > More > WCS** in the **Ribbon** if not already displayed.

3. Invoke the Sketch environment by using the XC-YC plane as the sketching plane.

Drawing the Sketch

1. Choose the **Profile** tool from the **Direct Sketch** group. Draw the outer profile of the sketch, refer to Figure 3-43. You can draw the first line with exact dimension and then draw the remaining sketched entities with dimension values close to the required dimension values. Note that the start point of line1 is at the origin.

   Note that after drawing the first line, you may need to modify the drawing display area by using the **Fit** tool from the **Operation** group of the **View** tab.

2. Next, choose the **Circle** tool from the **Direct Sketch** group. Move the cursor over the arc that is numbered 3 in Figure 3-43; the center point of the arc is highlighted.

Note
If the center of the arc is not highlighted, choose the ***Arc Center*** *button from the* ***Selection Group*** *of the* ***Top Border Bar****.*

3. Once the center point gets highlighted, move the cursor over it and press the left mouse button to specify the center point of the circle. Now, move the cursor away from the center point and specify the diameter of the circle by clicking the left mouse button or by entering the diameter value in the diameter input box. The circle is created, refer to Figure 3-43.

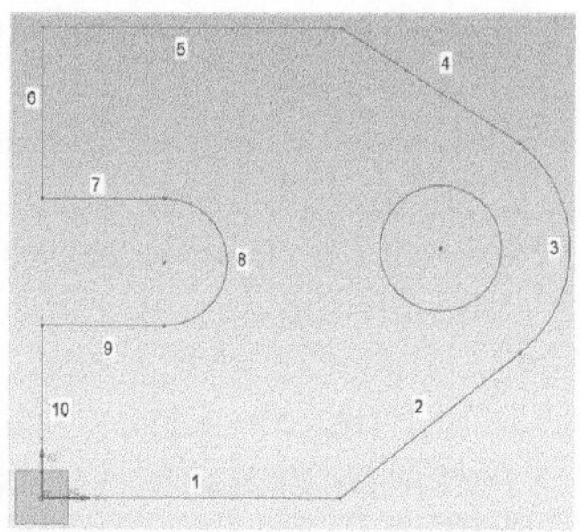

Figure 3-43 *The sequence to be followed for drawing the sketch*

Adding Constraints to the Sketch

1. Choose the **Geometric Constraints** tool from the **More** gallery of the **Direct Sketch** group; the **Geometric Constraints** dialog box is displayed.

2. Choose the **Horizontal** button from the **Geometric Constraints** dialog box and select line 1 to apply the Horizontal constraint if this constraint has not already been applied. Similarly, apply the Horizontal constraint to lines 5, 7, and 9.

3. Similarly, apply the Vertical constraint to lines 6 and 10 if this constraint has not already been applied.

4. Choose the **Concentric** button from the **Geometric Constraints** dialog box. Next, select the circle and arc 3 from the drawing area to apply the Concentric constraint.

5. Choose the **Equal Length** button from the **Geometric Constraints** dialog box and select lines 1 and 5 to apply the Equal Length constraint.

6. Similarly, apply the Equal Length constraint between lines 2 and 4, 6 and 10, and 7 and 9.

7. Choose the **Tangent** button from the **Geometric Constraints** dialog box and select Line 4 and arc 3, and Line 2 and arc 3 to apply the Tangent constraint between them if not already applied.

   The sketch after applying all the constraints is shown in Figure 3-44.

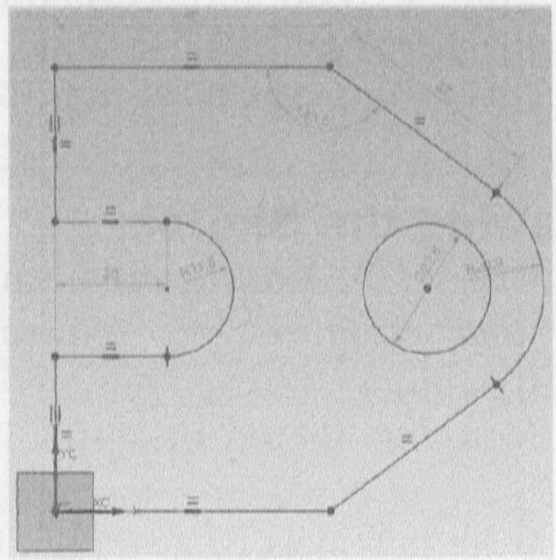

Figure 3-44 The sketch displayed after adding the required constraints

Modifying Dimensions of the Sketch

Next, you need to modify the dimensions of the sketch.

1. Double-click on the dimension of line 7; a dynamic edit box is displayed. Modify the value of the dimension to **20** and press ENTER. Next, drag and place the dimension below the line, refer to Figure 3-45.

2. Double-click on the dimension of the arc 8; a dynamic edit box is displayed. Modify the value of the dimension to **10** and press ENTER.

3. Double-click on the dimension of the arc 3; a dynamic edit box is displayed. Modify the value of the dimension to **10** and press ENTER.

   Next, you need to add some dimensions which are not added automatically.

4. Choose the **Rapid Dimension** tool from the **Direct Sketch** group.

5. Select line 6 and the center point of the circle. Place the dimension above the sketch and modify the dimension value to **80**. Press the ENTER key.

6. Select line 6 and place the dimension on the left of the sketch. Next, modify the dimension value to **20** and press ENTER.

7. Select the circle and place the dimension, refer to Figure 3-45. Next, modify the dimension value to 12 and press ENTER.

8. Choose the **Fit** tool from the **View** tab.

   The final sketch after adding the required dimensions is shown in Figure 3-45.

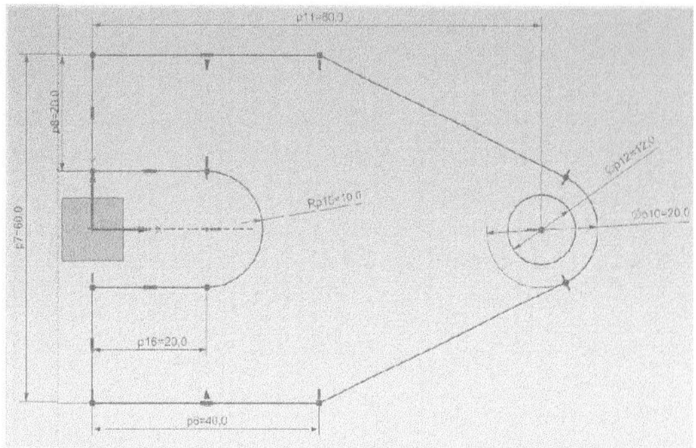

Figure 3-45 *The final sketch after adding the required dimensions*

Saving and Closing the File

1. Choose the **Save** button from the **Quick Access** toolbar to save the sketch. Note that the name and the location of the document has already been specified when you started the new file.

2. Exit the sketching environment and then choose **Menu > File > Close > All Parts** from the **Top Border Bar** to close the file.

Tutorial 3

In this tutorial, you will create the profile of the revolved model shown in Figure 3-46. The profile is shown in Figure 3-47. You will use the geometric and dimensional constraints to complete this sketch. **(Expected time: 30 min)**

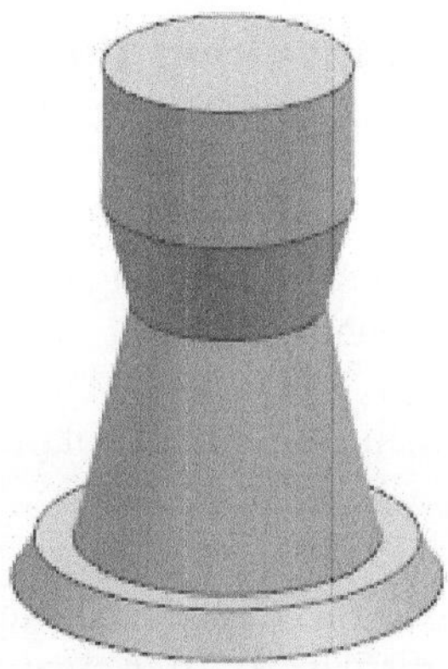

Figure 3-46 *Model for Tutorial 3*

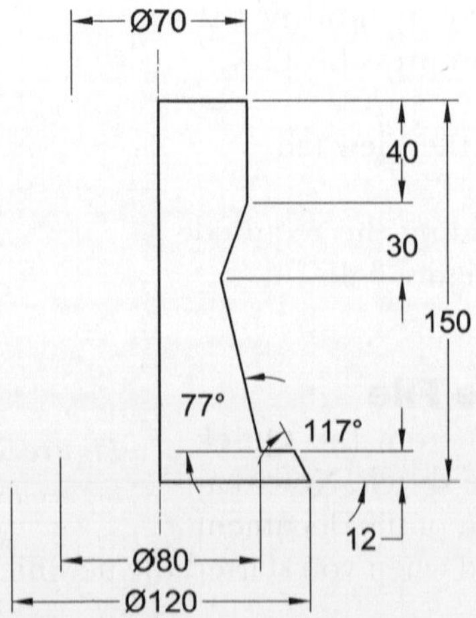

Figure 3-47 Sketch for Tutorial 3

The following steps are required to complete this tutorial:

a. Start a new file in NX and invoke the Sketch environment.
b. Draw the required profile of the sketch using the **Profile** tool, refer to Figure 3-48.
c. Add the geometric and dimensional constraints to the sketch, refer to Figure 3-49 and 3-50.
d. Save the sketch and close the file.

Starting a New File in NX and Invoking the Sketch Environment

1. Start a new file with the name *c03tut3.prt* using the **Model** template and specify its location as *C:\NX\c03*.

   If required turn on the display of WCS by choosing the **Display WCS** tool from the **Tools > Utilities > More > WCS** in the **Ribbon**.

2. Invoke the Sketch environment using the XC-ZC plane as the sketching plane.

Drawing the Sketch

It is recommended that you create the first sketch member of exact measurement by entering the value in the edit box displayed. After creating the first sketch member, you can create rest of the sketch members by taking the first entity as the reference. After creating the entire sketch, you can modify the values by using the dimensioning tools.

1. Choose the **Profile** tool from the **Direct Sketch** group; you are prompted to specify the first point of the line. Specify the start point of the line at the origin. Next, move the cursor horizontally toward the right and enter **60** in the **Length** edit box and **0** in the **Angle** edit box. Next, press ENTER.

2. Follow the sequence given in Figure 3-48 for drawing the sketch. Draw the rest of the entities of the sketch. For better understanding, the sketch has been numbered and temporary dimensions have been hidden.

Adding Geometric Constraints to the Sketch

After completing the sketch, you need to apply constraints to it.

1. Choose the **Geometric Constraints** tool from the **More** gallery of the **Direct Sketch** group of the **Home** tab; the **Geometric Constraints** dialog box is displayed. Choose the **Vertical** button from this dialog box and select line 8 to apply the vertical dimension if not applied automatically while the sketch is drawn.

2. Similarly, apply the horizontal constraint to lines 1, 3, and 7 if this constraint is not applied automatically.

3. Apply the vertical constraint to line 6 if not applied automatically.

4. After applying the constraints, choose the **Display Sketch Constraints** tool from the **Sketch Constraints** gallery of the **More** gallery in the **Direct Sketch** group if not already chosen. The resulting sketch is shown in Figure 3-49.

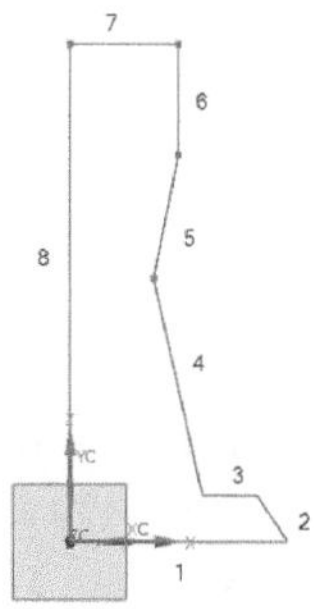

Figure 3-48 The sequence for drawing the profile

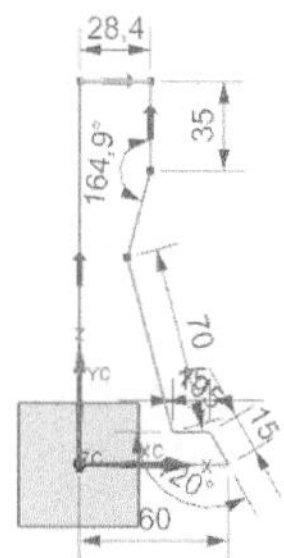

Figure 3-49 The resulting sketch displayed after adding the constraints

Modifying Dimensions of the Sketch

Next, you need to modify the dimensions of the sketch.

1. Double-click on the dimension of line 6; a dynamic edit box is displayed. Modify the value of the dimension to **40** and press ENTER. Next, drag and place the dimension on the right of the sketch, refer to Figure 3-50.

   Next, you need to add some dimensions which are not added automatically.

2. Choose the **Rapid Dimension** tool from the **Direct Sketch** group; the **Rapid Dimension** dialog box is displayed.

3. Select line 8 and then place the dimension on the left of the sketch; an edit box with default value is displayed. Enter **150** in this edit box and press the ENTER key; the dimension value is modified, refer to Figure 3-50.

4. Select line 5 and then place the dimension on the right of the sketch. Next, modify the dimension value to **30** and press the ENTER key, refer to Figure 3-50.

5. Select line 7 and place the dimension above the sketch. Next, modify the dimension value to **35** and press ENTER, refer to Figure 3-50.

6. Select line 2 and then line 1; an angular dimension gets attached to the cursor. Move the cursor outside the sketch towards right and click the left mouse button to place the dimension. Next, modify the dimension value to **117** and press ENTER, refer to Figure 3-50.

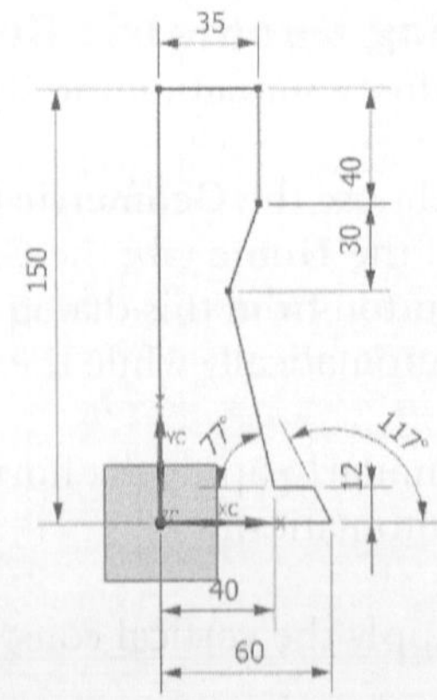

Figure 3-50 The completed sketch displayed after adding required constraints and dimensions

7. Select lines 3 and 4; an angular dimension is attached to the cursor. Move the cursor inside the sketch and place the dimension. Next, modify the dimension value to **77** and press ENTER, refer to Figure 3-50.

8. Select the lower endpoint of line 4 and then select line 8; the dimension value is attached to the cursor. Place the dimension value below the sketch and then modify this value to **40**. Next, press ENTER.

9. Select line 2 and place the dimension on the right of the line. Next, modify the dimension value to **12** and press ENTER, refer to Figure 3-50. Press the ESC key.

10. Choose the **Fit** tool from the **Operation** group of the **View** tab. The resulting sketch after adding all the dimensions is shown in Figure 3-50.

Note

*In Figure 3-50, the display of constraints is turned off to get a better display of dimensions. You can turn off the display of constraints by choosing the **Display Sketch Constraints** tool.*

Saving and Closing the File

1. Choose the **Save** button from the **Quick Access** toolbar to save the sketch. Note that the name and location of the document has already been specified when you started the new file.

2. Exit the sketching environment by choosing the **Finish Sketch** tool from the **Direct Sketch** group of the **Home** tab and choose **Menu > File > Close > All Parts** from the **Top Border Bar** to close the file.

Self-Evaluation Test

Answer the following questions and then compare them to those given at the end of this chapter:

1. The __________ constraint is used to force two curves to share same center point.

2. The __________ tool is used to dimension the radius of an arc.

3. The __________ tool is used to animate a fully constrained sketch.

4. The __________ tool is used to show all the constraints applied to a sketch.

5. In NX, you can add all types of geometric constraints by choosing the **Geometric Constraints** tool from the **Direct Sketch** group of the **Home** tab. (T/F)

6. The **Auto Constrain** tool allows you to apply all possible geometric constraints automatically to an entire sketch. (T/F)

7. The **Rapid Dimension** tool in the **Direct Sketch** group is used to add all possible dimension types. (T/F)

8. In NX, the **Radial Dimension** tool is used to add the diameter dimension to the sketch members. (T/F)

Review Questions

Answer the following questions:

1. Which of the following tools is used to apply geometric constraints to a sketch?

   (a) **Geometric Constraints** (b) **Automatic Constraints**
   (c) **Rapid Dimensions** (d) None of these

2. Which of the following tools is used to add a radial dimension to a sketch?

   (a) **Radial** (b) **Automatic Constraints**
   (c) **Rapid Dimension** (d) None of these

3. Which of the following tools is used to make the endpoints of selected objects coincident?

   (a) **Coincident** (b) **Concentric**
   (c) **Horizontal** (d) None of these

4. Which of the following tools is used to apply the constant length constraint between sketch members?

   (a) **Equal Length** (b) **Automatic Constraints**
   (c) **Vertical** (d) None of these

5. Which of the following tools is used to apply an angular dimension to a sketch member?

(a) **Angular** (b) **Constant Length**
(c) **Rapid Dimensions** (d) None of these

6. Which of the following tools is used to convert a sketch member into a reference element?

(a) **Convert To/From Reference** (b) **Automatic Constraints**
(c) **Geometric Constraints** (d) None of these

7. In NX, the degree of freedom arrows are displayed on the points that are free to move. (T/F)

8. The **Direct Sketch** group contains all the tools required to draw a sketch. (T/F)

9. The **Sketch** tool in the **Home** tab is chosen to switch to the Sketch in Task environment. (T/F)

10. The **Finish Sketch** tool in the **Home** tab is used to exit the Sketch environment. (T/F)

EXERCISES

Exercise 1

Draw the base sketch of the model shown in Figure 3-51. The sketch to be drawn is shown in Figure 3-52. Use the geometric and dimensional constraints to complete this sketch.

(Expected time: 15 min)

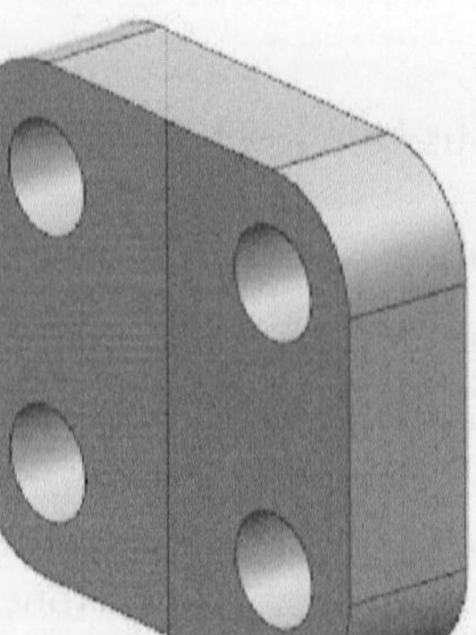

Figure 3-51 Model for Exercise 1

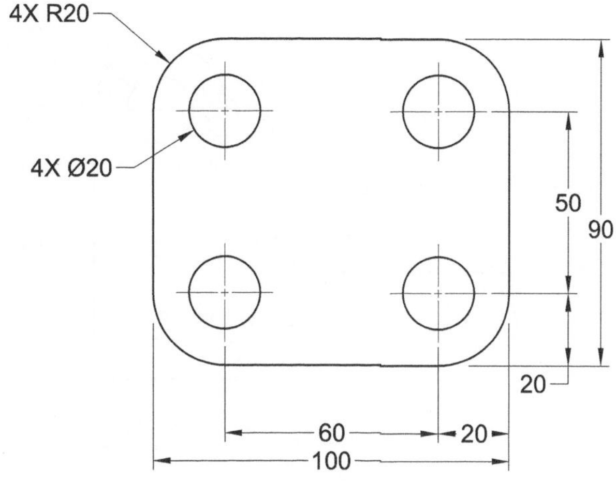

Figure 3-52 *Sketch for Exercise 1*

Exercise 2

Draw the base sketch of the model shown in Figure 3-53. The sketch to be drawn is shown in Figure 3-54. Use the geometric and dimensional constraints to complete this sketch.

(Expected time: 15 min)

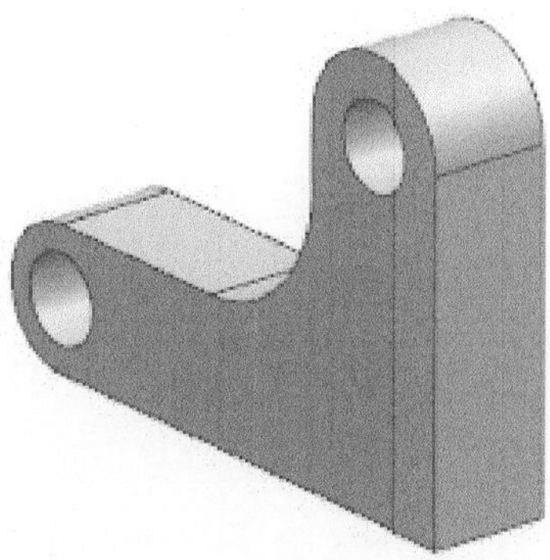

Figure 3-53 *Model for Exercise 2*

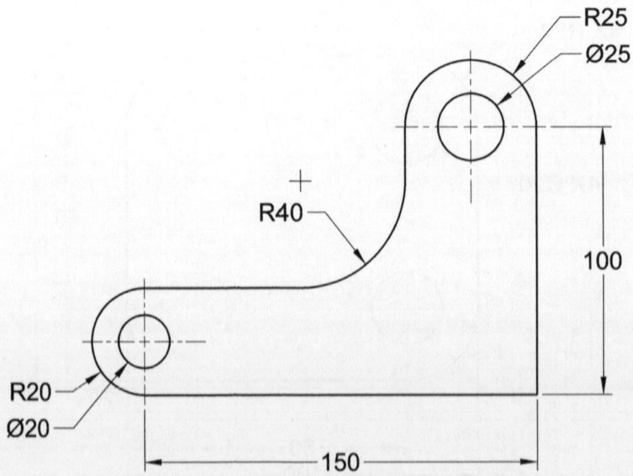

***Figure 3-54** Sketch for Exercise 2*

Answers to Self-Evaluation Test

1. Concentric, **2. Radial**, **3. Animate Dimension**, **4. Display Sketch Constraints, 5.** T, **6.** T, **7.** T, **8.** T

Chapter 4

Editing, Extruding, and Revolving Sketches

Learning Objectives

After completing this chapter, you will be able to:

- *Edit sketches using the editing tools*
- *Edit sketched entities by dragging*
- *Convert sketches into base features by extruding and revolving them*
- *Hide and show objects*
- *Rotate the view of a model dynamically in 3D space*
- *Change the view and display of models*

EDITING SKETCHES

Editing is a very important part of sketching in any design or manufacturing program. You need to edit the sketches during various stages of a design. NX provides you with a number of tools that can be used to edit sketched entities. These tools are discussed next.

Trimming Sketched Entities

Ribbon:	Home > Direct Sketch > Sketch Curve Gallery > Quick Trim
Menu:	Edit > Sketch Curve > Quick Trim

The **Quick Trim** tool is used to remove a portion of a sketch by chopping it off. Figure 4-1 shows the sketched entities to be trimmed and Figure 4-2 shows the sketch after performing the trimming operation. Note that when used on an isolated entity, this tool deletes the entity.

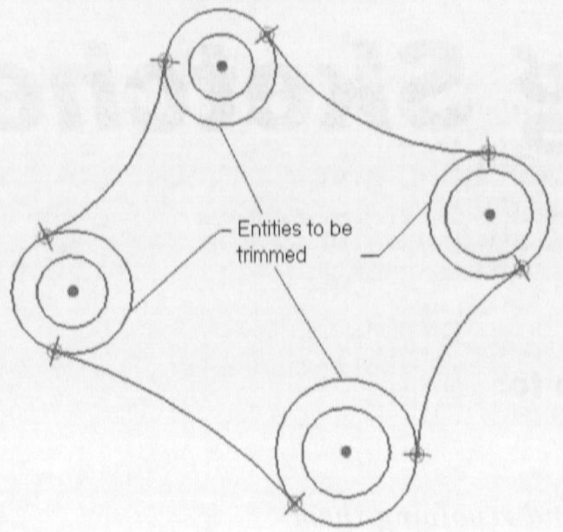

Figure 4-1 Selecting the entities to be trimmed

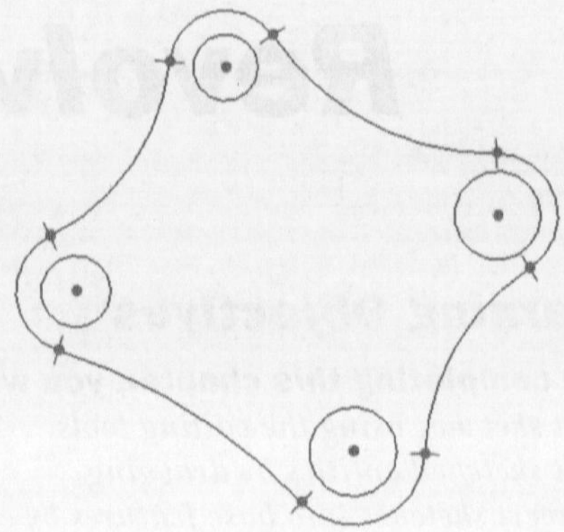

Figure 4-2 Sketch after trimming entities

To trim entities, invoke the **Quick Trim** tool from the **Sketch Curve** gallery of the **Direct Sketch** group of the **Home** tab; the **Quick Trim** dialog box will be displayed, as shown in Figure 4-3. Also, you will be prompted to select a curve to trim.

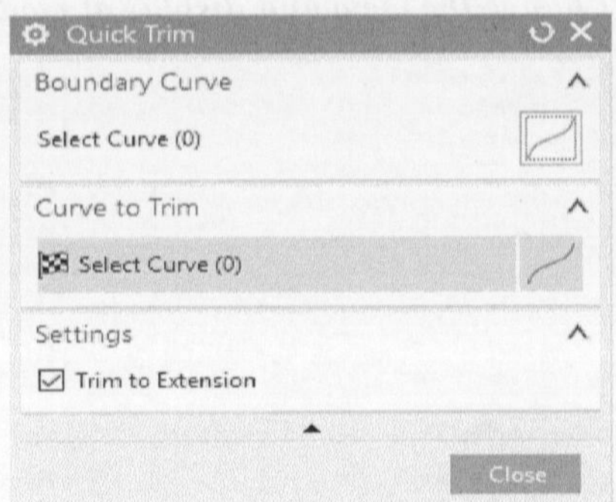

*Figure 4-3 The **Quick Trim** dialog box*

Move the cursor over the portion to be trimmed; it will be highlighted. Click to trim the highlighted portion. You will be prompted again to select the entity to be trimmed. After trimming all entities, press ESC to exit this tool.

To trim multiple entities, press and hold the left mouse button and drag the cursor over the entities to be trimmed. As you move the cursor over them, all the selected entities will be trimmed. Figure 4-4 shows multiple entities being trimmed by dragging the cursor over them and Figure 4-5 shows the resulting sketch.

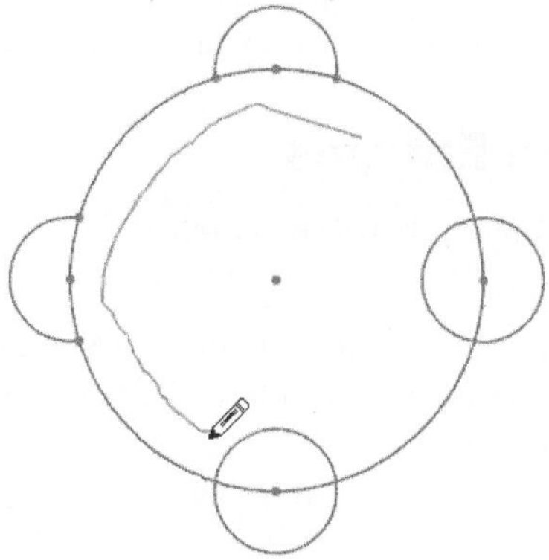

Figure 4-4 Dragging the cursor to trim multiple entities

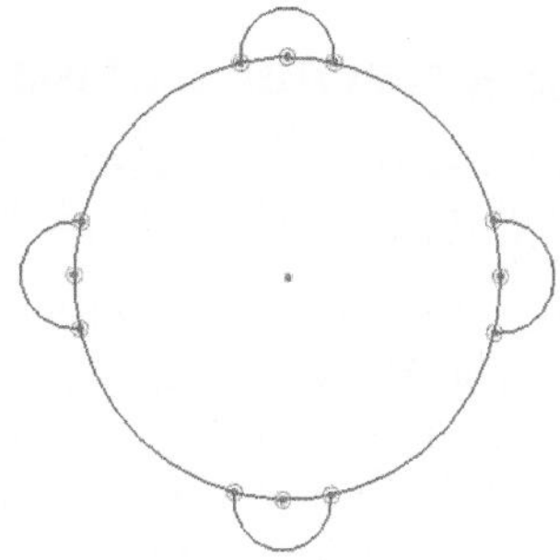

Figure 4-5 The resulting sketch

NX also allows you to select a sketched entity as a knife edge and then trim the other entities using this cutting edge. To trim entities using the cutting edge, choose the **Boundary Curve** button from the **Boundary Curve** rollout in the **Quick Trim** dialog box; you will be prompted to select the boundary curve. Select the curve from the drawing window; the curve becomes a knife edge. Next, choose the **Curve to Trim** button from the **Curve to Trim** rollout in the **Quick Trim** dialog box; you will be prompted to select the curve to be trimmed. Select the curve to be trimmed from the drawing area; the selected curve will be trimmed with respect to the knife edge specified. Similarly, select other curves that intersect the boundary curve; the selected curves will be trimmed. If the **Trim to Extension** check box is selected in the **Settings** rollout and the curve to be trimmed intersects the virtual boundary then the curve will be trimmed on the selected side of the virtual boundary.

Extending Sketched Entities

Ribbon:	Home > Direct Sketch > Sketch Curve Gallery > Quick Extend
Menu:	Edit > Sketch Curve > Quick Extend

The **Quick Extend** tool is used to extend or lengthen an open sketched entity upto the next entity that it intersects. Figure 4-6 shows the sketched entity before extending and Figure 4-7 shows the sketch after extending the entity. Note that this tool will not work on an entity that does not intersect with any existing sketched entity when extended.

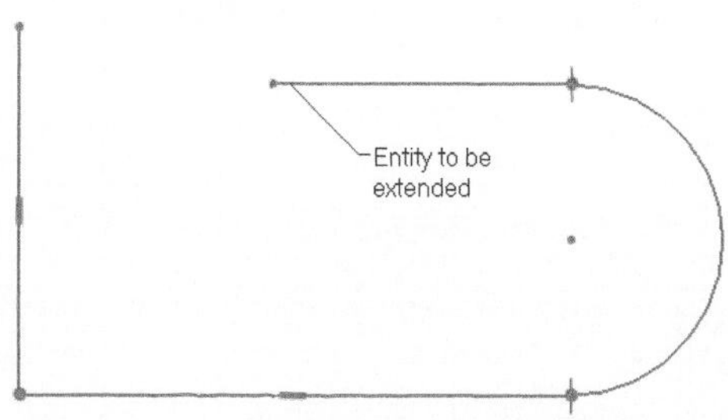

Figure 4-6 Selecting the entity to be extended

Figure 4-7 Sketch after extending the entity

You can also extend multiple entities by pressing and holding the left mouse button and dragging the cursor over them. All the other options of this tool are same as the **Quick Trim** tool.

Creating a Corner between Sketched Entities

Ribbon:	Home > Direct Sketch > Sketch Curve Gallery > Make Corner
Menu:	Edit > Sketch Curve > Make Corner

You can create a corner between two existing sketched entities by using the **Make Corner** tool. The **Make Corner** tool will work both as quick trim as well as quick extend tool. Depending on the object this tool can trim the object as well as extend the object to make the corner. To create a corner between two sketched entities, invoke the **Make Corner** tool from the **Sketch Curve** gallery of the **Direct Sketch** group of the **Home** tab; the **Make Corner** dialog box will be displayed, as shown in Figure 4-8. In this dialog box, the **Curve** button in the **Curve** rollout is chosen by default. Select the first curve, refer to Figures 4-9 and 4-11; you will be prompted to select the second curve. Select the second curve, refer to Figures 4-9 and 4-11; a corner will be created between the two sketched entities, refer to Figures 4-10 and 4-12. Next, exit the dialog box by choosing the **Close** button from it.

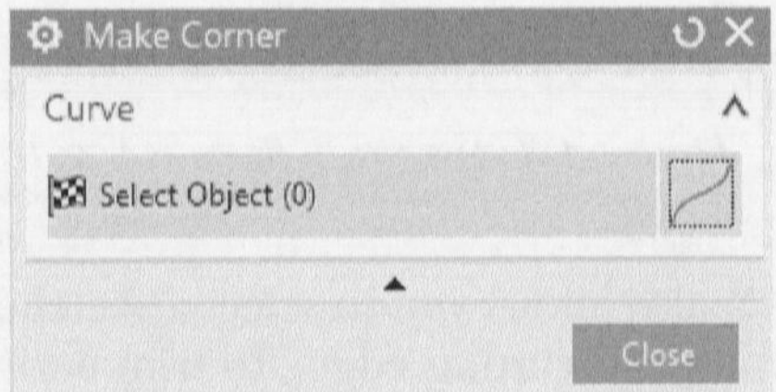

***Figure 4-8** The **Make Corner** dialog box*

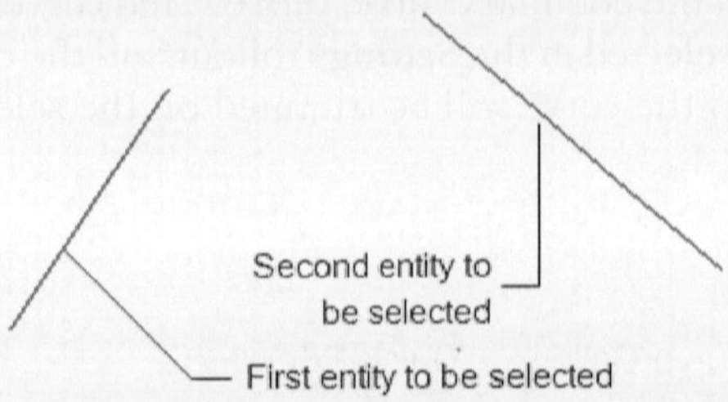

***Figure 4-9** Two entities selected for creating a corner*

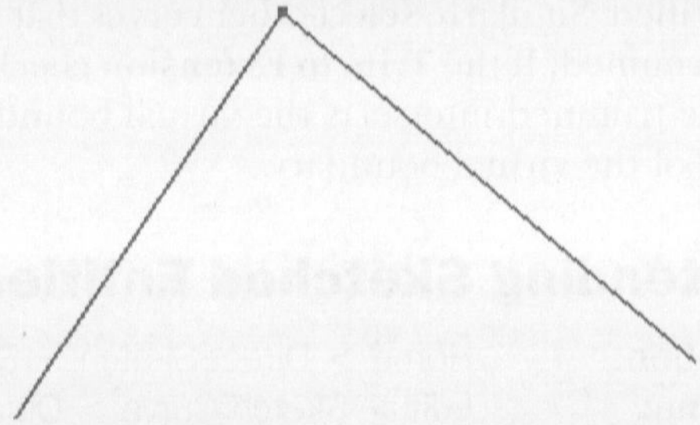

***Figure 4-10** Corner created between the selected entities*

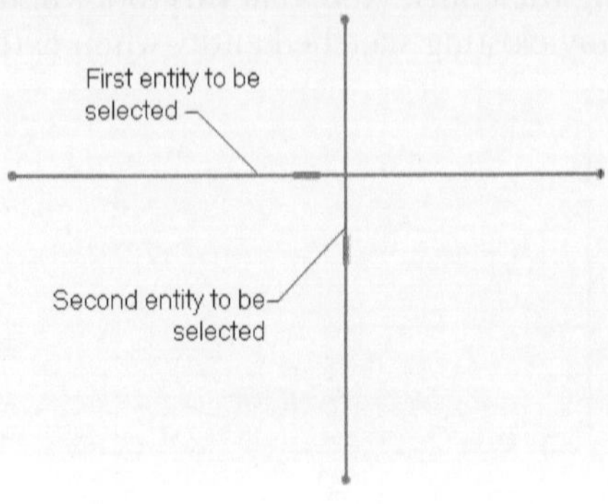

***Figure 4-11** Two entities selected for creating a corner*

***Figure 4-12** Corner created between the selected entities*

Moving Sketched Entities by Using the Move Curve Tool

Ribbon:	Home > Direct Sketch > Sketch Curve Gallery > Move Curve
Menu:	Edit > Sketch Curve > Move Curve

You can dynamically translate and rotate single or multiple curves by using the **Move Curve** tool. To move curves, invoke the **Move Curve** tool from the **Sketch Curve** gallery of the **Direct Sketch** group of the **Home** tab; the **Move Curve** dialog box will be displayed, as shown in Figure 4-13 and you will be prompted to select the curves to move or rotate. Select the curves to move or rotate from the drawing window. Next, enter the value in the **Distance** edit box available in the **Transform** rollout; a preview will be displayed, as shown in Figure 4-14. You can also enter the distance and angle values in the dynamic edit box displayed in the drawing area. You can use the **Reverse Direction** button to reverse the direction of translated curve. The other options available in the **Move Curve** dialog box are discussed next.

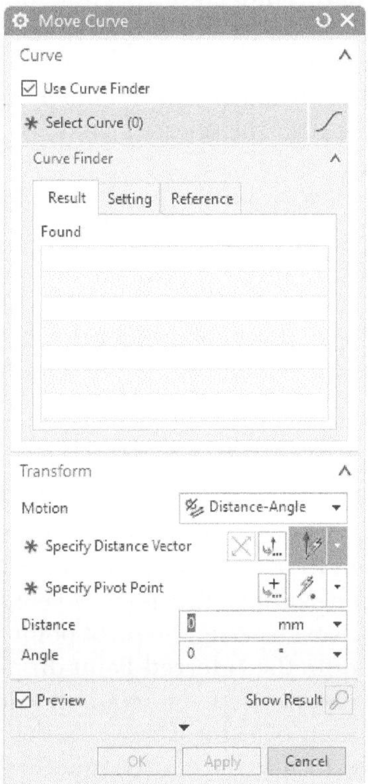

*Figure 4-13 The **Move Curve** dialog box*

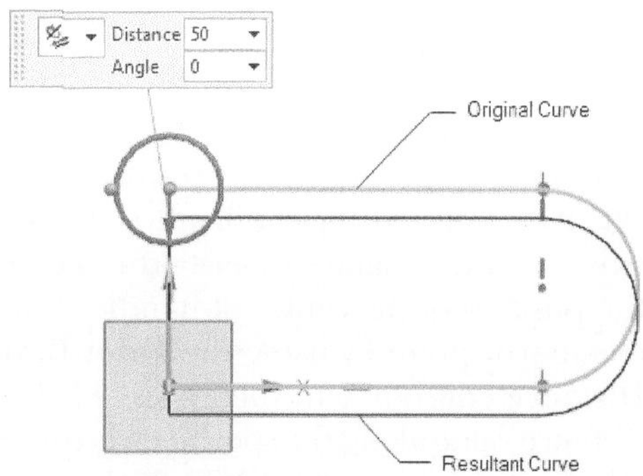

Figure 4-14 Preview of moved curve

Curve Rollout

By default, the **Use Curve Finder** check box is selected in this rollout. As a result, the curves in the sketch that meet specific geometric conditions relative to the curve selected are found. By default, the **Curve or control point to be recognized** button is chosen. As a result, you will be prompted to select the curves to move or rotate. While selecting the curves, you can use the options in the **Curve Rule** drop-down from the **Top Border Bar** to select a single curve or chain of curves. Just below the **Curve** rollout of the dialog box, the **Curve Finder** sub-rollout is available. The tabs available in the **Curve Finder** sub-rollout are discussed next.

Result Tab
This tab shows the curves found by using **Curve Finder** for each geometric condition type. When you move the cursor over the option listed in the **Result** tab, the corresponding curves will be highlighted in the drawing window. Depending on the requirement select the corresponding check box from the **Result** tab.

Setting Tab
This tab shows the list of geometric conditions that **Curve Finder** can use to select the related curves. When you select a geometric condition from this list, the corresponding condition is selected by default in the **Result** tab. To find the curve, first select the geometric condition from the list in the **Setting** tab and then select the curve from the drawing window.

Reference Tab
The options in this tab are used to define how **Curve Finder** works. These options are discussed next.

Find Scope: The **Find Scope** option is used to specify whether **Curve Finder** has to find curves in the entire sketch, or find only those that are near the selected curve.

Symmetry Lines: The **Symmetry Lines** option is used to specify the type of object to be used as a symmetry line.

Transform Rollout
The **Transform** rollout is used to specify method to transform objects. The **Motion** drop-down list in this rollout is used to specify the transform method to be used. The options in this drop-down list are discussed next.

Distance-Angle
This option is used to move and rotate the selected object by a specified distance and angle along the direction of the selected vector. By default, this option is selected in the **Motion** drop-down list. As a result, you are prompted to specify the direction vector along which the selected object will move and rotate. Select an existing edge, sketched entity, datum axis, or datum plane to specify the vector direction. Next, specify the pivot point to define the position of the center of handle. Select a point from the **Inferred Point** drop-down or create new point by using the **Point Dialog** button. Next, enter the required value in the **Distance** edit box and then press ENTER; the selected object will move by the specified distance value along the specified vector direction. Next, enter the desired value in the **Angle** edit box and then press ENTER; the selected object will rotate by the specified angle from the specified point, as shown in Figure 4-15. You can also flip the direction of the vector by choosing the **Reverse Direction** button. Next, choose the **OK** button.

Distance
This option is used to move the selected object by a specified distance along the direction of the selected vector. When you select this option from the **Motion** drop-down list; you will be prompted to specify the direction vector along which the selected object will be moved or copied. Select an edge, sketched entity, datum axis, or datum plane to specify the direction. Next, enter the required value in the **Distance** edit box and then press ENTER; the selected

object will move by the specified distance value along the specified direction, as shown in Figure 4-16. You can also flip the direction of the vector by choosing the **Reverse Direction** button. Next, choose the **OK** button.

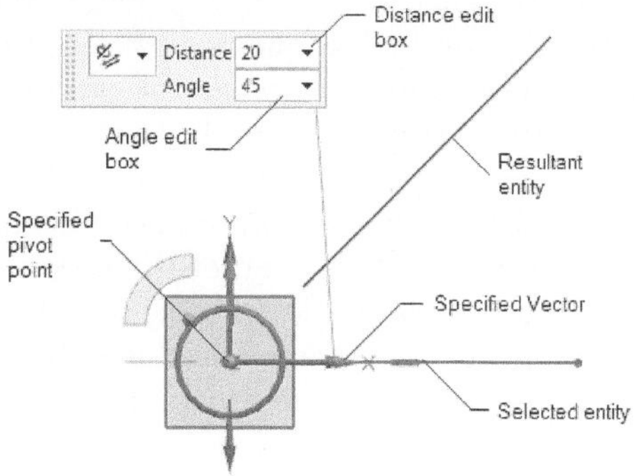

Figure 4-15 *Entity transformed by using the* ***Distance-Angle*** *option*

Angle

The **Angle** option in the **Motion** drop-down list is used to rotate the selected entity with respect to the specified point. Select this option from the **Motion** drop-down list; you will be prompted to select the curves to move. Select the curve or curves you want to move from the drawing area. Next, click in the **Specify Axis Point** area of the **Transform** rollout of the dialog box; you will be prompted to select the object to infer point. Select the point with respect to which you want to change the orientation of the object. Next, enter the angle value in the **Angle** edit box and press ENTER; the selected object will orient by the specified angle with respect to the specified point, as shown in Figure 4-17. Next, choose the **OK** button.

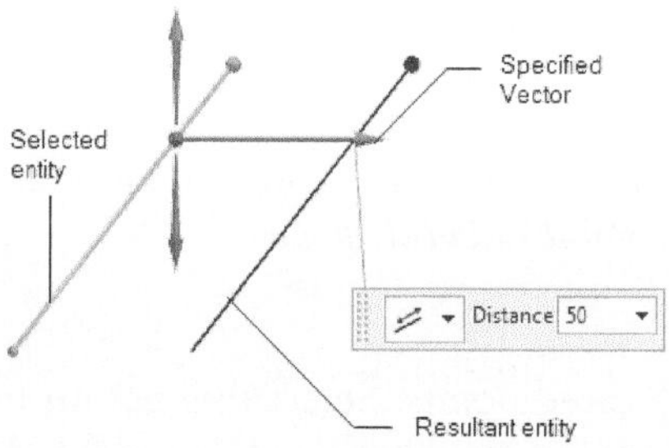

Figure 4-16 *Entity transformed by using the* ***Distance*** *option*

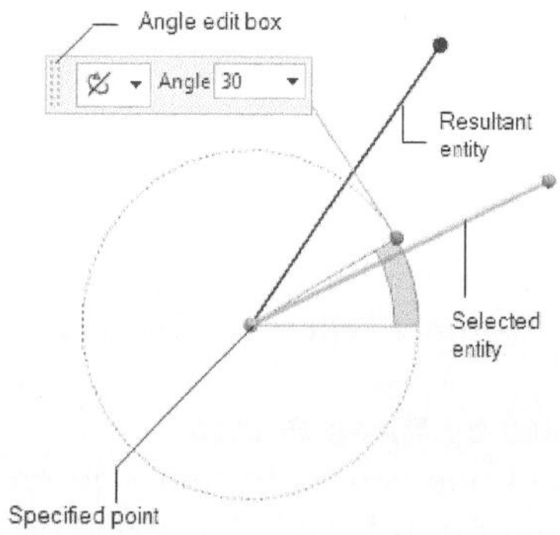

Figure 4-17 *Entity transformed by using the* ***Angle*** *option*

Distance between Points

This option is used to move an entity from one specified point to another along a specified vector. Select this option from the **Motion** drop-down list; you will be prompted to select the object to infer point. Also, the **Specify Origin Point** area will be highlighted in the **Transform** rollout. Select a point to define the origin; the **Specify Measurement Point** area will be highlighted in the **Transform** rollout. Specify the measurement point by selecting another point; the **Specify Vector** area will be highlighted in the **Transform** rollout. Also, a triad of vectors will be displayed in the drawing window. Select an existing edge, a sketched entity, or a datum axis to specify the vector direction; you will be prompted to select the object. Also, the **Distance** input edit box will be displayed attached to the specified measurement point. Select the object that you want to move. Next, enter the distance value in the **Distance** input edit box to define the driven distance of the selected object along the specified vector. You can also enter the distance value in the **Distance** edit box of the dialog box. Note that the selected object will move by the difference between the origin point and the measurement point, along the direction of the vector specified. For example, if the distance between the origin point and the measurement point along the direction vector is 100 mm and you want to move the object to a distance of 50 mm, then you need to enter the distance value of 150 mm in the **Distance** edit box. As you enter the distance value, the preview of the selected entity will be displayed in the graphics window, refer to Figure 4-18. You can flip the direction of the vector by choosing the **Reverse Direction** button. You can also dynamically move the selected object by dragging the arrowhead displayed in the graphics area.

Point to Point

This option is used to move the selected entity from one specified point to another. Select this option from the **Motion** drop-down list; you will be prompted to select the object to infer point. Also, the **Specify From Point** option will be highlighted in the **Transform** rollout. Specify the start point of the moving entity; you will be prompted to select the object to infer point. Also, the **Specify To Point** option will be highlighted in the **Transform** rollout. Next, specify the point upto which you want to move the entity; you will be prompted to select the object to move. Select the entity that you want to move; the selected entity will move to the specified point and the preview of the entity will be displayed in the graphics window, as shown in Figure 4-19.

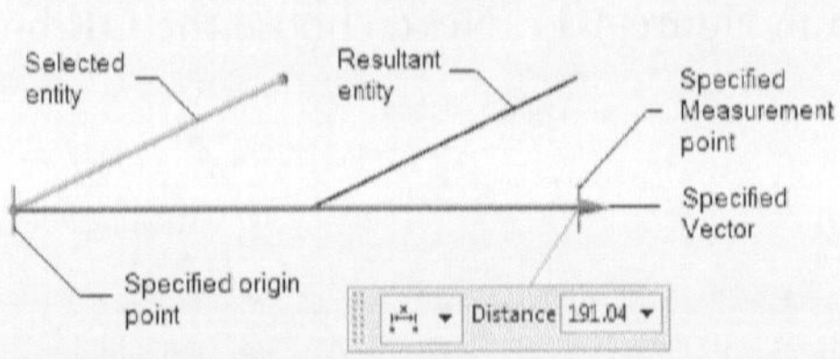

*Figure 4-18 Entity transformed by using the **Distance between Points** option*

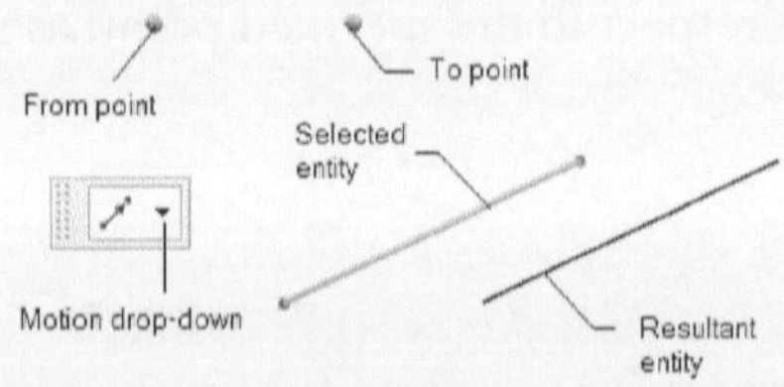

*Figure 4-19 Entity transformed by using the **Point to Point** option*

Rotate by Three Points

This option is used to rotate an entity by using three points. Select this option from the **Motion** drop-down list; you will be prompted to select the object to infer point. Also, the **Specify Pivot Point** option will be highlighted in the **Transform** rollout. Next, specify the pivot point relative to which the entity will change its orientation; the **Specify Start Point** area will be highlighted in the **Transform** rollout. As a result, you will be prompted to select the object to infer point. Specify the point from where the change in orientation will start; you will be prompted to select the object to infer point. The **Specify End Point** option will also be highlighted in the **Transform** rollout. Specify the end point; you will be prompted to select the object to move. Select the entity to be moved; the preview of the resultant entity will be displayed in the graphics window, as shown in Figure 4-20.

Align Axis to Vector

This option is used to rotate an object from one specified vector to another specified vector about the specified pivot point. Select this option from the **Motion** drop-down list; you will be prompted to select the object to infer vector. Specify the reference vector from which the rotation angle will be measured. After specifying the reference vector for the rotation angle, the **Specify Pivot Point** area will be highlighted in the **Transform** rollout. As a result, you will be prompted to select the object to infer the point. Specify the pivot point in the graphics window; you will be prompted to select the object to infer a vector. Specify the reference vector for the rotation angle; you will be prompted to select the object to be moved. After selecting the object, the preview of the resultant entity will be displayed in the graphics window, as shown in Figure 4-21.

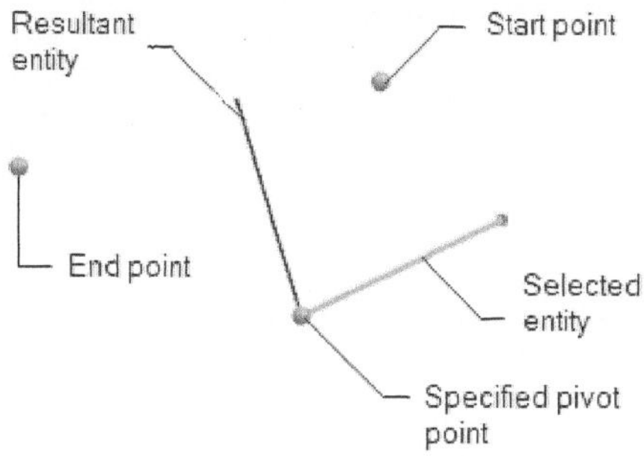

*Figure 4-20 Entity transformed by using the **Rotate by Three Points** option*

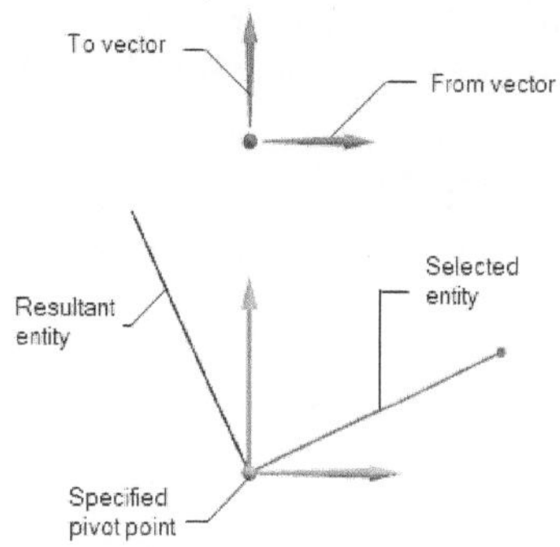

*Figure 4-21 Entity transformed by using the **Align Axis to Vector** option*

Dynamic

This option is used to move or rotate an object dynamically. Select this option from the **Motion** drop-down list; a dynamic dyad will be displayed at the origin, refer to Figure 4-22. Choose the **Curve or control point to be recognized** button from the **Curve** rollout and select the object to move or rotate; the dyad will be placed at the center of the selected object. You can use this dyad to move or rotate the selected entity dynamically by using its handles or angular handles. If you drag the handles, the object will move linearly. If you drag the angular handles, the object will move angularly. Also, you can place the selected object from one point to another by selecting the center of the dyad and then clicking at the point where you want to place the object. Note that instead of dragging the handles, you can also specify the values in their respective edit boxes, refer to Figure 4-23. You can select the **Move Handles Only** check box in the **Transform** rollout to move the dynamic dyad only.

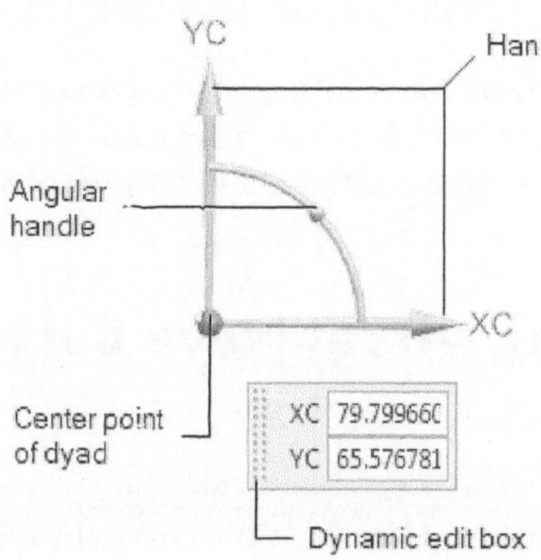

Figure 4-22 Dynamic dyad

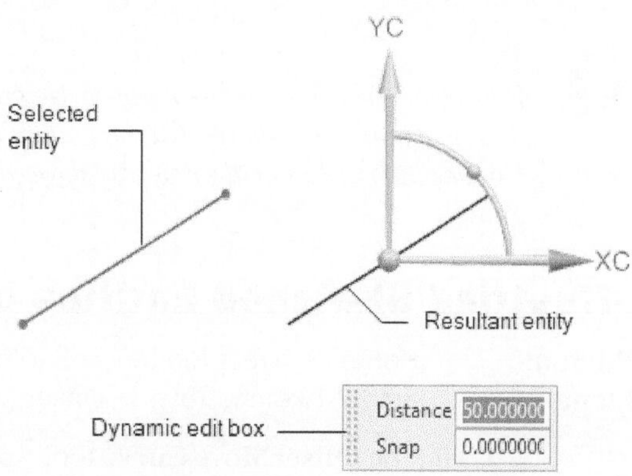

*Figure 4-23 Entity transformed by using the **Dynamic** option*

Delta XYZ

This option is used to move a selected entity from one position to another with respect to the X, Y, and Z coordinates. Select the **Delta XYZ** option from the **Motion** drop-down list; you will be prompted to select the object to be moved. Select the object to be moved. Next, enter the required coordinate values in the **XC**, **YC**, and **ZC** edit boxes in the **Transform** rollout of the dialog box, and then press ENTER; the preview of the resultant entity will be displayed in the graphics window. Note that the specified coordinate values are relative to the reference coordinate system that can be the Absolute Coordinate System or the World Coordinate System. You can select the required reference coordinate system from the **Reference** drop-down list in the **Transform** rollout of the dialog box.

Settings Rollout

The options in this rollout are discussed next.

Size

This area contains two radio buttons, **Trim and Extend** and **Maintain**, which are discussed next.

Trim and Extend: This radio button is used to trim or extend the curves as you move them.

Maintain: This radio button is used to keep the original size of the selected curve and to adjust adjacent curves.

Keep Tangent

This area contains two radio buttons: **Automatic** and **Fix Center**, which are discussed next.

Automatic: You can select this radio button to allow the center location of the adjacent tangent fillets to move, as you drag a curve.

Fix Center: You can select this radio button to keep the center location of the adjacent tangent fillets fixed, as you drag a curve.

The **Distance Tolerance** option available in this rollout is used to define the accuracy of the **Curve Finder** selection. This option does not affect the accuracy of the curves that you move.

> **Tip**
>
> *If tools to be invoked are not visible by default in the **Direct Sketch** group of the **Home** tab, you need to expand the **Sketch Curve** gallery of the **Direct Sketch** group. To expand the **Sketch Curve** gallery, click on the down arrow available at the lower right corner in the **Direct Sketch** group.*

Offsetting Sketched Entities by Using Offset Move Curve

Ribbon: Home > Direct Sketch > Sketch Curve Gallery > Offset Move Curve
Menu: Edit > Sketch Curve > Offset Move Curve

Using the **Offset Move Curve** tool, you can move single or multiple curves by offsetting the curves to a specified distance. To move or offset curves, invoke the **Offset Move Curve** tool from the **Sketch Curve** gallery of the **Direct Sketch** group of the **Home** tab; the **Offset Move Curve** dialog box will be displayed, as shown in Figure 4-24, and you will be prompted to select the curves to offset. Select the curves to offset from the drawing window. Next, enter the offset distance value in the **Distance** edit box available in the **Offset** rollout; the preview of offset moved curves will be displayed, as shown in Figure 4-25. You can also flip the direction of the vector by choosing the **Reverse Direction** button or by double-clicking on the blue arrowhead displayed in the graphics area. The other options available in the **Offset Move Curve** dialog box are same as those discussed earlier in the **Move Curve** dialog box.

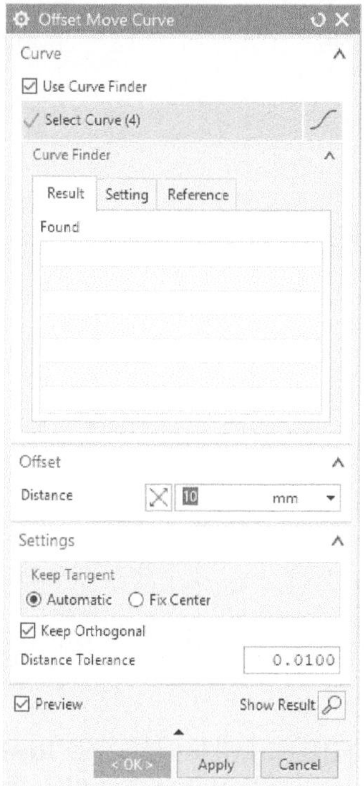

*Figure 4-24 The **Offset Move Curve** dialog box*

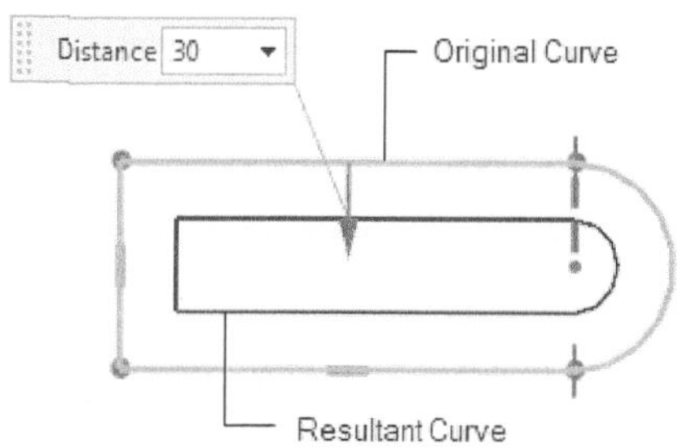

Figure 4-25 Preview of offset moved curve

Modifying Entities by Using the Resize Curve Tool

Ribbon:	Home > Direct Sketch > Sketch Curve Gallery > Resize Curve
Menu:	Edit > Sketch Curve > Resize Curve

Using the **Resize Curve** tool, you can modify the radius of the curves to a specified radius value. You can resize multiple curves together by using the **Use Curve Finder**. To modify the radius of curves, invoke the **Resize Curve** tool from the **Sketch Curve** gallery of the **Direct Sketch** group of the **Home** tab; the **Resize Curve** dialog box will be displayed, as shown in Figure 4-26, and you will be prompted to select the curves to resize. Select the curves to resize from the drawing window. If two curves have the same radius and you want to resize them together, you can select both the curves together by selecting the **Select Equal Radius** check box in the **Setting** tab under the **Curve Finder** sub-rollout in the **Curve** rollout before selecting the curves from the drawing window. Next, enter the value in the **Diameter** or **Radius** edit box of the **Size** rollout. The preview of resized curve will be displayed as shown in Figure 4-27.

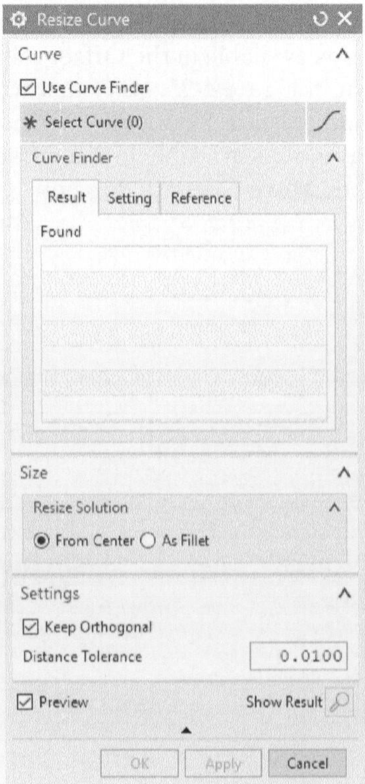

*Figure 4-26 The **Resize Curve** dialog box*

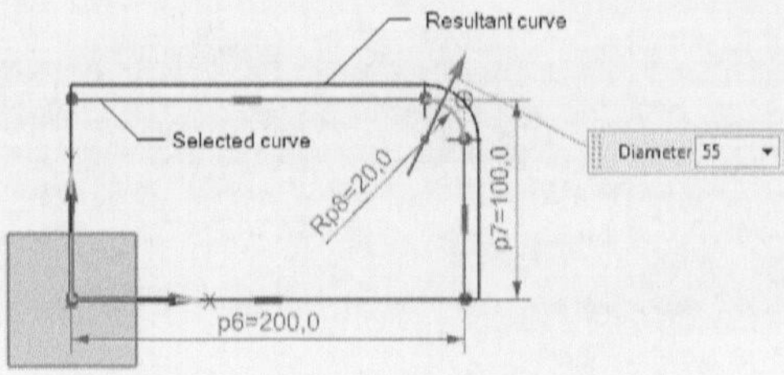

Figure 4-27 Preview of resized curve

There are two radio buttons **From Center** and **As Fillet** available in the **Resize Solution** sub-rollout under the **Size** rollout. Depending on the radio button selected from the **Resize Solution** sub-rollout of the **Size** rollout, the **Diameter** or **Radius** edit box will be available. If you select the **From Center** radio button then while resizing the curves, it will maintain the location of the arc center by changing the size of entire curve, as shown in Figures 4-28 and 4-29. If you select the **As Fillet** radio button to resize, it will maintain the adjacent tangent curve position, as shown in Figures 4-30 and 4-31.

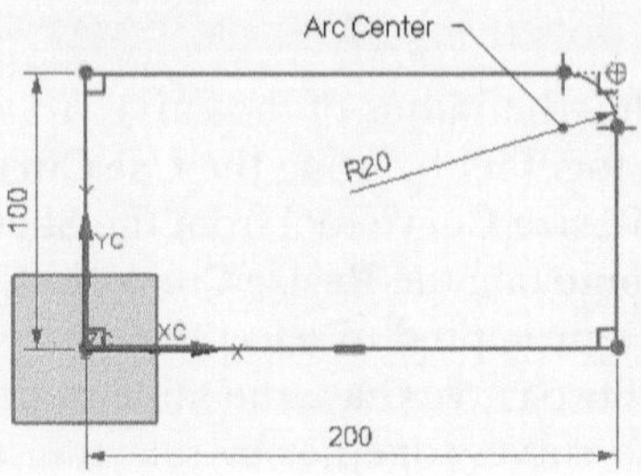

Figure 4-28 Curve before resizing

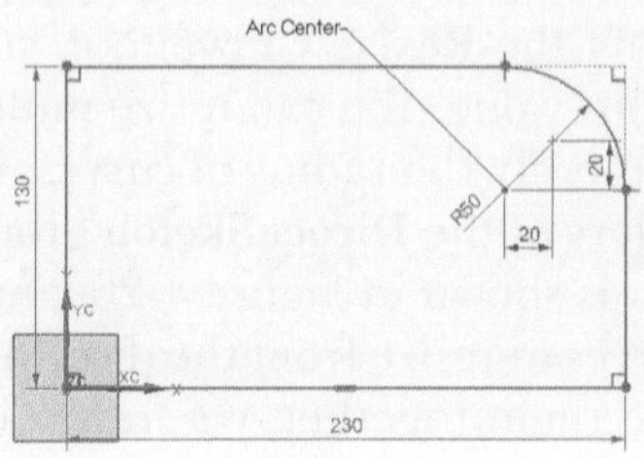

*Figure 4-29 Resized curve after using the **From Center** option*

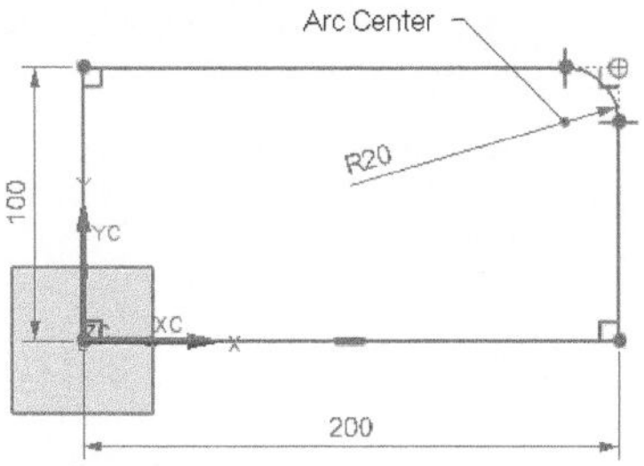

Figure 4-30 Curve before resizing

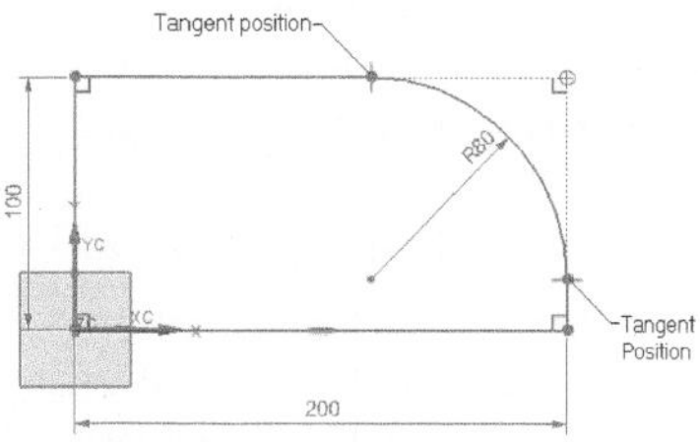

*Figure 4-31 Resized curve after using the **As Fillet** option*

Modifying Chamfer in Sketched Entities by Using Resize Chamfer Curve Tool

Ribbon: Home > Direct Sketch > Sketch Curve Gallery > Resize Chamfer Curve
Menu: Edit > Sketch Curve > Resize Chamfer Curve

Using the **Resize Chamfer Curve** tool, you can resize one or more chamfers in a sketch. To resize chamfer, choose the **Resize Chamfer Curve** tool from the **Sketch Curve** gallery of the the **Direct Sketch** group of the **Home** tab; the **Resize Chamfer Curve** dialog box will be displayed, as shown in Figure 4-32, and you will be prompted to select the chamfer curves to resize the chamfer. Select the curves to resize from the drawing window. Next, enter the offset distance value in the **Distance** edit box available in the **Offset** rollout; a preview of resized curves will be displayed, as shown in Figure 4-33. Next, choose the **OK** button to create a new chamfer.

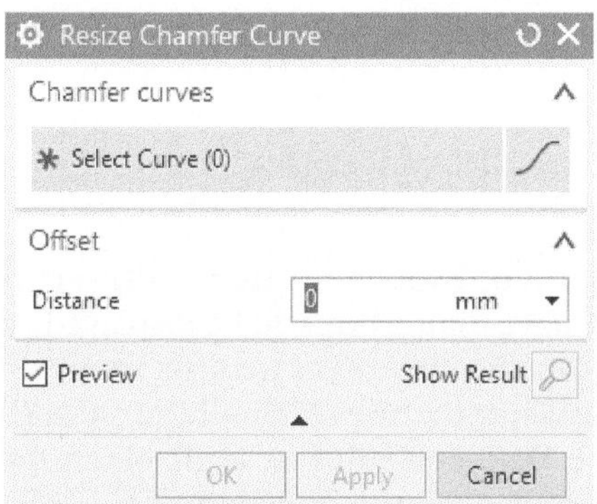

*Figure 4-32 The **Resize Chamfer Curve** dialog box*

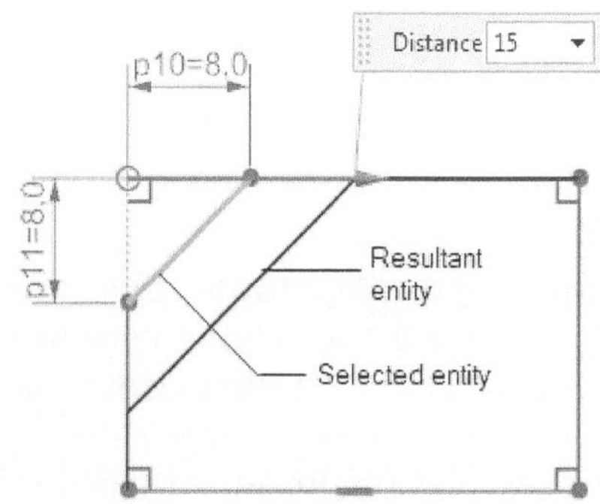

Figure 4-33 Preview of resize chamfer curve

Deleting Sketched Entities by Using Delete Curve Tool

Ribbon: Home > Direct Sketch > Sketch Curve Gallery > Delete Curve
Menu: Edit > Sketch Curve > Delete Curve

Using the **Delete Curve** tool, you can delete single or multiple curves. You can also heal the sketch by reconnecting the gap created by deleted curves. To delete curves, choose the **Delete Curve** tool from the **Sketch Curve** gallery of the **Direct Sketch** group of the **Home** tab; the **Delete Curve** dialog box will be displayed, as shown in Figure 4-34, and you will be prompted to select the curves to delete. Select the curves to delete from the drawing window and then choose the **Apply** button; the selected curves will be deleted from the drawing window.

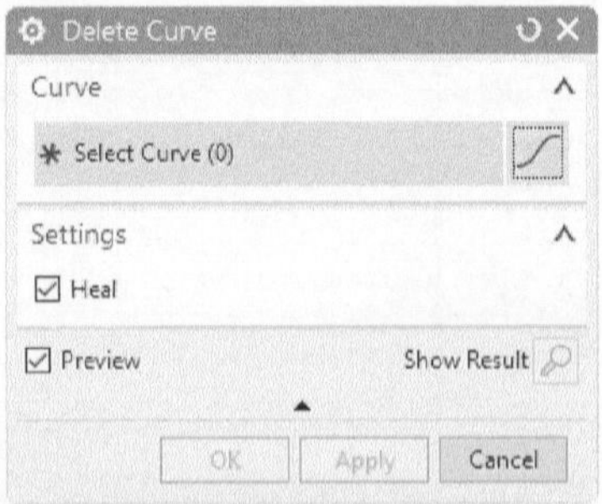

*Figure 4-34 The **Delete Curve** dialog box*

In the **Settings** rollout, the **Heal** check box is available. If you select the **Heal** check box, then after deleting the curve, NX will reconnect the gap in the sketch. For example, if you select the fillet radius to be deleted with the **Delete Curve** tool while the **Heal** check box is selected then the resulting sketch will reconnect the gap, as shown in Figure 4-35, and if you disable the **Heal** check box, then after deleting the curves, gap will be retained, as shown in Figure 4-36. To exit the dialog box, choose the **OK** button.

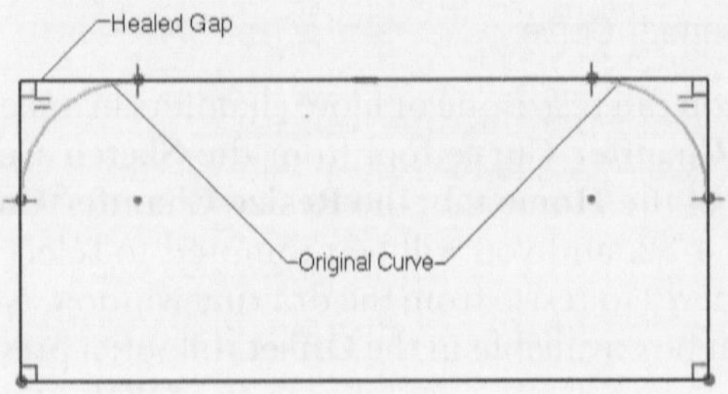

*Figure 4-35 The sketch when the **Heal** check box is selected*

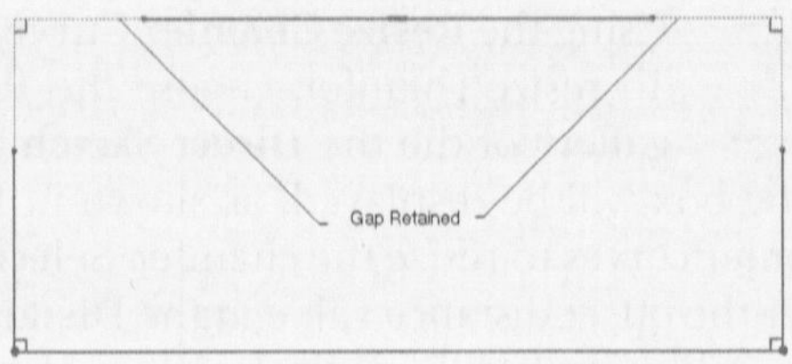

*Figure 4-36 The sketch when the **Heal** check box is cleared*

Offsetting Sketched Entities

Ribbon:	Home > Direct Sketch > Sketch Curve Gallery > Offset Curve
Menu:	Insert > Sketch Curve > Offset Curve

To offset sketched entities, choose the **Offset Curve** tool from **Menu > Insert > Sketch Curve** in the **Top Border Bar**; the **Offset Curve** dialog box will be displayed, as shown in Figure 4-37. Also, you will be prompted to select the curves to offset from the **Curves to Offset** rollout. Select the curves from the drawing window; the preview of the offset curve will be displayed. Next, enter the offset distance in the **Distance** edit box available in the **Offset** rollout. You can use the **Reverse Direction** button to reverse the direction of the offset curve. The other options available in the **Offset Curve** dialog box are discussed next.

Offset Rollout

The options in this rollout are used to specify the parameters of the offset curve.

Create Dimension

This check box is selected by default. As a result, a dimension is displayed between the input curve and the offset curve. If you clear this check box, the dimension will not be displayed. Note that the dimension constraint is created in both the cases.

Symmetric Offset

This check box is used to create the offset curve in both the directions of the input curve.

Number of Copies

This spinner is used to specify the number of offset curves to be created.

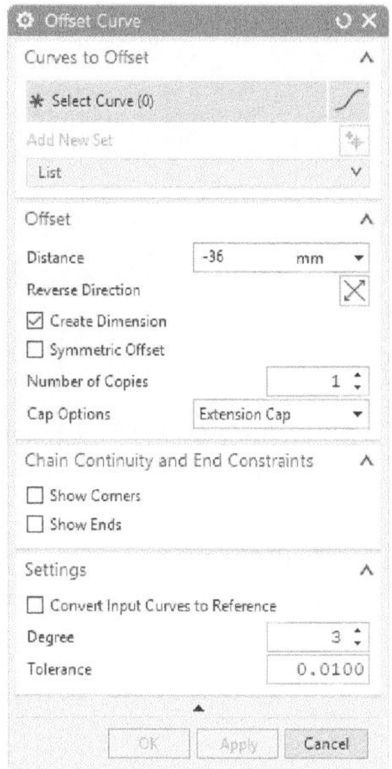

Figure 4-37 The ***Offset Curve*** *dialog box*

Cap Options

The options in this drop-down list are used to specify the types of caps to close the ends. If you select the **Extension Cap** option, offset entities will extend and intersect to create an end cap, as shown in Figure 4-38. On selecting the **Arc Cap** option, the arcs will be applied at the intersection point of the two offset entities, as shown in Figure 4-39.

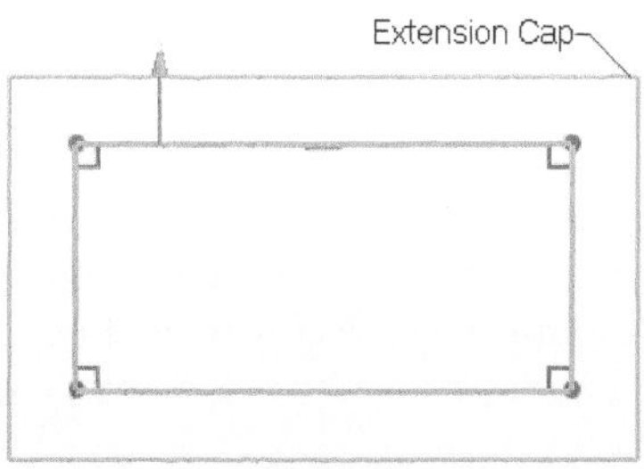

Figure 4-38 *Offset curve created with the* ***Extension Cap*** *option selected*

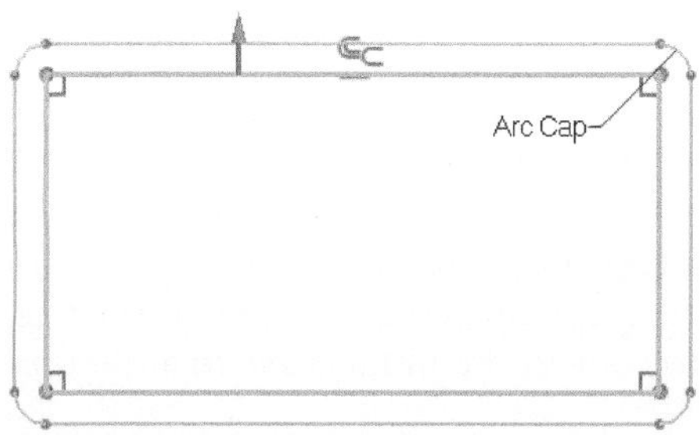

Figure 4-39 *Offset curve created with the* ***Arc Cap*** *option selected*

Chain Continuity and End Constraints Rollout

The options in this rollout are used to display the corner handles and the end constraints of the curves. Note that you need to expand this rollout by clicking on the down arrow.

Show Corners

On selecting this check box, the corner handles are displayed at the corners of the sketch, as shown in Figure 4-40. When you double-click on a handle, the respective corner will be opened, refer to Figure 4-41.

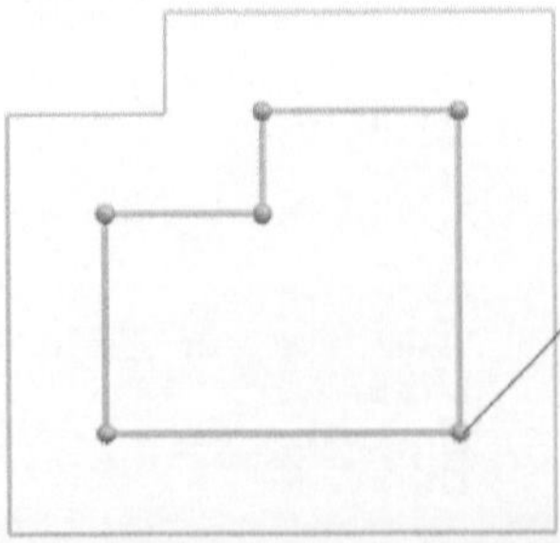

Figure 4-40 The corner handles displayed at the corners

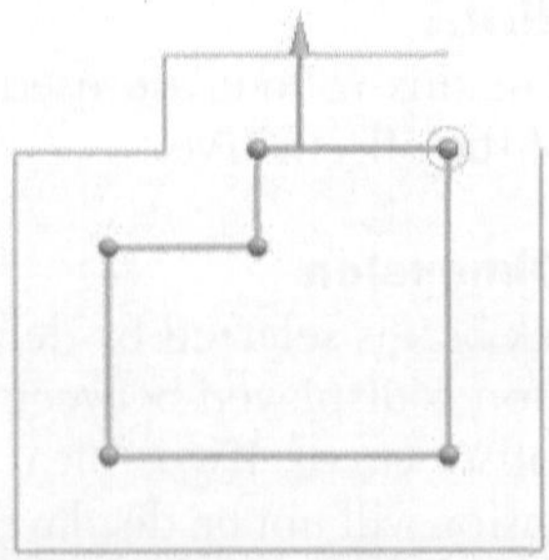

Figure 4-41 The offset curve with the open corner

Show Ends

On selecting this check box, the end constraints are displayed at the end points of the curves, refer to Figure 4-42. You can delete an end constraint by right-clicking on it and then choosing the **Delete** option from the shortcut menu displayed.

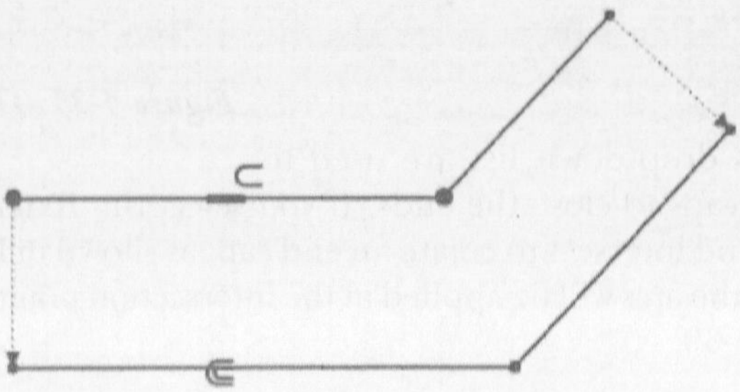

*Figure 4-42 The end constraints displayed on selecting the **Show Ends** check box*

Settings Rollout

The options in this rollout are used to modify the settings for creating offsets. In this rollout, the **Degree** and **Tolerance** edit boxes are used to specify the degree and tolerance values while offsetting a spline, conic, or an ellipse. The **Convert Input Curves to Reference** check box is used to convert the input curve to a reference element.

Mirroring Sketched Entities

Ribbon:	Home > Direct Sketch > Sketch Curve Gallery > Mirror Curve
Menu:	Insert > Sketch Curve > Mirror Curve

The **Mirror Curve** tool is used to create mirrored copies of the selected sketched entities. Before invoking this tool, you need to draw a line that will be the mirror line. This line will be converted into a reference line after the mirroring operation is completed. To mirror the sketched entities, choose **Menu > Insert > Sketch Curve > Mirror**

Curve from the **Top Border Bar**; the **Mirror Curve** dialog box will be displayed, as shown in Figure 4-43. The **Curve** button is chosen by default in the **Curve to Mirror** rollout of this dialog box. Also, you will be prompted to select the curves to mirror. Select the curves to be mirrored. Next, choose the **Centerline** button from the **Centerline** rollout; you will be prompted to select a linear object or a plane for the centerline. Select the centerline and choose the **OK** button; the selected entities will be mirrored and the centerline will be converted into a reference line. Figure 4-44 shows the mirror line and entities to be mirrored and Figure 4-45 shows the sketch after mirroring the selected entities.

Figure 4-43 *The **Mirror Curve** dialog box*

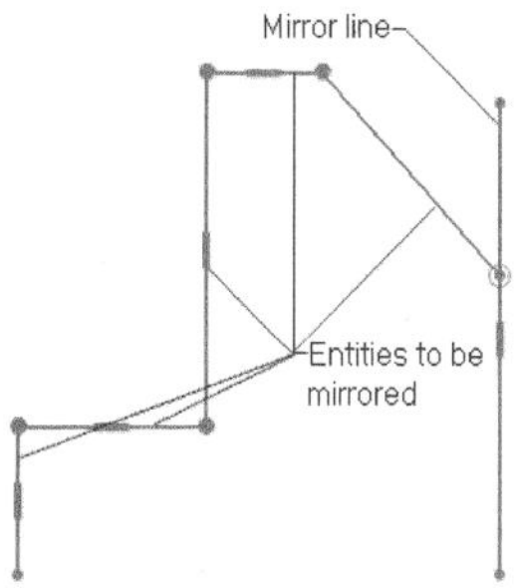

Figure 4-44 *Mirror line and entities selected to be mirrored*

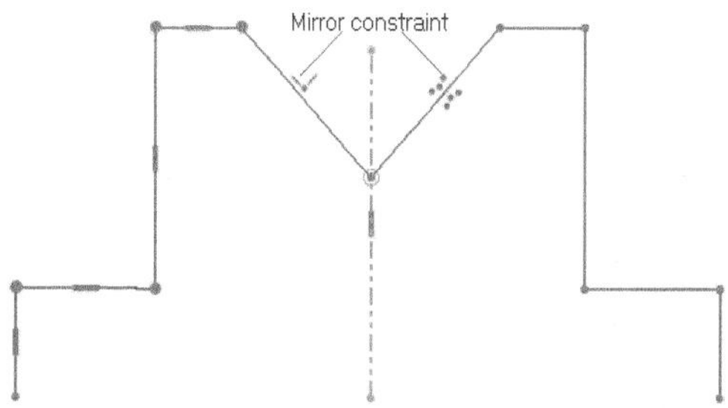

Figure 4-45 *Sketch after mirroring the selected entities*

Tip

1. After mirroring, if you select and drag any entity from its original object, the same change will also be reflected dynamically in its mirrored object. However, this relationship will end if you delete the mirror centerline.

*2. By default, the **Convert Centerline to Reference** check box is selected in the **Settings** rollout of the **Mirror Curve** dialog box. As a result, the mirror line automatically converts into a reference line. However, if you clear this check box, then the mirror line will not be converted into a reference line.*

Creating a Linear Sketch Pattern

Ribbon: Home > Direct Sketch > Sketch Curve Gallery > Pattern Curve
Menu: Insert > Sketch Curve > Pattern Curve

You can pattern the curve linearly by using the linear pattern. To create a linear sketch pattern, choose the **Pattern Curve** tool from **Menu > Insert > Sketch Curve** of the **Top Border Bar**; the **Pattern Curve** dialog box will be displayed, as shown in Figure 4-46, and you will be prompted to select the curves to be patterned. Also, the **Linear** option is selected by default in the **Layout** drop-down list in the **Pattern Definition** rollout of the **Pattern Curve** dialog box, refer to Figure 4-46. Select the sketched entity to be patterned. Next, click in the

Select Linear Object area of the **Direction 1** sub-rollout and then select a linear object to define the first direction, refer to Figure 4-47. Next, specify the instant count and pitch distance values in the **Count** and **Pitch Distance** edit boxes available in the **Direction 1** sub-rollout. Note that you can specify the instance number and the pitch distance by using the options available in the **Spacing** drop-down list. These options are discussed later in Chapter 7.

After specifying the parameters in the **Direction 1** sub-rollout, you can select the **Use Direction 2** check box available in the **Direction 2** sub-rollout to create the linear sketch pattern along the second direction as well. Next, specify the parameters in this sub-rollout. The options in the **Direction 2** sub-rollout are similar to the **Direction 1** sub-rollout. Next, choose the **OK** button to close the dialog box. The **Create Pitch Expressions** check box is selected by default. As a result, an expression is created from the specified values to define the pitch.

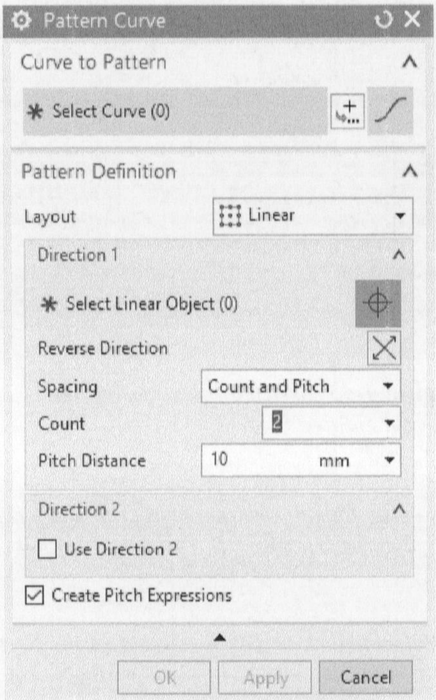

*Figure 4-46 The **Pattern Curve** dialog box*

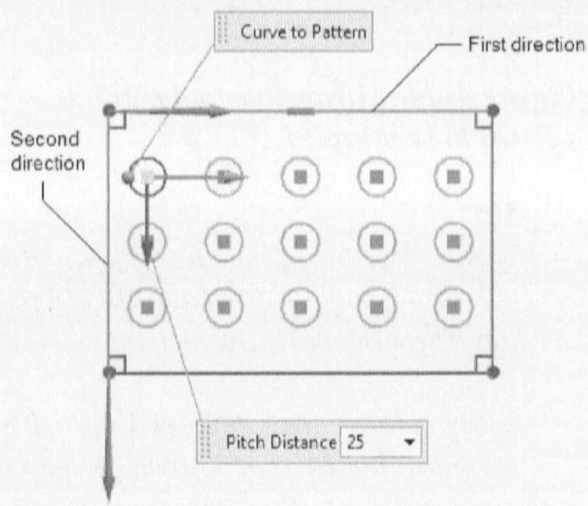

Figure 4-47 The linear sketch pattern created along directions

Creating a Circular Sketch Pattern

You can create circular pattern of the curves by using the **Pattern Curve** tool. To create a circular sketch pattern of the selected features, invoke the **Pattern Curve** tool; the **Pattern Curve** dialog box will be displayed. Select the **Circular** option from the **Layout** drop-down list in this dialog box; the **Pattern Curve** dialog box will be modified, as shown in Figure 4-48, and you will be prompted to select sketched entities to pattern. Select the entities to be patterned from the drawing window. Next, click in the **Specify Point** area in the **Rotation Point** sub-rollout; you will be prompted to select an object to infer a point. Now, you can infer the center point of the circle to specify the rotation point of the pattern, refer to Figure 4-49.

Next, you need to define the number of instances and the angular spacing between them by using the options listed in the **Spacing** drop-down list in the **Angular Direction** sub-rollout. In this case, select the **Count and Span** option from the **Spacing** drop-down list and then specify the count and span angle values in the **Count** and **Span Angle** edit boxes, respectively. Next, choose the **OK** button to create the circular pattern. The other options in the **Spacing** drop-down list are discussed later in Chapter 7.

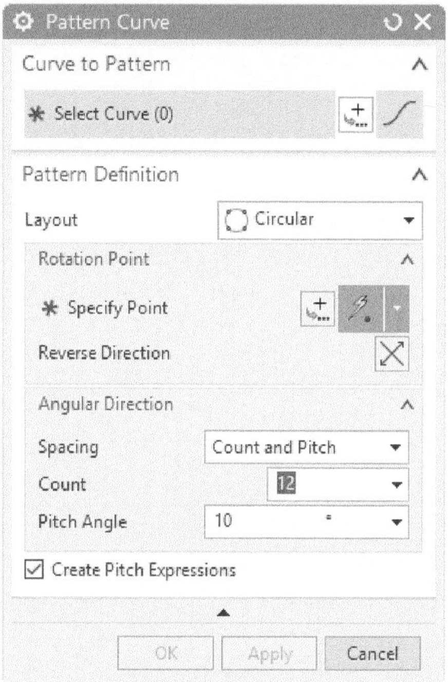

*Figure 4-48 The **Pattern Curve** dialog box to create a circular pattern*

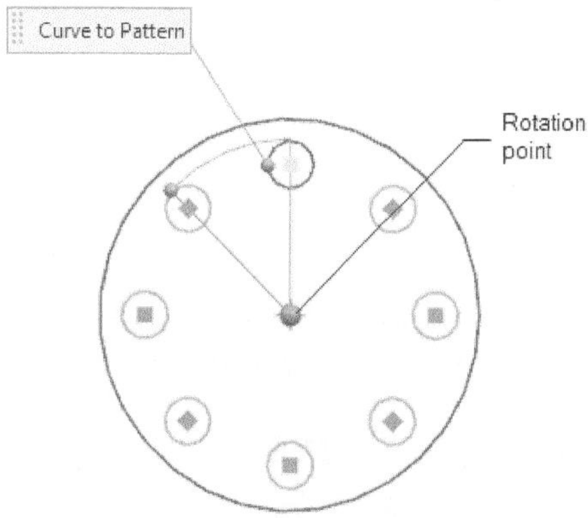

Figure 4-49 The circular sketch pattern

Creating a General Sketch Pattern

Using the **General** option, you can pattern the curves at specified points. To create a general sketch pattern of the selected entities, invoke the **Pattern Curve** tool; the **Pattern Curve** dialog box will be displayed. Select the **General** option from the **Layout** drop-down list in this dialog box; the **Pattern Curve** dialog box will be modified, as shown in Figure 4-50 and you will be prompted to select the sketched entities to pattern. Select the entities to be patterned from the drawing window. Next, select the **Point** option from the **Location** drop-down list if it is not selected by default and then click in the **Specify Point** area in the **From** sub-rollout; you will be prompted to select an object to infer a point. Now, select the point of the object to specify the pattern origin, refer to Figure 4-51. Next, you will be prompted to specify points for pattern locations. Also, the **Specify Point** area will be activated in the **To** sub-rollout. Next, you need to define the instance points in the drawing area to define the instances. After specifying the instance points, choose the **OK** button to create the general pattern. You will learn more about patterning features in Chapter 7.

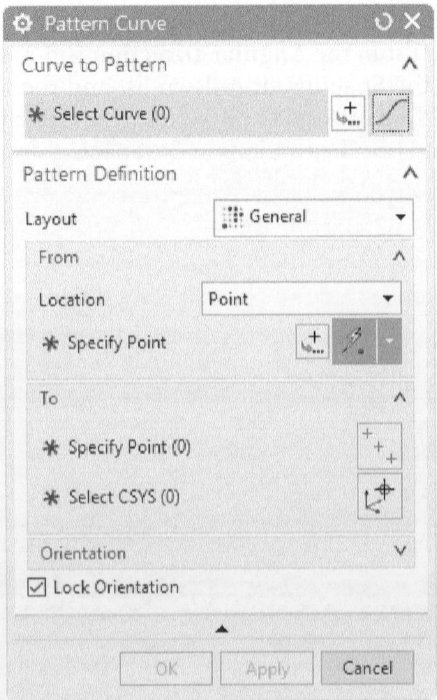

*Figure 4-50 The **Pattern Curve** dialog box to create a general pattern*

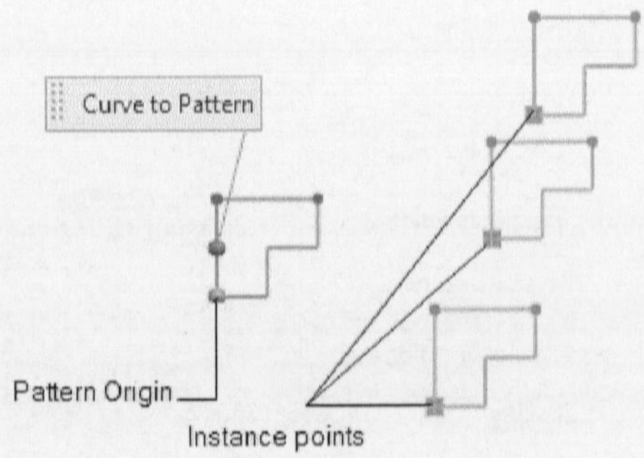

Figure 4-51 The general sketch pattern

Trim Recipe Curve

Ribbon: Home > Direct Sketch > Sketch Curve Gallery > Trim Recipe Curve
Menu: Edit > Sketch Curve > Trim Recipe Curve

This tool is used to trim the recipe curves (projected or intersected) between the selected boundaries. You can access this tool from the **Sketch Curve** gallery of the **Direct Sketch** group of the **Home** tab. When you choose this tool, the **Trim Recipe Curve** dialog box is displayed, refer to Figure 4-52. The rollouts and their options available in this dialog box are discussed next:

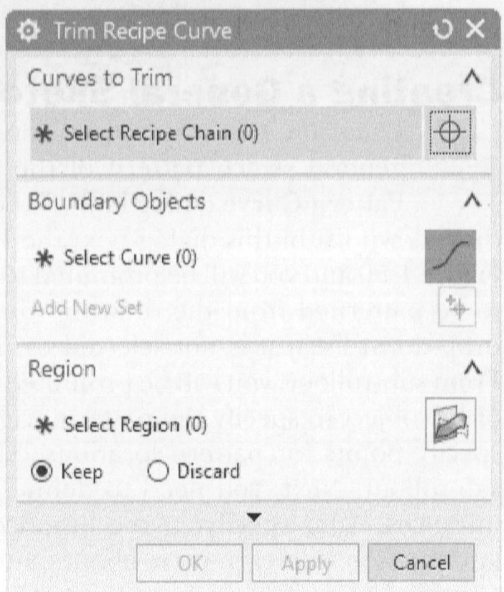

*Figure 4-52 The **Trim Recipe Curve** dialog box*

Curves to Trim Rollout

In this rollout, the **Recipe Curve** button is chosen by default and you are prompted to select the non-intersecting recipe chain to trim. Select the recipe curve to be trimmed from the drawing area.

Boundary Objects Rollout

This rollout contains two buttons, and they are discussed next.

Curve

Using this button, you can specify one or more sets of boundary curves that intersect the recipe chain.

Add New Set

Using this button, you can create a new set of boundary objects. Also, you can specify separate boundary sets.

Region Rollout

This rollout contains two radio buttons, **Keep** and **Discard**. Using these buttons, you can specify whether to keep or discard the region or regions in the current recipe chain.

Scale Curve

Ribbon: Home > Direct Sketch > Sketch Curve Gallery > Scale Curve
Menu: Edit > Sketch Curve > Scale Curve

The **Scale Curve** tool is used to manually scale the selected curves or all the curves from a selected scale point. NX automatically adjusts adjacent curves as required. Using this tool, you can scale curves dynamically by a percentage, by a fixed value, or with respect to a selected dimension. You can access this tool from the **Edit Curve** gallery of the **Sketch Curve** gallery in the **Direct Sketch** group of the **Home** tab. When you choose this tool, the **Scale Curve** dialog box will be displayed, as shown in Figure 4-53. The rollouts and their respective options available in this dialog box are discussed next.

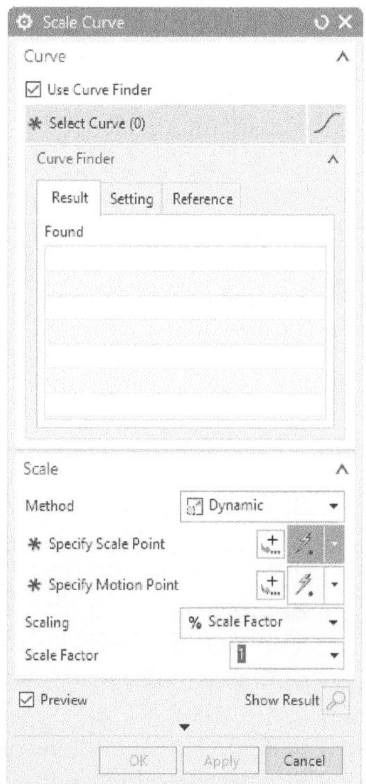

*Figure 4-53 The **Scale Curve** dialog box*

Curve Rollout

This rollout contains various options which allow you to select the curves to be scaled. These options are discussed next.

Use Curve Finder

You can select this check box to find curves in the sketch that share geometric conditions with the curves you selected.

Select Curve

In the **Scale Curve** dialog box, the **Curve or control point to be recognised** button is chosen by default and you are prompted to select the curves to scale. Select the curves to scale from the drawing area.

Curve Finder Sub-Rollout

This sub-rollout appears only when the **Use Curve Finder** check box is selected in the **Curve** rollout. It contains three tabs: **Result**, **Setting**, and **Reference**. These tabs are discussed next.

Result Tab: This tab lists the number and type of constraints between the curves found in a selection, and allows you to specify which curves to scale. When you hover the cursor over a geometric condition, the corresponding curves are highlighted in the graphics window.

Setting Tab: This tab allows you to select the geometric conditions that Curve Finder uses to find related curves.

Reference Tab: The Curve Finder finds the curves based on the options selected in this tab. The options in the **Find Scope** drop-down list are used for specifying as to whether the Curve Finder would find the curves only near the selected curve or from the entire sketch and the options in the **Symmetry Lines** drop-down list are used for selecting the type of objects that you want to use as symmetry lines. The **Select Object** area appears when the **Selected Object** option is selected in the **Symmetry Lines** drop-down list and is used to select the object to be taken as the symmetry line.

Scale Rollout

This rollout has various options which enable you to scale the curves as per your requirement. These options are discussed next:

Method

This drop-down list contains two options, **Dynamic** and **Dimension** and they are discussed next.

Dynamic: This option allows you to scale a set of curves by dragging the scale handle or by specifying a scale factor or distance.

Dimension: This option allows you to scale a set of curves by editing one of its existing dimensions.

Specify Scale Point

This area is used to select a point with respect to which you want to scale the sketch.

The following options appear when the **Dynamic** option is selected from the **Method** drop-down list:

Specify Motion Point

This option allows you to specify a point to determine the scaling direction.

Scaling

The **Scaling** drop-down list contains two options: **% Scale Factor** and **Distance**. These options are discussed next.

% Scale Factor: When you select this option, the **Scale Factor** edit box appears in the dialog box. In this edit box, you can specify the scale factor for the curves to be scaled, with 1 being the original size.

Distance: When you select this option, the **Distance** edit box appears in the dialog box using which you can set the distance between the scale point and the motion point.

Transforming Sketched Entities

Menu:	Edit > Transform

NX allows you to perform editing operations on sketches using the **Transform** tool. To do so, choose the **Transform** tool from **Menu > Edit** in **Top Border Bar**; the **Transform** dialog box will be displayed, as shown in Figure 4-54, and you will be prompted to select objects to transform.

The **Transform** dialog box is used to select objects to perform a particular operation. Various rollouts in this dialog box are discussed next.

Objects Rollout

The options in this rollout are used to define the selection methods which are discussed next.

Select Objects

This button is used to select the objects one by one.

Select All

This button is used to select all objects in the drawing window such as sketching entities, datum coordinate systems, work planes, and so on.

Invert Selection

This button is used to invert the selection.

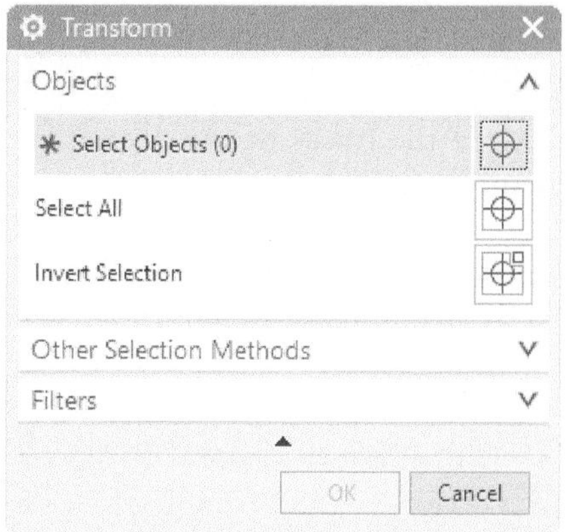

*Figure 4-54 The **Transform** dialog box*

Other Selection Methods Rollout

This rollout provides some additional selection methods.

Select by Name

You can enter the name of the sketch that you need to select in this text box and press the ENTER key; the specified sketch will be selected. Note that you need to assign the name to the sketch using sketch property. To assign name to the sketch, select and right-click on the sketch name displayed in the **Part Navigator**; a shortcut menu will be displayed. Choose **Properties** from the shortcut menu, the **Sketch Properties** dialog box will be displayed. Next, define the name in the **Name** edit box of the **General** tab, then choose the **OK** button. Note that you cannot use the name that has already been defined as the Feature name.

Select Chain

This check box is used to select the curves in the chain. You need to select the first and the last curve from the sketch; all the sketched entities of the sketch (lines, arcs, and fillets) between these two specified curves will be selected.

Filters Rollout

This rollout is used to filter out the selection procedure. Select the entities to be transformed and choose the **OK** button; the **Transformations** dialog box will be displayed, as shown in Figure 4-55.

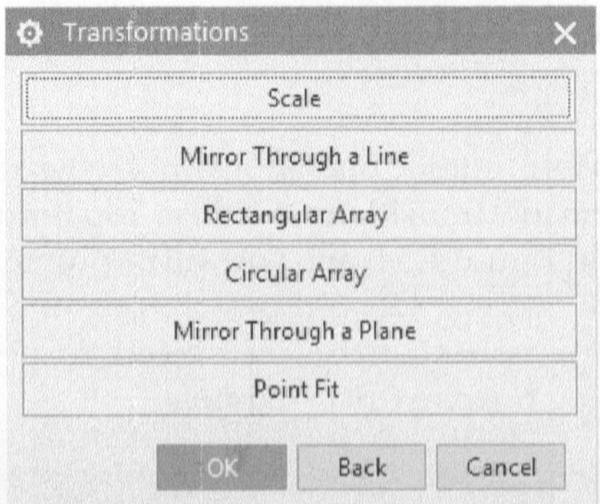

*Figure 4-55 The **Transformations** dialog box*

Some of the transformation tools in this dialog box are discussed next and the rest will be discussed in the later chapters.

Scaling the Copied Entities Using the Transformations Dialog Box

The **Scale** option is used to create scaled copies of the selected objects. If required, you can also scale the objects non uniformly in the X, Y, and Z directions.

The steps required to scale the sketched entities using the **Transform** dialog box are discussed next.

1. Choose the **Transform** tool from **Menu > Edit** in the **Top Border Bar** and then select entities using the **Transform** dialog box. Choose the **OK** button in this dialog box; the **Transformations** dialog box will be displayed.

2. Choose the **Scale** button in the **Transformations** dialog box; the **Point** dialog box will be displayed and you will be prompted to select the object to infer point.

3. Select a base point for scaling. You can select any point on the screen or any inferred point from the sketch. On selecting the base point, the modified **Transformations** dialog box will be displayed.

4. Enter the scale factor in the **Scale** edit box. If you need to scale the sketched entities non-uniformly, choose the **Non-uniform Scale** button; the dialog box will be modified and the edit boxes to specify different values of scale factor in the X, Y, and Z directions will be displayed.

5. After entering the required values, choose the **OK** button; the **Transformations** dialog box will expand. Choose the **Copy** button; the scaled copy of the selected entities will be displayed. Next, choose the **Cancel** button to exit from the dialog box. Figure 4-56 shows a uniformly scaled copy of the original sketch. The scale factor in this case is 1.5.

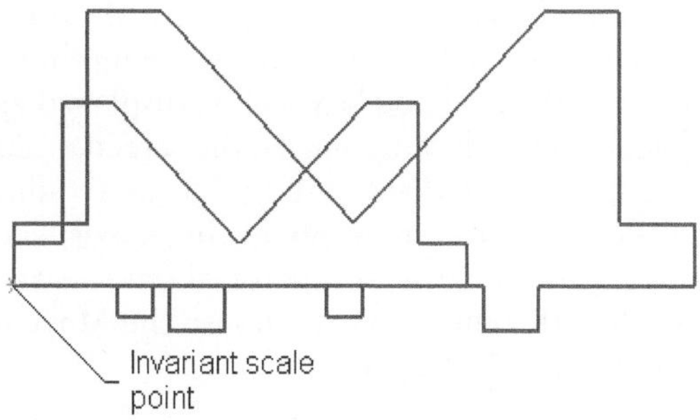

Figure 4-56 Uniformly scaled entities

Mirroring Entities Using the Transformations Dialog Box

The **Transformations** dialog box allows you to mirror the sketched entities using three methods. These methods are discussed next.

Mirroring Using Two Points

Invoke the **Transform** dialog box by choosing the **Transform** tool from the **Menu > Edit** in the **Top Border Bar**. Next, select the entity to be transformed and then choose the **OK** button in this dialog box; the **Transformations** dialog box will be displayed. Choose the **Mirror Through a Line** button from this dialog box; the **Transformations** dialog box will get modified. In the modified dialog box, choose the **Two Points** button; the **Point** dialog box will be displayed. Specify two points on the screen to define an imaginary line about which the sketch will be mirrored and then choose the **OK** button. Next, choose the **Move** button in the **Transformations** dialog box, if you want to delete the original sketch after mirroring it. Choose the **Copy** button, if you want to retain the original sketch along with the mirrored copy. Next, choose the **Cancel** button to exit the dialog box.

Note

*You cannot mirror an object by using the **Move** button in the **Transformations** dialog box, if dimensions are applied between the selected object and the origin.*

Mirroring Using an Existing Line

Invoke the **Transformations** dialog box and choose the **Mirror Through a Line** button; the **Transformations** dialog box will be modified. In the modified dialog box, choose the **Existing Line** button; the **Transformations** dialog box will be modified again and you will be prompted to enter the name of the mirror line. Enter the name of the mirror line or simply click on the mirror line in the drawing area. After selecting the line about which the sketch will be mirrored, choose the **Move** or **Copy** button. Next, choose the **Cancel** button to exit the dialog box.

Mirroring Using a Point and a Vector

Invoke the **Transformations** dialog box and choose the **Mirror Through a Line** button; the **Transformations** dialog box will be modified. In the modified dialog box, choose the **Point and Vector** button; the **Point** dialog box will be displayed and you will be prompted to select the object to infer point. Select a point on the screen or an inferred point from the sketch; the **Vector** dialog box will be displayed. Select the required option from the Type drop-down list in the dialog box. To mirror about the X-axis, choose the **XC-axis** option from the Type drop-down list. Similarly, to mirror about the Y-axis, choose the **YC-axis** option and then choose the **OK** button. Next, choose the **Move** or **Copy** button and exit from the dialog box by choosing the **Cancel** button.

Editing Sketched Entities by Dragging

You can also edit the sketched entities by dragging them. Depending upon the type of entity selected and the point of selection, the object will be moved or stretched. For example, if you select a line at any point other than the endpoints and drag the mouse, the line will be moved. However, if you select a line at its endpoint, it will be stretched to a new size. Similarly, if you select an arc at its circumference or its endpoints, it will be stretched. But, if you select the arc at its center point, it will be moved. Therefore, editing the sketched entities by dragging depends entirely upon their selection points. The following table gives the details of the operation that will be performed when you drag various entities. Note that while editing the sketched entities using the keypoints, all the related entities will also be moved or stretched.

Entity	Selection point	Operation
Circle	On circumference	Stretch
	Center point	Move
Arc	On circumference/endpoints	Stretch
	Center point	Move
Isolated line or multiple lines selected together	Anywhere other than the endpoints	Move
	Endpoints	Stretch
Curve	Any point other than the keypoints	Move
	Keypoints	Stretch
Rectangle	All lines selected together	Move
	Any of the lines or any endpoints	Stretch
Ellipse	Anywhere on the circumference or the center point	Move

EXITING THE SKETCH ENVIRONMENT

Finish Sketch

After drawing and dimensioning the sketch, you need to exit the sketching environment and invoke the Modeling environment to convert the sketch into a feature. To exit the sketching environment, choose the **Finish Sketch** tool from the **Home** tab in the **Ribbon**. On exiting the sketching environment and entering the Modeling environment, you will notice that only the sketch curve tools of the **Direct Sketch** group are available. Also, the dimensions of the sketch are hidden.

As mentioned in the earlier chapters, most designs are a combination of various sketched, placed, and reference features. The first feature, generally, is a sketched feature. Already you have learned to draw sketches for these base features and add constraints and dimensions to them. After drawing and dimensioning a sketch, you need to convert it into a base feature. NX provides you with a number of tools such as **Extrude**, **Revolve**, and so on to convert these base sketches into base features. In this chapter, you will learn to use the **Extrude** and **Revolve** tools. The remaining tools will be discussed in the later chapters. The base features are created in the Modeling environment.

CHANGING THE VIEW OF THE SKETCH

Sometimes you need to change the view of the sketch for better visualization. To change the view, choose the required tool from the **Orient View Drop-down** of the **View** group in the **Top Border Bar**; a flyout will be displayed with various view options. Select the required option from this flyout; the current view will change into the selected view.

CREATING BASE FEATURES BY EXTRUDING

Ribbon:	Home > Feature > Design Feature Drop-down > Extrude
Menu:	Insert > Design Feature > Extrude

Extrude is defined as the process of creating a feature from a sketch by adding the material along the direction normal to the sketch or any other specified direction. Figure 4-57 shows the isometric view of a closed sketch and Figure 4-58 shows the extruded feature created using this sketch.

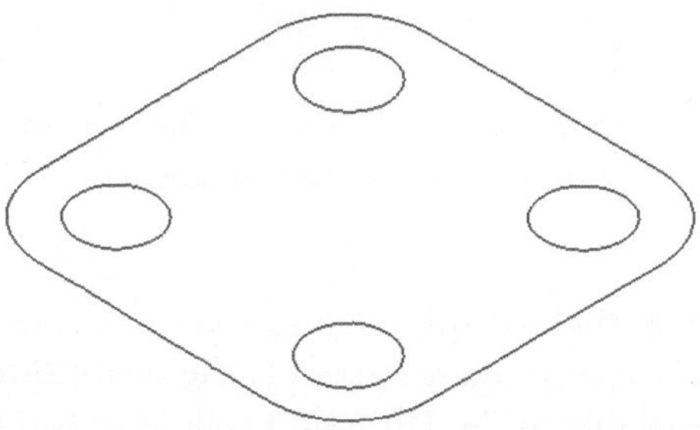

Figure 4-57 *Sketch for the extrude feature*

Figure 4-58 *Resulting extruded feature*

When you choose the **Extrude** tool from the **Feature** group of the **Home** tab; the **Extrude** dialog box will be displayed, as shown in Figure 4-59. Also, you will be prompted to select the planar face to sketch or the section geometry to be extruded. If you select the sketch at this stage, the preview of the extruded feature created using the default values will be displayed on the screen. If you select the sketch plane, the Sketch in Task Environment will be invoked. Draw the sketch and exit the Sketch in Task Environment; the preview of the extruded feature will be displayed in the Modeling environment. You can also draw the sketch in Sketch in Task Environment using the **Sketch Section** button available at the left of the **Curve** button in the **Section** rollout.

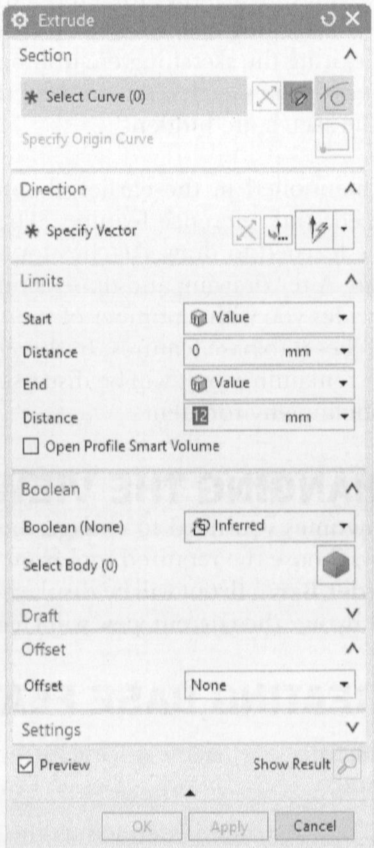

*Figure 4-59 The **Extrude** dialog box*

Extrude Dialog Box Options

The options in this dialog box are discussed next.

Section Rollout

The options in this rollout are used to sketch the section or to select the section. By default, both the **Sketch Section** and **Curve** buttons will be chosen in this rollout and you will be prompted to select the planar face to sketch or the section geometry to be extruded. These options are discussed next.

Sketch Section

This button is used to draw the sketch for extrusion. By default, this button is chosen in the **Section** rollout and it is used to select the planar face to sketch. When you choose this button, the **Create Sketch** dialog box will be displayed and you will be prompted to select the object for the sketch plane. You can select a datum plane or the face of a solid body as the sketching plane.

Curve

By default, this button is also chosen from the **Section** rollout and it is used to select the already drawn section sketch.

Direction Rollout

By default, the direction of extrusion will be normal to the selected section. The options in this rollout are used to define the direction of extrusion. These options are discussed next.

Vector Dialog

If you choose this button, the **Vector** dialog box will be displayed and you will be prompted to select objects to infer vector. Select the face, curve, or edge to specify the vector direction. You can use the **Reverse Direction** button available in the **Direction** rollout to reverse the extrude direction.

Inferred Vector Drop-down List

This drop-down list is used to specify the direction of extrusion. The default direction is normal to the selected section.

Reverse Direction

This button is chosen to flip the current extrusion direction.

Limits Rollout

The options in this rollout are used to specify the start and termination of the extrusion. These options are discussed next.

Start Drop-down List

This drop-down list is used to specify the start point of the extrusion. You can select the **Value** and **Symmetric Value** options from this drop-down list. The **Value** option allows you to specify the distance from the sketching plane at which the extruded feature will start. You need to enter this value in the **Distance** edit box. If you enter a positive value, it will be taken as the offset value between the sketch and the start of the extrusion feature. If you enter 0, the extruded feature will start from the sketch plane. If you enter a negative value, the extruded feature will start below the sketch plane. The **Symmetric Value** option allows you to extrude the sketch symmetrically in both directions of the current sketching plane. When you select this option, the preview will also be modified dynamically. Figure 4-60 shows the preview of a sketch being extruded symmetrically in both directions.

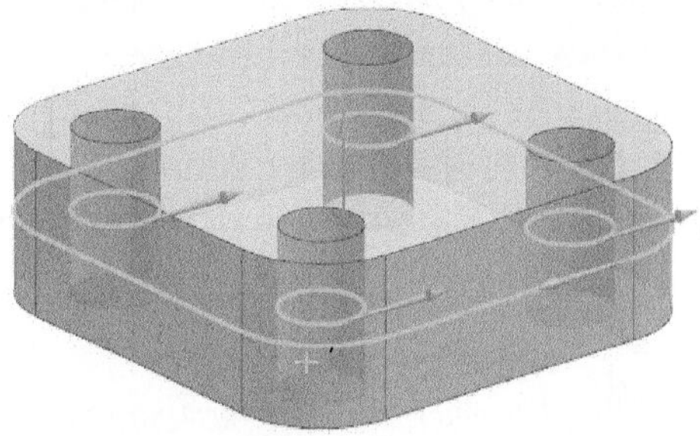

Figure 4-60 *Preview of the symmetric extrusion*

The other options available in this drop-down are discussed next:

Until Next: This option determines the limit of extrusion by finding an intersection with the next face in the model.

Until Selected: Using this option, you can extend the extrude feature to a selected face, datum plane, or body.

Until Extended: This option trims the extrude feature (if it is a body) to a selected face when the section extends beyond its edges. If the extrude section extends past or does not completely intersect the selected face, NX extends the selected face mathematically when possible, and then applies trimming.

Through All: This option extends the extrude feature completely through all selectable bodies along the path of the specified direction.

End Drop-down List

This drop-down list allows you to specify the extrusion termination in the direction of extrusion. For the base feature, only the **Value** and **Symmetric Value** options will be active in this drop-down list. By default, the **Value** option will be selected and the value entered last will be displayed in the **Distance** edit box. As a result, the sketch will be extruded only in the specified direction.

Figure 4-61 shows the preview of the extrusion only in one direction and Figure 4-62 shows the preview of the extrusion with different values in both directions. In this figure, the extrusion value in the upward direction is 10 and in the downward direction is -5.

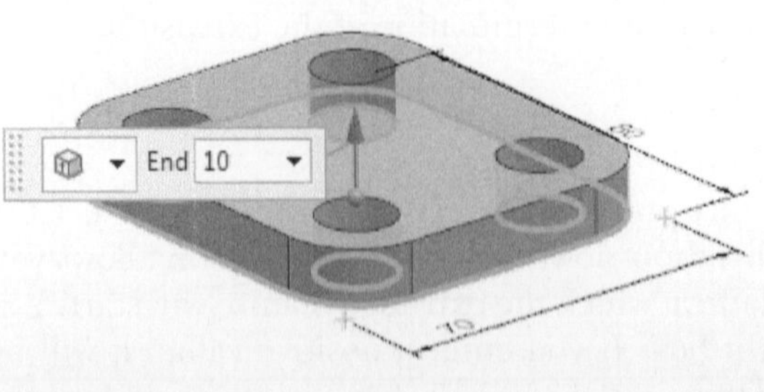

Figure 4-61 *Preview of the extrusion only in one direction*

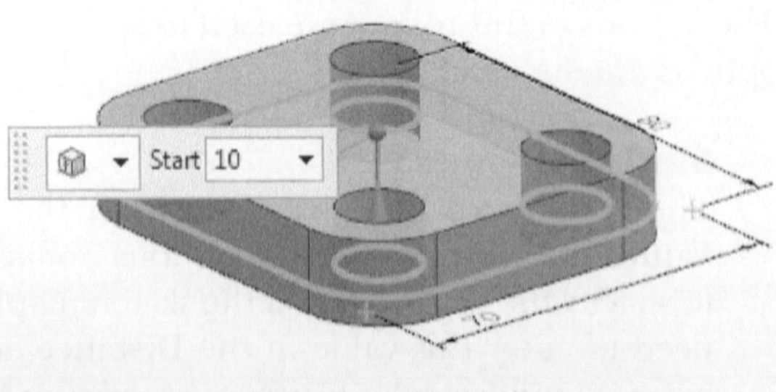

Figure 4-62 *Preview of the extrusion in two opposite directions with different values*

Open Profile Smart Volume

After selecting this check box, you can extend open profile geometry along open end points to find closure with the target body.

Note

The other extrusion termination options are discussed in the next chapter.

Tip

You can also use the start and end drag handles in the preview of the extruded feature to modify the extrusion values in the start and end directions.

Boolean Rollout

The options in this rollout are used to select the boolean operation that you need to perform. These options are discussed in the next chapter.

Draft Rollout

The options in this rollout are used to apply a draft angle to the extrusion feature. The options in this area will be available only when you select the section to extrude. Various draft options in this rollout are discussed next.

Draft

This drop-down list is used to specify the type of draft to be applied to the feature. The options in this drop-down list are discussed next.

From Start Limit

This option adds the draft from the start section to the end section of the extruded feature. As a result, the dimension of the feature at the start section is the same as that of the original sketch and it tapers toward the end section. Figure 4-63 shows the preview of the extruded feature drafted using this option. It is evident from this figure that the bottom section of the extruded feature is the same as that of the original sketch and the feature tapers as it goes toward the top section.

From Section
This option is used to taper the extruded surface in such a way that the cross-section of the extruded feature remains the same at the sketching plane, as shown in Figure 4-64.

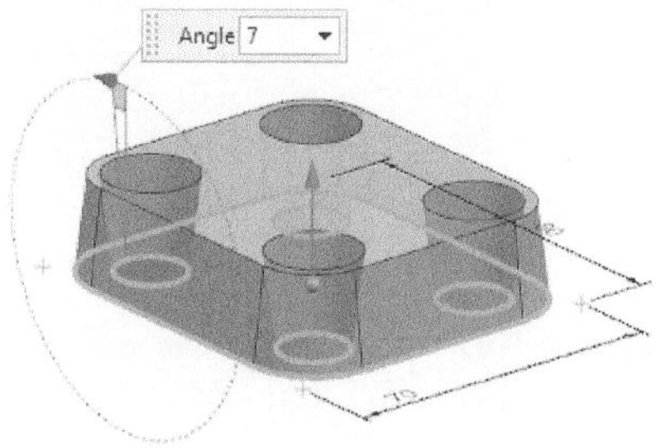

Figure 4-63 Preview of the extrusion tapered using the ***From Start Limit*** *option*

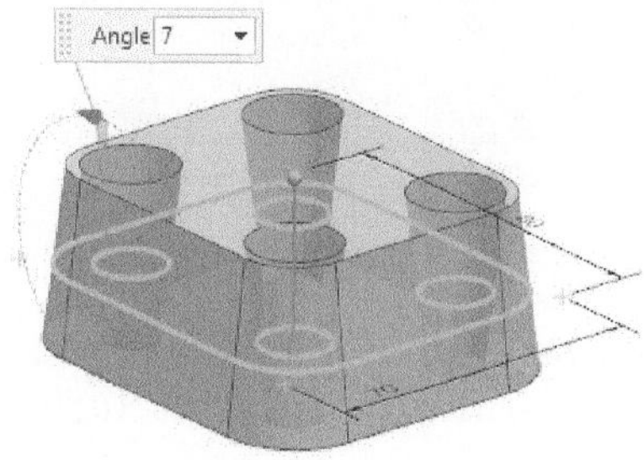

Figure 4-64 Preview of the extrusion tapered using the ***From Section*** *option*

From Section - Asymmetric Angle
This option is available only when you select the **Symmetric Value** option from the **Limits** rollout or specify values for both the start and the end directions. This option adds different tapers in both directions of the sketch, as shown in Figure 4-65. When you select this option, the **Front Angle** and **Back Angle** edit boxes will be available in the **Draft** rollout. The front and back angle values will be applied at the front and back sides of the sketching plane.

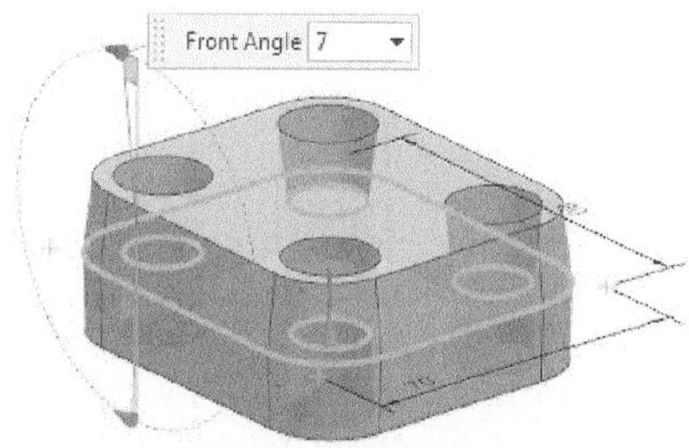

Figure 4-65 Preview of the extrusion tapered using the ***From Section - Asymmetric Angle*** *option*

From Section - Symmetric Angle
This option is available only when you select the **Symmetric Value** option from the **Limits** rollout or specify the values for both the start and the end directions. This option adds a symmetric taper in both directions of the sketch, as shown in Figure 4-66. In this draft type, if the distance value in one of the directions is more than the other, the section in that direction will also be smaller in size.

From Section - Matched Ends
This option is also available only when you select the **Symmetric Value** option from the **Limits** rollout or specify the values in both the start and the end directions. This option tapers the model such that the end sections in both the directions are of similar size, irrespective of the distance values in both directions, as shown in Figure 4-67.

Angle
This edit box allows you to specify the draft angle.

Angle Option
This drop-down list is used to specify the faces to draft. This drop-down will be available only when the **From Section** and **From Section- Asymmetric Angle** options are selected from the **Draft** drop-down list. The options in this drop-down list are discussed next.

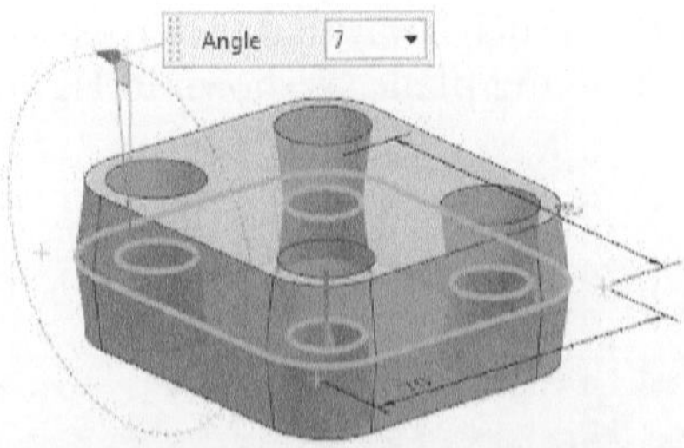

Figure 4-66 Preview of the extrusion tapered using the ***From Section-Symmetric Angle*** *option*

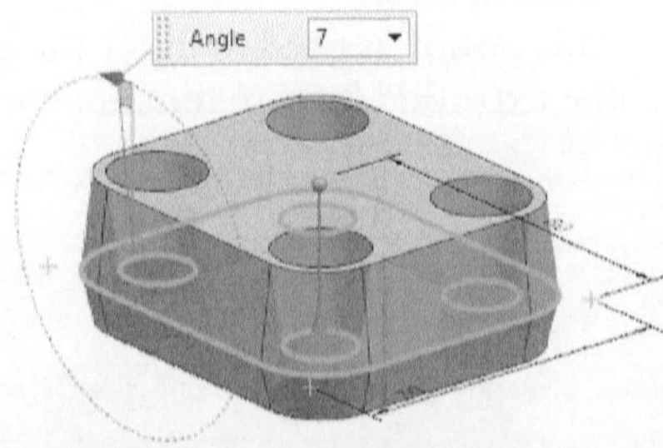

Figure 4-67 Preview of the extrusion tapered using the ***From Section - Matched Ends*** *option*

Single: This option adds the single draft angle value on all faces of the extruded feature.

Multiple: This option allows you to add unique draft angle value to each face of the extruded feature. On selecting this option, the **Angle** edit box and **List** sub-rollout will be displayed in the **Draft** rollout. You can edit the angles by selecting them from the displayed **List** box and entering values in the **Angle** edit box. You can also edit them by selecting the handles from the drawing window and entering the angle value in the **Angle** edit box.

Offset Rollout

The options in this rollout are used to specify the offset value to the extrusion feature, refer to Figure 4-68. You can specify the offset value in the edit box displayed or by dragging the handles displayed on the model. You can also create thin base features by extruding open or closed sketches. For example, refer to the closed sketch shown in Figure 4-69. A thin feature created using this sketch is shown in Figure 4-70. Similarly, Figure 4-71 shows an open sketch and Figure 4-72 shows the resulting thin feature.

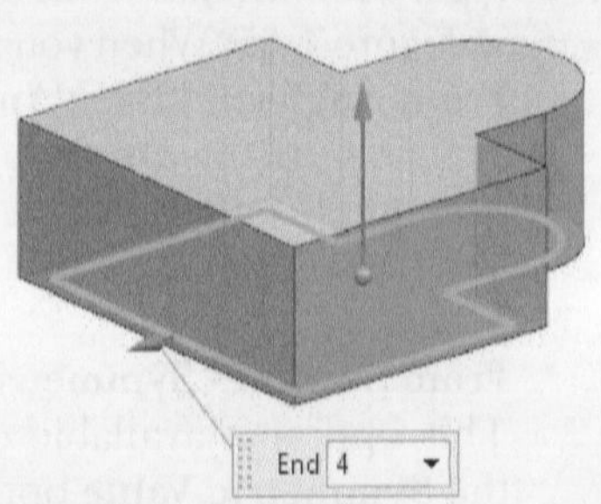

Figure 4-68 Extrusion feature created at an offset from the sketch

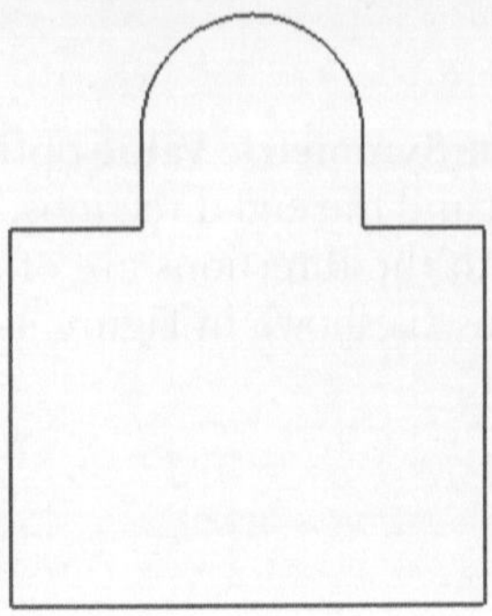

Figure 4-69 Top view of a single closed sketch

Figure 4-70 Isometric view of the resulting thin extruded feature

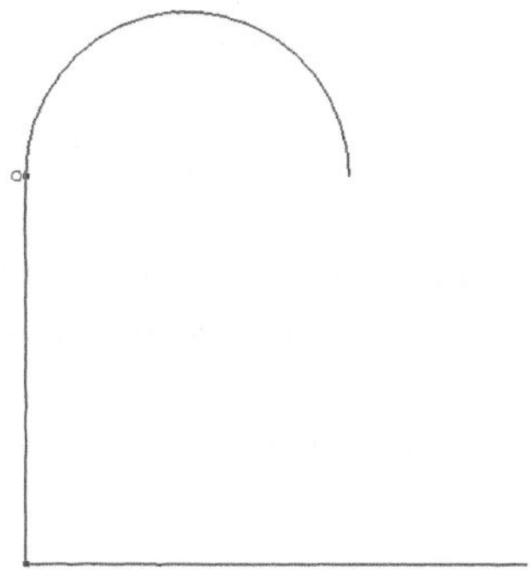

Figure 4-71 Front view of an open sketch

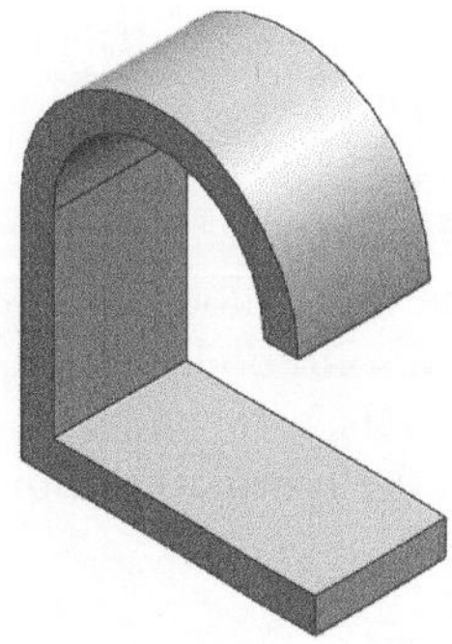

Figure 4-72 Isometric view of the resulting thin extruded feature

To create thin features, expand the **Offset** rollout in the **Extrude** dialog box; the **Offset** drop-down list will be displayed. This drop-down list contains three offset methods. These methods are discussed next.

Single-Sided

This option will be enabled only when you create a thin feature using a closed sketch with no nested closed sketch in it. If you select this option, the inner portion of the sketch will be filled automatically. As a result of this, there will be no cavity inside the model. It will be similar to the solid extrusion from inside. However, you can also add some offset to the outer side of the sketch.

Two-Sided

This option is used to create a thin feature by offsetting the sketch in two directions. Select this option; the **Start** and **End** edit boxes will be displayed. If you enter the positive value in the **End** edit box, the sketch will offset outward and vice-versa. Figure 4-73 shows the preview of a thin feature with an offset only in the end direction and Figure 4-74 shows the preview of the same feature with an offset in both the directions.

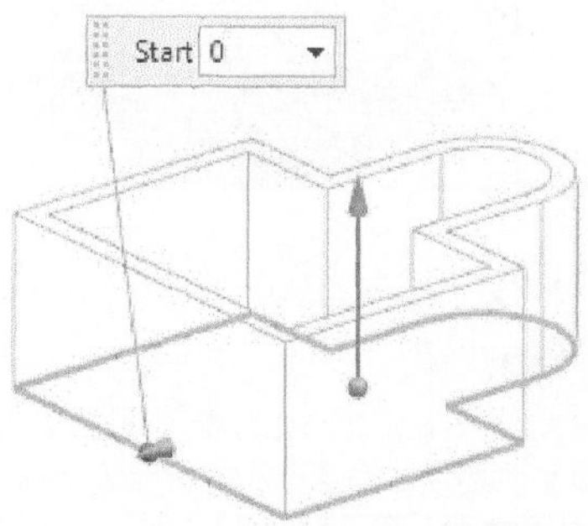

Figure 4-73 A thin feature with an offset only in the end direction

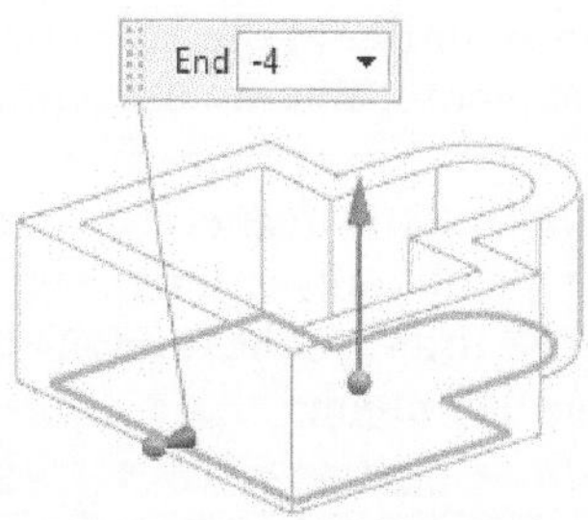

Figure 4-74 A thin feature with an offset in the end and start directions

Symmetric

This option is used to offset the material symmetrically on both sides of the sketch to create the thin feature.

Settings Rollout

The options in this rollout are used to specify whether you need the extruded feature to be a sheet body or a solid body. To get a solid body, the section must be a closed profile or an open profile with an offset. If you use the **Single-Sided** offset, you will not be able to get a sheet body. You can select the required option from the **Body Type** drop-down list.

Note

The display type of models in Figures 4-73 and 4-74 is changed. You will learn more about changing the display type later in this chapter.

Preview

This area is used to preview the model dynamically while modifying the values in the **Extrude** dialog box. On selecting the **Preview** check box, you can dynamically preview the changes in the model as you modify the values of the extrusion. The **Show Result** button is used to view the final model. The **Undo Result** button is used to go back to the preview mode.

After setting the values in the **Extrude** dialog box, choose the **OK** button to create the extruded feature and exit the dialog box. If you need to extrude more than one sketch, choose the **Apply** button; the selected sketch will be extruded and the dialog box will be retained. Also, you will be prompted to select the section geometry. Select the other sketch to extrude and choose the **OK** button.

You can also set and modify the values of extrusion using the drag handles that will be displayed in the preview of the extrusion feature, refer to Figure 4-75. The start drag handle will be a filled circle and the end drag handle will be an arrow. To modify the start limit, end limit, or draft angle values, click on their respective drag handles, and then press and hold the left mouse button and drag the mouse. You can also enter the new values in the edit boxes that will be displayed after clicking on the respective handles. To modify the type of limits or taper, right-click on their respective drag handles and select the type from the shortcut menu.

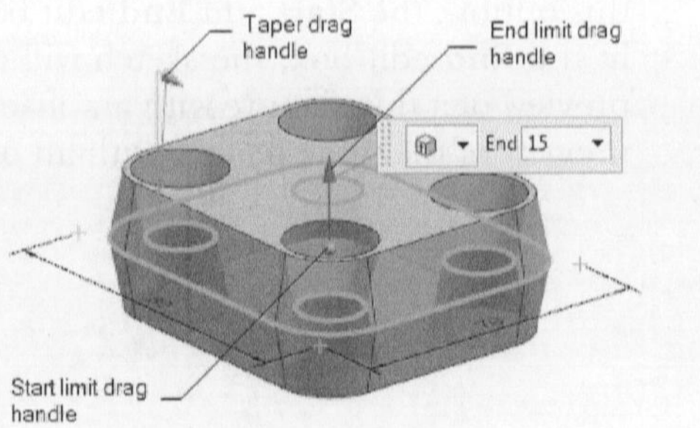

***Figure 4-75** Various drag handles in the preview of the extrusion feature*

CREATING SOLID REVOLVED BODIES

Ribbon:	Home > Feature > Design Feature Drop-down > Revolve
Menu:	Insert > Design Feature > Revolve

The **Revolve** tool is used to create a solid body by revolving a sketch around the revolution axis which could be a sketched line or an edge of an existing feature. Figure 4-76 shows a sketch for creating a revolved feature and Figure 4-77 shows the isometric view of the resulting feature revolved through an angle of 270 degrees. To convert a sketch into a revolved body, you need to invoke the **Revolve** tool. This tool works in the following three steps:

Step 1: Select the sketch to be revolved
Step 2: Select the revolution axis
Step 3: Specify the revolution parameters

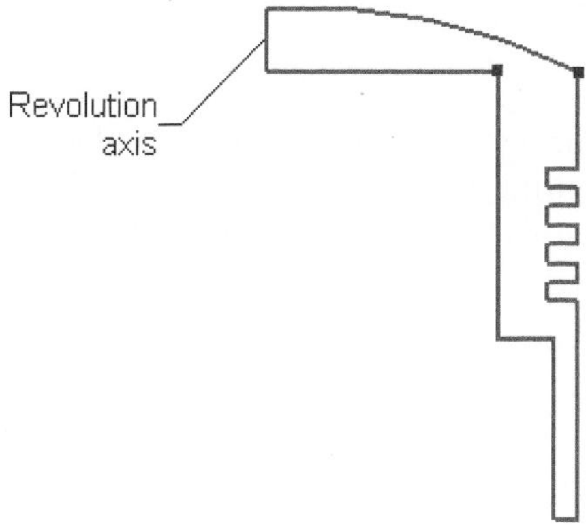

Figure 4-76 *Sketch for creating the revolved feature with the revolution axis*

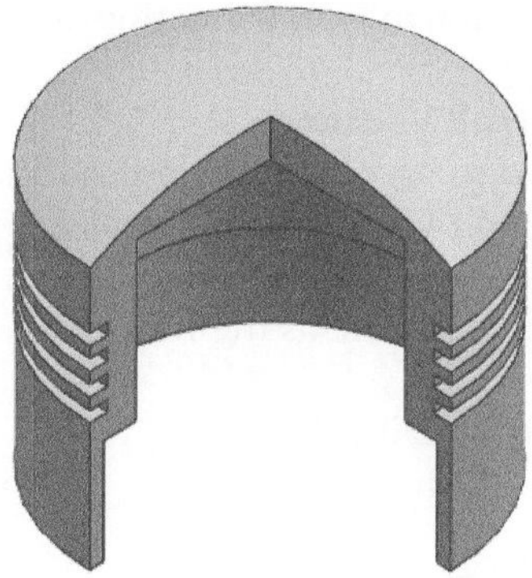

Figure 4-77 *Isometric view of the resulting feature revolved through an angle of 270 degrees*

To create a solid body, choose the **Revolve** tool from the **Design Feature Drop-down** of the **Feature** group; the **Revolve** dialog box will be displayed. Figure 4-78 shows the expanded view of the **Revolve** dialog box. The options in this dialog box are explained next.

Section Rollout

The options in this rollout are used to sketch the section or select the section created earlier. By default, both the **Sketch Section** and **Curve** buttons are chosen in this rollout and you are prompted to select the planar face to sketch or the section geometry to be revolved. The other options in this rollout are discussed next.

Specify Origin Curve

This option is used to select the origin curve of the selected profile.

Reverse Direction

This button is used to reverse the direction of the origin curve.

Axis Rollout

The options in this rollout are used to specify the revolution axis. These options are discussed next.

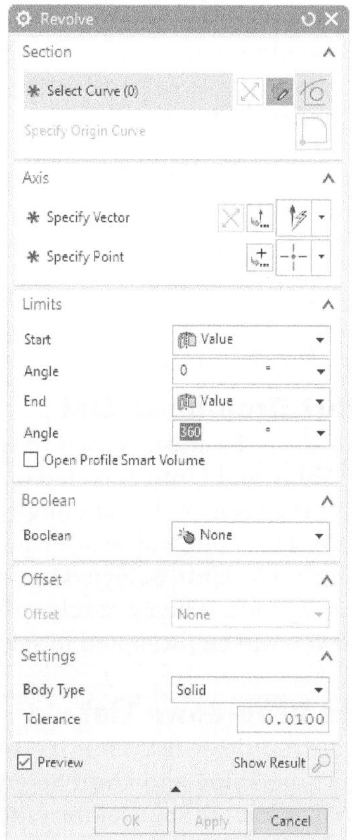

Figure 4-78 *The **Revolve** dialog box*

Specify Vector

The options in this area are used to specify the revolution axis using the **Vector Dialog** button or the **Inferred Vector** drop-down list.

Vector Dialog

When you choose this button, the **Vector** dialog box will be displayed. You can specify the revolution axis by using this dialog box.

Inferred Vector

The options in this drop-down list are used to specify the revolution axis. By default, the **Inferred Vector** option is selected in this drop-down list. As a result, you will be prompted to select the object to infer vector. You can select a sketched line, an axis, or an edge of an existing feature as the revolution axis.

Reverse Direction

You can choose this button to flip the direction of revolution.

Specify Point

The options in this area are used only when you use the vector method to specify the revolution axis.

Point Dialog

When you choose this button, the **Point** dialog box will be displayed. You can specify the point to define the revolution axis using this dialog box.

Inferred Point

This drop-down list contains the snap point options that are used to automatically snap the keypoints of the previously sketched entities or features.

Limits Rollout

The options in this rollout are used to specify the start and termination angles of revolution. These options are discussed next.

Start Drop-down List

This drop-down list is used to specify the start angle of the revolution feature. You can select the **Value** and **Until Selected** options from this drop-down list. The **Value** option allows you to enter the value of the start angle in the **Angle** edit box. You need to enter a positive value of the angle. This value will be taken as the offset value between the sketch and the start of the revolved feature. The **Until Selected** option allows you to start the revolve feature from the selected plane, face, or body. When you select this option, the **Face, Body, Datum Plane** button will be chosen and you will be prompted to select the face, body, or datum plane to start the revolved feature.

End Drop-down List

This drop-down list is used to specify the termination angle of the revolution feature. You can select the **Value** and **Until Selected** options from this drop-down list. The **Value** option allows you to enter the value of the end angle in the **Angle** edit box. You need to enter a positive value for the angle. This value will be taken as the offset value between the sketch and the end of the revolved feature. The **Until Selected** option allows you to terminate the revolve feature using the selected plane, face, or body. When you select this option, the **Face, Body, Datum Plane** button will be chosen and you will be prompted to select the face, body, or datum plane to start the revolved feature.

The default value of the end angle is the one that you have used to create the last revolved feature. Figure 4-79 shows a revolved feature with the start angle as 30 degrees and the end angle as 180 degrees. The sketch used to create this feature is also displayed.

Note that NX uses the right-hand thumb rule to determine the direction of revolution. This rule states that if the thumb of your right hand points in the direction of the axis of revolution, then the direction of the curled fingers will define the direction of revolution, refer to Figure 4-80. Figure 4-81 shows the sketch and an arrow pointing in the direction of the axis of revolution and Figure 4-82 shows the resulting feature revolved through an angle of 180 degrees.

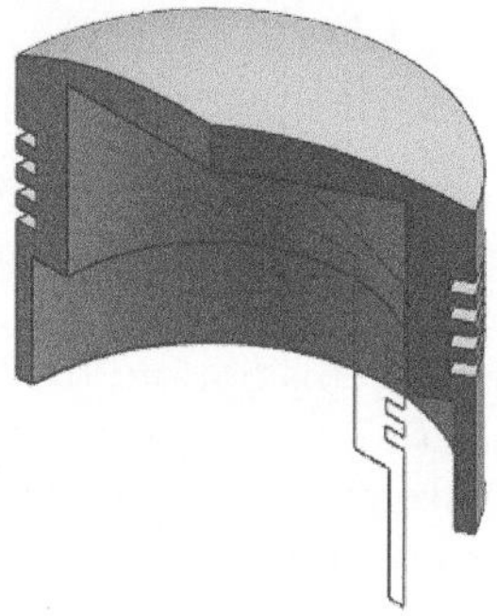

Figure 4-79 *Sketch revolved with start angle as 30 degrees and end angle as 180 degrees*

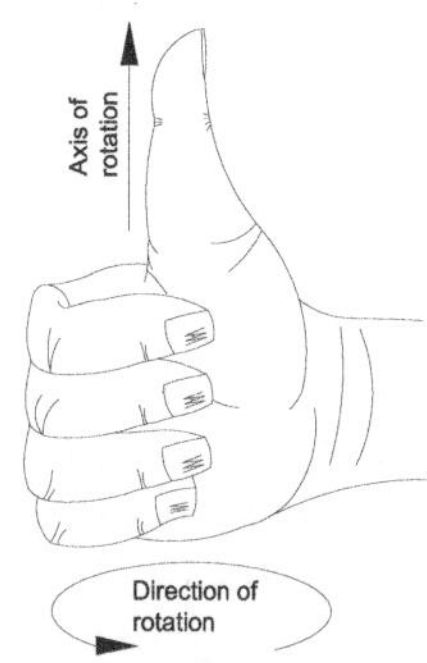

Figure 4-80 *The right-hand thumb rule*

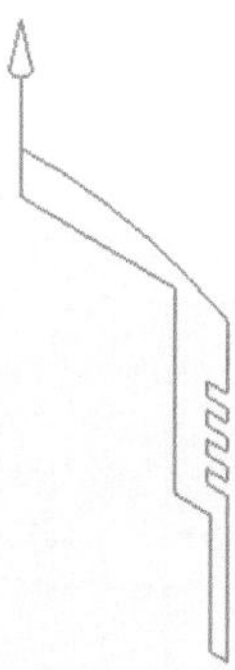

Figure 4-81 *Sketch for creating the revolved feature and the direction of the revolution axis*

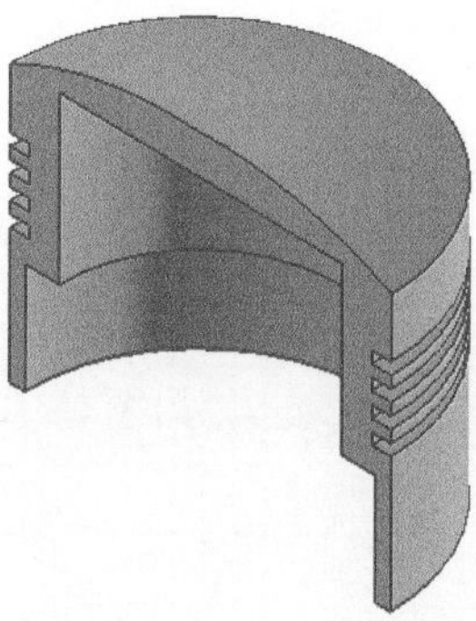

Figure 4-82 *Isometric view of the resulting feature revolved through an angle of 180 degrees*

Figure 4-83 shows the sketch and an arrow pointing in the direction of the axis of revolution and Figure 4-84 shows the resulting feature revolved through an angle of 180 degrees.

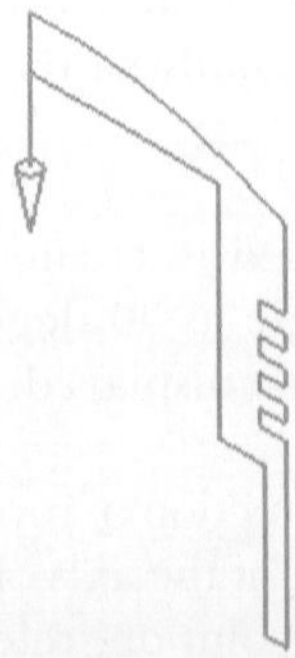

Figure 4-83 Sketch for creating the revolved feature and the direction of the revolution axis

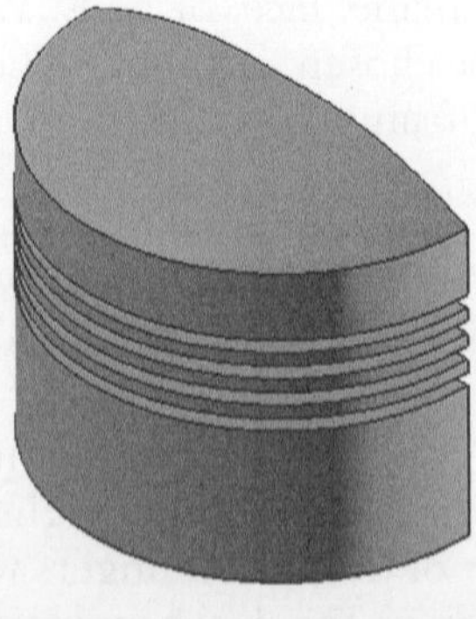

Figure 4-84 Isometric view of the resulting feature revolved through an angle of 180 degrees

Offset Rollout

NX also allows you to create thin revolved bodies using the open and closed sketches. This process is similar to that of creating thin solid extruded features. Click on the **Offset** rollout in the **Revolve** dialog box; the rollout will expand and display the **Offset** drop-down list. There is only one option, **Two-Sided**, available in this drop-down list. Select this option; the **Start** and the **End** edit boxes will be available. Enter the start and end offset values in the respective edit boxes. Figure 4-85 shows a thin revolved model with the open sketch and the revolution axis used to create it. In this model, the start angle is 30 degrees, the end angle is 180 degrees, and the start offset value is 2.

Figure 4-86 shows a thin revolved model with the closed sketch and the revolution axis used to create it. In this model, the start angle is 45 degrees, the end angle is 270 degrees, and the start offset value is 2.

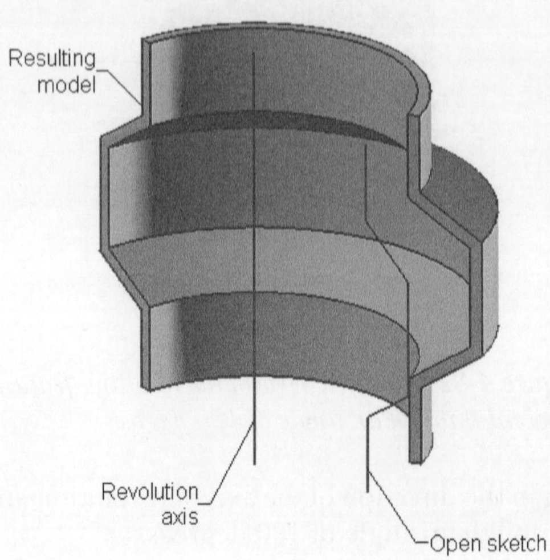

Figure 4-85 A thin revolved feature with the original open sketch and the axis of revolution

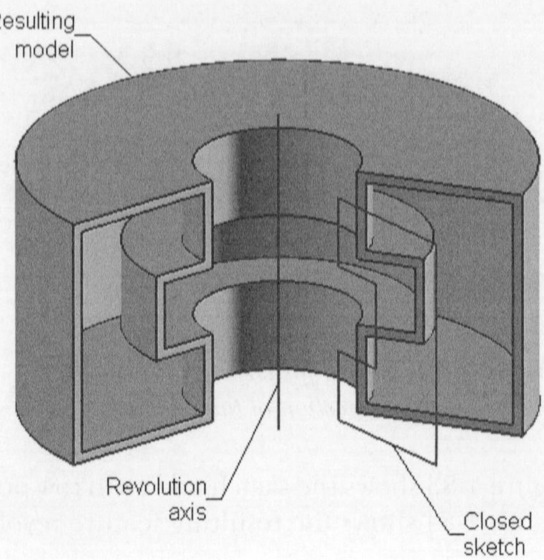

Figure 4-86 A thin revolved feature with the original closed sketch and the axis of revolution

Copying, Moving, and Rotating Objects

Ribbon:	Tools > Utilities > Move object
Menu:	Edit > Move Object

In NX, you can dynamically move, rotate, or copy solid objects as well as sketched entities by using the **Move Object** tool. To invoke this tool, choose **Menu > Edit > Move Object** from the **Top Border Bar**; the **Move Object** dialog box will be displayed, as shown in Figure 4-87. The options in this dialog box are discussed next.

Objects Rollout

In this rollout, the **Object** button is chosen by default. As a result, you will be prompted to select the objects to move. Select the entity that you want to move, rotate, or copy.

Transform Rollout

The **Transform** rollout is used to transform object using various methods. The **Motion** drop-down list in this rollout is used to specify the transform method to be used. The options in the **Transform** rollout keep on changing according to the options selected from the **Motion** drop-down list. These options are discussed next.

Distance

This option is used to move the selected object by a specified distance along the direction of the selected vector. Select this option from the **Motion** drop-down list; you will be prompted to specify the direction vector along which the selected object will be moved or copied. Select an existing edge, sketched entity, datum axis, or datum plane to specify the vector direction. Next, enter the required value in the **Distance** edit box and then press ENTER; the selected object will move by the specified distance value along the specified vector direction, as shown in Figure 4-88. You can also flip the direction of the vector by choosing the **Reverse Direction** button or by double-clicking on the arrowhead displayed in the graphics area. Next, choose the **OK** button.

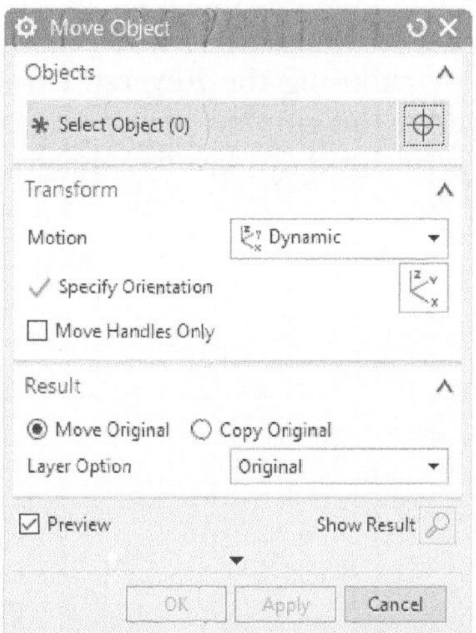

***Figure 4-87** The **Move Object** dialog box*

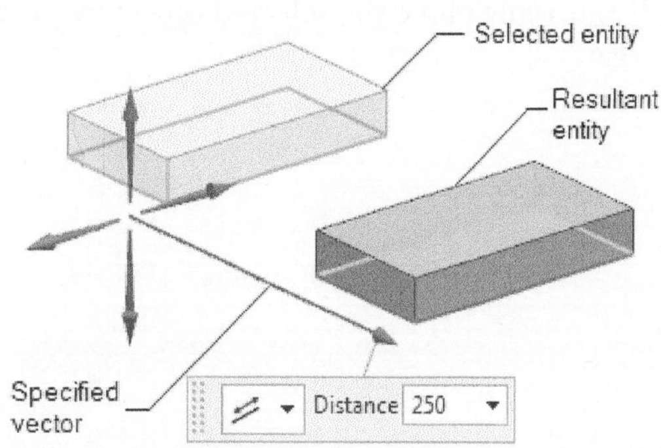

***Figure 4-88** Entity transformed by using the **Distance** option*

Angle

The **Angle** option in the **Motion** drop-down list is used to rotate the selected entity with respect to the specified point. Select this option from the **Motion** drop-down list; you will be prompted to select the objects to infer vector. Also, the **Specify Vector** area will be highlighted in the dialog box and a triad will be displayed in the drawing window. Specify the vector about which you want to change the orientation of the object; you will be prompted to select the objects to infer point. Also, the **Specify Axis Point** area will be highlighted in the dialog box. Specify the axis point at which you want to locate the axis vector. Next, enter the angle value in the **Angle** edit box and press ENTER; the **Select Object** area will be highlighted in the dialog box. Next, select the required object to orient from the drawing window, a preview of the transformed object will be displayed, as shown in Figure 4-89. Next, choose the **OK** button to exit the dialog box.

Distance between Points

This option is used to move an entity from one specified point to another specified point along a specified vector. Select this option from the **Motion** drop-down list; you will be prompted to select the object to infer point. Also, the **Specify Origin Point** area will be highlighted in the **Transform** rollout. Select a point to define the origin; the **Specify Measurement Point** area will be highlighted in the **Transform** rollout. Specify the measurement point by selecting another point; the **Specify Vector** area will be highlighted in the **Transform** rollout. Also, a triad of vector will be displayed in the drawing window. Select an existing edge, a sketched entity, or a datum axis to specify the vector direction; you will be prompted to select the object. Also, the **Distance** input edit box will be displayed attached to the specified measurement point. Select the object that you want to move. Next, enter the distance value in the **Distance** input edit box to define the driven distance of the selected object along the specified vector. You can also enter the distance value in the **Distance** edit box of the dialog box. Note that the selected object will move by the difference between the origin point and the measurement point along the direction of the vector specified. For example, if the distance between the origin point and the measurement point along the direction vector is 100 mm and you want to move the object to a distance of 50 mm, in this case, you need to enter the distance value of 150 mm in the **Distance** edit box. As you enter the distance value, the preview of the selected entity will be displayed in the graphics window, refer to Figure 4-90. You can flip the direction of the vector by choosing the **Reverse Direction** button or by double-clicking on the arrowhead displayed in the graphics area. You can also dynamically move the selected object by dragging the arrowhead displayed in the graphics area.

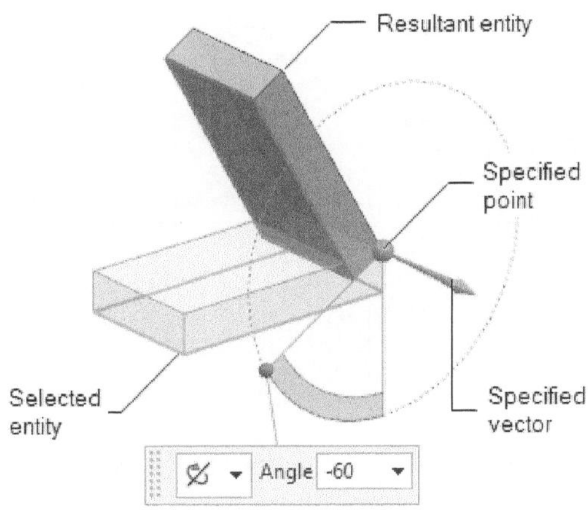

Figure 4-89 Entity transformed by using the ***Angle*** *option*

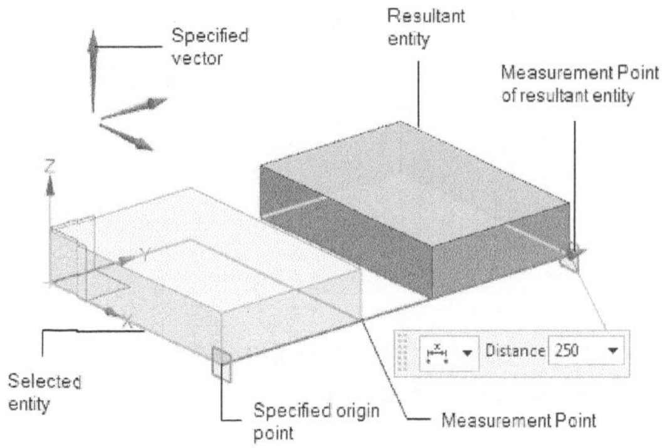

Figure 4-90 Entity transformed by using the ***Distance between Points*** *option*

Radial Distance

This option is used to move an entity by using the measurement point and axis. The distance will be measured normal to the axis. Select this option from the **Motion** drop-down list; you will be prompted to select the objects to infer vector. Also, the **Specify Vector** area will be highlighted in the **Transform** rollout; you will be prompted to specify the direction vector perpendicular to which the selected object will be moved or copied. Select an existing edge, a sketched entity, a datum axis, or a datum plane to specify the direction vector. Next, specify the axis point relative to which the entity will be moved or copied; the **Specify Measurement Point** area will be highlighted in the **Transform** rollout. As a result, you will be prompted to select the object to infer point. Next, specify the measurement point; the distance between the specified axis point and the measurement point will be displayed in the **Distance** edit box of the **Transform** rollout. Note that you need to add the distance value by which you want to move the object to the current value displayed in the **Distance** edit box of the dialog box. Next, enter the required distance value in the **Distance** edit box and press ENTER, you will be prompted to select the objects to move. Next, select the object to be moved from the drawing area; a preview of the resultant entity will be displayed in the drawing window, refer to Figure 4-91. Next, choose the **OK** button to exit the dialog box. The selected object will be moved by the specified distance value and perpendicular to the specified vector direction.

Point to Point

This option is used to move the selected entity from one specified point to another. Select this option from the **Motion** drop-down list; you will be prompted to select the object to infer point. Also, the **Specify From Point** area will be highlighted in the **Transform** rollout. Specify the start point of the moving entity; you will be prompted to select the object to infer point. Also, the **Specify To Point** area will be highlighted in the **Transform** rollout. Next, specify the point upto which you want to move the entity; you will be prompted to select the object to move. Select the entity that you want to move; the selected entity will be moved to the specified point and the preview of the entity will be displayed in the graphics window, as shown in Figure 4-92.

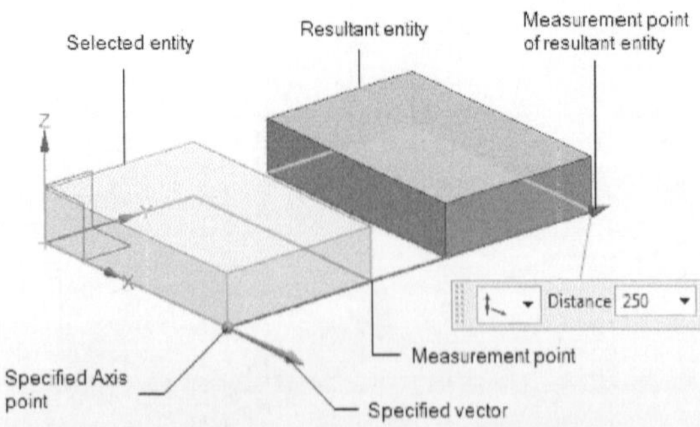

*Figure 4-91 Entity transformed by using the **Radial Distance** option*

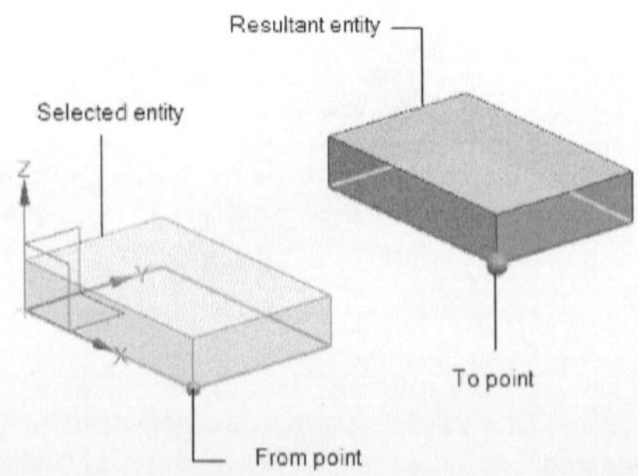

*Figure 4-92 Entity transformed by using the **Point to Point** option*

Rotate by Three Points

This option is used to rotate an entity by using three points. Select this option from the **Motion** drop-down list; you will be prompted to select the object to infer vector. Also, the **Specify Vector** area will be highlighted in the **Transform** rollout. Specify the direction vector along which the selected object will be rotated. Also, the **Specify Pivot Point** area will be highlighted in the **Transform** rollout. Next, specify the pivot point relative to which the entity will change its orientation; the **Specify Start Point** area will be highlighted in the **Transform** rollout. As a result, you will be prompted to select the object to infer point. Specify the start point from where the orientation will start; you will be prompted to select the object to infer point and also the **Specify End Point** area will be highlighted in the **Transform** rollout. Specify the end point; you will be prompted to select the object to rotate. Select the entity to be rotated; the preview of the resultant entity will be displayed in the graphics window, as shown in Figure 4-93.

Align Axis to Vector

This option is used to rotate an object from one specified vector to another specified vector about the specified pivot point. Select this option from the **Motion** drop-down list; you will be prompted to select the objects to infer vector. Specify the reference vector from which the rotation angle will be measured. After specifying the reference vector for the rotation angle, the **Specify Pivot Point** area will be highlighted in the **Transform** rollout. As a result, you will be prompted to select the object to infer point. Specify the pivot point in the graphics window; you will be prompted to select the object to infer vector. Specify the reference vector for the rotation angle; you will be prompted to select the object to be moved. After selecting the object, the preview of the resultant entity will be displayed in the graphics window, as shown in Figure 4-94.

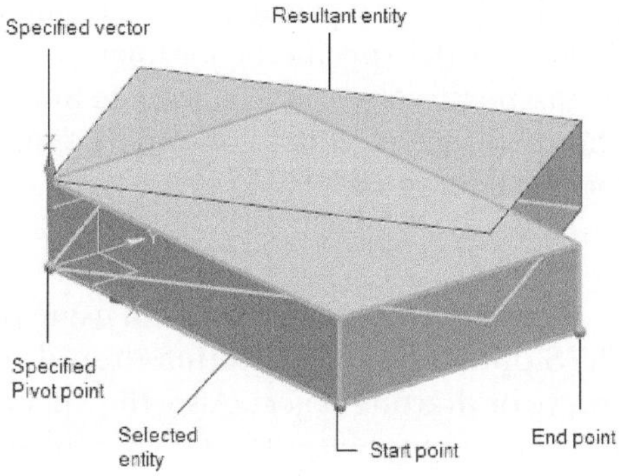

*Figure 4-93 Entity transformed by using the **Rotate by Three Points** option*

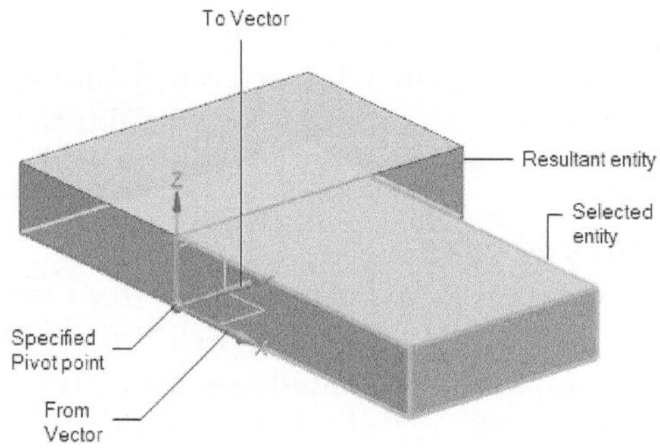

*Figure 4-94 Entity transformed by using the **Align Axis to Vector** option*

Dynamic

This option is used to move or rotate an object dynamically. Select this option from the **Motion** drop-down list; a dynamic triad will be displayed at the origin, refer to Figure 4-95. Select the object to move or rotate; the triad will be placed at the center of the selected object. You can use this triad to move or rotate the selected entity dynamically by using its handles or angular handles. If you drag the handles, the object will move linearly. If you drag the angular handles, the object will move angularly. Also, you can place the selected object from one point to another by selecting the center of the triad and then clicking at the point where you want to place the object. Note that instead of dragging the handles, you can also specify the values in their respective edit boxes, refer to Figure 4-96. You can select the **Move Handles Only** check box in the **Transform** rollout to move the dynamic triad only.

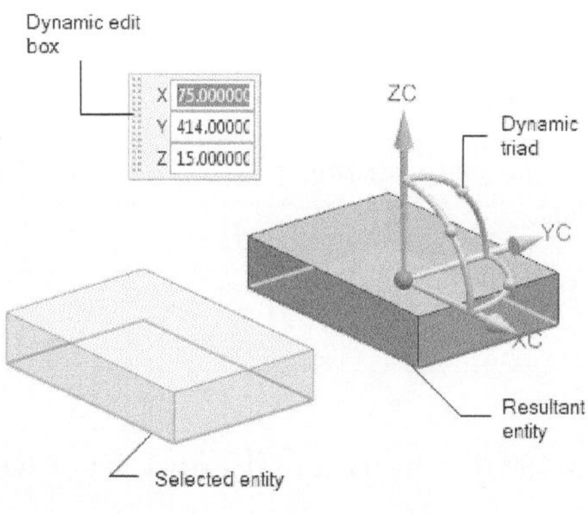

*Figure 4-95 Entity transformed by using the **Dynamic** option*

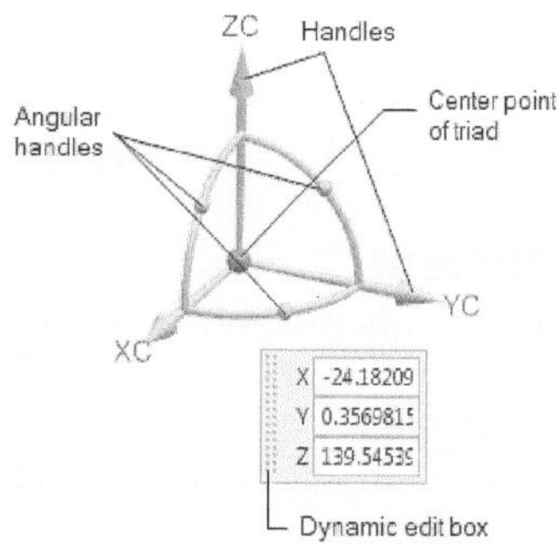

Figure 4-96 Dynamic triad

Delta XYZ

This option is used to move a selected entity from one position to another position with respect to the X, Y, and Z coordinates. Select the **Delta XYZ** option from the **Motion** drop-down list; you will be prompted to select the object to be moved. Select the object to be moved. Next, enter the required coordinate values in **XC**, **YC**, and **ZC** edit boxes in the **Transform** rollout of the dialog box, and then press ENTER; the preview of the resultant entity will be displayed in the graphics window. Note that the specified coordinate values are relative to the reference coordinate system that can be the Absolute Coordinate System or the Work Coordinate System. You can select the required reference coordinate system from the **Reference** drop-down list in the **Transform** rollout of the dialog box.

CSYS to CSYS

This option is used to move a selected entity from one position to another position using the Datum coordinate systems. Select the **CSYS to CSYS** option from the **Motion** drop-down list; you will be prompted to select a plane, planar curve or drafting object. Also, the **Specify From CSYS** area will be highlighted in the **Transform** rollout. Select the CSYS, a planar object or any plane of the CSYS; you will be prompted to select a plane, planar curve or drafting object again and the **Specify To CSYS** area will be highlighted in the **Transform** rollout. Select the target CSYS, a planar object or any plane of the target CSYS where you want the object to be moved; you will be prompted to select the object to move. Also, the **Select Object** area will be highlighted in the **Objects** rollout. Select the object to be moved; the preview of the resultant entity will be displayed in the graphics window, refer to Figure 4-97. Next, choose the **OK** button to exit the dialog box.

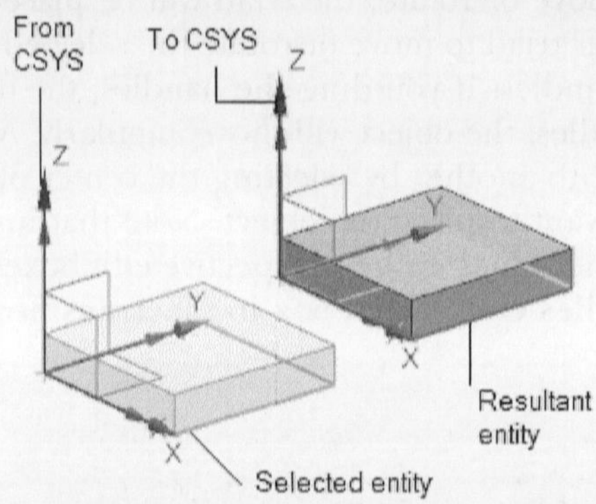

*Figure 4-97 Entity transformed by using the **CSYS to CSYS** option*

Result Rollout

The options in this rollout are discussed next.

Move Original

This radio button is selected by default. As a result, the original entity itself will be transformed.

Copy Original

This radio button toggles with the **Move Original** radio button. Select the radio button, if you want to create multiple copies of the entity such that the original entity is retained in its position.

Distance/Angle Divisions

This edit box is used to divide the specified distance or the angle value according to the numbers specified in it.

Note

*The **Distance/Angle Divisions** edit box will not be available if you choose the **Dynamic** or **CSYS to CSYS** options from the **Motion** drop-down list in the **Transform** rollout of the **Move Object** dialog box.*

Number of Non-associative Copies

This edit box will be available only when the **Copy Original** radio button is selected. In this edit box, you can specify the number of instances to be created, excluding the original one.

Settings Rollout

In this rollout, the **Create Trace Lines** check box is clear by default. If you select this check box, the trace lines of object will be created whenever the object shifts from one position to another, as shown in Figure 4-98.

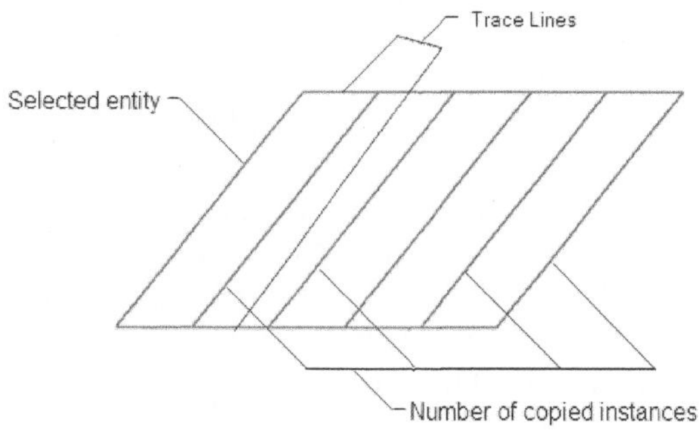

Figure 4-98 *Trace lines created*

HIDING ENTITIES

Ribbon:	View > Visibility > Show Hide Gallery (Customize to add) > Hide
Menu:	Edit > Show and Hide > Hide

Whenever you create a sketch-based feature, the sketch used to create it is retained on the screen even after the feature is created. NX allows you to hide the sketches or any other entity on the screen using the **Hide** tool. To invoke this tool, press the CTRL+B keys; the **Class Selection** dialog box will be displayed. Alternatively, you can invoke the **Hide** tool from the **Visibility** group in the **View** tab. Select the sketch or any other entity from the screen using this dialog box and choose the **OK** button; the selected entities will be hidden.

Note

*You can also use the **Immediate Hide** tool from the **Visibility** group to immediately hide the selected sketches.*

SHOWING HIDDEN ENTITIES

Ribbon:	View > Visibility > Show Hide Gallery (Customize to add) > Show
Menu:	Edit > Show and Hide > Show

The **Show** tool is used to restore the display of the hidden entities. To do so, invoke the **Show** tool by pressing the SHIFT+CTRL+K keys; the **Class Selection** dialog box and the hidden entities will be displayed. Also, you will be prompted to select the objects to be displayed. Select the entities to be displayed and then choose the **OK** button. Alternatively, you can invoke the **Show** tool from the **Visibility** group.

HIDING ALL ENTITIES USING A SINGLE TOOL

Ribbon:	View > Visibility > Show and Hide
Menu:	Edit > Show and Hide > Show and Hide

Show and Hide

NX allows you to hide or show all the entities (all datum planes, coordinate systems, sketches, faceted bodies, solid bodies, and so on) from the drawing window using a single tool. To do so, choose the **Show and Hide** tool from the **Visibility** group; the **Show and Hide** dialog box will be displayed, refer to Figure 4-99.

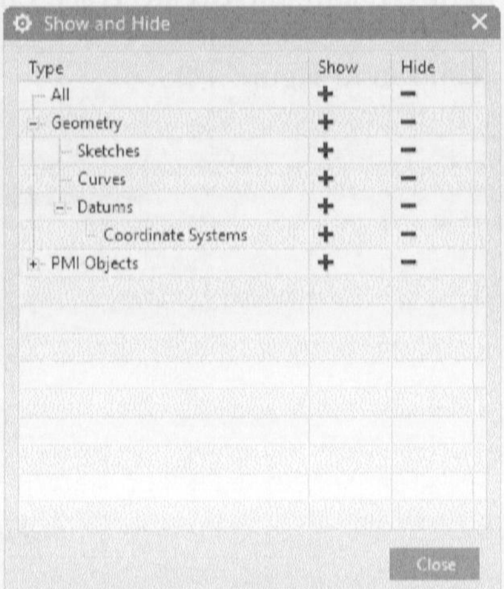

*Figure 4-99 The **Show and Hide** dialog box*

All entities are divided into three categories: Bodies, Sketches, and Datums. Select the minus sign (-) from the respective rows; the corresponding entities will be hidden. For example, if you need to hide all the sketches in the drawing window, select the minus sign (-) from the **Sketches** row; all the sketches will be hidden.

Similarly, to show hidden entities, select the plus sign (+) from the respective row; all the entities under that category will be redisplayed in the drawing window.

Note

*1. The **Show and Hide** tool is very useful while working with complicated models and assemblies where datum planes, coordinate systems, and sketches are in large numbers.*

2. You can also invoke this tool by pressing the CTRL+W keys.

ROTATING THE VIEW OF A MODEL IN 3D SPACE

Ribbon:	View > Operation (Customize to add) > Rotate

NX provides you with an option of rotating the view of a solid model freely in the 3-dimensional (3D) space. This enables you to visually maneuver around the solid model and view it from any direction. To do so, choose the **Rotate** tool from the **Operation** group in the **View** tab; the cursor changes into a rotate view cursor and you will be prompted to drag the cursor to rotate the model. Next, press and hold the left mouse button and drag the cursor; the view of the model will be rotated and you can visually maneuver around it.

You can also rotate the view around the X, Y, or Z axis of the current view. To rotate the view around the X-axis of the current view, invoke the **Rotate** tool and move the cursor close to the left or right edge of the drawing window; the cursor changes into a X-rotate cursor. Press and hold the left mouse button and drag the cursor; the view will be rotated around the X-axis of the current view. Move the cursor close to the bottom edge of the drawing window and drag the cursor to rotate the view around the Y-axis of the current view. Similarly, move the cursor close to the top edge of the drawing window and drag the cursor to rotate the view around the Z-axis of the current view. Figure 4-100 shows the X, Y, and Z rotate cursors.

***Figure 4-100** The X, Y, and Z rotate cursors*

You can also rotate the view by selecting any existing edge of the model. To do so, invoke the **Rotate** tool and move the rotate cursor toward the edge of the model about which you want to rotate the model; the edge will be highlighted. Select the edge by clicking the left mouse button. Next, press and hold the left mouse button and drag the cursor; the view of the model will rotate about the selected edge of the model.

Note

*You can restore any standard view by choosing its corresponding button from the **Orient View Drop-down** that is displayed when you click on the down arrow on the right of the **Trimetric** button of the **View** group in the **Top Border Bar**.*

SETTING DISPLAY MODES

You can set the display modes for the solid models using the buttons in the **View** group of the **Top Border Bar**. Figure 4-101 shows the partial display of the **View** group with various buttons and flyout options that you can use to set the display modes of the model.

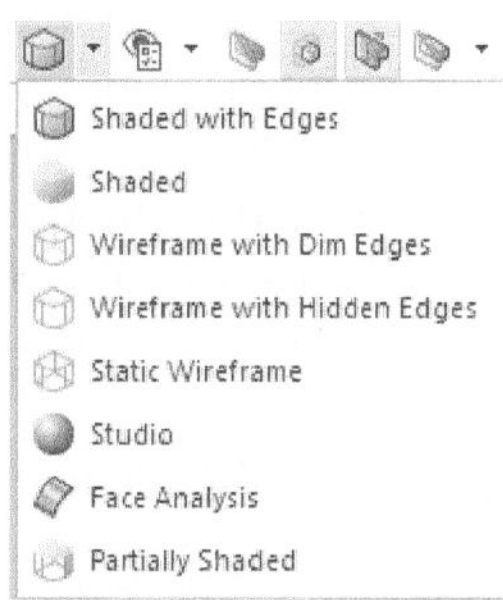

***Figure 4-101** Partial view of the **View** group displaying various options to set the display modes*

TUTORIALS

Tutorial 1

In this tutorial, you will create the model shown in Figure 4-102. The dimensions of the model are shown in Figure 4-103. The depth of extrusion of the model is 45.

(Expected time: 30 min)

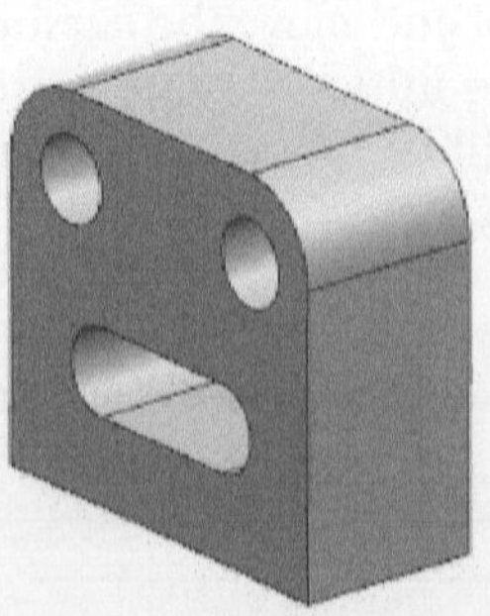

Figure 4-102 Model for Tutorial 1

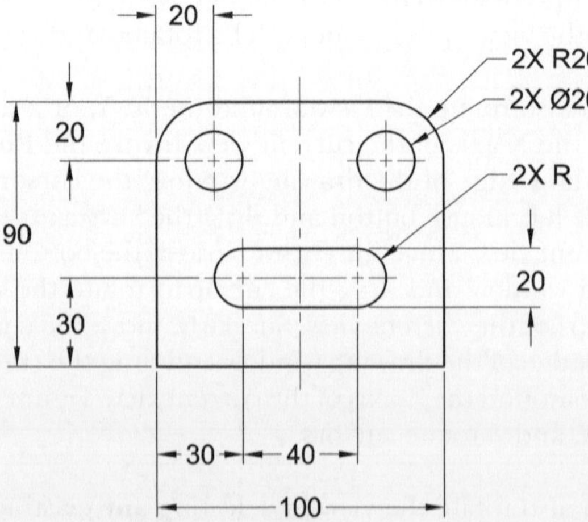

Figure 4-103 Dimensions of the model

The following steps are required to complete this tutorial:

a. Start a new part file using the **Model** template and then draw the profile of the outer loop. Next, add the required constraints, refer to Figure 4-104.
b. Draw the inner loops and add the required dimensions to them, refer to Figure 4-105.
c. Exit the sketching environment and invoke the **Extrude** tool. Define the depth of extrusion to create the final model.
d. Rotate the view in 3D space.
e. Save the file and close it.

Drawing the Sketch of the Model

The sketch of this model will be created on the XC-ZC plane. As mentioned earlier, when you extrude the sketch with nested closed loops, the inner loops are automatically subtracted from the outer sketch.

1. Start a new file with the name *c04tut1.prt* using the **Model** template and specify its location as *C:\NX\c04*.

2. Invoke the sketching environment using the XC-ZC plane as the sketching plane.

3. Draw the sketch of the outer loop and add the required geometric and dimensional constraints to it, as shown in Figure 4-104.

4. Draw the inner loops and then add the required geometric and dimensional constraints to them, as shown in Figure 4-105.

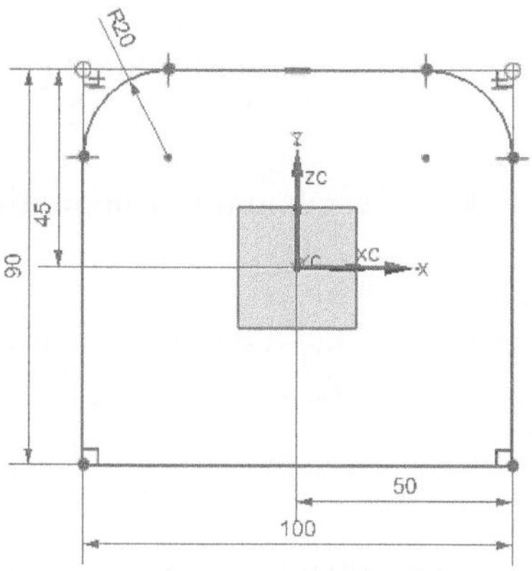

Figure 4-104 Dimensioned sketch of the outer loop

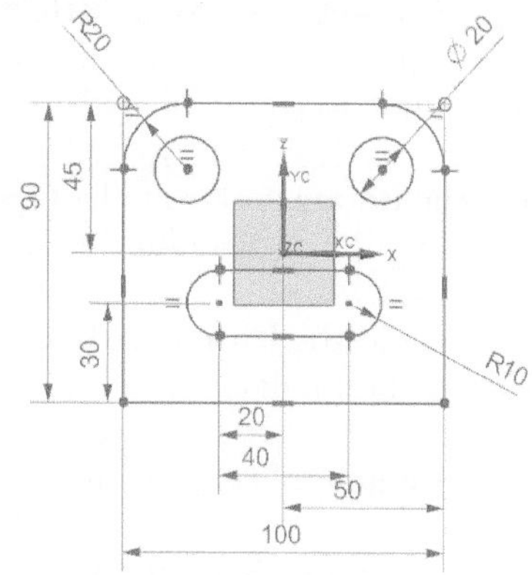

Figure 4-105 Final sketch of the base feature

Converting the Sketch into Base Feature

Next, you need to convert the sketch into base feature by using the **Extrude** tool.

1. Choose the **Finish Sketch** tool from the **Direct Sketch** group to exit the sketching environment.

2. Right-click in the drawing area; a shortcut menu is displayed. Choose the **Fit** option from the shortcut menu to fit the sketch in the screen.

3. Invoke the **Extrude** tool from the **Feature** group; the **Extrude** dialog box is displayed and you are prompted to select the planar face to sketch or select the section geometry. 

4. Select the sketch from the drawing window; the preview of the extruded feature is displayed. Also, the **End** dynamic input box is displayed in the drawing window.

5. Enter **45** in the **End** dynamic input box and press the ENTER key; the preview is modified accordingly.

6. Choose the **OK** button in the **Extrude** dialog box; the extrude feature is created and displayed in the drawing window.

7. Press the CTRL+B keys; the **Class Selection** dialog box is displayed. Select the sketch of the extruded feature to hide it. Next, choose the **OK** button from the dialog box. Figure 4-106 shows the extruded feature after hiding its sketch.

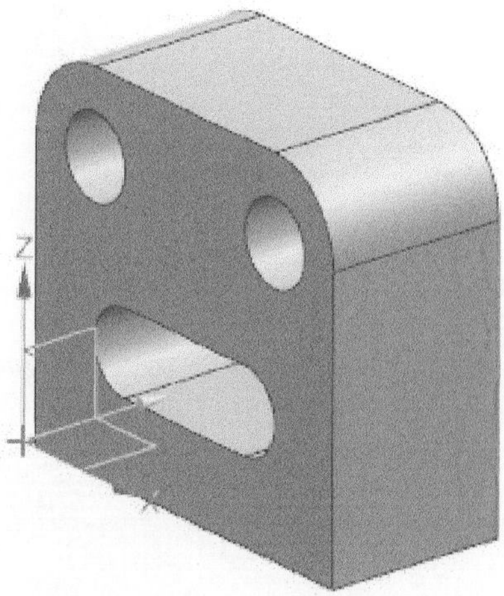

Figure 4-106 Extruded model for Tutorial 1

Rotating the View of the Model

Next, you need to rotate the view of the model so that you can maneuver and view it from different directions.

1. Choose the **Rotate** tool from the **Operation** group of the **View** tab in the **Ribbon**; the cursor changes into a rotate view cursor. 

2. Press and hold the left mouse button and drag the cursor in the drawing window to rotate the view of the model.

3. Exit the **Rotate** tool by pressing the ESC key.

4. Choose the **Trimetric** button from the **Orient View Drop-down** in the **View** group in the **Top Border Bar** to restore the Isometric view.

5. Right-click in the drawing window and choose the **Fit** option from the shortcut menu; the model fits in the drawing window.

Saving and Closing the File

1. Choose **Menu > File > Close > Save and Close** from the **Top Border Bar** to save and close the file.

Tutorial 2

In this tutorial, you will create the model shown in Figure 4-107. Its dimensions are given in the drawing views shown in Figure 4-108. **(Expected time: 30 min)**

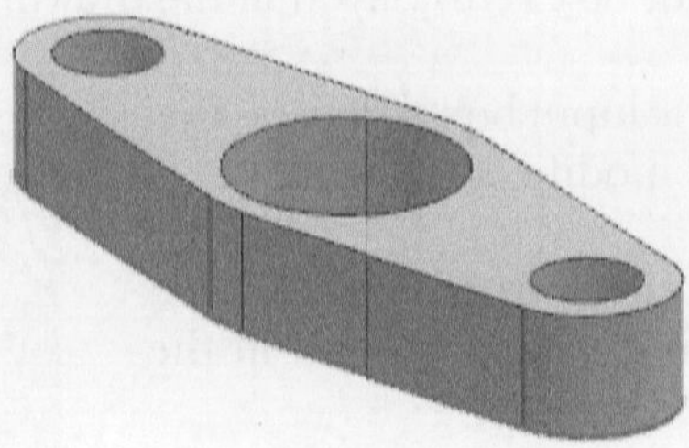

Figure 4-107 *Model for Tutorial 2*

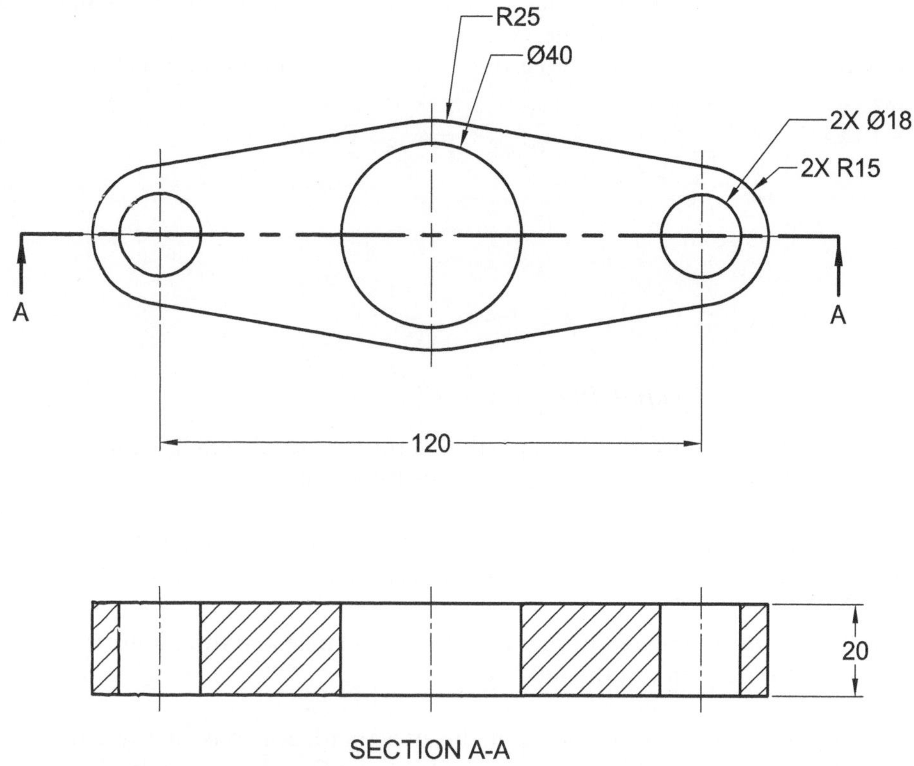

Figure 4-108 *Top and sectioned front views showing the dimensions of the model*

The following steps are required to complete this tutorial:

a. Start a new part file using the **Model** template and then draw the profile of the outer loop, refer to Figure 4-109.
b. Add the required dimensions and constraints to the profile, refer to Figure 4-111.
c. Draw the inner circles and add the required dimensions to them, refer to Figure 4-112.
d. Exit the sketching environment and invoke the **Extrude** tool. Define the depth of extrusion to create the final model.
e. Rotate the view in 3D space, save the file, and close it.

Drawing the Sketch of the Model

The sketch of this model can be created by using the **Sketch** tool. The inner circles will be automatically subtracted from the outer profile on extruding.

1. Start NX and then start a new file with the name *c04tut2.prt* using the **Model** template and specify its location as *C:\NX\c04*.

2. Invoke the sketching environment by choosing the **Sketch** tool from the **Direct Sketch** group using the XC-YC plane as the sketching plane.

3. Draw the sketch using the **Circle** tool and the **Line** tool, as shown in Figure 4-109. Make sure that the **Tangent** and **Point On Curve** constraints are applied between the lines and

the circles at all the points where the lines intersect the circles. The **Tangent** constraint is represented by a small line and the **Point On Curve** constraint is represented by a small circle, refer to Figure 4-109. Note that the dimensions are hidden for a clear view.

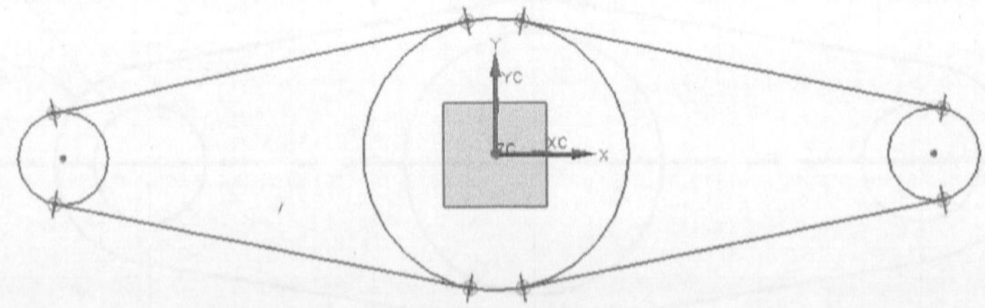

***Figure 4-109** Initial sketch for the base feature*

Next, you need to trim the unwanted portion of the circles to retain the outer profile of the model. The sketch is trimmed using the **Quick Trim** tool.

4. Choose the **Quick Trim** tool from the **Direct Sketch** group; the **Quick Trim** dialog box is displayed. Also, you are prompted to select the curve to be trimmed. 

5. Press and hold the left mouse button inside the right circle and drag it horizontally toward the left, close to the center of the left circle.

6. Release the left mouse button to trim the unwanted portions of the circles, refer to Figure 4-110. Next, choose the **Close** button from the **Quick Trim** dialog box.

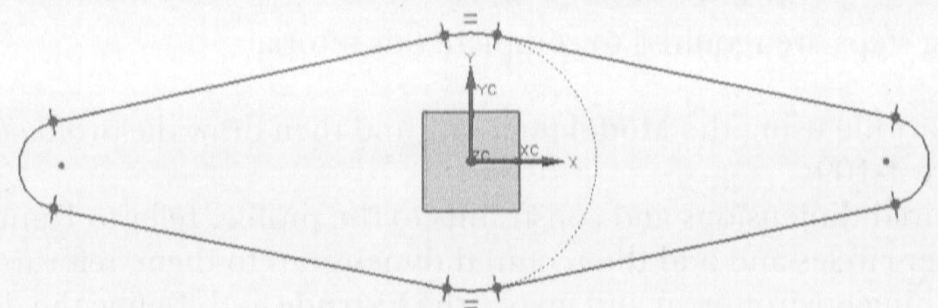

***Figure 4-110** Sketch after trimming the unwanted portion of circles*

Note

*If the **Point On Curve** and **Tangent** constraints are not applied automatically while drawing the sketch, then you need to manually add these constraints to the circles and the lines of the sketch.*

Next, you need to add constraints to the sketch.

7. Choose the **Geometric Constraints** tool from the **Direct Sketch** group of the **Home** tab and make the radius of the left arc equal to that of the right arc. Similarly, make all the lines equal using the Equal Length constraint. Note that you also need to add the Point On Curve constraint between the center of the left arc and the XC axis. Similarly, you need to apply the Point On Curve constraint between the right arc and the XC axis.

Next, you need to add dimensions to the sketch.

8. Add dimensions to the sketch using the **Rapid Dimensions** tool, refer to Figure 4-111.

> **Note**
>
> *In this tutorial, the dimension style of the dimensions has been changed for clarity. To change the dimension style, you need to invoke sketching environment by choosing the* ***Open in Sketch Task Environment*** *from the* ***Sketch Feature*** *gallery in the* ***More*** *gallery of the* ***Direct Sketch*** *group. Next, choose* ***Menu > Task > Sketch Settings*** *from the* ***Top Border Bar****. On doing so, the* ***Sketch Settings*** *dialog box is displayed. Select the* ***Value*** *option from the* ***Dimension Label*** *drop-down list. Next, choose the* ***OK*** *button to close the dialog box.*

Next, you need to draw the inner circles. You can use the center points of the arcs to draw them.

9. Next, draw three circles using the center points of the arcs, refer to Figure 4-112.

10. Add the Equal Radius constraint to the left and right circles. Now, add the required dimensions to the circles to complete the sketch. The final sketch of the model is shown in Figure 4-112.

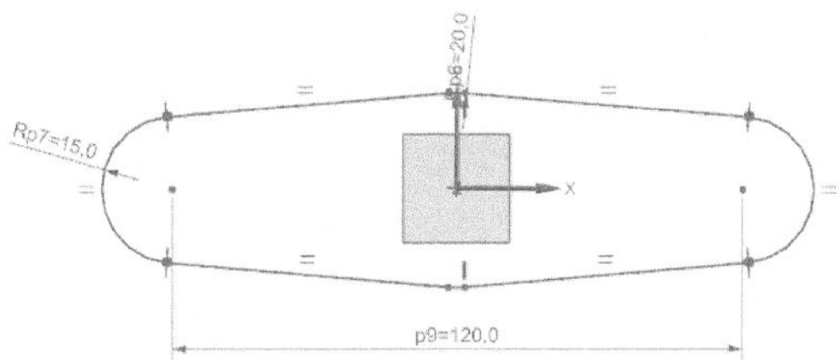

Figure 4-111 *Sketch after adding relationships and dimensions*

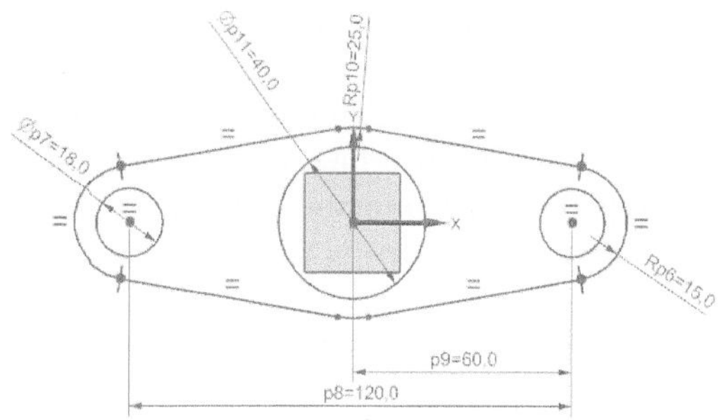

Figure 4-112 *Final sketch for Tutorial 2*

Converting the Sketch into the Base Feature

Next, you need to convert the sketch into the base feature by using the **Extrude** tool.

1. Choose the **Finish Sketch** tool from the **Direct Sketch** group to exit the sketching environment.

2. Invoke the **Extrude** tool from the **Feature** group; the **Extrude** dialog box is displayed and you are prompted to select the planar face to sketch or select the section geometry to extrude.

3. Select the sketch from the drawing window; the preview of the extruded feature is displayed. Also, the **End** dynamic input box is displayed.

4. Enter **20** in the **End** dynamic input box and press the ENTER key; the preview is modified accordingly.

5. Choose the **OK** button in the **Extrude** dialog box; the extruded feature is created. Next, select the **Trimetric** option from the **Orient View Drop-down** of the **Top Border Bar**; the extruded feature is displayed in the drawing window, as shown in Figure 4-113.

   Notice that the datum plane, sketch, and datum axes are still displayed in the sketch. For a better visualization of the model, you can turn off the display of these entities.

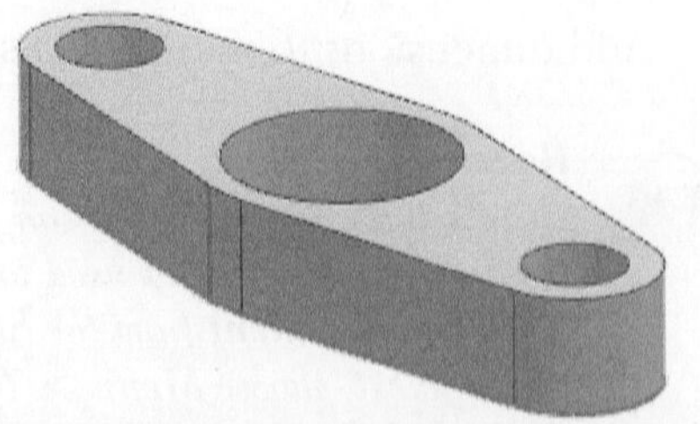

Figure 4-113 Model after extruding the sketch

6. Press the CTRL+B keys; the **Class Selection** dialog box is displayed. Select all the unwanted entities and then choose the **OK** button.

Rotating the View of the Model

Next, you need to rotate the model to view it from different directions.

1. Choose the **Rotate** tool from the **Operation** group of the **View** tab in the **Ribbon**; the cursor changes into a rotate view cursor.

2. Press and hold the left mouse button and drag the cursor in the drawing window. Figure 4-114 shows a model being rotated using the **Rotate** tool. Next, exit the **Rotate** tool by pressing the ESC key.

   Next, you need to restore the Isometric view of the model which has been changed by using the **Rotate** tool.

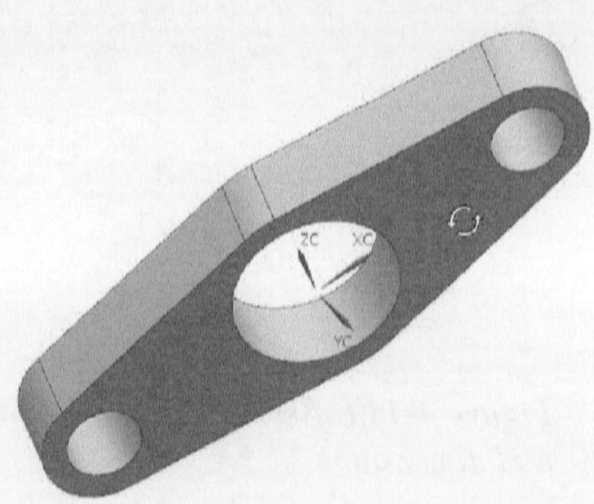

Figure 4-114 Rotating the model in 3D space

3. Choose the **Trimetric** button from the **Orient View Drop-down** in the **View** group of the **Top Border Bar** to restore the Isometric view.

4. Now, right-click in the drawing window and choose the **Fit** option from the shortcut menu; the model fits in the drawing window.

Saving and Closing the File

1. Choose **Menu > File > Close > Save and Close** from the **Top Border Bar** to save and close the file.

Tutorial 3

In this tutorial, you will create the model of a revolved body shown in Figure 4-115. You can create this model using the sketch shown in Figure 4-116. **(Expected time: 30 min)**

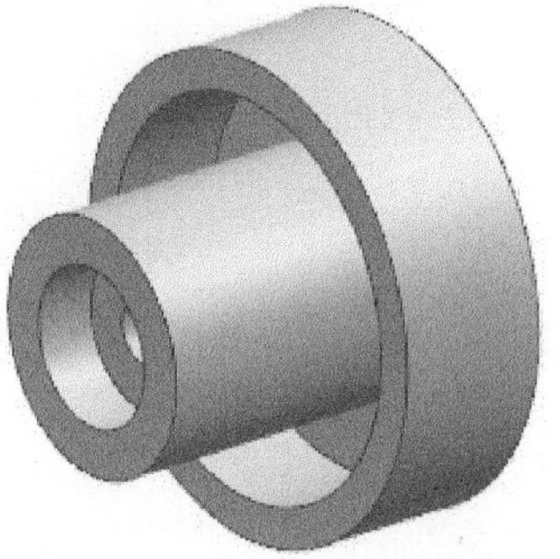

Figure 4-115 Model for Tutorial 3

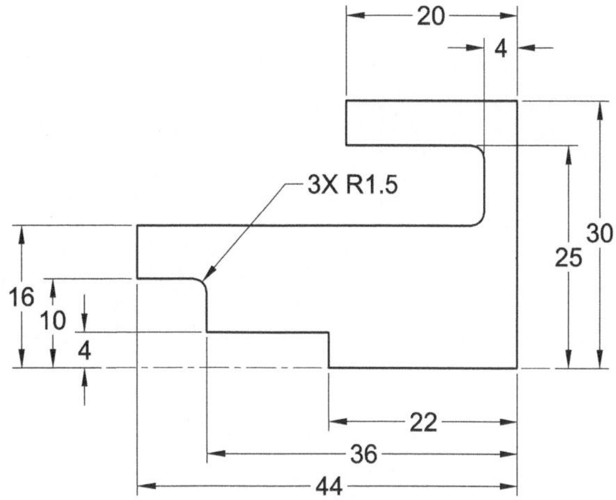

Figure 4-116 Dimensions of the model

The following steps are required to complete this tutorial:

a. Start a new part file using the **Model** template and draw the sketch of the revolved model. Next, add the required geometric and dimensional constraints.
b. Exit the sketching environment and invoke the **Revolve** tool. Select the sketch to be revolved and then the direction of the axis of revolution.
c. Define the other revolution parameters to create the final model.
d. Rotate the view in 3D space.
e. Save and close the file.

Drawing the Sketch of the Model

The sketch of the revolved model will be created on the YC-ZC plane.

1. Start a new file with the name *c04tut3.prt* using the **Model** template and specify its location as *C:\NX\c04*.

2. Invoke the sketching environment by using the YC-ZC plane as the sketching plane.

3. Draw the sketch of the revolved feature and add the required geometric and dimensional constraints to it, as shown in Figure 4-117.

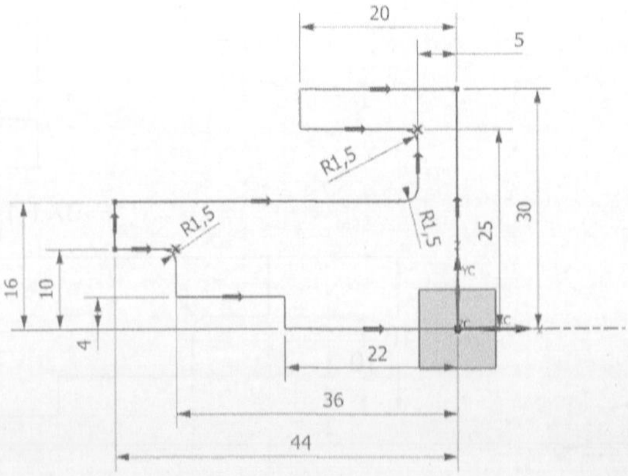

Figure 4-117 Dimensioned sketch of the revolved feature

Converting the Sketch into the Revolved Feature

Next, you need to convert the sketch into a revolved feature by using the **Revolve** tool.

1. Choose the **Finish Sketch** tool from the **Direct Sketch** group to exit the sketching environment.

2. Right-click in the drawing window; a shortcut menu is displayed. Choose the **Fit** option from the shortcut menu to fit the sketch in the screen.

3. Invoke the **Revolve** tool from the **Feature** group; the **Revolve** dialog box is displayed and you are prompted to select the planar face to sketch or select the section geometry.

4. Select the sketch drawn and choose the **Inferred Vector** button from the **Axis** rollout of the dialog box; you are prompted to select the objects to infer the vector.

5. Select the bottom horizontal line as the axis of revolution; the preview of the revolved body is displayed.

6. Accept the default options in the **Revolve** dialog box and choose the **OK** button; the revolved feature is created. Make sure that the angle of revolution of the model is 360 degrees.

7. Choose the **Show and Hide** tool from the **Visibility** group of the **View** tab; the **Show and Hide** dialog box is displayed. Click on the minus sign (-) in the **Datums** and **Sketches** rows to hide the sketch, axes, and sketching plane, and then close the dialog box. Next, fit the model to the screen. The revolved model after hiding the sketch, the axes, and the sketching plane is shown in Figure 4-118.

***Figure 4-118** Revolved model of Tutorial 3*

Rotating the View of the Model

Next, you need to rotate the model to maneuver and view it from different directions.

1. Choose the **Rotate** tool from the **Orientation** group of the **View** tab of the **Ribbon**; the cursor changes into a rotate view cursor.

2. Press and hold the left mouse button and drag the cursor in the drawing window to rotate the view of the model. Next, exit from the **Rotate** tool by pressing the ESC key.

3. Choose the **Trimetric** button from the **Orient View Drop-down** of the **View** group in the **Top Border Bar** to restore the Isometric view.

Saving and Closing the File

1. Choose **Menu > File > Close > Save and Close** from the **Top Border Bar** to save and close the file.

Self-Evaluation Test

Answer the following questions and then compare them to those given at the end of this chapter:

1. After invoking the **Quick Trim** tool, you can drag the cursor to trim _________ entities.

2. The _________ option is used to extrude the sketch symmetrically on both sides of the plane on which the sketch is created.

3. The _________ option is used to add the draft that is aligned with the profile.

4. NX uses the _________ rule to determine the direction of revolution.

5. You can create thin features using the _________ or _________ sketches.

6. You can restore standard views by using buttons from the _________ group in the **Top Border Bar**.

7. The **Quick Trim** tool is used to remove a portion of the sketch by chopping it off. (T/F)

8. In NX, while extruding a sketch, you can add a draft to it. (T/F)

9. The **Quick Extend** tool is used to extend or lengthen an open sketched entity up to infinity. (T/F)

10. You can set the display modes for solid models using the buttons in the **View** group in the **Top Border Bar**. (T/F)

Review Questions

Answer the following questions:

1. Which of the following tools in NX allows you to dynamically move, rotate, or copy the solid objects and the sketched entities?

   (a) **Transform** (b) **Modify**
   (c) **Move Object** (d) None of these

2. Which one of the following views is the default view in NX?

   (a) Trimetric (b) Isometric
   (c) Top (d) None of these

3. Which of the following rollouts is used to create a thin extruded feature by offsetting the sketch in two directions?

   (a) **Offset** (b) **Symmetric**
   (c) **Two Sided** (d) None of these

4. Which one of the following paths is used to invoke the **Move Object** tool?

   (a) **Menu > Edit** (b) **Menu > Insert**
   (c) **Menu > Preference** (d) **Menu > Tool**

5. Which one of the following rules is used to determine the direction of revolution?

   (a) Right-hand rule (b) Right-hand thumb rule
   (c) Left-hand rule (d) Left-hand thumb rule

6. In which of the following groups, you can set the display modes for solid models?
   (a) **Standard** (b) **Sketch**
   (c) **Visible** (d) **View**

7. If you choose the **Finish Sketch** tool from the **Direct Sketch** group to exit the sketching environment, the Modeling environment will be invoked. (T/F)

8. When you mirror various entities using the **Mirror Curve** tool, by default a mirrored copy of the selected entities is created and the original entities are deleted. (T/F)

9. In the **Results** rollout of the **Move Object** dialog box, you can specify whether you want to move the original entity or its copy by using the **Move Original** or **Copy Original** radio button. (T/F)

10. You can rotate a model in 3D space using the **Rotate** tool. (T/F)

EXERCISES

Exercise 1

Open the sketch drawn in Tutorial 3 of Chapter 3 and convert it into a fully revolved body. After creating the model, use the **Rotate** tool to rotate its view. Save the file with a different name in the folder of this chapter. **(Expected time: 15 min)**

Exercise 2

Create the model shown in Figure 4-119. The dimensions of the model are shown in Figure 4-120. The depth of extrusion is 30. After creating the model, use the **Rotate** tool to rotate its view. Before closing the file, restore the Isometric view of the model.

(Expected time: 30 min)

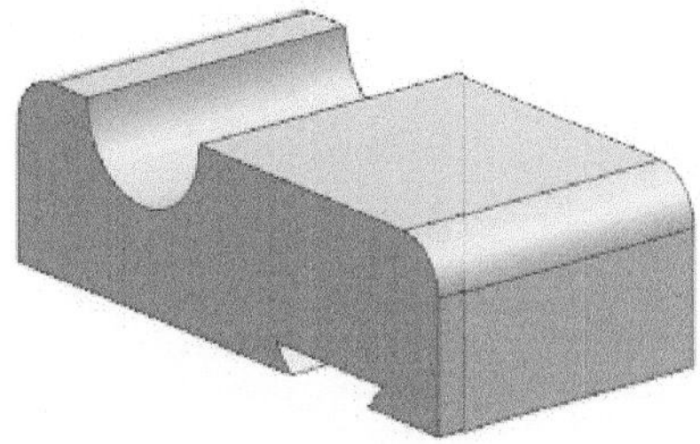

Figure 4-119 *Model for Exercise 2*

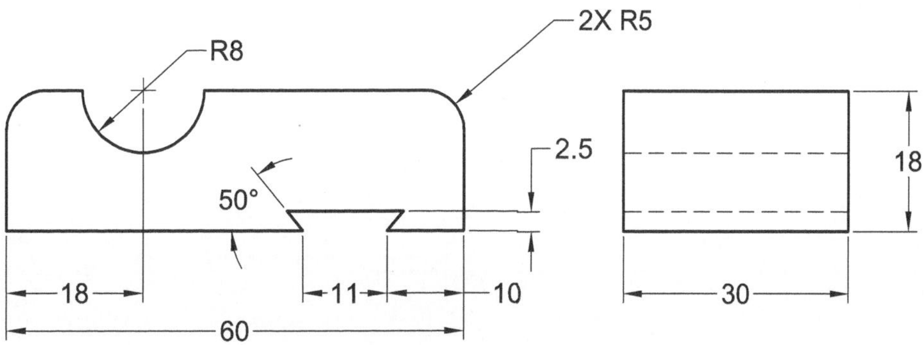

Figure 4-120 *Dimensions of the model*

Answers to Self-Evaluation Test

1. multiple, **2. Symmetric Value**, **3. From Section**, **4.** Right-hand thumb, **5.** open, close, **6. View**, **7.** T, **8.** T, **9.** F, **10.** T

Chapter 5

Working with Datum Planes, Coordinate Systems, and Datum Axes

Learning Objectives

After completing this chapter, you will be able to:

- *Understand the usage of reference geometries in NX*
- *Understand different types of datum planes in NX*
- *Create fixed and relative datum planes*
- *Understand the usage of CSYS (coordinate system)*
- *Create coordinate systems using different methods*
- *Understand the usage of datum axis*
- *Create datum axis using different methods*
- *Use additional extrude and revolve options*
- *Project existing elements on the current sketching plane*

ADDITIONAL SKETCHING AND REFERENCE PLANES

In the previous chapters, you learned to create basic models which had features placed on one of the three datum planes of the Datum Coordinate System (YC-ZC, XC-ZC, or XC-YC). All the models were created by selecting one of the three datum planes of the Datum Coordinate System. Most real world models consist of multiple sketched features, reference geometries, and placed features. In NX, features can be added to base features by using the boolean operations such as subtract, unite, and intersect. These boolean operations are available in all tools. When you invoke the sketching environment by choosing the **Sketch** tool from the **Direct Sketch** group of the **Home** tab, the **Create Sketch** dialog box is displayed and you are prompted to select a sketching plane. You can select any one of the three datum planes of the Datum Coordinate System as the sketching plane. You can also create a new datum plane by using the **Datum Plane** dialog box. On the basis of design requirement, you can select any plane as the sketching plane for the base feature. Also, you can create additional planes by taking reference of existing planes, faces, surfaces, sketches, or a combination of these objects. Figure 5-1 shows a model with multiple features.

The base feature for this model is shown in Figure 5-2. The sketch for the base feature is drawn on the XC-YC datum plane of the Datum Coordinate System. As mentioned earlier, after creating the base feature, you need to create the other sketched features, placed features, and reference features, refer to Figure 5-3. The extrude features shown in Figure 5-3 require additional sketching planes on which the sketch for the other features will be created.

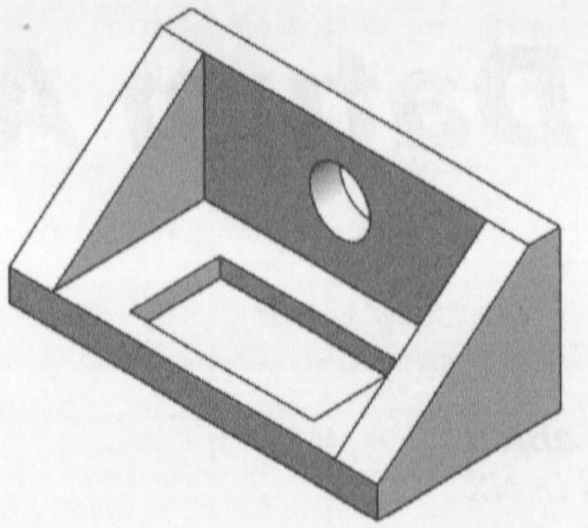

Figure 5-1 *Model with multiple features*

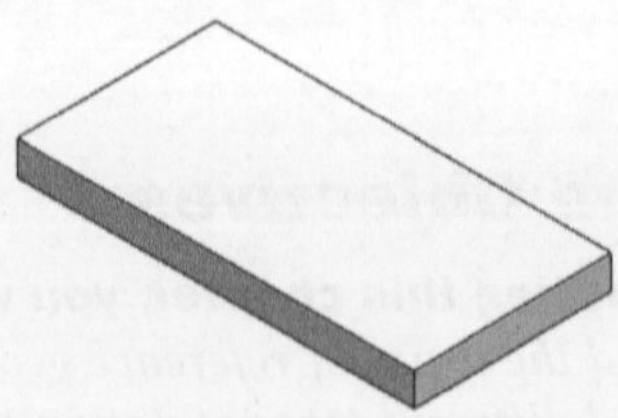

Figure 5-2 *The base feature for the model*

It is evident from Figure 5-3 that the additional features created on the base feature do not lie on the same sketching plane. They are created by defining additional sketching planes. Also, appropriate boolean operations are selected at the time of creating these features.

As mentioned earlier, if you invoke a new part file by using the **Model** template, the Datum Coordinate System containing three datum planes, three datum axes, and a point will be displayed in the drawing window. You can select any of these datum planes as the sketching plane or you can create new datum planes by using the **Datum Plane** dialog box.

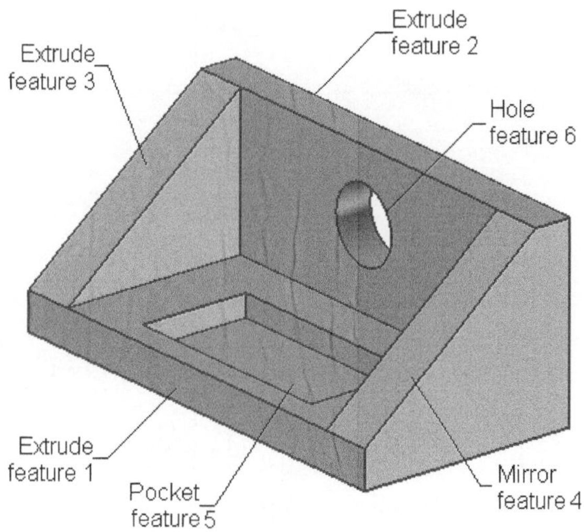

Figure 5-3 Various features in the model

TYPES OF DATUM PLANES

There are three types of datum planes in NX: datum planes of the Datum Coordinate System, fixed datum planes, and relative datum planes. Fixed datum planes are the ones that pass through the origin. Relative datum planes are created in addition to fixed datum planes by taking the reference of objects such as curves, sketches, edges, faces, surfaces, and points. The methods for creating these datum planes are discussed next.

Creating Three Fixed (Principle) Datum Planes

In NX, the principle datum planes are called fixed datum planes. The detailed procedure for creating the fixed datum planes is discussed in Chapter 2.

Creating Relative Datum Planes

Ribbon:	Home > Feature > Datum/Point Drop-down > Datum Plane
Menu:	Insert > Datum/Point > Datum Plane

As mentioned earlier, relative datum planes are the additional planes used for assisting you in completing a design. You can select objects such as curves, sketches, edges, faces, surfaces, datum planes of the Datum Coordinate System, and points as reference to create relative datum planes. To create relative datum planes, choose the **Datum Plane** tool from the **Datum/Point Drop-down** of the **Feature** group in the **Home** tab; the **Datum Plane** dialog box will be displayed, as shown in Figure 5-4. In NX, you can create relative datum planes using different options. You can access these options from the Type drop-down list available in the dialog box, as shown in Figure 5-5. Some of these options are discussed next.

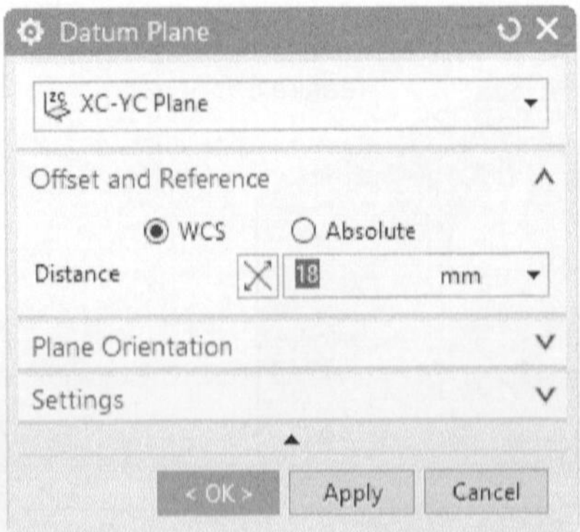

Figure 5-4 The ***Datum Plane*** *dialog box*

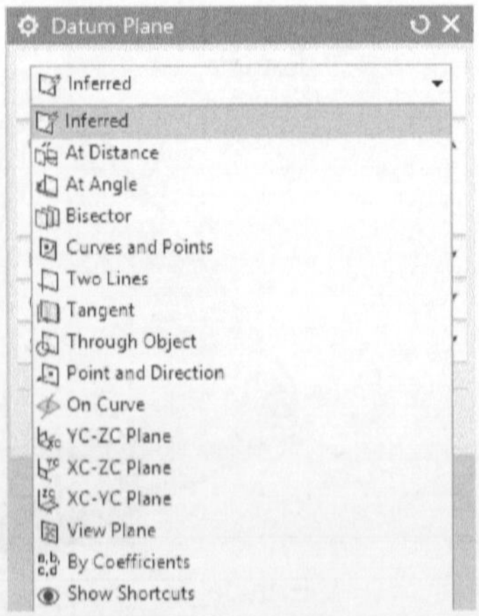

Figure 5-5 The Type drop-down list of the ***Datum Plane*** *dialog box*

Inferred

The **Inferred** option is used to create various types of planes, depending on the reference objects selected and the sequence in which they are selected. To create planes using this tool, select the **Inferred** option from the Type drop-down list if it is not selected by default. Depending on the reference objects selected and the sequence in which you select them, appropriate planes will be created. For example, if you select two parallel planes, then the plane will be created at the center of two selected planes. However, if you select a cylindrical surface and an edge, then the plane created will be tangent to the cylinder and it will pass through the selected edge.

At Distance

The **At Distance** option is used to create a plane offset to an existing planar face, a surface, or an existing datum plane.

To create an offset plane, you need to follow two steps. First, select the **At Distance** option from the Type drop-down list. Next, select a planar face, a surface, or a datum plane to which the new plane will be parallel. After selecting the reference object, the preview of the plane will be displayed, as shown in Figure 5-6. Also, an arrow will be displayed on the newly created plane, along with the **Distance** edit box.

The second step is to specify the offset distance. To do so, enter the offset distance in the **Distance** edit box and press ENTER; the preview of the plane will be modified accordingly. The arrow displayed on the plane indicates the positive direction of the offset. If you need to offset the plane in the opposite direction, enter a negative distance value. Also, you can double-click on this arrow or choose the **Reverse Direction** button from the **Offset** rollout of the **Datum Plane** dialog box to change the offset direction. To create multiple offset planes at specified distance, enter the number of planes in the **Number of Planes** edit box of the **Offset** rollout. After entering the appropriate offset distance, choose the **OK** button from the **Datum Plane** dialog box to create a plane, as shown in Figure 5-7.

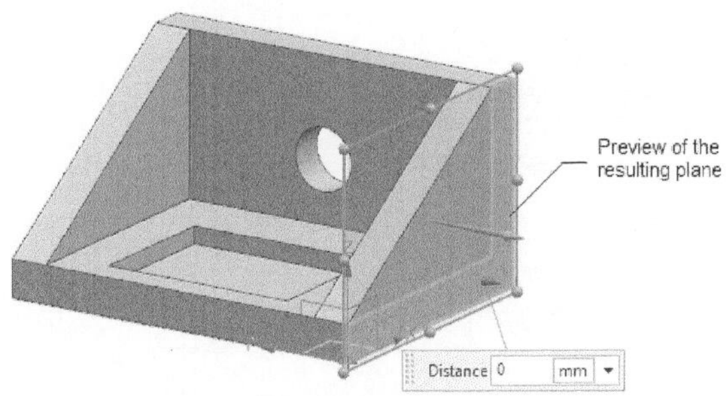

Figure 5-6 The preview of the plane

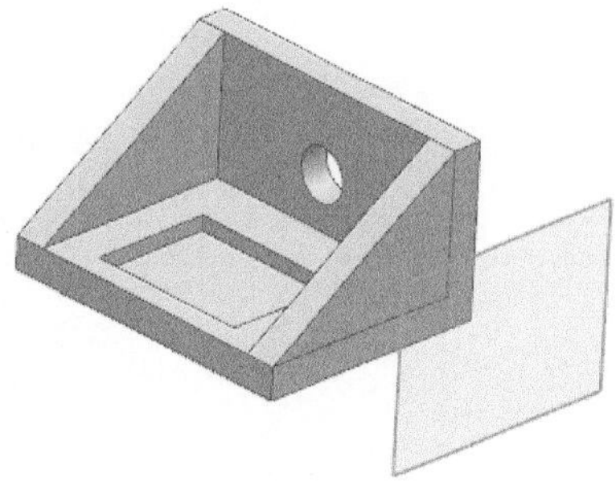

Figure 5-7 The resulting parallel plane

Note
While creating parallel planes, you can select only a planar face or surface as the reference object, not a non-planar face or surface.

At Angle

The **At Angle** option is used to create a plane at an angle to another plane passing through an edge, a linear sketched segment, or an axis. To create an angular plane, select the **At Angle** option from the Type drop-down list. Next, select a planar face or a datum plane to which the resulting plane will be at angle. Next, you need to select an edge or a linear sketch through which the resulting plane will pass. On selecting both the references, the preview of the plane will be displayed in the graphic window. Also, the **Angle** edit box will be displayed along with an angular handle, as shown in Figure 5-8. You need to enter the required value in the **Angle** edit box. Figure 5-9 shows the datum plane created at an angle of 65 degrees.

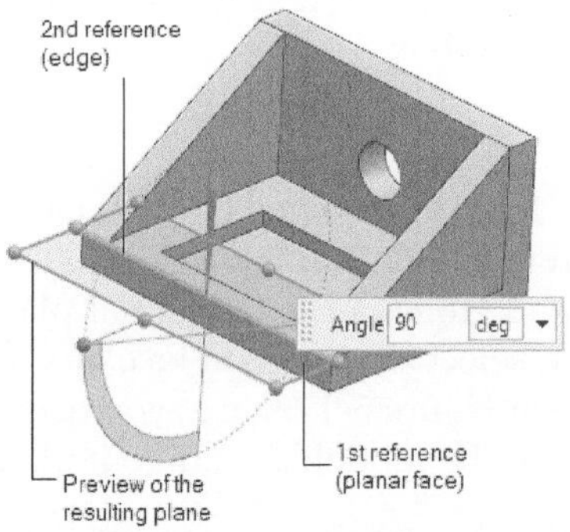

*Figure 5-8 The preview of the angular plane displayed along with the **Angle** edit box*

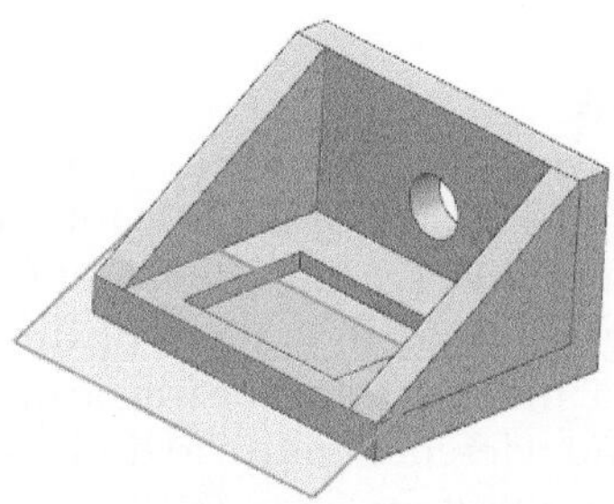

Figure 5-9 The plane created at an angle of 65 degrees

Bisector

The **Bisector** option is used to create a relative plane at the center of two specified planes or planar faces. To create a bisector plane, select the **Bisector** option from the Type drop-down list. Then, one by one, select two planes or planar faces; the preview of the resulting plane placed at the center of the two selected planes or planar faces will be displayed, refer to Figure 5-10. Next, choose the **OK** button from the **Datum Plane** dialog box to create this plane.

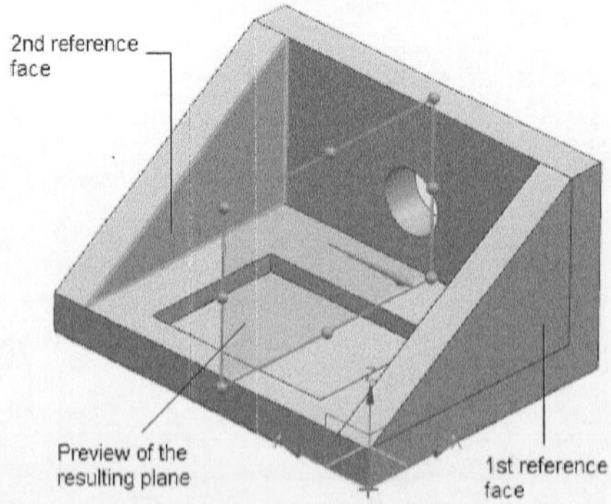

Figure 5-10 References selected to create the center plane and the resulting plane

Curves and Points

The **Curves and Points** option is used to create a plane using a line, a planar edge, a datum axis, a planar face, or various combinations of points, for example, two points, three points, a point and a curve, a point, and a face etc. You can use the options available in the **Subtype** drop-down list of the **Curves and Points Subtype** rollout to specify the type of combination you want to use for creating a plane.

Two Lines

The **Two Lines** option is used to create a plane using a combination of any two linear curves, linear edges, or datum axes. To create a plane using this option, select the **Two Lines** option in the Type drop-down list of the **Datum Plane** dialog box; the **First Line** and **Second Line** rollouts will be displayed in the dialog box. Also, you will be prompted to select a linear object. Select a linear curve, linear edge, or a datum axis to specify the first line. Similarly, specify the second line by selecting a linear curve, linear edge, or a datum axis; a preview of the plane will be displayed. Next, choose the **OK** button to exit the dialog box.

Tangent

The **Tangent** option is used to create a tangential plane. To do so, you need to select a cylindrical face and the second reference entity. The second reference entity can be a point, linear edge, line, datum axis, second cylindrical face, or datum plane. To create a tangential plane, select the **Tangent** option from the Type drop-down list. Next, select a cylindrical face or surface; the preview of the tangent plane will be displayed, as shown in Figure 5-11. Next, you need to select the second reference entity. To do so, select the edge from the model; the tangent plane will be created, as shown in Figure 5-12.

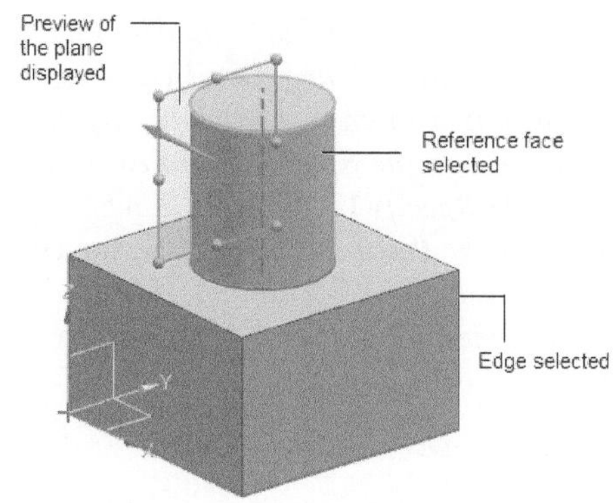

Figure 5-11 The preview of the tangent plane

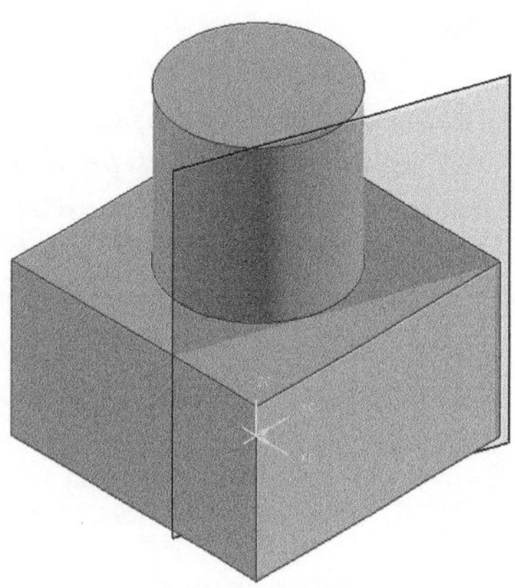

Figure 5-12 The tangent plane created after specifying the edge

Point and Direction

The **Point and Direction** option is used to create a plane at a specified point and is oriented normal to the selected direction. You need to specify a fix point and define the normal direction to create the plane. The direction can be defined using an edge or linear sketch. If you select an edge or a linear sketch to define the direction, the plane will be created normal to it and it will pass through the specified point.

To create this type of plane, select the **Point and Direction** option from the Type drop-down list; you will be prompted to select the object to infer point. Specify the point at which the plane is to be created. Use the **Selection Group** for an easy selection of the point. After specifying the point, the preview of the plane will be displayed.

Next, you need to define the direction of the plane by selecting a linear edge, sketch, planar face, or surface. You can also select a cylindrical face to define the direction. If you select a cylindrical face as the reference for defining the direction, the plane will be placed perpendicular to the axis of the cylindrical face selected. Figure 5-13 shows the reference selected to create this type of plane and Figure 5-14 shows the resulting plane.

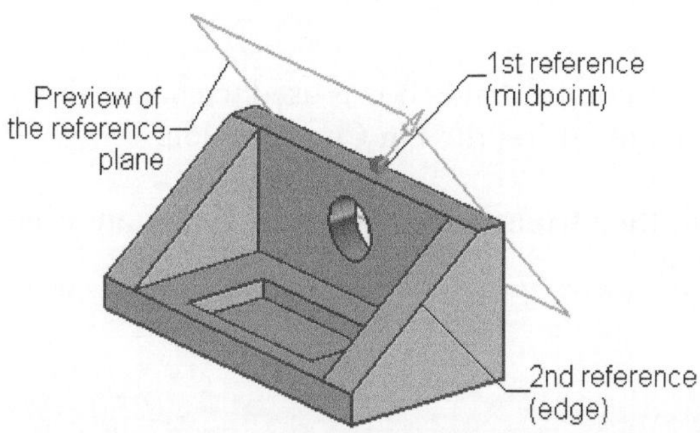

***Figure 5-13** The preview of the plane created using the **Point and Direction** option*

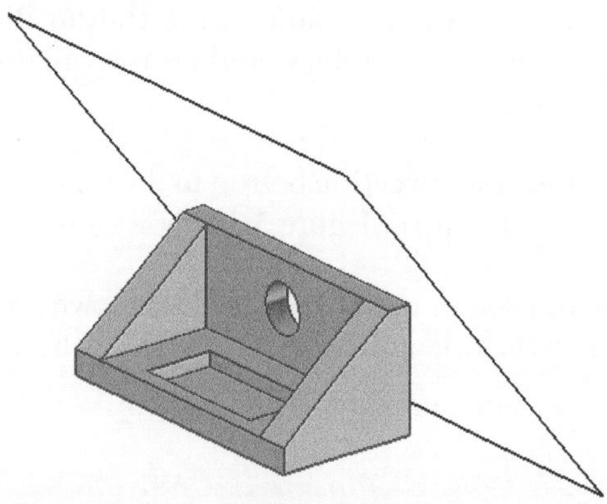

***Figure 5-14** The plane created using the **Point and Direction** option*

Note

*After selecting the **Point and Direction** option, two drop-down lists will be available at the right of **Specify Point** and **Specify Vector** areas in the **Datum Plane** dialog box. These drop-down lists contain the options for defining the point and direction to create the plane. By default, the **Inferred Point** option is selected in the drop-down list in the **Specify Point** area and the **Inferred Vector** option is selected in the drop-down list in the **Specify Vector** area. To define a point or direction by constructing a new point and vector, choose the **Point Dialog** and **Vector Dialog** buttons, respectively. Note that the plane creation shown in Figures 5-13 and 5-14 is created by selecting **Inferred Point** and **Inferred Vector** options from the drop-down lists in the **Specify Point** and **Specify Vector** areas, respectively.*

On Curve

The **On Curve** option is used to create a plane passing through a selected curve and located at a specified distance. To create a plane using this option, select the **On Curve** option from the Type drop-down list. Next, select a curve or an edge to create the plane; the preview of the plane along with the **Arc Length** or **% Arc Length** edit box will be displayed, refer to Figure 5-15. The current positional value of the plane will be displayed in the **Arc Length** or **% Arc Length** edit box. The **Arc Length** or **% Arc Length** edit box will be displayed depending upon the option selected from the **Location** drop-down list.

Next, you need to specify the location of the resulting plane on the selected curve. Select the **Arc Length** option from the **Location** drop-down list in the **Location on Curve** rollout; the **Arc Length** edit box will be displayed. Now, you can locate the plane on the curve by entering the arc length value in the **Arc Length** edit box. This value will be taken from the start point of the curve. By default, the nearest point where you select the curve will be defined as the start point. You can also locate the plane by percentage of arc length. To do so, select the **% Arc Length** option from the **Location** drop-down list in the **Location on Curve** rollout; the **Arc Length** edit box will change to the **% Arc length** edit box. Enter the percent of arc length between 0 and 100 in the **% Arc Length** edit box and press the ENTER key; the plane will move to a new location. Note that you can also drag the preview plane to modify its location on the curve.

You can also specify the location of the plane on the curve by specifying the coordinates of the plane. To do so, select the **Through Point** option from the **Location** drop-down list in the **Location on Curve** rollout of the **Datum Plane** dialog box; the coordinate edit boxes will be displayed in the graphics window. You can use these edit boxes to specify the coordinates of the required plane.

The **Reverse Direction** button in the **Curve** rollout of the dialog box is used to change the start point of the curve. Figure 5-16 shows a plane created using the **On Curve** option.

The options in the **Direction** drop-down list in the **Orientation on Curve** rollout are used to specify the orientation of the plane on the curve.

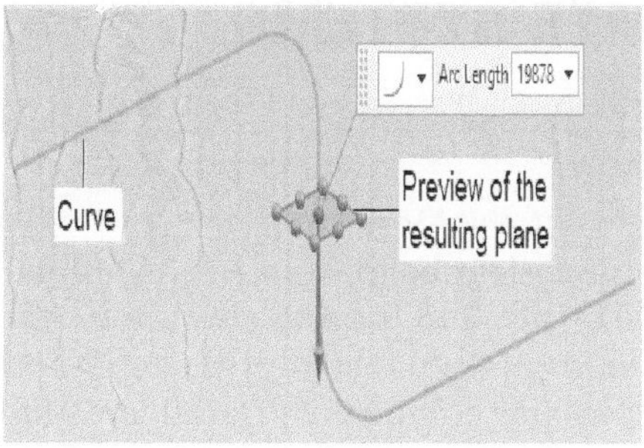

*Figure 5-15 The preview of the plane displayed while using the **On Curve** option*

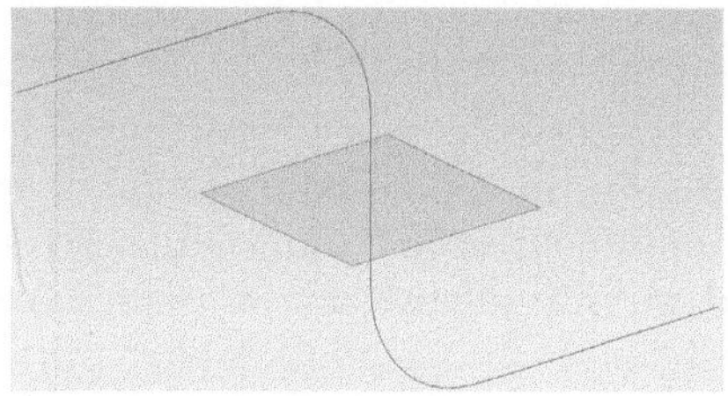

*Figure 5-16 The plane created using the **On Curve** option*

Other Options in the Datum Plane Dialog Box

The other rollouts in this dialog box are discussed next.

Plane Orientation Rollout

This rollout is used to define the orientation of the plane. The options in this rollout are discussed next.

Alternate Solution

This button allows you to preview all possible orientations of a plane based on its selected entities. Alternatively, you can use the Page Down and Page Up keys to preview all possible orientations of the plane. Note that this option will be available only when you select the **At Angle**, **Two Lines, or Tangent** option from the Type drop-down list.

Reverse Direction

This button is used to change the direction of the plane normal by 180 degrees.

Offset Rollout

If you select the **Offset** check box in this rollout, the **Distance** edit box will be displayed and the datum plane will be created at the default offset distance specified in this edit box. Specify the offset distance in **Distance** edit box to create the datum plane. You can reverse the offset direction by choosing the **Reverse Direction** button. This rollout will not be available when the **By Coefficients**, **YC-ZC Plane**, **XC-ZC Plane**, **XC-YC Plane**, or **View Plane** options are selected from the Type drop-down list.

Settings Rollout

If you select the **Associative** check box in this rollout, the datum plane created will be associative with its parent features.

Note

*For an associative datum plane, the name will be displayed as **Datum Plane** in the **Part Navigator**. For a non-associative datum plane, the name will be displayed as **Fixed Datum Plane** in the **Part Navigator**.*

CREATING DATUM COORDINATE SYSTEMS

Ribbon: Home > Feature > Datum/Point Drop-down > Datum CSYS
Menu: Insert > Datum/Point > Datum CSYS

As discussed earlier, on starting a new file using the **Model** template, you will only have the Datum Coordinate System at the origin. The handles of this coordinate system represent the X, Y, and Z directions in 3D space and form the basis for creating both the fixed and the relative datum planes. You can also create new coordinate systems for the separate features in a model. A part may contain any number of coordinate systems. The coordinate system can be used as a reference for creating features, sketches, and curves. Also, it can be used for assembling the parts in the assembly. The coordinate system is also treated as a feature and is displayed in the **Model History** section of the **Part Navigator**. The coordinate system is always associative with the object members or feature operation to which it is related.

To create the Datum Coordinate System, choose the **Datum CSYS** tool from the **Datum/Point Drop-down** of the **Feature** group in the **Home** tab; the **Datum CSYS** dialog box will be displayed, as shown in Figure 5-17. By default, the **Dynamic** option is selected in the Type drop-down list. As a result, you will be prompted to drag or select a handle for direct entry. There are different methods by which you can create a Datum Coordinate System. The options to use these methods are discussed next.

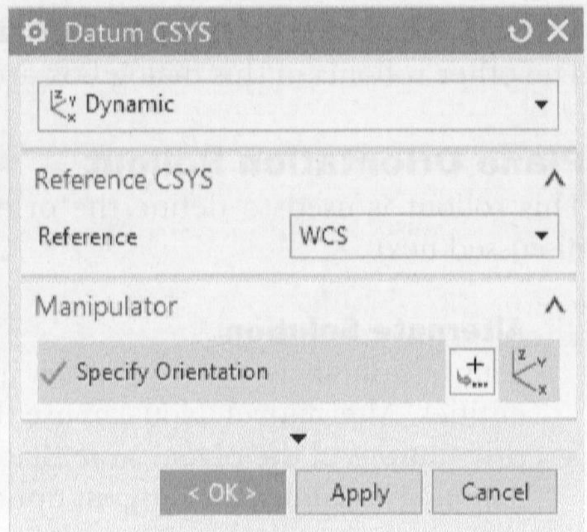

*Figure 5-17 The **Datum CSYS** dialog box*

Dynamic

This option is used to create the Datum Coordinate System by dragging it or entering the X, Y, and Z coordinates values. When you invoke the **Datum CSYS** tool, this option will be selected by default and you will be prompted to drag or select a handle for direct entry. Also, the preview of the Datum Coordinate System will be displayed at the origin in the drawing window, refer to Figure 5-18.

Select the sphere displayed at the center of new Datum Coordinate System, and then press and hold the left mouse button. Next, drag the mouse to position the new Datum Coordinate System. Alternatively, enter the X, Y, and Z coordinates values in the respective edit boxes to position the Datum Coordinate System.

Also, you can move the new Datum Coordinate System in a particular direction (X, Y, or Z). To do so, click on the respective arrow handle; the **Distance** and **Snap** edit boxes will be displayed, as shown in Figure 5-19. Enter the required distance value in the **Distance** edit box and press ENTER; the Datum Coordinate System will move in the specified direction to the specified distance.

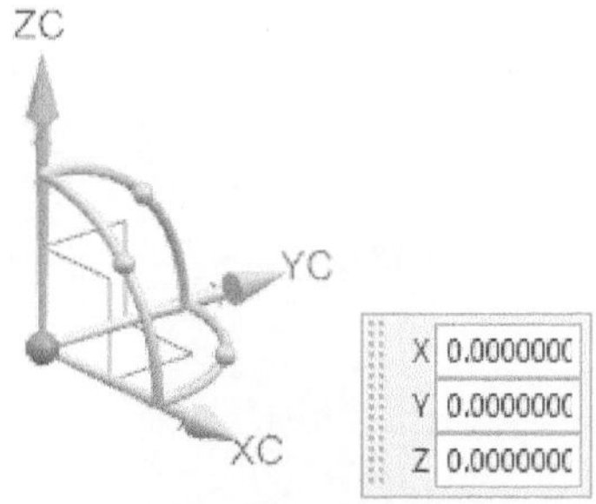

Figure 5-18 *Preview of the datum coordinate system*

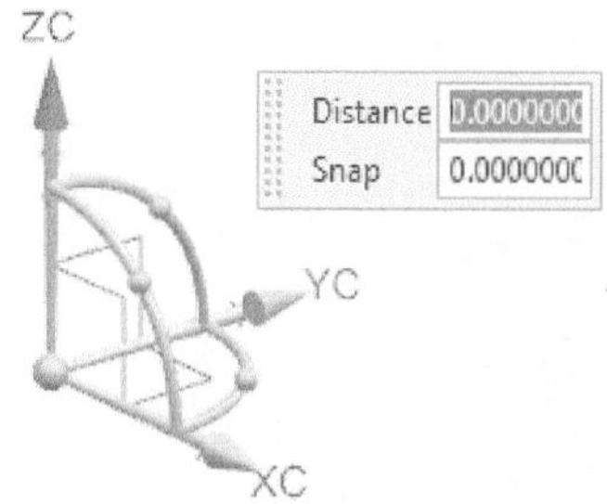

Figure 5-19 *The **Distance** and **Snap** edit boxes*

Similarly, you can rotate the new Datum Coordinate System along a particular axis (X, Y, or Z). To do so, click on the respective angular handle; the **Angle** and **Snap** edit boxes will be displayed. Enter the required angle value in the **Angle** edit box and press ENTER; the Datum Coordinate System will rotate along the specified axis as per the specified angle value.

Note

You can also move and rotate the new Datum Coordinate System dynamically. To do so, press and hold the left mouse button on the respective handle of the new Datum Coordinate System and then drag it.

Inferred

You can use the **Inferred** option to create different types of datum coordinate systems. The resulting datum coordinate system will depend on the reference objects selected and the sequence of their selection.

Origin, X-point, Y-point

To create a Datum Coordinate System by using this option, select the **Origin, X-point, Y-point** option from the Type drop-down list; you will be prompted to select the object to infer point. Next, you need to specify the origin point. Select the point on which you need to fix the origin of the Datum Coordinate System. While specifying the origin point, turn on the required snap button in the **Selection Group** to select points easily. Next, you need to specify the points along the X and Y directions. Specify the X and Y points. Note that the X point is used to specify the X-axis direction of the Datum Coordinate System and the Y point is used to define the orientation of the XY plane.

After specifying the origin, X point and Y point, preview of the Datum Coordinate System will be displayed, as shown in Figure 5-20. Choose the **OK** button from the **Datum CSYS** dialog box to accept the Datum Coordinate System. Figure 5-21 shows the resulting Datum Coordinate System.

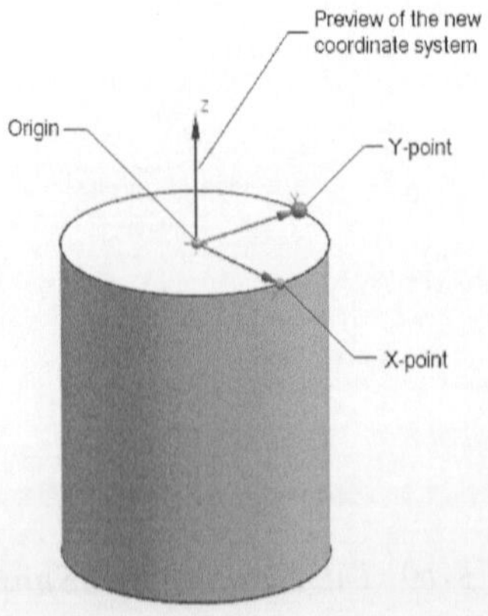

*Figure 5-20 Preview of the CSYS created by using the **Origin, X-point, Y-point** option*

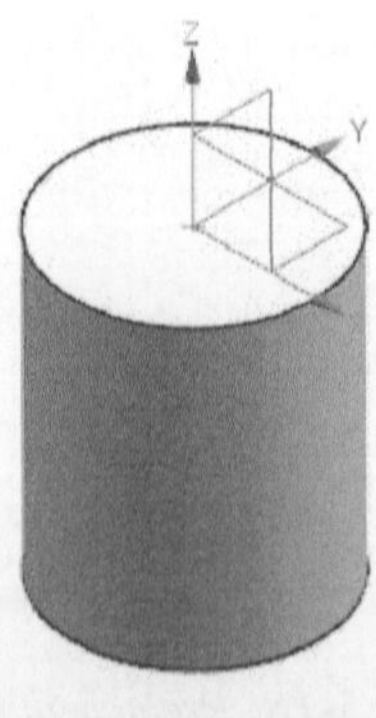

*Figure 5-21 The CSYS created by using the **Origin, X-point, Y-point** option*

Three Planes

To create a coordinate system by using this option, you need to select three reference objects that are mutually perpendicular to each other. You can only select faces or planes as reference objects.

Select the **Three Planes** option from the Type drop-down list; you will be prompted to select a planar object. Select the type of reference object from the **Type Filter** drop-down list in the **Selection Group**. This allows you to customize the process of selecting a particular type of reference object. Next, select three reference objects. If the selected reference objects are not mutually perpendicular, then the **Alerts** message box will be displayed, informing that the parallel planes are selected or no intersection found between the planes. After selecting the three reference objects, the preview of the Datum Coordinate System will be displayed, refer to Figure 5-22. Choose the **OK** button from the **Datum CSYS** dialog box to accept the Datum Coordinate System. The resulting Datum Coordinate System is shown in Figure 5-23.

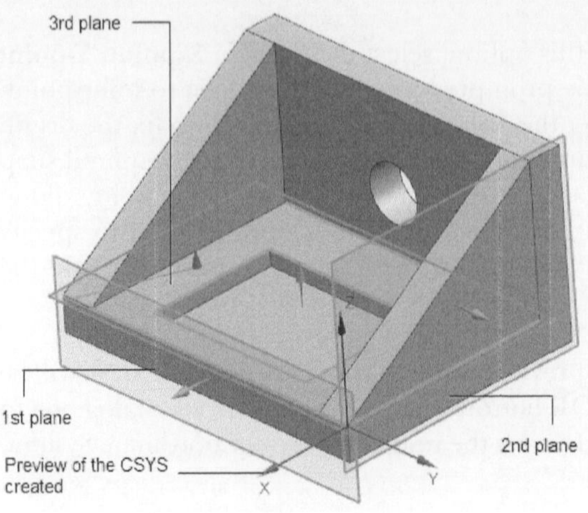

*Figure 5-22 The preview of the CSYS created by using the **Three Planes** option*

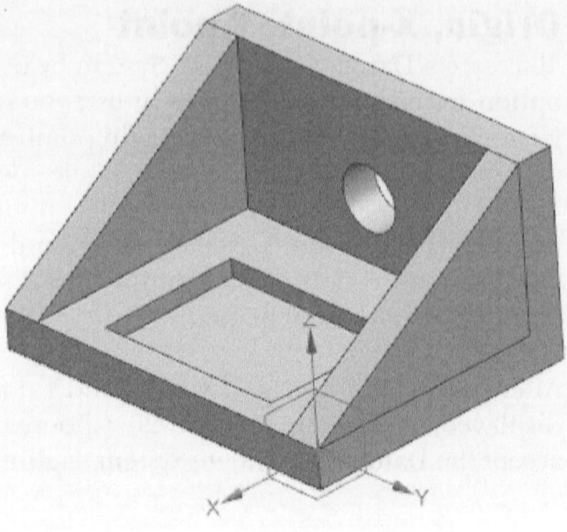

*Figure 5-23 The resulting CSYS created by using the **Three Planes** option*

CSYS of Current View

The **CSYS of Current View** option can be used to create a Datum Coordinate System such that the Z-axis is normal to the current view on the screen. To create a Datum Coordinate System using this tool, orient the model to the required position and then select the **CSYS of Current View** option from the Type drop-down list. Choose the **OK** button; the coordinate system for the modified orientation will be created.

Offset CSYS

This option is used to create a Datum Coordinate System offset to an existing Datum Coordinate System. Select the **Offset CSYS** option from the Type drop-down list; the **X**, **Y**, **Z**, **Angle X**, **Angle Y**, and **Angle Z** edit boxes will be displayed in the **Offset from CSYS** rollout. Next, select the **Selected CSYS** option from the **Reference** drop-down list of the **Reference CSYS** rollout; you will be prompted to select the existing coordinate system. On selecting the existing coordinate system, you will be prompted to enter the translate or rotation values. By default, the **0** value will be displayed in all edit boxes. Next, enter the offset and angle values along the X, Y, and Z directions in the corresponding edit boxes to position the coordinate system. Next, choose the **OK** button from the **Datum CSYS** dialog box; the coordinate system will be created, as shown in Figure 5-24.

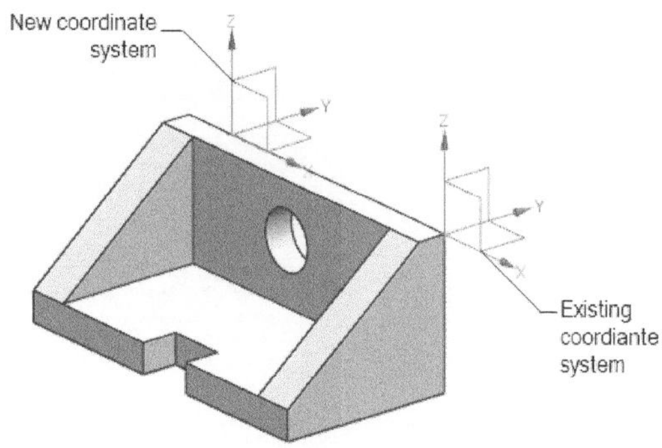

Figure 5-24 *The coordinate system created by using the* ***Offset CSYS*** *option*

Note

After creating the coordinate system, you can modify its location by double-clicking on it. On doing so, the ***Datum CSYS*** *dialog box will be displayed. Now, change the values entered in the edit boxes and choose the* ***OK*** *button; the modifications made in the coordinate system will be reflected in the drawing window.*

Other Options in the Datum CSYS Dialog Box

To display the other options in the **Datum CSYS** dialog box, expand the **Settings** rollout. The options in this rollout are discussed next.

Scale Factor

This edit box is used to change the size of the Datum Coordinate System, while creating it. You can use the scale factor value to change the size. By default, this value is **1.2500**. If you enter **0.625** as the scale factor value, the size of the Datum Coordinate System created will be half of the normal size (default size).

Associative
If you select this check box, the Datum Coordinate System created will be associative with its parent features.

CREATING FIXED AND RELATIVE DATUM AXES

Ribbon: Home > Feature > Datum/Point Drop-down > Datum Axis
Menu: Insert > Datum/Point > Datum Axis

The datum axis can be used as a reference object while creating a sketch-based feature such as a revolved feature or while creating the feature-based operations such as the draft feature. There are two types of datum axes in NX: fixed datum axis and relative datum axis. A fixed datum axis can be created without specifying any reference object. When you start a new file by using the **Model** template, by default, three fixed datum axes will be present in that file, as shown in Figure 5-25.

However, for creating a relative datum axis, you need to select the reference object. To create the relative datum axis, choose the **Datum Axis** option from the **Datum/Point Drop-down** of the **Feature** group of the **Home** tab; the **Datum Axis** dialog box will be displayed, as shown in Figure 5-26. The Type drop-down list of this dialog box contains the options to create the relative datum axes. These options are discussed next.

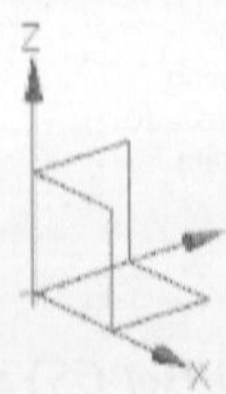

Figure 5-25 Fixed datum axes

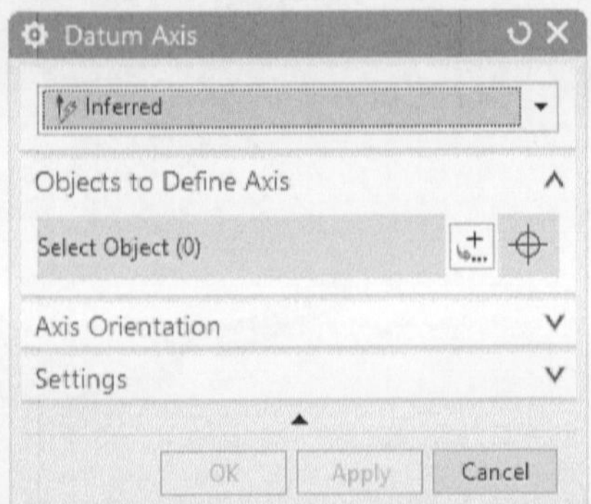

*Figure 5-26 The **Datum Axis** dialog box*

Inferred
You can use the **Inferred** option from the Type drop-down list to create the datum axis. The resulting datum axis will depend on the reference objects selected and the sequence of their selection.

On Curve Vector
The **On Curve Vector** option is used to create a datum axis passing through a point on a specified curve. To create relative datum axis by using this option, select the **On Curve Vector** option from the Type drop-down list of the dialog box; you will be prompted to select a point on the curve or the edge. On selecting the point on the curve or edge, the preview of the datum axis will be displayed. Next, you need to locate the datum axis on the selected curve by entering a value in the **Arc Length** edit box of the dialog box. Note that as soon as you enter the arc length in this edit box of the dialog box, the **Arc Length** edit box will also be displayed in the graphics window,

as shown in Figure 5-27. You can also enter the arc length in order to locate the datum axis in this edit box. You can also locate the datum axis by percentage of arc length. To do so, select the **% Arc Length** option from the **Location** drop-down list in the **Location on Curve** rollout; the **Arc Length** edit box will change to the **% Arc Length** edit box. Enter the percent of arc length between 0 to 100 in the **% Arc Length** edit box and press the ENTER key; the datum axis will move to a new location. The options from the **Orientation** drop-down list in the **Orientation on Curve** rollout are used to orient the datum axis. These options are discussed next.

Tangent
Select this option to create the datum axis tangent to the selected curve or edge.

Normal
Select this option to create the datum axis normal to the selected curve or edge.

Bi-normal
Select this option to create the datum axis bi-normal to the selected curve or edge.

Perpendicular to Object
This option allows you select an object to which the axis is oriented perpendicularly. You can select a curve, edge, planar face, or a datum plane.

Parallel to Object
This option allows you to select an object to which the axis is oriented in a parallel direction. You can select a curve, an edge, or a non-planar face.

Figure 5-28 shows a datum axis created by using 73 as the arc length value.

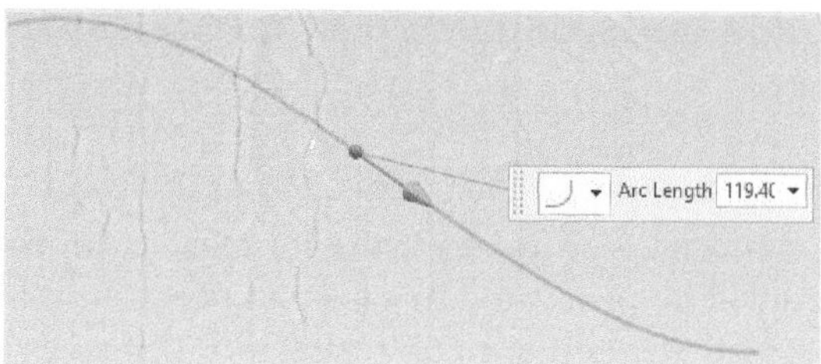

Figure 5-27 *The preview of the relative datum axis created by using the **On Curve Vector** option*

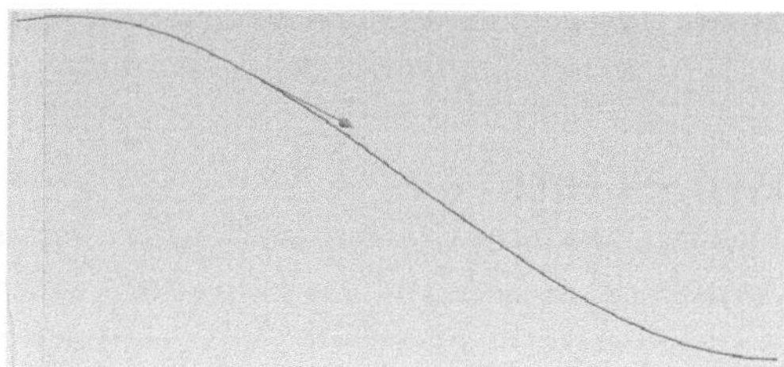

Figure 5-28 *The datum axis created by using 73 as the arc length value*

Point and Direction
The **Point and Direction** option is used to create a datum axis on a point along the defined direction. Select this option from the Type drop-down list; you will be prompted to select an object to infer point. Select the fixed point, refer to Figure 5-29. You can choose the required buttons from the **Selection Group** to enable an easy selection of the points. After specifying the fixed point, you will be prompted to select objects to infer vector. Also, a triad will be displayed in the drawing window. Next, you need to define the direction along which the datum axis will point. To define the direction, you can use the **Vector Dialog** button or the **Inferred Vector** drop-down list in the **Direction** rollout. Also, you can select an edge or a face for defining the

direction. If you select an edge as the reference, the axis will be created coincident or parallel to the selected edge. If you select a face as the reference, the axis will be created perpendicular to it. You can also select a direction vector from the triad. Figure 5-29 shows the preview of the datum axis after selecting an edge as the reference vector. The resulting datum axis is shown in Figure 5-30.

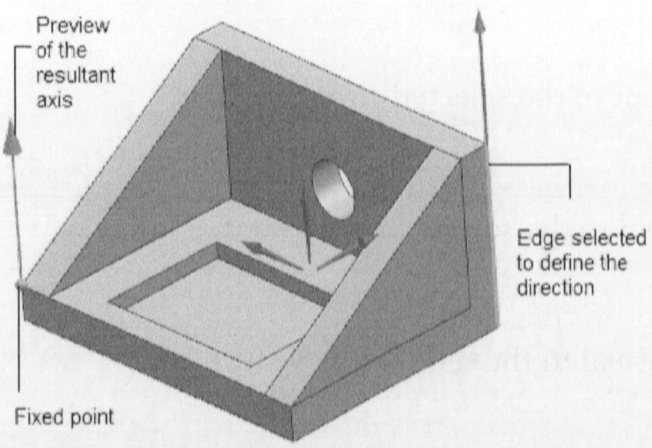

Figure 5-29 The preview of the relative datum axis

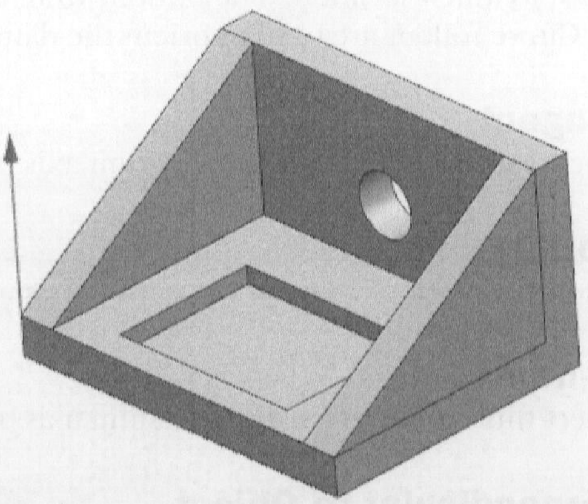

Figure 5-30 The resulting relative datum axis

By default, the **Parallel to Vector** option is selected from the **Orientation** drop-down list in the **Direction** rollout. As a result, the resulting axis will be created parallel to the reference vector. If you select the **Perpendicular to Vector** option, then the resulting axis will be created normal to the reference vector.

Note

You can also select an existing axis, a linear curve, or a linear sketch member as a reference object for defining the direction of the datum axis.

Two Points

The **Two Points** option is used to create a datum axis between two selected points. Select the **Two Points** option from the Type drop-down list; you will be prompted to select an object to infer point. Specify the first point. Next, you need to specify the endpoint towards which the axis will point. After you specify the second point, the preview of the datum axis will be displayed, as shown in Figure 5-31. Choose **Apply** and then the **Cancel** button from the **Datum Axis** dialog box to accept the axis created. The datum axis will be created, as shown in Figure 5-32.

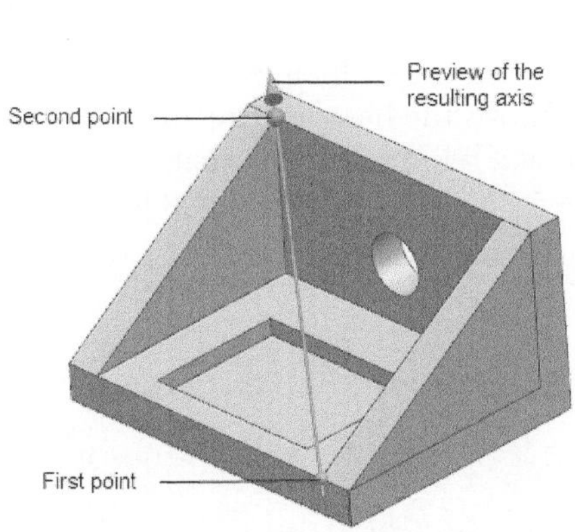

*Figure 5-31 The preview of the relative datum axis created using the **Two Points** option*

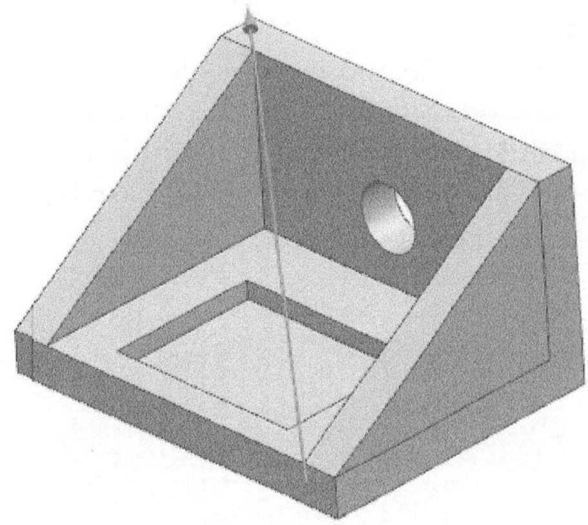

*Figure 5-32 The relative datum axis created using the **Two Points** option*

Other Options in the Datum Axis Dialog box

To display the other options in the **Datum Axis** dialog box, expand the **Axis Orientation** and **Settings** rollouts. The options in these rollouts are discussed next.

Axis Orientation Rollout

The **Reverse Direction** button in this rollout is used to reverse the direction of the axis.

Settings Rollout

If you select the **Associative** check box in this rollout, the datum axis created will be associative with its parent features.

OTHER EXTRUSION OPTIONS

In the previous chapter, you learned about the basic extrude options. In this chapter, you will learn about additional extrude options available in the **Extrude** dialog box.

Specifying the Boolean Operation

After creating the base feature, you can create additional features by using four types of boolean operations. These operations are available in the **Boolean** drop-down list, as shown in Figure 5-33. In order to perform a boolean operation, first you need to draw the sketch for the additional feature. Next, invoke the **Extrude** dialog box.

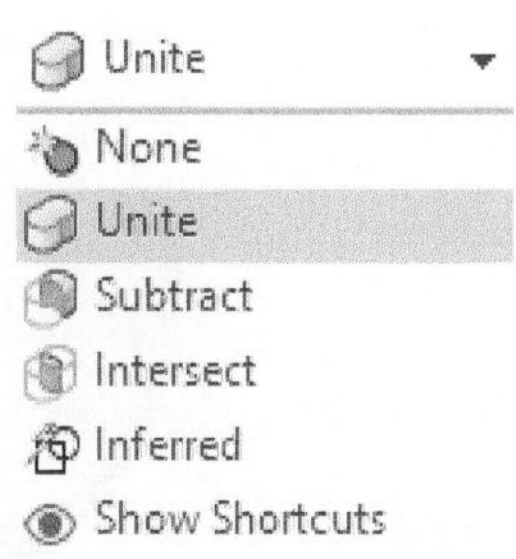

Figure 5-33 Various boolean operations

None

This option allows you to create a new body, which is independent of the existing feature.

Unite

The Unite boolean operation allows you to join the new feature with an existing feature. In this case, no additional solid body is created. Figure 5-34 shows the base feature and the sketch for the additional feature. Note that this sketch is created at a reference plane that is at some offset distance from the top face of the base feature. Figure 5-35 shows an additional feature created using the Unite boolean operation.

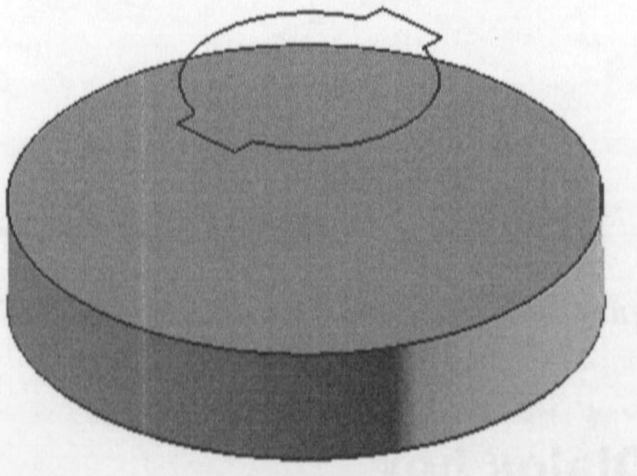

Figure 5-34 Base feature and sketch for the additional feature

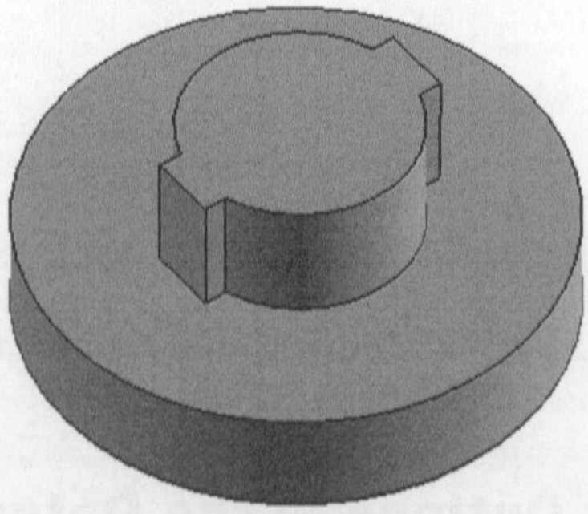

Figure 5-35 3D view of the feature created using the Unite boolean operation

In NX, you can also join a new feature to an existing feature of the model by extruding an open profile. To do so, select the **Open Profile Smart Volume** check box from the **Limits** rollout. Next, select an open profile from the drawing area, refer to Figure 5-36; the preview of the feature will be displayed, as shown in Figure 5-37. You can reverse the material side of the feature by double-clicking on the arrow displayed on the selected profile. Figure 5-38 shows the extrusion created on the other side of the profile.

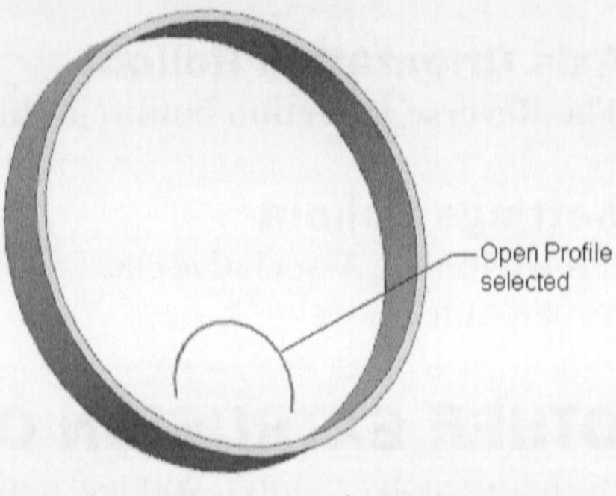

Figure 5-36 Open profile selected to create the extrusion

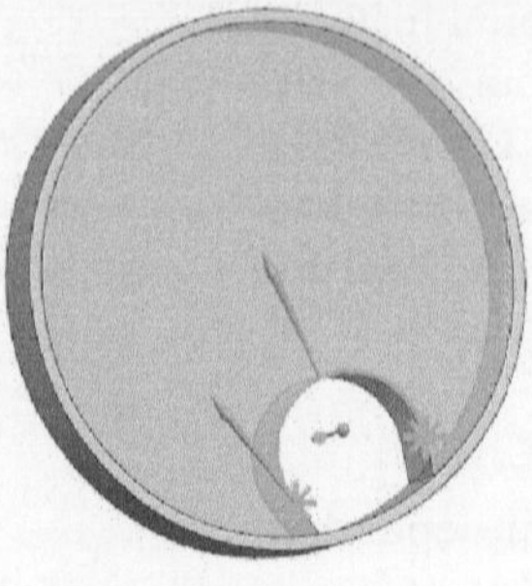

Figure 5-37 Preview of the extruded feature

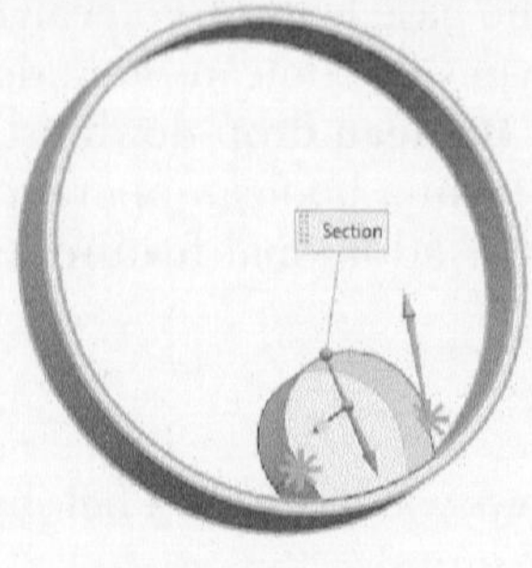

Figure 5-38 Extrusion created on the other side of the profile

Subtract

The Subtract boolean operation is used to create an extruded feature by removing material from the existing feature. The material to be removed will be defined by the sketch you have drawn. Figure 5-39 shows an extruded cut feature created using the Subtract boolean operation.

Intersect

The Intersect boolean operation is used to create an extruded feature by retaining the material common to the existing feature and the feature being created, refer to Figure 5-40. In this case, the material of the base feature that lies outside the boundary of the sketch is removed.

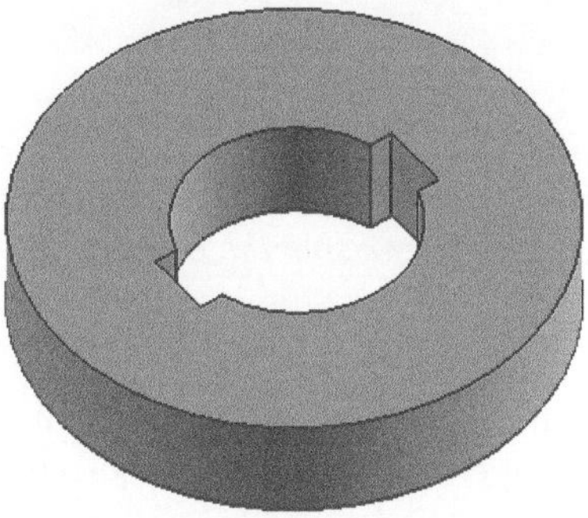

Figure 5-39 *Extruded cut feature created using the Subtract boolean operation*

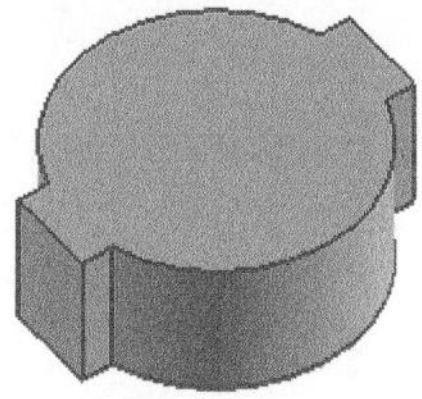

Figure 5-40 *Extruded cut feature created using the Intersect boolean operation*

Note

The models shown in Figures 5-39 and 5-40 are created using the sketch shown in Figure 5-34.

Inferred

You can also use the **Inferred** option to perform any of the boolean operations mentioned previously. The resulting feature will depend on the direction vector selected and the position of the sketch. This option is selected by default.

Other Extrusion Termination Options

In the previous chapter, you learned about the **Value** and **Symmetric Value** termination options. In this chapter, you will learn about the remaining termination options available in the **Start** and **End** drop-down lists in the **Limits** rollout of the **Extrude** dialog box.

Until Next

The **Until Next** option is used to extrude a sketch from the sketching plane to the next surface that intersects the feature in the specified direction. Figure 5-41 shows the sketch to be extruded and Figure 5-42 shows the sketch extruded up to the next face using the **Until Next** option.

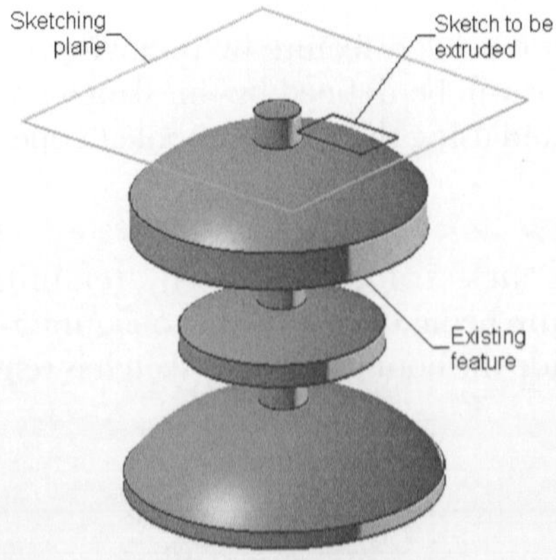

Figure 5-41 The existing feature and the sketch to be extruded

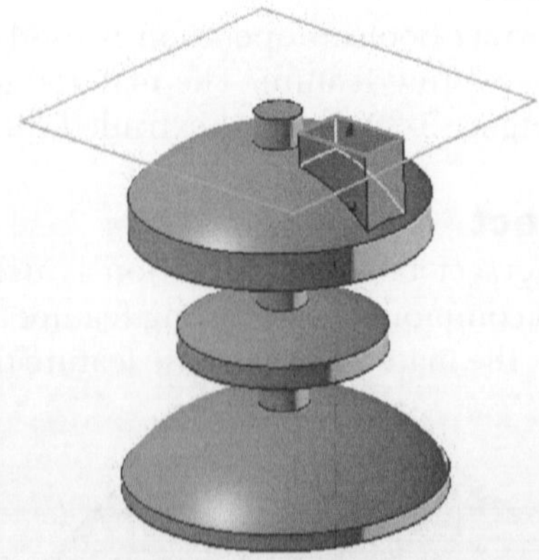

*Figure 5-42 Preview of the sketch being extruded up to the next surface using the **Until Next** option*

Until Selected

The **Until Selected** option is used to extrude the sketch up to a specified face, a datum plane, or a body. Figure 5-43 shows the preview of the sketch being extruded up to the selected face.

Until Extended

The **Until Extended** option is used to extrude the sketch up to a specified face, which does not intersect the sketch in its current size and shape. However, when extended, this face will intersect the extruded sketch. Figure 5-44 shows the preview of the sketch being extruded using this option.

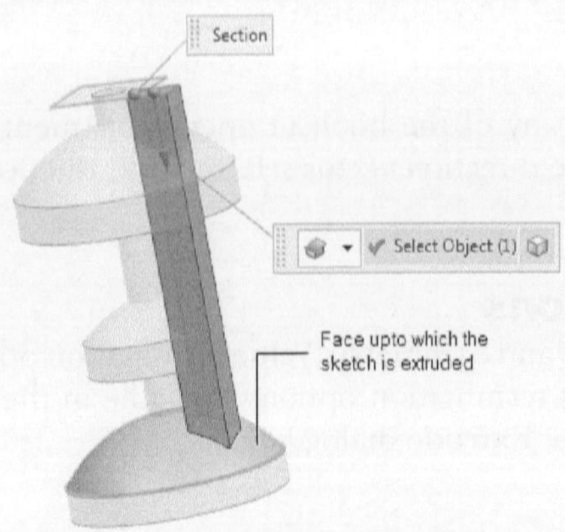

*Figure 5-43 Preview of the sketch being extruded up to the selected surface using the **Until Selected** option*

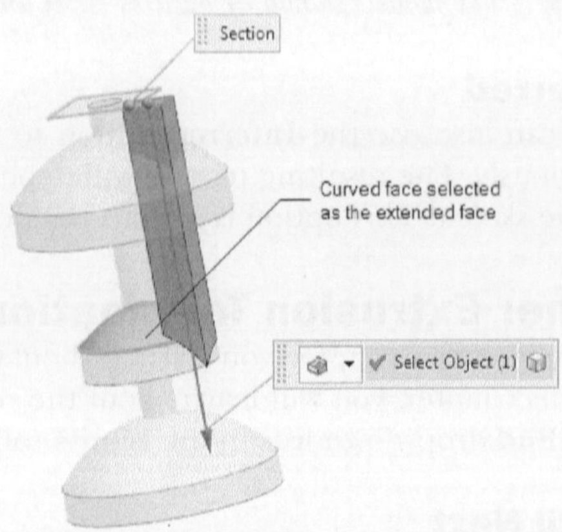

*Figure 5-44 Preview of the sketch being extruded up to the extended surface using the **Until Extended** option*

Through All

The **Through All** option is used to extrude the sketch through all the features and bodies that are in the path of the sketch. Figure 5-45 shows preview of the feature extruded using this option.

PROJECTING EXTERNAL ELEMENTS

Ribbon: Home > Direct Sketch > Sketch Curve gallery > More Curve > Project Curve
Menu: Insert > Sketch Curve > Project Curve

While sketching, you may sometimes need to use some elements of the existing features in the current sketch. NX facilitates this by allowing you to project external elements as sketched entities on the current sketching plane. This helps you create features that are similar to other features created on a different sketching plane. Figure 5-46 shows a model which has a cylindrical base feature and another feature created at the bottom face of the base feature. Now, if you want to create the same feature on the top face of the cylindrical feature, you can simply define a new sketching plane on the top face of the base feature and then project the top face of the second feature. On doing so, the entities will be automatically placed on the current sketching plane, as shown in Figure 5-47.

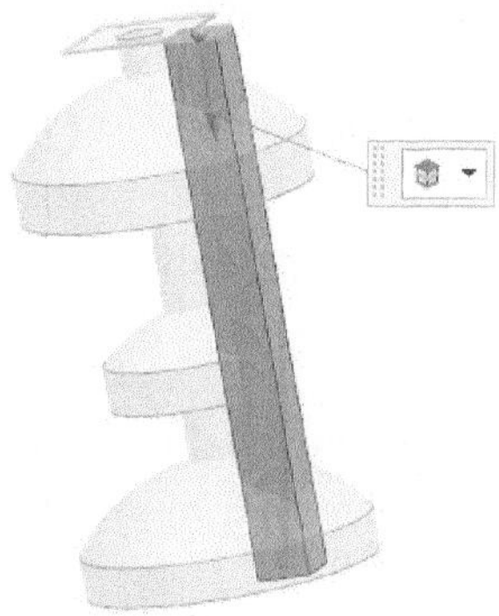

Figure 5-45 *Preview of the sketch being extruded up to the last surface using the* ***Through All*** *option*

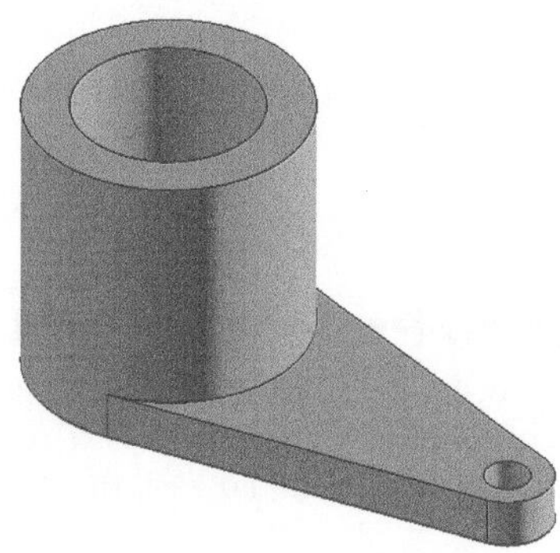

Figure 5-46 *Model with two features*

To project external elements, invoke the sketching environment by choosing the **Sketch** tool from the **Direct Sketch** group. Next choose **Menu > Insert > Sketch Curve > Project Curve** from the **Top Border Bar**; the **Project Curve** dialog box will be displayed, as shown in Figure 5-48.

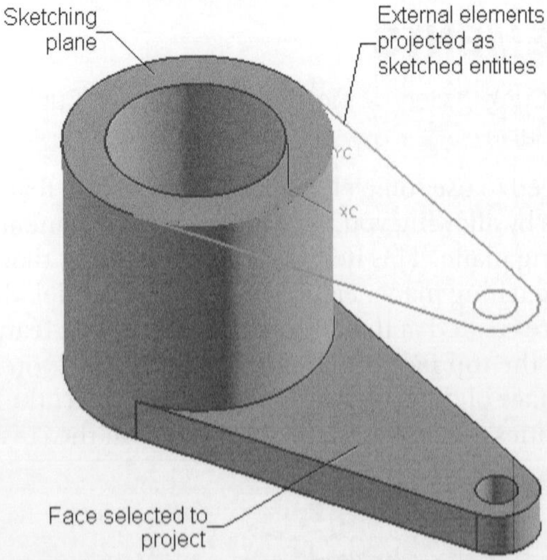

Figure 5-47 Face selected to be projected and the resulting sketch

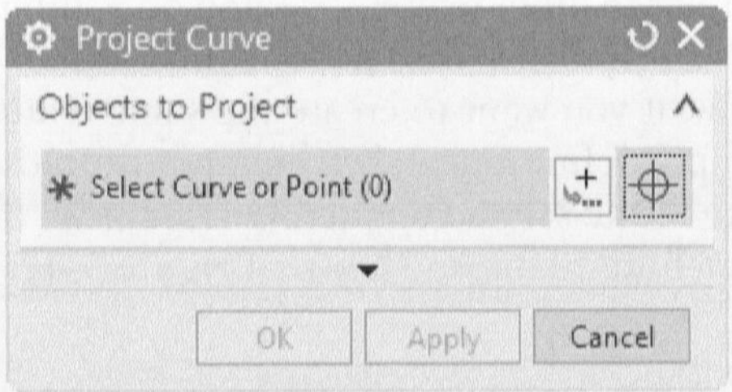

*Figure 5-48 The **Project Curve** dialog box*

The options in various rollouts of the **Project Curve** dialog box are discussed next.

Objects to Project Rollout

This rollout is used to the select the objects to be projected. By default, the **Objects to Project** button is chosen in this rollout. As a result, you will be prompted to select curve or point to project. You can select the curves, points, or edges of a model.

Settings Rollout

The options in the **Settings** rollout are discussed next.

Associative

If you select this check box, the projected sketched entities will be forced to be associative with the original entities from which they were projected. As a result, if the original entities are modified, the projected entities also get modified accordingly.

Output Curve Type

The options in this drop-down list are used to specify the projection output type. These options are discussed next.

Original

By default, the **Original** option is selected. As a result, the projected entities are similar to the original entities. This means that if the original sketch is a combination of lines, the projected sketch will also be a combination of lines only.

Spline Segment

This option is used to project the external elements as spline segments. Each external element is represented by a spline segment in the projected sketch. This means that if you select six original elements to project, the projected sketch will also comprise of six spline segments.

Single Spline

This option is used to project the external elements as a single continuous spline. As a result, irrespective of the number of entities you select to project, the projected sketch will have a single continuous spline.

Note

For editing the projected entities, you may need to break their associativity with the original elements.

Tolerance

This edit box is used to specify the gap upto which the entities will be considered as continuous entities in the projected sketch. If the gap between the original entities is more than that specified in this edit box, they will appear as noncontinuous entities in the projected sketch.

After specifying options in various rollouts, select the elements to be projected. You can select curves, points, or edges of the model. Next, choose the **OK** button from the **Project Curve** dialog box; the selected elements will be projected.

TUTORIALS

Tutorial 1

In this tutorial, you will create the model shown in Figure 5-49. The dimensions of the model are shown in Figure 5-50. **(Expected time: 30 min)**

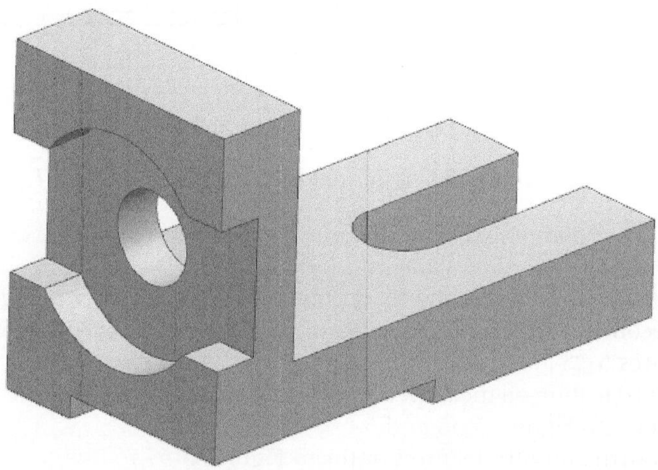

Figure 5-49 *Model for Tutorial 1*

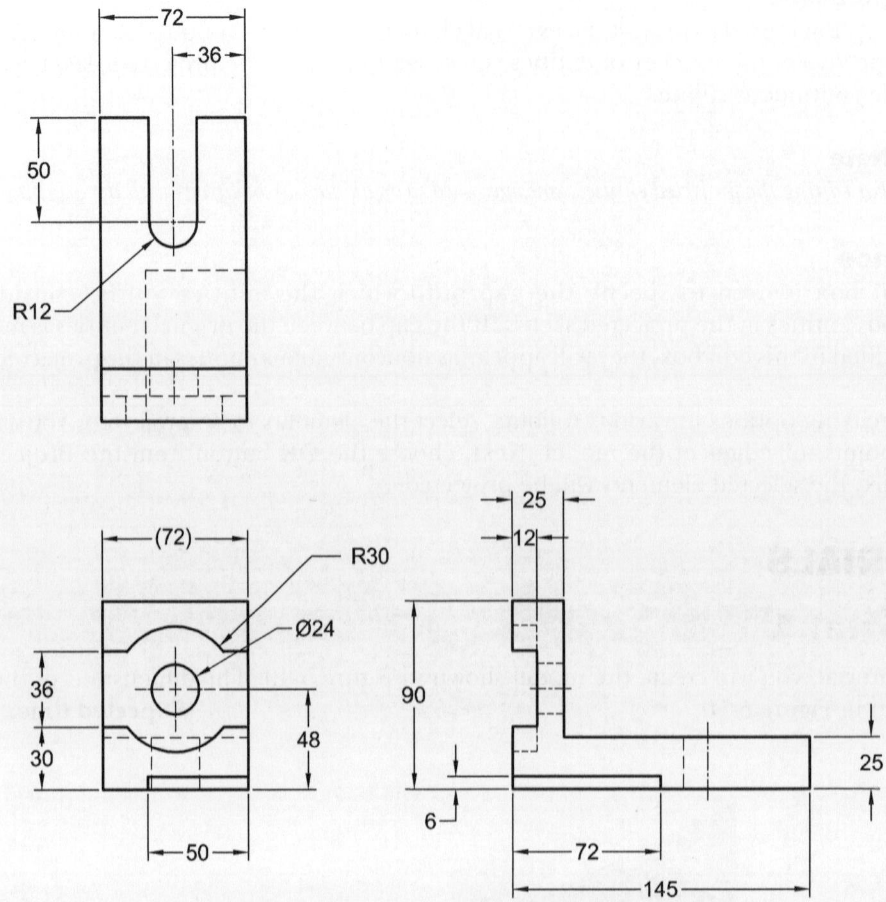

Figure 5-50 Dimensions of the model for Tutorial 1

The following steps are required to complete this tutorial:

a. Create the base feature of the model on the YC-ZC plane, refer to Figures 5-51 and 5-52.
b. Create the second feature on the front face of the base feature by using the **Subtract** operation, refer to Figures 5-53 and 5-54.
c. Create the third feature on the upper horizontal face of the base feature by using the **Subtract** operation, refer to Figures 5-55 and 5-56.
d. Create the fourth and fifth features, refer to Figures 5-57 to 5-59.

Creating the Base Feature

First, you need to create the base feature of the model.

1. Invoke the **New** dialog box and specify the location of the document as *C:\NX\c05* and name it as *c05tut1.prt*. Next, choose the **OK** button from it.

2. Invoke the sketching environment by using the YC-ZC plane and draw an open sketch, as shown in Figure 5-51.

3. Exit the sketching environment and invoke the **Extrude** dialog box. Select the sketch and then select the **Symmetric Value** option from the **Start** drop-down list in the **Limits** rollout; the **Start** drop-down list is converted into the **End** drop-down list. Enter **36** in the **Distance** edit box located below the **End** drop-down list and then press ENTER.

   Note that by default, only few rollouts are expanded in the **Extrude** dialog box.

4. Expand the **Offset** rollout and select the **Two-Sided** option from the **Offset** drop-down list; the **Start** and **End** edit boxes are displayed.

5 Enter **25** in the **Start** edit box. Also, make sure that the value entered in the **End** edit box is **0**.

6. Choose the **OK** button from the dialog box to create the base feature. Turn off the display of the sketch. The base feature of the model is shown in Figure 5-52.

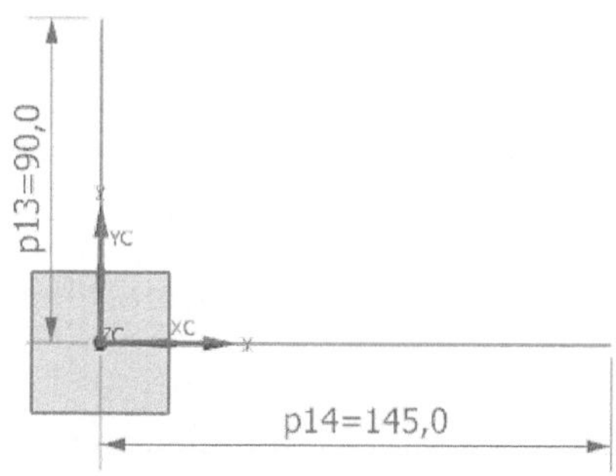

Figure 5-51 *Open sketch for the base feature*

Figure 5-52 *Base feature of the model*

Creating the Second Feature

The second feature is an extruded feature that can be created by using the **Subtract** option. The sketch of this feature is drawn on the front face of the base feature.

1. Invoke the sketching environment by selecting the right face of the base feature as the sketching plane. Make sure that the X-axis of the new sketching plane points toward the edge which measures 145 mm.

2. Draw the rectangular sketch of the cut feature. Make the bottom line and the left line of the rectangle collinear with the edges of the base feature. Add the required dimensions to the sketch, refer to Figure 5-53.

3. Exit the sketching environment and then invoke the **Extrude** dialog box. Now, select the sketch; the preview of the feature is displayed in the graphics window.

4. Select the **Subtract** option from the **Boolean** drop-down list and reverse the direction of extrusion by choosing the **Reverse Direction** button from the **Direction** rollout of the dialog box, if required. Enter **50** in the **Distance** edit box which is available below the **End** drop-down list of the **Limits** rollout and then choose the **OK** button from the **Extrude** dialog box.

5. Press CTRL+B; the **Class Selection** dialog box is displayed. Select the sketch of the second feature from the graphics window and choose the **OK** button from this dialog box; the selected sketch is hidden. The model with the cut feature created is shown in Figure 5-54.

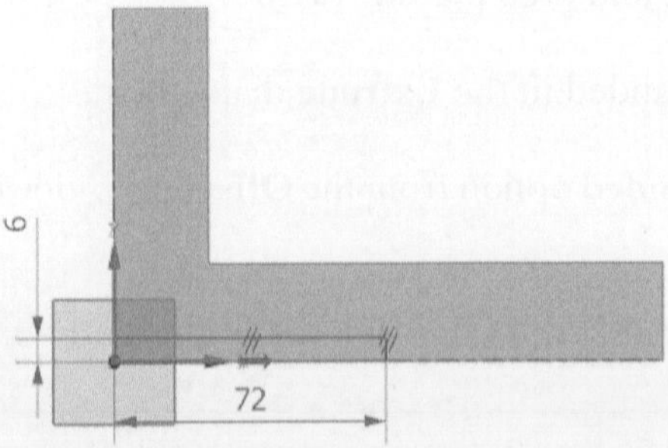

Figure 5-53 Sketch created for the second feature

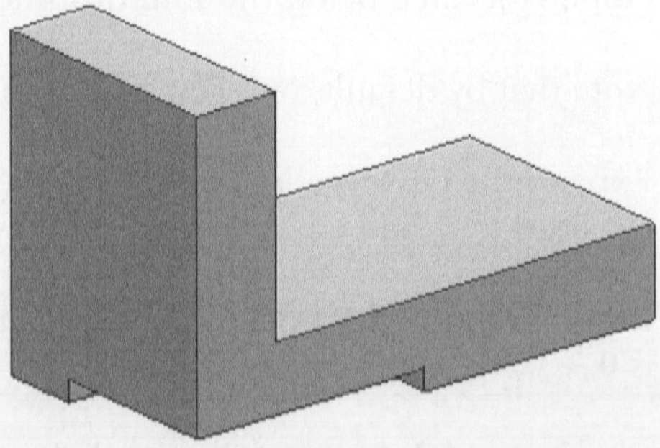

Figure 5-54 Model with the cut feature

Creating the Third Feature

The third feature is also an extruded feature which will be created by using the **Subtract** option. The sketch of this feature will be drawn on the top lower face of the base feature.

1. Invoke the sketching environment by selecting the top upper face of the base feature as the sketching plane. Make sure that the X-axis of the new sketching plane points toward the edge which measures 145 mm.

2. Draw the sketch of the feature and add the required constraints and dimensions to it, as shown in Figure 5-55.

3. Exit the sketching environment and then invoke the **Extrude** dialog box. Select the sketch; the preview of the feature is displayed in the drawing window.

4. Select the **Subtract** option from the **Boolean** drop-down list if not already selected and reverse the direction of extrusion.

5. Select the **Through All** option from the **End** drop-down list and choose the **OK** button from the dialog box.

6. Hide the sketch. The model with the cut feature is shown in Figure 5-56.

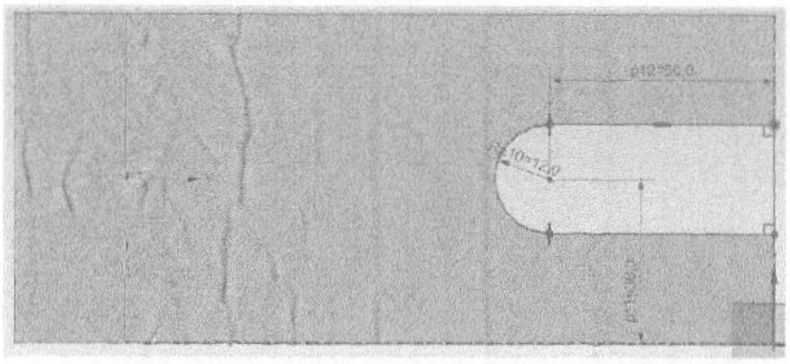

Figure 5-55 Sketch created for the third feature

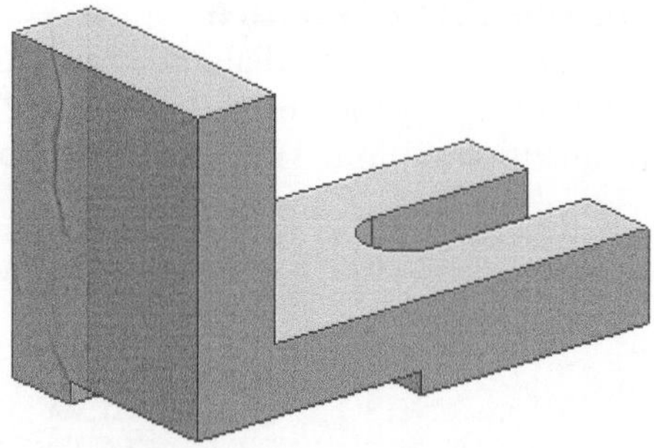

Figure 5-56 Model with the cut feature

Creating the Fourth Feature

The sketch of this feature will be drawn on the front face of the base feature and will be extruded upto a depth of 12 mm by using the **Subtract** option.

1. Invoke the sketching environment by selecting the left face of the base feature as the sketching plane. Make sure that the X-axis of the new sketching plane points toward the right.

2. Draw the sketch of the feature and add the required constraints and dimensions to it, as shown in Figure 5-57.

3. Exit the sketching environment and then invoke the **Extrude** dialog box. Select the sketch.

4. Select the **Subtract** option from the **Boolean** drop-down list if not already selected and reverse the direction of extrusion.

5. Enter **12** in the **Distance** edit box that is available below the **End** drop-down list, and then choose the **OK** button from the dialog box.

6. Hide the sketch. The model with the cut feature is shown in Figure 5-58.

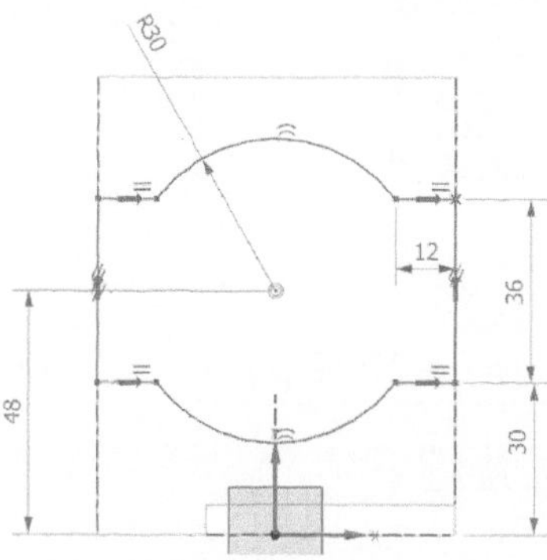

Figure 5-57 Sketch created for the fourth feature

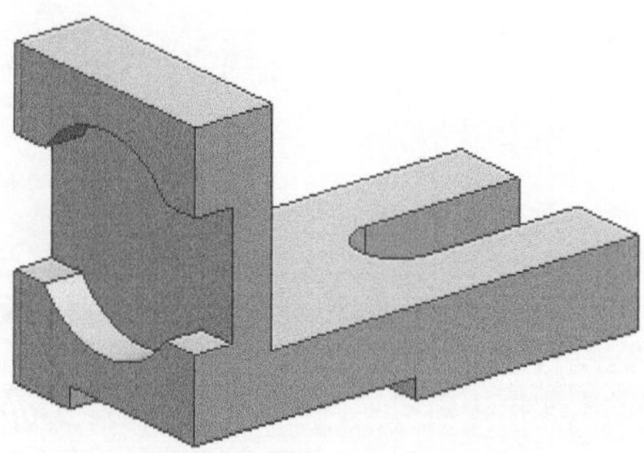

Figure 5-58 Model with the cut feature

Creating the Fifth Feature

1. Similarly, draw a circle of diameter 24 units on the new face that is exposed because of the last cut feature and then extrude the circle by using the **Subtract** option and the **Through All** termination option. The final model for Tutorial 1 is shown in Figure 5-59.

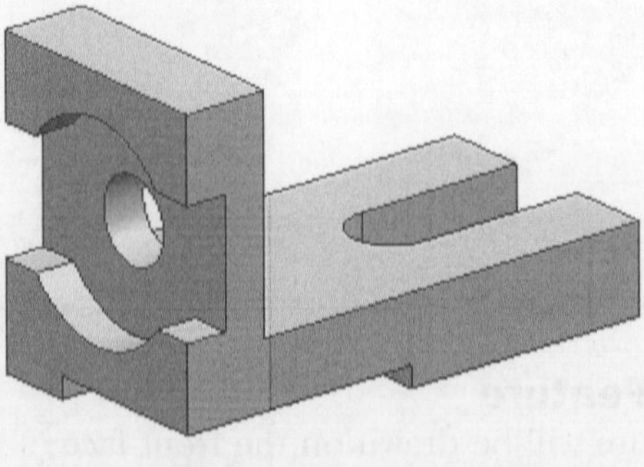

Figure 5-59 Final model for Tutorial 1

Saving and Closing the File

1. Choose **Menu > File > Close > Save and Close** from the **Top Border Bar** to save and close the file.

Tutorial 2

In this tutorial, you will draw the model shown in Figure 5-60. The dimensions of the model are given in Figure 5-60(a). **(Expected time: 30 min)**

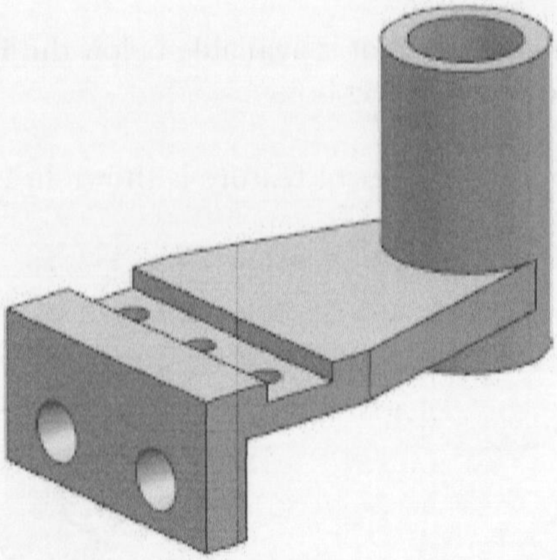

Figure 5-60 Model for Tutorial 2

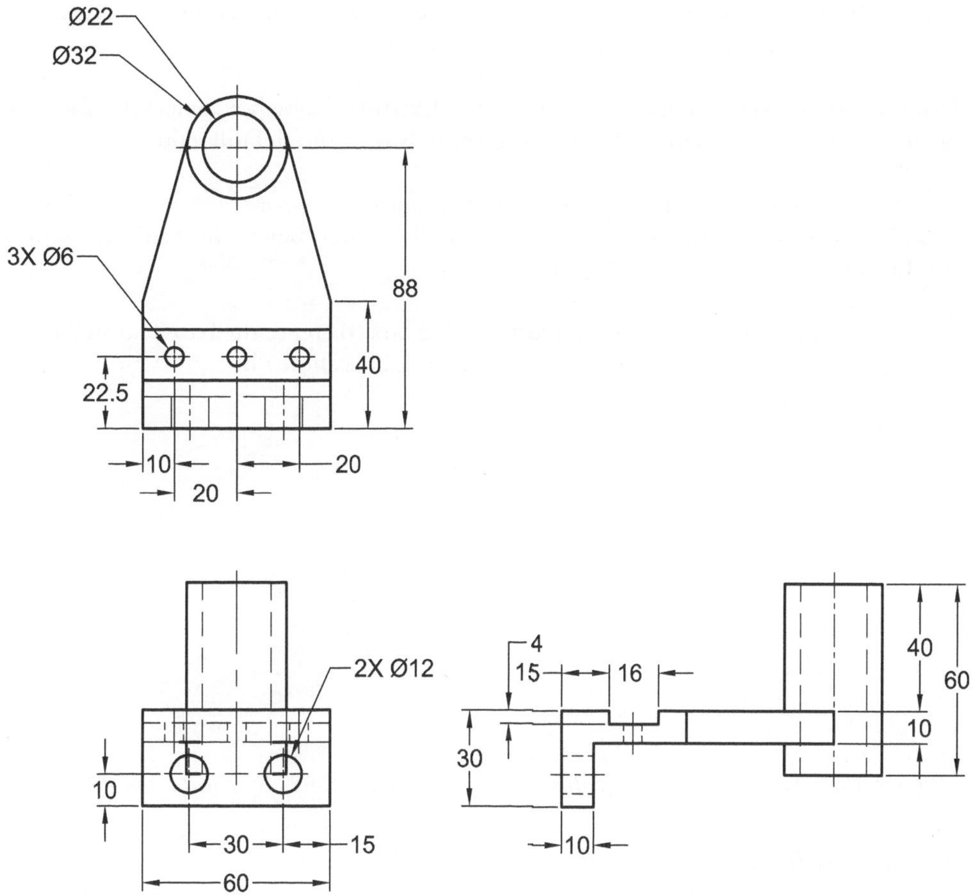

Figure 5-60(a) Views and dimensions of the model

The following steps are required to complete this tutorial:

a. Create the base feature of the model on the YC-ZC plane, refer to Figures 5-61 and 5-62.
b. Create the second feature using the **Unite** option. The sketch of this feature will be drawn on the top face of the base feature, refer to Figures 5-63 and 5-64.
c. Create a new datum plane at an offset of 40 mm from the top face of the second feature.
d. Draw the sketch of the third feature on the offset plane and extrude it by using the **Unite** option, refer to Figure 5-65.
e. Create holes in the model, refer to Figure 5-66.

Creating the Base Feature

First, you need to create the base feature of the model.

1. Start a new file with the name *c05tut2.prt* using the **Model** template and specify its location as *C:\NX\c05*.

2. Invoke the sketching environment by using the YC-ZC plane as the sketching plane and draw a sketch similar to the one shown in Figure 5-61.

3. Exit the sketching environment and invoke the **Extrude** dialog box. Select the sketch; preview of the feature is displayed in the drawing window with the default value.

4. Select the **Symmetric Value** option from the **Start** drop-down list in the **Limits** rollout. Next, enter **30** in the **Distance** edit box which is located below the **End** drop-down list in the **Limits** rollout and press ENTER.

5. Choose the **OK** button from the **Extrude** dialog box to create the base feature. Turn off the display of the sketch. The base feature of the model is shown in Figure 5-62.

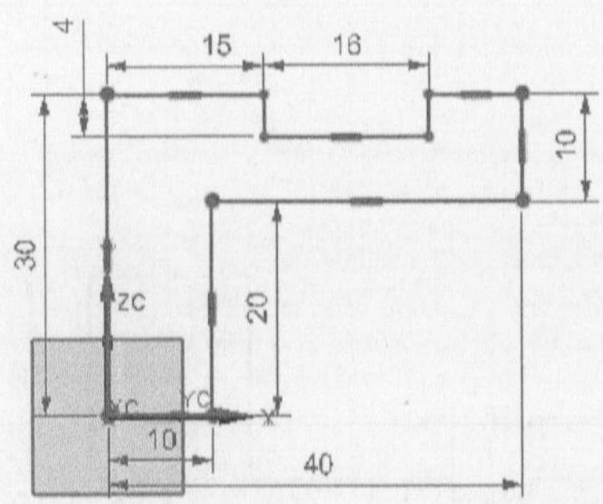

Figure 5-61 *Sketch for the base feature*

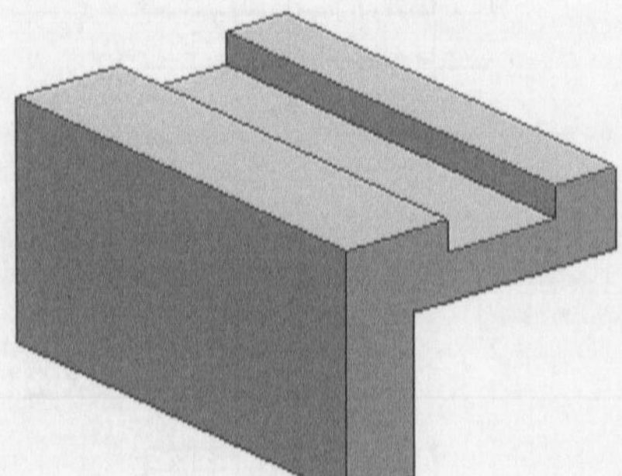

Figure 5-62 *Base feature of the model*

Creating the Second Feature

The second feature is also an extruded feature which will be created by using the **Unite** option. The sketch of this feature will be drawn on the top face of the base feature and will be extruded by using the **Until Extended** option.

1. Invoke the sketching environment by selecting the top face of the base feature as the sketching plane. Make sure that the X-axis of the new sketching plane points toward the right of the drawing window.

2. Draw the sketch of the feature and add the required constraints and dimensions to it, as shown in Figure 5-63.

3. Exit the sketching environment and then invoke the **Extrude** dialog box. Next, select the sketch; preview of the extruded feature is displayed in the drawing window.

4. Select the **Unite** option from the **Boolean** drop-down list in the **Boolean** rollout of the dialog box.

5. Select the **Until Extended** option from the **End** drop-down list in the **Limits** rollout of the dialog box. Hold the middle mouse button and then rotate the view of the model such that its lower faces are visible. Next, select the bottom horizontal face shown in Figure 5-64 to define the termination of the second feature.

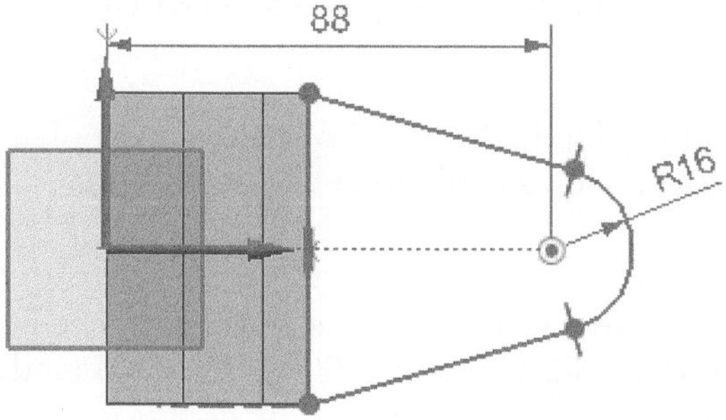

Figure 5-63 Sketch created for the second feature

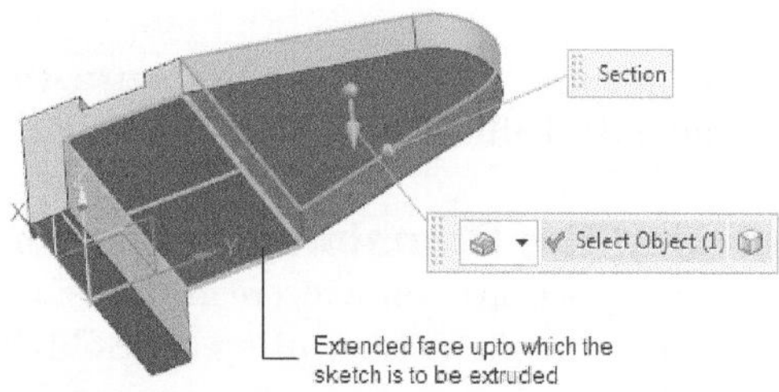

Figure 5-64 Face to be selected to terminate the second feature

6. Choose the **OK** button from the **Extrude** dialog box; the feature is created.

7. Change the current view to the isometric view and hide the sketch.

Creating the Third Feature

You need to create the third feature on a datum plane created at an offset of 40 mm from the top face of the second feature.

1. Choose the **Datum Plane** tool from the **Feature** group in the **Home** tab; the **Datum Plane** dialog box is displayed.

2. Select the **At Distance** option from the Type drop-down list and then select the top face of the second feature.

3. Enter **40** in the **Distance** edit box and make sure that the value entered in the **Number of Planes** edit box is 1. Next, choose the **OK** button from the **Datum Plane** dialog box; a new plane is created.

4. Invoke the sketching environment by using the new datum plane. You can define the orientation of the X-axis of the sketching plane by using any one of the straight edges of the model.

5. Draw a circle for the third feature. Next, make the circle concentric with the curve in the second feature and then make the curve and the circle of equal radius by using the **Equal Radius** tool. Now, as radii of both the curve and the circle are equal, you do not need to apply any dimensions to the sketch.

6. Exit the sketching environment and then invoke the **Extrude** dialog box. Select the sketch; preview of the feature is displayed in the drawing window.

7. Select the **Unite** option from the **Boolean** drop-down list in the **Extrude** dialog box and choose the **Reverse Direction** button if required. Note that the feature creation is in the downward direction.

8. Enter **60** in the **End** edit box and then choose the **OK** button from the **Extrude** dialog box; the feature is created.

9. Change the current view to isometric view and then hide the sketch and the datum plane. The model after creating the cylindrical feature is shown in Figure 5-65.

Creating the Remaining Features

1. In this section, you will create holes on the model. To create these holes, you need to extrude the sketches by using the **Subtract** option, refer to Figure 5-60(a). The final model for Tutorial 2 is shown in Figure 5-66.

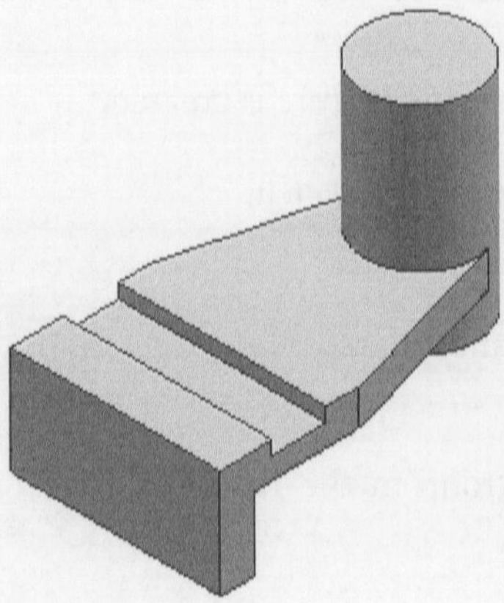

Figure 5-65 *Model after creating the cylindrical feature*

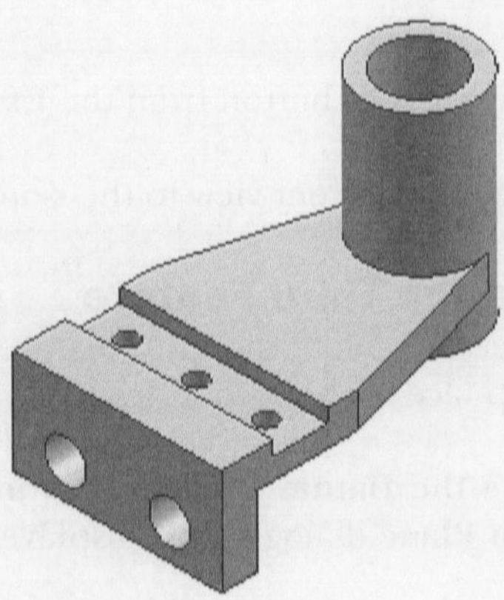

Figure 5-66 *Final model for Tutorial 2*

Saving and Closing the File

1. Choose **Menu > File > Close > Save and Close** from the **Top Border Bar** to save and close the file.

Tutorial 3

In this tutorial, you will create the model shown in Figure 5-67. The dimensions of the model are given in Figure 5-68. **(Expected time: 30 min)**

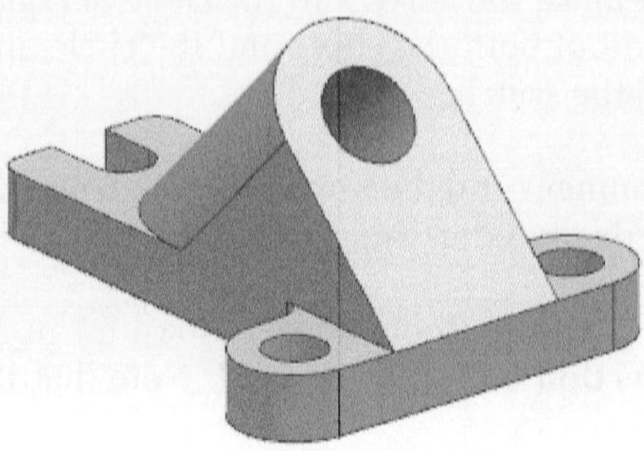

Figure 5-67 *Model for Tutorial 3*

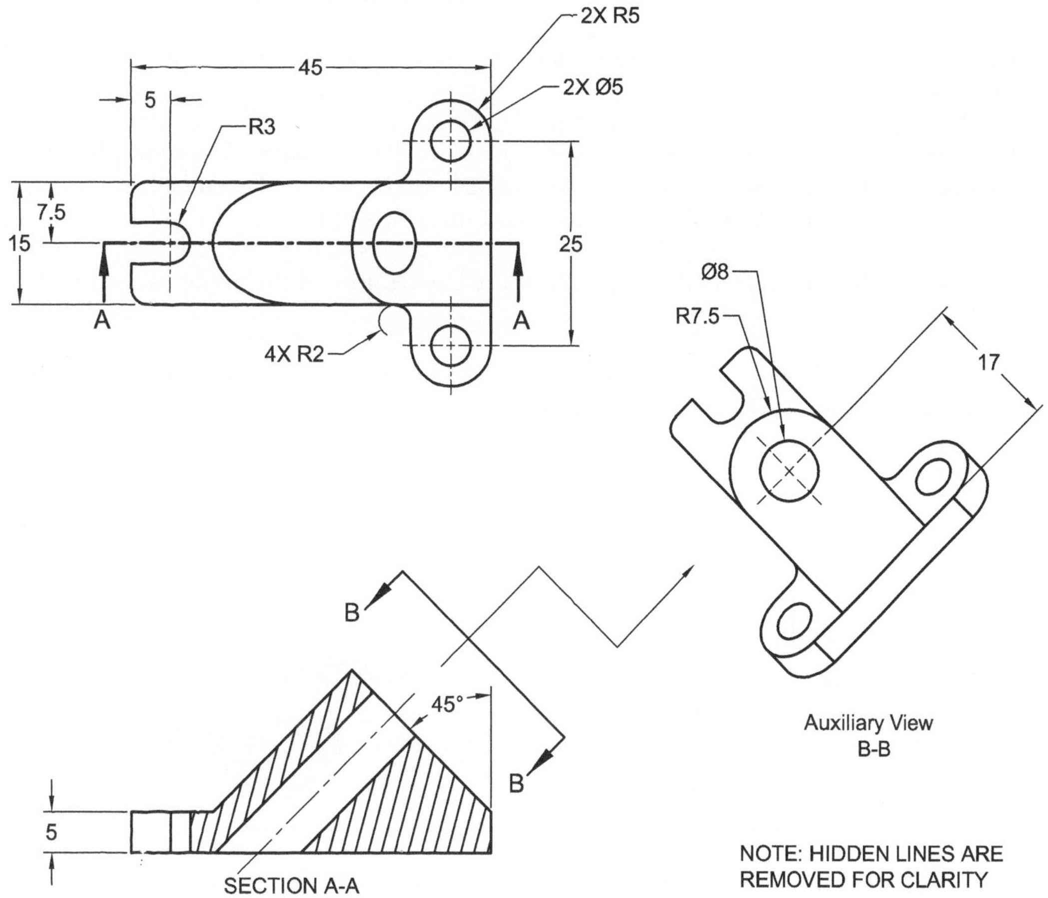

Figure 5-68 *Dimensions of the model for Tutorial 3*

The following steps are required to complete this tutorial:

a. Create the base feature of the model on the XC-YC plane, refer to Figures 5-69 and 5-70.
b. Create the second feature. In this process, you will create a new datum plane at an angle of 45 degrees and draw the sketch of the next extrude feature by using the new datum plane, refer to Figures 5-71 and 5-72.
c. Create a third feature on the inclined face of the second feature, refer to Figure 5-74.

Creating the Base Feature

First, you need to create the base feature of the model.

1. Start a new file with the name *c05tut3.prt* using the **Model** template and specify its location as *C:\NX\c05*.

2. Invoke the sketching environment by using the XC-YC plane as the sketching plane and draw a sketch similar to the one shown in Figure 5-69.

3. Exit the sketching environment by choosing the **Finish Sketch** tool.

4. Invoke the **Extrude** dialog box and select the sketch; preview of the extrude feature is displayed.

5. Enter **0** in the **Distance** edit box that is available below the **Start** drop-down list in the **Limits** rollout of the **Extrude** dialog box. Similarly, enter **5** in the **Distance** edit box which is available below the **End** drop-down list. Next, press ENTER.

6. Choose the **OK** button from this dialog box; the base feature of the model is created, refer to Figure 5-70.

7. Hide the sketch and the default datum planes. The base feature after hiding the sketch and the default planes is shown in Figure 5-70.

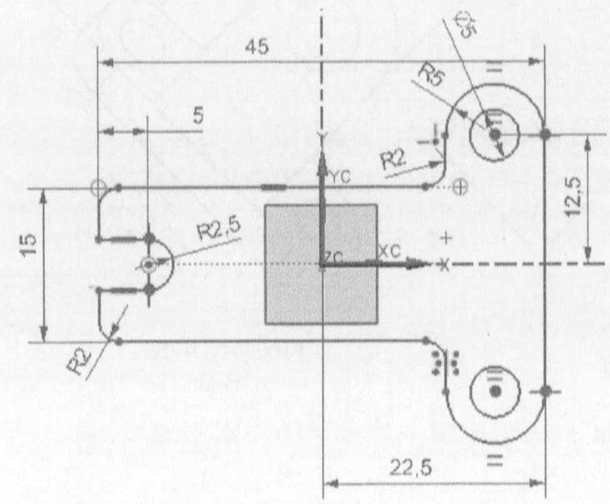

Figure 5-69 Sketch created for the base feature

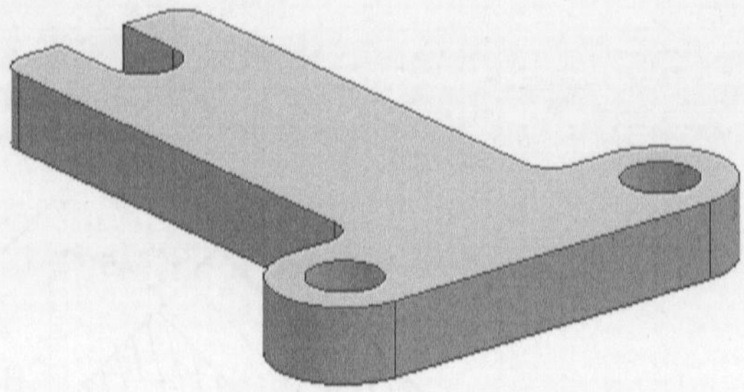

Figure 5-70 Base feature of the model

Creating the Second Feature

The second feature is also an extruded feature. However, to create the sketch of this feature, first you need to create a new datum plane at an angle of 45 degrees from the right face of the base feature.

1. Choose the **Datum Plane** tool from the **Feature** group of the **Home** tab; the **Datum Plane** dialog box is displayed.

2. Select the **At Angle** option from the Type drop-down list of this dialog box.

3. First, select the right face of the base feature and then the edge to define the new datum plane, refer to Figure 5-71. On doing so, the **Angle** edit box is displayed.

4. Enter **45** in the **Angle** edit box, as shown in Figure 5-71, and then choose the **OK** button from the **Datum Plane** dialog box.

5. Draw the sketch of the second feature on the newly created datum plane, as shown in Figure 5-72. You need to apply collinear constraints between the lines in the sketch and the edges of the base feature to place the sketch at the desired location.

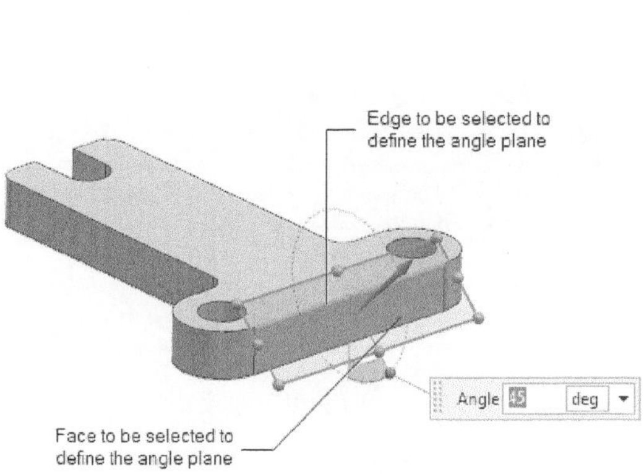

Figure 5-71 *Defining a new datum plane*

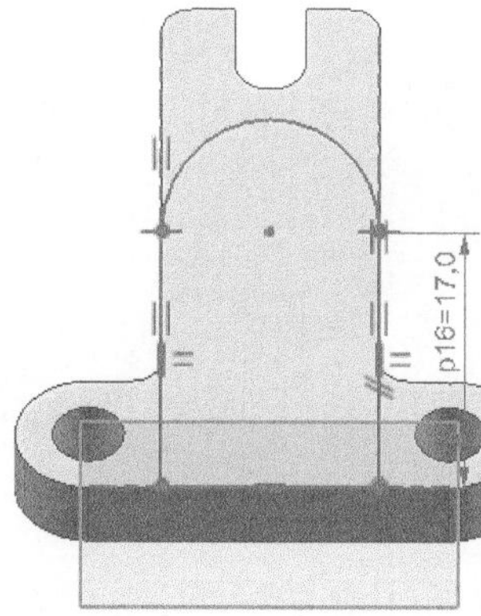

Figure 5-72 *Sketch created for the second feature*

6. Exit the sketching environment and then invoke the **Extrude** dialog box.

7. Select the sketch and then select the **Unite** option from the **Boolean** drop-down list in the dialog box.

8. Select the **Until Next** option from the **End** drop-down list in the **Limits** rollout of the dialog box.

9. Choose the **OK** button from the dialog box; the feature is created.

10. Hide the sketch and the datum plane. Figure 5-73 shows the model after creating the second feature.

Creating the Third Feature

The third feature is an extruded feature and will be created by using the **Subtract** boolean option. The sketch of this feature will be created on the inclined face of the second feature.

1. Select the inclined face of the second feature as the sketching plane and then draw the sketch for the hole. Add the required dimensions and constraints to the circle, refer to Figure 5-68.

2. Exit the sketching environment and then invoke the **Extrude** dialog box.

3. Select the circle and then select the **Subtract** option from the **Boolean** drop-down list in the **Extrude** dialog box.

4. Choose the **Body** button from the **Boolean** rollout if it is not selected by default and then select the existing body from the drawing window; preview of the feature is displayed in the drawing window.

5. Select **Through All** from the **Start** drop-down list in the **Limits** rollout.

6. Choose the **OK** button; the feature is created. Hide the sketch of the circle and then choose the **Fit** tool to fit the model into the screen. The final model for this tutorial is shown in Figure 5-74.

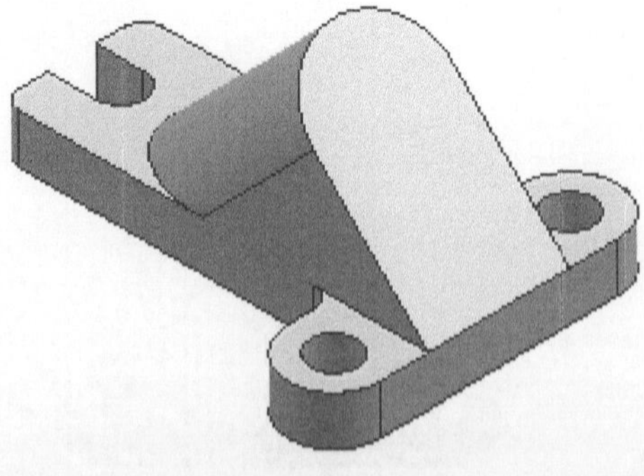

Figure 5-73 Model after creating the second feature on the inclined datum plane

Figure 5-74 Final model for Tutorial 3

Saving and Closing the File

1. Choose **Menu > File > Close > Save and Close** from the **Top Border Bar** to save and close the file.

Self-Evaluation Test

Answer the following questions and then compare them to those given at the end of this chapter:

1. Fixed datum planes are also termed as __________ datum planes.

2. The __________ boolean operation is used to create an extruded feature by removing material from an existing feature.

3. The __________ option is used to create a revolved feature that terminates at a specified face.

4. The __________ option is used to extrude the sketch up to a specified face which does not intersect the sketch in its current size and shape.

5. The __________ option is used to create a plane at an angle to another plane passing through an edge, linear sketched segment, or axis.

6. The __________ boolean operation is used to create an extruded feature by retaining the material common to the existing feature and the sketch.

7. In mechanical designs, all features are created on a single plane. (T/F)

8. When you start a new part file, the fixed datum planes are provided by default. (T/F)

9. You can turn off the display of additional datum planes. (T/F)

10. In NX, you can extrude a sketch to perform only the **Unite** operation. (T/F)

Review Questions

Answer the following questions:

1. Which of the following tools allows you to create additional datum planes?

   (a) **Plane** (b) **Datum Plane**
   (c) **Reference Plane** (d) None of these

2. Which of the following options in the **Insert** menu allows you to project existing entities on the current sketching plane?

   (a) **Project Curve** (b) **Project Edges**
   (c) **Divert** (d) None of these

3. Which of the following operations allows you to join a new feature with an existing feature?

   (a) **Join** (b) **Unite**
   (c) **Combine** (d) None of these

4. Which of the following options allows to you to extrude a sketch from the sketching plane to the next surface that intersects a feature in the specified direction?

   (a) **Until Selected** (b) **Until Next**
   (c) **Value** (d) None of these

5. Which of the following projection output types project external elements as a single continuous spline?

   (a) **Spline** (b) **Spline Segment**
   (c) **Single Spline** (d) None of these

6. If you create an associative datum plane, its name will be displayed as **Fixed Datum Plane** in the **Part Navigator**. (T/F)

7. While creating parallel planes, you can select only a planar face or a surface as reference object. (T/F)

8. After creating a coordinate system, you cannot modify its location. (T/F)

9. The **Until Selected** option is used to extrude a sketch up to a specified face, a datum plane, or a body. (T/F)

10. NX allows you to make the projected sketched entities associative with the original entities. (T/F)

EXERCISES

Exercise 1

Create the model shown in Figure 5-75. The dimensions of the model are shown in Figure 5-75(a). **(Expected time: 30 min)**

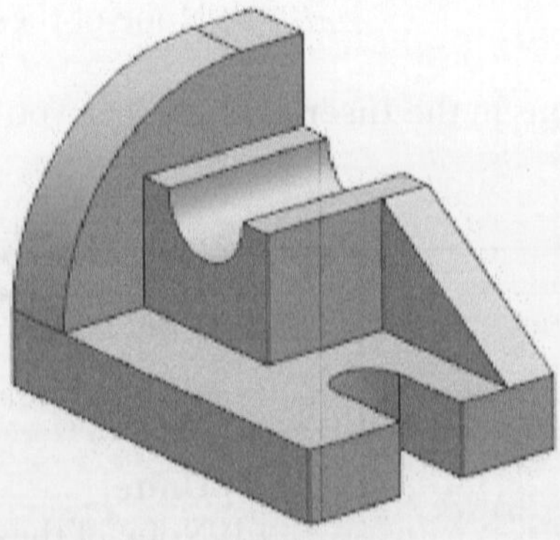

Figure 5-75 *Model for Exercise 1*

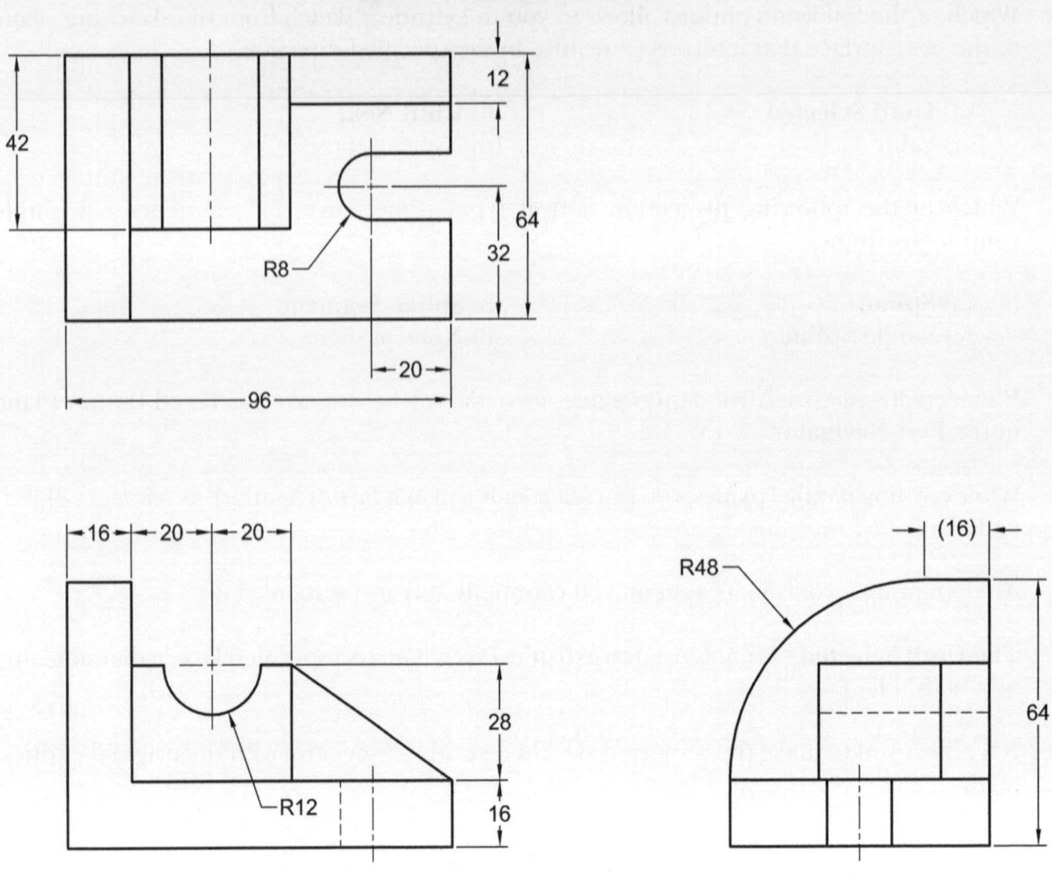

Figure 5-75(a) *Views and dimensions of the model*

Exercise 2

Create the model shown in Figure 5-76. The dimensions of the model are shown in Figure 5-76(a). **(Expected time: 30 min)**

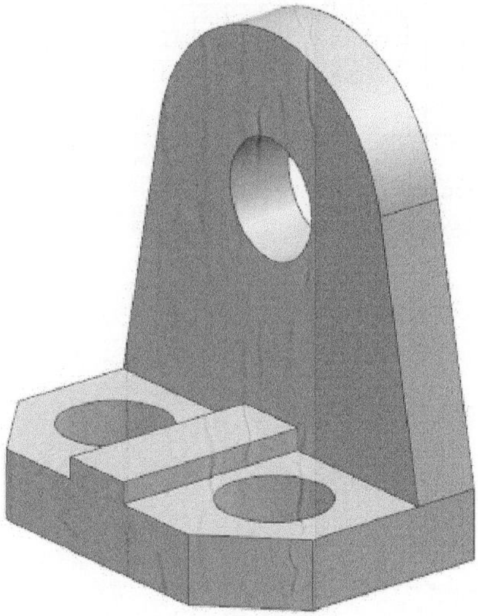

Figure 5-76 *Model for Exercise 2*

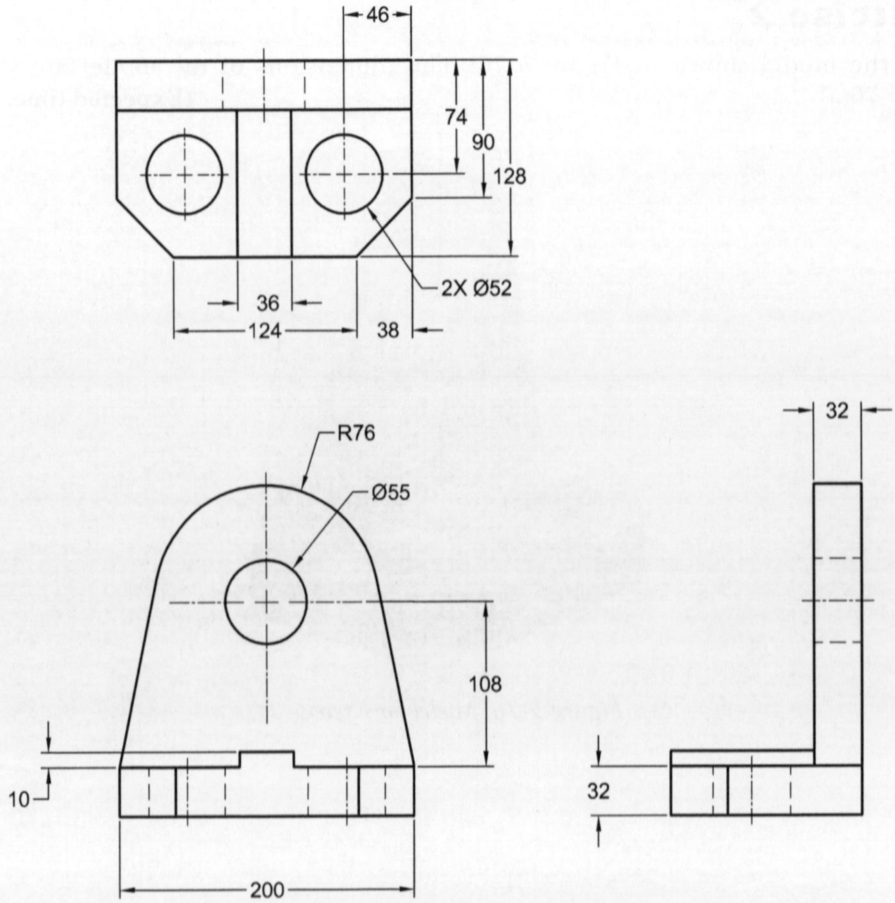

Figure 5-76(a) Views and dimensions of the model

Exercise 3

Create the model shown in Figure 5-77. The dimensions of the model are given in Figure 5-77(a). **(Expected time: 30 min)**

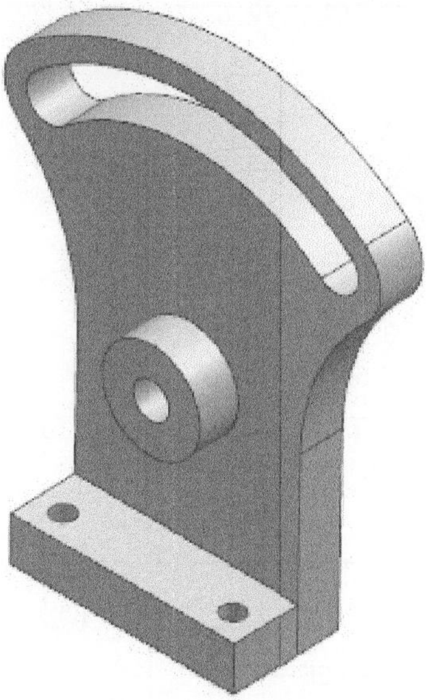

Figure 5-77 *Model for Exercise 3*

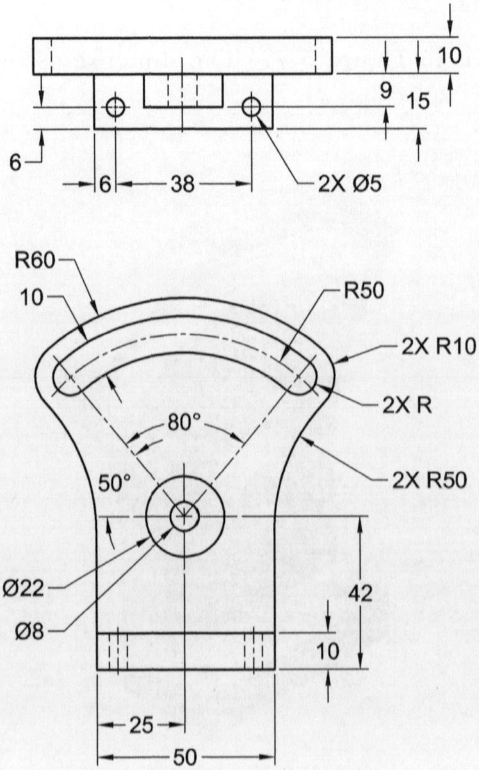

Figure 5-77(a) Dimensions of the model for Exercise 3

Answers to Self-Evaluation Test

1. Principle, **2. Subtract**, **3. Until Selected**, **4. Until Extended**, **5. At Angle**, **6. Intersect**, **7.** F, **8.** F, **9.** T, **10.** F

Chapter 6

Advanced Modeling Tools-I

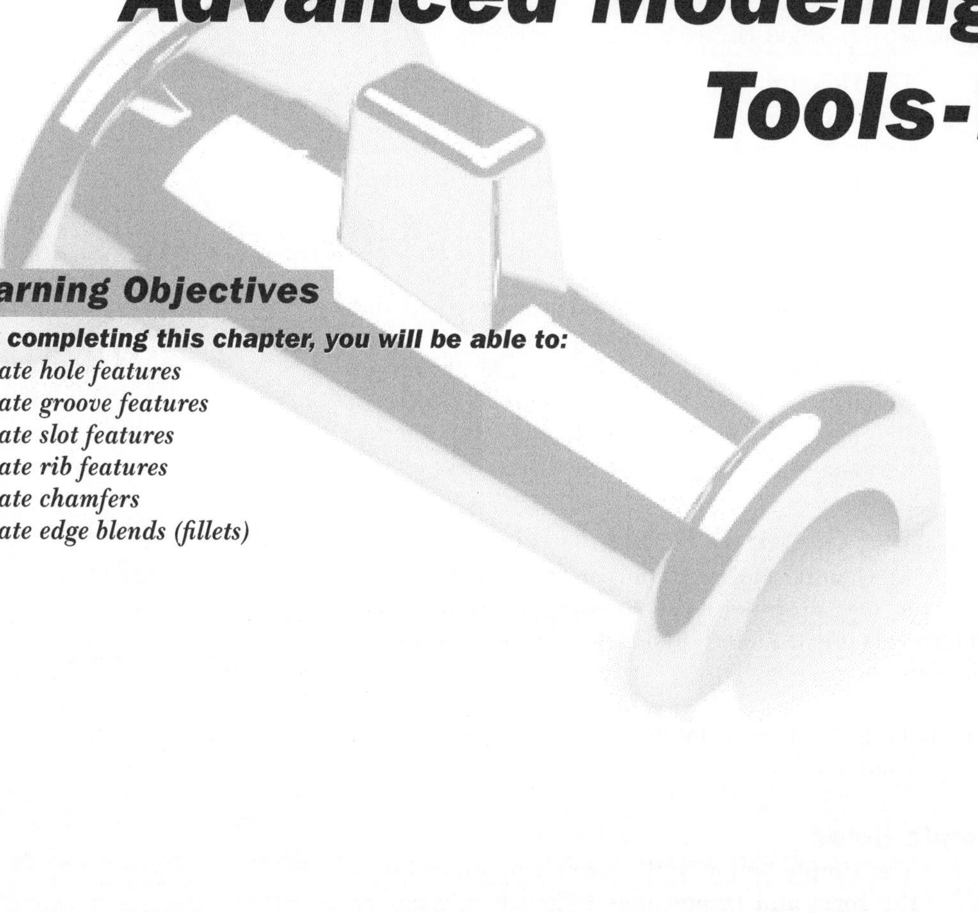

Learning Objectives

After completing this chapter, you will be able to:

- *Create hole features*
- *Create groove features*
- *Create slot features*
- *Create rib features*
- *Create chamfers*
- *Create edge blends (fillets)*

ADVANCED MODELING TOOLS

Advanced modeling tools are mostly used to place different types of standard and user-defined features in a model. Each advanced modeling tool has its specific use in designing a real-world model. Most of the mechanical designs are created using the advanced modeling features such as simple/counterbore/countersink holes, pocket, groove, slot, dart, and so on. NX provides you with a number of advanced modeling tools that assist in creating these advanced features. Note that these features are parametric in nature and can be modified or edited any time. The advanced feature tools are used to reduce the time taken in creating the design. Also, you can create and save user-defined features in NX. These features can be placed any number of times on a model.

CREATING HOLES BY USING THE HOLE TOOL

Ribbon:	Home > Feature > Hole
Menu:	Insert > Design Feature > Hole

The **Hole** tool is used to create a through, blind cylindrical, or conical cutout in a model. A hole can be threaded or non-threaded. To invoke this tool, choose **Home > Feature > Hole** from the **Ribbon**; the **Hole** dialog box will be displayed, as shown in Figure 6-1.

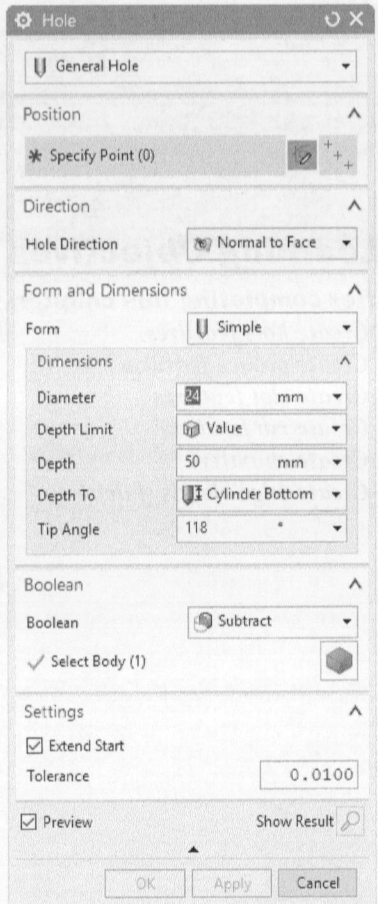

*Figure 6-1 The **Hole** dialog box*

By default, the **General Hole** option is selected in the Type drop-down list and the **Simple** option is selected in the **Form** drop-down list. As a result, you are prompted to select a planar face to sketch or specify points. You can create different types of holes. The different types of holes and the methods to create them are discussed next.

Creating General Holes

The **General Hole** option is selected by default in the Type drop-down list. By using this option, you can create simple, counterbored, countersunk, or tapered hole features.

The methods of creating different types of general holes are discussed next.

Simple Holes

The **Simple** option in the **Form** drop-down list of the **Form and Dimensions** rollout is selected by default. As a result, you are prompted to select a planar face to sketch or specify points. You need to follow two steps to create a simple hole. The first step is to select a face or a point on a face. If you select a point on a face, the preview of the hole will be displayed. If you select a face or a datum plane for the hole feature, the Sketch in Task environment will be invoked and the **Sketch Point** dialog box will be displayed. Also, you will be prompted to define a point. Specify a point at the desired location and choose the **Close** button from the **Sketch Point** dialog box. Next, you can apply the required dimensions to the specified point by using the tools available in the Sketch in Task environment. After applying the dimensions to the specified point, exit from the Sketch in Task environment; the preview of the hole feature will be displayed at the specified point. You can also define multiple points using the **Sketch Point** dialog box to create multiple simple holes at a time.

The second step is to specify the dimensions and parameters of the hole. To do so, enter the diameter of the hole to be created in the **Diameter** edit box of the **Dimensions** sub-rollout of the **Form and Dimensions** rollout. The **Value** option in the **Depth Limit** drop-down list is used to specify the depth and tip angle of the hole in their respective edit boxes. NX allows you to create an angular tip of the hole. By default, **118** is accepted as an ISO tip angle value in the **Tip Angle** edit box. You can enter a different tip angle value in the **Tip Angle** edit box to create an angular tip. To create a through hole in the component, select the **Through Body** option from the **Depth Limit** drop-down list. You can also use the **Until Next** or **Until Selected** option from the **Depth Limit** drop-down list to create a hole as explained in the previous chapter.

In the **Direction** rollout of the dialog box, you can specify the direction of the hole. By default, the **Normal to Face** option is selected in the **Hole Direction** drop-down list. As a result, the hole will be created normal to the selected face. To change the hole direction, select the **Along Vector** option in the **Hole Direction** drop-down list; the **Specify Vector** area will be displayed in the **Direction** rollout. Use this area to specify the hole direction.

After specifying the hole parameters, choose the **Apply** button; the hole will be created based on the specified parameters. Next, choose the **Cancel** button to exit from the dialog box.

Counterbored Holes

To create a counterbored hole, invoke the **Hole** dialog box by choosing the **Hole** tool from the **Feature** group of the **Home** tab. Select the **Counterbored** option from the **Form** drop-down list in the **Hole** dialog box and follow the first step as explained earlier; the preview of the counterbored hole will be displayed. Also, its parameters will be displayed below the **Form** drop-down list. Next, enter the c-bore diameter, c-bore depth, and diameter in their respective edit boxes in the **Dimensions** sub-rollout. The other options are similar to the options discussed earlier in this chapter.

Countersunk Holes

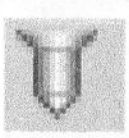

To create a countersunk hole, invoke the **Hole** dialog box by choosing the **Hole** tool from the **Feature** group of the **Home** tab. Select the **Countersunk** option from the **Form** drop-down list and follow the first step as explained earlier; the preview of the countersunk hole will be displayed. Also, its parameters will be displayed below the **Form** drop-down list. Next, enter the c-sink diameter, c-sink angle, and diameter in their respective edit boxes in the **Dimensions** sub-rollout. The other options are similar to those discussed earlier in this chapter.

Tapered Holes

To create a tapered hole, select the **Tapered** option from the **Form** drop-down list in the **Hole** dialog box and follow the first step as explained earlier; the preview of the tapered hole will be displayed. Also, its parameters will be displayed below the **Form** drop-down list. You can specify the taper angle in the **Taper Angle** edit box.

Creating Drill Size Hole

The **Drill Size Hole** option of the Type drop-down list is used to create a simple drill size hole feature using the ANSI or ISO standard by specifying its respective parameters in the **Standard** drop-down list of the **Settings** rollout. To create a drill size hole, select this option from the Type drop-down list and specify the placement point of the hole as discussed in the first step of creating general holes. Note that as soon as you select the **Drill Size Hole** option, the **Form and Dimensions** rollout will be modified. The options in this rollout are discussed next. Figure 6-2 shows various parameters associated with the drill size hole.

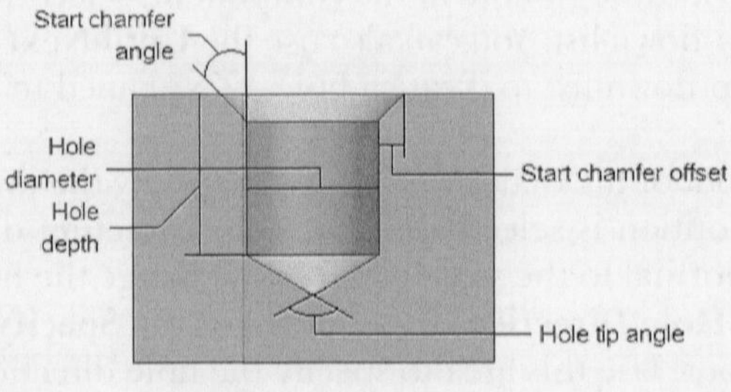

***Figure 6-2** Various parameters of the drill size hole*

Form and Dimensions Rollout

You can select a standard diameter for the drill size hole in the **Size** drop-down list of this rollout. The specified dimension in this drop-down list will apply only if the **Exact** option is selected in the **Fit** drop-down list which is available below the **Size** drop-down list of this rollout. In this rollout, three more sub-rollouts **Dimensions, Start Chamfer**, and **End Chamfer** are available. These sub-rollouts are discussed next.

Dimensions

The **Diameter** edit box of this sub-rollout will be activated only if the **Custom** option is selected in the **Fit** drop-down list. This edit box is used to specify the diameter of the hole. You can also specify the depth and tip angle of the hole by using their respective edit boxes in this sub-rollout.

Start Chamfer

The options of this sub-rollout will be available only when the **Custom** option is selected in the **Fit** drop-down list. If you clear the **Enable** check box in this sub-rollout, all options in this rollout will be deactivated and a sharp edge will be generated at the starting plane of the resultant hole. In the **Offset** edit box, you can specify the chamfer depth. In the **Angle** edit box, you can specify the chamfer angle of the resultant hole at the starting plane of the hole.

End Chamfer

The options in this sub-rollout are similar to the options of the **Start Chamfer** sub-rollout with the only difference that the options in this sub-rollout are used to specify chamfer settings at the end of the hole.

After specifying all required parameters for the drill size hole, choose the **OK** button in the **Hole** dialog box; the hole will be created.

Creating Screw Clearance Hole

On selecting the **Screw Clearance Hole** option from the drop-down list in the **Type** rollout, you can create simple, counterbore, or countersunk screw clearance hole features according to the standard specified in the **Standard** drop-down list of the **Settings** rollout. If you choose this option from the Type drop-down list, the **Form and Dimensions** rollout will be modified. Most of the options in this rollout are the same as those discussed earlier in this chapter. You can select the required screw type option from the **Screw Type** drop-down list in the **Form and Dimensions** rollout. The options in the **Screw Type** drop-down list are displayed based on the option selected in the **Form** drop-down list. In the **Fit** drop-down list, you can specify the required fit for the hole such as interference (press) fit, transition fit, or loose fit by selecting the **Close(H12)**, **Normal(H13)**, or **Loose(H14)** option, respectively. You can specify the neck chamfer for the counterbore hole in the **Neck Chamfer** sub-rollout and relief depth for the countersunk hole in the **Relief** sub-rollout, respectively.

Creating Threaded Hole

The **Threaded Hole** option in the Type drop-down list is used to create a threaded hole. The standard of a threaded hole depends on the option selected in the **Standard** drop-down list of the **Settings** rollout. You can specify the required size of the standard threaded hole by selecting the options from the **Size** drop-down list available in the **Thread Dimensions** sub-rollout of the **Form and Dimensions** rollout. In the **Radial Engage** drop-down list available below the **Size** drop-down list, you can specify the percentage of radial engagement which is used to calculate the tap drill diameter, refer to Figures 6-3 and 6-4. The **Tap Drill Diameter** edit box will be activated only when the **Custom** option is selected from the **Radial Engage** drop-down list. In this edit box, you can specify the customized value of the tap drill diameter. Similarly, you can specify the standard thread depth by selecting the required option from the **Depth Type** drop-down list. To enter the customized thread depth value, select the **Custom** option from the **Depth Type** drop-down list if not already selected; the **Thread Depth** edit box will be displayed below the **Depth Type** drop-down list. In this edit box, you can specify the thread depth value of the hole. In the **Handedness** area of the **Form and Dimensions** rollout, you can specify the right hand thread or the left hand thread by selecting the **Right Handed** or **Left Handed** radio button, respectively.

Note

If the threaded holes are created by using the ***Threaded Hole*** *option, then the threads are represented by dashed lines. These threads are known as symbolic threads. Figures 6-3 and 6-4 are for your reference only. To view these symbolic threads, change the display of the model to Static Wireframe.*

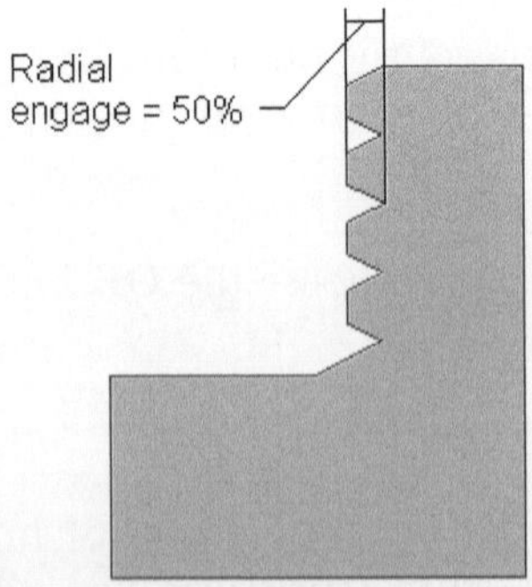

Figure 6-3 Radial engage = 50%

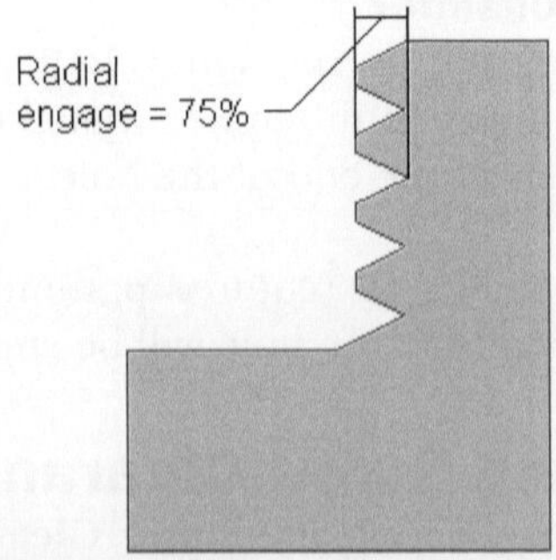

Figure 6-4 Radial engage = 75%

Creating Hole Series

You can use the **Hole Series** option to create an aligned series of holes in multiple bodies, refer to Figure 6-5. If you select this option from the Type drop-down list, the **Specification** rollout will be displayed with three tabs. These tabs are discussed next.

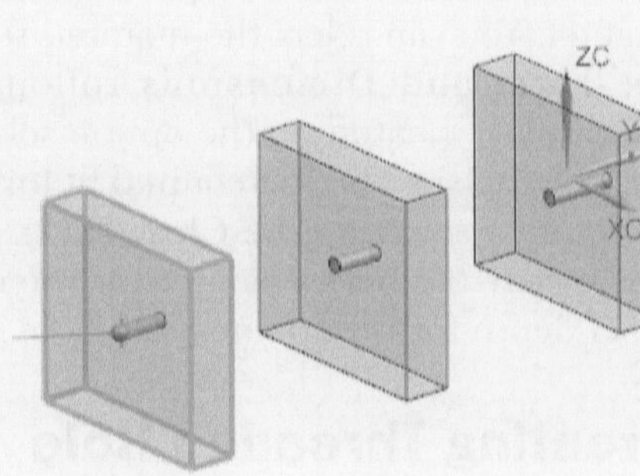

Figure 6-5 Aligned series of holes

The Start Tab

This tab is used to specify the parameters of a hole in the first body. The options in this tab are similar to those discussed earlier in this chapter.

The Middle Tab

This tab is used to specify the parameters of a hole in the middle body. The middle body hole is defined as the hole that lies in the middle body. By default, the **Match Dimensions of Start Hole** check box is chosen in this tab. As a result, all dimensions of the hole match to the hole in the first body. To create a user-defined hole, clear this check box and select the **Custom** option from the **Fit** drop-down list; all parameters in this tab will be activated.

The End Tab

This tab is used to specify the parameters of the hole on the last body.

Boolean Rollout

This rollout is used to specify the boolean operations on a body. By default, the **Subtract** option is selected in the **Boolean** drop-down list of this rollout. As a result, the material is removed from the body based on the specification of the hole in the resultant body. You can also deselect the selected body for a boolean operation. To do so, choose the **Body** button from the **Select Body** area; the selected body will be highlighted in the graphic area. Next, press the SHIFT key and select the highlighted body; the selected body will not be considered while performing the boolean operation.

Settings Rollout

You can select the desired standard option from the **Standard** drop-down list of this rollout. The **Standard** drop-down list is available for all options other than the **General Hole** option of the Type drop-down list. Also, you can specify the predefined tolerance value in the **Tolerance** edit box in this rollout.

CREATING GROOVES

Ribbon:	Home > Feature > Design Feature Drop-down > Groove *(Customize to Add)*
Menu:	Insert > Design Feature > Groove

Grooves are the channels that are created on the outer surface of a cylinderical part or a conical feature. The groove operation can only be performed on the features that have their own center axis. To create grooves, choose the **Groove** tool from the **Design Feature Drop-down** of the **Feature** group in the **Home** tab; the **Groove** dialog box will be displayed, as shown in Figure 6-6. Also, you will be prompted to choose the required groove type. In NX, you can create three types of grooves. The procedures for creating these grooves are discussed next.

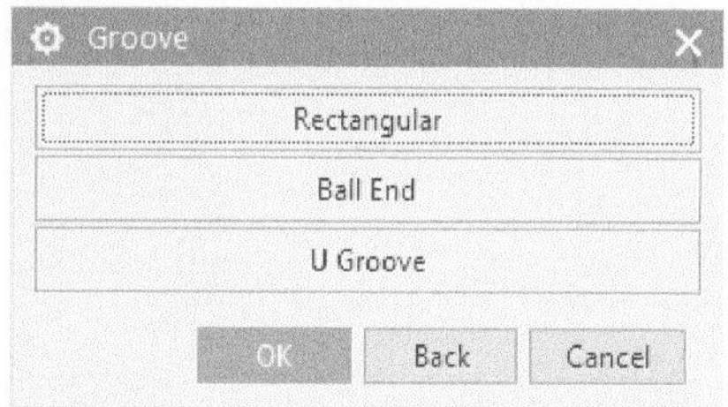

*Figure 6-6 The **Groove** dialog box*

Creating Rectangular Grooves

To create a rectangular groove, choose the **Rectangular** button from the **Groove** dialog box; the **Rectangular Groove** dialog box will be displayed, as shown in Figure 6-7, and you will be prompted to select the placement face.

You can only select a conical or cylindrical face as the placement face. Select the placement face; the **Rectangular Groove** dialog box will be modified, refer to Figure 6-8. Next, you need to specify the groove diameter. The diameter value entered in the **Groove Diameter** edit box is always maintained from the central axis of the model. The remaining portion, which is left out from the placement face, will be removed from the channel. Also, you need to enter the width value for the channel in the **Width** edit box of the dialog box.

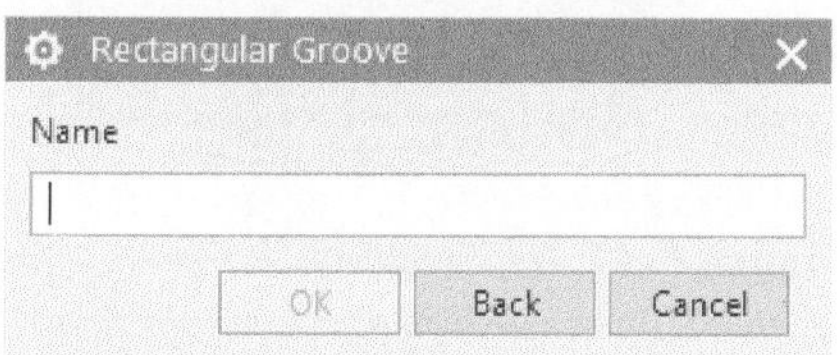

*Figure 6-7 The **Rectangular Groove** dialog box*

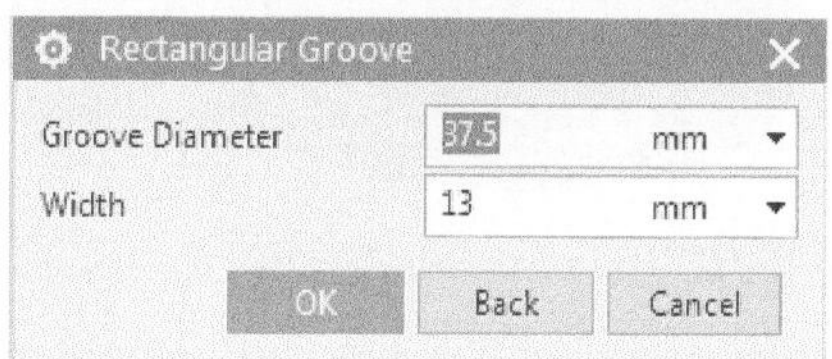

*Figure 6-8 The modified **Rectangular Groove** dialog box*

After specifying the width and diameter for the groove, choose the **OK** button from the **Rectangular Groove** dialog box; the **Position Groove** dialog box along with a preview of the groove feature will be displayed. Also, you will be prompted to select the target edge or choose the **OK** button to accept the initial position. Now, you can choose the **OK** button from the dialog box to create a groove at the current position. You can also position the groove at some other desired location. To do so, select an edge from the model, refer to Figure 6-9. On doing so, you will be prompted to select the tool edge. Select the edge from the tool (groove), refer to Figure 6-9. On selecting the tool edge, the **Create Expression** dialog box will be displayed. Enter the distance value in the edit box and choose the **OK** button; the groove feature will be created. The value specified in the **Create Expression** dialog box is the distance between the target edge and the tool edge. Once the feature is created, close the dialog box. Figure 6-10 shows a rectangular groove feature created using the selections made in Figure 6-9. Figure 6-11 shows the groove feature created by specifying 0 mm as the distance between the target edge and the tool edge.

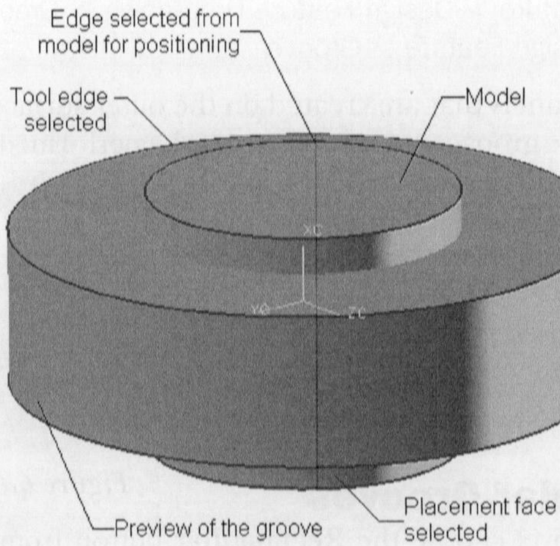

***Figure 6-9** Preview of the groove feature with the edges and model to be selected*

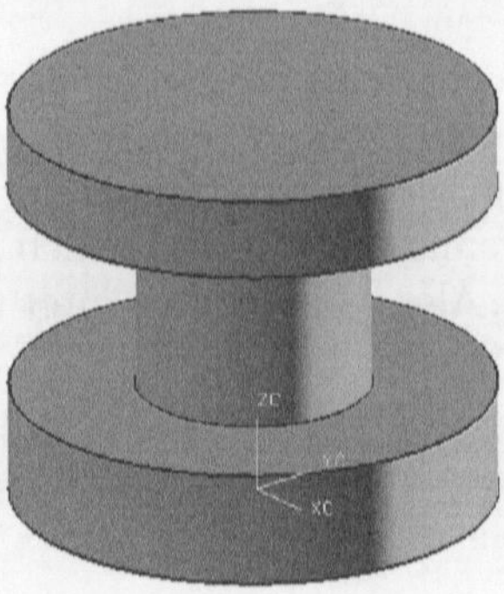

***Figure 6-10** The rectangular groove feature*

***Figure 6-11** The rectangular groove feature created with the distance between the target edge and the tool edge as 0*

Note

*1. If you enter 0 mm value in the **Groove Diameter** edit box, the **Message** window will be displayed and you will be informed that you have entered an invalid rectangular groove diameter. Similarly, if you enter a value larger than or equal to the diameter of the model in the **Groove Diameter** edit box, again the **Message** window will be displayed and you will be informed that the original face cannot be replaced.*

2. You can modify the parameters defined for the groove even after creating it. To edit the groove parameters, double-click on the groove feature; the ***Edit Parameters*** *dialog box will be displayed. You can also invoke the* ***Edit Parameters*** *dialog box by right-clicking on the feature name in the* ***Part Navigator*** *area. Choose the* ***Feature Dialog*** *button to edit the parameters.*

Creating Ball End Grooves

To create a ball end groove, invoke the **Groove** dialog box and choose the **Ball End** button from it; the **Ball End Groove** dialog box will be displayed and you will be prompted to select the placement face. You can select only a conical or a cylindrical face as the placement face. Planar faces cannot be selected for this feature. Select the placement face; the modified **Ball End Groove** dialog box will be displayed, as shown in Figure 6-12, and you will be prompted to enter the groove parameters.

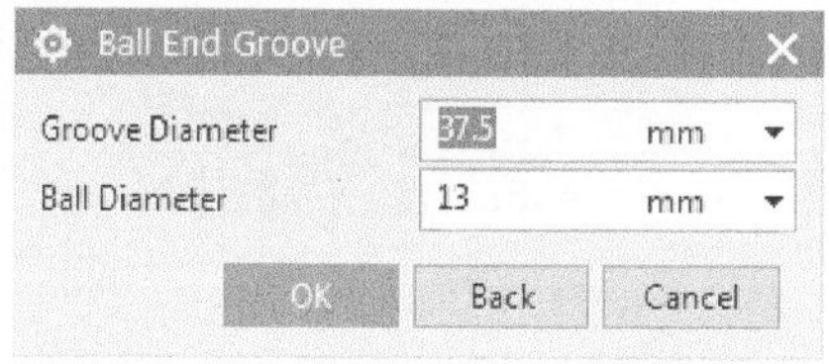

Figure 6-12 *The modified* ***Ball End Groove*** *dialog box*

In this dialog box, you need to specify the groove and ball diameters. The value entered in the **Groove Diameter** edit box is always maintained from the central axis of the model. The remaining portion of the selected placement face is removed from the channel. Enter the ball end diameter in the **Ball Diameter** edit box and choose the **OK** button; the **Position Groove** dialog box along with the preview of the groove feature will be displayed. Also, you will be prompted to select the target edge. Figure 6-13 shows a preview of the groove feature. To position the groove, select an edge from the model, refer to Figure 6-13; you will be prompted to select the tool edge (groove). Select an edge from the tool, refer to Figure 6-13; the **Create Expression** dialog box will be displayed. Enter the distance value in its respective edit box and choose the **OK** button to create the groove feature. Once the feature is created, close the dialog box. Figure 6-14 shows a ball end groove feature created using the selections made in Figure 6-13. Figure 6-15 shows the groove feature created by specifying the distance between the target edge and the tool edge as 0 mm.

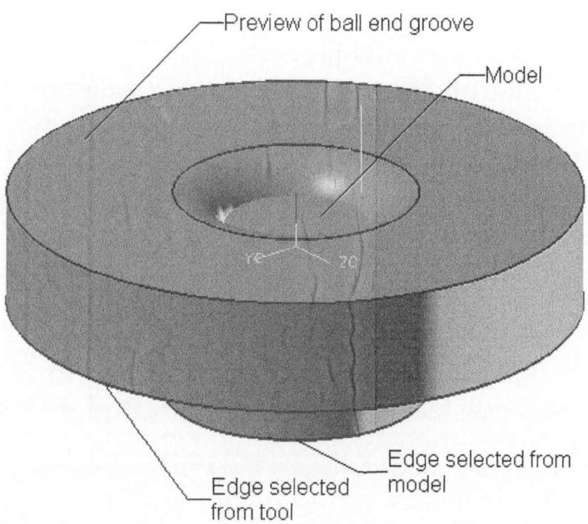

Figure 6-13 *The preview of the ball end groove feature with the edges and model to be selected*

Figure 6-14 The ball end groove feature created

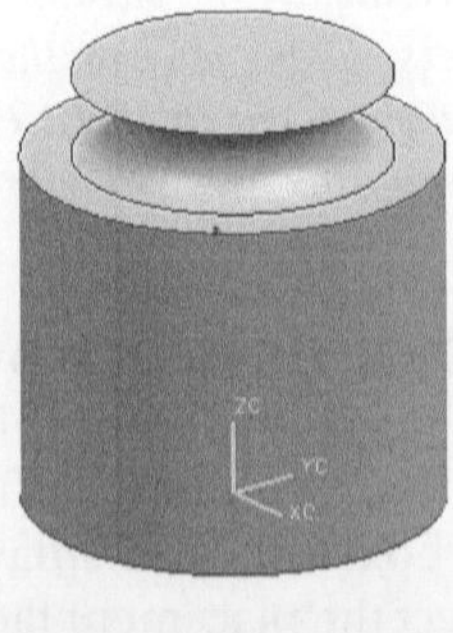

Figure 6-15 The ball end groove feature created with the distance between the target and tool edge as 0 mm

Creating U Grooves

To create a U groove, choose the **U Groove** button in the **Groove** dialog box; the **U Groove** dialog box will be displayed and you will be prompted to select the placement face. You can select a conical or a cylindrical face as the placement face. Select the placement face; the modified **U Groove** dialog box will be displayed, as shown in Figure 6-16 and you will be prompted to enter the groove parameters.

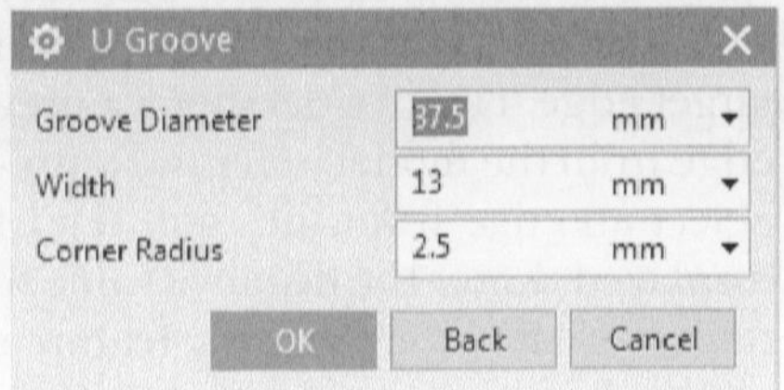

*Figure 6-16 The modified **U Groove** dialog box displaying the groove parameters*

Enter the diameter value of the U groove in the **Groove Diameter** edit box. The value entered for the groove diameter is always maintained from the central axis of the model and the remaining portion of the selected placement face is removed from the channel. Next, you need to specify the width value and the corner radius for the groove. Enter the values for the width and the corner radius of the groove in their respective edit boxes in the dialog box. The width value must be greater than twice the corner radius value. The edges formed between the normal faces due to the formation of this groove will automatically be filleted. The value entered in the **Corner Radius** edit box will be used as the fillet radius. After you specify the groove parameters, choose the **OK** button; the **Position Groove** dialog box will be displayed. A preview of the groove feature will be displayed in the graphic window, refer to Figure 6-17. Also, you will be prompted to select the target edge from the model.

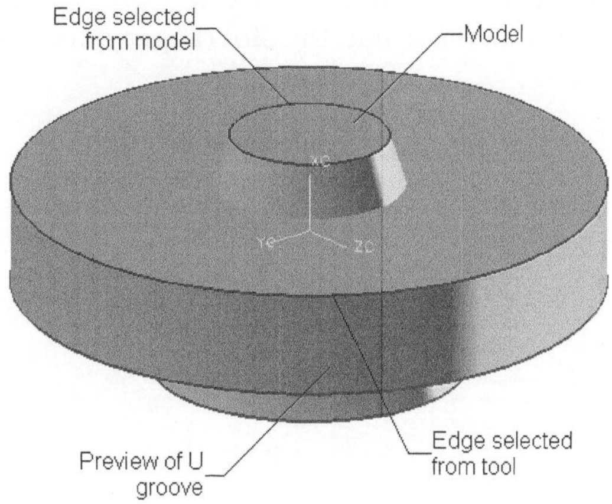

Figure 6-17 *The preview of the U groove feature*

To position the groove, select an edge from the model, refer to Figure 6-17; you will be prompted to select the tool edge (groove). Select the edge from the tool, refer to Figure 6-17; the **Create Expression** dialog box will be displayed. Enter the distance value in its respective edit box and choose the **OK** button to create the groove feature, refer to Figure 6-18. Once the feature is created, close the dialog box. Figure 6-19 shows the groove feature created by specifying the distance between the target edge and the tool edge as 0 mm.

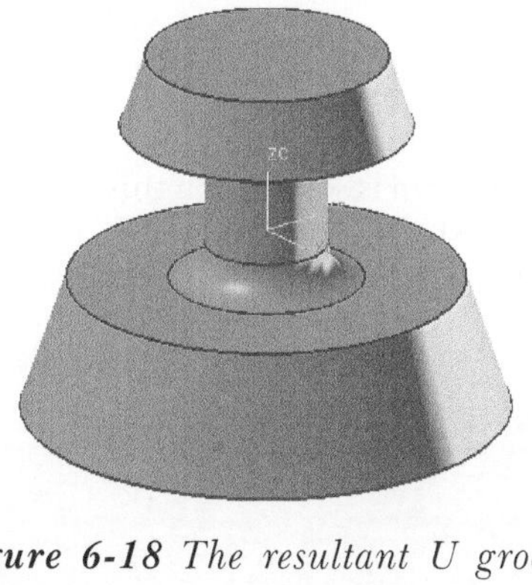

Figure 6-18 *The resultant U groove feature*

Figure 6-19 *The U groove feature created with the distance between the target edge and the tool edge as 0 mm*

CREATING SLOTS

Slots are the cutout features created on the planar surface of a model which can be used as a guide way for another component to slide over it. Note that you need to customize the **Slot** tool to add it to your desired location as it is currently hidden in this release of NX. To do so, type **Slot** in the **Command Finder** and press ENTER; the **Command Finder** dialog box will be displayed with a list of tools in the **6 Matches for: Slot** area, refer to Figure 6-20(a). Next, drag the cursor over the **Slot (Legacy)** tool which is the last tool displayed in this list; it will be highlighted in blue color. Also, a down arrow will be displayed at the right of the highlighted window. Click on the down arrow; a flyout will be displayed. Next, choose **Add to Ribbon Tab > Home** from the flyout; the **Slot (Legacy)** tool will be added to the **Home** tab of the **Ribbon**.

*Figure 6-20(a) The **Command Finder** dialog box*

Choose the **Slot (Legacy)** tool; the **Slot** dialog box will be displayed, refer to Figure 6-20(b). By default, the **Rectangular** radio button will be selected in this dialog box. In NX, you can create five different types of slots. The procedure to create these different type of slots is discussed next.

Creating Rectangular Slots

Rectangular slots are the ones that have a rectangular cross-section. To create a rectangular slot, invoke the **Slot** dialog box. By default, the **Rectangular** radio button is selected in this dialog box. Choose the **OK** button from the dialog box; the **Rectangular Slot** dialog box will be displayed, as shown in Figure 6-21, and you will be prompted to select a planar placement face.

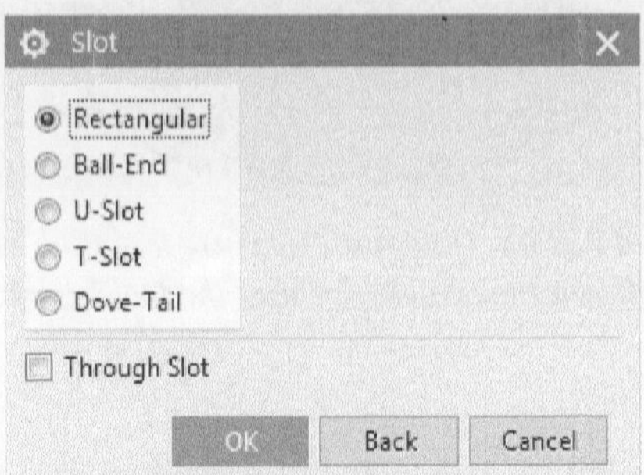

*Figure 6-20(b) The **Slot** dialog box*

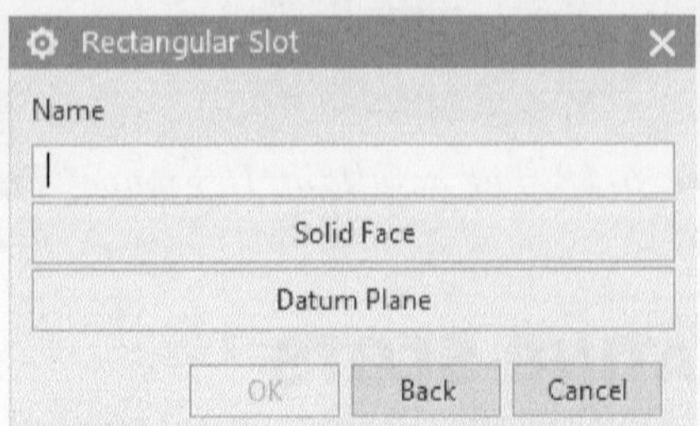

*Figure 6-21 The **Rectangular Slot** dialog box*

You can specify a datum plane or a planar face as the placement face for the slot. To specify a datum plane as the placement face, choose the **Datum Plane** button in this dialog box and select a datum plane. Otherwise, choose the **Solid Face** button from the dialog box and select a planar face.

After specifying the placement face, the **Horizontal Reference** dialog box will be displayed, as shown in Figure 6-22. Next, you need to define the reference object, which will determine the orientation of the slot. You can use various options in this dialog box to select a particular reference object for defining the orientation of the slot. The slot is always oriented parallel to the direction of the selected reference object. Specify the reference object for the slot; the **Rectangular Slot** dialog box will be displayed, as shown in Figure 6-23. The default parameters for the slot will be displayed in the **Rectangular Slot** dialog box. Enter the required slot parameter values such as the length, width, and depth in their respective edit boxes in the dialog box.

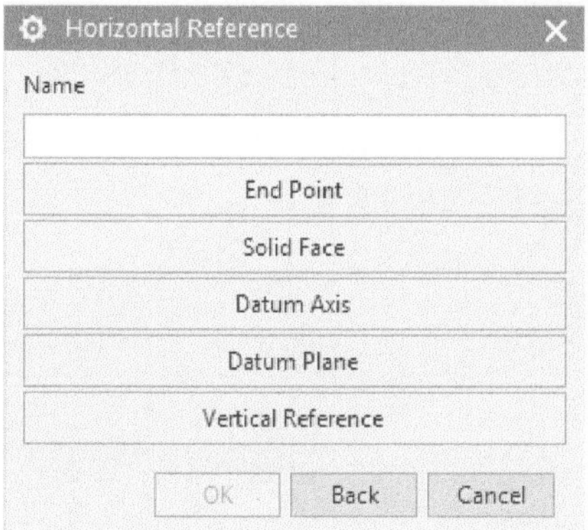

*Figure 6-22 The **Horizontal Reference** dialog box*

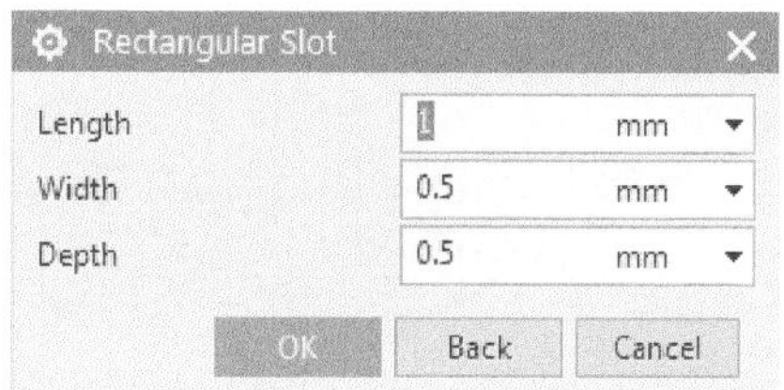

*Figure 6-23 The modified **Rectangular Slot** dialog box*

Note

*To create a through-slot along length, you need to select the **Through Slot** check box from the **Slot** dialog box. As a result, you need to define the start and end faces for defining the length value. The faces selected to define the through-width should always be normal to the placement face. Select two faces that are parallel to each other and perpendicular to the placement face. Next, choose the **OK** button; the **Rectangular Slot** dialog box will be displayed. Specify the slot parameters in the respective edit boxes. In this case, the **Length** edit box will not be available. Figure 6-24 shows the faces selected to define the length of the through-slot. Figure 6-25 shows the through-slot created on a model.*

After specifying the slot parameters, choose the **OK** button from this dialog box; a preview of the slot will be displayed, refer to Figure 6-26. Also, the **Positioning** dialog box will be displayed. Next, position the slot using the **Positioning** dialog box and then choose the **OK** button from the same dialog box; the slot will be created, refer to Figure 6-27. Next, exit from the **Rectangular Slot** dialog box by choosing the **Cancel** button.

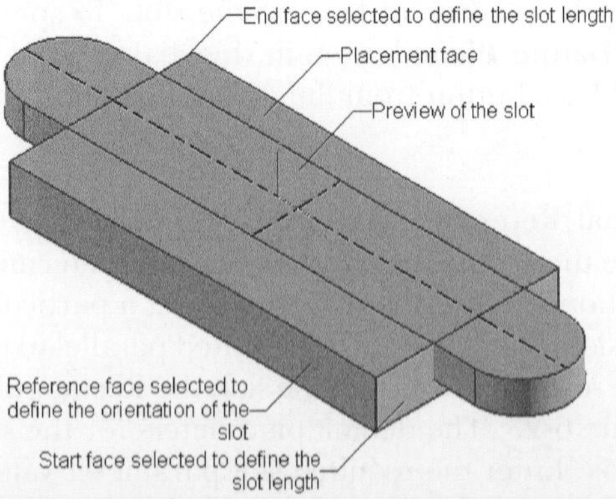

Figure 6-24 The preview of the through-slot

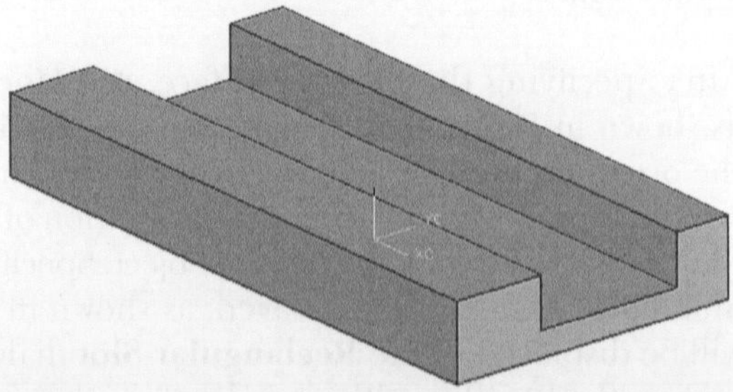

Figure 6-25 Model with a through-slot feature

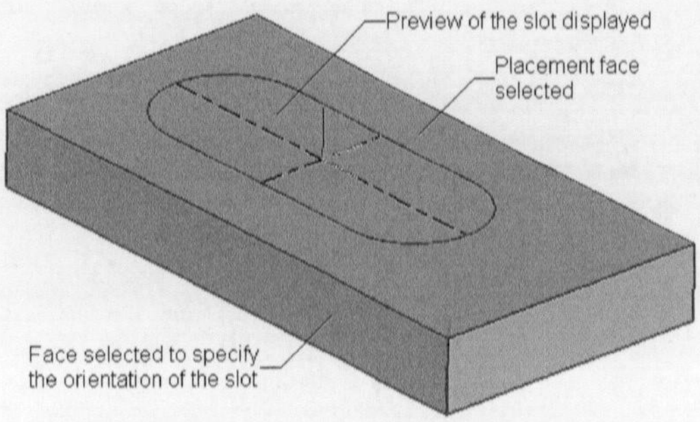

Figure 6-26 The preview of the slot feature

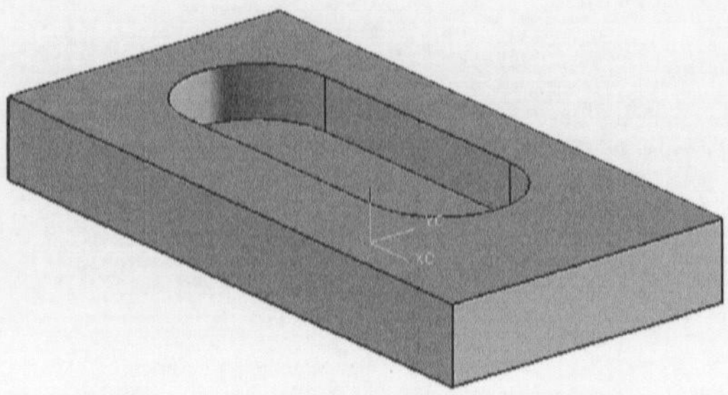

Figure 6-27 Model with a slot feature

Creating Ball-End Slots

The ball-end slots are the ones that have the rectangular cross-section with the filleted base and filleted side edges. The fillet radius will be half the width of the slot. To create this type of slot, select the **Ball-End** radio button from the **Slot** dialog box and then choose the **OK** button; the **Ball Slot** dialog box will be displayed and you will be prompted to select a planar placement face. You can specify a datum plane or a planar face as the placement face for the slot. To specify a datum plane as the placement face, choose the **Datum Plane** button from this dialog box and select a datum plane. Otherwise, choose the **Solid Face** button from this dialog box and select a planar face. As soon as you specify the placement face; the **Horizontal Reference** dialog box will be displayed. You need to define the reference object that will determine the orientation of the slot. You can use the options in this dialog box to select a particular reference object for defining the orientation of the slot. The slot is always oriented parallel to the direction of the reference object selected. Specify the orientation for the slot; the **Ball Slot** dialog box will be displayed with the default slot parameters, as shown in Figure 6-28.

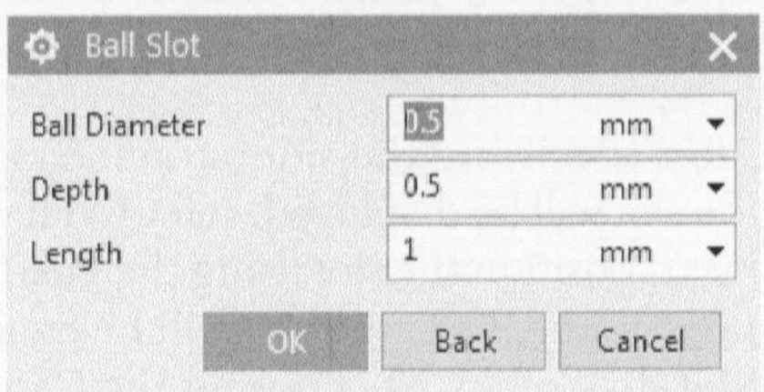

*Figure 6-28 The **Ball Slot** dialog box*

Enter the slot parameter values such as ball diameter, length, and depth in their respective edit boxes in the **Ball Slot** dialog box. Note that the value of slot depth must be greater than the ball radius value.

Note

If you have selected the ***Through Slot*** *check box from the* ***Slot*** *dialog box, you need to define the start and end faces for defining the length value. The faces selected to define the through-width should always be normal to the placement face. Select the two faces that are parallel to each other and normal to the placement face. After selecting the parallel faces, the* ***Ball Slot*** *dialog box will be displayed. Next, specify the slot parameters in their respective edit boxes. In this case, the* ***Length*** *edit box will not be available. Figure 6-29 shows the faces selected to define the length of the through-slot.*

After specifying the slot parameters, choose the **OK** button from this dialog box; a preview of the slot will be displayed, as shown in Figure 6-30, and the **Positioning** dialog box will be displayed. The tools in this dialog box are used to position the slot.

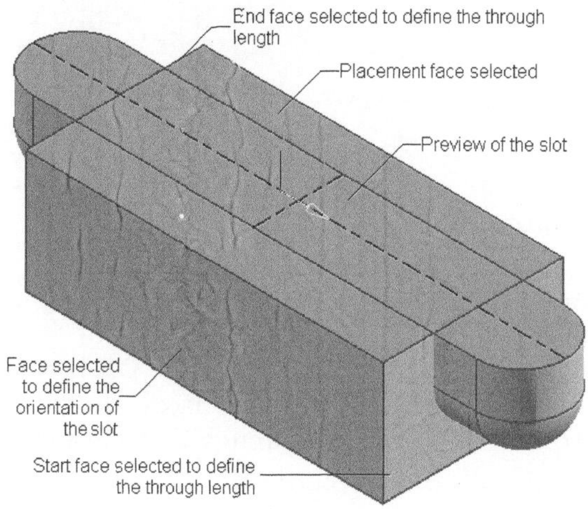

Figure 6-29 *Objects selected to create a through-slot feature*

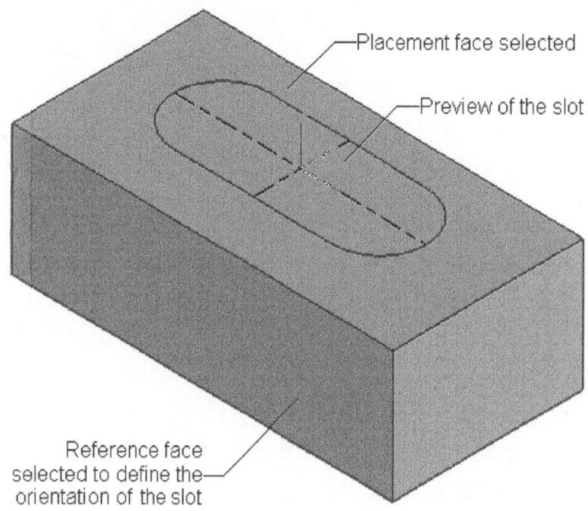

Figure 6-30 *Preview of the ball-end slot feature*

After positioning the slot, choose the **OK** button in the dialog box to create the slot. Figure 6-31 shows the ball-end slot. Figure 6-32 shows the through ball-end slot created on the model.

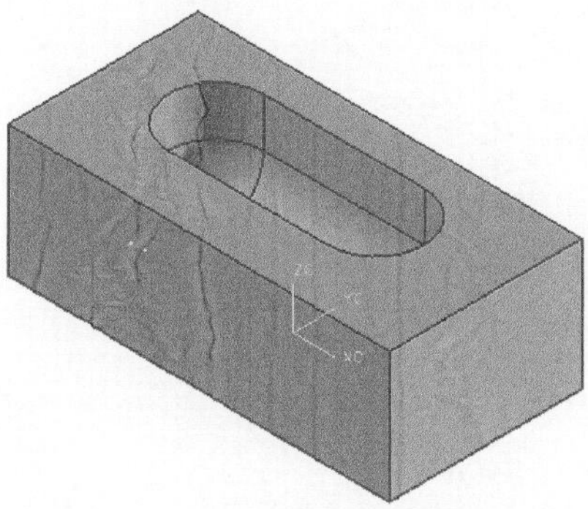

Figure 6-31 *The ball-end slot feature*

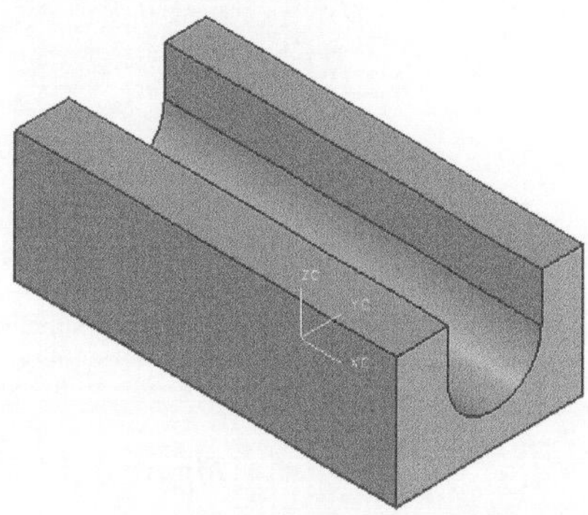

Figure 6-32 *The through ball-end slot feature*

Creating U-Slots

To create a U-slot, select the **U-Slot** radio button in the **Slot** dialog box and then, choose the **OK** button; the **U Slot** dialog box will be displayed and you will be prompted to select a planar placement face. You can specify a datum plane or a planar face as the placement face for the slot. If you need to specify a datum plane as the placement face, choose the **Datum Plane** button and select a datum plane. Otherwise, choose the **Solid Face** button and select a planar face. After you have specified the placement face, the **Horizontal Reference** dialog box will be displayed. You need to define the reference object that will determine the orientation of the slot. You can use the options listed in this dialog box to select a particular reference object for defining the orientation of the slot. The U-slot is always oriented parallel to the direction of the reference object selected. Specify the orientation for the slot; the **U Slot** dialog box will be displayed with default slot parameters, refer to Figure 6-33. Enter the slot parameter values such as corner radius, length, width, and depth in their respective edit boxes in this dialog box. Note that the corner radius of the U-slot must be less than half of its width. Also, it should be less than the depth of slot.

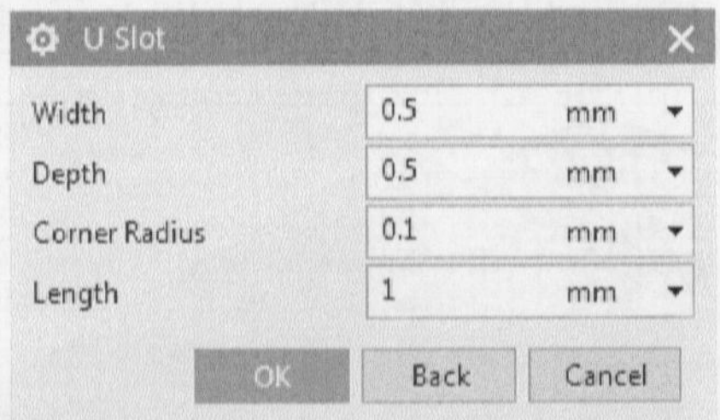

Figure 6-33 *The* ***U Slot*** *dialog box displaying the slot parameters*

After specifying the slot parameters, choose the **OK** button from the **U Slot** dialog box; a preview of the U-slot will be displayed, refer to Figure 6-34. Also, the **Positioning** dialog box will be displayed. The options in this dialog box are used to position the slot. After positioning the slot, choose the **OK** button to create the slot. Figure 6-35 shows the preview of the through U-slot with the faces selected to define the length of the slot. Figures 6-36 and 6-37 show the U-slot and through U-slot features, respectively.

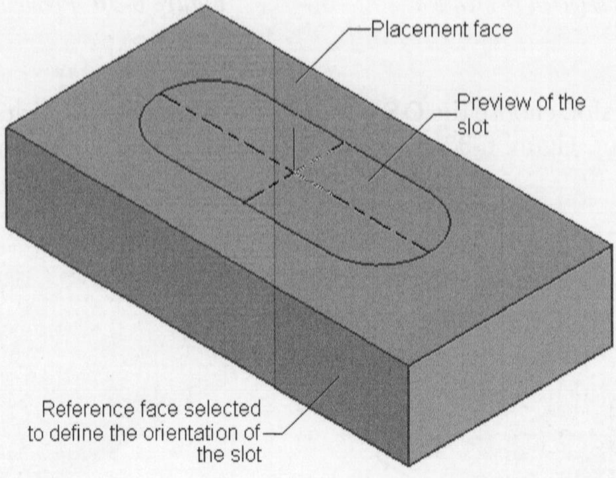

Figure 6-34 *Preview of the U-slot feature*

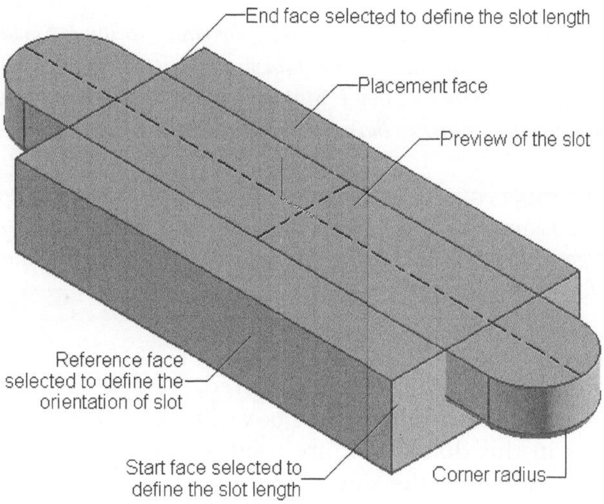

Figure 6-35 *Preview of the through U-slot feature*

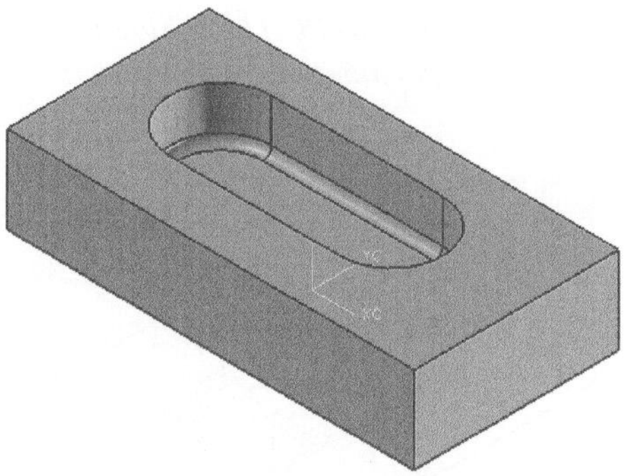

Figure 6-36 *The U-slot feature*

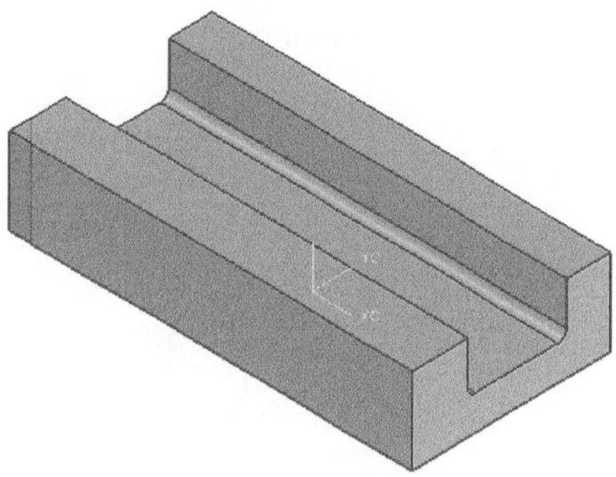

Figure 6-37 *The through U-slot feature*

Creating T-Slots

To create a T-slot, select the **T-Slot** radio button from the **Slot** dialog box and then choose the **OK** button; the **T Slot** dialog box will be displayed and you will be prompted to select a planar placement face. You can specify a datum plane or a planar face as the placement face for the slot. If you need to specify a datum plane as the placement face, choose the **Datum Plane** button and select a datum plane. Otherwise, choose the **Solid Face** button to select a planar face. After you have specified the placement face, the **Horizontal Reference** dialog box will be displayed. You need to define the reference object that will determine the orientation of the slot. You can use different options available in this dialog box to select a particular reference object for defining the orientation of the slot. The slot is always oriented parallel to the direction of the reference object selected. On specifying the orientation of the slot, the slot parameters will be displayed in the **T Slot** dialog box, as shown in Figure 6-38. Enter the slot parameter values such as the top width, top depth, bottom width, bottom depth, and length in their respective edit boxes.

Note

*1. If you enter the bottom width value less than or equal to the top width value, the **Message** window will be displayed and you will be informed about the same. To fix this error, choose the **OK** button from the same window; the **T Slot** dialog box will be displayed. Now, again enter the bottom width value which is larger than the top width value.*

*2. If you enter the length value less than or equal to the bottom width value, the **Message** window will be displayed and you will be informed about the same. To fix this error, choose the **OK** button from the **Message** window; the **T Slot** dialog box will be displayed. Now, again enter the length value which is larger than the bottom width value.*

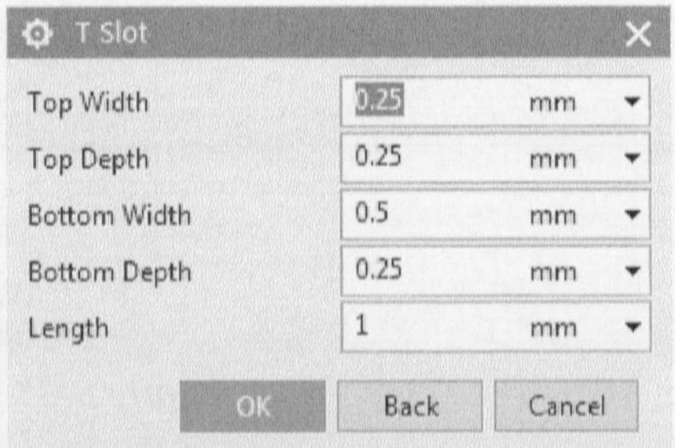

***Figure 6-38** The **T Slot** dialog box displaying the slot parameters*

After specifying the slot parameters, choose the **OK** button in this dialog box; a preview of the slot will be displayed, refer to Figure 6-39. Also, the **Positioning** dialog box will be displayed. The tools in this dialog box are used to position the slot. After positioning the slot, choose the **OK** button to create the T-slot, refer to Figure 6-40. Figure 6-41 shows the faces selected to define the length of the through T-slot. Figure 6-42 shows the through T-slot created in the model.

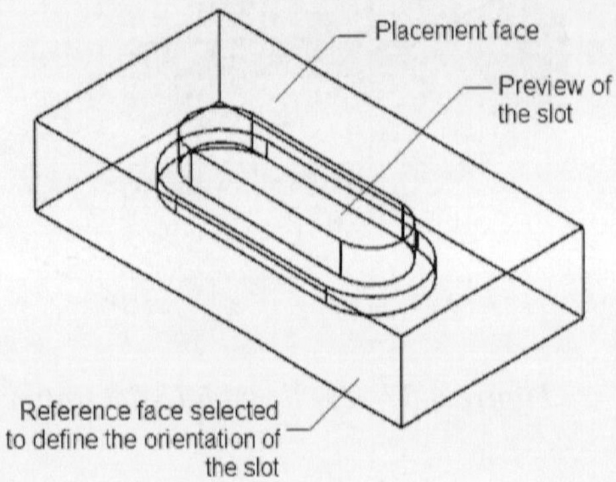

***Figure 6-39** The preview of the T-slot feature*

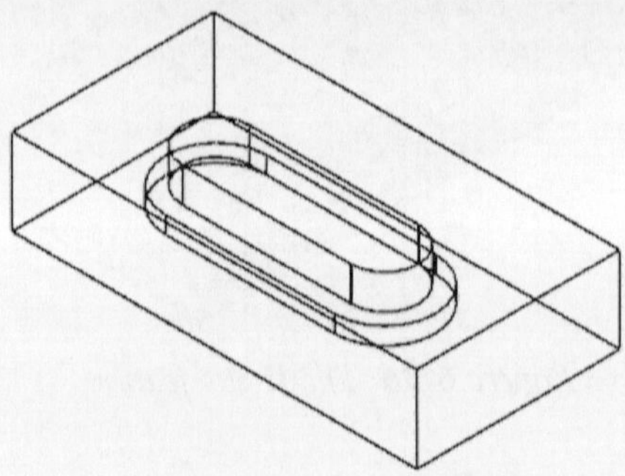

***Figure 6-40** The T-slot feature*

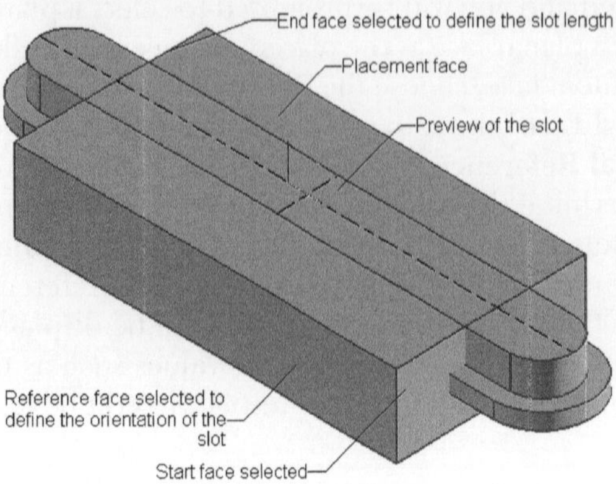

***Figure 6-41** The preview of the through T-slot*

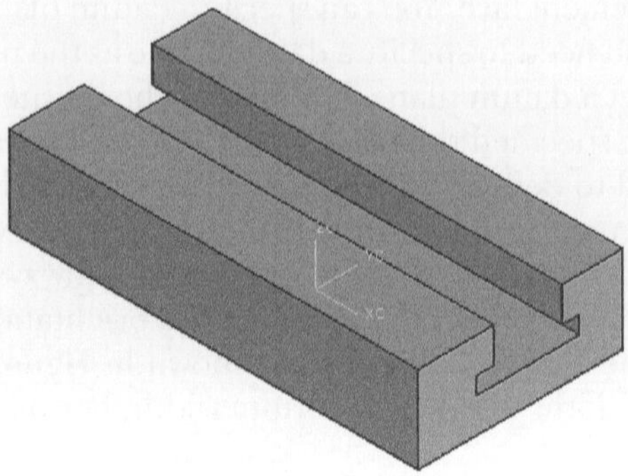

***Figure 6-42** The through T-slot feature*

Creating Dove-Tail Slots

To create a dove-tail slot, invoke the **Slot** dialog box and select the **Dove-Tail** radio button and then choose the **OK** button; the **Dove Tail Slot** dialog box will be displayed. You will be prompted to select a planar placement face. You can specify a datum plane or a planar face as the placement face for the slot. After you specify the placement face,the **Horizontal Reference** dialog box will be displayed. You can use the options in this dialog box to select a particular reference object for defining the orientation of the slot. The slot is always oriented parallel to the direction of the reference object selected. On specifying the orientation of the slot, the default slot parameters will be displayed in the **Dove Tail Slot** dialog box, as shown in Figure 6-43. Enter the slot parameter values such as the width, depth, angle, and length in their respective edit boxes.

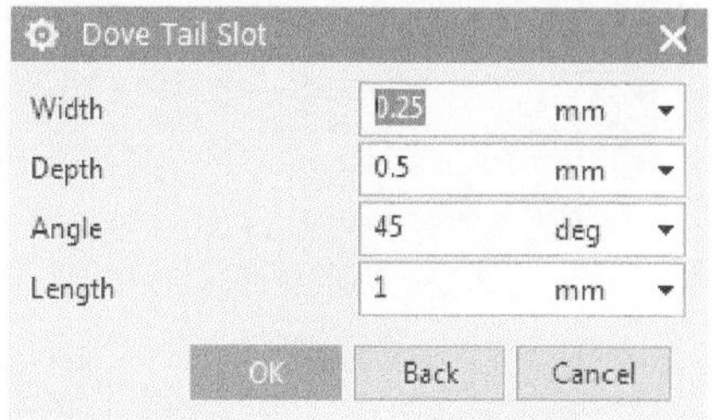

***Figure 6-43** The **Dove Tail Slot** dialog box displaying the slot parameters*

Note

*1. If you enter an angle value that is greater than or equal to 90, the **Message** window will be displayed and you will be informed that the dove-tail slot angle is invalid. To fix this error, choose the **OK** button from the same window; the **Dove Tail Slot** dialog box will be displayed. Next, enter the angle value that is less than or equal to 89.*

*2. If you enter a width value greater than the length value, the **Message** window will be displayed and you will be informed that the slot distance is less than or equal to width. To fix this error, choose the **OK** button from the **Message** window; the **Dove Tail Slot** dialog box will be displayed. Next, enter length value greater than the width value.*

After specifying the slot parameters, choose the **OK** button; a preview of the dove-tail slot feature will be displayed, as shown in Figure 6-44. Also, the **Positioning** dialog box will be displayed. The tools in this dialog box are used to position the slot. After positioning the slot, choose the **OK** button to create the dove-tail slot, as shown in Figure 6-45. Figure 6-46 shows the objects to be selected to create the through dove-tail slot feature and its preview. Figure 6-47 shows the through slots created in the model. Once the slot is created, choose **Cancel** to exit the dialog box.

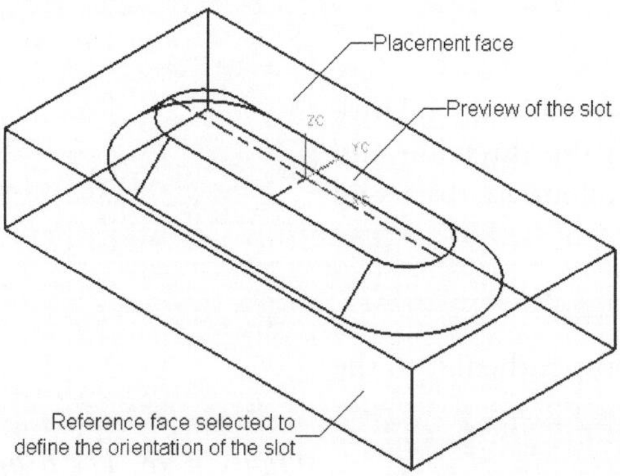

***Figure 6-44** The preview of the dove tail slot feature*

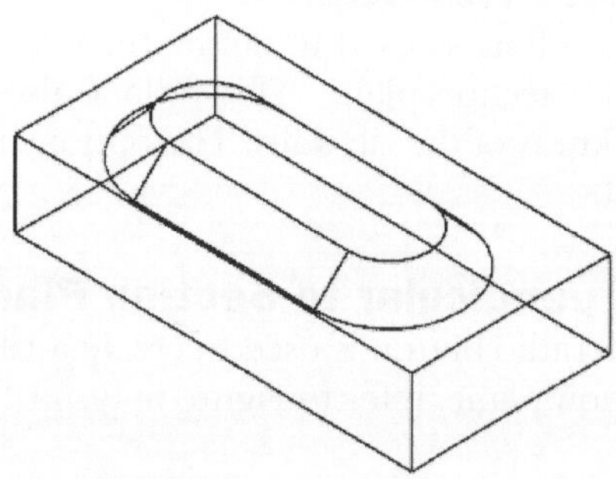

***Figure 6-45** The dove-tail slot feature*

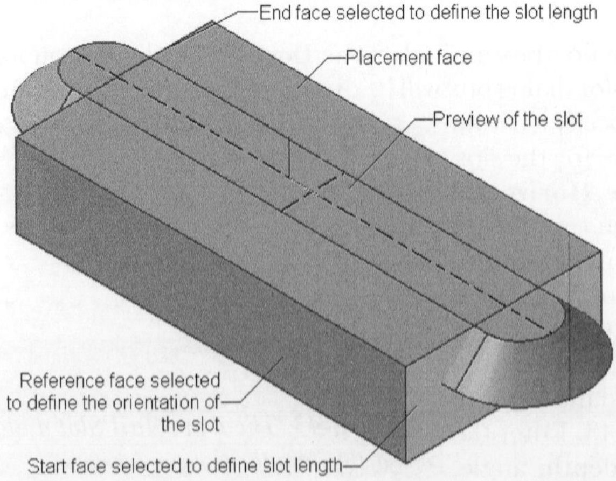

Figure 6-46 The preview of the through dove-tail slot feature

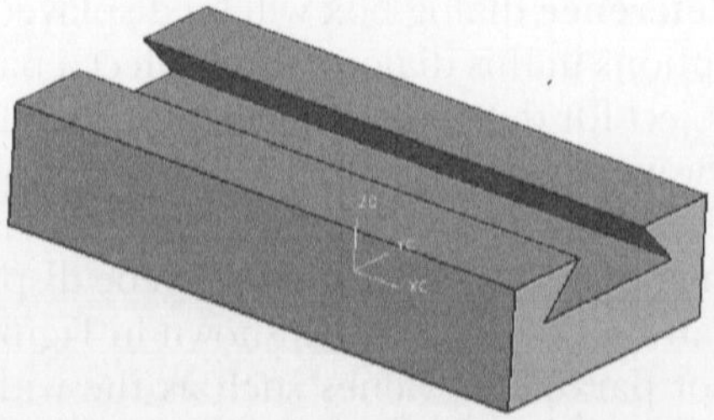

Figure 6-47 The through dove-tail slot feature

CREATING RIBS

Ribbon:	Home > Feature > Design Feature Drop-down > Rib *(Customize to add)*
Menu:	Insert > Design Feature > Rib

Ribs are defined as the thin-walled structures that are used to increase the strength of the entire structure of a component so that it does not fail under an increased load. In NX, the ribs are created using an open curve as well as a closed curve. To create a rib feature, choose the **Rib** tool from the **Design Feature Drop-down** of the **Feature** group in the **Home** tab; the **Rib** dialog box will be displayed, refer to Figure 6-48. In this dialog box, by default, the solid body will be selected as the target body. Also, you will be prompted to select a curve or create a curve to create the rib feature. Select the curve from the graphic area. Next, you need to enter the thickness value of thin wall in the **Thickness** edit box of the **Walls** rollout. After specifying values, choose the **OK** button to create the rib. Other rollouts in the **Rib** dialog box are discussed next.

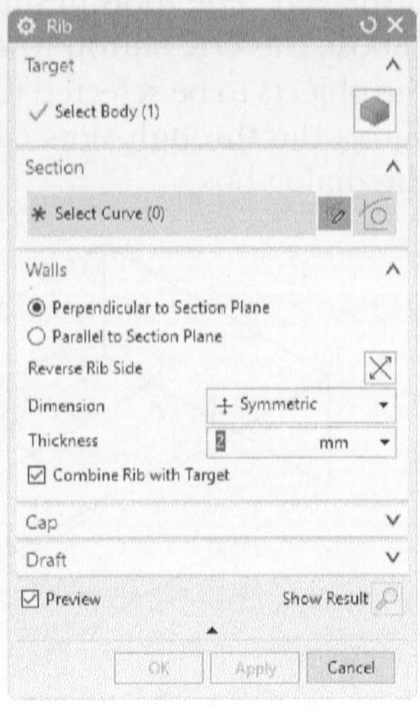

Figure 6-48 The ***Rib*** *dialog box*

Walls Rollout

This rollout is used to define the orientation of rib walls relative to the section plane. This rollout also defines the direction and thickness of the rib walls. The options in this rollout are discussed next.

Perpendicular to Section Plane

This radio button is used to create a rib wall perpendicular to the section plane, refer to Figure 6-49.

Parallel to Section Plane

This radio button is used to create the rib wall parallel to the section plane. This option is available only for single chain of curve, refer to Figure 6-50.

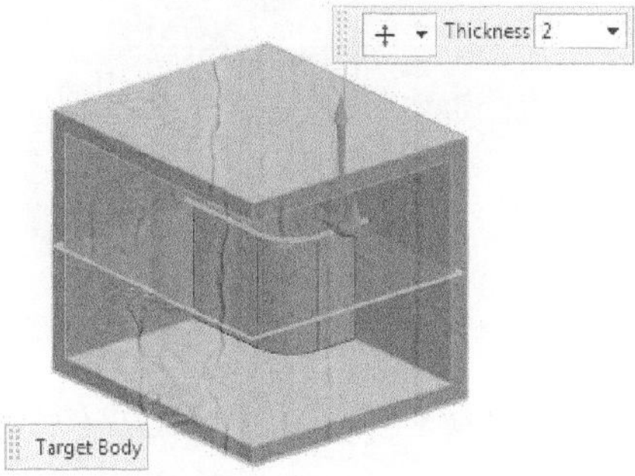

Figure 6-49 Thin wall rib created perpendicular to section plane

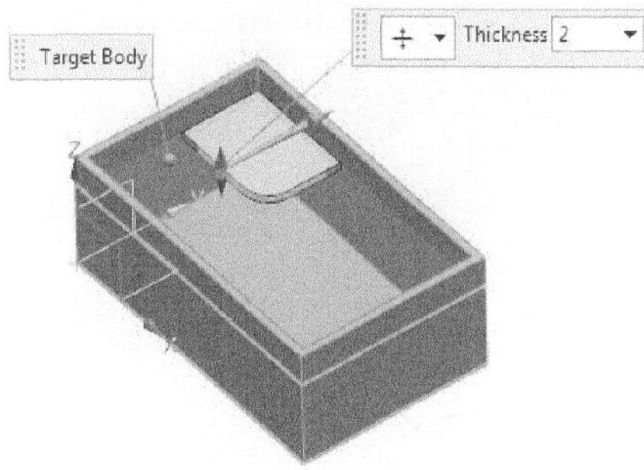

Figure 6-50 Thin wall rib created parallel to section plane

Reverse Rib Side

This button is used to reverse the direction of the rib creation, refer to Figure 6-51 and 6-52.

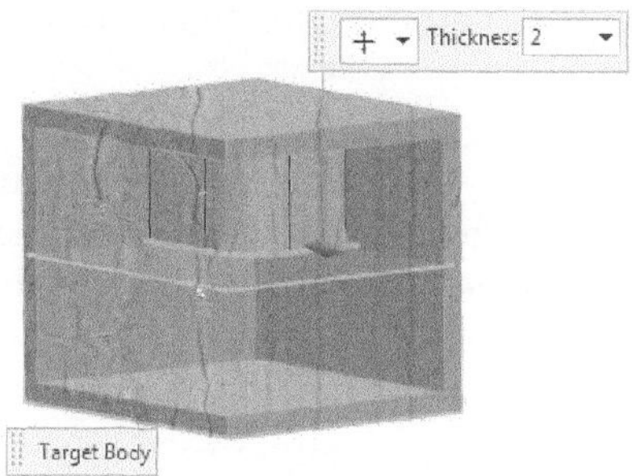

Figure 6-51 Perpendicular rib created by reversing the direction of rib creation

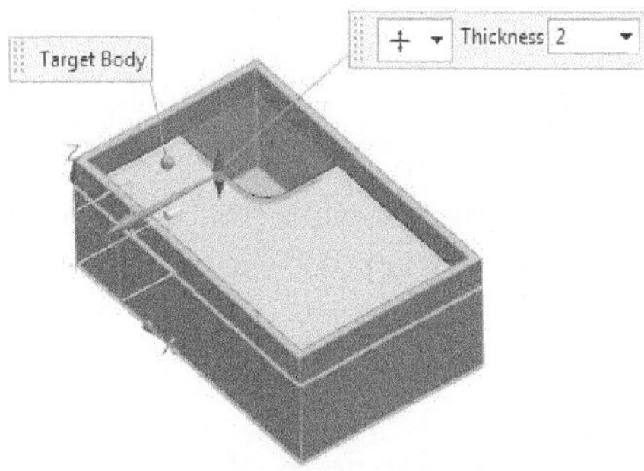

Figure 6-52 Parallel rib created by reversing the direction of rib creation

Dimension

This drop-down list is used to specify the side on which thickness is to be applied. This drop-down list consists of the **Symmetric** and **Asymmetric** options. The **Symmetric** option is used to offset the rib thickness symmetrically about the section curves, refer to Figure 6-53. The **Asymmetric** option is used to offset the rib thickness on one side of the section curves, refer to Figure 6-54. Note that the **Asymmetric** option is available only for single curve chain.

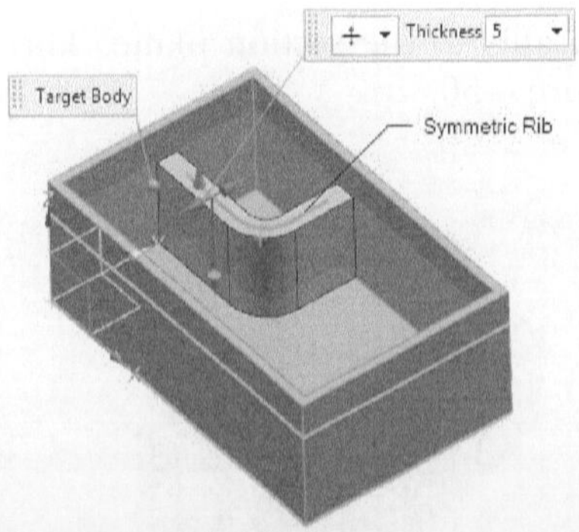

Figure 6-53 *Symmetric rib created*

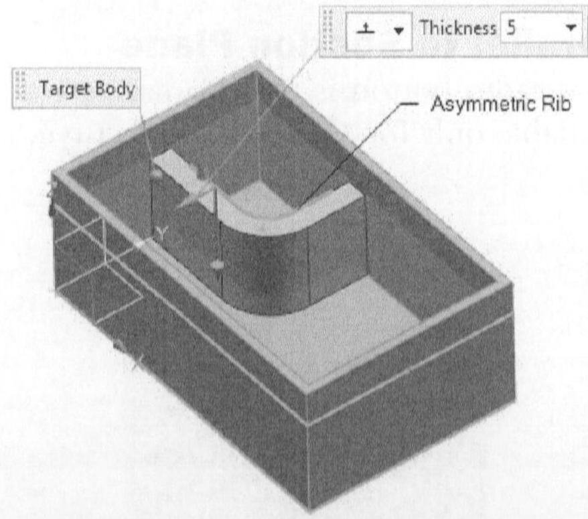

Figure 6-54 *Asymmetric rib created*

Combine Rib with Target

This check box is used to create a united feature with the target body. If this check box is selected, the rib feature created will be united with the target body.

Cap Rollout

The options in this rollout will be activated only when the **Perpendicular to Section Plane** radio button is selected in the **Walls** rollout. The options in this rollout are discussed next.

Geometry

This option is used to cap the rib. This drop-down list has two options, **From Section** and **From Selected**. The **From Section** option is used to cap the rib with respect to the section plane. The **From Selected** option is used to cap the rib with respect to the selected face chain or the datum plane.

Offset

This edit box is used to define the offset distance of the rib. If the **From Section** option is selected in the **Geometry** drop-down list then the offset distance will be calculated from the section plane. If the **From Selected** option is selected in the **Geometry** drop-down list then the offset distance is calculated from the selected face chain or the datum plane.

Draft Rollout

This rollout is used to define the draft angle on the rib walls. This rollout will be activated only when the **Perpendicular to Section Plane** is selected. You can select the **From Cap** option from the **Draft** drop-down list to draft the rib walls by keeping the cap section stationary. You can specify the draft angle value in the **Angle** edit box.

Preview

This check box is used to display the preview of the thin-wall rib.

Show Result / Undo Result

The **Show Result** button is used to display the resultant rib feature. After choosing this button, it will change into the **Undo Result** button, which can be used to rollback to the preview of the rib feature.

CREATING CHAMFERS

Ribbon:	Home > Feature > Chamfer
Menu:	Insert > Detail Feature > Chamfer

A chamfer feature is created on the sharp corners of a model to reduce stress concentration and to prevent accidental injuries due to sharp corners. To create a chamfer feature, choose the **Chamfer** tool from the **Feature** group of the **Home** tab; the **Chamfer** dialog box will be displayed, refer to Figure 6-55. In NX, there are three methods to create a chamfer feature: Symmetric, Asymmetric, and Offset and Angle. These three methods are discussed next.

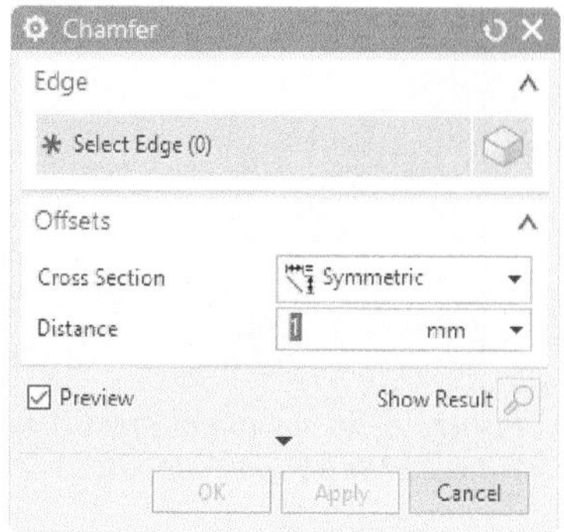

***Figure 6-55** The **Chamfer** dialog box*

Creating a Chamfer Feature Using the Symmetric Method

This method is used to create chamfers whose distance from the selected edge is equal along both the faces. You need to specify a single positive value for both distances. To create the chamfer feature using the Symmetric method, invoke the **Chamfer** dialog box. By default, the **Symmetric** option is selected in the **Cross Section** drop-down list of the **Offsets** rollout in the dialog box. Also, you will be prompted to select the edges to chamfer. Select any number of edges to create the chamfer feature. Next, enter the distance value in the **Distance** edit box, which is available below the **Cross Section** drop-down list of the dialog box. This value is taken as the distance value on both sides of the edges. Other rollouts in the **Chamfer** dialog box are discussed next.

Settings Rollout

Expand the **Settings** rollout to define the offset options. These options determine how the offset will be used to create the chamfer. These options are available in the **Offset Method** drop-down list of this rollout and are discussed next.

Offset Edges along Faces

This method is used to create chamfers for simple shapes. The offset values are measured along the faces from the edge being chamfered, refer to Figure 6-56. In this figure, a chamfer is created using the **Offset Edges along Faces** option with the **Distance** value taken as 10 mm.

Offset Faces and Trim

This method is used to create chamfers for complex shapes. A chamfer is created by offsetting two surfaces virtually by the specified chamfer distance and dropping normal from the intersection point of the offset surface on the original surface. The chamfer will be created between the two points where the normal will intersect with the original surface, refer to Figure 6-57. In this figure, the chamfer is created using the **Offset Faces and Trim** option and with the **Distance** value taken as 10 mm.

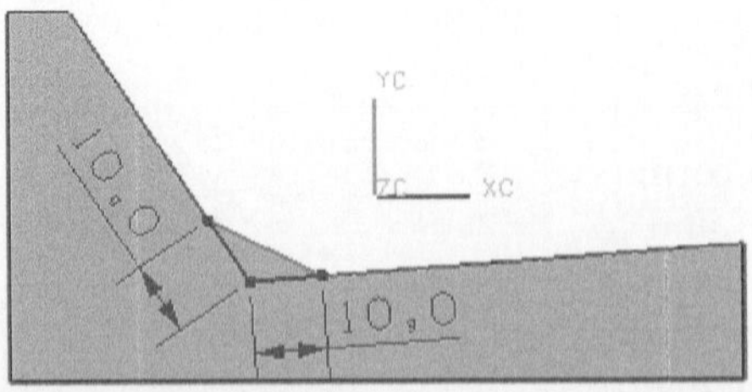

*Figure 6-56 Chamfer created using the **Offset Edges along Faces** option*

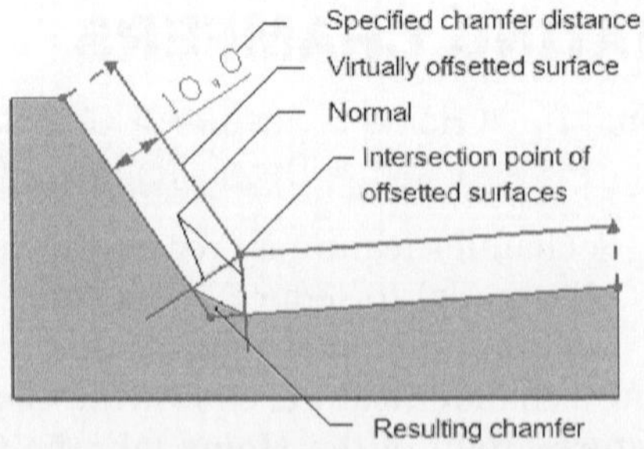

*Figure 6-57 Chamfer created using the **Offset Faces and Trim** option*

Preview

This check box is used to preview the chamfer in wireframe.

Show Result / Undo Result

The **Show Result** button is used to preview the chamfer when you create it. When you choose this button, it will get converted into the **Undo Result** button that can be used to undo the chamfer.

After selecting appropriate options, choose the **OK** button. Figure 6-58 shows the edges selected for creating the chamfer feature and Figure 6-59 shows the resultant chamfer feature created on the edges of the model.

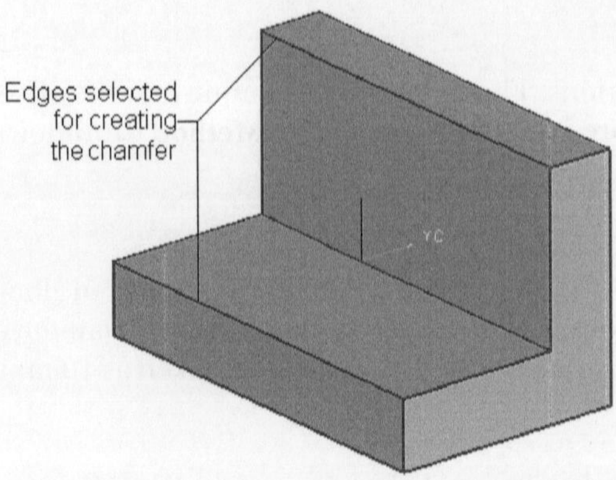

Figure 6-58 The edges selected for creating the chamfer feature

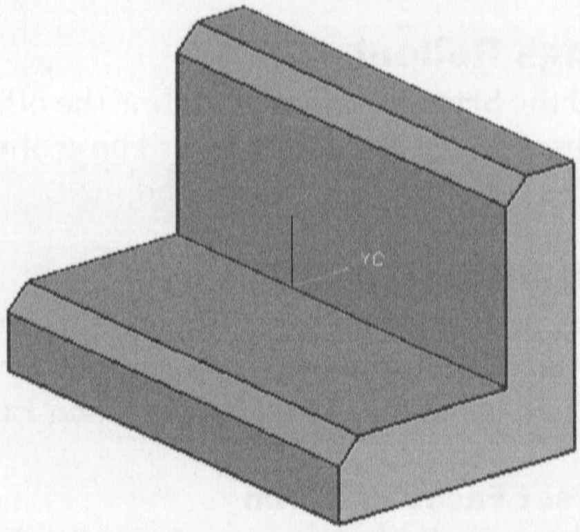

Figure 6-59 The resultant chamfer feature created on the edges of the model

Creating a Chamfer Feature Using the Asymmetric Method

This method is used to create the chamfer feature by specifying two different offset values along either side of the edge. To create the chamfer feature using the Asymmetric method, select the **Asymmetric** option from the **Cross Section** drop-down list in the **Offsets** rollout of the **Chamfer** dialog box; the **Chamfer** dialog box will be modified and you will be prompted to select the edges. Select any number of edges to create the chamfer feature. This dialog box contains the **Distance 1** and **Distance 2** edit boxes for entering two offset values. Enter the offset values in these edit boxes; the preview of the chamfer feature will be displayed. The **Reverse**

Direction button is used to reverse the chamfer distance. On choosing this button, the offset values of the two sides of the edge will get interchanged.

After selecting the appropriate options, choose the **OK** button. Figure 6-60 shows the edges selected for creating the chamfer and Figure 6-61 shows the resulting chamfer feature created on the edges of the model with two different offset values.

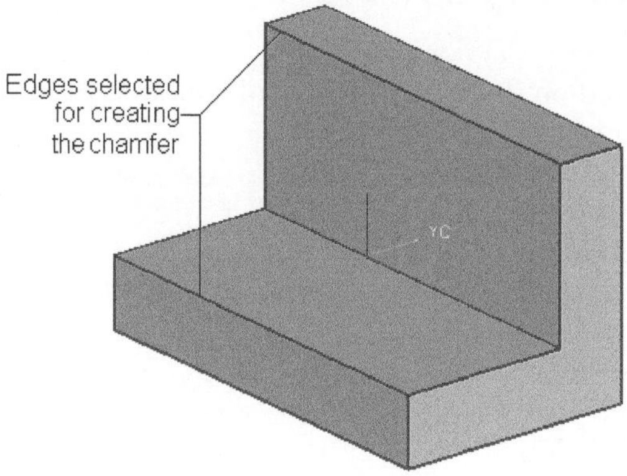

Figure 6-60 The edges selected for creating the chamfer feature

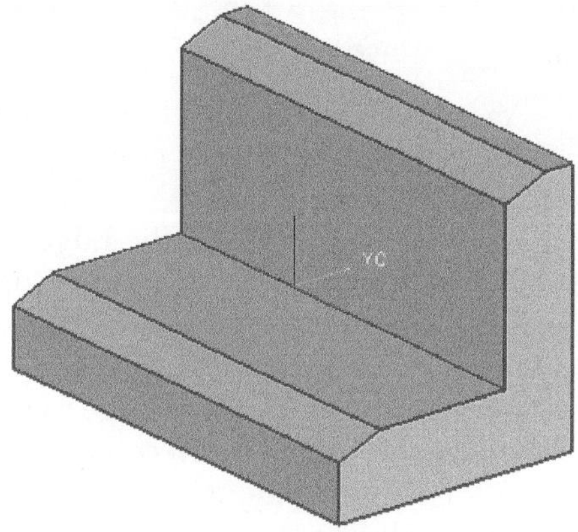

Figure 6-61 The resulting chamfer feature created on the edges with two different offset values

Creating a Chamfer Feature Using the Offset and Angle Method

This method is used to create a chamfer feature by defining an offset value and an angle value. The angle value is used to calculate the second offset value. To create the chamfer feature using the Offset and Angle method, select the **Offset and Angle** option from the **Cross Section** drop-down list; you will be prompted to select the edges. Also, the **Distance** and **Angle** edit boxes are displayed in the **Offsets** rollout. You can select any number of edges to create the chamfer feature. After selecting the edges, enter the values in the **Distance** and **Angle** edit boxes and choose the **OK** button. Figure 6-62 shows the edges selected for creating the chamfer feature and Figure 6-63 shows the resulting chamfer feature with an offset and an angle value.

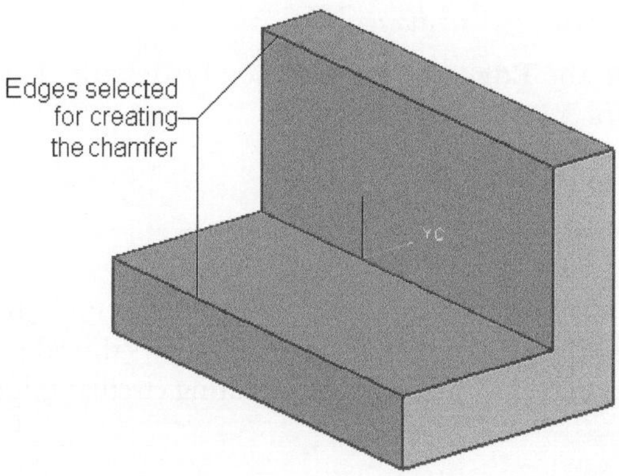

Figure 6-62 The edges selected for creating the chamfer feature

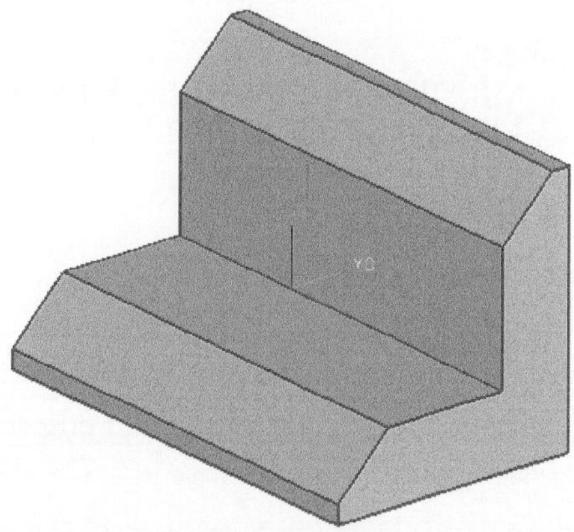

*Figure 6-63 The chamfer feature created using the **Offset and Angle** option*

Note

To reverse the chamfer, choose the ***Reverse Direction*** *button; the offset and angle values get applied to the other side of the edge.*

CREATING AN EDGE BLEND

Ribbon:	Home > Feature > Blend Drop-down > Edge Blend
Menu:	Insert > Detail Feature > Edge Blend

An edge blend is a fillet operation performed on the sharp corners of a model. In NX, you can create different types of fillets using this tool.

To create an edge blend, choose the **Edge Blend** tool from the **Blend Drop-down** of the **Feature** group of the **Home** tab; the **Edge Blend** dialog box will be displayed, as shown in Figure 6-64. By default, the **Circular** option is selected in the **Shape** drop-down list of the **Edge** rollout in the dialog box and you are prompted to select the edges to fillet. The options in the various rollouts of the **Edge Blend** dialog box are discussed next.

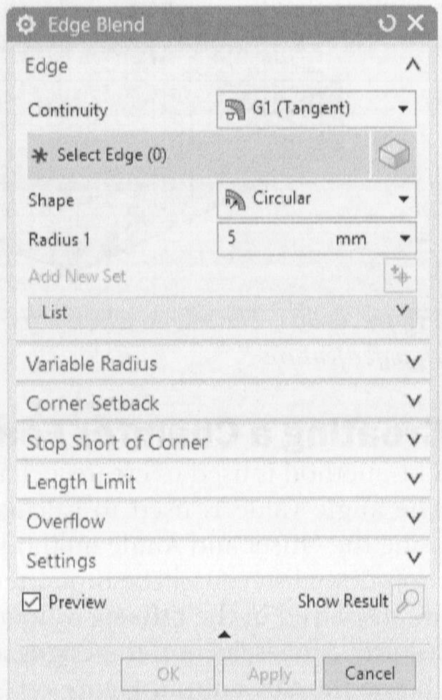

Figure 6-64 The ***Edge Blend*** *dialog box*

Edge Rollout

The options in this rollout will be modified depending upon the option selected in the **Shape** drop-down list of this rollout. The **Shape** drop-down list contains two options, namely **Circular** and **Conic**. The options in this rollout are discussed next.

Circular Blend Options

The options to create circular edge blend are discussed next.

Edge

When you invoke the **Edge Blend** tool, the **Edge** button is chosen by default. This button allows you to select the edges for an edge blend.

Radius 1

This edit box is used to enter the radius value to create a circular edge blend.

To create a circular fillet, select any number of edges to create the fillet. Next, enter the radius value in the **Radius 1** edit box and choose the **OK** button. Figure 6-65 shows the edges selected for creating the circular edge blend and Figure 6-66 shows the resulting circular edge blend feature.

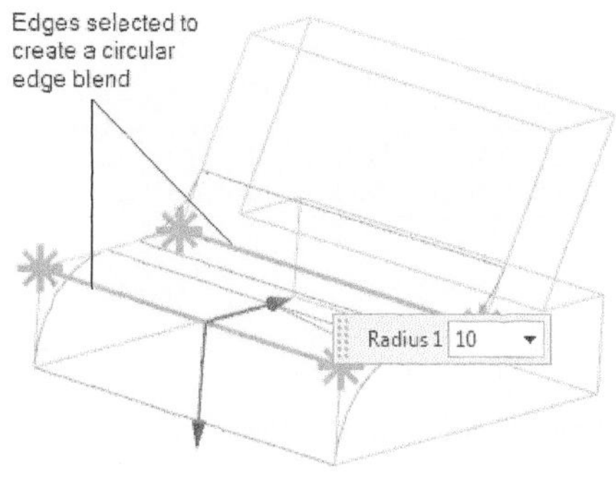

Figure 6-65 Edges selected for edge blend

Figure 6-66 The resulting edge blend feature

Conical Blend Options

To create a conical edge blend, select the **Conic** option from the **Shape** drop-down list in the **Edge** rollout of the **Edge Blend** dialog box; the **Edge** rollout will be modified and you are prompted to select the edges. Select any number of edges to create an edge blend. The **Conic Method** drop-down list in the **Edge** rollout contains three options to create a conical edge blend. These three methods are discussed next.

Boundary and Center

To create a conical blend using this option, select the **Boundary and Center** option from the **Conic Method** drop-down list. Next, enter values in the **Boundary Radius 1** and **Center Radius1** edit boxes and choose the **OK** button.

Boundary and Rho

To create the conical blend using the **Boundary and Rho** option, select the **Boundary and Rho** option from the **Conic Method** drop-down list. Next, enter values in the **Boundary Radius 1** and **Rho 1** edit boxes and choose the **OK** button.

Center and Rho

To create the conical blend using the **Center and Rho** option, select **Center and Rho** option from the **Conic Method** drop-down list. Next, enter values in the **Center Radius 1** and **Rho 1** edit boxes and choose the **OK** button. Figure 6-67 shows the edge selected for creating the conical edge blend and Figure 6-68 shows the resulting conical edge blend feature.

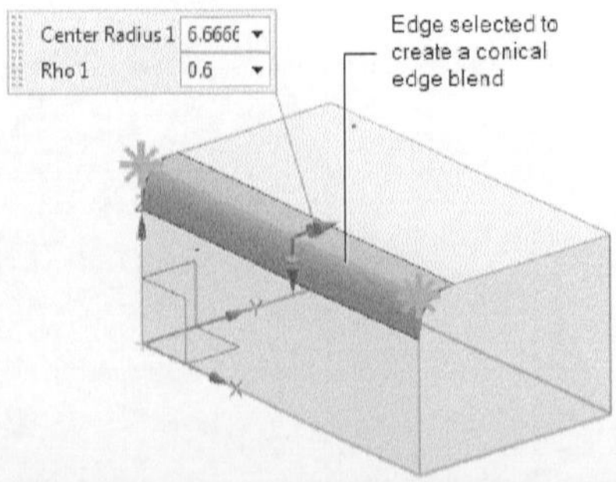

Figure 6-67 Edges selected for creating the conical edge blend

Figure 6-68 The resulting conical edge blend

Add New Set

This button is used to create a set of edges with the same radius value. After selecting edges for one set, choose the **Add New Set** button to create a new set and then select the required edges for the active set; these sets of edges will be listed in the **List** sub-rollout of the **Edge** rollout in the dialog box. You can modify the radius value of each edge set. To do so, expand the **List** sub-rollout; all edge sets will be displayed. Next, select the set of edges whose parameters are to be changed; the corresponding edges will be highlighted in the model. Enter the new values in the input boxes and press ENTER. Alternatively, you can enter new values of the respective parameters in the dialog box. As you press ENTER, a preview of the modified fillets will be displayed in the drawing window. The **Remove** button in the **List** sub-rollout is used to remove the selected edge set.

Note

You can complete an edge set by pressing the middle mouse button. The edge set can be identified by a spherical handle in the drawing window.

The other rollouts in the **Edge Blend** dialog box are discussed next:

Variable Radius Rollout

This rollout allows you to create the fillet with variable radii specified at different key points on an edge. To create the variable radius fillets, you need to follow three steps. The first step is to select the placement edge, second is to specify the key points for defining the multiple radii, and the third is to specify the radius value at each key point. Follow the steps given below to create the variable radii fillet:

1. Select the edge to create the variable radii edge blend and expand the **Variable Radius** rollout. This rollout has different options for specifying the keypoints.

2 Choose the **Point Dialog** button; the **Point** dialog box will be displayed and you will be prompted to select the object to infer a point.

3. You can locate the point using the options in the **Location** drop-down list of the **Location on Curve** rollout of the **Point** dialog box. These options have already been discussed earlier.

4. Select a point on the edge and choose the **OK** button; the **Variable Radius** rollout will be modified. Next, click on the specified point on the edge, the **V Boundary Radius 1, V Center Radius 1,** and **% Arc length** input edit boxes will be displayed on the model, refer to Figure 6-69.

5. Enter the radius value for this point in the **V Boundary Radius 1** and **V Center Radius 1** edit boxes.

6. Similarly, specify multiple points and then radius value at each point. Figure 6-70 shows the variable radii fillet created on the edge.

Note

1. You can also specify points by using the ***Inferred Point*** *drop-down list. All the specified points will be listed in the* ***List*** *sub-rollout. You can modify the radius value at each point. To do so, expand the* ***List*** *sub-rollout; all the specified points will be displayed. Next, select the point at which the radius value is to be changed and enter a new radius value in the respective edit box. The* ***Remove*** *button in the* ***List*** *sub-rollout is used to remove the specified points.*

2. If you select the ***Circular*** *option from the* ***Shape*** *drop-down list then the* ***V Radius*** *edit box will become available but if you select the* ***Conic*** *option from the* ***Shape*** *drop-down list then the* ***V Boundary Radius*** *edit box will become available.*

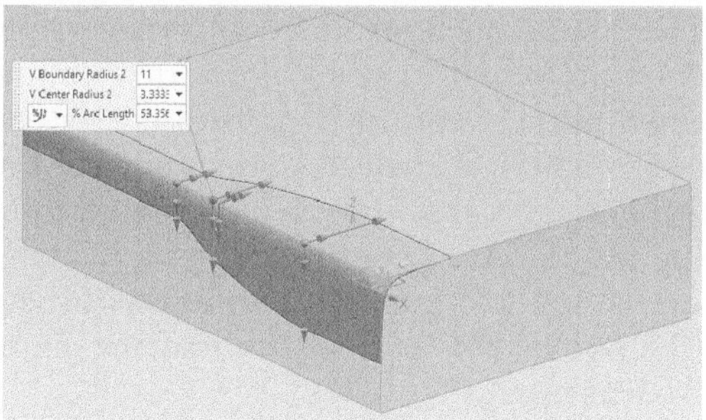

Figure 6-69 *The* ***V Boundary Radius 1, V Center Radius 1,*** *and* ***% Arc length*** *edit boxes displayed on the model*

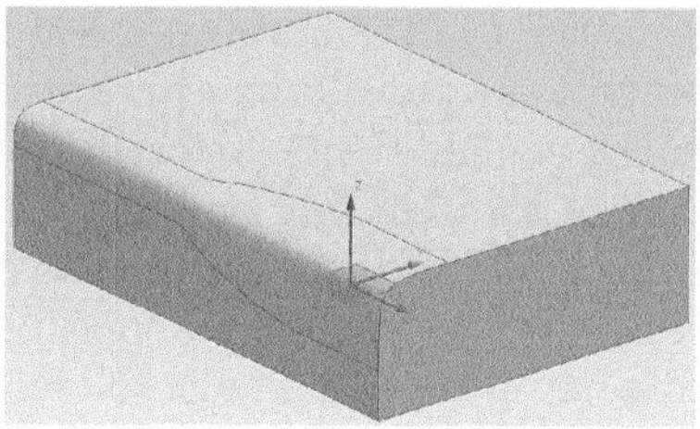

Figure 6-70 *The variable radii fillet*

Corner Setback Rollout

The **Corner Setback** rollout is used to create a corner blend by smoothening the corner. To do so, you need to select three or more edges that meet at a corner and then expand the **Corner Setback** rollout. Next, click in the **Select End Point** area in the **Corner Setback** rollout; you will be prompted to select the vertex point to specify the setback distance. Select the corner point by using the left mouse button; the drag handles will be displayed along with the input edit boxes, refer to Figure 6-71. These drag handles are used to smoothen corners. By default, all the handles are equally spaced and placed. You can modify this distance by dynamically dragging the handles or by entering the setback values in the respective edit boxes. To accept the corner edge blend, choose the **OK** button in the **Edge Blend** dialog box; the resultant corner edge blend will be displayed, as shown in Figure 6-72.

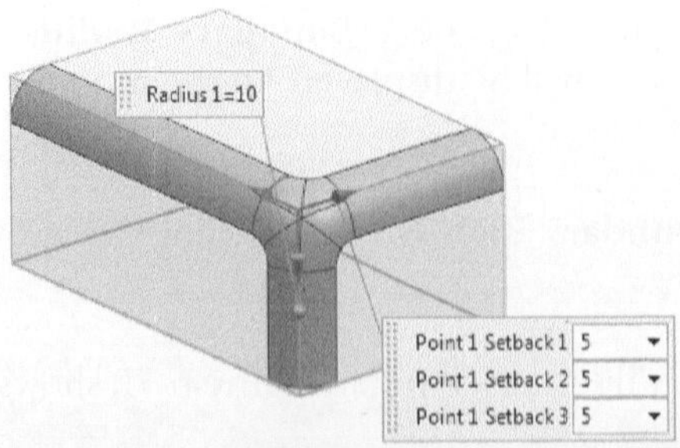

Figure 6-71 *Drag handles with input boxes*

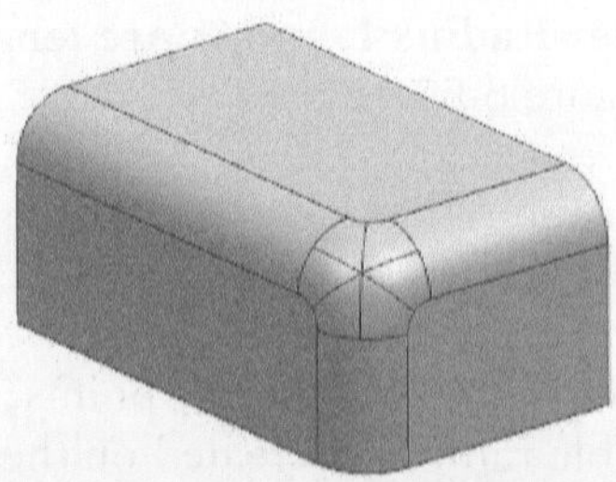

Figure 6-72 *The resultant corner edge blend*

Note

To specify same offset value for all the three drag handles, select the corner point; three input edit boxes will be displayed. Enter same offset value in all the three edit boxes and press the ENTER key.

Stop Short of Corner Rollout

This rollout is used to create a fillet that is limited to a desired distance on the selected edge. The specified length will be ignored and not filleted. Remember that the length can be ignored only from the endpoints of the selected edge and not at any intermediate portion.

Select an edge to create the stop short fillet and expand the **Stop Short of Corner** rollout. Next, click in the **Select End Point** area; you will be prompted to select the vertex for specifying stop short. Also, the **Distance** option is selected in the **Limit** drop-down list. As a result, you need to specify the point from where you need to limit the fillet. Note that only the **End Point** button will be available in the **Selection Group**. This is because you can only select the endpoints from the edge. On selecting one of the endpoints, the **Arc Length** edit box will be displayed. Also, a stop short handle will be displayed on the selected endpoint. Enter the distance value in the **Arc Length** edit box. You can specify the distance value dynamically by dragging the stop short handle to a point on the selected edge. Note that you can specify the stop-short distance from both the ends of the selected edge. After entering the stop short value, press the ENTER key; the preview of the stop short fillet will be dynamically modified. To accept the stop short fillet, choose the **OK** button from the **Edge Blend** dialog box. The resulting stop short fillet is shown in Figure 6-73. You can also select the intersection point of multiple fillets as the limiting point. To do so, select the **Blend Intersection** option from the **Limit** drop-down list and then select the point at which multiple fillets intersect.

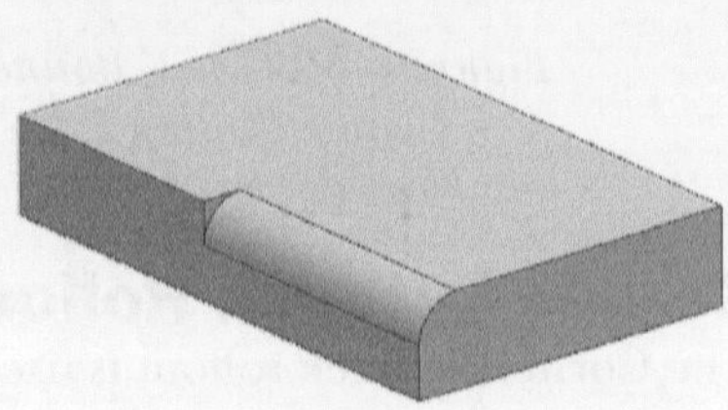

Figure 6-73 *The resulting stop short fillet*

Note

If there are two separate bodies and you are creating a fillet at one edge of a body, then the resulting fillet will be convex shaped, as shown in Figure 6-74. If you are creating a fillet at the common edge of two features of a solid body, then the resulting fillet will be concave shaped, as shown in Figure 6-75.

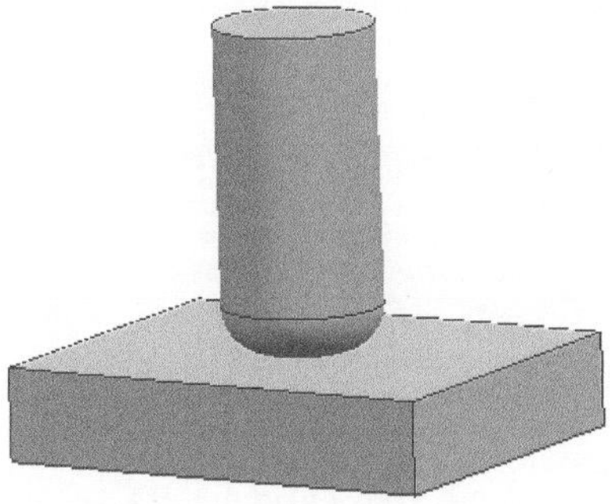

Figure 6-74 Resulting fillet between two separate part bodies

Figure 6-75 Resulting fillet between the united part body

Length Limit Rollout

The options in this rollout are used to trim the creation of fillets by selecting a plane or planar face. To do so, select the edges to fillet and then expand the **Length Limit** rollout. Next, select the **Enable Length Limit** check box to activate all the options in the **Length Limit** rollout. Now you can choose the **Plane**, **Face** or **Edge** option from the **Limit Object** drop-down list to specify the method for trimming the edge blend. On choosing the **Plane** option from the **Limit Object** drop-down list, you will be prompted to specify the plane to define the trim position of edge blend. Specify the plane by using the **Plane dialog** button or the options in the **On Curve** drop-down list, refer to Figure 6-76. As you specify the position of the plane on the selected edge, the **Arc Length** edit box will be displayed in the graphics window. Specify the length value in this edit box to determine the position of the trimming plane and then choose **OK** button. The **Reverse direction** button is used to reverse the direction of the edge blend. Similarily, you can choose the **Face** or **Edge** options from the **Limit Object** drop-down list to specify faces or edges to trim the blend, refer to Figures 6-77 and 6-78.

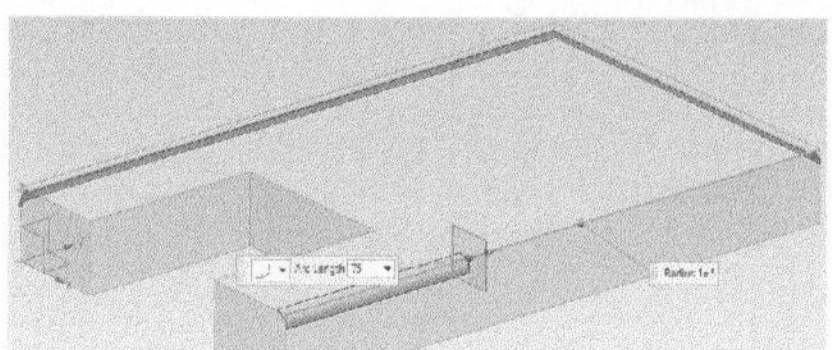

*Figure 6-76 Edge blend created with the **Plane** option selected from the **Limit Object** drop-down list*

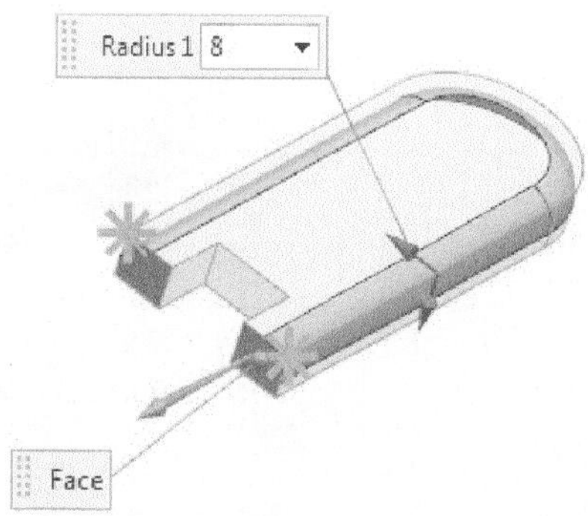

*Figure 6-77 Edge blend created with the **Face** option selected from the **Limit Object** drop-down list*

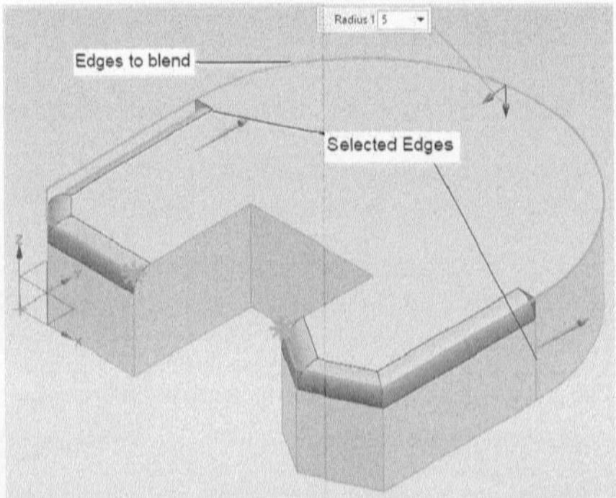

*Figure 6-78 Edge blend created with the **Edge** option selected from the **Limit Object** drop-down list*

TUTORIALS

Tutorial 1

In this tutorial, you will create the model shown in Figure 6-79(a). The dimensions of the model are shown in Figure 6-79(b). After creating the model, save it with the name *c06tut1.prt* at the following location: *\NX\c06.* **(Expected time: 30 min)**

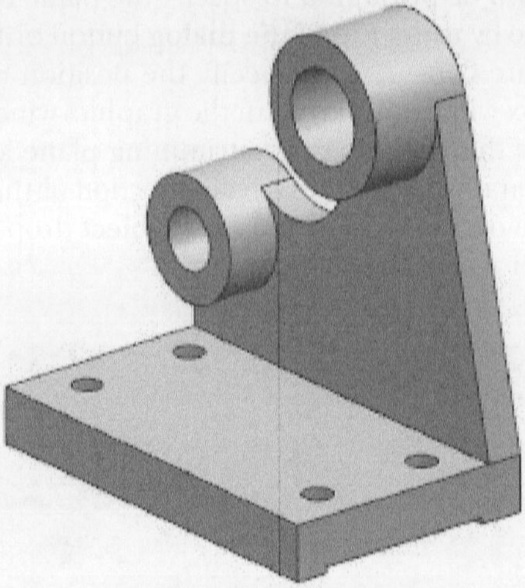

Figure 6-79(a) Model for Tutorial 1

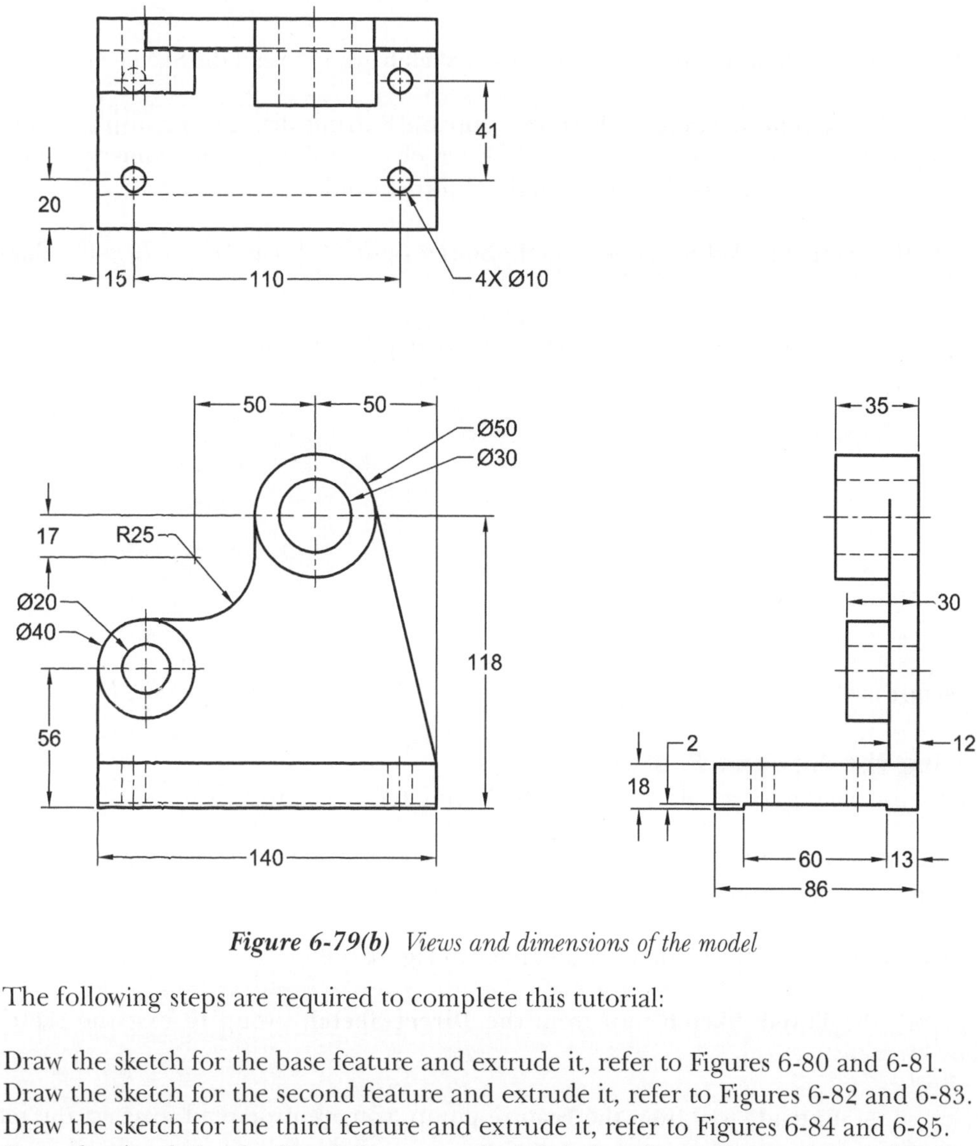

Figure 6-79(b) Views and dimensions of the model

The following steps are required to complete this tutorial:

a. Draw the sketch for the base feature and extrude it, refer to Figures 6-80 and 6-81.
b. Draw the sketch for the second feature and extrude it, refer to Figures 6-82 and 6-83.
c. Draw the sketch for the third feature and extrude it, refer to Figures 6-84 and 6-85.
d. Draw the sketch for the fourth feature and extrude it, refer to Figures 6-86 and 6-87.
e. Create two holes on the side face of the model using the **Hole** tool, refer to Figures 6-88 and 6-89.
f. Create four holes on the top face of the base feature using the **Hole** tool, refer to Figures 6-90 through 6-92.
g. Save and close the file.

Creating the Base Feature of the Model

The base feature will be created using the profile of the right face of the model.

1. Start a new file with the name *c06tut1.prt* using the **Model** template and specify its location as *C:\NX\c06*.

2. Draw the sketch by using the YC-ZC plane as shown in Figure 6-80.

3. Choose the **Finish Sketch** tool from the **Direct Sketch** group to exit the Sketch environment.

4. Choose the **Extrude** tool from the **Feature** group; the **Extrude** dialog box is displayed and you are prompted to select the planar face to sketch or select the section geometry. Select the sketch created for the base feature from the drawing window.

5. Select the **Symmetric Value** option from the **Start** drop-down list and enter **70** in the **Distance** edit box.

6. Choose the **Apply** button and then close the dialog box by choosing the **Cancel** button. The resulting base feature is shown in Figure 6-81.

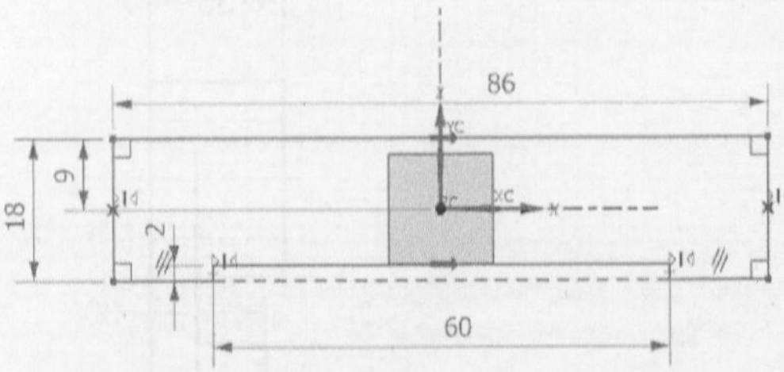

Figure 6-80 Sketch for the base feature

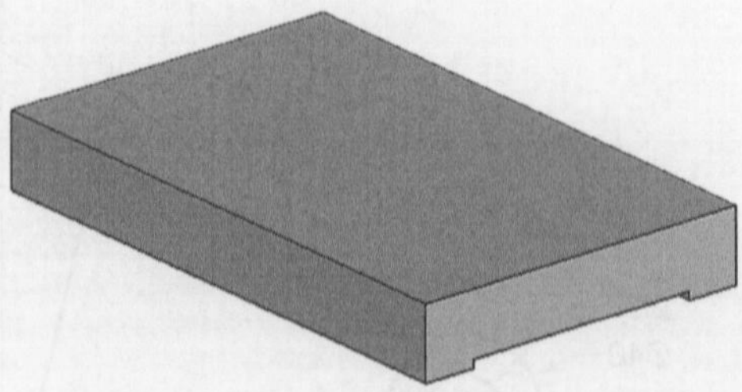

Figure 6-81 The resulting base feature

Creating the Second Feature

Next, you need to create the second feature using the steps given next.

1. Invoke the **Create Sketch** dialog box by choosing the **Sketch** tool from the **Direct Sketch** group. Next, select the back face of the base feature as the sketching plane.

2. Draw the sketch for the second feature, refer to Figure 6-82.

3. Choose the **Finish Sketch** tool from the **Direct Sketch** group to exit the sketching environment.

4. Choose the **Extrude** tool from the **Feature** group; you are prompted to select the planar face to sketch or select the section geometry.

5. Select the sketch created for the second feature. Next, in the **Limits** rollout of the dialog box enter **0** and **12** in the **Distance** edit boxes available below the **Start** and **End** drop-down lists, respectively. Make sure the sketch is extruded in the front direction.

6. Select the **Unite** option from the **Boolean** drop-down list in the **Boolean** rollout of the dialog box.

7. Choose the **Apply** button and then close the dialog box by choosing the **Cancel** button. The resulting model after creating the second feature is shown in Figure 6-83.

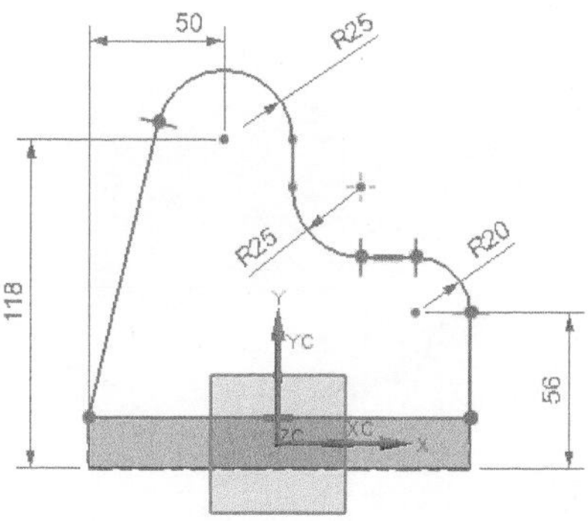

Figure 6-82 Sketch for the second feature

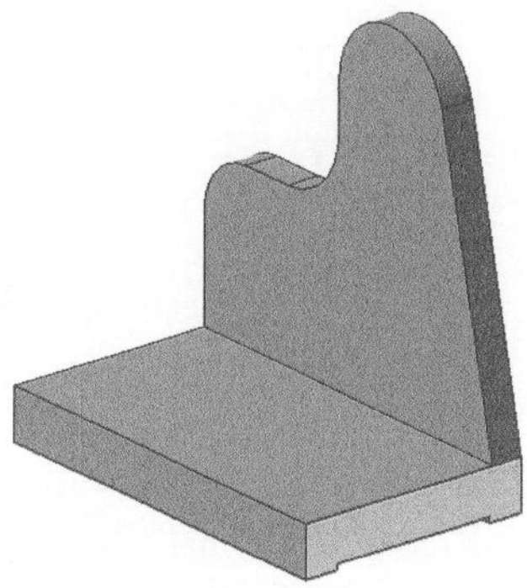

Figure 6-83 Model after creating the second feature

Creating the Third Feature

Now, you need to create the third feature, which is an extrude feature.

1. Invoke the **Create Sketch** dialog box by choosing the **Sketch** tool from the **Direct Sketch** group. Next, select the front face of the second feature as the sketching plane.

2. Draw a circle of **50** mm diameter as shown in Figure 6-84 as the sketch for the third feature.

3. Choose the **Finish Sketch** tool from the **Direct Sketch** group to exit the sketching environment.

4. Choose the **Extrude** tool from the **Feature** group; the **Extrude** dialog box is displayed and you are prompted to select the planar face to sketch or select the section geometry.

5. Select the sketch created for the third feature and enter **23** in the **Distance** edit box below the **End** drop-down list in the **Limits** rollout of the dialog box. Make sure the sketch is being extruded toward the screen.

6. Select the **Unite** option from the **Boolean** drop-down list in the **Boolean** rollout of the dialog box.

7. Choose the **OK** button from the dialog box. The model after creating the third feature is shown in Figure 6-85.

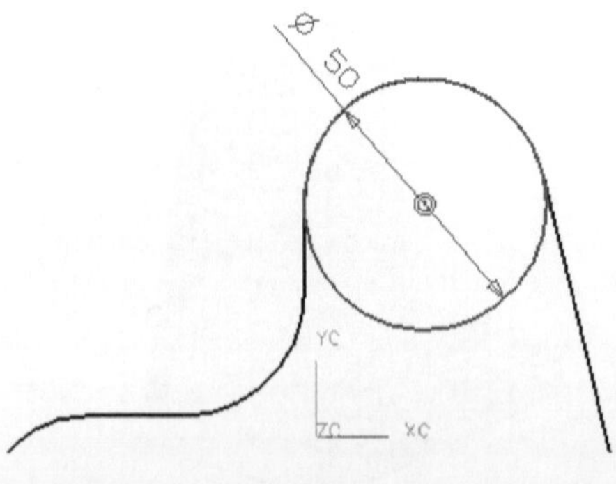

Figure 6-84 Sketch for the third feature

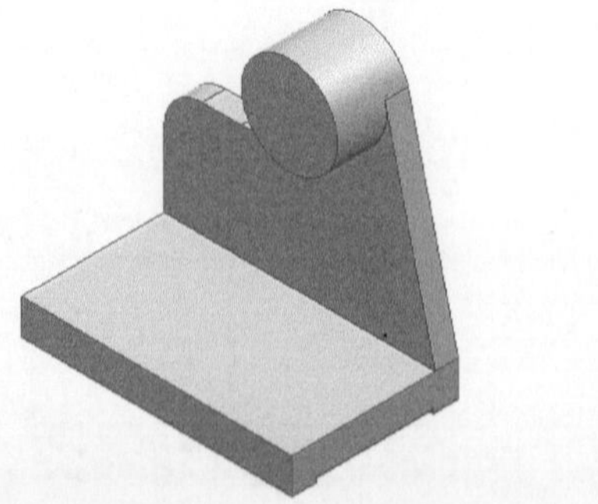

Figure 6-85 Model after creating the third feature

Creating the Fourth Feature

The steps given next are required to create the fourth feature.

1. Invoke the sketching environment by selecting the front face of the second feature as the sketching plane.

2. Draw a circle of **40** mm diameter, as shown in Figure 6-86 as the sketch for the fourth feature.

3. Choose the **Finish Sketch** tool from the **Direct Sketch** group to exit the sketching environment.

4. Choose the **Extrude** tool from the **Feature** group; the **Extrude** dialog box is displayed and you are prompted to select the planar face to sketch or select the section geometry.

5. Select the sketch created for the fourth feature and enter **18** in the **Distance** edit box available below the **End** drop-down list. Make sure the sketch is extruded toward the front.

6. Select the **Unite** option from the **Boolean** drop-down list in the **Boolean** rollout of the dialog box.

7. Choose the **OK** button from the dialog box. The resulting model after creating the fourth feature is shown in Figure 6-87.

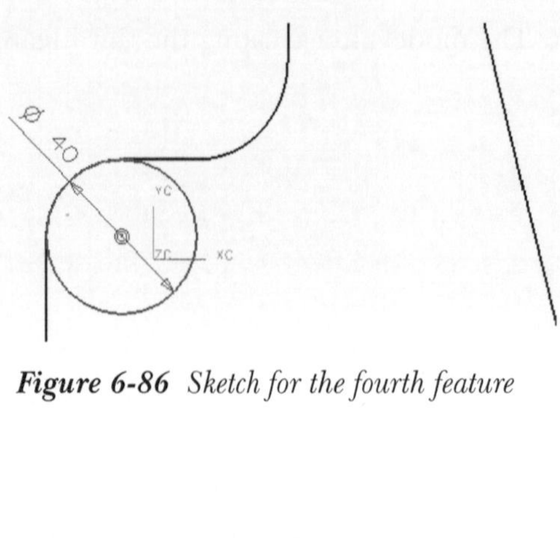

Figure 6-86 Sketch for the fourth feature

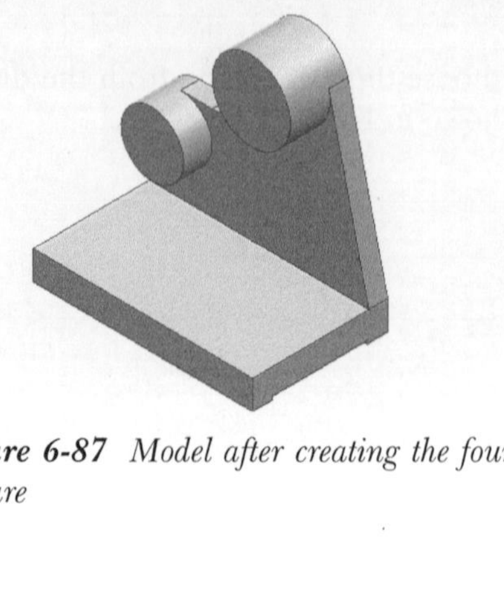

Figure 6-87 Model after creating the fourth feature

Creating a Hole in the Third Feature

Follow the steps given next to create a hole in the third feature.

1. Choose the **Hole** tool from the **Feature** group; the **Hole** dialog box is displayed and you are prompted to select the planar face to sketch or specify points.
2. Select the **General Hole** option from the drop-down list in the **Type** rollout and the **Simple** option from the **Form** drop-down list in the **Form and Dimensions** rollout of the dialog box if they are not selected by default.
3. Move the cursor over the center point of the circular face of the third feature. Click the left mouse button when the cursor snaps to the center point and the coincident constraint is displayed below the cursor; preview of the hole feature is displayed in the drawing window.
4. Enter **30** in the **Diameter** edit box of the **Dimensions** sub-rollout.
5. Select the **Through Body** option from the **Depth Limit** drop-down list in the **Dimensions** sub-rollout of the **Form and Dimensions** rollout. Next, select the **Subtract** option from the **Boolean** drop-down list.
6. Accept the other default settings and choose the **OK** button from the dialog box; a hole is created in the third feature, as shown in Figure 6-88.

Creating a Hole in the Fourth Feature

In this section, you will create a hole in the fourth feature using the following steps:

1. Choose the **Hole** tool from the **Feature** group; the **Hole** dialog box is displayed and you are prompted to select a planar face to sketch or specify points.
2. Move the cursor over the center point of the circular face of the fourth feature; the center point is highlighted. Now, select it; a preview of the hole is displayed in the drawing window.
3. Enter **20** in the **Diameter** edit box in the **Dimensions** sub-rollout.
4. Select the **Through Body** option from the **Depth Limit** drop-down list in the **Dimensions** sub-rollout of the dialog box.
5. Accept other default settings and choose the **OK** button from the **Hole** dialog box; a hole is created in the fourth feature, as shown in Figure 6-89.

Figure 6-88 Model after creating a hole in the third feature

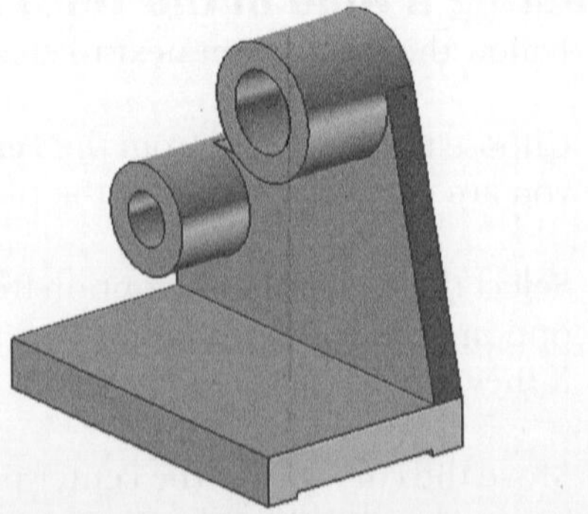

Figure 6-89 Model after creating a hole in the fourth feature

Creating Four Holes in the Base Feature

To complete the model, you need to create four holes in the base feature by using the steps discussed next.

1. Choose the **Hole** tool from the **Feature** group; the **Hole** dialog box is displayed and you are prompted to select a planar face to sketch or specify points.

2. Select the top face of the base feature as the planar placement plane; the **Sketch Point** dialog box is displayed and you are prompted to define a point. Also, the Sketch in Task environment is invoked and a point is placed on the top face of base feature.

3. Choose the **Close** button from the **Sketch Point** dialog box. Now, apply dimension to the point, as shown in Figure 6-90.

4. Choose the **Finish** tool from the **Sketch** group of the **Home** tab to exit the Sketch in Task environment. As you exit the Sketch in Task environment, the **Hole** dialog box is displayed again. Also, a preview of the hole is displayed. Note that the center of the hole is at the point that you have specified using the **Point** dialog box.

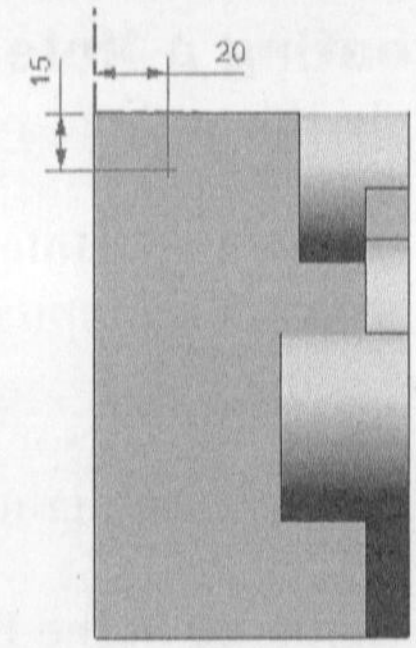

Figure 6-90 Point after applying the dimension

5. Enter **10** as the diameter of the hole in the **Diameter** edit box of the **Dimensions** sub-rollout of the **Form and Dimensions** rollout in the **Hole** dialog box.

6. Select the **Through Body** option from the **Depth Limit** drop-down list in the **Dimensions** sub-rollout of the **Form and Dimensions** rollout of the dialog box.

7. Accept other default settings and choose the **OK** button from the dialog box; a hole is created in the base feature, as shown in Figure 6-91.

8. Similarly, create the remaining three holes. Refer to Figure 6-79(b) for dimensions. The final model for this tutorial is shown in Figure 6-92.

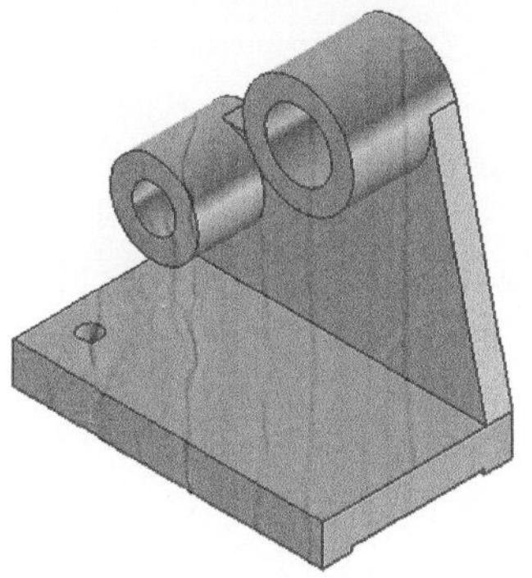

Figure 6-91 *Model after creating the first hole in the base feature*

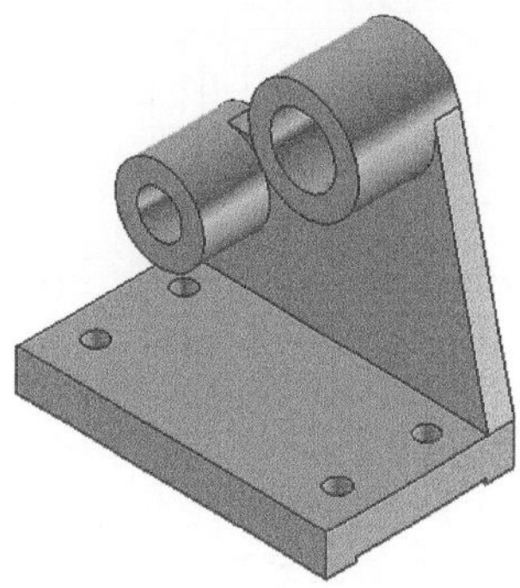

Figure 6-92 *Final model after creating all the four holes in the base feature*

Saving and Closing the File

1. Choose **Menu > File > Close > Save and Close** from the **Top Border Bar** to save and close the file.

Tutorial 2

In this tutorial, you will create the model shown in Figure 6-93. The drawing views and the dimensions are shown in Figure 6-94. After creating the model, save it with the name *c06tut2.prt* at the following location: *\NX\c06*. **(Expected time: 30 min)**

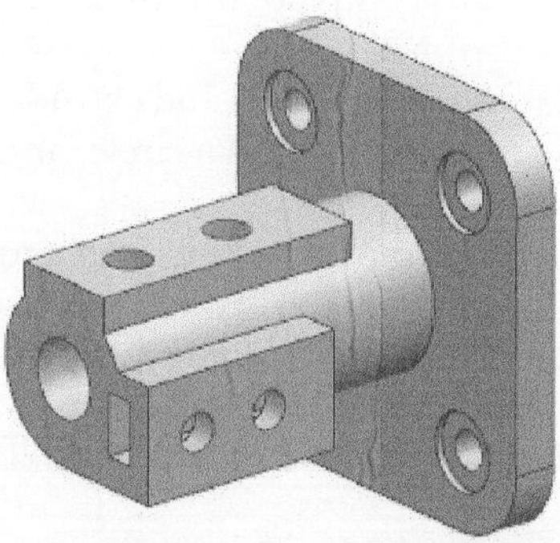

Figure 6-93 *Model for Tutorial 2*

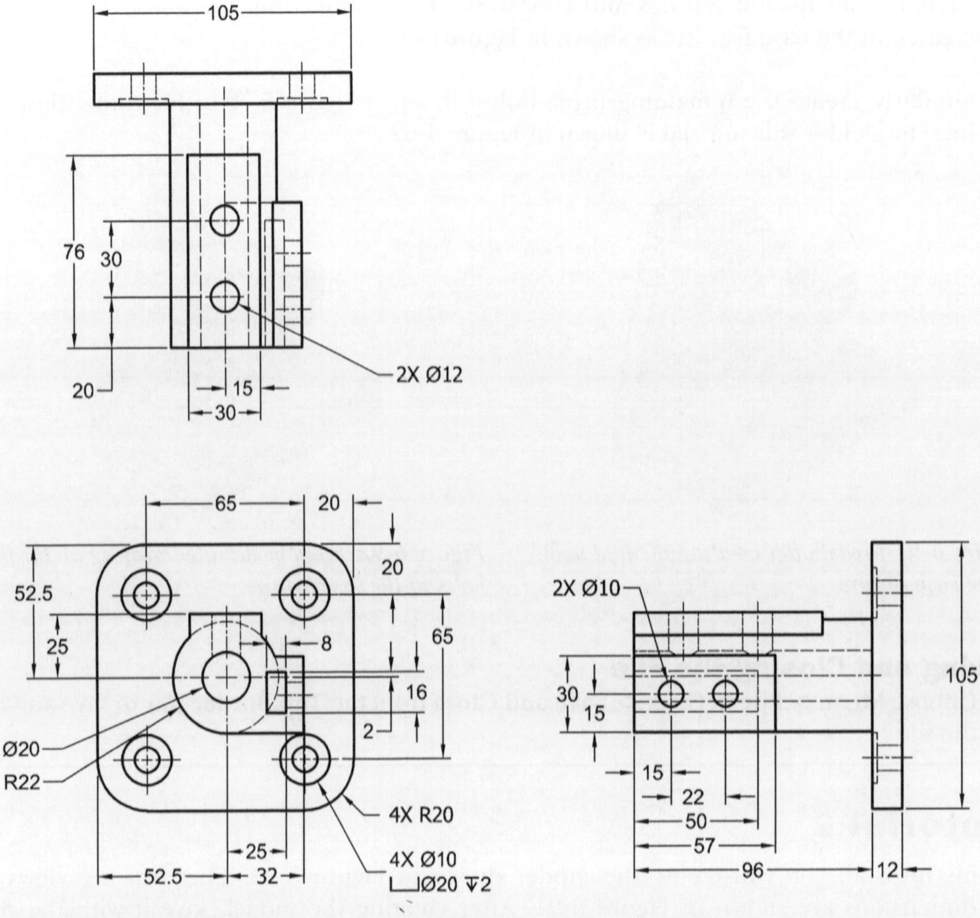

Figure 6-94 The drawing views and the dimensions of the model for Tutorial 2

The following steps are required to complete this tutorial:

a. Draw the sketch of the base feature of the model and extrude it, refer to Figures 6-95 and 6-96.
b. Draw the sketch of the second feature, which is a circle, and extrude it, refer to Figures 6-97 and 6-98.
c. Draw the sketches of the third and fourth features and extrude them, refer to Figures 6-99 and 6-100.
d. Create the simple hole on the left face of the model using the **Hole** tool, refer to Figure 6-101.
e. Create the rectangular cut extrude feature, refer to Figure 6-102.
f. Create holes on the top and front faces of the model using the **Hole** tool, refer to Figures 6-103 to 6-106.
g. Create four counterbore holes in the base feature using the **Hole** tool, refer to Figures 6-107 and 6-108.
h. Save and close the file.

Creating the Base Feature of the Model

After starting a new file, you need to create a sketch of the base feature of the model by following the steps given next.

1. Start a new file with the name *c06tut2.prt* using the **Model** template and specify its location as *C:\NX\c06*.

2. Draw sketch of the base feature by using the XC-ZC plane as the sketching plane, as shown in Figure 6-95. Next, exit the sketching environment.

3. Choose the **Extrude** tool from the **Feature** group; the **Extrude** dialog box is displayed and you are prompted to select the sketch to be extruded. Select the sketch created for the base feature.

4. Enter **12** in the **Distance** edit box available below the **End** drop-down list in the **Limits** rollout of the **Extrude** dialog box.

5. Choose the **OK** button from the **Extrude** dialog box; the base feature is created, as shown in Figure 6-96.

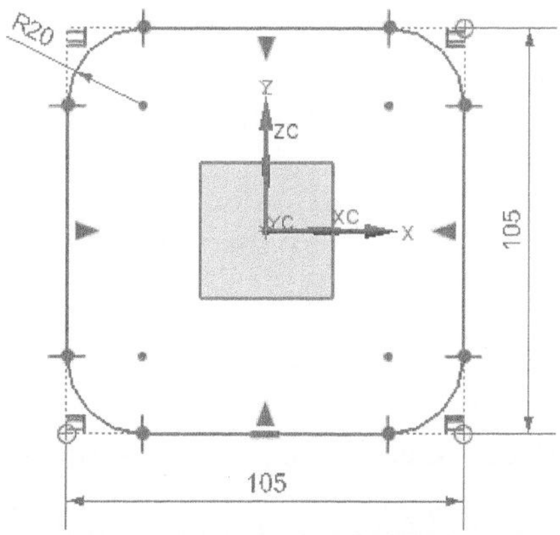

Figure 6-95 *The sketch of the base feature*

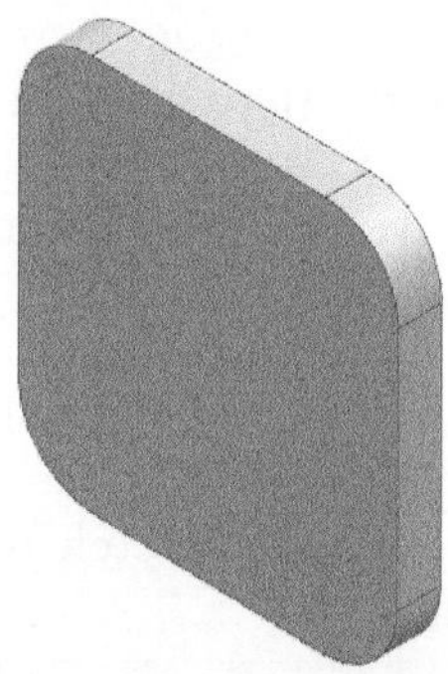

Figure 6-96 *The base feature*

Creating the Second Feature

The second feature of the model is a cylindrical extrude feature. The following steps explain the procedure to create this feature:

1. Invoke the sketching environment by selecting the front face of the base feature as the sketching plane.

2. Draw the sketch for the second feature which is a circle of diameter 44, refer to Figure 6-97. Next, choose the **Finish Sketch** tool from the **Direct Sketch** group to exit the sketching environment.

3. Choose the **Extrude** tool from the **Feature** group; the **Extrude** dialog box is displayed and you are prompted to select a sketch.

4. Select the sketch created for the second feature and enter **96** in the **Distance** edit box available below the **End** drop-down list in the **Limits** rollout of the **Extrude** dialog box.

5. Select the **Unite** option from the **Boolean** drop-down list in the **Boolean** rollout.

6. Choose the **OK** button from the dialog box; the cylindrical extrude feature is created. The model after creating the second feature is shown in Figure 6-98.

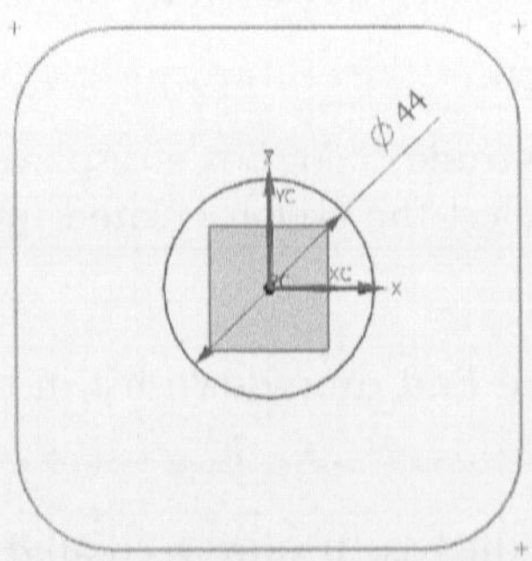

Figure 6-97 *The sketch for the second feature*

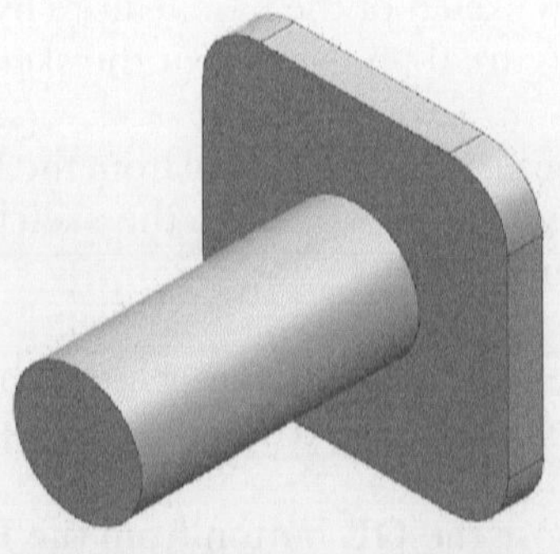

Figure 6-98 *Model after creating the second feature*

Creating the Third and Fourth Features

In this section, you need to create the third and fourth features which are extrude features, by following the steps given next.

1. Invoke the sketching environment by selecting the front face of the second feature as the sketching plane.

2. Draw a rectangular sketch for the third feature by using the dimensions given in Figure 6-94.

3. Choose the **Finish Sketch** tool from the **Direct Sketch** group to exit the sketching environment.

4. Choose the **Extrude** tool from the **Feature** group; the **Extrude** dialog box is displayed. Select the sketch created for the third feature; a preview of the feature is displayed in the drawing window.

5. Reverse the direction of extrusion by choosing the **Reverse Direction** button from the **Direction** rollout of the dialog box.

6. Enter **76** as the depth value in the **Distance** edit box available below the **End** drop-down list of the **Limits** rollout in the dialog box. Also, select the **Unite** option from the **Boolean** drop-down list in the **Boolean** rollout. Make sure that the value in the **Distance** edit box available below the **Start** drop-down list is 0.

7. Choose the **OK** button from the dialog box; the extruded feature is created. The resulting model after creating the third feature is shown in Figure 6-99.

8. Similarly, create the fourth extruded feature by using the dimensions given in Figure 6-94. The model after creating the fourth feature is shown in Figure 6-100.

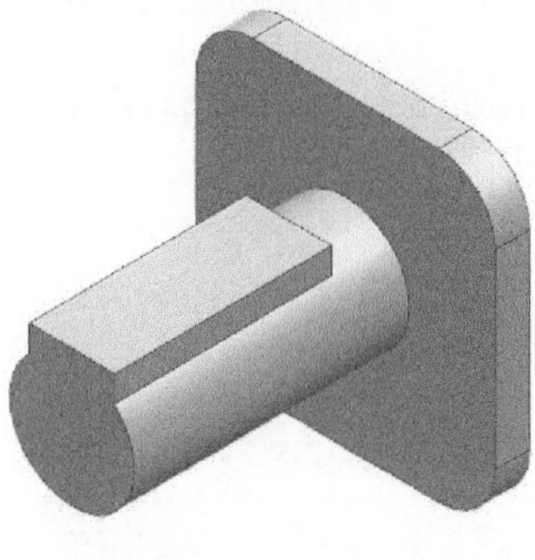

Figure 6-99 *The resulting model after creating the third feature*

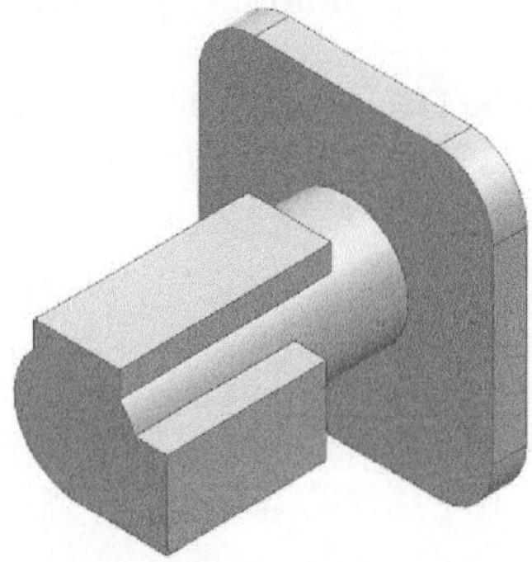

Figure 6-100 *The model after creating the fourth feature*

Creating a Hole in the Second Feature

In this section, you need to create a hole in the second feature.

1. Choose the **Hole** tool from the **Feature** group; the **Hole** dialog box is displayed and you are prompted to specify a point.

2. Select the center point of the front circular face of the second feature as the placement point; a preview of the hole feature is displayed in the drawing window. Make sure that the **General Hole** and **Simple** options are selected in the **Type** and **Form** drop-down lists, respectively in their rollouts.

3. Enter **20** in the **Diameter** edit box. Next, select the **Value** option from the **Depth Limit** drop-down list and enter **96** in the **Depth** edit box. Also, enter **0** in the **Tip Angle** edit box in the **Dimensions** sub-rollout of the **Hole** dialog box.

4. Accept other default settings and choose the **OK** button from the dialog box; a hole is created, as shown in Figure 6-101.

Creating the Rectangular Cut Extrude Feature

In this section, you need to create the rectangular cut extrude feature by following the steps given next.

1. Invoke the sketching environment by selecting the front face of the fourth feature which is merged with the front face of the second feature as the sketching plane.

2. Draw the sketch of this feature by using the dimensions given in Figure 6-94. Choose the **Finish Sketch** tool from the **Direct Sketch** group to exit the sketching environment.

3. Choose the **Extrude** tool from the **Feature** group and select the sketch created for the feature; a preview of the feature is displayed in the drawing window. Reverse the direction of feature creation by using the **Reverse Direction** button, if required.

4. Enter the depth value **50** in the **Distance** edit box available below the **End** drop-down list. Make sure the value in the **Distance** edit box available below the **Start** drop-down list is 0. Next, select the **Subtract** option from the **Boolean** drop-down list in the **Boolean** rollout.

5. Choose the **OK** button from the dialog box; the cut extrude feature is created. The resulting model after creating this feature is shown in Figure 6-102.

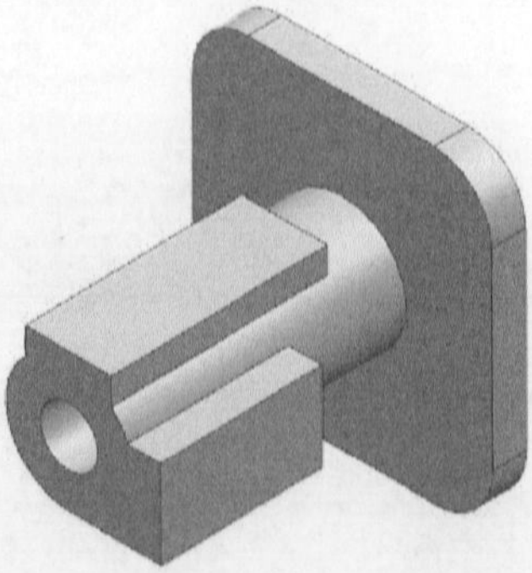

Figure 6-101 Model after creating the hole feature

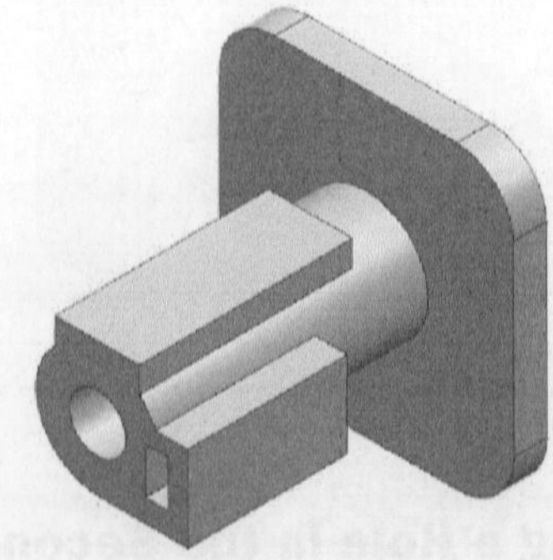

Figure 6-102 Model after creating the rectangular cut feature

Creating Holes in the Third and Fourth Features

In this section, you need to create holes in the third and fourth features by following the steps given next.

1. Choose the **Hole** tool from the **Feature** group; the **Hole** dialog box is displayed and you are prompted to select a planar face to sketch or specify a point. Make sure the **General Hole** and **Simple** options are selected in the **Type** and **Form** drop-down lists, respectively.

2. Select the top planar face of the third feature as a placement face; the **Sketch Point** dialog box is displayed. Also, the Sketch in Task environment is invoked. Now, place the point anywhere on the face and then exit the **Sketch Point** dialog box.

3. Apply dimensions to the point, refer to Figure 6-103. Next, exit the Sketch in Task environment; the **Hole** dialog box is displayed. Also, a preview of the hole is displayed in the drawing window.

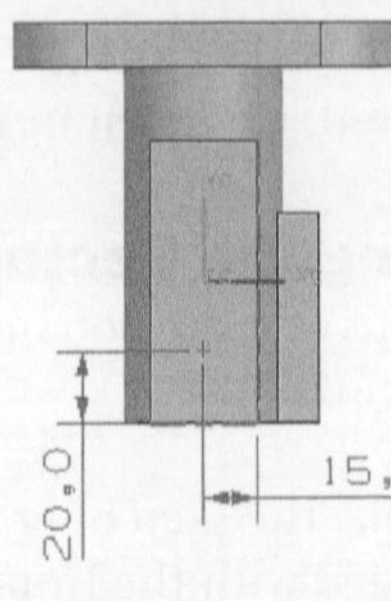

Figure 6-103 Point after applying the dimensions

4. Enter **12** as the hole diameter in the **Diameter** edit box in the **Dimensions** sub-rollout of the dialog box.

5. Select the **Until Selected** option from the **Depth Limit** drop-down list in the **Dimensions** sub-rollout of the dialog box; you are prompted to select a face or a datum plane on which the hole is to be created.

6. Select the cylindrical face of the hole created on the second feature as the face on which the hole is to be created.

7. Accept other default settings and choose the **OK** button from the dialog box; a hole is created, as shown in Figure 6-104.

8. Similarly, create the second hole on the third feature of the model using the **Hole** dialog box. The model after creating the second hole is shown in Figure 6-105.

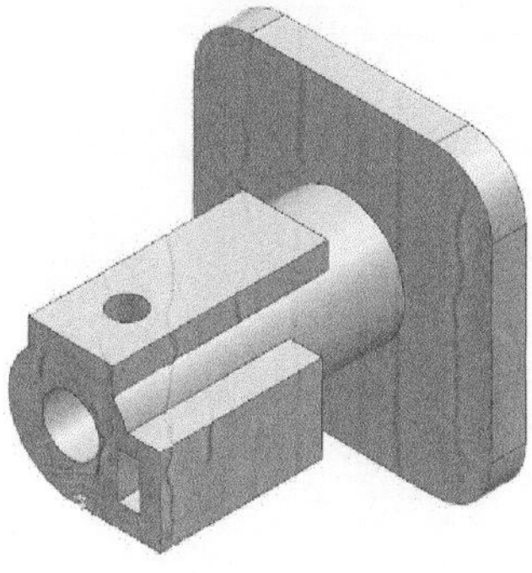

Figure 6-104 *Model after creating the first hole*

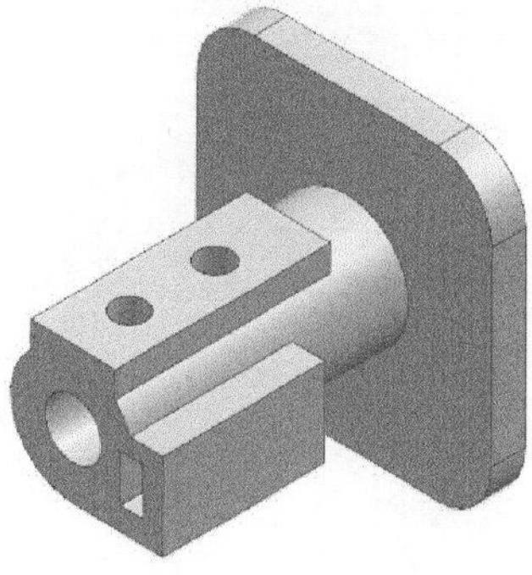

Figure 6-105 *Model after creating both holes*

After creating holes on the third feature, create holes on the fourth feature of the model by using the **Hole** dialog box. These holes will be created on the right face of the fourth feature. For dimensions of the holes, refer to Figure 6-94. The model after creating the holes in the fourth feature is shown in Figure 6-106.

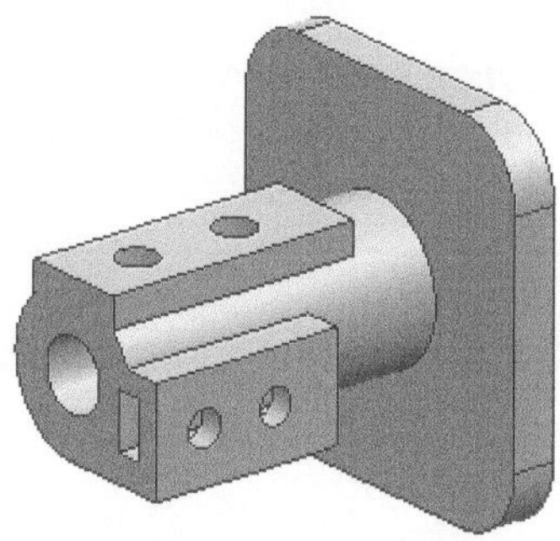

Figure 6-106 *Model after creating holes in the fourth feature*

Creating Counterbore Holes in the Base Feature

Next, create four counterbore holes in the base feature by following the steps given next.

1. Choose the **Hole** tool from the **Feature** group; the **Hole** dialog box is displayed. Next, you need to specify a point to define the hole location.

2. Move the cursor over the lower right round edge of the base feature and specify a point when the cursor snaps to its center point.

3. Select the **Counterbored** option from the **Form** drop-down list in the **Form and Dimensions** rollout of the dialog box. Make sure **General Hole** is selected in the **Type** drop-down list of the **Type** rollout in the dialog box.

4. Enter **20** in the **C-Bore Diameter** edit box, **2** in the **C-Bore Depth** edit box, and **10** in the **Diameter** edit box of the **Dimensions** sub-rollout of the **Form and Dimensions** rollout.

5. Select the **Until Selected** option from the **Depth Limit** drop-down list of the **Dimensions** sub-rollout in the dialog box and select the back face of the base feature to define the through face.

6. Choose the **OK** button from the dialog box; the counterbore hole is created, as shown in Figure 6-107.

7. Similarly, create the other three counterbore holes in the base feature of the model. The model after creating all counterbore holes is shown in Figure 6-108.

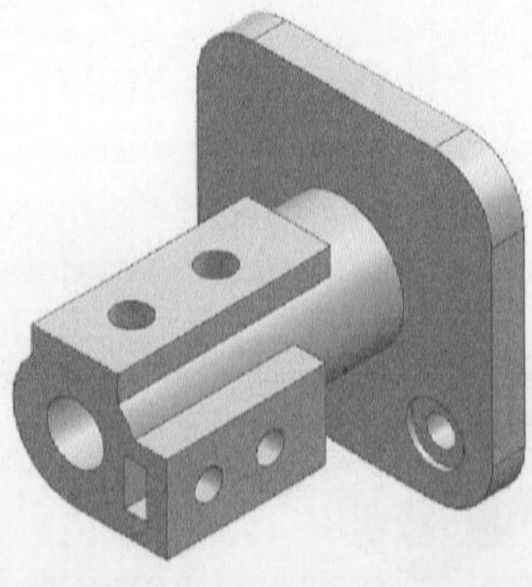

Figure 6-107 *The model after creating one counterbore hole*

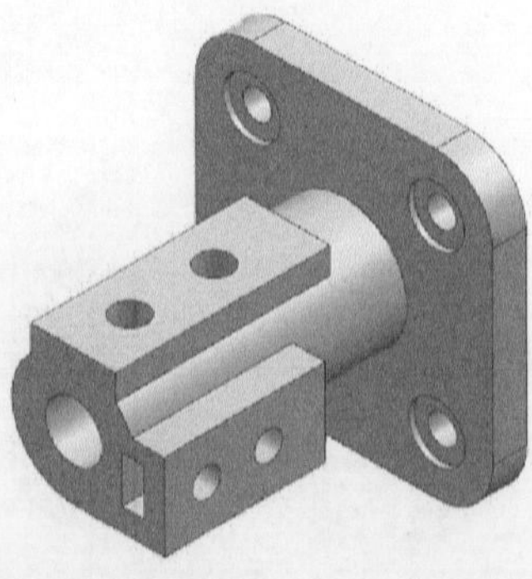

Figure 6-108 *The model after creating all counterbore holes*

Saving and Closing the File

1. Choose **Menu > File > Close > Save and Close** from the **Top border Bar** to save and close the current file.

Self-Evaluation Test

Answer the following questions and then compare them to those given at the end of this chapter:

1. Grooves can be created on both ________ and ________ faces.

2. In NX, you can create ________ types of grooves.

3. Slots are ________ features.

4. Slot features cannot be placed on a ________ face.

5. Slots are used as a ________ for sliding a member in practical models.

6. You can invoke the **Hole** tool by choosing **Menu > Insert > Design Feature > Hole** from the **Top border Bar**. (T/F)

7. In NX, you can create an aligned series of holes in multiple bodies. (T/F)

8. The placement face selected for holes cannot be a nonuniform surface. (T/F)

9. In NX, you can create a number of holes at a time using the **Hole** tool. (T/F)

10. While creating counterbore holes, the counterbore diameter must be greater than the hole diameter. (T/F)

Review Questions

Answer the following questions:

1. Which one of the following is not a hole type in NX?

   (a) **Counterbore** (b) **Countersink**
   (c) **Simple** (d) **Sectional**

2. Which of the following tools is used to create a chamfer feature?

   (a) **Chamfer** (b) **Edge Blend**
   (c) **Datum Plane** (d) None of these

3. Which of the following tools is used to create a blend (fillet) feature?

   (a) **Edge Chamfer** (b) **Edge Blend**
   (c) **Datum Plane** (d) None of these

4. Which of the following rollouts in the **Edge Blend** dialog box is used to create the variable radii blend feature?

   (a) **Variable Radius Points** (b) **Variable Radius**
   (c) **Variable Radius Blend** (d) None of these

5. Which of the following rollouts in the **Edge Blend** dialog box is used to create a corner blend feature?

   (a) **Corner Blend** (b) **Blend Setback**
   (c) **Corner Setback** (d) None of these

6. In T-slots, the bottom width value must be greater than the top width value. (T/F)

7. The **Stop Short of Corner** rollout of the **Edge Blend** dialog box is used to restrict the distance of the blend in the selected edge. (T/F)

8. You can chamfer circular edges. (T/F)

9. A counterbore hole has a uniform diameter throughout its length. (T/F)

10. Hole features can be placed on surfaces (sheet bodies). (T/F)

EXERCISES

Exercise 1

Create the model shown in Figure 6-109. The drawing views and dimensions of the model are given in Figure 6-110. After creating the model, save it with the name *c06exr1.prt* at the following location: *\NX\c06.* **(Expected time: 30 min)**

Figure 6-109 *Model for Exercise 1*

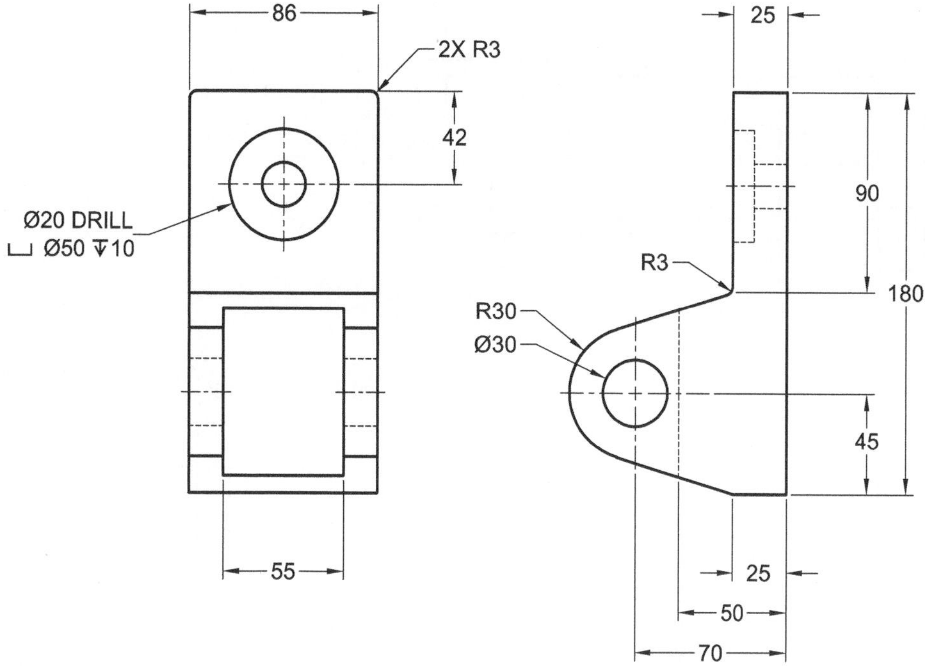

Figure 6-110 Dimensions and drawing views of the model for Exercise 1

Exercise 2

Create the model shown in Figure 6-111. The drawing views and dimensions of the model are given in Figure 6-112. After creating the model, save it with the name *c06exr2.prt* at the following location: *\NX\c06.* **(Expected time: 30 min)**

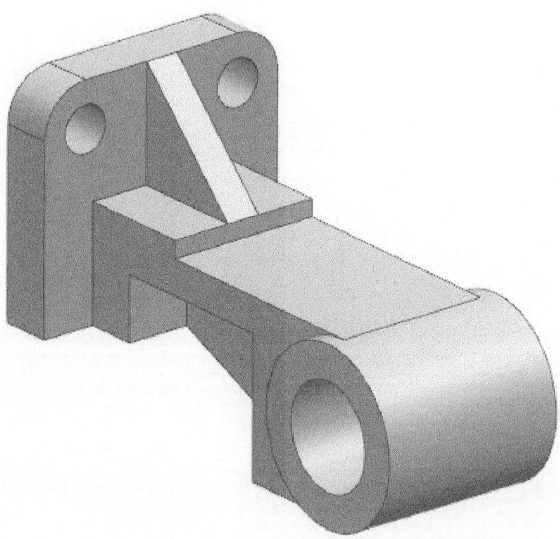

Figure 6-111 Model for Exercise 2

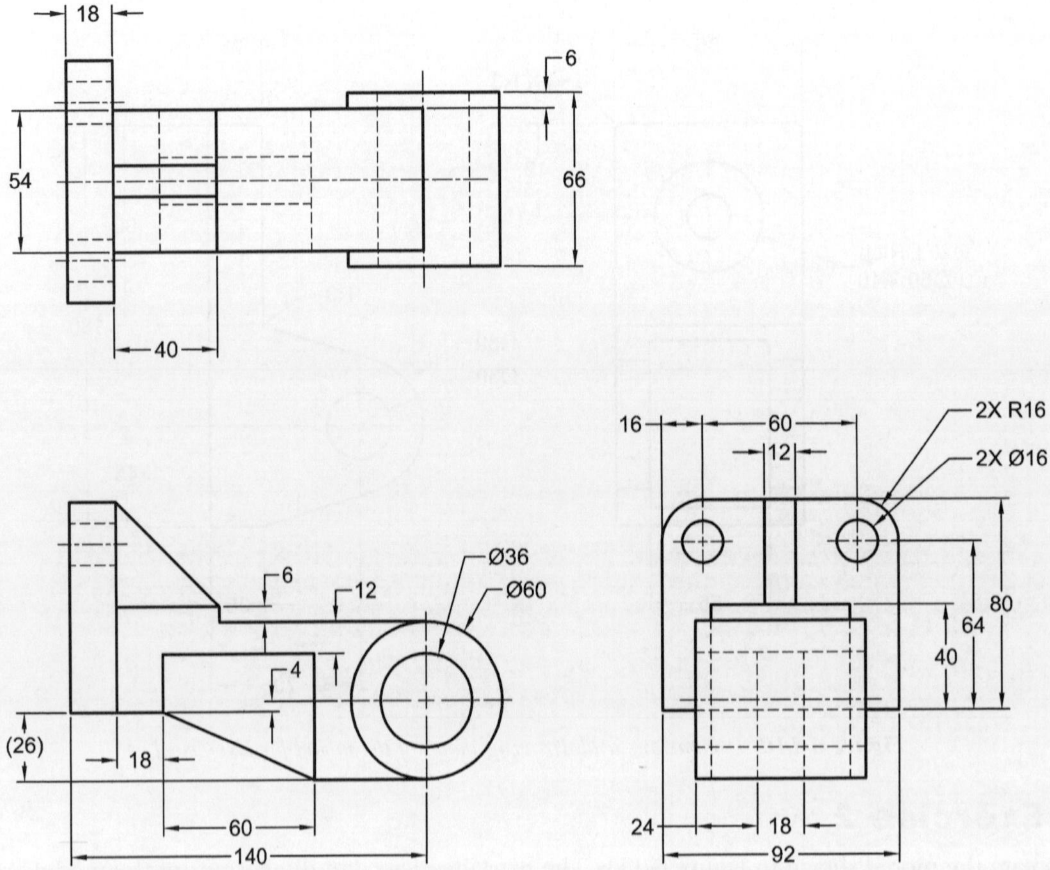

Figure 6-112 *Drawing views and dimensions of the model for Exercise 2*

Exercise 3

Create the model shown in Figure 6-113. The drawing views and dimensions of the model are given in Figure 6-114. After creating the model, save it with the name *c06exr3.prt* at the following location: *\NX\c06*. **(Expected time: 30 min)**

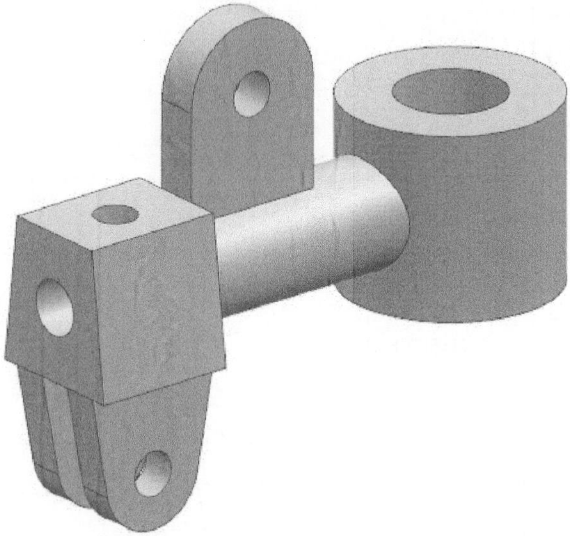

Figure 6-113 *Model for Exercise 3*

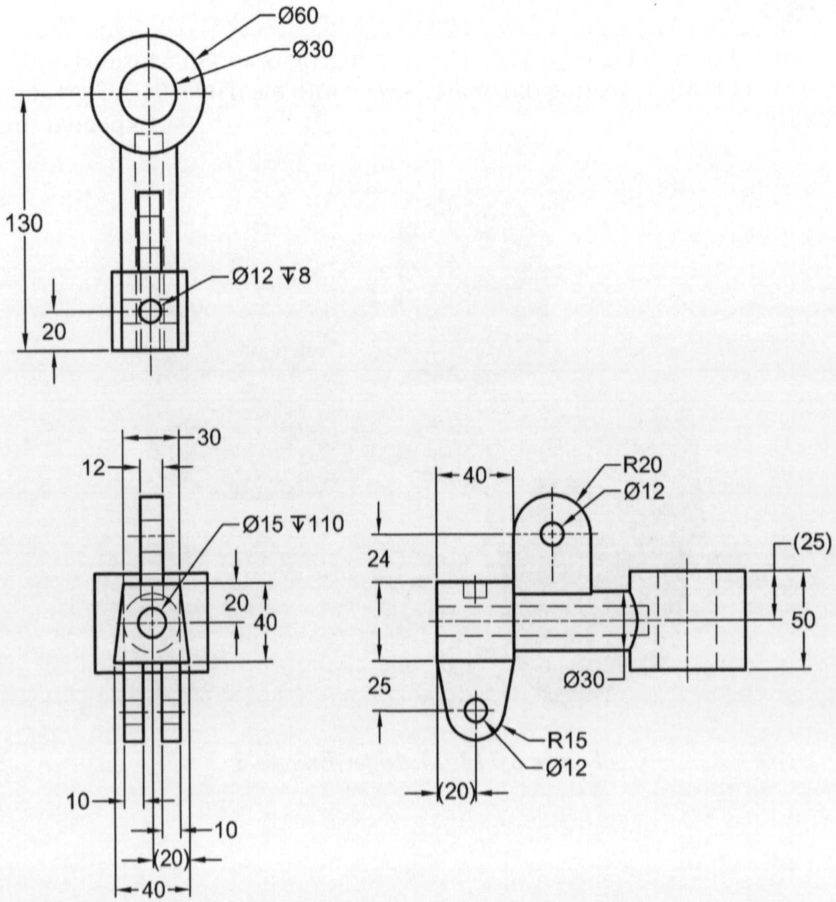

Figure 6-114 Drawing views and dimensions of the model for Exercise 3

Answers to Self-Evaluation Test

1. cylindrical, conical, **2.** three, **3.** placed, **4.** conical, **5.** guide way, **6.** T, **7.** T, **8.** T, **9.** T, **10.** T

Chapter 7

Advanced Modeling Tools-II

Learning Objectives

After completing this chapter, you will be able to:

- *Create the rectangular and circular arrays of a feature*
- *Mirror selected features and bodies*
- *Mirror selected faces and geometry*
- *Create sweep features*
- *Use the Swept tool to create lofted features*
- *Create tube features*
- *Create threads*
- *Convert solid features into hollow features*
- *Edit hole features*
- *Edit the positioning of groove features*
- *Edit the positioning of slot features*
- *Edit the parameters of features*
- *Edit the parameters of features with rollback*
- *Reorder features*
- *Create draft features*
- *Create lattice features*

ADVANCED MODELING TOOLS

In this chapter, you will learn about the following advanced modeling tools:

1. Pattern Feature
2. Mirror Feature
3. Mirror Body
4. Sweep along Guide
5. Swept
6. Tube
7. Thread
8. Shell

PATTERN FEATURE TOOL

Ribbon:	Home > Feature > Pattern Feature
Menu:	Insert > Associative Copy > Pattern Feature

The **Pattern Feature** tool is a very versatile tool in NX. This tool is used to create the linear and circular patterns of features. It is also used to create the polygon, spiral, along, general, reference, and helix patterns. The uses of this tool are discussed next.

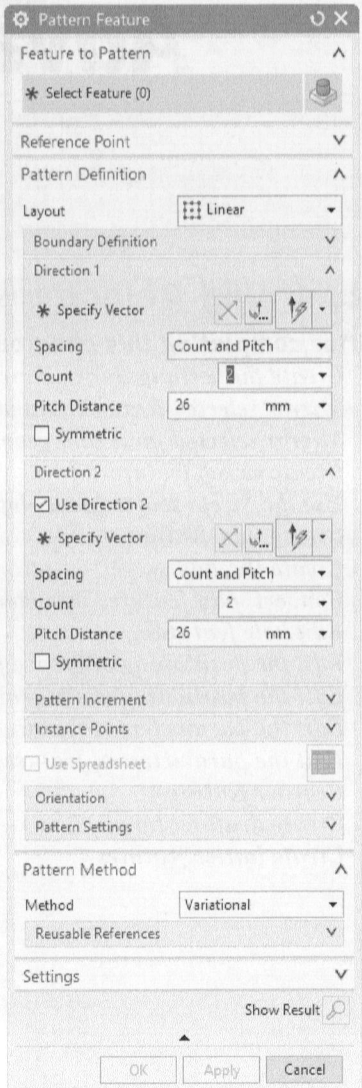

*Figure 7-1 The **Pattern Feature** dialog box for creating a linear pattern*

Creating a Linear Pattern

Linear pattern of a feature is created by placing the instances of that feature along the two directions of the work coordinate system (WCS). To create a linear pattern, choose the **Pattern Feature** tool from the **Feature** group of the **Home** tab; the **Pattern Feature** dialog box will be displayed, refer to Figure 7-1. The **Linear** option is selected by default in the **Layout** drop-down list of the **Pattern Definition** rollout of the dialog box. Click in the **Specify Vector** area of the **Direction 1** sub-rollout in the **Pattern Definition** rollout; a triad will be displayed in the graphics window and you will be prompted to select an object to define the first direction. Select an edge to define the first direction of the pattern creation. You can also use the triad to define the direction. Next, you need to define the number of instances and the spacing between them. There are four options to define the number of instances and spacing between them, which are listed in the **Spacing** drop-down list in the **Direction 1** sub-rollout. These options are discussed next.

Count and Pitch

On selecting this option, the **Count** and **Pitch Distance** edit boxes will be displayed. You need to specify the number of instances in the **Count** edit box and the distance between the instances in the **Pitch Distance** edit box.

Count and Span

On selecting this option, the **Count** and **Span Distance** edit boxes will be displayed. You need to specify the number of instances in the **Count** edit box and the total length of the pattern in the **Span Distance** edit box.

Pitch and Span

On selecting this option, the **Pitch Distance** and **Span Distance** edit boxes will be displayed. You need to specify the distance between two consecutive instances in the **Pitch Distance** edit box and the total length of the pattern in the **Span Distance** edit box.

List

On selecting this option, a table will be displayed in the **Direction1** sub-rollout. Also, the **Spacing Value** edit box will be displayed. You need to enter a value in the **Spacing Value** edit box. You can choose the **Add New Set** button located next to the table to add a new spacing value. You can remove a spacing value from the table using the **Remove** button.

After specifying the count and spacing of the pattern, you can select the **Symmetric** check box to create the pattern on both sides of the feature. Figure 7-2 shows the preview of the pattern created on both sides of the feature.

You can also create a linear pattern in two directions. To do so, select the **Use Direction 2** check box in the **Direction 2** sub-rollout; the options in this sub-rollout will be displayed. Next, specify the parameters in the **Direction 2** sub-rollout. The options in this sub-rollout are same as in the **Direction 1** sub-rollout. Figure 7-3 shows a model with a linear pattern created in two directions.

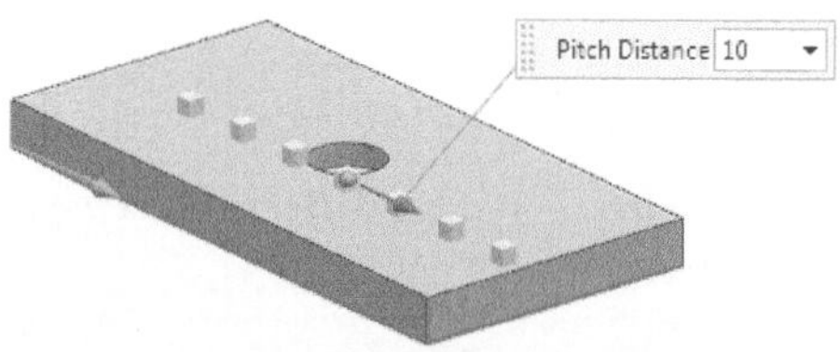

***Figure 7-2** Preview of the pattern created on both sides of the feature*

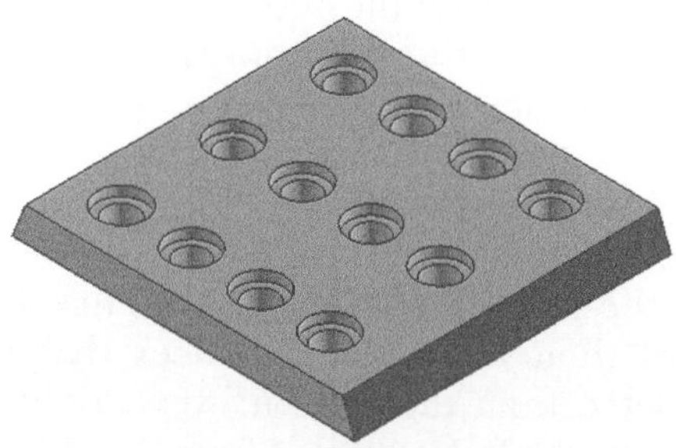

***Figure 7-3** Linear pattern created in two directions*

The advanced options of the **Pattern Feature** dialog box are discussed next.

Pattern Increment Sub-rollout

This sub-rollout is used to specify an increment value for the parameters of a pattern. To do so, choose the **Pattern Increment** button; the **Pattern Increment** dialog box will be displayed, as shown in Figure 7-4. The **Parameters** rollout in this dialog box displays the pattern and feature parameters. For example, if you want to specify an increment value for the offset distance along Direction 1, double-click on **Direction 1: Offset Distance** in the **Parameters** rollout or right-click on **Direction 1: Offset Distance** and choose the **Add to Direction 1** option; the **Increment** edit box will be displayed in the **Direction 1** rollout. Next, specify an increment value in the **Increment** edit box.

You can also specify an increment value for a particular parameter of the feature. To do so, double-click on the parameter in the **Parameters** rollout or right-click on the parameter and choose the **Add to Direction 1** option from the shortcut menu. Next, enter the increment value in the **Increment** edit box displayed. Figure 7-5 shows a pattern after specifying an increment value for the height of the feature. To exit the **Pattern Increment** dialog box, choose the **OK** button.

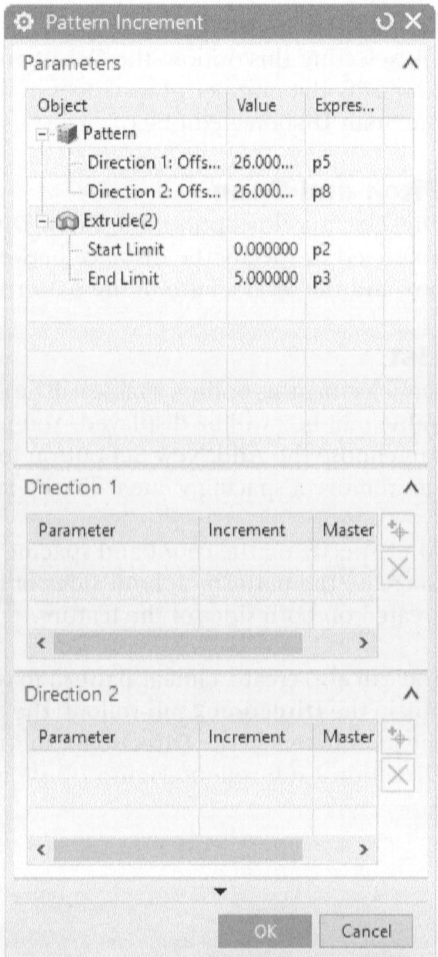

Figure 7-4 The ***Pattern Increment*** *dialog box*

Instance Points Sub-rollout

The button available at the right of the **Select Instance Point** area in this sub-rollout is used to suppress, delete, move, or change the parameters of an instance. The various uses of this option are discussed next.

Suppressing Instances

To suppress instances, choose the button available at the right of the **Select Instance Point** area and then select the instances that are to be suppressed. Next, right-click and choose the **Suppress** option from the shortcut menu displayed; the selected instances will be suppressed. Figure 7-6 shows a pattern with some suppressed instances. You can also unsuppress the suppressed instances. To do so, right-click on the dots displayed on them and then choose the **Unsuppress** option from the shortcut menu.

Deleting Instances

To delete instances, choose the button available at the right of the **Select Instance Point** area and then select the instances that are to be deleted from the pattern. Next, right-click and choose the **Delete** option from the shortcut menu displayed; the selected instances will be deleted.

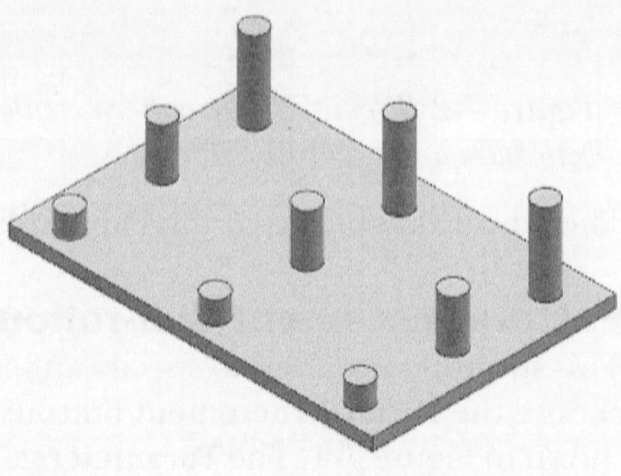

Figure 7-5 Pattern with height increment

Clocking or Moving Instances

To clock instances, choose the button available at the right of the **Select Instance Point** area and then select the instances from the pattern. Next, right-click and choose the **Clock** option from the shortcut menu displayed; the **Clock** dialog box will be displayed. You can clock the instances by using the **Within Pattern Definition** or the **User Defined** option available in the drop-down list in the **Type** rollout. On selecting the **Within Pattern Definition** option, you need to enter distance values in the **Direction 1** and **Direction 2** edit boxes. The instances will be moved to the specified location based on the values specified in the respective edit boxes. If you select the **User Defined** option, a dynamic triad will be displayed on the pattern. You can use the handles available on the triad to move the instances. You can also specify the coordinate values in the **X**, **Y** and **Z** edit boxes which are displayed on choosing the **Manipulator** button in the **Clocking Delta** rollout. Figure 7-7 shows a linear pattern after clocking some of the instances.

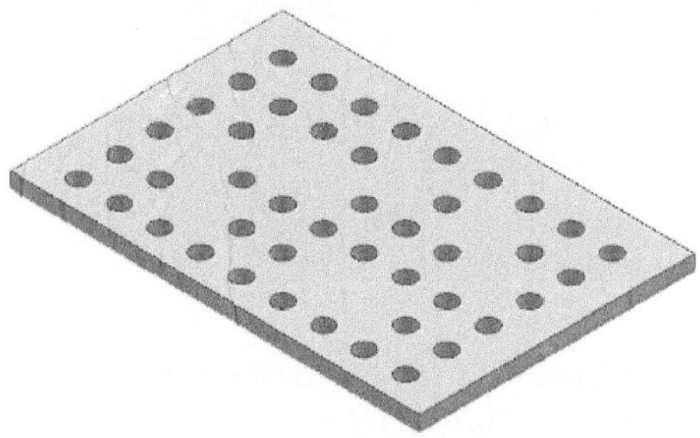

Figure 7-6 *Pattern with some instances suppressed*

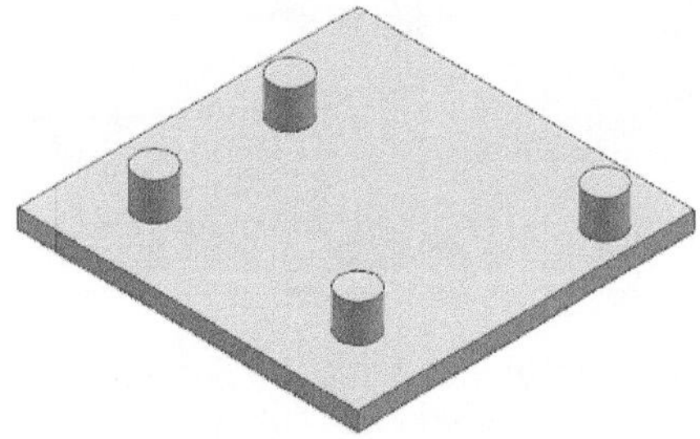

Figure 7-7 *Pattern after clocking some of the instances*

You can also unclock the clocked instances. To do so, choose the button available at the right of the **Select Instance Point** area and then select the instances that are to be unclocked. Next, right-click and choose the **Unclock** option from the shortcut menu displayed; the selected instances will be unclocked.

Note

*You can clock a pattern instance without invoking the **Pattern Feature** dialog box. To do so, expand the **Pattern Feature** node from the **Part Navigator** and right-click on the instance to be clocked; a shortcut menu will be displayed. Choose the **Clock** option from the shortcut menu; the **Instance Feature** dialog box will be displayed. Specify the clocking distance in the **Direction 1** and **Direction 2** edit boxes available in this dialog box and then choose the **OK** button; the instance will be clocked.*

Specifying Variant Parameters for an Instance

To specify variant parameters for a particular instance in the pattern, choose the button available at the right of the **Select Instance Point** area and then select the instances from the pattern. Next, right-click and choose the **Specify Variance** option from the shortcut menu displayed or double-click on the instance; the **Variance** dialog box will be displayed. The parameters of the instance will be displayed in the **Parameters** rollout in this dialog box. To edit a parameter, you need to double-click on it in the **Parameters** rollout. Next, enter a new value for the parameter in the **Value** edit box available in the **Values** rollout. Then, choose the **OK** button to close the **Variance** dialog box. Next, choose the **OK** button from the **Pattern Feature** dialog box; variant parameters will be applied to the selected instance. Figure 7-8 shows a pattern with a variant instance located in the middle.

Pattern Settings Sub-rollout

The options in this rollout are used to specify the settings of the pattern layout.

Frame Only

On selecting this check box, only the frame of the pattern will be created, as shown in Figure 7-9.

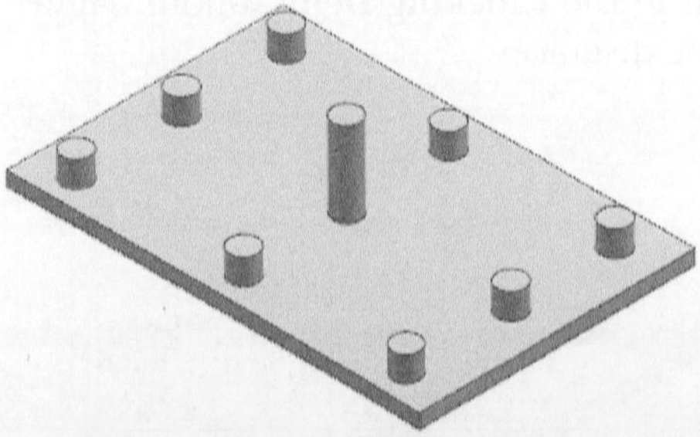

Figure 7-8 Pattern with a variant instance placed in the middle

Figure 7-9 The pattern created with the ***Frame Only*** *check box selected*

Stagger

The options in this drop-down list are used to create a stagger pattern. If you select the **Direction1** option, the stagger pattern will be created along the first direction. On selecting the **Direction 2** option, the stagger pattern will be created in the second direction. Figures 7-10 and 7-11 show the stagger patterns created along the first and second directions, respectively.

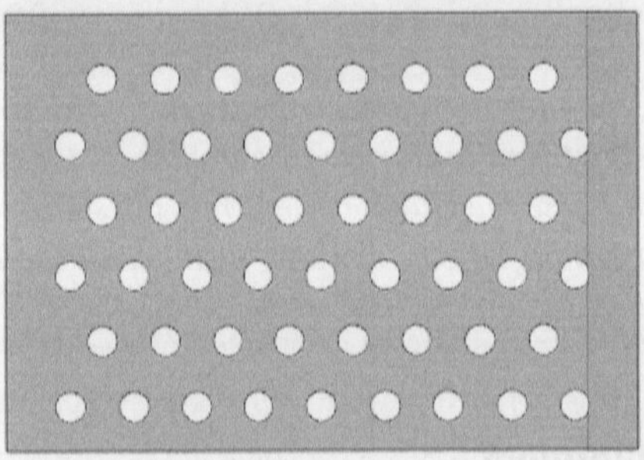

Figure 7-10 Stagger pattern created in the first direction

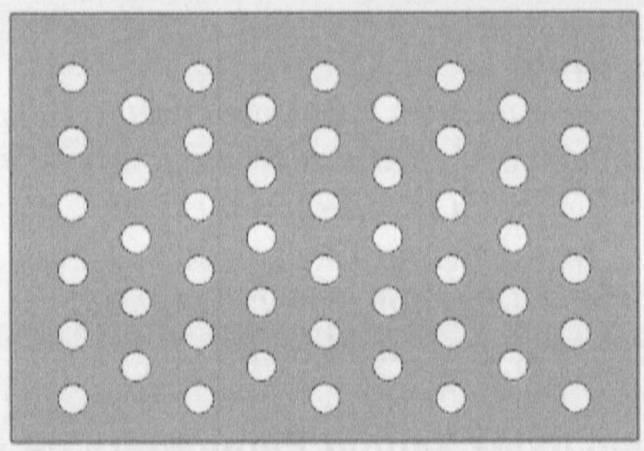

Figure 7-11 Stagger pattern created in the second direction

Show Last Line of Instances

On selecting this check box, the instances in the last line of the stagger pattern will be displayed.

Pattern Method Rollout

This rollout is used to specify the method for creating a pattern. These methods are available in the **Method** drop-down list and they are discussed next.

Variational

This method is used to pattern features with details such as rounds and chamfers, refer to Figure 7-12. You can also pattern multiple features using this method.

Simple

This method is used to pattern simple features such as holes, extruded features, and so on, refer to Figure 7-13. Also, you can only pattern a single feature at one time. If you select multiple features, a master pattern of first feature will be created and all the other features will be patterned as reference patterns. You will learn more about reference pattern later in this chapter.

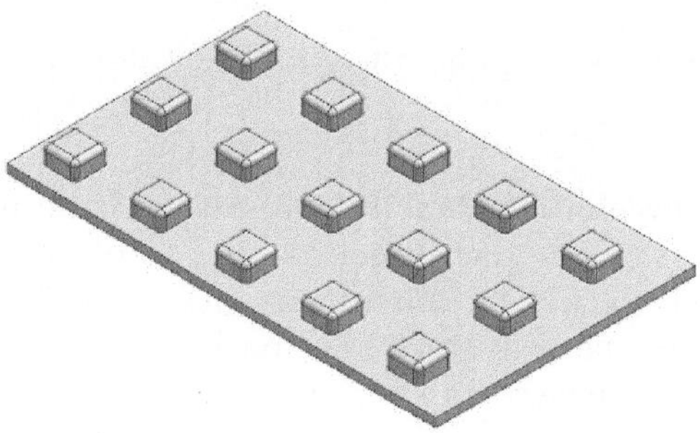

Figure 7-12 *Pattern created using the **Variational** method*

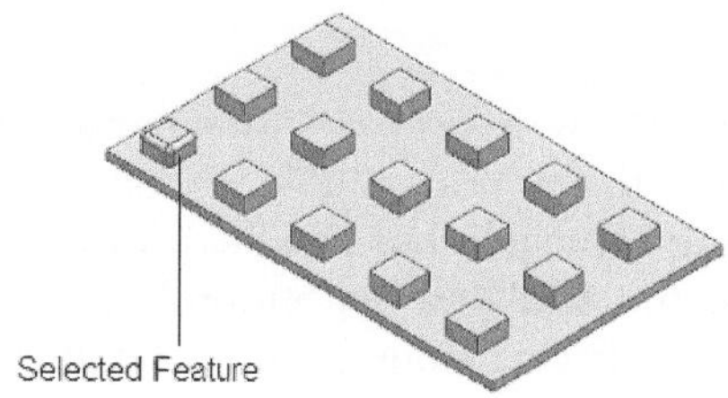

Figure 7-13 *Pattern created using the **Simple** method*

Note

You can change the pattern method while editing it.

Creating a Circular Pattern

To create a circular pattern of the selected features, invoke the **Pattern Feature** tool; the **Pattern Feature** dialog box will be displayed. Select the **Circular** option from the **Layout** drop-down list in this dialog box; the **Pattern Definition** rollout in this dialog box will be modified, as shown in Figure 7-14, and you will be prompted to select features to pattern. Select the features to be patterned from the drawing window. Next, click in the **Specify Vector** area in the **Rotation Axis** sub-rollout of the **Pattern Definition** rollout; a triad will be displayed in the drawing window and you will be prompted to select an object to infer vector. Use the triad to specify the axis of rotation. Note that you need to select the axis perpendicular to the face on which the pattern is to be created, refer to Figure 7-15. Next, you need to specify the center of the circular pattern. You can infer to center point of the circular face to specify the center of the pattern. Next, you need to define the number of instances and the angular spacing between them. There are four options to define the number of instances and spacing between them. These options are listed in the **Spacing** drop-down list in the **Angular Direction** sub-rollout and they are discussed next.

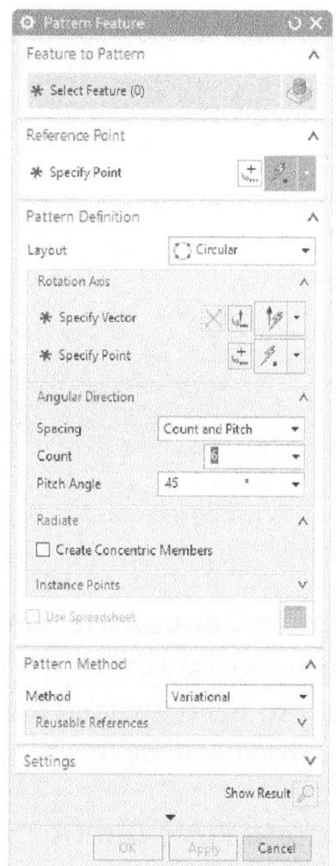

Figure 7-14 *The **Pattern Definition** rollout for creating a circular pattern*

Count and Pitch
This option is used to specify the instance count and the angle between the instances.

Count and Span
This option is used to specify the instance count and the span angle of the pattern.

Pitch and Span
This option is used to specify the angle between the instances and the span angle of the pattern.

List
This option is used to specify separate angle between individual instances of the pattern. On selecting this option, a table will be displayed in the **Angular Direction** sub-rollout. Also, the **Spacing Value** edit box will be displayed in which you need to enter an angular value. You can choose the **Add New Set** button located next to the table to add a new spacing value. You can remove a spacing value from the table using the **Remove** button.

The other options that are useful to create a circular pattern are discussed next.

Radiate Sub-rollout
This sub-rollout is used to create circular patterns which are concentric to the first pattern, as shown in Figure 7-16. The options in this sub-rollout are discussed next.

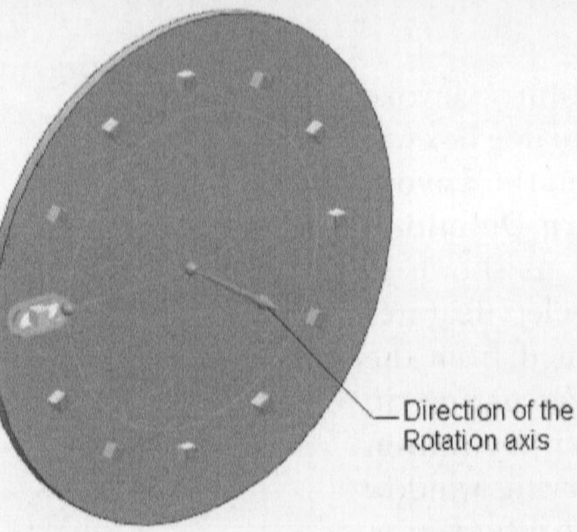

Figure 7-15 Preview of the circular pattern with the rotation axis selected

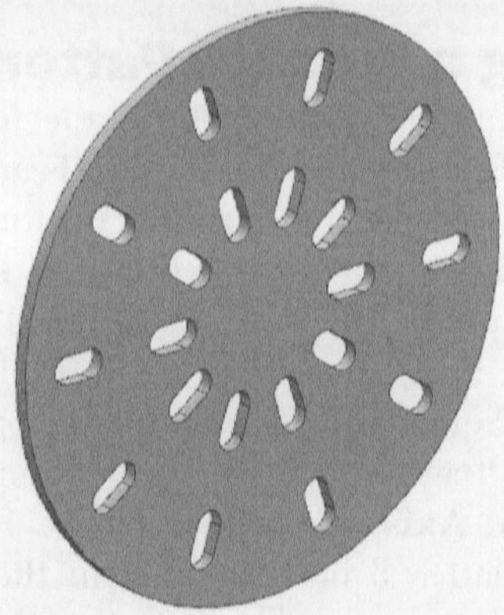

Figure 7-16 Two concentric circular patterns

Create Concentric Members
On selecting this check box, a preview of the other circular pattern is displayed. Also, the options to create concentric patterns are displayed in the **Radiate** sub-rollout. These options are discussed next.

Include First Circle
This check box is selected by default. If you clear this check box, the first circular pattern will not be included.

Spacing

In this drop-down list, there are four options to define the number of circular patterns and radial spacing between them. These four options have been discussed earlier in the chapter.

Orientation Sub-rollout

The options in this rollout are used to define the orientation of the pattern feature. These options are available in the **Orientation** drop-down list and are discussed next.

Same as Input

On selecting this option, the orientation of all the instances will become the same as that of the input feature, refer to Figure 7-17.

Follow Pattern

On selecting this option, the orientation of the instances will become as per the layout, refer to Figure 7-18.

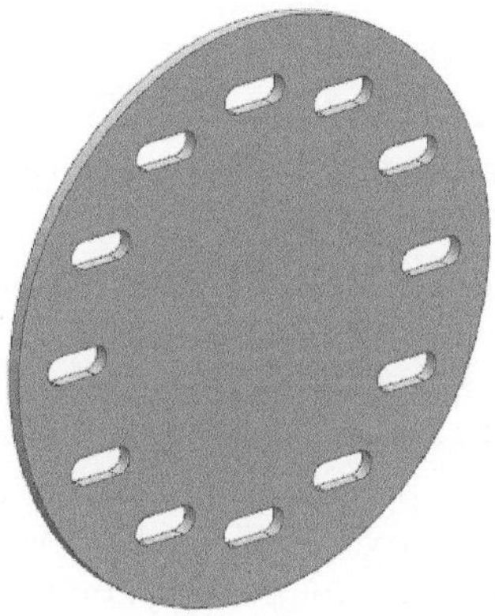

Figure 7-17 *Pattern orientation on selecting the* ***Same as Input*** *option*

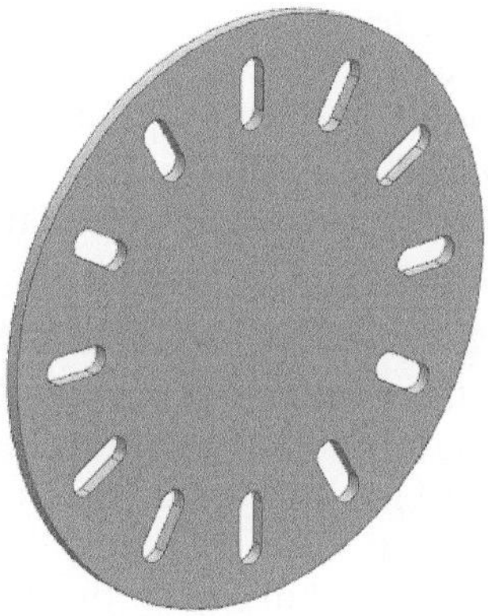

Figure 7-18 *Pattern orientation on selecting the* ***Follow Pattern*** *option*

CSYS to CSYS

This option is used to define the orientation of the instances from one coordinate system to another. On selecting this option, you will be prompted to select objects to infer CSYS. You can select an existing CSYS or create a new one by choosing the **CSYS Dialog** button available in the **Orientation** sub-rollout. After selecting the first CSYS, you will be prompted again to select objects to infer CSYS. Select an existing CSYS or create a new one. Note that the orientation of the second CSYS should be different from the first CSYS. Figure 7-19 shows two coordinate systems selected and Figure 7-20 shows the pattern instances oriented based on the second coordinate system.

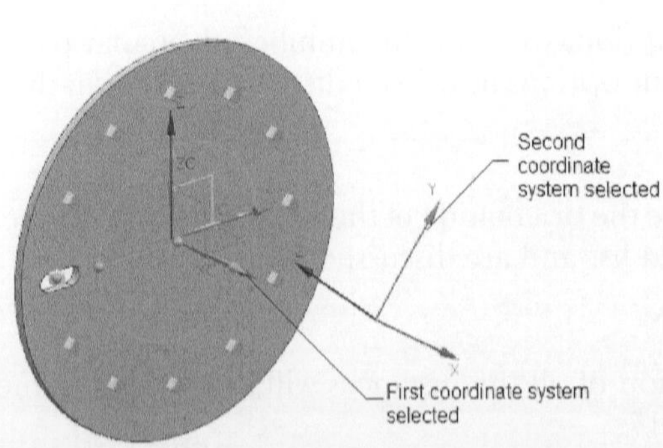

Figure 7-19 Two coordinate systems selected to specify the orientation

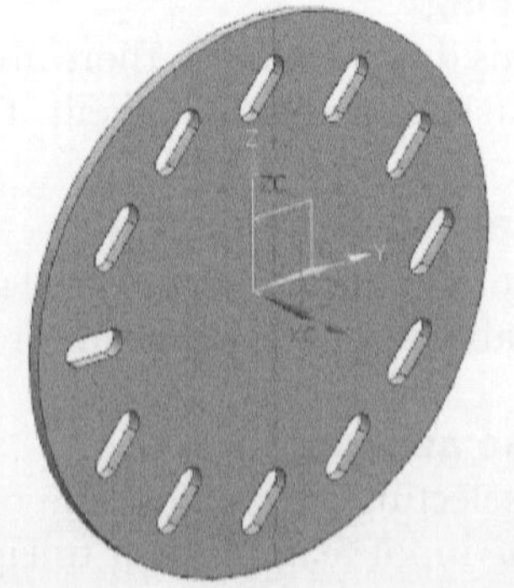

Figure 7-20 Pattern instances oriented based on the orientation of the second coordinate system

Follow Face

This check box is used to specify a face on the body. The instances will be oriented normal to the specified face. This check box is available when you select the **Same as Input** or **Follow Pattern** options from the **Orientation** drop-down list.

Creating a Polygon Pattern

The procedure to create a polygon pattern is similar to that of a circular pattern. To create a polygon pattern, invoke the **Pattern Feature** dialog box and select the **Polygon** option from the **Layout** drop-down list; various options to create a polygon pattern are displayed, as shown in Figure 7-21. Next, select the feature to be patterned from the drawing window. After selecting the feature, you need to specify the rotation axis and the center of the polygon pattern. Next, you need to specify the number of instances and spacing between them. The options to specify the instance count and the spacing are available in the **Polygon Definition** sub-rollout.

Polygon Definition Sub-rollout

The options in this sub-rollout are discussed next.

Number of Sides

This edit box is used to specify the number of sides of the polygon pattern.

Spacing

This drop-down list contains options to specify the spacing between the instances. The options in this drop-down list are discussed next.

Count per Side: On selecting this option, the **Count** edit box will be displayed below the spacing drop-down list. You need to specify the number of instances per side and the total span.

Pitch along Side: On selecting this option, you need to specify the pitch and total span in their respective edit boxes.

Radiate Sub-rollout

The options in this sub-rollout are used to create more patterns concentric to the first one, as shown in Figure 7-22. To do so, select the **Create Concentric Members** check box; the options to create a concentric pattern will be displayed.

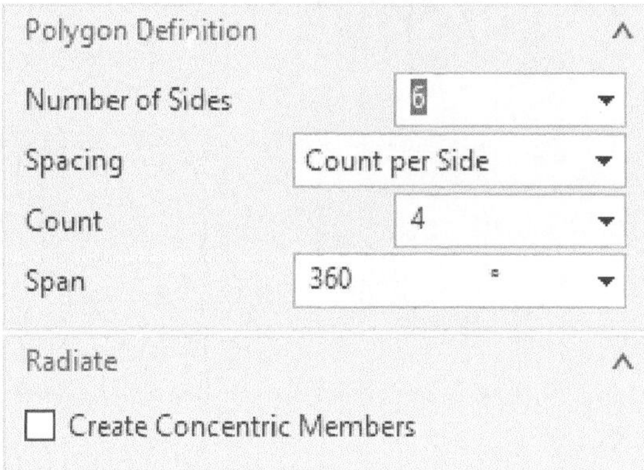

Figure 7-21 Options to create a polygon pattern

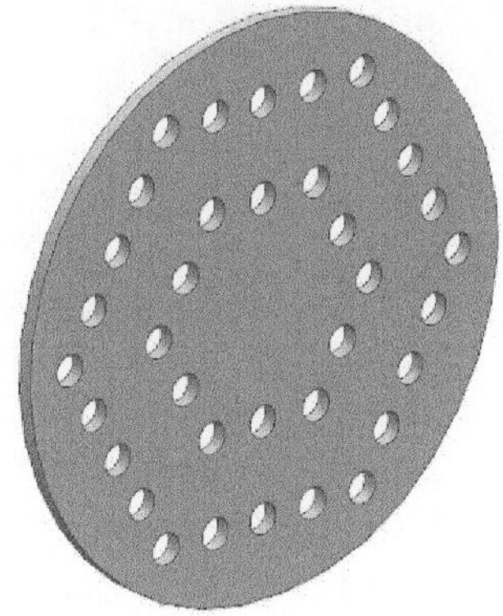

Figure 7-22 Concentric polygon patterns

The **Size** drop-down list contains the options to define the size of the polygon. You can select the **Inscribed** or the **Circumscribed** option from this drop-down list.

All the other options in this sub-rollout are same as discussed earlier in the chapter.

Creating a Spiral Pattern

To create a spiral pattern, invoke the **Pattern Feature** dialog box and select the **Spiral** option from the **Layout** drop-down list; the options to create a spiral pattern will be displayed in the **Spiral** sub-rollout, as shown in Figure 7-23. Also, you will be prompted to select the feature to be patterned. Select the feature to be patterned. Next, click in the **Specify Plane Normal** area in the **Spiral** sub-rollout and then select the plane or face on which the pattern is to be created; the **Reference Vector** area will get activated and you will be prompted to select object to infer vector. Use the vector triad displayed to specify the reference vector, refer to Figure 7-24. The total angle and the radial pitch will be calculated from the specified reference vector. Note that the reference vector should be parallel to the face on which the pattern is created. The other options related to creating spiral pattern are discussed next.

Direction

The options in this drop-down list are used to specify the direction of the spiral pattern. You can select the **Left Hand** option or the **Right Hand** option from this drop-down list to specify the direction.

Spiral Size By

This drop-down list is used to specify the method for calculating the size of the spiral pattern. The spiral size can be calculated by specifying the **Total angle** or **Number of Turns**.

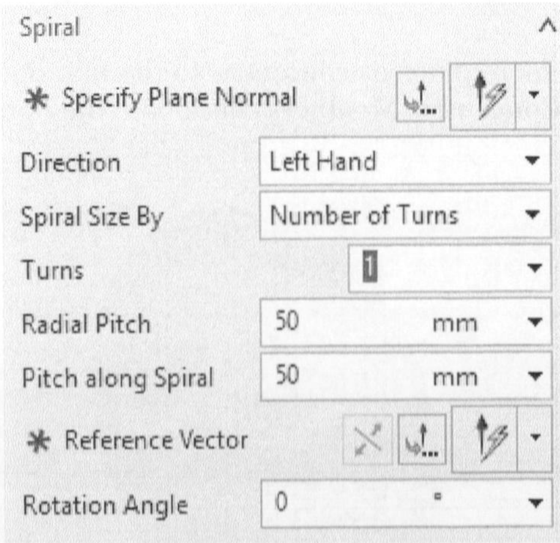

Figure 7-23 Options to create a spiral pattern

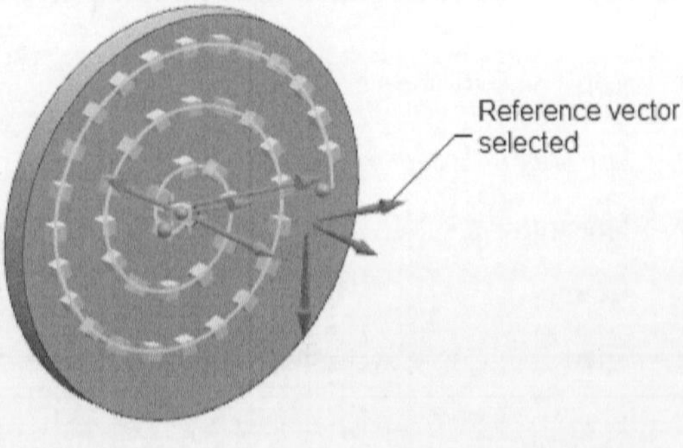

Figure 7-24 Reference vector to be selected

Turns

This edit box is used to specify the number of turns of the spiral pattern. This edit box is available only when you select the **Number of Turns** option from the **Spiral Size By** drop-down list.

Angle

The **Angle** edit box is used to specify the total angle of the spiral pattern. This edit box is available only when you select the **Total Angle** option from the **Spiral Size By** drop-down list. You need to specify an angle value greater than 360 in order to create turns greater than one.

Radial Pitch

This edit box is used to specify the distance between the consecutive turns of the spiral pattern.

Pitch along Spiral

This edit box is used to specify the distance between the consecutive instances of the pattern.

Rotation Angle

This edit box is used to specify an offset angle from the specified reference point.

After specifying the parameters in the **Spiral** sub-rollout, choose the **OK** button; the spiral pattern will be created, as shown in Figure 7-25.

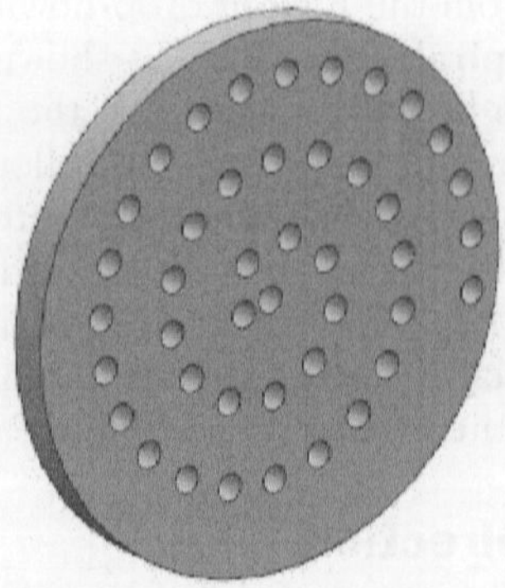

Figure 7-25 Spiral pattern

Creating a Pattern Along a Curve

In NX, you can pattern features along a selected curve or edge, as shown in Figure 7-26. A curve can be a sketched entity, an edge, an open profile, or a closed profile. To create a pattern along a curve, invoke the **Pattern Feature** dialog box and select the **Along** option from the **Layout** drop-down list; the options related to the along curve pattern will be displayed in the **Pattern**

Feature dialog box. Also, you will be prompted to select a feature to pattern. Select a feature from the drawing area. Next, choose the **Curve** button from the **Direction 1** sub-rollout and select the path along which the feature will be patterned. You can select an edge, a curve, or a sketched entity. Next, you need to define the alignment with the specified path. You can define the alignment of instances with the path using the **Rigid**, **Offset**, and **Translate** options that are available in the **Path Method** drop-down list. Next, you need to specify the orientation using the options in the **Orientation** sub-rollout.

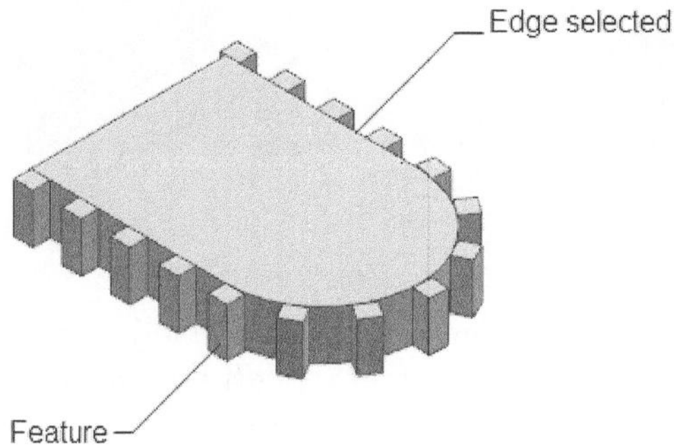

Figure 7-26 *Along curve pattern*

After specifying the alignment and orientation, you need to specify the spacing between the instances. There are four options to specify the spacing: **Count and Pitch**, **Count and Span**, **Pitch and Span**, and **List**. These options are available in the **Spacing** drop-down list.

Count and Pitch

This option is used to specify the instance count and the distance between the instances along the curve. Enter the number of instances in the **Count** edit box. Next, select an option from the **Location** drop-down list. If you select the **Arc Length** option, the **Pitch By** edit box is displayed. Enter the distance between the instances in the **Pitch By** edit box. Similarly, if you select the **% Arc Length** option, the **% Pitch By** edit box will be displayed. Enter the percentage of arc length between 0 and 100 in the **% Pitch By** edit box.

Count and Span

This option is used to specify the instance count and the span length of the pattern along the curve. You can specify the span length in the **Span By** or **% Span By** edit box.

Pitch and Span

This option is used to specify distance between the instances and the span length of the pattern along the curve.

You can also specify the parameters in the second direction. To do so, select the **Use Direction 2** check box; the options in the **Direction 2** sub-rollout will become available. You can specify the second direction by using the **Vector** or **Curve** options available in the **Direction by** drop-down list. On selecting the **Vector** option from this drop-down list, the vector triad will be displayed and you will be prompted to select objects to infer vector. You can also use the vector triad to define the direction. On selecting the **Curve** option, you can define the second direction by selecting a curve. All the other options in the **Direction 2** sub-rollout are same as discussed earlier.

Figure 7-27 shows a curve pattern feature created along the curve, with the pattern defined in the first and second directions.

Select the **Input Feature Only for Direction 2** option in the **Pattern settings** sub-rollout if you want to pattern only the input feature along the second direction, as shown in Figure 7-28.

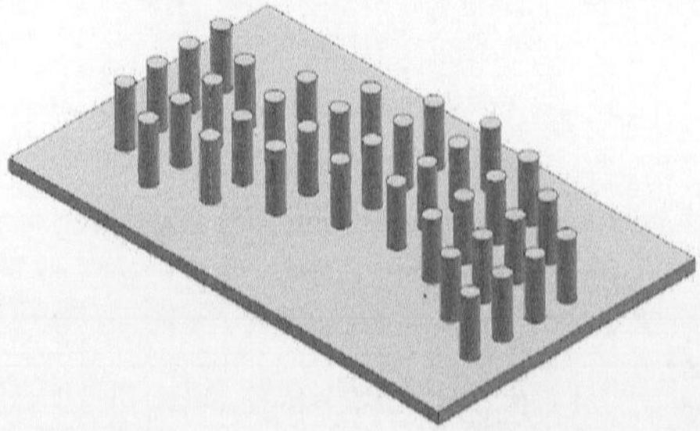

Figure 7-27 *Along curve pattern created by specifying parameters in both the directions*

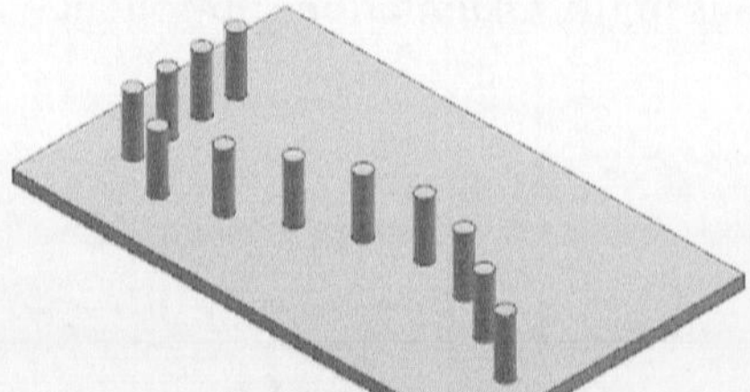

Figure 7-28 *Along curve pattern created with the* ***Input Feature only for Direction 2*** *check box selected*

Creating a General Pattern

In NX, you can create general pattern features by using points and coordinate system, as shown in Figure 7-29. To create a general pattern, invoke the **Pattern Feature** dialog box and then select the **General** option from the **Layout** drop-down list; the options related to the general pattern will be displayed in the **Pattern Feature** dialog box. Also, you will be prompted to select a feature to pattern. Select a feature from the drawing area. Next, select the **Point** or **Coordinate System** option from the **Location** drop-down list to define the position of instances. Now, click on the **Specify Point** area of the **From** sub-rollout; you will be prompted to specify point. Select an object to infer a point or you can create a point by using the **Point dialog** button. On doing so, you will be prompted to specify points in the **To** sub-rollout. Select the existing points or you can create points by using the **Sketch Section** button. Next, you need to define the orientation of instances using the options in the **Orientation** sub-rollout. The options in this sub-rollout are same as discussed earlier. Next, choose the **OK** button to create a general pattern.

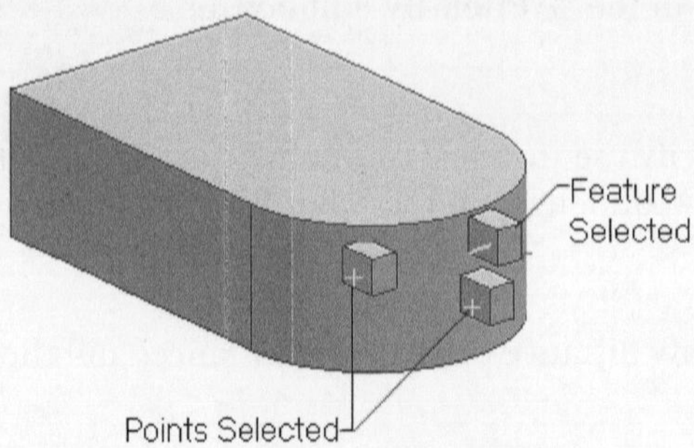

Figure 7-29 *The* ***General*** *pattern*

Creating a Reference Pattern

In NX, you can create a pattern of a new feature using an existing pattern. To do so, invoke the **Pattern Feature** dialog box and select the **Reference** option from the **Layout** drop-down list; the **Pattern Feature** dialog box will be modified and you will be prompted to select the feature to be patterned. After selecting the feature, click in the **Select Pattern** area of the **Reference** sub-rollout and then select an existing pattern. Next, click in the **Select Base Instance Handle** area and then select an instance from the existing pattern. The selected instance will be taken as the reference for the base point of the new pattern. Next, choose the **OK** button to create a reference pattern. Figure 7-30 shows a new pattern created using an existing pattern.

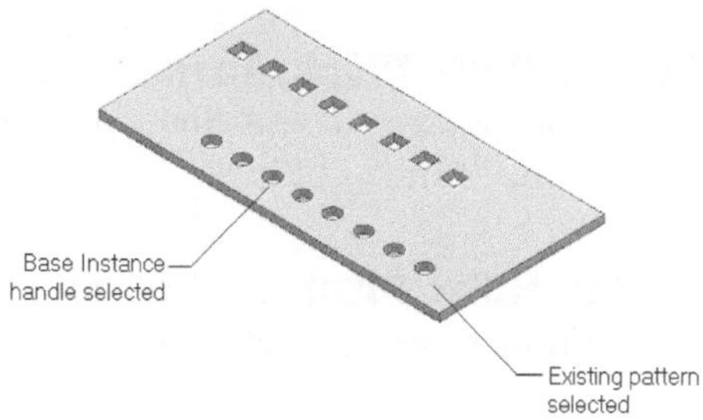

Figure 7-30 *A new pattern created using an existing pattern*

Creating a Helix Pattern

In NX, you can create a pattern of a feature using helical path. To do so, invoke the **Pattern Feature** dialog box and select the **Helix** option from the **Layout** drop-down list; the modified **Pattern Feature** dialog box will be displayed and you will be prompted to select the feature to be patterned. After selecting the feature, click in the **Specify Vector** area in the **Rotation Axis** sub-rollout of the **Pattern Definition** rollout; a triad will be displayed in the drawing window and you will be prompted to select an object to define the axis. Use the triad to specify the axis of rotation. Next, you will be prompted to specify the point to define the center of the helical pattern. You can select an object to infer a point or you can create a point using the **Point Dialog** button. Next, you need to define the direction by using the options in the **Direction** drop-down list. This drop-down list consist of the **Right Hand** and **Left Hand** options. The **Right Hand** option is used to define anti-clockwise direction and the **Left Hand** option is used to define clockwise direction. Next, you need to define the helix size by using the options given in the **Helix Size By** drop-down list in the **Helix Definition** sub-rollout. After specifying the size, choose the **OK** button to create the Helix Pattern, as shown in Figure 7-31. The options in the **Helix Size By** drop-down list are discussed next.

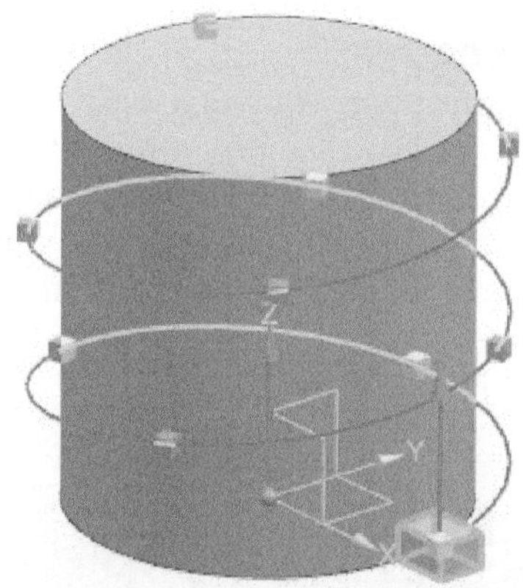

Figure 7-31 *Helix Pattern*

Count, Angle, Distance

This option is used to create helix pattern by specifying the instance count, angle between the instances, and distance between instances.

Count, Helix Pitch, Turns

This option is used to create helix pattern by specifying the instance count, helix pitch, and number of turns of helix.

Count, Helix Pitch and Span
This option is used to create helix pattern by specifying the instance count, helix pitch, and total span distance of helical path.

Angle, Helix Pitch, Turns
This option is used to create helix pattern by specifying the angle between instances, helix pitch, and number of turns of helix.

Angle, Helix Pitch and Span
This option is used to create helix pattern by specifying the angle between instances, helix pitch, and total distance of helix.

Creating Patterns by Defining Boundary
In NX, you can create patterns by using the options available in the **Boundary** drop-down list. This drop-down list is available in the **Boundary Definition** sub-rollout of the **Pattern Definition** rollout. This sub-rollout is not available for the **Along**, **General**, **Reference**, and **Helix** options of the **Layout** drop-down list. The options available in the **Boundary** drop-down list are discussed next.

None
On selecting this option, you can create a pattern without any boundary.

Face
This option is used to select a face to define the boundary of the pattern. On selecting this option, you will be prompted to select curves to define the boundary of the pattern. Select the face on which the pattern is to be created. You can specify an offset value for the boundary using the **Margin Distance** edit box. Select the **Apply Margin to Internal Boundaries** check box to apply an offset value to the internal boundary, refer to Figure 7-32 and Figure 7-33.

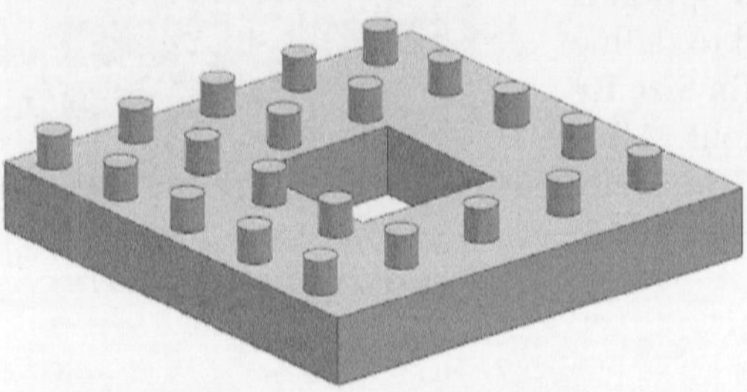

Figure 7-32 Pattern created with the ***Apply Margin to Internal Boundaries*** *check box selected*

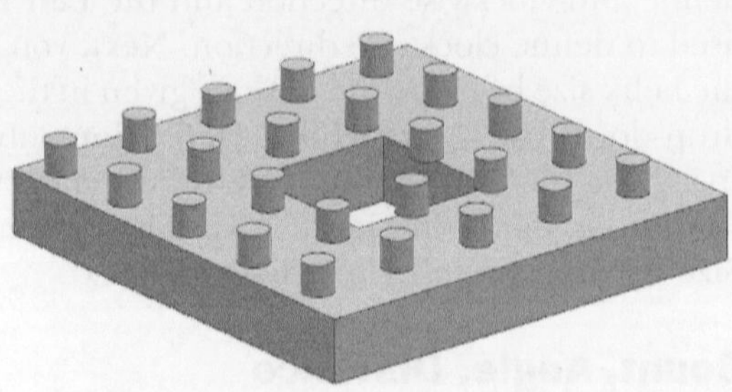

Figure 7-33 Pattern created with the ***Apply Margin to Internal Boundaries*** *check box cleared*

Curve
This option is used to select a curve to define the boundary of the pattern, refer to Figure 7-34.

Exclude

On selecting this option, the pattern is created outside the selected boundary, as shown in Figure 7-35.

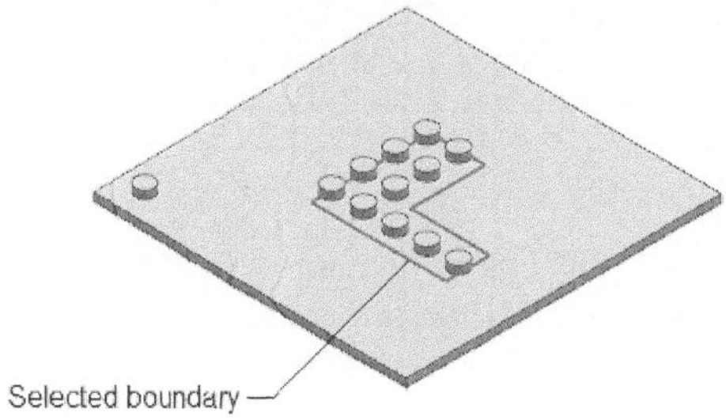

*Figure 7-34 Boundary defined using the **Curve** option*

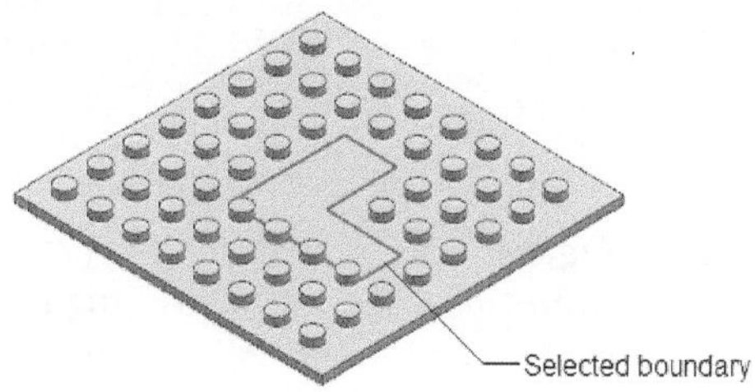

*Figure 7-35 Boundary defined using the **Exclude** option*

Creating a Fill Pattern

In NX, you can also create a fill pattern using the **Pattern Feature** tool. The methods to create fill pattern in different layouts are discussed next. Note that you cannot create a fill pattern using the **Along**, **General**, **Reference**, and **Helix** options.

Creating a Linear Fill Pattern

To create a linear fill pattern, invoke the **Pattern Feature** dialog box and select the **Linear** option from the **Layout** drop-down list. Next, select the feature to be patterned from the drawing window. Select the **Face** option from the **Boundary** drop-down list; the **Select Curve** area will become active in the **Boundary Definition** sub-rollout. Next, select the face to define the boundary of the pattern. Next, select the **Simplified Boundary Fill** check box from the **Boundary Definition** sub-rollout; the **Simplified Layout** sub-rollout will be displayed. The options in this sub-rollout are used to define the spacing between the instances. The **Layout** drop-down list contains three options: **Square**, **Triangle**, and **Diamond**. These options can be used to define the layout of the fill pattern. Select the required option from this drop-down list and then enter a value in the **Pitch Distance** edit box. Figures 7-36, 7-37, and 7-38 show linear fill patterns created on selecting the **Square**, **Triangle**, and **Diamond** options, respectively.

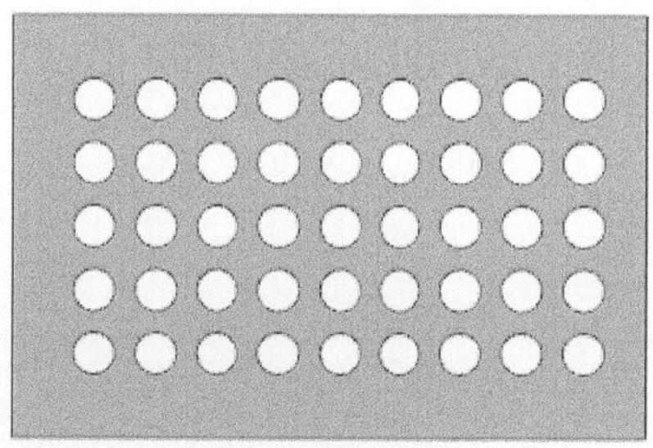

*Figure 7-36 Linear fill pattern created on selecting the **Square** option*

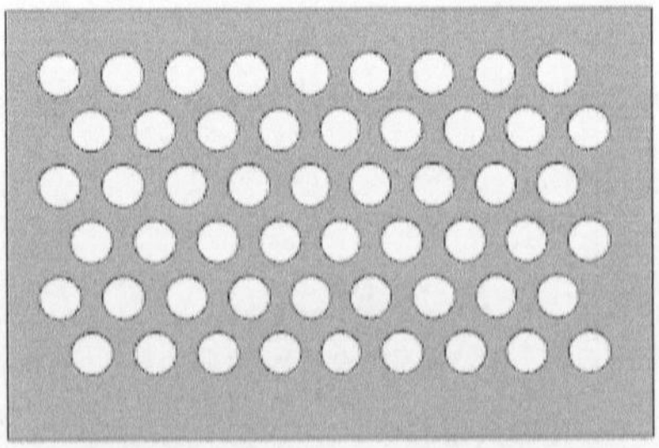

*Figure 7-37 Linear fill pattern created on selecting the **Triangle** option*

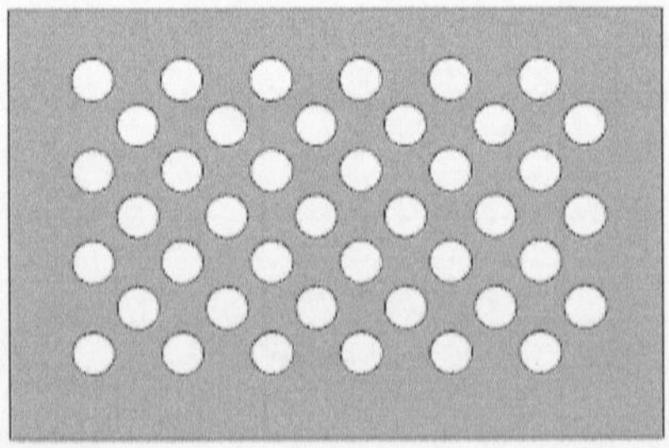

*Figure 7-38 Linear fill pattern created on selecting the **Diamond** option*

Creating a Circular Fill Pattern

To create a circular fill pattern, select the **Circular** option from the **Layout** drop-down list. Next, select the feature to be patterned from the drawing window. Select the **Face** option from the **Boundary** drop-down list; the **Select Curve** area will become active in the **Boundary Definition** sub-rollout. Select the face on which the pattern is to be created to define the boundary of the pattern. Next, select the **Simplified Boundary Fill** check box from the **Boundary Definition** sub-rollout; the **Simplified Layout** sub-rollout will be displayed. The **Circular Spacing** drop-down list in this sub-rollout contains two options: **Angle** and **Distance**. These options define the distance between the instances. On selecting the **Angle** option, you need to specify the pitch angle and the radial pitch in the respective edit boxes. On selecting the **Distance** option, you need to specify the pitch distance and the radial pitch in the respective edit boxes. Figures 7-39 and 7-40 show circular fill patterns created using the **Angle** and **Distance** options, respectively.

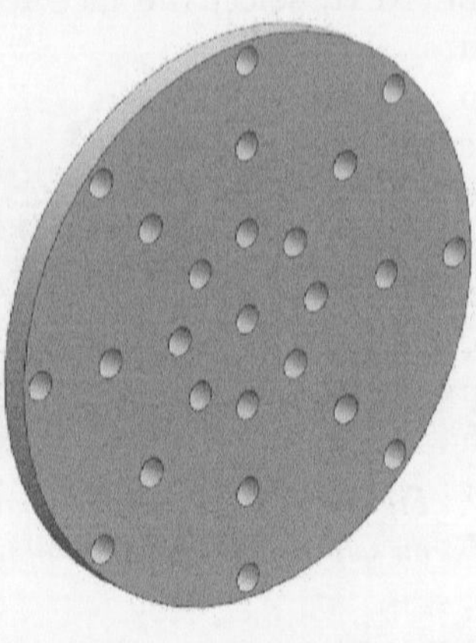

*Figure 7-39 A circular fill pattern created using the **Angle** option*

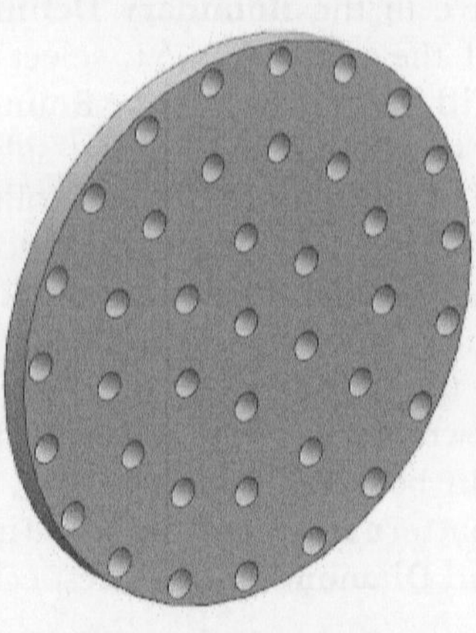

*Figure 7-40 A circular fill pattern created using the **Distance** option*

Creating a Polygon Fill Pattern

To create a polygon fill pattern, select the **Polygon** option from the **Layout** drop-down list. Next, select the feature to be patterned from the drawing window. Select the **Face** option from the **Boundary** drop-down list; the **Select Curve** area will become active in the **Boundary Definition** sub-rollout. Select the face on which the pattern is to be created to define the boundary of the pattern. Next, select the **Simplified Boundary Fill** check box from the **Boundary Definition** sub-rollout; the **Simplified Layout** sub-rollout will be displayed. The options in this sub-rollout are same as that in the polygon pattern. In addition, you need to specify a value in the **Radial Pitch** edit box. Figure 7-41 shows a polygon fill pattern.

Figure 7-41 *A polygon fill pattern*

Creating a Spiral Fill Pattern

The procedure to create a spiral fill pattern is similar to that of a spiral pattern. In this case, you do not need to specify the number of turns or the total angle of the spiral pattern.

MIRROR FEATURE TOOL

Ribbon: Home > Feature > More Gallery > Associative Copy > Mirror Feature
Menu: Insert > Associative Copy > Mirror Feature

The **Mirror Feature** tool is used to mirror selected features from a model. You can mirror features about a selected datum plane or a planar face. To do so, choose the **Mirror Feature** tool from the **Associative Copy** gallery of the **More** gallery in the **Feature** group; the **Mirror Feature** dialog box will be displayed, refer to Figure 7-42.

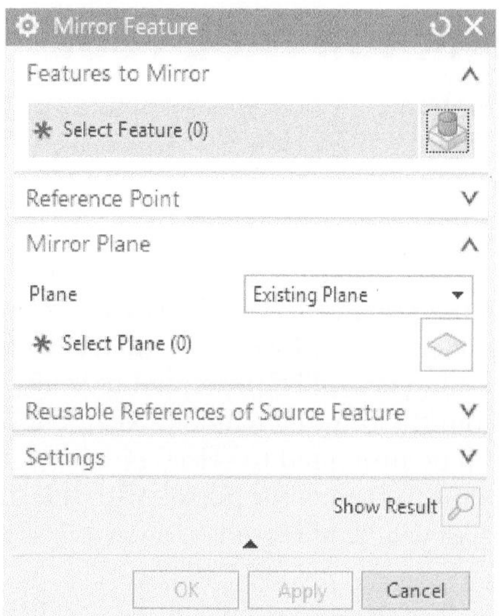

Figure 7-42 *The* ***Mirror Feature*** *dialog box*

By default, the **Features to Mirror** button is chosen in the **Features to Mirror** rollout of this dialog box. As a result, you will be prompted to select the features to be mirrored. Select the features to be mirrored from the drawing window. Next, choose the **Plane** button from the **Mirror Plane** rollout; you will be prompted to select a planar face or a datum plane. Select the planar face or the datum plane as the mirror plane. Next, choose the **OK** button; the selected features will be mirrored. Figure 7-43 shows the features selected to be mirrored and the datum plane selected as the mirror plane. Figure 7-44 shows the resulting mirrored feature, after turning off the display of the mirror plane. In this case, the mirror plane is passing through the center of the semicircular base feature.

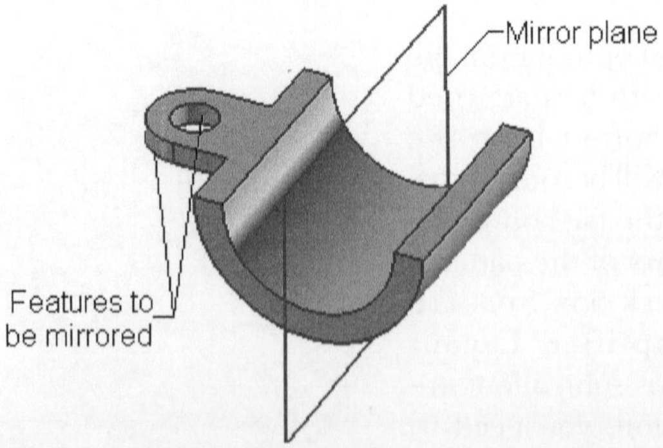

Figure 7-43 *The mirror plane and the features to be mirrored*

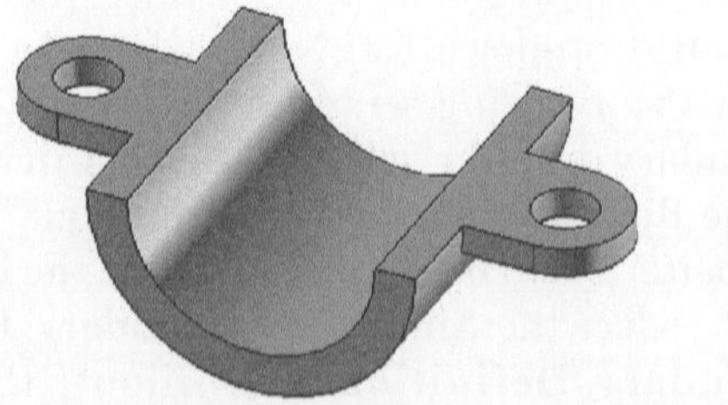

Figure 7-44 *The resulting mirrored feature*

Note

*The **Plane** drop-down list is used to select an existing datum plane or create a new datum plane as mirror plane.*

Tip

In NX, you can also mirror curves, reference geometries, and pattern features. Also, while mirroring a threaded or a helical feature, you can specify whether to maintain their originality or not.

MIRROR FACE TOOL

Ribbon: Home > Feature > More > Associative Copy > Mirror Face
Menu: Insert > Associative Copy > Mirror Face

The **Mirror Face** tool is used to mirror a set of selected faces of a model. You can mirror faces which define a feature. You can mirror faces about a selected datum plane or a planar face. To do so, choose the **Mirror Face** tool from the **Associative Copy** gallery of the **More** gallery in the **Feature** group; the **Mirror Face** dialog box will be displayed, as shown in Figure 7-45. By default, the **Face** button is chosen in the **Face** rollout of this dialog box. As a result, you will be prompted to select the faces to be mirrored. Select the faces to be mirrored from the drawing window. Next, choose the **Plane** button from the **Mirror Plane** rollout; you will be prompted to select a planar face or a datum plane. Select the planar face or the datum plane as the mirror plane. After selecting the mirror plane, choose the **OK** button; the selected faces will be mirrored, as shown in Figure 7-46.

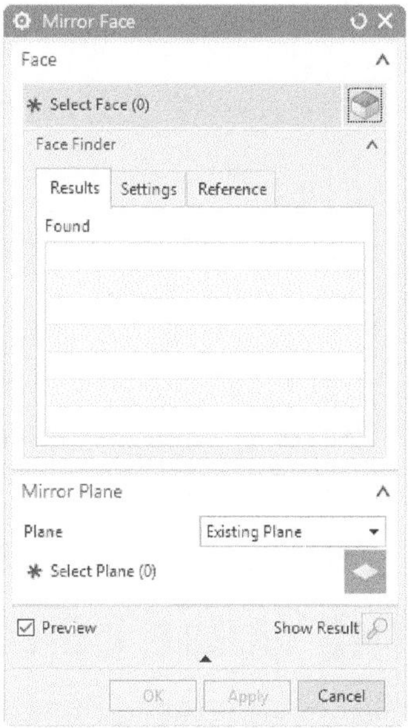

Figure 7-45 The ***Mirror Face*** *dialog box*

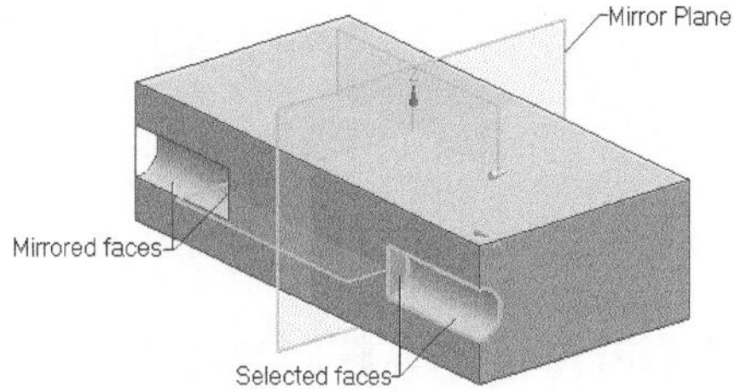

Figure 7-46 Mirrored faces

MIRROR GEOMETRY TOOL

Ribbon: Home > Feature > More > Associative Copy > Mirror Geometry *(Customize to Add)*
Menu: Insert > Associative Copy > Mirror Geometry

The **Mirror Geometry** tool is used to create an associative or non-associative mirror copy of the selected geometry. You can mirror the geometry about a selected datum plane or a planar face. To do so, choose the **Mirror Geometry** tool from the **Associative Copy** gallery of the **More** gallery in the **Feature** group of the **Home** tab; the **Mirror Geometry** dialog box will be displayed, as shown in Figure 7-47. By default, the **Object** button is chosen in the **Geometry to Mirror** rollout of this dialog box. As a result, you will be prompted to select the geometry to be mirrored. Select the geometry to be mirrored from the drawing window. After you have selected the geometry to be mirrored, click on the **Specify Plane** area in the **Mirror Plane** rollout; you will be prompted to select a planar face or a datum plane. Select the planar face or the datum plane as the mirror plane. Next, you need to define whether to create associative mirror geometry or non-associative mirror geometry in the **Settings** rollout. If you select the **Associative** check box, then after creating the mirrored geometry, any change made in the selected geometry will also be reflected in the mirrored geometry. If the **Associative** check box is cleared, then changes will not be reflected in the mirrored geometry. Next, choose the **OK** button; the selected geometry will be mirrored, as shown in Figure 7-48. You can mirror the geometries such as curve, edge, face, datums, solid body, point, CSYS, plane, and sheet body using this tool.

Figure 7-47 *The* ***Mirror Geometry*** *dialog box*

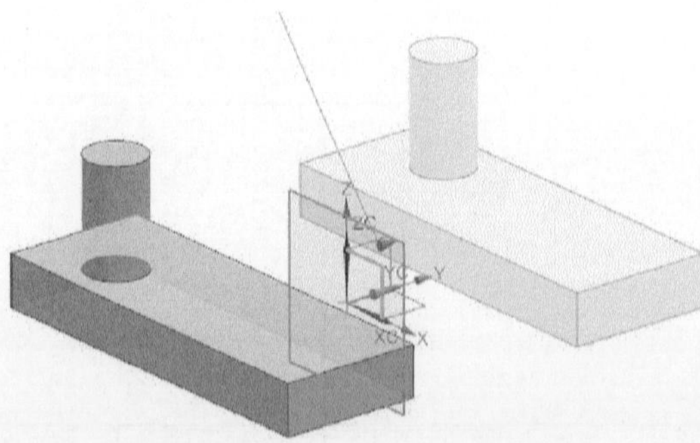

Figure 7-48 *Mirrored geometry*

SWEEPING SKETCHES ALONG THE GUIDE CURVES

Ribbon: Home > Feature > More Gallery > Sweep > Sweep along Guide
Menu: Insert > Sweep > Sweep along Guide

The **Sweep along Guide** tool is used to create sweep features by sweeping an open or a closed section about a guide string. Figure 7-49 shows an open section and the guide string and Figure 7-50 shows the resulting sweep feature.

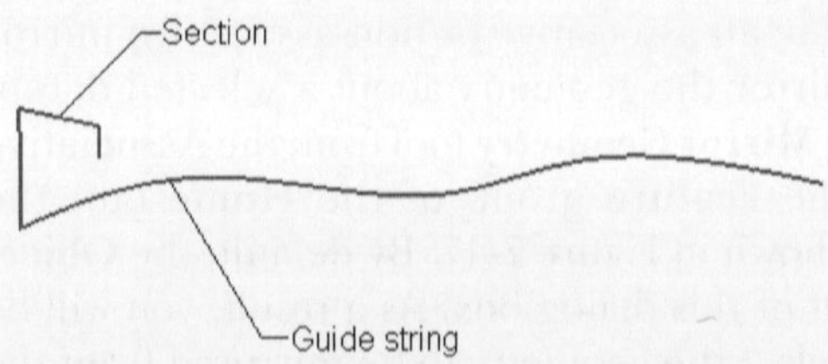

Figure 7-49 *An open section and a guide string to create a sweep feature*

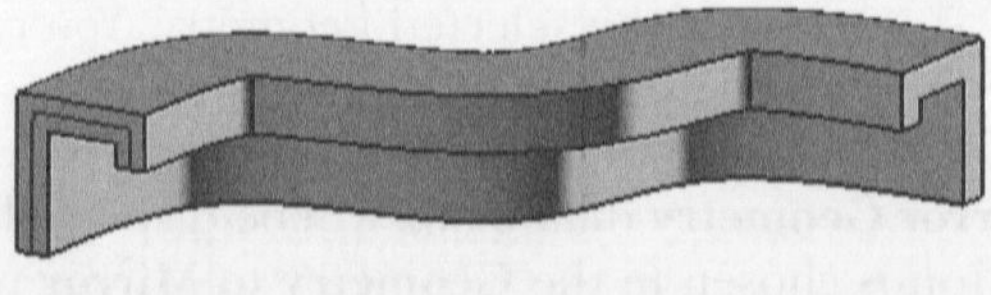

Figure 7-50 *The resulting sweep feature*

To invoke this tool, choose **Menu > Insert > Sweep > Sweep along Guide** from the **Top Border Bar**; the **Sweep Along Guide** dialog box will be displayed, as shown in Figure 7-51, and you will be prompted to select the chain of curves for the section. Select the chain of curves from the drawing window. Next, choose the **Curve** button from the **Guide** rollout; you will be prompted to select the chain of curves for the guide. Note that if the guide has multiple strings, they all should be end-connected to each other. After selecting the guide curve, enter values for the first and second directions in the **First Offset** and **Second Offset** edit boxes of the **Offsets** rollout, respectively. Note that these values should not be the same; it means one value must be greater than the other. Also, an arrow will be displayed in the graphics window, pointing toward the second offset direction. You can use this arrow to dynamically increase or decrease the values of the first and second offset directions.

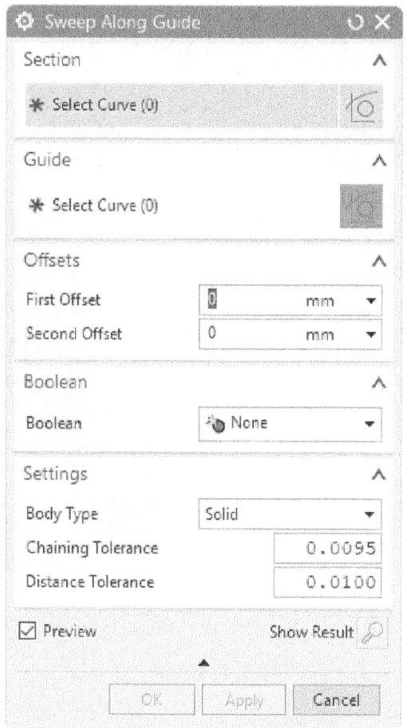

Figure 7-51 *The* ***Sweep Along Guide*** *dialog box*

Select the required boolean operation from the **Boolean** drop-down list in the dialog box. Note that if the sweep feature is the base feature in the model, then only the **None** option will be available in the **Boolean** drop-down list. Next, choose the **OK** button from the **Sweep Along Guide** dialog box; the sweep feature will be created.

Note

If the section for the sweep feature consists of nested closed loops, the guide string should only be drawn by using lines and arcs.

Tip

To create features that are swept along a guide curve, first draw the guide curve and then define a datum plane at one of the ends of the guide curve. Next, use this datum plane to draw the sketch of the section.

CREATING SWEPT FEATURES

Ribbon: Home > Feature > More Gallery > Sweep > Swept
Menu: Insert > Sweep > Swept

Swept features are created by sweeping one or more sections along one or more guide curves such that all the sections are blended together. Figure 7-52 shows three section strings (ellipse, circle, and ellipse) and two guide strings (splines). Figure 7-53 shows the resulting swept feature.

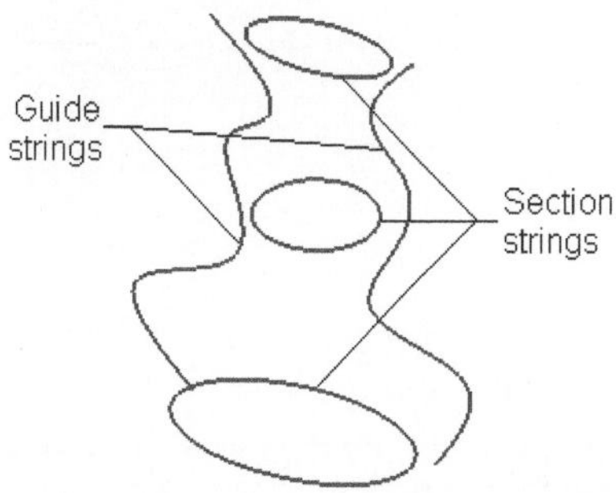

Figure 7-52 *Section strings and guide strings to create a sweep feature*

To create swept features, choose **Menu > Insert > Sweep > Swept** from the **Top Border Bar**; the **Swept** dialog box will be displayed and you will be prompted to select the section curves. On selecting the section curve, an arrow will be displayed on it. Press the middle mouse button to accept the curve. Similarly, select all the remaining section curves one by one. Note that while selecting the section curves, you need to be careful about the point from where you select them. It is recommended that multiple sections should be selected from the same quadrant. For example, if you need to select circles or ellipses, it is recommended that you select them from the same quadrant.

Otherwise, a twist will be introduced in the swept model. Figure 7-54 shows the arrows displayed on the three sections that are selected to be swept. Notice that all arrows point in the same direction, thereby avoiding any twist in the model. You can change the direction of any arrow by double-clicking on it.

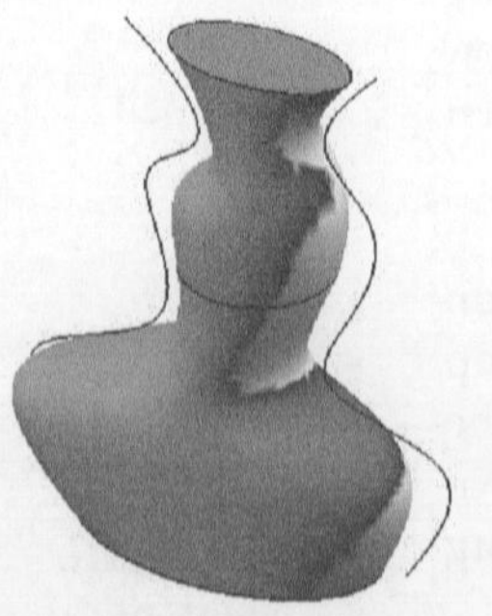

Figure 7-53 *The resulting swept feature*

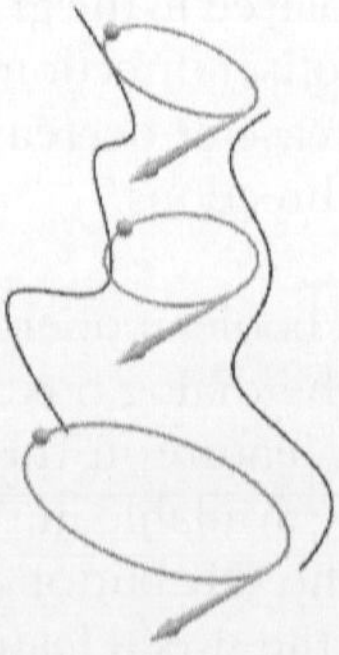

Figure 7-54 *Arrows displayed on the sections to be swept*

Note

After selecting each section curve, you need to press the middle mouse button to accept it. You can select any number of section curves.

After selecting the section curves, choose the **Guide** button from the **Guides** rollout; you will be prompted to select the guide curves. Select the guide curve; an arrow will be displayed at the end of the guide curve. Press the middle mouse button to accept the guide curve. Similarly, select the remaining guide curves one by one. You can select maximum of three guide curves. Note that all arrows should point in the same direction. After selecting all guide curves, choose the **OK** button from the **Swept** dialog box; the swept feature will be created.

Figure 7-55 shows the sections in which the arrows point in different directions and Figure 7-56 shows the resulting swept feature.

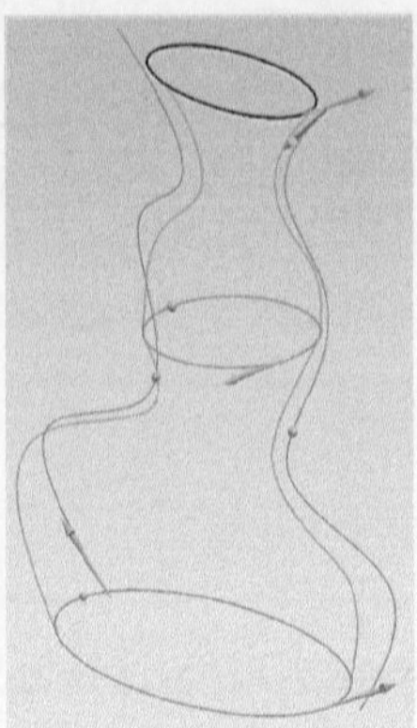

Figure 7-55 *Arrows on the section strings pointing in different directions*

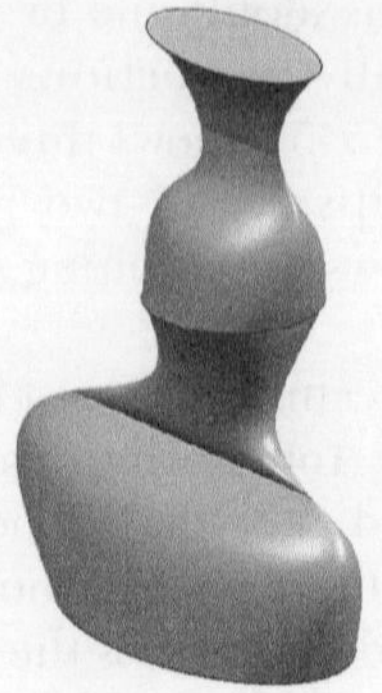

Figure 7-56 *The resulting swept feature*

After selecting all the section and guide curves, you can use the **Interpolation** drop-down list in the **Section Options** rollout to specify the type of blending between the sections. There are three options in this drop-down list, **Linear**, **Cubic**, and **Blend**. If you select the **Linear** option, a linear blending will be created between the sections. However, if you select the **Cubic** option, the blending between the sections will be smooth. If you select the **Blend** option, the blending between the sections will be continuous and a single face will be created across all strings. Figure 7-57 shows the sketch for a swept feature. In this sketch, the vertical line passing through the centers of the three sections has been used as the guide curve. Figures 7-58 through 7-60 show the features created with the **Linear**, **Cubic**, and **Blend** options selected respectively.

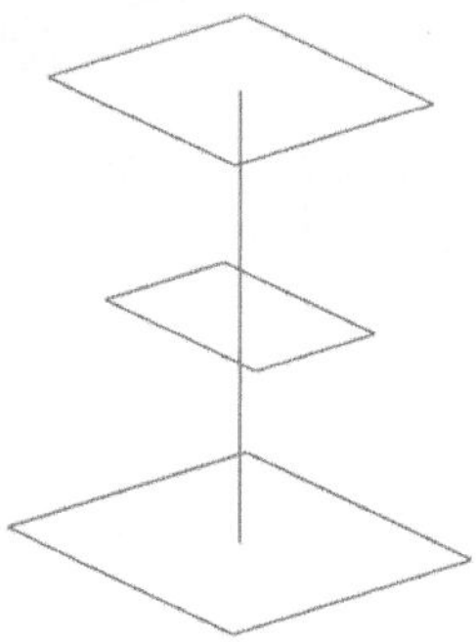

Figure 7-57 *Section and guide strings for the swept feature*

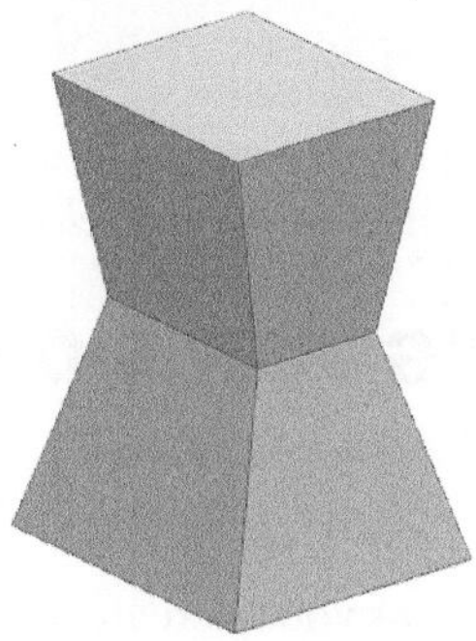

Figure 7-58 *Swept feature created with the* ***Linear*** *option selected*

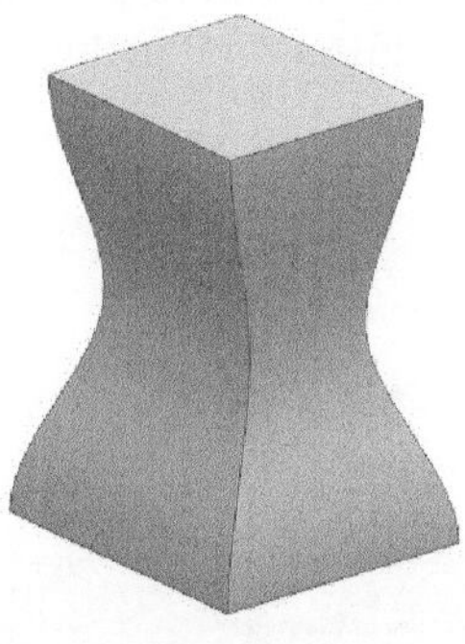

Figure 7-59 *Swept feature created with the* ***Cubic*** *option selected*

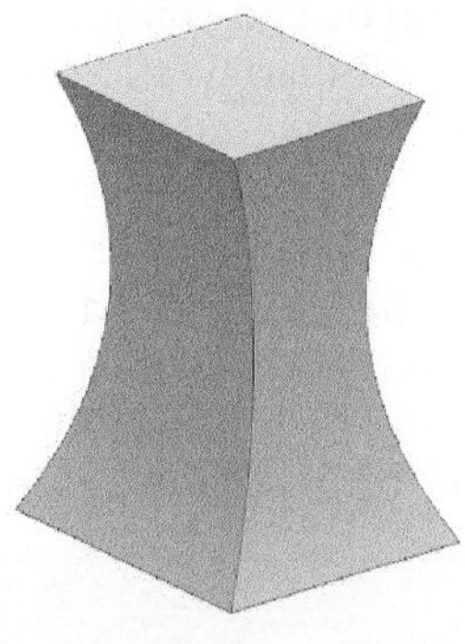

Figure 7-60 *Swept feature created with the* ***Blend*** *option selected*

Note

1. The ***Interpolation*** *drop-down list will be available only if you select more than one section.*

2. You need to select the ***Blend*** *option before selecting the guide curves; otherwise the option will not be available in the* ***Interpolation*** *drop-down list.*

In NX, you can create a swept feature with a split output. To do so, select the **Split Output along Guide** check box from the **Settings** rollout; the resultant feature will be a split feature. Figures 7-61 and 7-62 show a sweep feature with the **Split Output along Guide** check box selected and cleared, respectively.

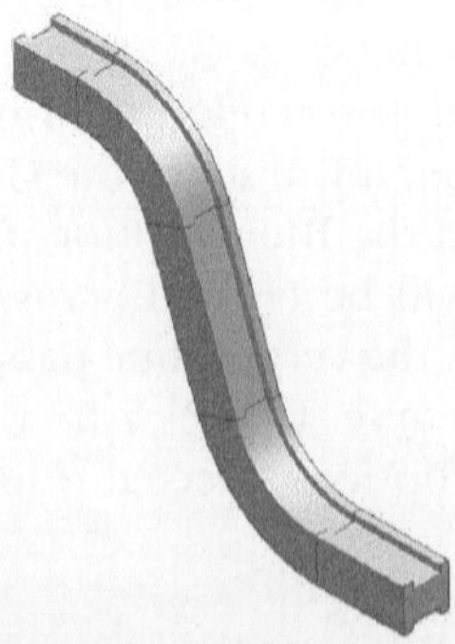

*Figure 7-61 Swept feature created with the **Split Output along Guide** check box selected*

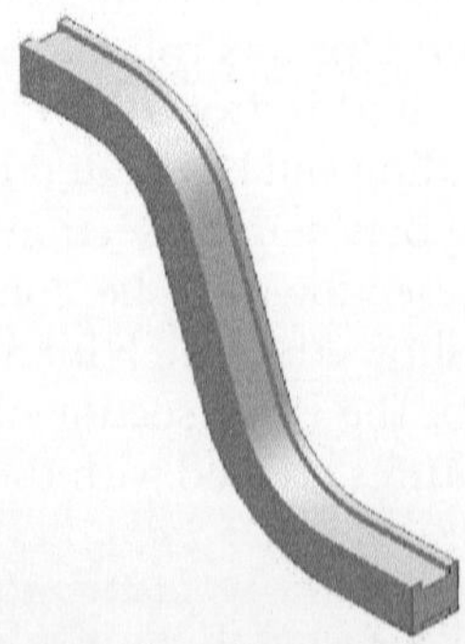

*Figure 7-62 Swept feature created with the **Split Output along Guide** check box cleared*

CREATING TUBES OR CABLES

Ribbon:	Home > Feature > More Gallery > Sweep > Tube *(Customize to Add)*
Menu:	Insert > Sweep > Tube

NX allows you to create tubes or cables using the **Tube** tool. To do so, you need to specify the guide curve about which the tube or cable will be created. To define the tube or cable section, enter its inner and outer diameters. To create a tube or a cable, first draw the sketch of the guide curve. Note that if the guide curve is a combination of multiple entities, all of them should be end-connected. Also, remember that there should be no sharp vertices in the guide curve. All sharp vertices should be filleted using the **Fillet** tool or the curve should be created using some other tool.

After drawing the sketch for the guide curve, invoke the **Tube** tool; the **Tube** dialog box will be displayed, as shown in Figure 7-63, and you will be prompted to select curves for tube centerline path. Select the sketch drawn for the guide curve. The different rollouts in the **Tube** dialog box are discussed next.

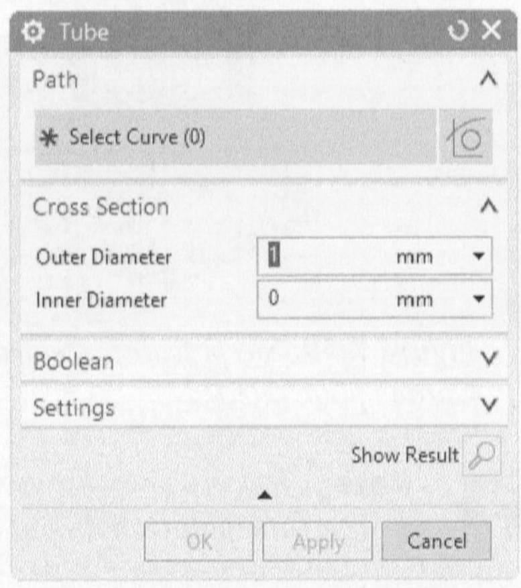

*Figure 7-63 The **Tube** dialog box*

Cross Section Rollout

The options in this rollout are used to define the cross-section of the tube. These options are discussed next.

Outer Diameter

This edit box is used to specify the outer diameter of the tube. Note that the value of outer diameter cannot be zero.

Inner Diameter

This edit box is used to specify the inner diameter of the tube. By specifying a value in this edit box, you can ensure that the tube is hollow. If you enter **0** in this edit box, the resulting tube will be solid filled.

Boolean Rollout

This rollout is used to specify the boolean operation to be performed.

Settings Rollout

This rollout is used to specify the output type and tolerance. The options in this rollout are discussed next.

Output

The options in this drop-down list are used to specify the output type for the tube feature. Select the **Multiple Segments** option if you need the tube to have multiple lateral faces. However, if you select the **Single Segment** option, the tube will have only one lateral face (if it is solid filled) or two lateral faces (if it is hollow).

Tolerance

The value in the **Tolerance** edit box is used to create a feature with the specified tolerance.

After setting the parameters in the **Tube** dialog box, choose the **OK** button; the tube will be created. Figure 7-64 shows the guide curve for the tube and Figure 7-65 shows the resulting hollow tube.

Figure 7-64 *Guide curve for the tube*

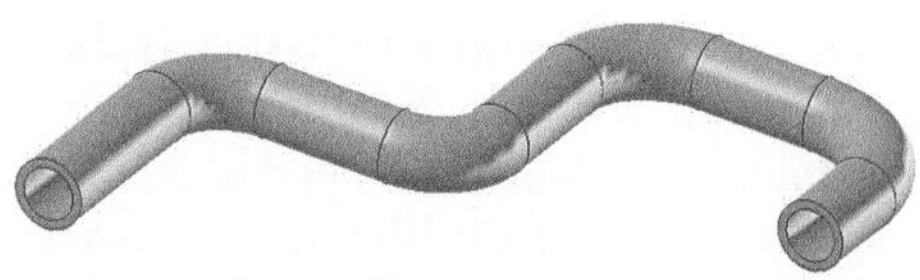

Figure 7-65 *The resulting hollow tube*

CREATING THREADS

Ribbon:	Home > Feature > More Gallery > Design Feature > Thread
Menu:	Insert > Design Feature > Thread

NX allows you to create internal or external threads on a cylindrical model. Internal threads are those that are created on the internal faces of a model, similar to a hole in a model. External threads are those that are created on the outer face of a model. Figure 7-66 shows the external threading on a bolt and Figure 7-67 shows the internal threading in a nut.

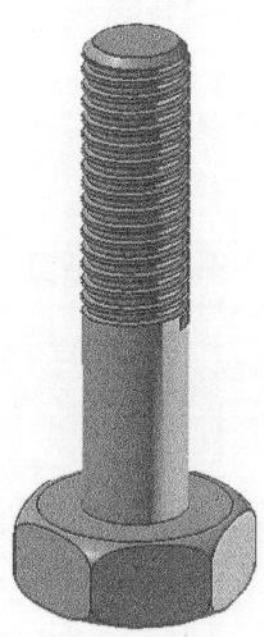

Figure 7-66 *External threading on a bolt*

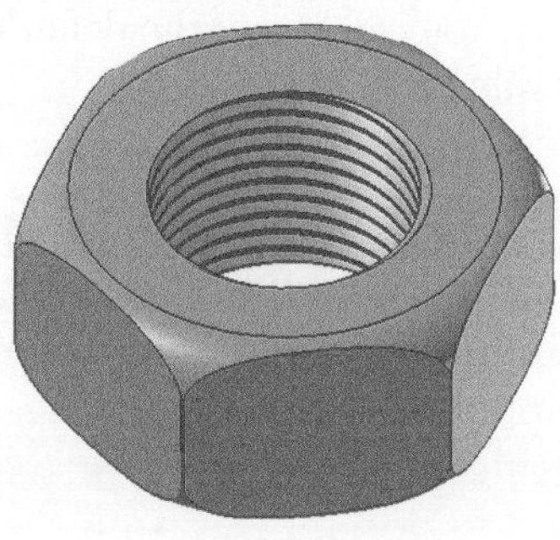

Figure 7-67 *Internal threading in a nut*

In NX, you can create detailed or symbolic threads. The detailed threads appear like actual threads, refer to Figures 7-66 and 7-67 whereas symbolic threads just display the thread convention in the form of dashed lines, as shown in Figure 7-68.

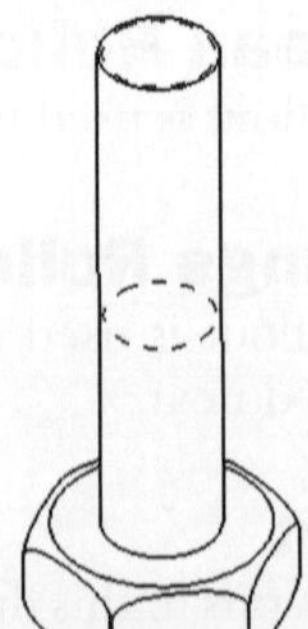

Figure 7-68 *Symbolic thread on a bolt*

Creating Symbolic Threads

To create symbolic threads, invoke the **Thread** tool; the **Thread** dialog box will be displayed. Select the **Symbolic** radio button, if it is not selected by default, to display the options to create symbolic threads, refer to Figure 7-69.

There are two methods of creating symbolic threads. In the first method, the system automatically defines the thread specifications for the selected face using a thread table. In the other method, some thread specifications are calculated and displayed in the edit box, but you can also modify these values individually. Both these methods are discussed next.

Creating Symbolic Threads Using Table

To create a symbolic thread using table, invoke the **Thread** dialog box and clear the **Manual Input** check box if it is already selected; the options to specify the parameters of the thread will be disabled. Next, select the cylindrical face on which you need to create the threads; the face will be highlighted and an arrow will be displayed at one of the ends of the face. The options that will be available in the dialog box at this stage are discussed next.

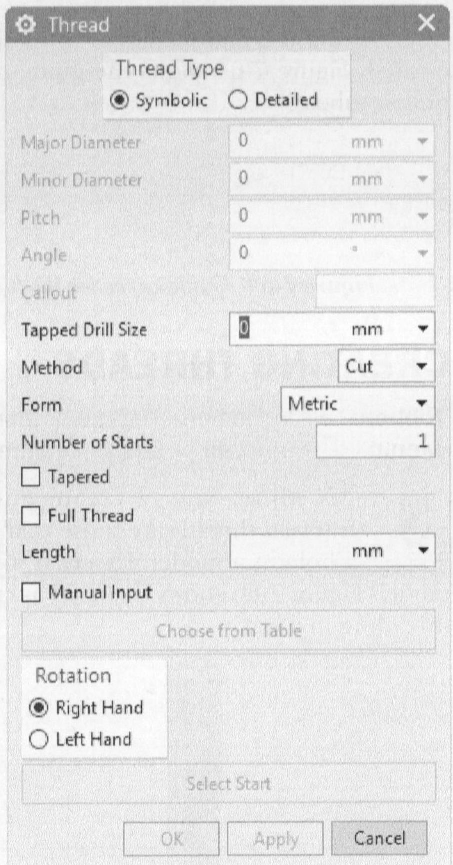

Figure 7-69 *The* ***Thread*** *dialog box*

Shaft Size / Tapped Drill Size

If you select an outer face to create threads, the **Shaft Size** edit box will be available. In this edit box, you can specify the size of the shaft. But if you select an interior face to create the thread, the **Tapped Drill Size** edit box will be available. Depending upon the face selected and the specifications from the table, a default value will be displayed in this edit box. You can accept the default value or enter a new value.

Method

This drop-down list is used to select the method that will be used to create threads. You can select the **Cut**, **Rolled**, **Ground**, or **Milled** option from this drop-down list.

Form

This drop-down list is used to select the form of the table, thus defining the type of table to be used to specify the thread parameters. The table that is used to create threads is called the lookup table. Note that the values of the hole parameters will be modified based on the form selected from this drop-down list.

Number of Starts

This edit box is used to specify the number of starts of the thread. If you specify more than one start, multiple threads will be created.

Tapered

This check box is selected to create tapered threads.

Full Thread

This check box is selected to create threads throughout the length of the selected cylindrical face.

Note

*If length of the cylindrical body is modified with the **Full Thread** option selected, the length of the thread will also get modified.*

Choose from Table

You can choose this button to select the thread type from the lookup table to create threads. When you choose this button, the **Thread** dialog box will be modified and will display the list of the holes that are available in the current lookup table.

Rotation

This area provides two radio buttons, **Right Hand** and **Left Hand**. These radio buttons are used to specify whether the resulting threads will be right hand threads or left hand threads. The right hand threads are those that allow the screw to get tightened when it is rotated in the clockwise direction. The left hand threads are those that allow the screw to get tightened when it is rotated in the counterclockwise direction.

Select Start

When you select a cylindrical face to create threads, an arrow is displayed at one of the ends of the face. This arrow specifies the start face and the direction of the threads. You can modify the start face and the direction of threads by choosing the **Select Start** button. When you choose this button, the **Thread** dialog box will be modified and you will be prompted to select the start face. On doing so, the **Thread** dialog box will display the options related to reversing the direction of the thread axis and start conditions. From the **Start Conditions** drop-down list, if you select the **Extend Through Start** option, a complete thread will be created even beyond the plane that you select as the start plane. However, on selecting the **Do Not Extend** option, the threads will start from the plane that you select as the start plane of the thread. After specifying these options, choose the **OK** button to return to the options to create the threads.

Creating Symbolic Threads Using Manual Inputs

To create a symbolic thread using the manual inputs, invoke the **Thread** dialog box and choose the **Manual Input** check box; the options to specify the parameters of the thread will be enabled. Next, select the cylindrical face on which you need to create the threads; some default values will be displayed in the edit boxes to define the parameters of the threads. The options that are enabled to create threads with manual inputs are discussed next.

Major Diameter

This edit box is used to specify the major diameter of threads. Note that the major diameter should be more than the diameter of the cylindrical face selected to create threads.

Minor Diameter

This edit box is used to specify the minor diameter of threads. Note that the minor diameter should be less than the diameter of the cylindrical face selected to create threads.

Pitch

This edit box is used to specify the pitch of threads.

Angle

This edit box is used to specify the angle of threads.

Creating Detailed Threads

To create the detailed thread, invoke the **Thread** tool; the **Thread** dialog box will be displayed. Select the **Detailed** radio button to display the options to create detailed threads; the dialog box will be modified and you will be prompted to select a cylindrical face, refer to Figure 7-70. Select the face on which you need to create threads; the options in the dialog box will be enabled. Most of the options in this dialog box are similar to those discussed while creating symbolic threads. The **Length** option is discussed next.

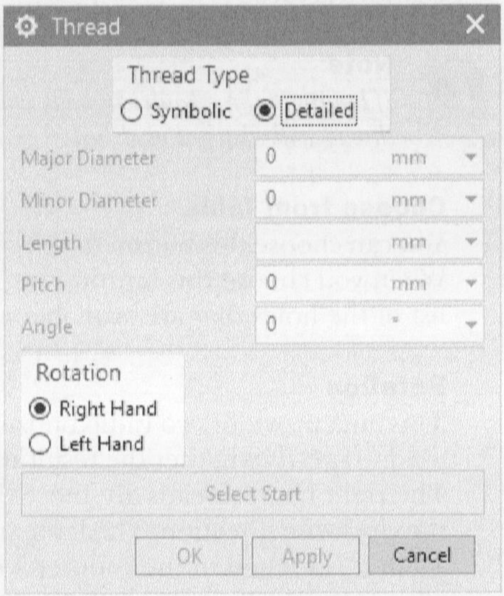

*Figure 7-70 The **Thread** dialog box*

Length

This edit box is used to specify the depth up to which the threads will be created. The default value that is displayed in this edit box is equal to the length of the cylindrical face that is selected to create threads. You can enter any other value in this edit box. Figure 7-71 shows a bolt with threads created throughout its length and Figure 7-72 shows a bolt with threads created up to a specified length.

Figure 7-71 *Threads created throughout the length of the bolt*

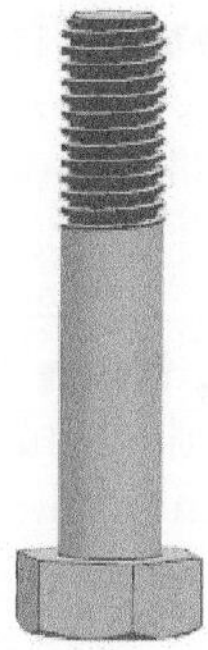

Figure 7-72 *Threads created up to a specified length*

CREATING SHELL FEATURES

Ribbon:	Home > Feature > Shell
Menu:	Insert > Offset/Scale > Shell

The **Shell** tool allows you to scoop out the material from a model and make it hollow. The resultant model will be a structure of walls with a cavity inside. You can remove some of the faces of the model and apply different wall thicknesses to them. Figure 7-73 shows a solid model before scooping out material and Figure 7-74 shows the model after shelling it.

Figure 7-73 *Solid model before scooping out material*

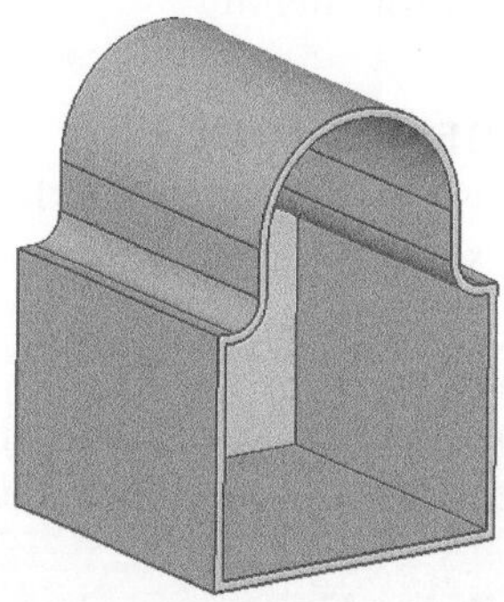

Figure 7-74 *Solid model after scooping out material using the* ***Shell*** *tool*

On invoking this tool, the **Shell** dialog box will be displayed, refer to Figure 7-75. You can hollow the models using various rollouts of this dialog box. These rollouts are discussed next.

Type Drop-down list

The drop-down list is used to specify the type of shell that you need to create. The options in this drop-down list are discussed next.

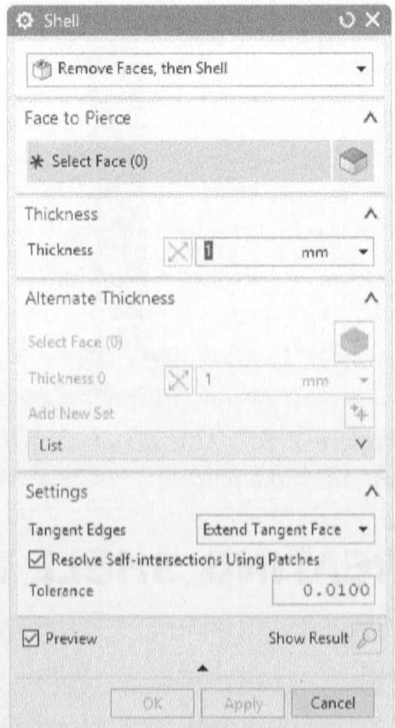

*Figure 7-75 The **Shell** dialog box*

Remove Faces, then Shell

If you select this option, then the faces selected to shell the model will be removed.

Shell All Faces

If you select this option, then all faces of the model will be shelled and none of the faces will be removed.

Face to Pierce and Body to Shell Rollouts

Depending upon the option selected from the Type drop-down list, the above mentioned rollouts will be available. For example, if you select the **Remove Faces, then Shell** option, the **Face to Pierce** rollout will be available. The **Face** button in this rollout is used to select the faces to be removed from the shelled body. However, if you select the **Shell All Faces** option, the **Body to Shell** rollout will be available. The **Body to Shell** button in this rollout is used to select the body for shelling.

Thickness Rollout

This rollout is used to define the thickness of the shelled walls. The options in this rollout are discussed next.

Thickness

This edit box is used to specify the thickness of the shelled walls. Alternatively, you can drag the thickness handle from the drawing area to specify the thickness.

Reverse Direction

This button is used to flip the direction of offset.

Alternate Thickness Rollout

This rollout is used to assign unique wall thicknesses to selected face-sets in a shell feature. The **Shell Set** button in this rollout is used to create a set of faces to assign unique thickness. The set may contain one or more faces. Select faces and enter the thickness value in the **Thickness** edit box, which is below the **Shell Set** button in this rollout. After completing one set, choose the **Add New Set** button to create another set. These sets are displayed in the **List** sub-rollout. You can modify the thickness value of a particular set by selecting it and entering a different value in the **Thickness** edit box.

Shelling the Entire Solid Body

To shell the entire solid body, select the **Shell All Faces** option from the Type drop-down list. Next, enter the thickness value in the **Thickness** edit box and select the solid body. Choose the **OK** button from the **Shell** dialog box; the entire solid body will be shelled.

EDITING FEATURES

Editing is one of the most important aspects of the product design cycle. Almost all designs require editing during or after their creation. As discussed earlier, NX is a feature-based parametric software. Therefore, the design created in NX is a combination of individual features integrated together to form a solid model. All these features can be edited individually. The editing operations that can be performed in NX are discussed next.

Editing a Hole Feature

After creating a hole, you may need to edit its parameters. The parameters that can be edited include diameters, depth, and positioning values of the hole. To modify the parameters of a simple hole, double-click on it; the **Hole** dialog box will be displayed. Also, the positioning values of the hole will be displayed on the model. Note that the **Hole** dialog box will be displayed on double-clicking only if the corresponding hole has been created by using the **Hole** tool. To edit the positioning values, click on the value that you want to edit; the input edit box will be displayed. Enter the required value in the input edit box and press ENTER; the position of the hole will be modified according to the value specified in the input edit box. You can also edit the positioning values of the hole by choosing the **Sketch Section** button from the **Position** rollout of the **Hole** dialog box. To edit the diameter and depth values of the hole, enter the required values in the respective edit boxes available in the **Dimensions** sub-rollout of the **Form and Dimensions** rollout in the **Hole** dialog box.

Editing the Positioning of a Groove Feature

You can edit the positioning of a groove feature. To do so, choose the **Part Navigator** tab from the **Resource Bar**; the **Part Navigator** will be invoked. Right-click on the groove feature displayed in the **Part Navigator**; a shortcut menu will be displayed. Choose the **Edit Positioning** option from the shortcut menu; the **Edit Positioning** dialog box will be displayed, as shown in Figure 7-76. Also, the edges selected for applying the positioning dimension will be displayed in the dashed line format. Next, choose the **Edit Dimension Value** button from the dialog box; the **Edit Expression** dialog box will be displayed. Enter the new positioning value in the edit box and choose the **OK** button; the **Edit Positioning** dialog box will be displayed again. Choose the **OK** button from this dialog box to reflect the changes made in the positioning value.

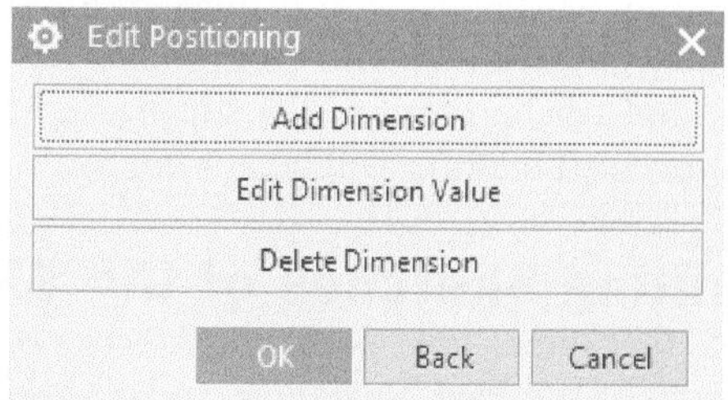

*Figure 7-76 The **Edit Positioning** dialog box*

You can also add or delete dimensions using the options in the **Edit Positioning** dialog box. These operations are discussed next.

Adding the Positioning Dimensions Using the Add Dimension Button

The **Add Dimension** button is used to add positioning dimensions to an already positioned feature. To add the new positioning dimensions, choose the **Add Dimension** button from the **Edit Positioning** dialog box; the **Position Groove** dialog box will be displayed. The tools in this dialog box can be used to create new positioning dimensions.

Deleting the Positioning Dimensions Using the Delete Dimension Button

The **Delete Dimension** button is used to delete the positioning dimensions. To delete the positioning dimensions, choose the **Delete Dimension** button; the **Remove Positioning** dialog box will be displayed, and you will be prompted to select the positioning dimension to be deleted. Select the positioning dimensions to be deleted and choose the **OK** button; the selected dimensions will be deleted.

Editing the Parameters of Features

Similar to editing the parameters of holes, NX allows you to edit the parameters of other features such as extruded features, revolved features, and so on. To edit the parameters of these features, right-click on the name of the feature in the **Part Navigator** and then choose the **Edit Parameters** from the shortcut menu displayed. Depending on the selected feature, the corresponding dialog box will be displayed. You can choose the required options from this dialog box to modify the parameters of the selected feature.

Editing the Parameters of Features with Rollback

In NX, you can edit parameters of features such as extrude features, edge blend features, face blend features, and so on with rollback. This editing operation is similar to the editing parameters, except that this option temporarily suppresses all features created after the feature to be edited. To do so, right-click on the required feature, and then choose the **Edit with Rollback** option from the shortcut menu displayed; a dialog box corresponding to the selected feature will be displayed, in which you can modify parameters. Also, the features created after the selected feature will be temporarily suppressed from the model. Once the editing is completed, the suppressed features will be automatically restored.

Editing Sketches of the Sketch-based Features

NX also allows you to edit the sketches of the sketch-based features. To do so, right-click on the sketch in the **Part Navigator** and choose **Edit** from the shortcut menu displayed; the selected sketch will be activated. Also, all dimensions of the sketch will be displayed. You can modify the dimensions of the sketch or remove the existing entities and add new entities to the sketch. However, you need to make sure that the sketch is closed after adding or removing the sketched entities.

Note

If the sketch of a feature is created by using the ***Sketch Section*** *button from the corresponding feature creation tool, then the sketch will not be displayed in the tree of the* ***Part Navigator****. In this case, right-click on the feature whose sketch is to be edited; a shortcut menu will be displayed. Choose the* ***Edit Sketch*** *option from the shortcut menu; the Sketch in Task environment will be invoked. Now, you can edit the sketch.*

Reordering Features

In NX, you can change the order of feature creation. The features can be reordered before or after the specified reference feature. To reorder a feature, right-click on the feature name in the **Part Navigator** and choose **Reorder Before** or **Reorder After** from the shortcut menu displayed; the cascading menu containing the names of the reference features will be displayed. Select the feature after or before which you need to reorder a selected feature.

Creating Drafts

Ribbon:	Home > Feature > Draft
Menu:	Insert > Detail Feature > Draft

This tool is used to create a draft on an existing model. To create the draft, choose the **Draft** tool from the **Feature** group of the **Home** tab; the **Draft** dialog box will be displayed, as shown in Figure 7-77. In NX, you can create four types of drafts: draft from face, draft from edges, draft tangent to faces, and draft to parting edges. The Type drop-down list contains four options to create the draft. The procedures to create different types of drafts are discussed next.

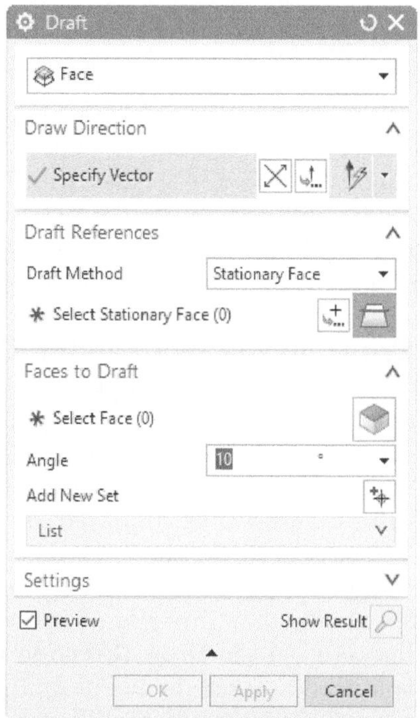

Figure 7-77 The ***Draft*** *dialog box*

Creating the Draft Using the Face Option

This type of draft is used to create a draft by selecting the stationary plane and faces of the model or a surface. To create the draft by using this option, choose the **Draft** tool from the **Feature** group; the **Draft** dialog box will be displayed.

In this dialog box, select the **Face** option from the Type drop-down list, if it is not selected by default. Note that the **Specify Vector** area is highlighted in the **Draw Direction** rollout of this dialog box. As a result, you will be prompted to specify the draw direction. Select an edge for the draw direction, refer to Figure 7-78. Alternatively, select the draw direction by using the **Inferred Vector** drop-down list. You can flip the draw direction by choosing the **Reverse Direction** button from the **Draw Direction** rollout. On doing so, you will be prompted to select the planar face. Select a face of the model as the stationary plane, refer to Figure 7-78. Next, choose the **Face** button from the **Faces to Draft** rollout; you will be prompted to select the faces to draft. Select the faces, refer to Figure 7-78. Enter the angle value in the **Angle1** edit box of the **Faces to Draft** rollout, and then choose the **OK** button from this dialog box; the draft will be created. The model after creating the draft feature is shown in Figure 7-79.

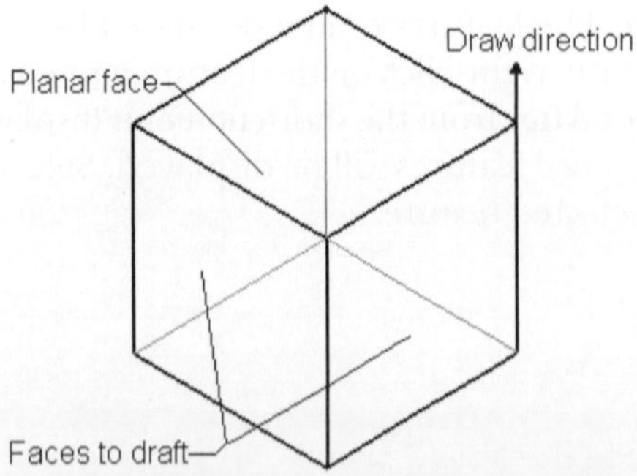

Figure 7-78 Objects to be selected

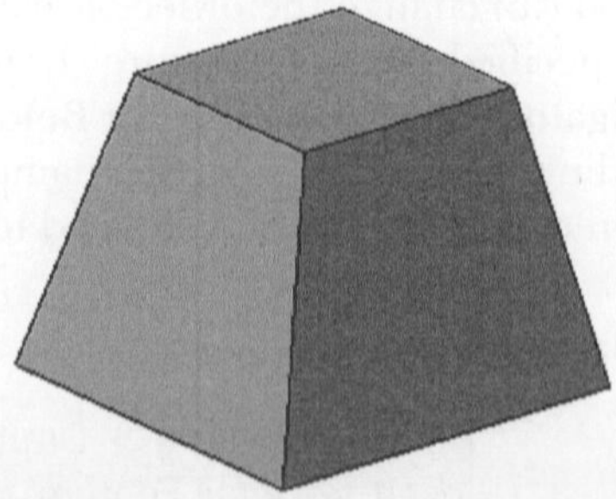

Figure 7-79 The model after creating the draft feature

You can create a set of faces to assign the unique angle value. The set may contain one or more faces to draft. To create a set of faces, select the faces to draft and enter the angle value in the **Angle 1** edit box of the **Faces to Draft** rollout. After completing one set, choose the **Add New Set** button to create another set and follow the same procedure. The list of sets created will be displayed in the **List** sub-rollout of the **Faces to Draft** rollout. You can also modify the angle value of a particular set by selecting it and then entering a new angle value in the respective edit box.

Creating the Draft Using the Edge Option

This option is used to create a draft by selecting the edges of a model. In such cases, you need to specify variable points and angles. This option is useful when the edges of the faces to be tapered are nonlinear. To create this type of draft, select the **Edge** option from the Type drop-down list; you will be prompted to select the objects to infer vector. Also, a triad will be displayed in the drawing area. Select the edge of the model or a datum axis to specify the draw direction, refer to Figure 7-80; you will be prompted to select the stationary edges. Alternatively, you can use the options in the **Inferred Vector** drop-down list to specify the draw direction. You can flip the draw direction by choosing the **Reverse Direction** button from the **Draw Direction** rollout. Next, select the edges, refer to Figure 7-80. Now, you need to select the points on the stationary edges to specify different draft angles. You can enter different angles for different selected points. To do so, expand the **Variable Draft Points** rollout and choose the **Inferred Point** button; you will be prompted to select the points. You can select any number of points on the edges to specify different angle values. Next, select the variable angle points, refer to Figure 7-80. Enter different angle values in the Pt A edit boxes, displayed after selecting the points. Next, choose the **OK** button to create the draft. The model after creating the draft feature is shown in Figure 7-81.

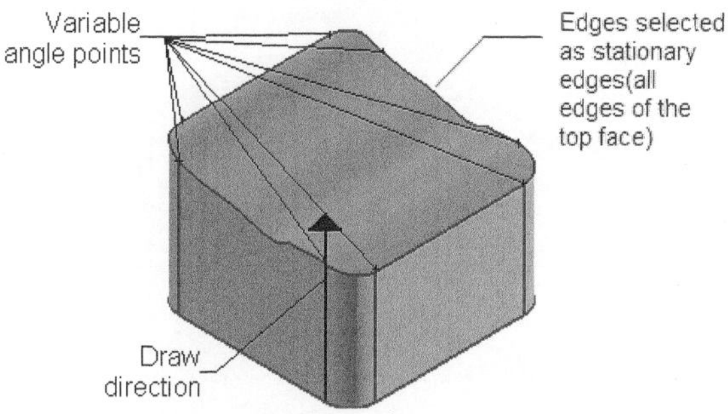

Figure 7-80 Objects to be selected

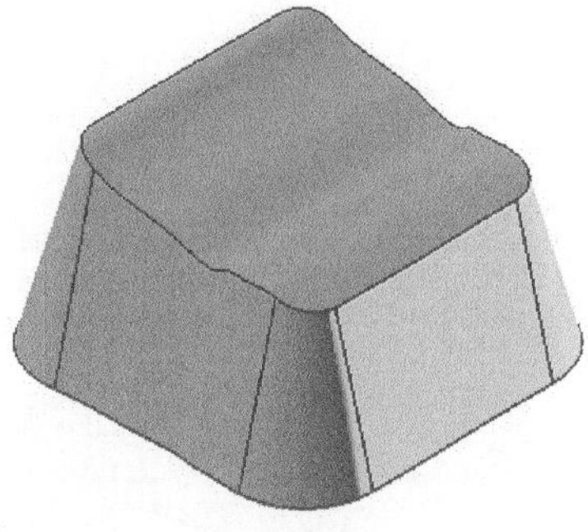

Figure 7-81 The draft created using the stationary edges

Creating the Draft Using the Tangent to Face Option

This option is used to create a draft that is tangent to the selected faces. In such cases, you need to specify the draw direction and the tangent face. To create this type of draft, select the **Tangent to Face** option from the Type drop-down list; you will be prompted to specify the draw direction. Select the edge of the model as the draft direction, refer to Figure 7-82; you will be prompted to select the tangent faces. Alternatively, you can use the options in the **Inferred Vector** drop-down list to select the draft direction. Next, select the face, refer to Figure 7-82. Enter the angle value in the **Angle 1** edit box. Choose the **Apply** button and then the **Cancel** button to create the draft. The resulting model after creating the draft feature is shown in Figure 7-83.

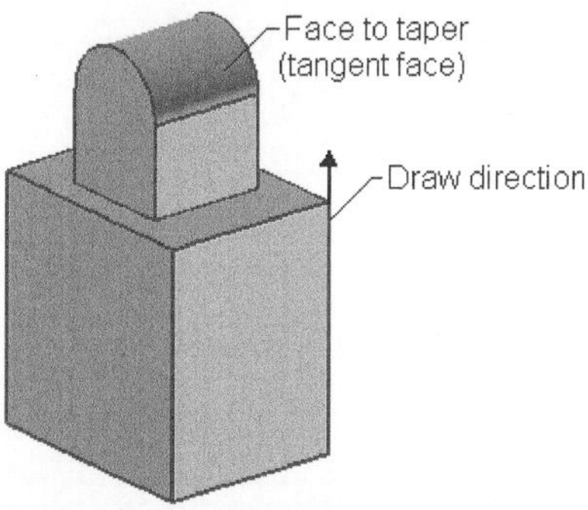

Figure 7-82 Objects to be selected

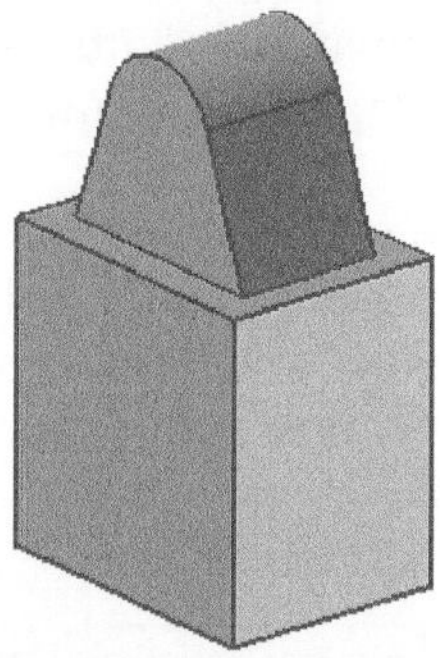

Figure 7-83 The draft created using the tangent faces

Creating the Draft Using the Parting Edge Option

This draft type is used to create a draft along the selected set of edges by specifying the angle, draw direction, stationary plane, and parting edges. To create this type of draft, select the **Parting Edge** option from the Type drop-down list; you will be prompted to specify the draw direction. Select an edge as the draw direction, refer to Figure 7-84. You can also use the options in the **Inferred Vector** drop-down list to specify the draw direction. After specifying the draw direction, you will be prompted to select a planar face. Select a planar face, refer to Figure 7-84. On doing so, you will be prompted to select parting edges. Select the parting edges, refer to Figure 7-84, and then enter the angle value in the **Angle 1** edit box. Next, choose the **Apply** button and then the **Cancel** button to create the draft. The resulting model after creating the draft feature is shown in Figure 7-85.

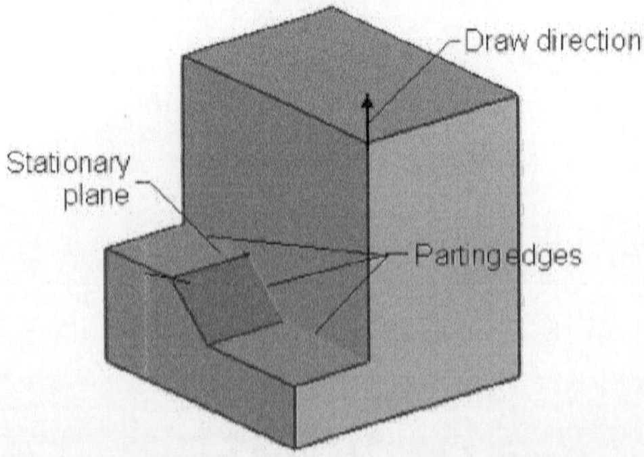

Figure 7-84 Objects to be selected

Figure 7-85 The draft feature created using the parting edges

Creating Lattice

Enhanced

Ribbon:	Home > Feature > More Gallery > Design Feature > Lattice
Menu:	Insert > Design Feature > Lattice

A lattice is a thin truss-like shape that you can use in additive manufacturing (3D printing) to create a lightweight part that still maintains its structural strength and integrity. It has a series of crisscrossed structures or supports that offer the strength and durability to a solid body while using significantly lesser material. Lattices reinforce designs to make them more structurally sound.

The **Lattice** tool allows you to set parameters and quickly generate a mesh or lattice to be used in a 3D printed part. To do so, choose the **Lattice** tool from the **Design Feature** area of the **More** gallery in the **Feature** group of the **Home** tab; the **Lattice** dialog box will be displayed, refer to Figure 7-86.

The various rollouts available in the **Lattice** dialog box and their subsequent options are discussed next.

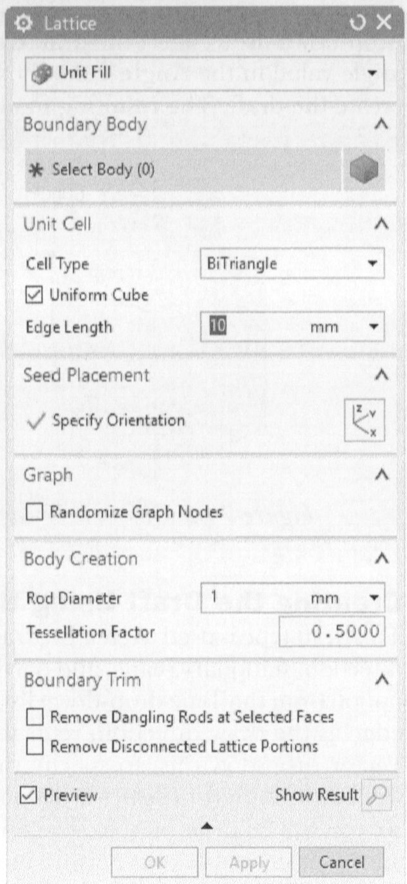

*Figure 7-86 The **Lattice** dialog box*

Type Drop-down list

The drop-down list contains four options, **Unit Fill**, **Unit Conformal**, **Surface**, and **Tetrahedron Fill**. The **Unit Fill** option is selected by default in this drop-down list and therefore, by using this option, you can specify a unit cell to be patterned, oriented, and trimmed upto the selected boundary body. On selecting the **Unit Conformal** option, you can specify a unit cell that is patterned and conformed to a selected face, and then trimmed in the lateral direction only. On selecting the **Surface** option, you can specify a lattice on faces by using their mesh facet edges as rods. On selecting the **Tetrahedron Fill** option, a boundary volume will be filled with a lattice by using its mesh facet edges as rods, and then tetrahedron structures are added inside. You can also offset the lattice from the selected face and create multiple layers. The options in the **Lattice** dialog box get modified depending upon the option selected from the Type drop-down list.

Boundary Body Rollout

This rollout is available only when the **Unit Fill** or **Tetrahedron Fill** option is selected from the Type drop-down list. The **Select Body** area in this rollout is activated by default which allows you to select a solid body as the boundary of the lattice.

If you select the **Unit Conformal or Surface** option from the Type drop-down list, the name of this rollout will be modified to **Base Face** rollout and the **Select Face** area in this rollout will be activated by default which enables you to select a face as the boundary of the lattice.

Unit Cell Rollout

The options in this rollout are discussed next.

Cell Type

This drop-down list allows you to select the cell geometry for thelattice. The expanded view of the **Cell Type** drop-down list is shown in Figure 7-87.

***Figure 7-87** The **Cell Type** drop-down list*

Uniform Cube

This check box is selected by default and allows you to specify a uniform edge length for the lattice cells. If you clear this check box, the **Size X**, **Size Y**, and **Size Z** edit boxes will become available in this rollout. You can specify different edge lengths for the X, Y, and Z directions using the respective edit boxes.

Edge Length

This edit box is available only when the **Uniform Cube** check box is selected and allows you to enter a uniform value for the edge length of the lattice.

Seed Placement Rollout

This rollout is available only when the **Unit Fill** option is selected from the Type drop-down list. The **Manipulator** button in this rollout allows you to locate and orient the unit cell.

Graph Rollout

The options in this rollout are discussed next.

Randomize Graph Nodes

If you select this check box, all the lattice nodes will be moved within a specified radius.

Layers

This edit box is available only if the **Unit Conformal** option is selected from the Type drop-down list. You can enter a value in this edit box to specify the number of layers for the graph.

Offset
This edit box is also available only if the **Unit Conformal** option is selected from the Type drop-down list. You can enter an offset value in this edit box to specify the offset distance for the graph.

Body Creation Rollout
In this rollout, you can enter diameter of the lattice rod and tessellation factor in the **Rod Diameter** and **Tessellation Factor** edit boxes, respectively. The tessellation factor value is multiplied with the rod diameter to define the tessellation tolerance for creating the lattice body.

Boundary Trim Rollout
This rollout is available only when the **Unit Fill** or **Unit Conformal** option is selected from the Type drop-down list and displays one or two check boxes depending upon the option selected in the Type drop-down list. On selecting the **Remove Disconnected Lattice Portions** check box, all the small disconnected lattice portions will be removed, keeping only the largest body. On selecting the **Remove Dangling Rods at Selected Faces** check box, all the rods from the lattice graph which are connected at one end to the lattice and touch one of the selected faces of the boundary body, will be removed.

Figure 7-88 shows a solid model and Figure 7-89 shows the lattice of the same model created using the **Unit Fill** option with the rod diameter value as **0.5**, tessellation factor value as **0.5**, and edge length value as **5**.

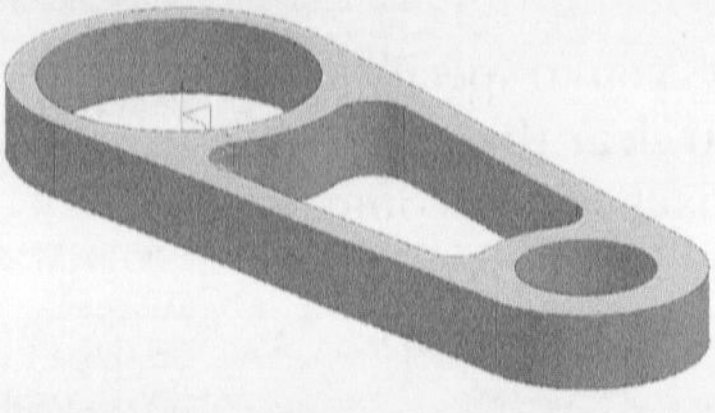

Figure 7-88 Solid model

Figure 7-89 Lattice created for the solid model

Figure 7-90 shows a solid model and Figure 7-91 shows the lattice of the same model created using the **Unit Conformal** option with the rod diameter value as **0.5**, tessellation factor value as **0.5**, and edge length value as **5**.

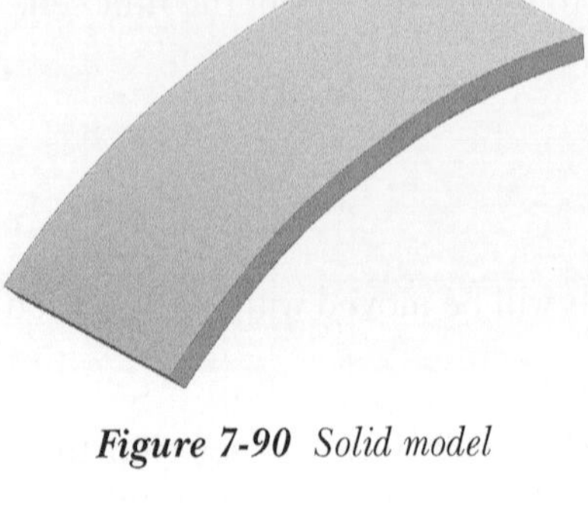

Figure 7-90 Solid model

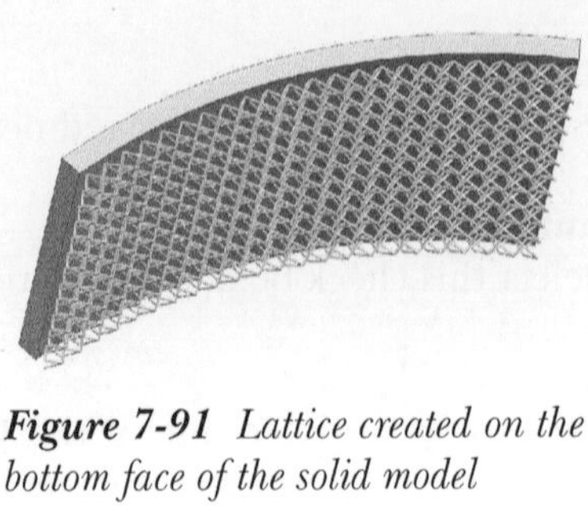

Figure 7-91 Lattice created on the bottom face of the solid model

MEASURING OBJECTS

Ribbon: Analysis > Measure > Measure
Menu: Analysis > Measure

The **Measure** tool is used to analyze a model and measure it. To measure an object, choose the **Measure** tool from the **Measure** group of the **Analysis** tab in the **Ribbon**; the **Measure** dialog box will be displayed, as shown in Figure 7-92. Various rollouts available in the **Measure** dialog box and their subsequent options are discussed next.

Object to Measure Rollout

This rollout contains various radio buttons. Depending upon the type of object selected, you can select different radio buttons. Some of the radio buttons in this rollout are discussed next.

Object

When this radio button is selected, you will be prompted to select the objects to measure. Select the face of the model, refer to Figure 7-93; you will get the information about the parameters of the selected face.

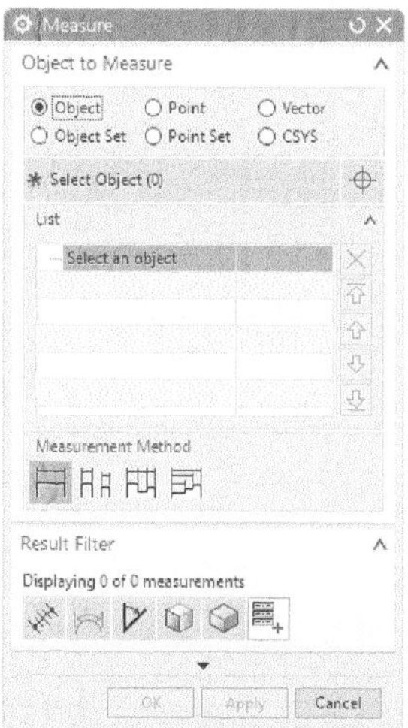

*Figure 7-92 The **Measure** dialog box*

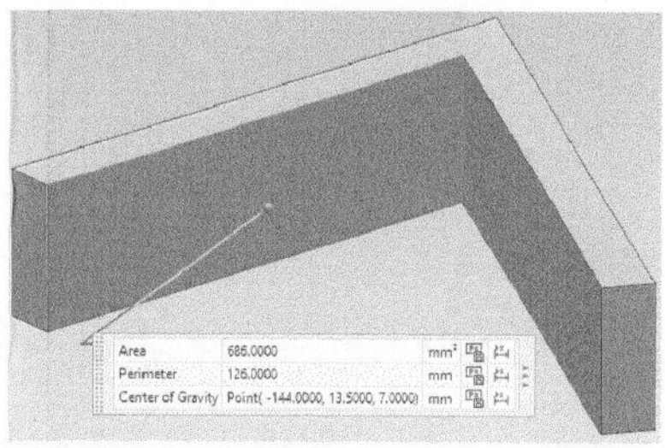

Figure 7-93 The face selected for model information

Point

When this radio button is selected, you will be prompted to select an object to infer point. Select the arc center, refer to Figure 7-94; you will get information for the point to be inferred.

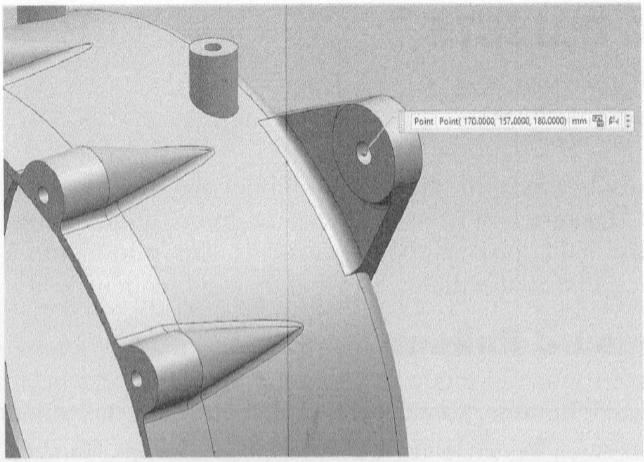

Figure 7-94 The arc center selected for model information

Vector

When this radio button is selected, you will be prompted to select objects to infer vector. Select the vector and the face, refer to Figure 7-95; you will get information about the angle between the selected vector and face.

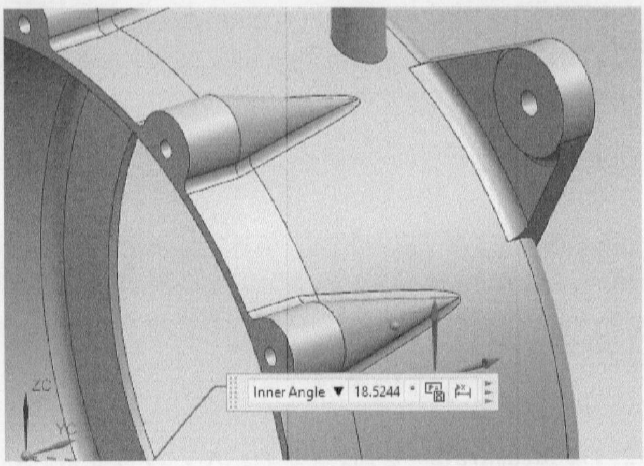

Figure 7-95 The vector and face selected for model information

Object Set

When this radio button is selected, you will be prompted to select objects to measure a new set. Select the faces, refer to Figure 7-96; you will get information about the parameters of the selected face.

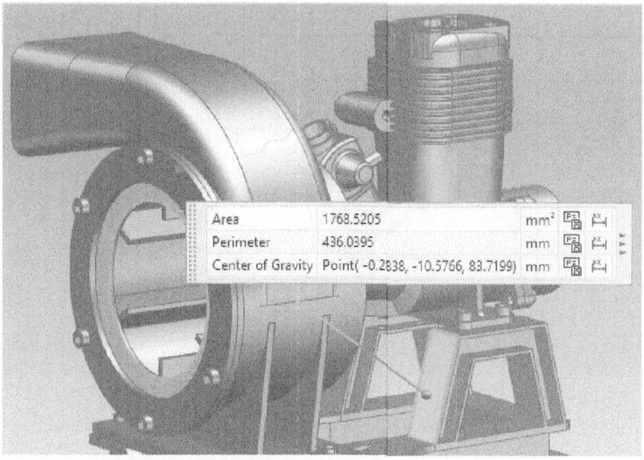

Figure 7-96 The faces selected for model information

TUTORIALS

Tutorial 1

In this tutorial, you will create a model of the Fixture Base shown in Figure 7-97. The dimensions of the model are shown in Figure 7-98. **(Expected time: 30 min)**

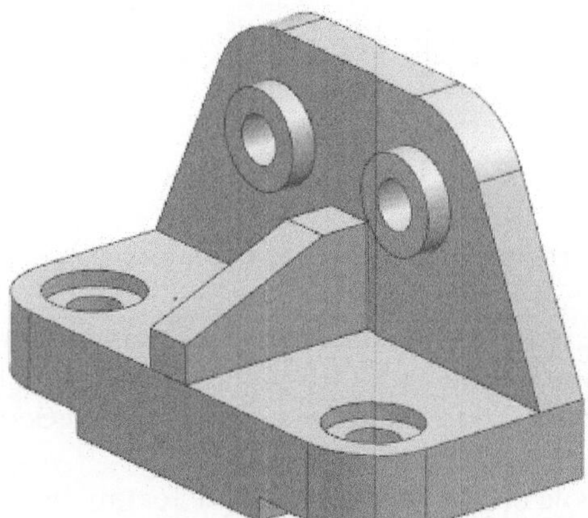

Figure 7-97 Model for Tutorial 1

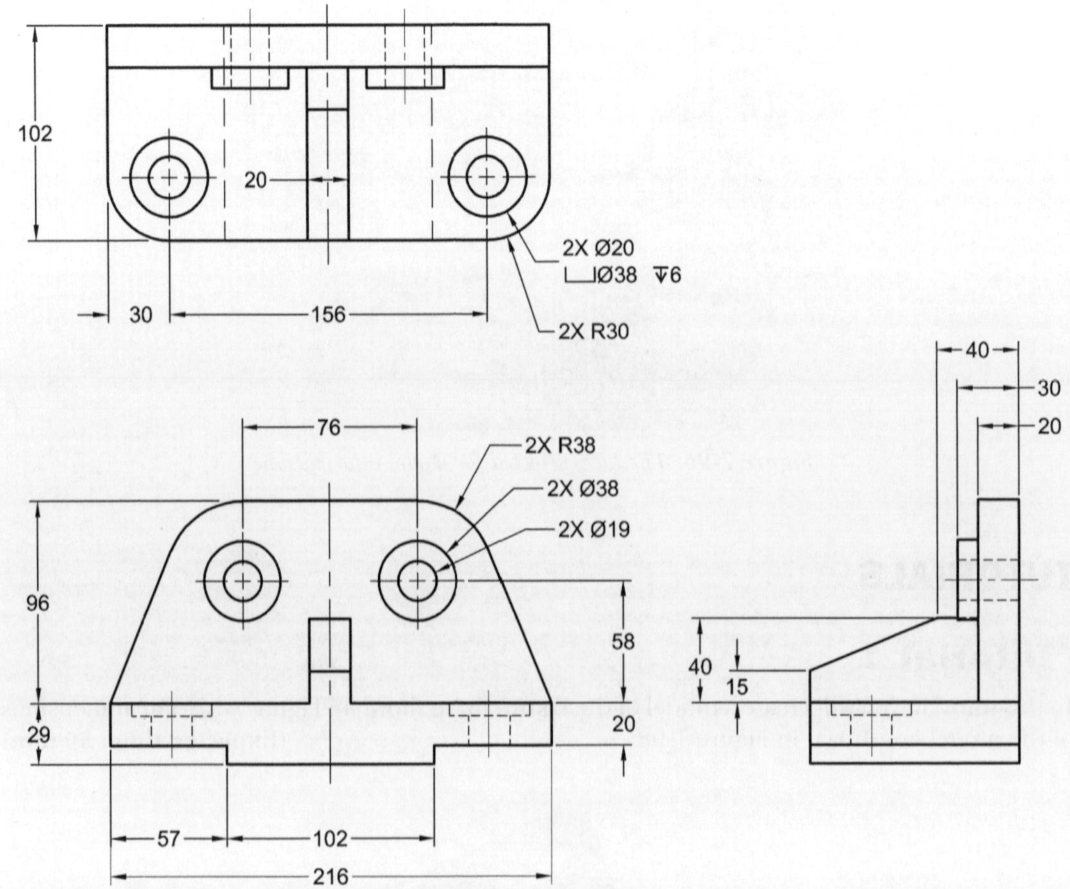

Figure 7-98 *Views and dimensions of the model*

The following steps are required to complete this tutorial:

a. Create the base feature of the model on the XC-ZC plane, refer to Figure 7-99.
b. Create the second feature on the back face of the base feature, refer to Figure 7-100.
c. Create the edge blend feature to fillet the two vertical edges of the base feature, refer to Figure 7-101.
d. Create a counterbore hole on the right of the base feature by using the center point of the edge blend on the right, refer to Figure 7-102.
e. Create the extruded join feature on the front face of the second feature and then create a hole on it, refer to Figures 7-103 and 7-104.
f. Mirror the two holes by using the YC-ZC plane, refer to Figure 7-105.
g. Create the central rib feature by drawing its sketch on the YC-ZC plane and extruding the sketch symmetrically in both directions, refer to Figure 7-106.

Creating the Base Feature

1. Start a new file with the name *c07tut1.prt* using the **Model** template and specify its location as *C:\NX\c07*.

2. Create the sketch for the base feature on the XC-ZC plane. For dimensions, refer to Figure 7-98. Make sure that the sketch is symmetric about the YC-ZC plane because it will be used as the mirror plane at a later stage. Extrude the sketch symmetrically on both sides of the sketching plane through a symmetric distance of **51**. The base feature of the model along the XC-ZC plane is shown in Figure 7-99.

Creating the Second Feature

1. Create the second feature, which is an extruded join feature, by using the back face of the base feature as the sketching plane, refer to Figure 7-100. For dimensions, refer to Figure 7-98.

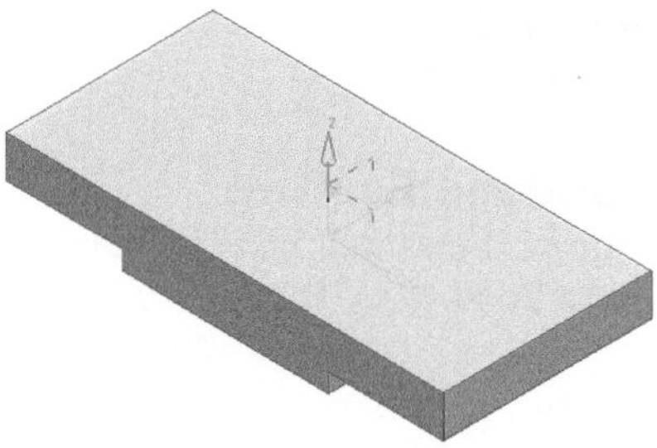

Figure 7-99 *Base feature of the model*

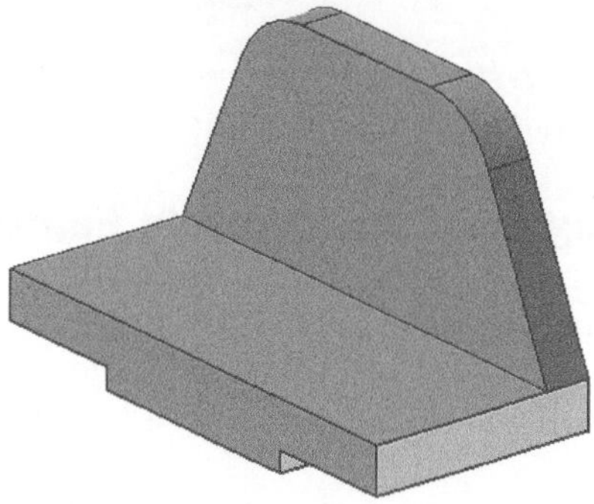

Figure 7-100 *Model after creating the second feature*

Creating the Edge Blend Feature

Next, you need to create the edge blend feature on the front vertical edges of the base feature. The center point of the right edge blend will be used to create the counterbore hole on the base feature.

1. Create the edge blend feature on the front vertical edges of the base feature, refer to Figure 7-101. For dimensions, refer to Figure 7-98.

Creating the Counterbore Hole

You need to create the counterbore hole on the right of the base feature and then mirror it on the other side. The center point of the edge blend on the right will be taken as the center point of the hole.

1. Invoke the **Hole** dialog box by choosing the **Hole** tool from the **Feature** group and specify the parameters of the counterbore hole in it. Refer to Figure 7-98 for parameters.

2. Use the center point of the edge blend feature to place the counterbore hole. The model after creating the counterbore hole is shown in Figure 7-102.

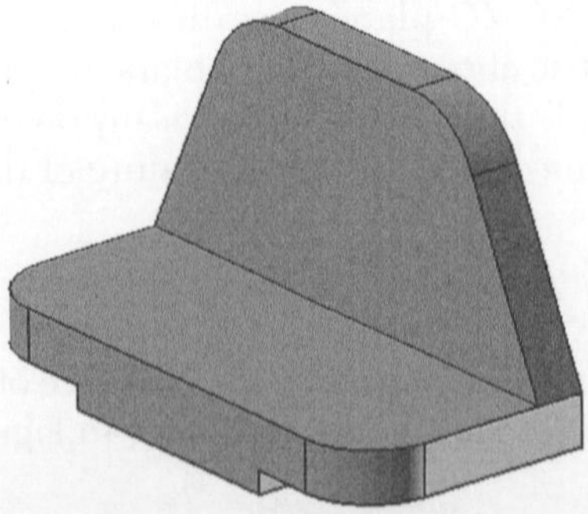

Figure 7-101 Model after creating the edge blend feature

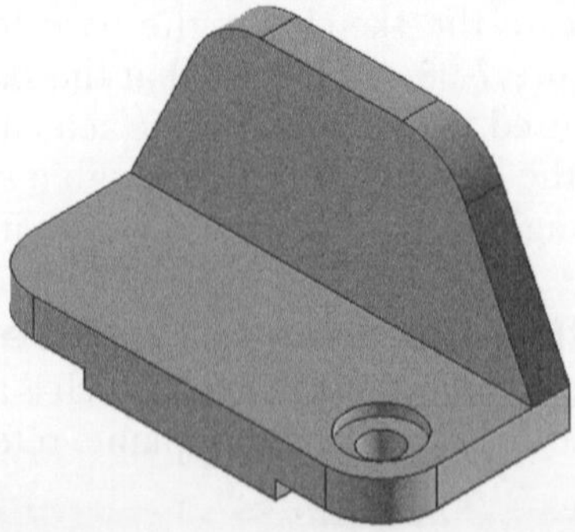

Figure 7-102 Model after creating the counterbore hole

Creating the Extruded Join Feature on the Second Feature

1. Select the front face of the second feature and then draw the sketch of the extruded join feature, which is a circle. For dimensions, refer to Figure 7-98.

2. Extrude the circle to create the join feature, refer to Figure 7-103.

Creating the Simple Hole

In this section, you need to create a simple hole on the front face of the last feature. The center point of the last feature will be used as the center point of the hole.

1. Invoke the **Hole** dialog box and specify the parameters of the simple hole in it, refer to Figure 7-98 for parameters.

2. Use the center point of the last feature to place the hole. The model after creating the simple hole is shown in Figure 7-104.

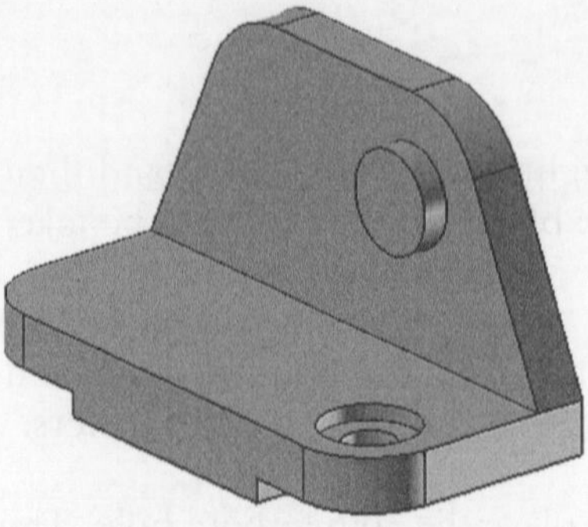

Figure 7-103 Model after creating the extruded join feature on the front face of the second feature

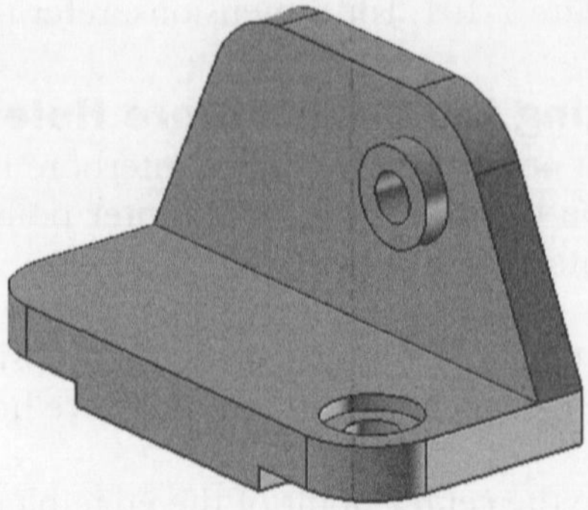

Figure 7-104 Model after creating the simple hole on the extruded join feature

Mirroring Features

The sketch of the base feature was created symmetric about the YC-ZC plane. Therefore, it will be used to mirror selected features.

2. Choose **Menu > Insert > Associative Copy > Mirror Feature** from the **Top Border Bar** to invoke the **Mirror Feature** dialog box.

2. Select the counterbore hole, the extruded feature on the second feature, and the simple hole from the model; these features get highlighted in the model.

3. Click in the **Select Plane** area of the **Mirror Plane** rollout of the **Mirror Feature** dialog box and then select the YC-ZC plane. To select this plane as the mirroring plane, you may need to zoom out the model by using the **Zoom In/Out** tool.

4. Choose the **OK** button from this dialog box; the features will be mirrored. The model after mirroring the features is shown in Figure 7-105.

Creating the Rib Feature

1. Create the last feature, which is also an extruded join feature. The sketch of this feature will be drawn on the YC-ZC plane and will be extruded symmetrically. For dimensions, refer to Figure 7-98. The final model after creating this feature is shown in Figure 7-106.

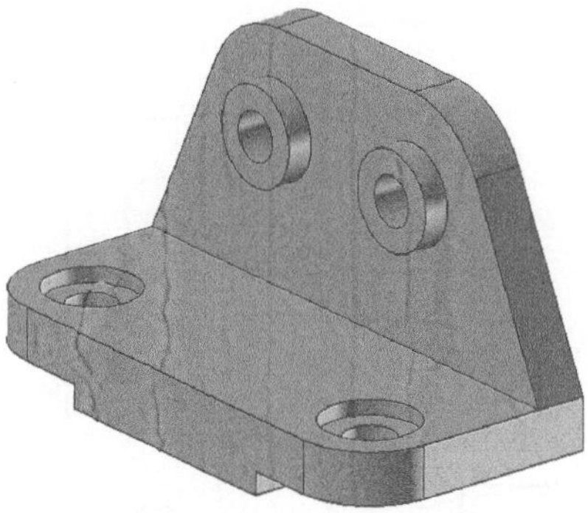

Figure 7-105 *Model after mirroring the features*

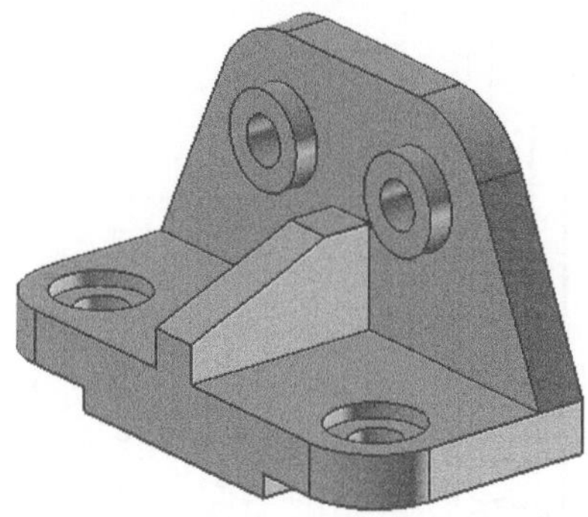

Figure 7-106 *Final model for Tutorial 1*

Saving and Closing the File

1. Choose **Menu > File > Close > Save and Close** from the **Top Border Bar** to save and close the file.

Tutorial 2

In this tutorial, you will create a model of the Joint shown in Figure 7-107. Its dimensions are shown in Figure 7-108. **(Expected time: 30 min)**

Figure 7-107 Model of the Joint for Tutorial 2

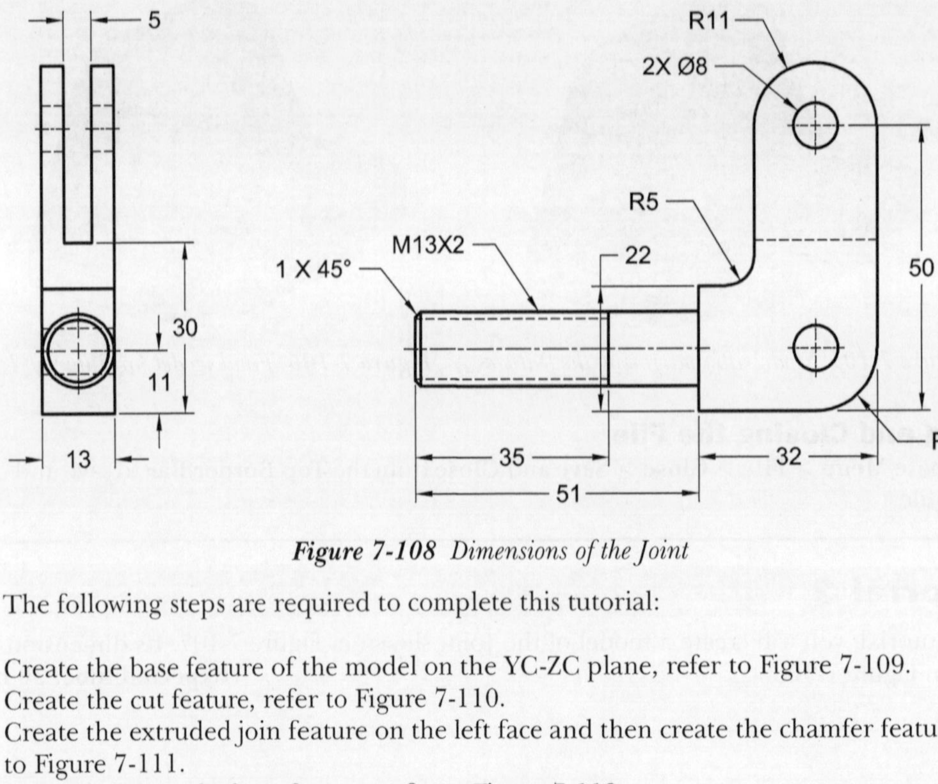

Figure 7-108 Dimensions of the Joint

The following steps are required to complete this tutorial:

a. Create the base feature of the model on the YC-ZC plane, refer to Figure 7-109.
b. Create the cut feature, refer to Figure 7-110.
c. Create the extruded join feature on the left face and then create the chamfer feature, refer to Figure 7-111.
d. Create holes on the base feature, refer to Figure 7-112.
e. Finally, create threads on the cylindrical join feature by using the **Thread** tool, refer to Figure 7-113.

Creating the Base Feature

1. Start a new file with the name *c07tut2.prt* using the **Model** template and specify its location as *C:\NX\c07*.

2. Create the base feature of the model on the YC-ZC plane, as shown in Figure 7-109. For dimensions, refer to Figure 7-108.

Creating the Cut Feature

1. Use the **Subtract** boolean option from the **Extrude** dialog box to create the cut feature in the base feature, refer to Figure 7-110. For dimensions of this cut feature, refer to Figure 7-108.

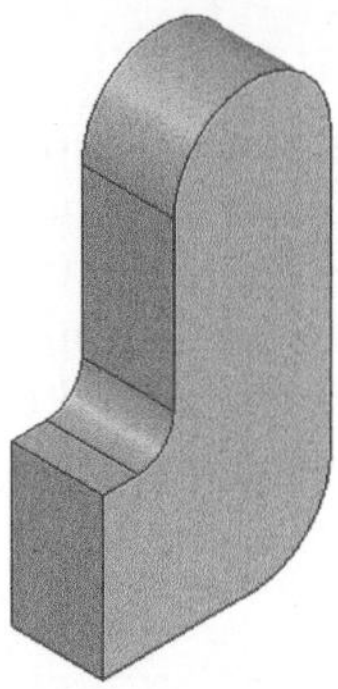

Figure 7-109 *Base feature of the model*

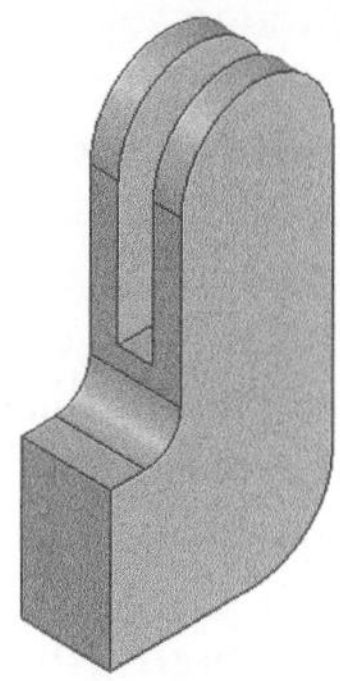

Figure 7-110 *Model after creating the cut feature*

Creating the Extruded Join Feature, Chamfer, and Holes

1. Use the **Unite** option of the **Extrude** dialog box to create the cylindrical feature on the front face of the base feature, refer to Figure 7-111. For dimensions of this extruded feature, refer to Figure 7-108.

2. Chamfer the front end of the cylindrical feature, refer to Figure 7-111. For its dimensions, refer to Figure 7-108.

3. Create two holes on the base feature, refer to Figure 7-112. For dimensions of the hole features, refer to Figure 7-108.

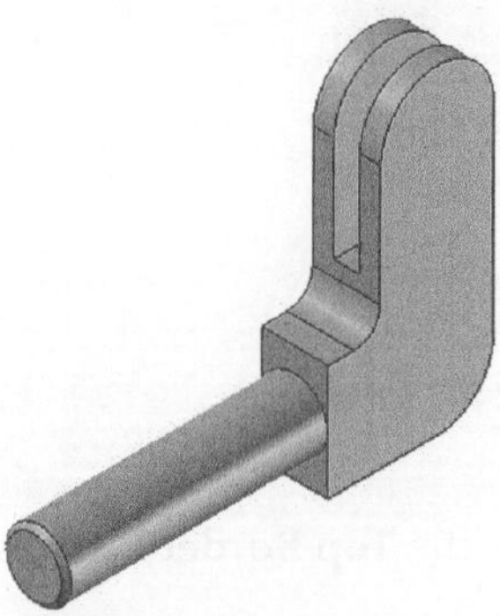

Figure 7-111 *Model after creating and chamfering the cylindrical join feature*

Figure 7-112 *Model after creating holes*

Creating Threads

Next, you need to create detailed threads on the cylindrical feature created on the front face of the base feature by using the **Thread** tool. When you invoke the **Thread** tool and select the cylindrical face, the thread parameters will automatically be defined in the edit boxes. You need to accept the default values for creating threads.

1. Choose **Menu > Insert > Design Feature > Thread** from the **Top Border Bar**; the **Thread** dialog box is displayed.

2. In this dialog box, select the **Detailed** radio button; the thread options are modified and you are prompted to select a cylindrical face.

3. Select the cylindrical face from the drawing area by clicking the left mouse button closer to its front face; the face is highlighted and an arrow is displayed on the front face of the cylindrical feature. If the arrow is not displayed on the front face of the cylindrical feature, then to display the arrow on the front face, choose the **Select Start** button from the **Thread** dialog box; the **Thread** dialog box is modified. Also, you are prompted to select the start face. Select the front face of the cylindrical face as the start face, and then choose the **OK** button from this dialog box.

4. Enter **35** in the **Length** edit box of the **Thread** dialog box.

5. Accept the other default values of thread parameters, which are displayed in various edit boxes of the **Thread** dialog box, and then choose the **OK** button; threads are created and the dialog box is closed. The final model of the Joint is shown in Figure 7-113.

Figure 7-113 Final model of the Joint

Saving and Closing the File

1. Choose **Menu > File > Close > Save and Close** from the **Top Border Bar** to save and close the file.

Tutorial 3

In this tutorial, you will create the model shown in Figure 7-114. The dimensions of the model are shown in Figure 7-115. **(Expected time: 30 min)**

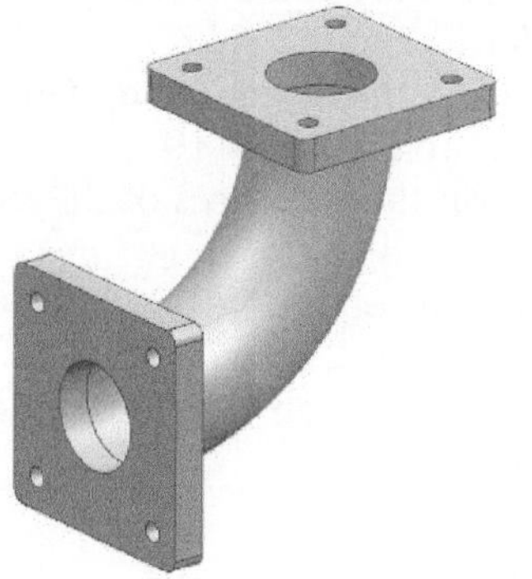

Figure 7-114 *Model for Tutorial 3*

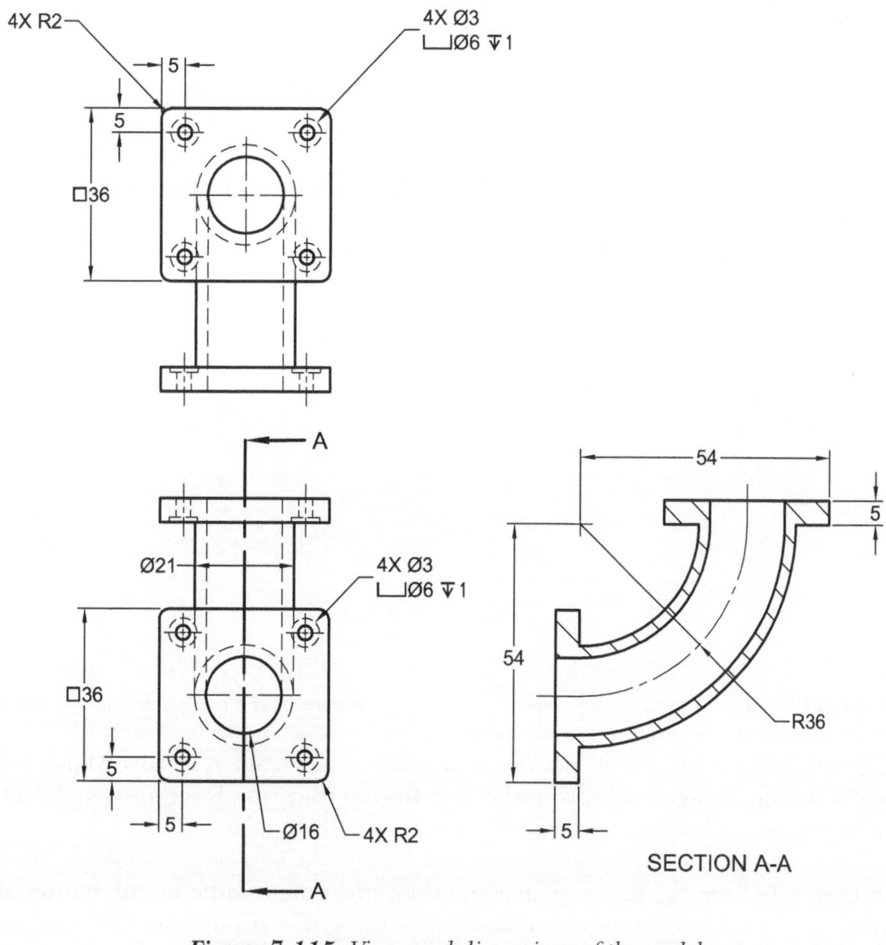

Figure 7-115 *Views and dimensions of the model*

The following steps are required to complete this tutorial:

a. Draw the sketch of the guide curve on the YC-ZC plane for the base feature, refer to Figure 7-116.
b. Create a new datum plane at the start point of the guide curve and then draw the sketch of the section on this plane, refer to Figure 7-117.
c. Create the sweep feature by using the **Sweep along Guide** tool, refer to Figure 7-118.
d. Hollow the sweep feature, refer to Figure 7-119.
e. Create extruded join features on the end faces of the sweep feature and then create holes on them, refer to Figures 7-120 and 7-121.
f. Create the counterbore hole on one of the extruded features and then create the rectangular pattern of holes, refer to Figures 7-122 and 7-123.
g. Similarly, create the counterbore hole on the other extruded feature and then create the pattern of holes, refer to Figure 7-124.

Creating the Base Feature

The base feature of this model is a sweep feature. First, you will draw the guide curve of the sweep feature and then create a datum plane at the lower end of the guide curve. You will use this datum plane as the sketching plane to sketch the section of the sweep feature.

1. Start a new file with the name *c07tut3.prt* using the **Model** template and specify its location as *C:\NX\c07*.

2. Draw the sketch of the guide curve on the YC-ZC plane, refer to Figure 7-116.

3. Create a datum plane normal to the curve at its lower end and then draw the sketch of the section on this plane, refer to Figure 7-117.

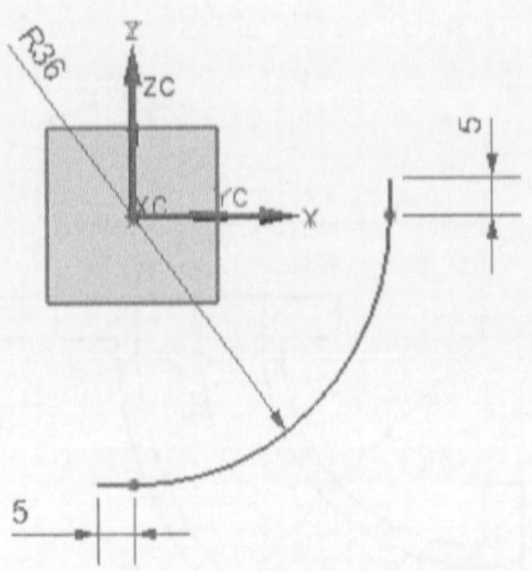

Figure 7-116 Sketch of the guide curve

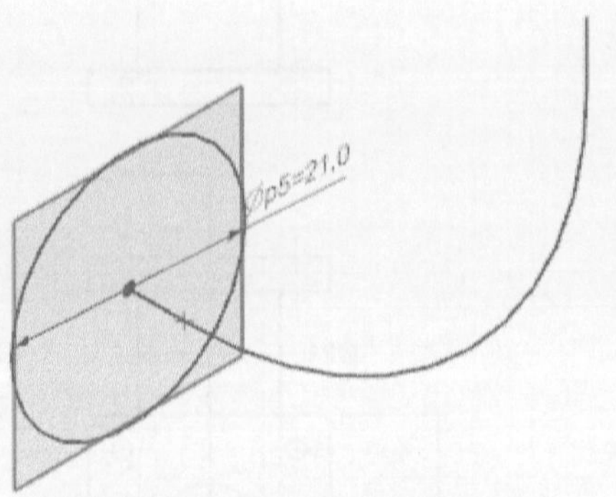

Figure 7-117 Sketch of the section

4. After creating the guide curve and a section of the sweep feature, choose **Menu > Insert > Sweep > Sweep along Guide** from the **Top Border Bar**; the **Sweep Along Guide** dialog box is displayed and you are prompted to select the section string.

5. Select the circle from the drawing area and then press the middle mouse button once; you are prompted to select the guide string. Select the guide curve from the drawing area; a

preview of the feature is displayed in the drawing window. Make sure the value **0** is entered in the **First Offset** and **Second Offset** edit boxes of the **Offsets** rollout in the dialog box.

6. Choose the **OK** button from this dialog box; the sweep feature is created, as shown in Figure 7-118.

Hollowing out the Base Feature

Next, you need to hollow out the base feature by using the **Shell** tool.

1. Invoke the **Shell** tool from the **Feature** group; the **Shell** dialog box is displayed and you are prompted to select the faces to be removed.

2. Enter **2.5** in the **Thickness** edit box and select the two end faces of the sweep feature.

3. Choose **Apply** and then the **Cancel** button to exit the dialog box. The model after hollowing out the base feature is shown in Figure 7-119.

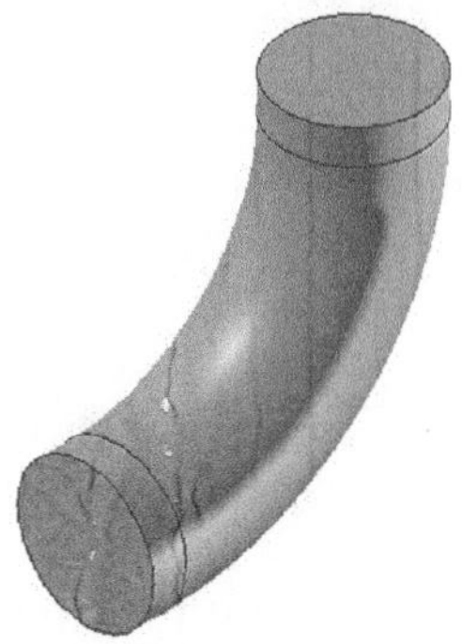

Figure 7-118 *Base feature of the model*

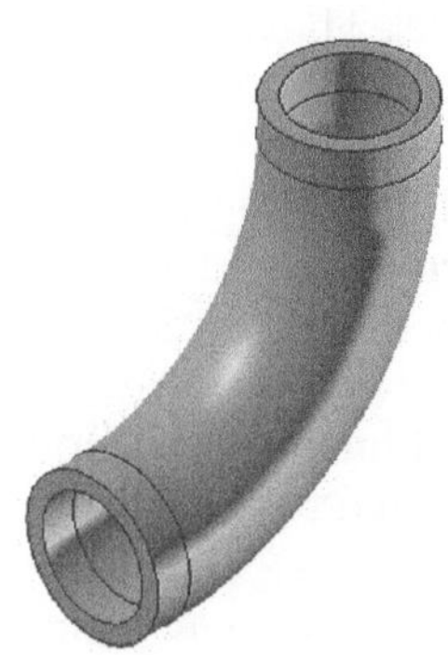

Figure 7-119 *Model after hollowing the base feature*

Note

*For hollowing the base feature, you can also enter **-2.5** in the **First Offset** edit box of the **Offsets** rollout in the **Sweep Along Guide** dialog box while creating the base feature.*

Creating Extruded Join Features

1. Create the extruded join features one by one on the two end faces of the base feature, as shown in Figure 7-120. Note that you need to reverse the direction of the feature creation. For dimensions, refer to Figure 7-120.

2. Create simple holes at the center of the extruded join features. Note that the holes need to be created only up to the back faces of the extruded features. For diameters of the holes, refer to Figure 7-115. Figure 7-121 shows the model after the holes have been created.

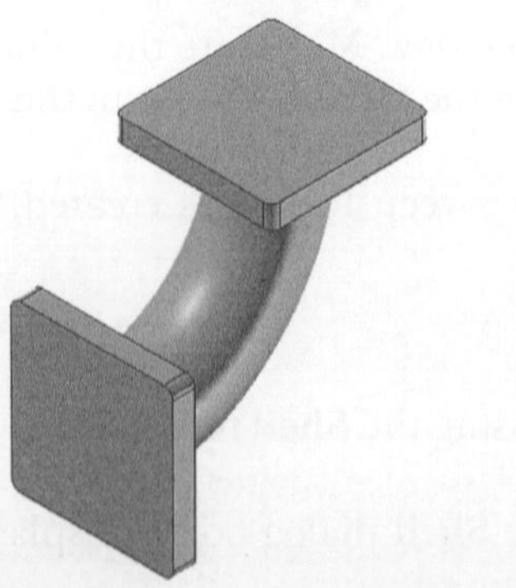

Figure 7-120 Extruded join features created on the two end faces of the base feature

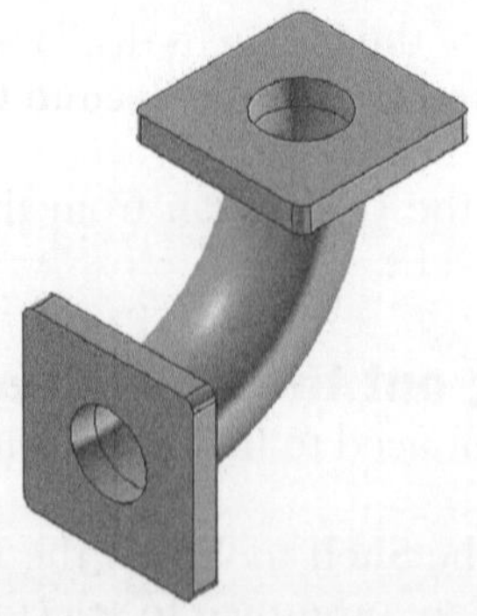

Figure 7-121 Model after creating holes

Creating Counterbore Holes

1. Create the counterbore hole on the lower right of the back face of the front extruded feature of the model. The rotated view of the model after creating the hole is shown in Figure 7-122. For dimensions of the counterbore hole, refer to Figure 7-115.

2. After creating the counterbore hole, choose the **Pattern Feature** tool from the **Feature** group; the **Pattern Feature** dialog box is displayed and you are prompted to select the features to be patterned.

3. Select the **Linear** option from the **Layout** drop-down list if it is not already selected; the options related to the linear pattern are displayed.

4. Select the counterbore hole from the drawing window and choose the **Specify Vector** option from the **Direction 1** sub-rollout in the **Pattern Feature** dialog box; the vector triad is displayed in the drawing window and you are prompted to select objects to infer vector.

5. Select the lower horizontal edge of the extruded join feature to define the first direction. Next, you need to define the second direction.

6. Select the **Use Direction 2** check box from the **Direction 2** sub-rollout; the options in the **Direction 2** sub-rollout are displayed and you are prompted to select objects to infer vector.

7. Select the vertical edge of the extruded join feature to define the second direction.

   Next, you need to define the number of instances and the spacing between them.

Note

If the direction arrows point in the directions opposite to what is required, then choose the ***Reverse Direction*** *button.*

8. Select the **Count and Pitch** option from the **Spacing** drop-down list in the **Direction 1** sub -rollout; the **Count** and **Pitch Distance** edit boxes are displayed.

9. Enter **2** in the **Count** edit box and **26** in the **Pitch Distance** edit box.

   Next, you need to define the parameters in the second direction.

10. Specify the same parameters in the **Direction 2** sub-rollout and choose the **OK** button from the **Pattern Feature** dialog box; a linear pattern of counterbore holes is created. The rotated view of the model after creating the linear pattern of the counterbore holes is shown in Figure 7-123.

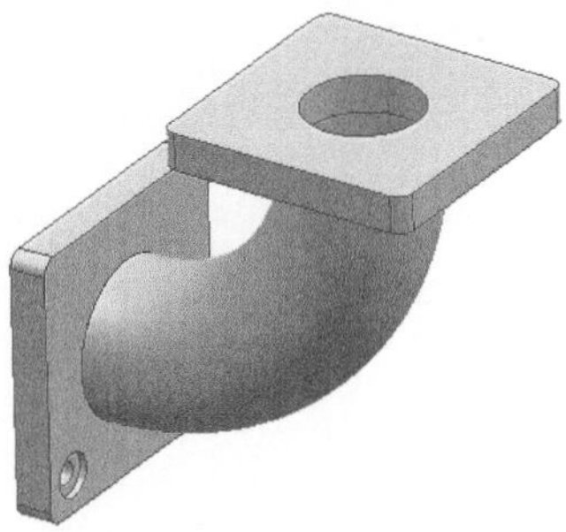

Figure 7-122 *One of the counterbore holes created on the front face of the model*

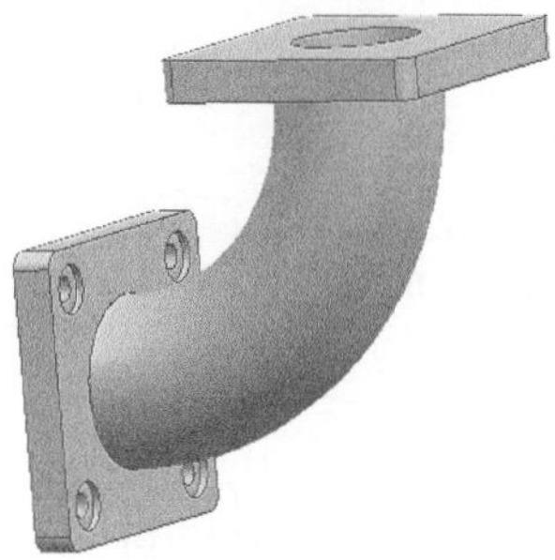

Figure 7-123 *Model after creating the linear pattern of counterbore holes*

11. Similarly, create the counterbore hole on the bottom face of the top extruded feature and then create a linear pattern of counterbore holes on the bottom face of the top extruded feature. The final model for this tutorial is shown in Figure 7-124.

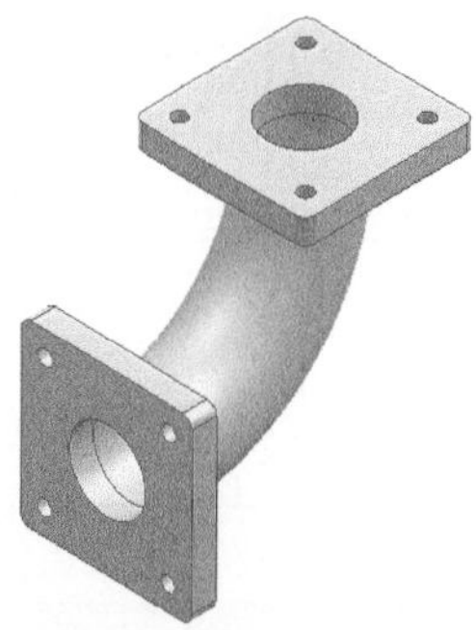

Figure 7-124 *Final model for Tutorial 3*

Saving and Closing the File

1. Choose **Menu > File > Close > Save and Close** from the **Top Border Bar** to save and close the file.

Tutorial 4

In this tutorial, you will create the model shown in Figure 7-125. The views and dimensions of the model are given in Figure 7-126. **(Expected time: 45 min)**

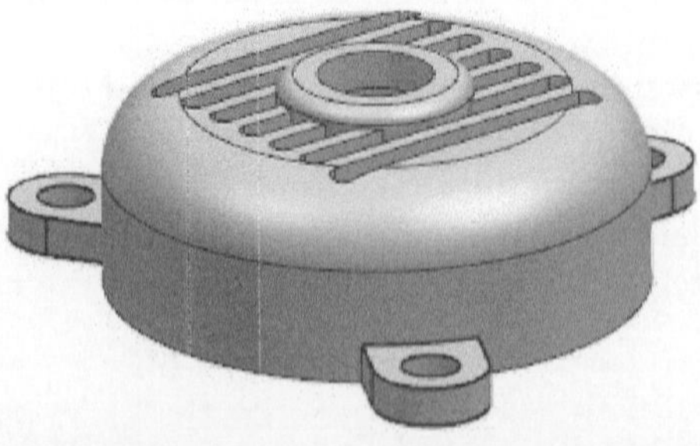

Figure 7-125 Model for Tutorial 4

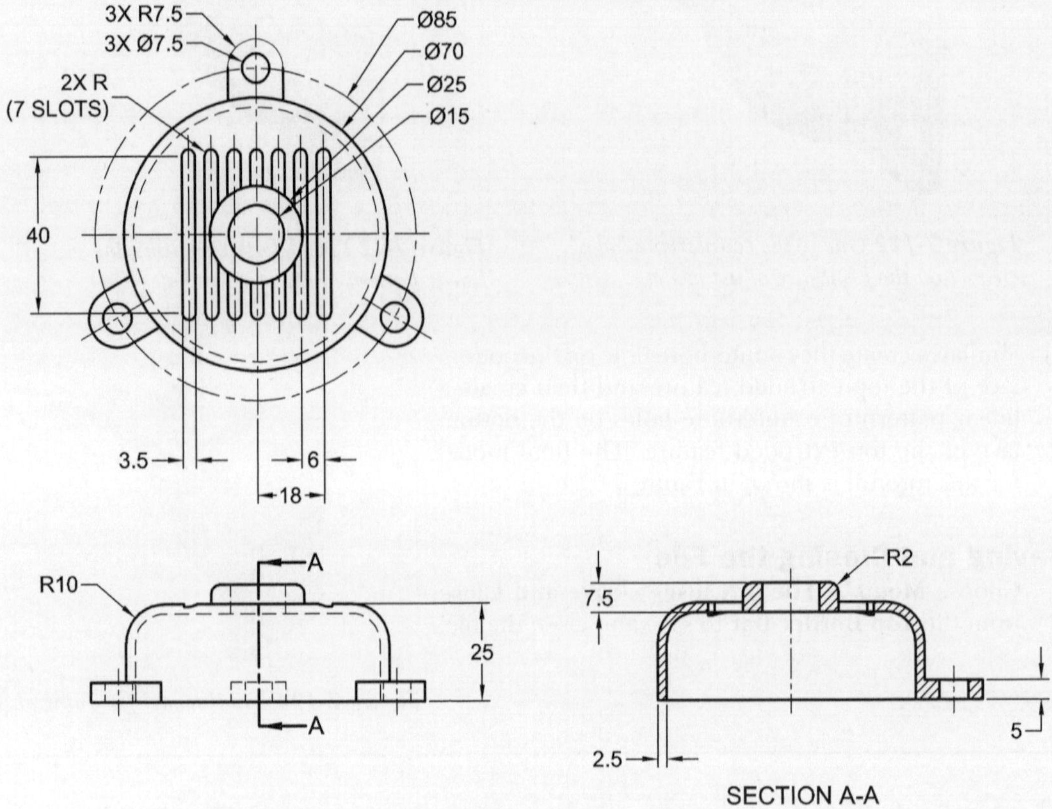

Figure 7-126 Views and dimensions of the model for Tutorial 4

The following steps are required to complete this tutorial:

a. Create the base feature of the model by revolving the sketch drawn on the YC-ZC plane, refer to Figures 7-127 and 7-128.
b. Shell the model using the **Shell** tool, refer to Figure 7-129.
c. Draw the sketch on the XC-YC plane and extrude it to a given distance, refer to Figure 7-130.

d. Pattern the extrude feature using the **Pattern Feature** tool, refer to Figures 7-131 and 7-132.
e. Create the slot on the top planar face and pattern it, refer to Figures 7-133 through 7-136.
f. Create the features on the top planar face, refer to Figures 7-137 and 7-138.
g. Save the model.

Creating the Base Feature

First, you need to create the base feature of the model by revolving the sketch created on the front plane.

1. Start a new file with the name *c07tut4.prt* using the **Model** template and specify its location as *C:\NX\c07*.

2. Invoke the **Revolve** tool and draw the sketch of the base feature on the YC-ZC plane, as shown in Figure 7-127.

3. Exit the Sketch in Task environment and create the base feature of the model, as shown in Figure 7-128.

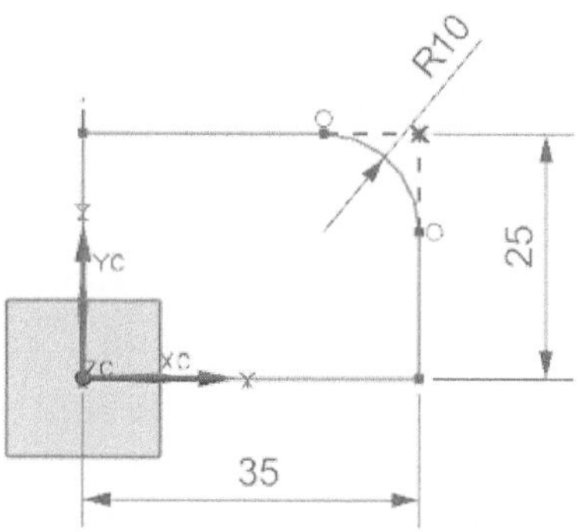

Figure 7-127 *Sketch of the base feature*

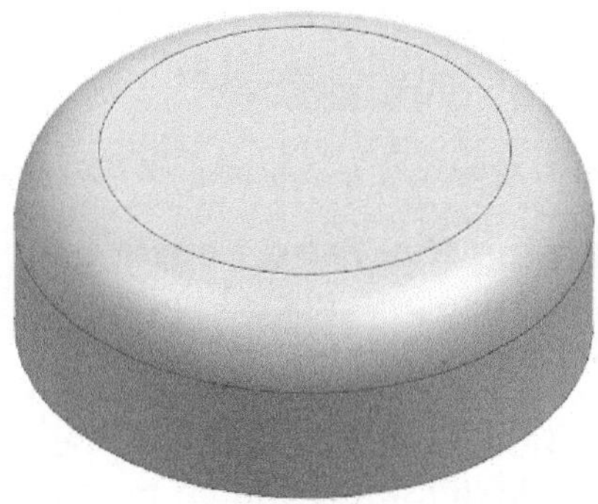

Figure 7-128 *Base feature of the model*

Hollowing out the Base Feature

After creating the base feature, you need to shell the model using the **Shell** tool. You also need to remove the bottom face of the base feature, leaving behind a thin-walled model.

1. Choose the **Shell** tool from the **Feature** group; the **Shell** dialog box is displayed. Set the value in the **Thickness** edit box to **2.5**.

2. Rotate the model and select its bottom face to remove it.

3. Choose the **OK** button to exit the dialog box. The model after hollowing out the base feature is shown in Figure 7-129.

Creating the Third Feature

After adding the shell feature to the model, you need to create the third feature, which is an extruded feature. The sketch for this feature will be drawn on the XC-YC plane.

1. Invoke the **Extrude** tool and select the XC-YC plane as the sketching plane.
2. Draw the sketch of the third feature, as shown in Figure 7-130.
3. Exit the Sketch in Task environment and extrude the sketch to a depth of 5 mm.

Figure 7-129 Shell feature added to the model

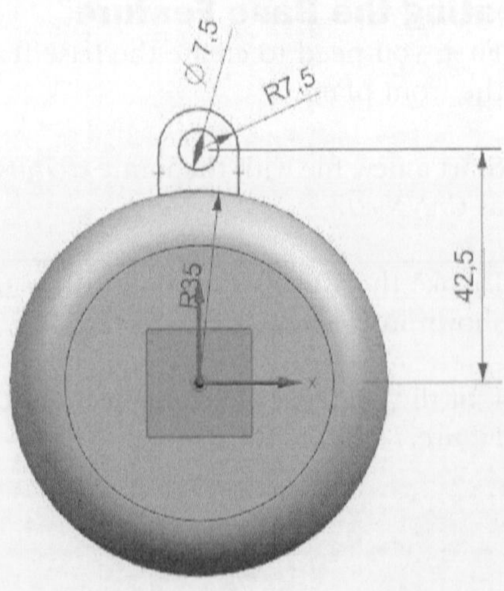

Figure 7-130 Sketch of the third feature

Patterning the Third Feature

You need to pattern the third feature after creating it. This feature will be patterned using the **Pattern Feature** tool.

1. Invoke the **Pattern Feature** dialog box and select the **Circular** option from the **Layout** drop-down list; the options to create a circular pattern are displayed. Next, you need to select the feature to be patterned.
2. Select the third feature from the drawing area.
3. Click in the **Specify Vector** area of the **Rotation axis** sub-rollout; a vector triad is displayed and you are prompted to select object to infer vector. Specify the vector, as shown in Figure 7-131; you are prompted to select object to infer point.
4. Select the center of the circular edge of the base feature; preview of the pattern is displayed. Next, you need to specify the number of instances and spacing between them.
5. Select the **Count and Span** option from the **Spacing** drop-down list.
6. Set the value to **3** in the **Count** edit box and **360** in the **Span Angle** edit box.
7. Select the **Follow Pattern** option from the **Orientation** drop-down list in the **Orientation** sub-rollout and choose **OK** from the **Pattern Feature** dialog box.

   The model after creating the pattern feature is displayed in Figure 7-132.

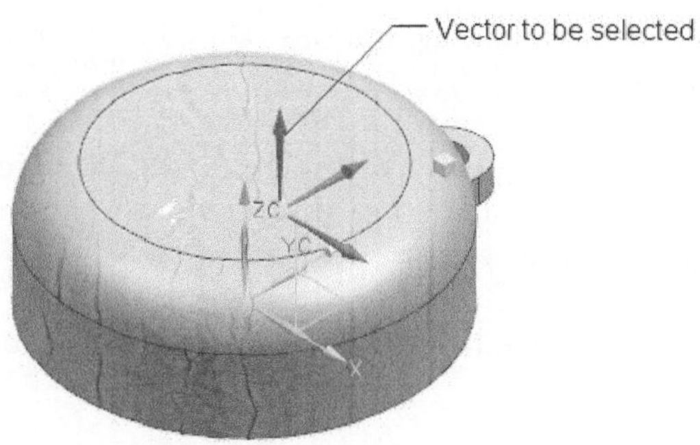

Figure 7-131 Vector to be selected

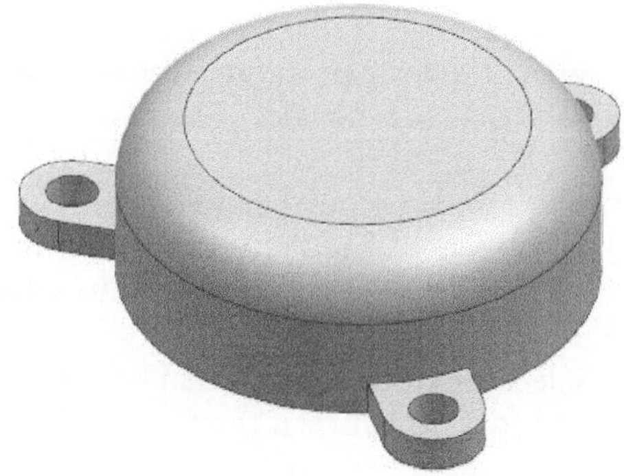

Figure 7-132 Model after creating the pattern

Creating the Slot Cut

Next, you need to create the slots on the top planar face of the base feature.

1. Invoke the **Extrude** tool and select the top planar face of the base feature as the sketching plane.

2. Draw the sketch of the slot and add required dimensions and constraints to it, as shown in Figure 7-133.

3. Exit the Sketch in Task environment and select the **Subtract** option from the **Boolean** drop-down list in the **Extrude** dialog box. On doing so, the preview of the feature is displayed in the drawing window.

4. Choose the **Reverse Direction** button to reverse the direction of the feature creation. Next, select the **Through All** option from the **End** drop-down list in the **Limits** rollout.

5. Choose the **OK** button; the slot feature is created, as shown in Figure 7-134.

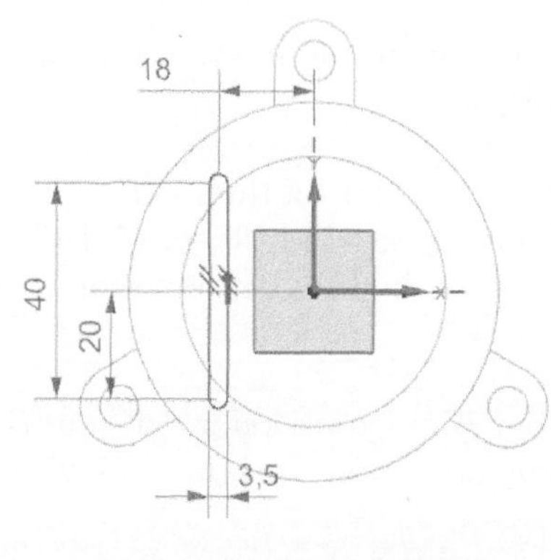

Figure 7-133 Sketch of the slot

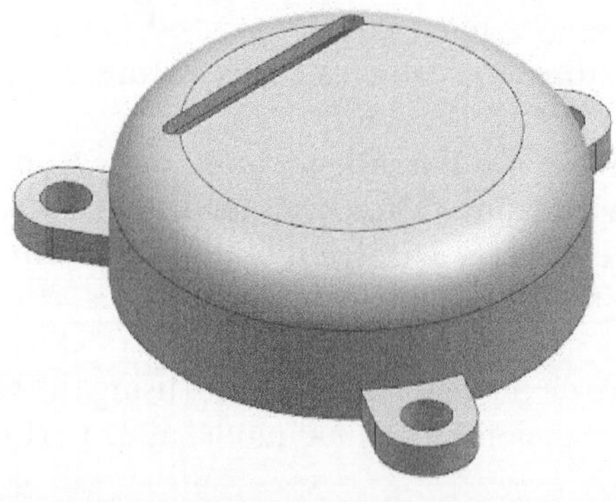

Figure 7-134 Model after creating the slot

6. After creating the slot feature, choose the **Pattern Feature** tool from the **Feature** group; the **Pattern Feature** dialog box is displayed and you are prompted to select features to pattern.

7. Select the **Linear** option from the **Layout** drop-down list; the options related to the linear pattern are displayed.

8. Select the slot from the drawing window and click in the **Specify Vector** area of the **Direction1** sub-rollout in the **Pattern Feature** dialog box; the vector triad is displayed in the drawing window and you are prompted to select objects to infer vector.

9. Select the vector, as shown in Figure 7-135. Next, you need to define the number of instances and spacing between them.

10. Select the **Count and Span** option from the **Spacing** drop-down list in the **Direction1** sub-rollout; the **Count** and **Span Distance** edit boxes are displayed.

11. Enter **7** in the **Count** edit box and **36** in the **Span Distance** edit box and then choose the **OK** button from the **Pattern Feature** dialog box; a linear pattern of slots is created, as shown in Figure 7-136.

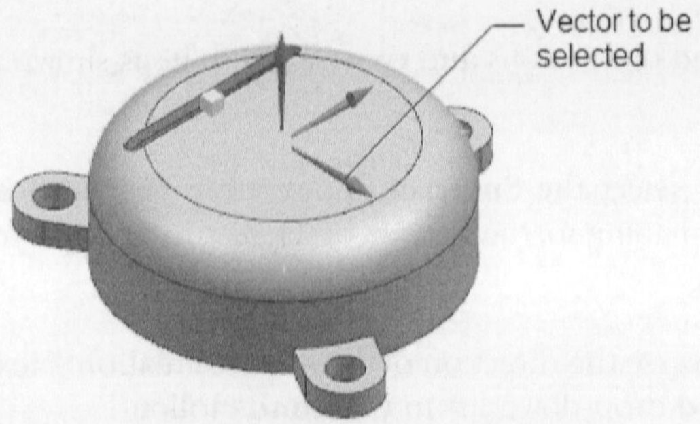

Figure 7-135 Vector to be selected

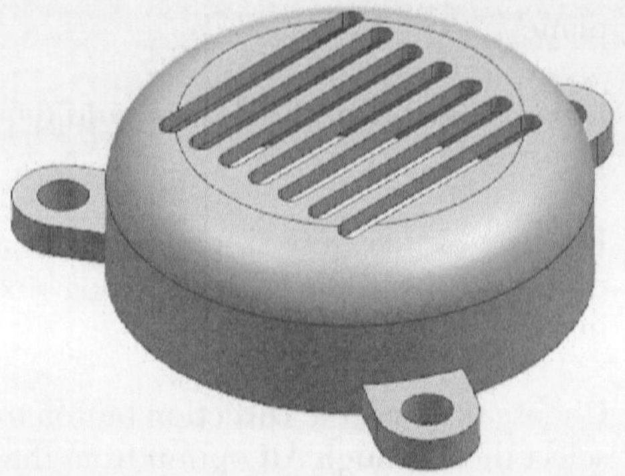

Figure 7-136 Model after patterning the slot

Creating the Remaining Features

The next feature that you need to create is the protrusion on the internal face of the base feature. You can create this feature using the **Extrude** tool.

1. Invoke the **Extrude** tool and draw a circle of **25** unit diameter on the internal face of the base feature. Then, extrude it to a distance of **7.5** mm, as shown in Figure 7-137. Choose the **Reverse Direction** button, if required and make sure that the **Unite** option is selected in the **Boolean** drop-down list.

2. Create the remaining features using the **Hole** and **Edge Blend** tools, refer to Figure 7-126 for dimensions. The final model after performing all the operations is shown in Figure 7-138.

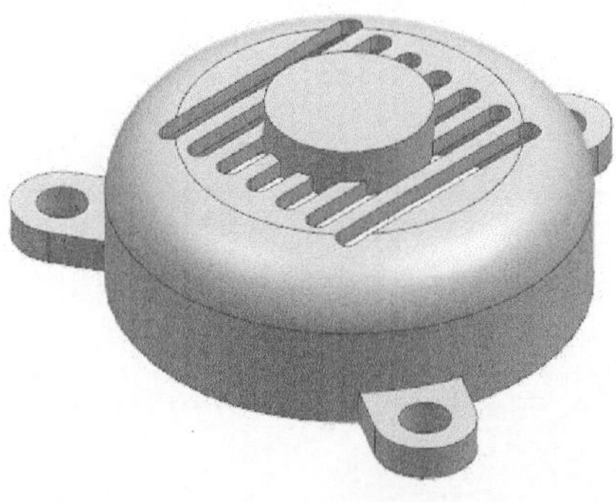

Figure 7-137 The extruded feature

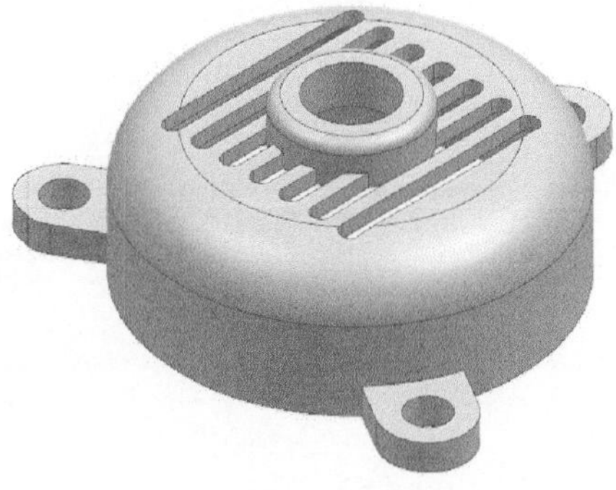

Figure 7-138 Model after creating other features

Saving and Closing the File

1. Choose **Menu > File > Close > Save and Close** from the **Top Border Bar** to save and close the file.

Tutorial 5

In this tutorial, you will download the model shown in Figure 7-139 from *https://www.cadcim.com*. The path of the file is as follows: *Textbooks > CAD/CAM > NX 2019 for Designers > Input Files*. Next, you will create the lattice for the model in the extruded cavity region, refer to Figure 7-140. After creating the lattice in the cavity region, save the model with the name *c07tut05.prt* at the location *\NX\c07*. **(Expected time: 15 min)**

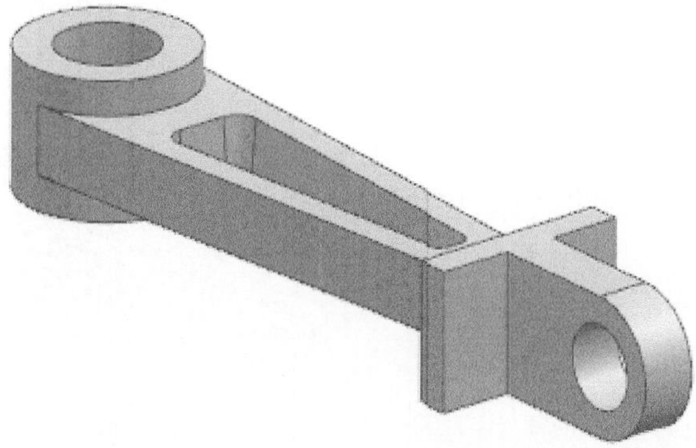

Figure 7-139 The solid model for Tutorial 5

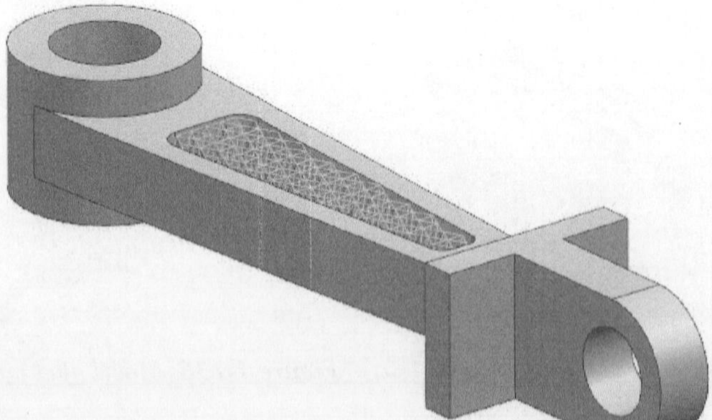

Figure 7-140 Model after creating the lattice

The following steps are required to complete this tutorial:

a. Download the model from the CADCIM website and open it in NX 2019.
b. Draw the sketch for the extrude feature and then extrude it, refer to Figures 7-142 and 7-143.
c. Change the display of the created extrude feature, refer to Figure 7-144.
d. Create the lattice of the created feature using the **Lattice** tool, refer to Figure 7-145.
e. Save the file.

Download the input model using the path mentioned above and open it in NX 2019. Next, follow the steps given below to create the lattice in the cavity region.

Creating the Extrude Feature

1. Select the top face of the model as the sketching plane, refer to Figure 7-141, and create the sketch for the extrude feature, refer to Figure 7-142.

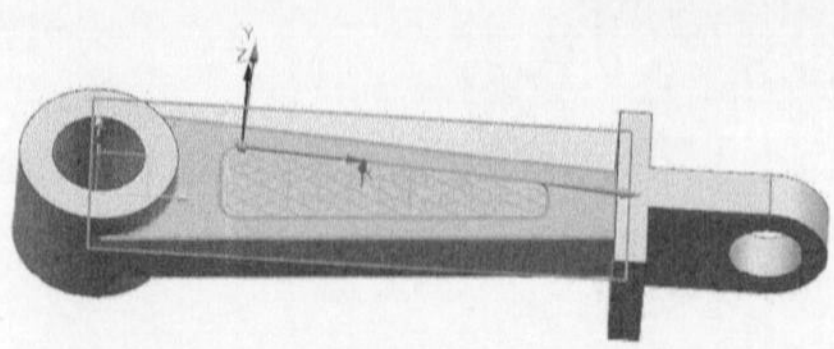

Figure 7-141 Face selected for drawing the sketch

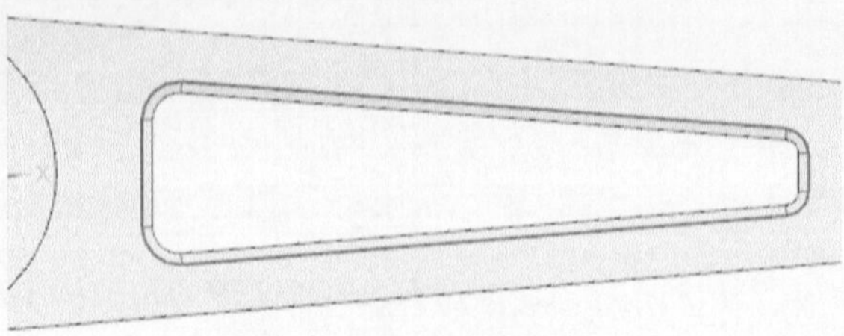

Figure 7-142 Sketch drawn for the extrude feature

2. Exit the sketching environment and extrude the sketch to a depth of **10** mm in the downward direction with a draft angle of **5** degrees using the **Extrude** tool. Make sure that the **From Start Limit** option is selected in the **Draft** drop-down list of the **Draft** rollout and the **None** option is selected in the **Boolean** drop-down list of the **Boolean** rollout in the **Extrude** dialog box. The model after extruding the sketch is shown in Figure 7-143.

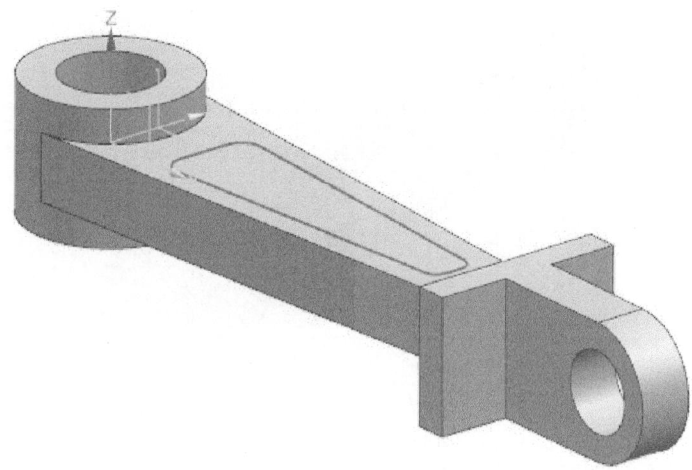

Figure 7-143 Model after creating the extrude feature

3. Hide the sketch drawn for the extrude feature.

Changing the Display of the Extrude Feature

Next, you need to change the display of the extrude feature so that the lattice you are going to create is clearly visible. To do so, follow the steps given below.

1. Select the extrude feature created in the previous step.

2. Choose **Menu > Edit > Object Display** from the **Top Border Bar**; the **Edit Object Display** dialog box is displayed. Set the translucency of the model to **35** using the **Translucency** slider bar available in the **Shaded Display** rollout of the dialog box. Next, choose the **OK** button to exit the dialog box.

Creating the Lattice of the Extrude Feature

1. Choose the **Lattice** tool from the **Design Feature** gallery of the **More** gallery in the **Feature** group of the **Home** tab; the **Lattice** dialog box is displayed.

2. Select the **Unit Fill** option from the Type drop-down list; you are prompted to select the solid body as the boundary of the lattice. Select the extrude feature created earlier. Next, select the **HexStar** option from the **Cell Type** drop-down list and enter **5** in the **Edge Length** edit box of the **Unit Cell** rollout.

3. Enter **0.2** in the **Rod Diameter** edit box of the **Body Creation** rollout.

4. Select the **Remove Dangling Rods at Selected Faces** check box in the **Boundary Trim** rollout if it is not already selected; the **Select Face** area becomes available.

5. Click in the **Select Face** area and select all the inner faces of the cavity region, refer to Figure 7-144.

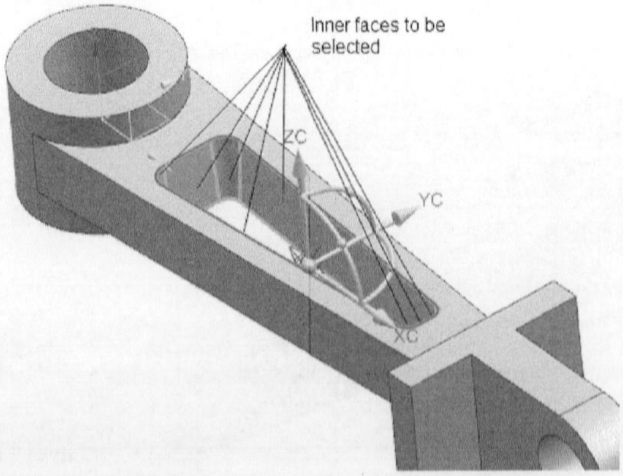

Figure 7-144 Inner faces to be selected

6. Next, choose the **Apply** button; the lattice is created, as shown in Figure 7-145. Choose the **Cancel** button to exit the **Lattice** dialog box. Figure 7-146 shows the top view of the model after creating the lattice.

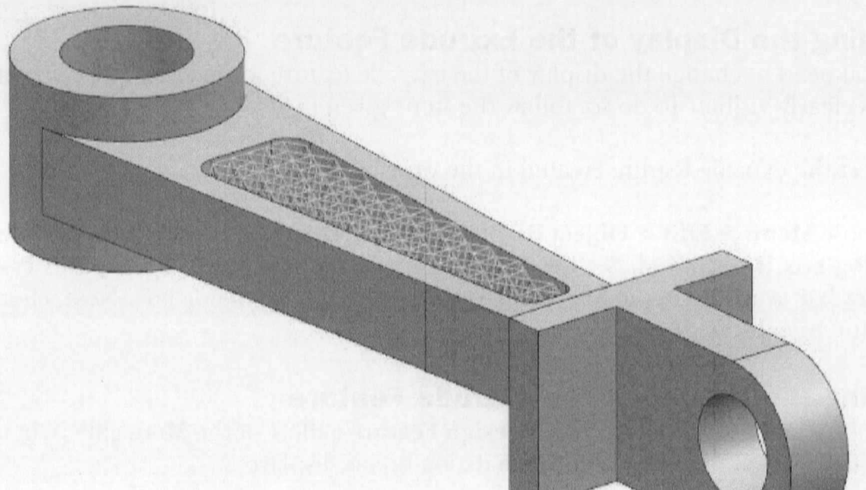

Figure 7-145 Model after creating the lattice

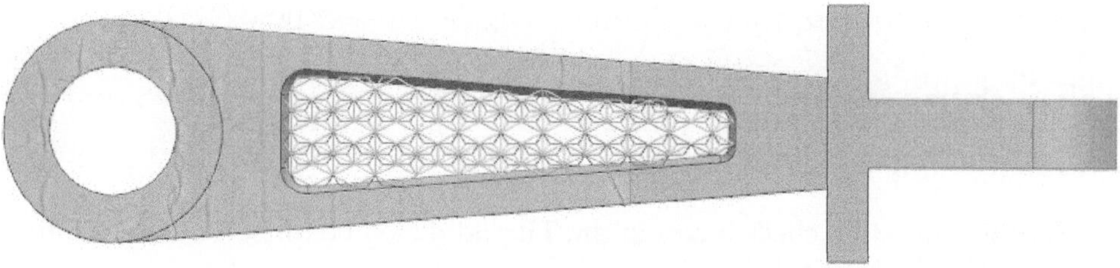

Figure 7-146 Top view of the model after creating the lattice

Saving the File

1. Choose **Menu > File > Save As** from the **Top Border Bar**; the **Save As** dialog box is displayed.

2. Browse to the location *C:\NX\c07* and enter *c07tut5.prt* in the **File name** edit box. Next, choose the **OK** button from the **Save As** dialog box; the part file is saved at the specified location.

Self-Evaluation Test

Answer the following questions and then compare them to those given at the end of this chapter:

1. The _________ tool is used to scoop out material from a model and make it hollow from inside.

2. The _________ features are created by sweeping one or more sections along one or more guide curves such that all sections are blended together.

3. The _________ radio button is selected from the **Thread** dialog box to create realistic threads.

4. The _________ pattern is created by placing the instances of the selected features along the circumference of an imaginary circle.

5. The _________check box is selected to create a fill pattern.

6. The _________ rollout in the **Shell** dialog box is used to specify the faces of a model that should not be displayed in the resultant model.

7. In NX, you can sweep an open section along a guide curve. (T/F)

8. You can use the **Linear** option from the **Pattern Feature** dialog box to create a linear pattern of features. (T/F)

9. In NX, you can create only realistic threads. (T/F)

10. The **Tube** tool is used to create a tube of rectangular cross-section. (T/F)

Review Questions

Answer the following questions:

1. Which of the following check boxes in the **Thread** dialog box is selected to create threads through the length of a selected face?

   (a) **Full** (b) **Full Thread**
   (c) **Complete** (d) None of these

2. Which of the following options is used to create a pattern of features with details such as rounds and chamfers?

   (a) **Simple** (b) **Variational**
   (c) **Identical** (d) None of these

3. Which of the following types of threads displays thread convention in the form of dashed lines?

   (a) Symbolic (b) Detailed
   (c) Convention (d) Improper

4. In the **Shell** dialog box, which of the following rollouts is used to select a face of a model to specify different wall thickness?

   (a) **Alternate Thickness** (b) **Thickness**
   (c) **Settings** (d) **Offset face**

5. Which of the following tools does not need a section to create a feature?

   (a) **Sweep along Guide** (b) **Swept**
   (c) **Tube** (d) None of these

6. Which of the following threads allows the screw to get tightened when rotated in the clockwise direction?

   (a) Right hand (b) Left hand
   (c) Downward (d) Upward

7. The _________ method is used to pattern features with details such as rounds and chamfers.

8. The **Shell** dialog box allows you to hollow models by using three methods. (T/F)

9. The **Thread** dialog box does not allow you to select the start and the end of threads. (T/F)

10. If you enter **0** in the **Inner Diameter** edit box, the resulting tube feature will be solid filled. (T/F)

EXERCISES

Exercise 1

Create the model shown in Figure 7-147. The dimensions of the model are given in Figure 7-148. Save the file with the name *c07exr1.prt* at the location */NX/c07.* **(Expected time: 30 min)**

Figure 7-147 *Model for Exercise 1*

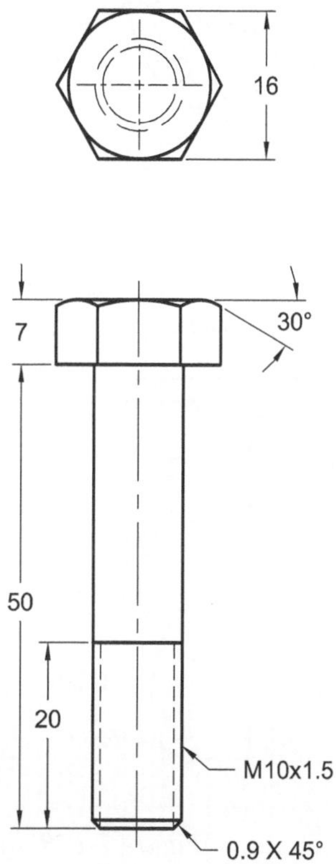

Figure 7-148 *Dimensions for Exercise 1*

Exercise 2

Create the model, as shown in Figure 7-149. The dimensions of the model are given in the same figure. Save the file with the name *c07exr2.prt* at the location */NX/c07*.

(Expected time: 30 min)

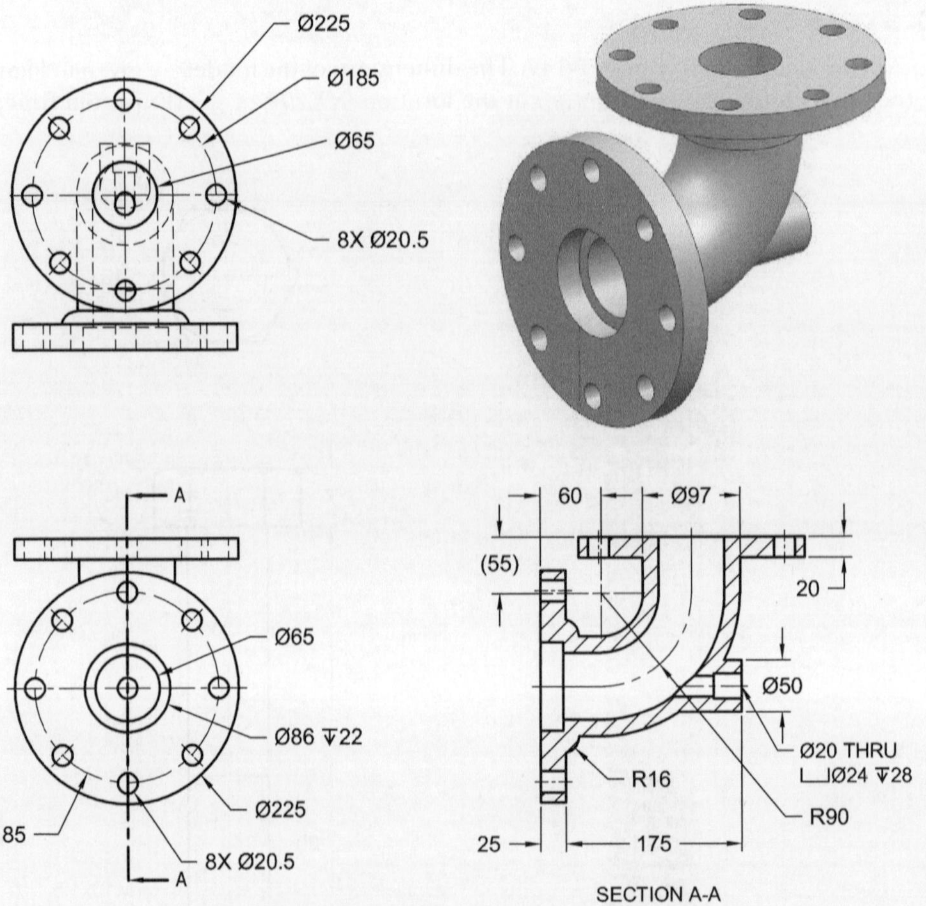

Figure 7-149 Model and dimensions for Exercise 2

Exercise 3

Create the model shown in Figure 7-150. The drawing views and dimensions of the model are shown in Figure 7-151. After creating the model, save it with the name *c07exr3.prt* at the following location *\NX\c07.* **(Expected time: 30 min)**

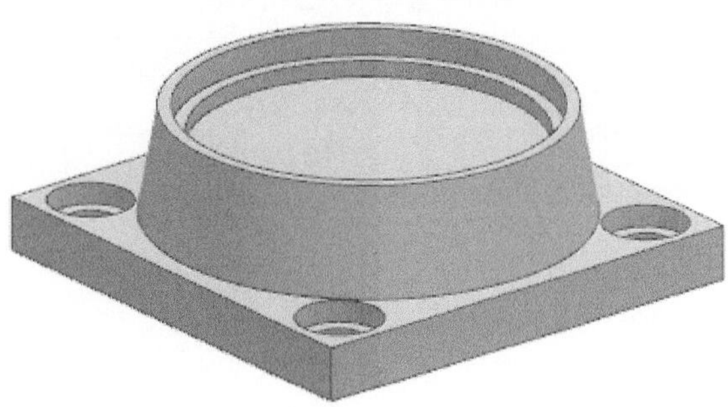

Figure 7-150 *The solid model for Exercise 3*

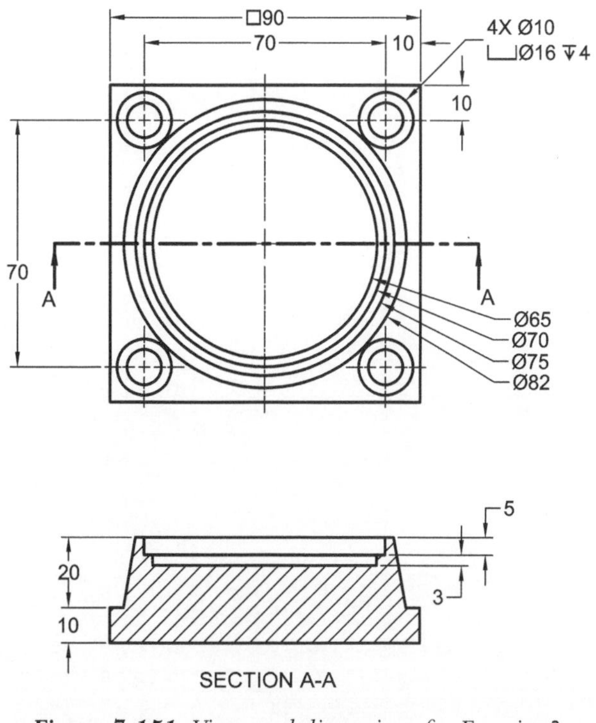

Figure 7-151 *Views and dimensions for Exercise 3*

Answers to Self-Evaluation Test

1. **Shell**, **2.** Swept, **3.** **Detailed**, **4.** circular, **5.** **Simplified Boundary Fill**, **6.** **Face to Pierce**, **7.** T, **8.** T, **9.** F, **10.** F

Chapter 8

Assembly Modeling-I

Learning Objectives

After completing this chapter, you will be able to:

- *Start the Assembly environment in NX*
- *Understand different types of assembly design approaches in NX*
- *Create assemblies using the Bottom-up assembly design approach*
- *Understand the meaning and usage of assembly constraints*
- *Create a pattern of components in an assembly*
- *Manipulate components in the Assembly environment*
- *Modify a component in the Assembly environment*

THE ASSEMBLY ENVIRONMENT

The Assembly environment is used to create interrelationship between the component parts which are assembled together by applying a parametric link, both in dimensional and positional aspects. The assembly constraints are parametric in nature so any types of modifications with the assembly constraints at any stage of the assembling procedure is possible. Figure 8-1 shows the Pipe Vice assembly created in the Assembly environment of NX. The assembly files in NX have the file name extension as .prt. The Assembly environment in NX is interactive and bidirectionally associative. The component can be modified in the assembly environment itself by setting the part to be modified as the work part. After assembling the components, you can also check the interference between them. This increases the efficiency of the assembly and also eliminates the errors while actually manufacturing the components. You can also create the exploded state of assembly. Creating this state of assembly helps the technician understand the sequence of components to be assembled better.

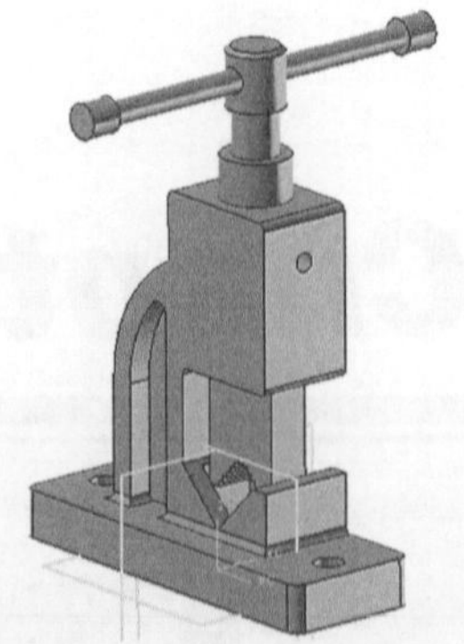

***Figure 8-1** The Pipe Vice assembly created in NX*

INVOKING THE ASSEMBLY ENVIRONMENT

You can invoke the Assembly environment by two methods:

1. Using the **Assembly** template from the **New** dialog box.
2. Invoking the Assembly environment in the current part file.

Invoking the Assembly Environment Using the New Dialog Box

To invoke the Assembly environment using the **Assembly** template, choose the **New** button from the **Standard** group of the **Home** tab; the **New** dialog box will be displayed. Choose the **Model** tab if it is not already chosen and Select the **Assembly** template from the **Templates** rollout of the dialog box. Next, choose the button on the right side of the **Name** text box; the **Choose New File Name** dialog box will be displayed. Enter the assembly name in the **File name** edit box. Also, to specify the location to save the assembly file, browse to the folder where you need to save the assembly file. Choose the **OK** button twice; the Assembly environment with the **Add Component** dialog box will be invoked. The use of the **Add Component** dialog box is discussed later.

Invoking the Assembly Environment in the Current Part File

Ribbon:	Application > Design > Assemblies

In the previous section, you learned to invoke the Assembly environment using the **New** dialog box. In this section, you will learn to invoke it in the current part file. To do so, choose the **Assemblies** tab from the **Ribbon**; the Assembly environment will be invoked. If the **Assemblies** tab is not already added to the **Ribbon**, then choose **Application > Design > Assemblies** from the **Ribbon**; the **Assemblies** tab will be added to the **Ribbon** and the **Assemblies** group will be added to the **Home** tab. The NX window with the Assembly environment is shown in Figure 8-2.

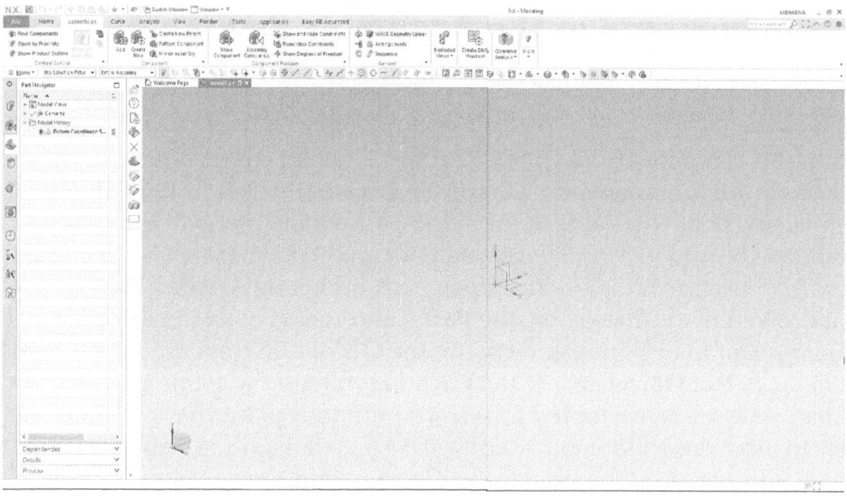

Figure 8-2 The NX window in the Assembly environment

Types of Assembly Design Approaches

In NX, the assemblies can be created using two types of design approaches, the bottom-up assembly design approach and the top-down assembly design approach. In this chapter, you will learn about the bottom-up assembly design approach. The top-down approach is discussed in the next chapter.

Bottom-up Assembly Design Approach

The Bottom-up assembly design approach is the most widely preferred traditional approach of assembly design. In this approach, all components are created as separate part files and placed in the assembly as external components. In this approach, you need to create components separately in the Modeling environment and save them as *.prt* files. After creating all components, you need to start a new file in the Assembly environment and place them in the assembly environment using the tools in the **Assemblies** group. Next, you need to assemble the components using assembly constraints.

The main advantage of using this approach is that you can pay more attention to the complexity of the component design as you create them before assembling. You can also capture the design intent easily. This approach is preferred while handling large assemblies or assemblies with complex components.

CREATING BOTTOM-UP ASSEMBLIES

As mentioned earlier, in the bottom-up assemblies, components are created as separate parts in the Modeling environment, and then they are placed in a new file that is started in the Assembly environment. In the assembly file, the parts are assembled using the assembly constraints. As discussed earlier, it is recommended that you first invoke the Modeling environment and then choose **Application** > **Design** > **Assemblies** from the **Ribbon** to invoke the Assembly environment.

Placing Components in the Assembly Environment

Ribbon:	Assemblies > Component > Add
Menu:	Assemblies > Components > Add Component

Add

In NX, the components are placed in the Assembly environment using the **Add** tool available in the **Component** group of the **Assemblies** tab in the **Ribbon**. To place the component, choose the **Add** tool from the **Component** group of **Assemblies** tab. You can also choose the **Add** tool from the **Assemblies** group of the **Home** tab; the **Add Component** dialog box will be displayed. Choose the **Open** button from the **Loaded Parts** sub-rollout of the **Part To Place** rollout of the dialog box; the **Part Name** dialog box will be displayed. Browse and select the component to be placed and choose the **OK** button from the **Part Name** dialog box. Next, click in the **Select Object** area of the **Location** rollout; the component will be attached to the cursor and you will be prompted to select location to place the component. Click in the drawing area to place the component. Once you click in the drawing area, a dynamic triad along with the input edit boxes will be displayed. You can enter the coordinate values in these edit boxes to place the component. The Assembly environment window with the **Add Component** dialog box is shown in Figure 8-3.

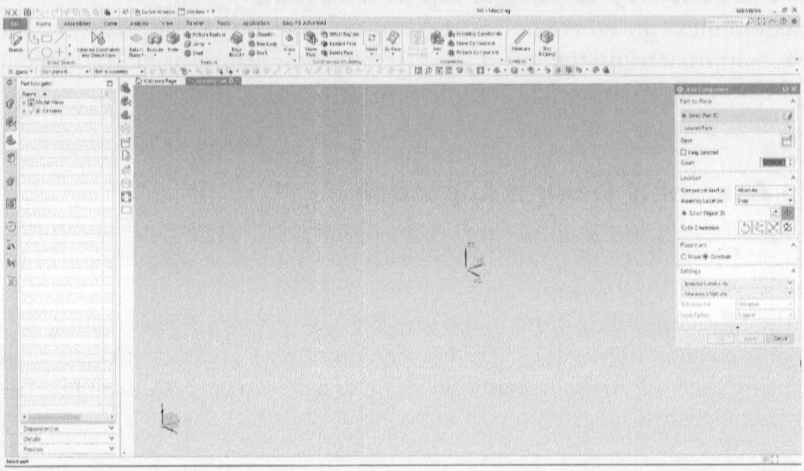

Figure 8-3 The Assembly environment window with the ***Add Component*** *dialog box*

Note

While placing the component in the drawing area, you are prompted to select the location to place the component. Select the plane to place the component; a dynamic triad along with the input edit boxes are displayed on the component. This is because the ***Move*** *radio button is selected in the* ***Placement*** *rollout of the* ***Add Component*** *dialog box. You can also select the* ***Constrain*** *radio button in the* ***Placement*** *rollout. On doing so, the* ***Constraint Type*** *sub-rollout will be displayed. You can use the constraint buttons available in this sub-rollout to place the components.*

The name of the component is displayed in the **File Name** list of the **Loaded Parts** sub-rollout of the **Part to Place** rollout of the **Add Component** dialog box.

Note

If the component to be assembled is already placed in the assembly, then for subsequent placements, you can directly retrieve the component from the ***File Name*** *list of the* ***Loaded Parts*** *sub-rollout* *of the **Part to Place** rollout. To do so, invoke the **Add Component** dialog box and then select the component to be placed from the **Loaded Parts** sub-rollout. Next, click in the **Select Object** area of the **Location** rollout and follow the same procedure explained before to place the component.*

You can add multiple instances of the same component to the assembly file. To do so, enter the number of instances in the **Count** edit box available in the **Part to Place** rollout. The remaining options in the **Add Component** dialog box are discussed next.

Location Rollout

The options available in this rollout are discussed next.

Component Anchor

This drop-down list lists all the possible anchors for the location of a component. By default, the **Absolute** option is selected in this drop-down list which takes the absolute origin of the component as the anchor.

Assembly Location

The options in this drop-down list enable you to locate the components in the drawing window. The **Snap** option allows you to select the placement face based on the orientation of the assembly and the location of the cursor. If you select the **Absolute - Work Part** option from this drop-down list, the component anchor will be placed at the absolute origin of the work part. If you select the **Absolute - Displayed Part** option, the component anchor will be placed at the absolute origin of the displayed part. The **WCS** option enables you to place the component anchor at the current WCS location and orientation.

Cycle Orientation

This area of the **Location** rollout contains four buttons which enable you to specify different component orientations based on the location settings of the component.

Placement Rollout

This rollout contains two radio buttons. The function of each radio button has been discussed earlier.

Settings Rollout

The options in this rollout are discussed next.

Enabled Constraints

This sub-rollout will be available only if the **Constrain** radio button is selected in the **Placement** rollout. Using this sub-rollout, you can control the availability of constraints in the **Constraint Type** sub-rollout of the **Placement** rollout. If you select the check box available on the left of any constraint in this sub-rollout, the corresponding constraint will be available in the **Constraint Type** sub-rollout of the **Placement** rollout.

Interaction Options

This sub-rollouts contains four check boxes. On selecting the **Scatter Components** check box, the components are automatically placed at different locations so that they do not overlap. The **Keep Constraints** check box is selected to create the constraints used to place the component. You can select these constraints from the **Assembly Navigator** and the **Constraint Navigator**. On selecting the **Preview** check box, the component is displayed in the drawing area while placing it. On selecting the **Preview Window** check box, a preview of the component is displayed in a separate **Component Preview** window.

Component Name

This edit box is used to display the name of the currently selected component in the **Add Component** dialog box.

Reference Set

The options in the **Reference Set** drop-down list are used to specify the state of the component that will occur in the assembly. If you select the **Model** option from the **Reference Set** drop-down list, only the model will be placed in the assembly file. If you select the **Entire Part** option, the model will be placed in the assembly file along with the datum planes and the sketches used for creating it. If you select the **Empty** option, the component will be placed in the assembly file as an empty part without the model or its reference sets.

Layer Option

The options in this drop-down list are used to specify different layers in the assembly file.

Tip
*It is recommended to assemble the base component by selecting the **Entire Part** option from the **Reference Set** drop-down list.*

Changing the Reference Set of a Component

Ribbon:	Assemblies > More Gallery > Other > Replace Reference Set
Menu:	Assemblies > Replace Reference Set

As mentioned earlier, when you place a component using the **Entire Part** option from the **Reference Set** drop-down list of the **Add Component** dialog box, datum planes and sketches used to create that component are also displayed in the assembly file. However, after assembling the component, you do not need these datum planes and sketches as they cause confusion in the assembly file and restrict the display of other components as well.

To change the reference set of a component, right-click on the component in the drawing window and choose **Replace Reference Set > MODEL**; the datum planes and sketches of the component will disappear. You can also select the model from the drawing window, and then select the **MODEL** option from the **Replace Reference Set** drop-down list available in the **General** group of the **Assemblies** tab (*Customise to Add*).

Alternatively, you can change the reference set of a component by using the **Replace Reference Set** tool. To do so, choose the **Replace Reference Set** tool from the **Other** gallery of **More** gallery in the **Assemblies** tab; the **Class Selection** dialog box will be displayed. Select a component from the drawing window and then choose the **OK** button from the dialog box; the **Replace Reference Set** dialog box will be displayed with a list of all reference sets. Select the required reference set for the selected component and then choose the **OK** button to apply it.

Applying Assembly Constraints to Components

In NX, assembly constraints can be applied to components by using the **Assembly Constraints** dialog box. To invoke this dialog box, choose the **Assembly Constraints** tool from the **Component Position** group of the **Assemblies** tab. Figure 8-4 shows the **Assembly Constraints** dialog box. Assembly constraints can also be applied to the components by using the **Add Component** dialog box. To apply constraints using **Add Component** dialog box, select the **Constrain** radio button from the **Placement** rollout of this dialog box. After loading the component, when you click in the **Select Object** area of the **Location** rollout and then click in the drawing window to place the component, the **Constraint Type** sub-rollout will be displayed in the **Placement** rollout. You can use the options available in this sub-rollout to apply constraints to the components. Figure 8-5 shows the **Constraint Type** sub-rollout.

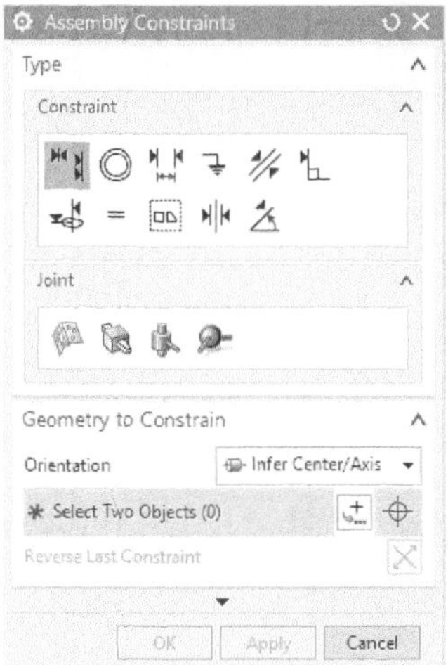

*Figure 8-4 The **Assembly Constraints** dialog box*

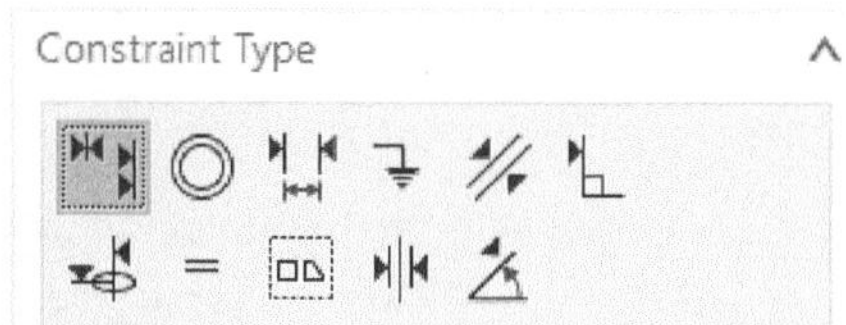

*Figure 8-5 The **Constraint Type** sub-rollout*

Assembly constraints are used to constrain the degree of freedom of a component in an assembly. By constraining the degrees of freedom of a component, you can restrict or determine the movement of the component. The options available in the **Constraint Type** sub-rollout of the **Add Component** dialog box are discussed next.

Touch Align

The Touch Align constraint is used to constrain the motion of two selected reference faces or reference planes of different components such that they touch or align with each other. This constraint is also used to make edges or axis of components collinear, or to make points of components coincident to each other. To apply this constraint, choose the **Touch Align** option from the **Constraint Type** sub-rollout of the **Placement** rollout of the **Add Component** dialog box; you will be prompted to select the first reference object from the component to be mated. Select a planar face, curved face, edge, datum axis, or point as the reference object from the component to be mated; you will be prompted to select the second reference object from the component to mate to.

Note

You can apply the Touch Align constraint to constrain the components tangentially.

Select a datum plane or any other reference object from the component displayed in the **Component Preview** window as the second reference object; the component will shift its position according to the constraint applied and a symbol of the constraint will be displayed on the component. Figure 8-6 shows the faces to be selected for applying the Touch Align constraint and Figure 8-7 shows the components after applying the Touch Align constraint to them.

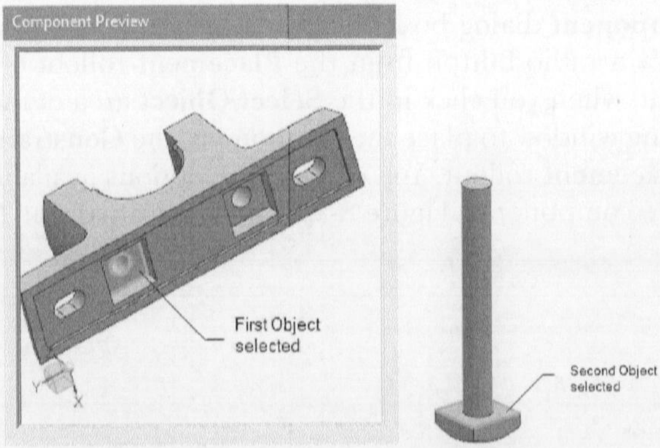

Figure 8-6 Faces selected as reference objects for applying the Touch Align constraint

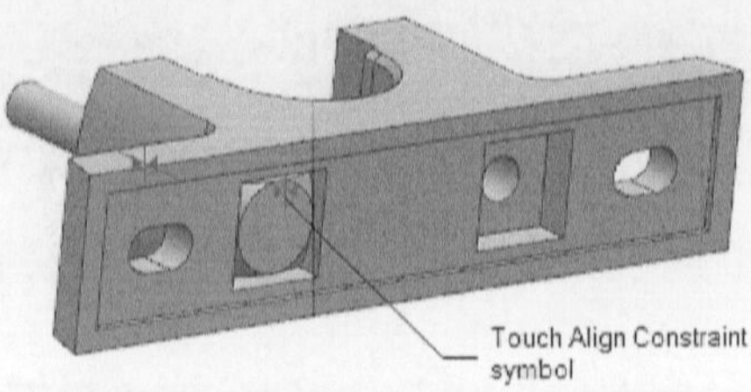

Figure 8-7 Components after applying the Touch Align constraint

Note
*The **Component Preview** window will be available only if the **Preview Window** check box is selected in the **Interaction Options** sub-rollout of the **Settings** rollout.*

Note that the options in the **Placement** rollout of the dialog box change depending upon the options selected from the **Constraint Type** sub-rollout. These options are discussed next.

Geometry to Constrain

The options in this sub-rollout are used to select geometries and set priorities for alternative solution of constraints among the selected geometries. Some of the options in this sub-rollout have been discussed in the earlier chapters and the other options are discussed next.

Orientation: This drop-down list will be available only when the **Touch Align** option is chosen in the **Constraint Type** sub-rollout. If you select the **Touch** option from the **Orientation** drop-down list, then the selected surfaces will face each other in the opposite direction. Also, both surfaces will become coplanar. Similarly, if you select the **Align** option from the **Orientation** drop-down list, then the selected surfaces will turn in the same direction. Also, both the surfaces will become coplanar. By default, the **Prefer Touch** option is selected in the **Orientation** drop-down list. As a result, the **Touch** option is preferred over the **Align** option when both the touch and align solutions are possible. If the touch solution over-constrains the selected surfaces, then the **Align** option gets the preference. You can make the axes of a selected cylindrical, conical, spherical face, or an edge coaxial using the **Infer Center/Axis** option from the **Orientation** drop-down list.

Tip
*The display of options available in the **Constraint Type** sub-rollout of the **Placement** rollout can be controlled by using the **Enabled Constraints** sub-rollout of the **Settings** rollout. You can select the check boxes for the constraints that you want to be displayed in the **Constraint Type** sub-rollout.*

Angle

The Angle constraint is applied to specify an angle between the two selected reference entities of components. To apply this constraint, select the **Angle** option from the **Constraint Type** sub-rollout of the **Placement** rollout in the **Add Component** dialog box; the **Geometry to Constrain** sub-rollout will be modified. By default, the **3D Angle** option will be chosen from the **Subtype** drop-down list in this sub-rollout. Also, you will be prompted to select the first object to apply the angle constraint. Select a face; you will be prompted to select the second object to apply constraint. Select the second face; two angular handles will be displayed in the drawing window. Also, the **Angle** sub-rollout will be displayed in the **Placement** rollout. Next, enter the required angle either in the dynamic input box or in the **Angle** edit box of the **Angle** sub-rollout. Figure 8-8 shows the faces selected as reference objects for applying the **Angle** constraint and Figure 8-9 shows the preview of the component after the constraint has been applied.

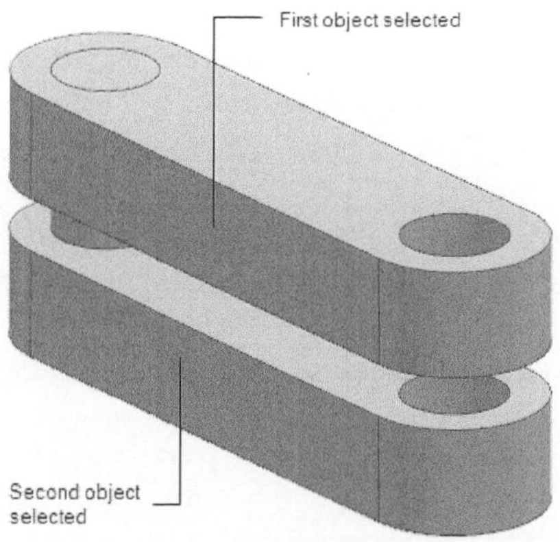

Figure 8-8 *Faces selected as reference objects for applying the Angle constraint*

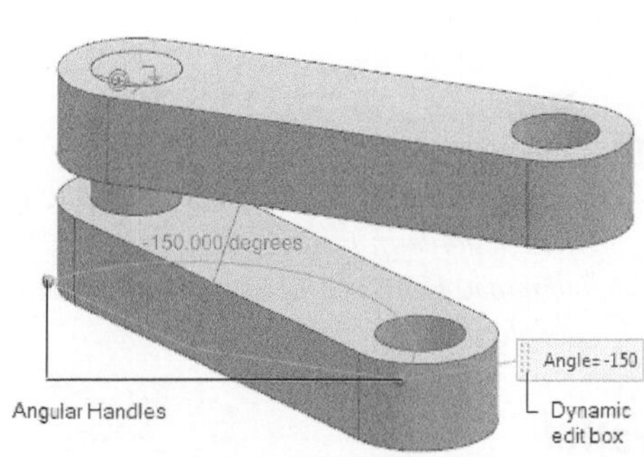

Figure 8-9 *Preview of the components after applying the Angle constraint*

If you select the **Orient Angle** option from the **Subtype** drop-down list, you will be prompted to select an axis for specifying the angle. Select an axis or an edge, refer to Figure 8-10; you will be prompted to select the first object for applying the Angle constraint. Select the first face; you will be prompted to select the second object for applying the Angle constraint. Select the second face of the object, refer to Figure 8-10; two angular handles will be displayed in the drawing window. You can use these angular handles to dynamically orient the component with respect to the selected axis (the distance between the selected axis and the selected face remains the same throughout the process). While dragging the handle, the angle value will be displayed in the **Angle** edit box. Alternatively, you can enter the angle value manually in the **Angle** edit box. Figure 8-10 shows the edge and faces selected for applying the Angle constraint using the **Orient Angle** option. Figure 8-11 shows the preview of components after applying the Angle constraint using the **Orient Angle** option.

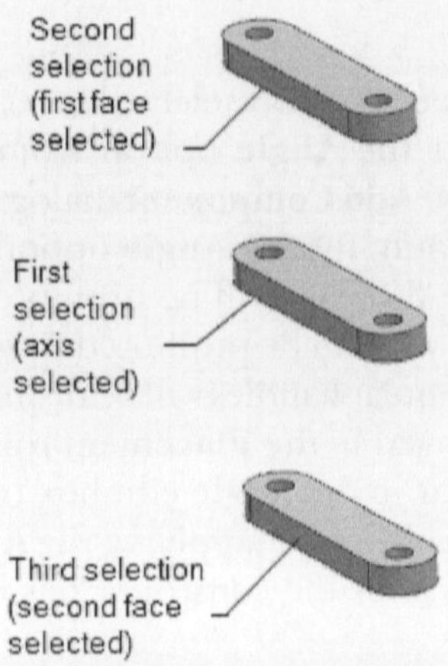

***Figure 8-10** Edge and faces selected for applying the Angle constraint*

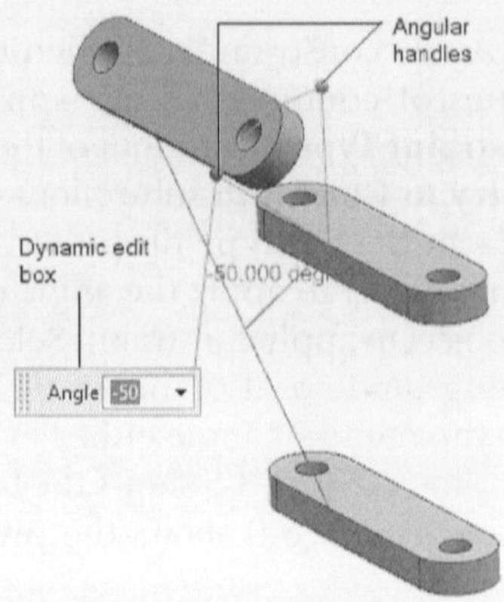

***Figure 8-11** Preview of the components after applying the Angle constraint*

Note

The number of handles displayed in the graphics window depend upon the objects selected for applying the constraint. For example, if the objects selected for applying the Angle constraint are free to move in the angular direction, then two angular handles will be displayed in the graphics window. However, in case one of the selected objects is fixed, then only one angular handle will be displayed in the graphics window.

Parallel

The Parallel constraint is applied to constrain the selected reference objects so that they become parallel to each other. To apply the Parallel constraint to objects, choose the **Parallel** option from the **Constraint Type** sub-rollout of the **Placement** rollout of the **Add Component** dialog box. Next, select the reference objects from the two given components, refer to Figure 8-12; the constraint will be applied and the resulting position of components will be displayed in the drawing window. You can also choose the **Reverse Last Constraint** button from the **Geometry to Constrain** sub-rollout of the **Placement** rollout, if you want to switch over to other possible solutions for applying constraint. Next, choose the **OK** button from the **Add Component** dialog box; the Parallel constraint will be applied to components, refer to Figure 8-13.

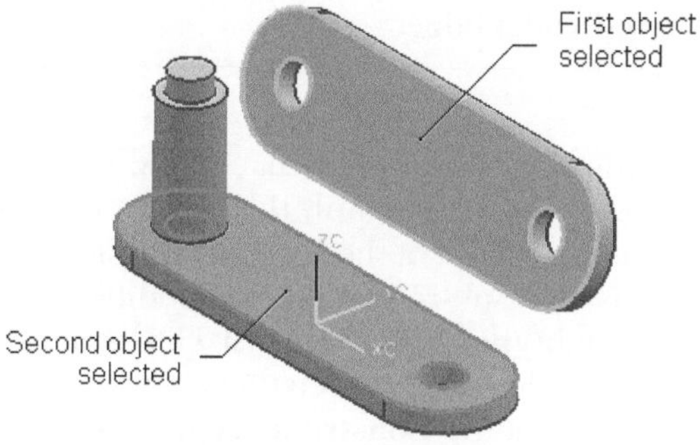

Figure 8-12 *Faces selected as reference objects for applying the Parallel constraint*

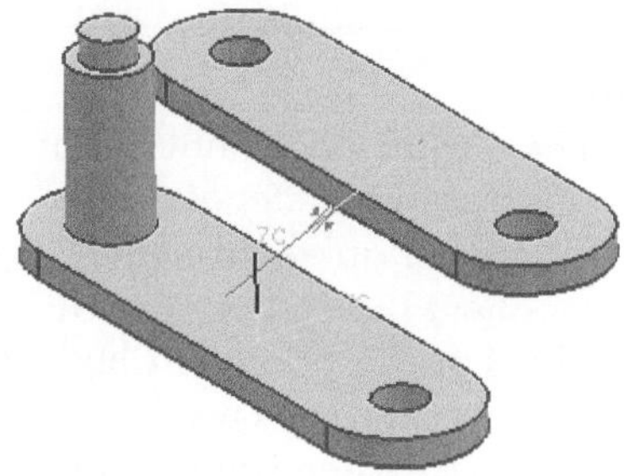

Figure 8-13 *Components after applying the Parallel constraint*

When you apply the Parallel constraint between the two cylindrical faces, the axes of the selected cylindrical faces become parallel to each other. However, if this constraint is applied between a cylindrical face and a planar face, the axis of the cylindrical face becomes parallel to the normal of the selected planar face.

Perpendicular

The Perpendicular constraint is applied to constrain the selected reference objects so that they become normal to each other. To apply this constraint, choose the **Perpendicular** option from the **Constraint Type** sub-rollout of the **Placement** rollout of the **Add Component** dialog box. Next, select the reference objects from the two given components, refer to Figure 8-14; the constraint will be applied and the resulting position of components will be displayed. You can also choose the **Reverse Last Constraint** button from the **Geometry to Constrain** sub-rollout of the **Placement** rollout to switch over to other possible solutions for the current selection set. Finally, choose the **OK** button from the **Add Component** dialog box. Figure 8-15 shows the final view of components after applying the Perpendicular constraint to them.

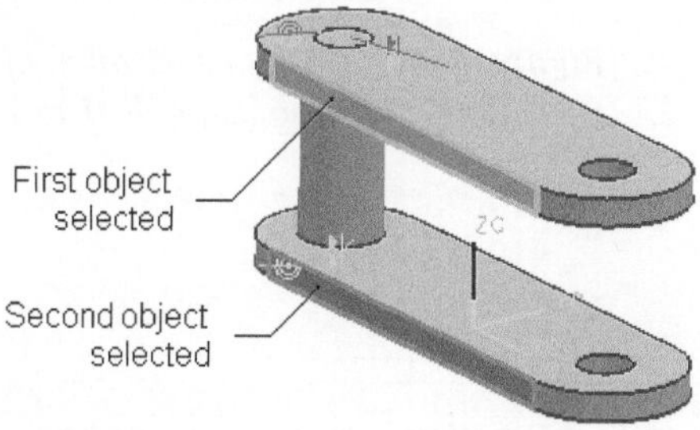

Figure 8-14 *Faces selected as reference objects for applying the Perpendicular constraint*

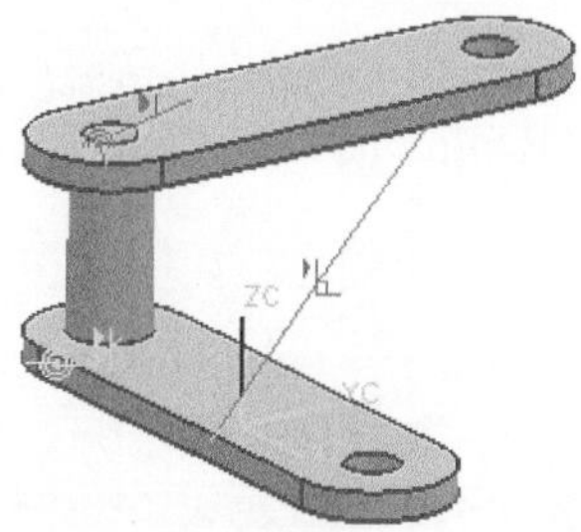

Figure 8-15 *Components after applying the Perpendicular constraint*

You can also apply the Perpendicular constraint between two cylindrical faces. In this case, the axes of the selected cylindrical faces become normal to each other. If you apply the Perpendicular constraint between a cylindrical face and a planar face, the axis of the cylindrical face will become normal to the selected planar face. If you apply this constraint between two selected curved edges, the selected curved edges will be placed normal to each other. If you apply the Perpendicular constraint between a linear edge and a curved edge, the curved edge will be pivoted about the linear edge. Also, it will be rotated about the selected linear edge.

Center

The Center constraint is applied to constrain an object such that it always remains exactly at the center of the two selected reference objects. To apply this constraint, choose the **Center** option from the **Constraint Type** sub-rollout of the **Placement** rollout of the **Add Component** dialog box; the **Geometry to Constrain** sub-rollout will be modified and by default, the **1 to 2** option will be selected in the **Subtype** drop-down list in **Geometry to Constrain** sub-rollout. As a result, the first selected object will shift between the other two selected reference objects. When you select the **Center** option from the **Constraint Type** sub-rollout of the **Placement** rollout, you will be prompted to select the first object that will be at the center of the other two selected objects. After selecting the first object, you will be prompted to select the first reference object. Select any face, edge, or axis of the object as the first reference object; you will be prompted to select the second reference object. Select the second reference object; the first selected object will shift between the two selected reference objects. Figure 8-16 shows the object and reference objects and Figure 8-17 shows the components after the Center constraint is applied to them.

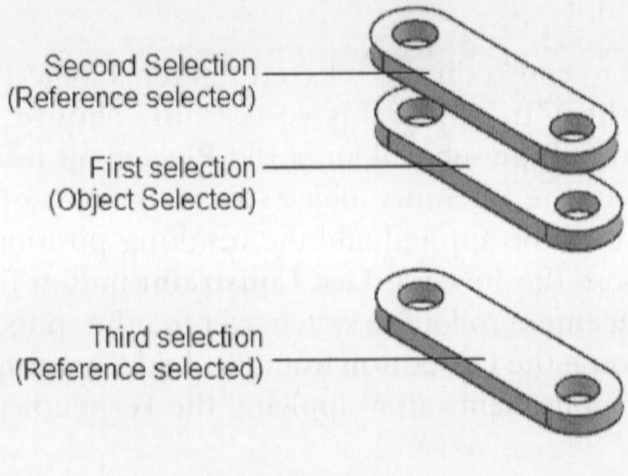

*Figure 8-16 Object and reference selection for applying the Center constraint using the **1 to 2** option*

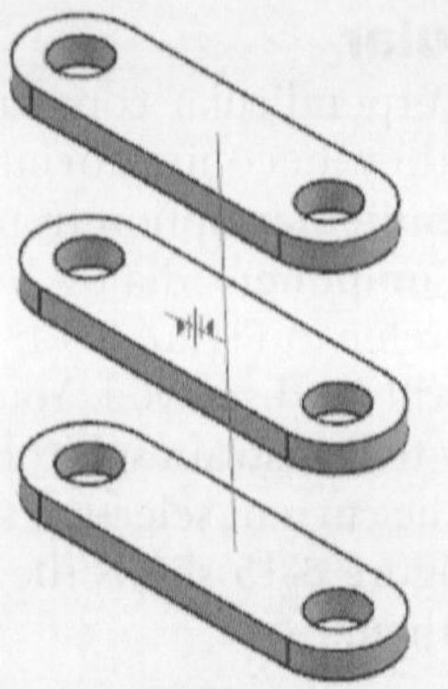

*Figure 8-17 Components after applying the Center constraint using the **1 to 2** option*

The **Subtype** drop-down list has two other options, **2 to 1** and **2 to 2**. You can use the **2 to 1** option from this drop-down list to shift the third selected object between the first two selected objects. Similarly, you can use the **2 to 2** option to bring the first two selected objects between the next two selected reference objects. Figures 8-18 and 8-19 show the first, second, and third selections for applying the Center constraint using the **2 to 1** option and the objects after applying the required constraints, respectively.

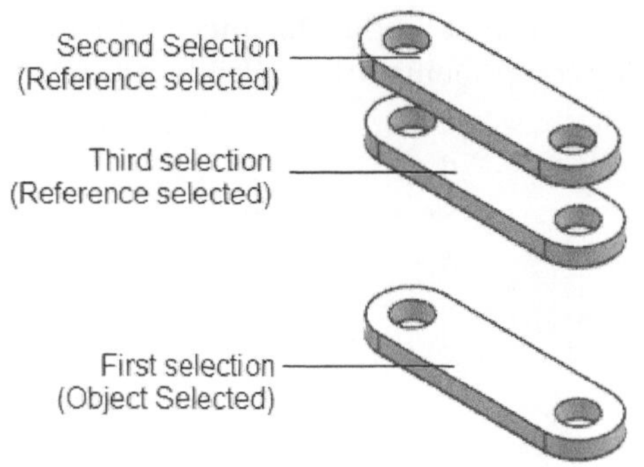

Figure 8-18 *Object and reference selection for applying the Center constraint using the **2 to 1** option*

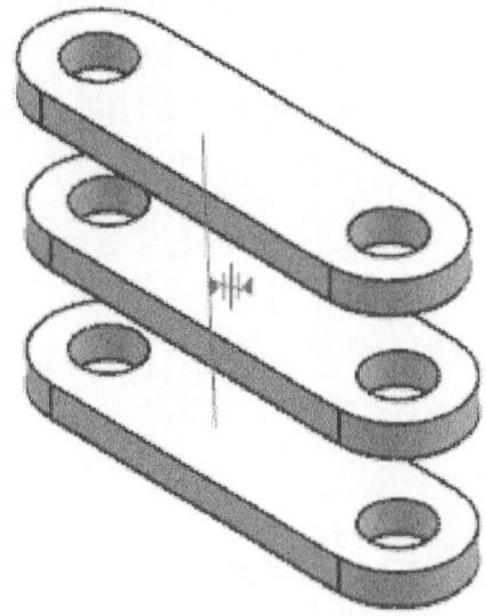

Figure 8-19 *Components after applying the Center constraint using the **2 to 1** option*

Figure 8-20 shows the first, second, third, and fourth selections of objects for applying the Center constraint using the **2 to 2** option and Figure 8-21 shows the objects after applying the Center constraint to them. When the **1 to 2** or **2 to 1** option is selected from the **Subtype** drop-down list, the **Axial Geometry** drop-down list is displayed in the **Geometry to Constrain** sub-rollout. If you select the **Use Geometry** option from the **Axial Geometry** drop-down list, the selected cylindrical faces will be used for applying the Center constraint. If you select the **Infer Center/Axis** option from the **Axial Geometry** drop-down list, the center or axis of the selected cylindrical faces will be used for applying the constraint.

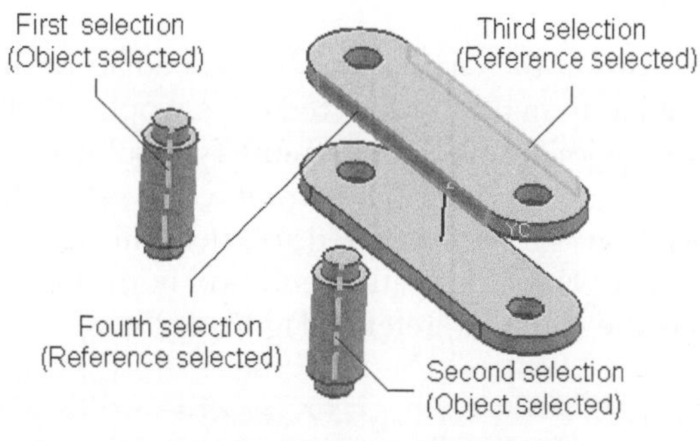

Figure 8-20 *Objects selected for applying the Center constraint using the **2 to 2** option*

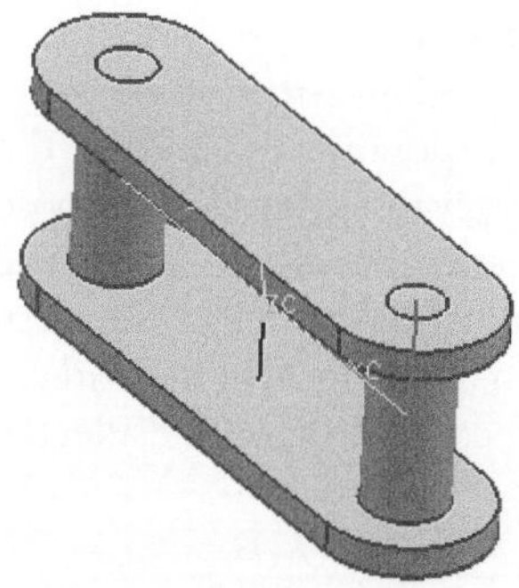

Figure 8-21 *Components after applying the Center constraint using the **2 to 2** option*

Distance

The Distance constraint is applied to maintain the required offset distance between the two selected reference objects. To apply this constraint, select the **Distance** option from the **Constraint Type** sub-rollout of the **Placement** rollout of the **Add Component** dialog box; you will be prompted to select the first object. Select the first reference object, refer to Figure 8-22; you will be prompted to select the second object. Select the second object; the **Distance** edit box will be displayed in the **Distance** sub-rollout and a handle with the dynamic input box will be displayed. Next, enter the required offset value in the **Distance** edit box and press ENTER; the preview of the resulting position of components will be displayed, refer to Figure 8-23.

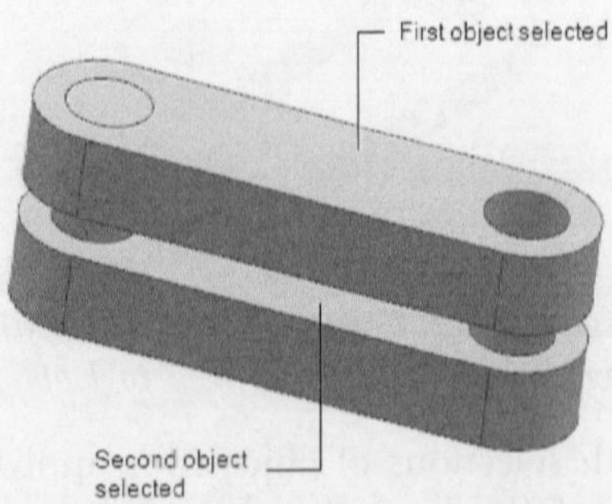

Figure 8-22 *Faces selected as reference objects for applying the Distance constraint*

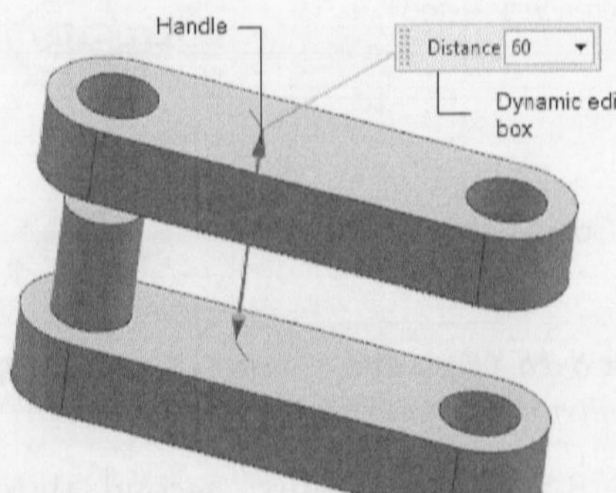

Figure 8-23 *Components after applying the Distance constraint*

You can also apply the Distance constraint between two cylindrical faces or circular edges. To do so, select the reference objects from both components and enter the required offset value in the **Distance** edit box; the constraint will be applied. Note that, in this case, the distance specified will be the distance between the axes of the selected objects.

Concentric

The Concentric constraint is applied to constrain the circular or elliptical edges of the components to coincide their centers as well as to make the selected edges coplanar. To apply this constraint, choose the **Concentric** option from the **Constraint Type** sub-rollout of the **Placement** rollout of the **Add Component** dialog box; you will be prompted to select the first circular object. Select the first circular object; you will be prompted to select the second circular object. Select the second circular object, refer to Figure 8-24; the centers of both circular edges will coincide and the selected edges will become coplanar, refer to Figure 8-25.

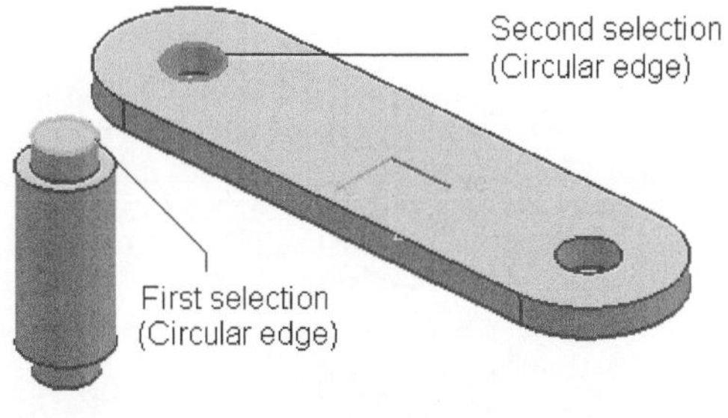

Figure 8-24 Selecting circular edges for applying the Concentric constraint

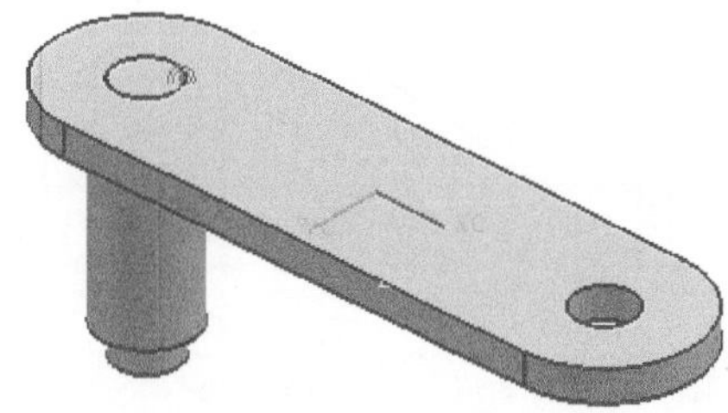

Figure 8-25 Components after applying the Concentric constraint

Fix

The Fix constraint is applied to fix the selected component at its current position in the 3D space. Once the component has been fixed, it cannot be changed and you can constrain other components with respect to the fixed component. To apply this constraint, choose the **Fix** option from the **Constraint Type** sub-rollout of the **Placement** rollout of the **Add Component** dialog box; you will be prompted to select the object to fix. Select the component; the selected component will be fixed at its current location and a small symbol will be displayed on it.

Bond

The Bond constraint is applied to fix the position of the selected components with respect to each other. Once the selected components are fixed using this constraint, they can be moved as a single component in such a way that the position of one component will remain the same with respect to the other component. To apply this constraint, choose the **Bond** option from the **Constraint Type** sub-rollout of the **Placement** rollout of the **Add Component** dialog box; you will be prompted to select the objects that you want to bond. Select two or more components; the **Create Constraint** button will be displayed in the **Geometry to Constrain** sub-rollout. Choose this button to apply the Bond constraint to the selected components. Next, choose the **OK** button to exit the dialog box.

Fit

The Fit constraint is applied to bring together two cylindrical faces of the same diameter. This constraint is useful for assembling nuts and bolts. To apply this constraint, choose the **Fit** option from the **Constraint Type** sub-rollout of the **Placement** rollout of the **Add Component** dialog box; you will be prompted to select the first object to fit. Select the first circular surface; you will be prompted to select the second object. Select the second circular surface of the same diameter; the axes of both components will coincide and they will become coaxial. Figure 8-26 shows components to apply the Fit constraint and Figure 8-27 shows components after applying the Fit constraint. Note that if the diameters of the selected surfaces (components) are not equal, the Fit constraint will become invalid.

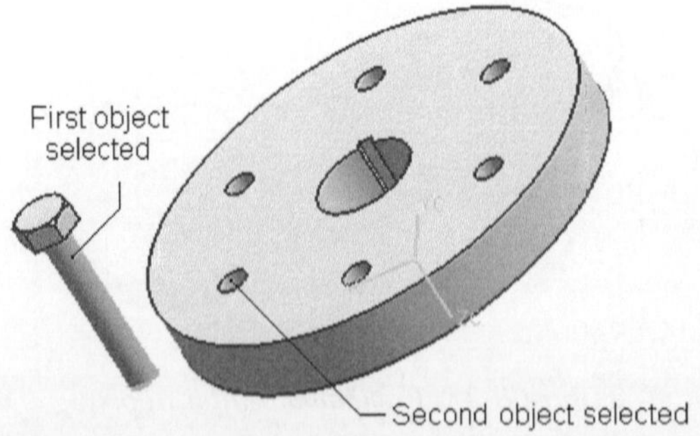

Figure 8-26 Selection of circular surfaces of equal diameter for applying the Fit constraint

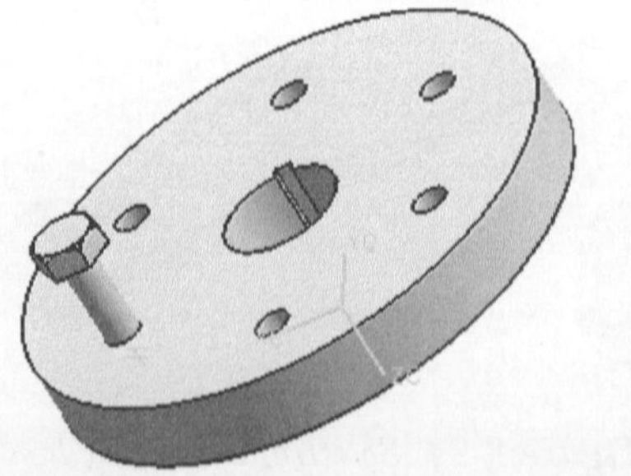

Figure 8-27 Components after applying the Fit constraint

Align/Lock

The Align/Lock constraint is used to align the axes of two different components and constrain the rotation of the components about the axis. In case of bolt, if you apply the Align/Lock constraint to bolt and hole, axes of the bolt and hole will be aligned and rotational movement of the bolt will be constrained. However, the bolt can move linearly along the axis. To apply this constraint, choose the **Align/Lock** option from the **Constraint Type** sub-rollout of the **Placement** rollout of the **Add Component** dialog box; you will be prompted to select the first circular object. Select the first circular object; you will be prompted to select the second circular object. Select the second circular object, refer to Figure 8-28; the axes of both the circular edges will be aligned and the rotation will be constrained about the axis and the selected edges will become coplanar, refer to Figure 8-29.

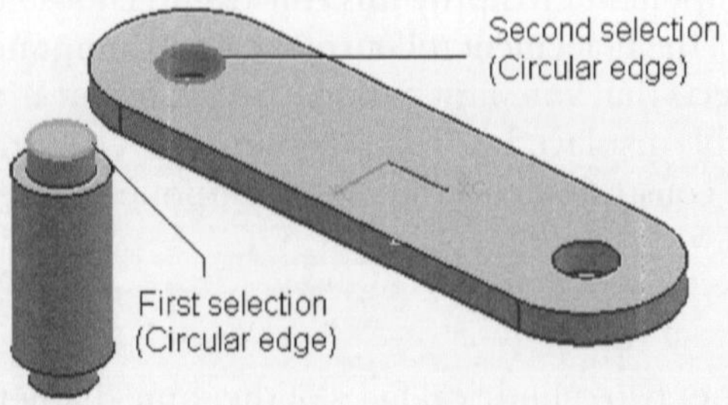

Figure 8-28 Circular edges selected for applying the Align/Lock constraint

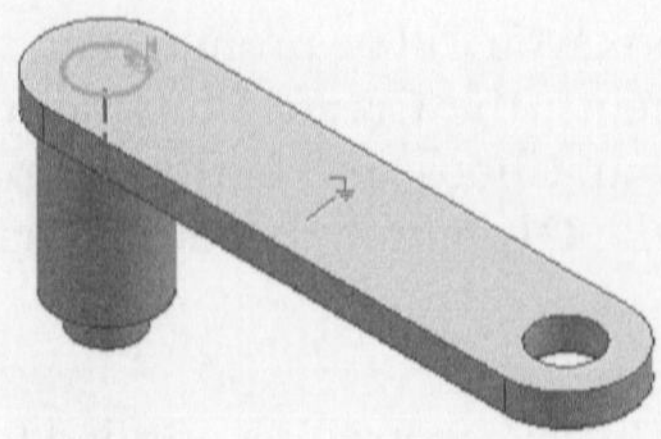

Figure 8-29 Components after applying the Align/Lock constraint

Applying Joints to Components in Assembly

In NX, Joints are used to constrain assembly components so that their range of motion is restricted to the desired directions and limits. The options available in the **Joint** rollout are discussed next.

Hinge

The **Hinge** joint between two bodies allows one rotational degree of freedom along an axis. This joint does not allow translational movement in any direction between the two bodies.

Slider

A **Slider** joint allows one translational degree of freedom between two bodies along a vector. This joint does not allow the bodies to rotate with respect to each other. You can set a distance value and limits for a slider joint.

Cylindrical

A **Cylindrical** joint between two bodies allows two degrees of freedom: one translational and one rotational. With a cylindrical joint, the two bodies are free to rotate and translate relative to each other about and along a vector. You can set distance and angle values as well as limits for a cylindrical joint.

Ball

A **Ball** joint between two bodies allows three rotational degrees of freedom. For a Ball joint, you can set an angle value but not the angle limits.

Points to Remember while Assembling Components

The following points should be kept in mind to work efficiently in the Assembly environment of NX:

1. The first component should be assembled in the assembly file using the datum planes.

2. It is important to make the components fully constrained using the assembly constraints before placing the next component. The component that is partially constrained will be displaced from its location while using it to assemble the other components.

3. If you have to place the same component at various positions in the same assembly, the second time onwards, you can directly select the component from the **File Name** list of the **Loaded Parts** sub-rollout of the **Part To Place** rollout of the **Add Component** dialog box and follow the same procedure explained before to place the component.

Creating a Pattern Component in an Assembly

Ribbon:	Assemblies > Component > Pattern Component
Menu:	Assemblies > Components > Pattern Component

The **Pattern Component** tool is used to pattern a component in an assembly. It is similar to the method of patterning a feature in a component. For example, if in an assembly, there are ten bolts to be assembled, you don't have to assemble them ten times. Instead, assemble one of the bolts in any one of the holes and pattern it using the **Pattern Component** tool. To do so, choose **Menu > Assemblies > Components > Pattern Component** from the **Top Border Bar**; the **Pattern Component** dialog box will be displayed, as shown in Figure 8-30, and you will be prompted to select the components. Select the components to pattern from the **Component To Pattern** rollout of the **Pattern Component** dialog box. You can create **Linear**,

Circular, and **Reference** associative patterns and **Polygon**, **Spiral**, **Along**, **General**, and **Helix** non-associative patterns by selecting the respective option from this dialog box. Note that the options for non-associative pattern will be available only when you clear the **Associative** check box under the **Settings** rollout.

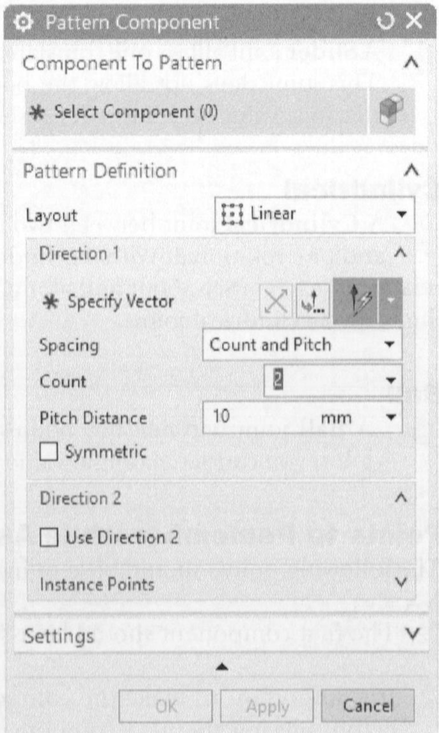

Figure 8-30 The ***Pattern Component*** *dialog box*

The procedure for creating the associative component pattern in an assembly is discussed next.

1. To create an associative circular pattern, select the **Circular** option from the **Layout** drop-down list of the **Pattern Definition** rollout; the **Pattern Component** dialog box will be modified, and you will be prompted to select components to pattern. Select the component to be patterned. Next, click on the **Specify Vector** area in the **Rotation Axis** sub-rollout of the **Pattern Definition** rollout; you will be prompted to select the objects to infer vector. You can select a cylindrical face, a datum axis, or an edge of the component to define the pattern axis. After selecting the pattern axis, you will be prompted to select the object to infer point. Specify the point about which you want to pattern the component. Next, select the **Count and Pitch** option from the **Spacing** drop-down list of **Angular Direction** rollout and enter the number of instances in the **Count** edit box and the angle of rotation in the **Pitch Angle** edit box of the **Pattern Component** dialog box. Next, choose the **OK** button from the dialog box.

Note

The angle value specified in the ***Pitch Angle*** *edit box of the* ***Pattern Component*** *dialog box is used to measure the angle between two instances.*

2. In case of an associative linear pattern, select the **Linear** option from the **Layout** drop-down list of the **Pattern Definition** rollout. You will be prompted to select objects to infer vector in the **Direction 1** sub-rollout. You can select a datum plane, edge, datum axis, a face normal to the object or triad from the graphic window to define the direction. Next, select the **Count and Pitch** option from the **Spacing** drop-down list; the **Count** and **Pitch Distance** edit boxes become available. Now, enter the number of instances in the **Count** edit box and distance between instances in the **Pitch Distance** edit box. Similarly, you can also define the second direction in the **Direction 2** sub-rollout by selecting the **Use Direction 2** check box. Next, choose the **OK** button from the dialog box.

3. The Reference pattern is used to create pattern of a component with reference to the pattern feature created in the component in the Modeling environment. For example, if you have created a circular pattern of the holes in a component in the Modeling environment, you can use it to assemble a bolt on each of the patterned holes. By using the pattern feature

created in the Modeling environment as a reference, you can create the pattern of a bolt in the Assembly environment. After assembling one of the instances of the bolt using the assembly constraints, refer to Figure 8-31, invoke the **Pattern Component** dialog box. Next, select the **Reference** option from the **Layout** drop-down list of the **Pattern Definition** rollout, and then choose the **OK** button from the **Pattern Component** dialog box to automatically pattern the selected component in the assembly with reference to the pattern created in the Modeling environment, refer to Figure 8-32.

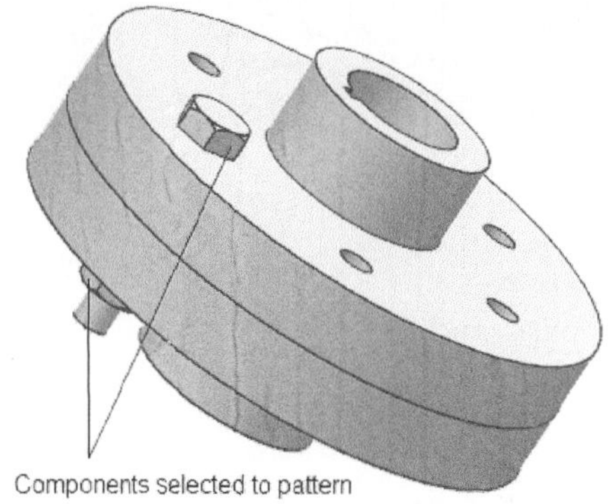

Figure 8-31 Components and the instance of the pattern feature to be selected

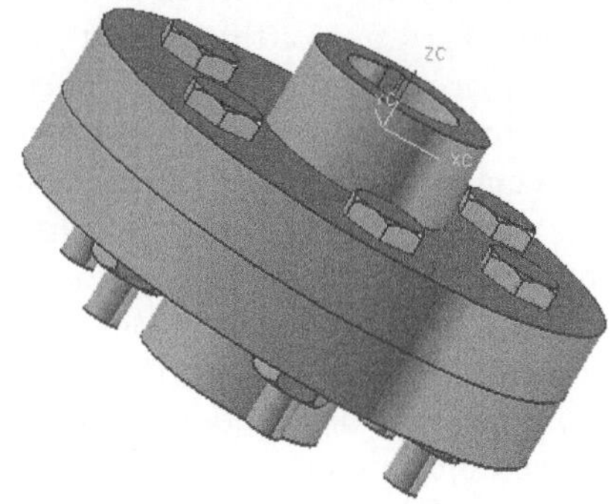

Figure 8-32 Assembly after creating the derived component pattern

Note
The options available for non-associative pattern are same as discussed in the earlier chapters.

Replacing a Component in an Assembly

Ribbon:	Assemblies > More Gallery > Component > Replace Component
Menu:	Assemblies > Components > Replace Component

The **Replace Component** tool is used to replace the component that is already placed in an assembly with the new component. If the new component has the same basic geometry as that of the original component, the new component will be placed exactly at the location where the original component was placed. To replace an existing component from an assembly, choose the **Replace Component** tool from **Menu > Assemblies > Components** in the **Top Border Bar**; the **Replace Component** dialog box will be displayed, as shown in Figure 8-33. The options in this dialog box are discussed next.

Note
The geometry of the new component should be in the same order to use the ***Replace Component*** *tool, otherwise, the replaced component will be placed arbitrarily in the space without any association with the location where the component was present earlier.*

Components To Replace Rollout

In this rollout, the **Select Components** area is activated by default. As a result, you will be prompted to select the components to be replaced. Select the components to be replaced, refer to Figure 8-34.

Replacement Part Rollout

In this rollout, you can select the required replacement component to replace the existing component of the assembly. To do so, click on the **Select Part** area of this rollout; you will be prompted to select the replacement part. You can select the replacement part either from the **File Name** list of the **Loaded Parts** sub-rollout of the **Replacement Part** rollout or by choosing the **Open** button from this rollout. If you choose the **Open** button to select the component, the **Part Name** dialog box will be displayed. Next, browse to the required location, select the required part, and then choose the **OK** button from the dialog box; the name of the selected part will be displayed in the **Unloaded Parts** list box of the **Replace Component** dialog box. After selecting the required part, choose the **OK** button from the **Replace Component** dialog box; the selected component in the assembly will be replaced by the replacement component. Figure 8-34 shows the parts to be replaced and Figure 8-35 shows the assembly after replacing parts.

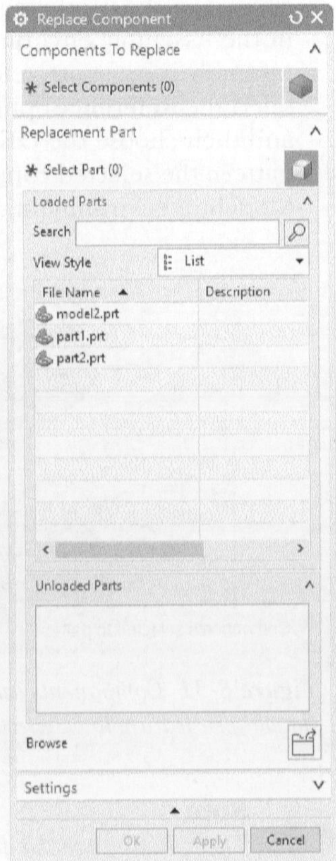

Figure 8-33 The ***Replace Component*** *dialog box*

Settings Rollout

In this rollout, the **Maintain Relationships** check box is selected by default. As a result, all applied constraints are maintained even after replacing a component. If you select the **Replace All Occurrences in Assembly** check box, all instances in the assembly will be replaced by the replacement component.

Component Properties

In this sub-rollout, you can change the name of the replaced component by specifying a new name in the **Component Name** edit box. You can also change the reference set of the replaced component by selecting an option from the **Reference Set** drop-down list. Additionally, you can change the layer of the replaced component by selecting an option from the **Layer Option** drop-down list in this rollout.

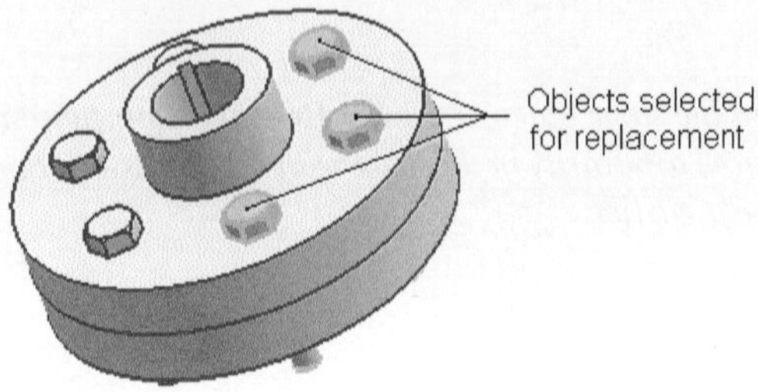

Figure 8-34 *Parts selected to be replaced*

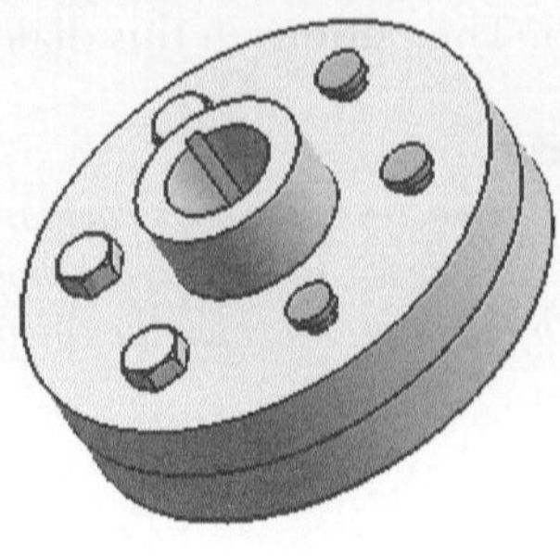

Figure 8-35 *Resultant model after replacement*

Moving a Component in an Assembly

Ribbon:	Assemblies > Component Position > Move Component
Menu:	Assemblies > Component Position > Move Component

You can move and reorient an assembled component in 3D space using available degrees of freedom. Note that a component cannot be reoriented along the constrained degree of freedom. To move a component, you need to invoke the Move Component dialog box. To do so, choose the **Move Component** tool from the **Component Position** group of the **Assemblies** tab; the **Move Component** dialog box will be displayed, refer to Figure 8-36. Also, you will be prompted to select the components to be moved. Select the component that you want to move. Now, you can move the selected component by using different options available in the Move Component dialog box. The options in this dialog box are discussed next.

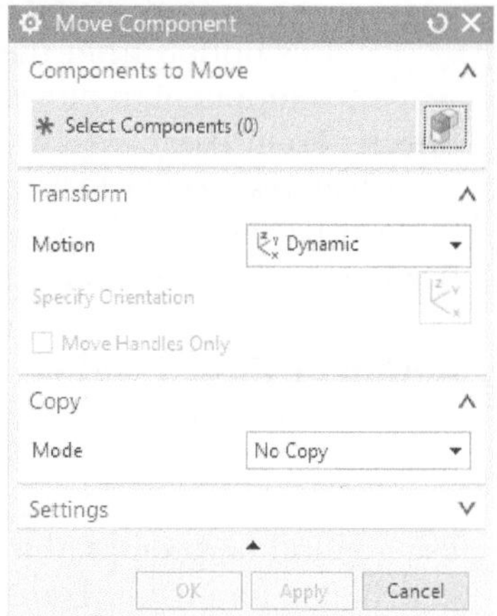

*Figure 8-36 The **Move Component** dialog box*

Transform Rollout

The options in the **Motion** drop-down list of the Transform rollout are used to specify the method for moving components. These methods are discussed next.

Dynamic

This option is selected by default in the **Motion** drop-down list. To move the selected component using this option, click in the **Specify Orientation** area in the **Transform** rollout; a dynamic triad will be displayed on the component. Move the component at available degrees of freedom by using the linear and angular handles of the triad. If you select the **Move Handles Only** check box, only the dynamic triad will move.

Distance

This option is used to move the selected component along the specified vector. If you select this option from the **Motion** drop-down list, you will be prompted to select the component to move. Select the component that you want to move; the **Transform** rollout will be modified. Next, click in the **Specify Vector** area of this rollout and specify the vector along which you want to move the selected component. Next, enter the required distance in the **Distance** edit box of the **Transform** rollout and press ENTER; the selected component will shift its position to the specified position along the specified vector.

Angle

This option is used to rotate the selected component about a specified axis and by a specified angle. If you select this option from the **Motion** drop-down list, you will be prompted to select the component to move. Select the component that you want to move; the **Transform** rollout will be modified. Next, click in the **Specify Vector** area of the **Transform** rollout and specify the direction vector about which the selected component will rotate. Next, click on the **Specify Axis Point** area in the **Transform** rollout and specify the point through which the axis will pass. Next, enter the required angle value in the

Angle edit box and press ENTER; the selected component will rotate about the specified axis and by the specified angle.

Point to Point

This option is used to move a component from one point to another. If you select this option from the **Motion** drop-down list, you will be prompted to select the component to move. Select the component that you want to move and click in the **Specify From Point** area; you will be prompted to select the object to infer point. Select the point with respect to which you want to move the selected component. The **Specify To Point** area will be highlighted. Now, select the destination point; the selected component will move from its original location to the newly specified location.

Rotate by Three Points

This option is similar to the **Angle** option of the **Move Component** dialog box, with the only difference being that in this case, you can just specify two points for rotation, instead of specifying the angle. If you select this option from the **Motion** drop-down list, you will be prompted to select the components to move. Select the components that you want to rotate; the **Transform** rollout will be modified. Click in the **Specify Vector** area and specify the axis of rotation. Also, click in the **Specify Pivot Point** area and specify the point from which the rotation axis will pass. After specifying a point, the **Inferred Point** button in the **Specify Start Point** area will be chosen automatically. Specify the point with respect to which the component will be measured and then specify the point upto which you want to rotate components. Figure 8-37 shows the component before using the **Rotate By Three Points** option and Figure 8-38 shows the component after rotating it using the **Rotate By Three Points** option. Choose the **Apply** or **OK** button to accept the resultant position.

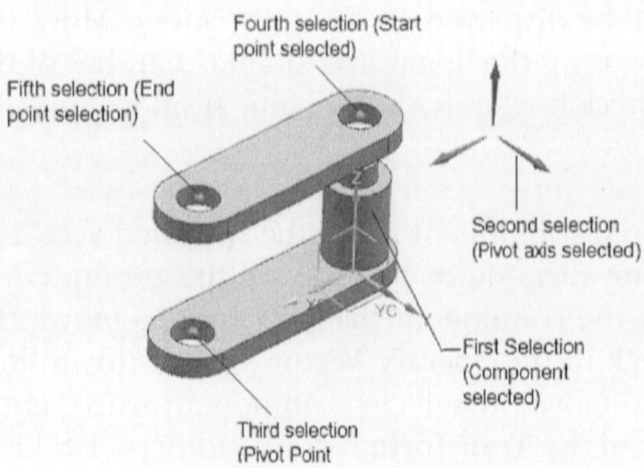

*Figure 8-37 Component and reference selection before using the **Rotate By Three Points** option*

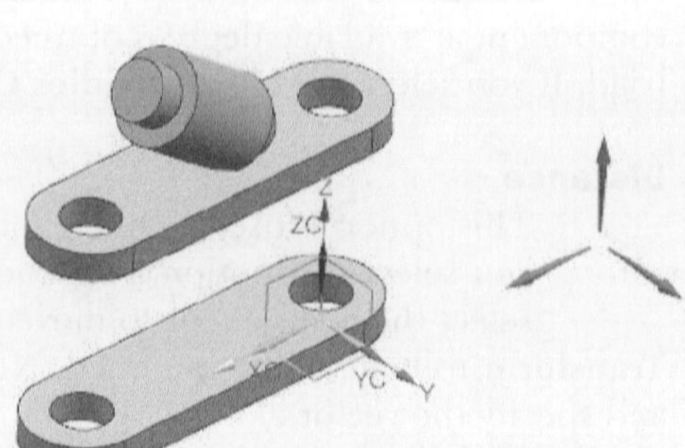

*Figure 8-38 Component after using the **Rotate By Three Points** option*

Align Axis to Vector

This option is used to rotate and move the selected components by specifying two direction vectors and an origin point. If you select this option from the **Motion** drop-down list, you will be prompted to select the component to move. Select the component that you want to rotate and move; the **Transform** rollout will be modified. Next, click in the **Specify From Vector** area and select the vector. The selected vector will align with the destination vector. Therefore, now you need to select the destination vector from the **Specify To Vector** area. Next, choose the **Inferred Point** button from the **Specify Pivot Point** and select a point; a displacement will occur with respect to the selected point. Figures 8-39 and 8-40 show components selected before using the **Align Axis to Vector** option and components after using the **Align Axis to Vector** option.

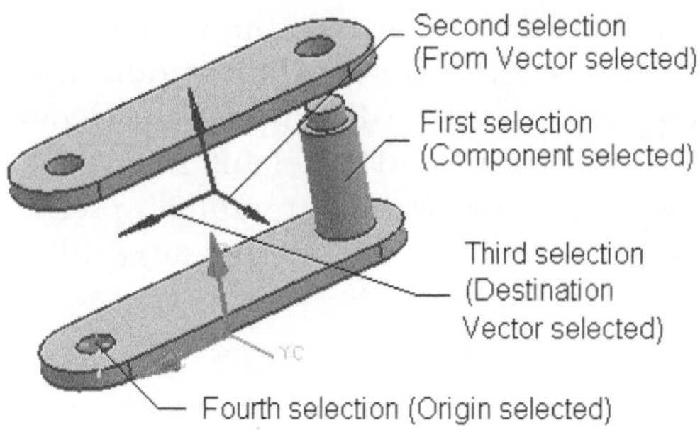

*Figure 8-39 Component and reference selection before using the **Align Axis to Vector** option*

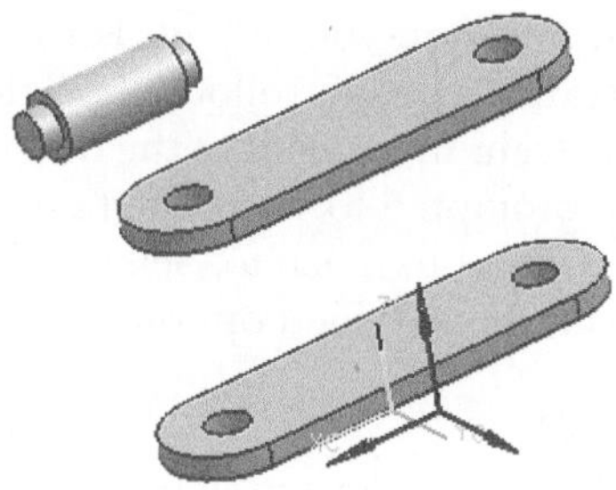

*Figure 8-40 Component after using the **Align Axis to Vector** option*

CSYS to CSYS

This option is used to reposition the selected components from one CSYS to another CSYS. If you select this option from the **Motion** drop-down list, you will be prompted to select the components to move. Select the component that you want to move. Next, click in the **Specify From CSYS** area and then select two edges to define CSYS or any face. The selected CSYS will align with the destination CSYS. After specifying the From CSYS, the **Specify To CSYS** area will be activated. Next, specify the destination CSYS by specifying two edges or any face or you can also create a new coordinate system by using the **CSYS Dialog** button; the selected component will be repositioned as specified. Figure 8-41 shows the component before using the **CSYS to CSYS** option and Figure 8-42 shows component after using the **CSYS to CSYS** option.

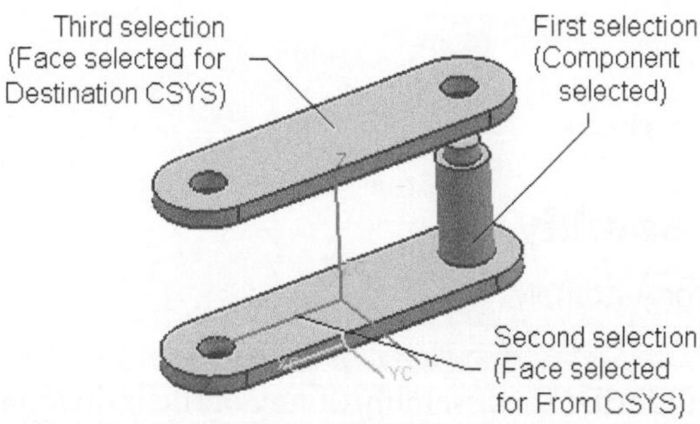

*Figure 8-41 Component and reference selection before using the **CSYS to CSYS** option*

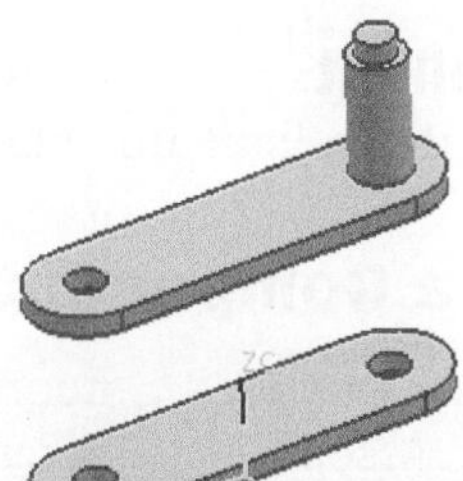

*Figure 8-42 Component after using the **CSYS to CSYS** option*

By Constraints

You can also move components by using the **By Constraints** option. If you select this option from the **Motion** drop-down list, the **Move Component** dialog will be modified and the **Constraint Type** sub-rollout will be displayed in it. Also, the **Geometry to Constrain** sub-rollout will be displayed. The **Constraint Type** sub-rollout is used to select the type of constraints. Select the required constraint from this sub-rollout; the **Geometry to Constrain** sub-rollout will be modified based on the option selected in the **Constraint Type** sub-rollout. For example, if you select the **Touch Align** option from the **Constraint Type** sub-rollout, the **Select Two Objects** area will be displayed in the **Geometry to Constrain** sub-rollout of the dialog box and it will be activated by default. As a result, you will be prompted to select the first object. Select a face; you will be prompted to select the second object to touch to. Select a face of another component; the selected faces will move based on the specified option.

Delta XYZ

This option is used to move the selected component from its position to the specified location with respect to the WCS or Absolute coordinate system. If you select this option from the **Motion** drop-down list, you will be prompted to select the component to move. Select the component that you want to move; the other options in the **Transform** rollout will be activated. Select the **WCS-Displayed Part** or **Absolute-Displayed Part** option from the **Reference** drop-down list to move the component with respect to the WCS or Absolute coordinate system. Next, enter the X, Y, and Z-coordinates in the **XC**, **YC**, and **ZC** edit boxes, respectively; the selected component will move according to the specified values.

Copy Rollout

In this rollout, the **No Copy** option is selected by default in the **Mode** drop-down list. As a result, a duplicate copy will not be created while moving the component. If you select the **Copy** option from this drop-down list, the original component will remain at its position and a duplicate copy of the component will be created at a new location. If you select the **Manual Copy** option from the **Mode** drop-down list, the **Create Copy** button will be displayed below the drop-down list. You need to choose the **Create Copy** button whenever you want to create a duplicate copy.

Settings Rollout

The options of this rollout are same as discussed earlier.

Mirroring a Component in an Assembly

Ribbon:	Assemblies > Component > Mirror Assembly
Menu:	Assemblies > Components > Mirror Assembly

The **Mirror Assembly** tool is used for mirroring the assembly or any of the individual components in the assembly about a reference plane. Note that you cannot select a planar face of a component for this purpose. When you choose the **Mirror Assembly** tool from the **Component** group in the **Assemblies** tab, the **Mirror Assemblies Wizard** will be displayed with the **Welcome** page, as shown in Figure 8-43.

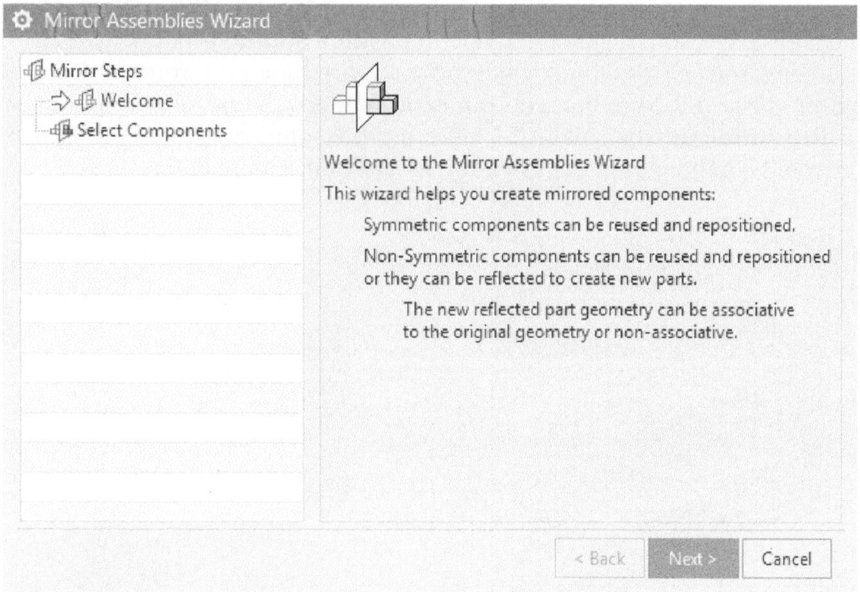

***Figure 8-43** The **Welcome** page of the **Mirror Assemblies Wizard** dialog box*

To select components of an assembly to mirror, choose the **Next** button; the **Select Components** page will be displayed and you will be prompted to select the components to be mirrored. Select the components that are to be mirrored and choose the **Next** button to proceed to the **Select Plane** page.

Select any of the reference planes as the mirroring plane. You can also create a mirroring plane, refer to Figure 8-44. To do so, choose the **Create Datum Plane** button from the **Select Plane** page; the **Datum Plane** dialog box will be displayed. Now, create a mirroring plane using the options available in this dialog box. After selecting the plane, choose the **Next** button to proceed to the **Naming Policy** page. Choose the **Next** button to proceed to the **Mirror Setup** page. There are three types of mirroring operations available. By default, the **Reuse and Reposition** type is chosen. If the mirroring operation is performed by using this type, the mirrored component will be the same part file. This means an associative link will be maintained between the parent and the mirrored components. Also, the name of the mirrored component will be the same as that of the parent component.

If the mirroring operation is performed by using the **Associative Mirror** option, the mirrored component will be a separate copy of the parent component and also an associative link will be maintained between the parent and mirrored components. Note that the **Associative Mirror** button will be available only after you select the components from the list box in this area. You can choose the **Exclude** button to exclude the selected component.

If the mirroring operation is performed by using the **Non Associative Mirror** option, the mirrored component will be a separate copy of the parent component with no link maintained between the parent and mirrored components.

After choosing the mirror type, choose the **Next** button; the **Mirror Review** page will be displayed. On this page, you can use the **Cycle Reposition Solutions** button to cycle through the possible solutions. You can also directly select the required solution from the **Cycle Reposition Solutions** drop-down list. Note that you can cycle through the possible solutions only for the **Reuse and Reposition** mirror type. After selecting the solution, choose the **Finish** button to view the mirrored component in the assembly, as shown in Figure 8-45.

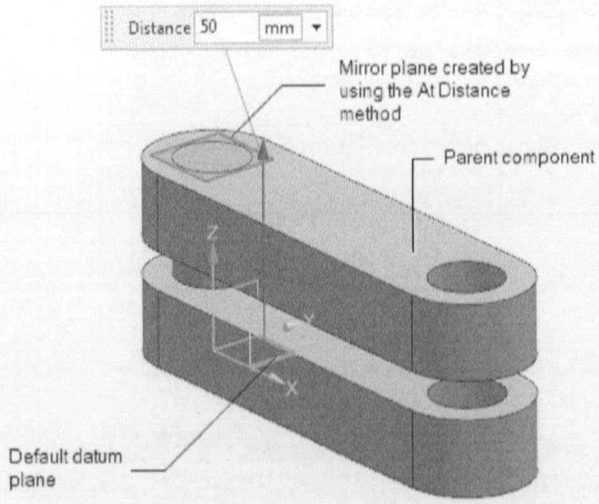

Figure 8-44 The parent part after creating the mirroring plane

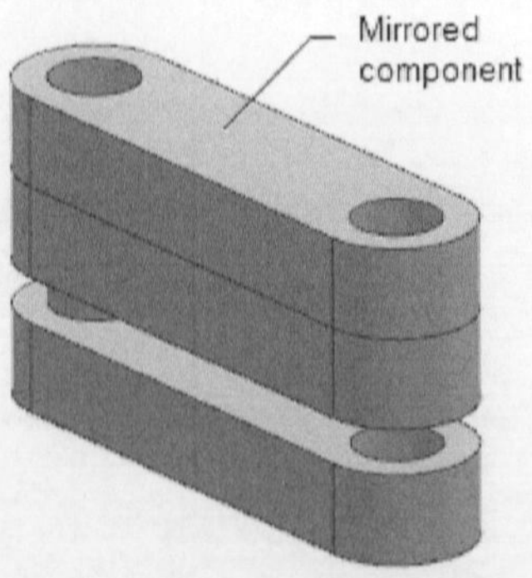

Figure 8-45 The assembly with the mirrored component

If you choose the **Associative Mirror** or **Non Associative Mirror** button from the **Mirror Setup** page and then choose the **Next** button, the **Mirror Components** message box will be displayed. Choose the **OK** button to close the message box; the **Mirror Review** page will be displayed. Choose **Next**; the **Name New Part Files** page will be displayed, as shown in Figure 8-46. Then, choose **Use the button to name the mirrored parts and set attributes**; the **Name Parts** dialog box appears. You can change the name and location of part in the **Name Parts** dialog box. Choose the **OK** button to close the **Name Parts** dialog box. Then, choose the **Finish** button to close the **Mirror Assemblies Wizard** dialog box.

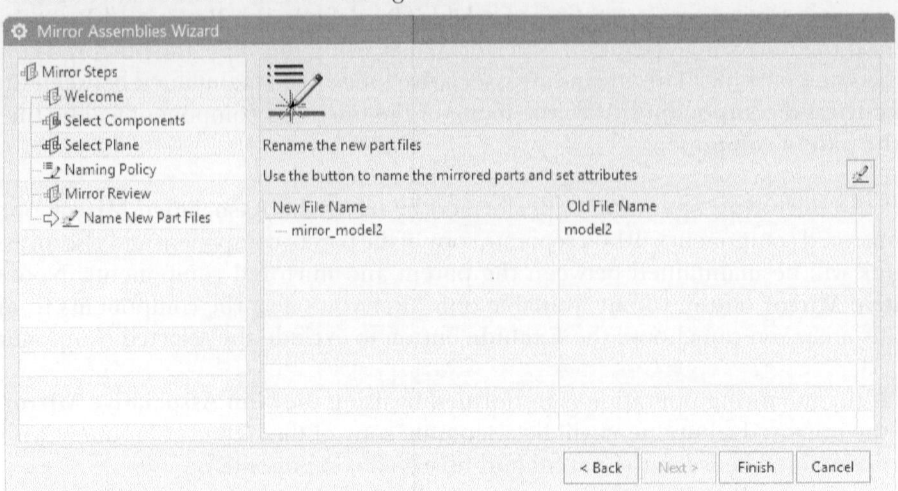

Figure 8-46 The ***Name New Part Files*** *page of the* ***Mirror Assemblies Wizard*** *dialog box*

Note

The mirrored components do not have assembly constraints. You need to manually add these constraints to the mirrored components.

Modifying a Component in the Assembly File

Ribbon: Assemblies > More > Context Control > Set Work Part (Customize to add)
Menu: Assemblies > Context Control > Set Work Part

The **Set Work Part** tool is used to modify or add sketches and features to the components that are placed in the assembly file by bringing the component into the current **Work Part** category. The procedure to modify the component in the assembly file is discussed next.

Choose the **Set Work Part** tool from **Menu > Assemblies > Context Control** in the **Top Border Bar**; the **Set Work Part** dialog box will be displayed, as shown in Figure 8-47, and you will be prompted to choose the option or select from view. Select the component from the assembly and choose the **OK** button. The components other than the selected ones will become faded. After converting the component into **Work Part**, you can perform any type of feature or sketch-based operation. The changes made in the component in the assembly are also updated in the part file of the component. After making the required modification in the component, choose the **Assembly Navigator** tab from the **Resource Bar**; a cascading menu will be displayed. Select the assembly name from the assembly node tree and right-click on it. Next, choose the **Make Work Part** option from the shortcut menu. When you select the assembly as a work part, the whole assembly will be displayed in the same color.

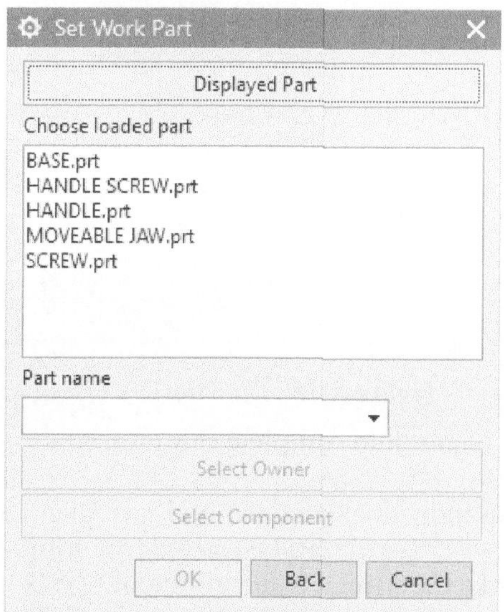

Figure 8-47 *The **Set Work Part** dialog box*

Note

*You can select only one component at a time in the **Work Part** category. The changes done in the component can be directly saved in the component file by saving the assembly file.*

TUTORIALS

Tutorial 1

In this tutorial, you will create all the components of the Pipe Vice assembly and then assemble them, as shown in Figure 8-48. The dimensions of the components are given in Figures 8-49 and 8-50. Save the file with the name *Pipe Vice.prt* at the location *NX \c08\Pipe Vice.*

(Expected time: 2.5 hr)

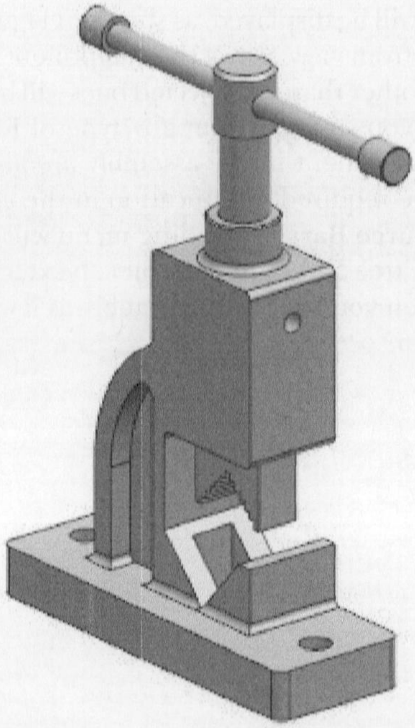

Figure 8-48 *The Pipe Vice assembly*

The following steps are required to complete this tutorial:

a. Create all components as individual part files and save them. Save the part files in the *Pipe Vice* folder at *\NX\c08*.
b. Start a new file and invoke the Assembly environment.

c. Insert the Base in the assembly window and make it fully-constrained by using the assembly constraints, refer to Figure 8-51.
d. Insert the Screw in the assembly window and apply the required assembly constraints to make it a fully-constrained part, refer to Figures 8-52 through 8-57.
e. Insert the Movable Jaw in the assembly window and apply the required assembly constraints, refer to Figures 8-58 through 8-62.
f. Insert the Handle into the assembly window and apply the required assembly constraints; refer to Figures 8-64 through 8-69.
g. Insert the Handle Screw into the assembly window and apply the required assembly constraints. Similarly, assemble the other instance of the Handle Screw with the assembly, refer to Figures 8-70 through 8-77.
h. Save and close the file.

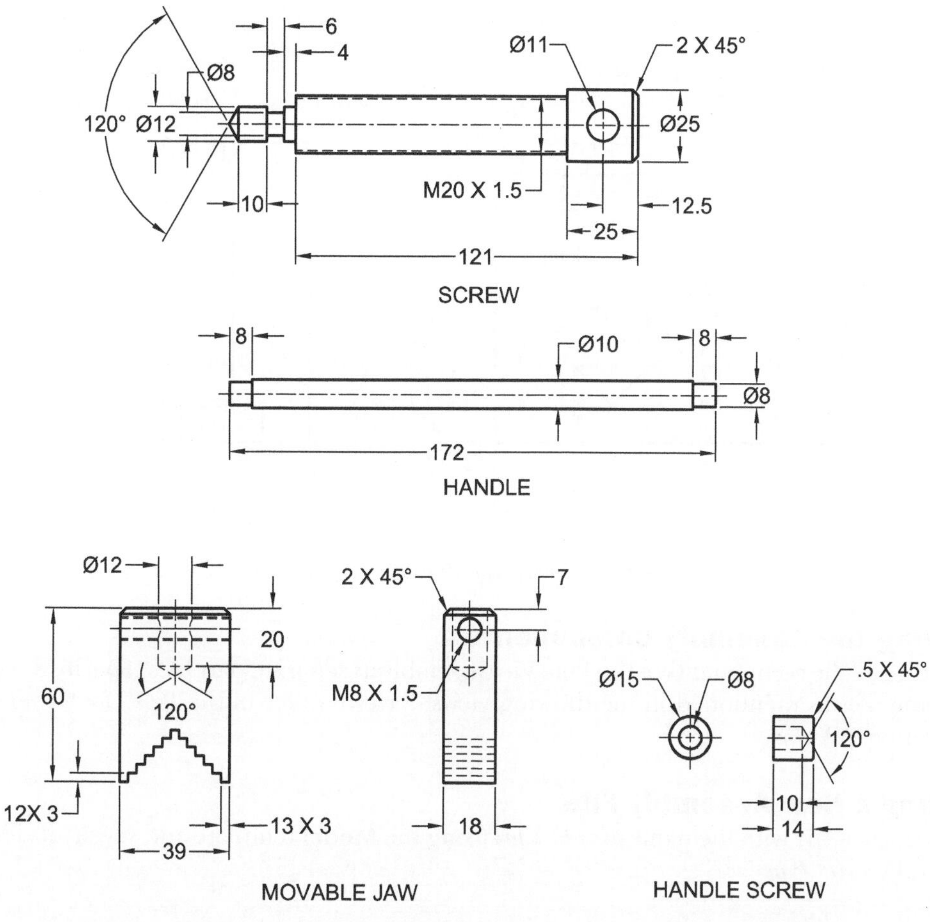

Figure 8-49 *Views and dimensions of the Screw, Handle, Movable Jaw, and Handle Screw*

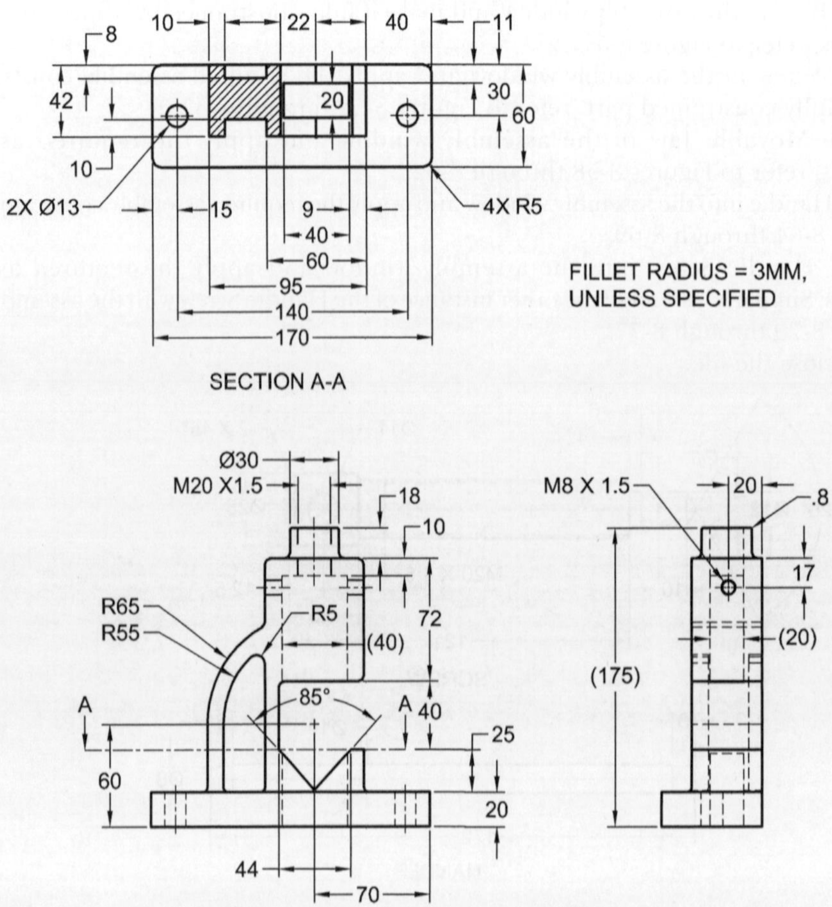

Figure 8-50 Views and dimensions of the Base

Creating the Assembly Components

1. Create all the components of the Pipe Vice assembly as separate part files. Specify the names of the files as mentioned in the drawing views. Save the files in the *Pipe Vice* folder at the location *\NX\c08*.

Starting a New Assembly File

1. Start a new file with the name *Pipe Vice.prt* using the **Model** template and specify its location as *C:\NX\c08\Pipe Vice.*

2. Choose **Application > Assemblies** from the **Ribbon** to invoke the Assembly environment.

3. Choose the **Assemblies** tab from the **Ribbon** to access the assembly tools.

Assembling the Base

The Base will be the first component to be placed in the assembly file. All other components will be assembled with the Base.

1. Choose the **Add** tool from the **Assemblies** tab to invoke the **Add Component** dialog box.

2. Choose the **Open** button from the **Add Component** dialog box; the **Part Name** dialog box is displayed.

3. Browse to *\NX\c08\Pipe Vice* and select Base from the **Part Name** dialog box, and then choose the **OK** button.

4. Select the **Entire Part** option from the **Reference Set** drop-down list in the **Settings** rollout, if not already selected.

5. Next, click in the **Select Object** area of the **Location** rollout; the Base is attached to the cursor and you are prompted to select location to place the component. Click anywhere in the drawing area to place the component. Select the **Move** radio button from the **Placement** rollout, if not already selected; the **X**, **Y**, and **Z** edit boxes are displayed in the drawing area. Enter **0**, **0**, and **0** in the respective edit boxes and then press ENTER; the absolute origin of the component is placed at the origin of the Datum CSYS.

6. Choose the **OK** button from the **Add Component** dialog box; the **Create Fix Constraint** message box is displayed. Choose the **Yes** button from it; the Fix constraint is applied to the Base and all its degrees of freedom are restricted.

   Next, you can change the reference set of the Base so that the datum planes and sketches used to create it are no more displayed.

7. Right-click on the Base and choose the **Replace Reference Set > MODEL** from the shortcut menu. The assembly after assembling the Base is shown in Figure 8-51.

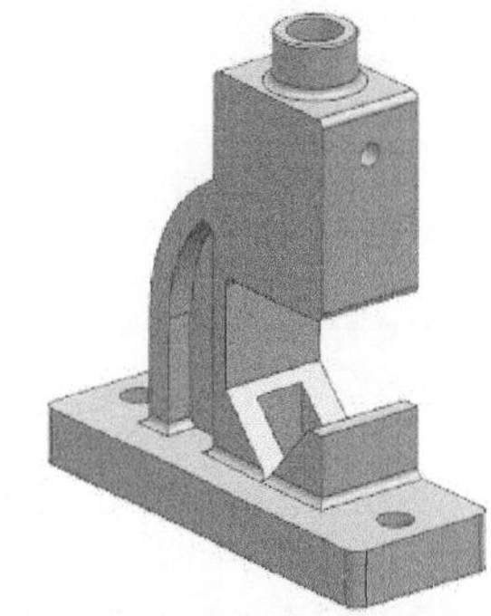

Figure 8-51 *The assembly after assembling the Base*

Note

1. It is recommended to use the selection group in case of complex assemblies for precise selection of components, planes, or entities.

*2. To orient the base in the assembly you can use the **Move Component** tool.*

Assembling the Second Component

The second component that you need to assemble is the Screw. This component will be assembled with the Base.

1. Choose the **Add** tool from the **Assemblies** tab to invoke the **Add Component** dialog box.

2. Choose the **Open** button from the **Add Component** dialog box; the **Part Name** dialog box is displayed. Select Screw from it and choose the **OK** button.

3. Next, click in the **Select Object** area of the **Location** rollout; the Screw is attached to the cursor and you are prompted to select location to place the component. Click anywhere in the drawing area to place the component. Select the **Constrain** radio button in the **Placement** rollout; the **Constrain Type** sub-rollout is displayed.

4. Choose the **Touch Align** option from the **Constraint Type** sub-rollout and then select the **Infer Center/Axis** option from the **Orientation** drop-down list in the **Geometry to Constrain** sub-rollout.

5. Select the cylindrical face of the Screw, refer to Figure 8-52. Next, select the cylindrical face of the Base, refer to Figure 8-53.

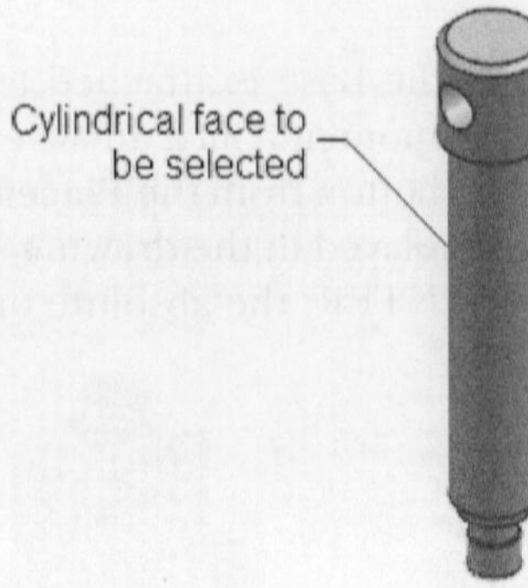

Figure 8-52 *Cylindrical face to be selected from the Screw*

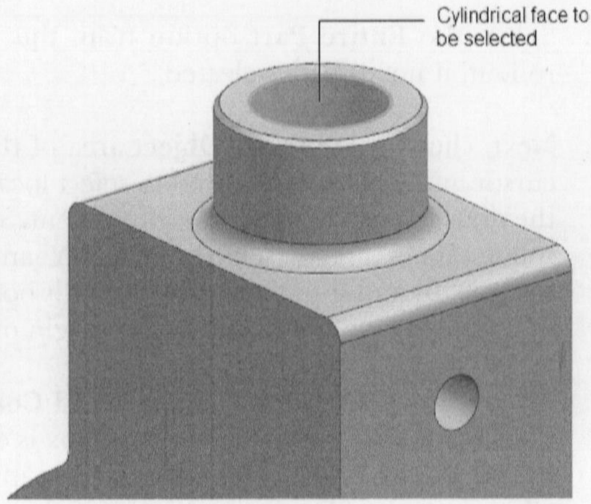

Figure 8-53 *Cylindrical face to be selected from the Base*

6. Now, choose the **Distance** option from the **Constraint Type** sub-rollout.

7. Select the planar face of the Screw, refer to Figure 8-54. Next, select the planar face of the Base component, refer to Figure 8-55.

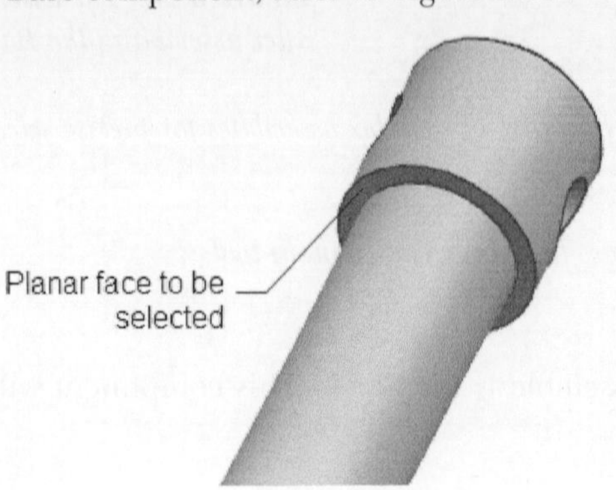

Figure 8-54 *Planar face to be selected from the Screw*

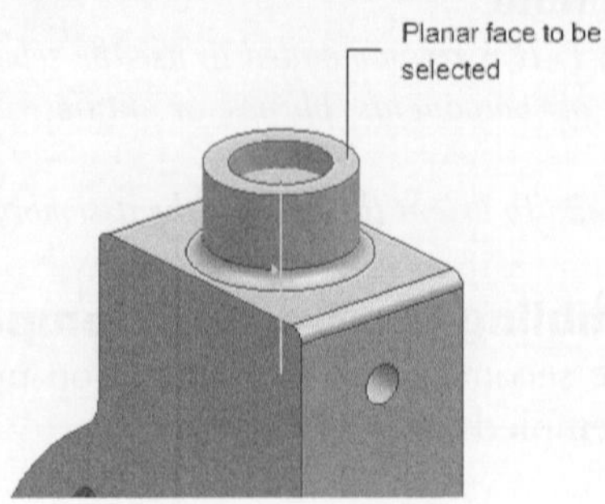

Figure 8-55 *Planar face to be selected from the Base*

8. Enter the offset value **35** in the **Distance** edit box of the **Distance** sub-rollout.

9. Next, choose the **Parallel** option from the **Constraint Type** sub-rollout.

10. Select the XC-YC plane from the Screw and then select the front face of the Base, refer to Figure 8-56 and then choose the **Apply** button. The assembly after assembling the Screw is shown in Figure 8-57.

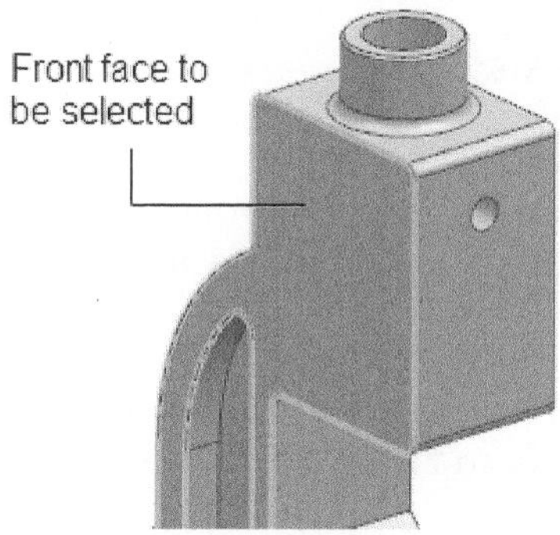

Figure 8-56 *Front face of the Base to be selected*

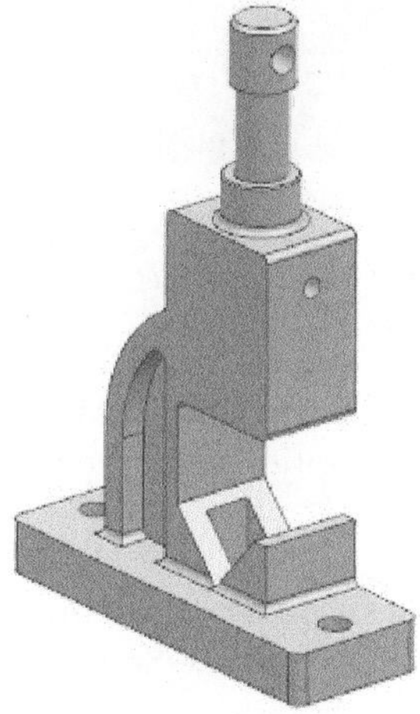

Figure 8-57 *The assembly after assembling the Screw*

Assembling the Third Component

Next, you need to assemble the Movable Jaw with the Screw. It is recommended that before assembling the Movable Jaw, you should hide the Base. This will provide a better display of the Screw.

1. Choose the **Assembly Navigator** tab from the **Resource Bar**; the **Assembly Navigator** cascading menu is displayed. Click on the check box on the left of the Base; the display of the Base is turned off.

2. Next, choose the **Open** button from the **Add Component** dialog box; the **Part Name** dialog box is displayed.

3. Select the Movable Jaw from the **Part Name** dialog box and then choose the **OK** button.

4. Next, click in the **Select Object** area of the **Location** rollout; the Movable Jaw is attached to the cursor and you are prompted to select location to place the component. Click anywhere in the drawing area to place the component.

5. Choose the **Fit** option from the **Constraint Type** sub-rollout. Select the cylindrical face of the Movable Jaw as the first object, refer to Figure 8-58. Next, select the cylindrical face of the Screw as the second object, refer to Figure 8-59.

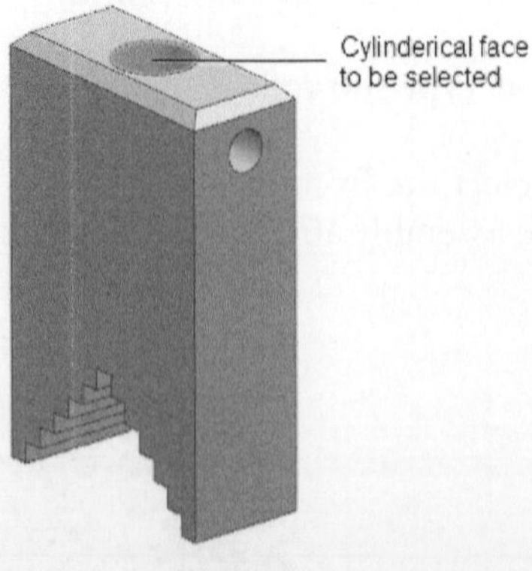

Figure 8-58 Cylindrical face to be selected from the Movable Jaw*

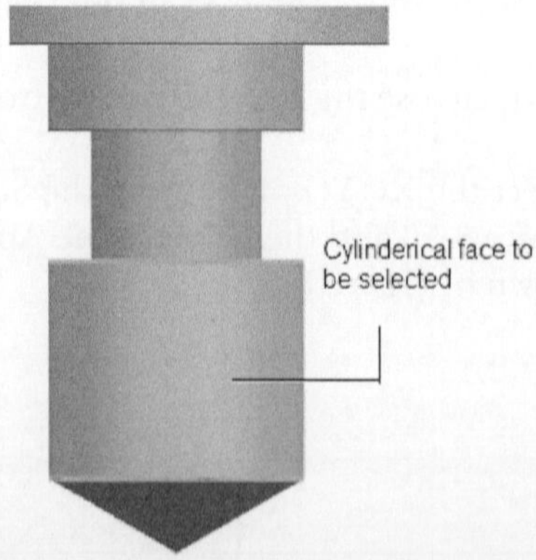

***Figure 8-59** Cylindrical face to be selected from the Screw*

6. Next, choose the **Touch Align** option from the **Constraint Type** sub-rollout and then the **Touch** option from the **Orientation** drop-down list in the **Geometry to Constrain** sub-rollout.

7. Select the top face of the Movable Jaw as the first object, refer to Figure 8-60 and select the planar face from the Screw as the second object, refer to Figure 8-61.

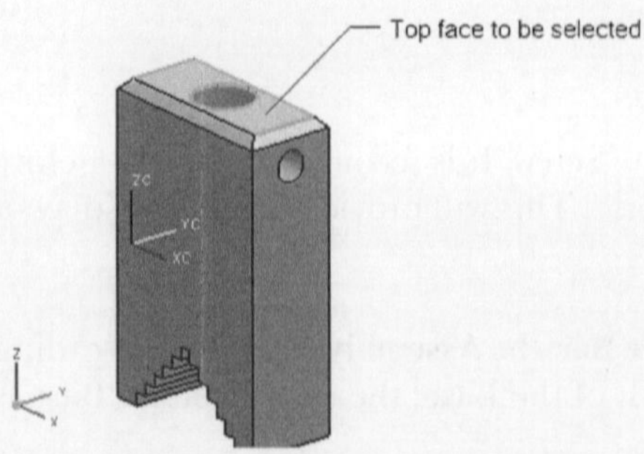

***Figure 8-60** Top face to be selected from the Movable Jaw*

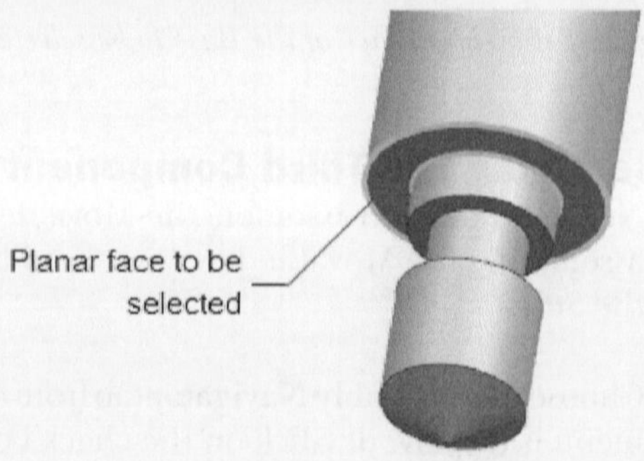

***Figure 8-61** Planar face to be selected from the Screw*

8. Select the **Parallel** option from the **Constraint Type** sub-rollout.

9. Select the front face of the Movable Jaw as the first object, refer to Figure 8-62. Next, select the XC-YC plane of the Screw as the second object to apply the **Parallel** constraint.

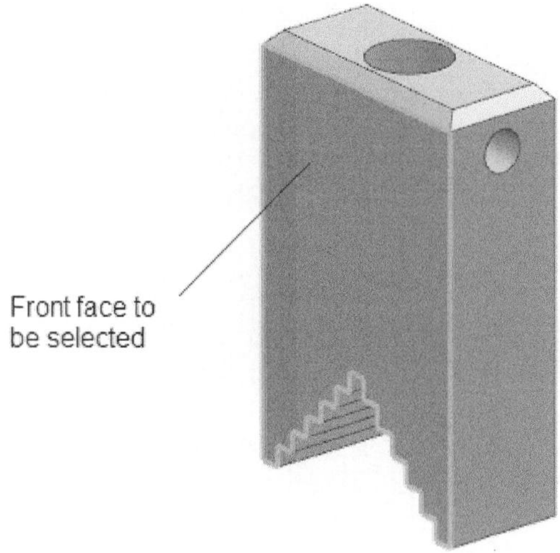

Figure 8-62 Front face of the Movable Jaw to be selected

10. Next, choose the **OK** button from the **Add Component** dialog box to exit it.

    After applying the three assembly constraints between the Movable Jaw and the Screw, you can cross check to ensure whether the component is fully-constrained or not using the **Move Component** tool from the **Component Position** group of the **Assemblies** tab.

    Next, you need to turn on the display of the Base.

11. Invoke the **Assembly Navigator** cascading menu. Select the check box on the left of the Base; the display of the Base is turned on.

    It is recommended that you change the texture of the Base component from solid to transparent. This is done to make those components visible that are assembled inside the Base such as the Movable Jaw and the Screw.

12. Choose **Menu > Edit > Object Display** from the **Top Border Bar**; the **Class Selection** dialog box is displayed and you are prompted to select the objects to edit. Select the Base and choose the **OK** button; the **Edit Object Display** dialog box is displayed.

    By dragging the **Translucency** sliding bar, you can change the transparency property of the Base from 0 to 100.

13. Drag the **Translucency** sliding bar to a value of **75** and choose the **OK** button. If the **Translucency Performance Warning** window is displayed, choose the **OK** button. This window informs you that enabling the translucency will decrease the performance of the graphics.

    The assembly after making the Base translucent is shown in Figure 8-63.

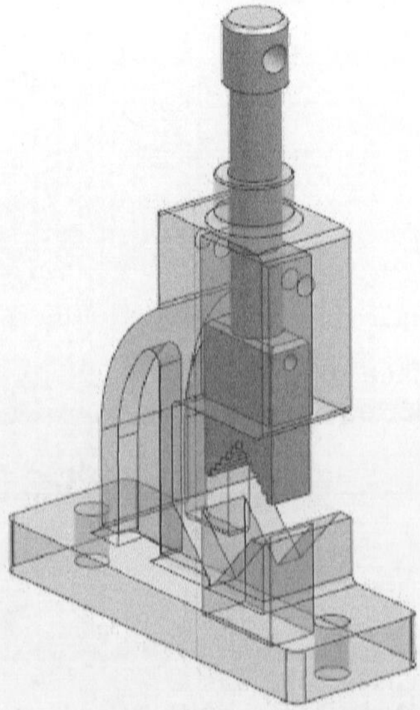

Figure 8-63 The assembly after making the Base translucent

Assembling the Handle

Next, you need to assemble the Handle with the Screw.

1. Choose the **Add** tool from the **Assemblies** tab; the **Add Component** dialog box is displayed.

2. Choose the **Open** button and select the Handle from the **Part Name** dialog box. Next, choose the **OK** button from this dialog box.

3. Next, click in the **Select Object** area of the **Location** rollout; the Handle is attached to the cursor and you are prompted to select location to place the component. Click anywhere in the drawing area to place the component.

4. Select the **Touch Align** option from the **Constraint Type** sub-rollout and then select the **Infer Center/Axis** option from the **Orientation** drop-down list in the **Geometry to Constrain** sub-rollout.

5. Select the cylindrical face of the Handle as the first object, refer to Figure 8-64. Next, select the cylindrical face of the Screw as the second object, refer to Figure 8-65.

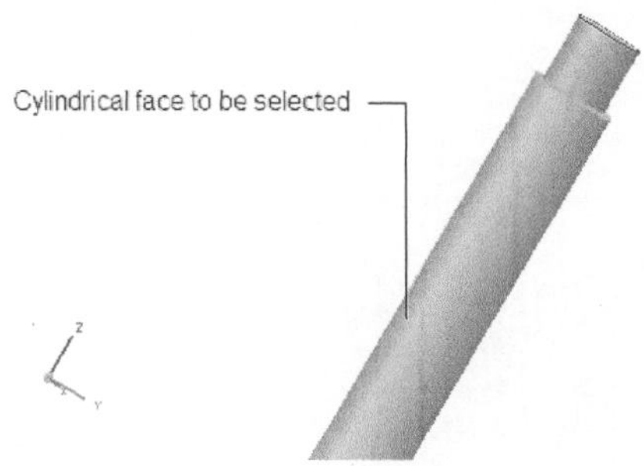

Figure 8-64 *Cylindrical face to be selected from the Handle*

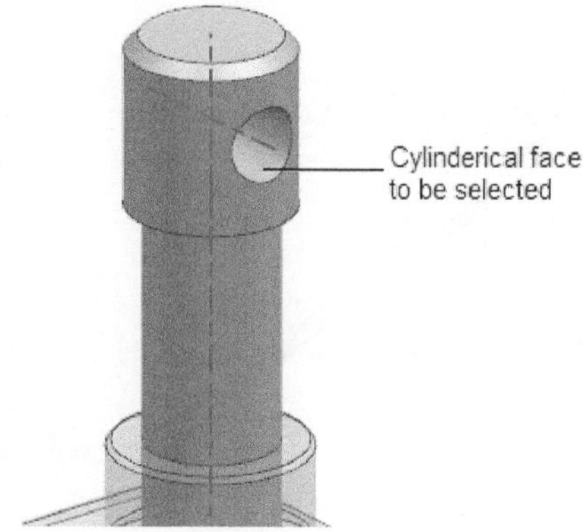

Figure 8-65 *Cylindrical face to be selected from the Screw*

6. Choose the **Distance** option from the **Constraint Type** sub-rollout. Select the YC-ZC plane of the Screw as the first object and the edge of the Handle as the second object, refer to Figure 8-66. Next, enter **86** as the distance value in the **Distance** edit box of the **Distance** sub-rollout and press ENTER.

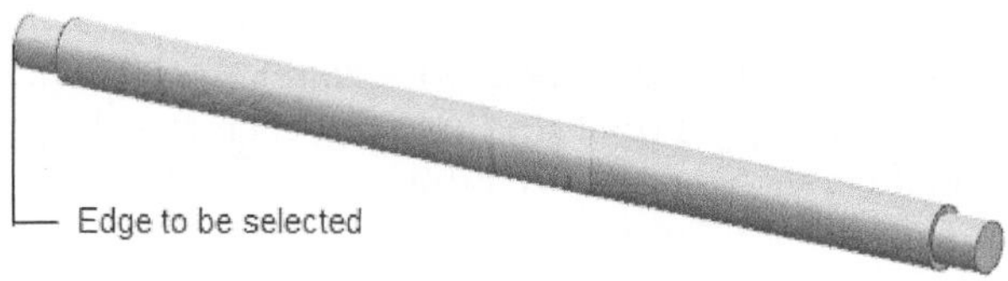

Figure 8-66 *Edge to be selected from the Handle*

7. Choose the **Parallel** option from the **Constraint Type** sub-rollout of the dialog box.

8. Select the datum plane of the Handle as the first object, refer to Figure 8-67. Next, select the top face of the Screw as the second object, refer to Figure 8-68.

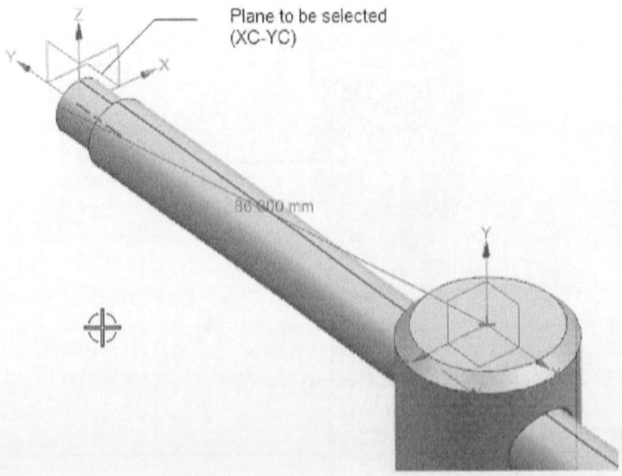

Figure 8-67 *Datum plane to be selected from the Handle*

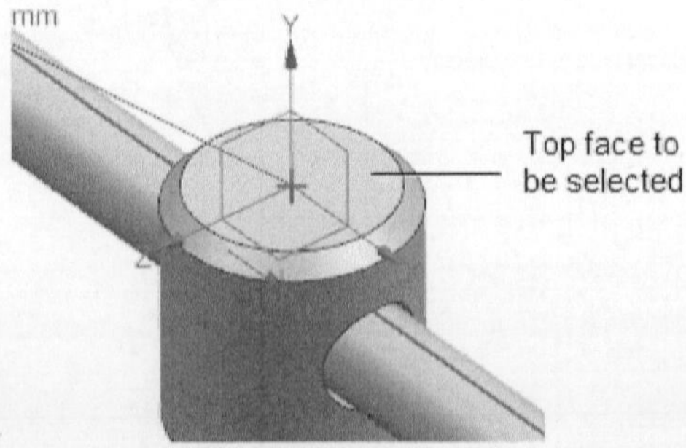

Figure 8-68 *Top face to be selected from the Screw*

9. Choose the **OK** button from the **Add Component** dialog box to exit the dialog box.

10. Choose the **Replace Reference Set** tool from the **More** drop-down of the **Assemblies** tab; the **Class Selection** dialog box is displayed. Select the Handle and the Screw from the assembly and choose the **OK** button from the **Class Selection** dialog box; the **Replace Reference Set** dialog box is displayed. 

11. Select the **MODEL** option from the list box of the dialog box. Next, choose the **OK** button; the display of the reference sets of the Handle and the Screw is changed. The assembly after assembling the Handle is shown in Figure 8-69.

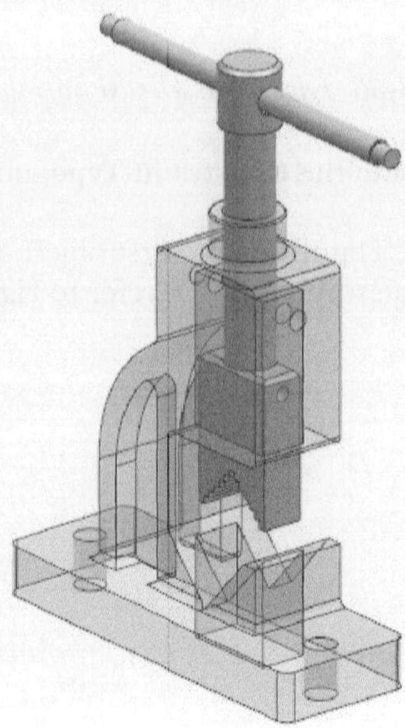

Figure 8-69 *The assembly after assembling the Handle*

Assembling the Handle Screw

Next, you need to assemble the Handle Screw.

1. Change the reference set of the Handle back to **Entire Part**.

2. Choose the **Add** tool from the **Assemblies** tab; the **Add Component** dialog box is displayed.

3. Choose the **Open** button from the **Add Component** dialog box and double-click on the Handle Screw in the **Part Name** dialog box.

4. Next, click in the **Select Object** area of the **Location** rollout; the Handle Screw is attached to the cursor and you are prompted to select location to place the component. Click anywhere in the drawing area to place the component.

5. Choose the **Touch Align** option from the **Constraint Type** sub-rollout and then the **Touch** option from the **Orientation** drop-down list in the **Geometry to Constrain** sub-rollout. 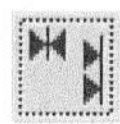

6. Next, select the planar face of the Handle Screw, refer to Figure 8-70, and then select the planar face of the Handle, refer to Figure 8-71.

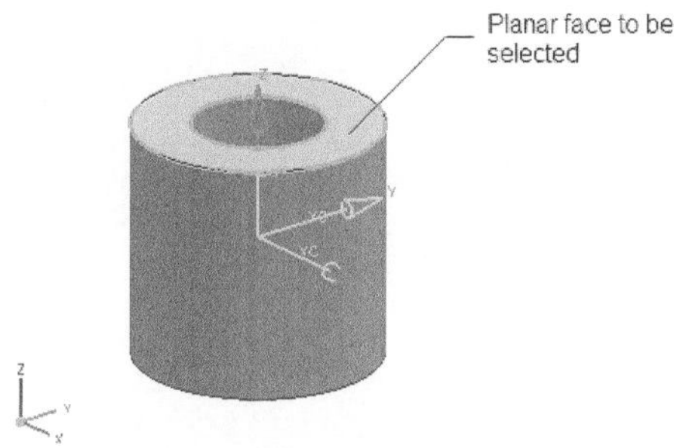

Figure 8-70 Planar face of the Handle Screw

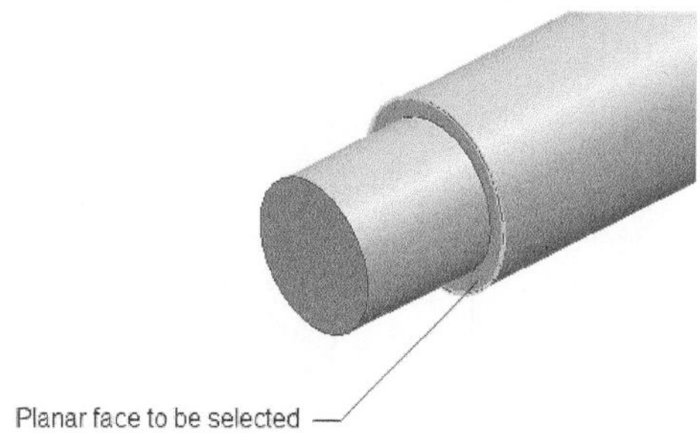

Figure 8-71 Planar face of the Handle

7. Now, select the **Infer Center/Axis** option from the **Orientation** drop-down list in the **Geometry to Constrain** sub-rollout.

8. Select the cylindrical face of the Handle Screw, refer to Figure 8-72, and then select the cylindrical face of the Handle, refer to Figure 8-73.

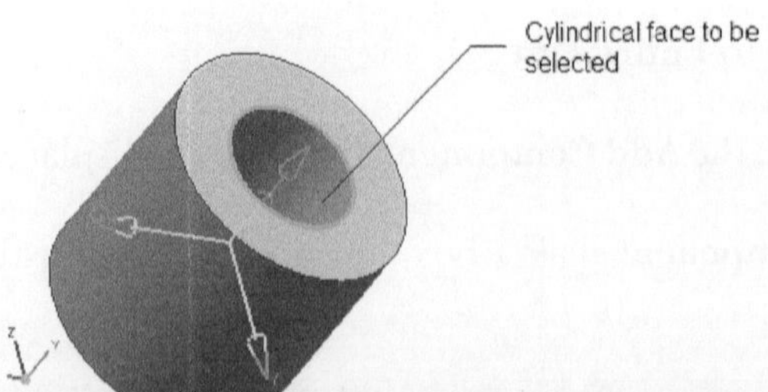

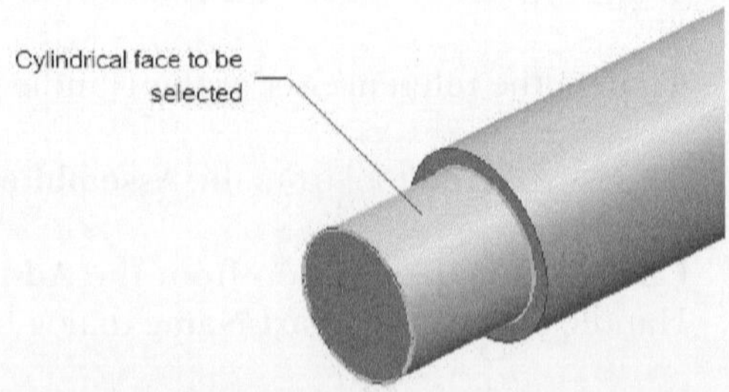

Figure 8-72 Cylindrical face of the Handle Screw

Figure 8-73 Cylindrical face of the Handle

9. Select the **Parallel** option from the **Constraint Type** sub-rollout of the dialog box.

10. Select the XC-YC datum plane of the Handle Screw, refer to Figure 8-74, and then select the XC-YC datum plane of the Handle, refer to Figure 8-75.

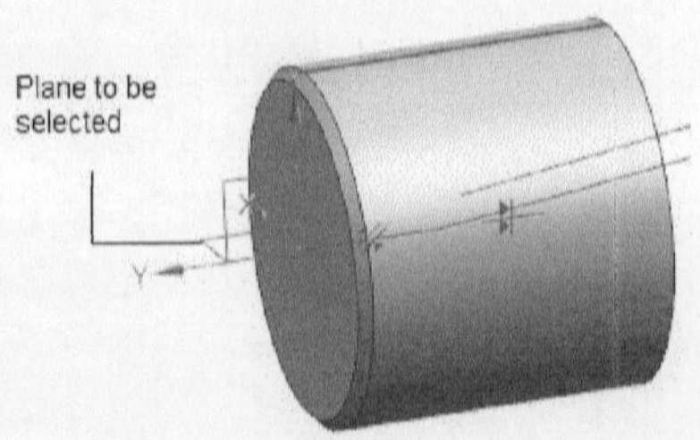

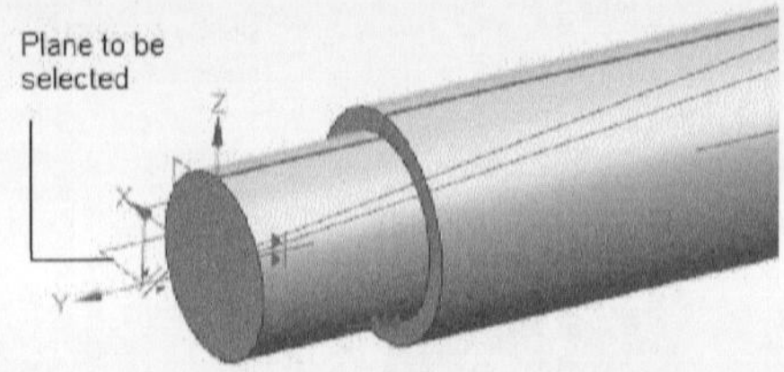

Figure 8-74 Datum plane of the Handle Screw

Figure 8-75 Datum plane of the Handle

11. Next, choose the **OK** button from the **Add Component** dialog box to exit it.
12. Change the reference set of the Handle Screw and the Handle to **MODEL**. The assembly after assembling one of the Handle Screws is shown in Figure 8-76.

13. Similarly, assemble the other instance of the Handle Screw at the other end of the Handle.

14. Change the reference set of all the components to **MODEL**. Also, change the texture of the Base component from transparent to solid. The final Pipe Vice assembly is shown in Figure 8-77.

Note

To turn off the display of the constraints, as shown in Figure 8-77, choose the ***Assembly Navigator*** *tab from the* ***Resource Bar****; the* ***Assembly Navigator*** *cascading menu is displayed. Next, right-click on the* ***Constraints*** *node; a shortcut menu is displayed. Next, clear the check mark on the left of the* ***Display Constraints in Graphics Window*** *option by choosing it.*

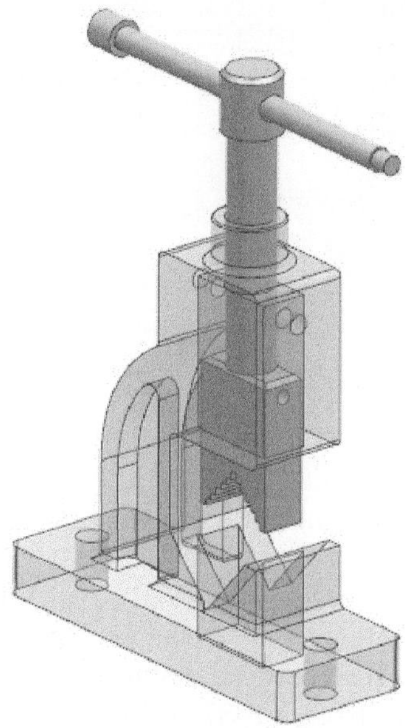

Figure 8-76 *The assembly after assembling the left side Handle Screw*

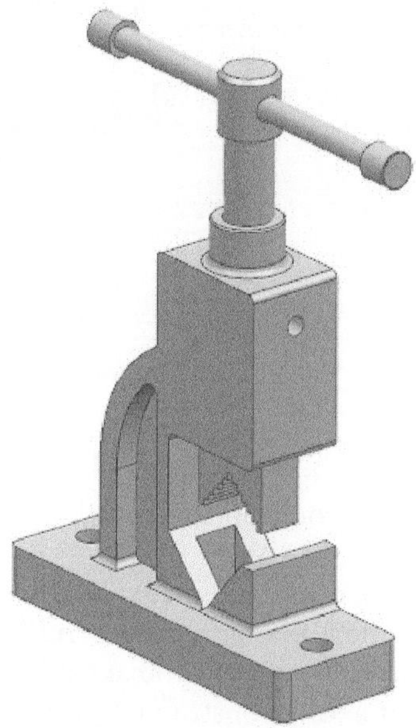

Figure 8-77 *The final Pipe Vice assembly*

Saving and Closing the File

1. Choose **Menu > File > Close > Save and Close** from the **Top Border Bar** to save and close the file.

Tutorial 2

In this tutorial, you will create the components of the Plummer Block assembly shown in Figure 8-78 and then assemble them. The dimensions of the components are given in Figures 8-79 through 8-81. Save the file with the name *Plummer Block.prt* at the location *NX\c08\Plummer Block.*

(Expected time: 2.5 hrs)

Figure 8-78 The Plummer Block assembly

The following steps are required to complete this tutorial:

a. Create all components as individual part files and save them in the *Plummer Block* folder at the location *|NX|c08*.
b. Start a new file and invoke the Assembly environment.
c. Insert the Casting in the assembly window and assemble it, refer to Figure 8-82.
d. Insert the Brasses in the assembly window and apply the required assembly constraints to make it a fully-constrained part, refer to Figures 8-83 through 8-87.
e. Insert the Cap in the assembly window and apply the required assembly constraints, refer to Figures 8-88 through 8-92.
f. Assemble the Bolts by using the required assembly constraints, refer to Figures 8-93 through 8-97.
g. Assemble the Nuts by using the required assembly constraints, refer to Figures 8-98 through 8-102.
h. Assemble the Lock Nuts by using the required assembly constraints, refer to Figures 8-103 through 8-106.

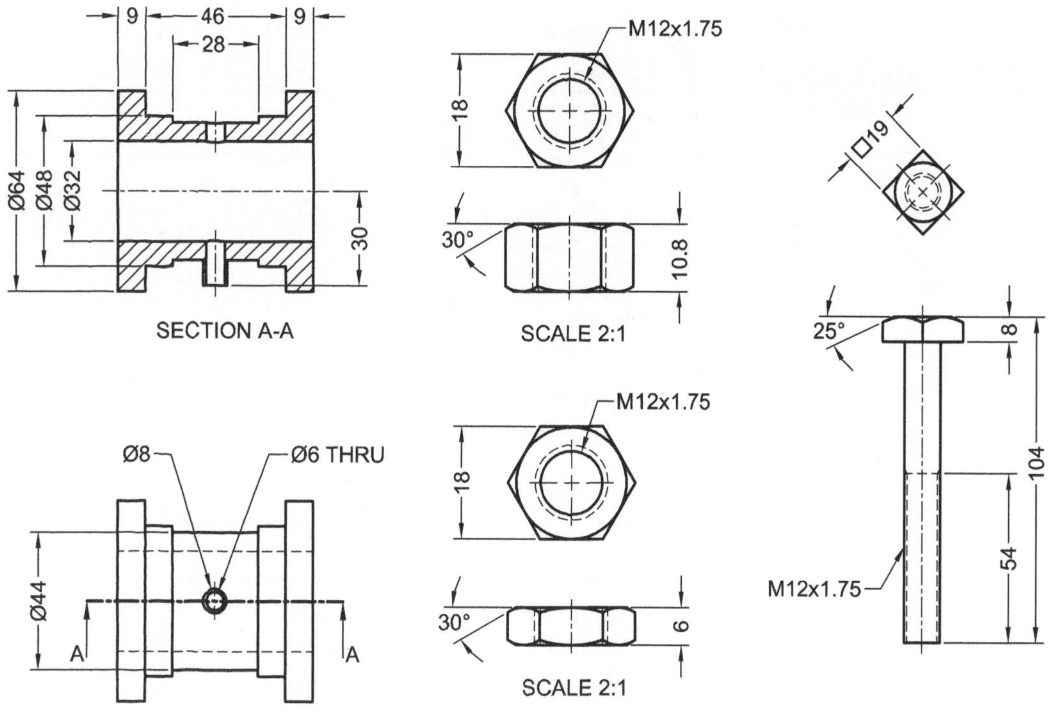

Figure 8-79 *Views and dimensions of Brasses, Nut, Lock Nut, and Bolt*

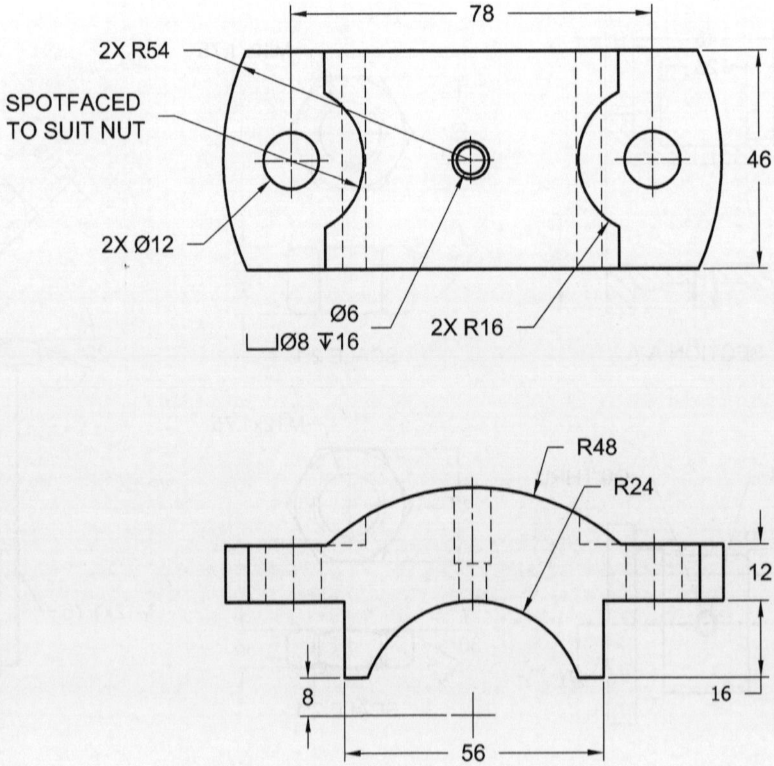

Figure 8-80 Views and dimensions of the Cap

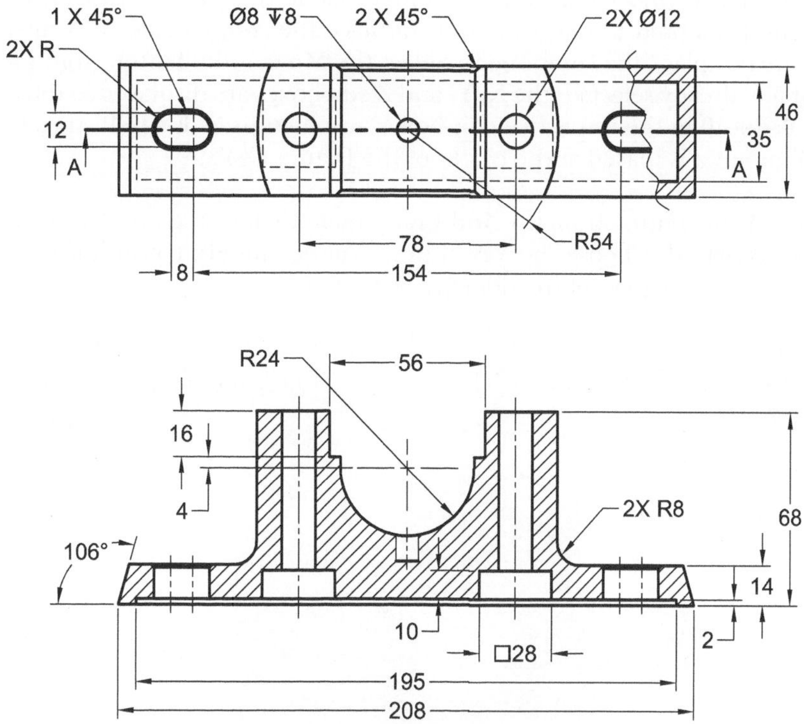

SECTION A-A

Figure 8-81 Views and dimensions of the Casting

Creating Assembly Components

1. Create all components of the Plummer Block assembly as separate part files. Specify the names of the files as mentioned in the drawing views. Save the files at the location *\NX\c08\Plummer Block.*

Starting a New Assembly File

1. Start a new file with the name *Plummer Block.prt* by using the **Model** template and specify its location as *C:\NX\c08\Plummer Block.*

2. Invoke the Assembly environment, if it is not already invoked, by choosing the **Assemblies** tab from the **Ribbon**.

Assembling the Casting with the Datum Planes

1. Choose the **Add** tool from the **Assemblies** tab; the **Add Component** dialog box is displayed.

2. Choose the **Open** button from the **Add Component** dialog box; the **Part Name** dialog box is displayed.

3. Double-click on the Casting in the **Part Name** dialog box. Next, select the **Entire Part** option from the **Reference Set** drop-down list in the **Settings** rollout.

4. Click in the **Select Object** area of the **Location** rollout; the Casting is attached to the cursor and you are prompted to select location to place the component. Click anywhere in the drawing area to place the component. Select the **Move** radio button from the **Placement** rollout, if not already selected; the **X**, **Y**, and **Z** edit boxes are displayed in the drawing area. Enter **0**, **0**, and **0** in the respective edit boxes and then press ENTER; the absolute origin of the component is placed at the origin of the Datum CSYS.

5. Choose the **Apply** button from the **Add Component** dialog box; the **Create Fix Constraint** window is displayed. Choose the **Yes** button from it; the **Fix** constraint is applied to the Casting and all its degrees of freedom are restricted.

6. Right-click on the Casting to display a shortcut menu. Next, choose **Replace Reference Set > MODEL** from the shortcut menu. The assembly after assembling the Casting is shown in Figure 8-82.

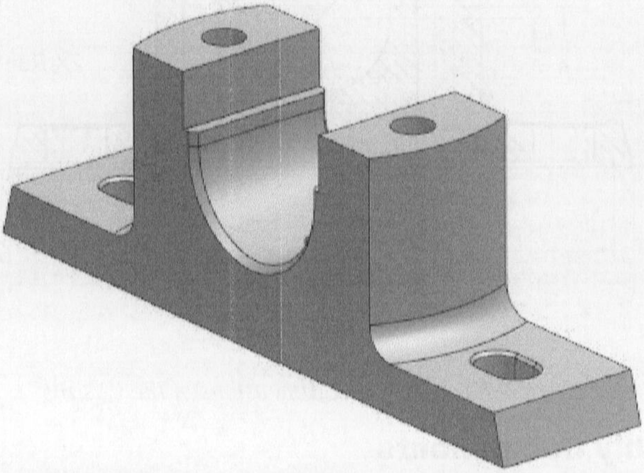

Figure 8-82 *Casting assembled in the Assembly environment*

Note

*In this tutorial, the display of the constraints has been turned off. To do so, click on the **Assembly Navigator** tab in the **Resource Bar**; the **Assembly Navigator** cascading menu is displayed. Right-click on the **Constraints** node; a shortcut menu is displayed. Next, clear the check mark on the left of the **Display Constraints in Graphics Window** option by choosing it.*

Assembling the Second Component

After inserting the Casting, you need to assemble Brasses as the second component.

1. Choose the **Add** tool from the **Assemblies** tab; the **Add Component** dialog box is displayed.

2. Choose the **Open** button from the **Add Component** dialog box; the **Part Name** dialog box is displayed.

3. Double-click on the Brasses in the **Part Name** dialog box. Next, select the **Model ("MODEL")** option from the **Reference Set** drop-down list in the **Settings** rollout.

4. Next, click in the **Select Object** area of the **Location** rollout; the Brasses is attached to the cursor and you are prompted to select location to place the component. Click anywhere in the drawing area to place the component. Select the **Constrain** radio button in the **Placement** rollout; the **Constrain Type** sub-rollout is displayed.

5. Choose the **Touch Align** option from the **Constraint Type** sub-rollout and then select the **Infer Center/Axis** option from the **Orientation** drop-down list in the **Geometry to Constrain** sub-rollout.

6. Select the cylindrical face of the Brasses, refer to Figure 8-83, and then select the cylindrical face of the Casting, refer to Figure 8-84.

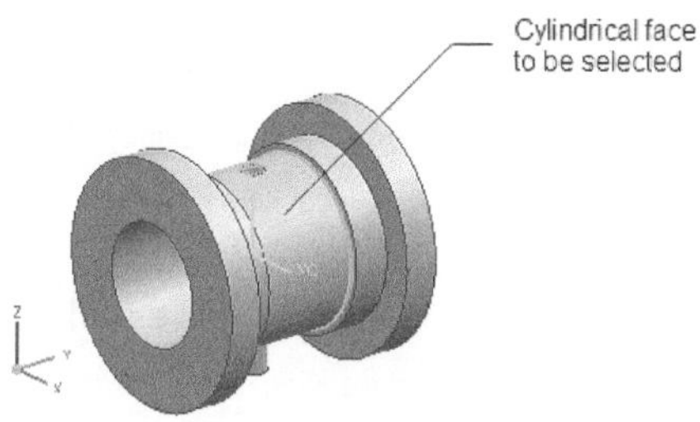

Figure 8-83 *Cylindrical face to be selected from the Brasses*

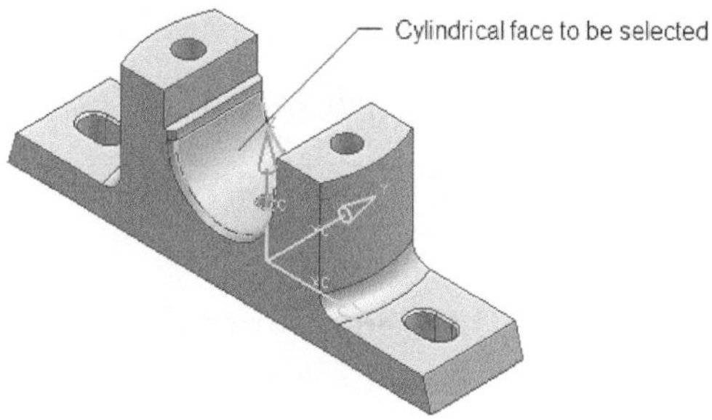

Figure 8-84 *Cylindrical face to be selected from the Casting*

7. Next, select the **Fit** option from the **Constraint Type** sub-rollout of the **Add Component** dialog box.

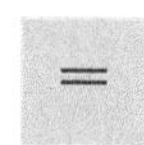

8. Select the cylindrical face of the Brasses, refer to Figure 8-85, and then select the cylindrical face of the Casting, refer to Figure 8-86.

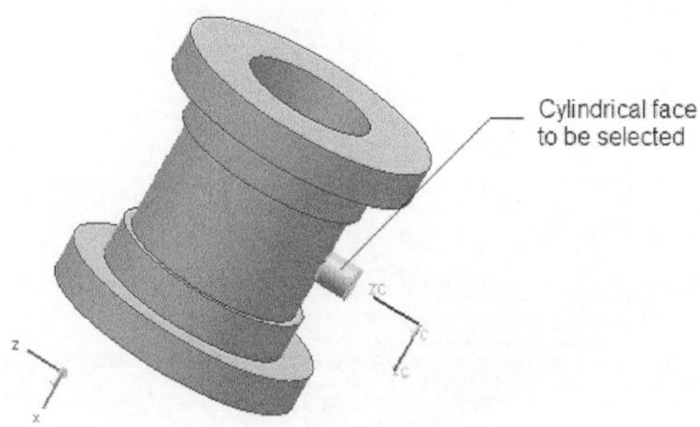

Figure 8-85 *Cylindrical face to be selected from the Brasses*

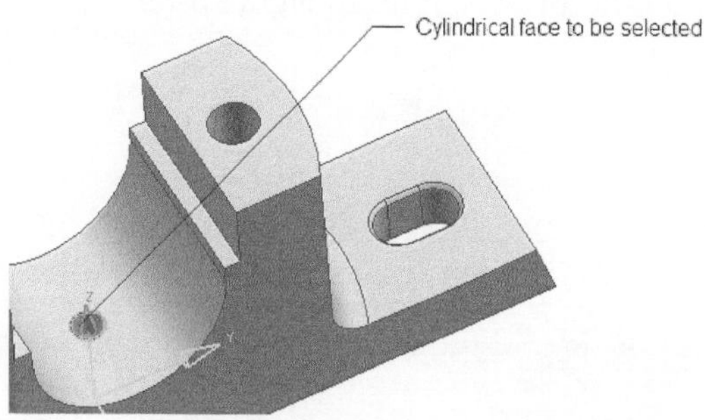

Figure 8-86 *Cylindrical face to be selected from the Casting*

9. Next, choose the **Apply** button from the **Add Component** dialog box.

   The assembly after assembling the Brasses is shown in Figure 8-87.

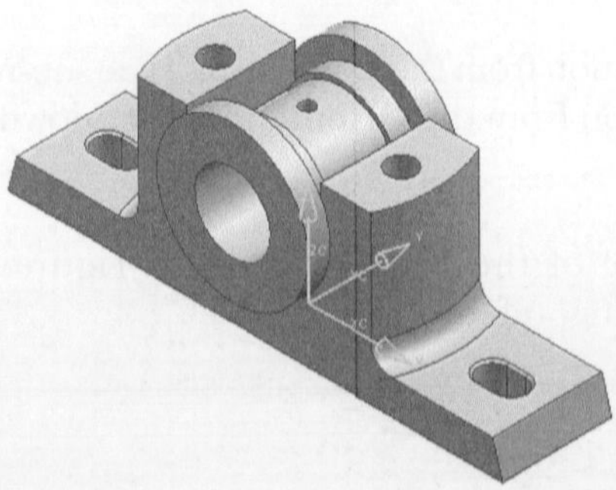

Figure 8-87 Assembly after assembling the Brasses

Assembling the Third Component

Next, you need to assemble the Cap.

1. Choose the **Open** button from the **Add Component** dialog box; the **Part Name** dialog box is displayed.

2. Double-click on the Cap in the **Part Name** dialog box.

3. Next, click in the **Select Object** area of the **Location** rollout; the Cap is attached to the cursor and you are prompted to select location to place the component. Click anywhere in the drawing area to place the component.

4. Choose the **Touch Align** option from the **Constraint Type** sub-rollout and then select the **Infer Center/Axis** option from the **Orientation** drop-down list in the **Geometry to Constrain** sub-rollout. 

5. Select the cylindrical face of the Cap, refer to Figure 8-88. Next, select the cylindrical face of the Brasses, refer to Figure 8-89.

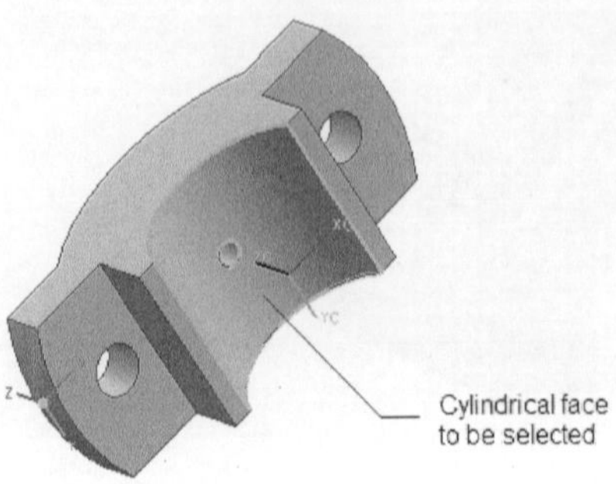

Figure 8-88 *Cylindrical face to be selected from the Cap*

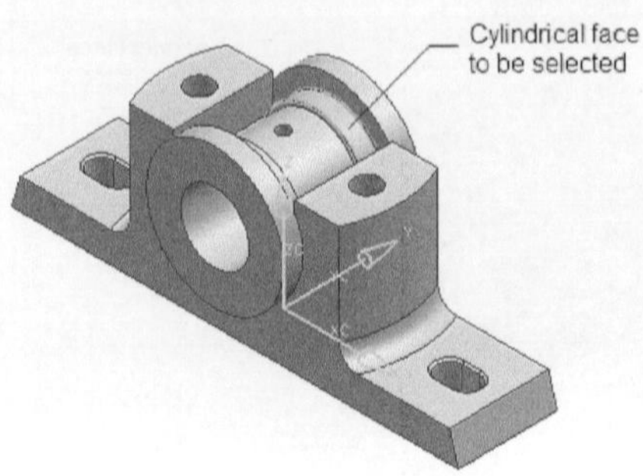

Figure 8-89 *Cylindrical face to be selected from the Brasses*

6. Select the cylindrical face of the Cap, refer to Figure 8-90. Next, select the cylindrical face of the Brasses, refer to Figure 8-91.

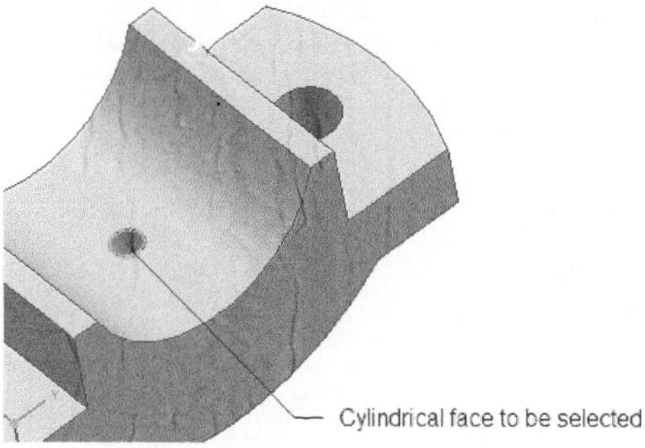

Figure 8-90 *Cylindrical face to be selected from the Cap*

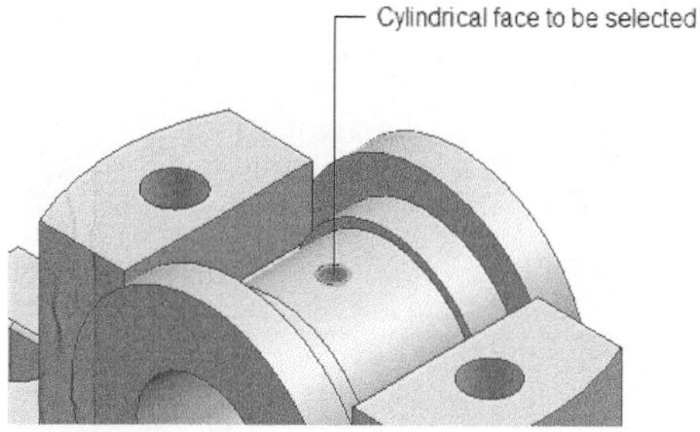

Figure 8-91 *Cylindrical face to be selected from the Brasses*

7. Next, choose the **Apply** button from the **Add Component** dialog box. The resulting assembly after assembling the Cap is shown in Figure 8-92.

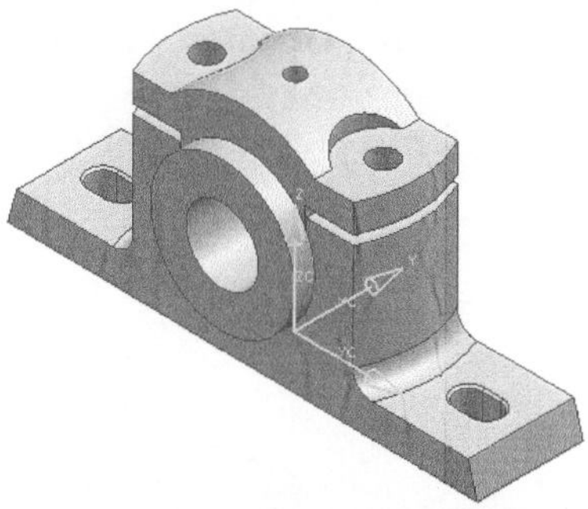

Figure 8-92 *The assembly after assembling the Cap*

Assembling the Bolts

Next, you need to assemble the Bolt as the fourth component.

1. Choose the **Open** button from the **Add Component** dialog box; the **Part Name** dialog box is displayed.

2. Double-click on the Bolt in the **Part Name** dialog box.

3. Next, click in the **Select Object** area of the **Location** rollout; the Bolt is attached to the cursor and you are prompted to select location to place the component. Click anywhere in the drawing area to place the component.

4. Choose the **Align/Lock** option from the **Constraint Type** sub-rollout.

5. Select the cylindrical face of the Bolt, refer to Figure 8-93. Next, select the cylindrical face from the Casting, refer to Figure 8-94.

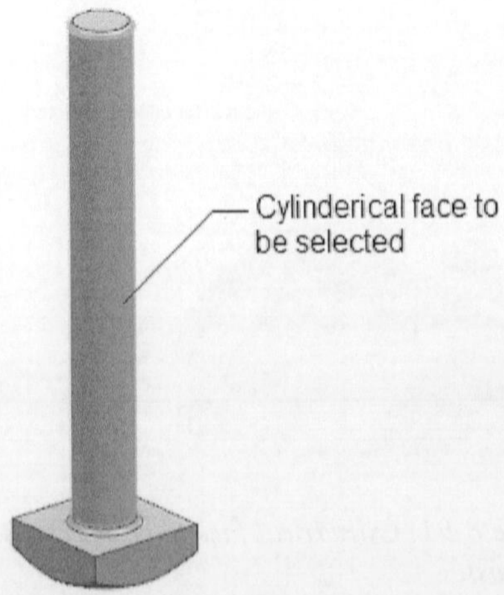

Figure 8-93 Cylindrical face to be selected from the Bolt

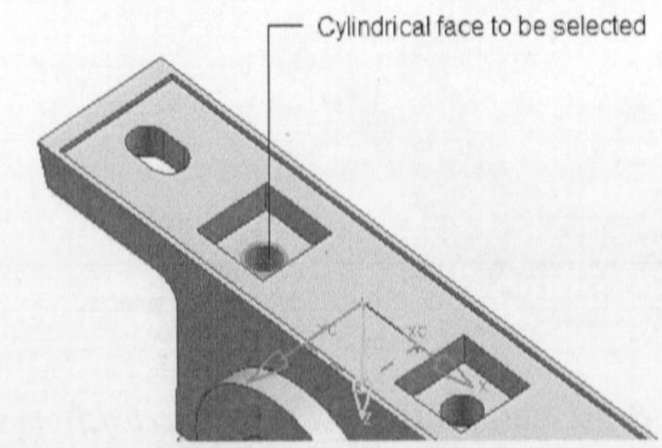

Figure 8-94 Cylindrical face to be selected from the Casting

6. Choose the **Touch Align** option from the **Constraint Type** sub-rollout and the **Touch** option from the **Orientation** drop-down list in the **Geometry to Constrain** sub-rollout.

7. Select the planar face of the Bolt, refer to Figure 8-95. Next, select the planar face of the Casting, refer to Figure 8-96.

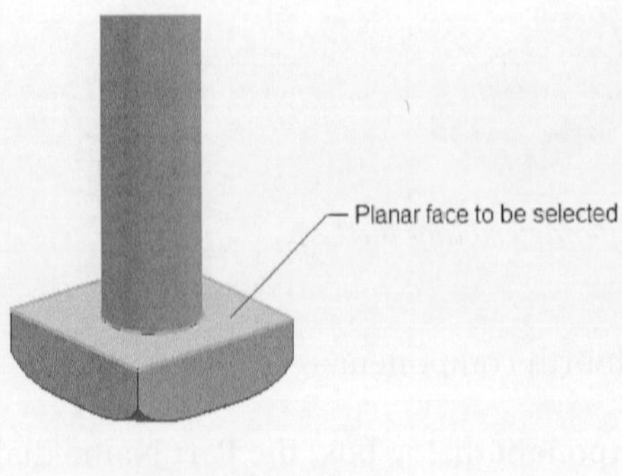

Figure 8-95 Planar face to be selected from the Bolt

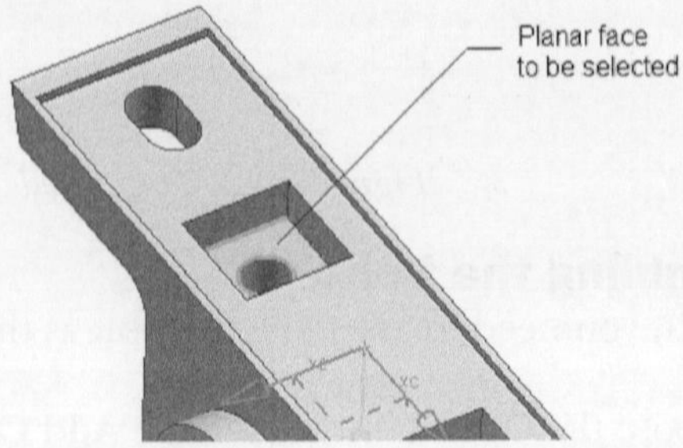

Figure 8-96 Planar face to be selected from the Casting

8. Next, choose the **Apply** button from the **Add Component** dialog box.

9. Similarly, assemble the second instance of the Bolt on the other side. The assembly after assembling the bolts is shown in Figure 8-97.

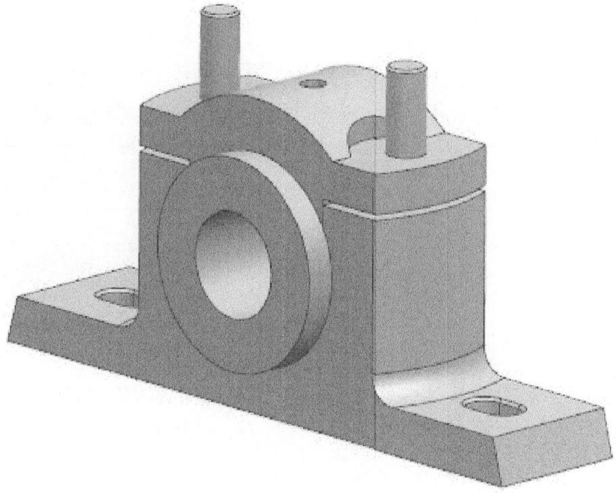

Figure 8-97 The assembly after assembling the Bolts

Note
*To align the bolt head in the casting rectangular slot, you can use the **Parallel** constraint.*

Assembling the Nuts

Next, you need to assemble the Nut as the fifth component.

1. Choose the **Open** button from the **Add Component** dialog box; the **Part Name** dialog box is displayed.

2. Double-click on the Nut in the **Part Name** dialog box.

3. Next, click in the **Select Object** area of the **Location** rollout; the Nut is attached to the cursor and you are prompted to select location to place the component. Click anywhere in the drawing area to place the component.

4. Choose the **Touch Align** option from the **Constraint Type** sub-rollout and then select the **Infer Center/Axis** option from the **Orientation** drop-down list in the **Geometry to Constrain** sub-rollout.

5. Select the cylindrical face of the Nut, refer to Figure 8-98. Next, select the cylindrical face of the Bolt, refer to Figure 8-99.

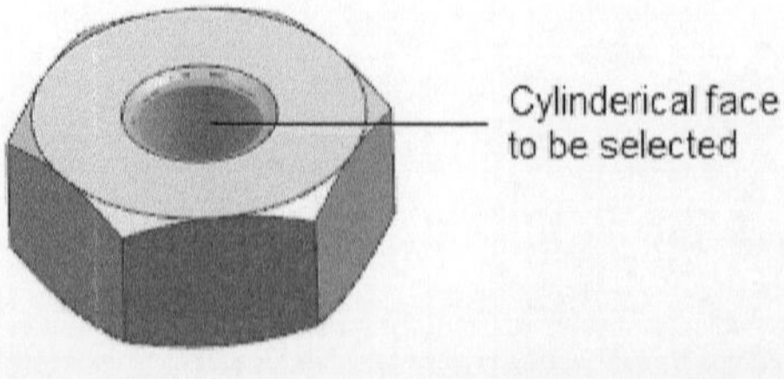

Figure 8-98 Cylindrical face to be selected from the Nut

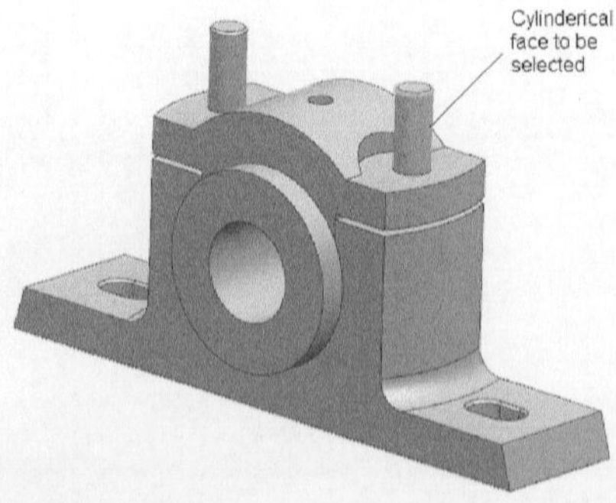

Figure 8-99 Cylindrical face to be selected from Bolt

6. Next, select the **Touch** option from the **Orientation** drop-down list.

7. Rotate the view of the Nut and select its bottom planar face, refer to Figure 8-100. Next, select the planar face from the Cap, refer to Figure 8-101.

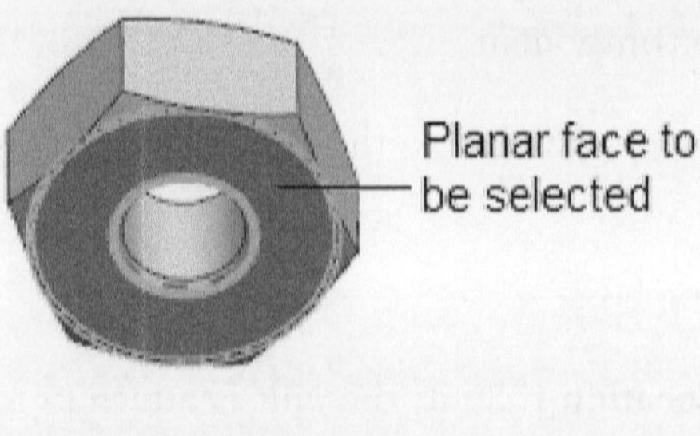

Figure 8-100 Bottom planar face to be selected from the Nut

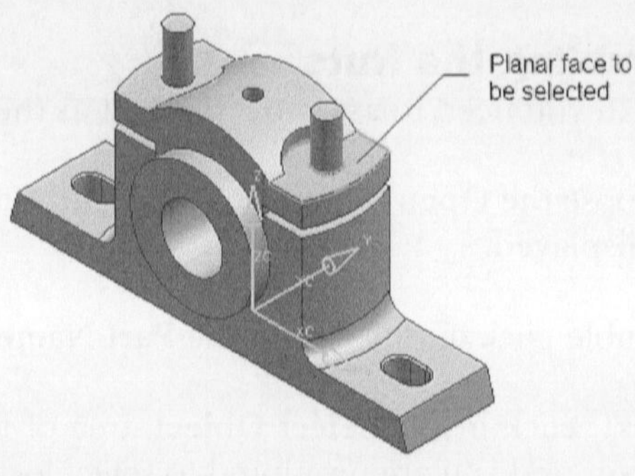

Figure 8-101 Planar face to be selected from the Cap

Note

You might need to turn off the display of the Casting while assembling the nut.

8. Choose the **Apply** button from the **Add Component** dialog box.

9. Similarly, assemble the second instance of the Nut on the other side. The assembly after assembling the Nuts is shown in Figure 8-102.

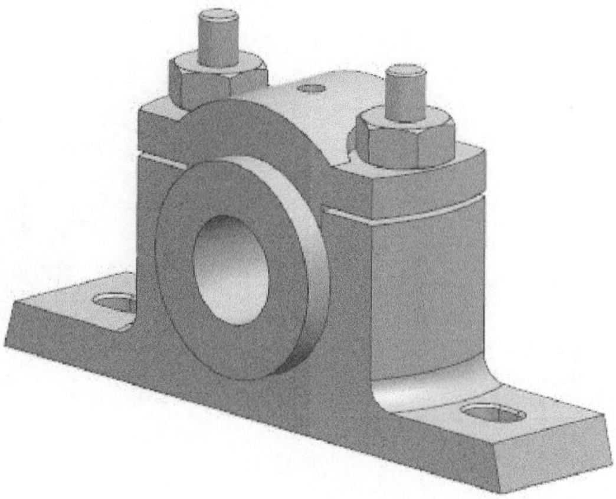

Figure 8-102 The assembly after assembling the Nuts

Tip

While assembling the Nut in the assembly, you should not constrain its rotational degree of freedom because on doing so, it will not be able to pass through the bolt threads to lock the Cap and Brasses with the Casting.

Assembling the Lock Nut

Next, you need to assemble the Lock Nut as the sixth component.

1. Choose the **Open** button from the **Add Component** dialog box; the **Part Name** dialog box is displayed.

2. Double-click on the Lock Nut in the **Part Name** dialog box.

3. Next, click in the **Select Object** area of the **Location** rollout; the Lock Nut is attached to the cursor and you are prompted to select location to place the component. Click anywhere in the drawing area to place the component.

4. Select the **Touch Align** option from the **Constraint Type** sub-rollout and then the **Touch** option from the **Orientation** drop-down list. 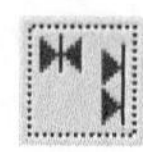

5. Select the planar face of the Lock Nut, refer to Figure 8-103. Next, select the planar face of the Nut, refer to Figure 8-104.

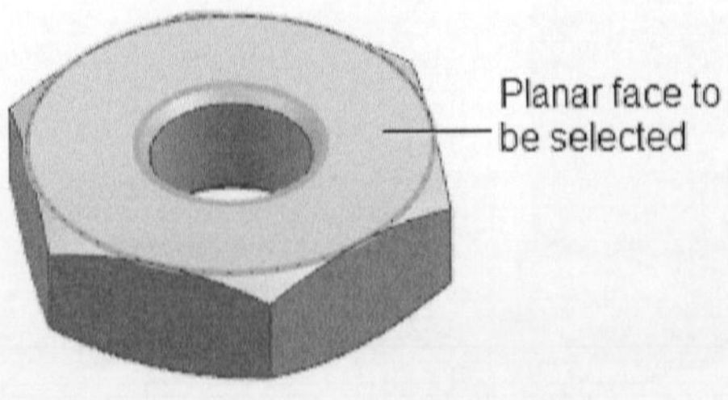

Figure 8-103 *Planar face to be selected from the Lock Nut*

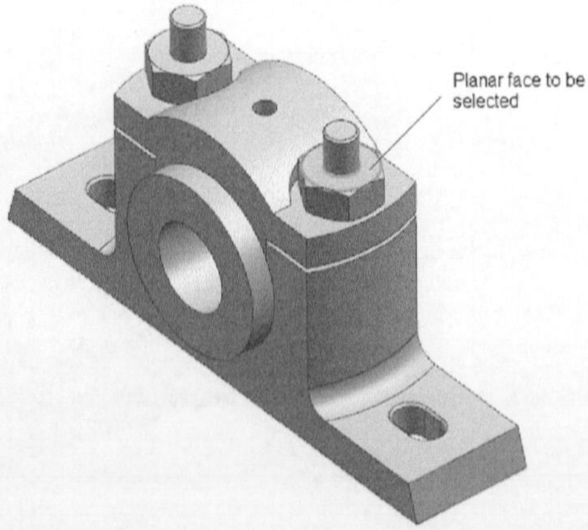

Figure 8-104 *Planar face to be selected from the Nut*

6. Select the **Infer Center/Axis** option from the **Orientation** drop-down list.

7. Select the cylindrical face of the Lock Nut, as shown in Figure 8-105. Next, select the cylindrical face of the Bolt, as shown in Figure 8-106.

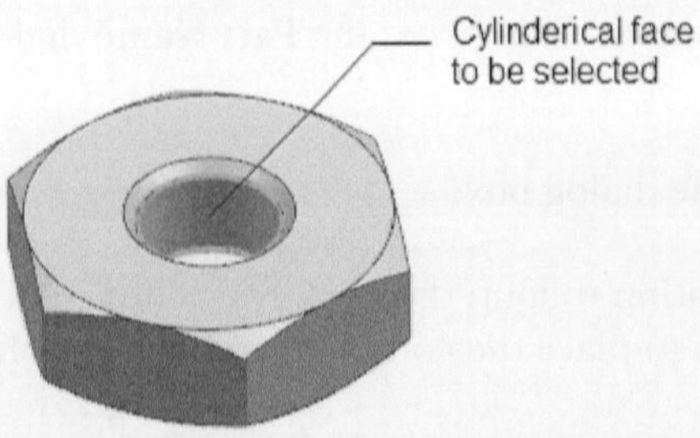

Figure 8-105 *Cylindrical face to be selected from the Lock Nut*

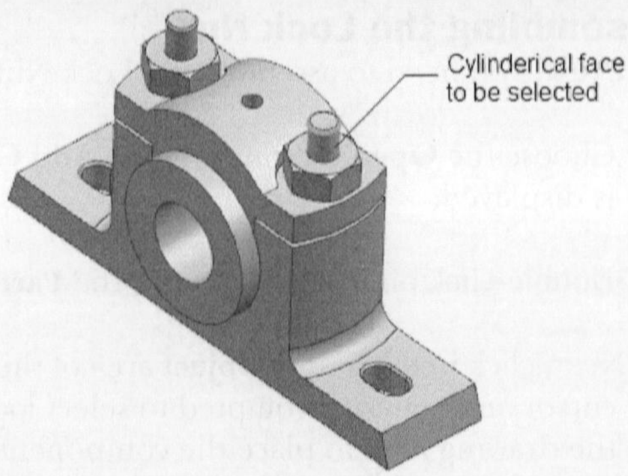

Figure 8-106 *Cylindrical face to be selected from the Bolt*

8. Choose the **Apply** button from the **Add Component** dialog box.

9. Similarly, assemble the second instance of the Lock Nut on the other side and then choose the **OK** button to exit the **Add Component** dialog box. The completed Plummer Block assembly is shown in Figure 8-107.

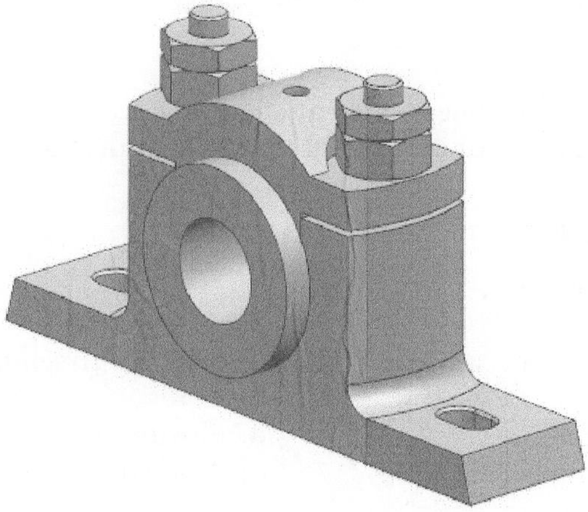

Figure 8-107 The final Plummer Block assembly

Saving and Closing the File

1. Choose **Menu > File > Close > Save and Close** from the **Top Border Bar** to save and close the file.

Self-Evaluation Test

Answer the following questions and then compare them to those given at the end of this chapter:

1. The _________ is the file name extension for the assembly files.

2. The _________ assembly constraint is used to maintain an offset value between the reference faces.

3. You can move and reorient an assembled component in 3D space along the available degrees of freedom using the _________ tool.

4. The _________ constraint is used to constrain two circular or elliptical edges of the components to coincide their centers as well as to make the selected edges coplanar.

5. In the top-down assembly design approach, all the components are created within the same assembly file. (T/F)

6. You can maintain an offset value between two faces by using the **Parallel** constraint. (T/F)

7. You cannot create a component in the Assembly. (T/F)

8. You can invoke the **Assembly Constraints** dialog box by choosing the **Assembly Constraints** tool from the **Assemblies** tab. (T/F)

9. The **Replace Reference Set** tool is used to change the reference set of the component assembled. (T/F)

10. For assembling the base component, it is mandatory to select the **Absolute Origin** option from the **Positioning** drop-down list in the **Add Component** dialog box. (T/F)

Review Questions

Answer the following questions:

1. Which of the following tools is used to invoke the **Mirror Assemblies Wizard** dialog box?

   (a) **Mirror Assembly** (b) **Create Component Array**
   (c) **Replace Reference Set** (d) None of these

2. Which of the following options is used to make the two faces of a component coplanar?

   (a) **Touch Align** (b) **Parallel**
   (c) **Angle** (d) None of these

3. Which of the following options is used to align the central axis of two cylindrical components?

   (a) **Infer Center/Axis** (b) **Perpendicular**
   (c) **Center** (d) None of these

4. The Angle constraint is used to specify an angle between two selected reference objects of the components. (T/F)

5. You cannot edit the Assembly constraints. (T/F)

6. The **Replace Component** tool is used to replace the component that is already placed in an assembly with the new component. (T/F)

7. The Fit constraint is used to bring together two cylindrical faces of different diameters. (T/F)

8. You can apply the Touch Align constraint to constrain the components tangentially. (T/F)

9. If you clear the **Associative** check box in the **Settings** rollout of the **Assembly Constraint** dialog box and choose the **OK** button, the constraint will not be applied. (T/F)

10. The Bond constraint is used to fix the position of the selected components with respect to each other. (T/F)

EXERCISES

Exercise 1

Create the components of the Butterfly Valve assembly and then assemble them, as shown in Figure 8-108. The dimensions of the components are shown in Figures 8-109 through 8-114. Create a folder with the name *\c08\Butterfly Valve Assembly* and save all component files and the assembly file in it. Assume the missing dimensions. **(Expected time: 4 hr)**

Figure 8-108 *The Butterfly Valve assembly*

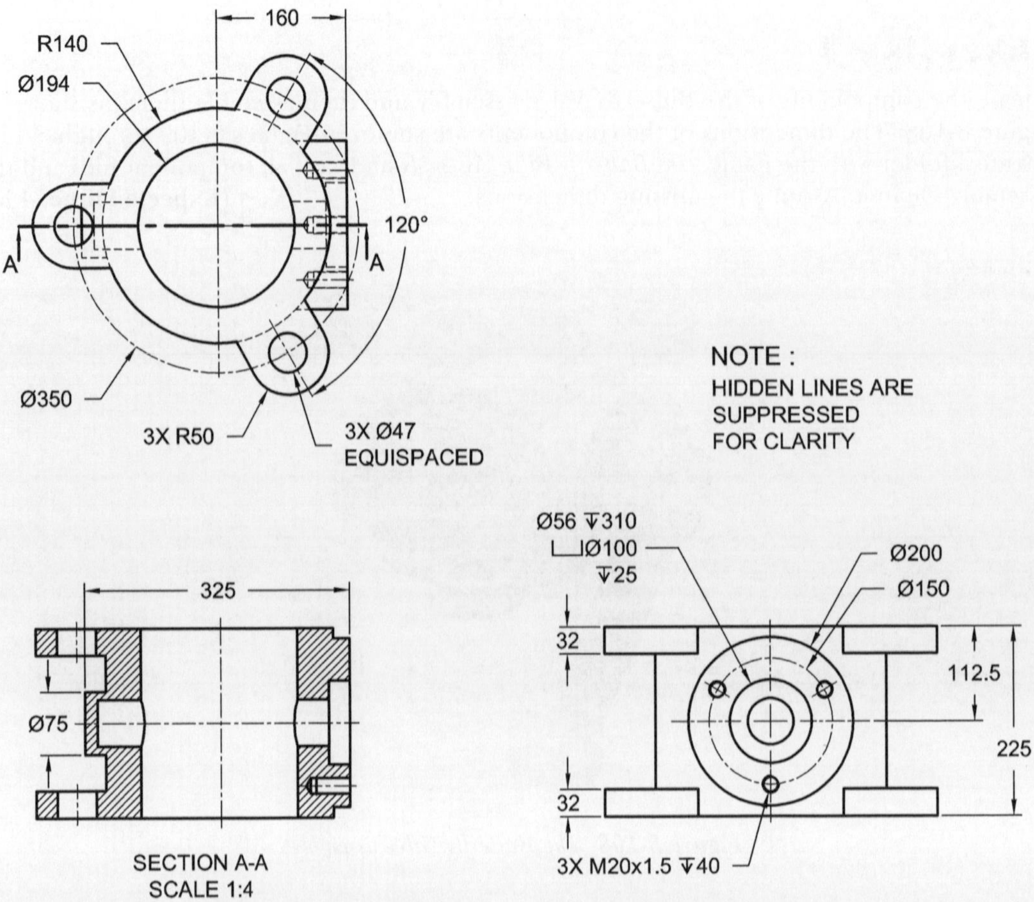

Figure 8-109 *Orthographic views and dimensions of the Body*

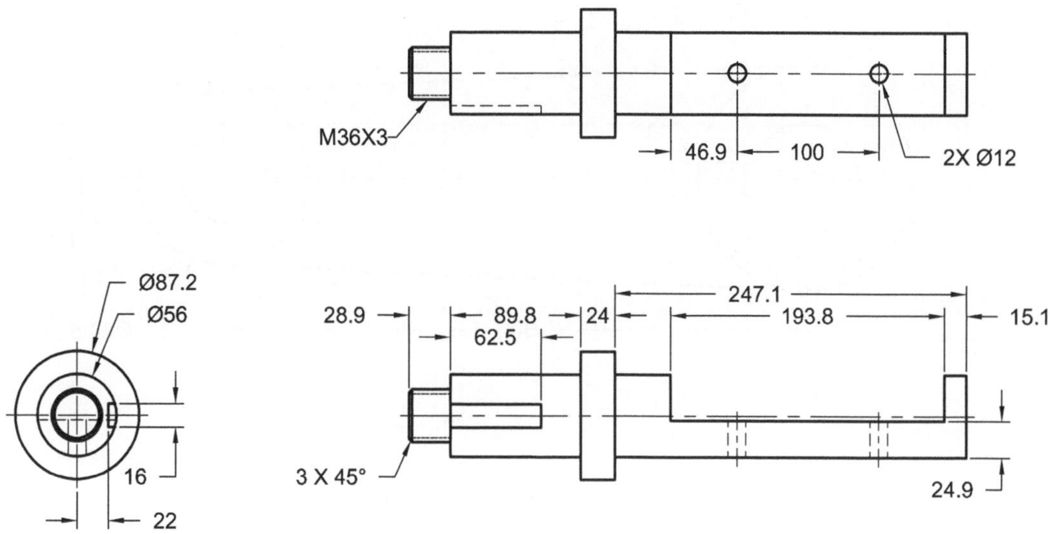

Figure 8-110 Dimensions of the Shaft

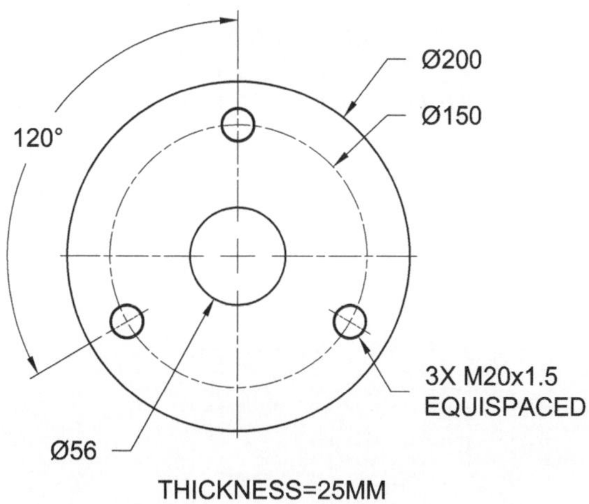

Figure 8-111 Dimensions of the Retainer

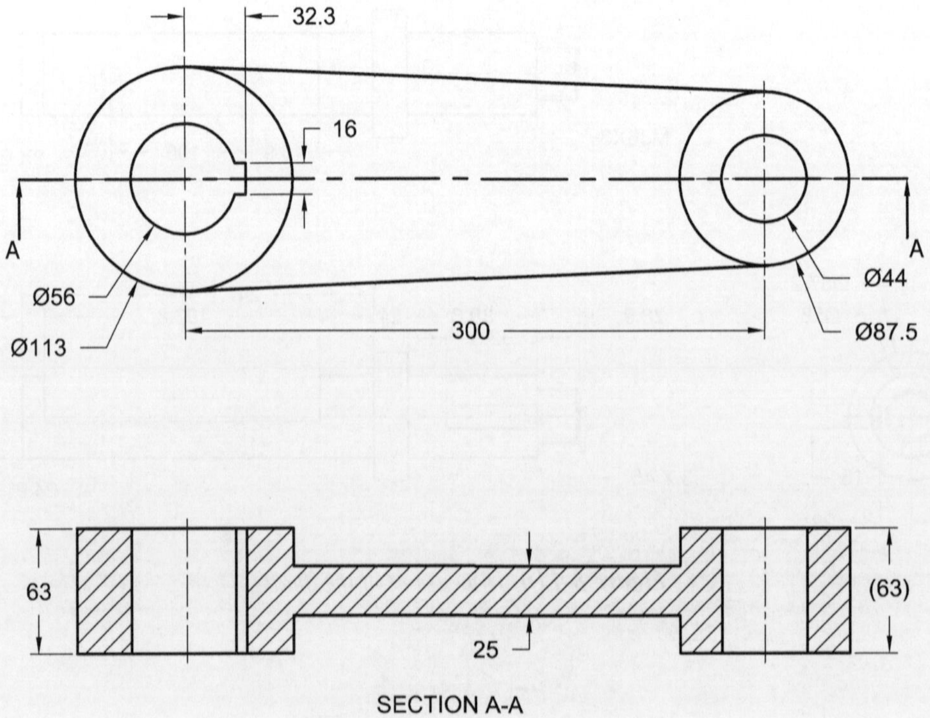

Figure 8-112 *Orthographic views and dimensions of the Arm*

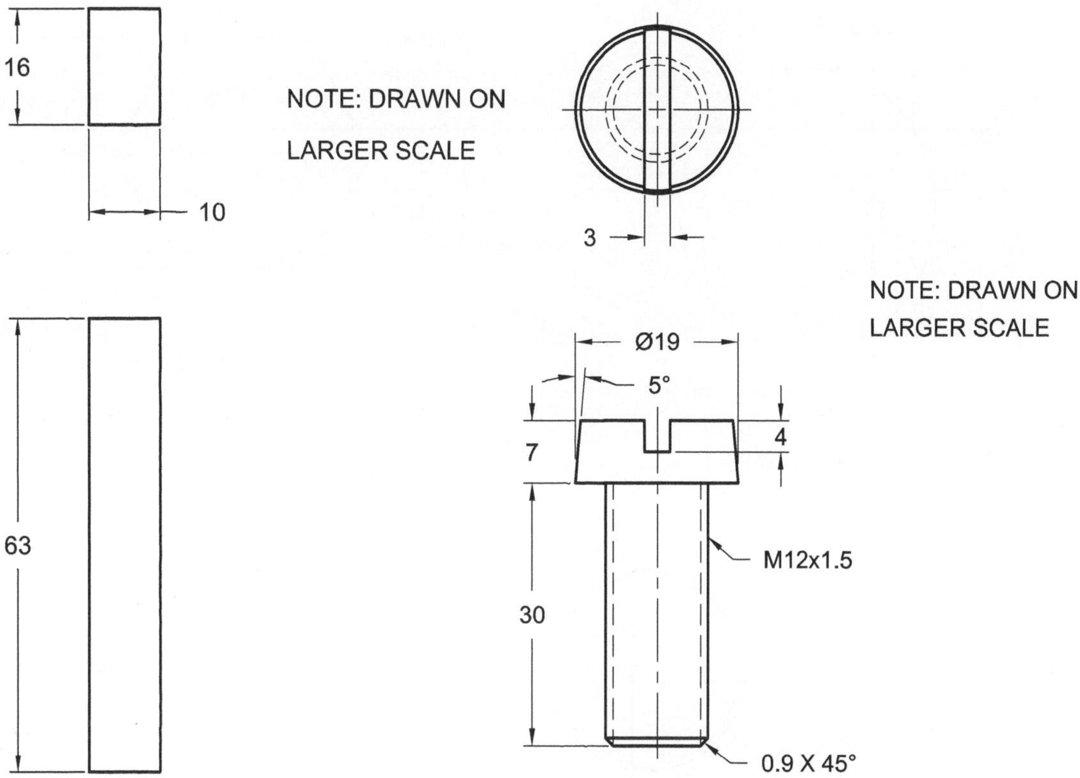

Figure 8-113 *Orthographic views and dimensions of the Parallel Key and the Screw 1*

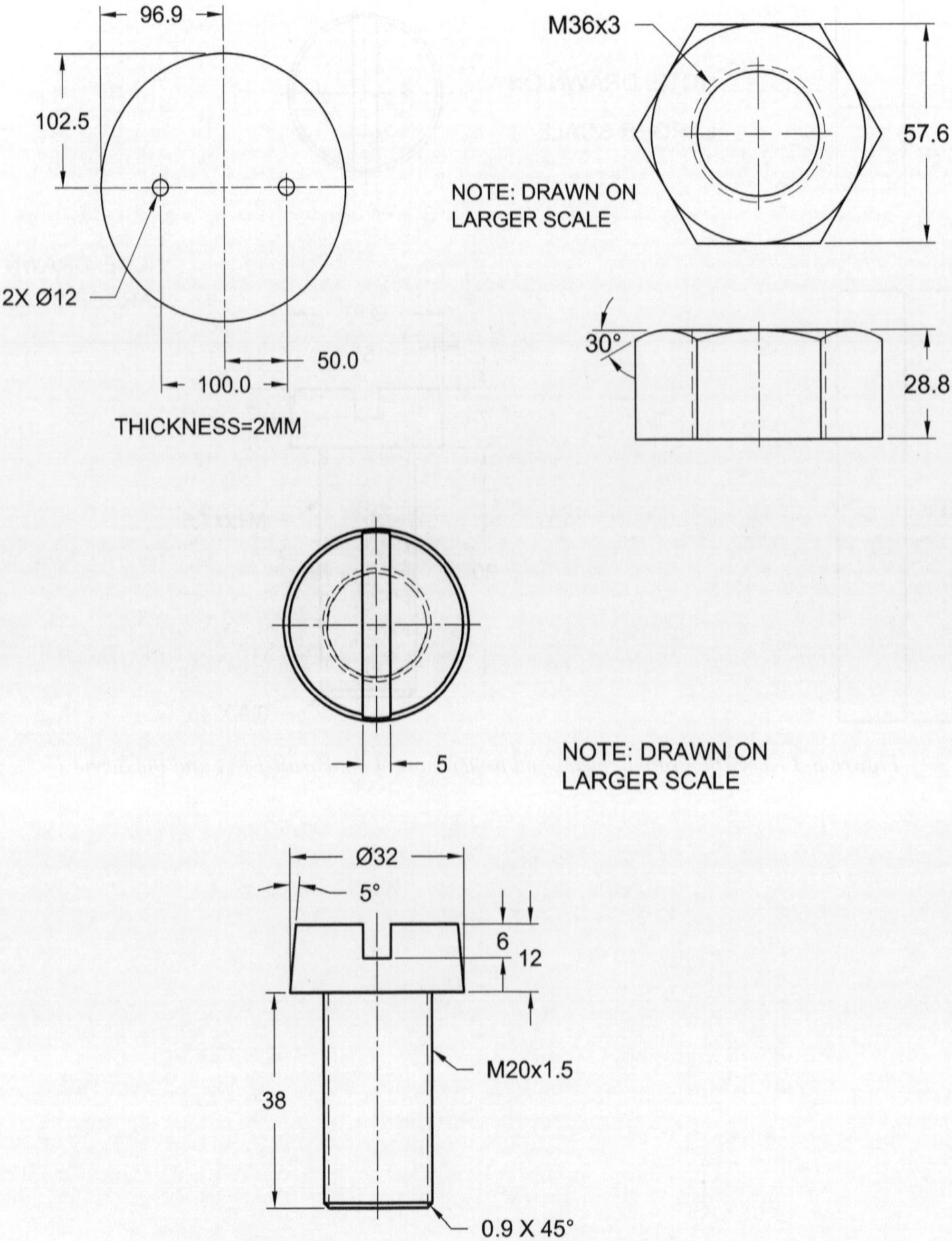

Figure 8-114 *Dimensions of the Plate, Nut, and Screw*

Exercise 2

Create components of the Pulley Support assembly and then assemble them, as shown in Figure 8-115. The exploded view and bill of material of the assembly is shown in Figures 8-116 and 8-117. The dimensions of the components are given in Figures 8-118 through 8-122.

(Expected time: 3 hrs)

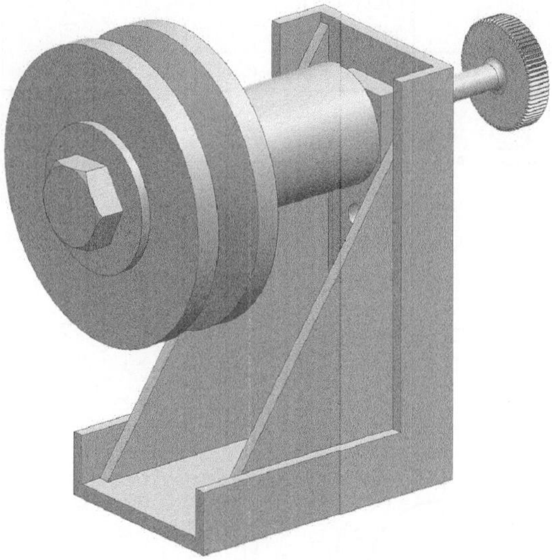

Figure 8-115 *The Pulley Support assembly*

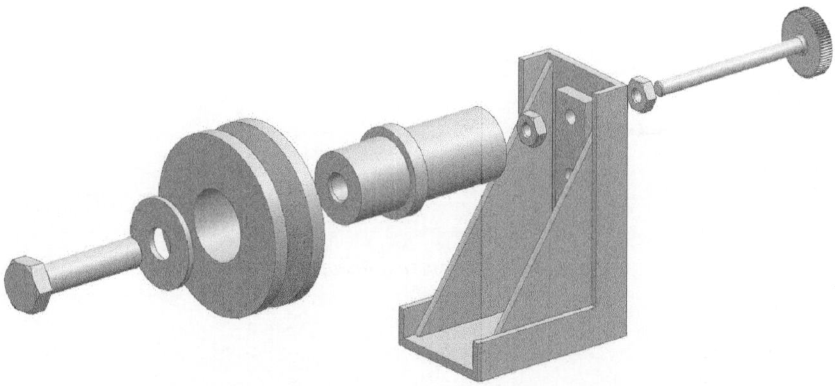

Figure 8-116 *Exploded view of the Pulley Support assembly*

7	THUMB SCREW	1
6	CAP SCREW M5X0.8-20 Hex Head	1
5	WASHER	1
4	NUT M2.5X0.45-2	2
3	BRACKET	1
2	BUSHING	1

Figure 8-117 *Parts list for the Pulley Support assembly*

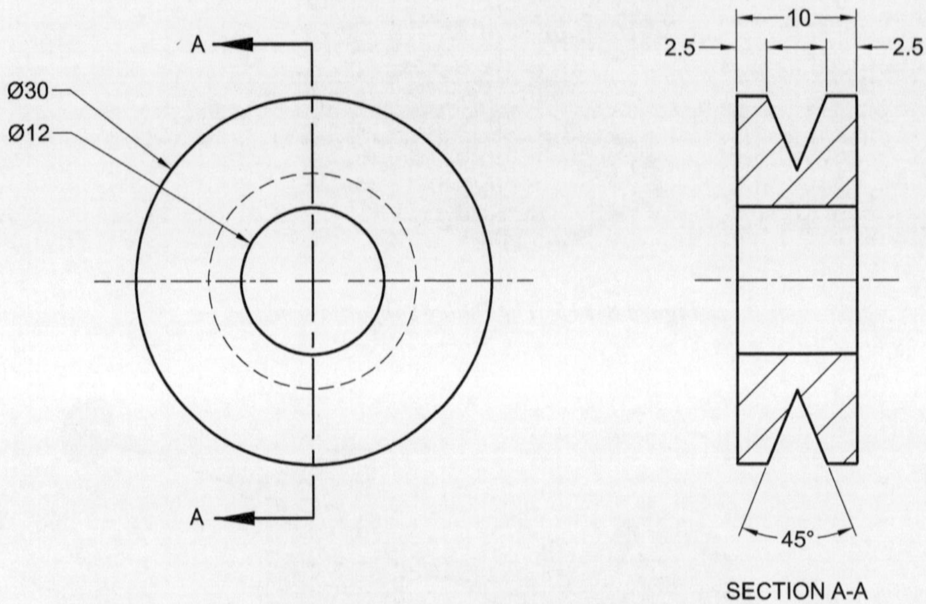

Figure 8-118 *Dimensions of the Pulley*

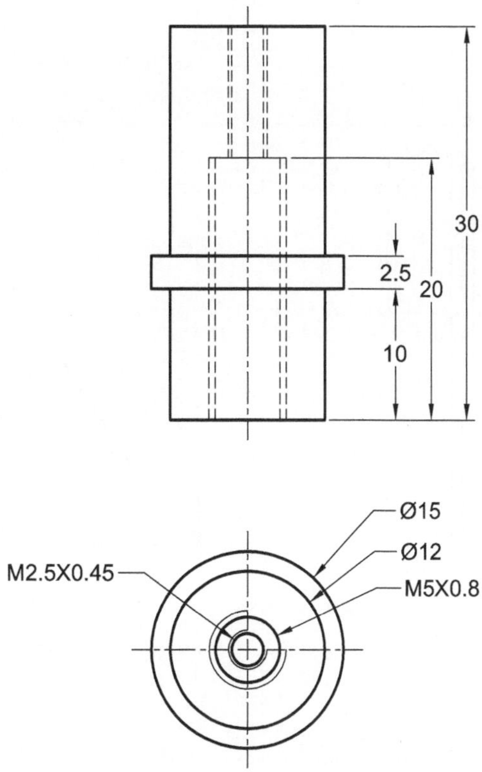

Figure 8-119 Dimensions of the Bushing

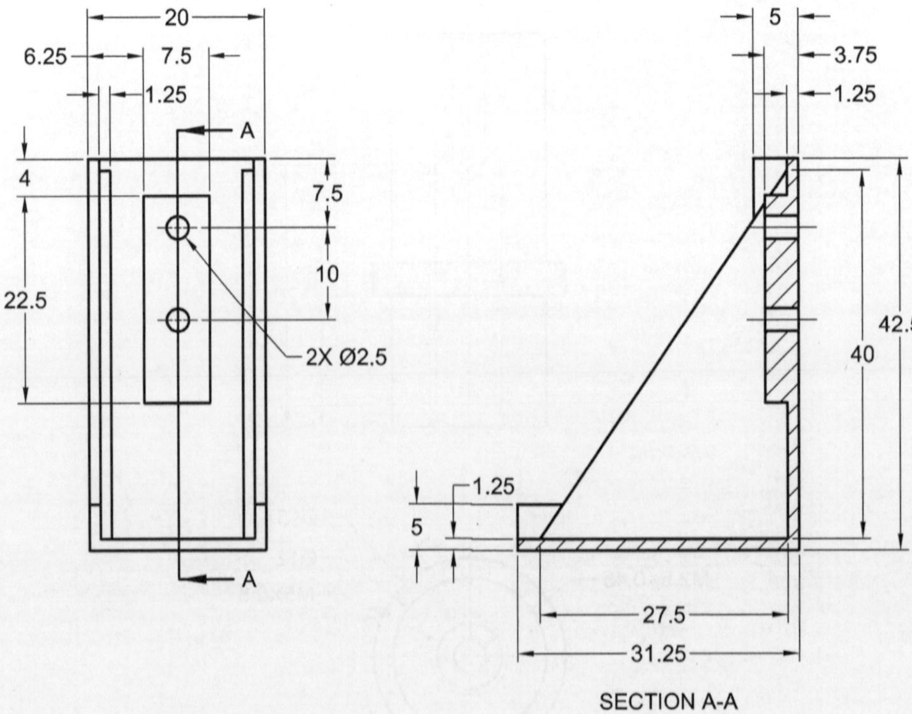

Figure 8-120 Orthographic views and dimensions of the Bracket

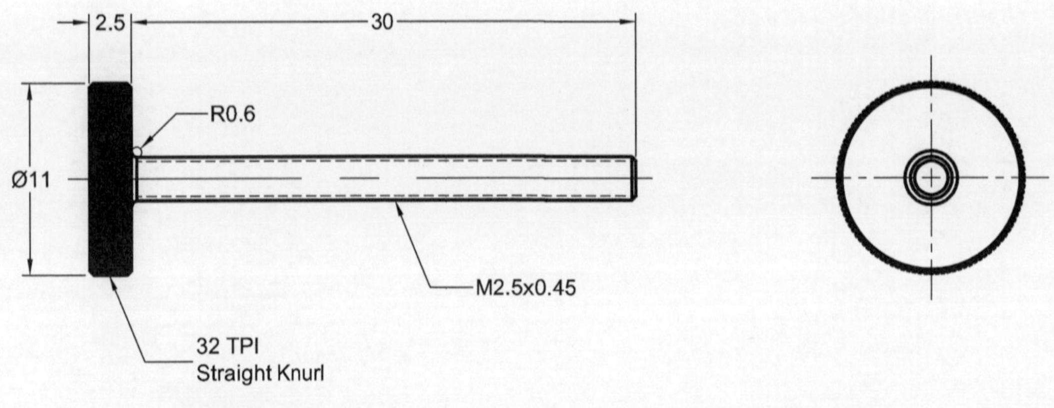

Figure 8-121 Dimensions of the Cap Screw, Nut, and Thumb Screw

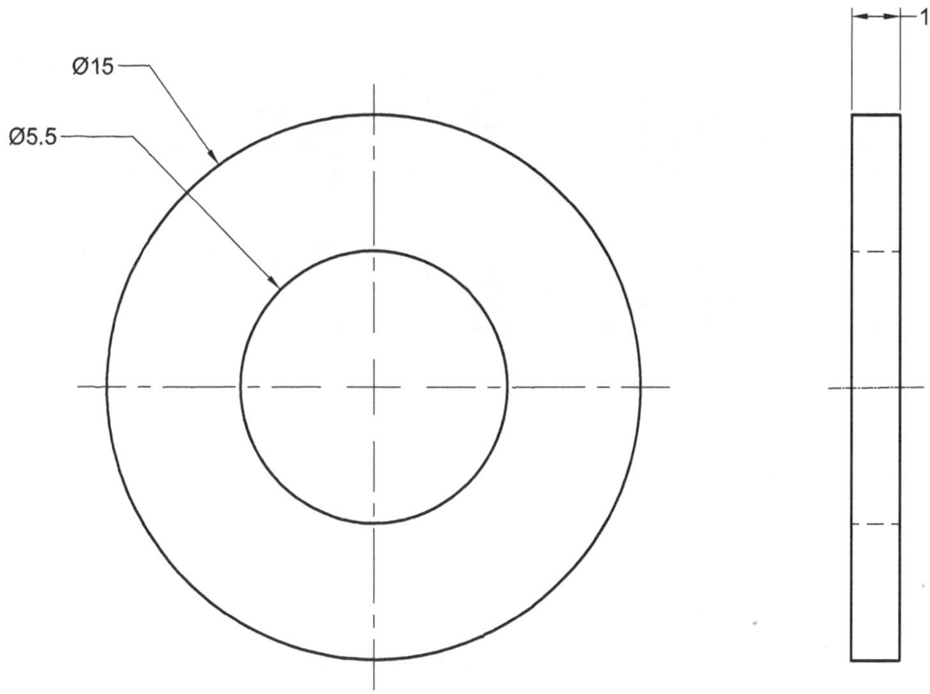

Figure 8-122 Dimensions of the Washer

Exercise 3

Create the Double Bearing assembly shown in Figure 8-123. The dimensions of the components of the assembly are given in Figures 8-124 through 8-127. **(Expected time: 4 hrs)**

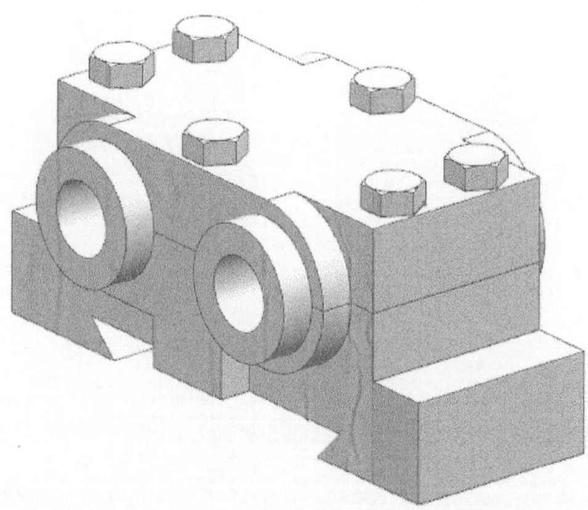

Figure 8-123 The Double Bearing assembly

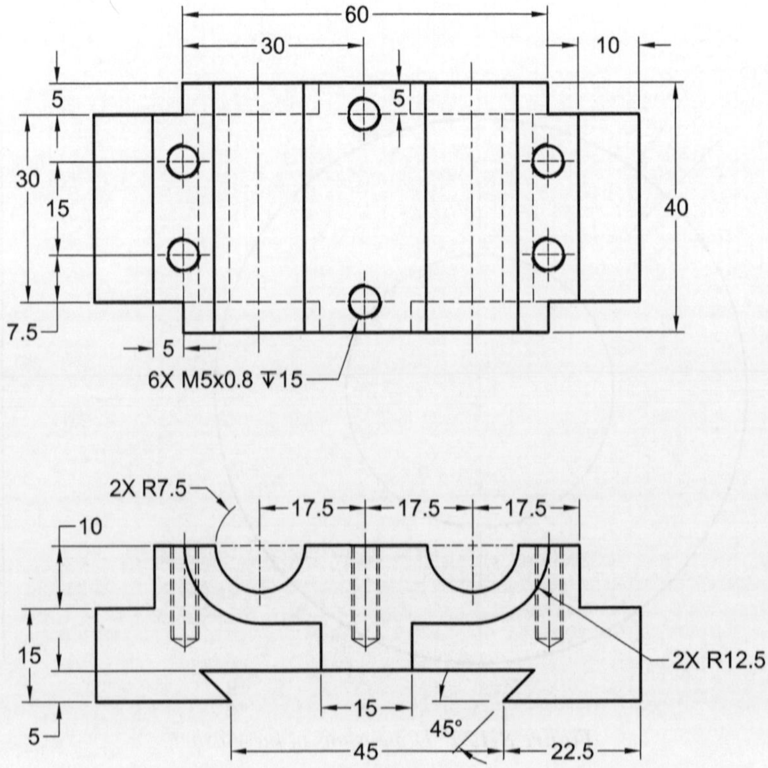

Figure 8-124 Orthographic views of the Base

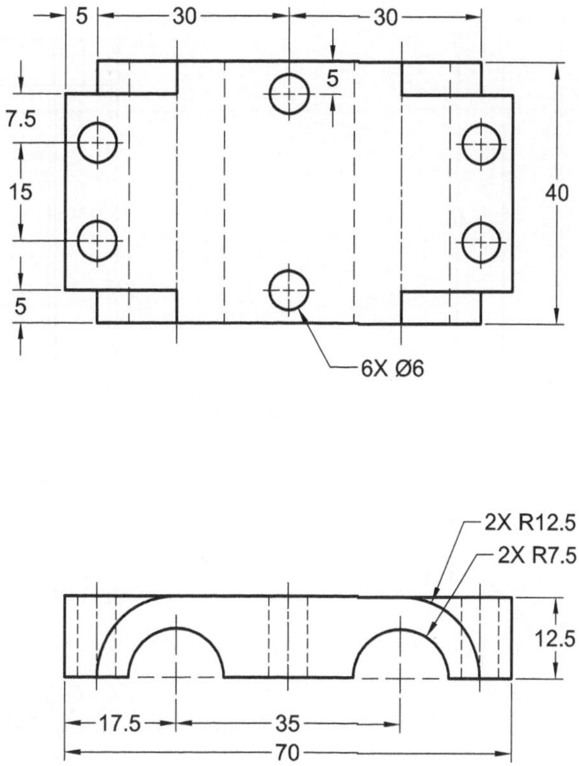

Figure 8-125 Orthographic views of the Cap

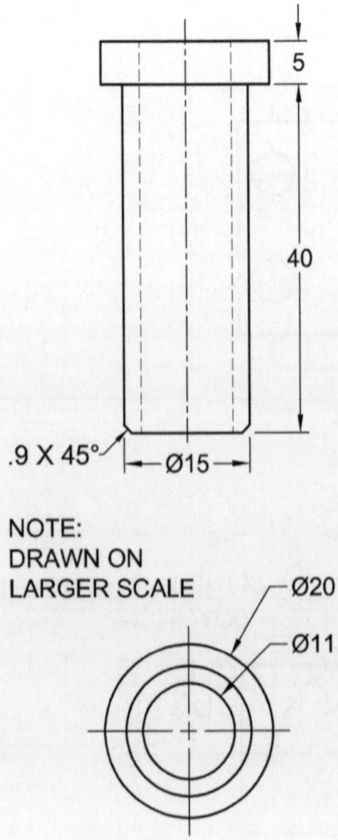

***Figure 8-126** Orthographic views of the Bushing*

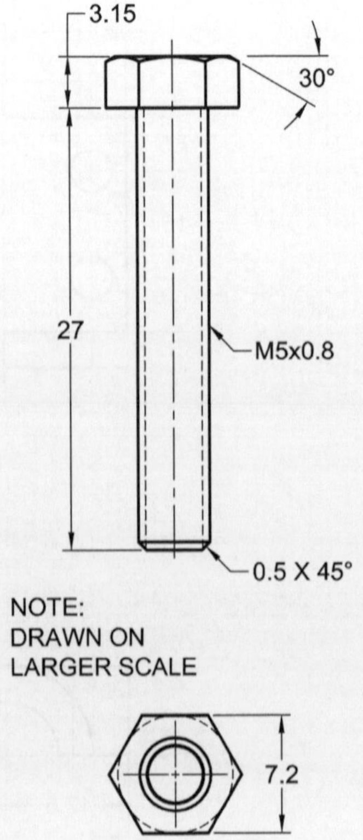

***Figure 8-127** Orthographic views of the Bolt*

Exercise 4

Create the Bench Vice assembly shown in Figure 8-128. The dimensions of the components of the assembly are given in Figures 8-129 through 8-132. **(Expected time: 3 hrs)**

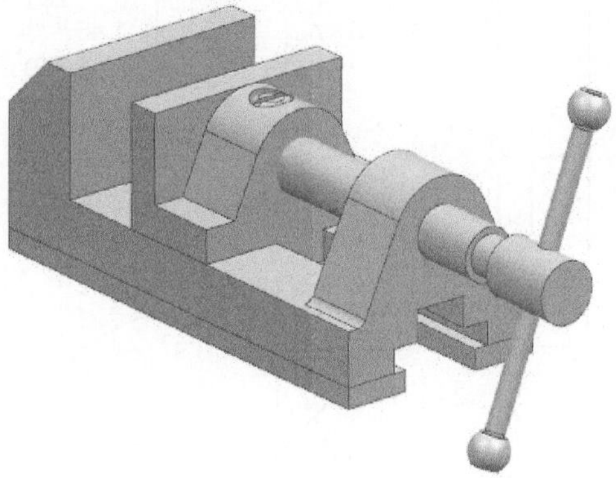

Figure 8-128 *Bench Vice assembly*

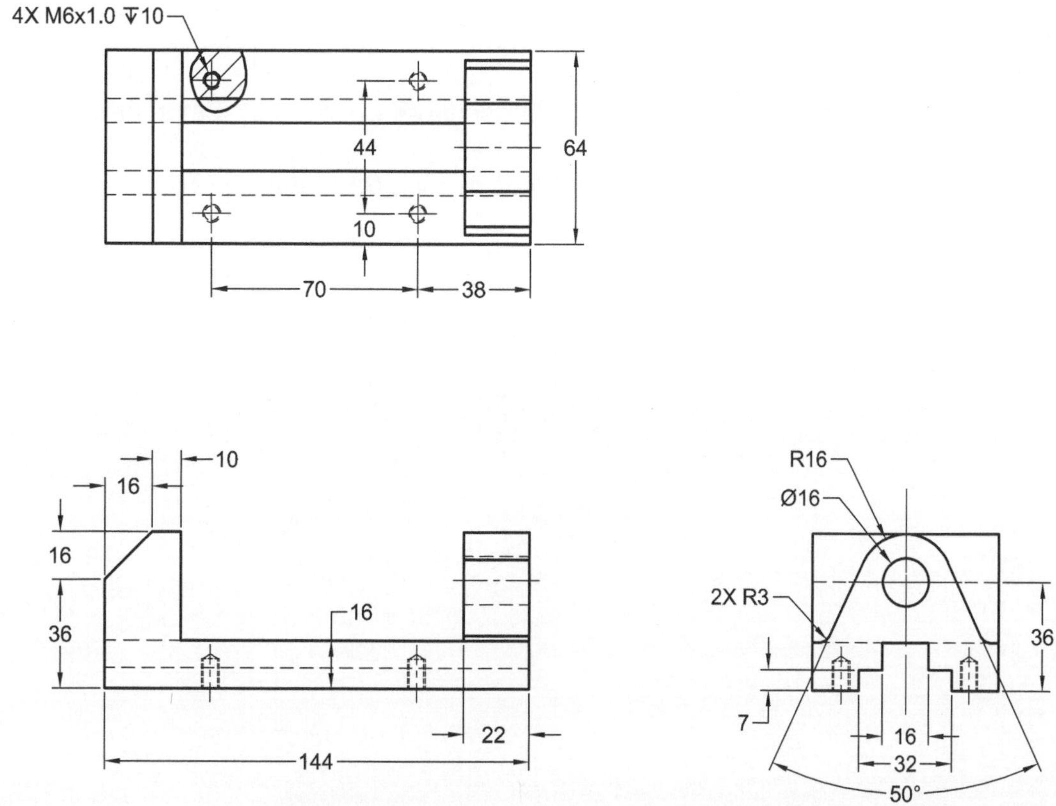

Figure 8-129 *Views and dimensions of the Vice Body*

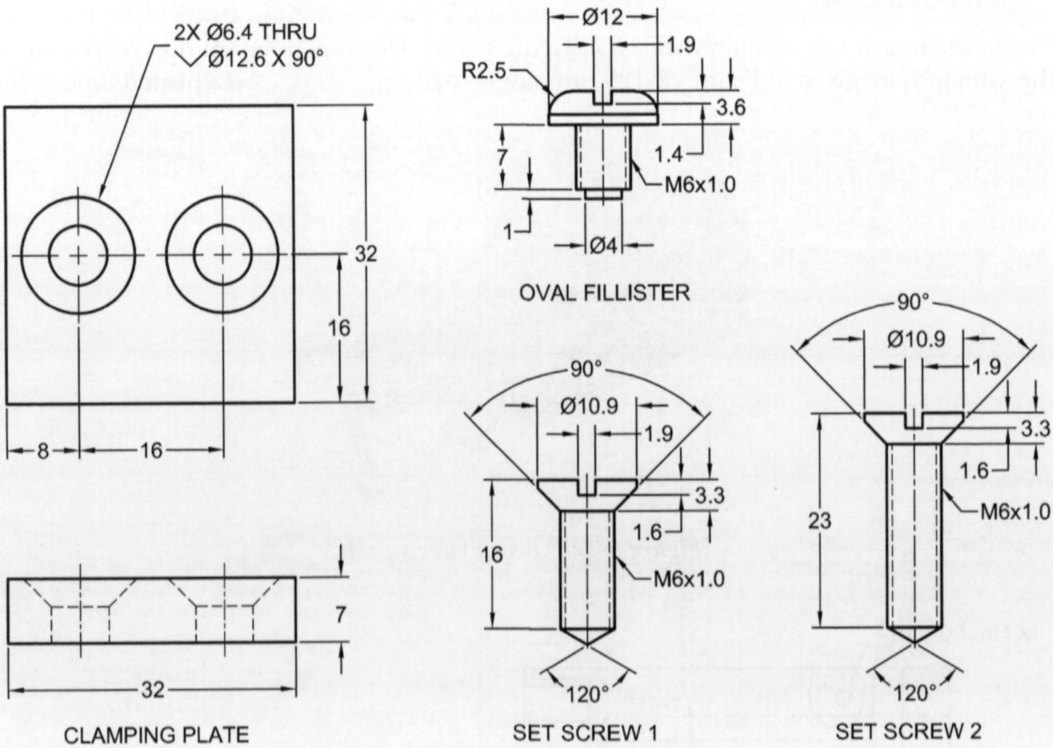

Figure 8-130 *Views and dimensions of the Clamping Plate, Oval Fillister, Set Screw 1, and Set Screw 2*

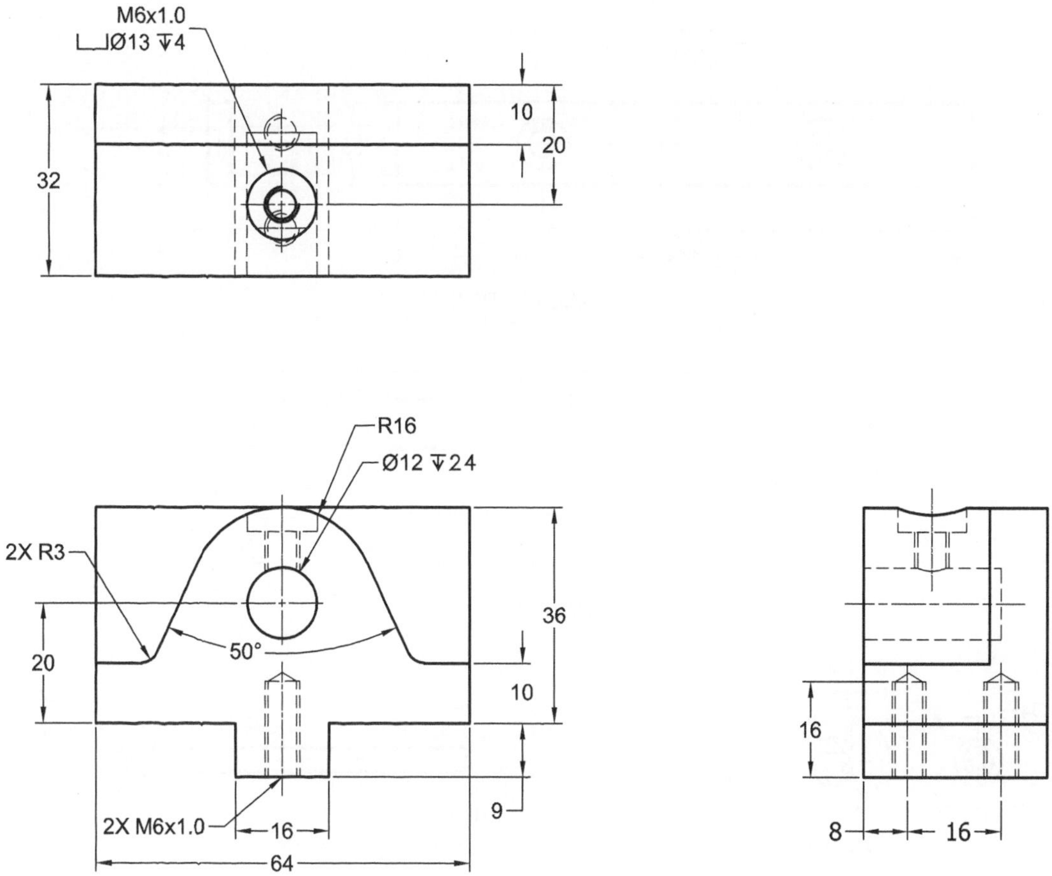

Figure 8-131 *Views and dimensions of the Vice Jaw*

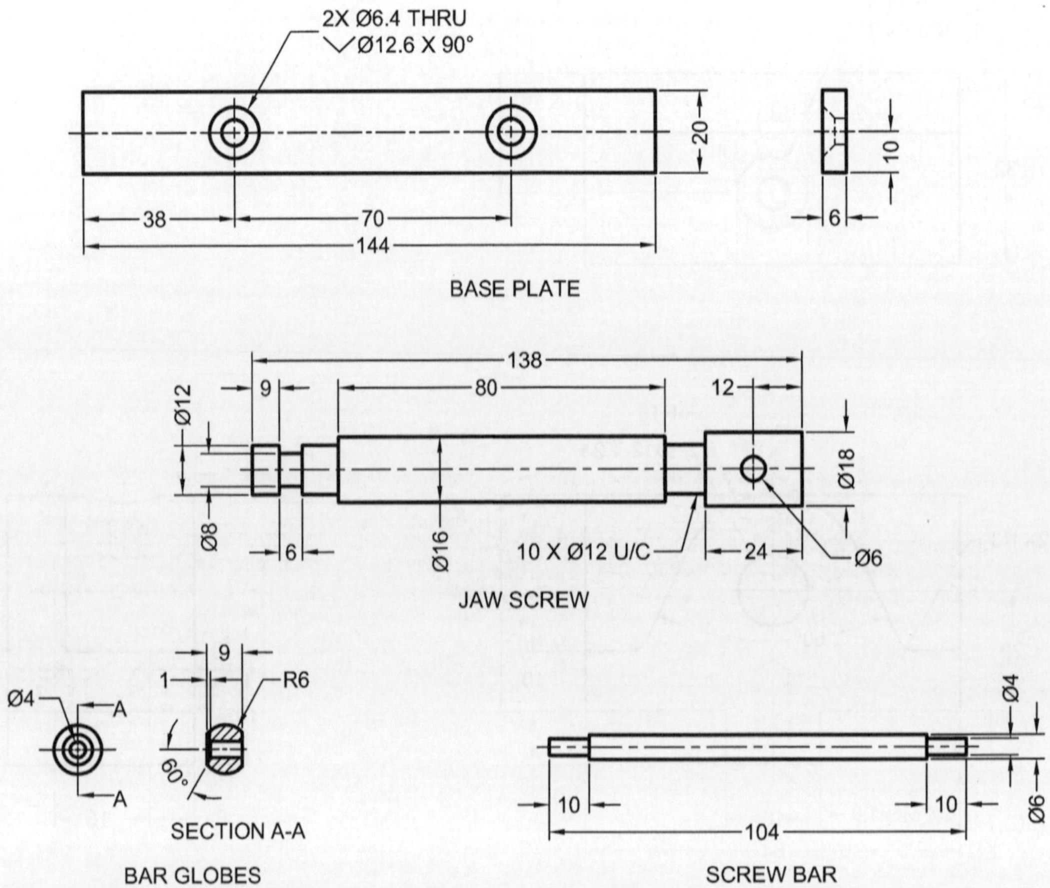

Figure 8-132 Views and dimensions of Base Plate, Jaw Screw, Screw Bar, and Bar Globes

Answers to Self-Evaluation Test

1. *prt*, **2. Distance**, **3. Move Component**, **4. Concentric**, **5.** T, **6.** F, **7.** F, **8.** T, **9.** T, **10.** F

Chapter 9

Assembly Modeling-II

Learning Objectives

After completing this chapter, you will be able to:

- *Create assemblies using the top-down assembly design approach*
- *Create subassemblies*
- *Check interference and clearance between the components of an assembly*
- *Create exploded views of an assembly*
- *Create and save snapshots of view orientations and component positions*

THE TOP-DOWN ASSEMBLY DESIGN APPROACH

As discussed in the previous chapter, you can also create all the components of an assembly in a single file as separate bodies or features and then save them as separate parts. This approach of creating an assembly is known as the top-down assembly design approach. In this approach, most of the dimensions are derived from other features and part bodies. The procedure for creating an assembly using the top-down assembly design approach is discussed next.

Creating Components Using the Top-down Assembly Design Approach

The procedure for creating an assembly using the top-down assembly design approach involves three steps. The first step is to create the features or part bodies. The second step is to save the features or part bodies as separate part files. The third step is to apply assembly constraints to the components and create the assembly. These steps are discussed next.

Creating Features in the Assembly File

1. Start a new part file.

2. Invoke the Assembly environment by choosing **Application > Design > Assemblies** from the **Ribbon** if not already invoked.

3. Choose the **Assemblies** tab from the **Ribbon.**

4. Create the features or part bodies that represent the components of the assembly.

5. Save the individual features or part bodies as separate parts.

6. Save the assembly file.

Note

You can create features as separate bodies or in union with an existing feature. For reorienting the WCS of the sketching plane, you should only use the datum axis of the assembly file as the reference entity. If you select reference entities such as an edge or a datum axis of the existing features, then the feature containing the reference entity will also be added to the feature created.

The procedure for saving the features created as separate part files is discussed next.

Creating Components in the Assembly File

Ribbon:	Assemblies > Component > Create New
Menu:	Assemblies > Components > Create New Component

Create New

You can create different components in the assembly environment and then save them as separate part files one by one. The procedure for creating and saving the components in assembly environment as separate part files is discussed next.

1. Choose the **Create New** tool from the **Component** group in the **Assemblies** tab; the **New Component File** dialog box will be displayed and you will be prompted to select a template. Select the **Model** template from the **Templates** rollout.

2. Specify the name and location of the file in the **New File Name** rollout of the **New Component File** dialog box.

3. Choose the **OK** button from the dialog box; the **Create New Component** dialog box will be displayed, as shown in Figure 9-1.

   By default, the file name that is specified in step 2 in the **New Component File** dialog box will be displayed in the **Component Name** text box of the **Settings** rollout.

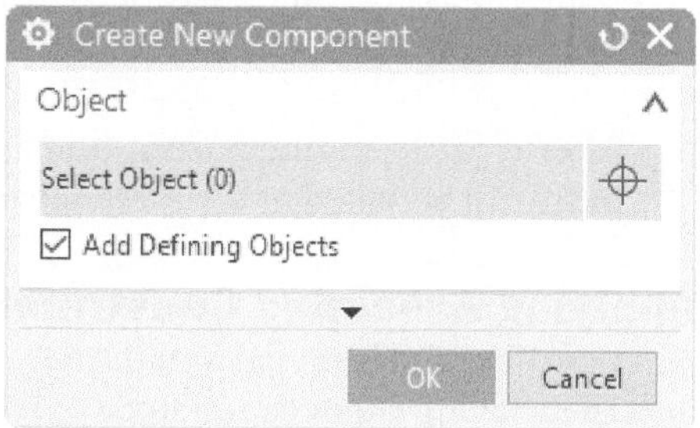

Figure 9-1 *The* ***Create New Component*** *dialog box*

4. By default, the **Select Objects** button is chosen in the **Create New Component** dialog box and you will be prompted to select objects for the new component. If you have created any object, you can select it to include in the new part file. Else, you can create an empty part file.

   Also, the **Add Defining Objects** check box is selected by default in the **Object** rollout of the **Create New Component** dialog box. As a result, the defined objects such as datum planes, axes, or points of the selected object will be included in the new part file. To exclude the defined objects from the new part file, clear the **Add Defining Objects** check box.

5. Now, you need to specify the required settings in the **Settings** rollout. Select the required reference set from the **Reference Set** drop-down list in the **Settings** rollout.

   In the **Component Origin** drop-down list, the **WCS** option is selected by default. As a result, the absolute coordinate system will be oriented exactly as the coordinate system of the displayed part. If you select the **Absolute** option from the **Component Origin** drop-down list, the absolute coordinate system will be oriented exactly as the coordinate system of the work part.

   In the **Settings** rollout, the **Delete Original Objects** check box is selected by default. As a result, the selected body will be saved as a new part file at the specified location, but it will be deleted from its original location. If you clear this check box, the selected body will be saved as a new part file at the specified location without being deleted from the original location in the part assembly.

6. After setting the required options in the **Create New Component** dialog box, choose the **OK** button; the name and node of the newly created part file will be displayed in the **Assembly Navigator** cascading menu below the parent assembly file node.

7. If you double-click on the name of the newly created part file in the **Assembly Navigator** cascading menu, the part will get activated, and the other parts as well as the parent assembly will get deactivated. You can modify the created part as per your requirement.

8. To activate the parent assembly, double-click on the name of the parent assembly in the **Assembly Navigator** cascading menu.

To create the remaining parts of the parent assembly, you need to follow the same procedure as mentioned above.

9. After creating all the parts of the assembly in the assembly file, choose the **Save** button; all parts will be saved as separate part files at the specified location.

Applying Assembly Constraints

After creating different parts in the Assembly file using the Top-down Assembly design approach and then saving them as separate part files, you need to apply the assembly constraints to the components by using the **Assembly Constraints** tool for making fully constrained assembly.

CREATING SUBASSEMBLIES

In the previous chapter, you learned to place components in the assembly file and apply assembly constraints to components. In this chapter, you will learn to create subassemblies and insert them in the main assembly.

Subassemblies are created in the assembly file of the Assembly environment of NX. After placing and assembling the components to be included in the sub-assembly, you need to save it. Open the master assembly file to place the instances of the sub-assembly and choose the **Add** tool from the **Component** group in the **Assemblies** tab; the **Add Component** dialog box will be displayed. Choose the **Open** button from this dialog box. Double-click on the sub-assembly file that is displayed in the **Part Name** dialog box. Place the instance of the sub-assembly and apply the assembly constraints using the **Constraint Type** sub-rollout of the dialog box. Figure 9-2 shows the sub-assembly of the Articulated Rod and Piston. Figure 9-3 shows the sub-assembly of the Master Rod and Piston. Figure 9-4 shows the main assembly that is created using the sub-assembly concept.

Figure 9-2 *A sub-assembly of the Articulated Rod and Piston*

Figure 9-3 *A sub-assembly of the Master Rod and Piston*

Figure 9-4 Main assembly created

EDITING ASSEMBLY CONSTRAINTS

Generally, after creating the assembly or during the process of assembling the components, you need to edit the assembly constraints. The editing operations that can be performed on an assembly are: modifying the angle and distance offset values, adding constraints to a partially constrained component and replacing an assembly constraint.

Note that whenever a constraint is applied to a component, the symbol of the applied constraint is displayed in blue color on the component in the drawing window. If you double-click on this symbol, the parameters of the constraint will be displayed in the **Assembly Constraints** dialog box. You can use this dialog box to redefine the parameters and modify the values of assembly constraints using the options in the **Constraint Type** sub-rollout. Alternatively, click on the plus (+) sign available at the left of the **Constraints** node in the **Assembly Navigator** cascading menu; names of all constraints applied to the component will be displayed under the **Constraints** node. If you right-click on any of the applied constraints, a shortcut menu will be displayed. Choose the **Redefine** option from the shortcut menu; the parameters of the respective constraint will be displayed in the **Assembly Constraints** dialog box. Now, you can modify the parameters as per your requirement.

CHECKING INTERFERENCE BETWEEN THE COMPONENTS OF AN ASSEMBLY

During the process of creating an assembly, the assembly constraints are applied between the components by selecting the corresponding reference object. In an assembly, the surface contact made between the mating components is equally important. In NX, you have the provision for checking the interferences between the components in an assembly. Checking the interference between the components is essential before sending the components for manufacturing. In NX, there are four methods to check interference: the simple interference, the check clearance analysis, the assembly clearance method, and the view section.

Checking Interference using the Simple Interference Tool

Menu: Analysis > Simple Interference

You can check the interference between the two bodies by using the **Simple Interference** tool. To do so, choose **Menu > Analysis > Simple Interference** from the **Top Border Bar**; the **Simple Interference** dialog box will be displayed, as shown in Figure 9-5, and you will be prompted to select the first body. Select the first body from the drawing window; you will be prompted to select the second body. Select the second body from the drawing window; the interfering faces of the two bodies will be highlighted, as shown in Figure 9-6. You can use the options available in the **Interference Check Results** rollout to change the type of result.

Figure 9-5 The ***Simple Interference*** *dialog box*

By default, the **Highlighted Face Pairs** option is selected in the **Resulting Object** drop-down list of the **Interference Check Results** rollout. As a result, the **Faces to Highlight** drop-down list is displayed below the **Resulting Object** drop-down list. By default, the **First Pair Only** option is selected in the **Faces to Highlight** drop-down list. As a result, the first pair of the interfering faces will be highlighted during the interference check. If you select the **Cycle Through All Pairs** option from the **Faces to Highlight** drop-down list, the **Display Next Pair** button will be displayed. You can use this button to highlight all interfering faces one after the other.

You can also create solid bodies at the intersection of the two selected bodies. To do so, select the **Interference Body** option from the **Resulting Object** drop-down list and then select the bodies one by one for which you need to check the intersection and then choose the **OK** button. The intersection body will be created between two selected bodies. Note that you need to hide the two selected bodies in order to view the intersection. Figure 9-7 shows the solid bodies created at the intersection of two selected bodies.

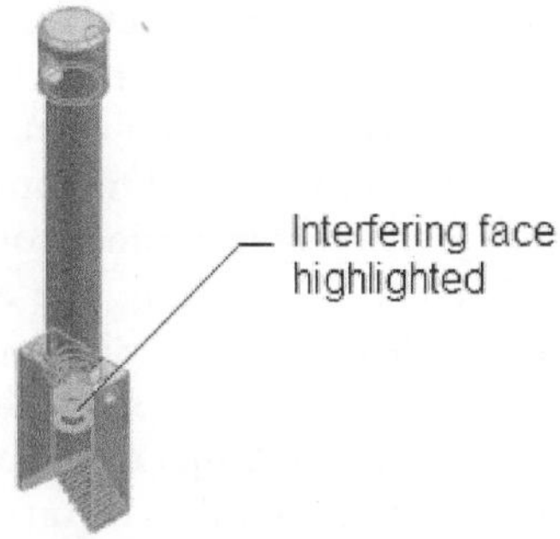

Figure 9-6 Interfering faces highlighted

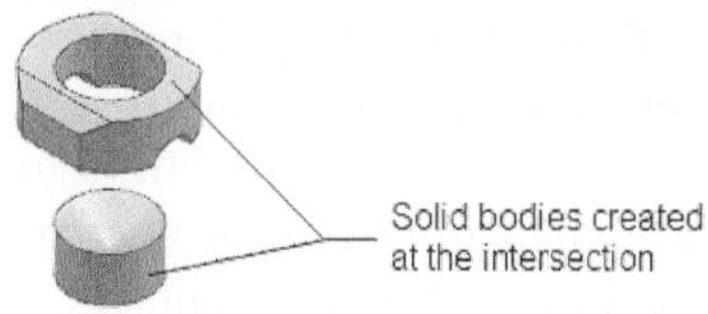

Figure 9-7 Solid bodies created at the intersection of two bodies

Checking Interference Between the Assembly Components

Ribbon: Assemblies > Clearance Analysis > Perform Analysis
Menu: Analysis > Assembly Clearance > Perform Analysis

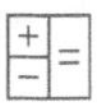
Perform Analysis

In NX, by using the **Perform Analysis** tool you can check the interference and clearance between all the components of an assembly. You can also check the interference and clearance between the selected components of an assembly by using this tool. However, to check interference and clearance, you first need to create or load an existing clearance set. A clearance set contains all the parameters for checking interference and clearance. An assembly can have multiple clearance sets. The method of creating and loading clearance set is discussed next.

Creating Clearance Set

After creating the assembly, choose **Assemblies** > **Clearance Analysis** > **New Set** from the **Ribbon**; the **Clearance Analysis** dialog box will be displayed, as shown in Figure 9-8. The options in this dialog box are discussed next.

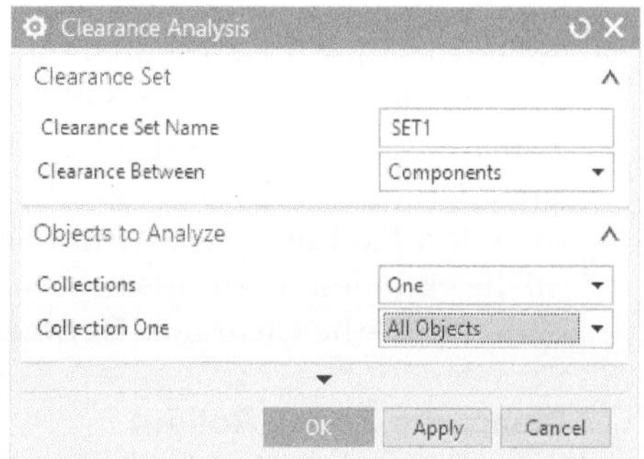

*Figure 9-8 The **Clearance Analysis** dialog box*

Clearance Set Rollout

In this rollout, you can enter the name for the clearance set in the **Clearance Set Name** edit box. The **Components** option is selected by default in the **Clearance Between** drop-down list, so the components will be included for the clearance check. If you select the **Bodies** option from this drop-down, the separate bodies of the components will be selected for the clearance check.

Objects to Analyze Rollout

The options available in this rollout are used to specify whether you want to analyze all the components of the assembly or a pair of components. By default, the **Collections** and **Collection One** drop-down lists are available in this rollout. Depending upon the options selected from these drop-down lists, the analysis check will take place. By default, the **One** option is selected in the **Collections** drop-down list and the **All Objects** options is selected in the **Collection One** drop-down list. As a result, the interference and clearance will be checked between all the components of the assembly. However, if you want to perform the analysis between the selected components only, make sure that the **One** option is selected in the **Collections** drop-down list and then select the **Selected Objects** option from the **Collection One** drop-down list. As soon as you select this option, the **Select Objects** area is displayed and you will be prompted to select clearance analysis objects. Select the components from the drawing area between which you want to perform the interference and clearance analysis. Similarly, on selecting the **All Visible Objects** option, the analysis will be performed between all the visible components of the assembly. If you want to exclude the selected components from the analysis check and include the components that are not selected, select the **All But Selected Objects** option from the **Collection One** drop-down list.

On selecting the **Two** option from the **Collections** drop-down list, the **Collection One** and **Collection Two** drop-down lists will be available in the rollout. Depending upon the options selected from these drop-down lists, the analysis will be performed. Also, the interference and clearance between the components will be checked based on the options selected from the **Collection One** and **Collection Two** drop-down lists.

Exceptions Rollout

In this rollout, you can add exceptions for a pair of objects. If you add an exception for more than two objects, then exceptions will be applied for all possible pairs of objects. If you select the **Exclude Pairs Within Selected Subassemblies** check box, then the selected sub-assembly will be excluded from the analysis. When you select this check box you are prompted to select the sub-assembly, and the **Select Unit Subassemblies** area will be highlighted. Now select the sub-assembly, the excluded sub-assemblies will not be included under the **Interferences** node of the **Clearance Browser** window. If you select **Exclude Pairs Within Same Subassembly** check box, then the first level sub-assembly from the displayed parts will be excluded from the analysis. If you select the **Exclude Pairs Within Same Group** check box, then the pair within the same object group will be excluded. If you select **Exclude Pairs Within Same Part** check box, then the pairs within the same part will be excluded. Both these check boxes will be available only when you select the **Bodies** option from the **Clearance Between** drop-down list of the **Clearance Set** rollout.

Clearance Zones Rollout

You can also check for the existence of the clearance value between the mating components using this rollout. To do so, enter the reference clearance value to be maintained in the **Default Clearance Zone** edit box. If the clearance value detected is less than or equal to the reference clearance value given in the **Default Clearance Zone** edit box, **Soft** will be displayed in the **Type** column of the **Clearance Browser** window. You can specify the zone by choosing the required option from the **Specify Zone** drop-down list. If you select the **Between Pairs** option from the drop-down list, then pair zone set will be created between the selected objects. If you select the **Around Objects** options from the drop-down list, then pair zone set will be created for the selected objects with the name and distance value as assigned in the **Name** and **Distance** edit boxes. You can add new clearance zones. To do so, select the objects and then click on the **Add New Clearance Zone** button from this rollout.

Settings Rollout

In this rollout, by selecting the **Save Interference Geometry** check box under the **Interference Geometry** sub-rollout, you can save the interference geometry of the specified layer, and the color generated by clearance analysis. The **Calculate Using** drop-down list will specify whether the clearance analysis is calculated either by **Exact**, **Exact if Loaded**, or **Lightweight** geometry. If you select the **Lightweight** option, then calculation will be faster but less accurate and if you select the **Exact** option then calculation will be slower but more accurate. If **Perform Analysis** check box is selected then it will perform the clearance analysis when the **OK** button is selected from the dialog box.

If the **Perform Analysis** check box is not selected in the **Settings** rollout then you need to run the analysis for the parameters defined in the clearance set. After defining the parameters for the clearance set, choose the **OK** button from the **Clearance Analysis** dialog box; the **Clearance Browser** window will be displayed without the analysis data, as shown in Figure 9-9. Right-click on the **Clearance Set** node and choose the **Perform Analysis** option from the shortcut menu displayed; the results will be generated in the **Clearance Browser** window, as shown in Figure 9-10. Alternatively, choose the **Perform Analysis** tool from the **Assemblies > Clearance Analysis** from the **Ribbon**.

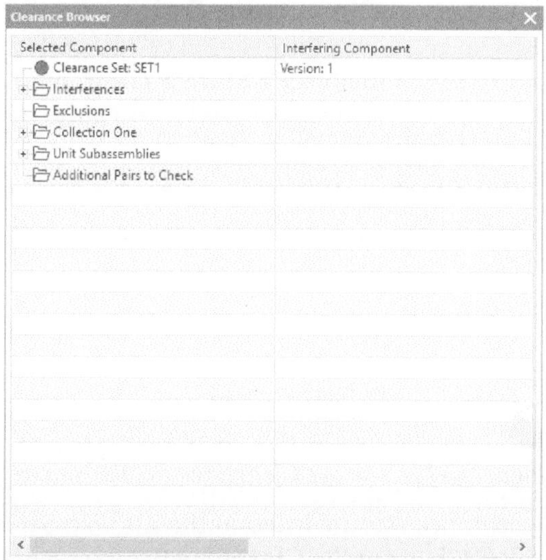

Figure 9-9 *The* ***Clearance Browser*** *window*

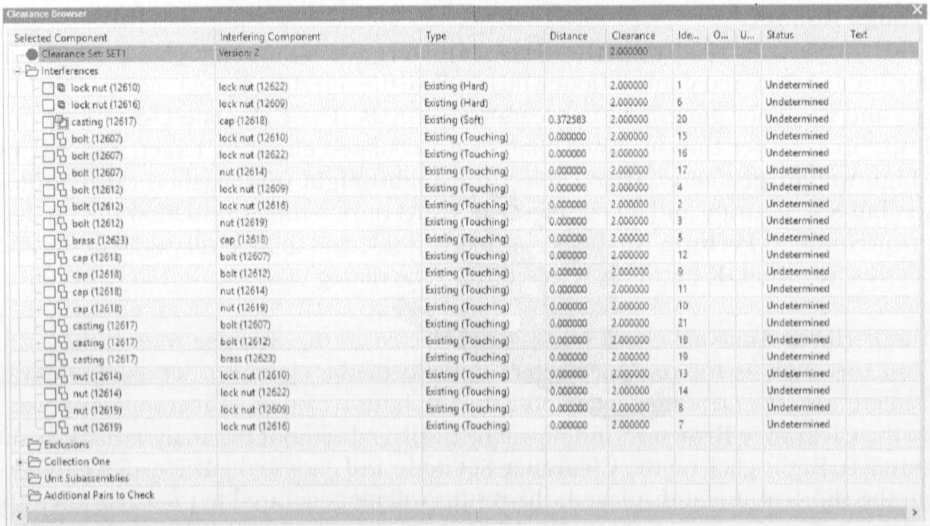

Figure 9-10 The ***Clearance Browser*** *window after performing analysis*

Loading an Existing Created Clearance Set

After creating the assembly, you have to load the clearance set before proceeding to the analysis part. Choose **Assemblies > Clearance Analysis > More > Clearance Set > Set** from the **Ribbon**; the **Set Clearance Set** dialog box will be displayed, refer to Figure 9-11.

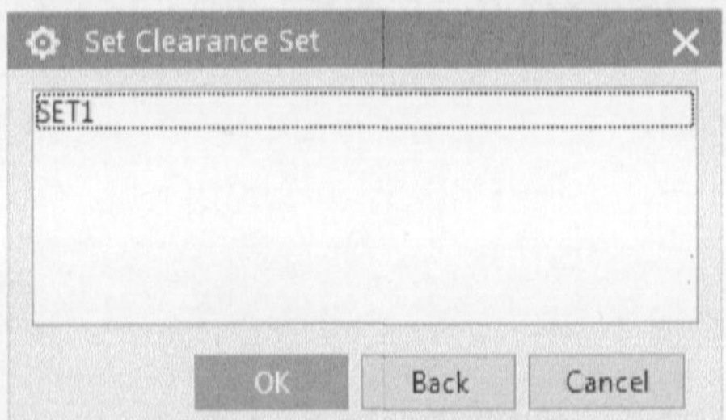

Figure 9-11 The ***Set Clearance Set*** *dialog box*

All the previously created clearance sets are listed in the list box. Select the clearance set name to be loaded and choose the **OK** button; the **Clearance Browser** window will be displayed with results, refer to Figure 9-12. The results are based on the parameters defined in the clearance set.

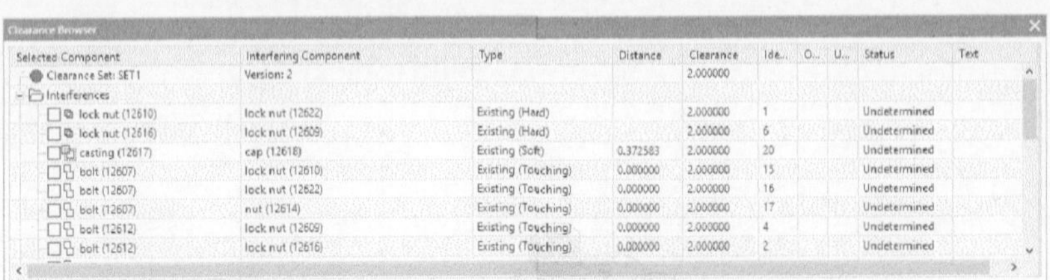

Figure 9-12 Partial view of the ***Clearance Browser*** *window*

Note

You can reorder the components listed in the columns in an alphabetical or reverse alphabetical order by clicking on the respective column.

Components of the Clearance Browser Window

The various components of the clearance browser window are discussed next.

Selected Component

The **Selected Component** column of the **Clearance Browser** window consists of the names of the components that are treated as the first object in the pair used for checking the interference or clearance.

Interfering Component

The **Interfering Component** column consists of the names of the components that are treated as the second object in the pair used for checking the interference or clearance.

Type

The **Type** column lists the result and the type of interference between the components.

Distance

In the **Distance** column, the distance between two object pairs is given in millimeters. The **Clearance** column displays the clearance value given in the **Default Clearance Zone** edit box of the **Clearance Analysis** dialog box.

Note

*1. The name of the clearance set loaded for analysis is displayed in the **Clearance Set** node of the **Clearance Browser** window. To make any changes in the parameters defined in the clearance set, double-click on the **Clearance Set** node from the **Clearance Browser** window; the **Clearance Analysis** dialog box will be displayed. Make the required changes and choose the **OK** button to reflect the changes. After updating the parameters in the **Clearance Analysis** dialog box, run the analysis once more to update the result. For updating the result, right-click on the **Clearance Set** node in the **Clearance Browser** window and choose the **Perform Analysis** option from the shortcut menu. The result will be updated for the modified clearance set.*

*2. To isolate an interference detected in the analysis, double-click on the interference result in the **Type** column; the interference will be isolated in the graphics window and the interference area will be marked with the interference color specified in the clearance set. Again, to retain whole assembly, right-click on the isolated interference result in the **Clearance Browser** window and then choose the **Restore Component Visibility** option from the shortcut menu.*

Exclusions Folder

The interference results in the **Exclusions** folder are ignored for the consecutive analysis. You can dynamically move the interference result by selecting and dragging it to the **Exclusions** folder. To include an ignored interference result in the consecutive analysis, select that result from the **Exclusions** folder of the **Clearance Browser** window and right-click on it. Choose the **List all pairs** from the shortcut menu; the interference result will be added to the analysis.

Saving the Report Generated

The generated interference report can be saved as a *.txt* file. To save it, right-click on the **Clearance Set** node from the **Clearance Browser** window to display a shortcut menu. Next, choose the **Save Report** option from the shortcut menu; the **Report File** dialog box will be displayed and you are prompted to specify the report file for the clearance analysis. Specify the directory and enter the file name in the **File name** edit box to save the report. Choose the **OK** button; the report will be saved in the specified directory as a *.txt* file.

Deleting a Clearance Set

To delete a clearance set, right-click on the **Clearance Set** node from the **Clearance Browser** window to display a shortcut menu. Choose **Clearance Set > Delete** from the shortcut menu; the **Delete Clearance Sets** dialog box will be displayed, as shown in Figure 9-13. Select the clearance set and then choose the **OK** button from the dialog box to delete the selected clearance set.

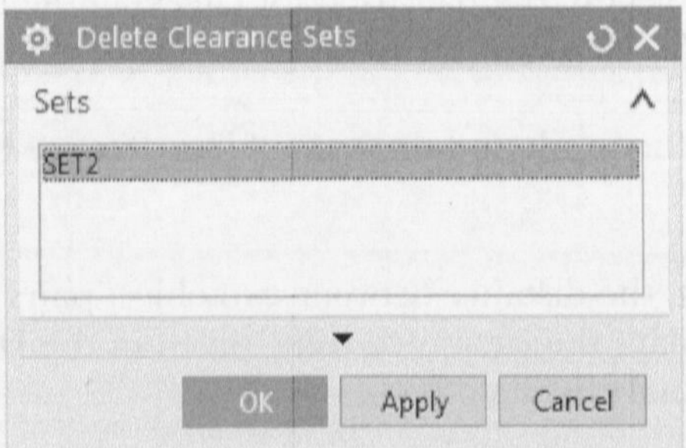

***Figure 9-13** The **Delete Clearance Sets** dialog box*

Checking Interference and Clearance, and Analyzing Cross-sections of Components Using the View Section Tool

Ribbon:	View > Visibility > Edit Section
Menu:	View > Section > Edit Section

Edit Section

You can check the interference and clearance between the components using the **View Section** dialog box. Using the options in this dialog box, you can dynamically view the cross-sections, interferences, and clearances as well as create section views of components. Moreover, you can use this dialog box to create datum planes. To invoke this dialog box, choose the **Edit Section** tool from the **Visibility** group of the **View** tab; the **View Section** dialog box will be displayed, refer to Figure 9-14. Note that as soon as you choose the **Edit Section** tool from the **View** tab, the **Clip Section** tool in the **Visibility** group of the **View** tab will be activated and a cross-section of the model will be displayed in the drawing window, refer to Figure 9-15. If you choose the **Clip Section** tool from the **Visibility** group, the cross-section will be turned off and the complete model will become visible. Various options in the **View Section** dialog box are discussed next.

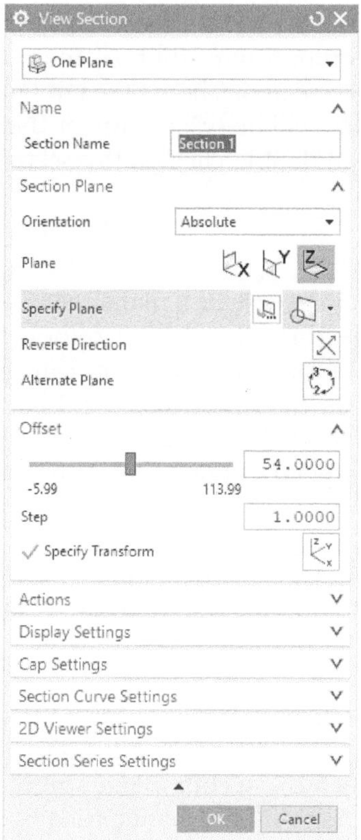

*Figure 9-14 The **View Section** dialog box*

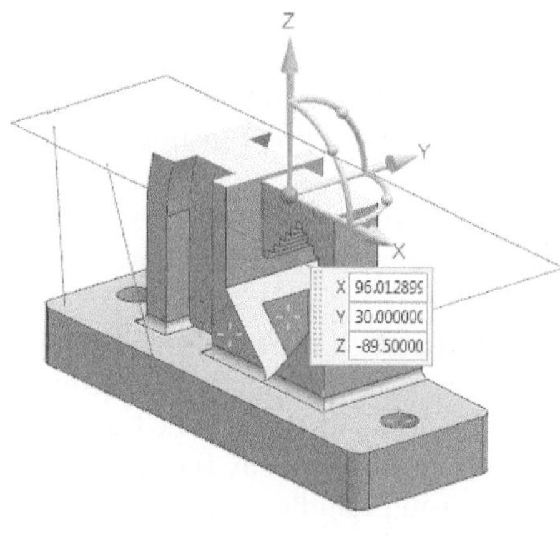

Figure 9-15 A cross-section of the assembly

Type drop-down

The **One Plane** option is selected by default in the type drop-down list. As a result, a single plane along with the triad of dynamic handles will be displayed in the drawing window that enables you to analyze the cross-section of the component. If you drag any of these handles, the plane of cross-section moves accordingly. If you drag any of the angular handles, the plane of cross-section will orient along with the movement of cursor.

If you select the **Two Parallel Planes** option from the type drop-down list, two parallel planes will be displayed in the drawing window to analyze the cross-section of the component. Also, a triad of dynamic handles will be displayed only on the activated plane. Note that out of the two planes, only one plane will be activated at a time. To activate the other plane, select the plane from the drawing window; the selected plane will be activated. Now, you can move this plane to view the cross-sections of various parts at different locations.

If you select the **Box** option from the type drop-down list, a box of planes will be displayed in the drawing window to analyze the cross-section of the component, and a triad of dynamic handles will be displayed only on the activated plane. Out of all the planes, only one plane will be active at a time. To activate the other plane, move the cursor over an edge of the box; the respective plane will be highlighted. Select the highlighted plane from the drawing window; the selected plane will be activated. Now, you can move this plane to view the cross-sections of various parts at different locations.

Name Rollout

In this rollout, **Section 1** is displayed by default in the **Section Name** edit box. You can use this edit box to specify a user-defined name for the section to be created. Choose the **OK** button from the **View Section** dialog box; the user-defined section view will be created under the **Sections** node in the **Assembly Navigator** cascading menu. You can double-click on this section view in the **Sections** node to display it in the drawing window.

Section Plane Rollout

This rollout is used to set the location and orientation of the selected plane. You can specify the orientation reference of the section plane by selecting the desired option from the **Orientation** drop-down list. After selecting the orientation reference, you can orient the section plane along the X, Y, or Z direction by choosing the **Set Plane to X**, **Set Plane to Y**, or **Set Plane to Z** button, respectively. These buttons are available below the **Orientation** drop-down list in the **Section Plane** rollout. Using the options in the **Specify Plane** area of this rollout, you can specify the user-defined section plane.

You can flip the direction of the active plane by using the **Reverse Direction** button. You can also cycle through the X, Y, or Z standard section planes by choosing the **Alternate Plane** button.

Offset Rollout

In this rollout, you can specify the offset distance of the active plane from its initial position using the slider bar or the edit box given on the right of the slider bar. The **Step** edit box in this rollout is used to specify the increment value by which the section plane will move while dragging it, using handles. You can also specify the position of the dynamic triad by choosing the **Manipulator** button from the **Offset** rollout.

Actions Rollout

You can create a datum plane at the current location of the section plane by choosing the **Create Datum Plane** button from the **Actions** rollout.

Box Rollout

This rollout will be available only when you select the **Box** option from the type drop-down list. In this rollout, you can define the settings for the box of section planes. If you select the **Lock to Plane** check box then the entire box of the section plane will move instead of the active plane. The **Thickness** slider bar in this rollout is used to define the size of the box along the normal axis of active plane. The **Reset Box** button is used to reset the box setting.

Display Settings Rollout

In this rollout, the **Type** drop-down list will be available only when the **One Plane** option is selected from the type drop-down list. By default, the **Section** option is selected in the **Type** drop-down list. As a result, a section of the selected part will be displayed in the drawing window, refer to Figure 9-15. If you select the **Slice** option from the **Type** drop-down list, only the sliced cross-section of the part will be displayed, as shown in Figure 9-16.

The **Show Manipulator** check box in this rollout is selected by default. As a result, a triad of dynamic handles is displayed in the drawing window. If you clear this check box, the triad of dynamic handles will not be visible. If the triad of dynamic handles is out of the drawing window, you can bring the triad in the drawing window by choosing the **Move Manipulator in View** button from this rollout. This option is very useful while handling large assemblies. If you choose the **Orient View to Plane** button, the section view will be oriented parallel to the screen. By default, the **Show Grid** check box in this rollout is cleared. As a result, the grid lines will not be displayed in the section plane. Select this check box, if you want the grid lines to be displayed in the section plane, as shown in Figure 9-17. The **Edit Grid Settings** button from this rollout is used to specify the grid setting. On choosing this button, the **Plane Grid** dialog box will be displayed. You can use this dialog box to change the grid settings.

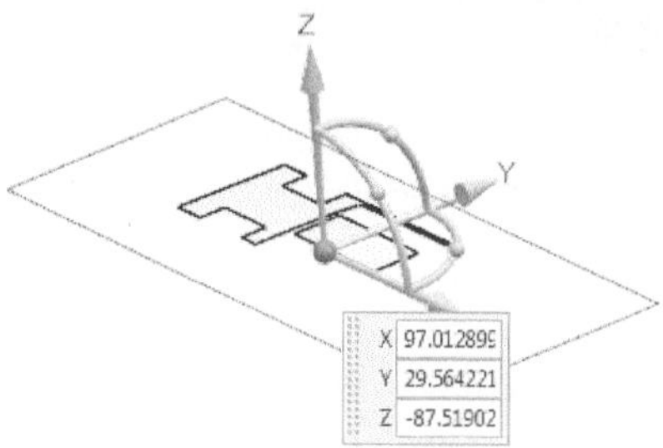

Figure 9-16 Cross-section of a part

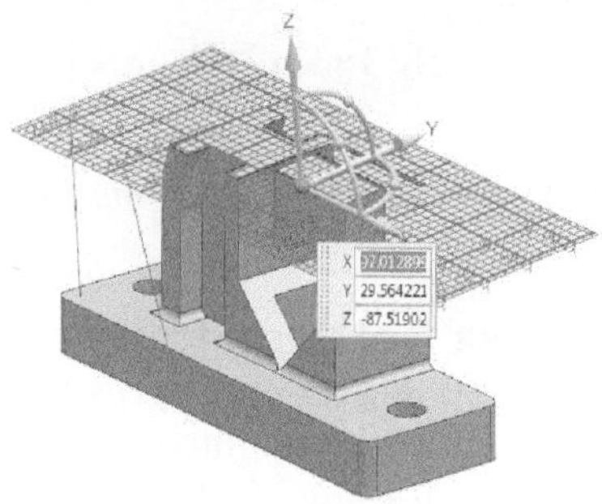

Figure 9-17 Cross-section with grid lines

Cap Settings Rollout

In this rollout, the **Show Cap** check box is selected by default. As a result, you can view the cross-section of a component in different colors. If you clear this check box, remaining options in this rollout will not be available and the cross-sectional surface will become transparent, as shown in Figure 9-18. The **Color Option** drop-down list in this rollout is used to specify the color of the cross-section of the component. By default, the **Specify Color** option is selected in this drop-down list. As a result, color of the cross-section of the component will be displayed in light green. You can also apply the user-defined colors to the cross-section. To do so, click on the **Cap Color** swatch from the **Cap Settings** rollout; the **Color** dialog box will be displayed. Select the required color from this dialog box and then choose the **OK** button; the selected color will be applied to the cross-section. If you select the **Body Color** option from the **Color Option** drop-down list, the cross-section of the component will be displayed in the same color as the color of the component. If you select the **Show Interference** check box, interference of components in the assembly at the currently active cross-section will be highlighted in the default color specified in the **Interference Color** swatch in this rollout, as shown in Figure 9-19. You can change this default color to any user-defined color by selecting the desired color from the **Color** dialog box that will be displayed after clicking on the **Interference Color** swatch.

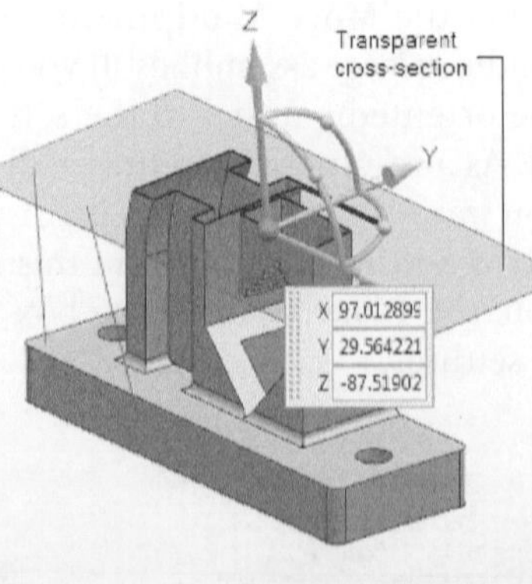

Figure 9-18 Transparent cross-section

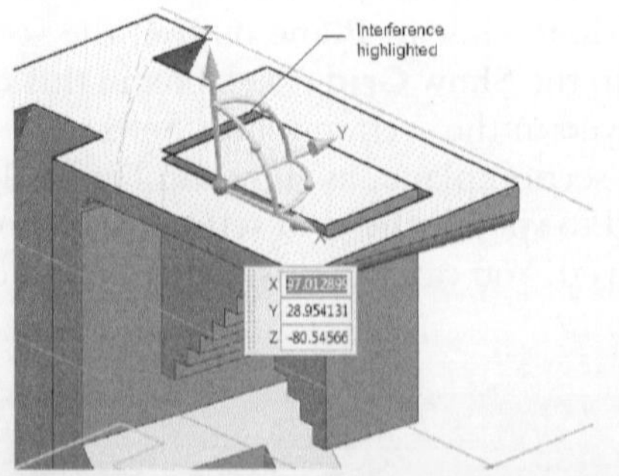

Figure 9-19 Interference highlighted at the active cross-section in the assembly

Section Curve Settings Rollout

If you select the **Show Section Curves Preview** check box from this rollout, the section curves of components will be highlighted in dark blue. You can also save the section curves that are highlighted in the drawing window. To do so, choose the **Save Copy of Section Curves** button from this rollout; the highlighted section curves will be saved at their respective places.

2D Viewer Settings Rollout

In this rollout, the **Show 2D Viewer** check box is cleared by default. If you select this check box, the **2D Section Viewer** window will be displayed, as shown in Figure 9-20, and the **2D Viewer Settings** rollout will be modified, refer to Figure 9-21. In the **2D Section Viewer** window, you can see that the section curves of the active cross-section are displayed in 2D view. If you select the **Shaded Cap Preview in 2D View** check box from the **2D Viewer Settings** rollout, the cross-section as well as its color will be displayed in the window. You can rotate the cross-section in the **2D Section Viewer** window according to your requirement using the **Rotate Right**, **Rotate Left**, **Reflect X-Axis**, or **Reflect Y-Axis** button from the **2D Viewer Settings** rollout.

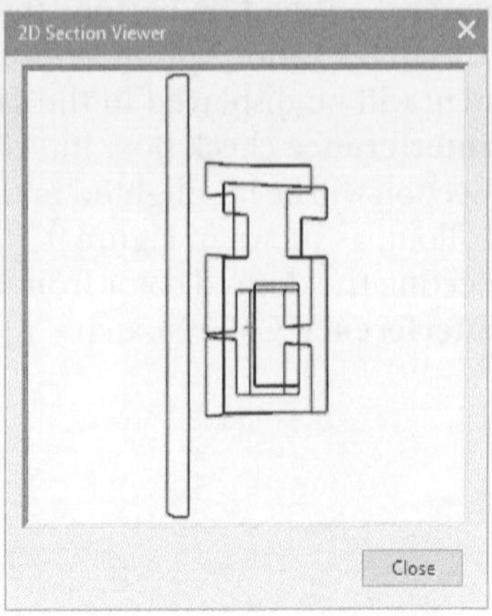

*Figure 9-20 The **2D Section Viewer** window*

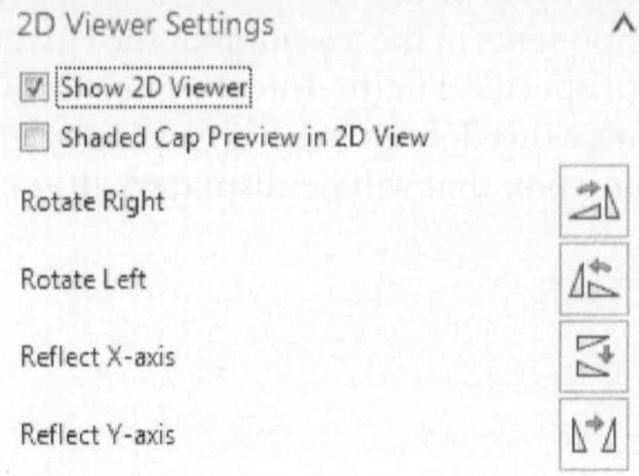

*Figure 9-21 The modified **2D Viewer Settings** rollout*

Section Series Settings Rollout

This rollout is used to view the number of section curves at different cross-sections. To view the section curves at different cross-sections, you can specify the number of sections in the **Number of Sections** edit box. Additionally, you can specify the distance between the section planes to be generated in the **Section Spacing** edit box. Choose the **Preview Series** button in the **Section Series Settings** rollout to preview the number of specified sections, as shown in Figure 9-22. To view the section curves in the opposite direction, select the **Reverse Series** check box and then choose the **Preview Series** button again from this rollout.

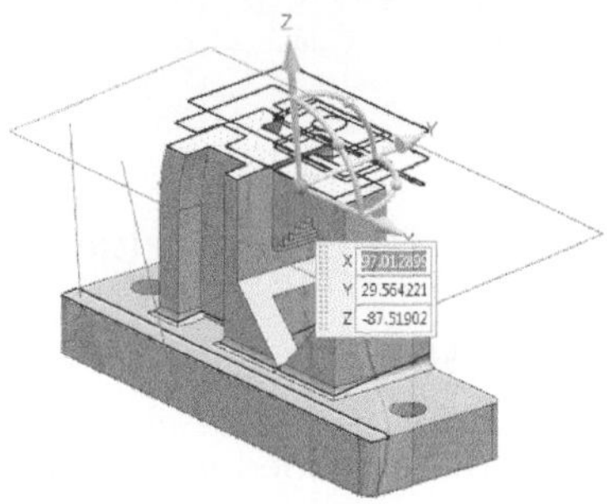

Figure 9-22 *Multiple section curves displayed at different cross-sections*

CREATING EXPLODED VIEWS OF AN ASSEMBLY

The exploded views of an assembly are created to expose the internal components of a complex assembly. The exploded views also provide a clear idea about the orientation of the components in an assembly. In a shop floor, the exploded views have their own uses. The assembly technicians use the exploded views for assembling the components of an assembly.

In NX, you have two methods for creating the exploded views of an assembly, automatic explosion method, and the manual explosion method. In automatic explosion, the component can only be exploded in the direction of the orientation of its center axis. In this case, you cannot specify the direction for the explosion. In manual explosion, you can explode the component in all directions. You can also specify a user-defined direction in this case. The exploded view of the Flange Coupling assembly is shown in Figure 9-23.

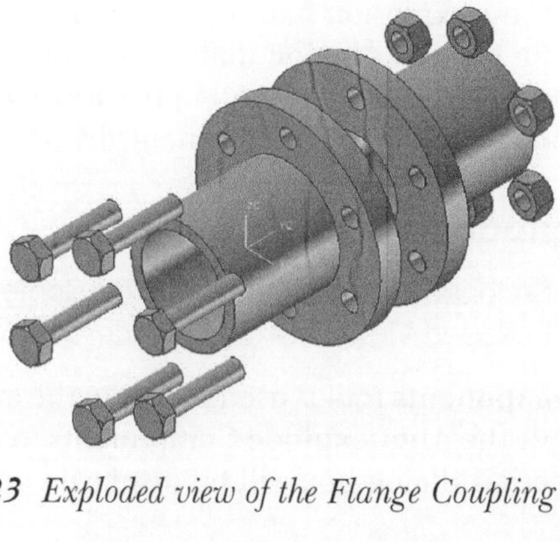

Figure 9-23 *Exploded view of the Flange Coupling assembly*

The **Exploded Views** group provides the tools for creating and editing various types of exploded views. Before creating the exploded views, you need to invoke the **Exploded Views** group. You can access the tools available in the **Exploded Views** group by clicking on the arrow available in the **Exploded Views** group of the **Assemblies** tab in the **Ribbon**, as shown in Figure 9-24.

*Figure 9-24 The **Exploded Views** group*

Exploding Views Automatically

In NX, you have to adopt two steps for creating the automatic exploded view. The first step comprises of creating the name for the exploded views. The second step is to explode the component automatically. The components selected for explosion are always exploded in the direction of orientation of their own center axis.

Assigning Names for Exploded Views

Ribbon:	Assemblies > Exploded Views > New Explosion
Menu:	Assemblies > Exploded Views > New Explosion

New Explosion

The explosion name is assigned to identify an exploded view in an assembly. All explosion names are listed in the **Work View Explosion** drop-down list of the **Exploded Views** group. The names assigned for exploded views are used to select the exploded view while editing. For assigning the explosion name, choose the **New Explosion** tool from the **Exploded Views** group; the **New Explosion** dialog box will be displayed, as shown in Figure 9-25.

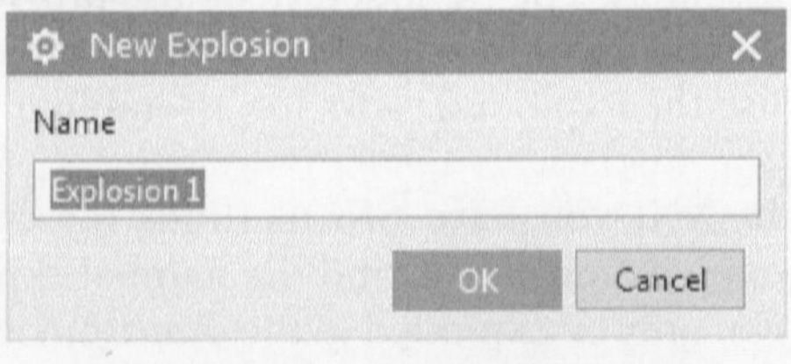

*Figure 9-25 The **New Explosion** dialog box*

By default, the name of the explosions will be displayed as **Explosion 1**, **Explosion 2**, **Explosion 3**, and so on. To change the name of the explosion state, enter a user-defined name for the explosion state in the **Name** edit box of the **New Explosion** dialog box and then choose the **OK** button. The **Auto-explode Components** tool will be activated in the **Exploded Views** group. Now, you can create the automatic exploded view for the components by using this tool.

Creating Automatic Exploded Views

Ribbon:	Assemblies > Exploded Views > Auto-explode Components
Menu:	Assemblies > Exploded Views > Auto-explode Components

Auto-explode Components

The **Auto-explode Components** tool is used to create the automatic exploded view for the components. Choose the **Auto-explode Components** tool from the **Exploded Views** group; the **Class Selection** dialog box will be displayed and you will be prompted to select the components. You can select individual components or a group of components from the assembly, as shown in Figure 9-26.

After selecting the components for exploding, choose the **OK** button from the **Class Selection** dialog box; the **Auto-explode Components** dialog box will be displayed, as shown in Figure 9-27.

Figure 9-26 Component selected from an assembly for automatic explosion

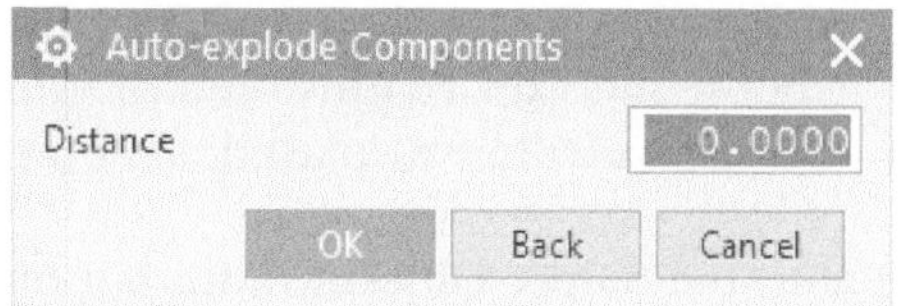

Figure 9-27 *The **Auto-explode Components** dialog box*

Enter the explosion distance value in the **Distance** edit box. Choose the **OK** button from the same dialog box to create the automatic explosion of the selected component, as shown in Figure 9-28.

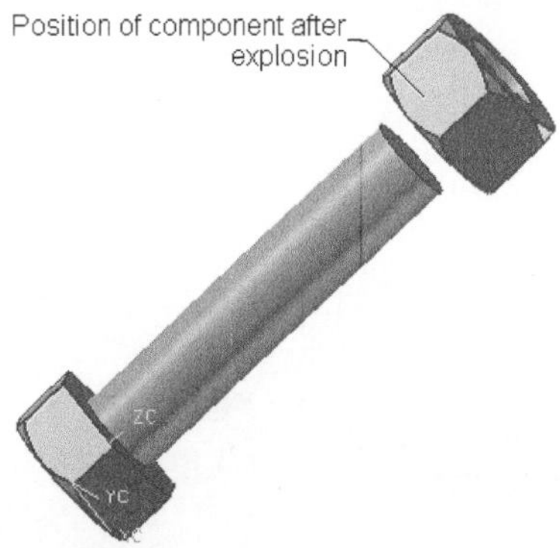

Figure 9-28 *Position of the component after explosion*

Note

*To edit the explosion distance after creating the automatic explosion, select the component and choose the **Auto-explode Components** tool from the **Exploded Views** group; the **Auto-explode Components** dialog box will be displayed with the previous explosion distance given in the **Distance** edit box. Enter the new explosion distance value in the **Distance** edit box and choose the **OK** button. You can enter both positive and negative values for the explosion distance. The component will be exploded in positive or negative direction with respect to the assembly WCS.*

Exploding Views Manually

After creating the automatic exploded views using the **Auto-explode Components** tool, you may need to explode the component manually to get the desired results. The components can be manually exploded even when the assembly constraints are applied to them. In NX, you have to adopt two steps to create the exploded views manually. The procedure for creating the exploded views manually is discussed next.

Creating Exploded Views Manually

Ribbon:	Assemblies > Exploded Views > Edit Explosion
Menu:	Assemblies > Exploded Views > Edit Explosion

The **Edit Explosion** tool is used to create exploded views manually. You can explode the component in any direction. You can also explode only the handles of the component. Choose the **Edit Explosion** tool from the **Exploded Views** group; the **Edit Explosion** dialog box will be displayed, as shown in Figure 9-29.

By default, the **Select Objects** radio button will be selected from the **Edit Explosion** dialog box and you will be prompted to select the components to explode. Select the components to be included in the exploded view and then select the **Move Objects** radio button; the selected component will be displayed, as shown in Figure 9-30. Select the direction of explosion for the selected component by clicking on the appropriate translation handle.

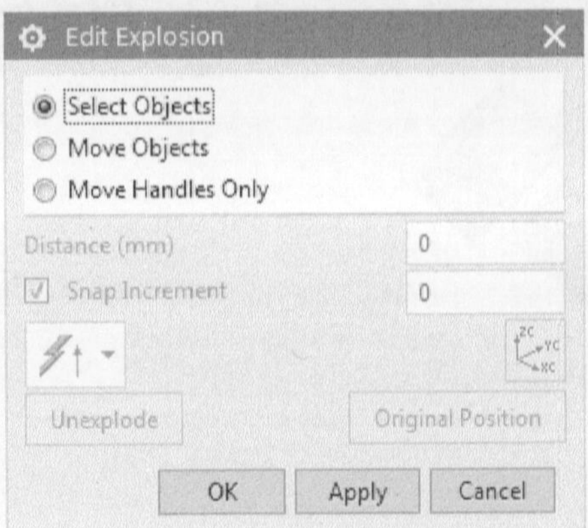

*Figure 9-29 The **Edit Explosion** dialog box*

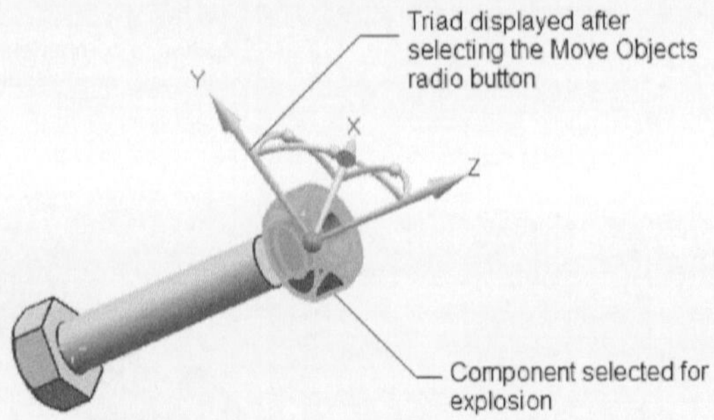

Figure 9-30 Component selected from the assembly for manual explosion

Note

*If you select the translation handle, the **Distance** edit box and the **Inferred Vector** drop-down list will be available in the **Edit Explosion** dialog box. If you select the angular handle, the **Angle** edit box will be available in the dialog box.*

The **Snap Handles to WCS** button from the **Edit Explosion** dialog box will be used for coinciding the handles of the selected component with the WCS of the assembly file. If you select the **Snap Increment** check box, then the **Snap Increment** edit box will be available in the **Edit Explosion** dialog box. The value entered in this edit box will be treated as a step increment value and considered whenever the selected objects are exploded dynamically by dragging the handles. After selecting the required options from the **Edit Explosion** dialog box, choose the **Apply** and then the **OK** buttons to create the exploded view, as shown in Figure 9-31.

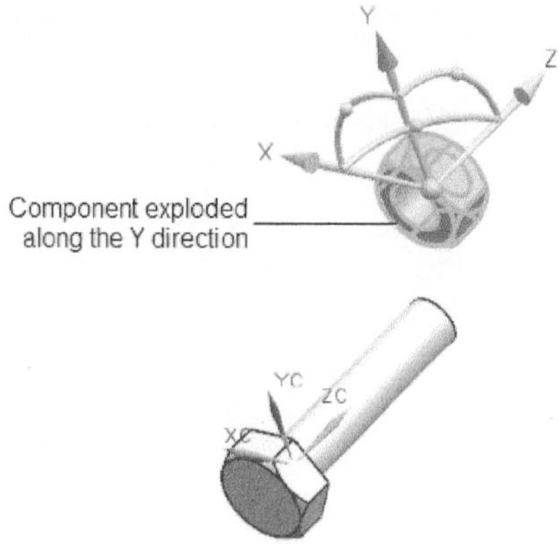

Figure 9-31 *Position of the component after exploding along the Y direction*

If you choose the **Unexplode** button from the **Edit Explosion** dialog box, which is enabled after exploding a selected component, the component will be unexploded. Also, the component will be retained to its original position in the assembly.

Note

*To move only the handles of the selected component, select the **Move Handles Only** radio button from the **Edit Explosion** dialog box and specify a value for the explosion distance in the **Distance** edit box. Note that you can modify an existing explosion distance only in the incremental mode. To modify the explosion distance, select the component whose explosion distance has to be modified and then choose the **Edit Explosion** tool from the **Exploded Views** group; the **Edit Explosion** dialog box will be displayed. Enter the new explosion distance value in the **Distance** edit box, which will be enabled after selecting the required translation or rotational handle. Choose the **Apply** button and then the **OK** button to apply the changes.*

DIGITAL MOCK UP APPLICATION (DMU)

Ribbon:	Assemblies > Create DMU Workset
Menu:	Assemblies > Create DMU Workset

Digital Mock Up (DMU) is an application in NX that provides tools to prepare for design reviews. In the DMU application, you can create a new DMU assembly type known as a workset. In a DMU assembly, you can save snapshots of view orientations, position of components, and of visibility of the components displayed in the drawing window. Without affecting the original design assembly, you can manipulate the components of a DMU assembly to take different snapshots. During the review process, you can click on your saved snapshots to quickly apply different views, orientations, and configurations of an assembly. To do so, open the assembly file in the Assembly environment and choose the **Create DMU Workset** tool from the **Assemblies** tab of the **Ribbon**; the **Create Workset** dialog box will be displayed, refer to Figure 9-32.

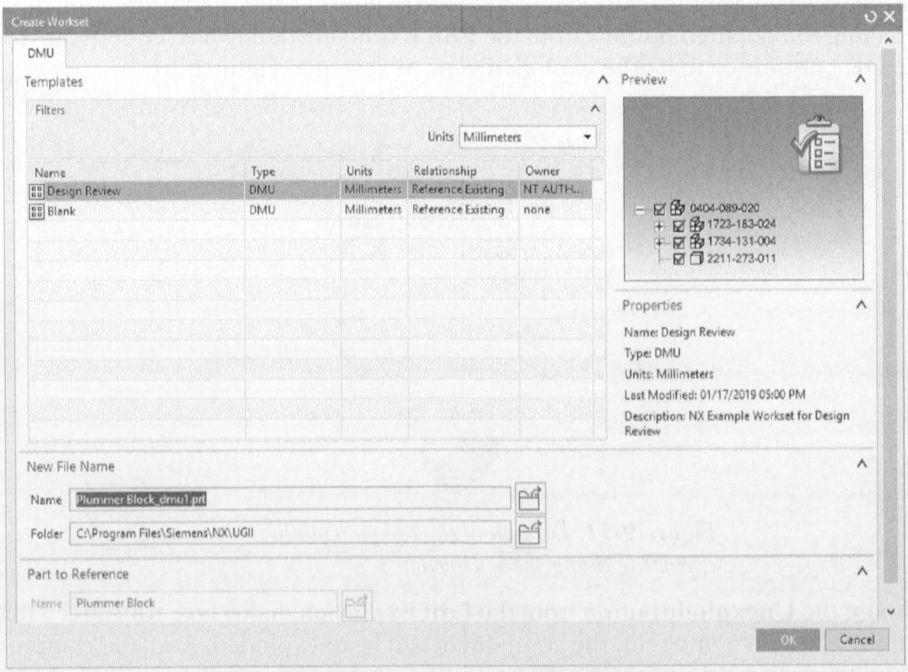

Figure 9-32 The ***Create Workset*** *dialog box*

The **Design Review** template is selected by default in the **Templates** rollout of the **Create Workset** dialog box. Choose the **OK** button to exit the dialog box; the **DMU** environment will be invoked, refer to Figure 9-33. Also, the **Snapshot Navigator** will be added to the **Resource Bar**, refer to Figure 9-33.

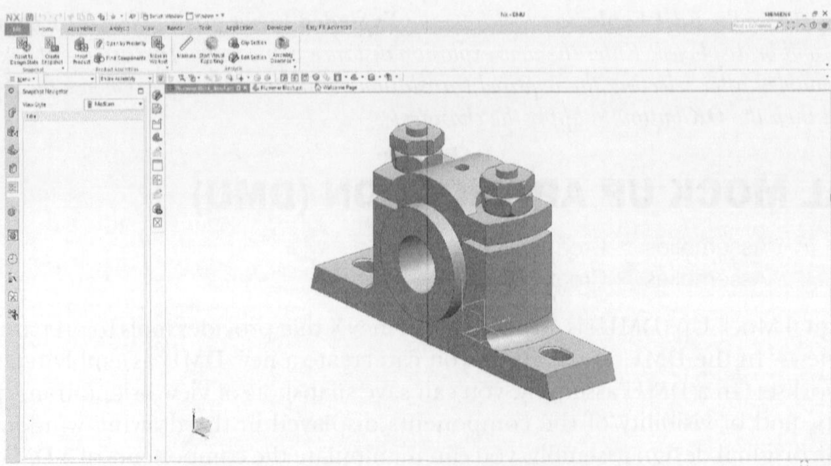

Figure 9-33 The DMU environment in NX

Now, to take the snapshots of the assembly in different orientations and positions, orient the model to the required view and then choose the **Create Snapshot** tool from the **Snapshot** group of the **Home** tab; the snapshot of the oriented assembly model will be loaded to the **Snapshot Navigator** palette. Figure 9-34 shows the **Snapshot Navigator** palette loaded with different snapshots of the same model in different orientations and with components hidden for better visualisation of the required component.

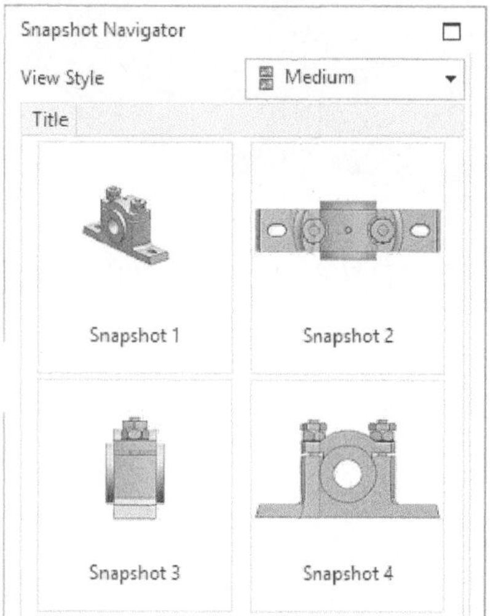

***Figure 9-34** The **Snapshot Navigator** palette loaded with snapshots*

By taking the snapshots of the assembly in any orientation or position, you are actually saving that view which can be used again later at any later stage of design. To do so, right click on any snapshot in the **Snapshot Navigator** palette; a shortcut menu will be displayed. Next, choose the **Apply** option from the shortcut menu; the assembly model will be displayed in the applied view. You can also choose the **Rename** option from the shortcut menu to rename and the **Delete** option to delete the snapshot. Also, you can replace any snapshot view with the current view of the assembly model. To do so, right click on the snapshot to be replaced and then choose the **Replace** option from the shortcut menu displayed. You can reset the assembly model to its original orientation by choosing the **Reset to Design State** tool from the **Snapshot** group of the **Home** tab.

TUTORIALS

Tutorial 1

In this tutorial, you will create exploded views of the Flange Coupling assembly. The exploded state of the Flange Coupling assembly is shown in Figure 9-35. The dimensions of the components are given in Figures 9-36 through 9-38. You will use the automatic explosion method for completing this tutorial. Save the configuration with the name *Flange Coupling.prt* at the location *\NX\c09\Flange Coupling.* **(Expected time: 1.5 hr)**

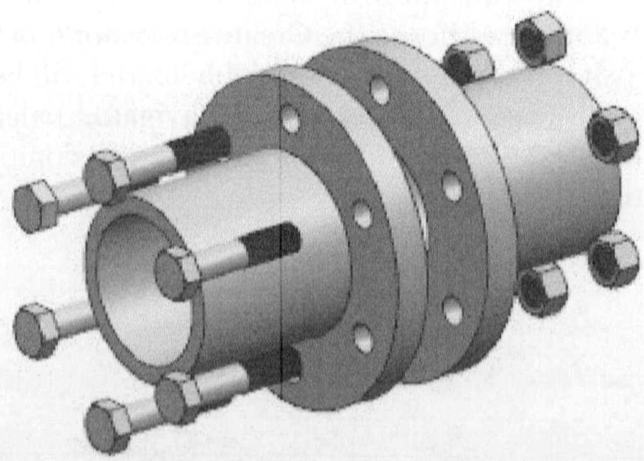

Figure 9-35 The exploded view of the Flange Coupling assembly

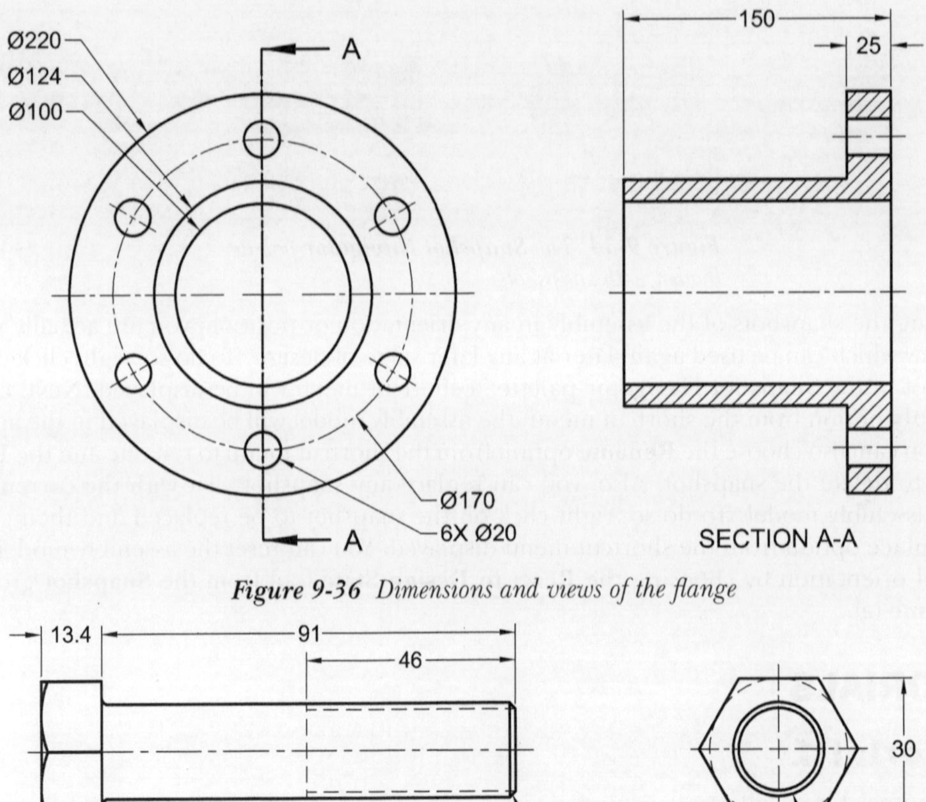

Figure 9-36 Dimensions and views of the flange

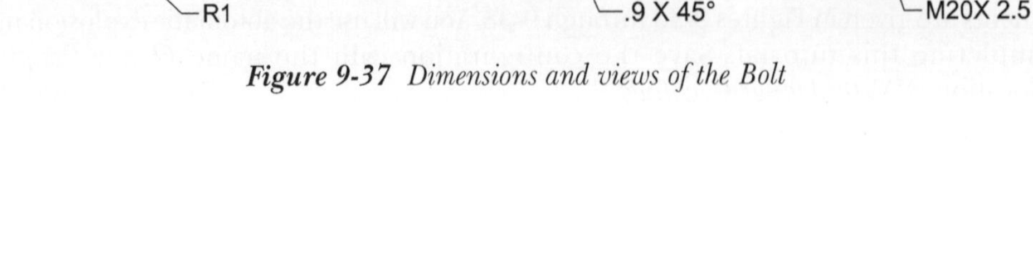

Figure 9-37 Dimensions and views of the Bolt

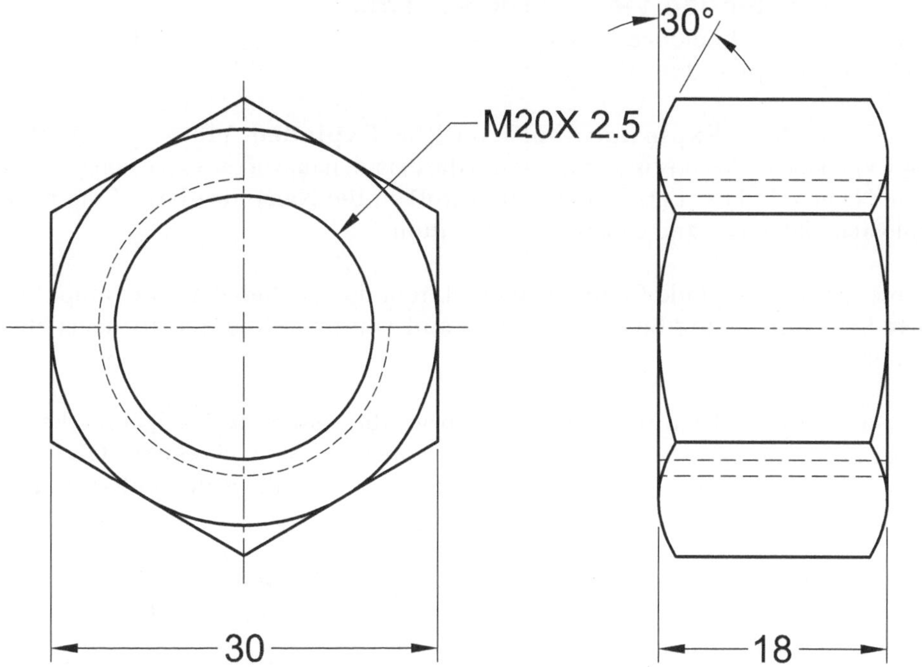

Figure 9-38 *Dimensions and the views of the nut*

The following steps are required to complete this tutorial:

a. Create all the components of the Flange Coupling assembly by using the dimensions given in Figures 9-36 through 9-38. Save the components in the specified folder.
b. Create a new assembly file and assemble all the components of the Flange Coupling by using the assembly constraints.
c. Expand the **Exploded Views** group of the **Assemblies** tab.
d. Create the exploded views of the Flange Coupling assembly, refer to Figure 9-44.
e. Save the exploded view of the Flange Coupling assembly in the configuration file.

Creating the Components of the Flange Coupling Assembly

1. Create all the components of the Flange Coupling assembly as separate part files and save them at the location *\NX\c09\Flange Coupling*. The views and dimensions of the components are given in Figures 9-36 through 9-38.

2. Start a new file and assemble all the components, refer to Figure 9-39. Save the assembly file in the same folder where the component files were saved.

Invoking the Exploded Views Group

1. Choose the **Exploded Views** group from the **Assemblies** tab; the **Exploded Views** group is displayed in the drawing window.

Creating the Exploded View of the Assembly

After invoking the **Exploded Views** group, you can explode the Flange Coupling assembly by following the procedure given next.

1. Choose the **New Explosion** tool from the **Exploded Views** group; the **New Explosion** dialog box is displayed with the default name of the explosion scheme in the **Name** edit box. Enter **Explosion Tut-01** in the **Name** text box of the **New Explosion** dialog box and choose the **OK** button.

2. Choose the **Auto-explode Components** tool from the **Exploded Views** group; the **Class Selection** dialog box is displayed and you are prompted to select the components.

3. Select all the Bolts from the assembly or from the **Assembly Navigator**; the Bolts are highlighted in the graphics window, refer to Figure 9-39. Next, choose the **OK** button from the dialog box; the **Class Selection** dialog box is closed and the **Auto-explode Components** dialog box is displayed.

4. Enter **150** in the **Distance** edit box of the **Auto-explode Components** dialog box and choose the **OK** button. The exploded view of the assembly after exploding all the Bolts from the assembly is shown in Figure 9-40.

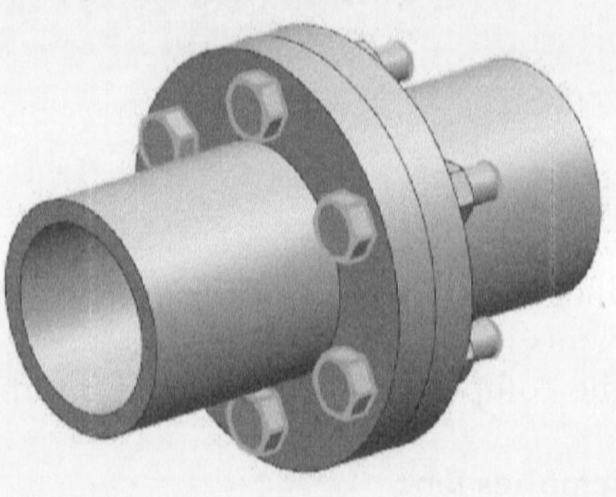

Figure 9-39 Bolts selected from the assembly for explosion

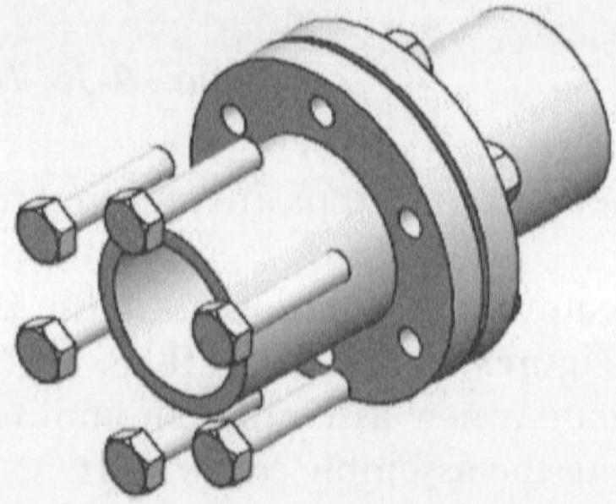

Figure 9-40 The assembly after exploding the Bolts

Note

In this tutorial, the display of the Datum Coordinate System is turned off.

5. Again, choose the **Auto-explode Components** tool from the **Exploded Views** group; the **Class Selection** dialog box is displayed and you are prompted to select the components.

6. Select all the Nuts from the assembly; the Nuts are highlighted in the graphics window, refer to Figure 9-41. Next, choose the **OK** button from the dialog box; the **Class Selection** dialog box is closed and the **Auto-explode Components** dialog box is displayed.

7. Enter **150** in the **Distance** edit box of the **Auto-explode Components** dialog box and choose the **OK** button; the Nuts are exploded. The assembly after exploding all the nuts is shown in Figure 9-42.

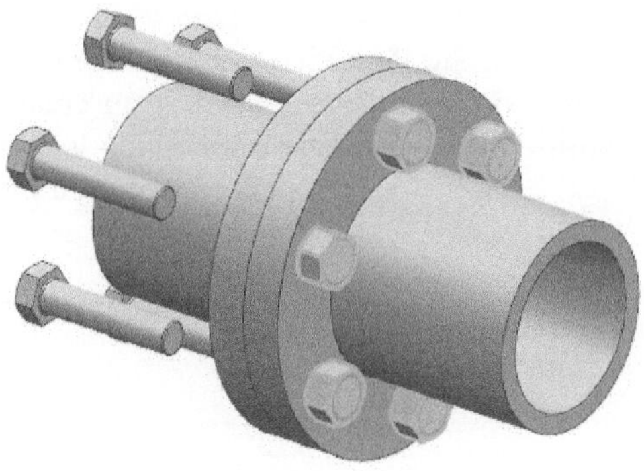

Figure 9-41 Nuts selected from the assembly for explosion

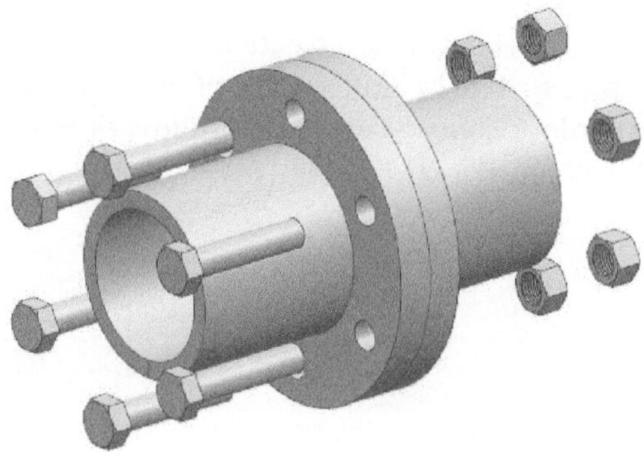

Figure 9-42 The assembly after exploding all Nuts

8. Choose the **Auto-explode Components** tool from the **Exploded Views** group; the **Class Selection** dialog box is displayed and you are prompted to select the components.

9. Select the back Flange from the assembly, refer to Figure 9-43. Next, choose the **OK** button from the dialog box; the **Class Selection** dialog box is closed and the **Auto-explode Components** dialog box is displayed.

10. Enter **-50** in the **Distance** edit box of the **Auto-explode Components** dialog box and choose the **OK** button; the Flange is exploded. The final exploded view of the Flange Coupling assembly is shown in Figure 9-44.

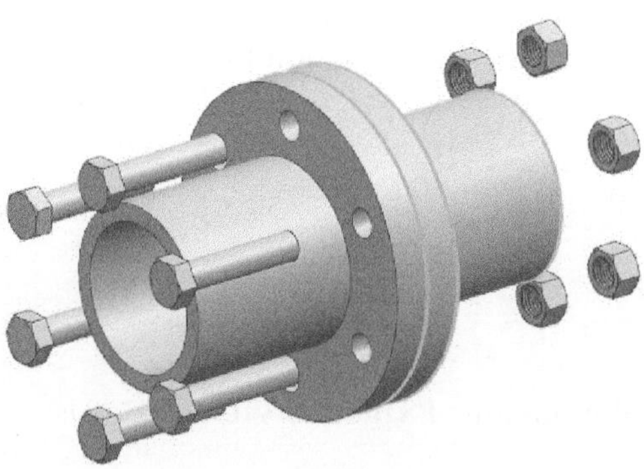

Figure 9-43 The Flange selected from the assembly for explosion

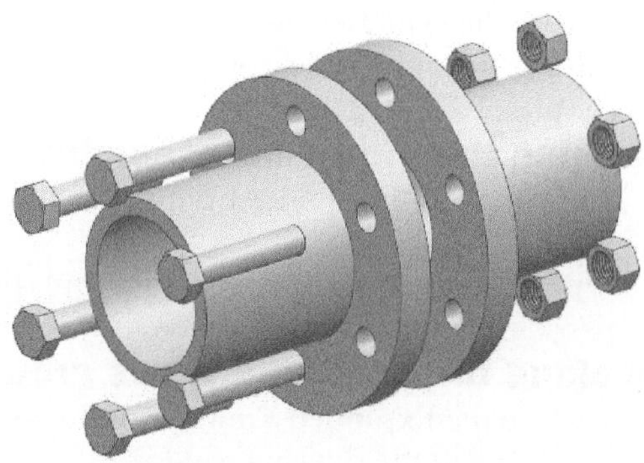

Figure 9-44 The final exploded view of the Flange Coupling assembly

Saving the Exploded View

1. Choose **Menu > File > Close > Save and Close** from the **Top Border Bar** to save and close the file.

Tutorial 2

In this tutorial, you will create the manually exploded view of the Pipe Vice assembly created in Chapter 8. The exploded view of the Pipe Vice assembly is shown in Figure 9-45. After creating the exploded view, save the configuration with the name *Pipe Vice.prt* at the following location *\NX\c09\Pipe Vice.* **(Expected time: 30 min)**

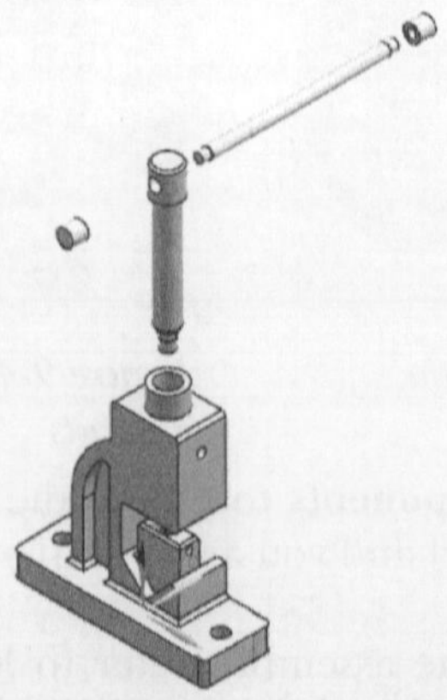

Figure 9-45 *The exploded view of the Pipe Vice assembly*

The following steps are required to complete this tutorial:

a. Copy the *Pipe Vice* folder from the *c08* folder to the *c09* folder.
b. Open the Pipe Vice assembly file.
c. Expand the **Exploded Views** group in the Assembly environment.
d. Create the exploded view of the Pipe Vice assembly using the **Edit Explosion** tool.
e. Save the exploded view of the Pipe Vice assembly in the configuration file.

Opening the Pipe Vice Assembly File

1. Copy the *Pipe Vice* folder from the *c08* folder to the *c09* folder.

2. Open the Pipe Vice assembly file from *c09/Pipe Vice*.

Invoking the Exploded Views group

1. Choose the **Exploded Views** from the **Assemblies** tab; the **Exploded Views** group is displayed in the drawing window.

Assigning a Name to the Exploded View

1. Choose the **New Explosion** tool from the **Exploded Views** group; the **New Explosion** dialog box is displayed with the default name of the explosion in the **Name** edit box.

2. Enter **Explosion Tut-02** as the name of the explosion in the **Name** text box of the **New Explosion** dialog box and choose the **OK** button; the **Edit Explosion** tool is enabled in the **Exploded Views** group.

Exploding the Screw, Handle Screw, and Handle Along the Z Direction

Next, you need to explode the Screw, Handle Screws, and Handle along the Z direction.

1. Choose the **Edit Explosion** tool from the **Exploded Views** group; the **Edit Explosion** dialog box is displayed. By default, the **Select Objects** radio button is selected in this dialog box and you are prompted to select the components to explode.

Edit Explosion

2. Select the Screw, Handle Screws, and Handle from the assembly and then select the **Move Objects** radio button from the dialog box; a dynamic triad is displayed, refer to Figure 9-46.

3. Click on the arrowhead of the Z handle of the dynamic triad; the **Distance** edit box is enabled in the **Edit Explosion** dialog box.

4. Enter **120** as the explosion distance in the **Distance** edit box.

5. Choose the **OK** button from the **Edit Explosion** dialog box; the selected components are exploded, as shown in Figure 9-47.

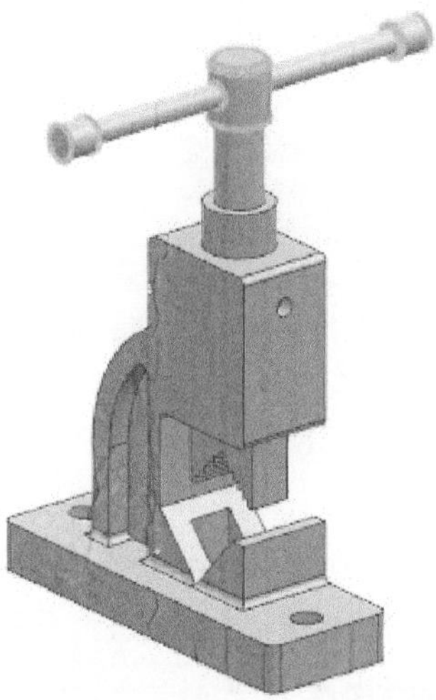

Figure 9-46 *The components selected for explosion*

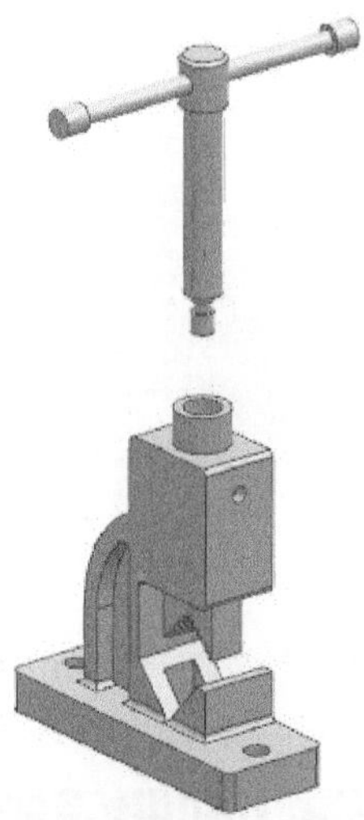

Figure 9-47 *The assembly after exploding the selected components*

Note

In this tutorial, the display of the Datum Coordinate System has been turned off.

Exploding the Movable Jaw

Now, you need to explode the Movable Jaw using the following steps:

1. Choose the **Edit Explosion** tool from the **Exploded Views** group; the **Edit Explosion** dialog box is displayed. By default, the **Select Objects** radio button is selected in this dialog box and you are prompted to select the components to explode.

Edit Explosion

2. Select the Movable Jaw from the assembly, as shown in Figure 9-48, and then select the **Move Objects** radio button from the **Edit Explosion** dialog box; a dynamic triad is displayed on the Movable Jaw.

3. Click on the arrowhead of the Z Handle of the dynamic triad; the **Distance** edit box is enabled in the **Edit Explosion** dialog box.

4. Enter **-30** as the explosion distance in the **Distance** edit box.

5. Choose the **OK** button from the **Edit Explosion** dialog box; the Movable Jaw is exploded. The resulting exploded view of the assembly is shown in Figure 9-49.

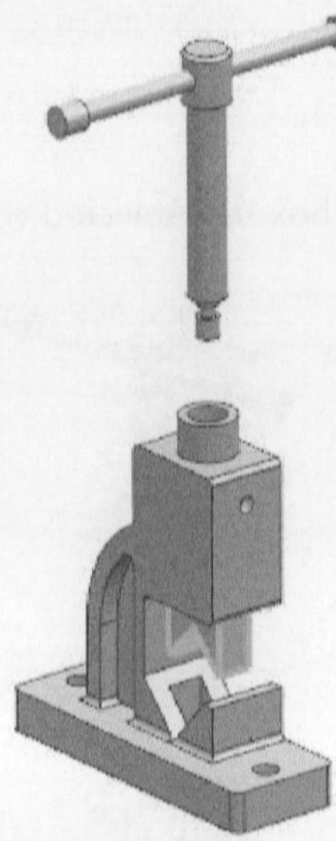

Figure 9-48 The Movable Jaw selected for explosion

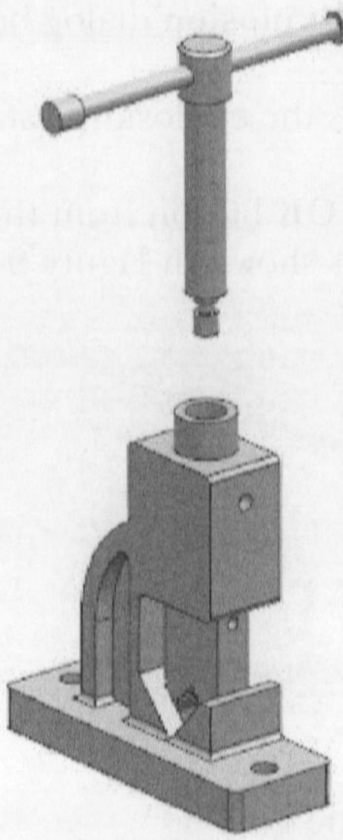

Figure 9-49 The assembly after exploding the Movable Jaw

Exploding the Handle Screw Along the Y Direction

Next, you need to explode the Handle screw.

1. Choose the **Edit Explosion** tool from the **Exploded Views** group; the **Edit Explosion** dialog box is displayed. By default, the **Select Objects** radio button is selected in this dialog box and you are prompted to select the components to explode.

2. Select the right Handle Screw from the assembly, as shown in Figure 9-50, and then select the **Move Objects** radio button from the **Edit Explosion** dialog box; a dynamic triad is displayed on the Handle Screw.

3. Click on the arrowhead of the Y Handle of the dynamic triad; the **Distance** edit box is enabled in the **Edit Explosion** dialog box.

4. Enter **140** as the explosion distance in the **Distance** edit box of the dialog box.

5. Choose the **OK** button from the **Edit Explosion** dialog box to exit it. The resulting exploded view of the assembly is shown in Figure 9-51.

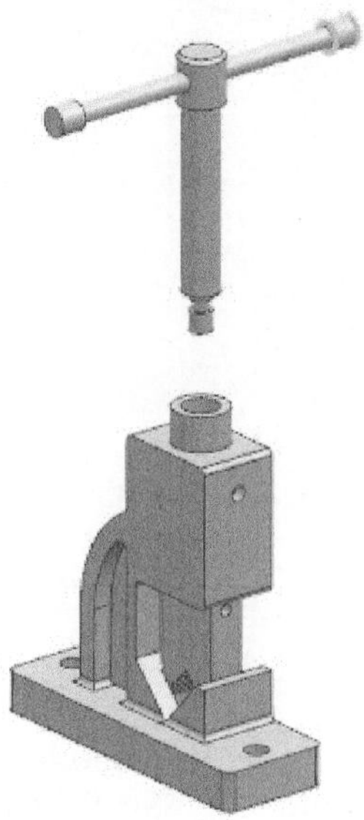

Figure 9-50 *The Handle Screw selected from the assembly for explosion*

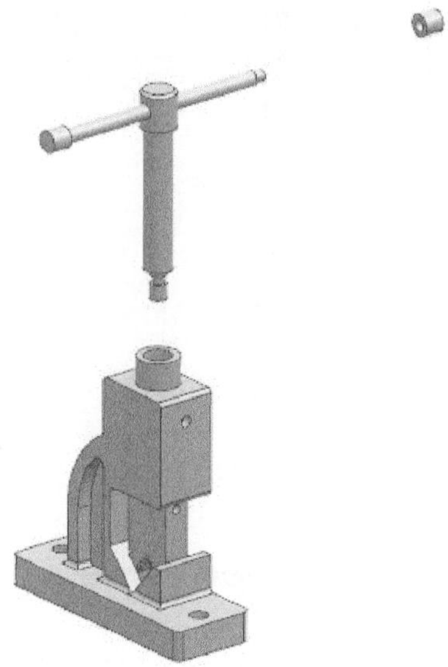

Figure 9-51 *The assembly after exploding the Handle Screw*

Exploding the Handle Along the Y Direction

Next, you need to explode the Handle.

1. Choose the **Edit Explosion** tool from the **Exploded Views** group; the **Edit Explosion** dialog box is displayed. By default, the **Select Objects** radio button is selected in this dialog box and you are prompted to select the components to explode.

2. Select the Handle from the assembly and then select the **Move Objects** radio button from the **Edit Explosion** dialog box; a dynamic triad is displayed on the Handle, refer to Figure 9-52.

3. Click on the arrowhead of the Y Handle of the dynamic triad; the **Distance** edit box is enabled in the **Edit Explosion** dialog box.

4. Enter **-115** as the explosion distance in the **Distance** edit box of the dialog box.

5. Choose the **OK** button from the **Edit Explosion** dialog box to exit. The resulting exploded view of the assembly is shown in Figure 9-53.

Figure 9-52 The Handle selected from the assembly for explosion

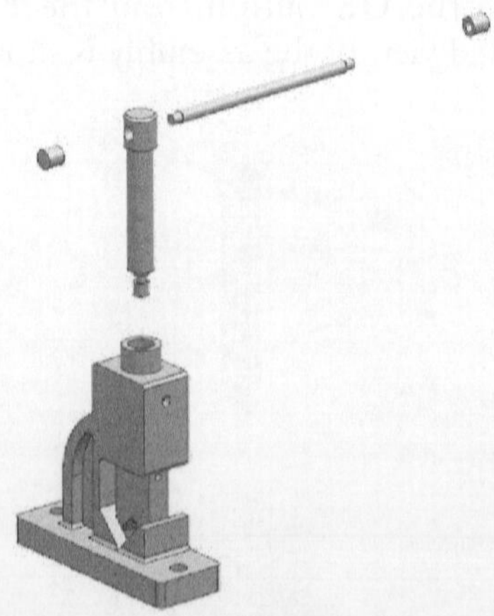

Figure 9-53 The assembly after exploding the Handle

Saving the Exploded Views

1. Choose **Menu > File > Save** from the **Top Border Bar** to save the exploded view. The final exploded view of the Pipe Vice assembly is shown in Figure 9-54. Next, close the file.

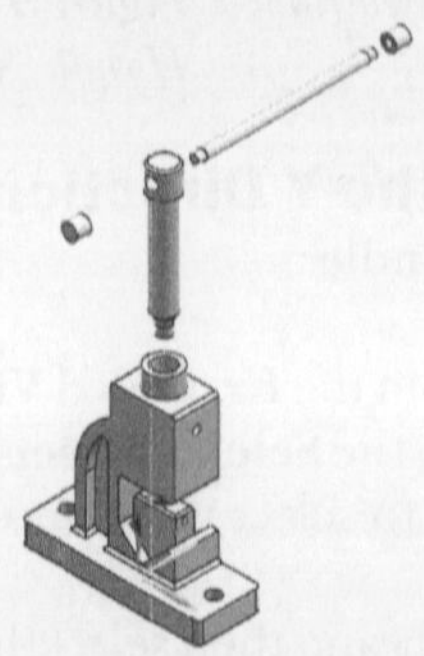

Figure 9-54 The final exploded view of the Pipe Vice assembly

Tutorial 3

In this tutorial, you will create the Radial Engine assembly shown in Figures 9-55 and 9-56. The Radial Engine assembly will be created in two parts, one will be the sub-assembly and the other will be the main assembly. The dimensions of the components of the Radial Engine assembly are shown in Figures 9-57 through 9-61. Save the assembly file with the name *Radial Engine.prt* at the location *\NX\c09\Radial Engine.* **(Expected time: 4 hr)**

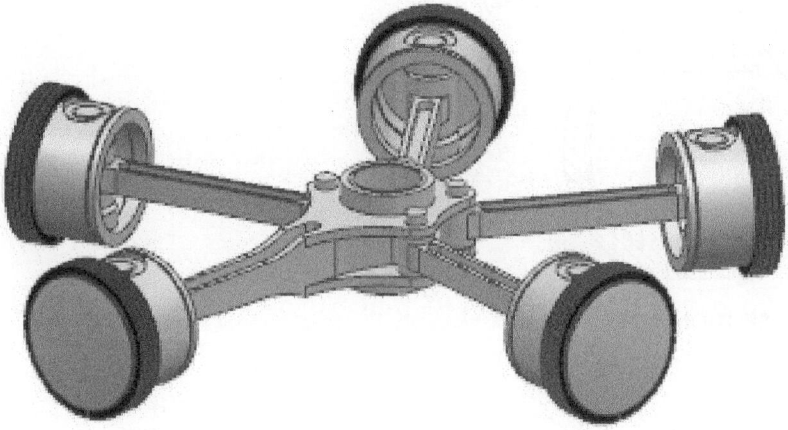

Figure 9-55 The Radial Engine assembly

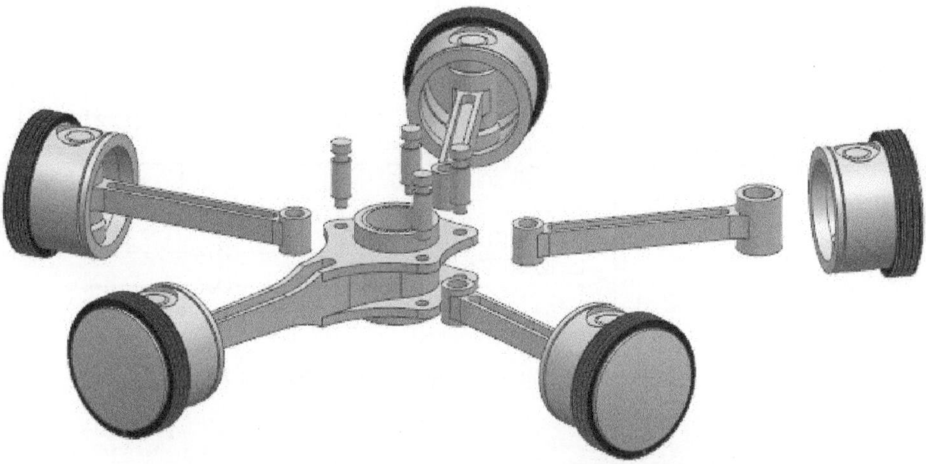

Figure 9-56 The exploded view of the assembly

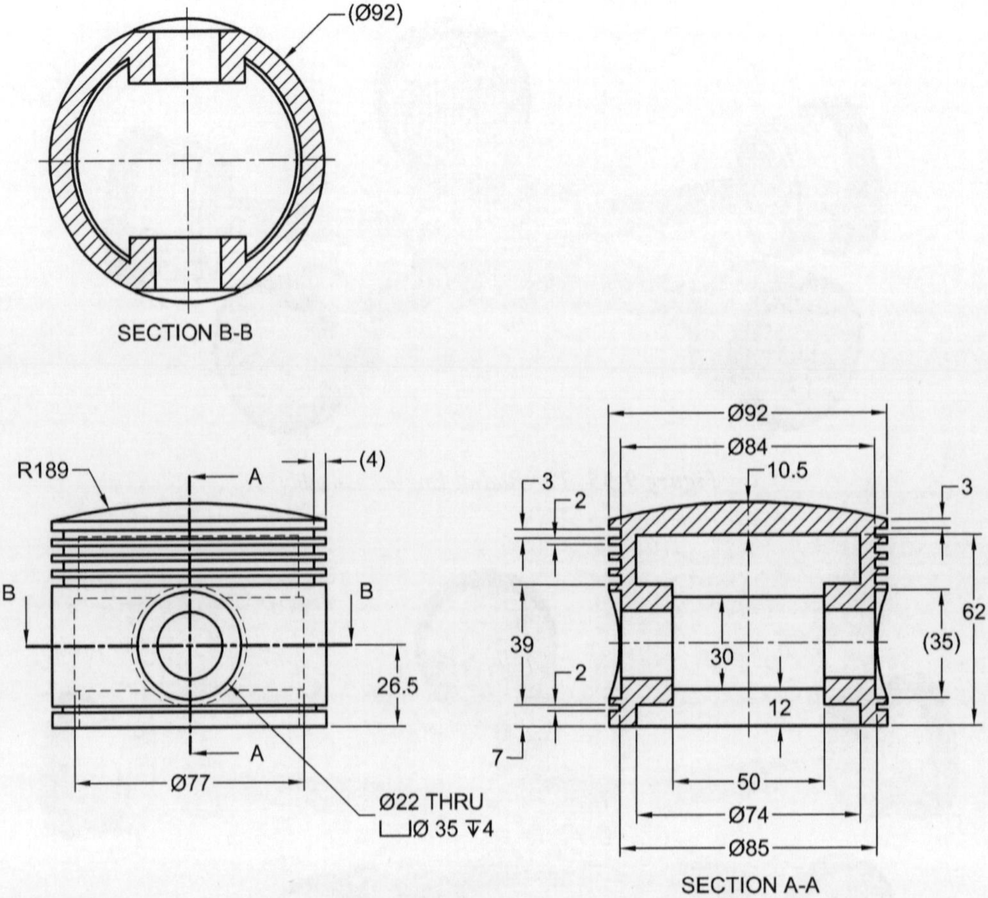

Figure 9-57 *Views and dimensions of the Piston*

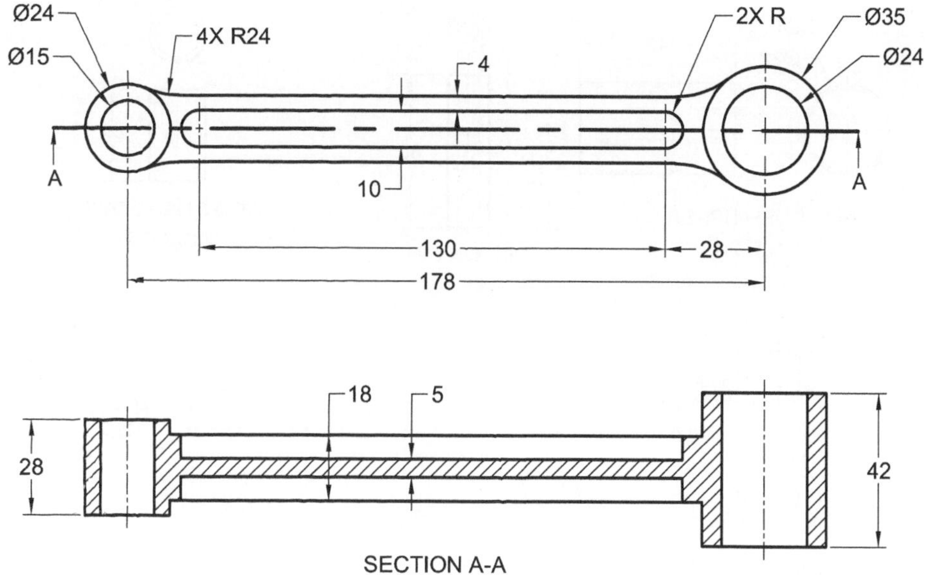

Figure 9-58 Views and dimensions of the Articulated Rod

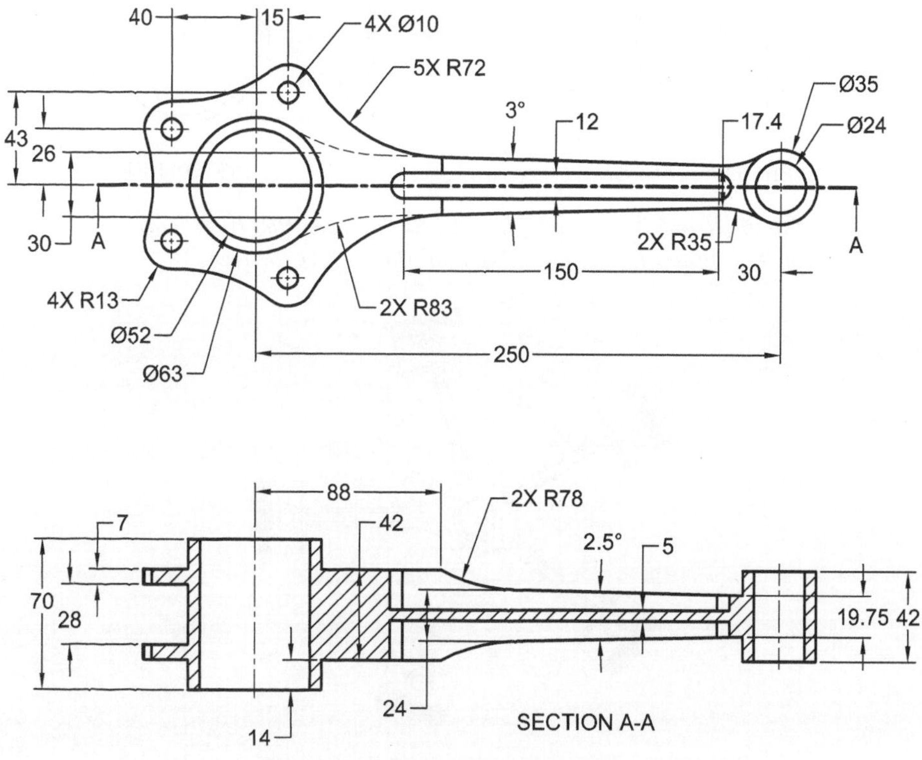

Figure 9-59 Views and dimensions of the Master Rod

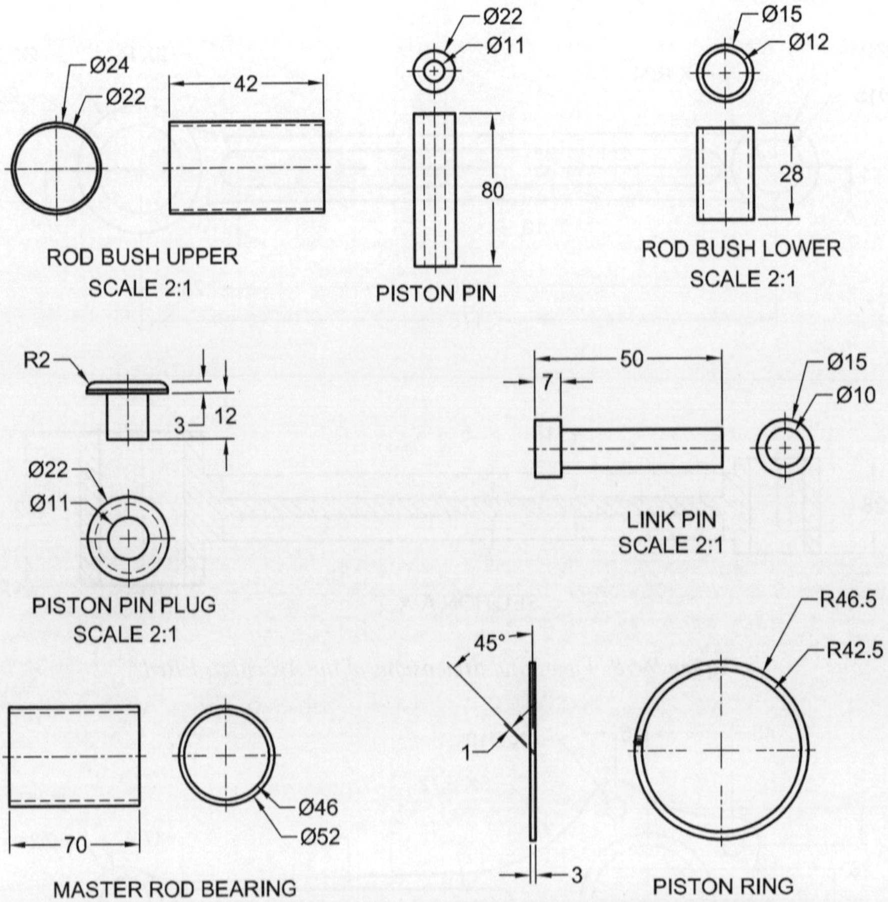

Figure 9-60 *Views and dimensions of the Rod Bush Upper, Rod Bush Lower, Piston Pin Plug, Piston Pin, Piston Rings, Link Pin, and Master Rod Bearing*

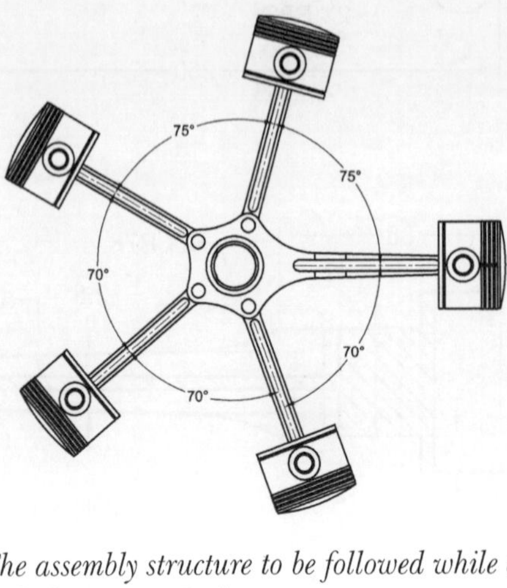

Figure 9-61 *The assembly structure to be followed while assembling the subassemblies with the Master Rod*

Since this is a large assembly, you need to create it in two steps. First, you need to create the sub-assembly that consists of the Articulated Rod, Piston, Rings, Piston Pin, Rod Bush Upper, Rod Bush Lower, and Piston Pin Plug. Next, you will create the main assembly by assembling the Master Rod with the Piston, Piston Rings, Piston Pin, Master Rod Bearing, and Piston Pin Plug, and the instances of the sub-assembly.

The following steps are required to complete this tutorial:

a. Create all the components of the Radial Engine assembly and save them in the *Radial Engine* folder.
b. Start a new file and create the sub-assembly, refer to Figures 9-62 through 9-64.
c. Start a new assembly and then assemble the sub-assembly and the individual components to create the main assembly, refer to Figures 9-67 and 9-68.
d. Save the file.

Creating the Components

1. Create a folder with the name *Radial Engine* at */NX/c09*. Create all the components of the Radial Engine as individual part files and save them in this folder. The views and dimensions of the components are given in Figures 9-57 through 9-61.

Creating the Sub-assembly

1. Start a new file with the name Articulated Rod_Piston and save it in the same folder where the parts were saved. Next, invoke the Assembly environment.

2. Assemble the components in the sequence as illustrated in Figure 9-62. The assembly after assembling the Rod Bush Upper, Rod Bush Lower, Piston, Piston Pin, and Piston Pin Plugs is shown in Figure 9-63.

3. Assemble the Piston Ring to the Piston by using the assembly constraints. The completed Articulated Rod_Piston sub-assembly is shown in Figure 9-64. Next, choose the **Save** button.

Note

*1. You can change the color of the Piston Rings for a better display. To do so, choose **Menu > Edit > Object Display** from the **Top Border Bar**; the **Class Selection** dialog box is displayed and you are prompted to select the objects to edit. Select the Piston Rings from the sub-assembly and choose the **OK** button; the **Edit Object Display** dialog box is displayed. Choose the **Color** swatch; the **Color** dialog box is displayed. Select the required color and then choose the **OK** button from the **Color** dialog box; the **Edit Object Display** dialog box is displayed again. Next, choose the **OK** button from it.*

*2. In Figure 9-63, the solid texture of the Piston has been changed to the transparent texture. This is done to view the components that are assembled inside the Piston. To change the texture of the Piston from solid to transparent, select the Piston from the drawing window and then invoke the **Edit Object Display** dialog box. Next, move the **Translucency** sliding bar to the value of 75 and then choose the **OK** button from the **Edit Object Display** dialog box. Note that the transparency value of the object ranges from 0 to 100.*

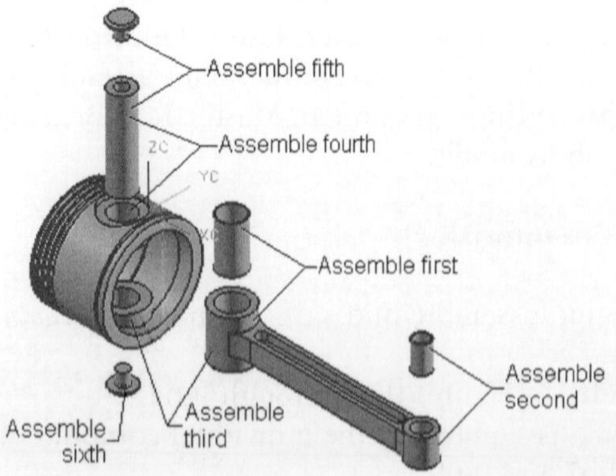

Figure 9-62 *Sequence for assembling the components to create the sub-assembly*

Figure 9-63 *The sub-assembly after assembling the Rod Bush Lower, Rod Bush Upper, Articulated Rod, Piston, Piston Pin, and Piston Pin Plug*

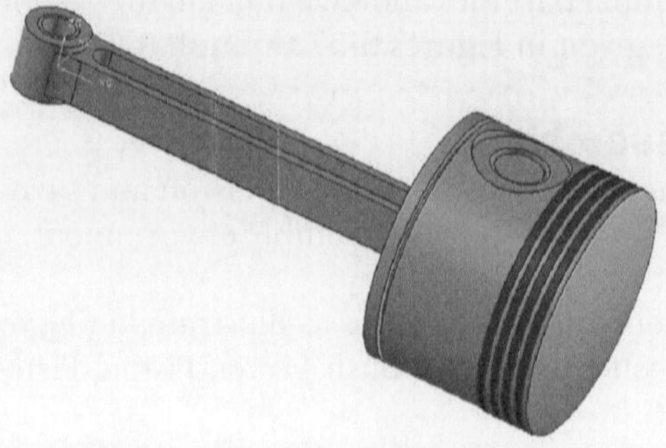

Figure 9-64 *The sub-assembly after assembling all instances of the Piston Rings*

Creating the Main Assembly

In this section, you need to create the main assembly by assembling the sub-assembly and the individual components.

1. Start a new file with the name Radial Engine and specify its location in the same folder where the components and the sub-assembly are saved. Next, invoke the Assembly environment.

2. Assemble the Master Rod, Rod Bush Upper, and Master Rod Bearing using the assembly constraints, refer to Figure 9-65.

3. Next, assemble the Piston, Piston Pin, and Piston Pin Plugs using the assembly constraints, refer to Figure 9-65.

4. Assemble the Piston Rings with the Piston. Change the color of the Piston Rings. The assembly after assembling these components is shown in Figure 9-65.

Figure 9-65 Components assembled in the main assembly

Assembling the Sub-assembly with the Main Assembly

Next, you need to assemble the instances of the Articulated Rod_Piston sub-assembly with the main assembly by using the assembly constraints.

1. Choose the **Add** tool from the **Assemblies** tab; the **Add Component** dialog box is displayed.

2. Choose the **Open** button from the **Add Component** dialog box; the **Part Name** dialog box is displayed. Select the Articulated Rod_Piston sub-assembly from the dialog box and choose the **OK** button.

3. Assemble the first instance of the Articulated Rod_Piston sub-assembly with the main assembly by using the assembly constraints. The assembly after assembling the first instance of the sub-assembly is shown in Figure 9-66.

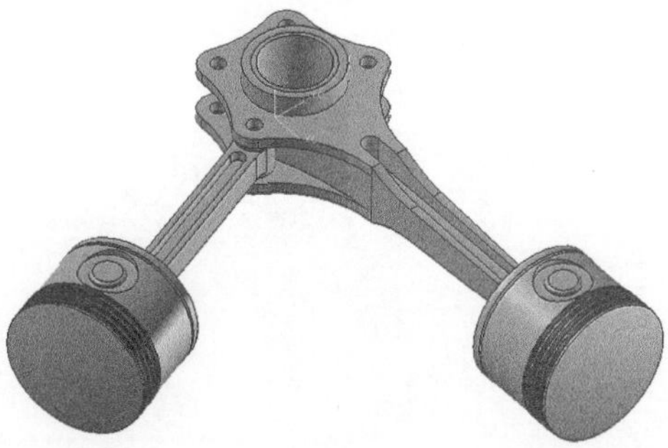

Figure 9-66 The main assembly after assembling the first instance of the sub-assembly

4. Similarly, assemble other instances of the sub-assembly with the main assembly by using the assembly constraints. The assembly structure to be followed while assembling the subassemblies with the main assembly is shown in Figure 9-61.

   The assembly after assembling all the instances of the sub-assembly is shown in Figure 9-67.

Assembling the Link Pin

1. Assemble four instances of the Link Pin with the Master Rod by using the assembly constraints. Modify the color of the Link Pins. The resulting assembly after assembling the Link Pins is shown in Figure 9-68.

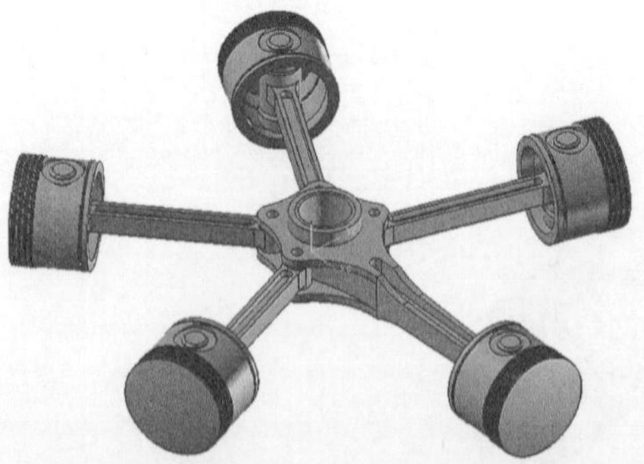

Figure 9-67 The assembly after assembling all instances of the sub-assembly with the main assembly

Figure 9-68 The final Radial Engine assembly

2. Choose **Menu > File > Save** from the **Top Border Bar** to save the assembly. Next, close the file.

Tutorial 4

In this tutorial, you will create the Press Tool assembly shown in Figure 9-69 by using the Top-down assembly design approach. The exploded state of the assembly is shown in Figure 9-70 and the dimensions of its various components are shown in Figures 9-71 through 9-73. After creating the assembly, save it with the name *Press Tool.prt* at the following location: *\NX\c09\Press Tool.*

(Expected time: 2 hrs)

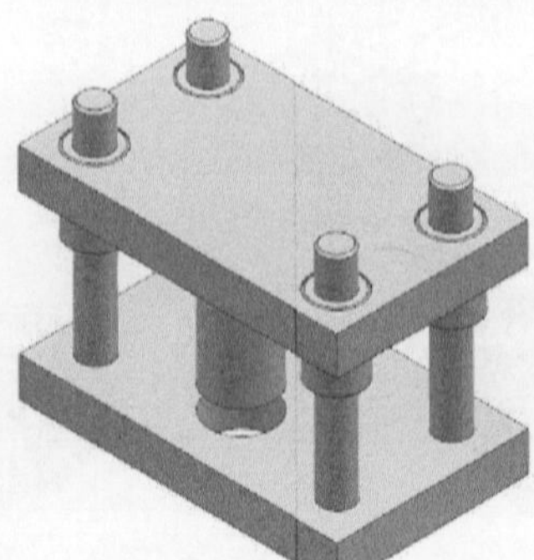

Figure 9-69 The completed Press Tool assembly after assembling the Top Plate with the assembly

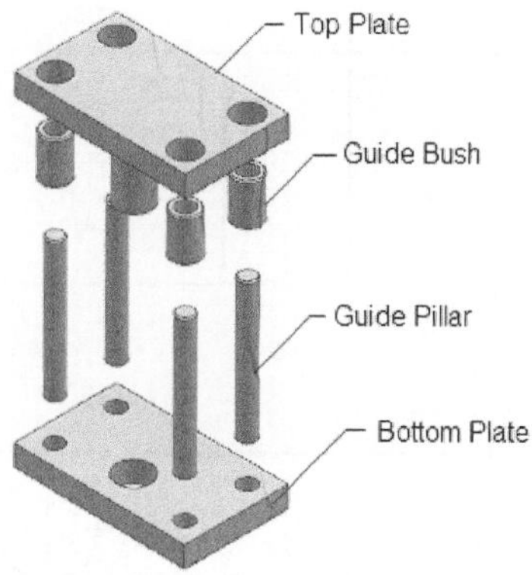

Figure 9-70 *The exploded view of the Press Tool assembly*

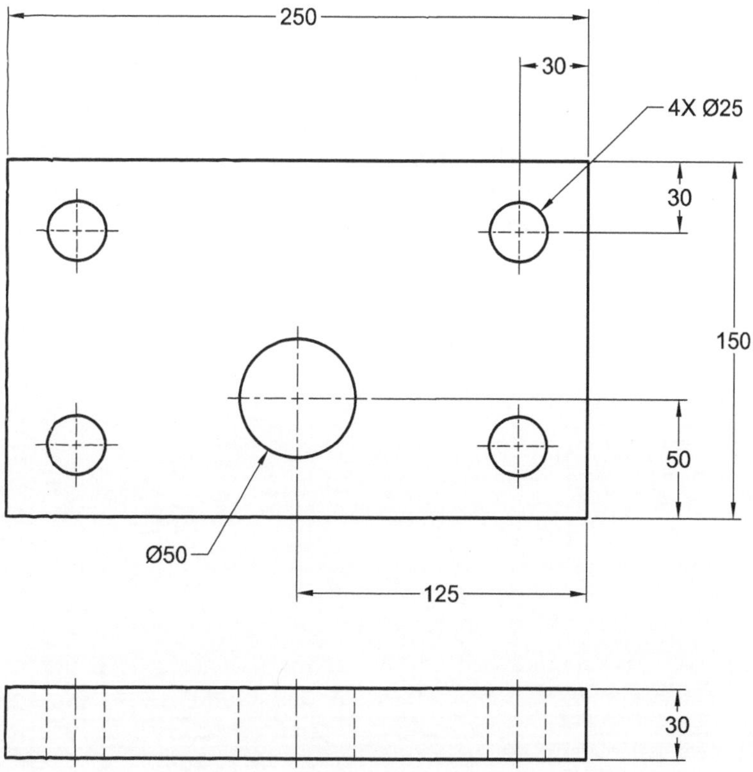

Figure 9-71 Dimensions and views of the Bottom Plate

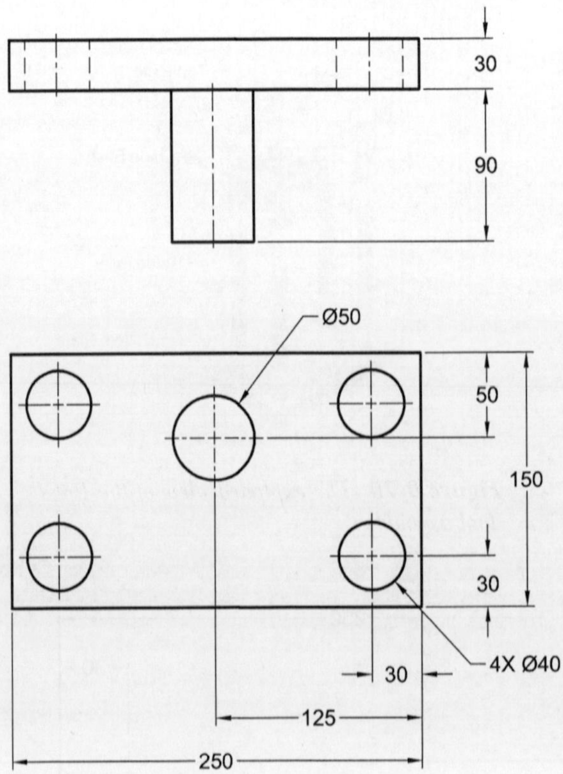

Figure 9-72 Dimensions and views of the Top Plate

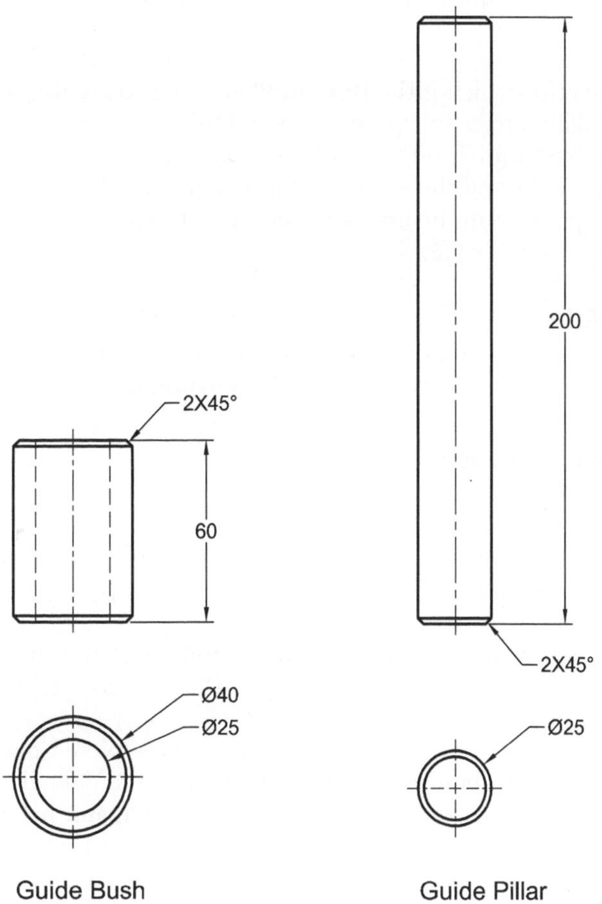

Figure 9-73 *Dimensions and views of the Guide Bush and Guide Pillar*

The following steps are required to complete this tutorial:

a. Start a new file.
b. Create the base feature, which is the Bottom Plate, refer to Figures 9-74 and 9-75.
c. Create the Guide Pillar, refer to Figures 9-76 and 9-77.
d. Create the Guide Bush and Top Plate, refer to Figure 9-78.
e. Save all the components and the assembly file as separate files.
f. Assemble the components in the assembly file, refer to Figure 9-79.
g. Save and close the assembly file.

Starting a New File

1. Start a new file with the name Press Tool using the **Model** template and specify its location as *\NX\c09\Press Tool*. Next, invoke the Assembly environment.

Creating the Bottom Plate

Next, you need to create the Bottom Plate.

1. Choose the **Create New** tool from the **Component** group in the **Assemblies** tab; the **New Component File** dialog box is displayed and you are prompted to select a template.

2. Select the **Model** template from the **Templates** rollout of the dialog box. Next, specify Bottom Plate as the name of the file and *\NX\c09\Press Tool* as the location of the file.

3. Choose the **OK** button from the dialog box; the **Create New Component** dialog box is displayed. Choose the **OK** button from this dialog box; the part file is created. The name and node of this part file is displayed in the **Assembly Navigator** below the parent assembly file node.

4. Choose the **Assembly Navigator** tab from the **Resource Bar**; the **Assembly Navigator** is displayed.

5. Double-click on the name **Bottom Plate** in the **Assembly Navigator**; the part gets activated.

6. Create sketch for the Bottom Plate on the XC-YC plane, as shown in Figure 9-74. Next, exit the sketch.

7. Extrude the sketch upto 30 mm in an upward direction; the Bottom Plate is created, as shown in Figure 9-75.

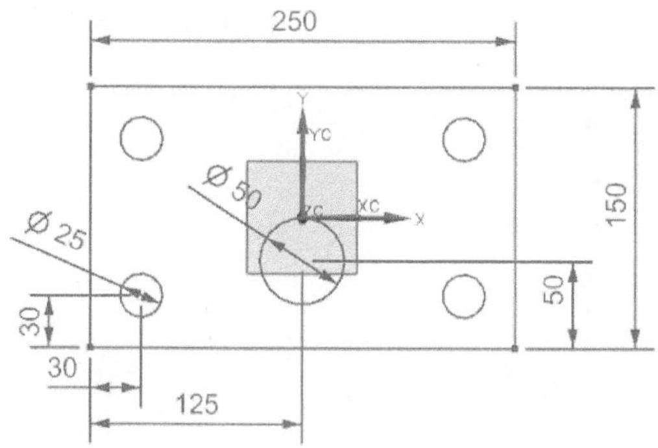

Figure 9-74 The sketch of the base feature

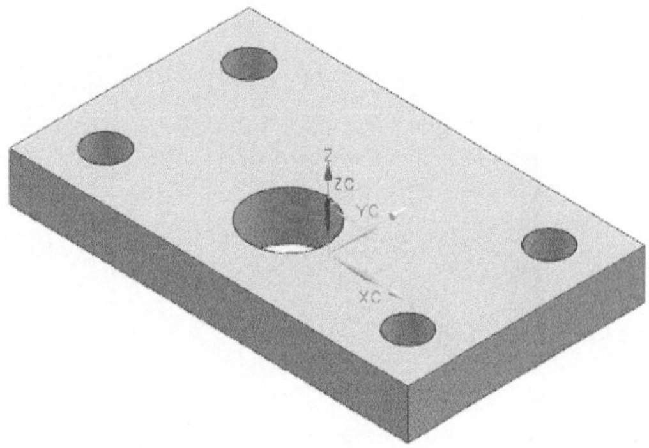

Figure 9-75 The base feature created

8. Double-click on the **Press Tool** (parent assembly) in the **Assembly Navigator** to activate it.

Creating the Guide Pillar

Next, you need to create the Guide Pillar.

1. Choose the **Create New** tool from the **Component** group of the **Assemblies** tab; the **New Component File** dialog box is displayed and you are prompted to select a template.

2. Select the **Model** template from the **Templates** rollout of the dialog box. Next, specify Guide Pillar as the name of the file and *\NX\c09\Press Tool* as the location of the file.

3. Choose the **OK** button from the dialog box; the **Create New Component** dialog box is displayed. In this dialog box, select the **Model ("MODEL")** option from the **Reference Set** drop-down list in the **Settings** rollout and then choose the **OK** button; the new part file is created.

4. Choose the **Assembly Navigator** tab from the **Resource Bar**; the **Assembly Navigator** is displayed.

5. Double-click on the name **Guide Pillar** in the **Assembly Navigator**; the part gets activated, and the Bottom Plate as well as the parent assembly get deactivated.

6. Invoke the sketching environment by selecting the XC-YC plane as the sketching plane. Next, create a circle of diameter 25 mm anywhere in the drawing window and then exit the Sketch in Task environment.

7. Extrude the sketch upto 200 mm in an upward direction, refer to Figure 9-76.

8. Choose the **Chamfer** tool from the **Feature** group; the **Chamfer** dialog box is displayed.

9. In this dialog box, select the **Offset and Angle** option from the **Cross Section** drop-down list of the **Offsets** rollout. Next, enter **2** in the **Distance** edit box and **45** in the **Angle** edit box.

10. Select the top and bottom circular edges of the feature to apply chamfer on it. Next, choose the **OK** button from the **Chamfer** dialog box; the Guide Pillar is created, refer to Figure 9-77.

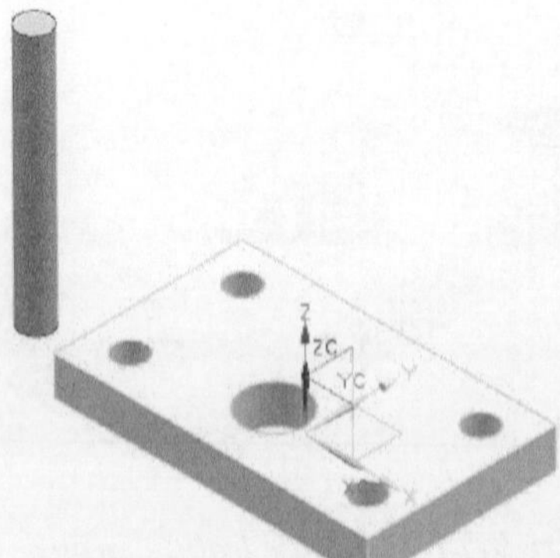

Figure 9-76 *Guide Pillar before creating the chamfer feature*

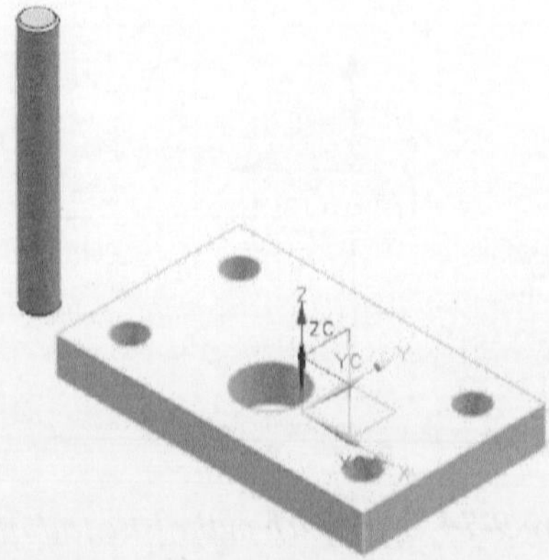

Figure 9-77 *Guide Pillar after creating the chamfer feature*

11. Double-click on the **Press Tool** (parent assembly) in the **Assembly Navigator** to activate it.

12. Create the Guide Bush and the Top Plate as you created the Guide Pillar, refer to Figure 9-78. For dimensions, refer to Figures 9-72 and 9-73.

Figure 9-78 *Bottom Plate, Guide Pillar, Guide Bush, and Top Plate*

Saving the Components

1. After creating all parts of the assembly in the assembly file, choose the **Save** button from the **Quick Access** toolbar; all parts and the assembly are saved as separate files at the specified location.

2. After saving all components and the assembly file, close the assembly file.

Assembling the Individual Components

1. Open the *Press Tool* assembly file.

2. Insert three instances of Guide Bush and Guide Pillar in the drawing window by using the **Add** tool.

3. Choose the **Assembly Constraints** tool from the **Assemblies** tab and apply the required assembly constraints to all components. The final Press Tool assembly is shown in Figure 9-79.

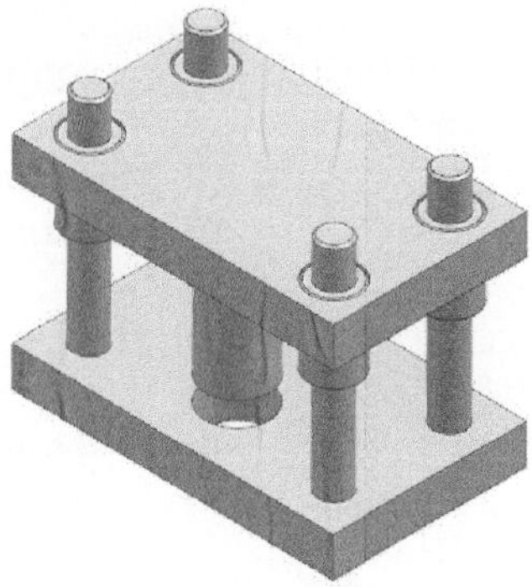

Figure 9-79 *The final Press Tool assembly*

4. Save the assembly file and then close it.

Self-Evaluation Test

Answer the following questions and then compare them to those given at the end of this chapter:

1. The ________________ group contains a set of tools for creating the exploded views.

2. The ________________ tool is used to save the solid bodies created as separate part files in the top-down assembly design approach.

3. The ________________ tool is used for editing an exploded view.

4. The ________________ tool is used for exploding the components automatically.

5. In NX, you have a separate tool for creating subassemblies. (T/F)

6. The sub-assembly files have the same file name extension as the assembly files. (T/F)

7. You can create datum planes using the **View Section** dialog box. (T/F)

8. Exploded views, once created, can be modified in the assembly application of NX. (T/F)

9. There is a separate tool for manually exploding the components in the **Exploded Views** group of the **Assemblies** tab. (T/F)

10. Clearance between the components can be checked by using the **Menu > Analysis > Assembly Clearance > Perform Analysis** option from the **Top Border Bar**. (T/F)

Review Questions

Answer the following questions:

1. Which of the following tools is used for replacing a component in an assembly?

   (a) **Substitute Component** (b) **Mate Component**
   (c) **Edit Explosion** (d) **Replace Component**

2. Which of the following groups contains the tools for creating the exploded views?

   (a) **Exploded Views** (b) **Assemblies**
   (c) **Assembly Sequencing Playback** (d) None of these

3. Which of the following tools is used for performing an interference check on an assembly?

   (a) **Exploded Views** (b) **Standard**
   (c) **Simple Clearance Check** (d) None of these

4. Which of the following tools is used to create the automatic exploded view of the components?

   (a) **Exploded Views** (b) **Assemble**
   (c) **Auto-explode Components** (d) None of these

5. One assembly can have only one exploded view. (T/F)

6. The **Delete Explosion** tool is used to delete an exploded view. (T/F)

7. You can modify the dimensions of a component in the Assembly environment. (T/F)

8. The **Check Clearance** tool is used to check the interference between the components in the assembly. (T/F)

9. You can set the transparency of a component in the assembly application for simplifying the assembly. (T/F)

10. Assembly constraints have no relation with the exploded views. (T/F)

EXERCISES

Exercise 1

Create the Shaper Tool Head assembly shown in Figure 9-80. After creating the assembly, create its exploded view, as shown in Figure 9-81. The dimensions of the components are given in Figures 9-82 through 9-86. Save the assembly file with the name *Shaper.prt* at the location *\NX\c09\Shaper Tool head.*

(Expected time: 4 hr)

Figure 9-80 The Shaper Tool Head assembly

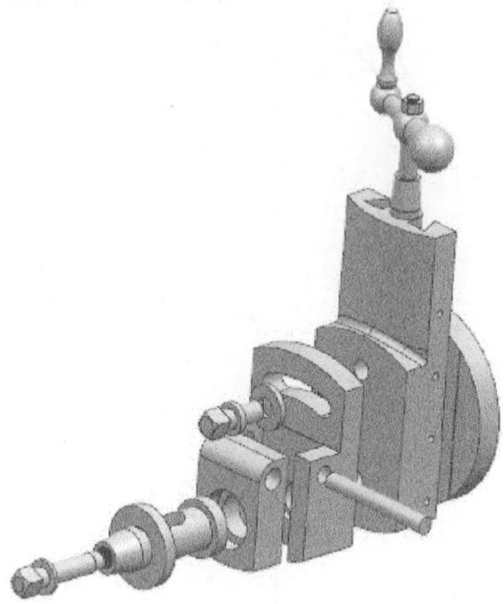

Figure 9-81 The exploded view of the Shaper Tool Head assembly

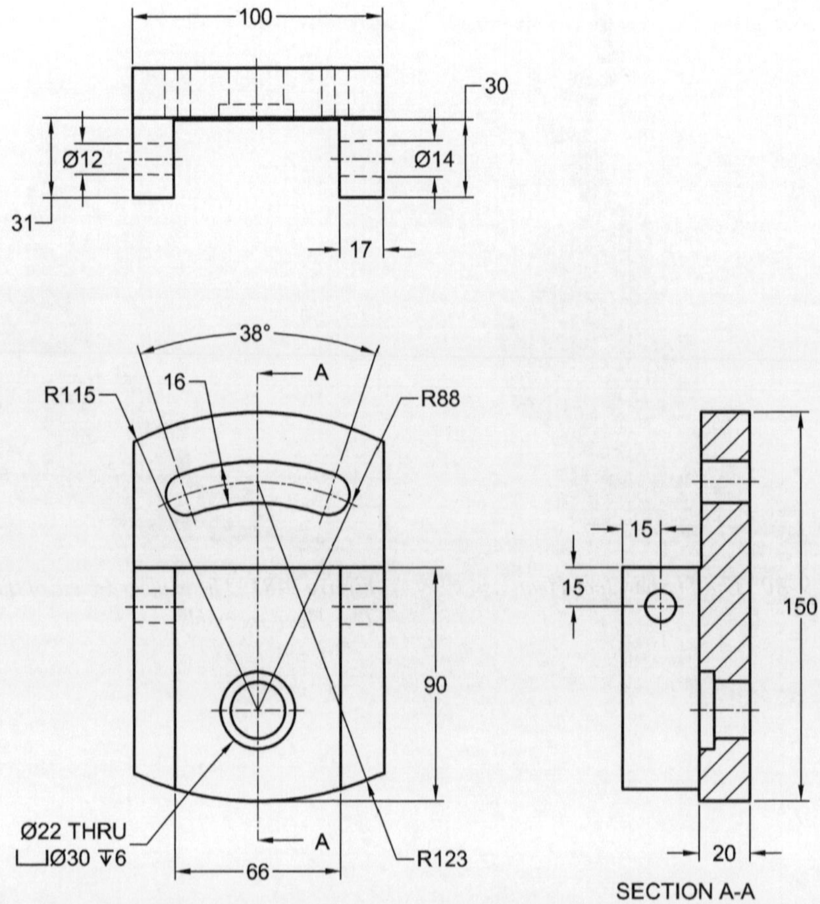

Figure 9-82 *Views and dimensions of the Swivel Plate*

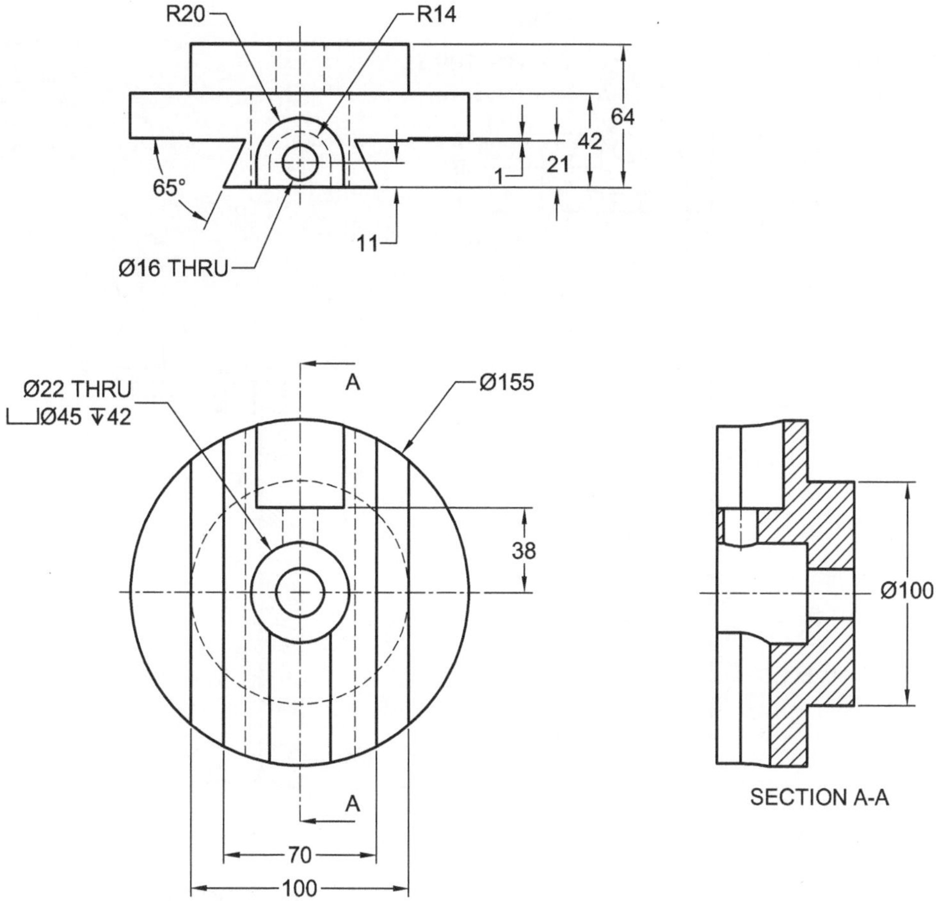

Figure 9-83 *Views and dimensions of the Back Plate*

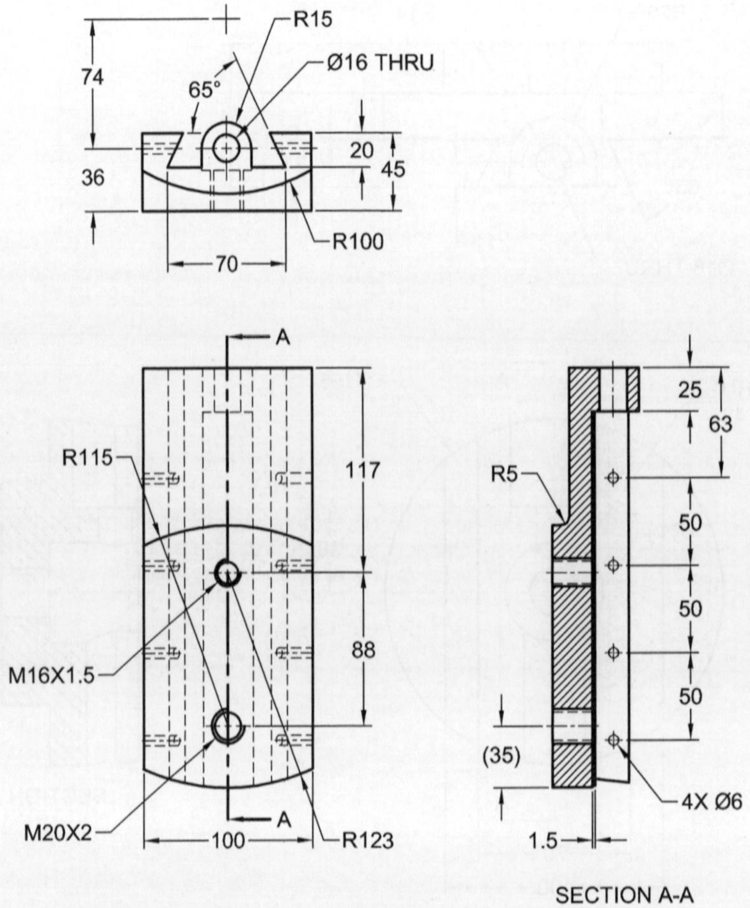

Figure 9-84 Views and dimensions of the Vertical Slide

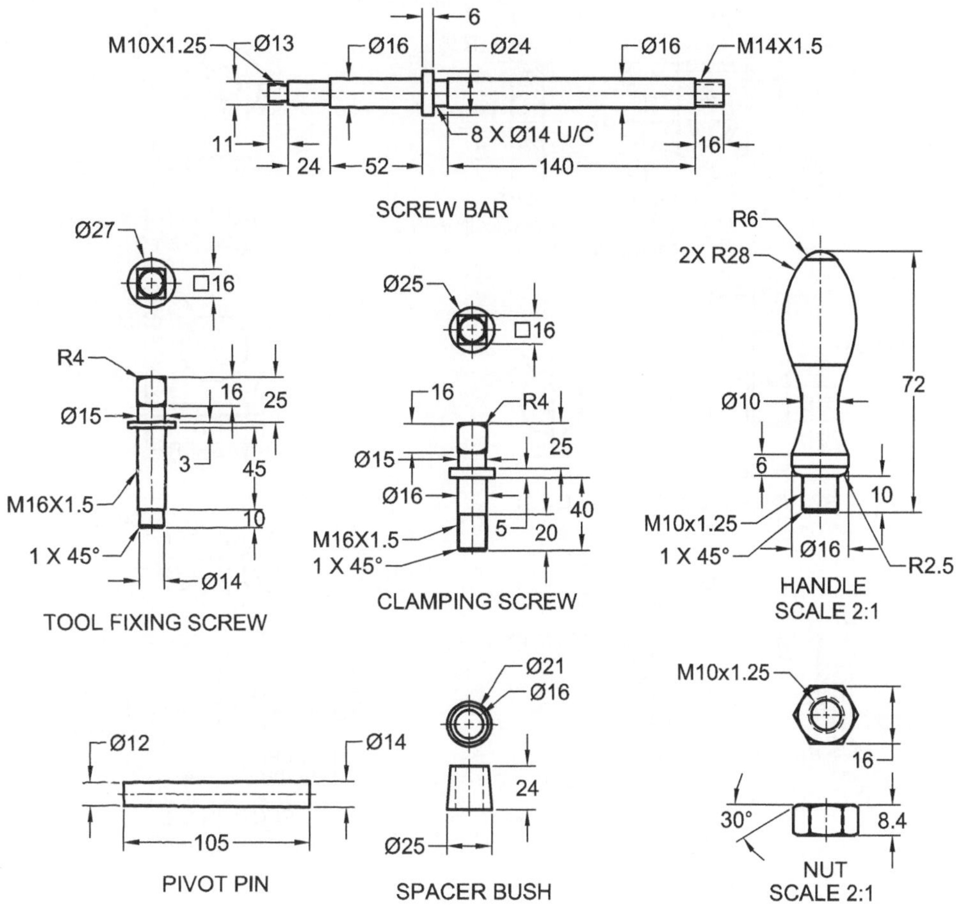

Figure 9-85 *Views and dimensions of various components*

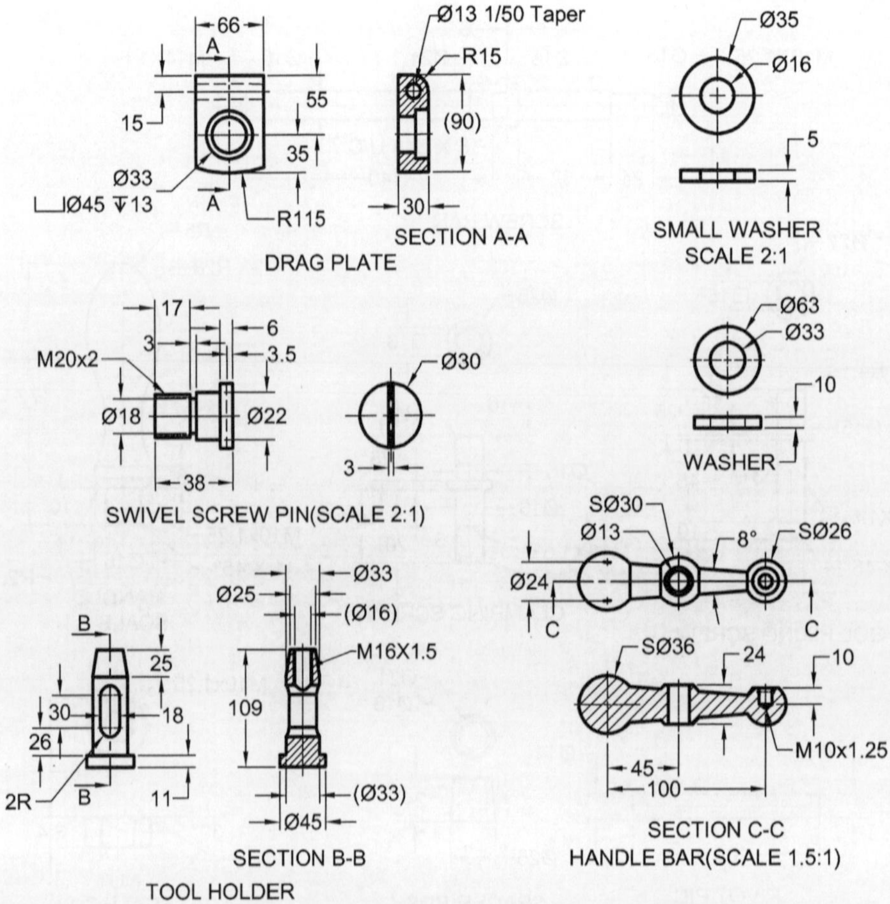

Figure 9-86 *Views and dimensions of various components*

Exercise 2

Create all components of the Blower assembly and assemble them. The Blower assembly is shown in Figure 9-87. The exploded view of the assembly is given in Figure 9-88 for reference. The dimensions of various components of this assembly are given in Figure 9-89 through 9-94. Note all dimensions are in inches. **(Expected time: 1 hr)**

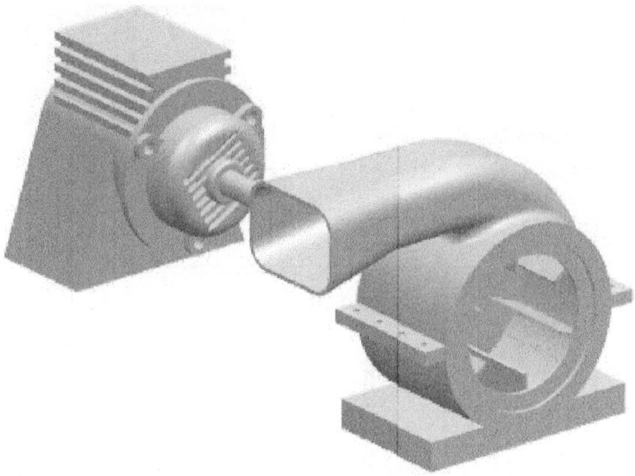

Figure 9-87 *Blower assembly*

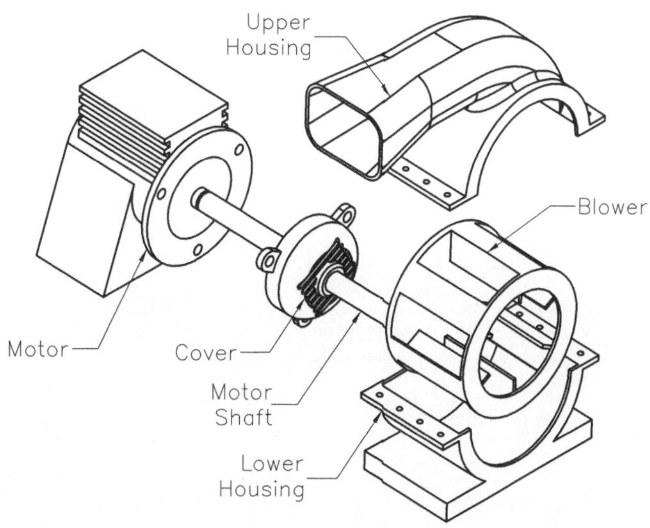

Figure 9-88 *Exploded view of the Blower assembly*

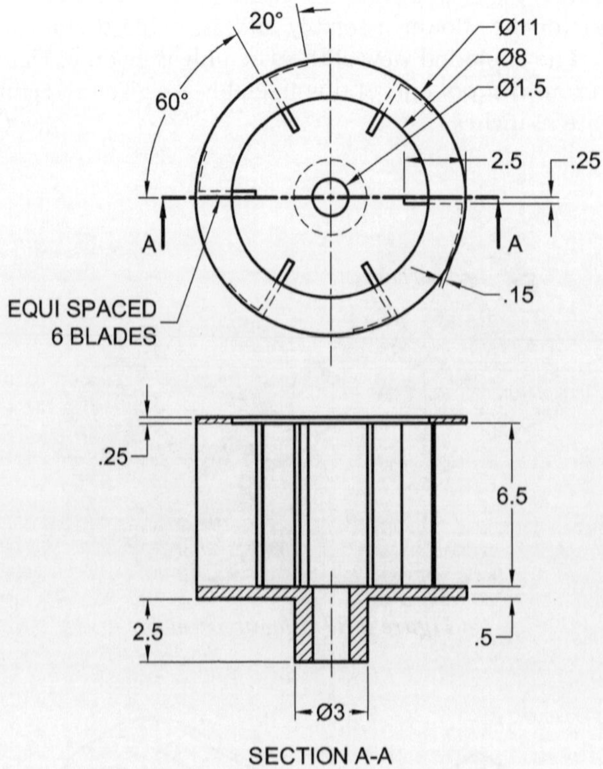

Figure 9-89 Dimensions of the Blower

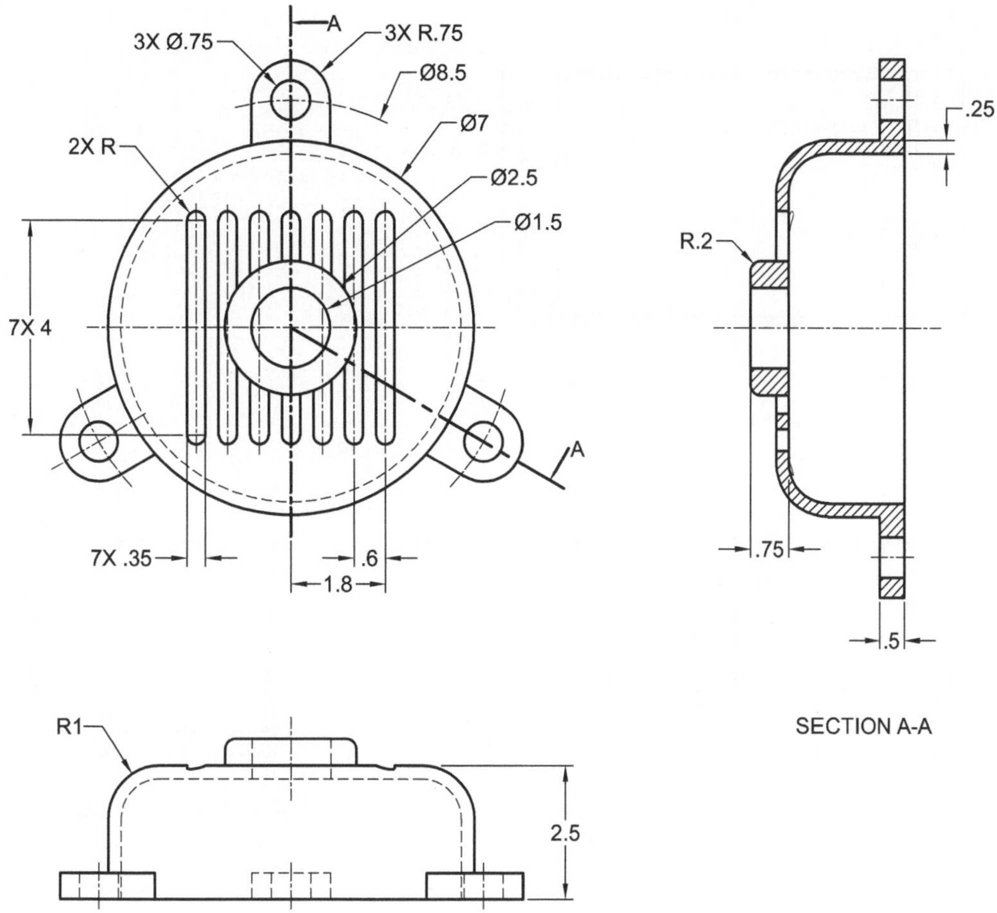

Figure 9-90 Dimensions of the Cover

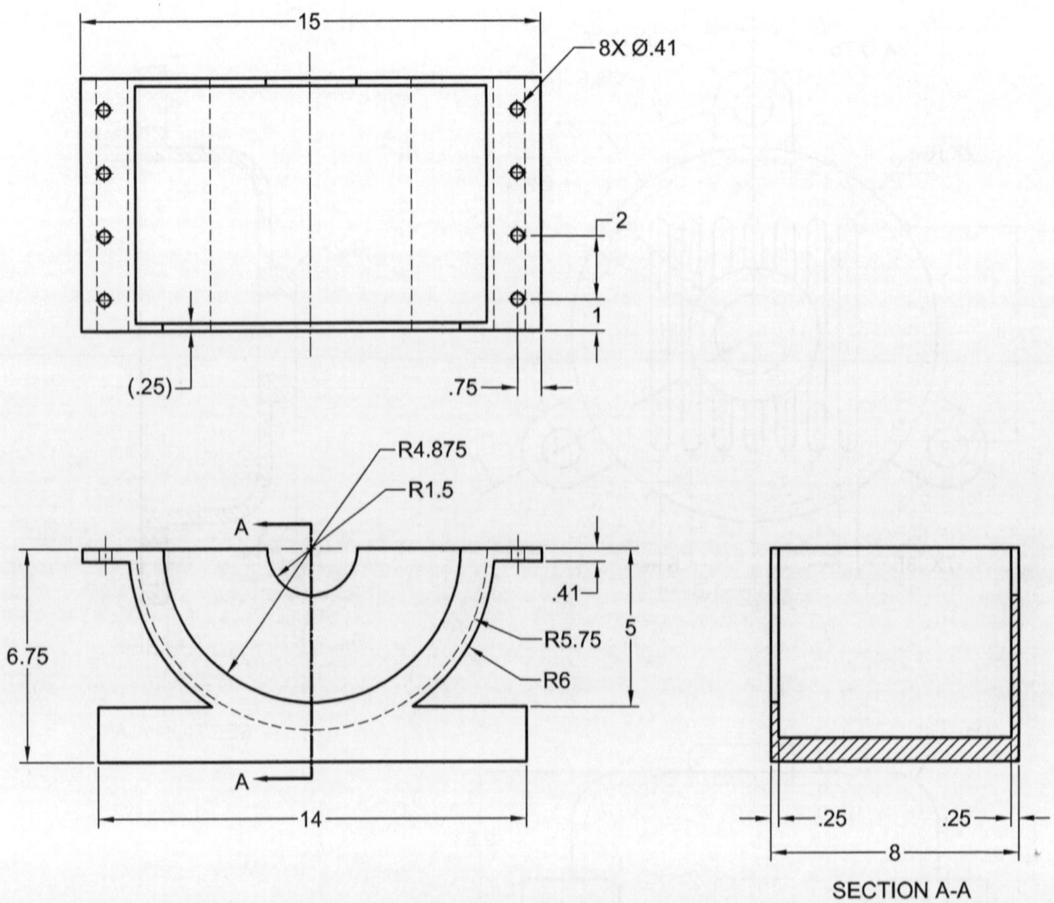

Figure 9-91 Dimensions of the Lower Housing

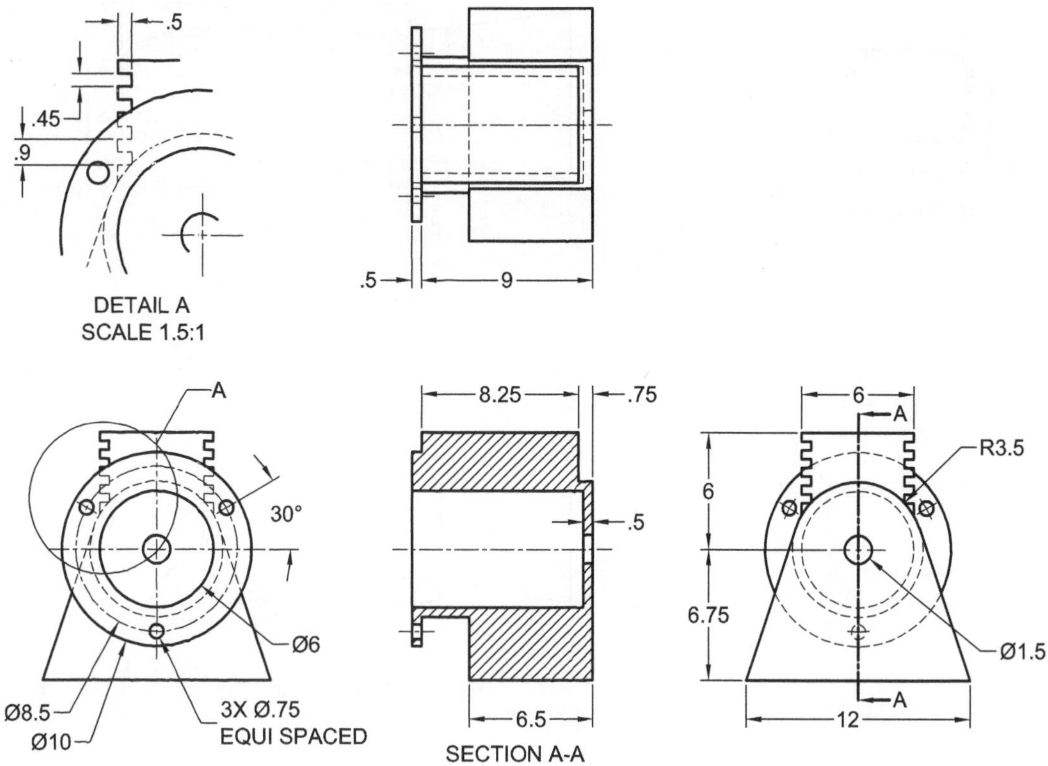

Figure 9-92 *Dimensions of the Motor*

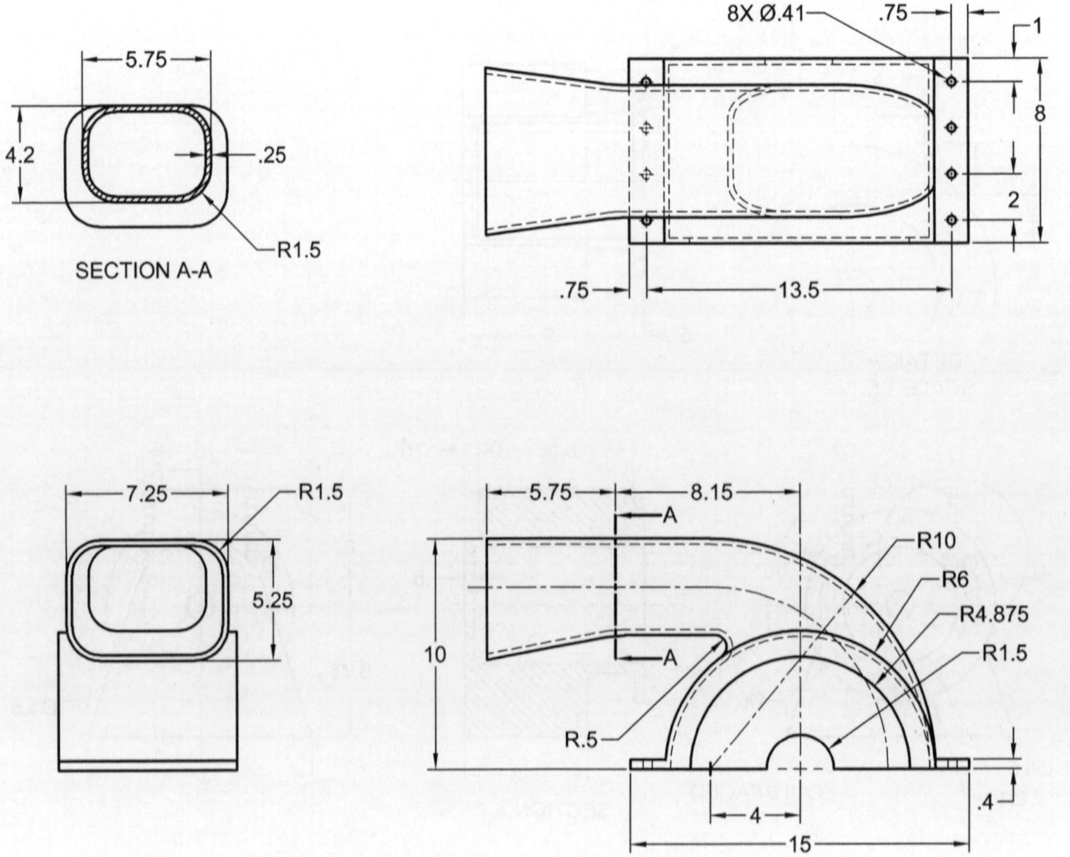

Figure 9-93 Dimensions of the Upper Housing

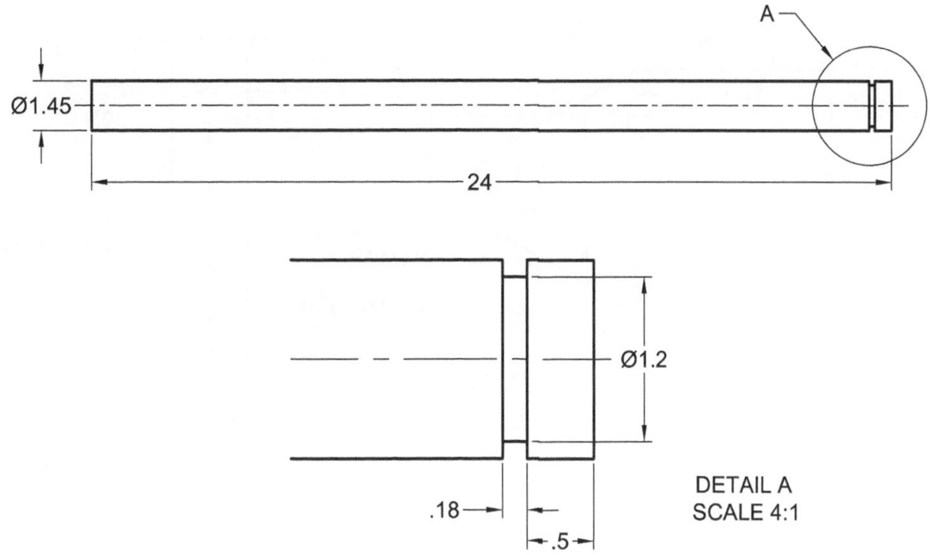

Figure 9-94 *Dimensions of the Motorshaft*

Exercise 3

Create all components of the Anti Vibration Mount assembly and assemble them. Its assembly is shown in Figure 9-95. The dimensions of various components of this assembly are given in Figures 9-96 through 9-99. Note that all dimensions are in mm. **(Expected time: 1 hr)**

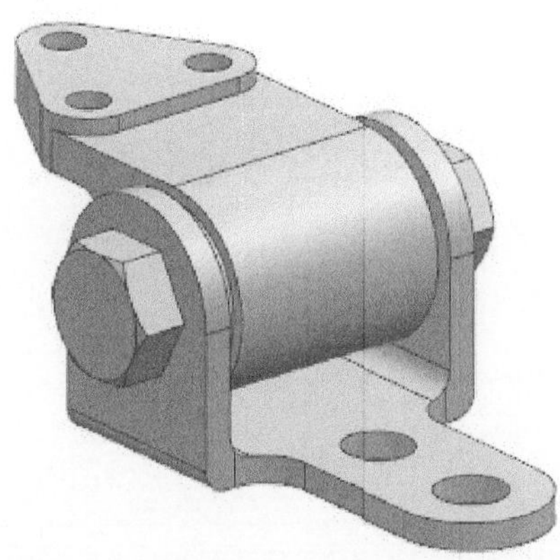

Figure 9-95 *Anti Vibration Mount*

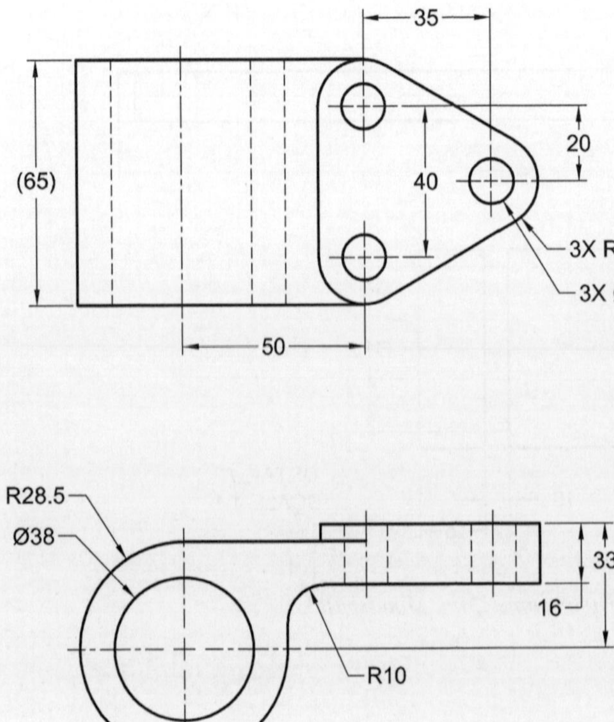

Figure 9-96 Top and front views of Body

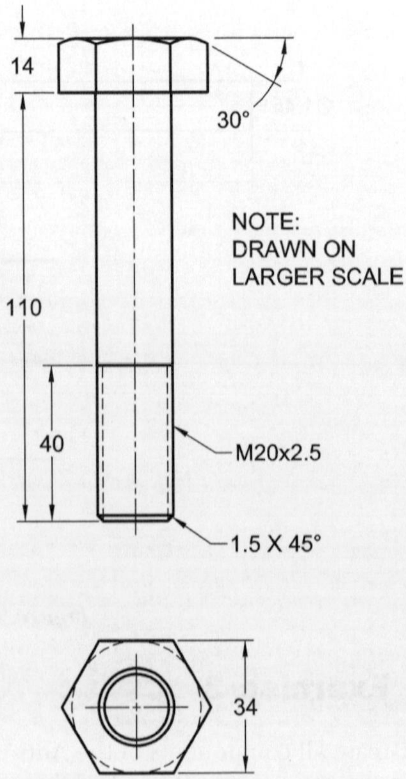

Figure 9-97 Top and front views of Hex Bolt

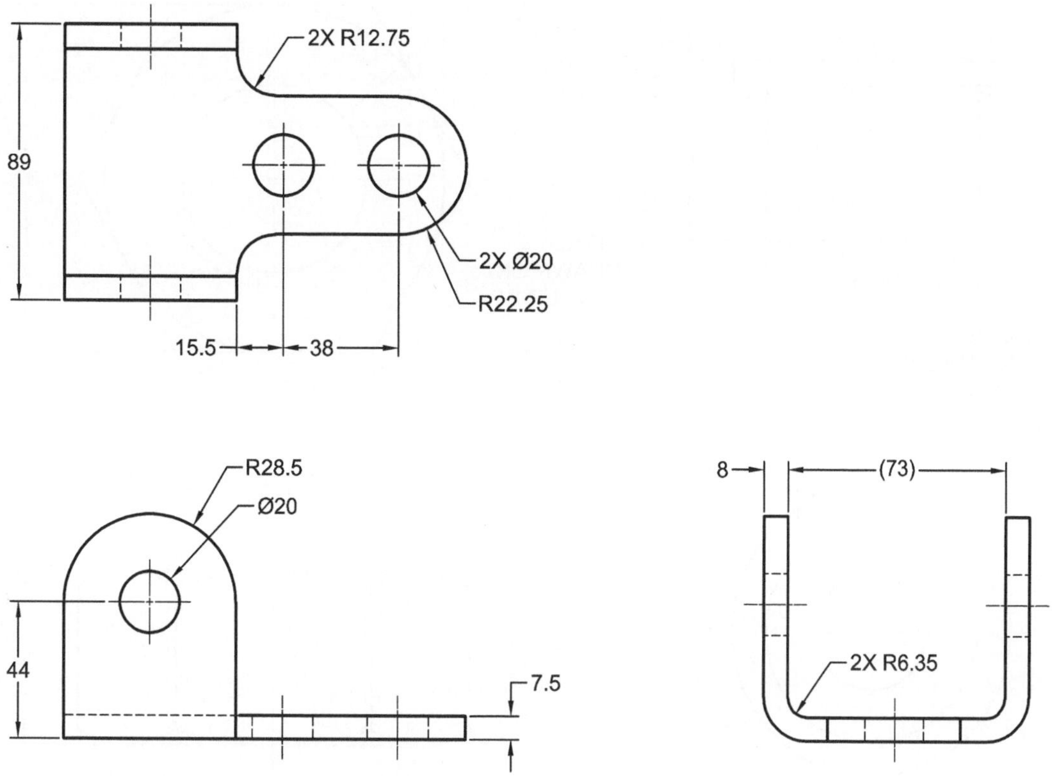

Figure 9-98 *Top, front, and side views of Yoke plate*

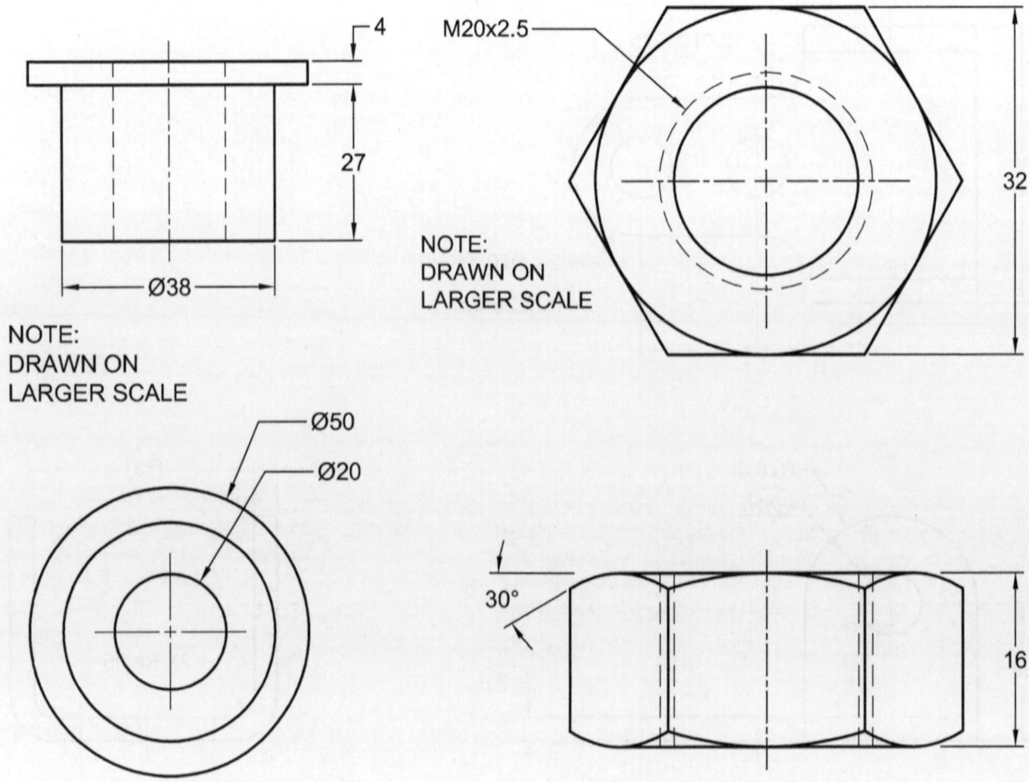

Figure 9-99 Orthographic views of the Bushing Rubber and Nut

Answers to Self-Evaluation Test

1. Exploded Views, **2.** Create New, **3.** Edit Explosion, **4.** Auto-explode Components, **5.** F, **6.** T, **7.** T, **8.** T, **9.** T, **10.** T

Chapter 10

Surface Modeling

Learning Objectives

After completing this chapter, you will be able to:

- *Create extrude, revolve, and combined surfaces*
- *Create surfaces using the Through Curves and Through Curve Mesh tools*
- *Create a surface by using four points*
- *Create a bounding plane surface*
- *Create an N-sided surface*
- *Create silhouette flange surfaces*
- *Extend and create a surface*
- *Create uniform and variable surface offsets*
- *Trim and extend a surface*
- *Create studio surface*
- *Create styled blend and styled sweep surfaces*
- *Sew individual surfaces into a single surface*
- *Add thickness to a surface*

INTRODUCTION TO SURFACE MODELING

Surfaces are three dimensional (3D) bodies with negligible thickness. They are used extensively for modeling complex features. A model or an assembly created using the surface body type has surface area but no volume or mass properties. In NX, surfaces are created in the form of single or multiple patches. With the increase in patches, the control over the shape of the surface also increases. In NX, surfaces are known as sheets and surface modeling is known as sheet modeling.

Most of the real world models are created using the solid modeling techniques. Only models that are complex in shape and have a non-uniform surface area are created with the help of the surface modeling techniques. The tools that are used to create solid models can also be used to create surface models. It becomes easy for the readers to learn surface modeling if they are familiar with the solid modeling tools. In NX, there is no separate application for surfaces. You need to create the surface model in the Shape Studio environment or Modeling environment. Before creating the surface model, you need to change the body type to sheet.

INVOKING THE SHAPE STUDIO ENVIRONMENT

To invoke the Shape Studio environment, choose the **New** tool from the **Standard** group of the **Home** tab; the **New** dialog box will be displayed. Choose the **Model** tab, if it is not already chosen and select the **Shape Studio** template from the **Templates** rollout of the dialog box. Next, choose the button on the right of the **Name** text box; the **Choose New File Name** dialog box will be displayed. Enter the file name in the **File name** edit box and then, choose the **OK** button to exit the dialog box. Also, to specify the location to save the file, browse to the folder where you need to save the file using the button on the right of the **Folder** edit box. After specifying the location of the file, choose the **OK** button twice; the Shape Studio environment will be displayed.

After invoking the Shape Studio or the Modeling environment, choose **Menu > Preferences > Modeling** from the **Top Border Bar**; the **Modeling Preferences** dialog box will be displayed, as shown in Figure 10-1. Choose the **General** tab, if it is not chosen by default, and then select the **Sheet** radio button from the **Body Type** area. Next, choose the **OK** button to exit this dialog box. All models created, henceforth, in the Modeling environment will be the sheet models.

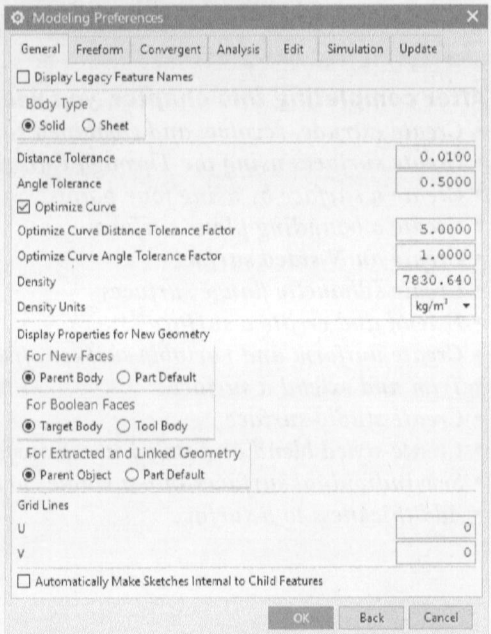

***Figure 10-1** The **Modeling Preferences** dialog box*

Creating an Extruded Surface

Ribbon:	Home > More Gallery > Design Feature > Extrude
Menu:	Insert > Design Feature > Extrude

As mentioned earlier, there is no separate tool available for creating an extruded surface. After invoking the Shape Studio environment, you can use the **Extrude** tool to create extruded sheets. The sketch drawn for creating an extruded surface may be an open or a closed entity. After creating the sketch, choose the **Extrude** tool from **Menu > Insert > Design Feature** in the **Top Border Bar**; the **Extrude** dialog box will be displayed and you will be prompted to select the section geometry to extrude. Select the sketch and enter the start and end extrusion values in their respective **Distance** edit boxes available below the **Start** and **End** drop-down lists of the **Limits** rollout in the dialog box. Next, choose the **OK** button from the **Extrude** dialog box; a sheet will be created. The options in the **Extrude** dialog box are the same as those discussed in Chapter 4. Figures 10-2 and 10-3 show the extruded surfaces created by using the open and closed sketches, respectively.

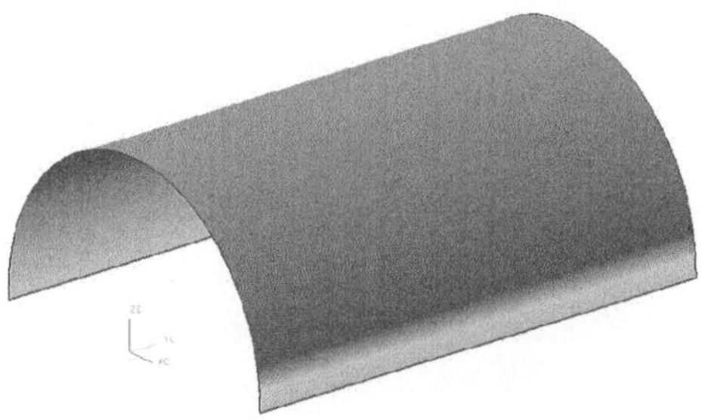

Figure 10-2 *Extruded surface created on an open sketch*

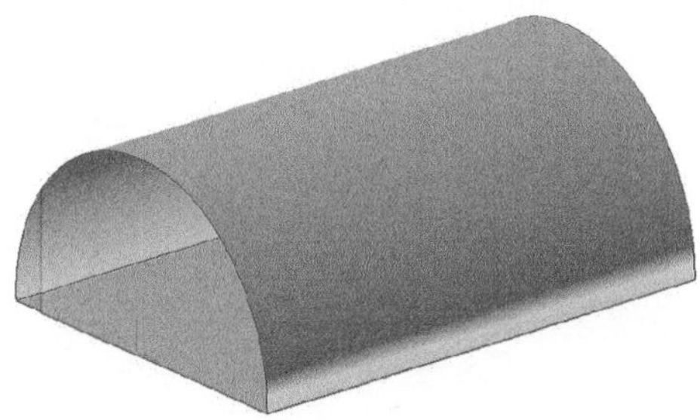

Figure 10-3 *Extruded surface created on a closed sketch*

Note

*You can use only the **None** and **Inferred** options from the **Boolean** drop-down list in the Shape Studio environment. The other options of this drop-down list are not available in this environment.*

Creating a Revolved Surface

Ribbon:	Home > More Gallery > Design Feature > Revolve
Menu:	Insert > Design Feature > Revolve

The **Revolve** tool is used to create a revolved surface. To create a revolved surface, first create a sketch, and then choose the **Revolve** tool from **Menu > Insert > Design Feature** in the **Top Border Bar**; the **Revolve** dialog box will be displayed. Also, you will be prompted to select the section geometry. Select the sketch drawn for the revolved surface. Next, click on the **Specify Vector** area in the **Axis** rollout of the dialog box and specify the axis of revolution; you will be prompted to select object to infer point. Specify the point where you want to locate the vector and then specify the start and end angles in the **Angle** edit boxes. Next, choose the **OK** button; a revolved surface will be created. The revolved surface models created by using an open sketch and a closed sketch are shown in Figures 10-4 and 10-5, respectively.

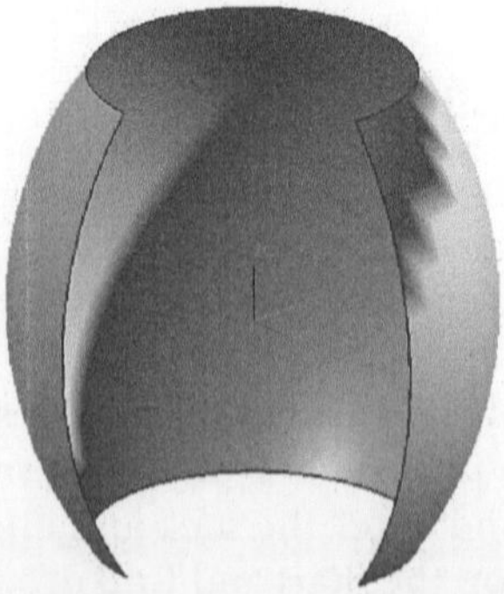

Figure 10-4 Revolved surface created using an open sketch

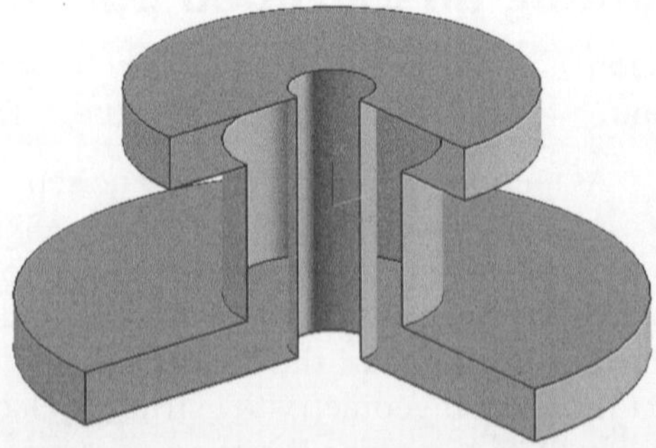

Figure 10-5 Revolved surface created using a closed sketch

Creating a Combined Surface

Menu: Insert > Combine > Combine

You can use the **Combine** tool to trim and join regions of multiple sheet bodies. To do so, choose **Menu > Insert > Combine** from the **Top Border Bar**; the **Combine** dialog box will be displayed, refer to Figure 10-6.

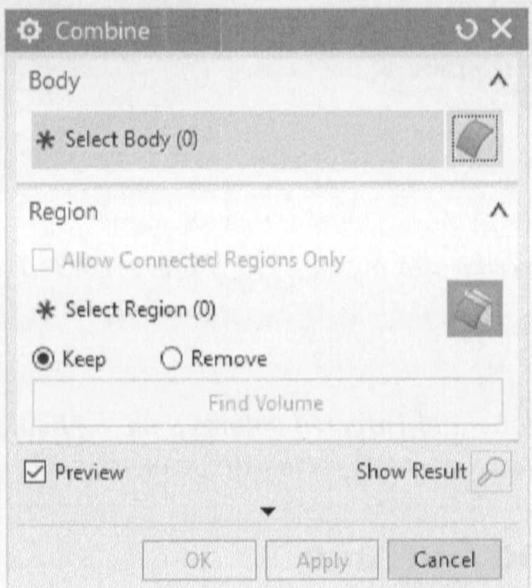

*Figure 10-6 The **Combine** dialog box*

The rollouts available in the **Combine** dialog box are discussed next.

Body Rollout

The **Body** button in this rollout is activated by default. As a result, you are prompted to select the bodies to be combined. Select the bodies to be combined using this rollout.

Region Rollout

The options available in this rollout are discussed next.

Allow Connected Regions Only

If this check box is selected, you can only select the bodies that are edge connected to a previously selected body. On clearing this check box, you can select any body created during the session.

Select Region

This area allows you to select the region of a body to keep or remove. If you select the **Keep** radio button, the selected side of the bodies will be retained and if you select the **Remove** radio button; the selected side of the bodies will be trimmed.

Find Volume

This button allows you to find and select regions that enclose a solid volume, or connected regions that form a volume-like sheet.

Figure 10-7 shows sheet bodies selected to be combined. Figure 10-8(a) shows the resulting body when the **Keep** radio button is selected and Figure 10-8(b) shows the resulting body when the **Remove** radio button is selected.

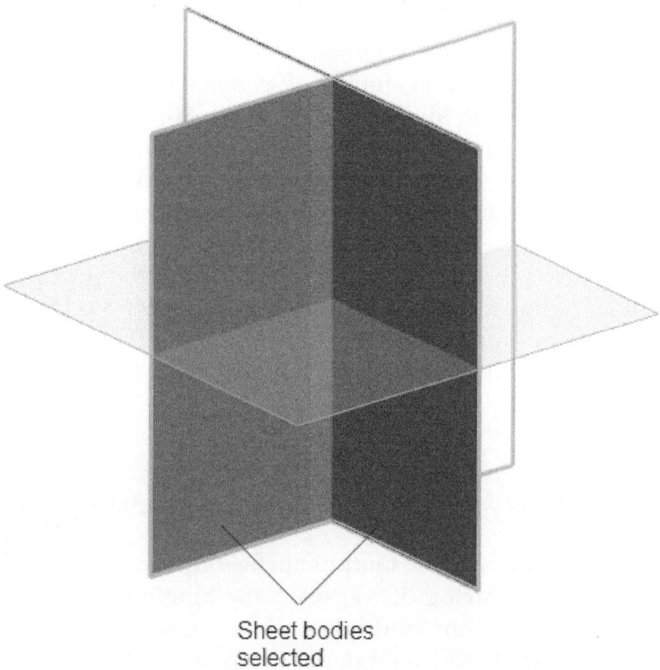

Figure 10-7 *Sheet bodies selected to be combined*

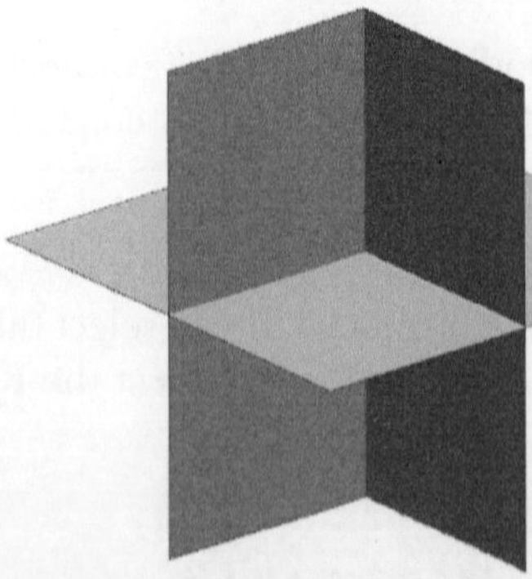

Figure 10-8(a) Resulting sheet body when the ***Keep*** *radio button is selected*

Figure 10-8(b) Resulting sheet body when the ***Remove*** *radio button is selected*

Creating a Surface Using the Through Curves Tool

Ribbon:	Home > More Gallery > Mesh Surface > Through Curves
Menu:	Insert > Mesh Surface > Through Curves

You can create surfaces with multiple section strings using the **Through Curves** tool. This method allows you to select any number of section strings. To do so, choose the **Through Curves** tool from the **Mesh Surface** gallery of the **More** gallery, refer to Figure 10-9; the **Through Curves** dialog box will be displayed, as shown in Figure 10-10, and you will be prompted to select the curve or point to section. Select the strings for first section and press the middle mouse button; you will be prompted again to select the curve or point to section. Likewise, you can select any number of section strings. After selecting section strings, make sure that all the arrows on the section strings point in the same direction. All the selected sections will be listed in the **List** sub-rollout of the **Sections** rollout. You can reorder a selected section by using the **Move Up** and **Move Down** buttons available on the right of the **List** sub-rollout. You can also delete a selected section by using the **Remove** button.

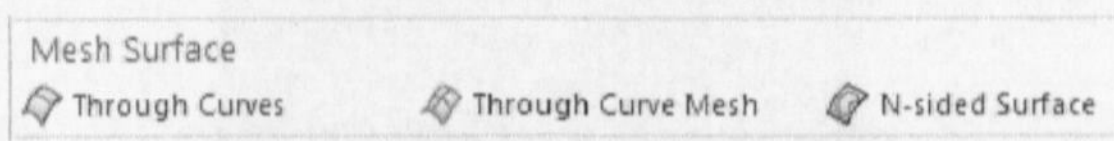

Figure 10-9 The ***Mesh Surface*** *gallery of the* ***More*** *gallery*

In the **Patch Type** drop-down list of the **Output Surface Options** rollout, there are three options, **Single**, **Multiple**, and **Match String**. If you select the **Single** option, a surface will be created with a single patch. If you select the **Multiple** option, the surface will be created with multiple patches. The number of patches formed depends upon the **Alignment** option selected from the **Alignment** rollout.

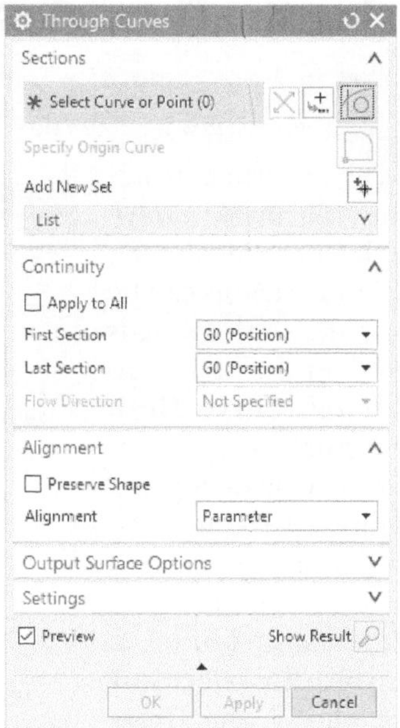

Figure 10-10 *The* ***Through Curves*** *dialog box*

When you select the **Multiple** option from the **Patch Type** drop-down list of the **Output Surface Options** rollout, the **Closed in V** and **Normal to End Sections** check boxes will be enabled. If you select the **Closed in V** check box, the surface body will be closed in the V direction and the **Normal to End Sections** check box will be deactivated. If you select the **Normal to End Sections** check box, the resultant surface will be normal to the two end sections and the options in the **Continuity** rollout will be deactivated. Figure 10-11 shows the section strings selected for creating a through curve surface and Figure 10-12 shows the resulting surface.

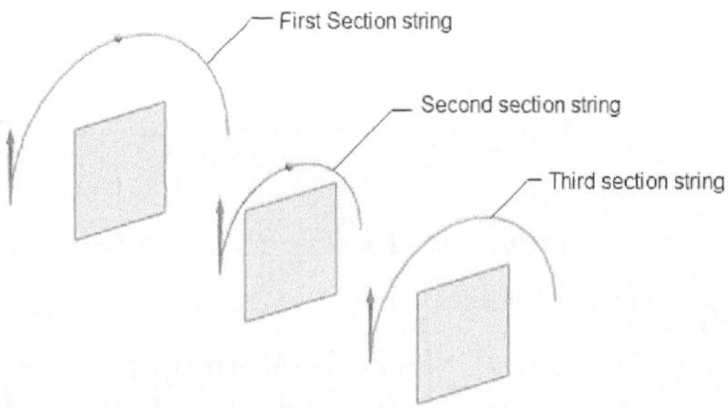

Figure 10-11 *Section strings selected for creating the Through Curves surface*

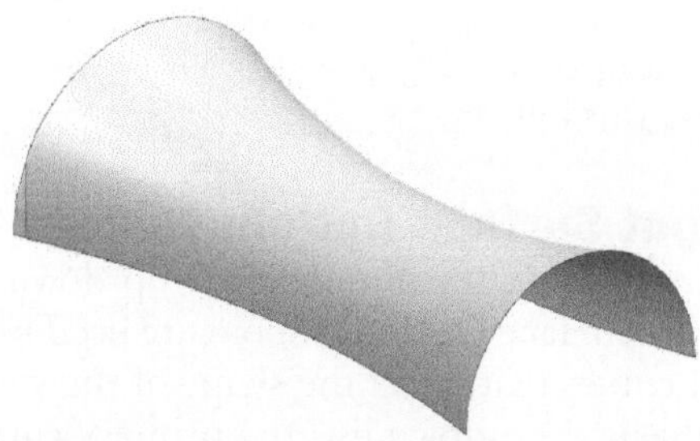

Figure 10-12 *The resulting surface*

Creating a Surface Using the Through Curve Mesh Tool

Ribbon:	Home > More Gallery > Mesh Surface > Through Curve Mesh
Menu:	Insert > Mesh Surface > Through Curve Mesh

You can create surfaces by specifying section strings and guide strings using the **Through Curve Mesh** tool. While using the **Through Curve Mesh** tool, any number of section strings and guide strings can be specified. For selecting multiple guide strings, it is required that they are connected end-to-end. To create a surface by using the **Through Curve Mesh** tool, invoke this tool from the **Mesh Surface** gallery of the **More** gallery; the **Through Curve Mesh** dialog box will be displayed, as shown in Figure 10-13, and you will be prompted to select primary curves. You need to select a collection of control curves. Select the first primary curve and press the middle mouse button to select the next curve. Similarly, you can select any number of primary curves. Next, choose the **Cross Curves** button from the **Cross Curves** rollout; you will be prompted to select cross curves. Select the first cross curve and press the middle mouse button to select the next curve. Similarly, you can select any number of cross curves.

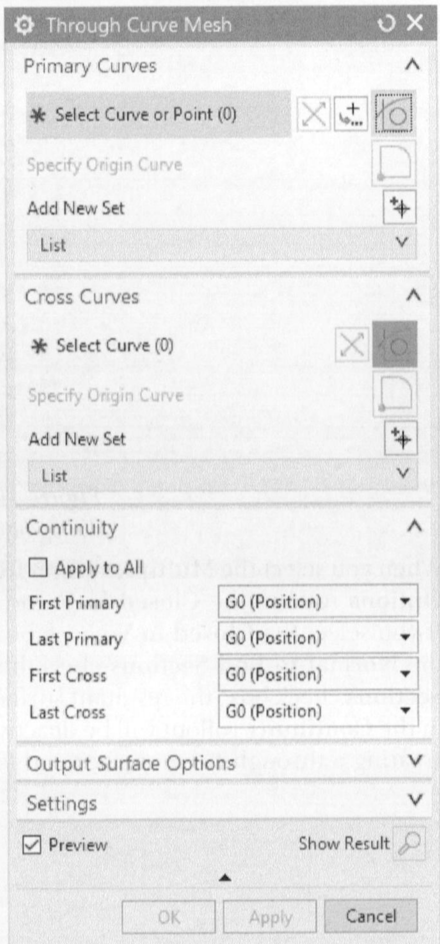

Figure 10-13 The Through Curve Mesh dialog box

Note that after selecting two primary curves, the **Spine** rollout will be added to the **Through Curve Mesh** dialog box. The **Spine** button in this rollout allows you to select the spine string. This spine string improves the smoothness of the surface and it must be normal to all primary strings. However, the selection of the spine string is optional. If you want to skip this step, do not choose this button.

Output Surface Options Rollout

The options in the **Emphasis** drop-down list of the **Output Surface Options** rollout are used to define the set of curves that affect the shape of the surface to be created. Select the **Both** option from the **Emphasis** drop-down list; the primary curves and cross curves will cast an equal effect. If you select the **Primary** option from the **Emphasis** drop-down list, the primary curves will cast more effect and if you select the **Cross** option from the **Emphasis** drop-down list, the cross curves will cast more effect. If you select the **Normal** option from the **Construction** drop-down list in the **Output Surface Options** rollout, the resulting surfaces will have more number of patches. If you select the **Spline Points** option, the resulting surface will have less number of patches. The surface is formed by reparameterizing curves into temporary curves. If you select the **Simple** option, the resulting surface will be created with or without specifying any constraints.

Settings Rollout

The options in the **Rebuild** drop-down list of the **Settings** rollout will only be enabled if you select the **Normal** option from the **Construction** drop-down list. You can use the options in the **Rebuild** drop-down list to join the mesh surface smoothly with the surrounding surfaces. You can rebuild the mesh surface by selecting the **Degree and Tolerance** option and entering the value in the **Degree** spinner. If you select the **Auto Fit** option, the **Maximum Degree** and **Maximum Segments** spinners will be enabled. You can set the values in these spinners to rebuild the mesh surface automatically.

Figure 10-14 shows the control strings selected for creating the through curve mesh surface and Figure 10-15 shows the resulting surface. You can enter the distance tolerance value between the curves in the **G0 (Position)** edit box and the angle tolerance value in the **G1 (Tangent)** edit box. The curvature tolerance value can be entered in the **G2 (Curvature)** edit box.

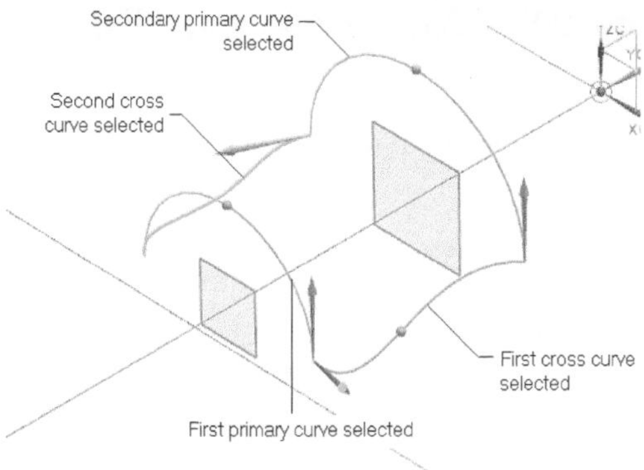

Figure 10-14 *The control strings selected for creating the through curve mesh surface*

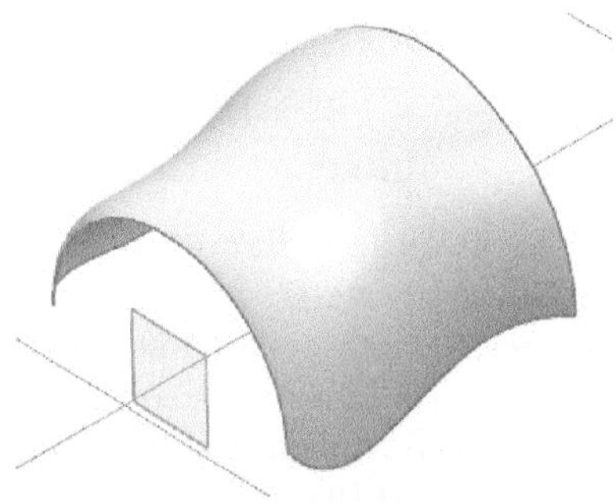

Figure 10-15 *The resulting through curve mesh surface*

Creating a Surface Using the Four Point Surface Tool

Ribbon: Home > Create > Surface Drop-down > Four Point Surface
Menu: Insert > Surface > Four Point Surface

The **Four Point Surface** tool is used to create a planar (2D) or non-planar (3D) surface. To create a surface by using this tool, choose the **Four Point Surface** tool from the **Surface Drop-down** of the **Create** group; the **Four Point Surface** dialog box will be displayed, as shown in Figure 10-16, and you will be prompted to select object to infer point. Specify the point for the first surface corner. Similarly, specify the other three surface corners and choose the **OK** button; the four point surface will be created. You can also redefine the previously selected corner points. To do so, choose the button corresponding to the point that you want to redefine from the **Surface Corners** rollout; the respective point will be highlighted in the drawing window. Again, specify the point for the corner.

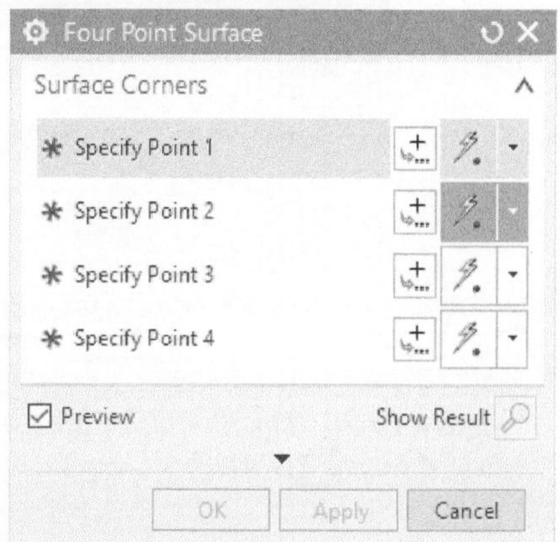

Figure 10-16 *The* ***Four Point Surface*** *dialog box*

Figure 10-17 shows the corner points to be selected for creating a surface. Figure 10-18 shows the resulting surface formed by enclosing the specified corner points.

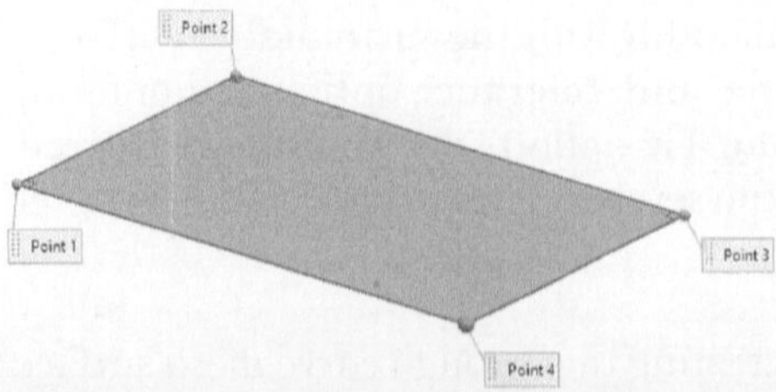

***Figure 10-17** The four corner points to be selected for creating a surface*

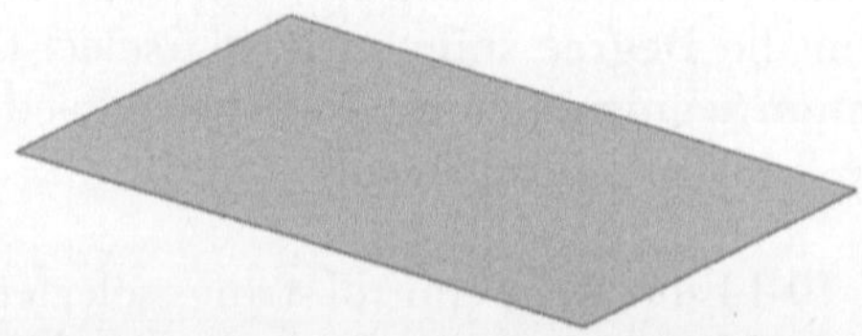

***Figure 10-18** The resulting surface*

Creating Planar Surfaces from 2D Sketches and Edges of Solid or Surface

Ribbon:	Home > More Gallery > Surface > Bounded Plane
Menu:	Insert > Surface > Bounded Plane

The **Bounded Plane** tool is used to create a surface from 2D sketches or closed coplanar edges. If you need to enclose a 2D sketch or closed coplanar edges with a surface, choose **Menu > Insert > Surface > Bounded Plane** in the **Top Border Bar**; the **Bounded Plane** dialog box will be displayed, as shown in Figure 10-19, and you will be prompted to select curves for the bounded plane. Select the closed coplanar edges of the object or the closed coplanar sketch and then choose the **OK** button; the bounded plane surface will be created. Figure 10-20 shows a bounded plane surface enclosing a 2D sketch and Figure 10-21 shows a bounded plane surface created from a circular edge. You can create a bounded plane surface by selecting the closed coplanar edges of the solid and surface bodies.

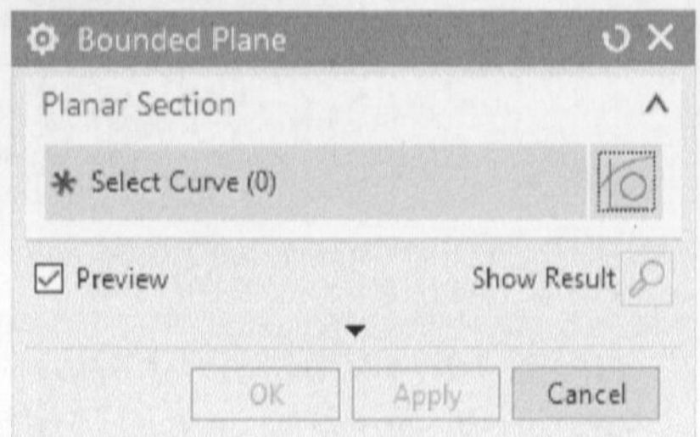

***Figure 10-19** The **Bounded Plane** dialog box*

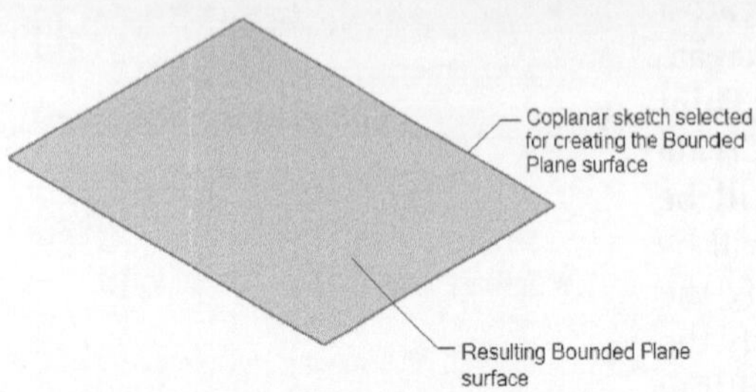

***Figure 10-20** The Bounded Plane surface formed from a 2D sketch*

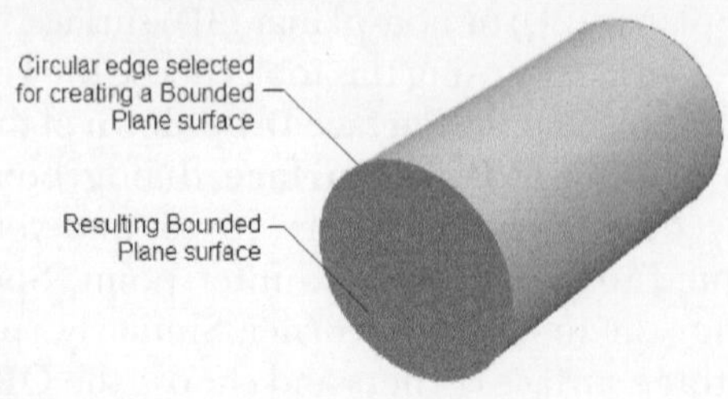

***Figure 10-21** The Bounded Plane surface formed from a circular edge*

Editing Surface Using the X-Form Tool

Ribbon: Home > More Gallery > Shape > X-Form *(Customize to add)*
Menu: Edit > Curve > X-Form

The **X-Form** tool is used to edit surfaces by dynamically manipulating the pole locations. To edit surfaces, choose the X-Form tool from **Menu > Edit > Curve** in the **Top Border Bar**; the X-Form dialog box is displayed, as shown in Figure 10-22 and you will be prompted to select a curve or surface to start editing. Select the surface, the poles and polylines will be displayed. Select these poles or polylines and drag them to get the desired shape of the surface. Refer to Figure 10-23(a) for the surface to be selected and Figure 10-23(b) for the pole and polyline displayed after selecting the surface. The surface gets modified after selecting and dragging the poles, as shown in Figure 10-24.

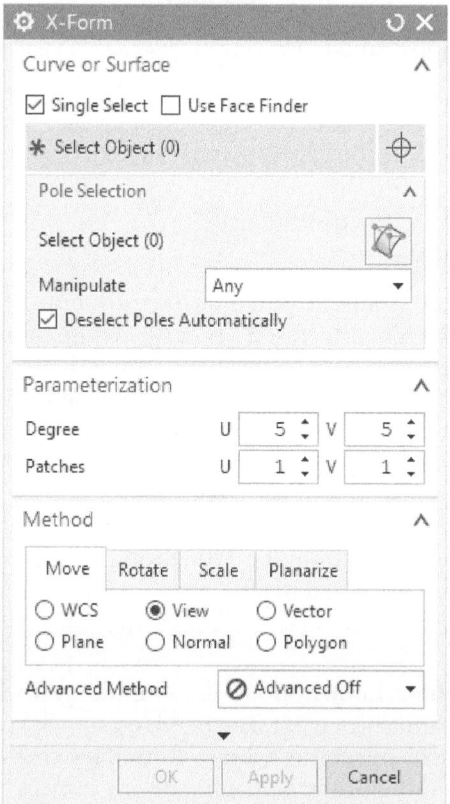

Figure 10-22 *The **X-Form** dialog box*

Figure 10-23(a) *The cylindrical surface selected*

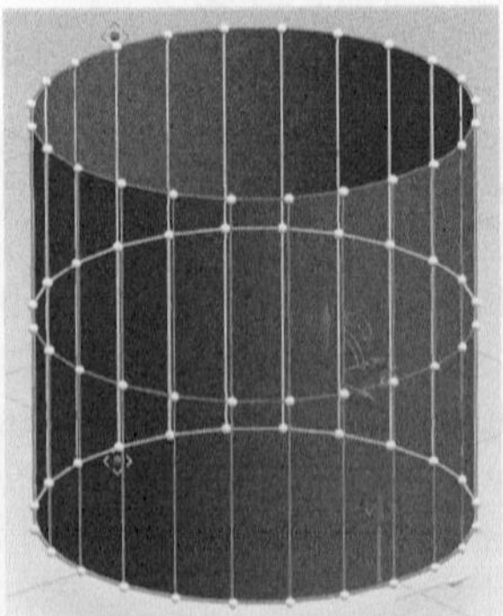

Figure 10-23(b) The pole and polyline display on cylindrical surface

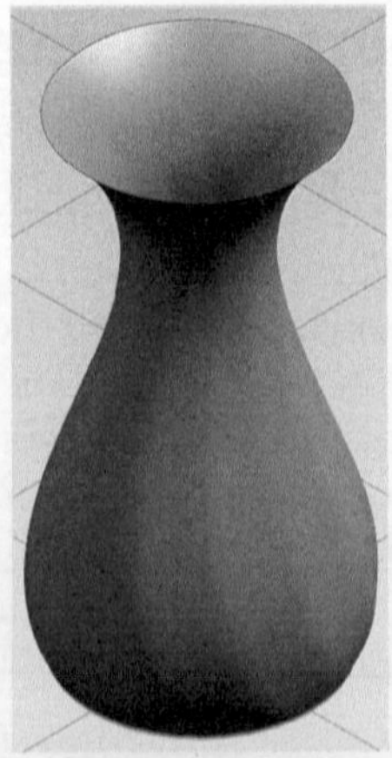

Figure 10-24 The surface after editing poles

Creating an N-sided Surface

Ribbon:	Home > More Gallery > Mesh Surface > N-sided Surface
Menu:	Insert > Mesh Surface > N-sided Surface

The **N-sided Surface** tool is used to create a single patch surface or multi-patch triangular surfaces that enclose a closed 2D sketch or a closed 3D curve. While doing so, an existing surface can optionally be selected as a reference for maintaining the shape of the surface to be created. To create an N-sided surface, choose the **N-sided Surface** tool from **Menu > Insert > Mesh Surface** in the **Top Border Bar**; the **N-sided Surface** dialog box will be displayed, as shown in Figure 10-25, and you will be prompted to select a closed loop of curves or edges. By default, the **Trimmed** option is selected in the Type drop-down list. As a result, a surface with a single patch will be created. To create a surface with multiple triangular patches, you need to select the **Triangular** option from the Type drop-down list. Both the options used for creating the N-sided surface are discussed next.

Trimmed

By default, the **Curve** button is chosen in the **Outer Loop** rollout. As a result, you will be prompted to select a closed loop. Select a closed boundary of a 2D sketch, edges, or a 3D curve; the preview of the new surface will be displayed. Next, select the **Trim to Boundary** check box from the **Settings** rollout; the surface created will automatically be trimmed with respect to the closed loop of the curve, as shown in Figure 10-26.

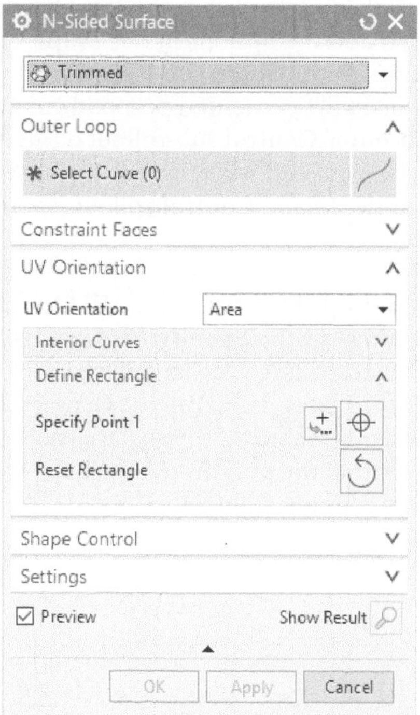

Figure 10-25 The ***N-Sided Surface*** *dialog box*

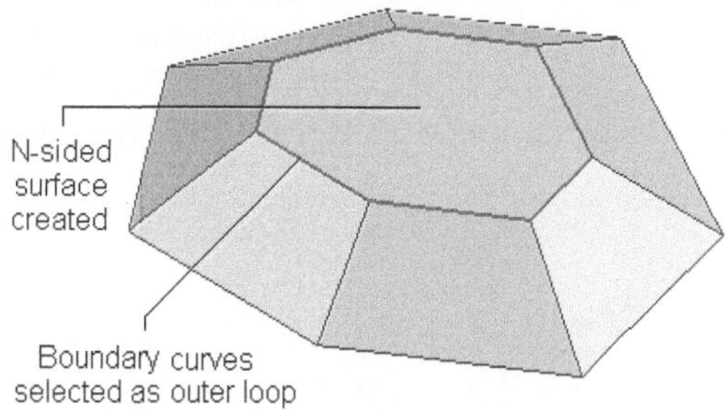

Figure 10-26 Single patch N-sided surface created for the selected boundary curve

By default, the **Area** option is selected in the **UV Orientation** drop-down list of the **UV Orientation** rollout. Click on the **Select Curve** area in the **Interior Curves** sub-rollout to activate it; you will be prompted to select a curve. Select the curve; the surface will be modified such that it passes through the selected interior curves; thereby, deforming the shape of the surface, as shown in Figure 10-27. In this figure, the **Trim to Boundary** check box is cleared for better understanding of the deformation of the surface. You can also define a rectangle by specifying two points as diagonally opposite corners of the rectangle so that the resultant surface is created in the specified rectangle. To do so, click on the **Specify Point 1** area in the **Define Rectangle** sub-rollout; the **Specify Point 1** area will be activated. Next, click in the drawing window; a rectangle will be attached to the cursor. Also, the **Specify Point 2** area will be activated in the **Define Rectangle** sub-rollout. Again, click in the graphics window to specify the second point of the rectangle; a square surface will be created in the graphics window. To reset the rectangle created, choose the **Reset Rectangle** button from the **Define Rectangle** sub-rollout.

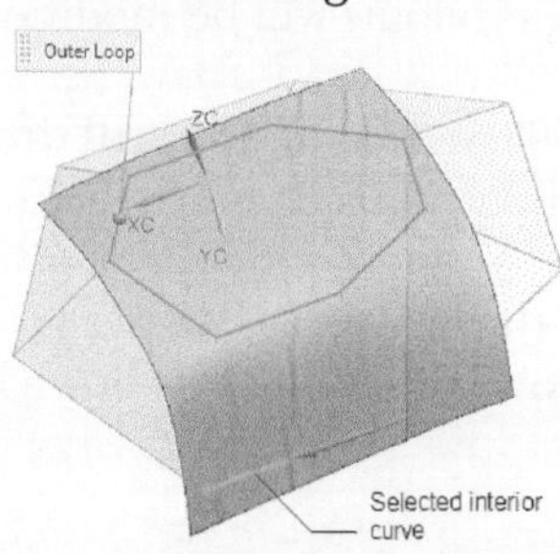

Figure 10-27 *Modified part with interior curve selected*

If you select the **Spine** option from the **UV Orientation** drop-down list in the **UV Orientation** rollout, then the **UV Orientation** rollout will be modified and the options in the **Shape Control** rollout will become active. Click on the **Select Curve** area of the **Spine** sub-rollout; you will be prompted to select a spine curve. Select a curve; the surface will be oriented perpendicular to the selected spine curve. The **Center Flat** slider bar in the **Center Control** sub-rollout of the **Shape Control** rollout is used to modify the shape of the surface created with respect to the selected curve, as shown in Figure 10-28. To reset the options in the **Shape Control** rollout, choose the **Reset Center Control** button from this rollout.

If you select the **Vector** option from the **UV Orientation** drop-down list in the **UV Orientation** rollout, the **UV Orientation** rollout will be modified. Click on the **Specify Vector** area of the **Vector** sub-rollout; you will be prompted to select the object to infer vector. Select a vector; the surface will follow the selected vector direction. The **Center Flat** slider bar in the **Center Control** sub-rollout of the **Shape Control** rollout is used to modify the shape of the surface created with respect to a specified vector, as shown in Figure 10-29. To reset the options in the **Shape Control** rollout, choose the **Reset Center Control** button from the **Shape Control** rollout.

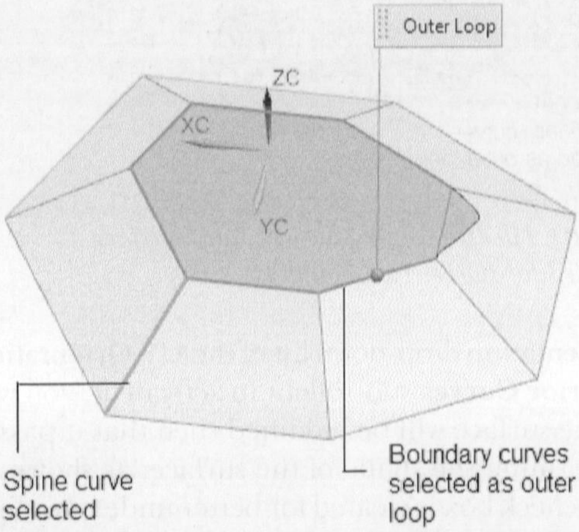

Figure 10-28 Modified part with the spine curve selected

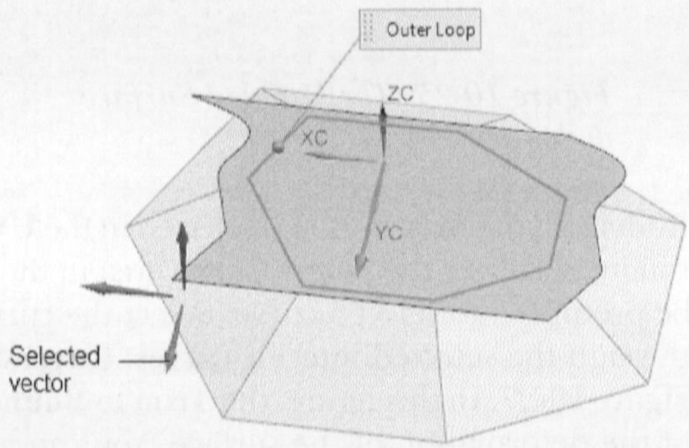

Figure 10-29 Modified part with the selected vector

Triangular

To create a triangular patch surface, select the **Triangular** option from the Type drop-down list; you will be prompted to select a chain of curves for outer loop. Select the closed entity; the preview of the selected surface will be displayed in the drawing window, as shown in Figure 10-30, and the **Shape Control** and **Settings** rollouts will be modified.

By default, the **Position** option is selected in the **Control** drop-down list of the **Center Control** sub-rollout in the **Shape Control** rollout. You can move the center point of the new surface in the X, Y, and Z directions by using the **X**, **Y**, and **Z** slider bars, respectively, as shown in Figure 10-31. You can specify the flow direction of the new surface as per your requirement by selecting any one of the following options from the **Flow Direction** drop-down list: **Not Specified**, **Perpendicular**, **Iso U/V Line**, or **Adjacent Edges**.

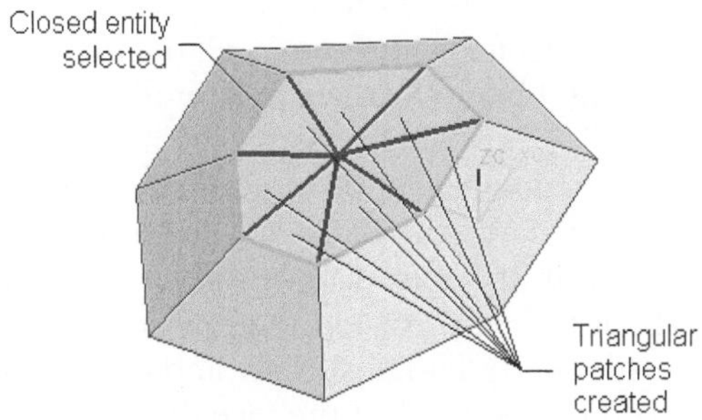

Figure 10-30 *Triangular patches created using the **Triangular** option*

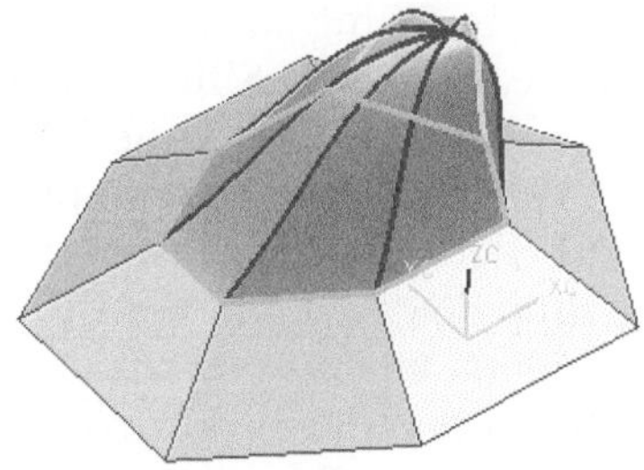

Figure 10-31 *Modified surface in the X, Y, and Z directions*

Select the **Tilting** option from the **Control** drop-down list and then use the **X** and **Y** slider bars to tilt the created surface in the X and Y directions, respectively, as shown in Figure 10-32. By default, the **Merge Faces if Possible** check box in the **Settings** rollout is clear. As a result, patches are created for each edge of the loop. If you select this check box, the patches of the loop will be removed by treating the tangent continuous edges as a single loop, as shown in Figure 10-33.

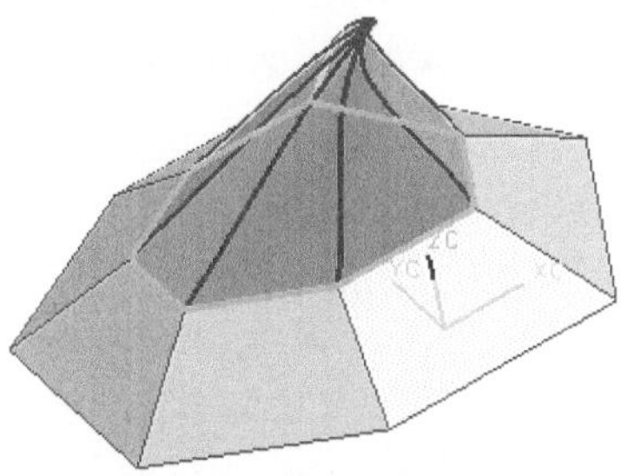

Figure 10-32 *The tilted surface in the X and Y directions*

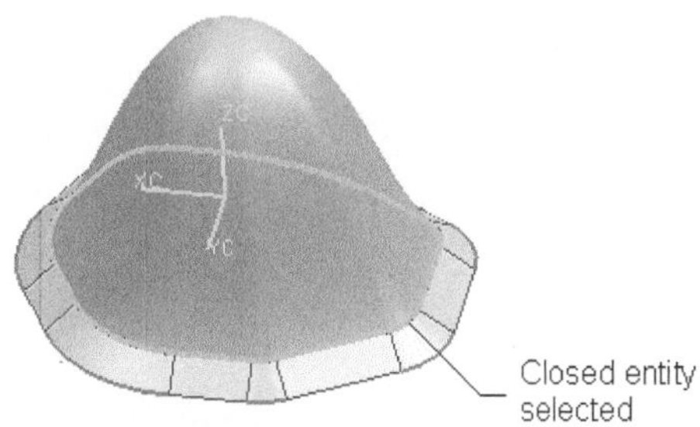

Figure 10-33 *The curves of the loop merged by selecting the **Merge Faces if Possible** check box*

Creating a Silhouette Flange Surface

Ribbon: Home > More Gallery > Flange Surface > Silhouette Flange
Menu: Insert > Flange Surface > Silhouette Flange

The silhouette flange surfaces are created with respect to an existing surface such that the aesthetic shape, quality, and the slope continuity of the existing surface are maintained.

The flange surface is created with a full round surface or a fillet at the start point. The flange created can be dynamically modified in shape and size. The silhouette flange surface can be created by using any of the three methods discussed next.

Creating a Silhouette Flange Surface Using the Basic Method

The **Silhouette Flange** tool is used to create silhouette flange surfaces on an edge or on a curve by taking any of the adjacent surfaces as reference. To create a silhouette flange surface, invoke the **Silhouette Flange** tool from the **Flange Surface** gallery of the **More** gallery, refer to Figure 10-34; the **Silhouette Flange** dialog box will be displayed, as shown in Figure 10-35, and you will be prompted to select curve or edges to define base curve. Select the curve or the edge on which you want to create a flange. By default, the **Basic** option is selected in the Type drop-down list and the **Curve** button is chosen in the **Base Curve** rollout. Selecting the **Basic** option enables you to create a flange without the help of any other existing flange surfaces. Select an edge or a curve for creating the silhouette flange surface and choose the **Face** button from the **Base Face** rollout; you will be prompted to select the face that will act as base face. Select the desired face. The other options in this dialog box are discussed next.

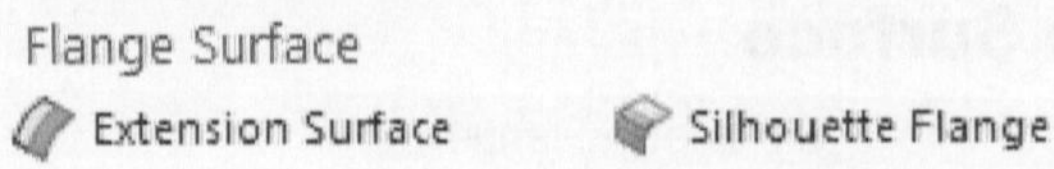

*Figure 10-34 The **Flange Surface** gallery of the **More** gallery*

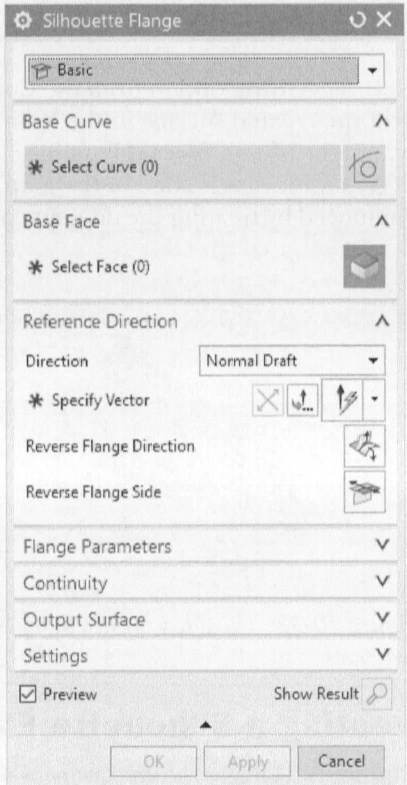

*Figure 10-35 The **Silhouette Flange** dialog box*

Reference Direction Rollout

In this rollout, you can specify the direction of a flange by selecting any one of the options from the **Direction** drop-down list. These options are **Face Normal**, **Vector**, **Normal Draft**, and **Vector Draft**. By default, the **Normal Draft** option is selected in the **Direction** drop-down list. Click on the **Specify Vector** area of this rollout to activate it, and then select the vector; the preview of the flange surface will be displayed, as shown in Figure 10-36. To change the direction of the flange to opposite direction, choose the **Reverse Flange Direction** button from this rollout; the direction of the flange will be reversed. To switch the flange extension to the opposite side of the bend, select the **Reverse Flange Side** button from this rollout. If you do not get the desired result after choosing this button, choose the **Reverse Direction** button from this rollout.

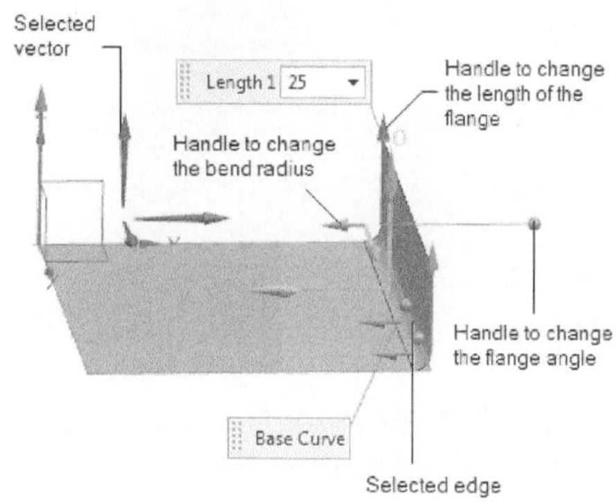

Figure 10-36 Preview of the flange surface

Flange Parameters Rollout

You can use the options in this rollout to control the parameters of a flange. Alternatively, you can control the parameters of the flange by using the handle and angular handles in the drawing window. If you select a handle from the drawing window, then the respective dynamic edit box will be displayed. You can enter value in the edit box or drag the handle to modify the respective parameters of the flange.

If you select the **Multi-transition** option from the **Law Type** drop-down list, the **Specify New Location** area is activated in the **Radius** sub-rollout. As a result, you will be prompted to select the object to infer point. Select the point on the base curve; a control point and a dynamic edit box will be displayed. Enter the desired value in this edit box to specify the location of the point on curve. To change the radius at this point, drag the handle pointing normal to the flange; the radius at that point will be changed. To change the length of the flange at the selected point, drag the handle pointing parallel to the flange. To change the bend angle of the flange, drag the angular handle; the bend angle of the flange will be changed.

You can change the transition type of the bend radius of the flange to modify the bend radius by selecting the options (**Constant**, **Linear**, **Blend**, and **Minimum/Maximum**) from the **Values along Spine** sub-rollout of the **Flange Parameters** rollout. You can change the transition type of the length of the flange by selecting the options (**Constant**, **Linear**, **Cubic**, **Multi-transition**) from the **Law Type** drop-down list of the **Length** sub-rollout, refer to Figure 10-37.

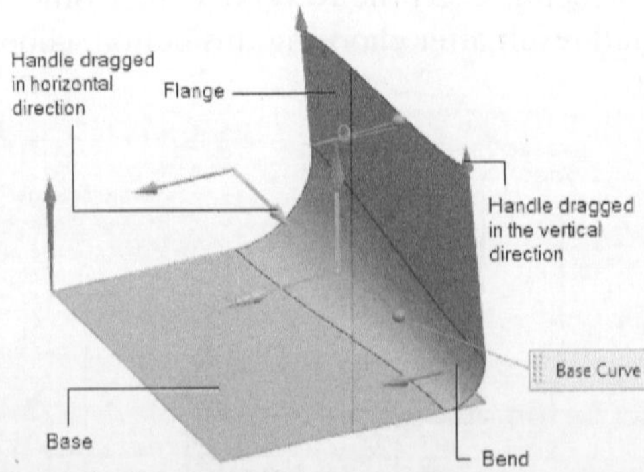

*Figure 10-37 Part modified using the **Flange Parameters** and **Continuity** rollouts*

Continuity Rollout

You can control the continuity between the base and the bent portion using the options in the **Base and Pipe** sub-rollout of the **Continuity** rollout. To do so, select the required **G1 (Tangent)**, **G2 (Curvature)**, and **G3 (Flow)** continuities in the **Continuity** drop-down list of the **Base and Pipe** sub-rollout. To control the amount of edge shift, you can use the **Lead-in** slider bar. Alternatively, you can use the **Lead-in** edit box to control the edge shift. Similarly, you can control the continuity between the flange and the bent portion in the **Flange and Pipe** sub-rollout of this rollout, refer to Figure 10-37.

Output Surface Rollout

In this rollout, the **Blend and Flange** option is selected by default in the **Output Options** drop-down list. If you select the **Pipe Only** option from this drop-down list, then only a pipe will be created. If you select the **Flange Only** option from the **Output Options** drop-down list, then only a flange will be created. By default, the **Trim Base Faces** check box is clear in this rollout. As a result, the portion extended beyond the flange will be retained, as shown in Figure 10-38. If you want to remove the unwanted portion of the flange, select the **Trim Base Faces** check box. The **Extend Flange** check box will be available only when the **Trim Base Faces** check box is clear. If you select this check box, the flange will be extended to cover the entire span of the base surface.

Settings Rollout

By default, the **Create Curves** check box is clear in this rollout. If you select this check box, two curves will be created along the center of the bend radius and at the intersection of the bend and the flange. If you select the **Show Pipe** check box in this rollout, the pipe of the bend radius will be displayed in the preview, as shown in Figure 10-39.

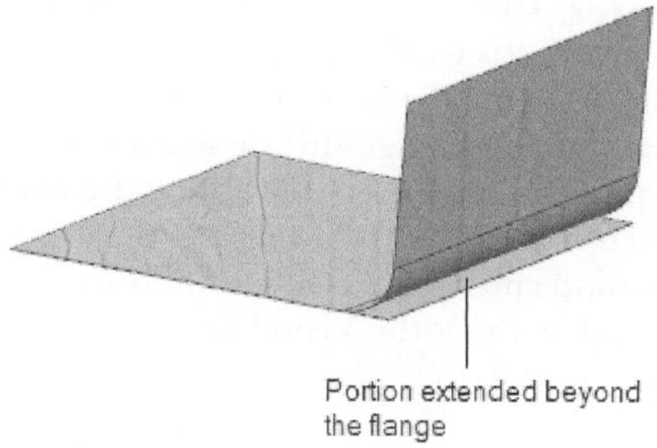

Figure 10-38 *Unwanted extended surface*

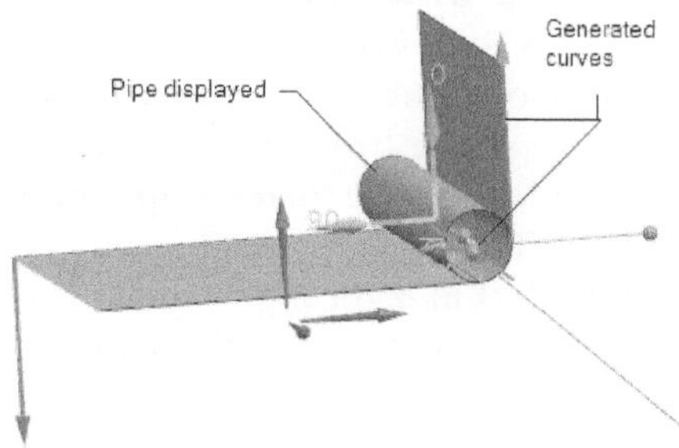

Figure 10-39 *Pipe of the bend radius displayed in the preview*

Creating a Silhouette Flange Surface Using the Absolute Gap Method

By selecting the **Absolute Gap** option from the Type drop-down list, you can create a silhouette flange surface relative to an existing silhouette flange surface and also maintain a predefined gap. The minimum gap is calculated by taking the center line of the bend radius of the two pipes and the nearest tangential distance between them. You can also maintain the predefined gap between two silhouette flange surfaces by entering a gap value in the **Gap** edit box.

If you select the **Absolute Gap** option from the Type drop-down list, the **Base Feature** rollout will be displayed. By default, the **Base Feature** button is chosen in the **Base Feature** rollout. As a result, you will be prompted to select the silhouette flange to define the base flange. Select the existing flange; you will be prompted to select the faces to define the base face. Select the reference face. Next, specify the reference direction in the **Reference Direction** rollout. To do so, choose the **Reverse Flange Side** button in the **Reference Direction** rollout; the preview of the resultant component will be displayed, as shown in Figure 10-40. To change the gap between the created flange and the existing selected flange, you can enter the required value in the **Gap** edit box, which is available at the bottom of the **Flange Parameters** rollout.

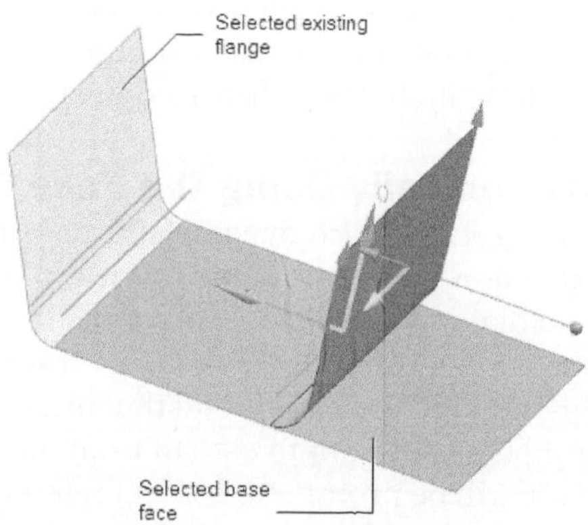

Figure 10-40 *The preview of the silhouette flange surface displayed along with handles and pipe*

Creating a Silhouette Flange Surface Using the Visual Gap Method

The **Visual Gap** option from the Type drop-down list is used to create a flange surface in accordance with an existing flange surface by specifying a visual gap attribute between the two flange surfaces. To create the silhouette flange surface using the visual gap method, select the **Visual Gap** option from the Type drop-down list of the **Silhouette Flange** dialog box. The selection procedure for reference objects is the same as discussed in the previous two methods. Enter the gap value in the **Gap** edit box and choose the **OK** button to create the surface. Figure 10-41 shows the silhouette flange created by using the **Visual Gap** method.

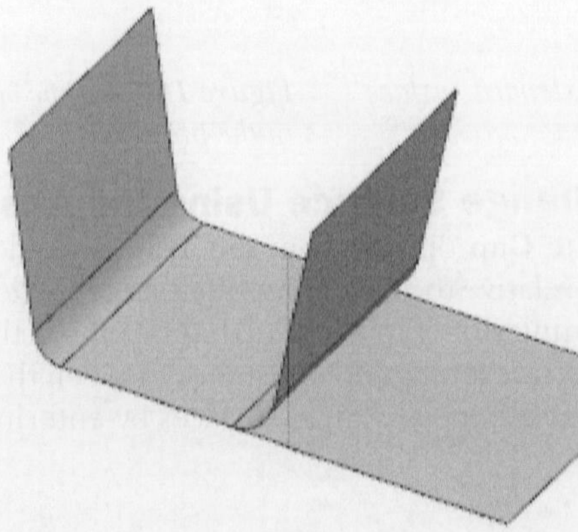

***Figure 10-41** The resultant silhouette flange surface created using the **Visual Gap** method*

Extending a Surface Using the Law Extension Tool

Ribbon: Home > More Gallery > Flange Surface > Law Extension *(Customize to add)*
Menu: Insert > Flange Surface > Law Extension

The **Law Extension** tool is used to extend a surface either dynamically or by defining different type of laws for an extension. The extension of the surface can be carried out in both the directions of the edge or the curve selected. The process of extending the surface by using each of these methods is discussed next.

Extending a Surface Dynamically Using the Face Option

As discussed earlier, you can extend a surface dynamically by using the **Law Extension** tool. To do so, choose the **Law Extension** tool from **Menu > Insert > Flange Surface** in the **Top Border Bar**; the **Law Extension** dialog box will be displayed, refer to Figure 10-42, and you will be prompted to select the base curve profile. By default, the **Face** option is selected from the Type drop-down list. Using this method, you can extend the surface by taking an existing face as reference. Select the curve string that you want to extend from the surface and choose the **Face** button from the **Face** rollout; you will be prompted to select reference faces. Select the required face as the reference face; the preview of the surface will be displayed, as shown in Figure 10-43.

*Figure 10-42 The **Law Extension** dialog box*

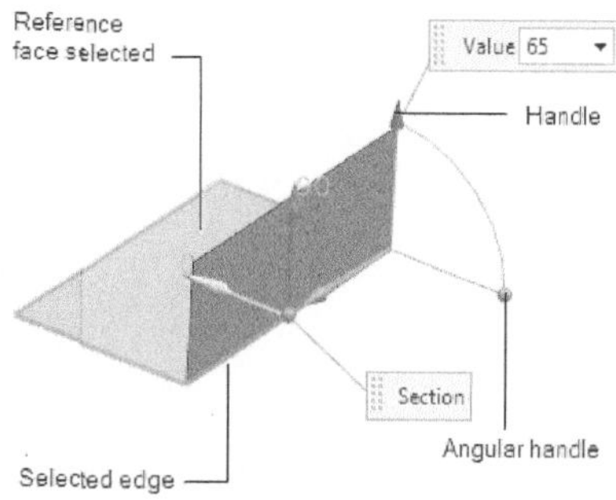

Figure 10-43 Preview of the component

Length Law and Angle Law Rollouts

The options in the **Length Law** and **Angle Law** rollouts are the same with the only difference that the length law is applicable for the length of the flange, whereas the angle law is applicable for the angle of the flange. By default, the **Constant** option is selected in the **Law Type** drop-down list in the **Length Law** as well as the **Angle Law** rollouts. As a result, you can specify a constant value of length in the **Value** edit box. On selecting the **Multi-transition** option from the **Law Type** drop-down list, you can change the length or angle of the flange regardless of the other control points. However, you can change the length and angle of the flange by applying other laws such as **Linear**, **Cubic**, **By Equation**, and **By Law Curve**. For example, select the **Linear** option from the **Law Type** drop-down list; the **Start** and **End** edit boxes will be displayed in this rollout. Enter the start and end values in the **Start** and **End** edit boxes, respectively, and then choose the **OK** button; the extended surface will be displayed.

Side Rollout

By default, the **One-sided** option is selected in the **Extension Side** drop-down list. If you select the **Symmetric** option from the **Extension Side** drop-down list; a symmetric flange will be created on the opposite side of the created flange. If you select the **Asymmetric** option from the **Extension Side** drop-down list, the **Length Law** sub-rollout will be displayed in this rollout. Also, the new flange will be created on the opposite side of the created flange.

You can modify this new flange by using the **Length Law** sub-rollout.

Spine Rollout

This rollout is used to define the spine of the law extension surface. To define a spine, select the **Curve** option from the **Method** drop-down list of the **Spine** rollout. Next, choose the **Curve** button from the **Spine** rollout if it is not already chosen and then select the curve, refer to Figure 10-44. An imaginary plane will be placed perpendicular to the selected curve, with respect to which the angle of the flange will be measured, refer to Figure 10-44. You can also define a spine by selecting a vector. To do so, select the **Vector** option from the **Method** drop-down list and then specify the required vector from the triad displayed in the drawing window.

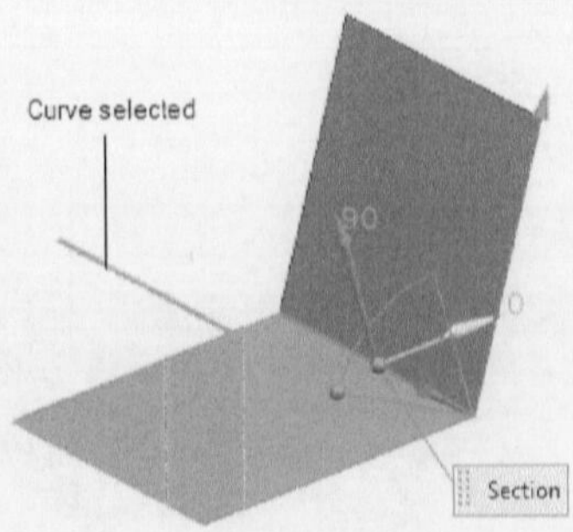

Figure 10-44 *Curve selected using the* ***Curve*** *button in the* ***Spine*** *rollout*

Miter Rollout

This rollout is used to create miter at the corner where two surfaces meet. When you select the **Sharp** option from the **Method** drop-down list of the **Miter** rollout, a sharp miter is created at the corner. Select the **Blend** option to create a blend at the corner. Figure 10-45 shows a corner with no miter. Figures 10-46 and 10-47 show corners with sharp and blend miters created, respectively.

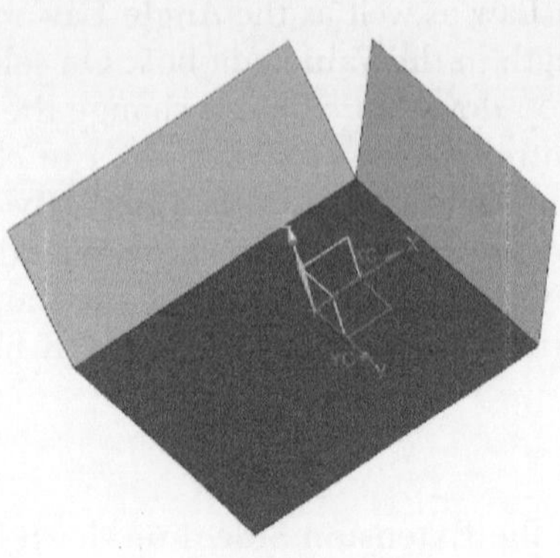

Figure 10-45 *Law extension surfaces with no miter at the corner*

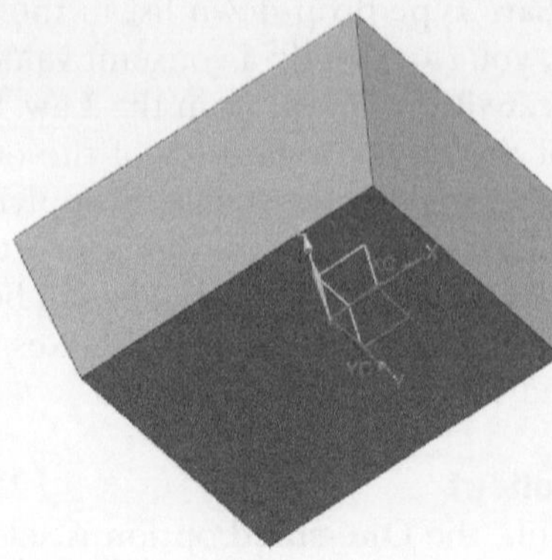

Figure 10-46 *Law extension surfaces with sharp miter at the corner*

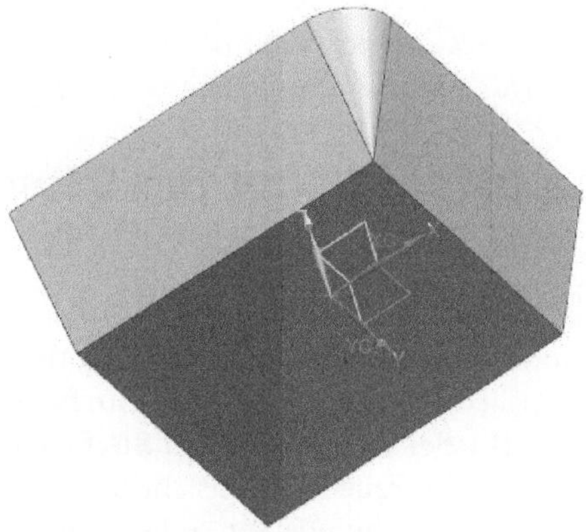

Figure 10-47 Law extension surfaces with blend miter at the corner

Settings Rollout

In this rollout, the **Lock End Length/Angle Handles** check box is clear by default. As a result, you can move handles and angular handles irrespective of each other, refer to Figure 10-48. If you select this check box, the end handles of the profile will be locked. As a result, if you drag the handles at the start point, the handle at the end point will be modified simultaneously. Note that this check box is available only when you select the **Multi-transition** option from the **Law Type** drop-down list.

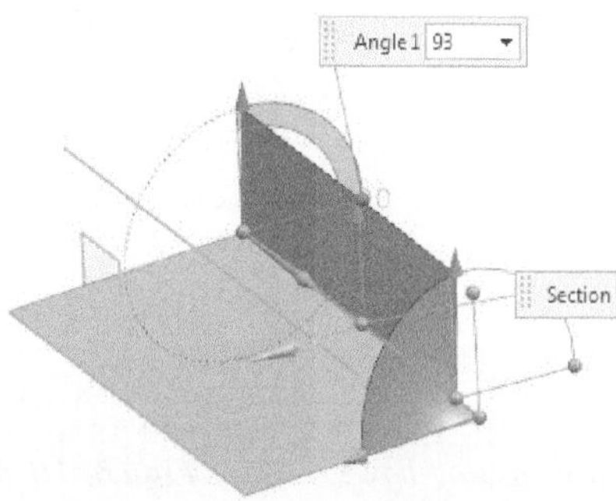

Figure 10-48 End handles dragged irrespective of each other

Extending a Surface Dynamically Using the Vector Option

To extend a surface dynamically by using the **Vector** option, select the **Vector** option from the Type drop-down list; the **Face** rollout will be replaced by the **Reference Vector** rollout and the rest of the options will remain the same. In this method, instead of selecting reference faces, you can select reference vector so that the extended surface is created along the normal of the selected vector. To do so, select the curve string that you want to extend from the surface and then click on the **Specify Vector** area in the **Reference Vector** rollout; you will be prompted to select a vector. Also, the triad of vector will be displayed. You can select an edge, a line, or an arrow from the triad as a vector. Alternatively, you can specify the vector by selecting the required option from the **Inferred Vector** drop-down list in the **Reference Vector** rollout.

Note

*In the **Face** method, a curve selected from a surface for extension should lie on the selected reference face. In the **Vector** method, a curve selected from a surface for extension need not lie on any face.*

Creating a Surface Offset Using the Offset Surface Tool

Ribbon: Home > Operations > Offset Surface
Menu: Insert > Offset/Scale > Offset Surface

The **Offset Surface** tool is used to offset a surface in the direction normal to a selected surface. To offset a surface, choose the **Offset Surface** tool from **Menu > Insert > Offset/Scale** in the **Top Border Bar**; the **Offset Surface** dialog box will be displayed, as shown in Figure 10-49. By default, the **Face** button is chosen in the **Face** rollout. As a result, you will be prompted to select the faces for the new set. Select the face, refer to Figure 10-50. Next, enter the offset value in the **Offset 1** edit box. If you want to create a new set, choose the **Add New Set** button from the **Face** rollout and select the faces for the second set. To flip the offset direction, choose the **Reverse Direction** button. Next, choose the **OK** button; the resulting offset surface will be created, as shown in Figure 10-50.

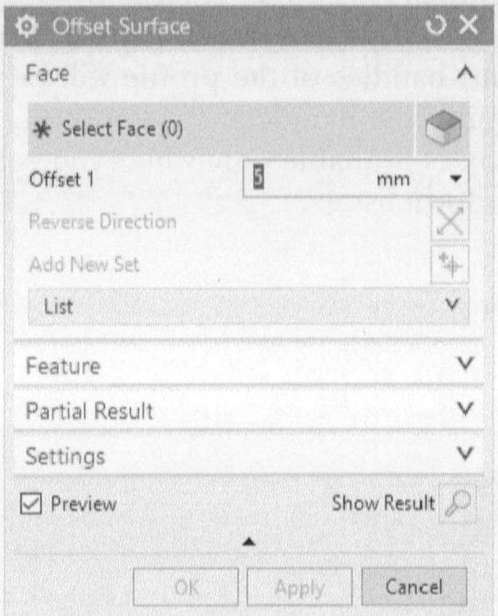

*Figure 10-49 The **Offset Surface** dialog box*

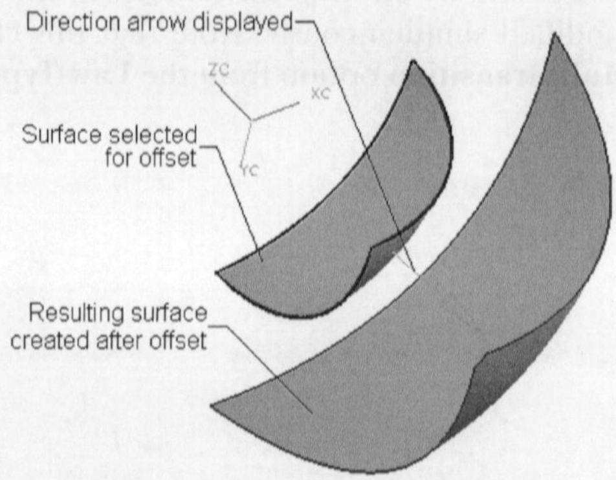

Figure 10-50 Offset surface created

Trimming and Extending a Surface Using the Trim and Extend Tool

Ribbon: Home > Operations > Operations Gallery > Trim and Extend
Menu: Insert > Trim > Trim and Extend

The **Trim and Extend** tool is used to trim or extend an open or a closed surface. To trim or extend a surface, choose the **Trim and Extend** tool from **Menu > Insert > Trim** in the **Top Border Bar**; the **Trim and Extend** dialog box will be displayed, as shown in Figure 10-51, and you will be prompted to select the face or edge to trim or extend. Select a single edge or multiple edges from the surface to be extended. When you select multiple edges for extending them, ensure that the selected edges are in continuity. If the **Preview** check box is selected, the preview of the extended surface will be displayed. The different rollouts in the **Trim and Extend** dialog box are discussed next.

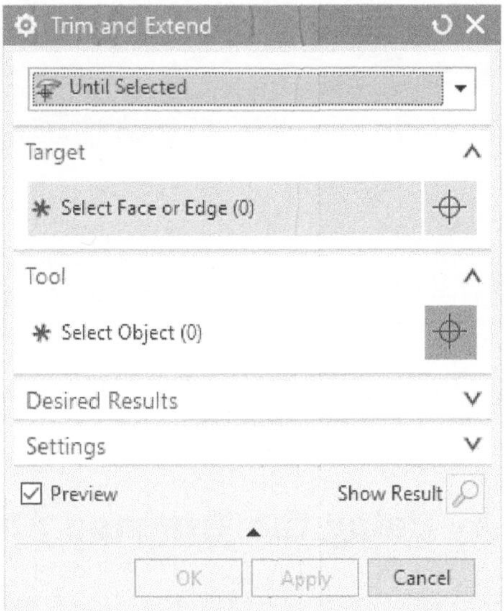

*Figure 10-51 The **Trim and Extend** dialog box*

Trim and Extend Type Drop-down

On selecting the **Until Selected** option from the Trim and Extend Type drop-down list, the surface will be extended up to a selected reference object. This option can also be used to trim a selected surface. If you select the **Make Corner** option, a corner will be created at the intersection of the extended surface with the tool body and the tool body will be trimmed.

Settings Rollout

The options in the **Surface Extension Shape** drop-down list of the **Settings** rollout are used to define the type of continuity of the extended surface with the existing surface. If you select the **Natural Curvature** option, the surface will be extended normally to the selected edge. If you select the **Natural Tangent** option, the surface will be extended by maintaining an angular curvature of 3 degree at the start point of the selected edge. If you select the **Mirrored** option, the surface will be extended along the curvature of the existing surface.

Note that if you select the **Until Selected** option from the Trim and Extend Type drop-down list, you need to select the tool body that serves as the boundary object after selecting the edge for extension. Choose the **Tool** button from the **Tool** rollout and select the boundary object. Next, choose the **OK** button to extend the surface up to the selected boundary object. The options in the **Arrow Side** drop-down list of the **Desired Results** rollout are used to retain or discard a selected tool body. If you select the **Retain** option, the selected tool body will be retained after trimming. If you select the **Delete** option, the material from the tool body will be removed in the direction of the arrow displayed on selecting the tool body. Figure 10-52 shows the preview of the extended surface after selecting the edges. Figure 10-53 shows the surface extended by using the **Make Corner** option.

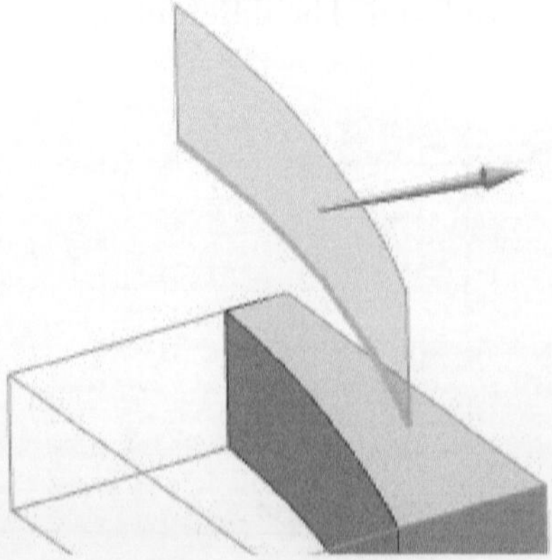

Figure 10-52 *The preview of the extended surface after selecting edges*

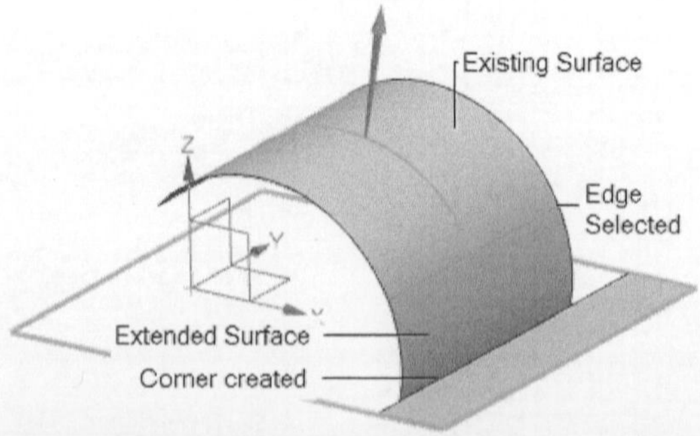

Figure 10-53 *The surface extended using the* ***Make Corner*** *option*

Trimming a Sheet by Using the Trimmed Sheet Tool

Ribbon:	Home > Operations > Trim Sheet
Menu:	Insert > Trim > Trim Sheet

The **Trim Sheet** tool is used to trim a sheet by defining the trim boundary. You can also trim a sheet by projecting a curve and then defining it as trim boundary. If the trim boundary is a surface, then the surface to be trimmed must be intersected completely with the trimming surface. Choose the **Trim Sheet** tool from **Menu > Insert > Trim** of the **Top Border Bar**; the **Trim Sheet** dialog box will be displayed, as shown in Figure 10-54, and you will be prompted to select sheet bodies to trim.

By default, the **Sheet Body** button is chosen in the **Target** rollout. Select the sheet to be trimmed and then press the middle mouse button. Next, you will be prompted to select the boundary objects. Select boundary objects. Next, choose the **Region** button from the **Region** rollout; the surface will be highlighted. The highlighted surface indicates whether this region is to be kept or discarded. You need to select the **Keep** or **Discard** radio button in the **Region** rollout to specify whether the area highlighted has to be kept or discarded. If you select the **Keep** radio button from this rollout, the highlighted region will be retained, and the other region will be removed. If you select the **Discard** radio button, the highlighted region will be removed (trimmed) and the other region will be retained.

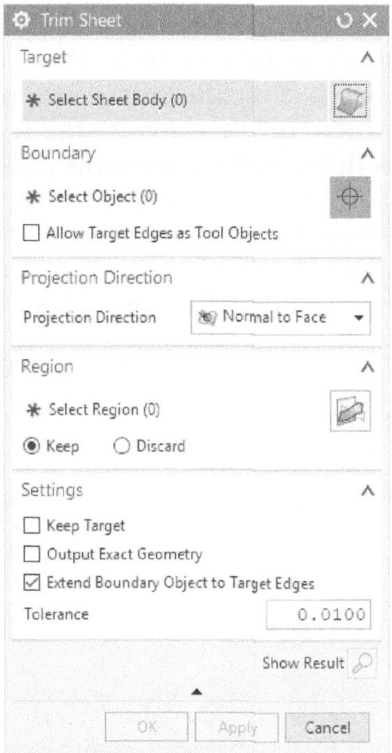

Figure 10-54 *The* ***Trim Sheet*** *dialog box*

Figure 10-55 shows the entities selected for trimming a surface. Figure 10-56 shows the resulting trimmed surface created after selecting the **Discard** radio button from the **Region** rollout.

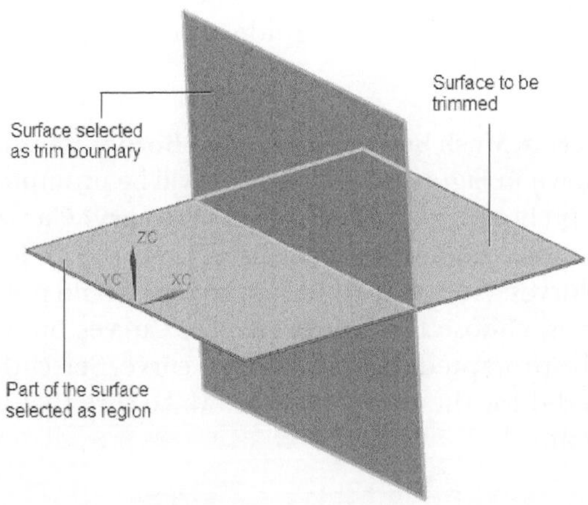

Figure 10-55 *Entities selected for trimming a sheet*

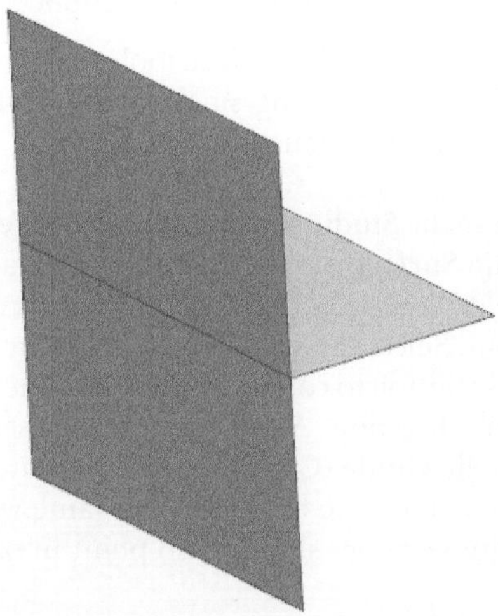

Figure 10-56 *The resulting trimmed sheet created after selecting the* ***Discard*** *radio button*

The **Projection Direction** drop-down list contains the options for projecting (imprinting) a curve or a sketch on the surface to be trimmed. The projection curve or sketch can be defined as the trimming boundary. Select the surface to be trimmed and press the middle mouse button. Next, select the curve or the sketch as the trim boundary. The selected curve or the sketch automatically gets imprinted on the surface to be trimmed and forms the trim boundary. The curve projected as the trim boundary should intersect the surface to be trimmed. Figure 10-57 shows the objects selected when the trim boundary is created by imprinting a curve on the surface to be trimmed. Figure 10-58 shows the resulting trimmed surface created after selecting the **Discard** radio button from the **Region** rollout.

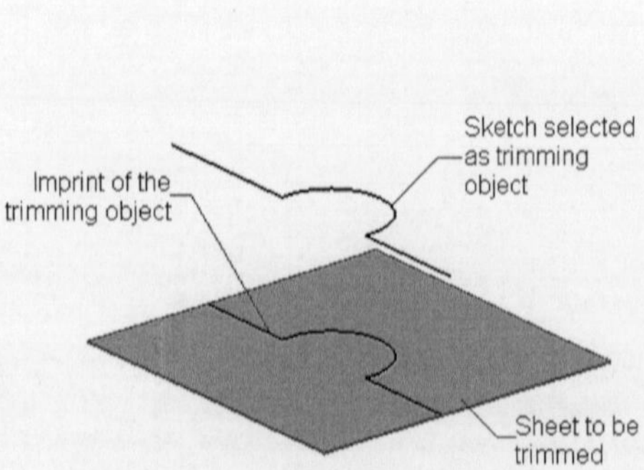

***Figure 10-57** Sketch selected for trimming a sheet*

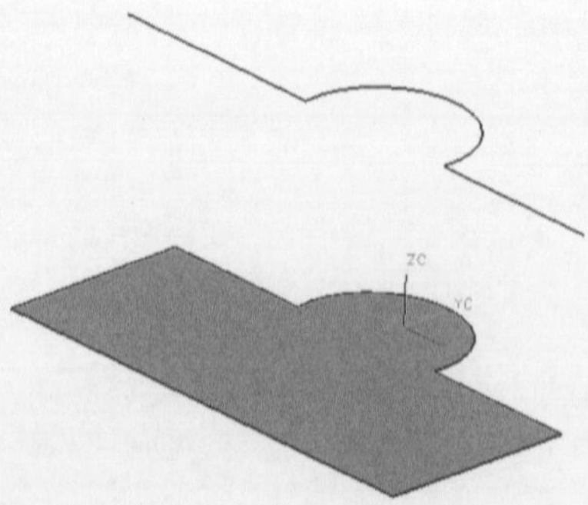

***Figure 10-58** The resulting trimmed sheet created after selecting the **Discard** radio button*

Creating a Surface Using the Studio Surface Tool

Ribbon:	Home > Create > Studio Surface
Menu:	Insert > Mesh Surface > Studio Surface

The **Studio Surface** tool is used to create a surface by sweeping a single section or multiple sections along single or multiple guide curves. The selected guide and section curves can be opened or closed.

Choose the **Studio Surface** tool from **Menu > Insert > Mesh Surface** in the **Top Border Bar**; the **Studio Surface** dialog box will be displayed, as shown in Figure 10-59, and you will be prompted to select a section. By default, the **Curve** button is chosen from the **Section (Primary) Curves** rollout. Select the section curves one by one. After selecting one section curve, press the middle mouse button to continue selecting other section curves. Note that all section curves should point in one direction. After selecting the section curves, choose the **Guide (Cross) Curves** button from the **Guide (Cross) Curves** rollout; you will be prompted to select a guide curve. Select the guide curves one by one in the same way as you did for the section curves. Make sure that all the guide curves should also point in one direction.

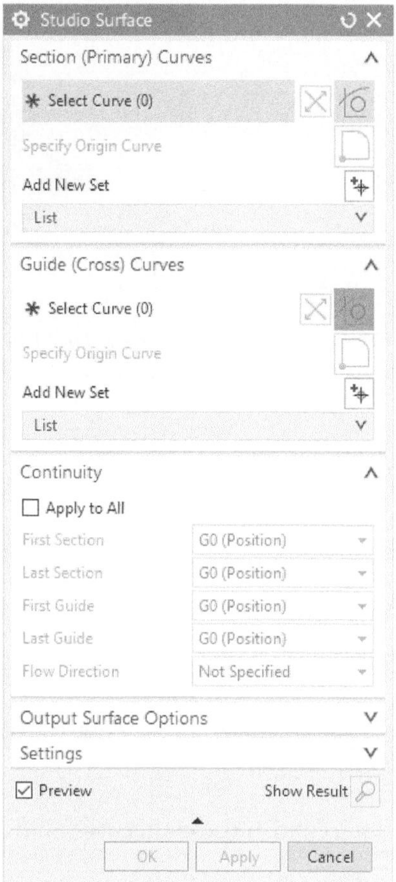

Figure 10-59 *The **Studio Surface** dialog box*

The other options in the dialog box have been discussed in the earlier tools. After selecting all parameters, choose the **OK** button; a surface will be created. Figure 10-60 shows the section and the guide curve selected for creating the studio surface. Figure 10-61 shows the preview of the resulting studio surface.

Figure 10-62 shows a single section and two guide curves selected for creating a studio surface and Figure 10-63 shows the resulting studio surface.

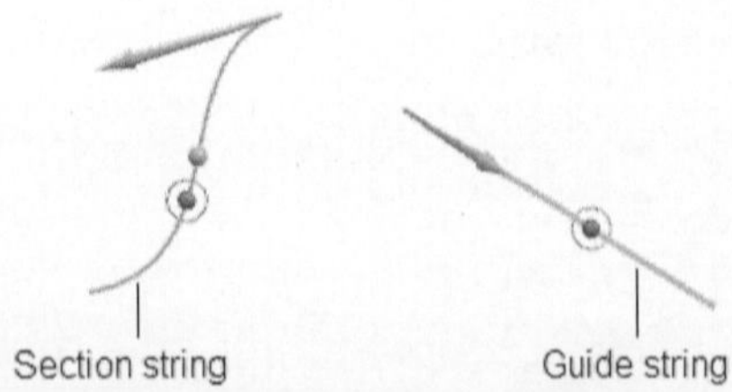

Figure 10-60 *The section string and the guide string selected for creating a studio surface*

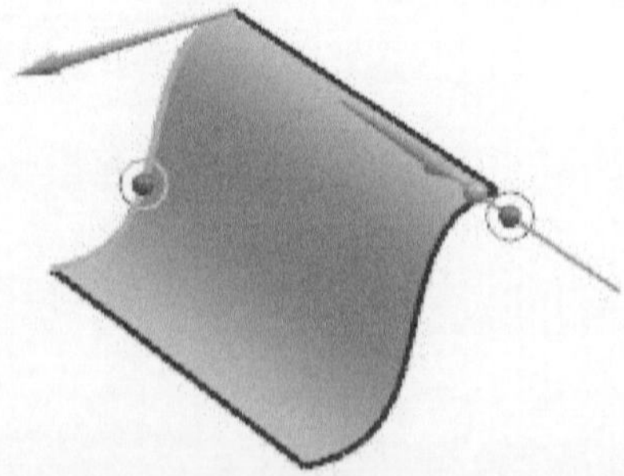

Figure 10-61 *The preview of the studio surface created using the* ***Studio Surface*** *tool*

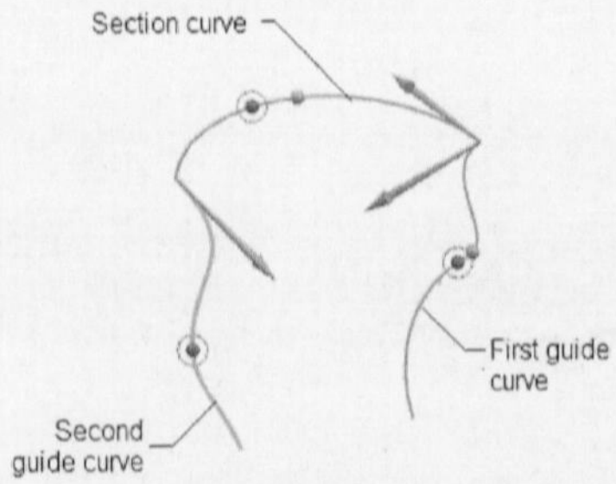

Figure 10-62 *The section curve and two guide curves selected for creating the studio surface*

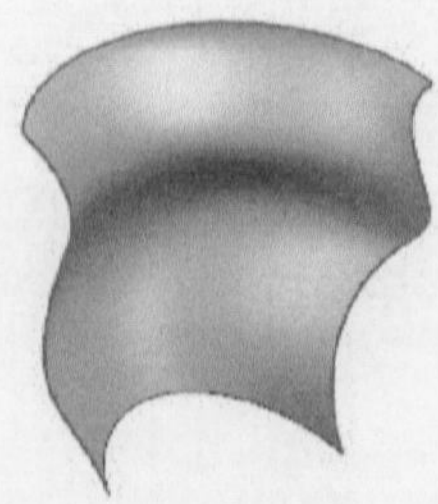

Figure 10-63 *The resulting studio surface*

Figure 10-64 shows the selected start and end section curves and Figure 10-65 shows the resulting studio surface.

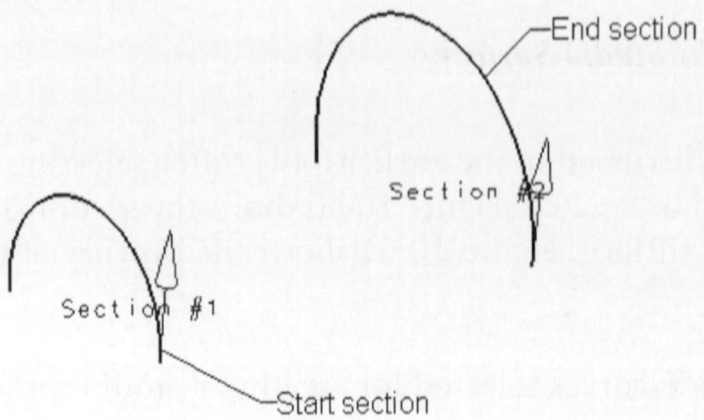

Figure 10-64 *The section curves selected for creating a studio surface*

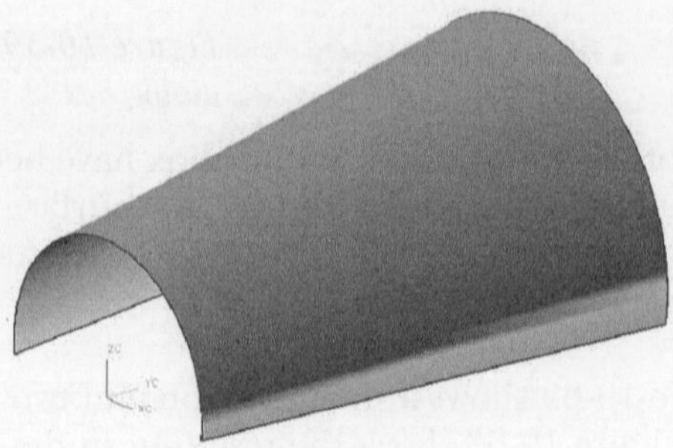

Figure 10-65 *The resulting studio surface created using the* ***Studio Surface*** *tool*

Figure 10-66 shows two section curves and two guide curves selected for creating a studio surface. Figure 10-67 shows the resulting studio surface.

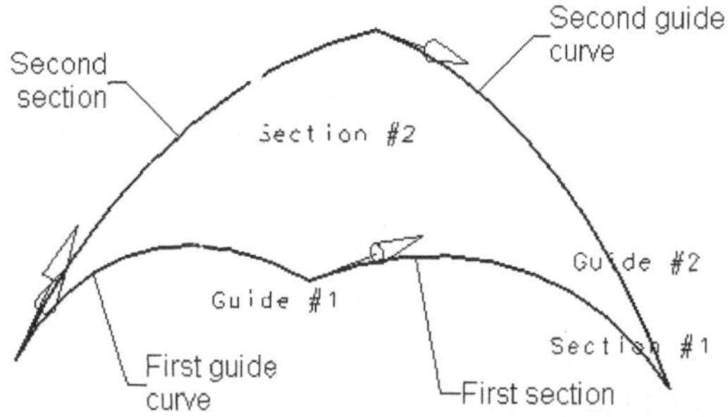

Figure 10-66 The section and guide curves selected for creating a studio surface

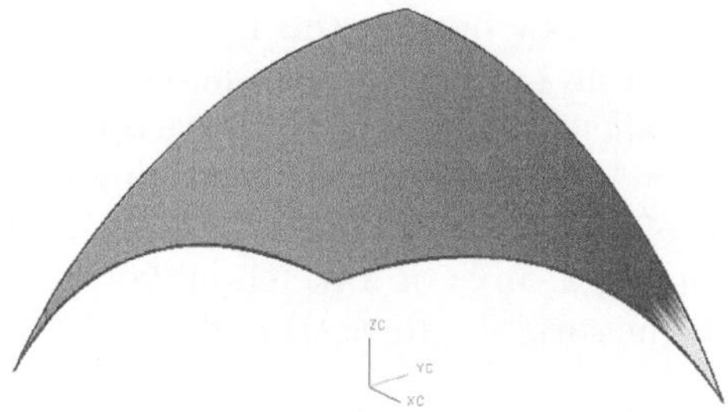

*Figure 10-67 The resulting studio surface created using the **Studio Surface** tool*

Figure 10-68 shows the selected section curves and guide curves. Figure 10-69 shows the resulting studio surface.

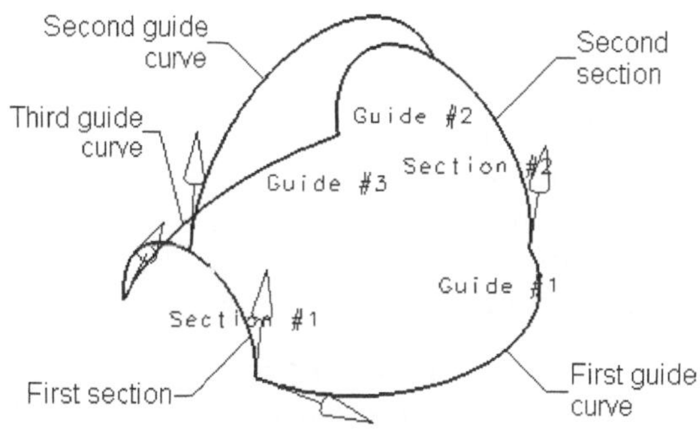

Figure 10-68 The section curves and the guide curves selected to create a studio surface

*Figure 10-69 The resulting studio surface created using the **Studio Surface** tool*

Creating a Surface between Two Walls Using the Styled Blend Tool

Ribbon:	Home > Create > Blend Gallery > Styled Blend
Menu:	Insert > Detail Feature > Styled Blend

The **Styled Blend** tool is used to create a fillet surface between two intersecting walls. While creating fillet surfaces, you can maintain a tangent or curvature continuity among walls. You can also create variable fillets using this tool. To create a fillet surface, choose the **Styled Blend** tool from **Menu > Insert > Detail Feature** in the **Top Border Bar**; the **Styled Blend** dialog box will be displayed, as shown in Figure 10-70, and you will be prompted to select the faces for face chain 1.

The method of formation of the blend surface is defined by the type of option you select from the Type drop-down list. If you select the **Law** option, the lines holding the tangent will automatically be created with respect to the pipe radius specified for the fillet. If you select the **Curve** option, you need to select the tangent holding curves for creating the fillet. If you select the **Profile** option, the tangent holding lines will be created by imprinting a curve or a sketch on both the surfaces between which the surface is to be created.

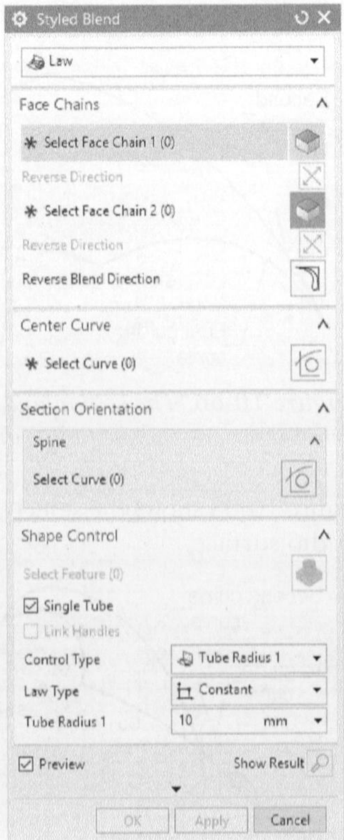

Figure 10-70 *Partial view of the* ***Styled Blend*** *dialog box*

Creating a Styled Blend Surface Using the Law Option

By default, the **Law** option is selected in the Type drop-down list and the **Select Face Chain 1** area is activated in the **Face Chains** rollout. Select the first face and then click on the **Select Face Chain 2** area in the **Face Chains** rollout. While selecting both the faces, you need to ensure that the arrow displayed on the faces are facing inward where the surface is to be created. You can use the **Reverse Direction** button in the **Face Chains** rollout to flip the direction of the arrow. Select the second face and press the middle mouse button; the preview of the fillet along with the handles and dynamic edit box will be displayed, as shown in Figure 10-71. You can view the alternate solutions of the displayed fillet by choosing the **Reverse Blend Direction** button in the **Face Chains** rollout. By default, the **Single Tube** check box is selected in the **Shape Control** rollout. As a result, the parameters of the fillet will change simultaneously for both the walls, as shown in Figure 10-72. If you clear this check box, the parameters of the fillet will change only for the wall 1, as shown in Figure 10-73. Also, the **Tube Radius 2** option will be activated in the **Control Type** drop-down list. By default, the **Tube Radius 1** option is selected in the **Control Type** drop-down list. As a result, you can change the radius of the fillet by using the **Tube Radius** edit box.

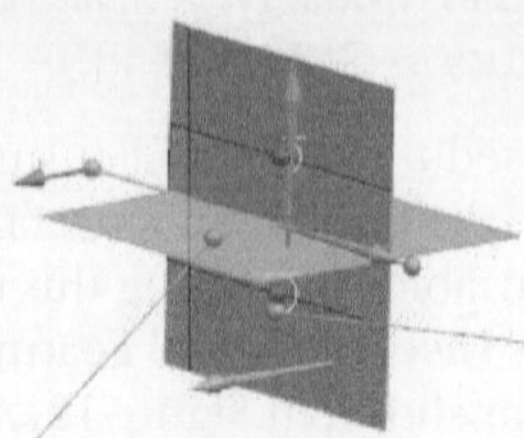

Figure 10-71 *Preview of the fillet created between two walls*

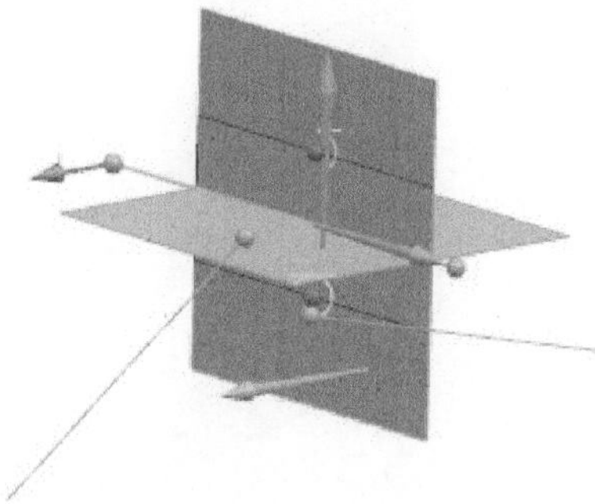

Figure 10-72 Fillet being created with the ***Single Tube*** *check box selected*

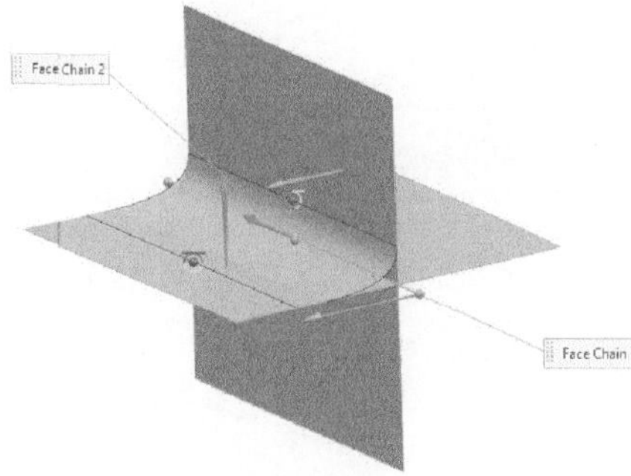

Figure 10-73 Fillet being created with the ***Single Tube*** *check box cleared*

If you select the **Depth** option in the **Control Type** drop-down list, you can create the blend by specifying its depth. If you select the **Skew** option, you can create the blend by specifying its skewness. If you select the **Tangent Magnitude** option, you can create the blend by specifying its tangent magnitude.

If you have already created a curve, as shown in Figure 10-74, then you can use that curve as the center of the blend. To do so, choose the **Curve** button from the **Center Curve** rollout and select the curve; the preview of the blend will be displayed by using the selected curve as the center, as shown in Figure 10-75. By default, line curve will be extended by 10% of its original length at the start point and end point. You can edit this value in the **Limits** sub-rollout.

You can restrict the length of the blend by using the **Section Orientation** rollout. To do so, choose the **Curve** button from the **Spine** sub-rollout; you will be prompted to select the curves for spine. Select a curve, as shown in Figure 10-76; the preview of the resultant model will be displayed, as shown in Figure 10-77. By default, the **Use Center Curve as Spine** check box is clear. If you select this check box, the center curve will be used as spine curve.

Figure 10-74 Existing curve to be selected as the center of the bend

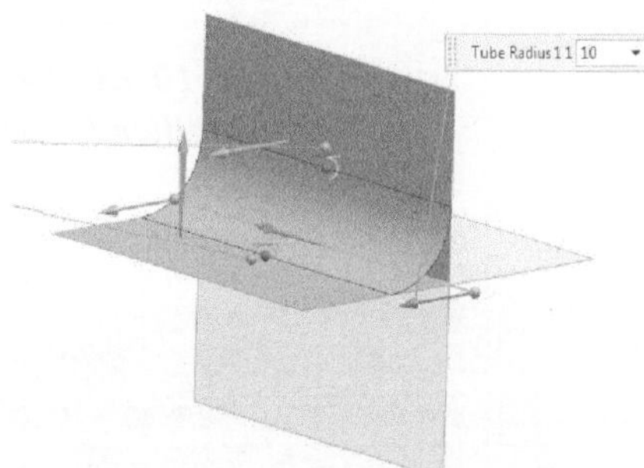

Figure 10-75 Preview of the resultant model

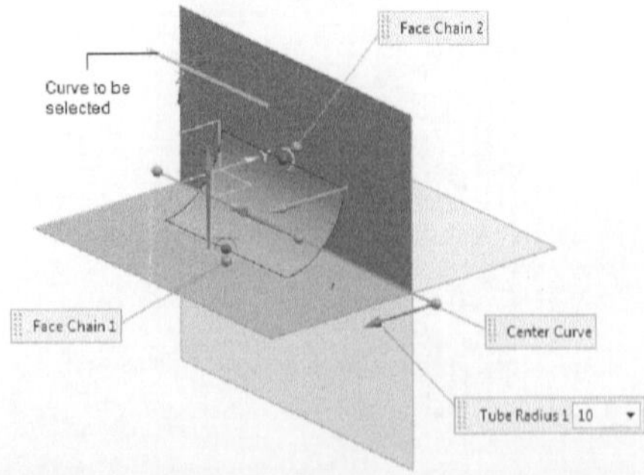

Figure 10-76 *The curve to be selected to restrict fillet*

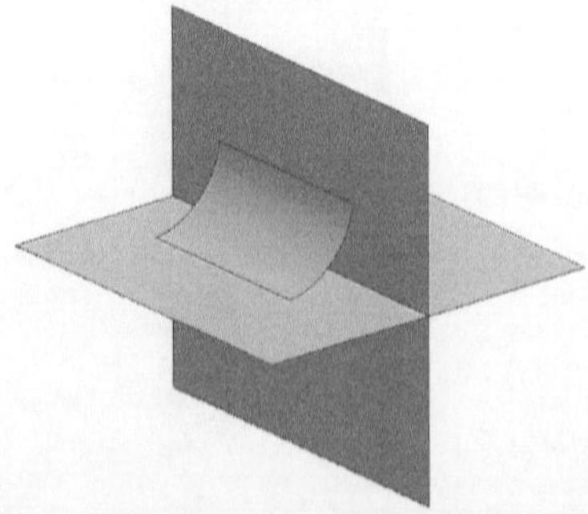

Figure 10-77 *Preview of the resultant model*

To enable the **Extend Blend** check box in the **Blend Output** rollout, select the **Use Center Curve as Spine** check box from the **Spine** sub-rollout in the **Section Orientation** rollout. If you select the **Extend Blend** check box, the fillet will extend throughout the center line, as shown in Figure 10-78. By default, the **No Trim** option is selected in the **Trimming Method** drop-down list of the **Blend Output** rollout, As a result, it keeps the extended portion after the blend in the resultant model. If you select the **Trim & Attach** option from this drop-down list, the extended portion of the wall after the blend and the extended portion of the blended curve after the boundary edges in the resultant model will be removed, as shown in Figure 10-79. If you select the **Trim Input Face Chains** option, only the extended portion of the wall after the blend will be removed, as shown in Figure 10-80.

Figure 10-78 *Preview of the fillet with the* ***Extend Blend*** *check box selected*

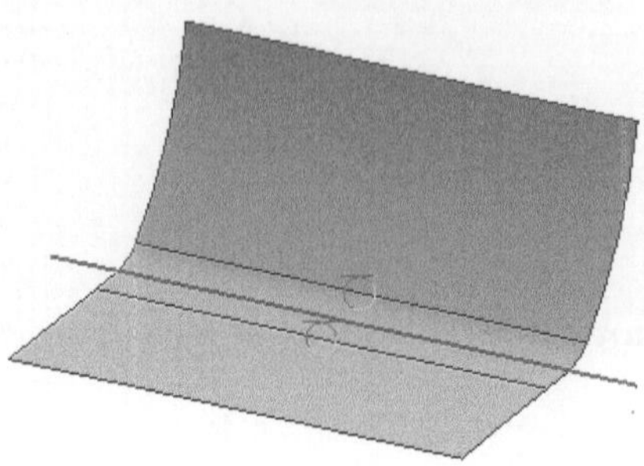

Figure 10-79 *The styled blend created using the* ***Trim and Attach*** *option*

Figure 10-80 *The styled blend created using the* ***Trim Input Face Chains*** *option*

If you select the **Show Tube** check box from the **Show** sub-rollout of the **Settings** rollout, the tube of specified radius will be displayed in the preview. If you select the **Show Depth Curve** check box, the depth of curvature will be displayed in the preview. You can reset the options in the **Settings** rollout by choosing the **Reset All** button in the **Settings** rollout.

The options in the **Constraint Options** rollout will be activated only when two adjacent blends are available in the component. The options in this rollout are used to maintain continuity between two adjacent blends.

Creating a Styled Blend Surface Using the Curve Option

To create a styled blend surface by using the **Curve** option, select the **Curve** option from the Type drop-down list; you will be prompted to select the faces for face chain 1. Select the first face and then click on the **Select Face Chain 2** area in the **Face Chains** rollout; you will be prompted to select the faces for face chain 2. Select the second face and press the middle mouse button; the **Select Curve Set 1** area in the **Tangent Curves** rollout will be activated and you will be prompted to select the curves for curve set 1. Select the first tangential curve from the first face selected and then click on the **Select Curve Set 2** area; you will be prompted to select the curves for curve set 2. Select the second tangential curve from the selected second wall, refer to Figure 10-81; the preview of the fillet will be displayed, as shown in Figure 10-82. Note that you may need to choose the **Reverse Direction** button to reverse the direction of surface creation.

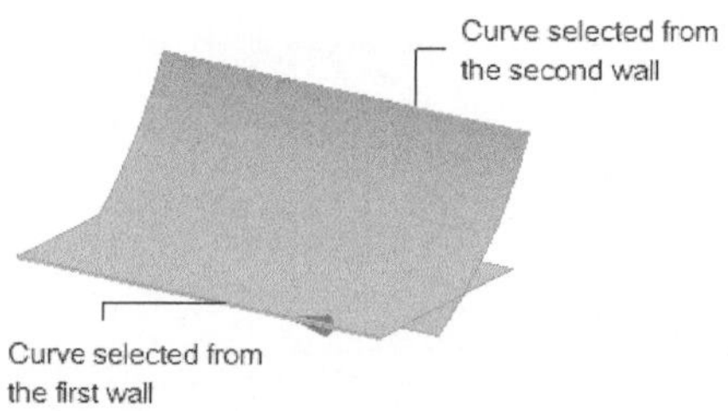

Figure 10-81 *Reference selection for the* ***Curve*** *option*

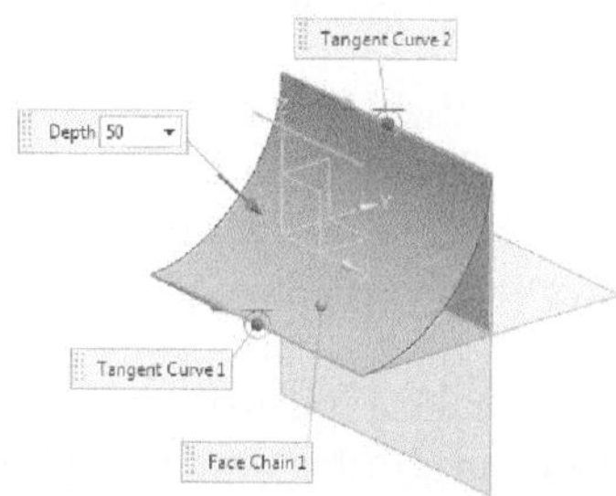

Figure 10-82 *Preview of the fillet*

Creating a Styled Blend Surface Using the Profile Option

To create a styled blend surface by using the **Profile** option, select the **Profile** option from the Type drop-down list; you will be prompted to select the faces for face chain 1. Select the first face and press the middle mouse button. Next, select the second face and press the middle mouse button; the **Select Curve** area in the **Profile** rollout will be activated. Also, you will be prompted to select the curves for profile curve. Select the curve, refer to Figure 10-83; the preview of the fillet will be displayed, as shown in Figure 10-84. Remaining options are the same as discussed earlier.

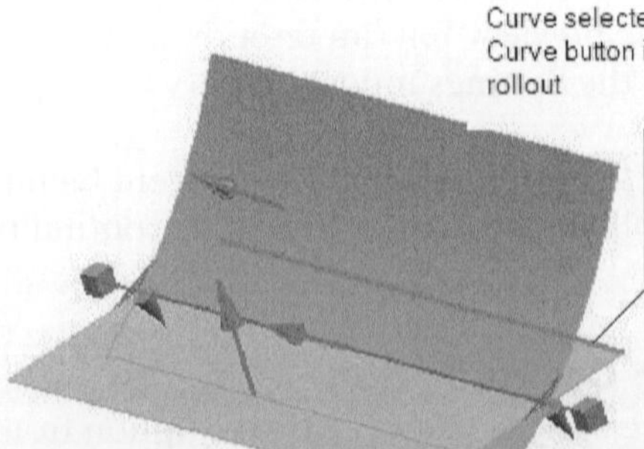

*Figure 10-83 The curve selected for creating the Styled Blend surface using the **Profile** option*

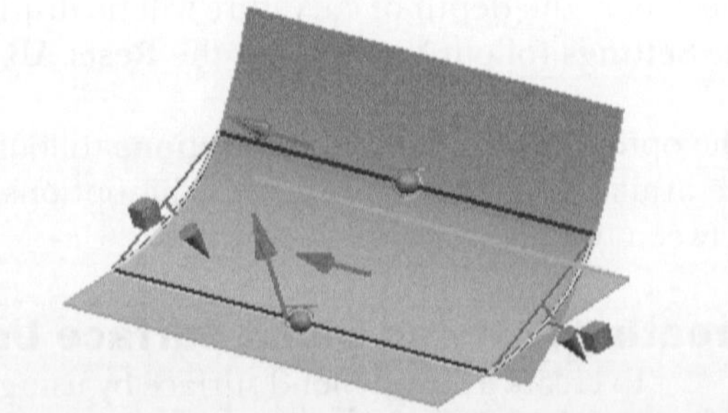

*Figure 10-84 The preview of the Styled Blend surface using the **Profile** option*

Creating Surfaces Using the Styled Sweep Tool

Ribbon:	Home > Create > Styled Sweep
Menu:	Insert > Sweep > Styled Sweep

The **Styled Sweep** tool is used to create surfaces by sweeping cross-sections along one or two guide curves. A surface created by using this tool can be modified dynamically by dragging the pivot point displayed along with the surface. To create a styled sweep surface, choose the **Styled Sweep** tool from **Menu > Insert > Sweep** in the **Top Border Bar**; the **Styled Sweep** dialog box will be displayed, as shown in Figure 10-85.

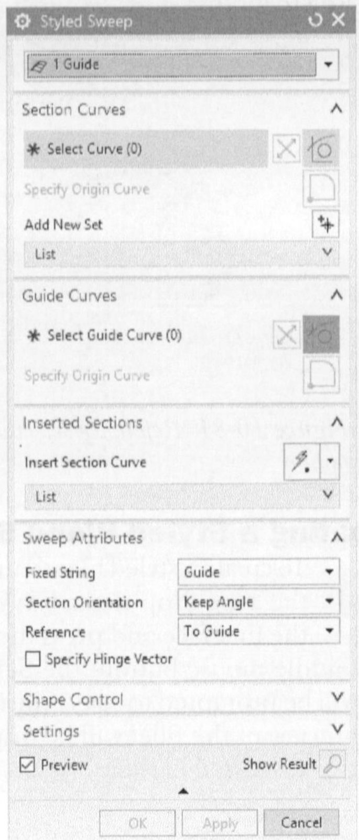

*Figure 10-85 The **Styled Sweep** dialog box*

The options in the Type drop-down list are used to specify the number of guide, touch, and orientation strings. These options are discussed next.

1 Guide
This option allows you to select only one guide string. However, you can select up to 150 section strings.

1 Guide, 1 Touch
This option allows you to select one guide string, one touch string, and one section string.

1 Guide, 1 Orientation
This option allows you to select one guide string and one orientation string.

2 Guides

This option allows you to select two guide strings only. However, you can select up to 150 section strings.

Select the required option from the Type drop-down list. Next, select the section and guide curves by using the **Section Curves** and **Guide Curves** rollouts, respectively. Note that you need to press the middle mouse button to add each section and guide string. Figure 10-86 shows the entities to be selected for creating the styled sweep surface by using the **1 Guide, 1 Touch** option. After selecting the section and guide strings, the preview of the surface along with the pivot point will be displayed, as shown in Figure 10-87.

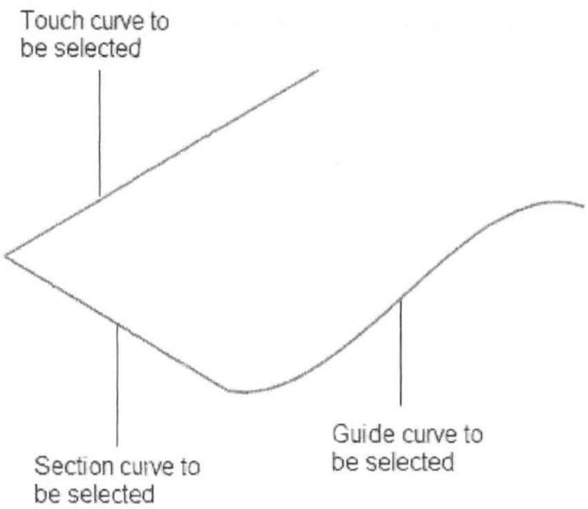

Figure 10-86 *Entities to be selected for creating the styled sweep surface*

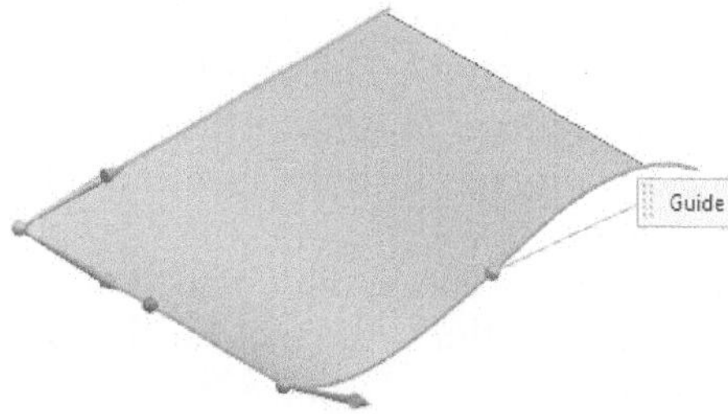

Figure 10-87 *Preview of the resulting styled sweep surface*

You can modify the shape and size of the surface by dragging the pivot point. Alternatively, you can use the slider bar in the **Shape Control** rollout to modify the shape and size of the surface. The options in the **Shape Control** rollout are used to display different types of handles for the surface created, and the handles can be used to modify the surface dynamically.

Sewing Individual Surfaces into a Single Surface

Ribbon:	Home > Operations > Sew
Menu:	Insert > Combine > Sew

The **Sew** tool is used to stitch individual surfaces into a single surface with a common edge. When a selected individual surface encloses a volume, it creates a solid body. A sheet to which all other individual sheets are to be stitched is known as target sheet, and the individual sheets to be stitched are known as the tool sheets. You cannot stitch the tool sheets that intersect a target sheet and extend beyond it.

To stitch individual surfaces to a single surface, choose **Menu > Insert > Combine > Sew** from the **Top Border Bar**; the **Sew** dialog box will be displayed, as shown in Figure 10-88. By default, the **Sheet** option is selected from the Type drop-down list and you are

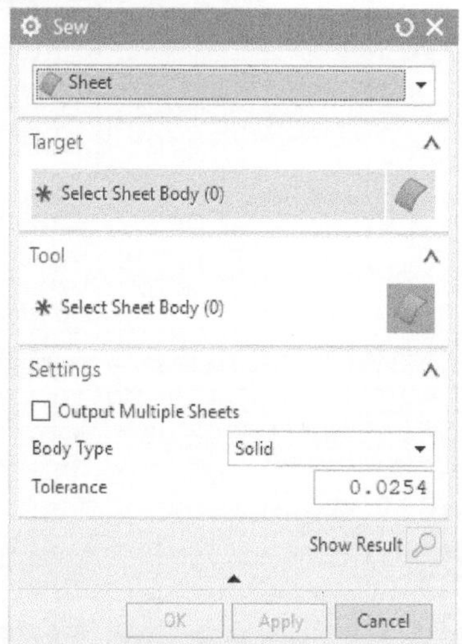

Figure 10-88 *The* ***Sew*** *dialog box*

prompted to select the target sheet body. Select the target sheet body; you will be prompted to select the tool sheet bodies to sew. The border of the selected tool sheets should lie within the target sheet boundary. Otherwise, the selected tool sheet will not get stitched to the target sheet. Select the tool sheet bodies and choose the **OK** button; the sheet bodies will be stitched.

Similarly, to combine solid bodies, select the **Solid** option from the Type drop-down list. Note that you can sew two solid bodies together only if they share one or more common (coincident) faces. You can also enter sew tolerance value in the **Tolerance** edit box of the **Settings** rollout.

Adding Thickness to a Surface

Ribbon:	Home > More Gallery > Offset/Scale > Thicken (Customize to add)
Menu:	Insert > Offset/Scale > Thicken

The **Thicken** tool is used to add thickness to a sheet. Once you add thickness to a sheet, it is converted into a solid. To add thickness to a sheet, choose **Menu > Insert > Offset/Scale > Thicken** from the **Top Border Bar**; the **Thicken** dialog box will be displayed, as shown in Figure 10-89, and you will be prompted to select faces to thicken. Select the sheet bodies to which the material is to be added.

Enter thickness value in the **Offset 2** edit box to add thickness along the direction of handle. Enter a negative thickness value in the **Offset 1** edit box to assign thickness on the other side of the surface.

The **Boolean** drop-down list in the **Boolean** rollout provides options to perform the boolean operations on an existing solid body. Select the required option from the **Boolean** drop-down list and choose the **Body** button from the **Boolean** rollout. Next, select the target solid body; the boolean operation will be performed.

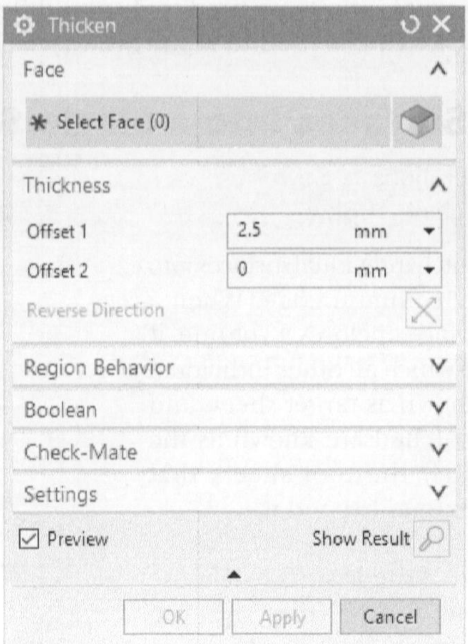

*Figure 10-89 The **Thicken** dialog box*

Figure 10-90 shows the sheet selected for adding thickness and Figure 10-91 shows the resulting solid body.

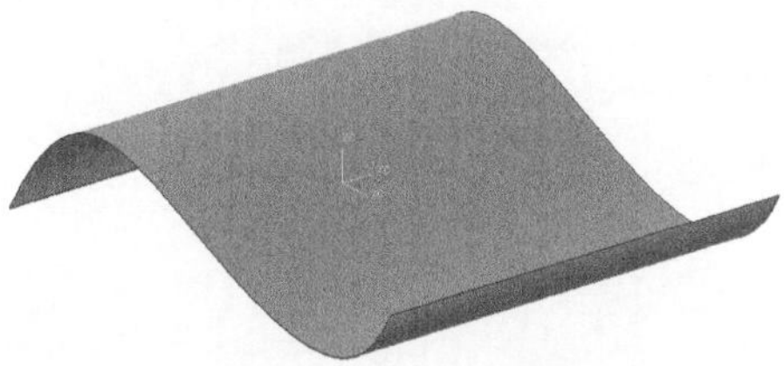

Figure 10-90 *The sheet selected for adding material*

Figure 10-91 *The sheet after adding thickness*

Adding a Draft

Ribbon:	Feature > Feature > Draft
Menu:	Insert > Detail Feature > Draft

In earlier chapters, you learned to add a draft using some of the options in the **Draft** dialog box. In this section, you will learn to add the split draft using the **Parting Face** option in the **Draft Method** drop-down list. Note that this option is available when the **Face** option is selected from the Type drop-down list. The procedure of adding the split draft and the step draft angle using the **Parting Face** option is discussed next.

Parting Face

The **Parting Face** option enables you to select a parting geometry that acts as a pivot for the draft to be added to the faces. To add a draft by using this option, invoke the **Draft** dialog box and then select the **Face** option from the Type drop-down list of the **Draft** dialog box. Next, select the **Parting Face** option from the **Draft Method** drop-down list in the **Draft References** rollout; you will be prompted to select the parting surface. Select the construction surface to be used as parting surface, as shown in Figure 10-92. Next, choose the **Face** button from the **Faces to Draft** rollout; you will be prompted to select the faces to be added to the draft. Select the faces. You need to enter the draft angle value in the **Angle 1** edit box; the preview of the draft will be displayed, as shown in Figure 10-93.

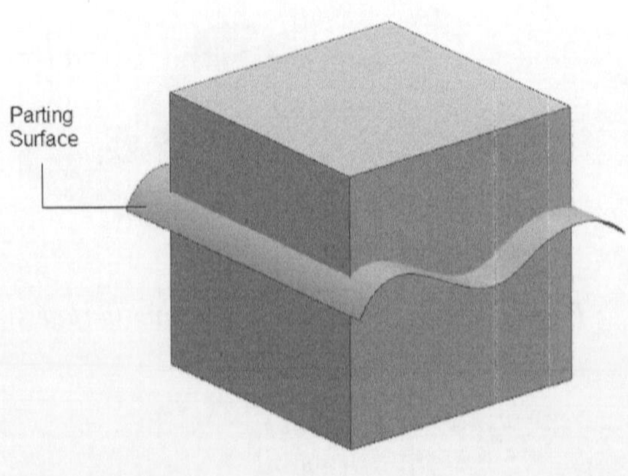

Figure 10-92 Construction surface to be used as the parting surface

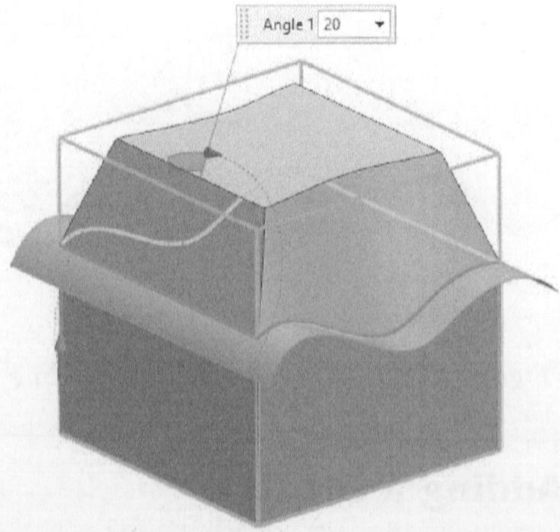

Figure 10-93 Preview of the draft added to the faces

To create two different drafts such that the face of a model is split using a surface, select the **Draft Both Sides** check box in the **Draft References** rollout. The parting surface acts as a hinge about which the draft angles will be added. Figure 10-92 shows the construction surface that is used as a parting surface. The parting surface splits the selected faces. As a result, two different draft angles are added to the faces, refer to Figure 10-94.

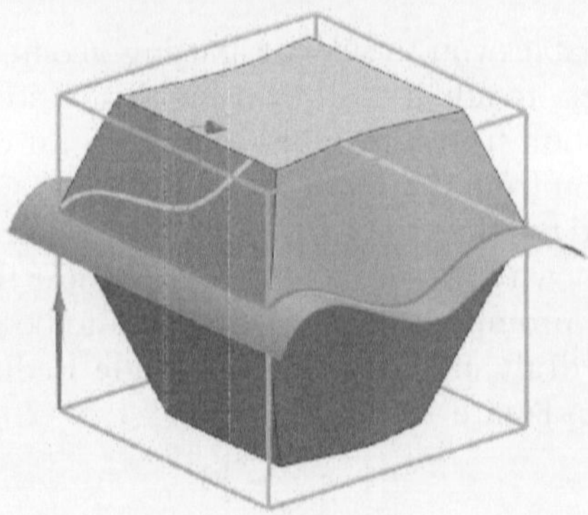

Figure 10-94 Two different drafts added to the faces

TUTORIALS

Tutorial 1

In this tutorial, you will create the surface model shown in Figure 10-95. The dimensions and orthographic views of the model are shown in Figure 10-96. After creating the surface, save it with the name *c10tut1.prt* at the location *\NX\c10.* **(Expected time: 30 min)**

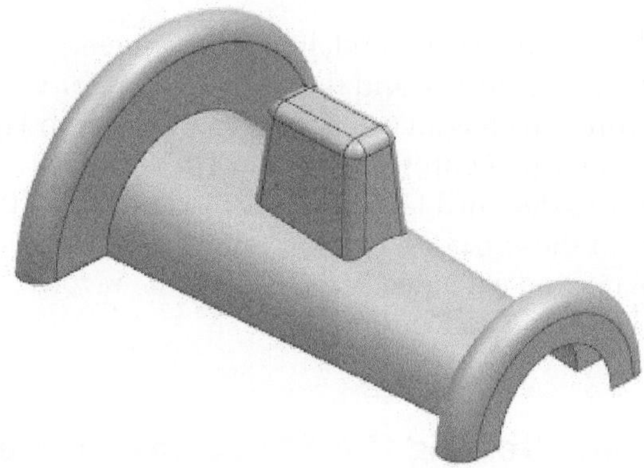

Figure 10-95 The isometric view of the surface model

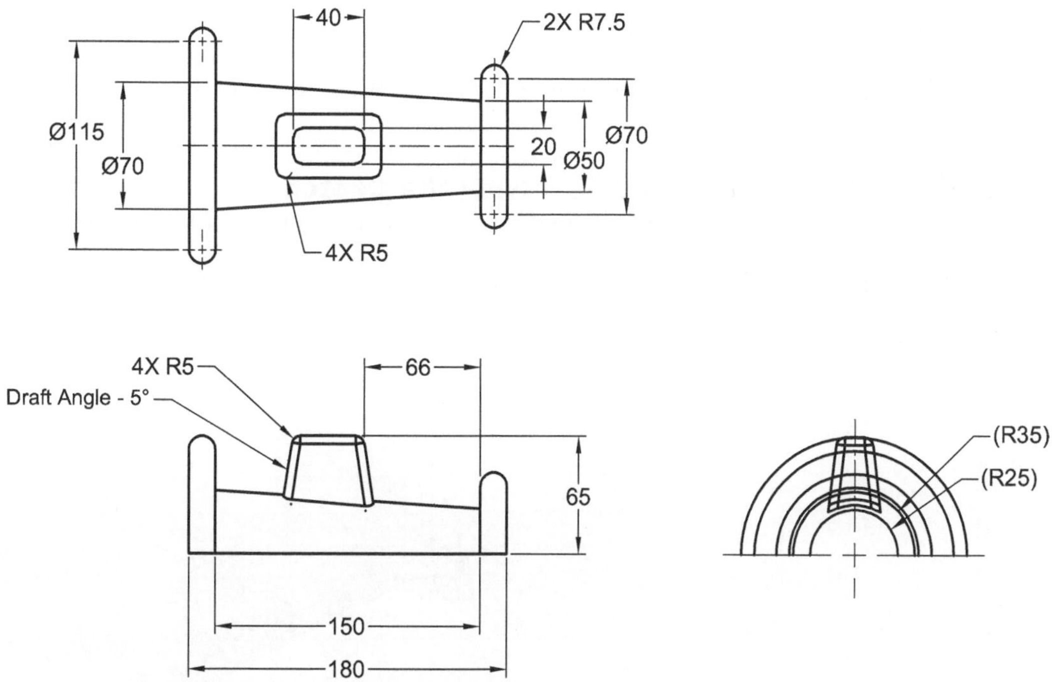

Figure 10-96 Dimensions and drawing views of the surface model

The following steps are required to complete this tutorial:

a. Start a new file and then set the sheet modeling environment.
b. Create the sketch for the base surface and then revolve it, refer to Figures 10-97 and 10-98.
c. Create the second feature, which is an extruded surface, refer to Figures 10-99 and 10-100.
d. Trim the base surface, refer to Figures 10-101 and 10-102.
e. Trim the extended part of the third feature, refer to Figures 10-103 and 10-104.
f. Create the top surface of the extruded feature, refer to Figures 10-105 and 10-106.
g. Stitch the bounded plane and extruded surfaces with the revolved surface.
h. Fillet the stitched surface, refer to Figures 10-107.
i. Save and close the file.

Starting a New File and Setting the Sheet Environment

1. Start a new file with the name *c10tut1.prt* using the **Shape Studio** template and specify its location at *C:\NX\c10.*

2. Choose **Menu > Preferences > Modeling** from the **Top Border Bar**; the **Modeling Preferences** dialog box is displayed.

3. In this dialog box, select the **Sheet** radio button from the **Body Type** rollout and choose the **OK** button.

Creating the Base Feature by Revolving the Sketch

1. Create the sketch for the base surface on the XC-YC plane, as shown in Figure 10-97.

2. Revolve the sketch about an angle of 180 degrees. The resulting revolved base feature created by using the **Sheet** option is shown in Figure 10-98.

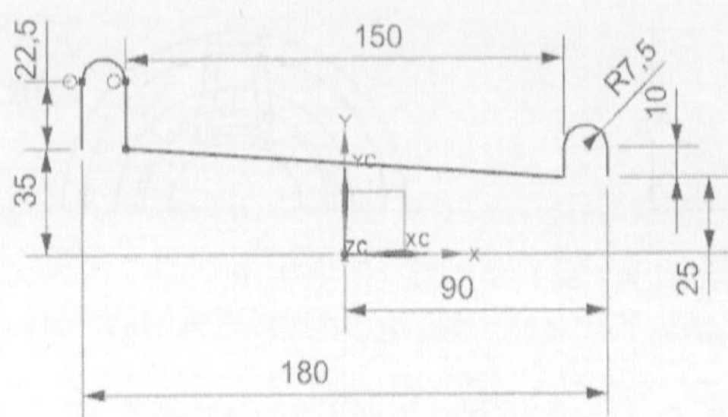

Figure 10-97 The sketch created for the base feature

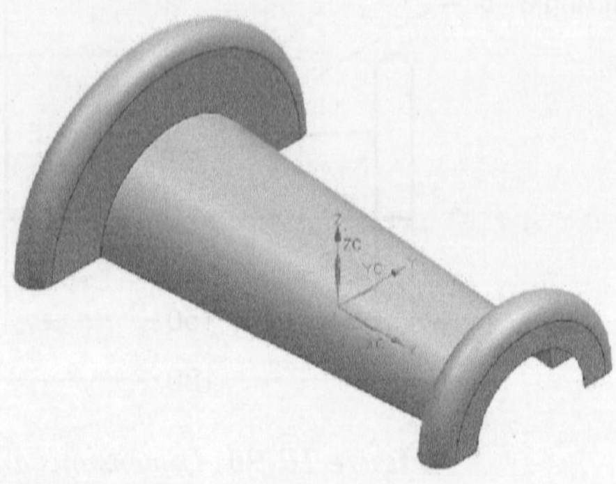

Figure 10-98 The base feature created by revolving the sketch

Creating the Second Feature by Extruding the Sketch

1. Create a datum plane in the upward direction at an offset of 65 mm from the XC-YC plane.

2. Create the sketch for the second feature by selecting the offset plane as the sketching plane, as shown in Figure 10-99.

3. Extrude the sketch through a distance of 50 mm in the downward direction and at the draft angle of -5 degrees by selecting the **From Start Limit** option from the **Draft** drop-down list. The resulting extruded surface model is shown in Figure 10-100.

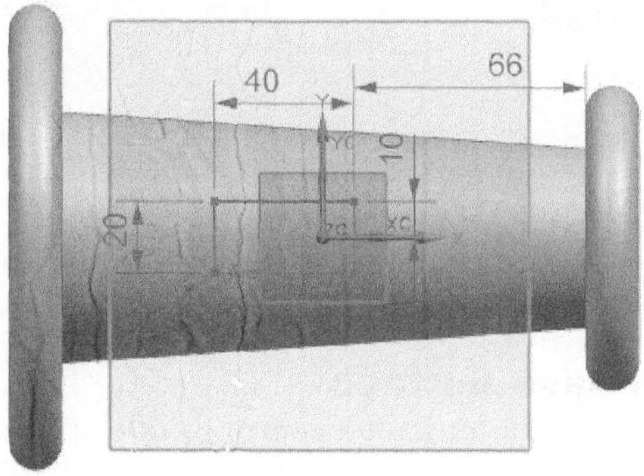

Figure 10-99 *The sketch drawn for creating the extruded feature*

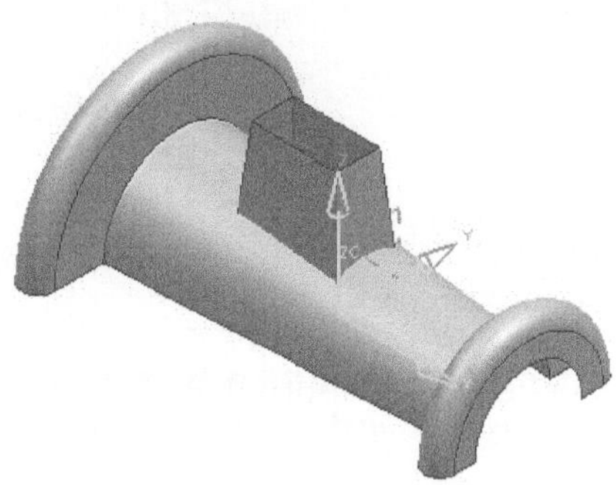

Figure 10-100 *The resulting extruded surface*

Trimming the Base Surface with Respect to the Second Surface

Next, you need to trim the base surface with respect to the second feature.

1. Choose the **Trim Sheet** tool from **Menu > Insert > Trim** in the **Top Border Bar**; the **Trim Sheet** dialog box is displayed and you are prompted to select the sheet bodies to trim.

2. Select the sheet to be trimmed, as shown in Figure 10-101. Make sure that you select the sheet by using the selection points shown in this figure. After selecting the target sheet body, press the middle mouse button; you are prompted to select the boundary objects.

3. Select the trimming surfaces, as shown in Figure 10-101. Make sure that you select the surfaces by using the points shown in this figure.

4. Select the **Keep** radio button from the **Region** rollout and then choose the **OK** button. The trimmed surface model is shown in Figure 10-102.

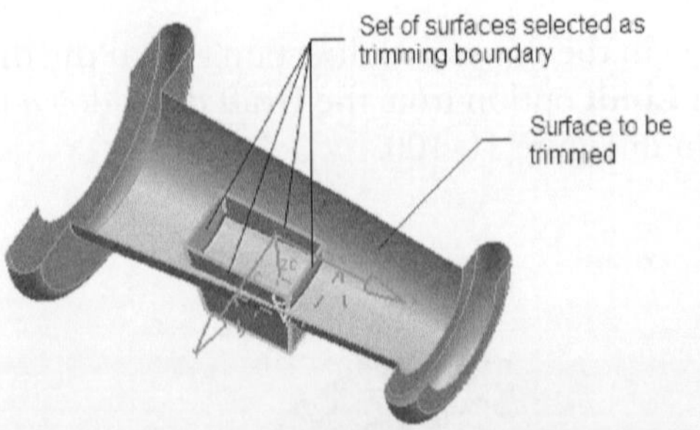

Figure 10-101 *The surface to be trimmed and the trimming surfaces*

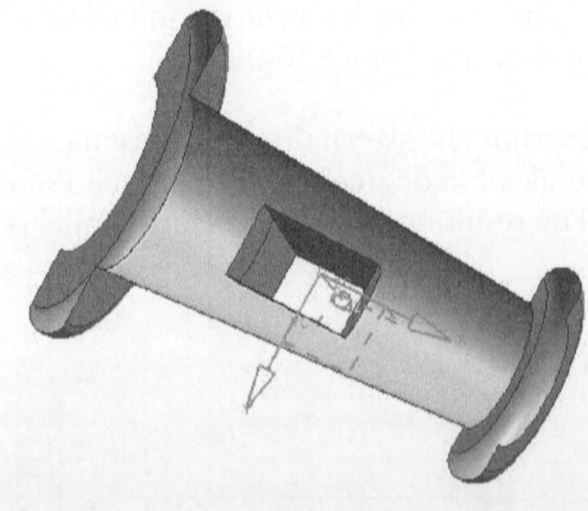

Figure 10-102 *The surface model after trimming the base surface with respect to the extruded surface*

Trimming the Second Surface with the Base Surface

After trimming the base surface, you need to trim the unwanted portions of the second feature.

1. Choose the **Trim Sheet** tool from **Menu > Insert > Trim** of the **Top Border Bar**; the **Trim Sheet** dialog box is displayed and you are prompted to select the sheet bodies to trim.

2. Select the sheet to be trimmed, as shown in Figure 10-103, and then press the middle mouse button; you are prompted to select the boundary objects.

3. Select the trimming surface, as shown in Figure 10-103. Select the **Keep** radio button from the **Region** rollout and then choose the **OK** button. The resulting surface after trimming the extended portion of the extruded surface is shown in Figure 10-104.

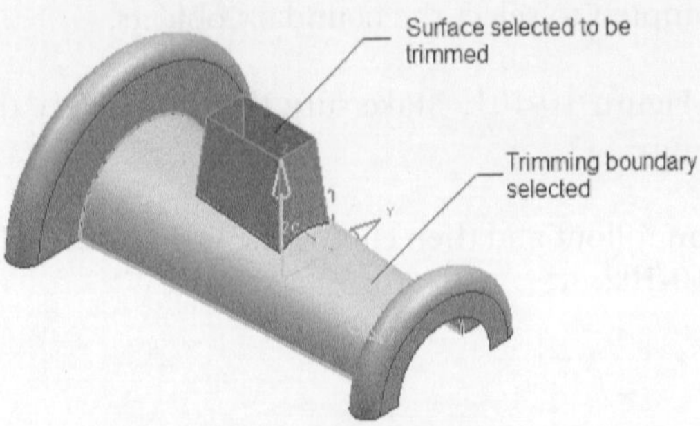

Figure 10-103 *The surface to be trimmed and the trimming surface*

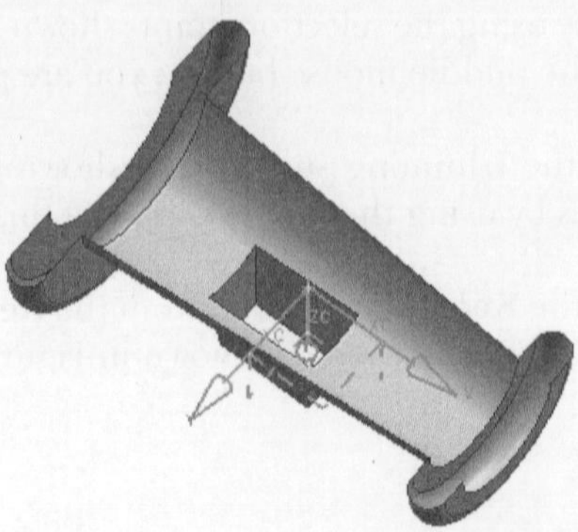

Figure 10-104 *The resulting surface after trimming the extended portion of the extruded surface*

Creating the Top Surface on the Extruded Feature

Next, you need to create the top surface of the extruded feature.

1. Choose the **Four Point Surface** tool from the **Surface Drop-down** in the **Create** group; the **Four Point Surface** dialog box is displayed and you are prompted to select object to infer point.

2. Select the vertices at the top of the extruded feature, refer to Figure 10-105, and then choose the **OK** button. The resulting surface is shown in Figure 10-106.

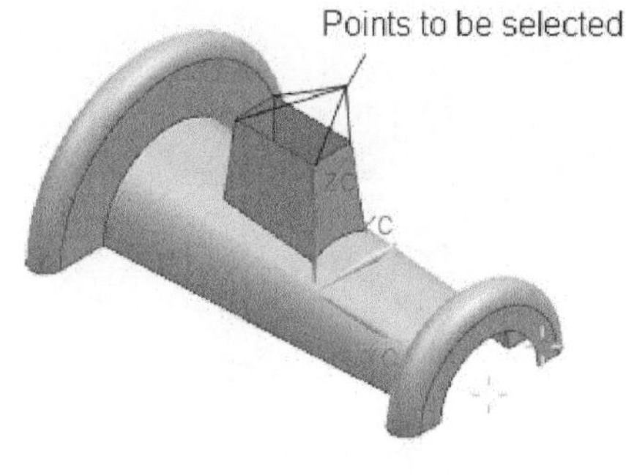

Figure 10-105 *Vertices to be selected*

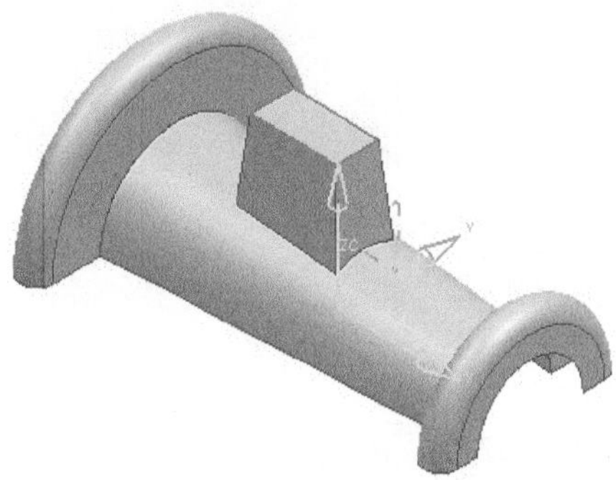

Figure 10-106 *The resulting surface*

Stitching the Extruded Surface and its Top Surface with the Revolved Surface

After creating all the surfaces, you need to stitch them together by using the **Sew** tool.

1. Choose the **Sew** tool from the **Menu > Insert > Combine** of the **Top Border Bar**; the **Sew** dialog box is displayed and you are prompted to select the target sheet to sew.

2. Select the revolved surface; you are prompted to select the tool sheets to sew.

3. Select the extruded surface and its top surface.

4. Choose the **OK** button; all the surfaces are stitched together.

Note

After stitching individual surfaces into a single surface, you can hide the sketch created for revolving the base feature, the sketch created for extruding the second feature, and the datum plane. To hide these entities, press CTRL+B; the ***Class Selection*** *dialog box is displayed. Select the entities and choose the* ***OK*** *button.*

Creating Fillets on Edges Using the Edge Blend Tool

Next, you need to fillet edges.

1. Choose the **Edge Blend** tool from **Menu > Insert > Detail Feature** of the **Top Border Bar**; the **Edge Blend** dialog box is displayed and you are prompted to select the edges for a new set.

2. Select the edges of the surface, refer to Figure 10-107. Enter **5** as the fillet radius value in the **Radius 1** edit box.

3. Choose the **OK** button from the **Edge Blend** dialog box. The completed surface model after adding fillets to edges is shown in Figure 10-108.

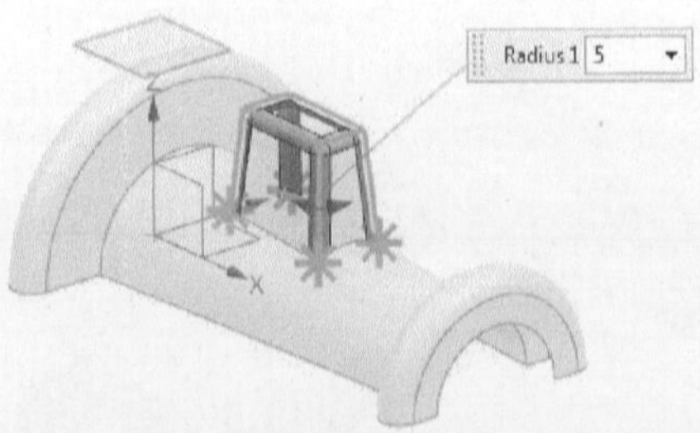

Figure 10-107 The preview of the fillets displayed after selecting the edges

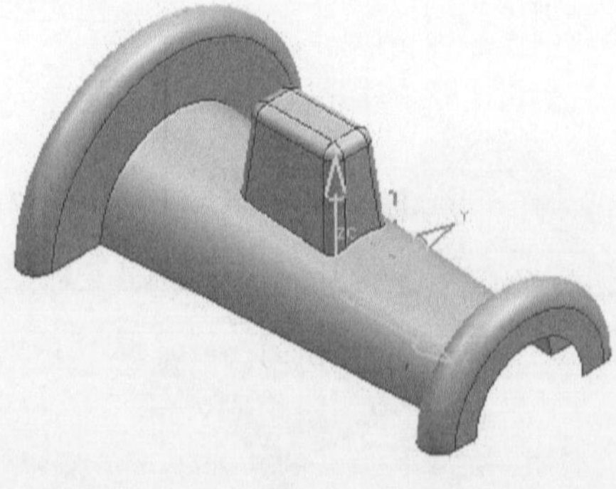

Figure 10-108 The final surface model

Saving and Closing the File

1. Choose **Menu > File > Close > Save and Close** from the **Top Border Bar** to save and close the file.

Tutorial 2

In this tutorial, you will create the surface model shown in Figure 10-109. The drawing views and dimensions of the surface model are shown in Figure 10-110. After creating the model, save it with the name *c10tut2.prt* at the location *\NX\c10.* **(Expected time: 45 min)**

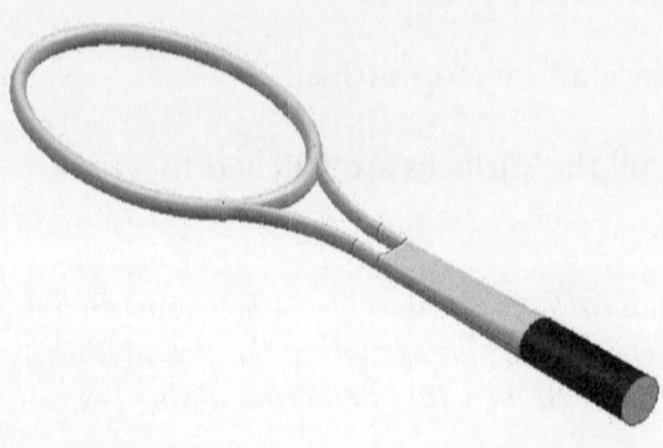

Figure 10-109 The isometric view of the surface model

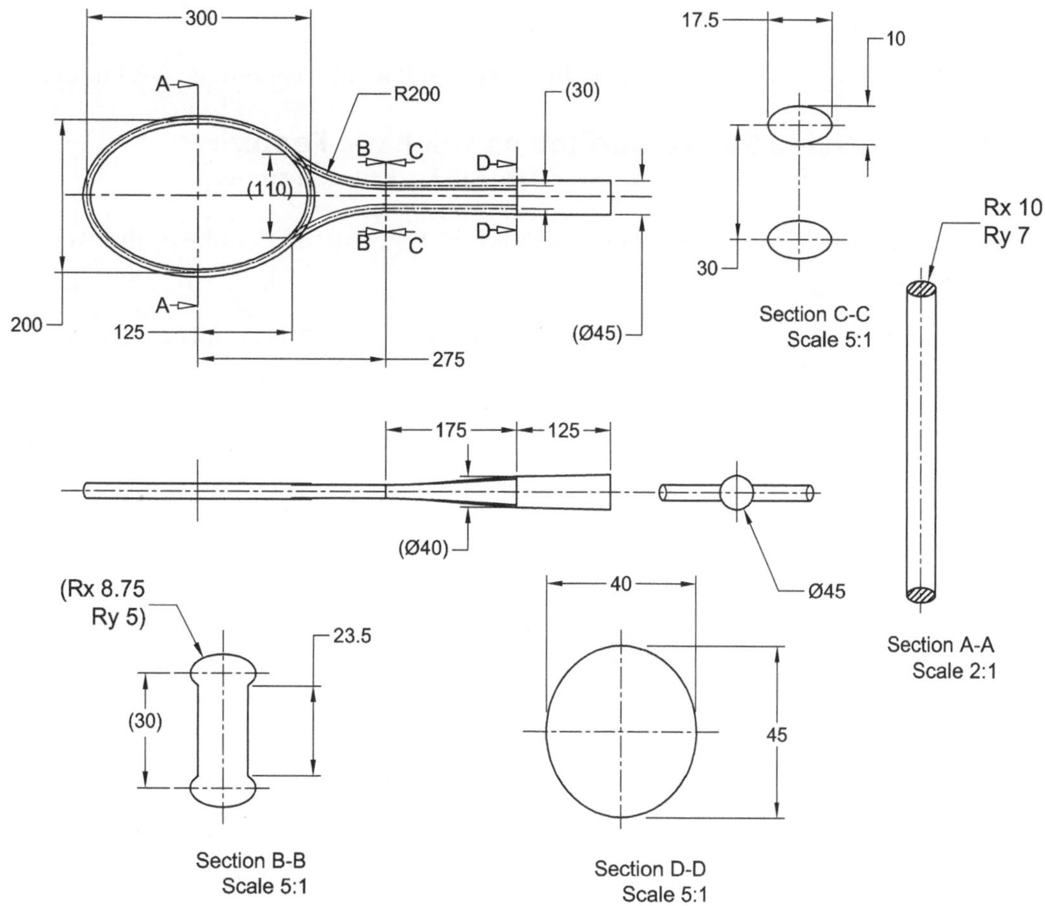

Figure 10-110 *The drawing views and dimensions of the surface model*

The following steps are required to complete this tutorial:

a. Start a new file and set the sheet environment.
b. Create the styled sweep surface as the base feature, refer to Figures 10-111 through 10-113.
c. Create the sweep surface as the second feature and mirror the surface, refer to Figures 10-114 through 10-117.
d. Create the studio surface as the third feature, refer to Figures 10-118 through 10-122.
e. Create the through curves surface as the fourth feature, refer to Figures 10-124 and 10-125.
f. Create the bounded plane surface as the fifth feature, refer to Figure 10-126.
g. Create another bounded plane surface as the sixth feature, refer to Figure 10-127.
h. Save and close the file.

Starting the New File and Setting the Sheet Environment

1. Start a new file with the name *c10tut2.prt* using the **Model** template and specify its location at *C:\NX\c10*.

2. Choose **Menu > Preferences > Modeling** from the **Top Border Bar**; the **Modeling Preferences** dialog box is displayed.

3. Select the **Sheet** radio button from the **Body Type** rollout and choose the **OK** button.

Creating the Styled Sweep Surface as the Base Feature

As mentioned earlier, the styled sweep surface will be the base feature.

1. Draw an ellipse on the XC-YC plane, as shown in Figure 10-111, and exit the sketching environment.

2. Draw another ellipse on the XC-ZC plane, as shown in Figure 10-112, and exit the sketching environment.

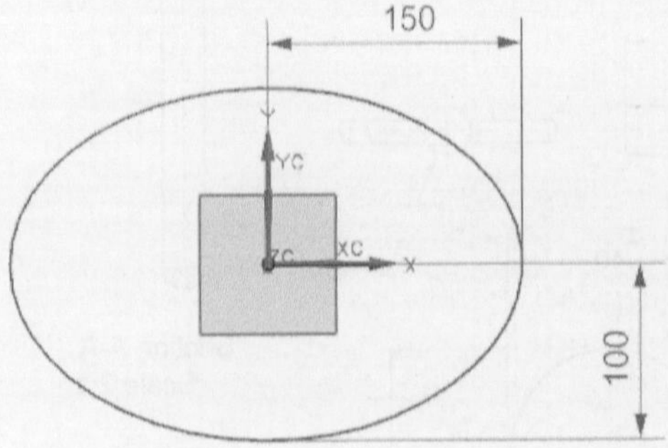

Figure 10-111 The sketch for the guide string

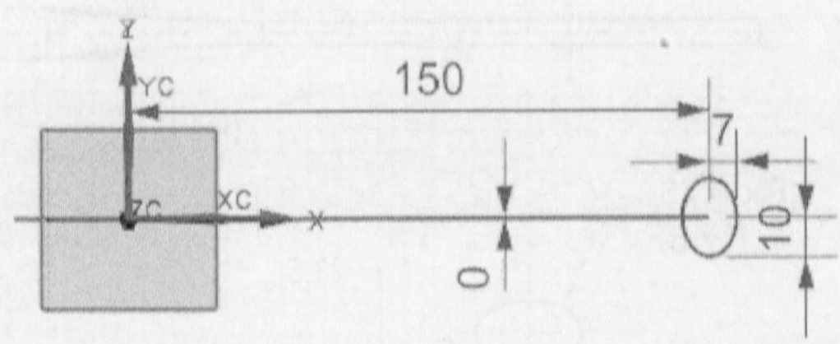

Figure 10-112 The sketch for the section string

3. Choose the **Styled Sweep** tool from **Menu > Insert > Sweep** of the **Top Border Bar**; the **Styled Sweep** dialog box is displayed and you are prompted to select the section curves.

4. Select the **1 Guide** option from the Type drop-down list in the dialog box, if it is not selected by default.

5. Select the section curve drawn on the XC-ZC plane and press the middle mouse button.

6. Choose the **Guide** button from the **Guide Curves** rollout and then select the guide curve drawn on the XC-YC plane; the preview of the styled sweep surface is displayed in the drawing window. Next, press the middle mouse button.

7. Select the **Guide and Section** option from the **Fixed String** drop-down list of the **Sweep Attributes** rollout in the dialog box.

8. Choose the **OK** button to create the styled sweep surface. Hide the sketches that are used to create the styled surface. The resulting styled sweep surface is shown in Figure 10-113.

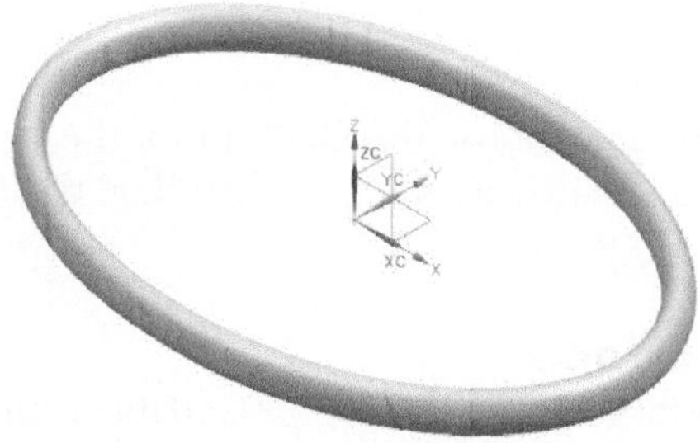

Figure 10-113 *The base feature of the surface model*

Creating the Sweep Surface

The second feature is a sweep surface.

1. Select the XC-YC plane as the sketching plane and draw the guide curve, as shown in Figure 10-114. Next, exit the sketching environment.

2. Create a new datum plane perpendicular to the guide curve by entering **0** as the arc length value.

Note

In this tutorial, the datum plane perpendicular to the guide curve is created by selecting the entity of the guide curve that measures 30 mm.

3. Draw the sketch by selecting the newly created plane as the sketching plane. Note that you may need to specify horizontal or vertical reference for the sketch in the **Create Sketch** dialog box to invoke the sketching environment. Next, draw the ellipse (section curve), refer to Figure 10-115, and then exit the sketching environment.

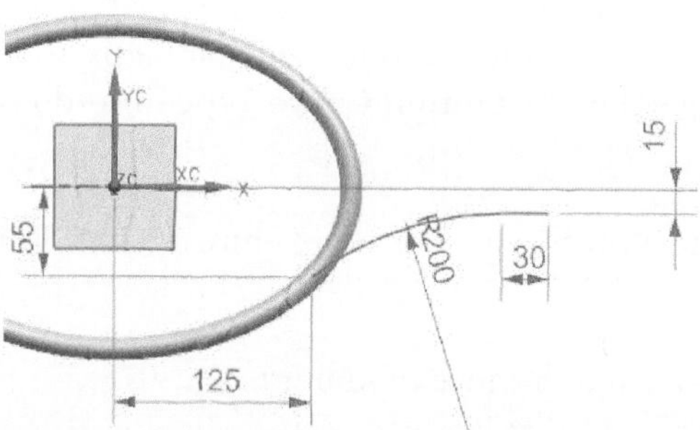

Figure 10-114 *The guide curve for creating the sweep surface*

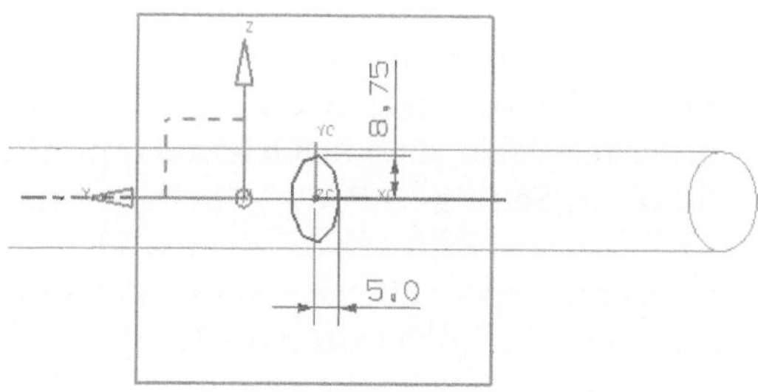

Figure 10-115 *The section curve drawn for creating the sweep surface*

4. Choose **Menu > Insert > Sweep > Sweep along Guide** from the **Top Border Bar**; the **Sweep Along Guide** dialog box is displayed and you are prompted to select the chain of curves for the section.

5. Select the section curve and then press the middle mouse button; you are prompted to select the guide curve.

6. Select the guide curve and then choose the **OK** button; the sweep surface is created. Hide the sketches that are used to create the sweep surface. The resulting surface model is shown in Figure 10-116.

Mirroring the Sweep Surface

1. Mirror the last created surface by using the XC-ZC plane as the mirror plane. The surface model after mirroring the sweep surface is shown in Figure 10-117.

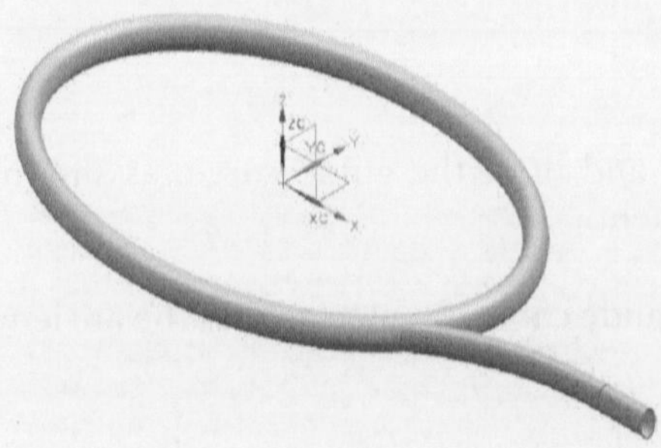

Figure 10-116 The surface model after creating the sweep surface

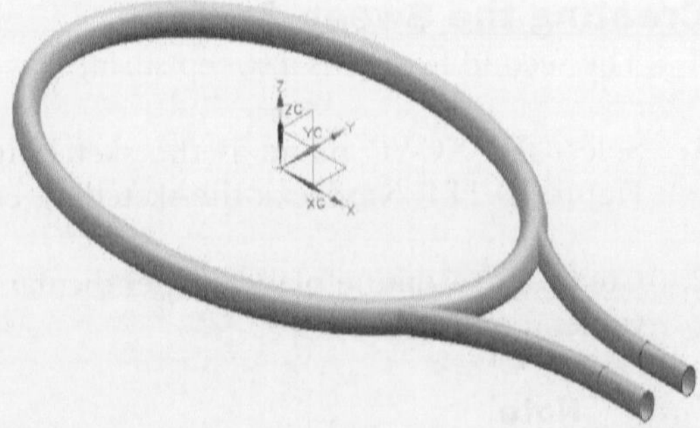

Figure 10-117 The surface model after mirroring the sweep surface

Creating the Studio Surface

The third feature is a surface and it will be created by using the **Studio Surface** tool.

1. Choose the **Sketch in Task Environment** tool to draw the section of the sweep surface by using the last datum plane.

2. Choose **Menu > Insert > Recipe Curve > Project Curve** from the **Top Border Bar**; the **Project Curve** dialog box is displayed and you are prompted to select the geometry to be projected. Make sure the **Original** option is selected in the **Output Curve Type** drop-down list of the **Settings** rollout.

3. Select the edges of the sweep surfaces and create a profile, as shown in Figure 10-118. Exit the Sketch in Task environment.

4. Create a datum plane parallel to the YC-ZC plane at a distance of **450** mm.

5. Select the newly created datum plane as the sketching plane and create the second section curve, as shown in Figure 10-119. For dimensions, refer to Figure 10-110.

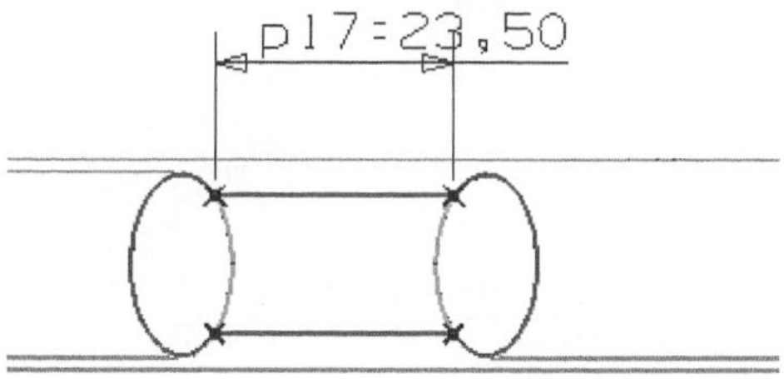

Figure 10-118 *The first section curve drawn to create the through curve mesh surface*

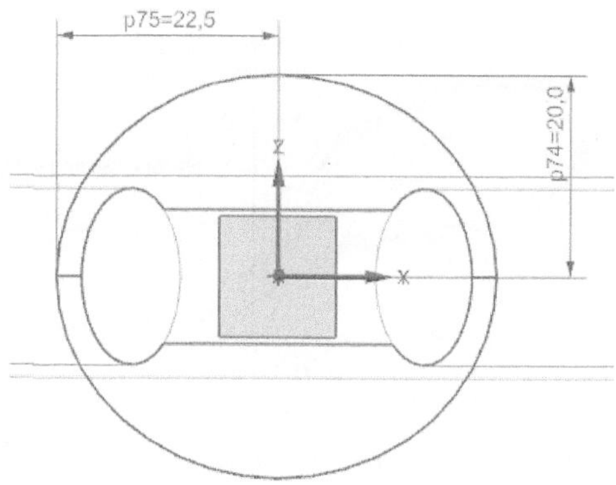

Figure 10-119 *The second section curve*

6. Select the XC-YC plane as the sketching plane and create the guide strings, as shown in Figure 10-120.

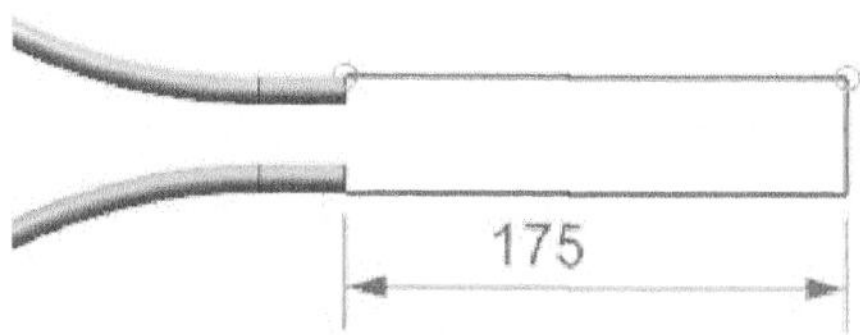

Figure 10-120 *Sketch for the guide strings*

7. Choose **Menu > Insert > Mesh Surface > Studio Surface** from the **Top Border Bar**; the **Studio Surface** dialog box is displayed and you are prompted to select the section.

8. Select all the elements from first section string, refer to Figure 10-121, and then press the middle mouse button; you are prompted to select the section again.

9. Select the second section string, refer to Figure 10-121, and then choose the **Guide (Cross) Curves** button from the **Guide (Cross) Curves** rollout; you are prompted to select the guide string.

10. Select the first guide curve, refer to Figure 10-121, and then press the middle mouse button; you are prompted to select the guide string again.

11. Select the second guide curve, refer to Figure 10-121. The preview of the studio surface after selecting the sections and the guide curves is shown in Figure 10-122. Next, choose the **Apply** button and then the **Cancel** button to create the studio surface.

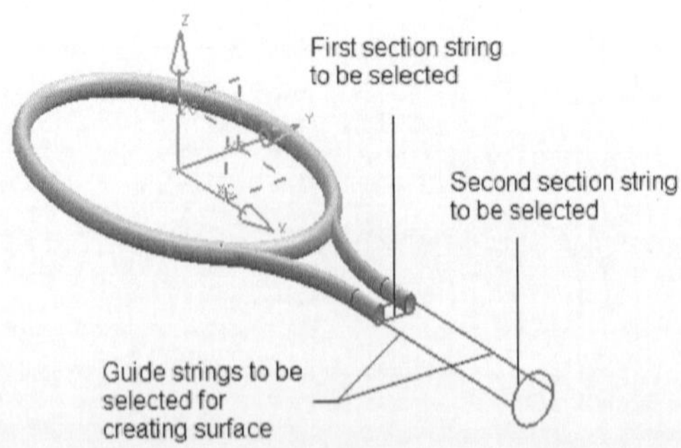

Figure 10-121 The second section curve and the guide strings to create a surface

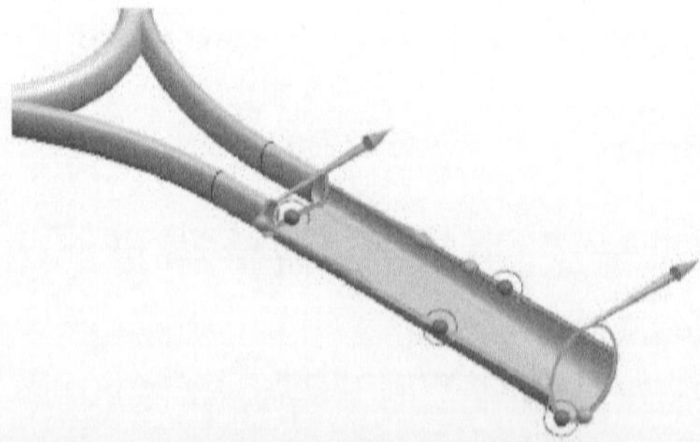

Figure 10-122 Entities to be selected for creating the studio surface

Mirroring the Studio Surface

1. Mirror the studio surface using the XC-YC plane as the mirror plane. The surface model after mirroring the studio surface is shown in Figure 10-123.

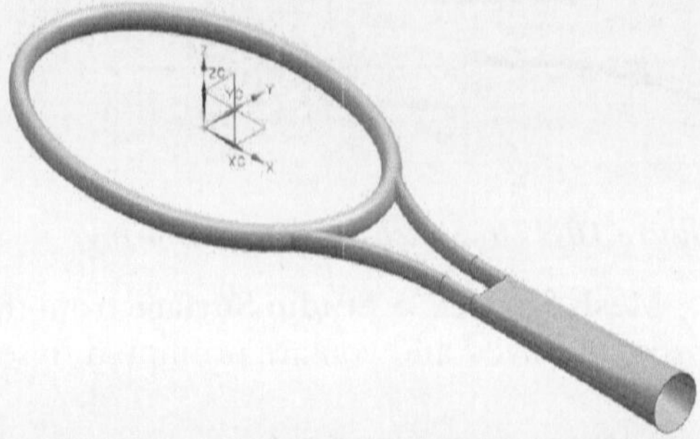

Figure 10-123 The surface model after mirroring the studio surface

Creating the Through Curves Surface

Next, you need to create the ruled surface.

1. Create a plane parallel to the YC-ZC plane at a distance of **575** mm.

2. Select the newly created plane as the sketching plane and draw the sketch, as shown in Figure 10-124.

3. Exit the Sketch in Task environment and choose **Menu > Insert > Mesh Surface > Through Curves** from the **Top Border Bar**; the **Through Curves** dialog box is displayed and you are prompted to select the curve or point to section.

4. Select the first section string, refer to Figure 10-125. Next, press the middle mouse button; you are again prompted to select the curve or point to section.

5. Select the second section string, which is the edge of the surface created earlier, refer to Figure 10-125. Note that the arrows should point in the same direction. Next, choose the **OK** button; the surface is created.

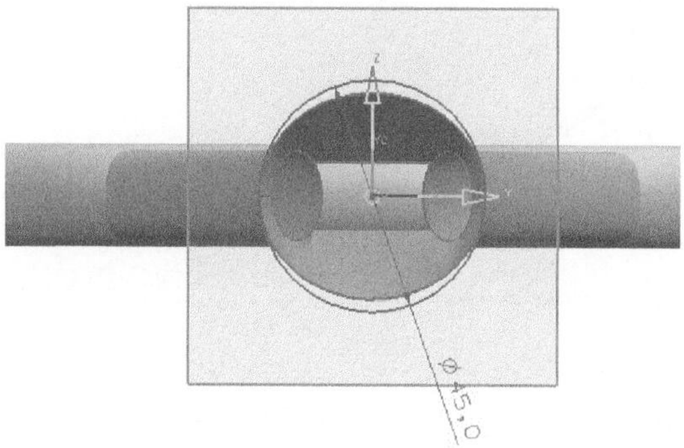

Figure 10-124 *The first section curve drawn to create the through curves surface*

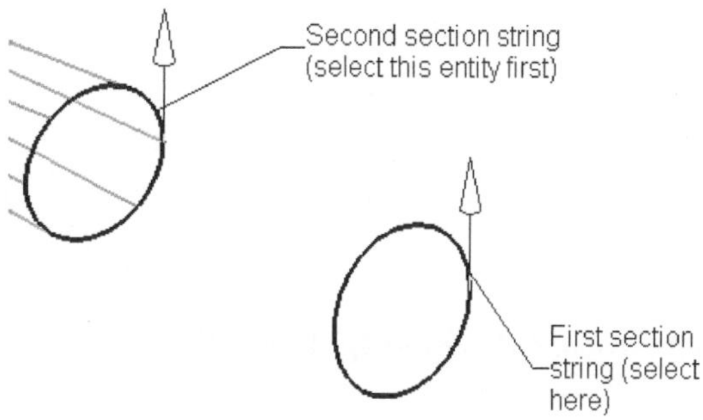

Figure 10-125 *The through curves surface created after selecting both cross-sections*

6. Change the color of the through surface to black.

Creating the N-sided Surface

1. Choose the **N-Sided Surface** tool from **Menu > Insert > Mesh Surface** of the **Top Border Bar**; the **N-Sided Surface** dialog box is displayed and you are prompted to select chain of curves for outer loop.

2. Select the **Trimmed** option from the Type drop-down list and then select the circular edge, refer to Figure 10-126. The preview of the bounded plane surface is displayed. Next, select the **Trim to Boundary** check box from the **Settings** rollout and choose the **OK** button from the dialog box; the fill surface is created.

3. Again, invoke the **N-Sided Surface** dialog box and select bounding string, refer to Figure 10-127. Make sure that the **Trim to Boundary** check box is selected. Next, choose the **OK** button from this dialog box. The bounded plane surface is created. The final surface model after hiding all the sketches and datum planes is shown in Figure 10-128.

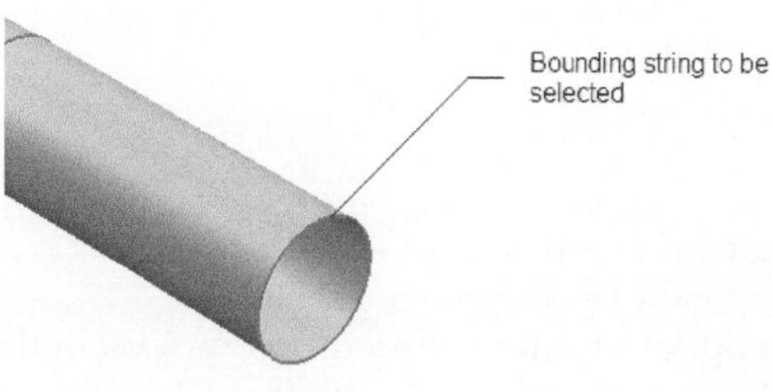

Figure 10-126 *The bounding string to be selected*

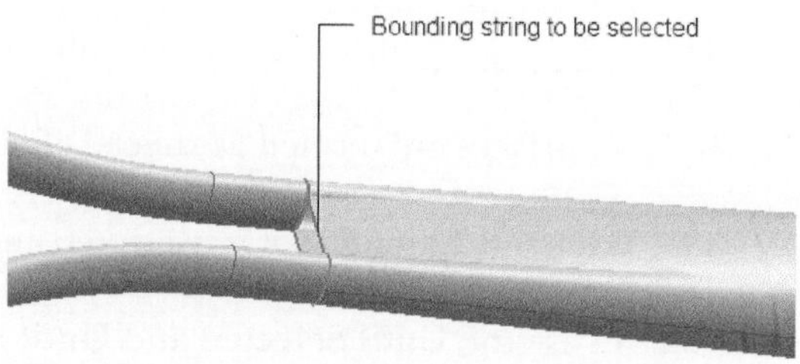

Figure 10-127 *The bounding string to be selected*

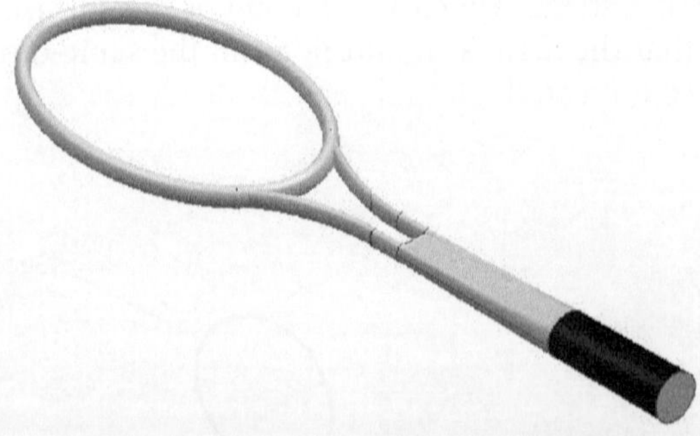

Figure 10-128 The final surface model

Saving and Closing the File

1. Choose **Menu > File > Close > Save and Close** from the **Top Border Bar** to save and close the file.

Self-Evaluation Test

Answer the following questions and then compare them to those given at the end of this chapter:

1. The __________ tool is used to create a revolved surface.

2. The __________ tool is used to create a sheet from *n* number of guide curves and *n* number of section curves.

3. The __________ tool is used to stitch individual surfaces into a single surface.

4. The __________ tool is used to trim and extend a surface.

5. The __________ tool is used to create a planar surface.

6. The __________ tool is used to extend a surface dynamically or by defining the laws for extension.

7. The __________ tool is used to create an offset surface.

8. In NX, surfaces are termed as sheets. (T/F)

9. The **Trim and Extend** tool is used to trim or extend an open or a closed surface. (T/F)

10. You can use the **Until Selected** and **Until Next** options from the **End** drop-down list of the **Extrude** dialog box to create a base sheet. (T/F)

11. You can create surfaces by specifying section strings and guide strings using the **Through Curves Mesh** tool. (T/F)

Review Questions

Answer the following questions:

1. How many points are required to create a surface while using the **Four Point Surface** tool?

   (a) Three (b) Four
   (c) Five (d) None of these

2. Which of the following tools is used to create a single patch surface or a multi-patch triangular surface that encloses a closed 2D sketch or a closed 3D curve?

   (a) **N-Sided Surface** (b) **Silhouette Flange**
   (b) **Law Extension** (d) None of these

3. Which of the following options is available in the **Type** rollout of the **Law Extension** rollout?

   (a) **Faces, Vector** (b) **Visual Gap, Absolute Gap**
   (c) **Basic, Absolute Gap** (d) None of these

4. Before adding a fillet at the intersection of two surfaces, the surfaces have to be:

   (a) Stitched using the **Sew** tool (b) Merged
   (c) Trimmed (d) None of these

5. The __________ tool is used to create a surface by sweeping a single section or multiple sections along single or multiple guide curves.

6. You can invoke the **Bounded Plane** tool by choosing **Menu > Insert > Surface > Bounded Plane** from the **Top Border Bar** in the Shape Studio environment. (T/F)

7. You can select an open sketch to create a bounded plane surface. (T/F)

8. Surface models do not have mass properties. (T/F)

9. You can create a surface from a closed or an open sketch. (T/F)

10. Once thickness has been added to a sheet, it is converted into a solid. (T/F)

11. You can create a hole feature on a planar surface by using the **Hole** tool. (T/F)

EXERCISES

Exercise 1

Create the surface model shown in Figure 10-129. The drawing views and dimensions of the surface model are shown in Figure 10-130. Save the model with the name *c10exr1.prt* at the location *\NX\c10.* **(Expected time: 30 min)**

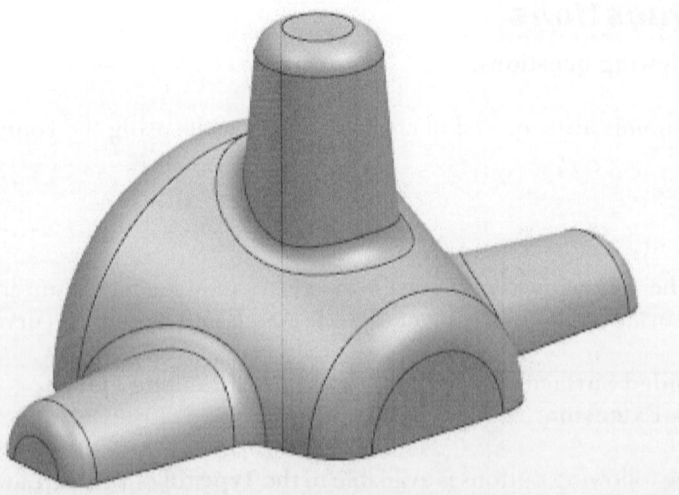

Figure 10-129 Surface model for Exercise 1

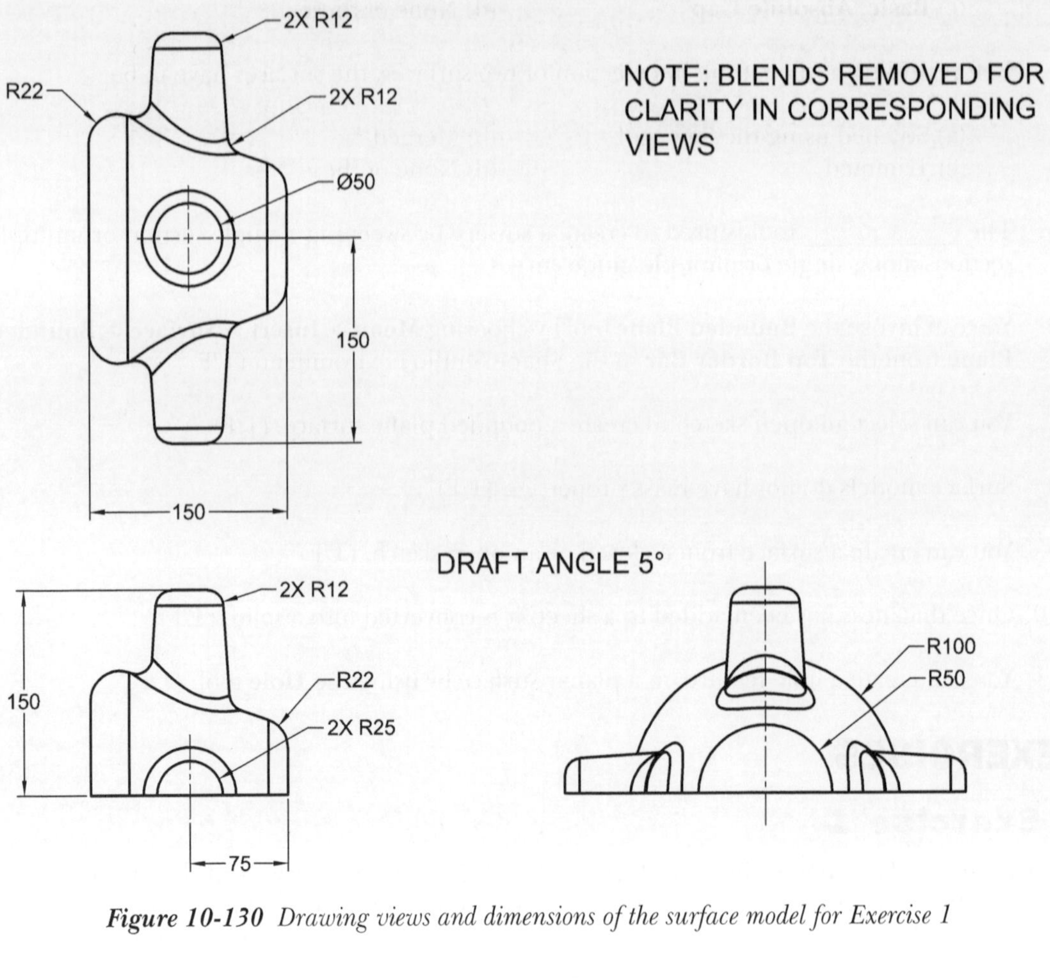

Figure 10-130 Drawing views and dimensions of the surface model for Exercise 1

Exercise 2

Create the surface model shown in Figure 10-131. The drawing views and dimensions of the surface model are shown in Figure 10-132. Save the model with the name *c10exr2.prt* at the location *\NX\c10.* **(Expected time: 30 min)**

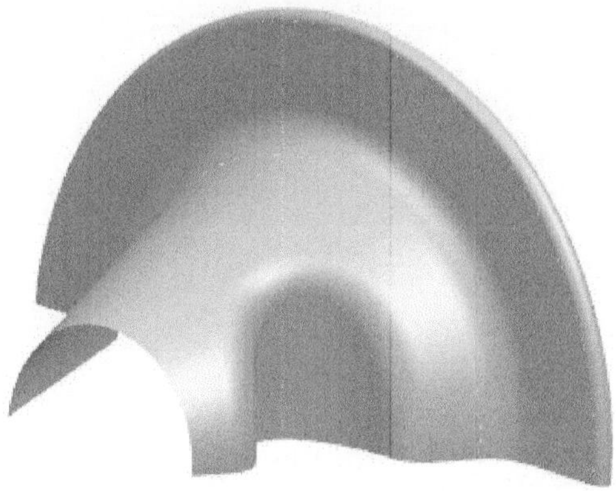

Figure 10-131 *The isometric view of the surface model for Exercise 2*

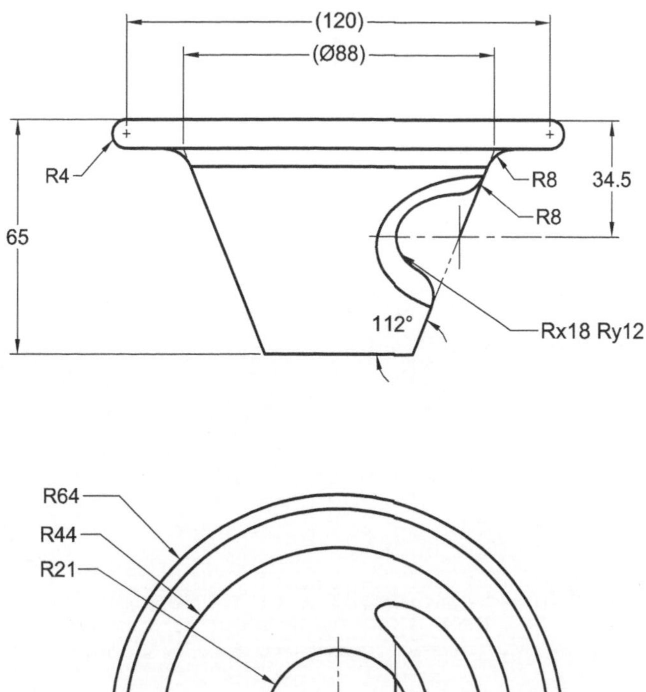

Figure 10-132 *The dimensions and drawing views of the surface model*

Answers to Self-Evaluation Test

1. Revolve, 2. Studio Surface, 3. Sew, 4. Trim and Extend, 5. Bounded Plane, 6. Law Extension, 7. Offset Surface, 8. T, 9. T, 10. F, 11. T

Chapter 11

Advanced Surface Modeling

Learning Objectives

After completing this chapter, you will be able to:

- *Create curves from bodies*
- *Create projected curves*
- *Create emboss sheet features*
- *Create face blend features*
- *Create fillet features*
- *Create bridge features*

CREATING CURVES FROM BODIES

In NX, you can create various types of curves using the existing bodies. These curves are further used to create surface bodies. The methods to create different types of curves are discussed next.

Creating Intersection Curves

Ribbon:	Home > Create > Curve Gallery > Intersection Curve
Menu:	Insert > Derived Curve > Intersection Curve

The **Intersection Curve** tool is used to create intersection curves between two sets of objects. The set of objects could be a solid, a sheet body, one or more faces, or a datum plane. To create the intersection curve, choose the **Intersection Curve** tool from the **Curve** gallery of the **Create** group in the **Home** tab, refer to Figure 11-1; the **Intersection Curve** dialog box will be displayed, as shown in Figure 11-2.

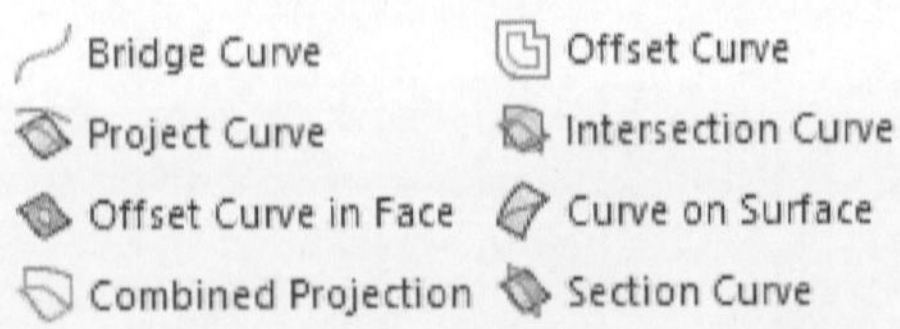

*Figure 11-1 Tools in the **Curve** gallery*

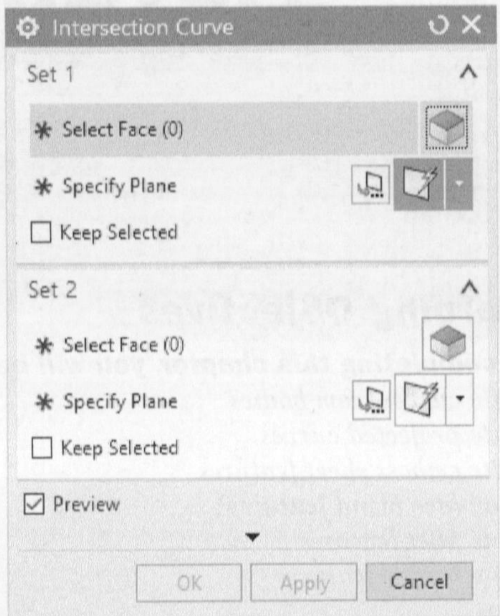

*Figure 11-2 The **Intersection Curve** dialog box*

Note

*If the tools in the **Curve** gallery are not visible by default, then you need to expand this gallery. To expand the **Curve** gallery, click on the down arrow available on its lower right corner.*

In this dialog box, by default, the **Face** button is chosen in the **Set 1** rollout. As a result, you are prompted to select the first set of faces to intersect. To select all the faces of the solid body, drag a box around it; all faces of the solid and sheet body will be selected, refer to Figure 11-3. Next, press the SHIFT key and select the sheet body to remove it from the selection and then release the SHIFT key. Choose the **Face** button from the **Set 2** rollout; you will be prompted to select the second set of faces to intersect. Select the sheet body, refer to Figure 11-3. The **Specify Plane** area that is available in both the **Set 1** and **Set 2** rollouts is used to create datum planes, which are selected as the first and second sets of intersection, respectively. However, after selecting the first set and second set of faces to intersect, this area will no longer will be available in the rollouts. Select the **Keep Selected** check box from the **Set 1** rollout to ensure that the first set of objects is automatically selected again to create the next intersection curve. Next, choose the **Apply** button. Similarly, the second set of objects can be selected automatically by selecting the **Keep Selected** check box from the **Set 2** rollout.

You need to expand the **Settings** rollout for some additional options. The **Associative** check box in this rollout allows you to specify whether the intersection curve is associative or not. An associative intersection curve will update automatically when changes are made to its source objects.

An intersection curve resulting from the selections made in Figure 11-3 is shown in Figure 11-4.

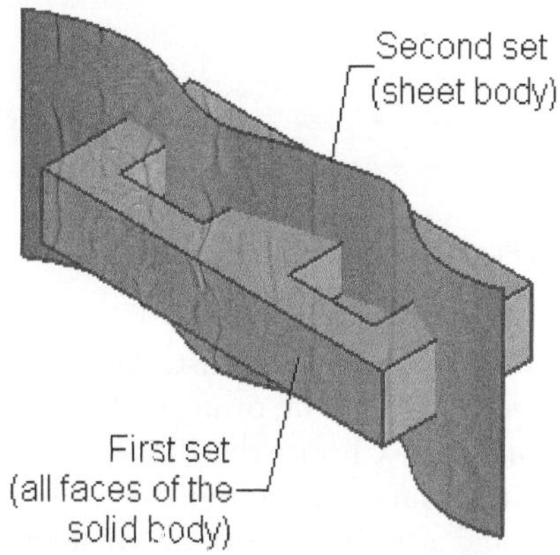

***Figure 11-3** Objects to be selected*

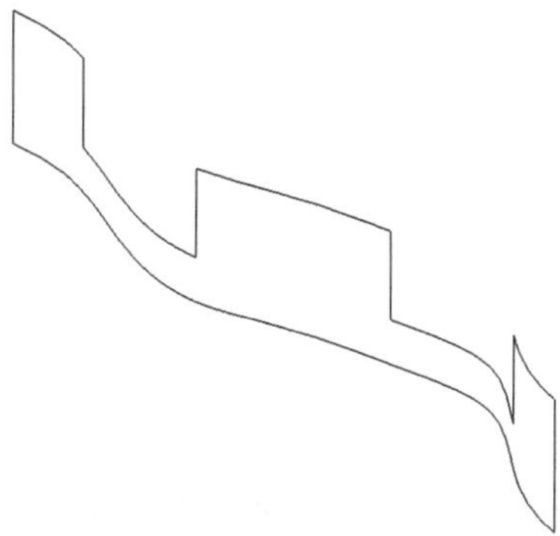

***Figure 11-4** Resulting intersection curve*

Creating Section Curves

Ribbon: Home > Create > Curve Gallery > Section Curve
Menu: Insert > Derived Curve > Section Curve

The **Section Curve** tool is used to create the section curves between specified planes and solid bodies, surfaces, or curves. The output curve can be associative. The section curves can be created in four ways: by using **Selected Planes**, **Parallel Planes**, **Radial Planes**, and **Planes Perpendicular to Curve** methods. The selection steps for each method are different. The methods for creating section curves are discussed next.

Creating Section Curves by Using the Selected Planes Method

This method is used to create section curves by specifying solid or sheet bodies and one or more section planes. To create section curve by selecting planes, choose the **Section Curve** tool from the **Curve** gallery of the **Create** group in the **Home** tab; the **Section Curve** dialog box will be displayed, as shown in Figure 11-5.

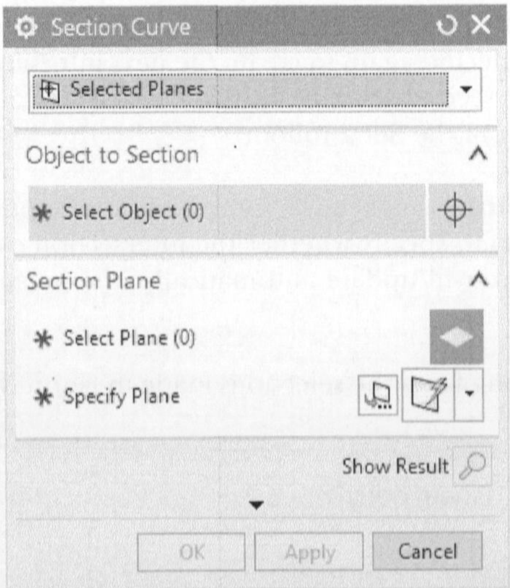

Figure 11-5 *The **Section Curve** dialog box*

By default, the **Selected Planes** option is selected in the Type drop-down list, and the **Object** button is chosen in the **Object to Section** rollout. As a result, you will be prompted to select the object to be sectioned. Select the solid body, refer to Figure 11-6. Choose the **Plane** button from the **Section Plane** rollout; you will be prompted to select the plane for section. Select the plane, refer to Figure 11-6. Expand the **Settings** rollout to use some additional options. By default, the **Associative** check box is selected in the **Settings** rollout. As a result, the section curve will be associative to the source object. Clear this check box; the **Non-associative Settings** sub-rollout will be displayed. In this sub-rollout, the **Group Objects** check box allows you to automatically group the output curves and the points that are created for each plane. In the **Non-associative Settings** sub-rollout, the **Output Sampled Points** check box is clear. If you select this check box, instead of curve, the points will be created in the resultant model. You can specify the distance between these points by using the **Sample Distance** edit box. The **Join Curves** drop-down list allows you to join a chain of curves to create a single B-spline curve. The resultant spline is either a polynomial cubic spline, a general spline, or a polynomial quintic. After specifying the required parameters, choose the **OK** button from the **Section Curve** dialog box; the section curves will be created, refer to Figure 11-7.

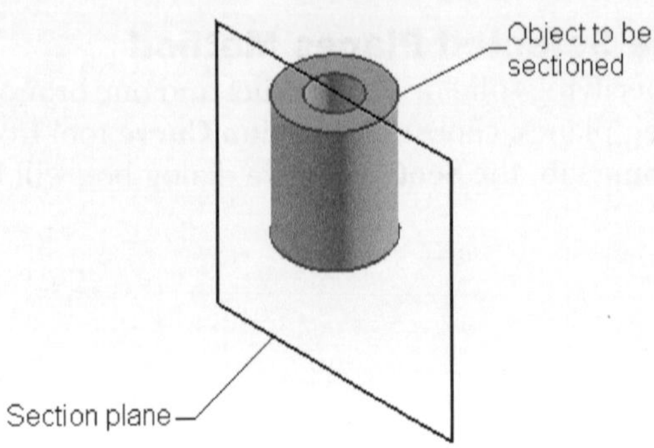

Figure 11-6 *Objects to be selected*

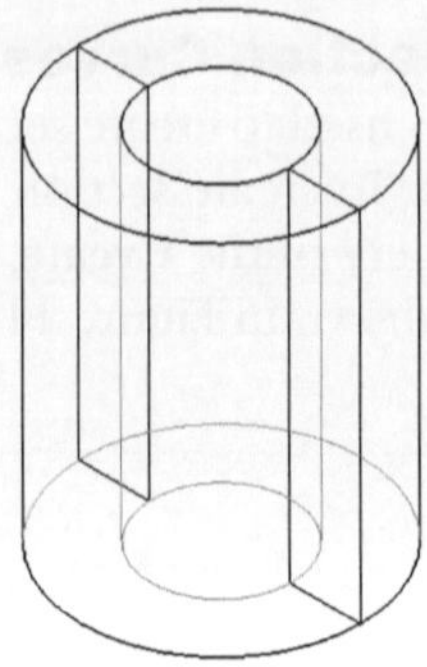

Figure 11-7 *Section curves created*

Creating Section Curves by Using the Parallel Planes Method

This method is used to create the section curves by specifying the base plane, step distance, start distance, and end distance. A series of parallel planes are spaced at the equal distances and are further used to create the section of the selected object. To create the section curves using this method, choose the **Section Curve** tool from the **Curve** gallery of the **Create** group in the **Home** tab; the **Section Curve** dialog box will be displayed. Select the **Parallel Planes** option from the Type drop-down list; you will be prompted to select the objects to be sectioned. Select the solid body, refer to Figure 11-8.

Now, choose the **Inferred** button from the **Base Plane** rollout; you will be prompted to select the objects to define a plane. Select the plane, refer to Figure 11-8. Next, enter the **Start**, **End**, and **Step** distance values in their corresponding edit boxes. The step distance is the distance between two parallel planes. The start and the end distances are measured from the base plane. The software generates as many planes as possible between the start and end distances by maintaining a step distance between the consecutive planes.

Next, choose the **OK** button to create curves. The section curves created using the selections made in Figure 11-8 are shown in Figure 11-9.

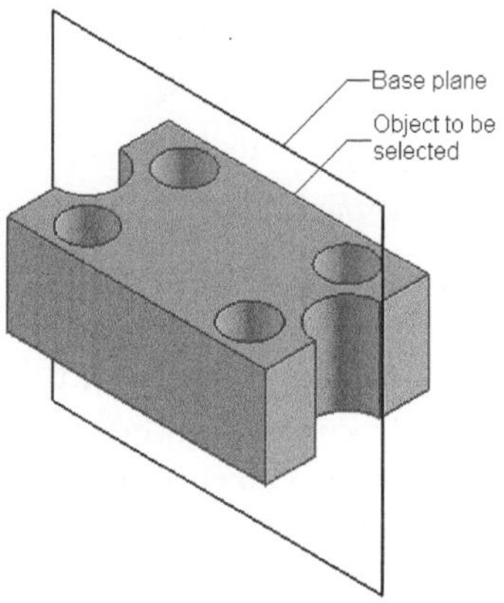

Figure 11-8 *Objects to be selected*

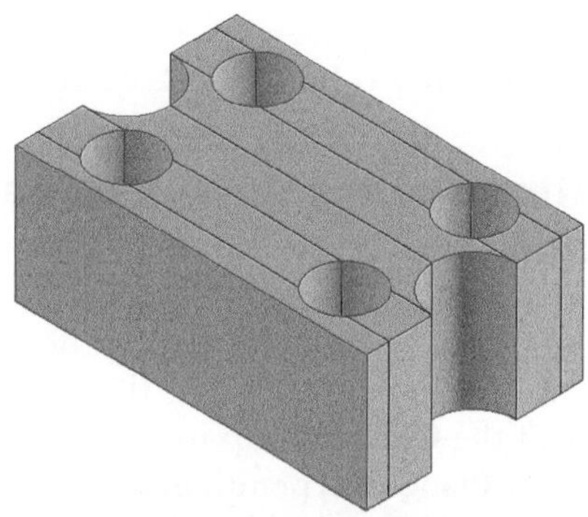

Figure 11-9 *Section curves created by using the Parallel Planes method*

Creating Section Curves by Using the Radial Planes Method

This method is used to specify the planes spaced at equal angles, which are further used to section the selected bodies. The planes are pivoted around a common axis. To create the section curves using this method, choose the **Section Curve** tool from the **Curve** gallery of the **Create** group in the **Home** tab; the **Section Curve** dialog box will be displayed. Select the **Radial Planes** option from the Type drop-down list; you will be prompted to select the objects to be sectioned. Select the solid body, refer to Figure 11-10. Next, choose the **Inferred Vector** button from the **Radial Axis** rollout; you will be prompted to select objects to infer vector. Select the edge of the object, refer to Figure 11-10. Alternatively, you can use the **Vector Dialog** button to create a vector. Choose the **Inferred Point** button from the **Point on Reference Plane** rollout; you will be prompted to select the object to infer point. Select the radial reference point, refer to Figure 11-10. Next, enter the values for the **Start**, **End**, and **Step** angles in their corresponding edit boxes. The step angle is the angle between two radial planes. The start and end angles are measured from the base plane. The base plane passes through the radial axis and the point on the reference plane. The software generates as many planes as possible between the start and end angles by maintaining the step distance between the consecutive planes.

The section curves resulted from the selections made in Figure 11-10 are shown in Figure 11-11.

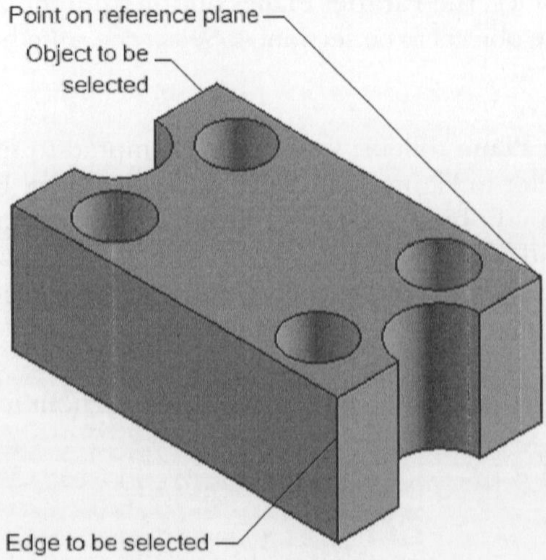

Figure 11-10 Objects to be selected

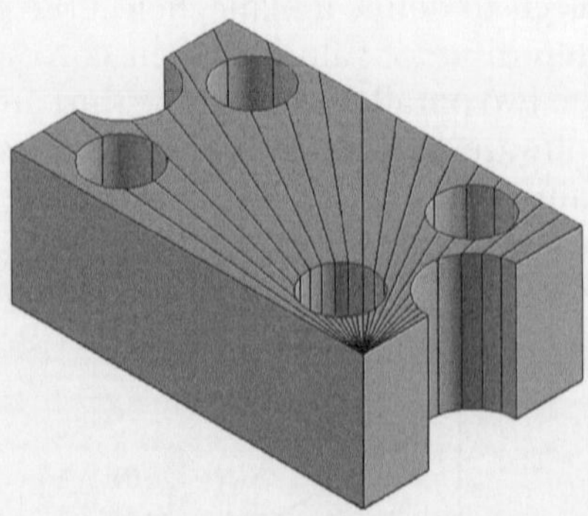

Figure 11-11 Section curves created by using the Radial Planes method

Creating Section Curves by Using the Planes Perpendicular to Curve Method

This method is used to create section curves along the planes perpendicular to the selected curve. You need to specify the solid or the sheet body, curve, and the spacing method. To create section curves using this method, choose the **Section Curve** tool from the **Curve** gallery of the **Create** group in the **Home** tab; the **Section Curve** dialog box will be displayed. Select the **Planes Perpendicular to Curve** option from the Type drop-down list; you will be prompted to select the objects to be sectioned. Select the solid body, refer to Figure 11-12. Next, choose the **Curve or Edge** button from the **Curve or Edge** rollout; you will be prompted to select the curve or the edge. Select the curve along which the perpendicular planes will be created, refer to Figure 11-12.

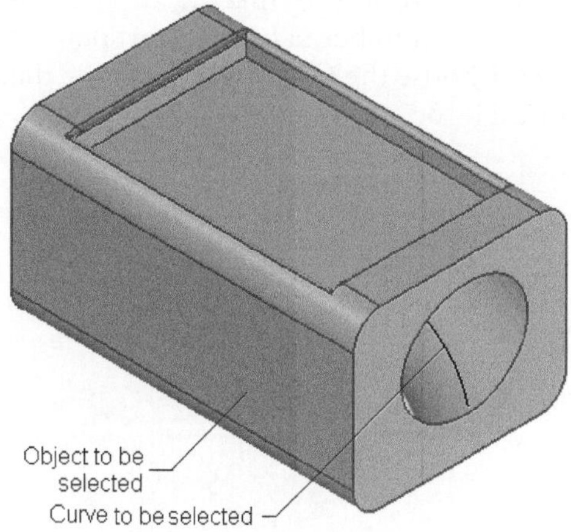

Figure 11-12 *Objects to be selected*

Next, you need to select the spacing method from the **Spacing** drop-down list in the **Plane Location** rollout. The section planes will be placed perpendicular to the curve. The distance between the planes will be determined by the spacing method. You can use one of the following spacing methods:

Equal Arc Length
This option allows you to create sections using the planes at equal arc lengths along the curve. You need to enter the values for the number of section planes on the curve. Similarly, enter the start and end percentage values relative to the arc length of the curve.

Equal Parameters
This option allows you to create sections using the planes based on the parameterization of the curve. You need to enter the values for the number of section planes on the curve. Similarly, enter the start and the end percentage values relative to the arc length of the curve.

Geometric Progression
This option allows you to create sections using the planes based on a geometric ratio. You need to enter the values for the number of section planes on the curve as well as the start and the end percentage values relative to the arc length of the curve. Similarly, enter a value in the **Ratio** edit box to determine the mathematical ratio for spacing the planes between the start and end percentage points.

Chordal Tolerance
This option allows you to create sections using the planes based on a chordal tolerance. In this case, you need to enter the value for the chordal tolerance.

Incremental Arc Length
This option allows you to create sections using the planes placed at increments along the curve. In this case, you need to enter the value for the arc length.

Select the **Equal Arc Length** option from the **Spacing** drop-down list of the **Plane Location** rollout. Next, enter the values for the number of copies, start percentage, and end percentage in their corresponding edit boxes. Choose the **OK** button from the dialog box. The section curves are created, as shown in Figure 11-13.

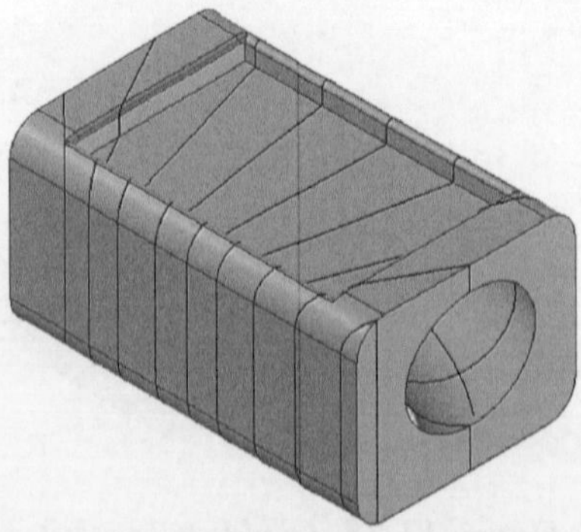

Figure 11-13 Section curves created by using the Planes Perpendicular to Curve method

Creating Isoparametric Curves

Ribbon:	Curve > Derived Curve > Derived Curve Gallery > Isoparametric Curve *(Customize to add)*
Menu:	Insert > Derived Curve > Isoparametric Curve

The isoparametric curves are created along the U/V parameters on a face. To create isoparametric curves, choose the **Isoparametric Curve** tool from **Menu > Insert > Derived Curve** in the **Top Border Bar**; the **Isoparametric Curve** dialog box will be displayed, as shown in Figure 11-14. In this dialog box, by default, the **Face** button is chosen in the **Face** rollout. As a result, you will be prompted to select a face of the model. Select the face of the model to create isoparametric curves on it. Next, you need to specify the parameters using the options in the **Iso Curve** rollout. The options in this rollout are discussed next.

Direction

The options in this drop-down list are used to specify the direction of the curves. You can specify the direction of the curves using the **U**, **V**, and **U and V** options.

Location

The options in this drop-down list are used to define the location of the curves and these are discussed next.

Uniform

This option is selected by default. As a result, the curves are created uniformly on the selected surface. Figure 11-15 shows curves created uniformly along the U and V directions.

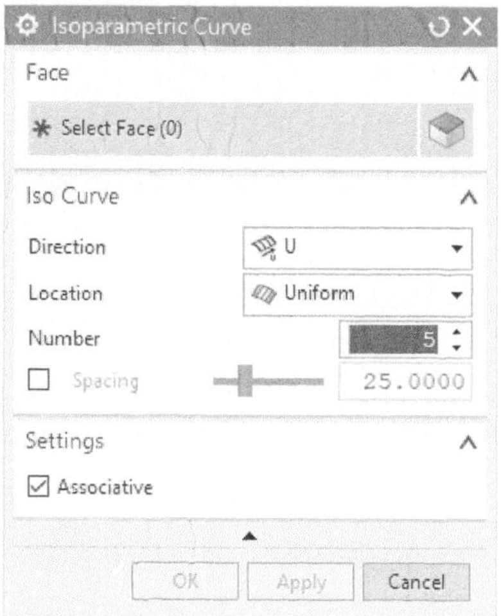

*Figure 11-14 The **Isoparametric Curve** dialog box*

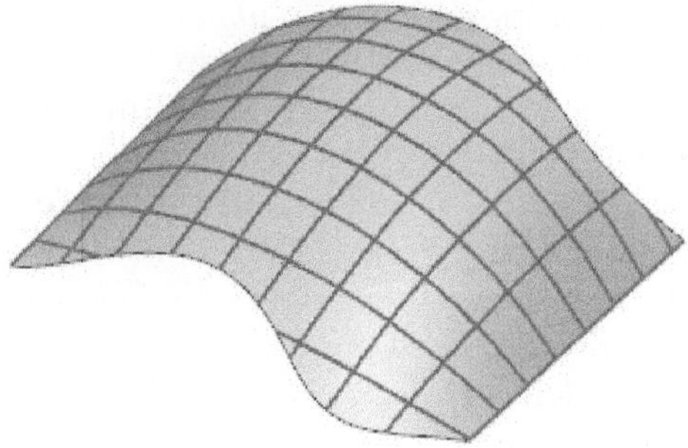

Figure 11-15 Curves created uniformly along the U and V directions

Through Points

On selecting this option, the **Specify Point** area is activated in the **Iso Curve** rollout. As a result, you will be prompted to select points to insert iso curves. Specify the points on the selected face; the curves will be created passing through the specified points, as shown in Figure 11-16.

Between Points

This option is used to create curves between two specified points on the face of a model. Select both the points on the face and then enter the number of curves to be created in the **Number** edit box; the specified number of curves will be created between the selected points, as shown in Figure 11-17.

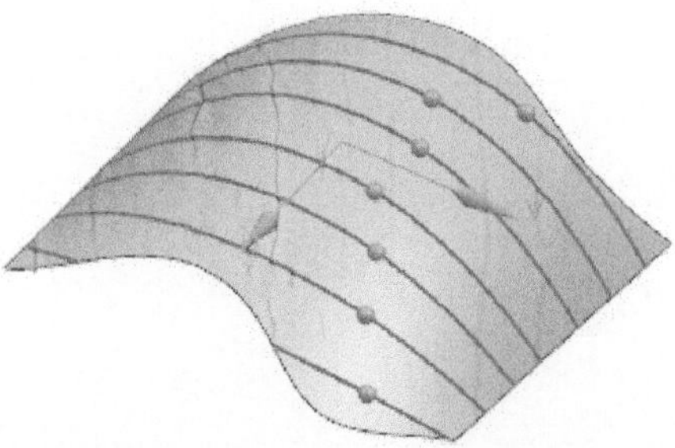

Figure 11-16 Curves passing through specified points

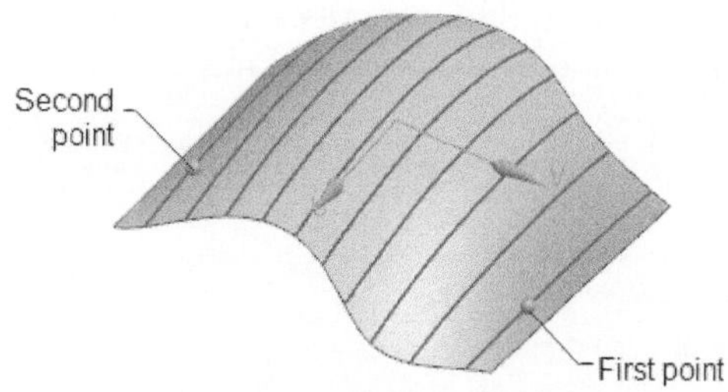

Figure 11-17 Curves created between two points

Projecting Curves

Ribbon:	Curve > Derived Curve > Project Curve
Menu:	Insert > Derived Curve > Project

Project Curve

You can project a closed or an open curve on one or more than one planar or curved faces. To do so, first create a feature and then draw a curve. Note that the curve and the feature should not be on the same plane. Next, choose the **Project Curve** tool from the **Derived Curve** group of the **Curve** tab; the **Project Curve** dialog box will be displayed, as shown in Figure 11-18. Select the curve from the drawing area and press the middle mouse button; the **Select Object** area in the dialog box will be activated and you will be prompted to select a face, facet body, or a datum plane onto which the curve is to be projected. Select the face on which you want the curve to be projected and then press the middle mouse button; the **Specify Vector** area will be activated in the **Projection Direction** rollout as the **Along Vector** option is selected by default in the **Direction** drop-down list. Also, you will be prompted to select the objects to infer vector and a vector triad will be displayed in the drawing area. Next, click on the required handle of the triad to specify the vector direction. You can also reverse the direction of the specified vector by using the **Reverse Direction** button available in the **Projection Direction** rollout. Next, choose the **OK** button from the dialog box; the selected curve will be projected on the specified face. Figure 11-19 shows the curve and the face to be selected. Figure 11-20 shows the resulting projected curve. The rollouts available in the **Project Curve** dialog box are discussed next.

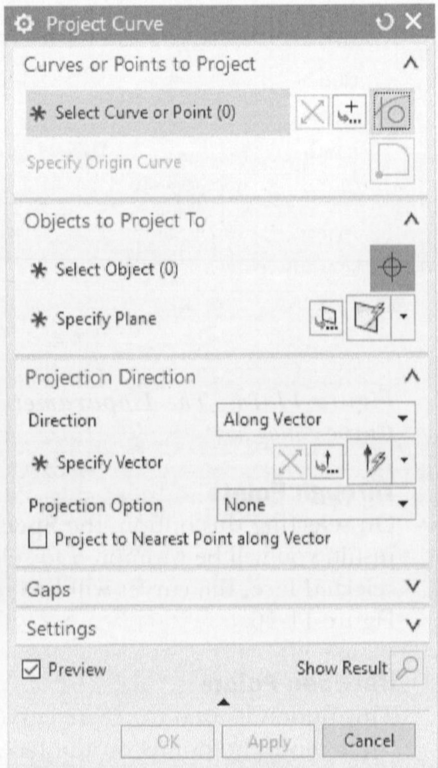

*Figure 11-18 The **Project Curve** dialog box*

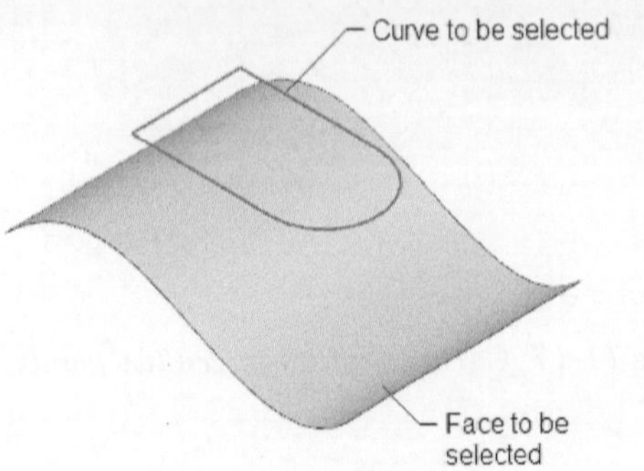

Figure 11-19 Curve and face to be selected

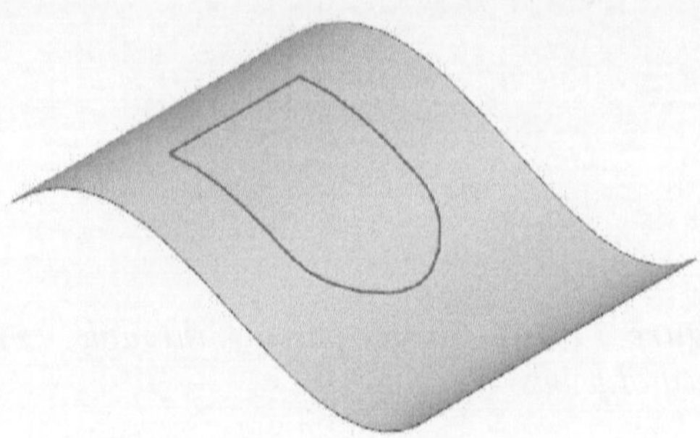

Figure 11-20 Resulting projected curve

Objects to Project To Rollout

The options in this rollout are used to select the objects onto which the selected curves will be projected. If you want to project the curve onto a plane, click in the **Specify Plane** area in the dialog box; you will be prompted to select objects to define a plane. You can also create a plane by choosing the **Plane Dialog** button in the **Specify Plane** area.

Projection Direction Rollout

The **Direction** drop-down list in this rollout contains the options to define the direction of curves to be projected and are discussed next.

Along Face Normal

On selecting this option, the selected curve will be projected along a direction normal to the selected face.

Toward Point

On selecting this option, you are prompted to select a point toward which the curve will be projected. Select a point from the graphics window, refer to Figure 11-21; the curve will be projected toward the selected point.

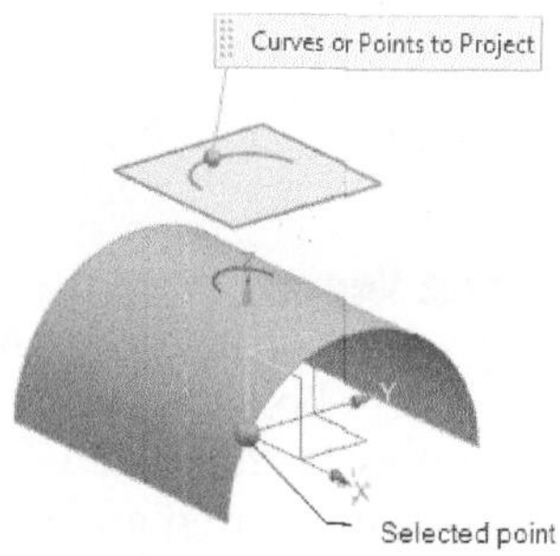

Figure 11-21 Curve projected toward the selected point

Toward Line

On selecting this option, you are prompted to select a line. Select a line from the drawing window, refer to Figure 11-22; the curve will be projected toward the selected line along the vector perpendicular to it.

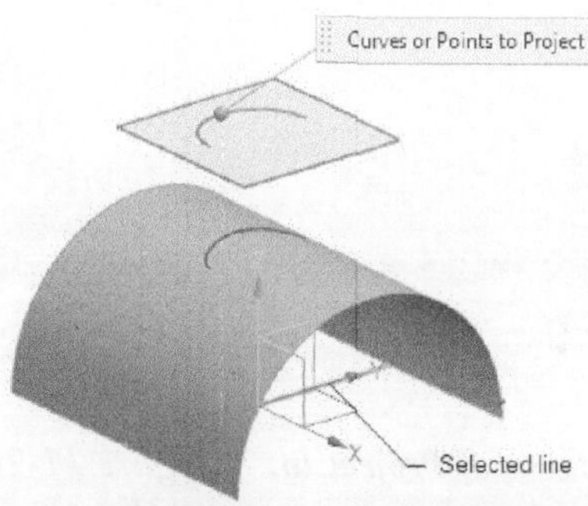

Figure 11-22 Curve projected along the vector perpendicular to the selected line

Along Vector

This option is used to project a curve along the selected vector, refer to Figure 11-23.

Angle to Vector

On selecting this option, you need to specify a vector using the vector triad displayed. Next, enter an angle value in the **Angle to Vector** edit box. As a result, the curve will be projected at an angle to the selected vector, as shown in Figure 11-24.

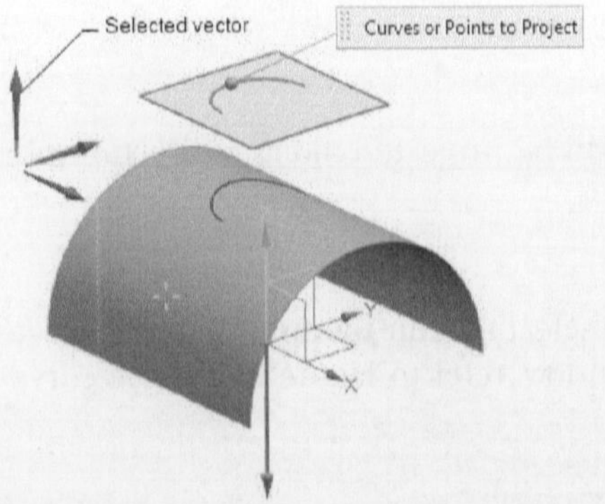

Figure 11-23 Curve projected along the selected vector

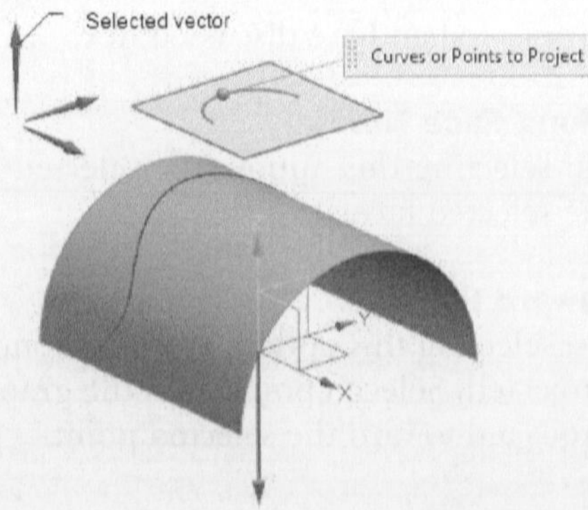

Figure 11-24 Curve projected at a specified angle to the specified vector

Project to Nearest Point along Vector

This check box is available only when you select the **Along Vector** option in the **Direction** drop-down list. If you select this check box, the curve will be projected to the surface, which is nearest to the input curve. Figures 11-25 and 11-26 show the curves projected with the **Project to Nearest Point along Vector** cleared and selected, respectively.

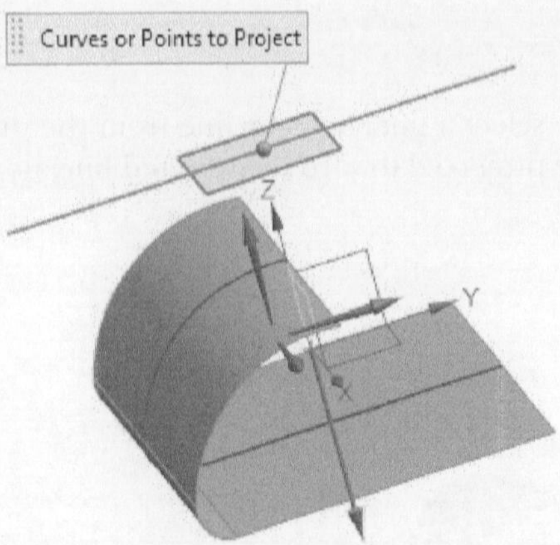

*Figure 11-25 Projected curve with **Project to Nearest Point along Vector** cleared*

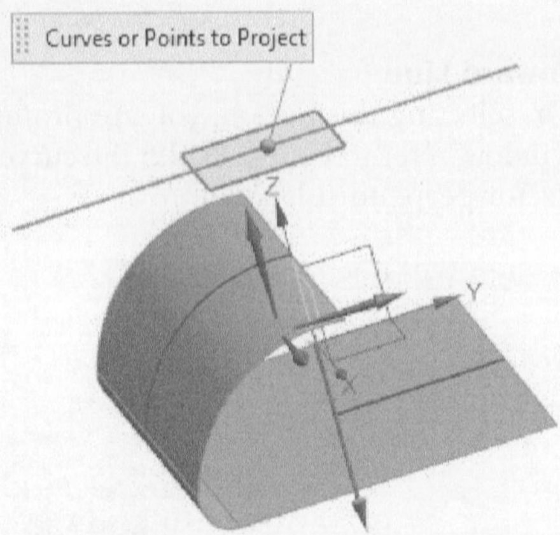

*Figure 11-26 Projected curve with **Project to Nearest Point along Vector** selected*

Gaps Rollout

The options in this rollout are used to bridge the gaps between two segments of a projected curve. To bridge the gap, select the **Create Curves to Bridge Gaps** check box; the **Maximum Bridged Gap Size** edit box will be activated. Next, enter a value in this edit box; the gaps between the curves will be bridged. Note that the input value should be greater than the gap length. The gap lengths of the individual gaps are displayed in the **Gap List** sub-rollout table. Figures 11-27(a) and 11-27(b) show the projected curve with the **Create Curves to Bridge Gaps** check box cleared and selected, respectively.

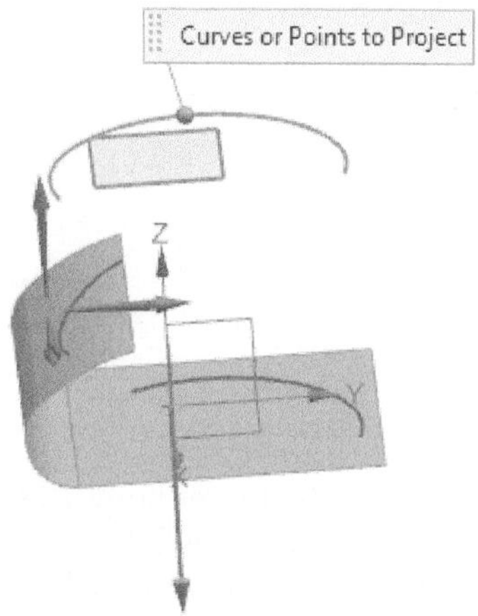

Figure 11-27(a) *Projected curve with the* ***Create Curves to Bridge Gaps*** *check box cleared*

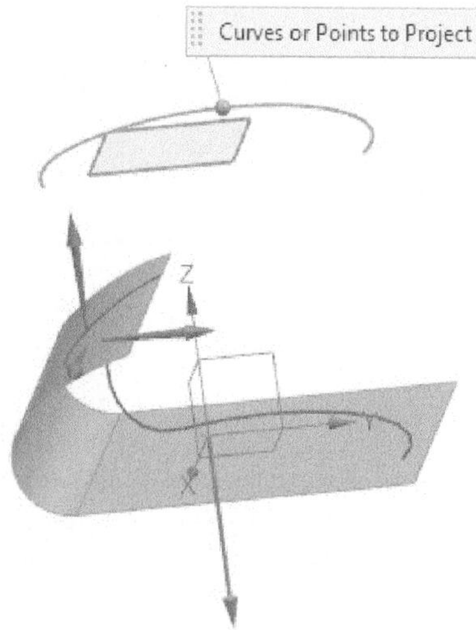

Figure 11-27(b) *Projected curve with the* ***Create Curves to Bridge Gaps*** *check box selected*

Settings Rollout

The **Associative** check box in this rollout is used to specify whether the projected curve is associative or not. Note that an associative projected curve is updated automatically when changes are made to its input curve. The options in the **Input Curves** drop-down list are used to keep or hide the input curves.

ADVANCED SURFACE MODELING TOOLS

These tools are used to create the basic and advanced surfaces and are discussed next.

Creating Emboss Body on a Sheet or Solid Body

Ribbon:	Feature > Feature > More Gallery > Combine > Emboss Body (Customize to Add)
Menu:	Insert > Combine > Emboss Body

The **Emboss Body** tool is used to emboss the shape of one solid body onto another solid or sheet body. To create the emboss body on a sheet, choose **Menu > Insert > Combine > Emboss Body** from the **Top Border Bar**; the **Emboss Body** dialog box will be displayed, as shown in Figure 11-28.

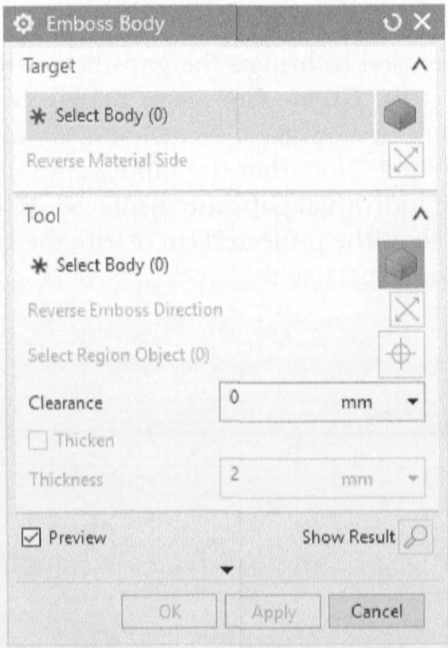

*Figure 11-28 The **Emboss Body** dialog box*

By default, the **Target** button is chosen in the **Target** rollout of this dialog box. As a result, you will be prompted to select the target body. Select the sheet as the target body, as shown in Figure 11-29; the **Tool** button in the **Tool** rollout will be activated and you will be prompted to select the tool bodies. Select a solid body from the drawing window as the tool body, as shown in Figure 11-29.

By default, the **Keep Target** and **Keep Tool** check boxes are clear in the **Settings** rollout. If you select the **Keep Target** check box, the target body will not be discarded from the resultant model. If you select the **Keep Tool** check box, the tool body will not be discarded from the resultant model.

Choose the **Show Result** button to preview the resultant model. Next, choose the **OK** button from the **Emboss Body** dialog box; the emboss body feature will be created. Figure 11-30 shows the emboss sheet body created by embossing the solid body. Note that the side of tool body is reversed in order to get this result.

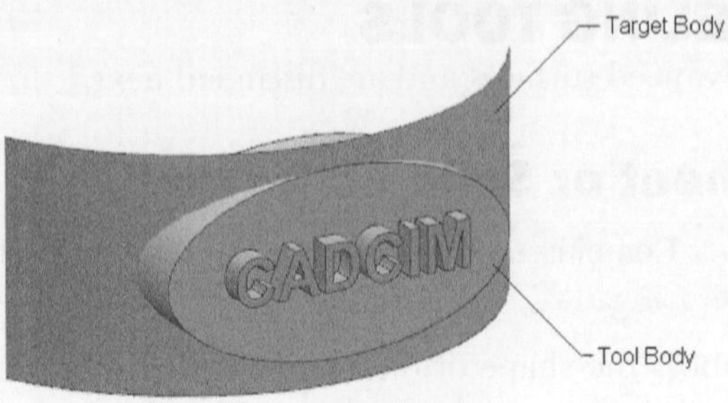

Figure 11-29 Objects to be selected

Figure 11-30 Resulting emboss body feature

Creating Face Blend Features

Ribbon:	Home > Create > Blend Gallery > Face Blend
Menu:	Insert > Detail Feature > Face Blend

The **Face Blend** tool is used to create complicated blends tangent to a specified set of faces. A face blend can be created between the faces of the solid or sheet bodies. The wall faces of the blend can be trimmed automatically. To create the face blend feature, choose the **Face Blend** tool from **Menu > Insert > Detail Feature** in the **Top Border Bar**; the **Face Blend** dialog box will be displayed, as shown in Figure 11-31. The options in various rollouts of this dialog box are discussed next.

Type Drop-down List

The drop-down list is used to select the blend type. The face blends are classified into two types based on the number of faces to be selected. The options in this drop-down list are discussed next.

Two-face

This option is selected by default and is used to create a face blend between two intersecting faces.

Three-face

This option is used to create a face blend between three intersecting faces.

Faces Rollout

This rollout is used to select set of faces for blending. There are two or three **Face** buttons available in this rollout depending upon the option selected in the Type drop-down list. When the **Two-face** option is selected from the Type drop-down list, two **Face** buttons will be available in the **Faces** rollout. The first **Face** button allows you to select the first set of faces for blending. You can also select edges, instead of faces. After selecting the faces, a vector will be displayed. This vector should point toward the center of the blend. Choose the **Reverse Direction** button to reverse the direction of the vector. The second **Face** button allows you to choose the second set of faces for blending. After selecting the second set of faces, again a vector will be displayed which should point toward the center of the blend.

On selecting the **Three-face** option from the Type drop-down list, the third **Face** button becomes available in the **Faces** rollout. After selecting the first face and the second face, the third **Face** button will be activated and you will be prompted to select middle faces to blend. Select the middle face and then press the middle mouse button to exit the dialog box. Figure 11-32 shows a preview of the face blend created using the **Three-face** option.

*Figure 11-31 The **Face Blend** dialog box*

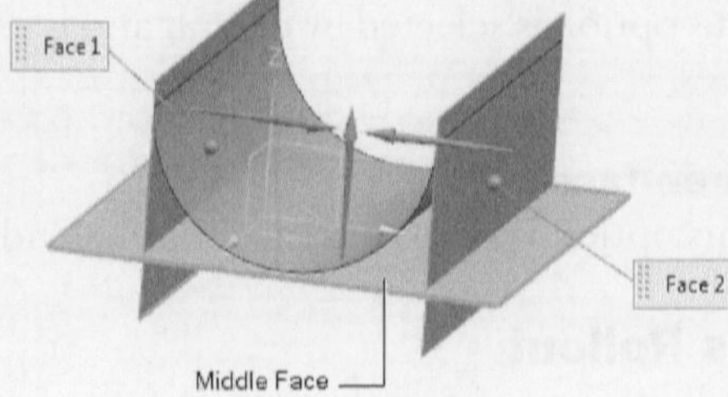

*Figure 11-32 Preview of the face blend created using the **Three-face** option*

Cross Section Rollout

This rollout is used to specify the cross-section radius of bend and its orientation. The options in this rollout are discussed next.

Orientation

The options in this drop-down list are used to define the orientation of the cross-section and are discussed next.

Rolling Ball: Using this option, you can create a face blend as if it was rolled by a ball which is in constant contact with the selected faces.

Swept Disc: This option is used to create a face blend whose surface is controlled by a tangent curve. This tangent curve is swept along a spine curve.

Width Method

The options in this drop-down list are used to control the width of the face blend.

Shape

On selecting the **Circular** option from this drop-down list, the following options will be available in the **Radius Method** drop-down list to control the cross-section:

Constant: On selecting this option, you can enter the values for the constant radius blends in the **Radius** edit box.

Variable: This option is used to define variable radii at two or more individual points along the spine curve based on the law type selected in the **Law Type** drop-down list.

Limit Curve: This option is used to set the blend radius based on the curves or edges selected for creating the face blend. On selecting this option from the **Radius Method** drop-down list, the **Select Sharp Limit Curve** area will be displayed in the **Width Limits** rollout and you will be prompted to select the sharp limit curve. Note that the curve must lie on one of the faces selected.

On selecting the **Tangent Symmetric** option from the **Shape** drop-down list, the following options will be available to control the cross-section:

Conic Method: By default, the **Boundary and Center** option is selected in the **Conic Method** drop-down list. As a result, you can define the shape of a cone by specifying its boundary and center. Alternatively, you can select the **Boundary and Rho** option or the **Center and Rho** option from this drop-down list to define the conic shape.

Boundary Method: By default, the **Constant** option is selected in the **Boundary Method** drop-down list. As a result, you can define a constant radius value of the boundary. Alternatively, you can select the **Law Controlled** option from this drop-down list to define the law to specify the boundary.

Boundary Radius: You can specify the radius value of the boundary by using this edit box. Note that this edit box is available only when you select the **Constant** option from the **Boundary Method** drop-down list.

Center Method: By default, the **Constant** option is selected in the **Center Method** drop-down list. As a result, you can define the constant center radius of the symmetric conic. Alternatively, you can select the **Law Controlled** option from this drop-down list to define the law to specify the center radius.

Center Radius: You can specify the center radius value of the symmetric conic by using this edit box.

On selecting the **Tangent Asymmetric** option from the **Shape** drop-down list, the following options will be available to control the cross-section:

Offset 1 Method: By default, the **Constant** option is selected in the **Offset 1 Method** drop-down list. As a result, you can define a constant offset value for the first face selected. Alternatively, you can select the **Law Controlled** option from this drop-down list to define the law.

Offset 1 Distance: This edit box is used to set the distance of the conic offset from the first face.

Offset 2 Method: By default, the **Constant** option is selected in the **Offset 2 Method** drop-down list. As a result, you can define a constant offset value for the second face selected. Alternatively, you can select the **Law Controlled** option from this drop-down list to define the law.

Offset 2 Distance: This edit box is used to set the distance of the conic offset from the second face.

Rho Method: The options available in the **Rho Method** drop-down list are used to specify the rho method for the conic cross-sections.

On selecting the **Curvature Symmetric** option from the **Shape** drop-down list, the **Curve** button will be activated in the **Cross Section** rollout and the following options will be available to control the cross-section:

Boundary Method: The options available in this drop-down list are same as discussed in the **Tangent Symmetric** option.

Boundary Radius: The options available in this drop-down list are same as discussed in the **Tangent Symmetric** option.

Depth Law Type: The options available in this drop-down list are used to define the depth of blend.

Depth: In this edit box, you can specify the value of depth according to the type of selection made from **Depth Law Type** drop-down list.

On selecting the **Curvature Asymmetric** option from the **Shape** drop-down list, the **Curve** button will be activated in the **Cross Section** rollout and the following additional options will be available to control the cross-section:

Shape Skew Law Type: The options available in this drop-down list are used to specify the skew type of the blend.

Shape Skew: In this edit box, you can specify the value for skew.

The remaining options in the **Cross Section** rollout are same as discussed in previous sections.

Width Limits Rollout

This rollout will be available on selecting the **Two-face** option from the Type drop-down list. This rollout is used to select the coincident edges and tangency control objects for the blend. The options in this rollout are discussed next.

Select Sharp Limit Curve

The **Curve** button in this area is used to specify the curve with which the blend remains coincident when the blend is large enough to encounter it.

Location

The options available in the **Location** drop-down list are used to specify whether the constraining curve is on the first face chain or the second face chain.

Select Tangent Limit Curve

The **Curve** button in this area is used to control the radius of the sphere, or an offset of the conic by maintaining a tangency between the blend surface and an underlying face set along a specified curve or edge.

Location

The options available in the **Location** drop-down list are used to specify whether the constraining curve is on the first face chain or the second face chain.

Trim Rollout

The options in this rollout are used to specify the trim and sew conditions for the blend. By default, the **To All** option is selected in the **Trim Blend** drop-down list.

The following steps explain the procedure to create a rolling ball face blend:

1. Choose the **Face Blend** tool from **Menu > Insert > Detail Feature** of the **Top Border Bar**; the **Face Blend** dialog box will be displayed. By default, the **Two-face** option is selected in the Type drop-down list and the **Face** button is chosen from the **Faces** rollout. Therefore, you will be prompted to select the faces or edges to blend.

2. Select the first chain face, refer to Figure 11-33 and make sure that the normal vector points in the upward direction.

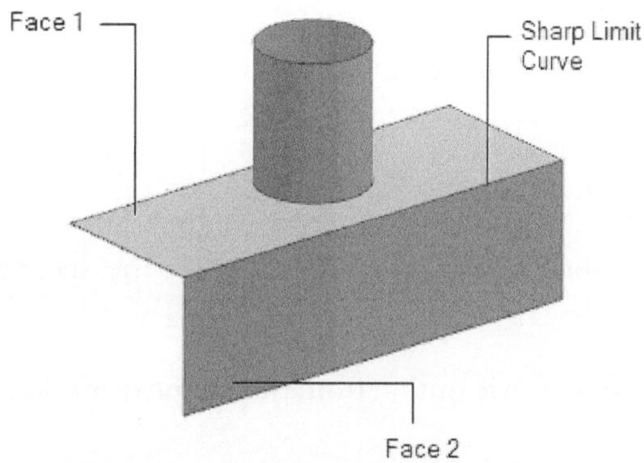

Figure 11-33 *Faces to be selected*

3. Choose the second **Face** button from the **Faces** rollout; you will be prompted to select the faces to blend. Select the second chain face, refer to Figure 11-33.

4. Choose the **Curve** button from the **Width Limits** rollout; you will be prompted to select the sharp limit curve. Select the limit curve, refer to Figure 11-33.

5. Enter the value of the radius in the **Radius** edit box of the **Cross Section** rollout.

6. Select the **To All** option from the **Trim Blend** drop-down list in the **Trim** rollout and choose the **OK** button. The resulting face blend feature is shown in Figure 11-34.

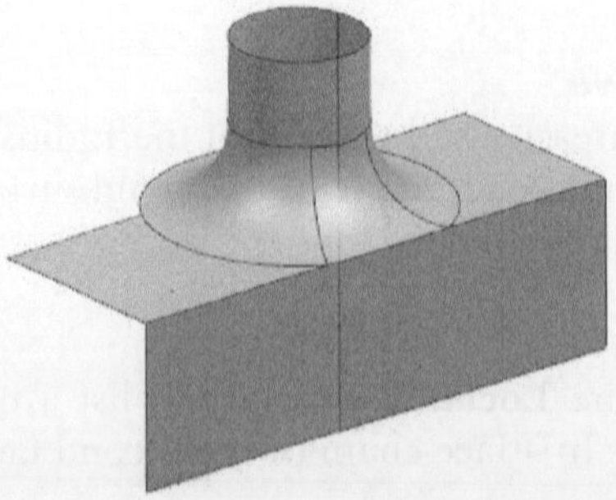

Figure 11-34 Resulting face blend feature

The following steps explain the procedure of creating a face blend:

1. Choose the **Face Blend** tool from **Menu > Insert > Detail Feature** in the **Top Border Bar**; the **Face Blend** dialog box will be displayed. Also, you will be prompted to select faces or edges to blend and the **Face** button in the **Select Face 1** area will be activated.

2. Select the first face set, refer to Figure 11-35. Choose the **Reverse Direction** button, if needed.

3. Choose the **Face** button in the **Select Face 2** area and then select the second face set, refer to Figure 11-35. Choose the **Reverse Direction** button, if needed.

4. Select the **Contact Curve** option from the **Width Method** drop-down list in the **Cross Section** rollout; the **Select Contact Curve 1** area will be activated. The **Contact Curve** option helps to maintain tangency between blends to be created and the surface selected as face chain1 and face chain 2.

5. Select the first contact curve, refer to Figure 11-35.

6. Click in the **Select Contact Curve 2** area and select the second contact curve, refer to Figure 11-35.

7. Select the **Curvature Asymmetric** option from the **Shape** drop-down list in the **Cross Section** rollout.

8. Click in the **Select Spine Curve** area and select the Spine string, refer to Figure 11-35.

9. Choose the **OK** button from the **Face Blend** dialog box to create the blend, refer to Figure 11-36.

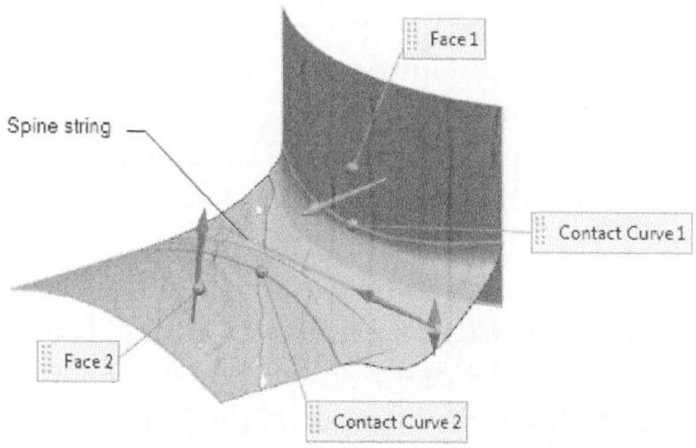

Figure 11-35 Objects to be selected

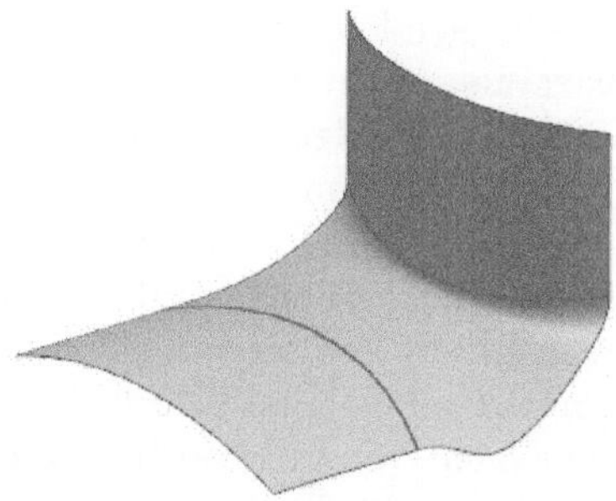

Figure 11-36 Resulting face blend feature

Creating Bridge Features

Ribbon:	Home > Create > Blend Gallery > Bridge
Menu:	Insert > Detail Feature > Bridge

The **Bridge** tool is used to create the bridge surface that joins the edges of the surfaces. You can specify a tangent or a curvature continuity between the bridge surface and the defining faces.

The following steps are required to create the bridge feature:

1. Choose **Menu > Insert > Detail Feature > Bridge** from the **Top Border Bar**; the **Bridge Surface** dialog box will be displayed, as shown in Figure 11-37.

2. By default, the **Select Edge 1** area is activated in the **Edges** rollout and you will be prompted to select a face near an edge or an edge. Select the first edge and the second edge, refer to Figure 11-38.

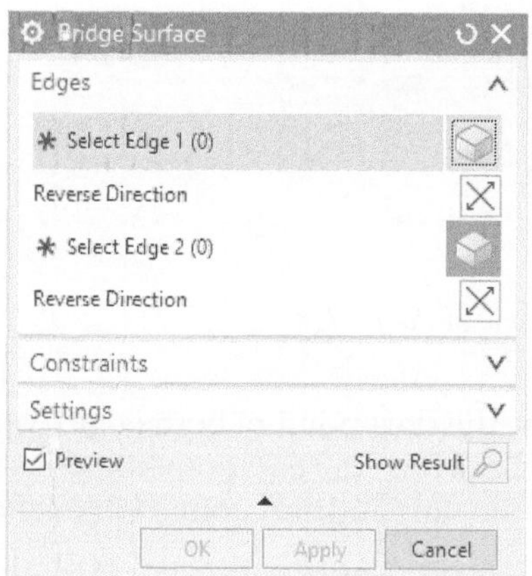

*Figure 11-37 The **Bridge Surface** dialog box*

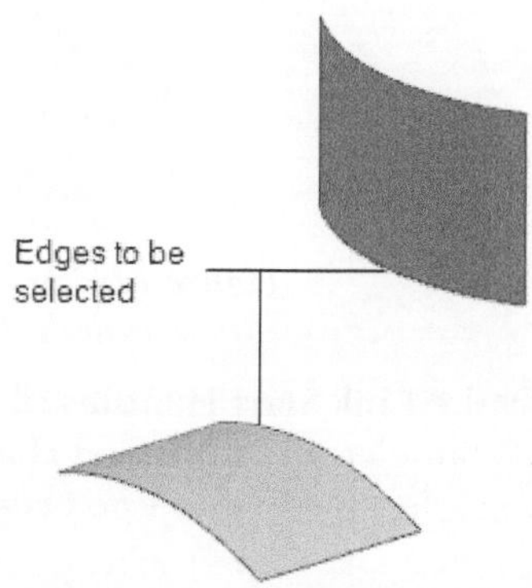

Figure 11-38 Edges to be selected

Note that you may need to use the **Reverse Direction** button, if needed.

3. Next, you need to choose the continuity type from the **Continuity** sub-rollout in the **Constraints** rollout. Choose the continuity type for the first edge and the second edge from the **Edge 1** and **Edge 2** drop-down lists. You can specify **G0 (Position)**, **G1 (Tangent)**, or **G2 (Curvature)** continuity between the selected faces and the bridge surface.

4. Next, you need to specify the tangent value to change the surface as per requirement. You can specify the tangent value using the **Edge 1** and **Edge 2** edit boxes in the **Tangent Magnitude** sub-rollout. Alternatively, use the **Edge 1** and **Edge 2** slider bars to specify the tangent value. You can also use the **Edge 1** and **Edge 2** handles to specify the tangent value, refer to Figure 11-39.

5. Specify the flow direction of the bridge surface using the **Edge 1 and 2** drop-down list in the **Flow Direction** sub-rollout. By default, the **Not Specified** option is selected. You can also select the **Isoparametric** or the **Perpendicular** option to define the flow direction.

You can use the handles displayed on the edges of the bridge surface to change its size and shape, refer to Figure 11-39. Alternatively, you can use the options available in the **Edge Limit** sub-rollout to modify the bridge surface. Choose the **Edge 1** tab from this sub-rollout to modify the Edge 1. The **%Start** and **%End** edit boxes in this tab are used to modify the start point and the end point of the edge. You can also modify the start point and end point of the edge by using the slider bars available below the respective edit boxes. The **%Offset** edit box is used to specify the offset value of the edge. You can also use the slider bar or the offset handle to offset the edge. Similarly, you can modify the second edge by choosing the **Edge 2** tab.

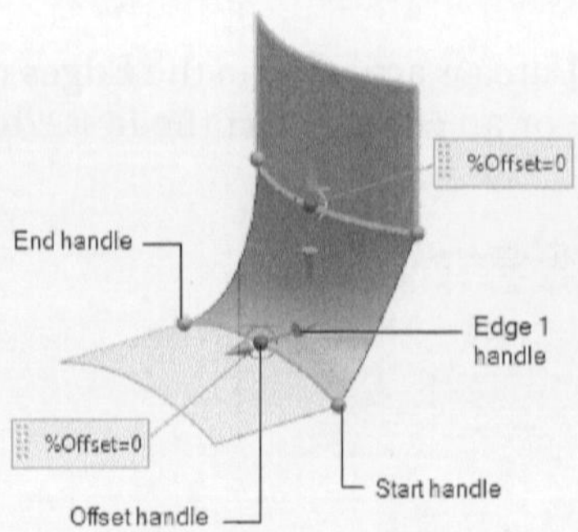

***Figure 11-39** The preview of the bridge surface with the handles*

If you select the **Link Start Handles** check box, the start point of both edges will be linked. Similarly, if you select the **Link End Handles** check box, the end point of both edges will be linked. If you select the **End to End** check box, the start and end points will not be modified.

TUTORIALS

Tutorial 1

In this tutorial, you will create the model shown in Figure 11-40. First, you need to create the surface model using the dimensions and orthographic views shown in Figure 11-41. After creating the surface model, you need to apply thickness of 1 mm in the outward direction. Assume the missing dimensions. Save the model with the name *c11tut1.prt* at the following location: *\NX\c11.*

(Expected time: 45 min)

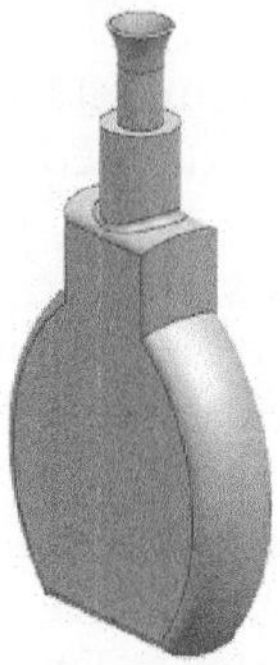

Figure 11-40 *Model for Tutorial 1*

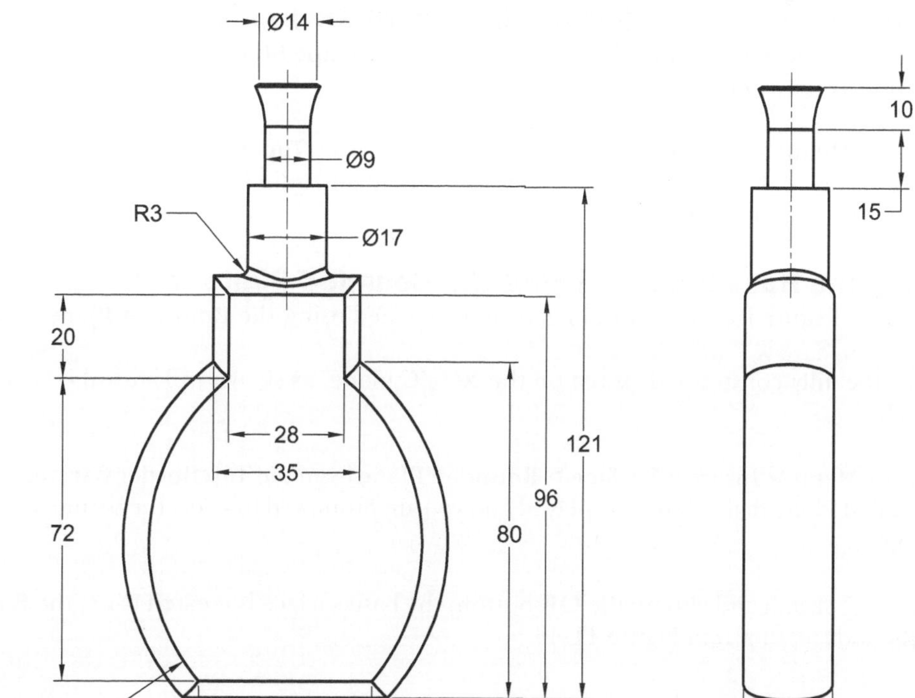

Figure 11-41 *Views and dimensions for Tutorial 1*

The following steps are required to complete this tutorial:

a. Start a new file and set the sheet environment.
b. Create the base feature using the **Bounded Plane** tool, refer to Figures 11-42 and 11-43.
c. Create the second feature using the **Bounded Plane** tool, refer to Figures 11-44 and 11-45.
d. Create the third feature using the **Bridge** tool that will join the two bounded surfaces, refer to Figures 11-46 and 11-47.
e. Mirror the bridge surface about the YC-ZC plane, refer to Figure 11-48.
f. Create the bottom surface of the model using the **Bridge** tool, refer to Figures 11-49 and 11-50.
g. Extrude edges of the model, refer to Figures 11-51 and 11-52.
h. Create the bridge surface over the extruded surface using the **Bridge** tool, refer to Figures 11-53 and 11-54.
i. Create the extrude feature using the **Extrude** tool, refer to Figures 11-55 and 11-56.
j. Create the face blend feature using the **Face Blend** tool, refer to Figures 11-57 and 11-58.
k. Create the surface using the **Bounded Plane** tool, refer to Figure 11-59.
l. Extrude the sketch, refer to Figures 11-60 and 11-61.
m. Create the surface by using the **Through Curve** tool, refer to Figures 11-62 through 11-64.
n. Sew the individual surfaces into a single surface, refer to Figure 11-65.
o. Add thickness to the surface model, refer to Figure 11-66.
p. Save and close the file.

Starting a New File and Setting the Sheet Environment

1. Start a new file with the name *c11tut1.prt* using the **Shape Studio** template, and specify its location as *C:\NX\c11*.

2. Choose **Menu > Preferences > Modeling** from the **Top Border Bar**; the **Modeling Preferences** dialog box is displayed. Select the **Sheet** radio button from the **Body Type** area and choose the **OK** button.

Creating the Base Feature Using the Bounded Plane Tool

The base feature for this tutorial needs to be created using the **Bounded Plane** tool.

1. Draw the fully constrained sketch on the XC-ZC plane, as shown in Figure 11-42. Exit the sketch.

2. Choose **Menu > Insert > Surface > Bounded Plane** from the **Top Border Bar**; the **Bounded Plane** dialog box is displayed and you are prompted to select the bounding string.

3. Select the sketch and choose the **OK** button; the base surface is created using the **Bounded Plane** tool, as shown in Figure 11-43.

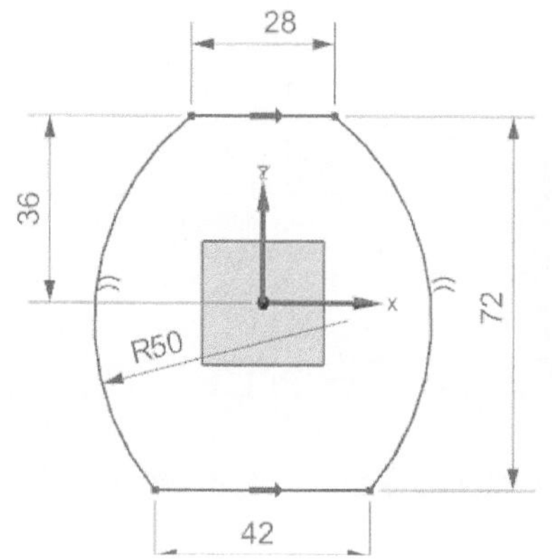

Figure 11-42 Sketch for the base feature

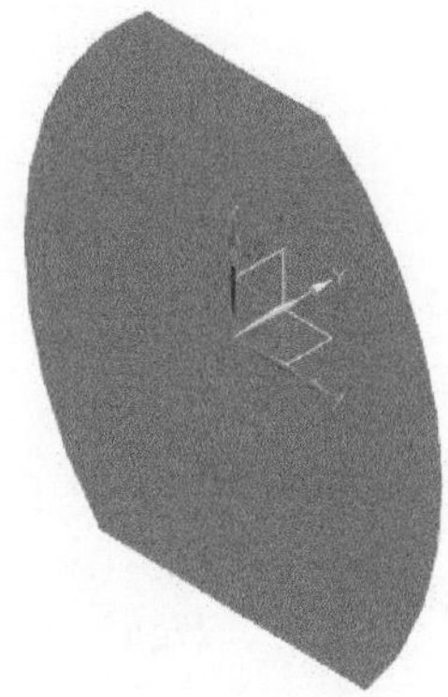

Figure 11-43 Base feature of the surface model

Creating the Second Feature Using the Bounded Plane Tool

The second feature for this tutorial will also be created using the **Bounded Plane** tool.

1. Create a plane at an offset of 20 mm from the XC-ZC plane.

2. Select the offset plane as the sketching plane and invoke the Sketch in Task environment.

3. Choose **Menu > Insert > Sketch Curve > Project Curve** from the **Top Border Bar**; the **Project Curve** dialog box is displayed and you are prompted to select the curve to project. Select the base feature and choose the **OK** button.

4. Exit the Sketch in Task environment; the curves are projected, refer to Figure 11-44.

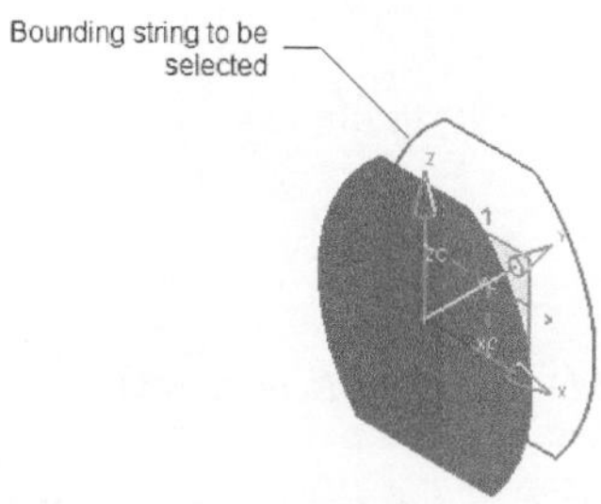

Figure 11-44 Projected curves

5. Choose **Menu > Insert > Surface > Bounded Plane** from the **Top Border Bar**; the **Bounded Plane** dialog box is displayed and you are prompted to select the bounding string. 

6. Select the projected curve, as shown in Figure 11-44, and choose the **OK** button; the second feature is created, as shown in Figure 11-45.

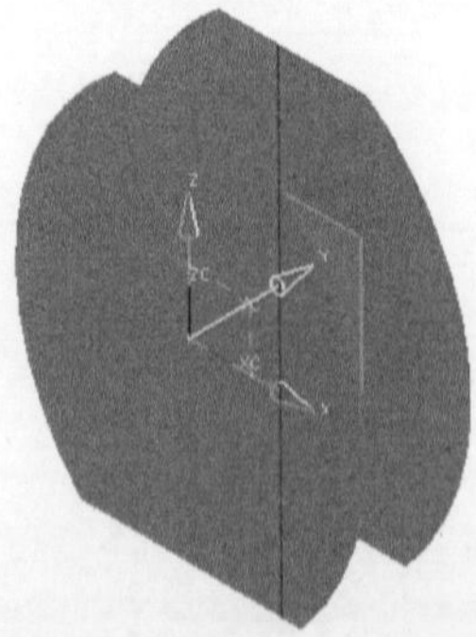

Figure 11-45 Second feature of the surface model

Creating the Bridge Surface Using the Bridge Tool

The third feature for this tutorial is a bridge surface. The procedure to create this feature is discussed next.

1. Choose **Menu > Insert > Detail Feature > Bridge** from the **Top Border Bar**; the **Bridge Surface** dialog box is displayed. By default, the **Select Edge 1** area is activated in the **Edges** rollout and you are prompted to select edges.

2. Select the edges, as shown in Figure 11-46.

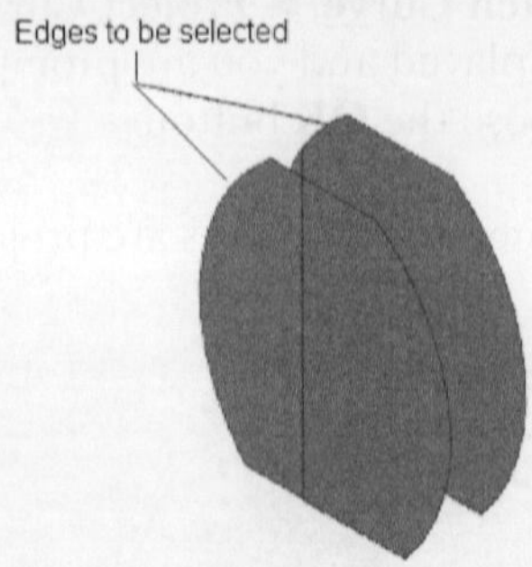

Figure 11-46 Edges to be selected

3. Next, select the **G1(Tangent)** option from the **Edge 1** and **Edge 2** drop-down lists in the **Continuity** sub-rollout of the **Constraints** rollout. Next, you need to choose the **Reverse Direction** button available below the **Edge 1** and **Edge 2** drop-down lists, if required.

4. Enter **1** in the **Edge 1** and **Edge 2** edit boxes available in the **Tangent Magnitude** sub-rollout. Make sure that the **Not Specified** option is selected in the **Edge 1 and 2** drop-down list in the **Flow Direction** sub-rollout.

5. Next, choose the **OK** button from the **Bridge Surface** dialog box. The surface created using the **Bridge** tool is shown in Figure 11-47.

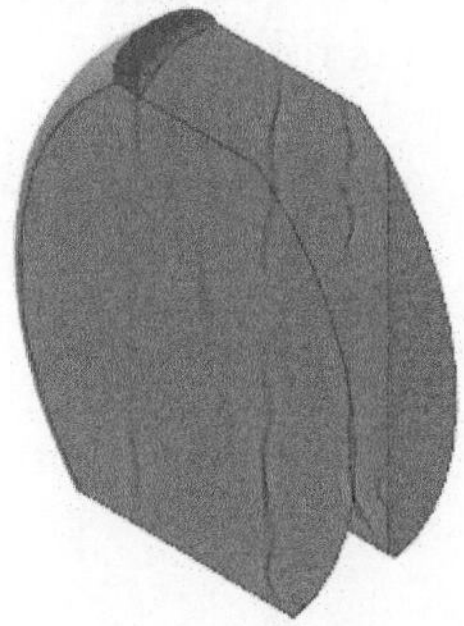

Figure 11-47 *Surface created using the* ***Bridge*** *tool*

Mirroring the Bridge Surface

1. After creating the bridge surface, mirror it about the YC-ZC plane. Turn off the display of the plane. The model after creating the mirror feature is shown in Figure 11-48.

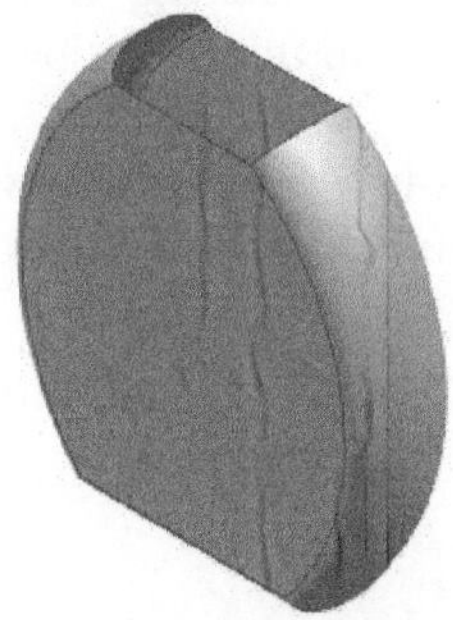

Figure 11-48 *The model after mirroring the bridge surface*

Creating the Bottom Face of the Model Using the Bridge Tool

The fifth feature for this tutorial is the bottom surface of the model.

1. Choose **Menu > Insert > Detail Feature > Bridge** from the **Top Border Bar**; the **Bridge Surface** dialog box is displayed. Select the first edge and then the second edge, refer to Figure 11-49.

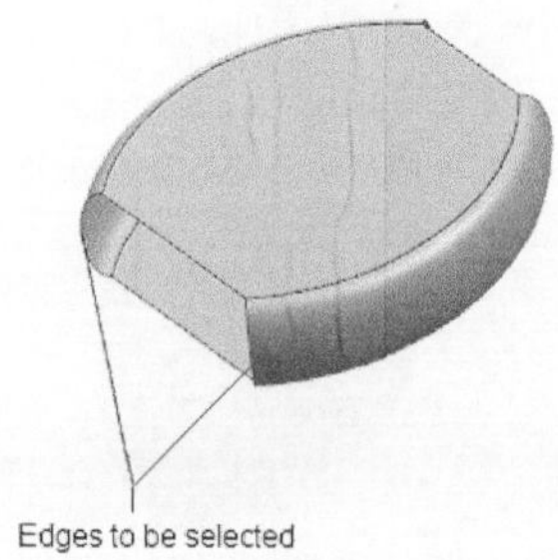

Figure 11-49 *Edges to be selected*

2. Select the **G0 (Position)** option from the **Edge 1** and **Edge 2** drop-down lists in the **Continuity** sub-rollout available in the **Constraints** rollout.

3. Choose the **OK** button; the surface created using the **Bridge** tool is shown in Figure 11-50.

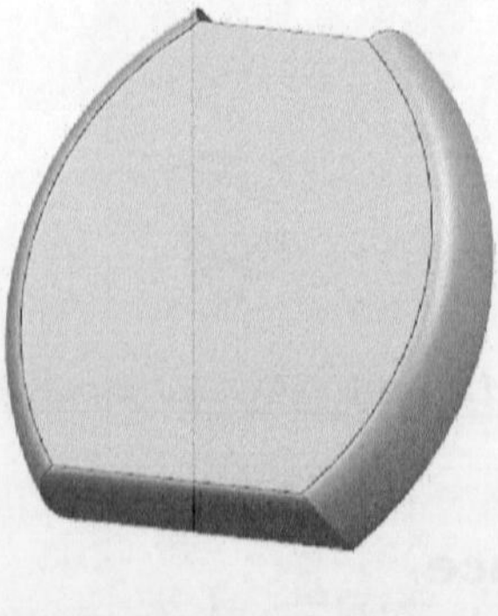

Figure 11-50 Resulting bridge surface

Creating the Sixth Feature by Extruding the Edges

In this section, you need to create the sixth feature by extruding the edges of the model.

1. Choose the **Extrude** tool from **Menu > Insert > Design Feature** in the **Top Border Bar** and select the edges of the model, refer to Figure 11-51.

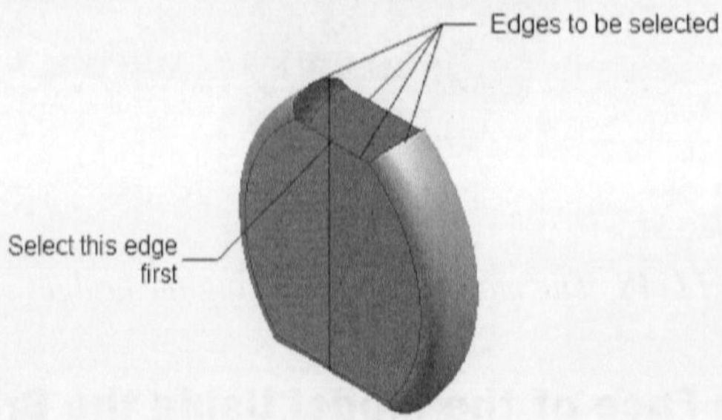

Figure 11-51 Edges to be selected

2. Enter the value **20** in the **Distance** edit box available below the **End** drop-down list and choose the **OK** button. The resulting surface model is shown in Figure 11-52.

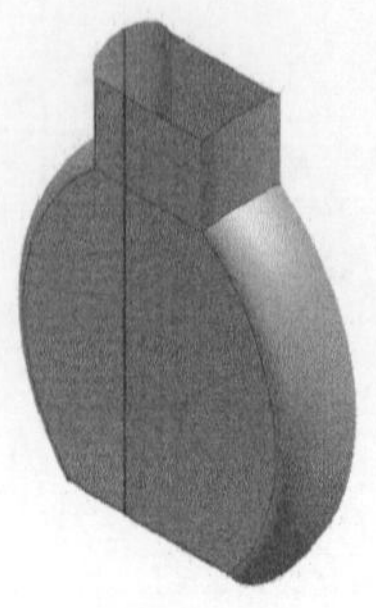

Figure 11-52 The surface model after creating the extrude feature

Creating the Surface Using the Bridge Tool

The seventh feature for this tutorial also needs to be created using the bridge surface.

1. Choose **Menu > Insert > Detail Feature > Bridge** from the **Top Border Bar**; the **Bridge Surface** dialog box is displayed. 

2. Select the first edge and then the second edge, refer to Figure 11-53. Choose the **Reverse Direction** button from the **Edges** rollout, if required.

3. Select the **G0 (Position)** option from the **Edge 1** and **Edge 2** drop-down lists in the **Continuity** sub-rollout available in the **Constraints** rollout. Next, choose the **OK** button. The surface created using the **Bridge** tool is shown in Figure 11-54.

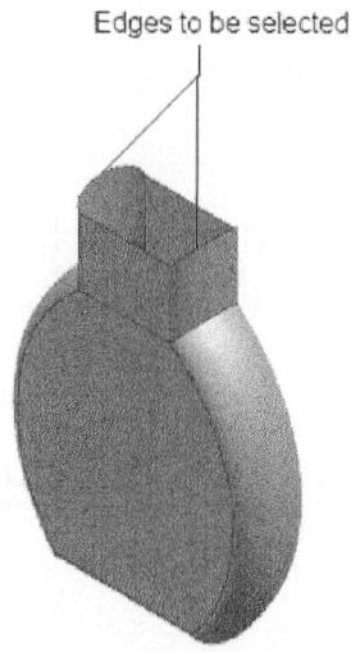

Figure 11-53 *Objects to be selected*

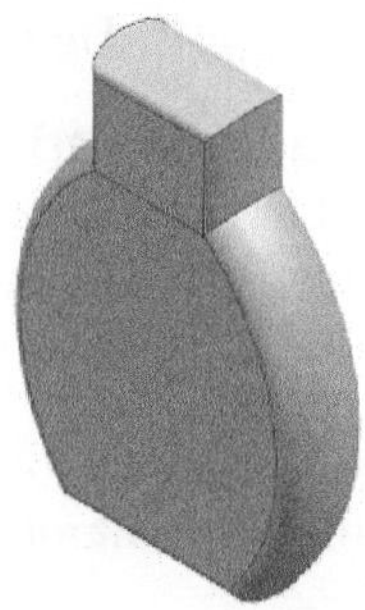

Figure 11-54 *Resulting bridge surface*

Creating the Extrude Feature

In this section, you need to create the eighth feature by extruding the sketch. You need to create the sketch for this feature on a plane that is at an offset of 81 mm from the XC-YC plane.

1. Create the datum plane at an offset of 81 mm from the XC-YC plane and create the sketch for the eighth feature by selecting the offset plane as the sketching plane, as shown in Figure 11-55.

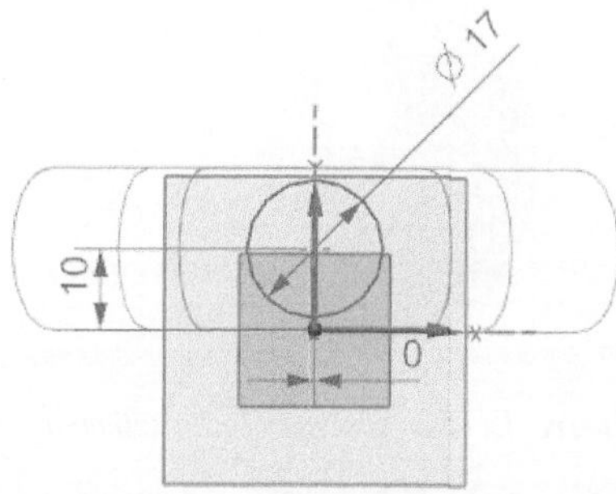

Figure 11-55 *Sketch drawn for the extrude feature*

2. Extrude this sketch through a distance of 25 mm in the downward direction. The resulting surface model is shown in Figure 11-56.

Figure 11-56 Resulting extruded surface

Creating the Face Blend Feature

Next, you need to create a face blend feature to blend the extruded surface created in the previous section with the bridge surface. The blending will also ensure that the portion of the extruded surface that extends below the bridge surface is removed.

1. Choose the **Face Blend** tool from **Menu > Insert > Detail Feature** of the **Top Border Bar**; the **Face Blend** dialog box is displayed.

2. By default, the **Two-face** option is selected in the Type drop-down list and the **Select Face 1** area is activated in the **Faces** rollout. As a result, you are prompted to select the faces to blend. Select the faces, refer to Figure 11-57; a arrow is displayed. Make sure the arrow points outward. If not, choose the **Reverse Direction** button to flip the direction.

3. Choose the second **Face** button from the **Faces** rollout and select the second face, refer to Figure 11-57. An arrow is displayed on selecting the face. If this arrow does not point upward, reverse the direction.

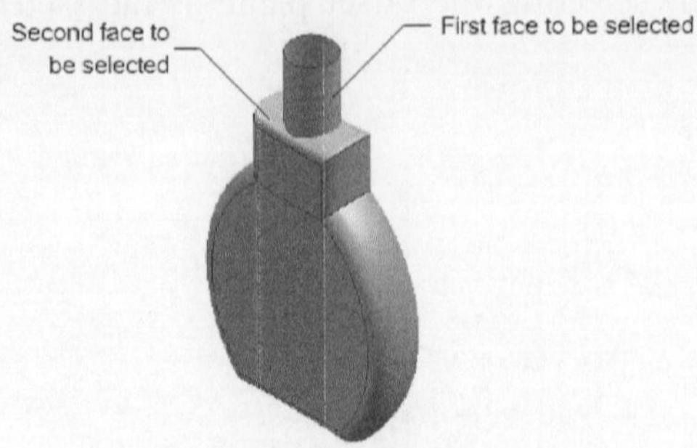

Figure 11-57 Entities to be selected

4. Select the **Rolling Ball** option from the **Orientation** drop-down list in the **Cross Section** rollout, if it is not selected by default. Make sure that the **Circular** option is selected in the **Shape** drop-down list.

5. Enter the value **3** in the **Radius** edit box and choose the **OK** button. The resulting face blend feature is shown in Figure 11-58.

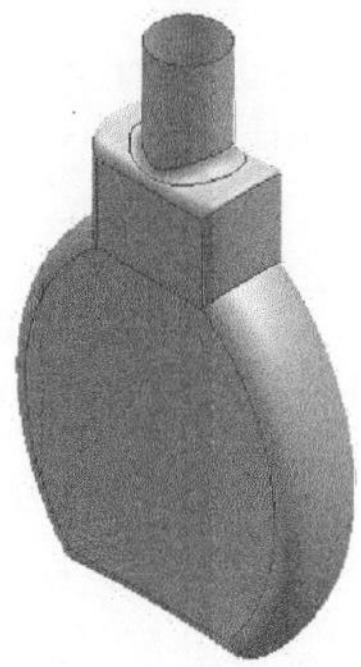

Figure 11-58 *Resulting face blend feature*

Creating the Tenth Feature Using the Bounded Plane Tool

In this section, you need to create the tenth feature using the **Bounded Plane** tool.

1. Choose the **Bounded Plane** tool from **Menu > Insert > Surface** of the **Top Border Bar**; the **Bounded Plane** dialog box is displayed and you are prompted to select the bounding string.

2. Select the circular edge of the extruded feature created earlier.

3. Choose the **OK** button. The surface model after creating the bounded plane feature is shown in Figure 11-59.

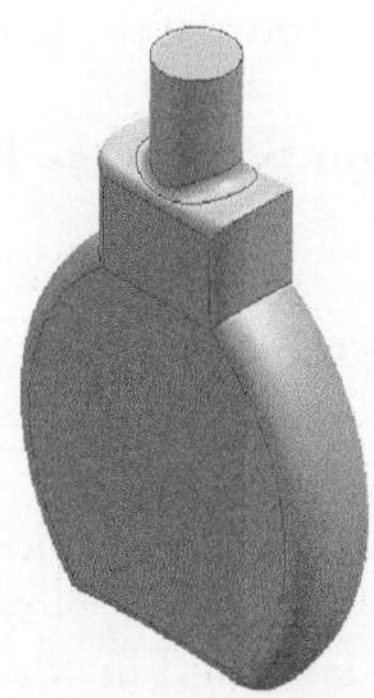

Figure 11-59 *The model after creating the bounded plane feature*

Creating the Extrude Feature

In this section, you need to create the eleventh feature by extruding the sketch. You need to create the sketch for this feature on the bounded surface created earlier.

1. Create the sketch for the eleventh feature by selecting the bounded surface created earlier as the sketching plane, refer to Figure 11-60.

2. Choose the **Extrude** tool from **Menu > Insert > Design Feature** in the **Top Border Bar**; the **Extrude** dialog box is displayed and you are prompted to select the section geometry to be extruded.

3. Select the sketch and enter the value **15** in the **Distance** edit box available below the **End** drop-down list. Next, choose the **OK** button from the **Extrude** dialog box. The resulting surface model is shown in Figure 11-61.

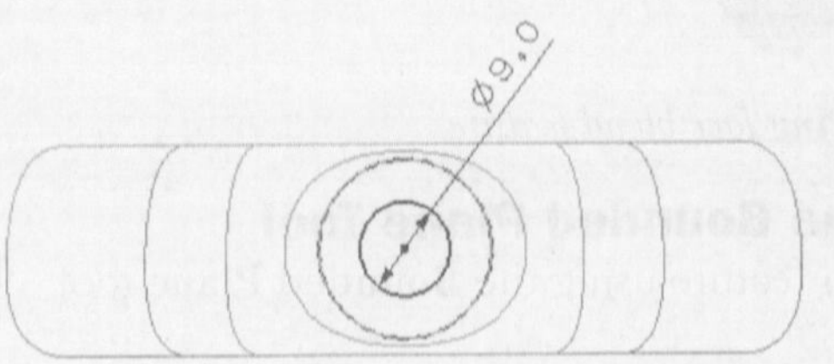

Figure 11-60 Sketch drawn for the eleventh feature

Figure 11-61 The surface model after creating the extrude feature

Trimming the Sheet

Next, you need to trim the unwanted portion of the surface model using the **Trim Sheet** tool.

1. Choose the **Trim Sheet** tool from **Menu > Insert > Trim** in the **Top Border Bar**; the **Trim Sheet** dialog box is displayed.

2. Select the tenth feature created using the **Boundary Plane** tool and then press the middle mouse button.

3. Select the extruded sheet feature created in the previous step and then select the **Keep** radio button from the **Region** rollout of the dialog box. Next, choose the **OK** button. The portion of the boundary plane surface that is enclosed inside the extruded surface is trimmed.

Creating the Through Curves Surface

This feature will be created using the **Through Curves** tool. You need to create the sketch for this feature on a plane at an offset of 106 from the XC-YC plane. The following steps are required to create the twelfth feature:

1. Create a datum plane at an offset of 106 mm from the XC-YC plane in the upward direction.

2. Create the sketch of the twelfth feature by selecting the offset plane as the sketching plane, refer to Figure 11-62.

3. Choose the **Through Curves** tool from **Menu > Insert > Mesh Surface** in the **Top Border Bar**; the **Through Curves** dialog box is displayed and you are prompted to select the curve or point to section. 

4. Select the edge as the first section string from the previous extruded feature, refer to Figure 11-63, and press the middle mouse button; you are again prompted to select the section.

5. Select the sketch as the second section string, refer to Figure 11-63 and press the middle mouse button. Make sure the arrows in both sections point in the same direction.

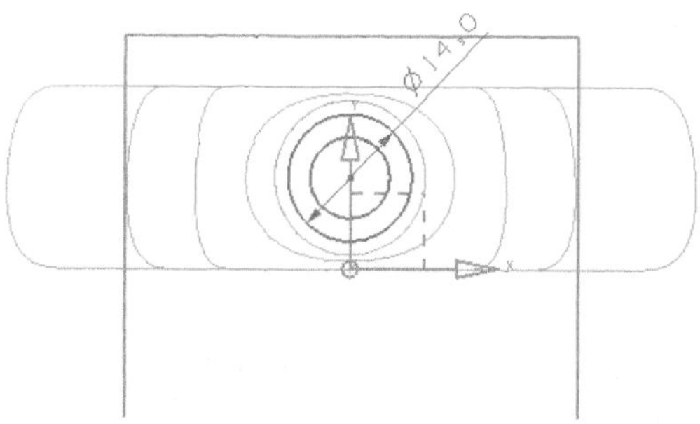

Figure 11-62 Sketch for the through curve surface

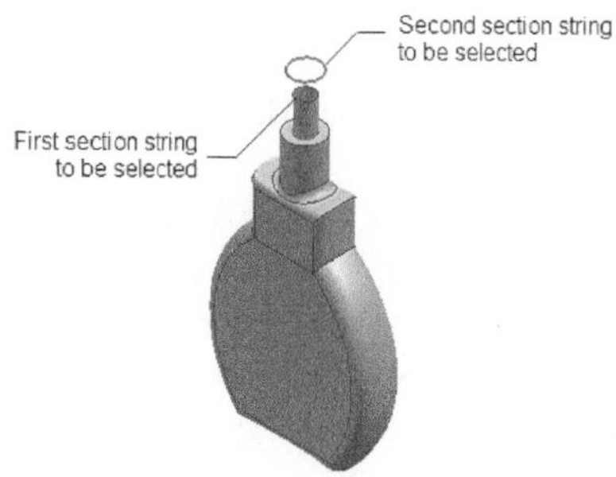

Figure 11-63 Edges to be selected

6. Next, select the **G1 (Tangent)** option from the **First Section** drop-down list in the **Continuity** rollout; the **Select Face** option is activated. As a result, you are prompted to select the continuity constraint face. Select the eleventh feature from the drawing window. Next, select the **Multiple** option from the **Patch Type** drop-down list of the **Output Surface Options** rollout, and then choose the **OK** button from the **Through Curves** dialog box.

The resulting surface model is shown in Figure 11-64.

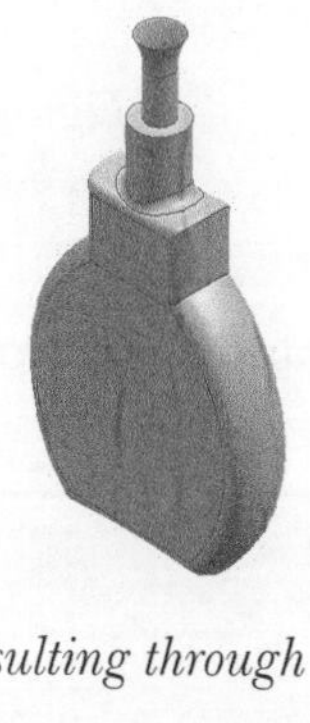

Figure 11-64 The resulting through curves surface feature

Sewing Individual Surfaces into a Single Surface

After creating the surface model, you need to sew individual surfaces into a single surface using the **Sew** tool.

1. Invoke the **Sew** tool by choosing **Menu > Insert > Combine > Sew** from the **Top Border Bar**; the **Sew** dialog box is displayed.

2. Select the **Sheet** option from the Type drop-down list, if it is not selected.

3. Select the base feature that is created using the **Bounded Plane** tool as the target body and then select all the remaining surfaces as the tool sheet bodies.

4. Choose the **OK** button. The resultant model after sewing individual surfaces into a single surface with a common edge is shown in Figure 11-65.

Adding Thickness to the Surface Model

Now, you need to add thickness to the surface model.

1. Choose **Menu > Insert > Offset/Scale > Thicken** from the **Top Border Bar**; the **Thicken** dialog box is displayed. Also, you are prompted to select the faces to thicken.

2. Select the surface model from the graphics window. Next, enter the thickness value as **0** and **1** in the **Offset 1** and **Offset 2** edit boxes, respectively.

3. Choose the **OK** button from the dialog box. The final model after applying the thickness is shown in Figure 11-66.

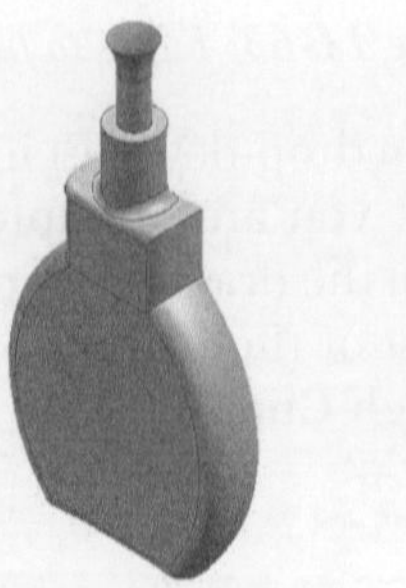

Figure 11-65 The surface model after sewing the surfaces

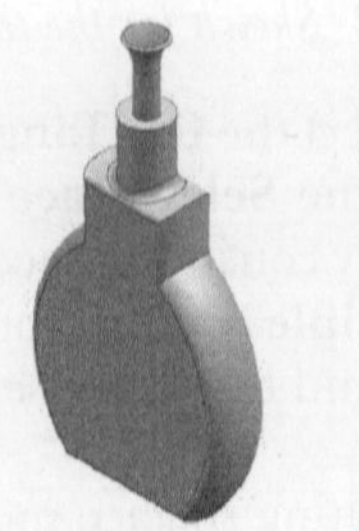

Figure 11-66 The final model after applying the thickness

Saving and Closing the File

1. Choose **Menu > File > Close > Save and Close** from the **Top Border Bar** to save and close the file.

Tutorial 2

In this tutorial, you will create the model shown in Figure 11-67. First, you need to create the surface model using the dimensions and orthographic views shown in Figure 11-68. After creating the surface model, you need to apply thickness of 1 mm in the outward direction. Assume the missing dimensions and then save the model with the name *c11tut2.prt* at the following location: *\NX\c11*. **(Expected time: 30 min)**

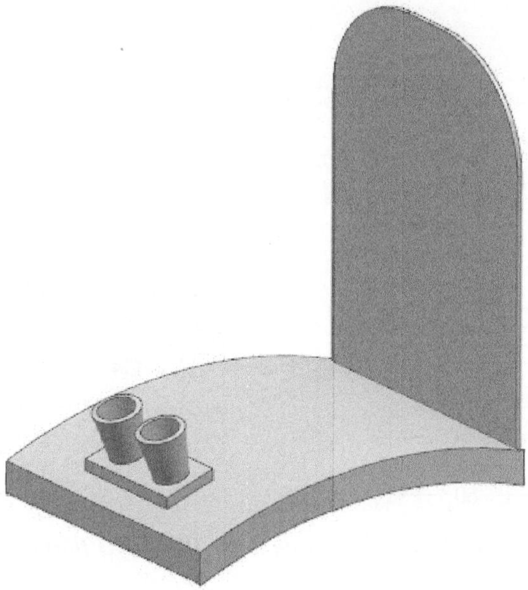

Figure 11-67 *Surface model for Tutorial 2*

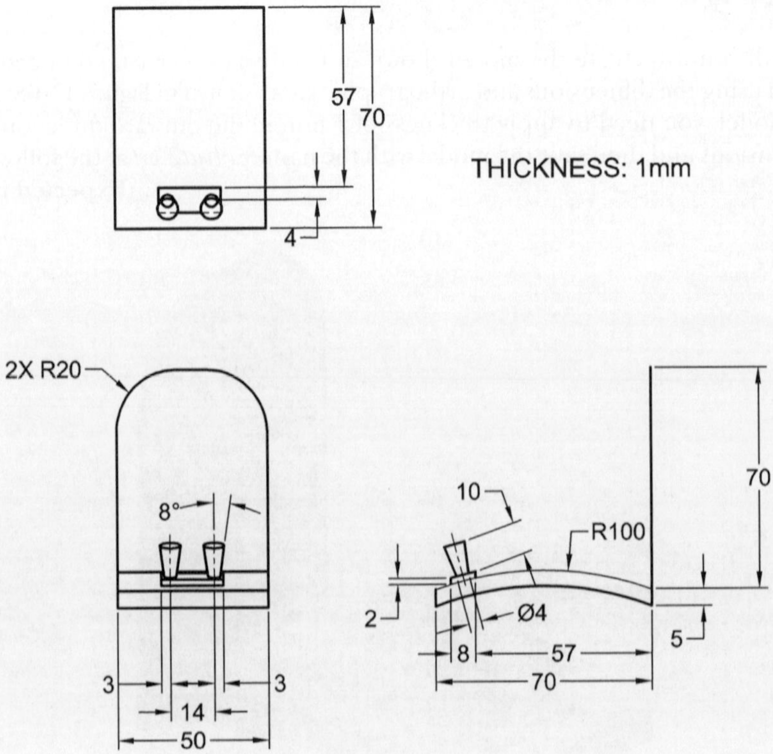

Figure 11-68 Views and dimensions for Tutorial 2

The following steps are required to complete this tutorial:

a. Start a new file and set the sheet environment.
b. Create the base feature by extruding the base sketch, refer to Figures 11-69 and 11-70.
c. Create the second feature by extruding the edges of the base feature, refer to Figures 11-71 and 11-72.
d. Create the third feature by extruding the sketch, refer to Figures 11-73 and 11-74.
e. Create the fourth feature by using the **Bounded** tool, refer to Figures 11-75 and 11-76.
f. Trim the fourth feature using the **Trimmed Sheet** tool, refer to Figures 11-77 and 11-78.
g. Create the fifth feature by extruding the sketch and mirror it, refer to Figures 11-79 through 11-82.
h. Create the feature by extruding the sketch and trim it, refer to Figures 11-83 through 11-86.
i. Sew individual surfaces into a single surface.
j. Add thickness to the surface model, refer to Figure 11-87.
k. Save and close the file.

Starting a New File and Setting the Sheet Environment

1. Start a new file with the name *c11tut2.prt* using the **Model** template, and specify its location as *C:\NX\c11*.

2. Choose **Menu > Preferences > Modeling** from the **Top Border Bar** and then select the **Sheet** radio button from the **Body Type** area of the **Modeling Preferences** dialog box. Next, choose the **OK** button.

Creating the Base Feature by Extruding the Sketch

In this section, you need to create the base feature for this tutorial by extruding the sketch.

1. Create the sketch of the base feature on the YC-ZC plane, as shown in Figure 11-69.

2. Extrude the sketch symmetrically on both sides of the sketching plane through a symmetric distance of 25 mm. The base feature of the surface model is shown in Figure 11-70.

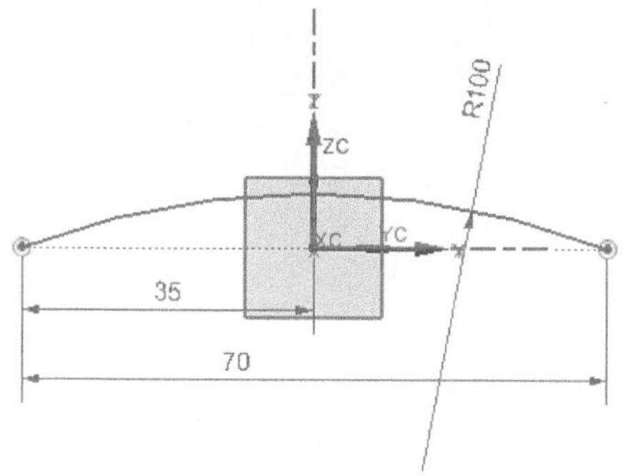

Figure 11-69 *Sketch of the base feature*

Figure 11-70 *Base feature of the surface model*

Creating the Second Feature by Extruding the Edges

The second feature will be created by extruding the edges of the base feature. The following steps are required to create the second feature:

1. Invoke the **Extrude** tool and then select the edges of the base surface, refer to Figure 11-71.

2. Define the -ZC-axis direction as the direction of extrusion using the **Inferred Vector** drop-down list. Enter **5** in the **Distance** edit box available below the **End** drop-down list.

3. Choose the **OK** button. The resulting surface model is shown in Figure 11-72.

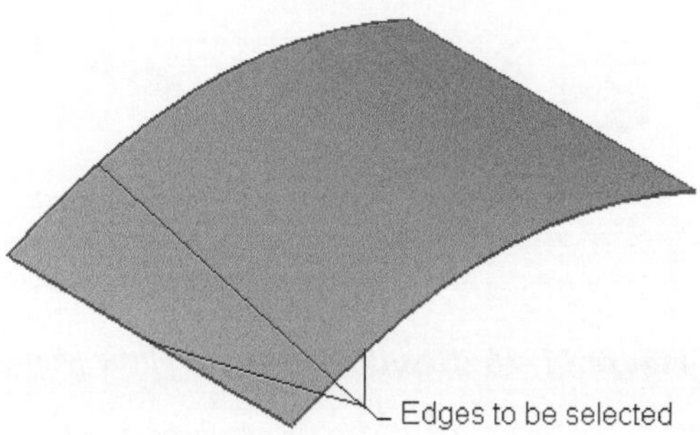

Figure 11-71 *Edges to be selected*

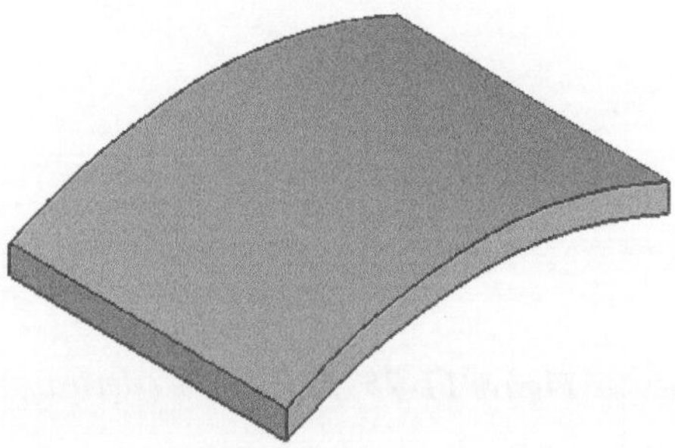

Figure 11-72 *The second feature created*

Creating the Third Feature by Extruding the Sketch

The third feature will be created by extruding a sketch. You need to create the sketch for the third feature on the YC-ZC plane.

1. Create the sketch for the third feature by selecting the YC-ZC plane as the sketching plane, as shown in Figure 11-73.

2. Extrude the sketch through a symmetric distance of 10 mm. The resulting surface model is shown in Figure 11-74.

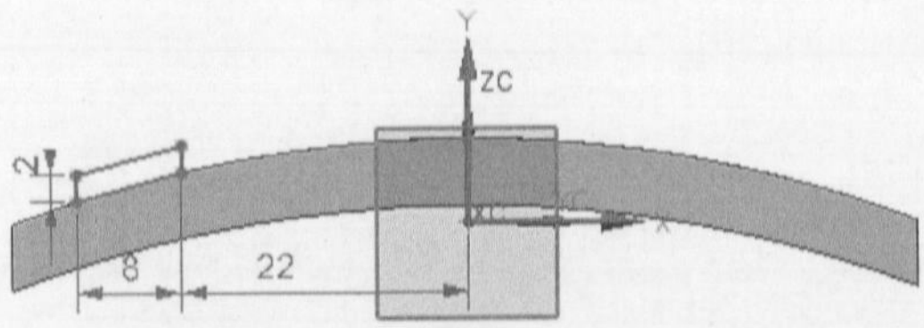

Figure 11-73 Sketch drawn for extrusion

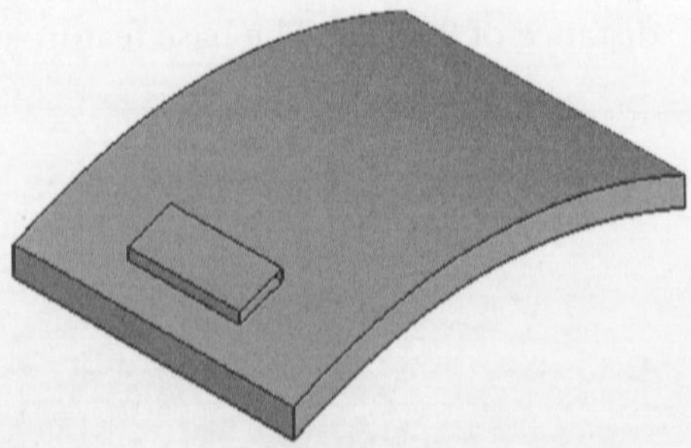

Figure 11-74 Resulting extruded feature

Creating the Bounded Plane Features

Now, you need to create the bounded plane features by using the **Bounded Plane** tool.

1. Choose **Menu > Insert > Surface > Bounded Plane** from the **Top Border Bar**; the **Bounded Plane** dialog box is displayed and you are prompted to select the bounding string.

2. Select the edges of the third feature to create a bounded plane, refer to Figure 11-75.

3. Choose the **OK** button from the dialog box; the bounded plane feature is created, refer to Figure 11-76.

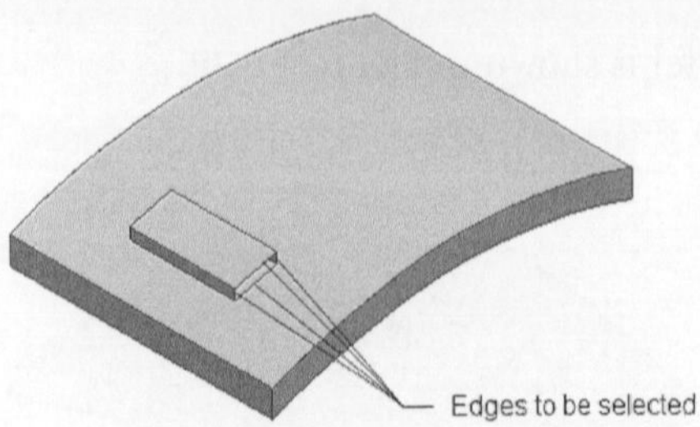

Figure 11-75 Edges to be selected

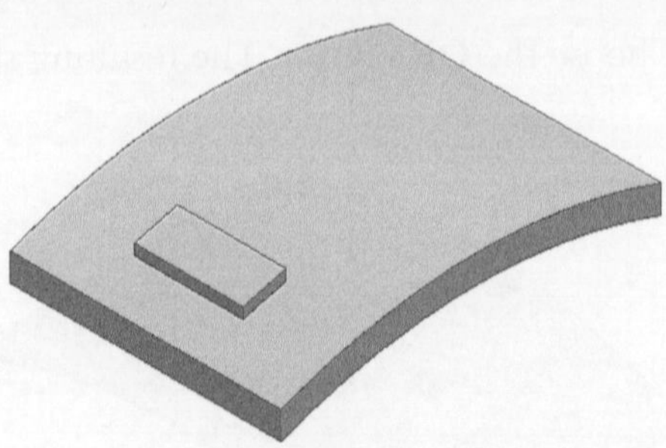

Figure 11-76 Resulting bounded plane feature

4. Similarly, create the bounded plane feature on the other side of the third extruded feature.

Trimming the Surfaces Using the Trim Sheet Tool

Now, the unwanted surfaces need to be trimmed using the **Trim Sheet** tool. The following steps are required to trim the unwanted surfaces.

1. Choose the **Trim Sheet** tool from **Menu > Insert > Trim** in the **Top Border Bar**; the **Trim Sheet** dialog box is displayed and you are prompted to select the target sheet body.

2. Select the third surface feature created and press the middle mouse button; you are prompted to select the trimming objects.

3. Select the base surface created, and then choose the **Apply** button; the third feature is trimmed. You are again prompted to select the sheet body to be trimmed.

4. Select the base surface created as the sheet body to be trimmed and then press the middle mouse button; you are prompted to select the trimming objects.

5. Select the surfaces as trimming objects, refer to Figure 11-77. Next, choose the **OK** button from the **Trim Sheet** dialog box. The rotated view of the resultant surface model is shown in Figure 11-78.

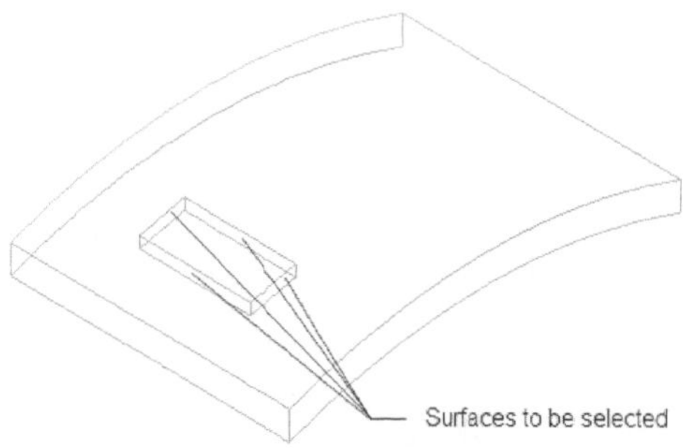

Figure 11-77 Surfaces to be selected

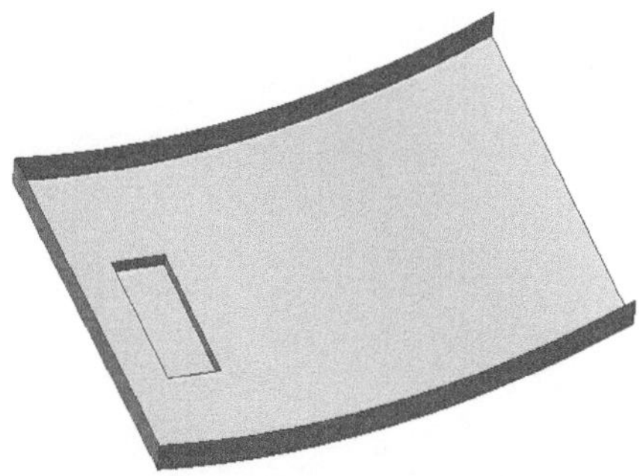

Figure 11-78 Resultant surface model

Creating the Next Feature by Extruding the Sketch

The next feature will be created by extruding the sketch. You need to create the sketch for this feature on the top face of the third feature.

1. Create the sketch for this feature by selecting the top face of the third feature as the sketching plane, as shown in Figure 11-79.

2. Extrude this sketch through a distance of 10 mm with -8 degrees as the draft angle by using the **From Start Limit** option. The resulting surface model is shown in Figure 11-80.

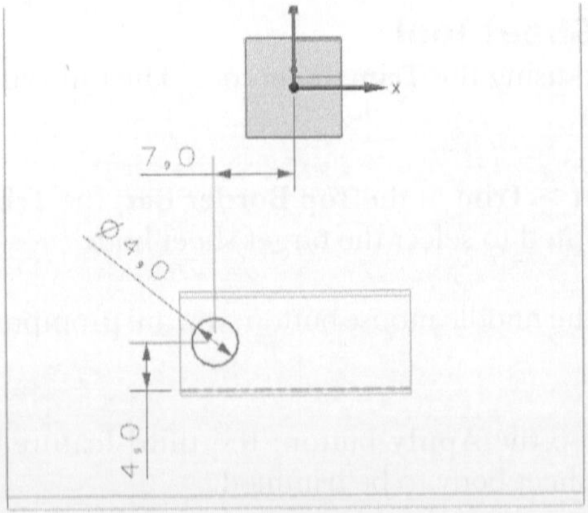

Figure 11-79 Sketch created

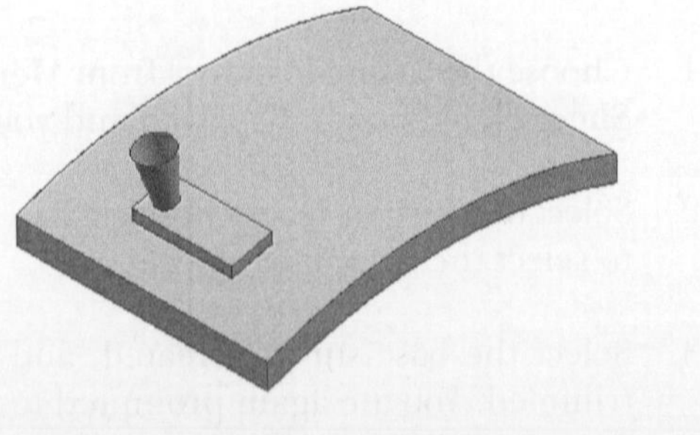

Figure 11-80 Resultant fourth feature

Mirroring the Feature

1. Invoke the **Mirror Feature** dialog box and then select the feature to mirror, refer to Figure 11-81.

2. Choose the **Plane** button from the dialog box and then select the YC-ZC plane as the mirroring plane. Next, choose the **OK** button; the mirror feature is created, refer to Figure 11-82.

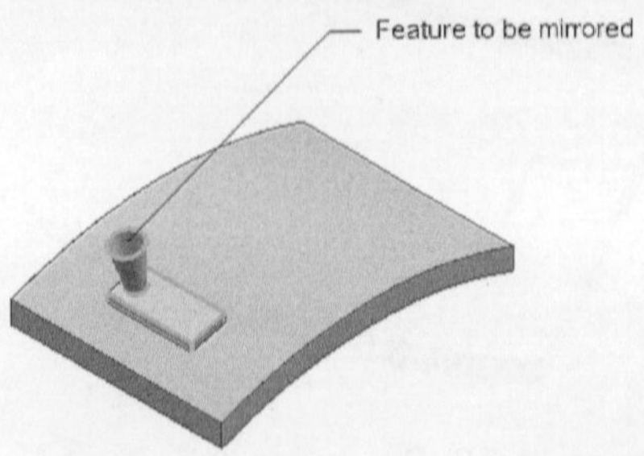

Figure 11-81 Feature to be mirrored

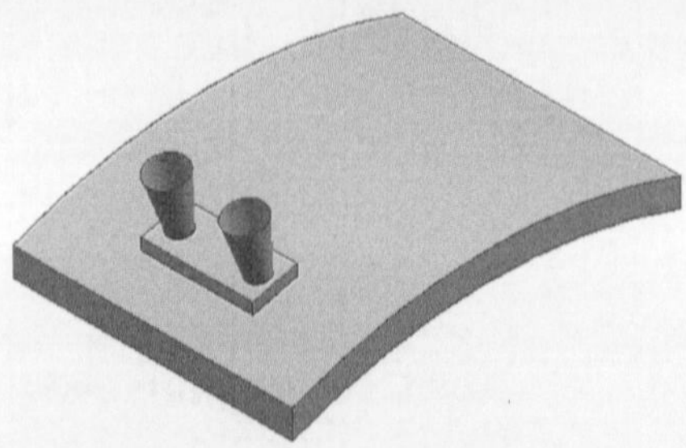

Figure 11-82 Resultant surface model with the mirrored feature

Trimming the Surface Using the Trim Sheet Tool

Now, the surface that is enclosed between the top face of the third feature and the previously created features will be trimmed using the **Trim Sheet** tool.

1. Choose the **Trim Sheet** tool from **Menu > Insert > Trim** in the **Top Border Bar**; the **Trim Sheet** dialog box is displayed and you are prompted to select the target sheet body.

2. Select the third surface feature created and press the middle mouse button; you are prompted to select the trimming objects.

3. Select the previously created extruded surface and its mirror feature and then choose the

OK button; the surface enclosed between the top face of the third feature and the previously created features is trimmed.

Creating the Next Feature by Extruding the Edge

The next feature will be created by extruding the edge of the base feature.

1. Invoke the **Extrude** dialog box and then select the edge, refer to Figure 11-83. Next, extrude it through a distance of 70 mm in the upward direction. The resulting surface model is shown in Figure 11-84.

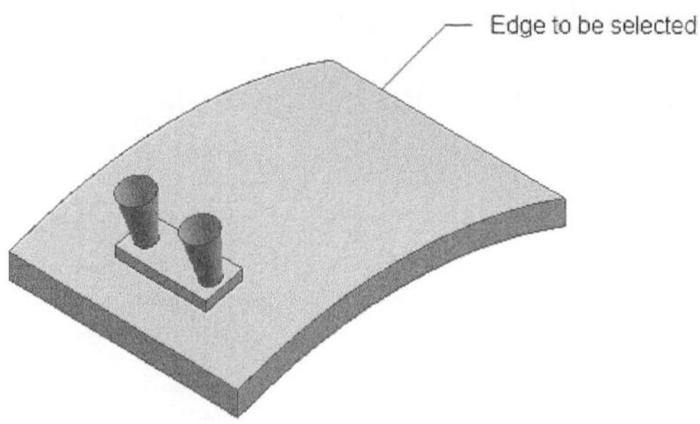

Figure 11-83 The edge to be selected

Figure 11-84 Resultant surface model

Trimming the Previously Created Extruded Surface

Now, the previously created extruded surface will be trimmed using the **Trim Sheet** tool.

1. Select the previously created surface as the sketching plane and draw the sketch, as shown in Figure 11-85.

2. Choose the **Trim Sheet** tool from **Menu > Insert > Trim** in the **Top Border Bar**; the **Trim Sheet** dialog box is displayed and you are prompted to select the target sheet body.

3. Select the previously created extruded surface and press the middle mouse button; you are prompted to select the trimming objects. Select the sketch created and then choose the **OK** button. The resulting surface model is shown in Figure 11-86.

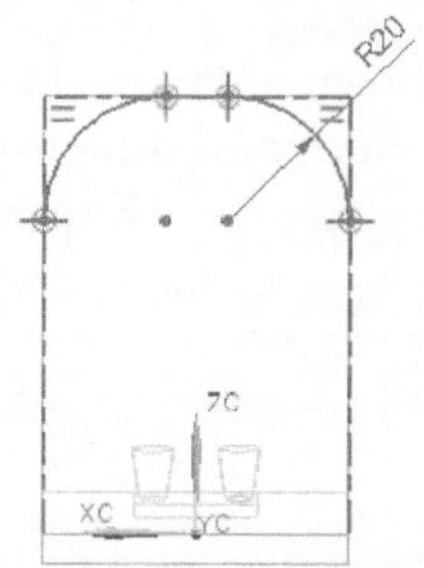

Figure 11-85 Sketch drawn for trimming

Figure 11-86 The resulting surface model after trimming the fifth feature

Sewing Individual Surfaces into a Single Surface

Now, you need to sew individual surfaces of the surface model into a single surface by using the **Sew** tool.

1. Invoke the **Sew** tool by choosing **Menu > Insert > Combine > Sew** from the **Top Border Bar**; the **Sew** dialog box is displayed.

2. Select the **Sheet** option from the Type drop-down list if it is not selected by default.

3. Select the base feature that is created using the **Extrude** tool as the target body and then select all the remaining surfaces as the tool sheet bodies.

4. Choose the **OK** button; all the individual surfaces get sewed into a single surface.

Adding Thickness to the Surface Model

Now, you need to add thickness to the surface model.

1. Choose **Menu > Insert > Offset/Scale > Thicken** from the **Top Border Bar**; the **Thicken** dialog box is displayed. Also, you are prompted to select the faces to thicken.

2. Select the surface model from the graphics window. Next, enter the thickness value as **0** and **1** in the **Offset 1** and **Offset 2** edit boxes, respectively.

3. Choose the **OK** button from the dialog box. The final model after adding the thickness is shown in Figure 11-87.

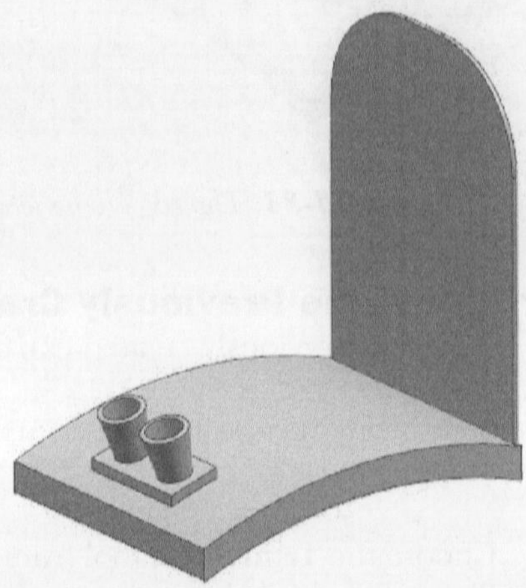

***Figure 11-87** Final surface model after adding the thickness*

Saving and Closing the File

1. Choose **Menu > File > Close > Save and Close** from the **Top Border Bar** to save and close the file.

Tutorial 3

In this tutorial, you will create the cover of a hair dryer, as shown in Figure 11-88. First, you will create the model by using surfaces and then thicken it. The views and dimensions of the model are displayed in Figures 11-89(a) and 11-89(b). **(Expected time: 1.5 hr)**

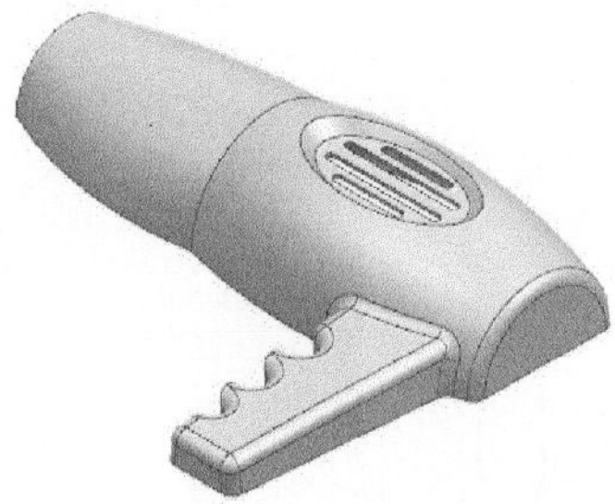

Figure 11-88 *Model for Tutorial 3*

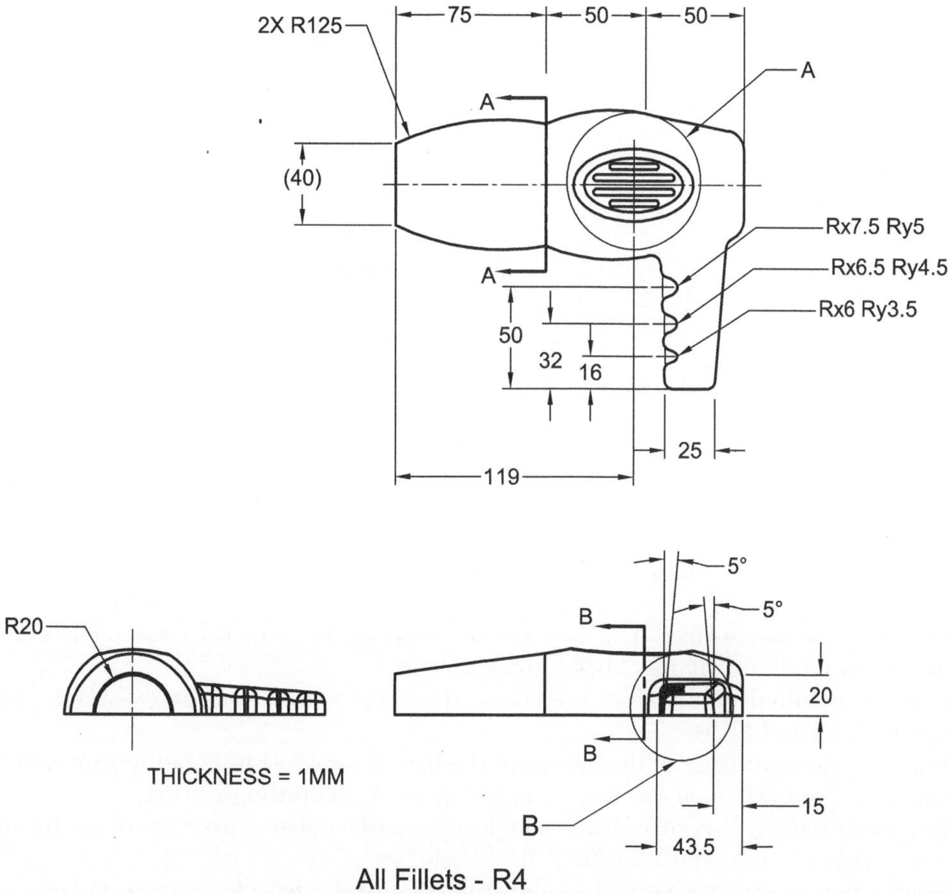

Figure 11-89(a) *Views and dimensions of the model*

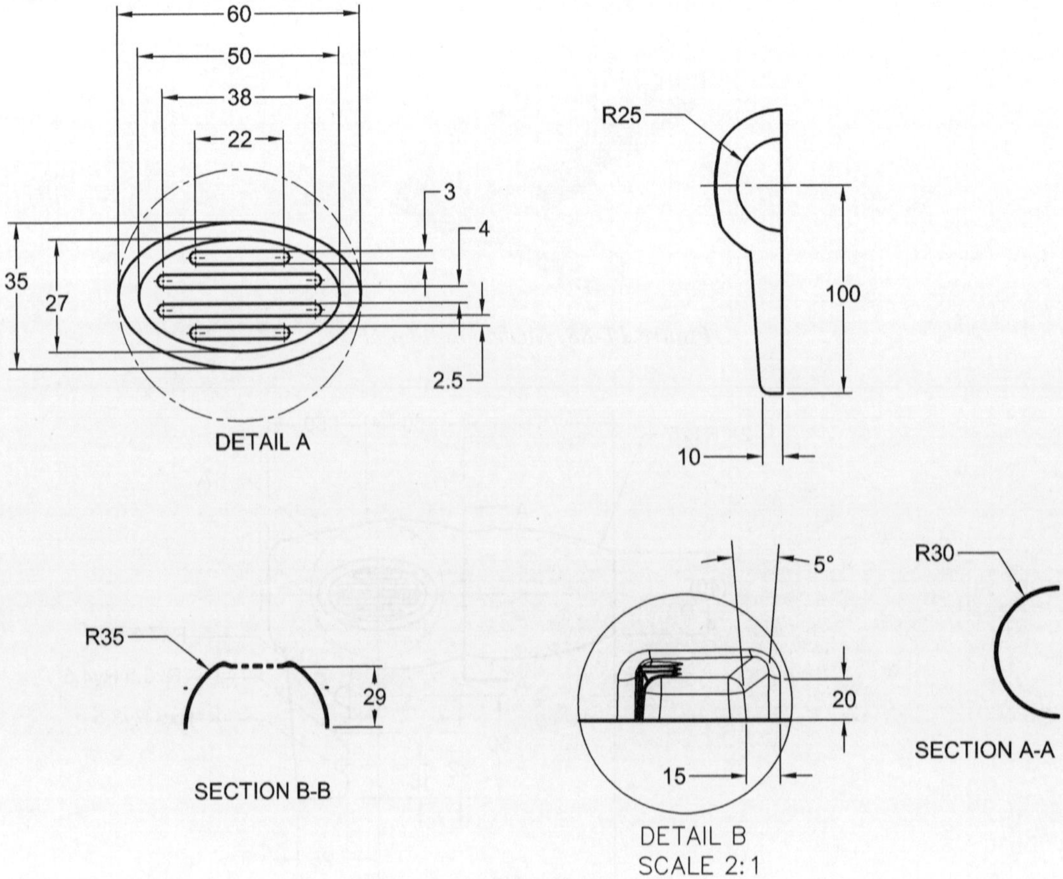

Figure 11-89(b) Section and Detail views of the model

The following steps are required to complete this tutorial:

a. First create the base surface. The base surface is created by using the open sections and the guide curves, refer to Figures 11-90 through 11-92.
b. Create a bounded plane surface to close the right face of the base surface, refer to Figures 11-93 and 11-94.
c. Create the basic structure of the handle of the hair dryer cover by creating a through curve surface between two open sections, refer to Figures 11-95 through 11-98.
d. Trim the unwanted portion of the through curve surface that is used to create the handle, refer to Figures 11-99 and 11-100.
e. Create a four point surface to close the front face of the handle, refer to Figures 11-101 and 11-102.
f. Create and extrude the elliptical sketches to create the grips of the handle and then trim the unwanted surfaces, refer to Figures 11-103 through 11-107.
g. Create a dip on the top surface of the hair dryer, refer to Figures 11-108 through 11-113.
h. Trim the surface to create air vents, refer to Figure 11-114.
i. Sew all surfaces together and add fillets to the model, refer to Figure 11-115.

j. Thicken the surface, refer to Figure 11-116.
k. Save and close the file.

Creating the Base Surface

To create the hair dryer cover, you first need to create the base surface of the model. The base surface will be created by lofting semicircular sections along guide curves. These sections will be created on different planes. Therefore, you first need to create three planes at an offset distance from the YC-ZC plane.

1. Start a new file with the name *c11tut3.prt* using the **Shape Studio** template and specify its location as *C:\NX\c11*.

2. Choose **Menu > Preferences > Modeling** from the **Top Border Bar** and select the **Sheet** radio button from the **Body Type** area of the **Modeling Preferences** dialog box. Next, choose the **OK** button to exit the dialog box.

3. Create three planes at an offset distance from the YC-ZC plane, as shown in Figure 11-90. For the offset distance of planes, refer to Figure 11-89(a).

4. Create sections and guide strings to create a studio surface, as shown in Figure 11-90. For dimensions, refer to Figure 11-89(a).

5. Choose the **Studio Surface** from **Menu > Insert > Mesh Surface** in the **Top Border Bar**; the **Studio Surface** dialog box is displayed and you are prompted to select a section.

6. Select Section 1, refer to Figure 11-91, and then press the middle mouse button; you are prompted to select a section again.

7. Select Section 2, refer to Figure 11-91, and then choose the **Guide (Cross) Curves** button from the **Guide (Cross) Curves** rollout; you are prompted to select a guide string. Note that you may need to choose the **Reverse Direction** button, if required.

8. Select the Guide Curve 1, refer to Figure 11-91, and then press the middle mouse button; you are prompted to select a guide string again.

9. Select the Guide Curve 2, refer to Figure 11-91. The preview of the studio surface after selecting the sections and the guide curves is shown in Figure 11-102. Next, choose the **Apply** button from the **Studio Surface** dialog box.

10. Select the Section 2, refer to Figure 11-91, and then press the middle mouse button; you are prompted to select a section again.

11. Select the Section 3, refer to Figure 11-91, and then press the middle mouse button; you are prompted to select a section again.

12. Select the Section 4, refer to Figure 11-91, and then choose the **Guide (Cross) Curves** button from the **Guide (Cross) Curves** rollout; you are prompted to select a guide string.

13. Select the Guide Curve 3, refer to Figure 11-91, and then press the middle mouse button; you are prompted to select a guide string again.

14. Select the Guide Curve 4, refer to Figure 11-91. A preview of the studio surface after selecting the sections and the guide curves is shown in Figure 11-92. Next, choose the **OK** button to create the studio surface.

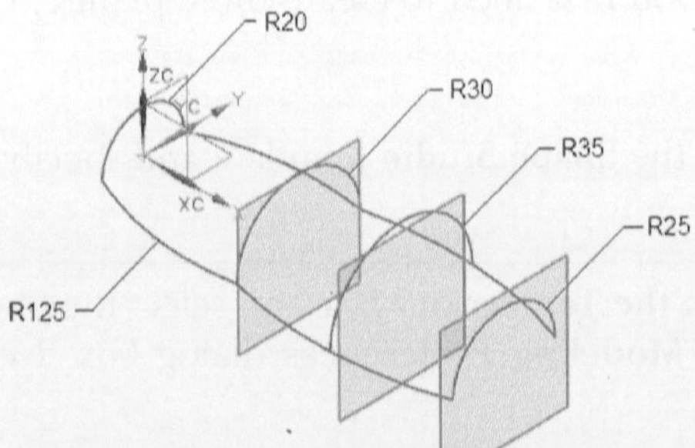

Figure 11-90 Dimensions of sections and guide curves

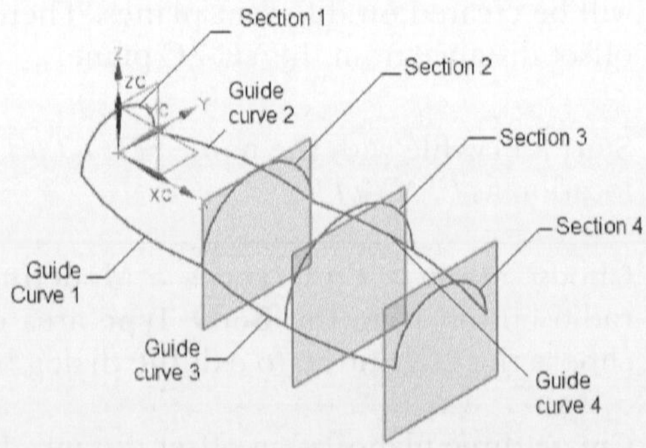

Figure 11-91 Sections and guide curves to create the studio surface

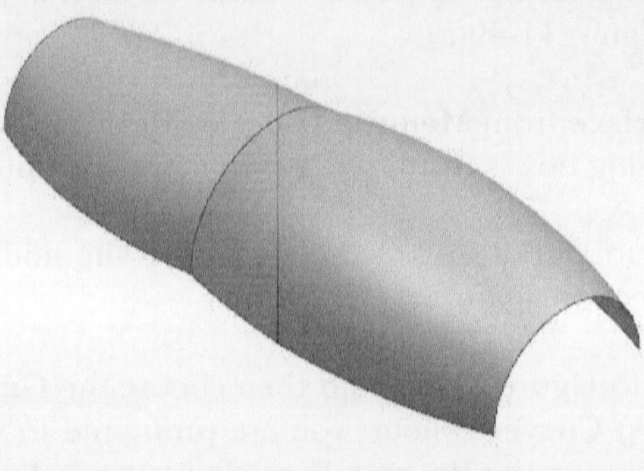

Figure 11-92 Resultant studio surface

Creating the Bounded Plane Surface

1. Invoke the Sketch in Task environment by selecting a plane created at an offset of 175mm.

2. Draw a closed sketch to create the bounded plane surface, as shown in Figure 11-93.

3. Invoke the **Bounded Plane** dialog box and then select the closed sketch from the drawing area. Next, choose the **OK** button from the **Bounded Plane** dialog box; the bounded plane surface is created, as shown in Figure 11-94.

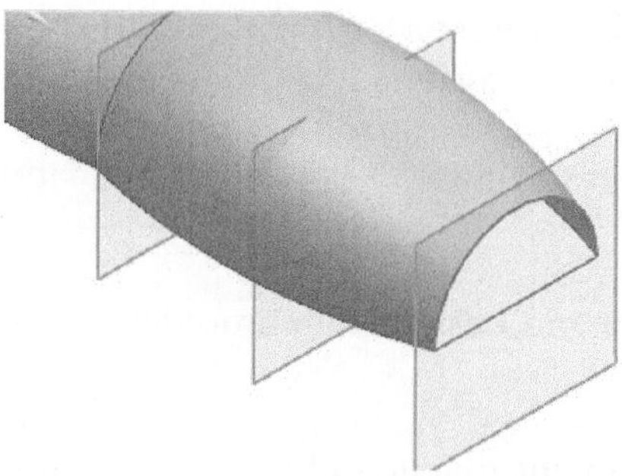

Figure 11-93 Closed sketch to create a bounded plane surface

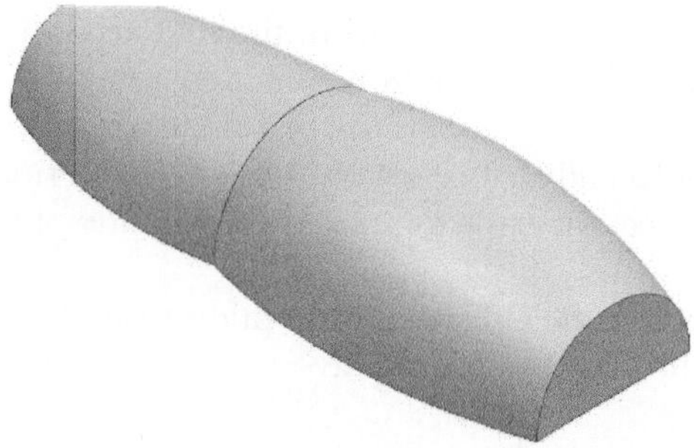

Figure 11-94 Resultant bounded plane surface

Creating the Base Surface for the Handle

Next, you need to create the base surface for the handle. The base surface for the handle will be created through two open sections.

1. Create a plane at an offset distance of 100 mm from the XC-ZC plane.
2. Invoke the Sketch in Task environment by using the newly created plane as the sketching plane.
3. Create an open sketch, as shown in Figure 11-95, and exit the Sketch in Task environment.
4. Next, invoke the Sketch in Task environment by using the XC-ZC plane as the sketching plane.
5. Again, create another open sketch, as shown in Figure 11-96, and exit the Sketch in Task environment.

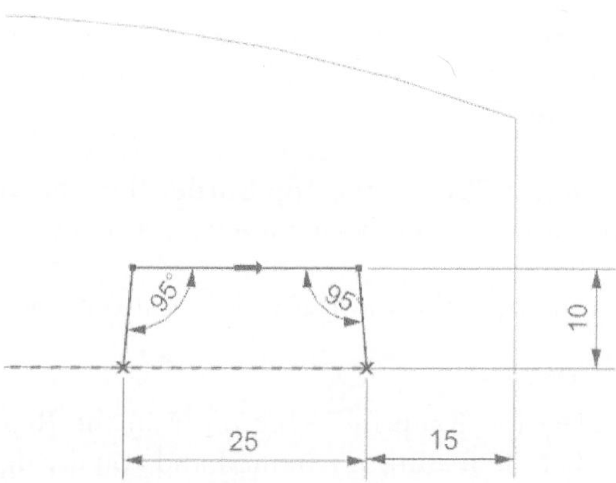

Figure 11-95 Open sketch created

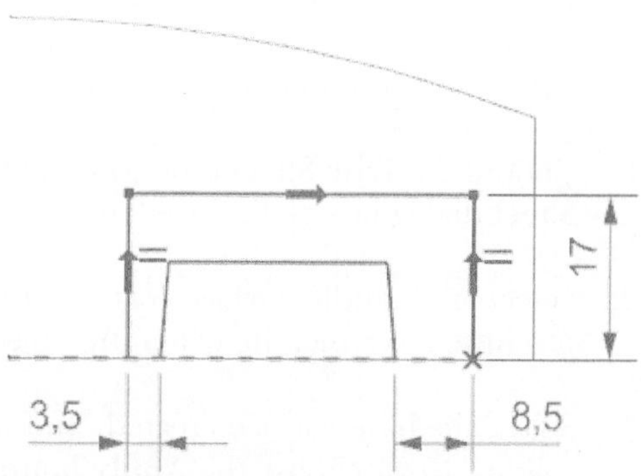

Figure 11-96 Open sketch created

6. Choose the **Through Curves** tool from **Menu > Insert > Mesh Surface** in the **Top Border Bar**; the **Through Curves** dialog box is displayed and you are prompted to select a section.

7. Select all elements from the first section string, refer to Figure 11-97, and then press the middle mouse button; you are prompted to select a section again.

8. Select all elements from the second section string, refer to Figure 11-98. Make sure that the direction arrows are on the same side of the sections.

9. Select the **G0 (Position)** option from the **First Section** and **Last Section** drop-down lists in the **Continuity** rollout.

10. Select the **Preserve Shape** check box from the **Alignment** rollout and make sure that the **Parameter** option is selected in the **Alignment** drop-down list.

11. Choose the **OK** button from the **Through Curves** dialog box; the handle surface is created, as shown in Figure 11-98.

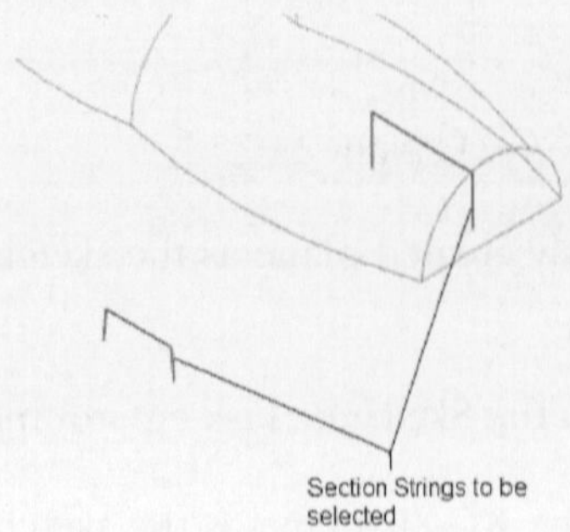

Figure 11-97 Sections to be selected

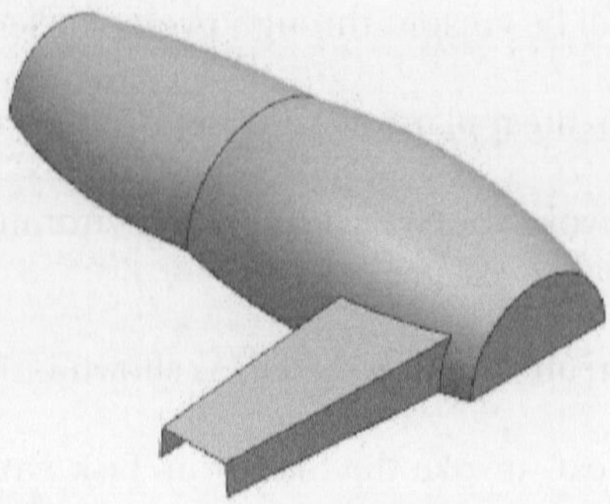

Figure 11-98 Resultant surface for the handle

Trimming the Unwanted Portion from the Surface of the Handle

If you rotate the model after creating the lofted surface for the handle, you will observe that a portion of the lofted surface needs to be trimmed.

1. Choose the **Trim Sheet** tool from **Menu > Insert > Trim** in the **Top Border Bar**; the **Trim Sheet** dialog box is displayed and you are prompted to select the target sheet body.

2. Select the handle surface feature created and press the middle mouse button; you are prompted to select the trimming objects.

3. Select the base surface created, and then select the **Keep** radio button from the **Region** rollout. Next, choose the **Apply** button; the handle feature is trimmed and you are again prompted to select the sheet body to be trimmed.

4. Select the base surface created as the sheet body to be trimmed, and then press the middle mouse button; you are prompted to select the trimming objects.

5. Select the surfaces shown in Figure 11-99 as the trimming objects. Next, choose the **OK** button from the **Trim Sheet** dialog box. The rotated view of the resultant surface model is created, as shown in Figure 11-100.

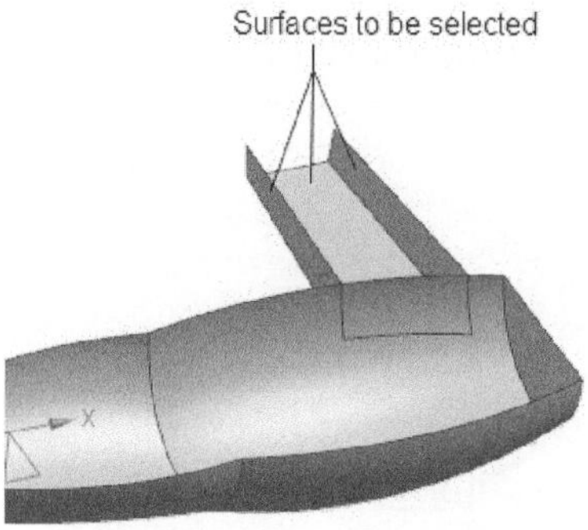

Figure 11-99 Surfaces to be selected

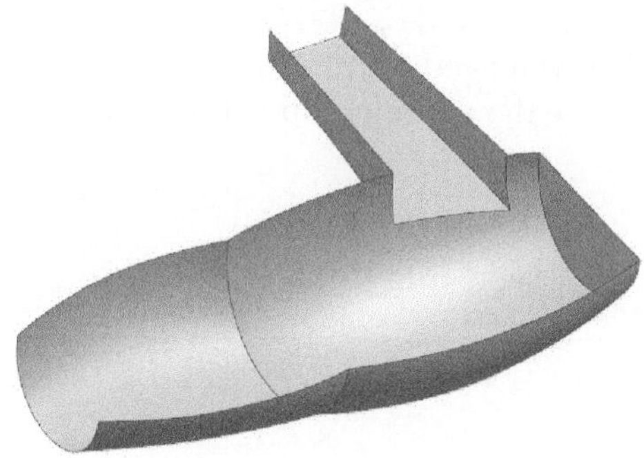

Figure 11-100 Resultant trimmed surface

Creating the Four Point Surface

Next, you need to create a planar surface to close the front face of the handle.

1. Choose the **Four Point Surface** tool from **Menu > Insert > Surface** in the **Top Border Bar**; the **Four Point Surface** dialog box is displayed and you are prompted to select objects to infer points.

2. Select the vertices on the front face of the handle, refer to Figure 11-101, and then choose the **OK** button; the planar surface is created. The model after closing the front face of the handle is shown in Figure 11-102.

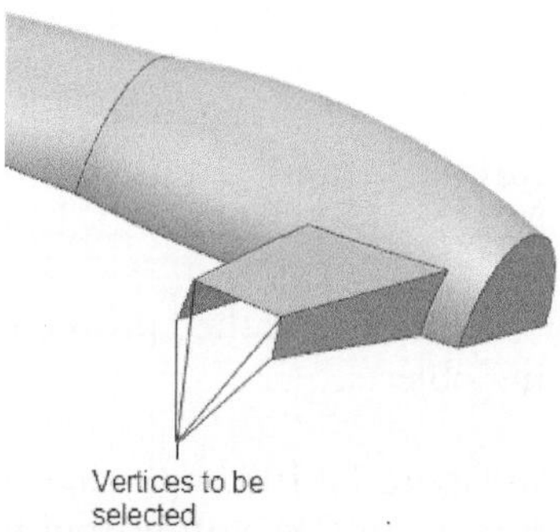

Figure 11-101 Vertices to be selected

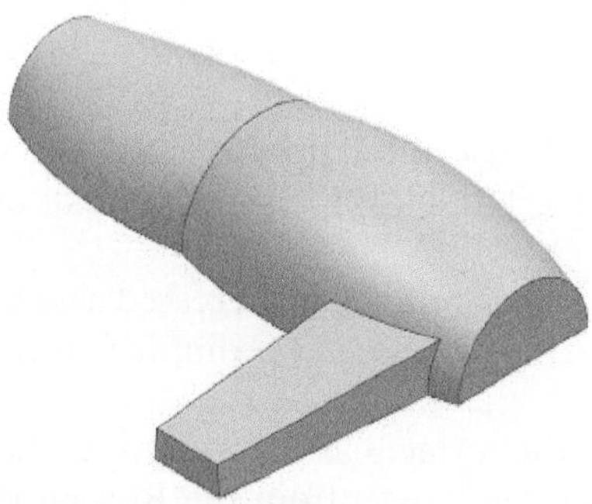

Figure 11-102 Model after closing the front face of the handle

Creating Grips on the Handle

Next, you need to create grips on the handle of the hair dryer. The grips will be created by extruding the elliptical surfaces and then trimming the unwanted portions of the surfaces.

1. Invoke the Sketch in Task environment using the XC-YC plane as the sketching plane.

2. Create a sketch for extruding the surface, as shown in Figure 11-103.

3. Extrude the sketch up to a depth of 25 mm. The extruded surface is displayed, as shown in Figure 11-104.

   Next, you need to trim the unwanted portions of the extruded surface and the handle to achieve the desired shape of the grips.

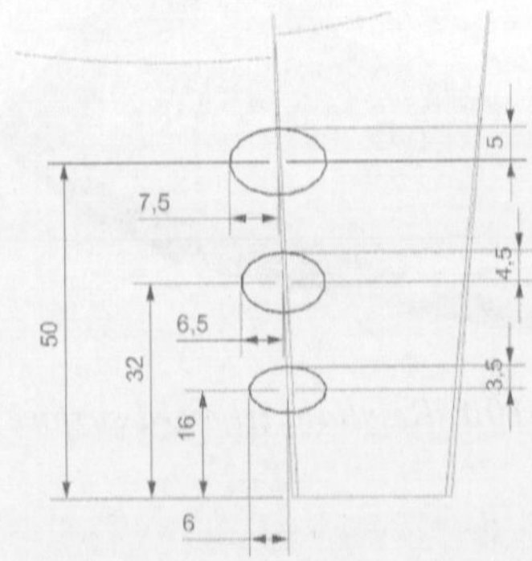

Figure 11-103 Sketch created for extruding the surface

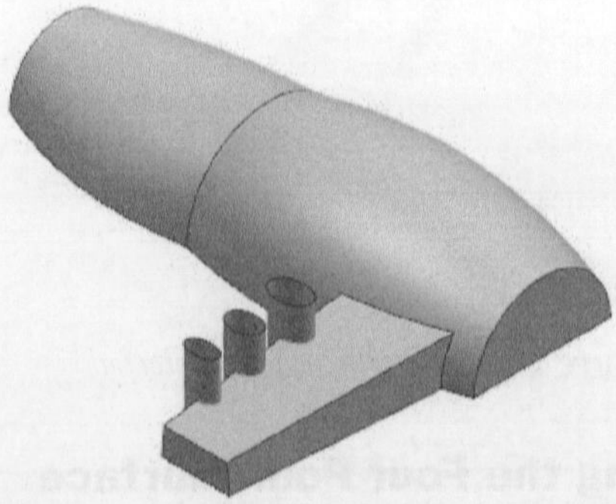

Figure 11-104 Resultant extruded surface

4. Choose the **Trim Sheet** tool from **Menu > Insert > Trim** in the **Top Border Bar**; the **Trim Sheet** dialog box is displayed and you are prompted to select the target sheet body.

5. Select the extruded surface features and press the middle mouse button; you are prompted to select the trimming objects.

6. Select the faces of the handle, refer to Figure 11-105, and then select the **Discard** radio button from the **Region** rollout.

7. Next, choose the **Apply** button; the extruded features are trimmed and you are again prompted to select the sheet body to be trimmed.

8. Select the handle surface created as the sheet body for trimming, and then press the middle mouse button; you are prompted to select the trimming objects.

9. Select the surfaces as the trimming objects, as shown in Figure 11-106 and then choose the **Keep** radio button from the **Region** rollout. Next, choose the **OK** button from the **Trim Sheet** dialog box. The rotated view of the resultant surface model is created, as shown in Figure 11-107.

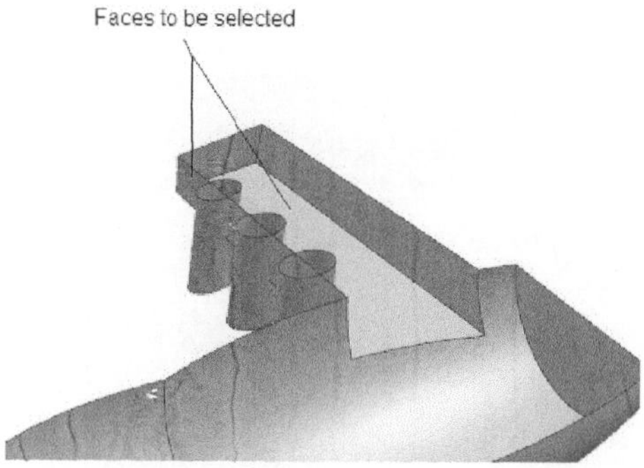

Figure 11-105 *Faces to be selected*

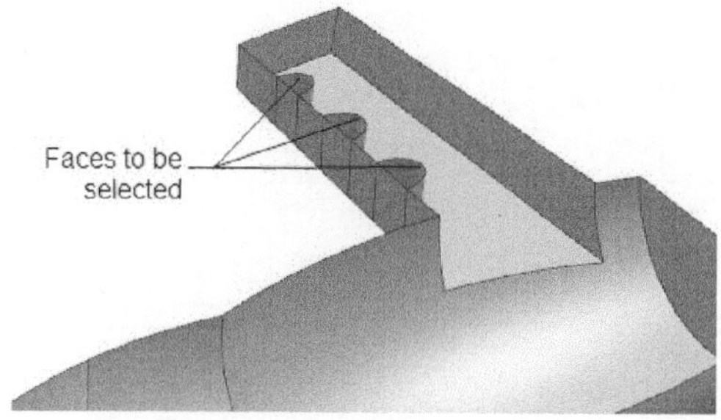

Figure 11-106 *Faces to be selected*

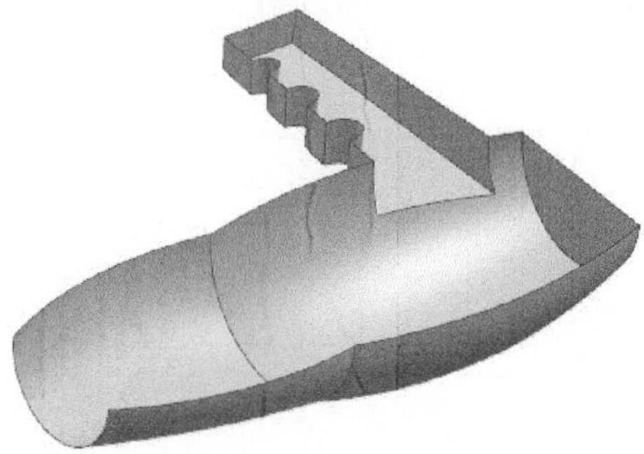

Figure 11-107 *Resultant trimmed surface*

Creating a Dip on the Base Surface

Next, you need to create a dip on the base surface. To do so, you need to use various tools for offsetting planes, creating lofted surface, trimming unwanted surfaces, and creating a bounded plane surface.

1. Create a plane at an offset distance of 35 mm from the XC-YC plane.

2. Invoke the Sketch in Task environment using the newly created plane as the sketching plane.

3. Create a sketch, as shown in Figure 11-108, and then exit the Sketch in Task environment.

4. Next, choose the **Project Curve** tool from the **Curve** gallery of the **Create** group and project the newly created sketch on the base surface; the model after projecting the sketch is displayed, as shown in Figure 11-109.

5. Create a plane at an offset distance of 6 mm from the newly created plane in the downward direction.

6. Next, invoke the Sketch in Task environment by using the newly created plane as the sketching plane and create a sketch, as shown in Figure 11-110. Next, exit the Sketch in Task environment.

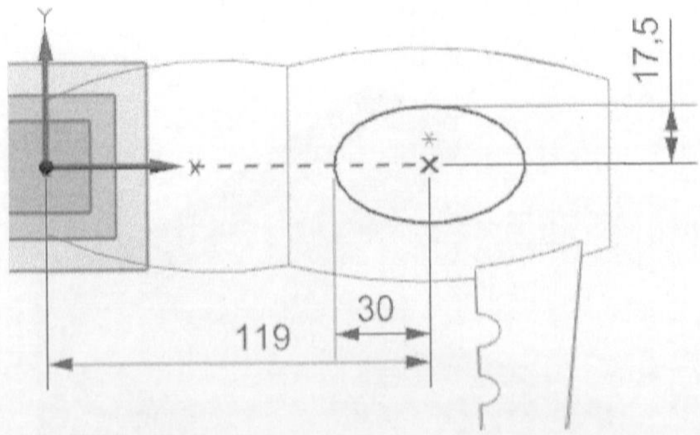

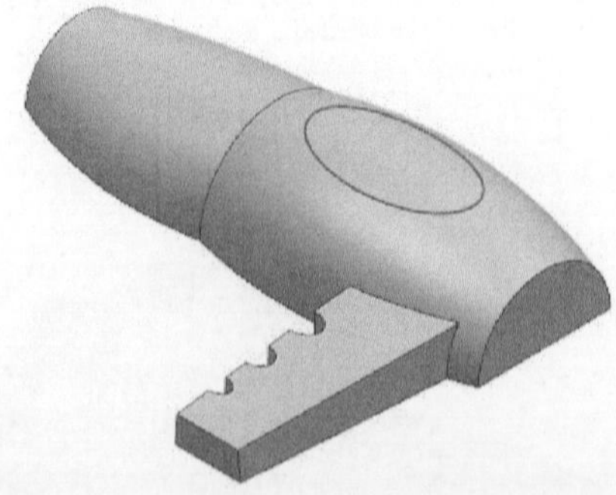

Figure 11-108 Sketch to be created *Figure 11-109 Resultant projected curve*

7. Invoke the **Studio Surface** tool and create a studio surface by using the sketch and the projected curve created earlier. The studio surface after hiding the base surface is shown in Figure 11-111.

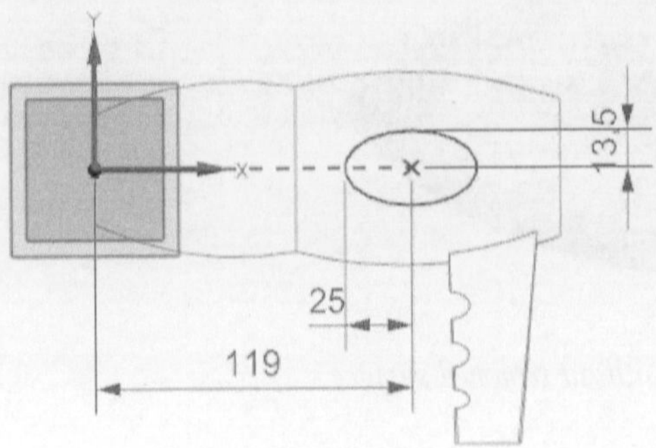

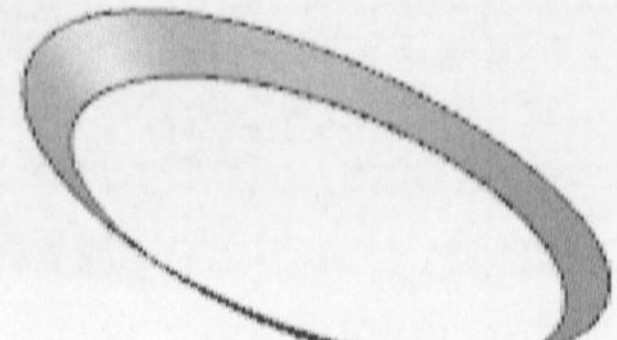

Figure 11-110 Sketch to be created *Figure 11-111 Resulting Studio surface*

8. Invoke the **Class Selection** dialog box and select the base feature. Next, choose the **OK** button; the selected surface is hidden.

9. Invoke the **Trim Sheet** tool and trim the base surface using the projected curve. The model after trimming the surface is shown in Figure 11-112.

10. Next, create the bounded plane surface by using the **Bounded Plane** tool, as shown in Figure 11-113.

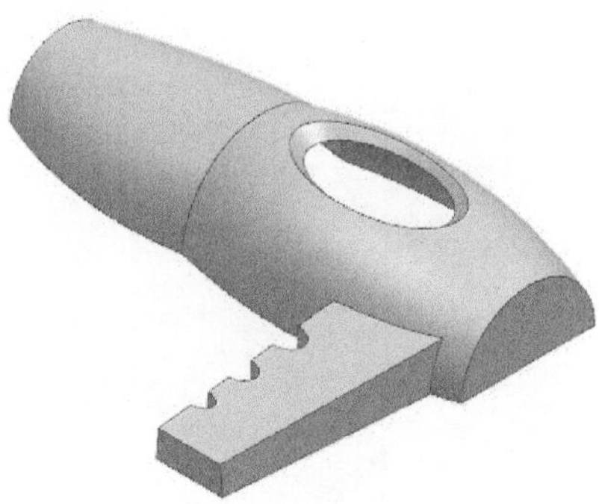

Figure 11-112 *Model after trimming the surface*

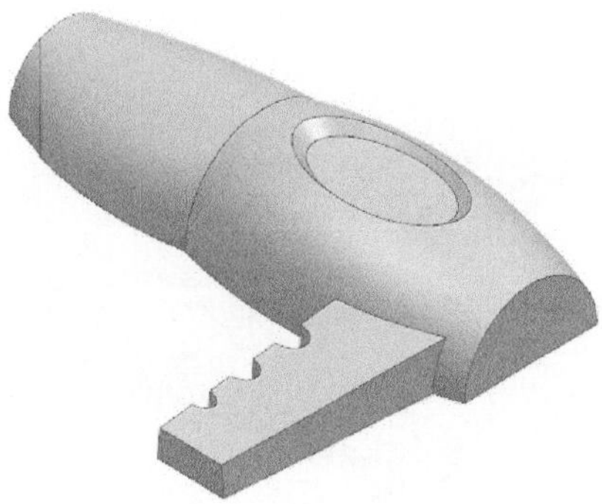

Figure 11-113 *Bounded plane surface*

Creating Air Vents

Next, you need to create air vents on the newly created bounded plane surface. Air vents are created by drawing the sketch on the bounded plane surface and then trimming the surface.

1. Select the newly created bounded plane surface as the sketching plane and then invoke the Sketch in Task environment.

2. Create the sketch of air vents. For dimensions, refer to Figure 11-89(b).

3. Invoke the **Trim Sheet** tool from **Menu > Insert > Trim** in the **Top Border Bar**. Then, select a sketch as the trimming tool to trim the bounded plane surface for creating air vents.

   The surface model after creating air vents is displayed in Figure 11-114.

Sewing all Surfaces

After creating all surfaces, you need to sew all surfaces together and then add fillets to surfaces and thicken the model.

1. Choose the **Sew** tool from **Menu > Insert > Combine** in the **Top Border Bar**; the **Sew** dialog box is displayed.

2. Select the **Sheet** option from the Type drop-down list, if it is not selected.

3. Select the base feature that is created using the **Studio Surface** tool as the target body and then select all the remaining surfaces as the tool sheet bodies.

4. Choose the **OK** button.

5. Add blends at the required places of the surface model. For dimensions, refer to Figure 11-89(a). The model after adding blends is displayed in Figure 11-115.

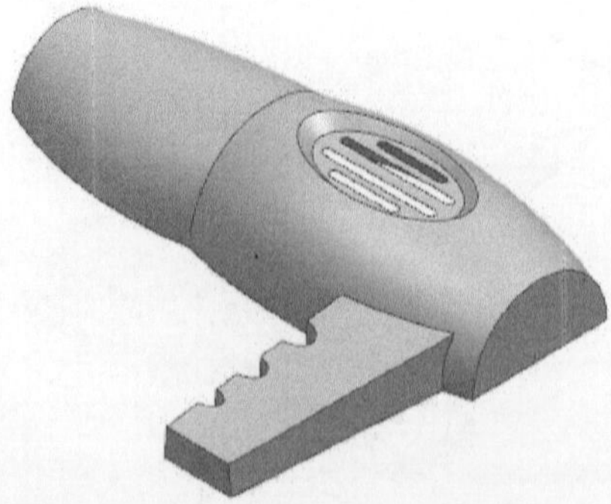

Figure 11-114 Surface model after trimming the bounded plane surface

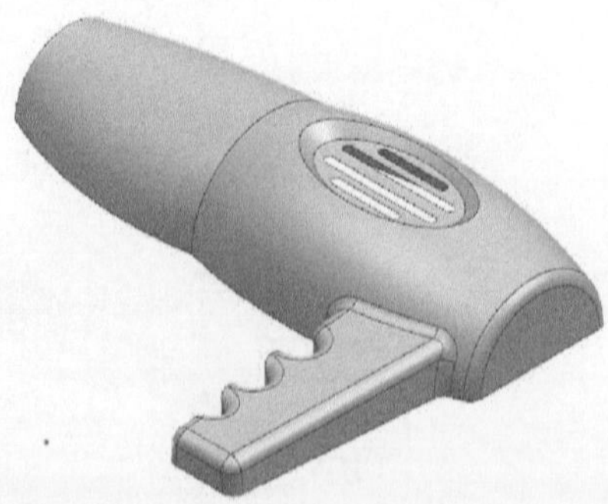

Figure 11-115 Surface model after adding blends

Adding Thickness to the Surface Model

After creating the entire model, you need to add thickness to the surface model.

1. Choose the **Thicken** tool from **Menu > Insert > Offset/Scale** in the **Top Border Bar**; the **Thicken** dialog box is invoked and you are prompted to select the surface to thicken.

2. Select the surface model from the graphics window. Next, enter the thickness value as **0** and **1** in the **Offset 1** and **Offset 2** edit boxes, respectively.

3. Choose the **OK** button from the dialog box. The final model after applying the thickness is shown in Figure 11-116.

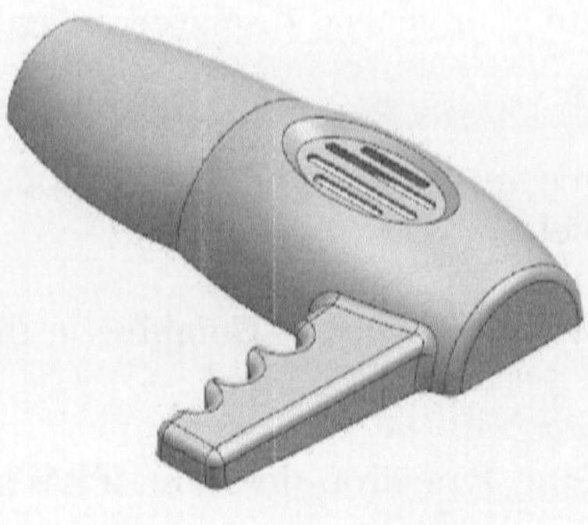

Figure 11-116 Final model

Saving and Closing the File

1. Choose **Menu > File > Close > Save and Close** from the **Top Border Bar** to save and close the file.

Self-Evaluation Test

Answer the following questions and then compare them to those given at the end of this chapter:

1. The __________ tool is used to create intersection curves between two sets of objects.

2. The __________ option creates a face blend as if it was subtended by a ball rolling in constant contact with two sets of input faces.

3. The __________ option is used to specify the planes spaced at equal angles which are further used to section the selected bodies.

4. The maximum number of primary faces that can be used to create the bridge surface is __________.

5. The __________ tool is used to create the section curves between specified planes and solid bodies, surfaces, and curves.

6. Select the __________ check box to bridge the gap between two segments of a projected curve.

7. The __________ tool is used to project a closed or an open curve on one or more than one planar or curved faces.

8. The __________ tool is used to create complicated blends tangent to the specified sets of faces.

9. The **Emboss Body** tool is used to emboss the shape of one solid body onto another solid or sheet body. (T/F)

10. You can project a curve onto a plane. (T/F)

Review Questions

Answer the following questions:

1. Which of the following tools is used to stitch the surfaces into a single surface?

   (a) **Face Blend** (b) **Emboss Body**
   (b) **Bridge** (d) **Sew**

2. Which of the following tools is used to create intersection curves between two sets of objects?

   (a) **Curve Intersection** (b) **Intersection Curve**
   (b) **Project Curve** (d) **Section Curve**

3. Which of the following tools is used to create the sheet body that joins the two edges of faces?

   (a) **Bridge** (b) **Fillet**
   (c) **Face Blend** (d) None of these

4. The __________ option is used to create a face blend between three faces.

5. The __________ option is used to create section curves along the planes perpendicular to the selected curve.

6. The isoparametric blend is used for turbine blades. (T/F)

7. You can create a surface body from a closed sketch. (T/F)

8. Using the **Three-face** option in the **Face Blend** dialog box, you can create a face blend between three faces. (T/F)

9. The **Emboss Body** tool is used to emboss the shape of one solid body onto another solid or sheet body. (T/F)

10. The **Project Curve** tool is used to project curves on planar or curved faces. (T/F)

EXERCISES

Exercise 1

Create the surface model shown in Figure 11-117. The drawing views and dimensions of the surface model are shown in Figure 11-118. Assume the missing dimensions. After creating the surface model, save it with the name *c11exr1.prt* at the location *\NX\c11*.

(Expected time: 45 min)

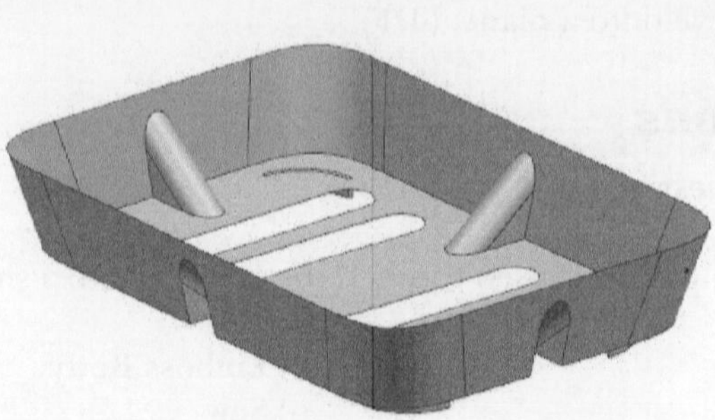

Figure 11-117 *Surface model for Exercise 1*

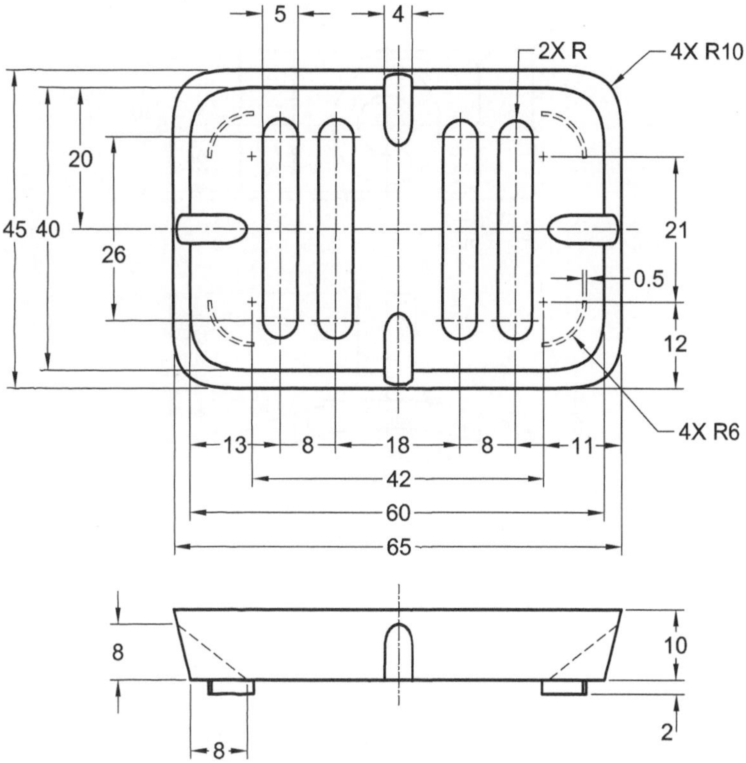

Figure 11-118 Views and dimensions for Exercise 1

Exercise 2

Create the surface model shown in Figure 11-119. The drawing views and dimensions of the surface model are shown in Figure 11-120. Assume the missing dimensions. After creating the surface model, save it with the name *c11exr2.prt* at the location *\NX\c11.*

(Expected time: 45 min)

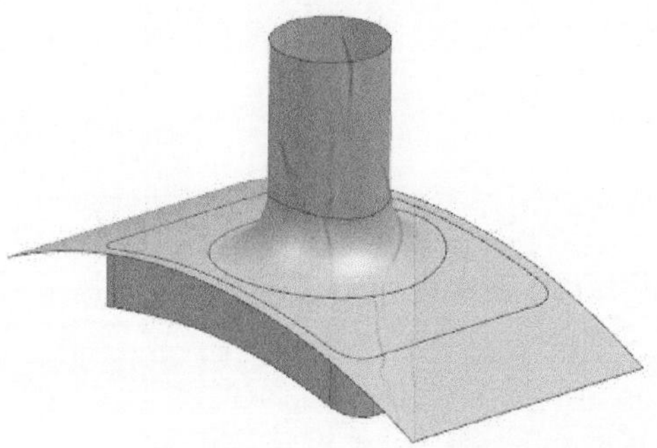

Figure 11-119 Surface model for Exercise 2

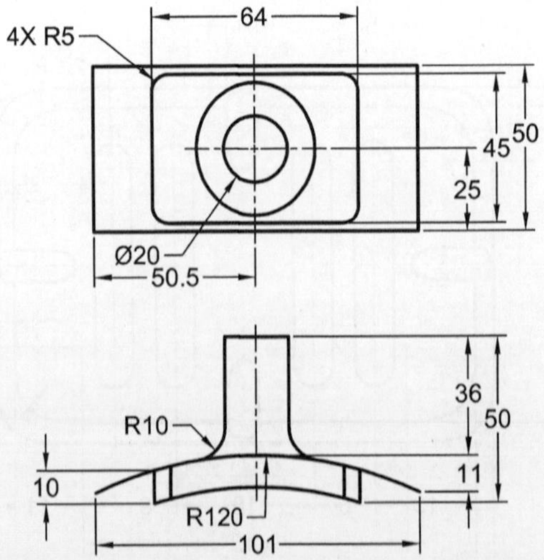

Figure 11-120 Views and dimensions for Exercise 2

Answers to Self-Evaluation Test

1. Intersection Curve, 2. Rolling Ball, 3. Radial Planes, 4. two, **5. Section Curve, 6. Create Curves to Bridge Gaps, 7. Project Curve, 8. Face Blend, 9.** T, **10.** T

Chapter 12

Generating, Editing, and Dimensioning the Drawing Views

Learning Objectives

After completing this chapter, you will be able to:

- *Understand the Drafting environment*
- *Understand the types of views that can be generated in NX*
- *Generate drawing views*
- *Manipulate drawing views*
- *Add annotation to drawing views*
- *Modify annotations created in drawing views*
- *Generate exploded drawing views of an assembly*
- *Create tabular notes and add them to the Tables palette*
- *Insert images into a drawing sheet*
- *Print drawing sheets*
- *Plot drawing sheets*

THE DRAFTING ENVIRONMENT

After creating a solid model or an assembly, you need to generate its drawing views and apply dimensions to it. In NX, there is a separate environment called Drafting environment for generating drawing views and orthographic projections. This environment contains tools to generate, edit, and modify drawing views.

INVOKING THE DRAFTING ENVIRONMENT

You can invoke the Drafting environment by using two methods:

1. Using the drawing template from the **New** dialog box.
2. Invoking the Drafting environment in the current part file.

These methods are discussed next.

Invoking the Drafting Environment Using the Drawing Template from the New Dialog Box

To invoke the Drafting environment, choose the **New** button from the **Standard** group of the **Home** tab; the **New** dialog box will be displayed. Choose the **Drawing** tab in the dialog box; the drawing templates will be displayed in the **Templates** rollout, as shown in Figure 12-1. These drawing templates are used to start a new drawing file in the Drafting environment for generating drawing views.

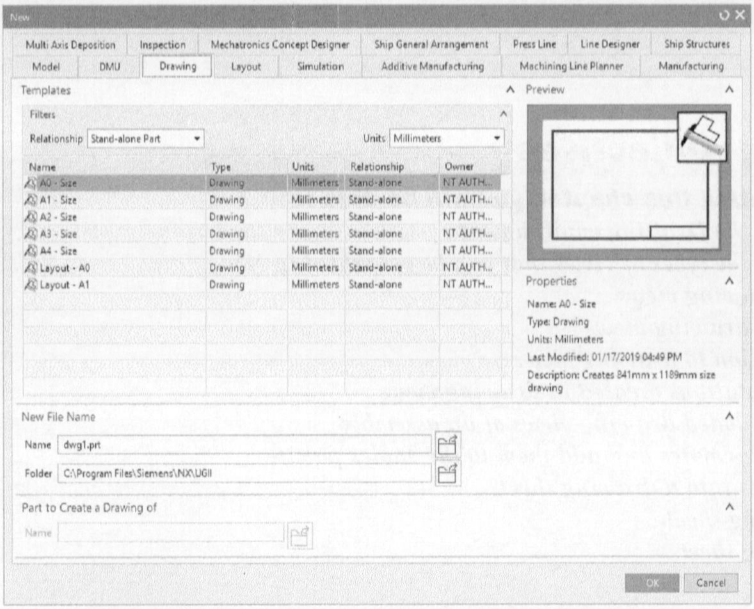

*Figure 12-1 The **Drawing** tab in the **New** dialog box*

These drawing templates are arranged according to the sheet size (A0, A1, A2, A3, and A4) in the **Drawing** tab. There are two types of templates for each sheet size: stand-alone and model based. If you select the stand-alone template, then the drawing will be created in a separate part file, without any reference to an existing part file. If you select the model based template, the drawing will be created with reference to an existing part file.

To create a drawing for a model based template, select the **Reference Existing Part** option from the **Relationship** drop-down list and then select the required drawing template. Now, you need to specify the part file for which you want to generate the drawing views. To do so, choose the button on the right of the **Name** edit box in the **Part to create a drawing of** rollout; the **Select Master Part** dialog box will be displayed. Choose the **Open** button; the **Part Name** dialog box will be displayed. Next, browse to the folder where you have saved the part file. Now, select the file and choose the **OK** button; the selected part file will be added to the **File Name** list of the **Loaded Parts** sub-rollout of the **Select Master Part** dialog box. Next, choose the **OK** button from this dialog box; the **New** dialog box will be displayed. Also, the name of the part file and its location will be displayed in the **New File Name** rollout. Choose the **OK** button from the dialog box; the Drafting environment along with the **Populate Title Block** dialog box will be displayed, refer to Figure 12-2.

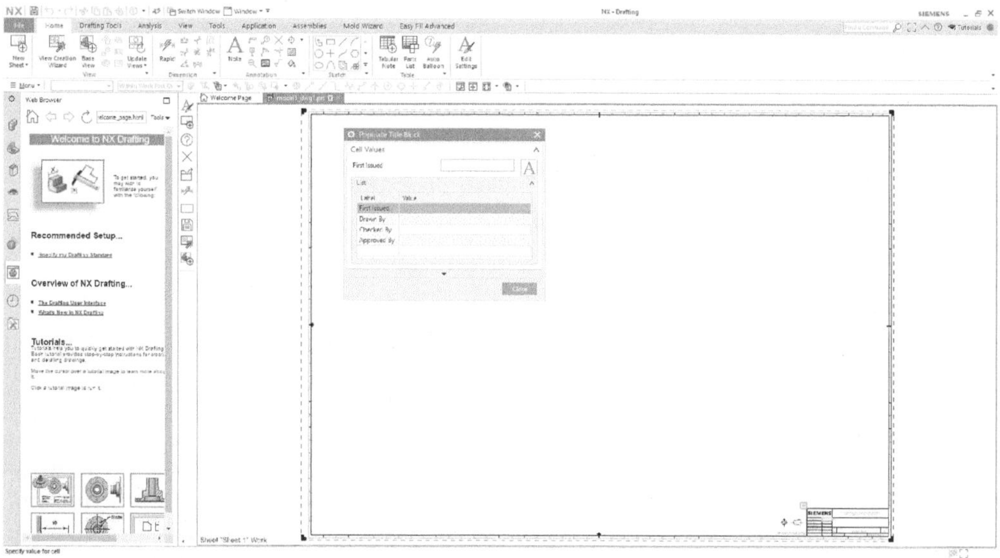

***Figure 12-2** The Drafting environment with the **Populate Title Block** dialog box displayed*

Specify the data in the **Populate Title Block** dialog box and choose the **Close** button; the **View Creation Wizard** dialog box will be displayed to generate the drawing views. The details about generation of the drawing views are discussed later in the chapter.

Invoking the Drafting Environment in the Current Part File

To invoke the Drafting environment in the current part file, open the part file and choose the **Drafting** tool from the **Design** group in the **Application** tab of the **Ribbon.** On doing so, the Drafting environment along with the **Sheet** dialog box will be displayed, refer to Figure 12-3. Note that at this stage some of the tools of the Drafting environment will not be active. These tools will become active only after generating the first drawing view. You need to set the required parameters in the **Sheet** dialog box before generating and dimensioning the drawing views. These parameters will then be used to generate and dimension the drawing views. Also, you can modify the defined parameters after generating and dimensioning the drawing views.

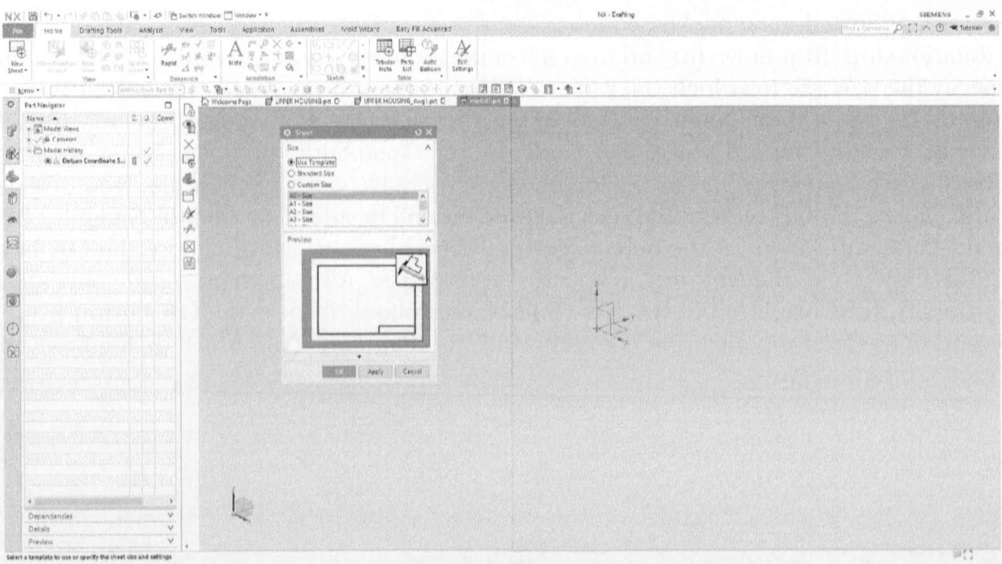

*Figure 12-3 The Drafting environment window of NX with the **Sheet** dialog box displayed*

The options in various rollouts of the **Sheet** dialog box are discussed next.

Size Rollout

This rollout is used to define the sheet size and the scale value of the drawing views. The options in this rollout are discussed next.

Use Template

If you select this radio button, the Drawing Sheet Templates list box and the **Preview** rollout will be displayed in the dialog box. You can select the required drawing template from the Drawing Sheet Templates list box. On doing so, the preview of the selected drawing template will be displayed in the **Preview** rollout.

Standard Size

If you select this radio button, the **Size** and **Scale** drop-down lists are displayed in the **Size** rollout. You can select the required drawing sheet size from the **Size** drop-down list. If you need to scale the drawing sheet, then select the required scale value from the **Scale** drop-down list.

Custom Size

This radio button is used to specify the user-defined drawing sheet size. If you select this radio button, the **Height**, **Length**, and **Scale** edit boxes will be displayed. You can enter the height and length values for a drawing sheet in the respective edit boxes. Also, if scaling is required, then select the required scale value from the **Scale** drop-down list.

Name Rollout

You can enter a name for the drawing sheet in the **Drawing Sheet Name** edit box of the **Sheet** dialog box.

Settings Rollout

This rollout is used to set units and projection method for generating drawing views. The dimensions of these views can be set in millimeters or inches by selecting the **Millimeters** or **Inches** radio button in the **Units** area of the **Settings** rollout. Similarly, you can set the first angle or third angle projection method for generating the drawing views by choosing the **1st Angle Projection** or **3rd Angle Projection** button, respectively in the **Projection** area of the **Settings** rollout. To start the view creation automatically, select the **Always Start View Creation** check box in this rollout. Next, select the **View Creation Wizard** or the **Base View Command** radio button. By default, the **View Creation Wizard** radio button is selected.

After setting the required parameters in the **Sheet** dialog box, choose the **OK** button; the **View Creation Wizard** dialog box will be displayed. In case you select the **Base View Command** radio button, then the **Base View** dialog box will be displayed and the base view of the part will be attached to the cursor, refer to Figure 12-4. Also, you will be prompted to specify the location to place the view. Specify the location to place the drawing view on the sheet; the drawing view (Top view) will be placed at the specified location and the **Projected View** dialog box will be displayed. Also, the projected view of the model will be attached to the cursor, depending upon the movement of the cursor. Specify the location to place the first projected view. Similarly, place all the required projected views on the sheet and then exit the dialog box by choosing the **Close** button.

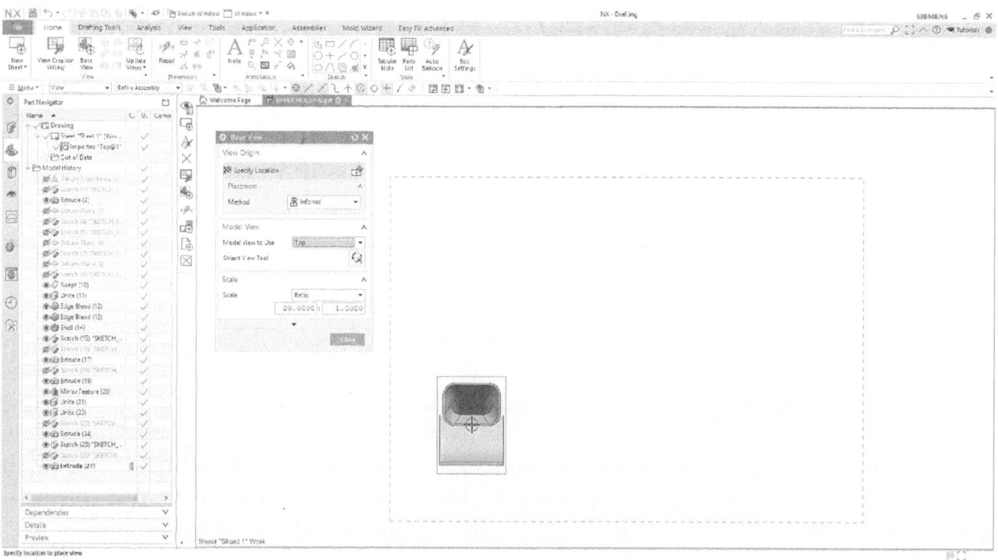

*Figure 12-4 The Drafting environment of NX with the **Base View** dialog box displayed*

Note

*1. If the display of the grid is turned on, choose **Menu > Preferences > Grid** from the **Top Border Bar**; the **Grid Preferences** dialog box will be displayed. Clear the **Show Grid** check box from the **Grid Settings** rollout and choose the **OK** button to exit the dialog box; the display of the grid will be turned off.*

*2. To change the background to white, choose **Menu > Preferences > Visualization** from the **Top Border Bar**; the **Visualization Preferences** dialog box will be displayed. In this dialog box, choose the **Color>Drawing Layouts** tab, select the **Monochrome Display** check box, and then select the **Background** swatch from the **Drawing and Layout Colors** rollout; the **Color** dialog box will be displayed. Select the white swatch from this dialog box, and then choose the **OK** button twice.*

EDITING THE DRAWING SHEET PARAMETERS IN THE DRAFTING ENVIRONMENT

After invoking the Drafting environment, you can edit the parameters of the drawing sheet in the **Sheet** dialog box by following the steps discussed next. Right-click on the drawing limits border represented by the dashed lines and choose the **Edit Sheet** option from the shortcut menu; the **Sheet** dialog box will be displayed. You can change the parameters in the **Sheet** dialog box and choose the **OK** button to reflect the changes.

INVOKING THE DRAFTING TOOLS

After invoking the Drafting environment, you need to invoke the drafting toolbars. By default, the **View** and **Dimension** groups are available in the **Home** tab of the **Ribbon**. The tools in the **View** and **Dimension** groups are used to generate the drawing views and add dimensions to them.

TYPES OF DRAWING VIEWS IN NX

In the Drafting environment of NX, you can generate different types of drawing views for a component or an assembly. The drawing views that can be generated in the Drafting environment of NX are discussed next.

Base View

The Base View is the parent drawing view generated from the model or assembly, which is currently open in the Modeling environment. This is an independent view which is not affected by the changes made in any other view in the drawing sheet. Most of the other views are generated by using the Base view as the parent drawing view. If the dimensional aspects of the parent model are modified, all the views need to be updated manually by right-clicking on the view boundary and choosing the **Update** option from the shortcut menu.

In NX, you can also create a drawing view from a model or an assembly, which is not currently opened in the Modeling environment. This enables you to have drawing views of different models without opening the corresponding models in the Modeling environment.

Projected View

The projected views are the orthographic projections generated from the base view. These views are used to understand the model from the drawing views in terms of shape and size.

Detail View

The detail view is used to magnify the congested area of the drawing view. The congested area is scaled to a greater value and elaborately defined at the side of the same drawing view. The scale value of the detail view will be higher than the one specified for the drawing view.

Section View

The section view is generated by chopping an existing view using a section line at any cross-section and viewing the parent view normal to it. The section views are used to display the internal features of the model at any cross-section.

Auxiliary View

The auxiliary view is generated by projecting the section exactly normal to the cutting member. This view is used to show the true dimensions of the features that are created on an inclined face. For example, an inclined circular hole feature will be displayed as an elliptical cross-section when viewed from the side. This error in viewing can be eliminated by viewing the same hole feature in a normal direction to its center axis. In NX, there is no separate tool for generating an auxiliary view. Instead, the **Projected View** tool can be used to generate the auxiliary view.

Half-Section View

The half-section view is generated by chopping a section of the drawing view and viewing the model normal to the cross-section. In NX, you can use the **Half** option to generate a section of a required length along the cutting plane. This section can be trimmed to a user-defined value when it is formed.

Revolved Section View

The revolved section view is generated for drawing views that can be revolved about an axis. Here, the first cutting plane is placed stationary at the base point and the second cutting plane is rotated at an angle around it.

Break-Out Section View

The break-out section view is used to remove a part of the existing view and display the area of the model or an assembly that lies behind the removed portion.

Broken View

The broken view is one in which a user-defined portion of the drawing view is removed, keeping the ends of the drawing view intact. The broken view is used for displaying the drawing view that has a high length to width ratio. By generating the broken view, you can shorten the length or width of the drawing view and accommodate it in the drawing sheet as a drawing view of normal size.

GENERATING DRAWING VIEWS

In NX, the base view is generated as the parent view from the model or an assembly. The other views are generated and projected directly from the base view. The steps for generating all the nine types of drawing views are discussed next.

Generating Views Using the View Creation Wizard Tool

Ribbon:	Home > View > View Creation Wizard
Menu:	Insert > View > View Creation Wizard

View Creation Wizard

In NX, you can generate all the drawing views of a model simultaneously. To generate the drawing views, choose the **View Creation Wizard** tool from the **View** group of the **Home** tab, refer to Figure 12-5; the **View Creation Wizard** dialog box with the **Part** page will be displayed. Figure 12-6 shows the wizard with a part file selected.

*Figure 12-5 The **View** group in the **Home** tab*

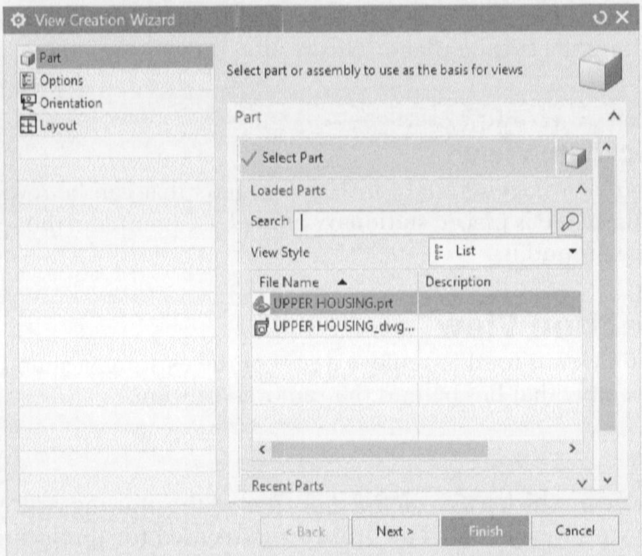

*Figure 12-6 The **Part** page of the **View Creation Wizard***

If you want to select another part, choose the **Open** button; the **Part Name** dialog box will be displayed. Next, browse to the part that you need to select and double-click on it; the part will be displayed in the **Loaded Parts** sub-rollout.

Options Page

When you choose the **Next** button from the **Part** page, the **Options** page will be displayed, as shown in Figure 12-7. The options in this page are discussed next.

View Boundary

The options in this drop-down list are used to specify the type of view boundary. If you select the **Automatic** option, the view boundary will automatically change with respect to the modified view. However, on selecting the **Manual** option, you need to manually modify the boundary with respect to the modified view.

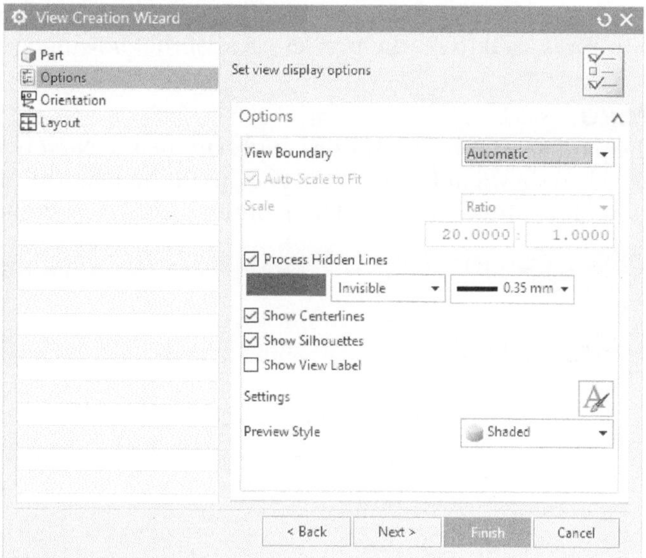

*Figure 12-7 The **Options** page of the **View Creation Wizard***

Auto-Scale to Fit

This check box is available only when the **Manual** option is selected from the **View Boundary** drop-down list. On selecting this check box, the drawing views will be scaled automatically to the size of the sheet.

Scale

This drop-down list is used to specify the scaling factor of the drawing views. Note that this drop-down list is active only when you clear the **Auto-Scale to Fit** check box.

Process Hidden Lines

On selecting this check box, the hidden lines are displayed as dashed lines. If you clear this check box, the hidden lines are displayed as continuous lines.

Show Centerlines

If you select this check box, the centerline symbol is displayed on the circular edges of the view.

Show Silhouettes

This check box is selected by default. As a result, the silhouette edges are displayed in the drawing view.

Show View Label

If you select this check box, the view labels are displayed based on the settings in the **Drafting Preferences** dialog box. You will learn about view labels later in the chapter.

Settings

On choosing this button, the **Settings** dialog box is displayed. You can specify the additional view settings in this dialog box.

Preview Style

This drop-down list is used to set the preview style of the drawing views.

Orientation Page

After specifying the parameters on the **Options** page, choose the **Next** button; the **Orientation** page will be displayed, as shown in Figure 12-8. The options in this page are used to specify the standard orientation of the drawing views. These options are discussed next.

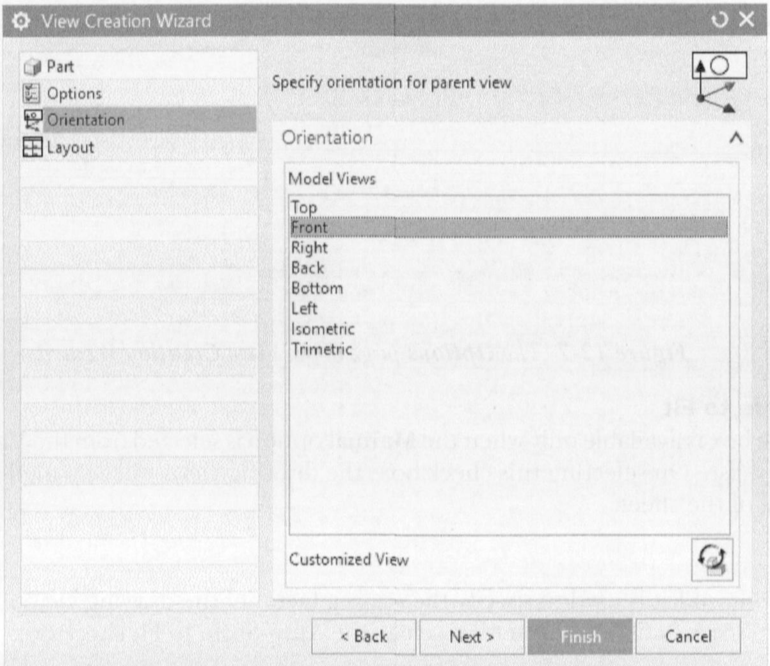

*Figure 12-8 The **Orientation** page of the **View Creation Wizard***

Model Views

This display box consists of various options used for generating views in the standard orientations.

Customized View

When you choose this button, the **Orient View Tool** dialog box and the **Orient View** window are displayed, refer to Figures 12-9 and 12-10. The **Orient View** window displays the part or the assembly that you had selected earlier. You can use the options available in the **Orient View Tool** dialog box to set the orientation of the model. You can also rotate the model using the middle mouse button. After setting the orientation, close the **Orient View Tool** dialog box by choosing the **OK** button from it.

Layout Page

When you choose the **Next** button from the **Orientation** page, the **Layout** page is displayed, as shown in Figure 12-11. The **Parent View** button located in the middle represents the orientation of the model that is selected in the **Model Views** list box. You can select multiple views from the **Layout** page. The options in this page are discussed next.

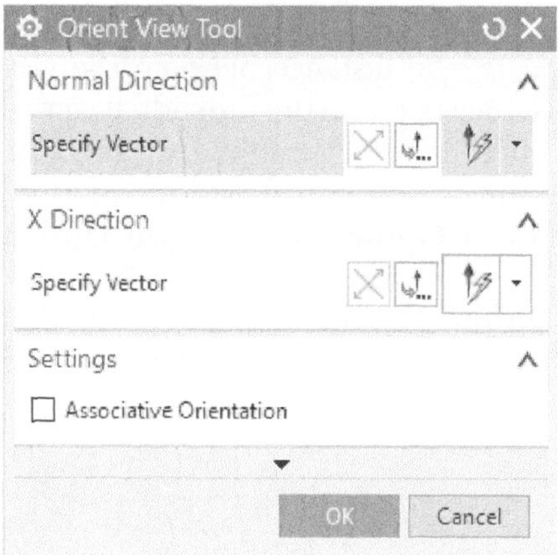

Figure 12-9 *The* ***Orient View Tool*** *dialog box*

Figure 12-10 *The* ***Orient View*** *window*

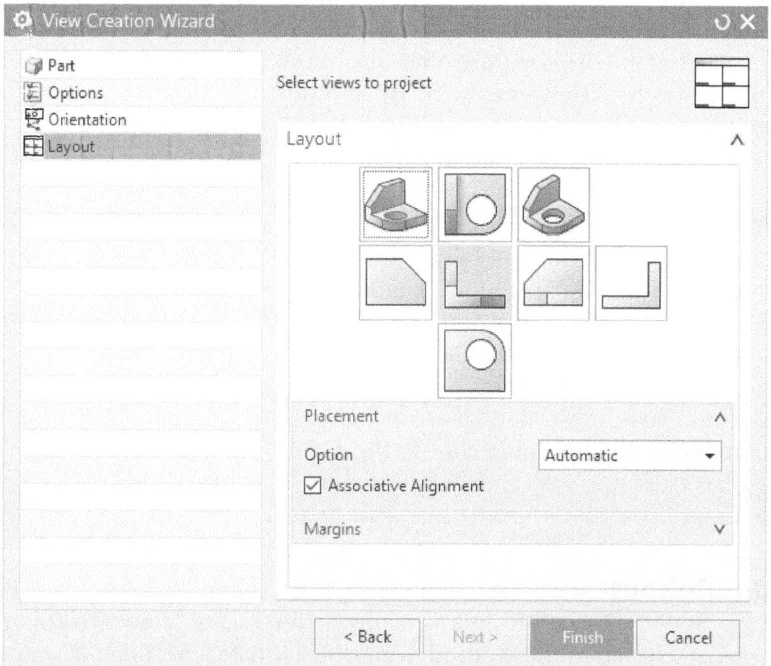

Figure 12-11 *The* ***Layout*** *page of the* ***View Creation Wizard***

Placement

The options in this sub-rollout are discussed next.

The **Option** drop-down list is used to define the location of the layout to be placed in the sheet. By default, the **Automatic** option is selected in this drop-down list. As a result, the layout is placed at the center of the sheet. You can select the **Manual** option to manually specify the location of the layout within the sheet. The **Associative Alignment** check box is selected by default. As a result, all the views are aligned associatively.

Margins

The options in this sub-rollout are used to specify the distance between the views. The **Between Views** edit box is used to specify the distance between the individual views. The **To Border** edit box is used to specify the distance between the view and the border of the sheet. Note that the options in this sub-rollout will become active only if you choose the **Manual** option from the **View Boundary** drop-down list in the **Options** rollout of the **Options** page.

After specifying all the settings, choose the **Finish** button from the wizard to place the views in the drawing sheet.

Generating the Base View

Ribbon:	Home > View > Base View
Menu:	Insert > View > Base

Base View

As mentioned earlier, the base view is created as the parent drawing view from a model or an assembly. To generate the base view of a model or an assembly, choose the **Base View** tool from the **View** group of the **Home** tab; the **Base View** dialog box will be displayed, as shown in Figure 12-12. The options in this dialog box are discussed next.

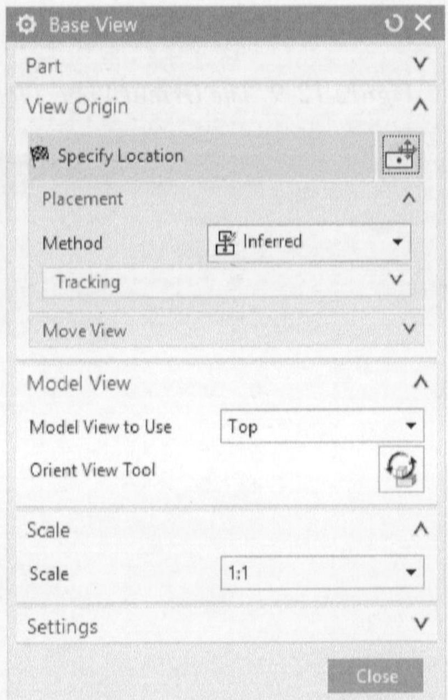

*Figure 12-12 The **Base View** dialog box*

Part Rollout

This rollout is used to select components for drafting. In this rollout, the **File Name** list area in the **Loaded Parts** sub-rollout lists the components that were opened in the current NX session before opening the new drawing sheet. You can select these components to create a base view. The **Recent Parts** sub-rollout lists the recently opened components. You can also choose the **Open** button in the **Part** rollout to select a new component to create a base view.

View Origin Rollout

By default, the **Specify Location** area remains active in the **View Origin** rollout. Also, the **Inferred** option is selected in the **Method** drop-down list. As a result, you can place the drawing view anywhere in the drawing sheet by clicking in the drawing sheet. You can specify the method of placement and the alignment of the new base view by selecting an option from the **Method** and **Alignment** drop-down lists, respectively. Note that the **Alignment** drop-down list will be displayed when you select an option other than the **Inferred** and **Hinge** option from the **Method** drop-down list. The options other than the **Inferred** option in the **Method** drop-down list will be activated only if any view is already placed in the drawing sheet. To place and align a base view horizontally to another view, select the **Horizontal** option from the **Method** drop-down list. Next, you need to specify the alignment of the resulting view. To do so, select an option from the

Alignment drop-down list. By default, the **To View** option is selected in this drop-down list. As a result, you will be prompted to select a view to which the resulting view has to be aligned. Select a view and place the new base view; the resulting view will be placed and aligned horizontally to the selected view.

To place a view horizontally and align it with respect to the specified point from the model, select the **Horizontal** option from the **Method** drop-down list and then select the **Model Point** option from the **Alignment** drop-down list; the **Specify Stationary View Point** area will be highlighted and you will be prompted to specify the point to which the resulting view has to be aligned. Specify the point from the view and place the new base view; the resulting view will be placed horizontally and aligned with respect to the selected point.

To place a view horizontally and align it with respect to two points, select the **Horizontal** option from the **Method** drop-down list. Next, select the **Point to Point** option from the **Alignment** drop-down list; the **Specify Stationary View Point** area will be highlighted and you will be prompted to specify the stationary point. Specify a point from the view; the **Specify Current View Point** area will be highlighted and you will be prompted to specify a point to which the resulting view has to be aligned. Specify a point from the view and place the new base view; the resulting view will be placed horizontally and will be aligned with respect to the two points.

Similarly, you can select other options from the **Method** drop-down list and specify its alignments by selecting different options from the **Alignment** drop-down list.

By default, the **Cursor Tracking** check box is clear in the **Tracking** sub-rollout. If you select this check box, the **Offset**, **X**, and **Y** edit boxes will be displayed in this sub-rollout. You can specify the location of the current drawing view by specifying values in these edit boxes.

You can also change the location of an existing created drawing view. To do so, click on the **Specify Screen Position** area in the **Move View** sub-rollout; you will be prompted to drag the view. Drag an existing drawing view and place it at the required location.

Model View Rollout

By default, the **Top** option is selected in the **Model View to Use** drop-down list. As a result, top view will be created. You can create front view, right side view, left hand side view, and so on by selecting the respective option from the **Model View to Use** drop-down list.

To change the orientation of the parent model, choose the **Orient View Tool** button from the **Model View** rollout; the **Orient View Tool** dialog box and the **Orient View** window will be displayed along with the parent model. You can dynamically reorient the model by pressing the middle mouse button and dragging the mouse. To accept the new orientation, press the middle mouse button.

Scale Rollout

This rollout is used to select the required scale ratio value from the **Scale** drop-down list.

Settings Rollout

This rollout is very useful for drafting the assembly with the desired effect. To do so, choose the **Settings** button; the **Base View Settings** dialog box will be displayed. You can use the options in the dialog box to set the appearance of the component, edges, threads and so on. The **Hidden Components** sub-rollout will be displayed while generating a drawing view of an assembly. You can hide the selected components of the assembly using the **Hidden Components** sub-rollout. To do so, click on the **Select Object** area in the **Hidden Components** sub-rollout; you will be prompted to select the components to hide. Select the components from the view; the selected components will not be displayed in the resultant view and the name of those components will be displayed in the list of the **Hidden Components** sub-rollout. To redisplay the component, select the name of that component from the list of the **Hidden Components** sub-rollout; the **Remove** button will be activated. Next, choose this button; the component will be redisplayed.

Standard parts such as nuts, bolts, washers, pins, and so on should be excluded from sectioning in the drawing. To exclude the selected part from sectioning, click on the **Select Object** area in the **Non-Sectioned** sub-rollout; you will be prompted to select components. Select the components from the resultant view; the selected components will not be considered for sectioning in the section view and the name of the selected components will be displayed in the list of the **Non-Sectioned** sub-rollout. To redisplay the component, select the name of that component from the list of the **Non-Sectioned** sub-rollout; the **Remove** button will be activated. Choose the **Remove** button; the component will be redisplayed. The **Section View** tool is discussed later in this chapter.

Note

*If the borders are generated along with the drawing views and you do not want them to be displayed, choose **Menu > Preferences > Drafting** from the **Top Border Bar**; the **Drafting Preferences** dialog box will be displayed. Expand the **Drawing View** node from the dialog box and select the **Workflow** sub-node from the displayed list. Now, clear the **Display** check box from the **Border** rollout. Next, choose the **OK** button; the borders will be cleared from the generated drawing views.*

Generating the Orthographic Drawing Views Using the Projected View Tool

Ribbon:	Home > View > Projected View
Menu:	Insert > View > Projected

The **Projected View** tool is used to generate the projection views of a model from the base view. After positioning the base view in the drawing sheet by using the **Base View** tool, the **Projected View** dialog box is displayed automatically and the projected view of the model is attached to the cursor and displayed in the drawing window. The display of hinge line from the base view confirms that the **Projected View** tool has been invoked. Apart from the base view, you can also generate the projection views from an existing drawing view. In the aforesaid case, you need to select the parent view and invoke the **Projected View** tool by choosing it from the **View** group of the **Home** tab. On doing so, the preview of the projected view will be displayed in the graphics window. Also, the **Projected View** dialog box will be displayed, as shown in Figure 12-13. You will notice that the hinge line is attached to the parent view and the appearance of the projection view changes as you move the cursor around the parent view. To place the projection view in the drawing sheet, click the left mouse button at the required location.

Hinge Line Rollout

By default, the **Inferred** option is selected in the **Vector Option** drop-down list. As a result, the hinge line rotates as you move the cursor around the parent view. Also, the appearance of the projection view changes according to the movement of the cursor. If you choose the **Reverse Projected Direction** button in this rollout, then the projection direction of the view will be reversed. You can generate any number of projection views at a time using the **Projected View** tool. For placing the generated projection view, click the left mouse button. Next, exit the **Projected View** tool by pressing the ESC key or the middle mouse button. Figure 12-14 shows the projected drawing views, hinge line, unpositioned drawing view, and drawing limits. If you select the **Associative** check box, the projected view will be associatively aligned to the base view.

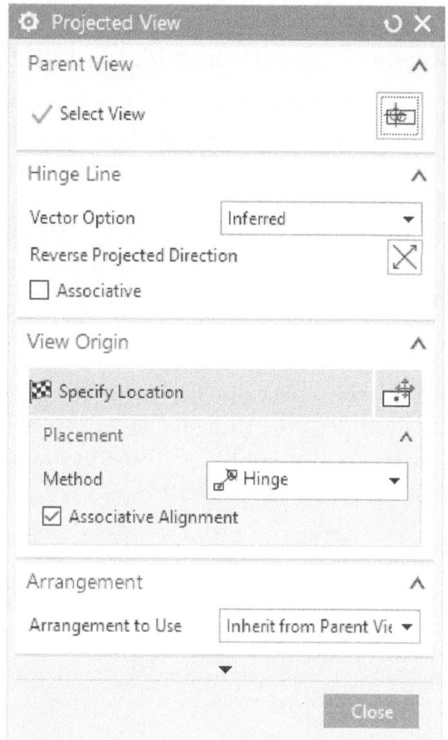

*Figure 12-13 The **Projected View** dialog box*

To create an auxiliary view with respect to the defined hinge line by using the **Projected View** tool, select the **Defined** option from the **Vector Option** drop-down list in this rollout; the **Specify Vector** area will be activated. Also, you will be prompted to select objects to infer vector. Specify the direction vector in the drawing sheet; the auxiliary view with respect to the direction vector specified will be displayed. Click at the required location in the drawing sheet to place the drawing view.

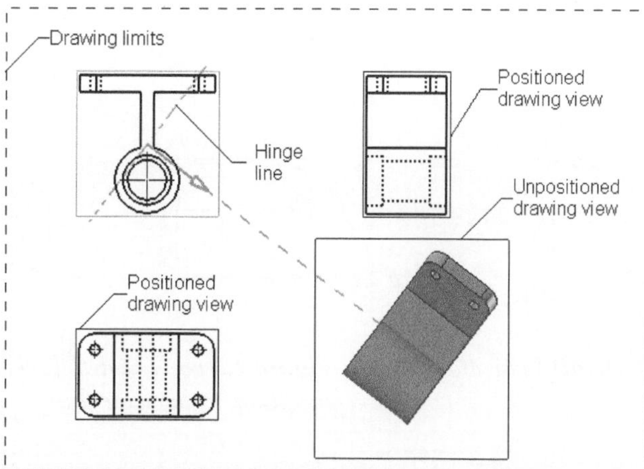

Figure 12-14 The hinge line emerging from the base view

The remaining options in this dialog box are the same as those of the **Base View** tool, as discussed earlier.

Generating the Detail View Using the Detail View Tool

Ribbon:	Home > View > Detail View
Menu:	Insert > View > Detail

The **Detail View** tool is used to generate the detail views for a drawing view. To do so, choose the **Detail View** tool from the **View** group of the **Home** tab; the **Detail View** dialog box will be displayed, as shown in Figure 12-15.

In the **Detail View** dialog box, select the **Circular** option from the Type drop-down list if it is not already selected; you will be prompted to select an object to infer point. Specify the center point for drawing the detail view boundary; you will be prompted to select an object to infer point. Specify the radius point. After you specify the radius for the circular boundary, the detail view will be generated and you will be prompted to specify location to place view. You can also define the scale value for the detail view from the **Scale** drop-down list in the **Scale** rollout. Next, position it in the drawing sheet by pressing the left mouse button. The detail view representing the cooling fins of the piston is generated and placed in the drawing sheet, along with the label, as shown in Figure 12-16.

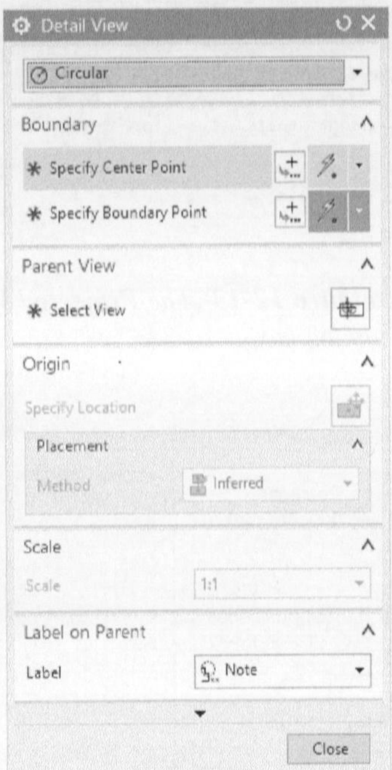

*Figure 12-15 The **Detail View** dialog box*

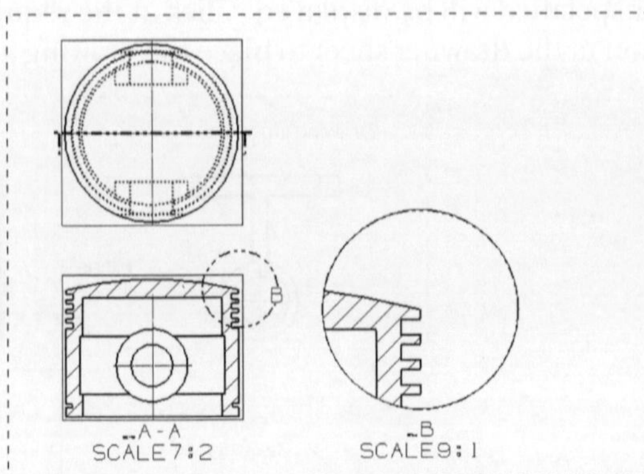

Figure 12-16 The detail view generated for the piston to show the fins

Note

*You can select a placement option from the **Method** drop-down list in the **Placement** sub-rollout. If you select a placement method other than the **Inferred** method, the **Associative Alignment** check box will be active. You can select this check box to align the detail view with one of the existing views in the drawing sheet.*

Instead of a circular boundary, you can define a rectangular boundary by using the **Rectangle by Corners** or **Rectangle by Center and Corner** option from the Type drop-down list. The process for generating the detail view using the rectangular boundary is the same as that of the circular boundary.

Label on Parent Rollout

The options in the **Label** drop-down list of the **Label on Parent** rollout are used for specifying the label style of the parent view. You can use any of these label styles to label the parent view. These label styles are discussed next.

None

If you select this option from the **Label** drop-down list, no boundary will be created in the parent view.

Circle

If you select this option from the **Label** drop-down list, a circular boundary will be created in the parent view.

Note

If you select this option from the **Label** drop-down list, a circular boundary with label, but without any leader, will be created in the parent view.

Label

If you select this option from the **Label** drop-down list, a circular boundary with label, and along with the leader, will be created in the parent view.

Embedded

If you select this option from the **Label** drop-down list, a circular boundary will be created with two arrow heads. Also, the label will be placed between these arrow heads in the parent view.

Boundary

If you select this option from the **Label** drop-down list, a circular boundary or rectangular boundary will be created in the parent view. This boundary depends upon the option selected in the drop-down list of the **Type** rollout.

Label on Boundary

If you select this option from the **Label** drop-down list, a copy of view boundary and the label is displayed.

Editing the Detail View Label

The detail view label generated at the bottom of the detail view can be modified according to your requirement. To do so, right-click on the detail view label and then choose the **Settings** option from the shortcut menu displayed; the **Settings** dialog box will be displayed. Choose the **Detail** node from the **Settings** dialog box, refer to Figure 12-17. To change the label name of the detail view, select the **Label** option of the **Detail** node. Next, select the **Letter** option from the **View Label Type** drop-down list in the **Label** rollout if it is not already selected; the **Letter** text box in the **View Label** option of the **Common** node of the **Settings** dialog box will be enabled. Enter a name in the **Letter** text box and choose the **Apply** button for reflecting the changes. Next, choose the **OK** button.

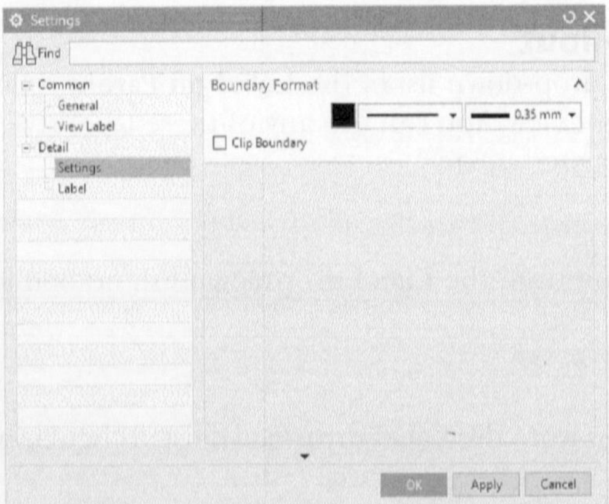

Figure 12-17 The ***Settings*** *dialog box*

Adding Prefix Text to the View Label

To define the prefix text for the view label, enter the text in the **Prefix** text box of the **Label** rollout in the **Label** option of the **Detail** node. The prefix text may contain alphabets, numeric values, and also special characters. A combination of these three is also possible. The label letter size can be modified by entering the scale value in the **Character Height Factor** edit box. The label created in the parent view is called the parent label. The options in the **Label on Parent** sub-rollout are used for defining the letter style of the parent label with respect to the detailing boundary specified.

If you require a prefix text for the parent label, enter text in the **Parent Label Prefix** text box in the **Label on Parent** sub-rollout. You can align the scale value above, below, after or before the label name by selecting the **Above**, **Below**, **After**, or **Before** options, respectively from the **Position** drop-down list in the **Scale** rollout.

The text for the prefix of the scale value can be entered in the **Prefix** text box in the **Scale** rollout. To change the format of the scale value, you can select the required format option from the **Value Format** drop-down list. To change the size of the scale value, enter the required scale value in the **Character Height Factor** edit box.

Creating a Section Line

Ribbon:	Home > View > Section Line
Menu:	Insert > View > Section Line

The **Section Line** tool is used for creating a section line that can be used for generating section views. To create a section line, choose the **Section Line** tool from **Menu > Insert > View > Section Line** in the **Top Border Bar**; the **Section Line** dialog box will be displayed, refer to Figure 12-18, and you will be prompted to select the view. Select the view;

the sketching environment will be invoked wherein you can draw the section line using the **Profile** tool. Create the section line and exit the sketching environment. Next, choose the **OK** button to close the dialog box. The options in this dialog box are discussed next.

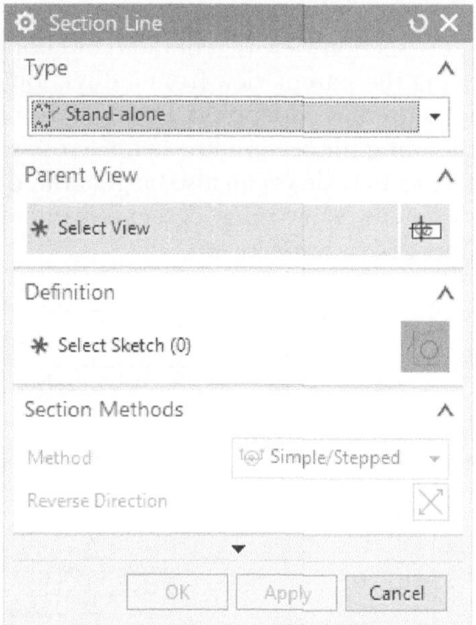

*Figure 12-18 The **Section Line** dialog box*

Parent View Rollout

The **View** button in this rollout is used to select the view in which you can create the section line.

Definition Rollout

You can create and edit a section using the **Sketch** and **Sketch Section** buttons from this rollout.

Section Methods Rollout

The **Method** drop-down list in this rollout consists of various options for specifying the type of section view that will be created from the section line.

Simple/Stepped

On selecting this option from the **Method** drop-down list, the selected drawing view gets fully sectioned.

Half

On selecting this option, you can create the section view with half of the part sectioned and the other half not sectioned.

Settings Rollout

In this rollout, you can set the options for changing the appearance of the section line by using **Settings** button.

Generating Section Views Using the Section View Tool

Ribbon:	Home > View > Section View
Menu:	Insert > View > Section

As mentioned earlier, the section view is generated by chopping the existing view at any cross-section and viewing the parent view from a direction normal to the cross-section. The **Section View** tool is used to generate the section view of a model or an assembly. A section view is generated by defining the section line at any cross-section of the drawing view of a model or an assembly. In NX, section views can also be generated by defining a multi segment section line. Full section views generated by using segmented and multi-segmented section lines are shown in Figures 12-19 and 12-20, respectively.

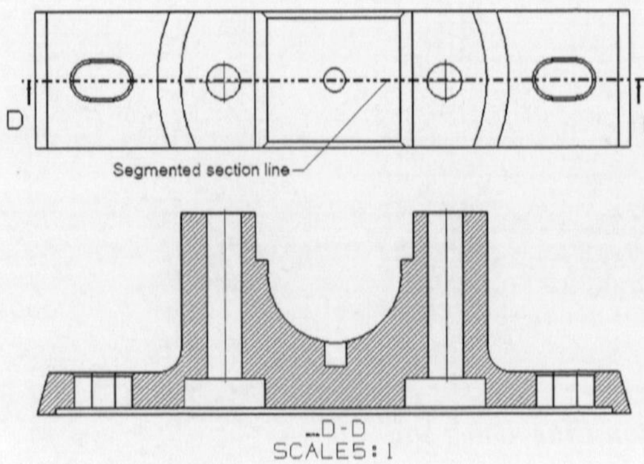

Figure 12-19 Section view generated using a segmented section line

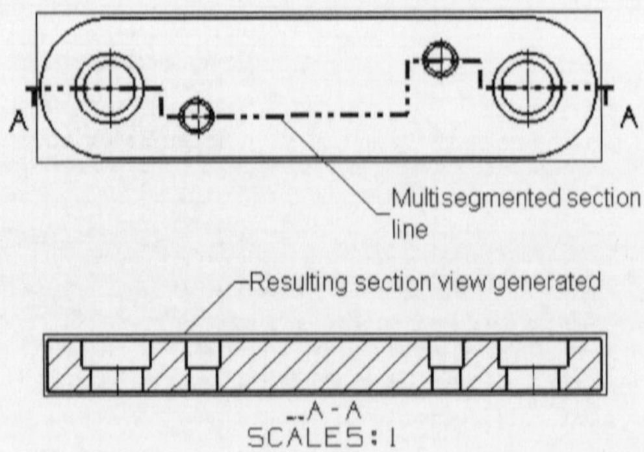

Figure 12-20 Section view generated using multi segmented section line

To generate the section view, choose the **Section** tool from **Menu > Insert > View > Section** in the **Top Border Bar**; the **Section View** dialog box will be displayed, as shown in Figure 12-21. The options in this dialog box are discussed next.

Section Line Rollout

In this rollout, you can set the definition and method for specifying the section line. In the **Definition** drop-down list, two options are available: **Dynamic** and **Select Existing**. These options are discussed next.

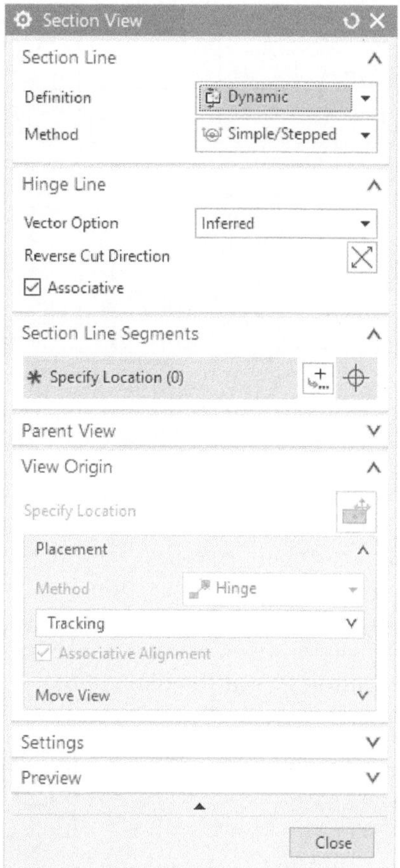

*Figure 12-21 The **Section View** dialog box*

Dynamic

Select this option from the **Definition** drop-down list to create interactive section line. On selecting the **Dynamic** option from the **Definition** drop-down list, the **Method** drop-down list will be available. The options in this drop-down list are discussed next.

Simple/Stepped: This option has been discussed earlier under the **Section Line** tool, refer to Figure 12-22 for simple section.

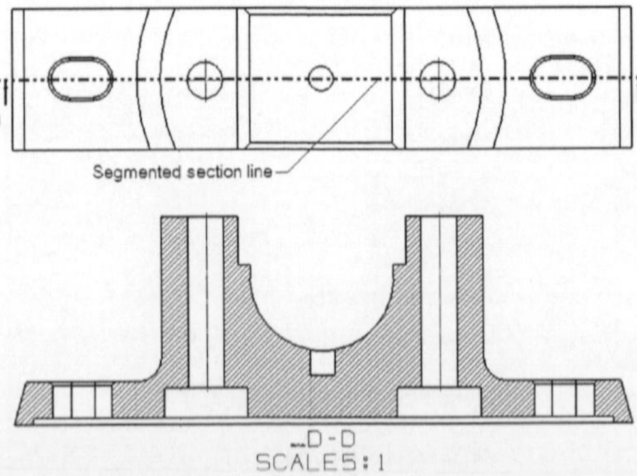

Figure 12-22 The full section view generated for Casting

Half: The **Half** option is used for generating the half section view of a drawing view. This option also helps you to generate section views of the required length from the parent drawing view. To generate the half section view, select the **Half** option from the **Method** drop-down list in the **Section Line** rollout of the **Section View** dialog box. Next, specify points for creating section line and then place the view, refer to Figures 12-23 and 12-24. Choose the **Close** button to exit the dialog box.

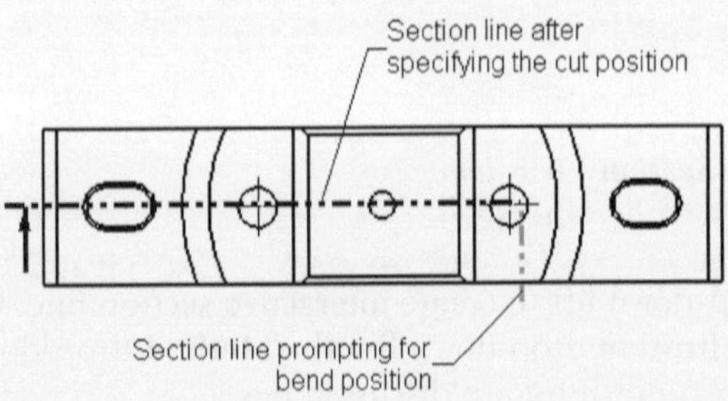

Figure 12-23 Section line prompting for the bend position

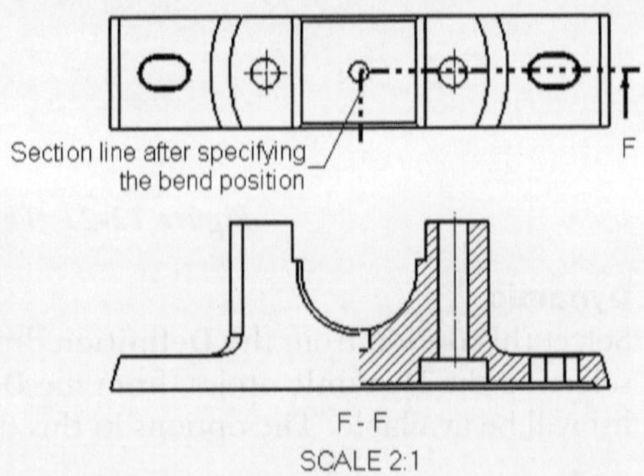

Figure 12-24 Half section view generated

Revolved: As mentioned earlier, a revolved section view is generated for the drawing views that are revolved about an axis. To create a revolved section view for an existing drawing view, select the **Revolved** option from the **Method** drop-down list in the **Section Line** rollout of the **Section View** dialog box; you will be prompted to select the object to infer point. After specifying the rotation point for the section line, you need to fix the angle of the first and second legs of the section line by moving the cursor dynamically. Next, you need to specify the location for placing the revolved section view, refer to Figure 12-25. Click the left mouse button at the required position to place the view; the revolved section view will be generated, refer to Figure 12-26.

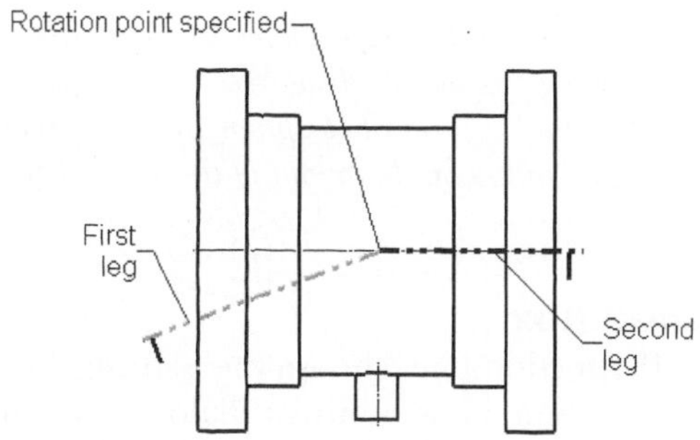

Figure 12-25 Section line after specifying the rotation point

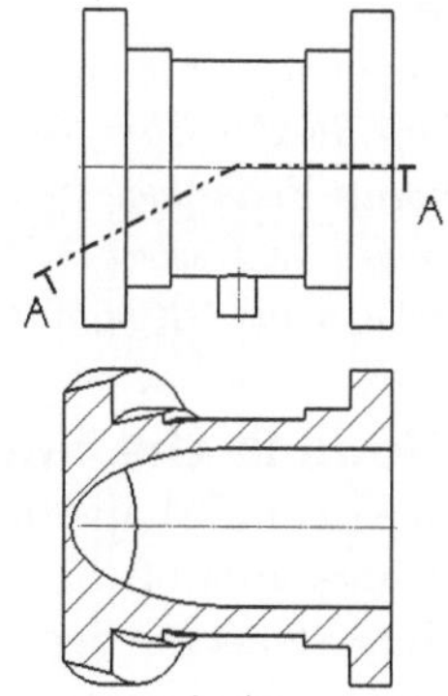

Figure 12-26 The revolved section view

Point to Point: Using this option, you can create a section line of desired shape by specifying points for locating the section line segment.

Select Existing

On selecting this option from the **Definition** drop-down list, you can create the section view by selecting existing section line that is created by using the **Section Line** tool.

Hinge Line Rollout

A hinge line is a reference line used to orient the section view. The options in this rollout are discussed next.

Vector Option

By using the options from this drop-down list, you can set the method for defining the hinge line. The options in this drop-down list are discussed next.

Inferred: On selecting this option, you can create a hinge line that is attached with the section line.

Defined: On selecting this option, you can define a hinge line based on the option selected from the **Specify Vector** list.

Reverse Cut Direction

On choosing this button, you can reverse the viewing direction.

Associative

On selecting this check box, you can create a section view that is associated to the orientation of section line.

Note

*To display the scale value in the view label, choose **Menu > Preferences > Drafting** from the **Top Border Bar**; the **Drafting Preferences** dialog box will be displayed. Now, expand the **Drawing View** node from the dialog box and then choose the **Label** option from the **Section** sub-node. Next, select the **Show View Scale** check box in the **Scale** rollout of the dialog box and then choose the **OK** button.*

Other Options in the Section View Dialog Box

To modify the size and shape of the arrow head of the section line, choose the **Settings** button from the **Settings** area of the **Settings** rollout; the **Section View Settings** dialog box will be displayed. Then, select the **Section Line** node from the **Section View Settings** dialog box. Make necessary changes and choose the **OK** button to reflect the changes. The options in the **Section View Settings** dialog box are discussed later in this chapter.

While generating section views for an assembly, you may need to avoid sectioning the assembled standard parts such as bolt, fasteners, nut, and so on. To avoid sectioning standard parts, choose the **Objects** button from the **Non-Sectioned** Sub-rollout of the **Settings** rollout. Select the components that are not to be sectioned and choose the **Close** button. Note that you need to select these components before placing the section view.

Note

*1. If the hatching is not displayed on the sectioned component, select the section view and then right-click on it. Then, choose the **Settings** option from the shortcut menu displayed; the **Settings** dialog box will be displayed. Next, choose the **Settings** option from the **Section** node of the dialog box and select the **Create Crosshatch** check box of the **Crosshatch** rollout if not selected by default. Next, choose the **OK** button; the hatching pattern will be displayed.*

2. The sectional view previously generated can also be used as a parent view for generating the next section view.

To move the views created earlier, expand the **Move View** sub-rollout of the **View Origin** rollout and then select the **View** button; you will be prompted to move selected view. Select the required view and drag it to the desired location.

Modifying the Properties of the Section View Label

Select the section line and right-click on it; a shortcut menu will be displayed. Choose the **Settings** option from the shortcut menu; the **Settings** dialog box will be displayed. Select the **View Label** option of the dialog box; you can change the label of the section line from the **Format** rollout. To do so, enter the new label name in the **Letter** edit box of the **Format** rollout.

Editing the Section Line

The section line created using the **Section Line** tool can be edited in order to attain perfect results in the section view. To edit the section line, right-click on the section line, and then choose the **Edit** option from the shortcut menu displayed; the **Section Line** dialog box will be displayed. Then, choose the **Sketch Section** button in the **Definition** rollout to edit the sketch of a section line. After editing the sketch, choose the **Finish** button from the **Sketch** group in the **Section Line** tab and then choose the **OK** button from the **Section Line** dialog box.

Editing the Hatching Lines

After creating the section view of a component, the lines that are displayed on the cross-section of the component are known as hatching lines. These lines can be edited in order to attain perfect results in the section view. To edit a hatching line, right-click on it, and then choose the **Edit** option from the shortcut menu; the **Crosshatch** dialog box will be displayed, as shown in Figure 12-27.

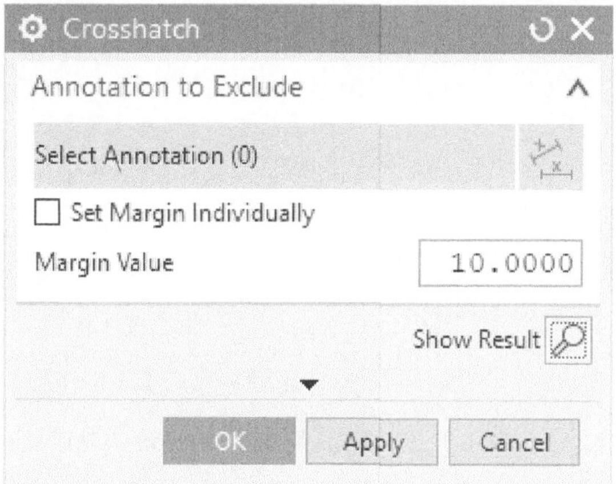

*Figure 12-27 The **Crosshatch** dialog box*

The **Select Annotation** area in the **Annotation to Exclude** rollout of this dialog box is activated by default. As a result, you will be prompted to select annotation to exclude. Select annotations to exclude. You can select the hatch patterns from the **Pattern** drop-down list in the **Settings** rollout. You can change the distance and angle between two hatch lines using the **Distance** and **Angle** edit boxes, respectively. You can change the thickness of the hatch lines using the **Width** drop-down list. Use this dialog box to apply predefined hatch patterns. The **.chx* files are used to save the predefined hatch patterns.

Generating the Break-Out Section View

Ribbon:	Home > View > Break-out Section View
Menu:	Insert > View > Break-out

As mentioned earlier, a break-out section view is generated to display the area of a model or an assembly that lies behind the material removed from the same. Before generating the break-out section, you need to create boundary curves for defining the material to be removed. To do so, right-click on the border of the parent view, and then choose the **Active Sketch View** option from the shortcut menu. Next, you need to draw boundary curves by using the sketching tools from the **Sketch** group. You can create a closed or an open boundary curve. After drawing the boundary curve, choose the **Break-out Section View** tool from the **View** group of the **Home** tab; the **Break-Out Section** dialog box will be displayed, as shown in Figure 12-28.

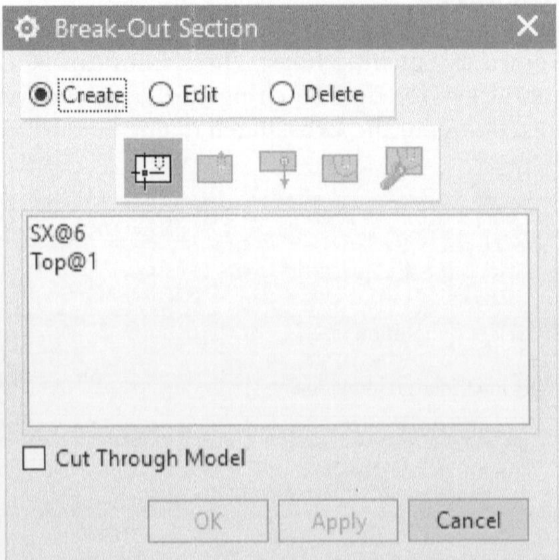

***Figure 12-28** The **Break-Out Section** dialog box*

To edit an already generated break-out section, select the **Edit** radio button. To delete an already defined break-out section view, select the **Delete** radio button. By default, the **Create** radio button is selected in the **Break-Out Section** dialog box. As a result, you can generate a new break-out section. Also, the **Select View** button will be enabled and you will be prompted to select a view for the break-out creation. Select the parent view; all the other buttons except the **Modify Boundary Curves** button will be enabled and you will be prompted to specify the inferred point. Specify the base point by using the curves in the drawing view. The base point is the reference point from which the boundary curve is swept through the model along the extrusion vector direction. Next, you will be prompted to define the extrusion vector. By default, the Z axis is selected for specifying the vector direction. To define the direction, define the vector by selecting the curves from the drawing view or by using the **Inferred Vector** drop-down list. The **Reverse Vector** button is used to reverse the direction of the extrusion vector. If the **Cut Through Model** check box is selected, then the boundary curve will be swept through the model in both directions. Choose the **Select Curves** button; you will be prompted to select a break line near the start of the line. Select the boundary curve created, as shown in Figure 12-29 and choose the **Apply** button; the break-out section view will be generated, as shown in Figure 12-30. Note that if you have created an open boundary curve, then on selecting the curve from the drawing area by using the **Select Curves** button, the **Modify Boundary Curves** button will be enabled. On choosing the **Modify Boundary Curves** button, a construction line connected to the end points of the selected curve will be automatically generated. To modify the boundary of the curves, select the construction line; a vertex point will be created at the position where you click to select the construction line. Drag the vertex point to modify the boundary.

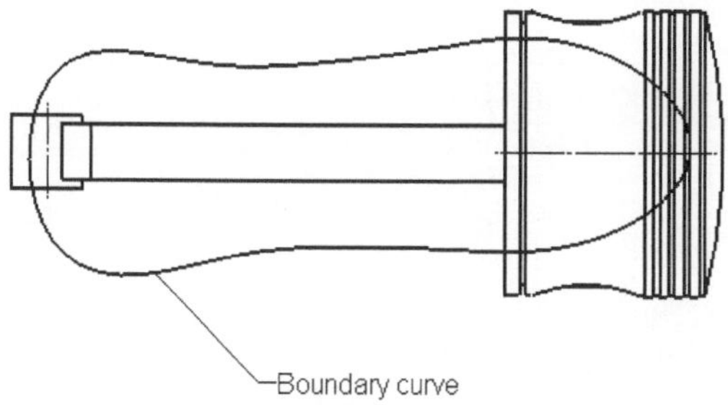

Figure 12-29 The boundary curve defined for generating the break-out section view

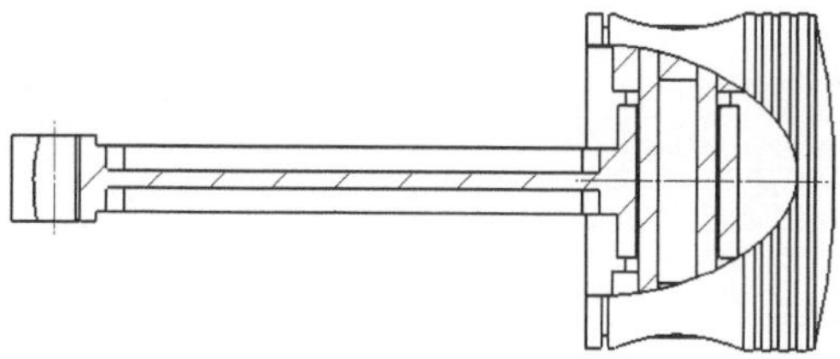

Figure 12-30 The resulting break-out section view

Generating the Broken View

Ribbon:	Home > View > View Break
Menu:	Insert > View > View Break

The **View Break** tool is used to generate a broken view for an existing drawing view that has a high length to width aspect ratio. In such cases, the view is broken at an intermediate distance to fit into the drawing sheet as a normal drawing view. Note that this tool does not create a separate drawing view.

To generate the broken view for a drawing view, choose the **View Break** tool from the **View** group of the **Home** tab; the **View Break** dialog box will be displayed, as shown in Figure 12-31. The methods of creating different types of broken views using the **View Break** dialog box are discussed next.

Creating a Regular Broken View

To create a regular broken view, select the **Regular** option from drop-down list in the **Type** rollout if it is not already selected; you will be prompted to select a view. Select a drawing view from the sheet; the **Specify Anchor Point** area of the **Break Line 1** rollout will be activated. As a result, you will be prompted to select an object to infer point. Select a point on the view; the first break line will be created and you will be prompted again to select an object to infer point. Specify an anchor point for the second break line. The **Offset** edit box in the **Break Line 1** and **Break Line 2** rollouts is used to set an offset distance between the anchor point and the break line. You can also use the handle available on the anchor point to move the break line.

The **Gap** edit box in the **Settings** rollout is used to specify the distance between the two break lines. You can select the break line style from the **Style** drop-down list. You can control the amplitude of a spline by entering the amplitude value in the **Amplitude** edit box. The **Extension 1** and **Extension 2** edit boxes are used to specify an extension value about both the sides of the model. The **Show Break Line** check box is used to display the break lines. If you clear this check box, the break lines will not be displayed in the broken view. You can specify the color and width of the break lines using the **Color** swatch and the **Width** drop-down list, respectively.

***Figure 12-31** The **View Break** dialog box*

Creating a Single-Sided Broken View

To create a single sided broken view, select the **Single-Sided** option from the drop-down list in the **Type** rollout and then select the view from the sheet. On doing so, you will be prompted to select an object to infer point. Select the point of the view and choose the **OK** button; only one side about the selected break point will be displayed. You can choose the **Reverse Direction** button in the **Direction** rollout to reverse the side to be displayed.

Figures 12-32 and 12-33 show the regular broken view and single sided broken view, respectively.

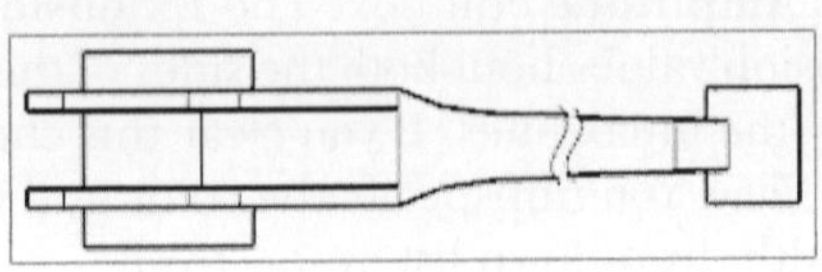

***Figure 12-32** Regular broken view*

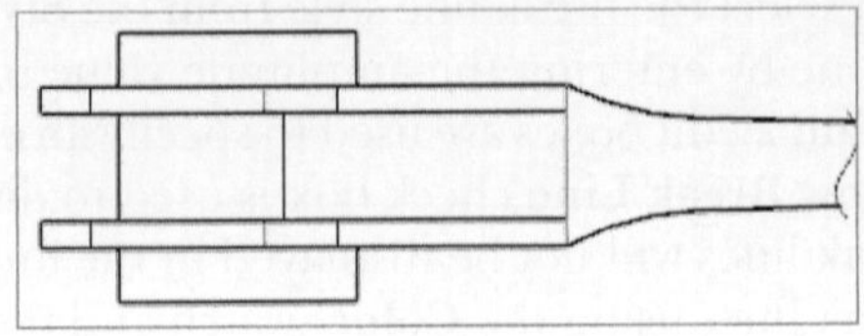

***Figure 12-33** Single sided broken view*

MANIPULATING THE DRAWING VIEWS

After the drawing views are created, it is important to learn how they can be modified or edited. There are various editing operations that can be performed on the existing drawing views. The tools to edit the drawing views are listed in the **Edit View Drop-down** of the **View** group in the **Home** tab, refer to Figure 12-34. These tools are discussed next.

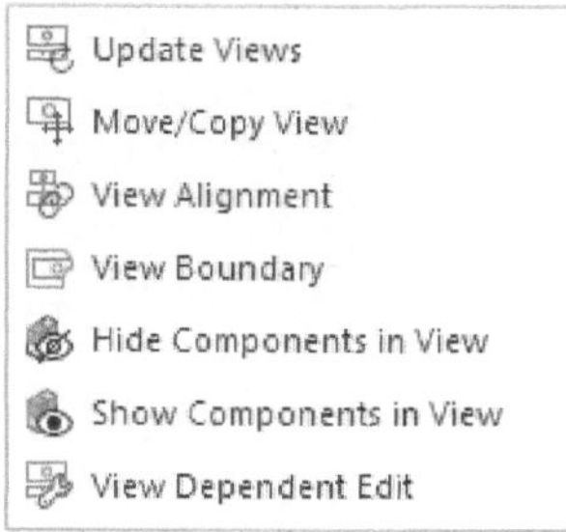

***Figure 12-34** The **Edit View** drop-down list*

Moving the Drawing Views Using the Move/Copy View Tool

Ribbon: Home > View > Edit View Drop-down > Move/Copy View
Menu: Edit > View > Move/Copy

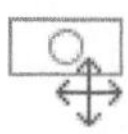

The **Move/Copy View** tool is used to move or copy the generated drawing views as per your requirement. To move the generated drawing views, choose the **Move/Copy View** tool from the **Edit View Drop-down** in the **View** group of the **Home** tab; the **Move/Copy View** dialog box will be displayed, refer to Figure 12-35. Also, you will be prompted to select the views to be moved. Select the views to be moved from the drawing sheet or the view list area of the dialog box. Now, you will be prompted to select the move method. Select the required option from the move/copy method area. After selecting the required method, you will be prompted to specify the new position of the selected view. Specify the new position of the selected view to move or copy in the drawing sheet. Choose the **Deselect Views** button to skip the view selection.

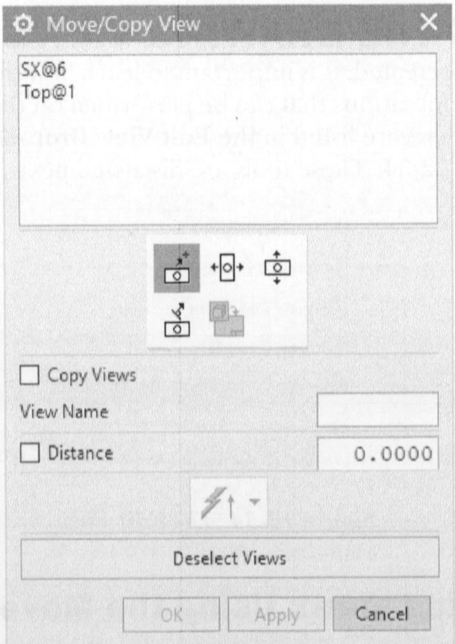

*Figure 12-35 The **Move/Copy View** dialog box*

If you select the **Copy Views** check box, the copy of the selected view will be created, and if the **Copy Views** check box is cleared, then the selected view will move. If the **Distance** check box is selected then the selected view will be moved or copied upto a distance specified in the **Distance** edit box. Note that if multiple views are selected then the views will move or copy with respect to the position of first view selected.

Aligning the Drawing Views Using the Align View Tool

Ribbon:	Home > View > Edit View Drop-down > View Alignment
Menu:	Edit > View > Alignment

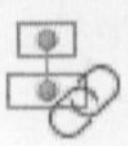

The **View Alignment** tool is used to align the generated drawing views as per your requirement. To align the generated drawing views, choose the **View Alignment** tool from the **Edit View Drop-down** in the **View** group; the **View Alignment** dialog box will be displayed, refer to Figure 12-36. Also, you will prompted to select the view to be aligned. Select the view to be aligned from the drawing sheet. Next, you need to specify the alignment method and options in the **View Alignment** dialog box. The options in this dialog box are discussed next.

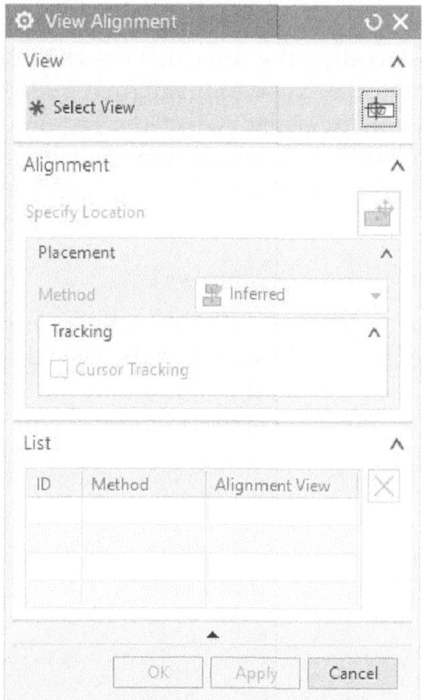

*Figure 12-36 The **View Alignment** dialog box*

Alignment Rollout

The **Method** drop-down list in this rollout consists of various options for specifying alignment. These options are discussed next.

Inferred

On selecting this option from the **Method** drop-down list, the selected drawing view will be moved to the point inferred on the drawing sheet.

Horizontal

The **Horizontal** option is used to align the drawing view horizontally with respect to the stationary view. To do so, select the drawing view to be aligned and then select the **Horizontal** option from the **Method** drop-down list. Next, you need to select the required alignment method from the **Alignment** drop-down list. The options in this drop-down list are used to align the views. If you select the **To View** option from the **Alignment** drop-down list and then select the stationary drawing view, the selected view will be aligned horizontally with respect to the stationary view. On selecting the **Model Point** option, the alignment point selected in the stationary view is considered as the alignment point for all the views that are to be aligned.

After selecting the required option from the **Alignment** drop-down list, select the stationary view from the drawing sheet; the selected drawing views will be aligned horizontally with respect to the stationary view as per the alignment points.

Vertical

The **Vertical** option is used to align the drawing view vertical with respect to the stationary view. To do so, select the drawing view to be aligned and then select the **Vertical** option from the **Method** drop-down list. Next, select the required option from the **Alignment** drop-down list and then select the stationary drawing view; the selected drawing views will be aligned vertically with respect to the stationary view as per the alignment option used to align the views.

Perpendicular to Line

The **Perpendicular to Line** option is used to align the drawing views normal to each other with respect to a reference line. To do so, select the view that needs to be aligned with the stationary view. Next, select the **Perpendicular to Line** option from the **Method** drop-down list; you will be prompted to select the object to infer vector. Specify the vector by using the **Inferred Vector** drop-down list or the **Vector dialog** button. Alternatively, you can specify the vector by creating a reference line using sketching tools available in the **Sketch** group. Next, select the required option from the **Alignment** drop-down list. As soon as you specify the alignment option, you will be prompted to select the view that is perpendicular to line alignment. Select the stationary view; the first selected view will be aligned normal to the reference line.

Overlay

The **Overlay** option from the **Method** drop-down list is used to superimpose the drawing views one over the other. To align the drawing views using this method, select the drawing view to be aligned and then select the **Overlay** option from the **Method** drop-down list. Next, select the required option from the **Alignment** drop-down list and then select the stationary view; the selected drawing view will be overlaid on the stationary view as per the alignment points.

Hinge

The **Hinge** option is used to align a projected view with the parent view by using the hinge line of the parent view. Note that this method is available only to align the projected views with the parent views. To align two views using this method, first select the drawing view and then select the **Hinge** option from the **Method** drop-down list; the selected drawing view will be aligned with the parent view.

Note

*To make the **Hinge** option available in the **Method** drop-down list of the **Alignment** rollout, you need to select it from the **List** rollout of the **View Alignment** dialog box.*

List Rollout

This rollout displays the information about the alignment. It displays the alignment ID, alignment method, and the view to which the selected view is aligned.

Note

*If you want to remove the view alignment between two views, select the drawing view whose view alignment is to be removed. Now, right-click on the selected view and choose the **View Alignment** option from the shortcut menu; the **View Alignment** dialog box will be displayed.*

*Select the existing view alignment from the **List** rollout. Clear the **Associative Alignment** check box or choose the remove button at the right side of the rollout to remove the alignment.*

View Boundary

Ribbon:	Home > View > Edit View Drop-down > View Boundary
Menu:	Edit > View > Boundary

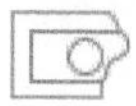

The **View Boundary** tool is used to create the outer boundary for enclosing the drawing views. To create the outer boundary, choose the **View Boundary** tool from the **Edit View Drop-down** in the **View** group of the **Home** tab; the **View Boundary** dialog box will be displayed, refer to Figure 12-37. The names of the drawing views in the drawing sheet will be displayed in the list box of this dialog box and you will be prompted to select a view to define the view boundary. Select the drawing view to define the view boundary; some of the buttons of the dialog box will be enabled. If you want to increase or decrease the diameter of the detail view boundary, select the **Break Line / Detail** option from the **View Boundary** Type drop-down list. Next, select the circle created using the **Detail View** tool; the circumference of the circle is attached with the cursor. Now, you can increase or decrease the diameter of the boundary of the detail view by moving the cursor away or toward the center point. If you select the **Automatic Rectangle** option, then a rectangular boundary will be created and it will enclose the selected drawing view. If you want to enclose the drawing view by drawing a rectangle manually, then select the **Manual Rectangle** option. In such a case, the rectangle drawn should not touch the other drawing views.

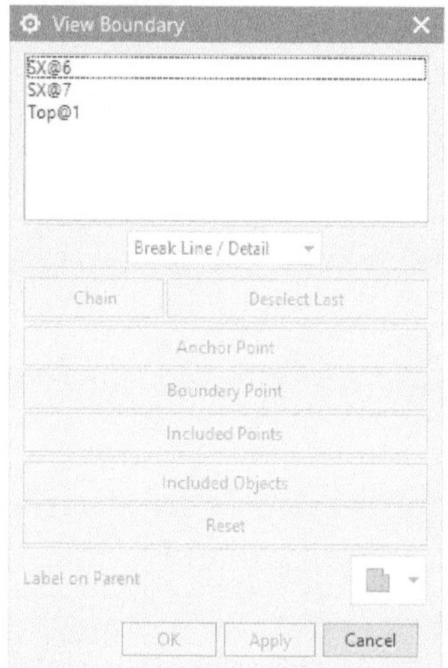

***Figure 12-37** The **View Boundary** dialog box*

Anchor Point

The **Anchor Point** button in the **View Boundary** dialog box is used to specify an anchor point for the drawing view. Generally, the anchor point is specified to fix the drawing view at a position. Any further changes made in the model will be updated in the drawing view with respect to the anchor point specified. To specify an anchor point, choose the **Anchor Point** button from the **View Boundary** dialog box. Next, specify the anchor point in the drawing view and choose the **Apply** button.

Section in View Tool

Ribbon:	Home > View > Edit View Drop-down > Section in View *(Customize to add)*

The **Section in View** tool is used to specify the sectioning properties such that you can exclude the components of an assembly from sectioning. To specify the sectioning properties, choose the **Section in View** tool from the **Edit View Drop-down** in the **View** group of the **Home** tab; the **Section in View** dialog box will be displayed, refer to Figure 12-38. Also, you will be prompted to select the view to be sectioned. Select the view from the drawing sheet. Next, click in the **Select Object** area in the **Body or Component** rollout of the dialog box, you will be prompted to select the bodies or components. Select the component of an assembly or solid from the drawing view; the selected component will be listed in the object list box of the **Body or Component** rollout. Next, choose the **Apply** button. Other rollouts in this dialog box are discussed next.

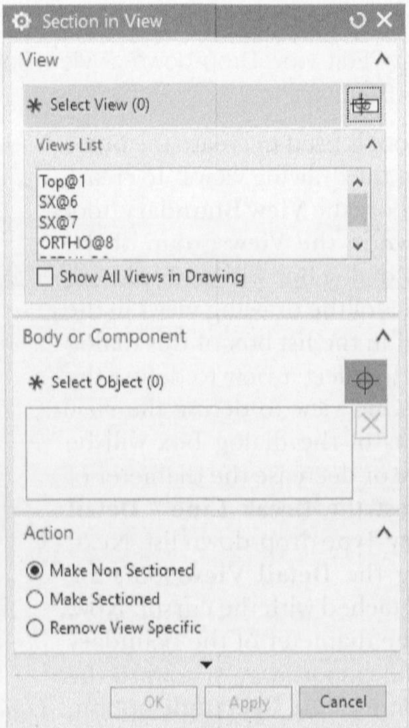

Figure 12-38 The ***Section in View*** *dialog box*

Action Rollout

This rollout has three radio buttons which are discussed next.

Make Non Sectioned

This radio button is used to make the selected components non-sectioned in the section view, as shown in Figure 12-39. In this figure, two bolts are selected to make them non-sectioned in the top view. As a result, when you generate section view of the assembly, these two selected bolts will not be sectioned.

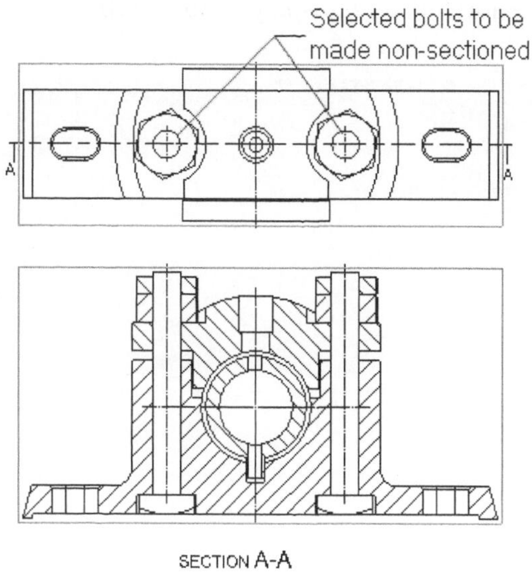

Figure 12-39 Bolts to be made non-sectioned

Make Sectioned

This radio button is used to make the selected components sectioned in the section view.

Remove View Specific

This radio button is used to remove the sectioning property specified by the above two options of the selected objects.

Inserting a Drawing Sheet Using the New Sheet Tool

Ribbon:	Home > Sheet Drop-down > New Sheet
Menu:	Insert > Sheet

In NX, you can add any number of drawing sheets to a drawing file. After generating the drawing views in the first drawing sheet, you may need to add a new drawing sheet. To add a new drawing sheet in the Drafting environment, choose the **New Sheet** tool from the **Sheet Drop-down** of the **Home** tab; the **Sheet** dialog box will be displayed. Enter the parameters for the new drawing sheet in their respective edit boxes and choose the **OK** button from the **Sheet** dialog box; the new sheet will be created and displayed in the Drafting environment.

MODIFYING THE PROPERTIES OF THE GENERATED DRAWING VIEW

The properties of the generated drawing views can be edited by using the methods discussed next.

Modifying the Scale Value of the Drawing View

By default, the scale value of a generated drawing view is 1:1. But you can change this value, if required. To modify the scale value, select the view and right-click on it. Next, choose the

Settings option from the shortcut menu displayed; the **Settings** dialog box will be displayed, as shown in Figure 12-40.

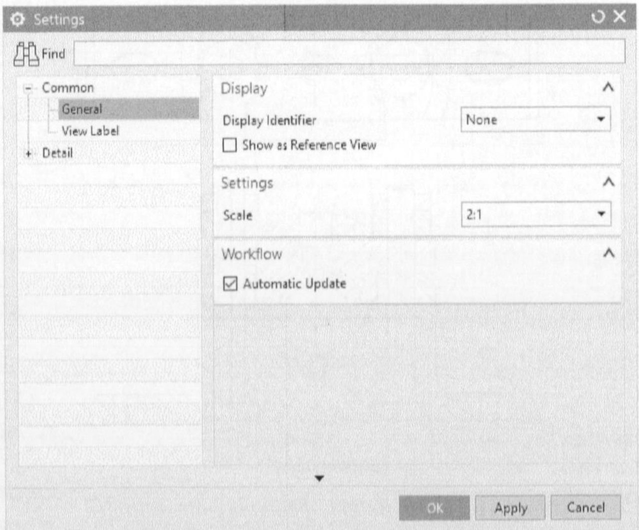

*Figure 12-40 The **Settings** dialog box*

Choose the **General** option of the **Common** node from the **Settings** dialog box. Choose the new scale value from the **Scale** drop-down list of the **Settings** rollout and choose the **Apply** button.

You can also align the drawing view at an angle in the view boundary by specifying the angle value in the **Angle** edit box of the **Angle** option of the **Common** node. Select the **Show View Label** check box from the **Label** rollout of the **Label** option in the **Section** node to display the view label for the drawing view. Next, select the **Show View Scale** check box from the **Scale** rollout to display the scale label for the drawing view selected.

Displaying Hidden Lines in a Drawing View

When the drawing views are generated from the model that has internal edges, then the internal edges will not be displayed in the view, unless it is a section view. To display the hidden lines as dashed lines or dotted lines, select the drawing view and right-click on it. Next, select the **Settings** option from the shortcut menu displayed; the **Settings** dialog box will be displayed. Choose the **Hidden Lines** option from the **Common** node, the parameters of the hidden lines in the drawing view will be displayed. The **Process Hidden Lines** check box is selected by default in the **Format** rollout. The Font and Width drop-down lists are used for modifying the style of the hidden lines. The Font drop-down list consists of various line types that are used at various places in the drawing view. The Width drop-down list consists of lines with various predefined line widths, and these are used at various places in the drawing views. Select the **Dashed** option from the Font drop-down list and the required line weight from the Width drop-down list. The color of the hidden line can be changed by using the Color swatch in the **Format** rollout of the **Hidden Lines** option. After selecting the parameters, choose the **Apply** button and then the **OK** button to exit the **Settings** dialog box.

Other Options in the Hidden Lines Option

To display the hidden edges, select the **Show Edges Hidden by Edges** check box. You can restrict the display of small features by selecting the **Simplify** option from the **Small Features** drop-down list, and then fixing the tolerance value by using the **Tolerance** slider. If you select the **Hide** option from the **Small Features** drop-down list, then the features in the selected tolerance limit will be hidden. If you select the **Show All** option from this drop-down list, all the hidden features will be displayed in the drawing view.

Moving the Drawing Views in the Drawing Sheet

The drawing views can be moved in the drawing limits area and positioned dynamically. To do so, select the drawing view and position the cursor over the view boundary; the drag cursor will be displayed. Drag the view by pressing the left mouse button and dynamically position it.

Displaying the Symbolic Thread Feature

You can also display the symbolic thread feature created in the model in the drawing view. To do so, select the drawing view and right-click on it. Next, choose the **Settings** option from the shortcut menu displayed; the **Settings** dialog box will be displayed. Choose the **Threads** option from the **Common** node; the **Type** drop-down list in the **Display** rollout will be displayed. Various thread standards are displayed in this drop-down list. You can select the required thread standard and choose the **Apply** button from the **Settings** dialog box. If you select the **None** option, the symbolic thread feature created in the model will not be displayed in the drawing view. You can also define a fake pitch value while representing the symbolic threads in the drawing view. To do so, enter the pitch value in the **Minimum** edit box of the **Pitch** rollout and choose the **Apply** button from the **Settings** dialog box; the new pitch value will be updated. Note that the pitch value entered while generating the drawing view is not associated with the pitch specified in the model. The original pitch specified in the model remains unchanged. If the threads are still not displayed in the drawing view, choose the **Hidden Lines** option and then clear the **Process Hidden Lines** check box from the **Format** rollout. Choose the **Apply** button; the threads will be displayed.

ADDING DIMENSIONS TO THE DRAWING VIEWS

After generating the drawing views, you need to add dimensions to them. The tools for dimensioning the drawing views manually are available in the **Dimension** group of the **Home** tab. These tools are the same as those discussed in the sketching environment. In addition to the dimensioning method in the sketching environment, there are few more methods of dimensioning in the Drafting environment. These methods are discussed next.

Chamfer Dimensioning

Ribbon:	Home > Dimension > Chamfer
Menu:	Insert > Dimension > Chamfer

The **Chamfer** tool in the **Dimension** group is used to dimension the chamfer feature. The method adopted for creating a chamfer feature in the model can be shown in the drawing view. To create the chamfer dimension, choose the **Chamfer** tool from the **Dimension** group; the **Chamfer Dimension** dialog box will be displayed, refer to Figure 12-41. Also, you will be prompted to select a chamfer for chamfer dimension. Select the linear edge (chamfer); the dimension of the chamfer gets attached to the cursor. Place the dimension at the required position. Note that if you want to change the orientation of the dimension, then you need to select the corresponding edge for orientation. To edit the chamfer dimension, right-click on it and choose the **Settings** option from the shortcut menu displayed; the **Settings** dialog box will be displayed. On choosing the **Chamfer** option from the **Settings** dialog box, various methods are displayed which can be used to modify the chamfer feature. You can select the required options from the drop-down list of the **Chamfer Format** and **Leader Format** rollouts and then choose the **Close** button from the **Settings** dialog box to exit the dialog box.

*Figure 12-41 The **Chamfer Dimension** dialog box*

Thickness Dimensioning

Ribbon:	Home > Dimension > Thickness
Menu:	Insert > Dimension > Thickness

The thickness dimensioning is defined as the method of generating dimensions between two curves including splines. To do so, choose the **Thickness** tool from the **Dimension** group; the **Thickness Dimension** dialog box will be displayed and you will be prompted to select the object for thickness dimension. Select the first object for thickness dimension; you will be prompted to select the second object for thickness dimension. Select the second object for thickness dimension; the **Specify Location** area will be highlighted. Also, you will be prompted to specify the origin to place the thickness dimension. Click in the drawing window to place the dimension. If the **Place Automatically** check box is selected in the **Origin** rollout then the dimension will be placed automatically in the drawing window. The **Thickness** dimension is used to measure the dimension normally from the point specified on the first curve.

Note

*If you want to change the text style of the text of dimension, then select the dimension and right-click on it. Now, choose the **Settings** option from the shortcut menu displayed; the **Settings** dialog box will be displayed. In this dialog box, different options are available under the **Text** node to change the text style. Choose the required option to change the text style.*

Arc Length Dimensioning

Ribbon: Home > Dimension > Arc Length
Menu: Insert > Dimension > Arc Length

The arc length dimensioning is defined as the method of generating perimeter dimension along a circular arc. To do so, choose the **Arc Length** tool from the **Dimension** group of the **Home** tab; you will be prompted to select an object for arc length dimension. Select the circular arc for the arc length dimension; the **Specify Location** area will be highlighted. Also, you will be prompted to specify the origin to place the arc length dimension. Click in the drawing window to place the dimension. If you select the **Place Automatically** check box in the **Origin** rollout, the dimension will get placed automatically in the drawing window after selecting the arc. If you want to change the style of the dimension, then choose the **Settings** button in the **Settings** rollout of the dialog box and choose the required options. If you want to inherit the dimension style of a existing dimension then choose the **Select Dimension to Inherit** button from the **Settings** rollout.

Ordinate Dimensioning

Ribbon: Home > Dimension > Ordinate
Menu: Insert > Dimension > Ordinate

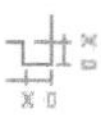

The ordinate dimensioning is defined as the method of creating dimensions by taking one origin point as a common reference. Generally, the ordinate dimensions are given in the drawing view by taking a reference in the horizontal or vertical direction. To create an ordinate dimension, choose the **Ordinate** tool from the **Dimension** group of the **Home** tab; the **Ordinate Dimension** dialog box will be displayed, as shown in Figure 12-42. Now, you can select the **Single Dimension** or **Multiple Dimensions** option from the Type drop-down list. These options are discussed next.

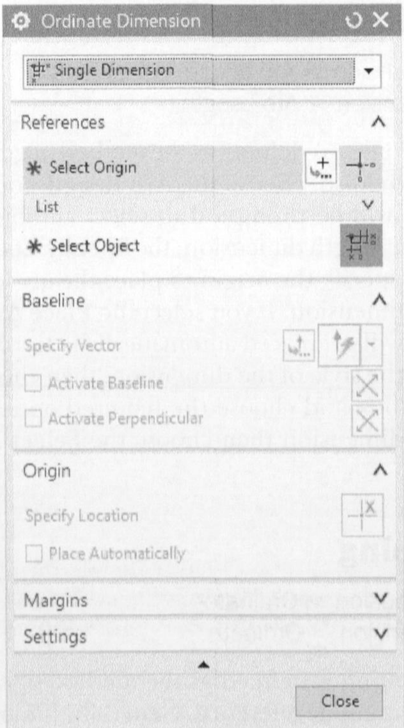

*Figure 12-42 The **Ordinate Dimension** dialog box*

Single Dimension

On selecting the **Single Dimension** option, you can create the ordinate dimensions by selecting points one by one. To create the single dimension, select the **Single Dimension** option from the Type drop-down list if it is not already selected; the **Select Origin** area will be highlighted in the **References** rollout and you will be prompted to select an object or point to define the ordinate origin or select existing origin to activate baselines. Select the origin point from the drawing view. Next, click in the **Specify Vector** area in the **Baseline** rollout; you will be prompted to select an object to infer vector. Specify the vector from the **Inferred Vector** drop-down list or select the vector direction from the direction vectors displayed in the drawing window. Next, click in the **Select Object** area of the **References** rollout; you will be prompted to select dimension measurement object or point. Select the point for baseline dimension. As you select the point for baseline dimension, the **Specify Location** area will be highlighted in the **Origin** rollout and you will be prompted to specify the origin. Click in the drawing window to specify the dimension location; again you will be prompted to select dimension measurement object or point. Select the points and specify their locations one by one to define the baseline dimensions. Note that if you select the **Place Automatically** check box from the **Origin** rollout, then the dimension will be placed automatically in the drawing window. Also, when you select a new point for dimension, it will automatically align the new dimension with the margin of the first dimension.

Note that the **Activate Baseline** check box is selected by default in the **Baseline** rollout which makes the primary baseline active. If you select the **Activate Perpendicular** check box then it makes the secondary baseline active, indicating that you can create a baseline dimension in the direction other than the specified vector direction. You can also define the margins for the baseline dimension by using the **Define Margins** button from the **Margins** rollout.

Multiple Dimensions

Using the **Multiple Dimensions** option, you can create dimensions by selecting multiple points simultaneously using the rectangle selection method. To create multiple dimensions, select the **Multiple Dimensions** option from the drop-down list in the **Type** rollout; the **Select Origin** area will be highlighted in the **References** rollout and you will be prompted to select an object or point to define the ordinate origin or select existing origin to activate baselines. Select the origin point from the drawing view. Next, click in the **Specify Vector** area of the **Baseline** rollout; you will be prompted to select an object to infer vector. Specify the vector from the **Inferred Vector** drop-down list or select the vector direction from the direction vectors displayed in the drawing window. Note that in multiple dimensions, you need to define the margins before selecting the points for the baseline dimension. Therefore, you need to click on the **Define Margins** button in the **Margins** rollout to define the margin for specifying multiple dimensions. On choosing the **Define Margins** button, the **Define Margins** dialog box will be displayed and you will be prompted to specify the location to define the margin. Select the point from the drawing window to specify the margin. Then, choose the **OK** button from the dialog box. Next, click in the **Select Objects** area of the **References** rollout; you will be prompted to select dimension measurement objects or points. Select the point for the baseline dimension or select multiple points simultaneously by pressing the left mouse button and dragging the mouse over the points.

If you select the **Select Only Arc Centers** check box from the **Rectangle Selection** sub-rollout of the **References** rollout, then it will allow you to select only the arc centers when you select multiple points by rectangle selection. If you select the **Allow Duplicates** check box of the **Multiple Dimension Creation** sub-rollout, then it will create multiple ordinate dimension of the same value while using the rectangle selection method.

Hole Callout

Ribbon:	Home > Dimension > Linear/Radial
Menu:	Insert > Dimension > Linear/Radial

In NX, you can generate associative callouts for holes and threads based on the hole feature. The hole callout can be applied to symbolic threads, general holes, drill size holes, screw clearance holes, and threaded holes. You can generate the hole callout for a hole while creating the linear or radial dimension. The **Hole Callout** option is available in the **Method** drop-down list of the **Measurement** rollout in both the **Linear Dimension** and **Radial Dimension** dialog boxes. To create a hole callout, choose the **Linear** or **Radial** tool from the **Dimension** group of the **Home** tab; the respective dialog box will be displayed. Next, select the **Hole Callout** option from the **Method** drop-down list of the **Measurement** rollout; you will be prompted to select the object for applying linear or radial dimension. Select the hole for creating the hole callout and click in the drawing window to specify the location for the hole callout. Note that the **Linear** tool generates cylindrical callouts and the **Radial** tool generates hole and diameter callouts.

GENERATING EXPLODED VIEWS OF AN ASSEMBLY

Ribbon:	Home > View > Base View
Menu:	Insert > View > Base

In NX, you can generate drawing view for the exploded state of an assembly. To generate the drawing view, choose the **Base View** tool from the **View** group; the **Base View** dialog box will be displayed. In this dialog box, select the **Trimetric** option from the **Model View to Use** drop-down list; the exploded view created in the Assembly environment will be generated as the drawing view. Next, place the exploded view in the drawing sheet, refer to Figure 12-43. Irrespective of the orientation of the assembly in the Assembly environment, the orientation of the drawing view generated for the exploded state of an assembly is always isometric. Note that before creating the base view, the assembly must be exploded in the Assembly environment and then directly opened in Drafting environment using the **Application** tab of the **Ribbon**.

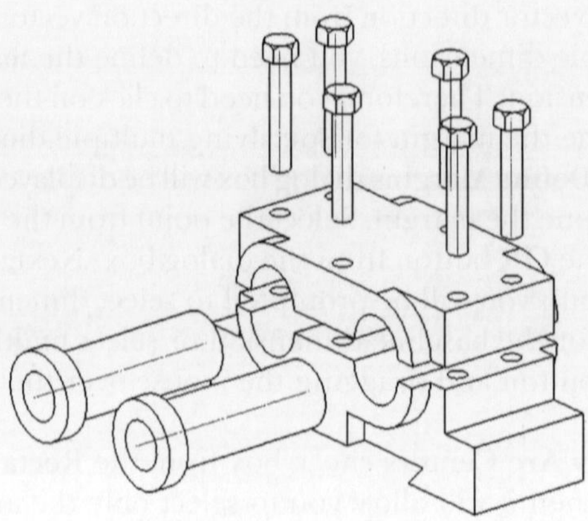

Figure 12-43 The drawing view generated for the exploded state of an assembly

CREATING PARTS LIST AND ASSOCIATIVE BALLOONS

For every assembly drawing, the details about the components such as the component name, number of the same components utilized in the assembly and material property of the components are listed in a tabular format known as the Bill of Materials. In NX, the Bill of Materials is called as the Parts List.

Creating a Parts List for an Assembly

Ribbon:	Home > Table > Parts List
Menu:	Insert > Table > Parts List

To create the parts list for an assembly, choose the **Parts List** tool from the **Table** group of the **Home** tab, refer to Figure 12-44; you will be prompted to indicate a position for the new parts list. Specify a point for placing the parts list. The generated parts list after increasing the cell size is shown in Figure 12-45. You can create the parts list for the assembly by using any drawing view of the assembly. You can dynamically modify the width and height of the cells of the parts list by dragging the cell borders with the left mouse button pressed. To edit the default text in the cells of the **Parts List**, double-click on cells; the **Attribute Cell**

Edit message box will be displayed. Choose the **OK** button from this message box and enter the text in the text box. To change the text size, choose the cell or collection of cells and right-click. Then, choose the **Settings** option from the shortcut menu; the **Settings** dialog box will be displayed. Enter the new text size in the **Height** edit box and press ENTER and then the **Close** button. The parts list will be created for the assembly opened in the Modeling environment of NX.

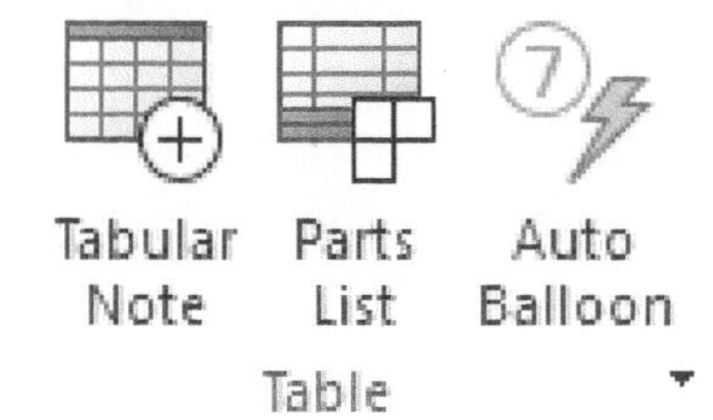

*Figure 12-44 The **Table** group*

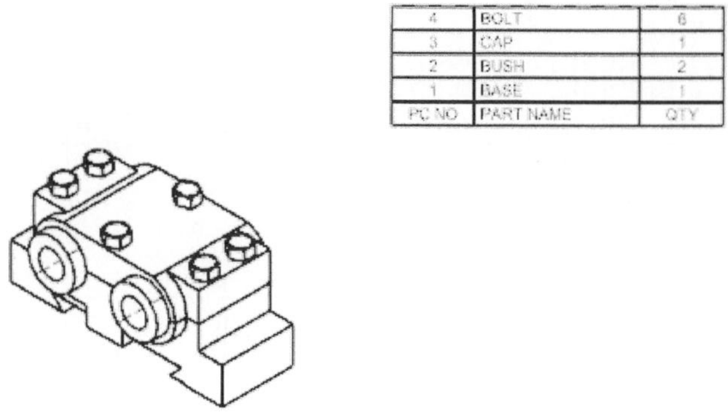

Figure 12-45 The resulting drawing sheet after generating the parts list

Creating Associative Balloons

Ribbon: Home > Table > Auto Balloon
Menu: Insert > Table > Auto Balloon

Associative balloons are created to identify the components in an assembly that are listed in the parts list. To create associative balloons, choose the **Auto Balloon** tool from the **Table** group of the **Home** tab, refer to Figure 12-44; the **Parts List Auto Balloon** dialog box will be displayed and you will be prompted to select the parts list to auto balloon. Select the parts list and choose the **OK** button; the **Parts List Auto Balloon** dialog box will be modified and the list of drawing views will be displayed in it. Select the view to which you want to add the balloons from the list area and choose the **OK** button; auto balloons will be added to the specified drawing views. Note that if a single drawing view is available in the drawing sheet, the auto balloons will be added automatically to the drawing view on selecting the part list. Figure 12-46 shows the auto balloons created after modifying their positions. You can also modify the position of a balloon. To do so, double-click on a balloon; the **Balloon** dialog box will be displayed, as shown in Figure 12-47. You can specify the location of the balloon by using the **Origin** rollout of this dialog box. To do so, click on the **Specify Location** area in the **Origin** rollout; you will be prompted to specify the new origin location. Click in the drawing sheet; the balloon will be placed at the specified location. You can modify the leader of a balloon by using the **Leader** rollout. Similarly, to modify the size ID symbol, enter a new value in the **Size** edit box in the **Settings** rollout. Next, choose the **Close** button to reflect the changes made. You can also navigate to the part listed in the parts list from the corresponding auto balloon. To do so, select the auto balloon and right-click on it. Next, choose the **Navigate to Parts List Row** option from the shortcut menu. The part name, corresponding to the selected auto balloon, will be zoomed to fit and displayed in the drawing sheet.

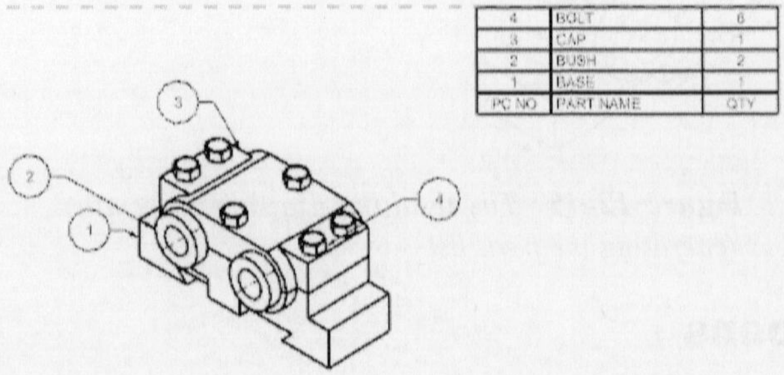

Figure 12-46 The drawing sheet with auto balloons created

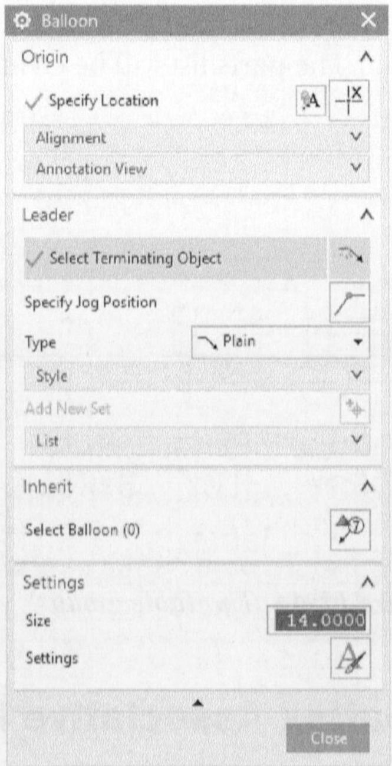

Figure 12-47 The ***Balloon*** *dialog box*

Creating a Tabular Note (Title Block)

Ribbon:	Home > Table > Tabular Note
Menu:	Insert > Table > Tabular Note

Tabular Note

The title block of a drawing sheet consists of details about a drafting work such as the name of the draftsman, date of drafting, name of the person who verified the drafting, the angle of projection method adopted, and so on. In NX, the title block is termed as the tabular note. The drawing sheet created for the shop floor also contains the name and logo of a company, and sheet number details. To create a user-defined tabular note, choose the **Tabular Note** tool from the **Table** group of the **Home** tab; the **Tabular Note** dialog box will be displayed and you will be prompted to specify origin. Specify a point for placing the tabular note; the default tabular note with five rows and columns will be attached to the cursor. Click in the drawing sheet at the required location to place it and press the ESC key. To enter text in the cells, double-click in the respective cell; a text box will be displayed. Enter the required text and press the ENTER key.

Resizing and Merging the Rows and Columns of the Tabular Note

You can dynamically resize the rows and columns by dragging the borders. If you want to merge two or more cells together, select the cells by dragging the cursor on them with the left mouse button pressed. The selected cells will be highlighted in orange. Right-click in the selection area and then choose the **Merge Cells** option from the shortcut menu. To delete a row or column, select the row or column and right-click on it. Then, choose the **Delete** option from the shortcut menu; the selected row or column will be deleted. To modify the size of the text in the tabular note, select the cell and right-click. Choose the **Settings** option from the shortcut menu displayed; the **Settings** dialog box will be displayed. Enter a new value for the text in the **Height** edit box and press ENTER to reflect the changes. Figure 12-48 shows a tabular note that is created and modified to be accommodated in the drawing sheet.

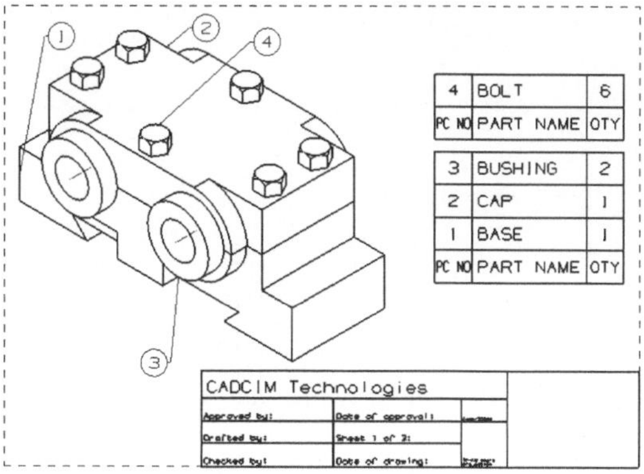

Figure 12-48 The drawing sheet with the tabular note (title block)

Adding a User-defined Tabular Note to the Tables Palette

After creating the required tabular note, you can add it to the library. To add a user-defined tabular note in the library, select the tabular note from the upper left corner and right-click on it. Next, choose the **Save As Template** option from the shortcut menu; the **Save As Template** dialog box will be displayed and you will be prompted to specify a name for the template. Enter the name in the **File name** edit box and choose the **OK** button; the tabular note will be saved. By default, the user-defined tabular notes are saved at: **Program Files > Siemens > NX > UGII > table_files**.

Inserting the Company Logo (Image) into the Tabular Note

Ribbon:	Home > Annotation > Image
Menu:	Insert > Image

After entering the required data in the cells of the tabular note, you may even insert the company logo in it. You can insert an image into the drawing sheet that has the file name extension as .JPG, .TIF, or .PNG. To insert the image, choose the **Image** tool from the **Annotation** group of the **Home** tab; the **Insert Image** dialog box will be displayed. Next, choose the **Choose Image File** button from the dialog box; the **Raster Image File** dialog box will be displayed. Browse to the image and choose the **OK** button; the image will be displayed in the drawing sheet along with the handles. As you choose the **OK** button, the **Size** rollout options becomes available to modify the size of image. By selecting the **Lock Aspect Ratio** check box from the **Size** rollout, you can lock the aspect ratio for the scaling so that further scaling will be uniform as per the locking made. Using the translational handles, you can position the image anywhere in the drawing sheet. The drawing sheet after inserting the company logo is shown in Figure 12-49.

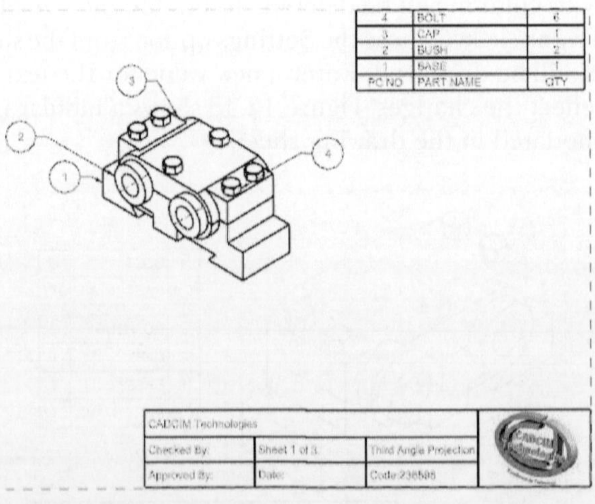

Figure 12-49 The drawing sheet after inserting the image

ADDING MULTILINE TEXT TO A DRAWING SHEET

Ribbon:	Home > Annotation > Note
Menu:	Insert > Annotation > Note

To enter a multiline text in the drawing, choose the **Note** tool from the **Annotation** group of the **Home** tab; the **Note** dialog box will be displayed. The expanded view of this dialog box is shown in Figure 12-50. Enter the text to be added in the drawing view in the text edit box in the **Text Input** rollout. After entering the text, you can place it by clicking in the drawing limits area. Press the middle mouse button to exit the tool.

You can specify the view and alignment of the text in the **Origin** rollout. The **Edit Text** and **Formatting** sub-rollouts of the **Text Input** rollout are used to edit and format the text written in the text box. You can add geometrical symbols to the multiline text using the **Symbols** sub-rollout. To insert the text from the already saved *. *txt* files, you can use the **Insert Text From File** button using the **Import/Export** sub-rollout. Similarly, you can save the created text in the *. *txt* file format using the **Save As** button in the **Import/Export** sub-rollout. To place the text vertically, select the **Vertical Text** check box in the **Settings** rollout. You can modify the parameters of the text using the **Settings** rollout.

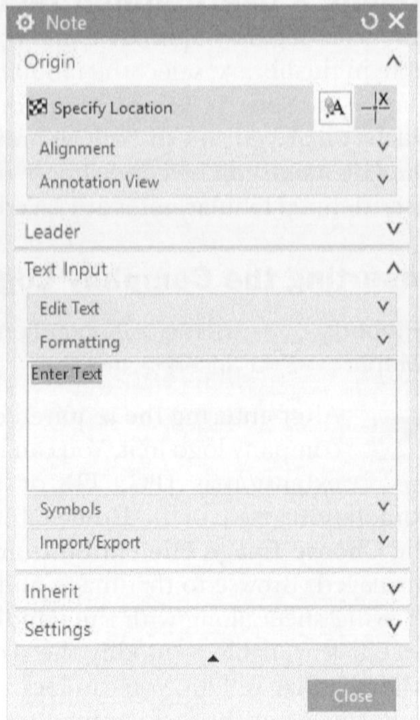

*Figure 12-50 The **Note** dialog box*

PRINTING TOOLS

After generating the required drawing views, you may need to print the drawing sheet to send it for manufacturing. Also, you need to create the quality print representations of your designs. This can be done using the following printing tools:

Print

Ribbon:	File > Print
Menu:	File > Print

The **Print** tool is used to print the entities displayed in the drawing window. The entity to be printed may be a solid model or drawing views of the solid model. To print the solid model, you need to invoke the Modeling environment. Similarly, to print the drawing sheet, you need to invoke the Drafting environment.

Invoke the Modeling or Drafting environment and choose **Menu > File > Print** from the **Top Border Bar**; the **Print** dialog box will be displayed, refer to Figure 12-51.

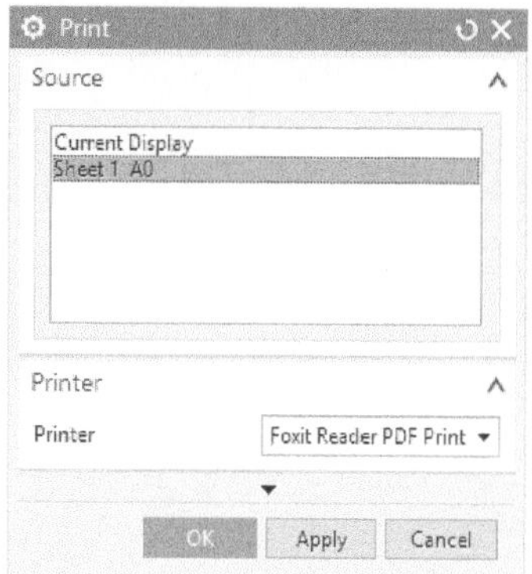

*Figure 12-51 The **Print** dialog box*

Select the name of the printer connected to your computer from the **Printer** drop-down list in the **Printer** rollout. Then, choose the **Properties** button from the **Details** sub-rollout; the **XYZ Printer Properties** dialog box will be displayed. You can use this dialog box to set the printing properties. After specifying the required options, choose the **OK** button from the **Printer Properties** dialog box.

To change color settings of the printer, you can use the options in the **Output** drop-down list of the **Settings** rollout. Enter the number of copies to be printed in the **Copies** spinner and select the required check box from the **Settings** area. To set the printing quality, select an option from the **Image Resolution** drop-down list.

After setting the required parameters, choose the **OK** button from the **Print** dialog box; the printer will start printing the file.

Plot

Ribbon:	File > Plot
Menu:	File > Plot

The **Plot** tool is used to create quality print representations of your designs. You can save the output of the file in the TIFF, JPEG, EMF, CGM, and PNG format. To plot a drawing sheet, choose **Menu > File > Plot** from the **Top Border Bar**; the **Plot** dialog box will be displayed, as shown in Figure 12-52.

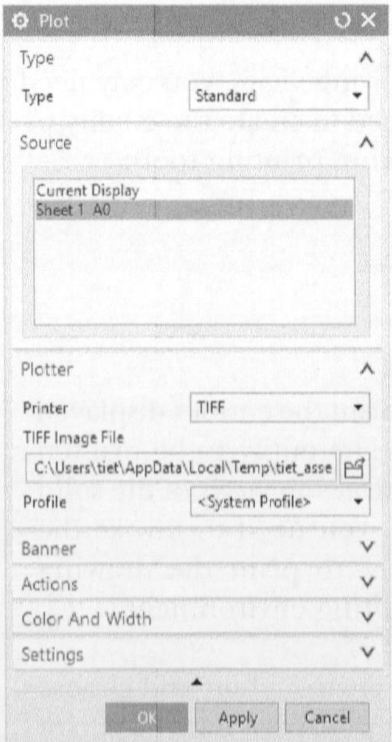

*Figure 12-52 The **Plot** dialog box*

Select the required output format of the file from the **Printer** drop-down list of the **Plotter** rollout. The options available in this drop-down list are **TIFF**, **JPEG**, **EMF**, **CGM**, and **PNG**. Next, choose the **Browse** button from the **Plotter** rollout and specify the location to save the output file. You can set advanced parameters and then specify them in the **Banner**, **Actions**, **Color And Width**, and **Settings** rollouts. After setting the required parameters, choose the **OK** button; the file will be plotted at the specified location.

TUTORIALS

Tutorial 1

In this tutorial, you will generate the top view, front view, right-side view, and isometric view of the model created in Exercise 2 of Chapter 6. Use the standard A2 landscape sheet format for generating the drawing views. You will also create a tabular note for the drawing sheet, add an image to it, and then save it as a template at the desired location. Figure 12-53 shows the drawing sheet after generating the drawing views of the model and creating the tabular note.

(Expected time: 1 hr)

The following steps are required to complete this tutorial:

a. Open the model created in Exercise 2 of Chapter 6 and then invoke the Drafting environment.
b. Generate the drawing views of the model, refer to Figure 12-55.
c. Add a tabular note to the drawing sheet, refer to Figure 12-56.
d. Insert the logo of a company into the tabular note, refer to Figure 12-57.
e. Save the tabular note as a template.

f. Print the drawing sheet.
g. Plot the drawing sheet.
h. Save the drawing file.

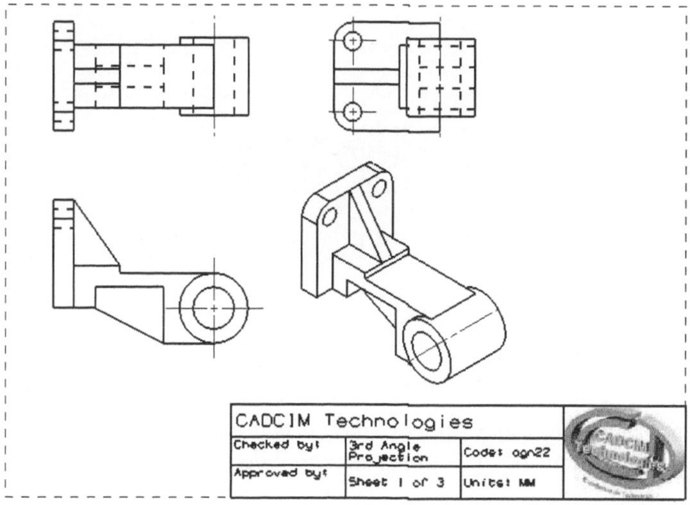

Figure 12-53 The drawing sheet after generating the drawing views and adding title block to it

Opening the Part File and Invoking the Drafting Environment

1. Open the part file created in Exercise 2 of Chapter 6. Next, choose **Application > Design > Drafting** from the **Ribbon**; the **Sheet** dialog box is displayed. Select the **Standard Size** radio button from the **Size** rollout.

2. Select the sheet size **A2 - 420 x 594** from the **Size** drop-down list. By default, the **3rd Angle Projection** button is chosen and the **Millimeters** radio button is selected in the **Settings** rollout. The default scale value selected in the **Scale** drop-down list is **1:1**. Select the **Base View Command** radio button from the **Settings** rollout. Note that you need to select the **Always Start View Creation** check box to make this radio button active. Accept default values for all other parameters and choose the **OK** button to invoke the Drafting environment.

   Now, you are in the Drafting environment and an empty drawing sheet along with the floating top view attached to the cursor is displayed. Also, the **Base View** dialog box is displayed, refer to Figure 12-54.

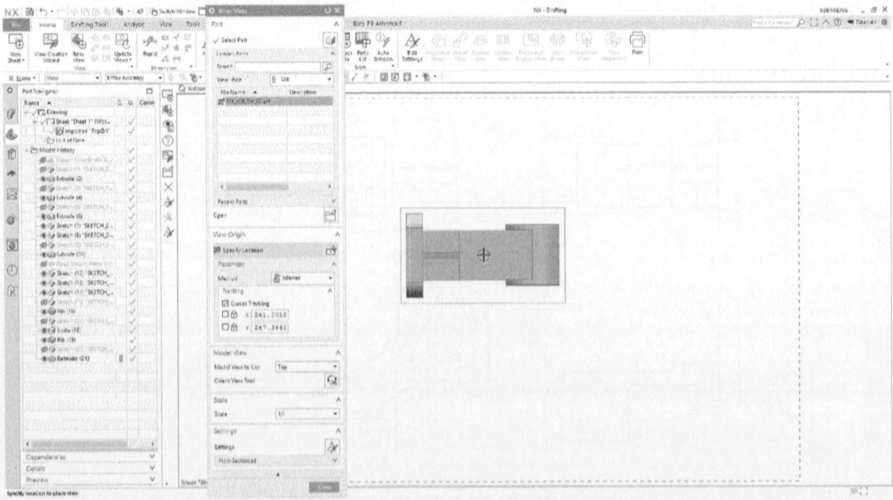

*Figure 12-54 The empty drawing sheet displayed with the floating top view and the **Base View** dialog box after invoking the Drafting environment*

Note

*For the purpose of printing, you should turn off the display of grids. To do so, choose **Menu > Preferences > Grid** from the **Top Border Bar**; the **Grid Preferences** dialog box is displayed. Clear the **Show Grid** check box from the **Grid Settings** rollout and choose the **OK** button; the display of grids is turned off.*

Generating the Top, Front, and Right-Side Views of the Model

1. Choose **Menu > Preferences > Drafting** from the **Top Border Bar**; the **Drafting Preferences** dialog box is displayed. Choose the **Drawing View** node and clear the **Display** check box in the **Border** rollout. Choose the **OK** button; the **Base View** dialog box is displayed again and you are prompted to specify the location to place the view on the sheet.

2. Specify the center point for the generated drawing view, refer to Figure 12-55. After generating the base view, the **Projected View** tool is automatically invoked from the **View** group and the **Projected View** dialog box is displayed.

3. Click on the right side of the base view and then at the bottom of the base view to generate the right-side view and the front view, respectively. Press the middle mouse button to exit the tool.

4. If the hidden lines are not displayed, select the drawing views and right-click on any of the selected views. Then, choose the **Settings** option from the shortcut menu displayed; the **Settings** dialog box is displayed.

5. Choose the **Hidden Lines** option from the **Common** node in the dialog box. The **Process Hidden Lines** check box is selected by default in the **Format** rollout. Select the **Dashed** option from the Font drop-down list and **0.13 mm** from the Width drop-down list.

6. Choose the **OK** button to exit the **Settings** dialog box; the hidden lines are displayed. The top view, the right-side view, and the front view of the model are shown in Figure 12-55.

Generating the Isometric View of the Model

1. Choose the **Base View** tool from the **View** group of the **Home** tab; the **Base View** dialog box is displayed. Also, the floating top view of the model attached to the cursor is displayed in the drawing sheet.

2. Select the **Isometric** option from the **Model View to Use** drop-down list of the **Model View** rollout; the isometric view of the model is displayed in the drawing sheet and you are prompted to specify the location to place the view on the sheet.

3. Specify the center point of the isometric view, refer to Figure 12-55. Then, press the middle mouse button to exit the tool. The resulting drawing sheet after generating the drawing views is shown in Figure 12-55.

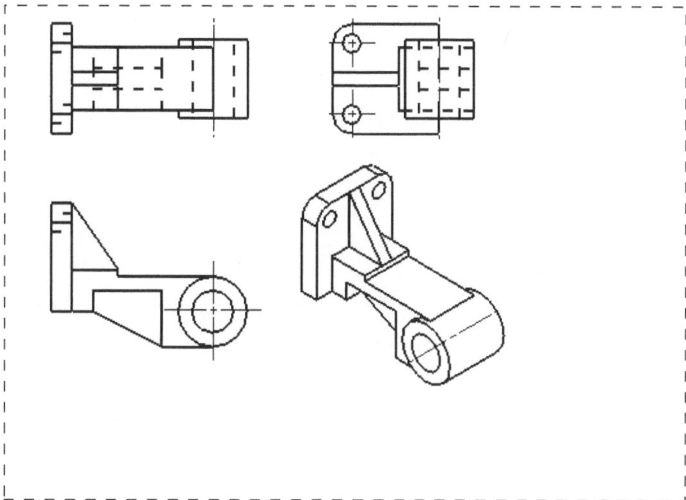

Figure 12-55 *The drawing sheet after creating the drawing views*

Creating the Tabular Note for the Drawing Sheet

1. Choose the **Tabular Note** tool from the **Table** group of the **Home** tab; the **Tabular Note** dialog box is displayed and the floating tabular note is attached to the cursor. Position the tabular note on the drawing sheet and then choose the **Close** button from the **Tabular Note** dialog box, refer to Figure 12-56.

2. Select the last two columns of the tabular note by moving the cursor on the columns with the left mouse button pressed; the two selected columns are displayed in orange.

3. Right-click in the selection area and then choose the **Merge Cells** option from the shortcut menu displayed; the selected cells are merged together.

4. Drag the cells dynamically to modify their size with the left mouse button pressed. The width and height of the cells should be 50 and 14, respectively.

5. Merge the cells of the first three rows and modify its height to 16, refer to Figure 12-56. Next, you need to enter the text in the cells, refer to Figure 12-56.

6. To enter the text in cells, double-click on them and enter the text in the text box.

7. Select the cell from the first row in which the text is entered and then right-click on it. Next, choose the **Settings** option from the shortcut menu displayed; the **Settings** dialog box is displayed.

8. Choose the **Lettering** node, enter **5** in the **Height** edit box, and then press ENTER to reflect the changes. The resulting drawing sheet after creating the tabular note is shown in Figure 12-56.

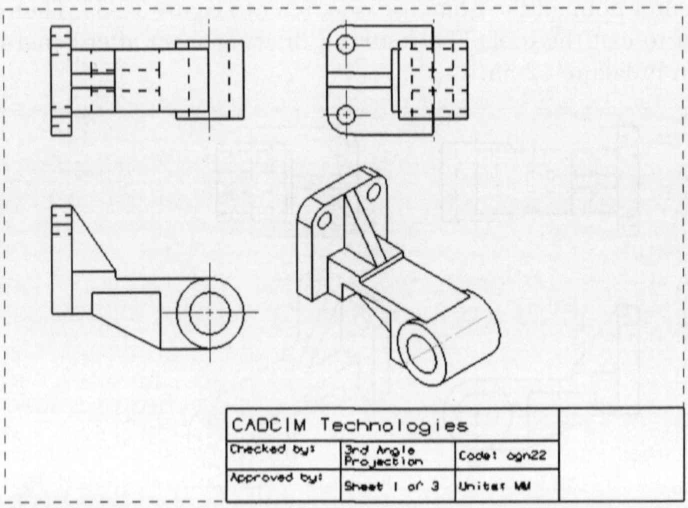

Figure 12-56 The drawing sheet after creating the drawing views and the tabular note

Inserting the Image

1. Choose the **Image** tool from the **Annotation** group; the **Insert Image** dialog box is displayed. Choose the **Choose Image File** button from this dialog box; the **Raster Image File** dialog box is displayed. Browse to the required image by using the **Look in** drop-down list and select it. Next, choose the **OK** button from the dialog box. The image along with the handles is displayed in the drawing sheet.

2. Position the image in the tabular note by using the handles. If necessary, choose the **Lock Aspect Ratio** check box from the **Size** rollout to maintain uniform scale of image. After positioning the image, Choose the **OK** button. The complete drawing sheet after inserting the image is shown in Figure 12-57.

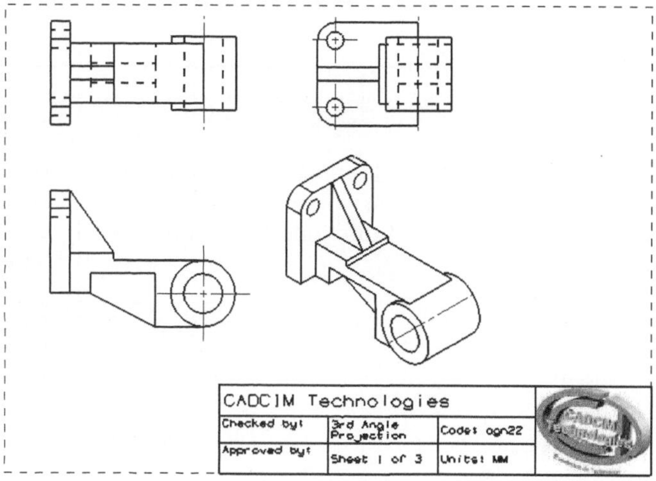

Figure 12-57 *The final drawing sheet*

Saving the Tabular Note as a Template

1. Move the cursor to the upper left corner of the tabular note; the **Tabular Note Section** is displayed. Select the **Tabular Note Section**. The complete tabular note is now displayed in orange color.

2. Right-click on the **Tabular Note Section** and then choose the **Save As Template** option from the shortcut menu; the **Save As Template** dialog box is displayed. Enter **Table-1** as the name of the tabular note in the **File name** text box and choose the **OK** button; the name of the tabular note is saved as **Table-1** and added as the tabular note at the specified location.

Printing the Drawing Sheet

1. Choose **File > Print** from the **Ribbon**; the **Print** dialog box is displayed. Select the printer connected to your computer from the **Printer** drop-down list in the **Printer** rollout.

2. Choose the **Properties** button from the **Details** sub-rollout and set the orientation of the paper to **Landscape**. Change the color settings, if required, and choose the **OK** button.

3. Set the value in the **Copies** spinner of the **Settings** rollout to **1** and choose the **OK** button; the drawing sheet is printed.

Plotting and Saving the Drawing Sheet

1. Choose **File > Plot** from the **Ribbon**; the **Plot** dialog box is displayed. Select **JPEG** from the **Printer** drop-down list of the **Plotter** rollout.

2. Choose the **Browse** button from the **Plotter** rollout and specify the location to save the output file. Enter the name of the output file in the **File name** edit box. Next, choose the **OK** button twice; the file is plotted at the specified location.

3. Choose **Menu > File > Save** from the **Top Border Bar**; the drawing file is saved. Next, close the file.

Tutorial 2

In this tutorial, you will generate the isometric and exploded views of the Double Bearing assembly created in Exercise 3 of Chapter 8. Also, you will generate the Parts List and Auto balloons, and insert the tabular note **Table-1** from the **Table** palette, as shown in Figure 12-58.

(Expected time: 2 hr)

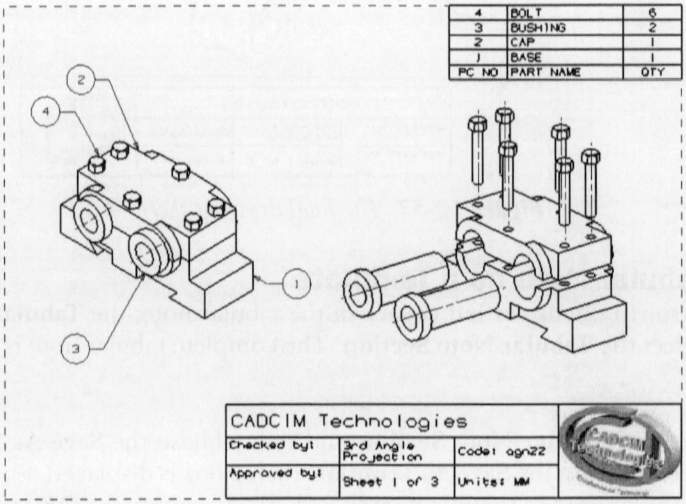

Figure 12-58 The drawing sheet after generating drawing views, parts list, auto balloons, and inserting the title block

The following steps are required to complete this tutorial:

a. Create the exploded view of the assembly in the assembly file.
b. Invoke the Drafting environment.
c. Create the isometric and exploded views of the assembly, refer to Figure 12-59.
d. Create the parts list and auto balloons, refer to Figure 12-60.
e. Insert the tabular note into the drawing sheet, refer to Figure 12-61.
f. Print the drawing sheet.
g. Plot the drawing sheet.
h. Save the drawing sheet.

Invoking the Drafting Environment

1. Open the assembly file and choose the **Explosion 1** option from the **Work View Explosion** drop-down list of the **Exploded Views** group, if not already chosen. Next, choose **Application > Design > Drafting** from the **Ribbon**; the **Sheet** dialog box is displayed.

2. Select the **Standard Size** radio button from the **Size** rollout.

3. Select the sheet size **A4 - 210 x 297** from the **Size** drop-down list. By default, the **3rd Angle Projection** button is chosen and the **Millimeters** radio button is selected in the **Settings** rollout. The default scale value selected in the **Scale** drop-down list of the **Size** rollout is **1:1**. Select the **Base View Command** radio button from the **Settings** rollout. Accept all default parameters and choose the **OK** button to exit the **Sheet** dialog box.

Generating the Isometric Drawing View of the Assembly

Once you choose the **OK** button from the **Sheet** dialog box, the **Base View** dialog box along with the floating top view of the model is displayed.

1. Select the **Isometric** option from the **Model View to Use** drop-down list. The floating isometric view of the assembly is displayed on the drawing sheet and you are prompted to specify location to place view. Position the drawing view generated in the drawing sheet by pressing the left mouse button, refer to Figure 12-59. Next, press the middle mouse button to exit the tool. The isometric view of the model is displayed in the drawing sheet, refer to Figure 12-59.

2. Next, choose the **Base View** tool from the **View** group; the **Base View** dialog box is displayed. Choose the **Trimetric** option from the **Model View to Use** drop-down list; the floating trimetric view of the assembly is displayed on the drawing sheet and you are prompted to specify location to place view. Position the drawing view generated in the drawing sheet by clicking the left mouse button, refer to Figure 12-59. Next, press the middle mouse button to exit the tool.

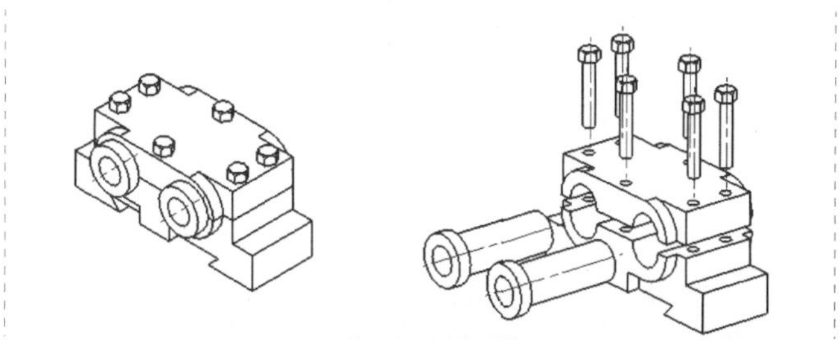

Figure 12-59 *The drawing sheet after generating the isometric and exploded drawing views of the assembly*

Generating the Parts List of the Assembly

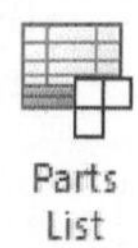

1. Choose the **Parts List** tool from the **Table** group of the **Home** tab; you are prompted to indicate a position for the new parts list. Also, the floating rectangle is displayed in the drawing sheet.

2. Position the parts list by pressing the left mouse button in the drawing sheet at the location shown in Figure 12-60.

Generating Associative Auto balloons for the Parts List

Auto Balloon

1. Choose the **Auto Balloon** tool from the **Table** group of the **Home** tab; the **Parts List Auto Balloon** dialog box is displayed and you are prompted to select the parts list to add auto balloon.

2. Select the parts list generated in the previous step and choose the **OK** button; the modified **Parts List Auto Balloon** dialog box is displayed and you are prompted to select views to auto balloon.

3. Select **Isometric** from the list box of the same dialog box; the selected view is enclosed in an orange color border. Choose the **OK** button; the auto balloons are generated. The drawing sheet after generating the auto balloons along with the drawing views, and the parts list is shown in Figure 12-60.

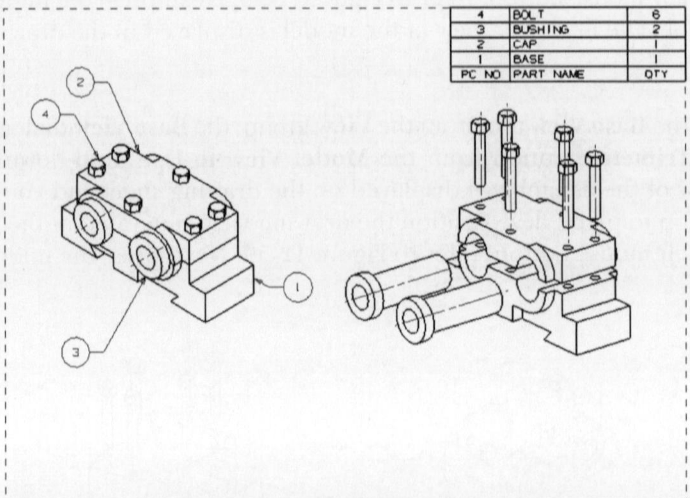

Figure 12-60 The drawing sheet after generating the drawing view, parts list, and auto balloons for the assembly

Inserting the Tabular Note (Table-1) from the Tables Palette

By default, the **Tables** palette is not present in the **Resource Bar**. You need to retrieve it from the **Palettes** option.

1. Choose **Menu > Preferences > Palettes** from the **Top Border Bar**; the **Palettes** dialog box is displayed.

2. Choose the **Open Palette** button from the **Palettes** dialog box; the **Open Palette** dialog box is displayed.

3. Choose the **Browse** button and browse to *C:\Program Files\Siemens\NX 2019\UGII\table_files.* Next, select the **tables.pax** file from the dialog box and choose the **OK** button twice; the **Tables** palette is added to the **Resource Bar**. Next, choose the **Close** button to exit the **Palettes** dialog box.

4. Next, choose the **Tables** tab from the **Resource Bar**; the **Tables** cascading menu is displayed.

5. Drag the tabular note named **Table-1** from the list of tables displayed and drop it in the drawing sheet. Then, position the tabular note in the drawing sheet, as shown in Figure 12-61. Add the company logo to the tabular note as discussed in the previous tutorial. Figure 12-61 shows the complete drawing sheet.

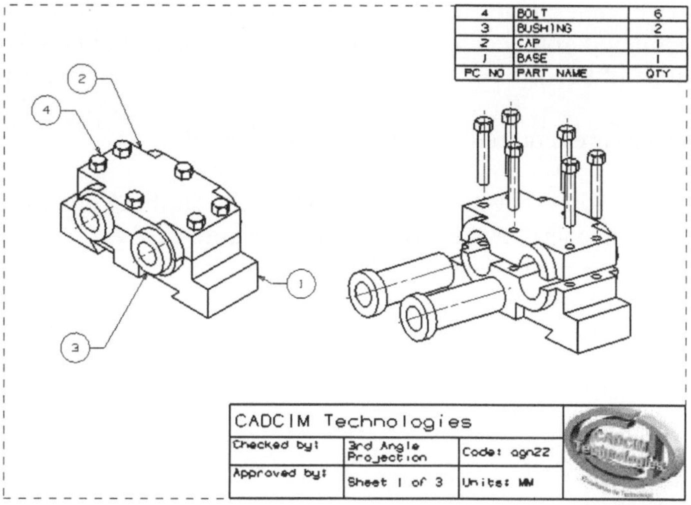

Figure 12-61 *The completed drawing sheet after generating the drawing view, parts list, auto balloons, and inserting the title block*

Printing the Drawing Sheet

1. Choose **Menu > File > Print** from the **Top Border Bar**; the **Print** dialog box is displayed. Select the printer connected to your computer from the **Printer** drop-down list.

2. Choose the **Properties** button from the **Details** sub-rollout and make the orientation of the paper to **Landscape**. Change the color settings, if required, and choose the **OK** button.

3. Set the value **1** in the **Copies** spinner of the **Settings** rollout and choose the **OK** button; the drawing sheet is printed.

Plotting the Drawing Sheet

1. Choose **Menu > File > Plot** from the **Top Border Bar**; the **Plot** dialog box is displayed.

2. Select **TIFF** from the **Printer** drop-down list of the **Plotter** rollout.

3. Choose the **Browse** button from the **Plotter** rollout. Specify the location and name to save the output file.

4. Choose the **OK** button twice; the file is plotted at the specified location.

Saving the Drawing Sheet

1. Choose **Menu > File > Save** from the **Top Border Bar**; the drawing sheet is saved. Next, close the file.

Tutorial 3

In this tutorial, you will generate the front view, left-side view, and top view of the model created in Tutorial 1 of Chapter 7. You need to manually add the required dimensions to the drawing views shown in Figure 12-62. **(Expected time: 30 min)**

The following steps are required to complete this tutorial:

a. Open the part file created in Chapter 7 and invoke the Drafting environment.
b. Generate the drawing views of the model, refer to Figure 12-64.
c. Create dimensions for all views, refer to Figure 12-68.
d. Save and close the drawing file.

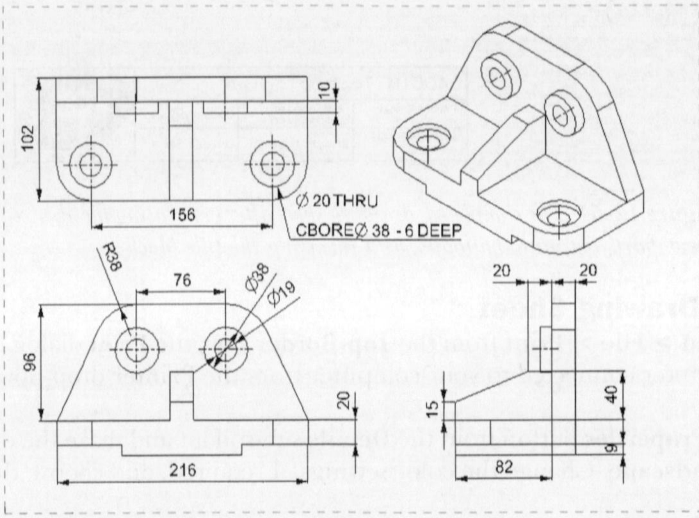

Figure 12-62 The drawing views of the model after retrieving and creating the dimensions

Opening the Part File and Invoking the Drafting Application

1. Open the part file created in Chapter 7 (Tutorial 1). Choose **Application > Design > Drafting** from the **Ribbon**; the **Sheet** dialog box is displayed.

2. Select **A2 - 420 x 594** as the sheet size from the **Size** drop-down list. By default, the **3rd Angle Projection** button is chosen and the **Millimeters** radio button is selected in the **Settings** rollout. The default scale value selected in the **Scale** drop-down list of the **Size** rollout is **1:1**. Select the **View Creation Wizard** radio button from the **Settings** rollout. Accept all default parameters and choose the **OK** button; the Drafting environment is invoked. Also, the **View Creation Wizard** dialog box is invoked and the selected part file is displayed in the **Loaded Parts** sub-rollout of the **Part** rollout.

Generating the Drawing Views of the Model

1. Choose the **Next** button from the **View Creation Wizard**; the **Options** page is displayed.

2. Select the **Manual** option from the **View Boundary** drop-down list and then select the **Process Hidden Lines** check box. Next, select the **Dashed** option from the Font drop-down list and **0.35 mm** option from the Width drop-down list. Also, select the **Show Centerlines** check box and make sure the scale factor is set to 1:1.

3. Choose the **Next** button; the **Orientation** page is displayed.

4. Select the **Front** view from the **Model Views** area and then choose the **Next** button; the **Layout** page is displayed.

5. In the **Layout** page, select the views shown in Figure 12-63 and then select the **Automatic** option from the **Option** drop-down list in the **Placement** rollout.

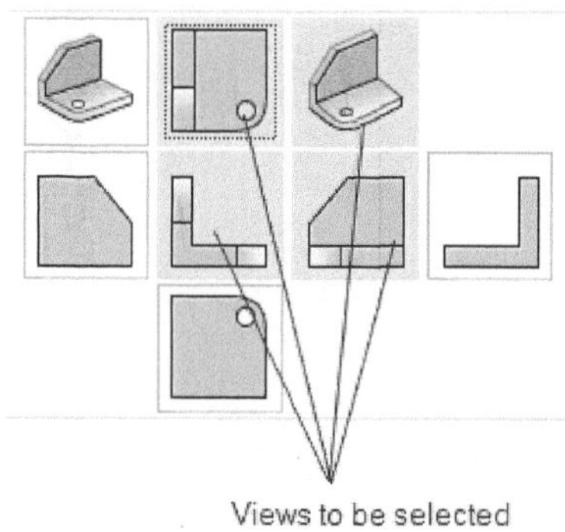

*Figure 12-63 Views to be selected from the **Layout** page*

6. Enter **20** in both the **Between Views** and **To Border** edit boxes of the **Margins** sub-rollout of the **Layout** rollout. Next, choose the **Finish** button; the views are created in the sheet.

   Next, you need to increase the view boundary of the isometric view.

7. Choose the **View Boundary** tool from the **Edit View Drop-down** in the **View** group; the **View Boundary** dialog box is displayed and you are prompted to select a view to define the view boundary.

8. Select the isometric view from the drawing sheet and then select the **Manual Rectangle** option from the View Boundary Type drop-down list.

9. Press the left-mouse button on the top-left corner of the isometric view, and then drag the cursor to define a rectangle. Note that the newly created view boundary should cover all the entities of the isometric view. Next, choose the **Cancel** button to exit the **View Boundary** dialog box.

   Next, you need to turn off the hidden lines of the isometric view.

10. Select the drawing view and then right-click on it to invoke the shortcut menu. Next, choose the **Settings** option from the shortcut menu; the **Settings** dialog box is displayed.

11. Choose the **Hidden Lines** option from **Common** node of the dialog box. The **Process Hidden Lines** check box is selected by default in the **Format** rollout. Select the **Invisible** option from the Font drop-down list and the **Original** option from the Width drop-down list.

12. Choose the **OK** button to exit the **Settings** dialog box; the hidden lines are not displayed in the drawing. Now, hide the borders of the views. The drawing sheet after generating the required drawing views is shown in Figure 12-64.

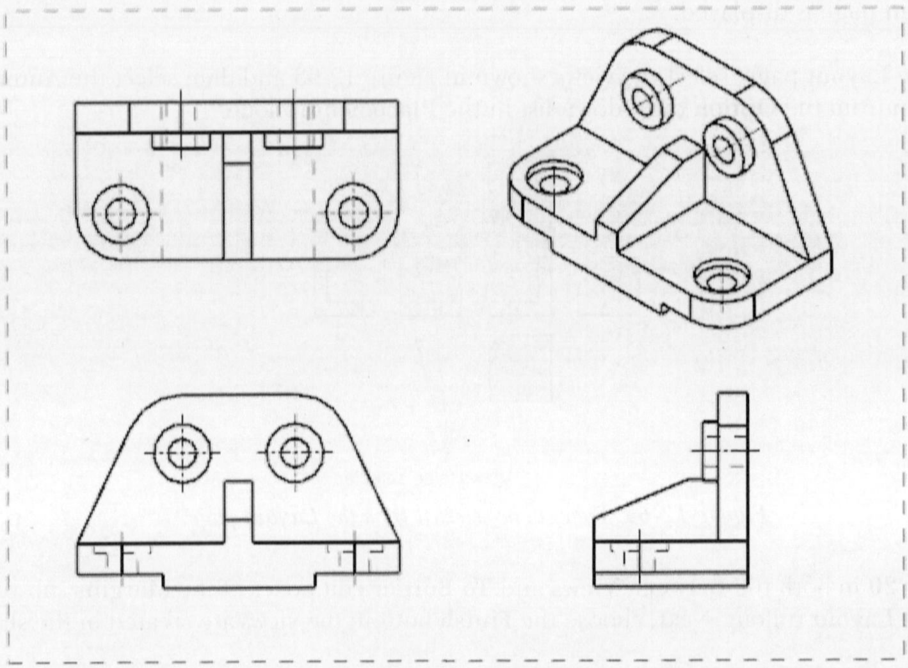

Figure 12-64 The drawing sheet after generating the drawing views of the model

Creating Dimensions for the Front View

Before creating dimensions, you need to set some dimensioning parameters.

1. Choose **Menu > Preferences > Drafting** from the **Top Border Bar**; the **Drafting Preferences** dialog box is displayed.

2. Choose the **Narrow** option from the **Dimension** node of the dialog box. Select the **No Leader** option from the **Style** drop-down list. Next, select the **Horizontal** option from the **Text Orientation** drop-down list in the **Format** rollout.

3. Choose the **Line/Arrow** option from the **Common** node. Next, select the **Filled Arrow** option from the **Type** drop-down list available in the **Leader and Dimension Side 1** rollout. Next, enter **10** in the **Length** edit box of the **Format** rollout.

4. Next, choose the **Dimension Text** option from the **Text** sub-node of the **Dimension** node of the dialog box and enter **10** in the **Height** edit box of the **Format** rollout.

5. Next, choose the **Lettering** option from the **Common** node and enter **4** in the **Height** edit box of the **Text Parameters** rollout. Next, choose the **OK** button to exit the **Drafting Preferences** dialog box. Now, you can create the dimensions.

6. Choose the **Rapid** tool from the **Dimension** group; the **Rapid Dimension** dialog box is displayed and you are prompted to select the first object for rapid dimension. Select the bottom left endpoint and then select the bottom right endpoint of the front view; a floating dimension measuring **216** is attached to the cursor and you are prompted to specify the origin. Drag the cursor below the front view and click at the desired location to place the dimension. Similarly, place other dimensions, as shown in Figure 12-65, using the **Rapid** tool. The front view after adding the required dimensions should look similar to the one shown in Figure 12-65.

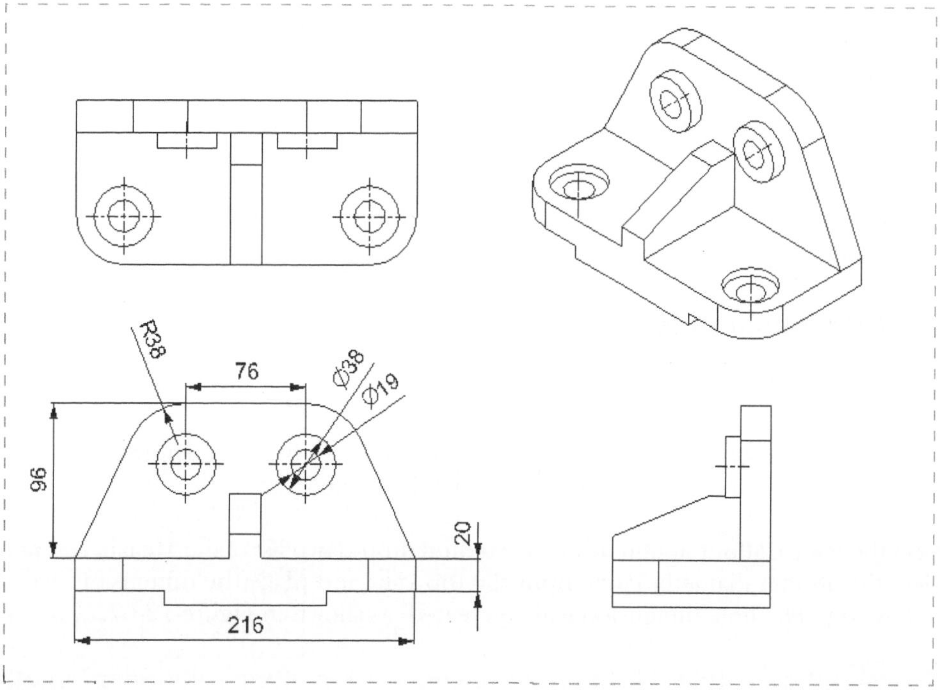

***Figure 12-65** The drawing view after creating the dimensions and placing them in the proper position*

Creating Dimensions for the Right-Side View

1. Again, choose the **Rapid** tool from the **Dimension** group and add the dimensions to the right side view. The right side view after adding the required dimensions should look similar to the one shown in Figure 12-66.

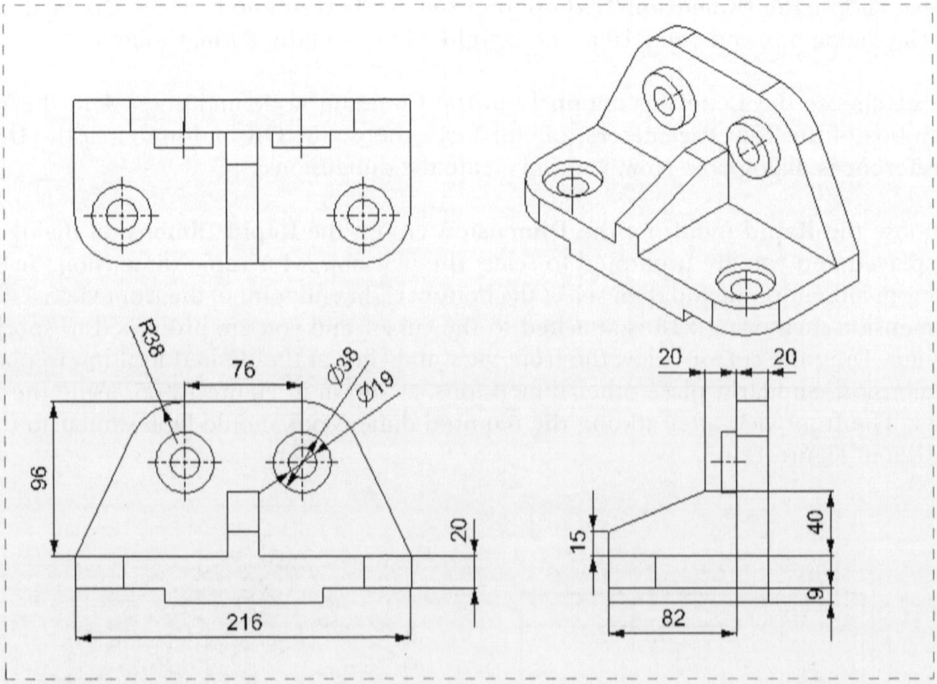

Figure 12-66 The drawing views after retrieving and creating the dimensions for the right side-view

Creating Dimensions for the Top View

1. Choose the **Rapid** tool from the **Dimension** group and create all the dimensions required for the top view, refer to Figure 12-67.

2. To add a counterbore dimension, choose the **Radial** tool from the **Dimension** group; you are prompted to select an object for the radial dimension.

3. Select the **Hole Callout** option from the **Method** drop-down list of the **Measurement** rollout. Select the **38** mm diameter circle from the top view and place the dimension. Next, press the ESC key. The hole dimension will be created, as shown in Figure 12-67.

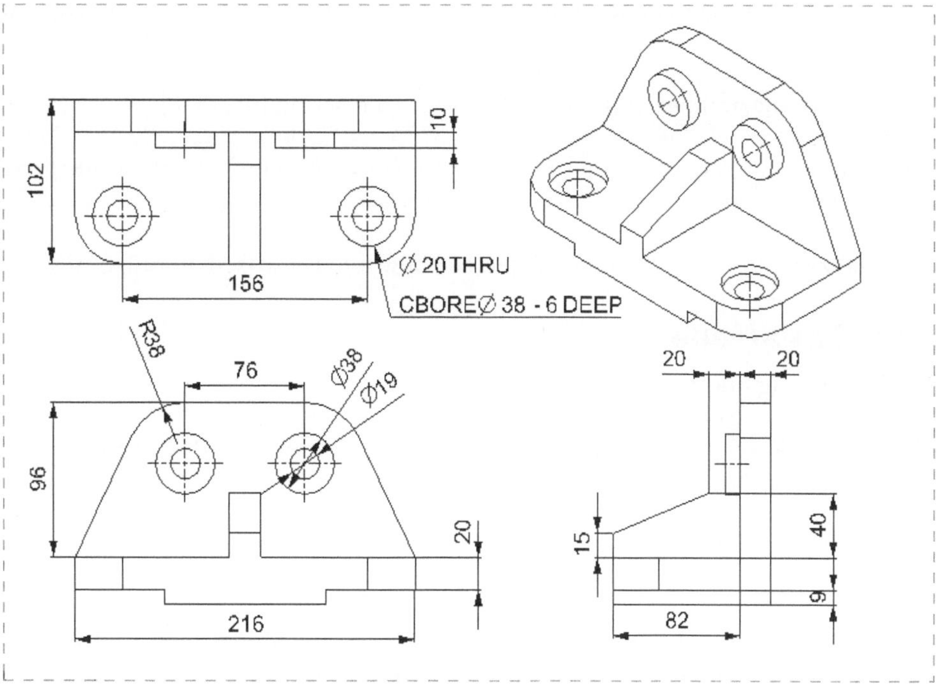

Figure 12-67 The complete drawing sheet after adding the counterbore dimension

Saving the Drawing Sheet

1. Choose **Menu > File > Save** from the **Top Border Bar**; the drawing sheet is saved. Next, close the file.

Self-Evaluation Test

Answer the following questions and then compare them to those given at the end of this chapter:

1. The ______ is the extension for the files created in the Drafting environment of NX.
2. The __________ is the parent drawing view generated from the model or assembly, which is currently opened in the modeling environment.
3. The __________ tool is used to insert a new drawing sheet into a drawing file.
4. To generate a section drawing view, you need choose the __________tool.
5. You can create two types of broken views using the **View Break** tool. (T/F)
6. By default, a grid exists in a drawing sheet. (T/F)

7. You cannot place the generated drawing views outside the drawing limits area of a drawing sheet. (T/F)

8. You can insert any number of drawing sheets into a drawing file. (T/F)

9. In the Drafting environment, you can change the orientation of a model while generating the drawing views. (T/F)

10. After generating the base view, the **Projected View** tool is invoked automatically. (T/F)

Review Questions

Answer the following questions:

1. Which of the following tools is used to automatically retrieve the dimensions created in a model in the drawing view?

   (a) **Feature Parameters** (b) **Insert Sheet**
   (c) **Add Base View** (d) None of these

2. Which of the following options should be selected from the **Model View to Use** drop-down list in the **Model View** area for generating an exploded drawing view?

   (a) **Isometric** (b) **Top**
   (c) **Trimetric** (d) None of these

3. Which of the following tools is used to create a title block in a drawing sheet?

   (a) **Tabular Note** (b) **Insert Parts List**
   (c) **Display Sheet** (d) None of these

4. Which of the following tools is used to insert an image into a drawing sheet?

   (a) **Image** (b) **ID Symbol**
   (c) **Custom Symbol** (d) None of these

5. Before creating part balloons, it is mandatory to create the Parts List of the assembly. (T/F)

6. A detail view can be generated directly from a model. (T/F)

7. After generating different drawing views, you can align them using the **View Alignment** tool. (T/F)

8. After invoking the Drafting environment, you can change the sheet specifications. (T/F)

9. The **Drafting Preferences** dialog box is used to set the dimension parameters. (T/F)

10. Part balloons can be modified dynamically. (T/F)

EXERCISES

Exercise 1

Create the exploded view and the isometric view of the assembly created in Tutorial 2 of Chapter 8, refer to Figure 12-68. Also, generate the parts list and auto balloons shown in the same figure. After completing the drawing sheet, print and plot it. **(Expected time: 30 min)**

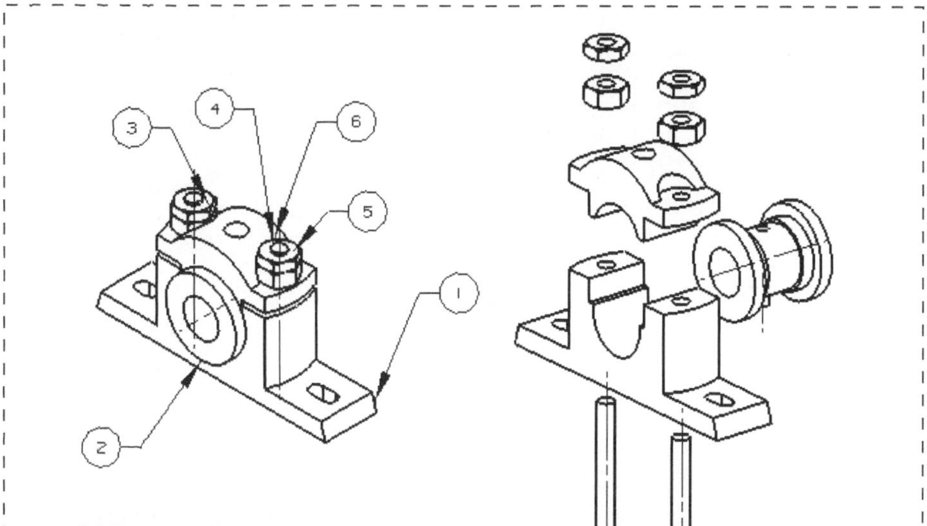

PC NO	PART NAME	QTY
6	LOCKNUT	2
5	NUT	2
4	BOLT	2
3	CAP	1
2	BRASSES	1
1	CASTING	1

Figure 12-68 *The drawing views of the assembly along with the parts list and auto balloons*

Exercise 2

Create the drawing views of the model created in Exercise 1 of Chapter 6. Generate the dimensions and add the required dimensions to the drawing views. Also, add the tabular note to the drawing sheet, as shown in Figure 12-69. After completing the drawing sheet, print and plot it. **(Expected time: 30 min)**

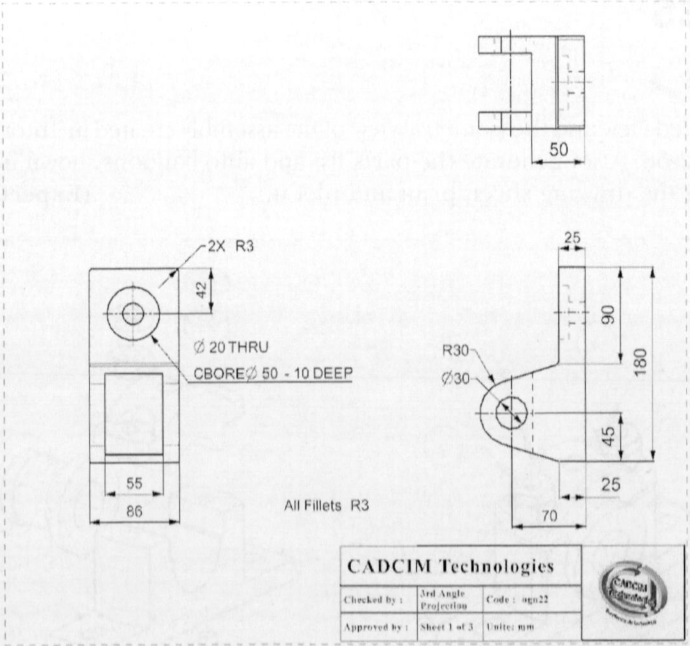

Figure 12-69 The drawing sheet displaying the drawing views after retrieving and adding the dimensions along with the tabular note

Answers to Self-Evaluation Test

1. *.prt,* **2. Base View, 3. New Sheet, 4. Section View, 5.** T, **6.** F, **7.** T, **8.** T, **9.** T, **10.** T

Chapter 13

Synchronous Modeling

Learning Objectives

After completing this chapter, you will be able to:

- *Modify Faces*
- *Modify Blends and Chamfers*
- *Reuse Faces*
- *Relate Faces*
- *Apply dimensions between faces*
- *Shell faces*
- *Group Faces*
- *Edit the cross-section of a model*

INTRODUCTION

Synchronous Modeling is a state-of-the-art technology used to modify the parts even if the modeling history is not available. As a result, the time required for rebuilding the sketches and converting them into the solid geometry will be saved. The parts to be modified can be made in NX or any other CAD package. Synchronous Modeling tools are used to modify and improve the already created design in the shortest period of time, regardless of its origin, associativity, or feature history. NX with Synchronous Modeling gets an edge over other modeling packages.

SYNCHRONOUS MODELING TOOLS

The Synchronous Modeling tools are available in the **Synchronous Modeling** group of the **Home** tab of the **Ribbon**. The tools in the **Synchronous Modeling** group are discussed next.

Move Face

Ribbon:	Home > Synchronous Modeling > Move Face
Menu:	Insert > Synchronous Modeling > Move Face

Move Face

You can move a set of selected faces of a model in the linear direction or orient them in the angular direction using the **Move Face** tool. On doing so, the adjacent chamfers or fillets will also get adjusted automatically. To move the face of a model, choose the **Move Face** tool from the **Synchronous Modeling** group; the **Move Face** dialog box will be displayed, refer to Figure 13-1. The options in this dialog box are discussed next.

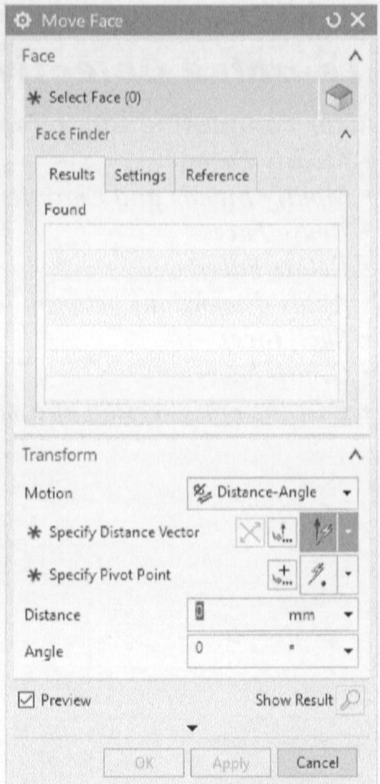

*Figure 13-1 The **Move Face** dialog box*

Face Rollout

In this rollout, the **Face** button is chosen by default. As a result, you will be prompted to select the faces to be moved. Select the faces that you want to move; a dimension handle, and a dynamic edit box will be displayed, refer to Figure 13-2. Components of the handle are shown in Figure 13-2. Click on the point located at the center of the handle, the OrientXpress tool will be displayed, as shown in Figure 13-3. Using this tool, you can choose the direction for moving the selected faces. Using the distance axis, you can drag the selected faces along the specified direction on the vector triad. Note that the component will be modified according to the movement of the cursor. Using the angle axis, you can change the angular direction of the selected face. You can also use the dynamic edit box for modifying the component. Figure 13-3 shows the selected faces, the OrientXpress tool, and the dynamic edit box and Figure 13-4 shows a preview of the dynamically updated model. Figure 13-5 shows the faces selected to rotate by using the angular axis and Figure 13-6 shows a preview of the dynamically updated model.

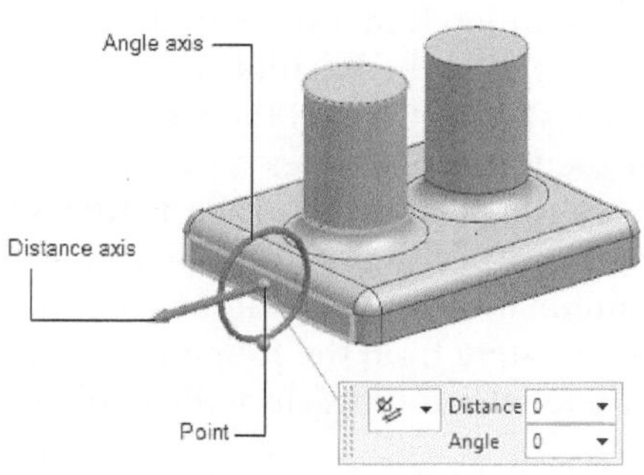

Figure 13-2 *The Dimension handle and its components*

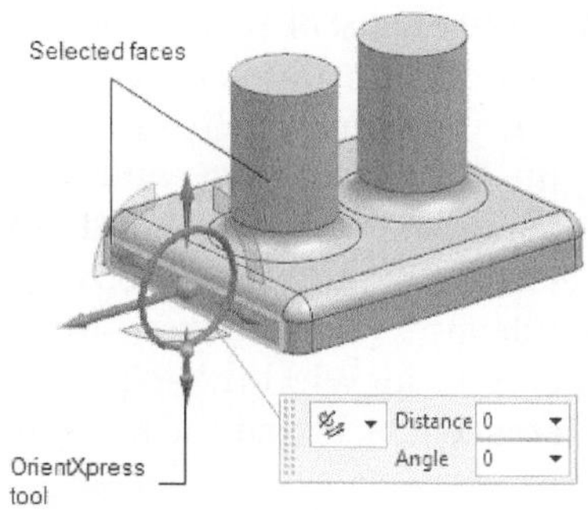

Figure 13-3 *Face selected to move in the linear direction*

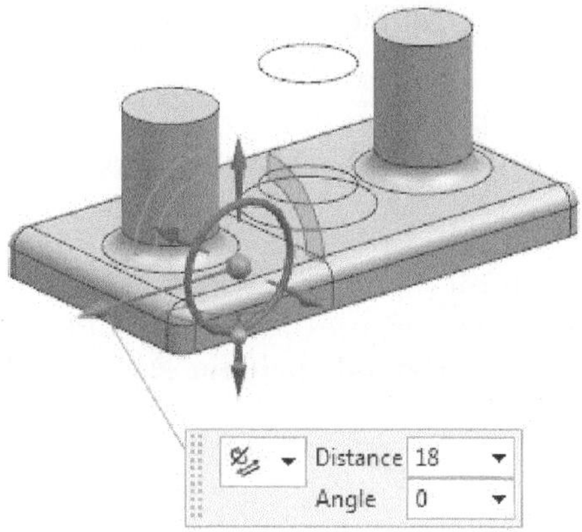

Figure 13-4 *Dynamically updated model*

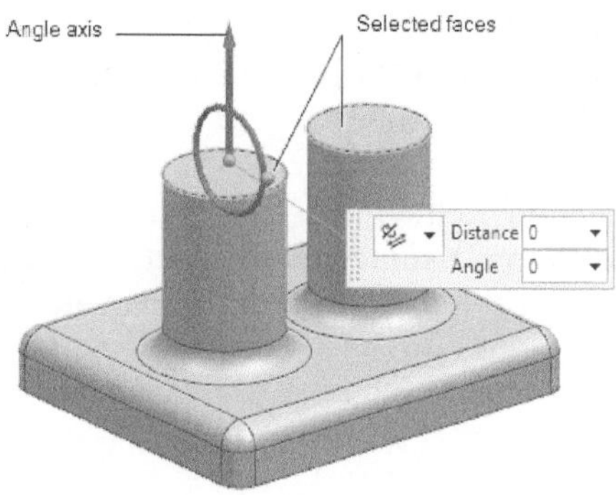

Figure 13-5 *Faces selected to rotate*

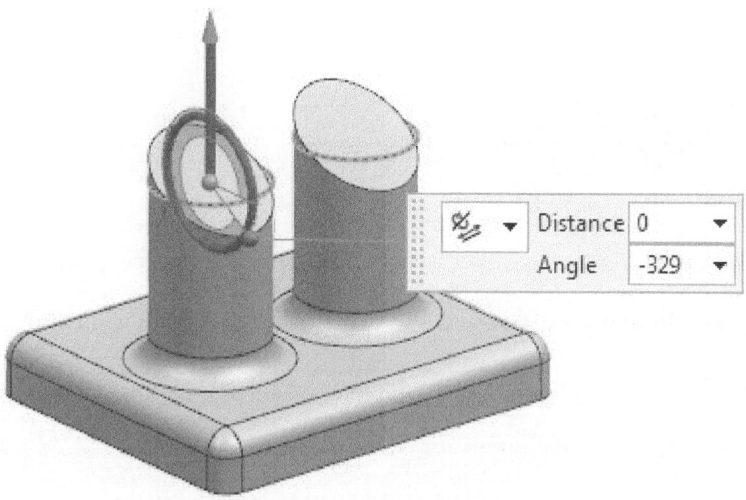

Figure 13-6 *Dynamically updated model*

If you select a face, a list of all possible geometrical conditions that can be applied to the selected face with respect to the unselected faces will be displayed in the **Results** tab of the **Face Finder** sub-rollout. If you move the cursor over a geometrical condition, all the faces related to it will be highlighted in the drawing window. To select the unselected faces, select the check box of the corresponding geometrical condition. In the **Settings** tab of the **Face Finder** sub-rollout, you can select the required check boxes of the geometrical conditions in such a way that if you select a single face, multiple faces are selected automatically according to the settings in the **Settings** tab. You can select the required coordinate system from the **Reference** drop-down list in the **Reference** tab, so that the faces move with reference to the selected coordinate system.

Transform Rollout

Instead of dragging the dimension handle or using the dynamic edit boxes to move the faces, you can use the **Transform** rollout to specify the values. The options in this rollout are similar to the options in the **Move Component** dialog box discussed in Chapter 8.

Settings Rollout

The **Move Behavior** drop-down list in the **Settings** rollout is used to specify the behavior of the faces while moving them.

The **Overflow Behavior** drop-down list is used to control the output, when an offset value is specified in the **Distance** edit box in the **Transform** rollout. Figures 13-7, 13-8, and 13-9 show the output of the model when the **Extend Change Face**, **Extend Incident Face**, and **Extend Cap Face** options are respectively selected.

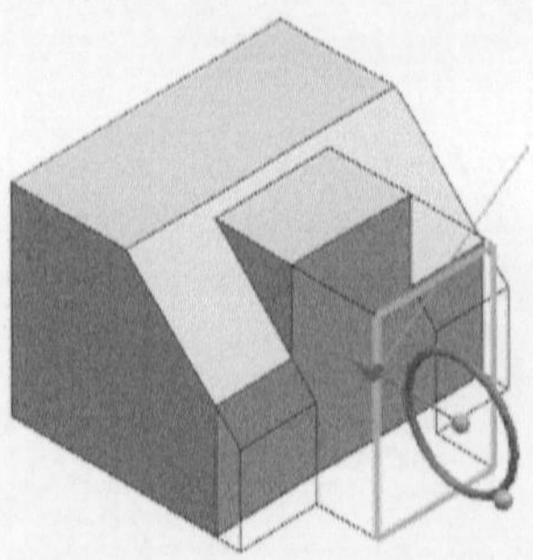

Figure 13-7 The model output with the ***Extend Change Face*** *option selected*

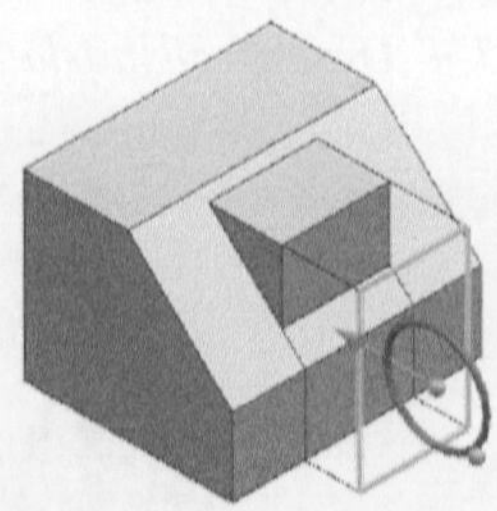

Figure 13-8 The model output with the ***Extend Incident Face*** *option selected*

The **Step Face** drop-down list is used to extend the neighboring faces while moving the selected face.

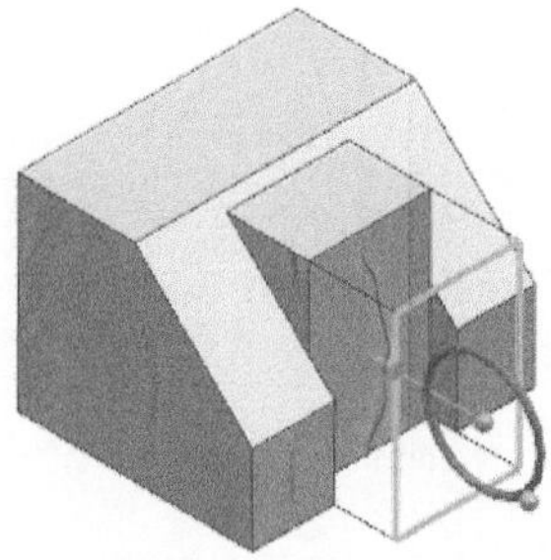

*Figure 13-9 The model output with the **Extend Cap Face** option selected*

Move Edge

Ribbon:	Home > Synchronous Modeling > More Gallery > Edge > Move Edge *(Customize to Add)*
Menu:	Insert > Synchronous Modeling > Edge > Move Edge

This tool is used to move the selected edges of a model. You can directly edit the shape of a model by moving the edges. To move an edge of a model, invoke the **More** Gallery of the **Synchronous Modeling** group and choose the **Move Edge** tool from the **Edge** Gallery; the **Move Edge** dialog box will be displayed, refer to Figure 13-10. The options in this dialog box are discussed next.

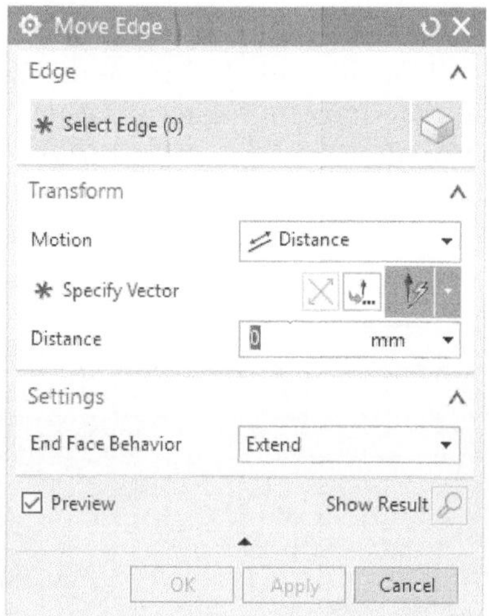

*Figure 13-10 The **Move Edge** dialog box*

Edge Rollout

In this rollout, the **Edge** button is chosen by default. As a result, you will be prompted to select the edges to be moved. Select the edges that you want to move; a direction handle, a distance axis, and a dynamic edit box will be displayed on the selected edges, refer to Figure 13-11. Using this handle, you can choose the direction for moving the selected edges. Using the distance axis, you can drag the selected edges along the specified direction. Note that the model will be modified according to the movement of the cursor. You can also use the dynamic edit box for modifying the model. Figure 13-12 shows the preview of the dynamically updated model.

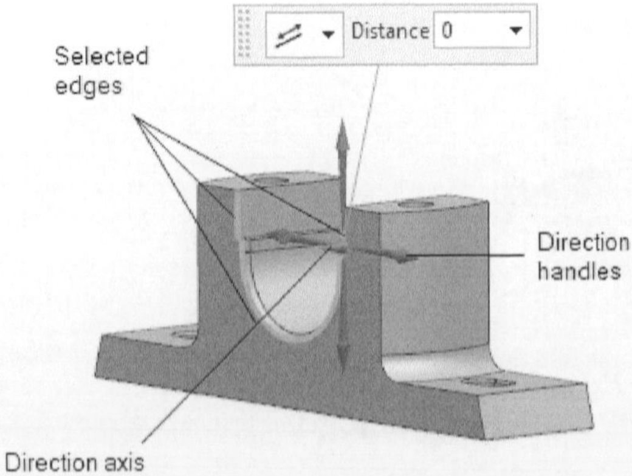

Figure 13-11 Model with selected edges

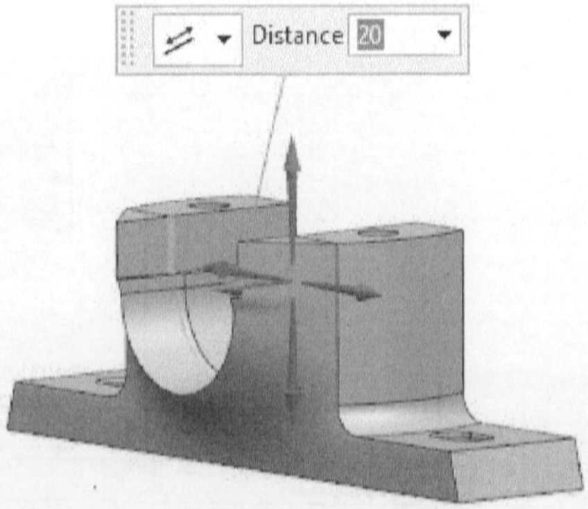

Figure 13-12 Dynamically updated model

Transform Rollout

Instead of dragging the dimension handle, or using the dynamic edit boxes to move the faces, you can move the faces by using the **Transform** rollout to specify the values. The options in this rollout are similar to the options of the **Move Component** dialog box discussed in Chapter 8.

Settings Rollout

The **End Face Behavior** drop-down list in the **Settings** rollout is used to specify the behavior of the adjacent faces or edges while moving the selected edges. If you choose the **Extend** option from the drop-down list, the shape of adjacent faces will remain unchanged, refer to Figure 13-13. If you choose the **Morph** option from the drop-down list, the shape of the adjacent faces will change according to the moved faces, refer to Figure 13-14.

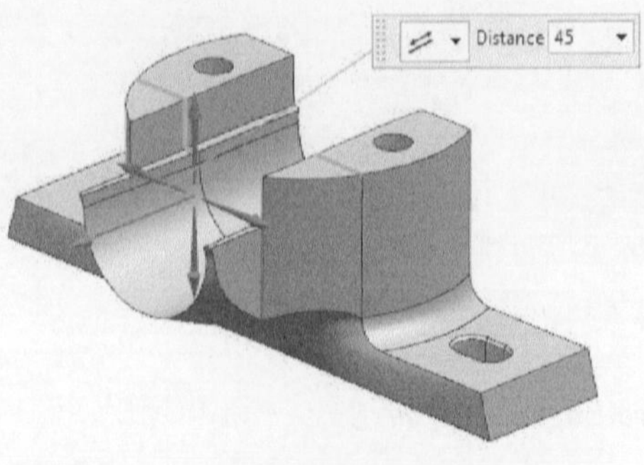

*Figure 13-13 The model output with the **Extend** option selected*

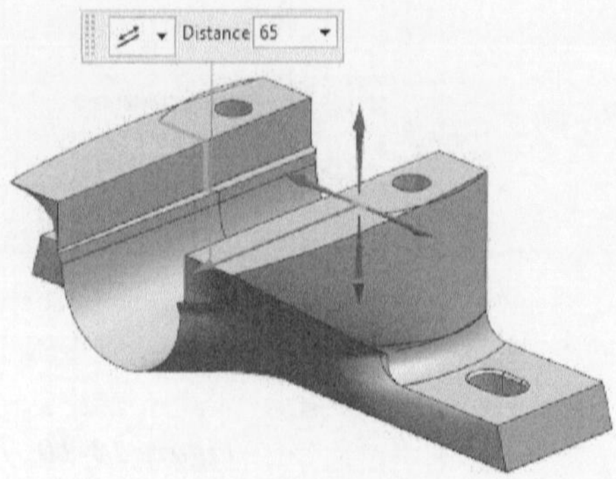

*Figure 13-14 The model output with the **Morph** option selected*

Note

The edges selected to be moved must form a connected chain.

Pull Face

Ribbon:	Home > Synchronous Modeling > Pull Face
Menu:	Insert > Synchronous Modeling > Pull Face

You can pull a set of selected faces of a model in the linear direction using the **Pull Face** tool, but you cannot orient them in the angular direction. While pulling the faces, the adjacent chamfers or fillets will be automatically adjusted. To invoke this tool, choose **Menu > Insert > Synchronous Modeling > Pull Face** from the **Top Border bar**; the **Pull Face** dialog box will be displayed, as shown in Figure 13-15. Also, you will be prompted to select the faces to pull. Select the faces; a handle, a dynamic edit box, and a vector triad will be displayed on one of the selected faces, as shown in Figure 13-16. Note that you may need to specify the direction vector after selecting the faces. Drag the handle; the model will be dynamically updated, as shown in Figure 13-17.

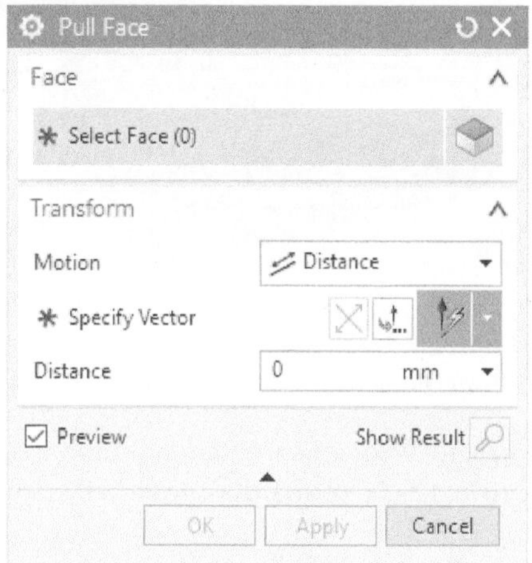

Figure 13-15 The ***Pull Face*** *dialog box*

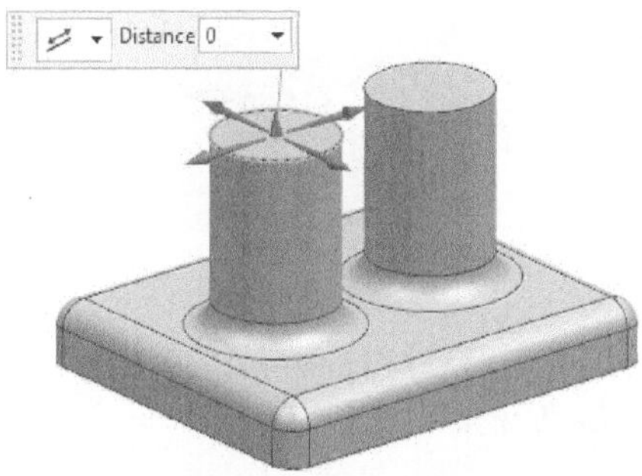

Figure 13-16 Face selected to be pulled

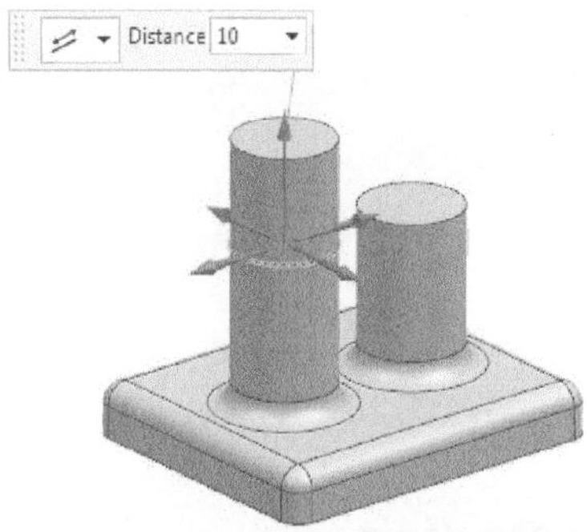

Figure 13-17 Dynamically updated model

The options in the **Pull Face** dialog box are the same as those in the **Move Face** dialog box with the only difference that the **Move Face** tool is used to move the selected faces with respect to the adjacent geometry, whereas the **Pull Face** tool is used to pull the selected faces regardless of the adjacent geometry. For example, Figure 13-18 shows the face moved using the **Move Face** tool and Figure 13-19 shows the face moved using the **Pull Face** tool.

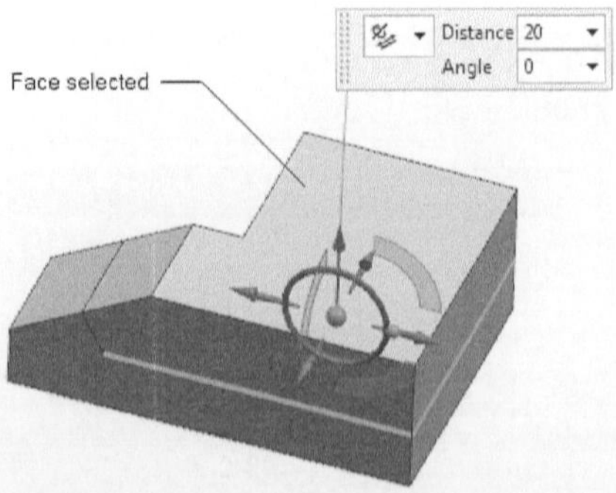

Figure 13-18 *Selected face moved using the* ***Move Face*** *tool*

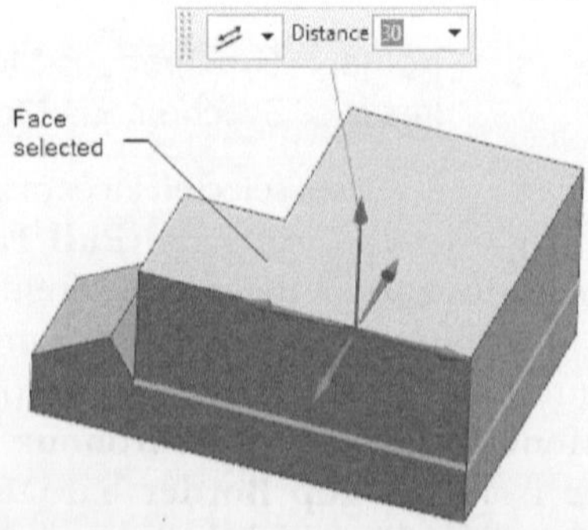

Figure 13-19 *Selected face moved using the* ***Pull Face*** *tool*

You can also select a sketch region to pull. Figure 13-20 shows a sketch region selected and Figure 13-21 shows the model after pulling the sketch region.

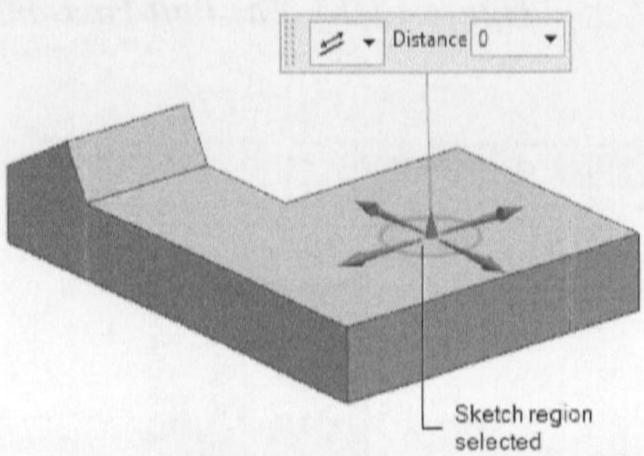

Figure 13-20 *Sketch region selected*

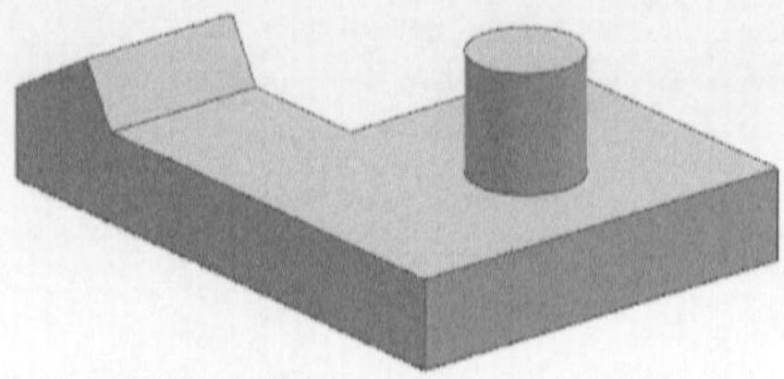

Figure 13-21 *Model after pulling the sketch region*

Offset Region

Ribbon:	Home > Synchronous Modeling > Offset Region
Menu:	Insert > Synchronous Modeling > Offset Region

The **Offset Region** tool is used to offset a set of selected faces of a model along the normal of the selected faces. To do so, choose the **Offset Region** tool from the **Synchronous Modeling** group; the **Offset Region** dialog box will be displayed, refer to Figure 13-22 and you will be prompted to select the faces to offset. Select the faces; a handle and a dynamic edit box will be displayed on the first selected face, refer to Figure 13-23. Drag the handle; the model will be updated, refer to Figure 13-24. The options of the **Offset Region** dialog box are the same as those in the **Move Face** dialog box.

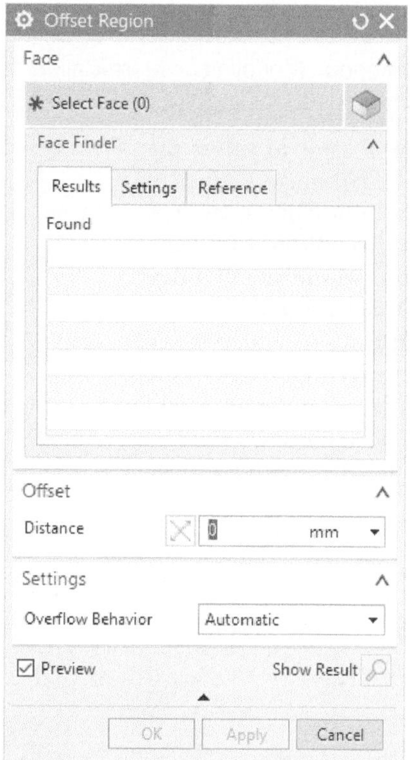

Figure 13-22 *The **Offset Region** dialog box*

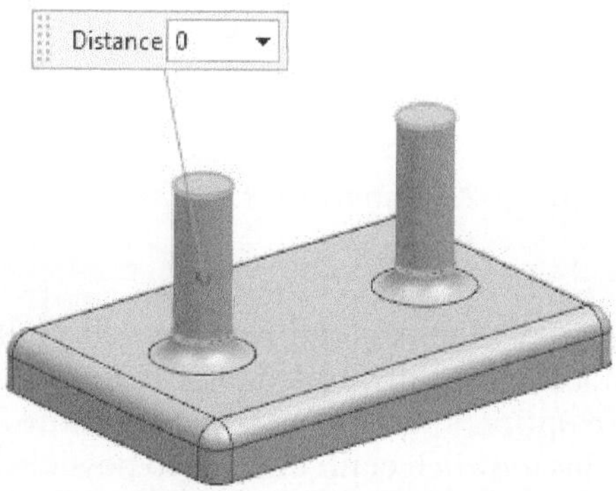

Figure 13-23 *Faces selected to offset*

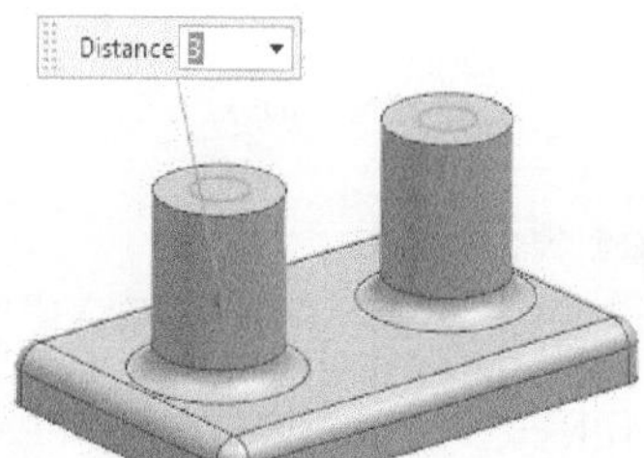

Figure 13-24 *Dynamically updated model*

Offset Edge

Ribbon: Home > Synchronous Modeling > More Gallery > Edge > Offset Edge
Menu: Insert > Synchronous Modeling > Edge > Offset Edge

The **Offset Edge** tool is used to offset the selected edge or a set of connected edges of a model along the plane or face of the selected edges. To do so, choose the **Offset Edge** tool from **Menu > Insert > Synchronous Modeling > Edge** in the **Top Border Bar**; the **Offset Edge** dialog box will be displayed, refer to Figure 13-25 and you will be prompted to select the edges to offset. Select the set of connected edges; a handle and a dynamic edit box will be displayed on the selected edges, refer to Figure 13-26. Drag the handle; the model will be updated, refer to Figure 13-27. The other options of the **Offset Edge** dialog box are discussed next.

*Figure 13-25 The **Offset Edge** dialog box*

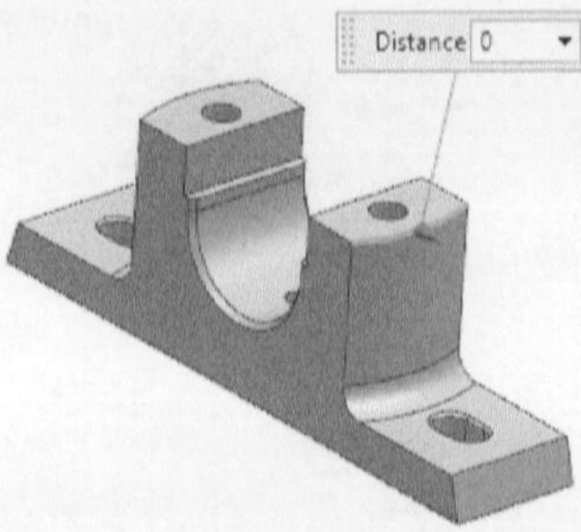

Figure 13-26 Edge selected to offset

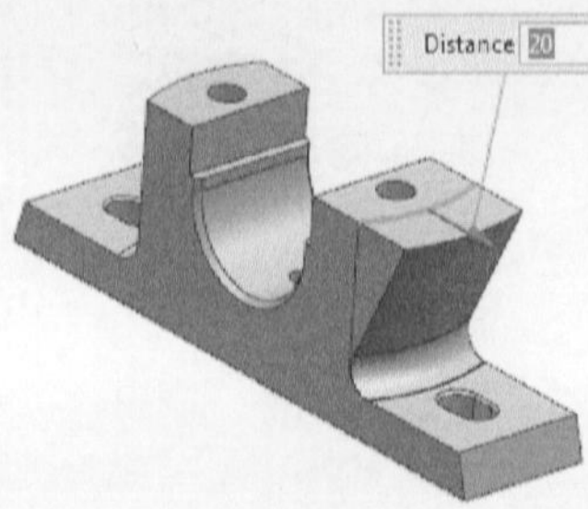

Figure 13-27 Dynamically updated model

Offset Rollout

In this rollout, the **Method** drop-down list is used to specify the side of the edge to offset. If you select the **Along Face** option from the drop-down list, the edge will offset along the adjacent face of the selected edge. When you select the **Along Face** option, the **Change which Face the Edge is Offset Along** button will be available. You can use this to switch between the two possible faces along which the edge can be offset, refer to Figures 13-28 and 13-29. If you select the **Along Plane of Edge** option from the drop-down list then the planar edge will offset along the plane of the selected edges. The **Reverse Offset Direction** button is used to reverse the direction of the offset either inside the boundary of the selected edges and face or outside the boundary.

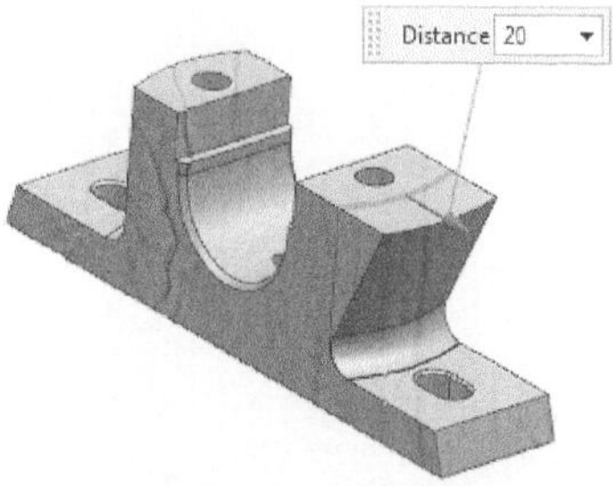

Figure 13-28 The edge offset without using the ***Change which Face the Edge is Offset Along*** *button*

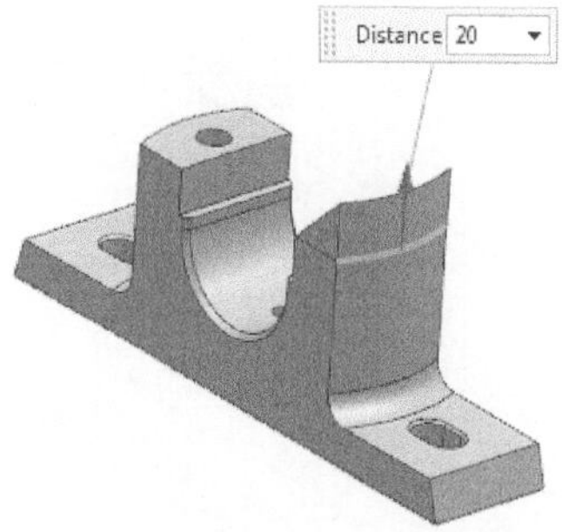

Figure 13-29 The edge offset using the ***Change which Face the Edge is Offset Along*** *button*

Replace Face

Ribbon:	Home > Synchronous Modeling > Replace Face
Menu:	Insert > Synchronous Modeling > Replace Face

The **Replace Face** tool is used to replace a selected face of a model with another face. Choose the **Replace Face** tool from the **Synchronous Modeling** group; the **Replace Face** dialog box will be displayed, as shown in Figure 13-30 and you will be prompted to select the faces to replace. Select the faces that you want to replace. Next, choose the **Face** button from the **Replacement Face** rollout; you will be prompted to select the replacement face. Select the replacement face; the face to be replaced will become coplanar with the replacement face. Also, a handle and a vector will be displayed on the replacement face. Next, click in the **Distance** edit box of the **Offset** sub-rollout of the **Replacement Face** rollout. Figure 13-31 shows the faces selected and Figure 13-32 shows preview of the resultant model along with the dynamic edit box, the handle, and the vector. You can further modify the selected face with respect to the replacement face by dragging the handle or by modifying the offset distance in the **Distance** edit box in the **Offset** sub-rollout. To change the direction of vector, choose the **Reverse Direction** button from the **Replacement Face** rollout and to change the direction of the handle, use the **Reverse Direction** button from the **Offset** sub-rollout. To apply the changes and close the **Replace Face** dialog box, choose the **OK** button.

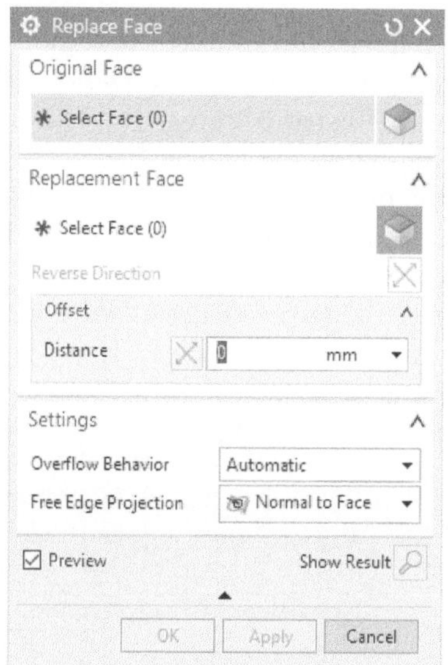

Figure 13-30 The ***Replace Face*** *dialog box*

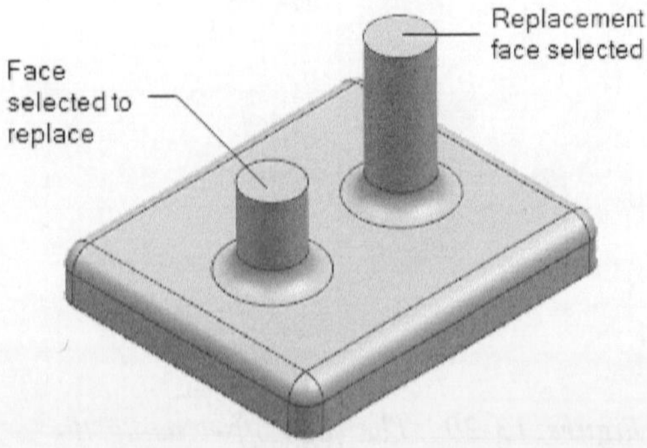

Figure 13-31 Faces to be selected

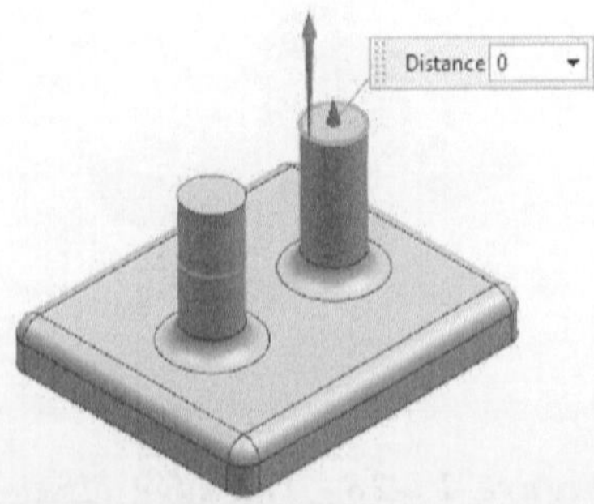

Figure 13-32 Dynamically updated model after selecting the faces

Resize Blend

Ribbon:	Home > Synchronous Modeling > More Gallery > Detail Feature > Resize Blend
Menu:	Insert > Synchronous Modeling > Detail Feature > Resize Blend

You can change the radius of a blend in a model using the **Resize Blend** tool. To do so, invoke the **More** Gallery of the **Synchronous Modeling** group and then choose the **Resize Blend** tool from the **Detail Feature** Gallery, refer to Figure 13-33; the **Resize Blend** dialog box will be displayed, as shown in Figure 13-34, and you will be prompted to select the blend to resize. Select a blend; the radius of the blend will be displayed in the **Radius** edit box of the **Radius** rollout. Also, a dynamic edit box with the radius of blend, and a handle will be displayed in the graphics window, refer to Figure 13-35. You can use these edit boxes to change the radius of the blend. Alternatively, you can change the radius of the blend dynamically by dragging the handle, refer to Figure 13-36.

Figure 13-33 The **More** Gallery

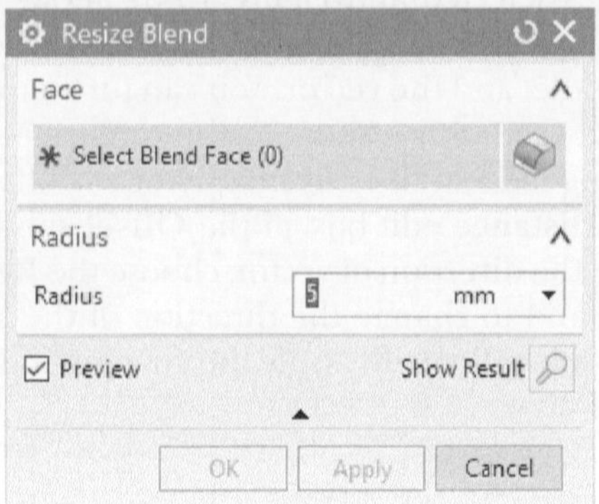

Figure 13-34 The **Resize Blend** dialog box

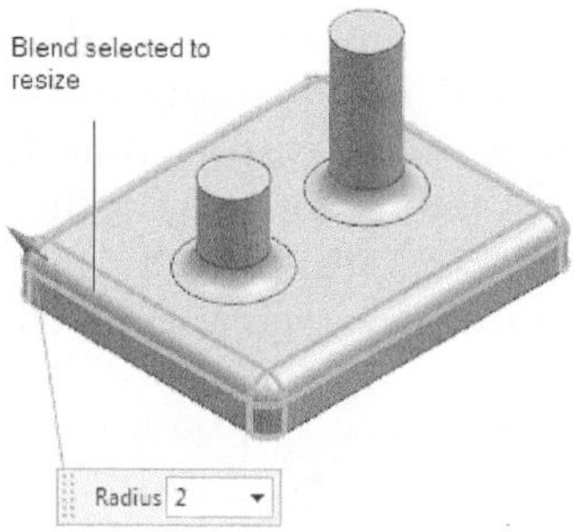

Figure 13-35 Blend selected to resize

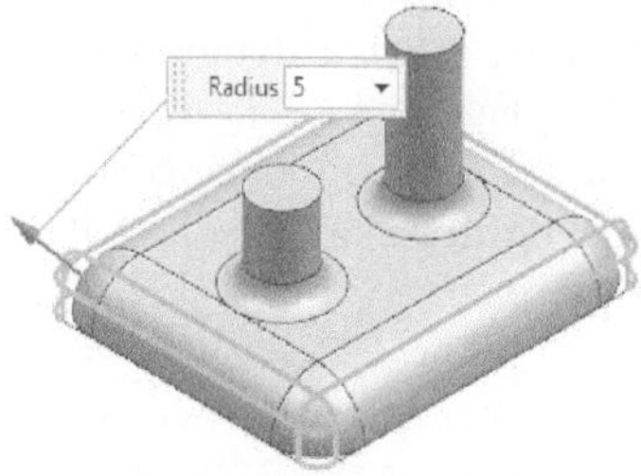

Figure 13-36 Dynamically updated model

Reorder Blends

Ribbon: Home > Synchronous Modeling > More Gallery > Detail Feature > Reorder Blends
Menu: Insert > Synchronous Modeling > Detail Feature > Reorder Blends

You can use the **Reorder Blends** tool to modify the shapes of the blends that are formed at the intersection of three blends. Note that the corner blend can be modified only if it is created by the combination of concave and convex shaped blends. To change the shape of a corner blend, invoke the **More** gallery of the **Synchronous Modeling** group and then choose the **Reorder Blends** tool from the **Detail Feature** gallery; the **Reorder Blends** dialog box will be displayed, and you will be prompted to select the corner blend to be modified. Select the corner blend, refer to Figure 13-37; the blend will be modified, as shown in Figure 13-38.

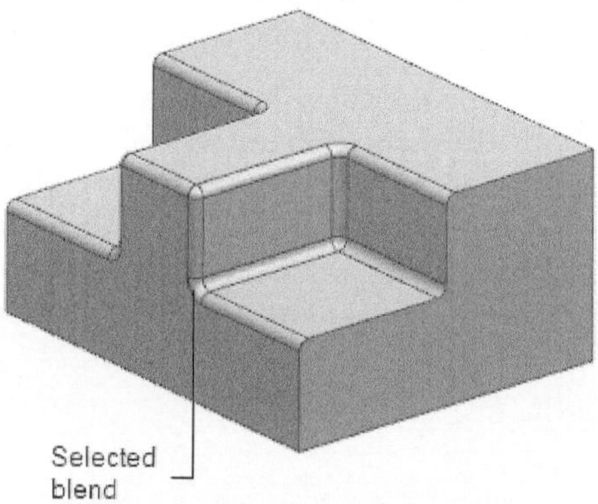

Figure 13-37 Intersecting blend to be selected

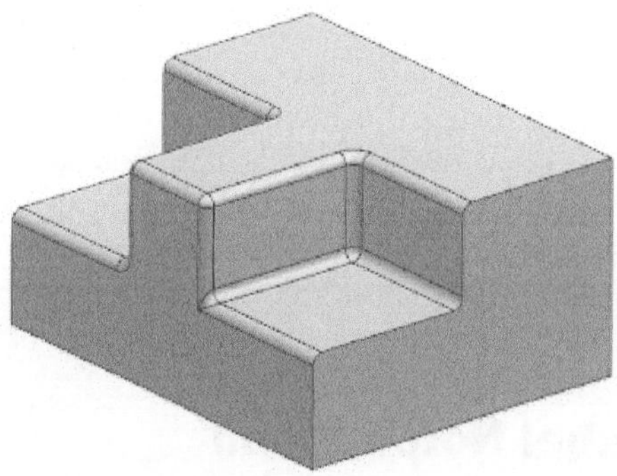

Figure 13-38 Model after reordering the blend

Resize Chamfer

Ribbon: Home > Synchronous Modeling > More Gallery > Detail Feature > Resize Chamfer
Menu: Insert > Synchronous Modeling > Detail Feature > Resize Chamfer

You can change the size of a chamfer in a model, regardless of its adjacent geometry, by using the **Resize Chamfer** tool. To do so, invoke the **More** gallery of the **Synchronous**

Modeling group and then choose the **Resize Chamfer** tool from the **Detail Feature** gallery; the **Resize Chamfer** dialog box will be displayed and you will be prompted to select the chamfer to resize. Select the chamfer; the chamfer values will be displayed in their respective edit boxes in the **Offsets** rollout. Also, a dynamic edit box, and a handle will be displayed in the graphics window, refer to Figure 13-39. You can change the size of the chamfer using the edit boxes available in the **Offsets** rollout or by using the dynamic edit box. Alternatively, you can change the size of the chamfer using the handles, refer to Figure 13-40. Next, choose the **OK** button to exit the dialog box.

Figure 13-39 *Model with a dynamic edit box, a handle*

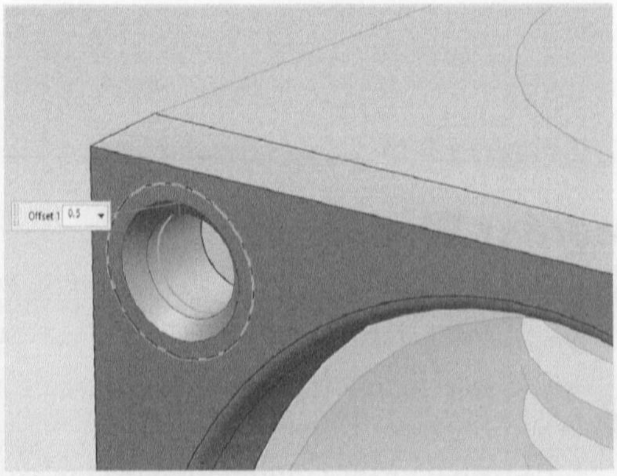

Figure 13-40 *Preview of the resultant model*

Label Chamfer

Ribbon: Home > Synchronous Modeling > More Gallery > Detail Feature > Label Chamfer
Menu: Insert > Synchronous Modeling > Detail Feature > Label Chamfer

You can label an angular face which is not created by using the **Chamfer** tool, as a chamfer by using the **Label Chamfer** tool. To do so, invoke the **Label Chamfer** tool and then select the angular face; the selected angular face will be labeled as a chamfer. After labeling the angular face as a chamfer, you can use the **Resize Chamfer** tool to resize it as a chamfer. Also, if you move its adjacent faces, it will move as a chamfer and its size will not change. However, if you move the faces adjacent to the angular face without labeling the angular face as a chamfer, the size of the angular face will change as you move the face using the **Move Face** tool.

Label Notch Blend

Ribbon: Home > Synchronous Modeling > More Gallery > Detail Feature > Label Notch Blend (Customize to Add)
Menu: Insert > Synchronous Modeling > Detail Feature > Label Notch Blend

You can label a curved face as a blend by using the **Label Notch Blend** tool. To do so, invoke the **Label Notch Blend** tool and then select the curved face; the selected curved face will be labeled as a blend. After doing so, you can use the **Resize Blend** tool to resize the curved face as a blend. Also, if you move its adjacent faces, it will move as a blend and its size will not change. However, if you move the faces adjacent to the curved face without labeling the curved face as a blend, the size of the curved face will change as you move the face using the **Move Face** tool. Figure 13-41 shows the labeled and unlabeled curved faces in a model and Figure 13-42 shows the preview of the resultant model after moving the adjacent faces of the labeled and unlabeled covered faces.

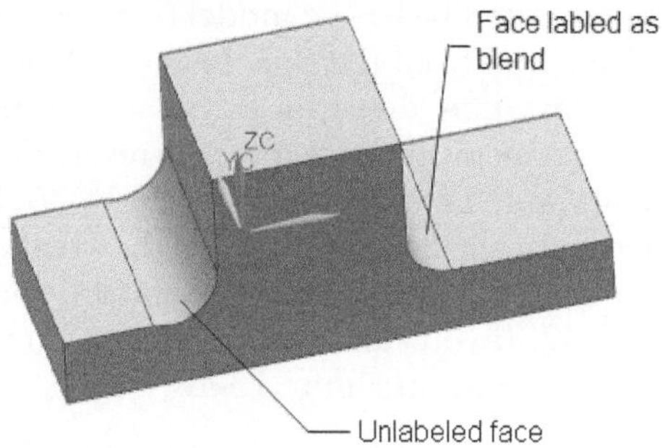

Figure 13-41 *Unlabeled and labeled faces*

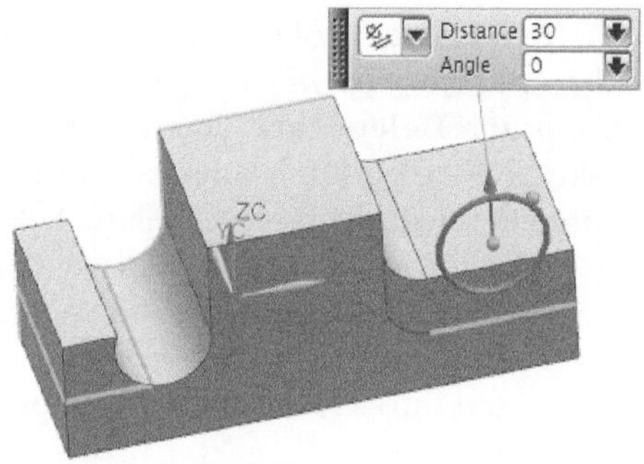

Figure 13-42 *Resulting model after moving the faces*

Resize Face

Ribbon:	Home > Synchronous Modeling > More Gallery > Move > Resize Face
Menu:	Insert > Synchronous Modeling > Resize Face

You can resize the selected cylindrical faces of a model using the **Resize Face** tool. To do so, invoke the **More** gallery of the **Synchronous Modeling** group and then choose the **Resize Face** tool from it; the **Resize Face** dialog box will be displayed and you will be prompted to select the faces to resize. Select the cylindrical face; the diameter of the selected cylindrical face will be displayed in the **Diameter** edit box of the **Size** rollout. Now, you can use this edit box to change the diameter of the selected cylindrical face. Figure 13-43 shows the face selected to resize and Figure 13-44 shows the model after resizing the selected face. The other options in this dialog box are the same as those discussed in the **Move Face** dialog box.

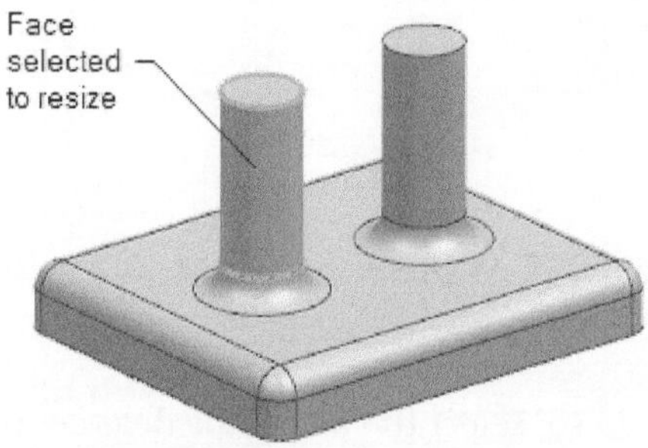

Figure 13-43 *Face selected to resize*

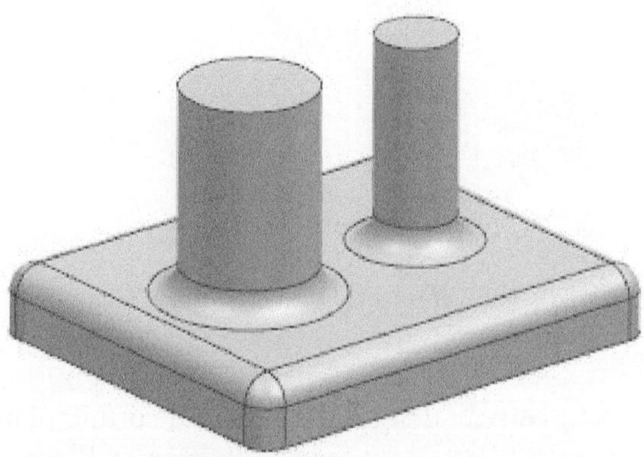

Figure 13-44 *Dynamically updated model*

Delete Face

Ribbon:	Home > Synchronous Modeling > Delete Face
Menu:	Insert > Synchronous Modeling > Delete Face

The **Delete Face** tool is used for deleting the unwanted faces of a model by projecting its adjacent faces. To do so, choose the **Delete Face** tool from the **Synchronous Modeling** group; the **Delete Face** dialog box will be displayed, as shown in Figure 13-45. In this dialog box, the **Face** option is selected by default in the type drop-down list. As a result, you will be prompted to select the faces to delete. Select the unwanted face, refer to Figure 13-46. Next, choose the **OK** button; the selected face will be deleted. In the **Settings** rollout, the **Heal** check box is selected by default. As a result, the neighbouring faces get extended and heal the opening created after deleting the face, as shown in Figure 13-47. If you clear this check box, the solid body is converted into a sheet body with open edges, as shown in Figure 13-48.

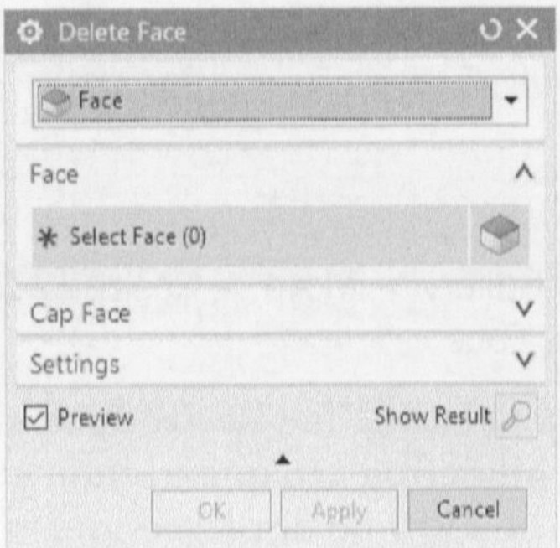

*Figure 13-45 The **Delete Face** dialog box*

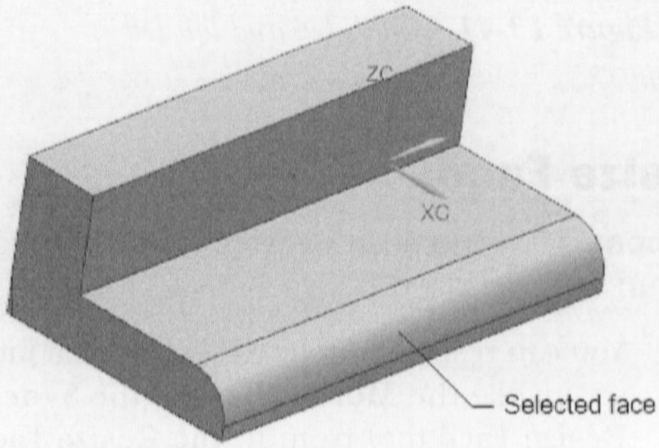

Figure 13-46 Face selected for deleting

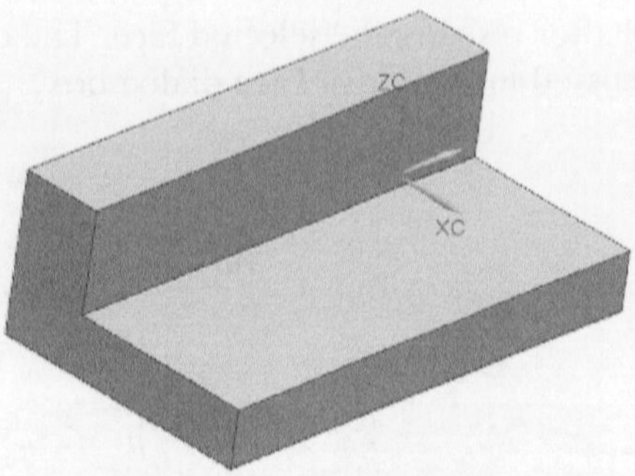

*Figure 13-47 Resultant model with the **Heal** check box selected*

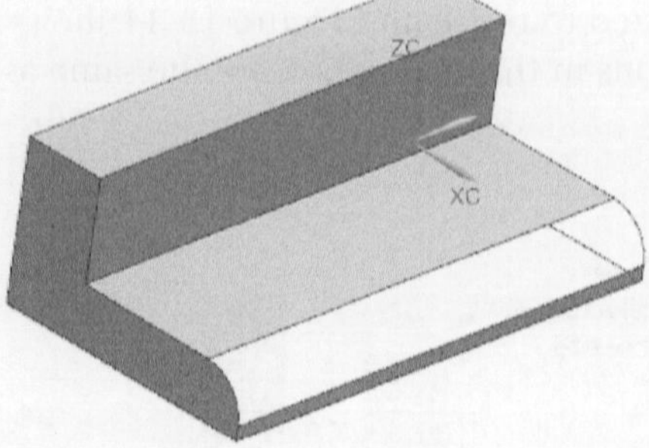

*Figure 13-48 Resultant model with the **Heal** check box cleared*

In NX, you can delete a face using a cutting plane. To do so, select the face to be deleted, refer to Figure 13-49. Next, select the **Face or Plane** option from the **Cap Option** drop-down list of the **Cap Face** rollout. Choose the **Face** button from the **Cap Face** rollout and then select a plane or face, refer to Figure 13-49. Make sure that the **Heal** check box is selected in the **Settings** rollout. Figure 13-50 shows the model after deleting the face.

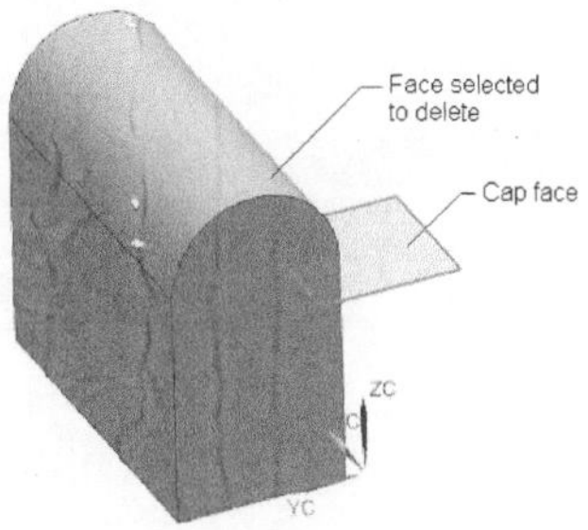

Figure 13-49 Face to be deleted and the cap face

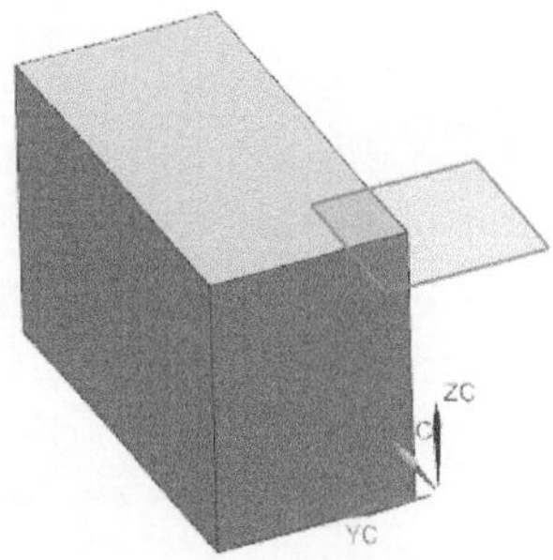

Figure 13-50 Resultant model

You can also delete a blend which is adjacent to another blend, refer to Figure 13-51. The **Delete Partial Blend** check box in the **Settings** rollout can be used for deleting a blend which is adjacent to another blend. If you select this check box, the **Setback** drop-down list is enabled. Next, select the **Selected Blend** or **Neighbor Blend** option from this drop-down list. Figures 13-52 and 13-53 show the blend deleted using the **Selected Blend** and **Neighbor Blend** options, respectively. Figure 13-54 shows a blend deleted with the **Delete Partial Blend** check box cleared.

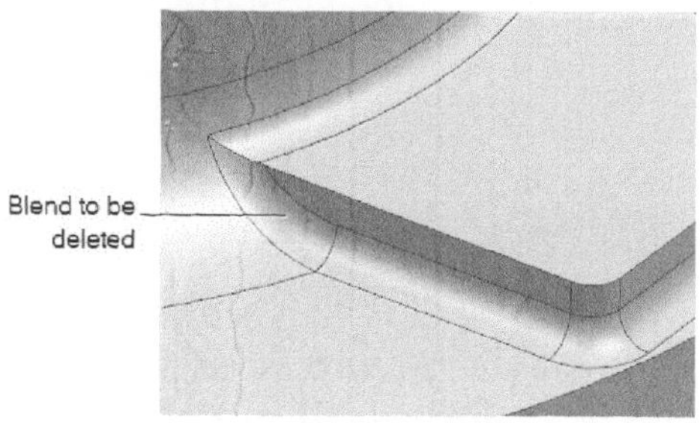

Figure 13-51 Example of blend adjacent to another blend

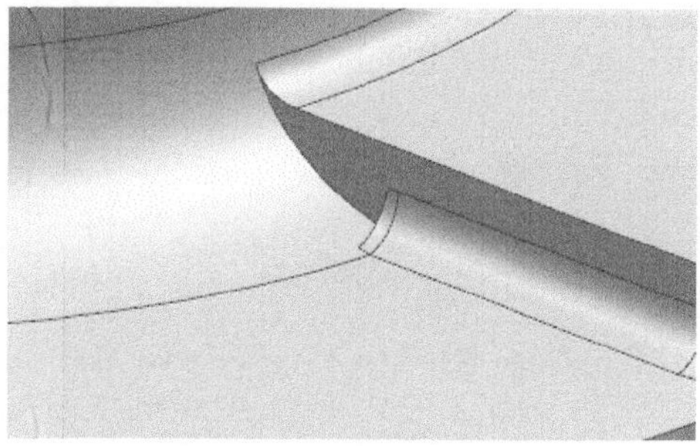

*Figure 13-52 Blend deleted with the **Selected Blend** option selected*

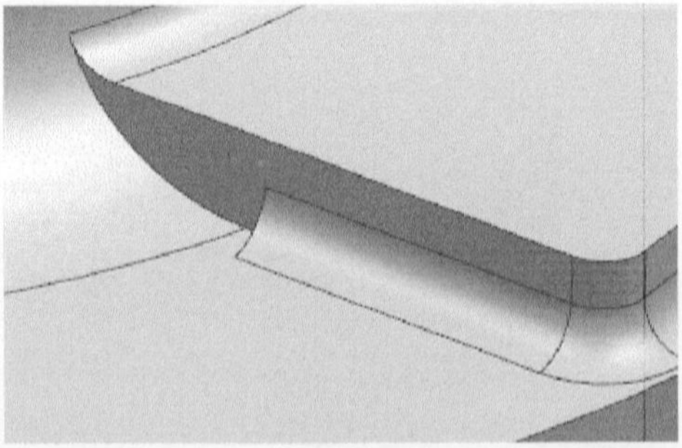

*Figure 13-53 Blend deleted with the **Neighbor Blend** option selected*

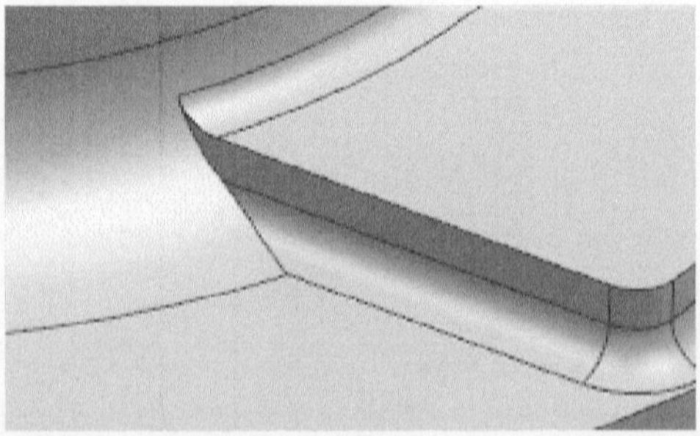

*Figure 13-54 Blend deleted with the **Delete Partial blend** check box cleared*

If you select the **Hole** option from the type drop-down list, you will be prompted to select the faces of the holes to be deleted. Select the holes to be deleted and then choose the **OK** button; the selected holes will be deleted. The **Select Holes by Size** check box available in the **Face** rollout is used to select the holes of the specified hole diameter. You can specify the required diameter of the hole in the **Hole Size** edit box available below the **Select Holes by Size** check box. For example, if you enter **6** in the **Hole Size** edit box, then you can only select the holes whose diameter is equal to or less than 6 mm. However, if you clear this check box, you can select holes of any diameter.

Copy Face

Ribbon:	Home > Synchronous Modeling > More Gallery > Reuse > Copy Face
Menu:	Insert > Synchronous Modeling > Reuse > Copy Face

The **Copy Face** tool is used to copy and place the selected faces of a solid or surface body. You can place the selected faces as a surface or as a solid body. To place them as a solid body, the selected faces must be in the form of a closed entity. To copy a face, invoke the **More** Gallery of the **Synchronous Modeling** group and then choose the **Copy Face** tool from the **Reuse** Gallery, refer to Figure 13-55; the **Copy Face** dialog box will be displayed, as shown in Figure 13-56 and you will be prompted to select the faces to copy. Select the faces; a handle, and an edit box will be displayed, refer to Figure 13-57. You can use the handle for moving the copied object, refer to Figure 13-58. Select the **Paste Copied Faces** check box from the **Paste** rollout and choose the **OK** button to generate a solid body. If you clear the **Paste Copied Faces** check box, the resulting surface generated will be a surface body. The remaining options in this dialog box are similar to those in the **Move Face** dialog box.

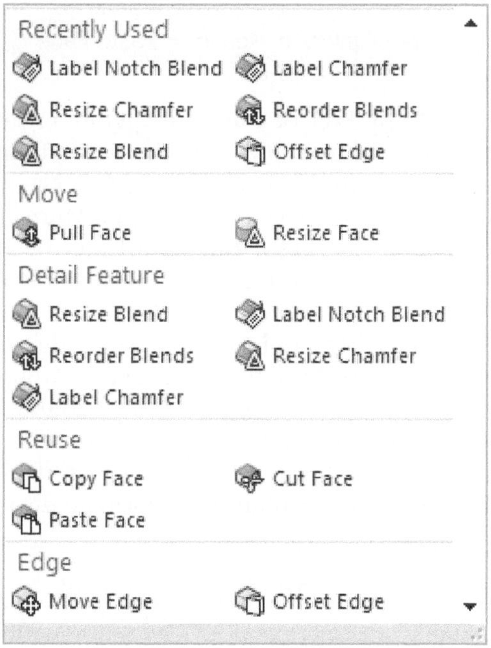

Figure 13-55 *The customized view of* ***More*** *Gallery*

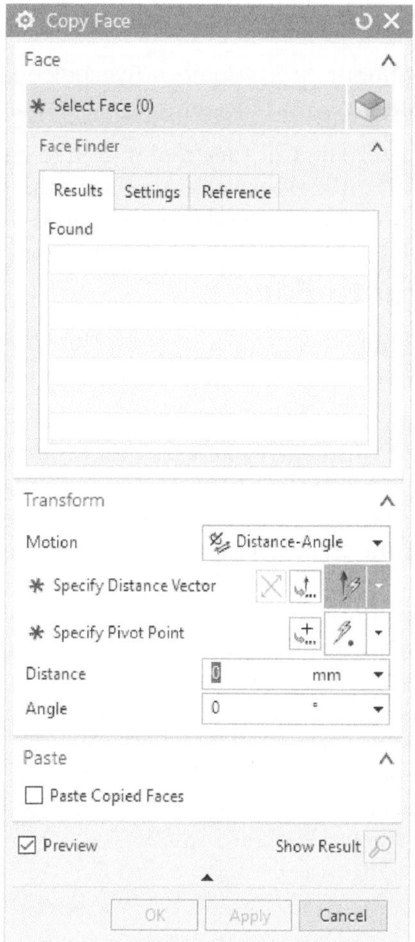

Figure 13-56 *The* ***Copy Face*** *dialog box*

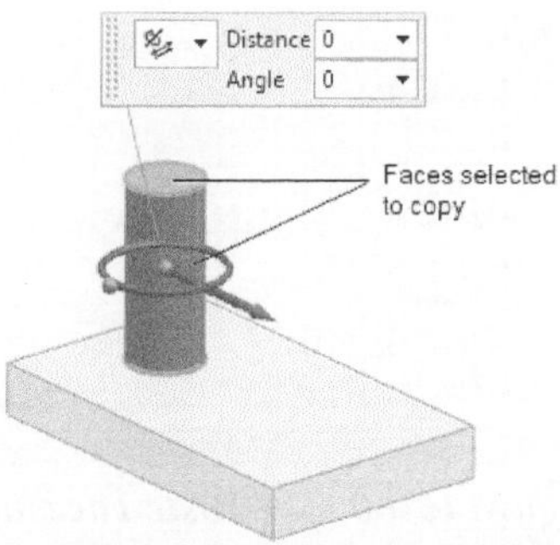

Figure 13-57 *Faces selected for copying*

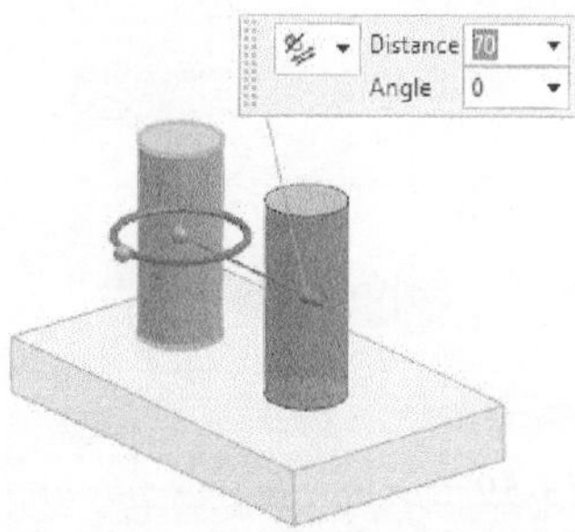

Figure 13-58 *Preview of the resultant model*

Cut Face

Ribbon:	Home > Synchronous Modeling > More Gallery > Reuse > Cut Face
Menu:	Insert > Synchronous Modeling > Reuse > Cut Face

The **Cut Face** tool is used to cut and place the selected faces of a solid or surface model. This tool works similar to the **Copy Face** tool with the only difference that in this case, the selected faces are moved to a new location.

Paste Face

Ribbon:	Home > Synchronous Modeling > More Gallery > Reuse > Paste Face
Menu:	Insert > Synchronous Modeling > Reuse > Paste Face

Once you create a surface by performing the **Copy Face** or **Cut Face** operation, you can use the **Paste Face** tool to add or subtract it from the attached body. For example, a copy face operation performed on a model, refer to Figure 13-59. In this figure, the circular surface of the hole is copied using the **Copy Face** tool. To paste a face, invoke the **More** gallery of the **Synchronous Modeling** group and then choose the **Paste Face** tool from the **Reuse** gallery; the **Paste Face** dialog box will be displayed, as shown in Figure 13-60, and you will be prompted to select the target body to paste the surface. Select the target body, refer to Figure 13-61; you will be prompted to select the surface body to be pasted. Select the surface created, refer to Figure 13-61. Next, select the **Subtract** option from the **Paste Option** drop-down list in the **Tool** rollout to subtract the material from the selected target body. If the original feature is created by adding material, then you need to select the **Add** option from the **Paste Option** drop-down list so that the resulting surface is also created by adding material. After specifying the required options, choose the **OK** button; the resultant model will be displayed, as shown in Figure 13-62.

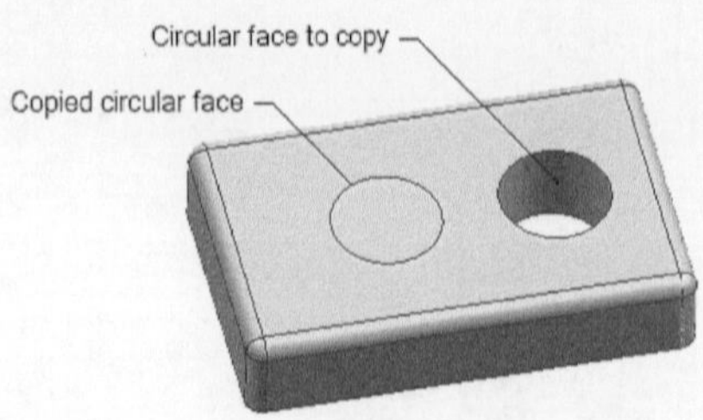

*Figure 13-59 Circular face to copy and resultant copied face after performing the **Copy Face** operation*

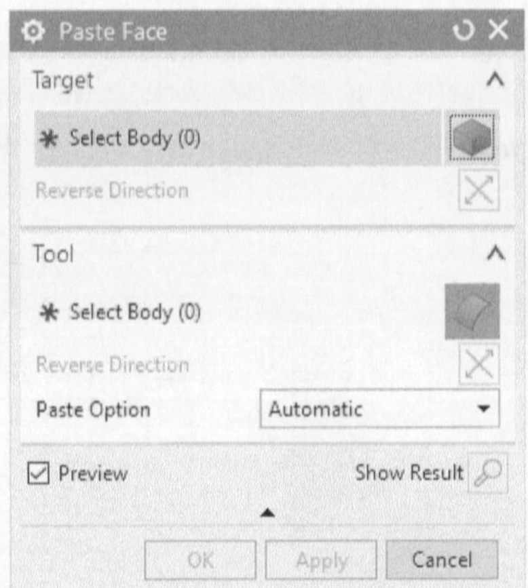

*Figure 13-60 The **Paste Face** dialog box*

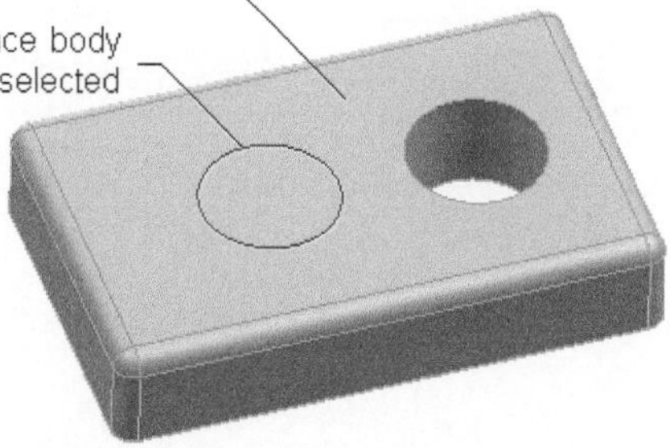

Figure 13-61 Surface and target bodies to be selected

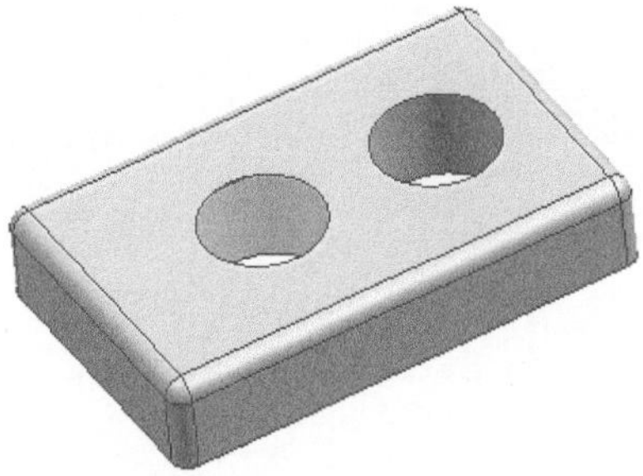

Figure 13-62 Resultant model

Mirror Face

Ribbon:	Home > Synchronous Modeling > More Gallery > Reuse > Mirror Face *(Customize to add)*
Menu:	Insert > Synchronous Modeling > Reuse > Mirror Face

The **Mirror Face** tool is used to mirror a set of faces in the same body about a selected plane. Invoke the **More** gallery of the **Synchronous Modeling** group and then choose the **Mirror Face** tool from the **Reuse** gallery; the **Mirror Face** dialog box will be displayed, as shown in Figure 13-63 and you will be prompted to select the faces to mirror. Select the faces, refer to Figure 13-64. Next, choose the **Plane** button from the **Mirror Plane** rollout; you will be prompted to select a planar face or a datum plane to mirror about. Select the required plane, as shown in Figure 13-64; a preview of the resultant model will be displayed, as shown in Figure 13-65. Choose the **OK** button; the selected set of faces will be mirrored about the selected plane.

*Figure 13-63 The **Mirror Face** dialog box*

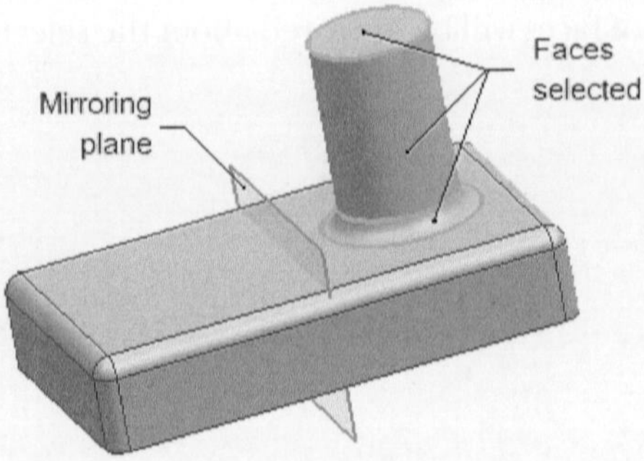

Figure 13-64 Faces and mirroring plane selected

Figure 13-65 Preview of the resultant model

Pattern Face

Ribbon:	Home > Synchronous Modeling > More Gallery > Reuse > Pattern Face *(Customize to add)*
Menu:	Insert > Synchronous Modeling > Reuse > Pattern Face

You can pattern the selected faces of a component using the **Pattern Face** tool. To do so, invoke the **More** gallery of the **Synchronous Modeling** group and then choose the **Pattern Face** tool from the **Reuse** gallery; the **Pattern Face** dialog box will be displayed. The options in the **Pattern Face** dialog box are similar to the options in the **Pattern Feature** tool discussed in Chapter 7.

Make Coplanar

Ribbon:	Home > Synchronous Modeling > More Gallery > Relate > Make Coplanar *(Customize to add)*
Menu:	Insert > Synchronous Modeling > Relate > Make Coplanar

You can make two different faces of a component coplanar to each other using the **Make Coplanar** tool. To do so, invoke the **More** gallery of the **Synchronous Modeling** group and then choose the **Make Coplanar** tool from the **Relate** gallery, as shown in Figure 13-66; the **Make Coplanar** dialog box will be displayed, as shown in Figure 13-67, and you will be prompted to select a planar face to make it coplanar. Select the faces that you want to make coplanar; you will be prompted to select a planar face or datum plane to remain stationary. Select the required plane or planar face so that the previously selected face becomes coplanar with it. Figure 13-68 shows the planar faces selected to make them coplanar to each other and Figure 13-69 shows preview of the resultant component. The other options of the **Make Coplanar** dialog box are similar to those in the **Move Face** dialog box.

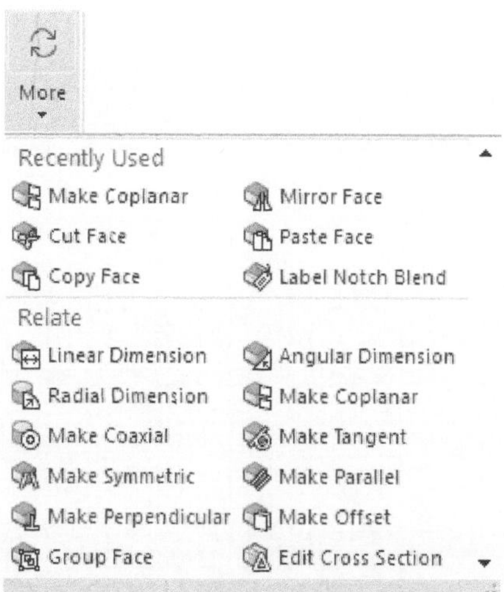

*Figure 13-66 The customized view of the **More** gallery showing the **Relate** gallery*

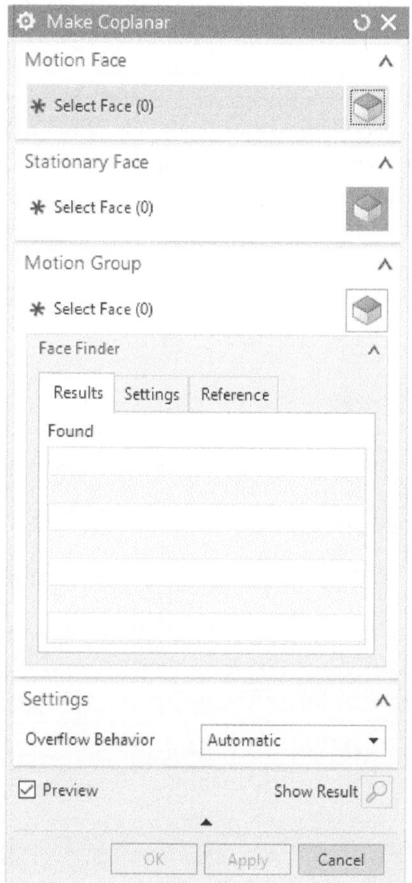

*Figure 13-67 The **Make Coplanar** dialog box*

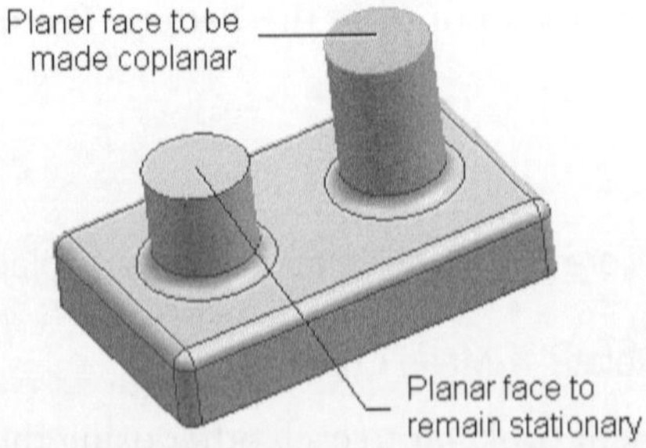

Figure 13-68 Faces selected to be made coplanar

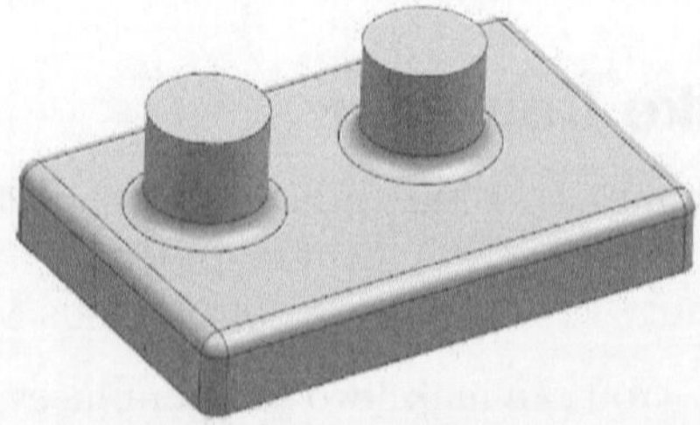

Figure 13-69 Preview of the resultant model

Make Coaxial

Ribbon:	Home > Synchronous Modeling > More Gallery > Relate > Make Coaxial *(Customize to add)*
Menu:	Insert > Synchronous Modeling > Relate > Make Coaxial

You can make two different cylindrical faces of a component coaxial using the **Make Coaxial** tool. To do so, invoke the **More** gallery of the **Synchronous Modeling** group and then choose the **Make Coaxial** tool from the **Relate** gallery; the **Make Coaxial** dialog box will be displayed, as shown in Figure 13-70, and you will be prompted to select a cylinder, cone, or torus to be made coaxial. Select the required cylinder, cone, or torus; the **Face** button in the **Stationary Face** rollout will be chosen automatically and you will be prompted to select another cylinder, cone, or torus that has to be made coaxial with the previously selected entity. Select the required cylinder, cone, or torus so that the entity selected earlier becomes coaxial to the entity selected later, refer to Figure 13-71, a preview of the resultant component will be displayed, as shown in Figure 13-72. The other options of the **Make Coaxial** dialog box are similar to those discussed in the **Move Face** dialog box.

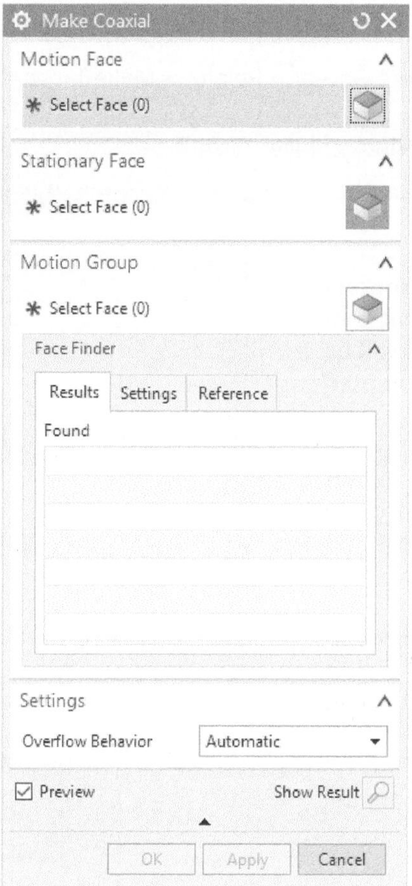

***Figure 13-70** The **Make Coaxial** dialog box*

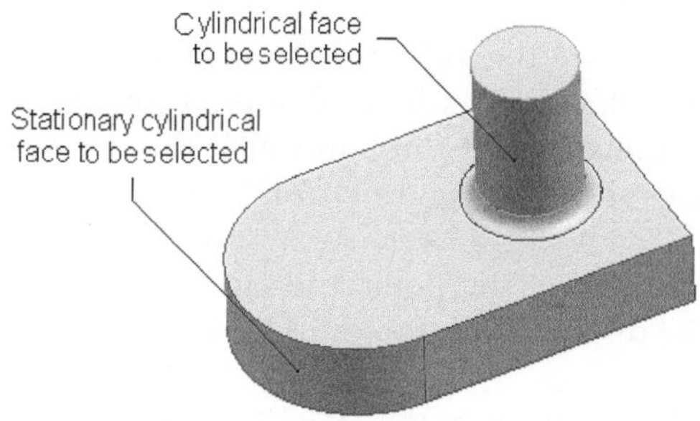

***Figure 13-71** Faces selected to be made coaxial*

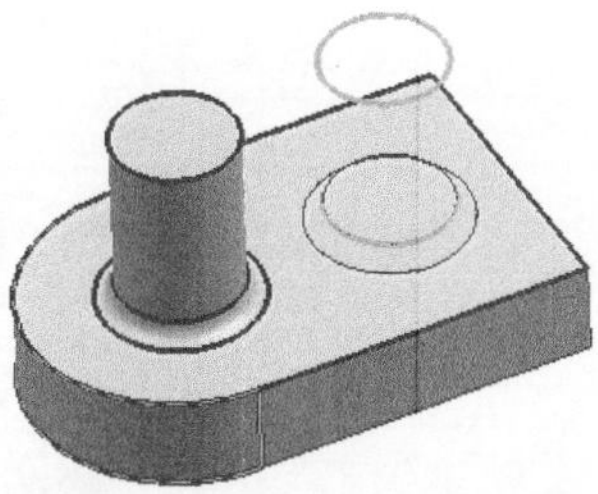

***Figure 13-72** Preview of the resultant model*

Make Tangent

Ribbon:	Home > Synchronous Modeling > More Gallery > Relate > Make Tangent *(Customize to add)*
Menu:	Insert > Synchronous Modeling > Relate > Make Tangent

You can make one face of component tangent to another face using the **Make Tangent** tool.

To do so, invoke the **More** gallery of the **Synchronous Modeling** group and then choose the **Make Tangent** tool from the **Relate** gallery; the **Make Tangent** dialog box will be displayed, as shown in Figure 13-73 and you will be prompted to select the face to be made tangent.

Select the face; the **Face** button in the **Stationary Face** rollout will be activated and you will be prompted to select a face or a datum plane that has to remain stationary. Select the required face or plane.

Next, choose the **Inferred Point** button from the **Through Point** rollout; you will be prompted to select a point. Select the required point through which the resultant face should pass, as shown in Figure 13-74.

After selecting the point and faces, a preview of the model will be displayed, as shown in Figure 13-75.

The other options in the **Make Tangent** dialog box are similar to those discussed in the **Move Face** dialog box.

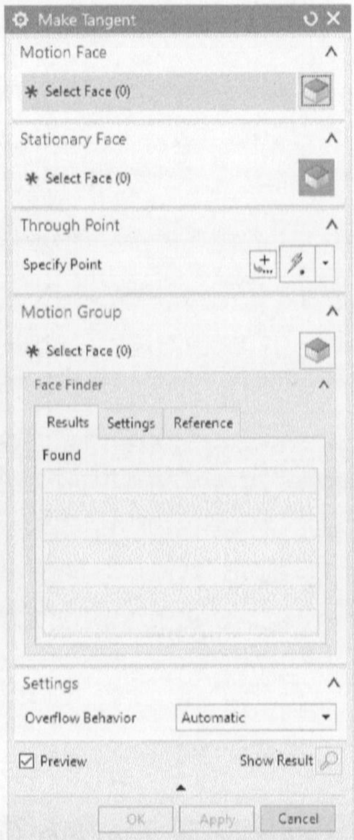

***Figure 13-73** The **Make Tangent** dialog box*

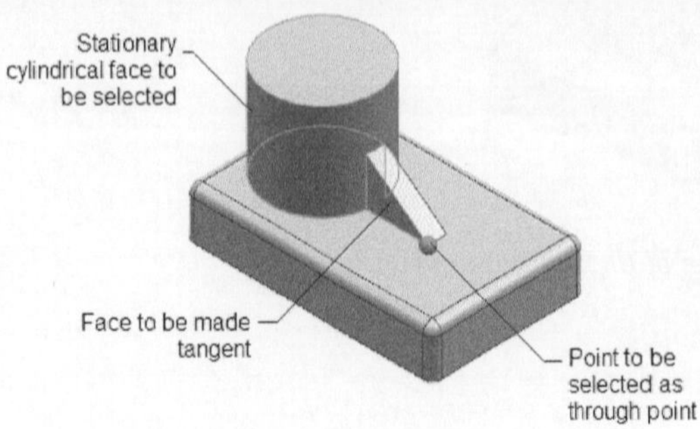

***Figure 13-74** Face selected to be made tangent*

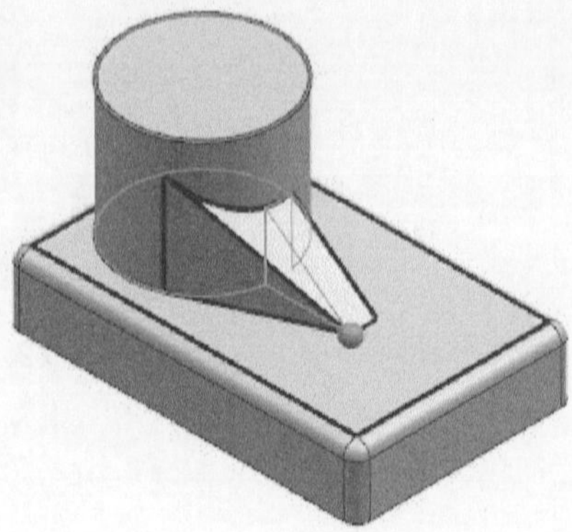

***Figure 13-75** Preview of the resultant model*

Make Symmetric

Ribbon:	Home > Synchronous Modeling > More Gallery > Relate > Make Symmetric *(Customize to add)*
Menu:	Insert > Synchronous Modeling > Relate > Make Symmetric

You can make one face of a component symmetric to another face about any specified plane using the **Make Symmetric** tool. To do so, invoke the **More** gallery of the **Synchronous Modeling** group and then choose the **Make Symmetric** tool from the **Relate** gallery; the **Make Symmetric** dialog box will be displayed, as shown in Figure 13-76, and you will be prompted to select the face to be made symmetric. Select the face; the **Plane** button in the **Symmetry Plane** rollout will be highlighted and you will be prompted to select a planar face or a datum plane to make the face symmetric about. Select the required planar face or plane; you will be prompted to select the face that has to remain stationary. Select the face to be kept stationary, refer to Figure 13-77, a preview of the resultant component will be displayed, as shown in Figure 13-78. Also, the **Face** button in the **Motion Group** rollout will be activated automatically. As a result, you can select multiple faces as per your requirement for modifying. The other options in the **Make Symmetric** dialog box are similar to options in the **Move Face** dialog box.

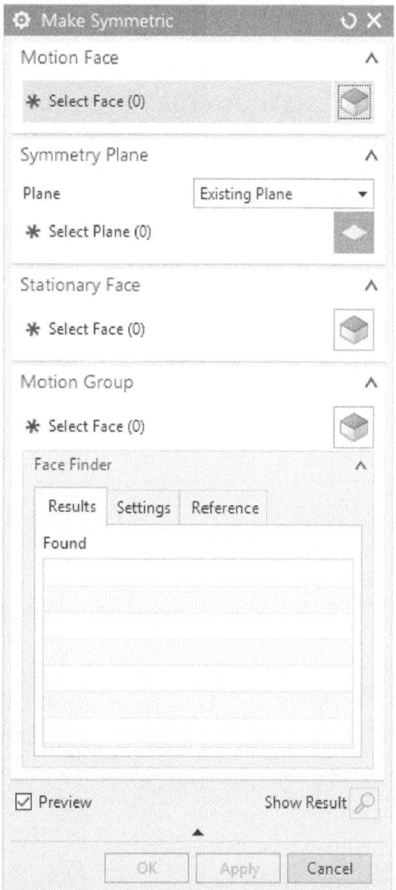

*Figure 13-76 The **Make Symmetric** dialog box*

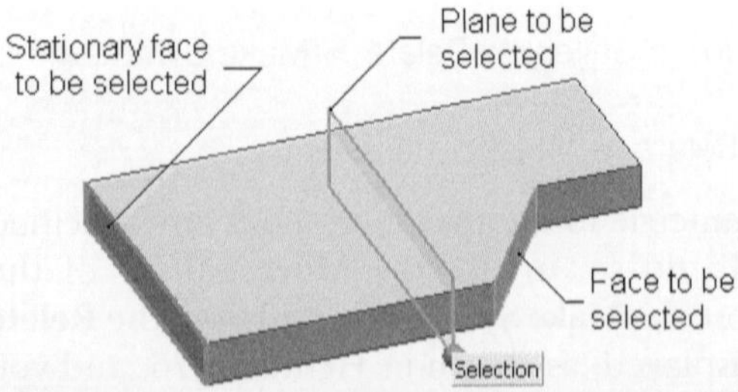

Figure 13-77 Faces and datum plane selected to be made symmetric

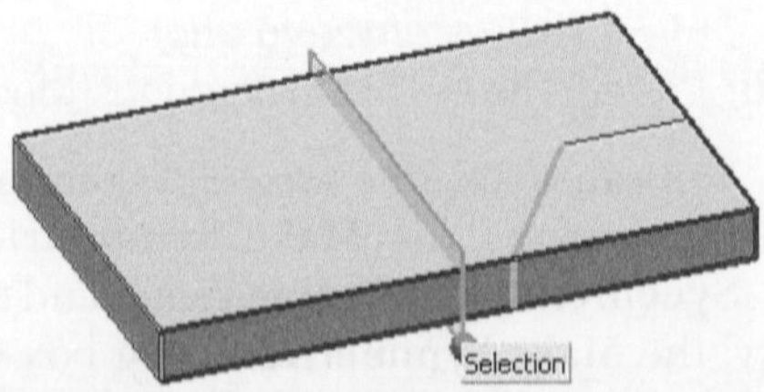

Figure 13-78 Preview of the resultant model

Make Parallel

Ribbon:	Home > Synchronous Modeling > More Gallery > Relate > Make Parallel *(Customize to add)*
Menu:	Insert > Synchronous Modeling > Relate > Make Parallel

You can make one planar face of a component parallel to another planar face using the **Make Parallel** tool. To do so, invoke the **More** gallery of the **Synchronous Modeling** group and then choose the **Make Parallel** tool from the **Relate** gallery; the **Make Parallel** dialog box will be displayed, as shown in Figure 13-79, and you will be prompted to select the planar faces to be made parallel. Select the planar face that you want to modify; the **Face** button from the **Stationary Face** rollout will be chosen automatically and you will be prompted to select the planar face or datum plane that has to remain stationary. Select the required planar face or plane. Next, choose the **Inferred Point** button from the **Through Point** rollout; you will be prompted to select a point. Select the point through which the face should pass, refer to Figure 13-80. On selecting the required point and faces, a preview of the resultant model will be displayed, as shown in Figure 13-81. The other options in the **Make Parallel** dialog box are similar to those discussed in the **Move Face** dialog box.

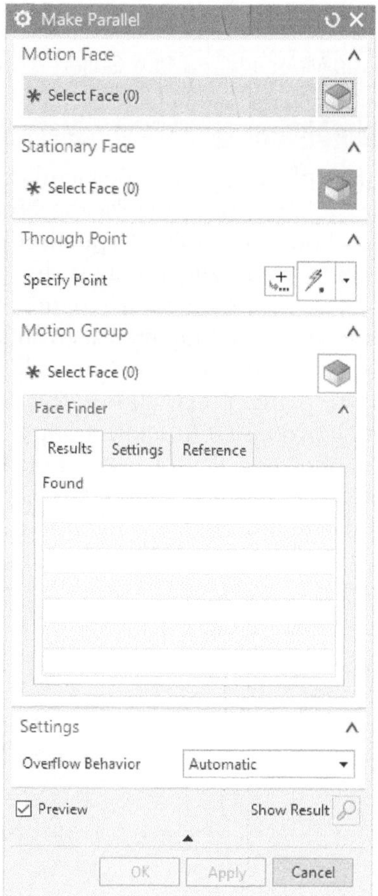

*Figure 13-79 The **Make Parallel** dialog box*

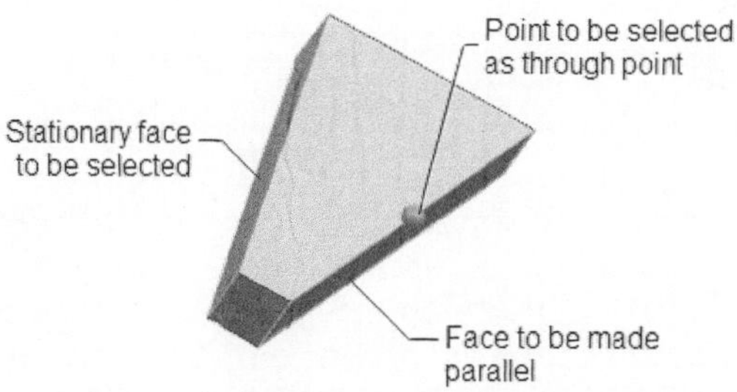

Figure 13-80 Faces selected to be made parallel

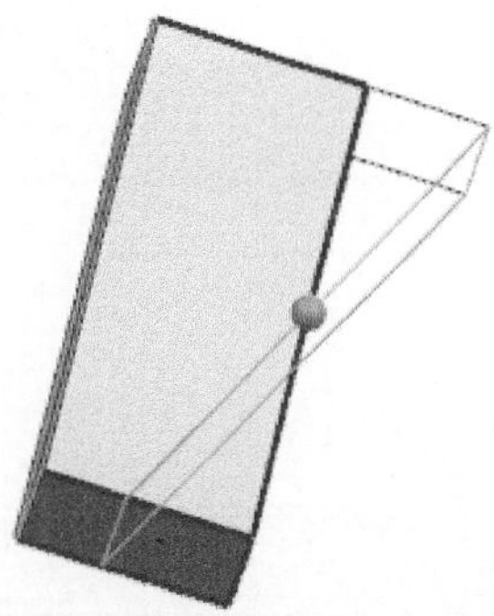

Figure 13-81 Preview of the resultant model

Make Perpendicular

Ribbon:	Home > Synchronous Modeling > More Gallery > Relate > Make Perpendicular *(Customize to add)*
Menu:	Insert > Synchronous Modeling > Relate > Make Perpendicular

You can make one planar face of a component perpendicular to another planar face using the **Make Perpendicular** tool. To do so, invoke the **More** gallery of the **Synchronous Modeling** group and then choose the **Make Perpendicular** tool from the **Relate** gallery; the **Make Perpendicular** dialog box will be displayed, as shown in Figure 13-82, and you will be prompted to select the planar faces to be made perpendicular. Select the required planar face to modify; the **Face** button from the **Stationary Face** rollout will be chosen automatically and you will be prompted to select the planar face or datum plane that has to be kept stationary. Select the required planar face or plane. Next, choose the **Inferred Point** button from the **Through Point** rollout; you will be prompted to select a point. Select the point through which the resultant face should pass, as shown in Figure 13-83. On selecting the required point and faces, a preview of the resultant model will be displayed, as shown in Figure 13-84. The other options in the **Make Perpendicular** dialog box are similar to those discussed in the **Move Face** dialog box.

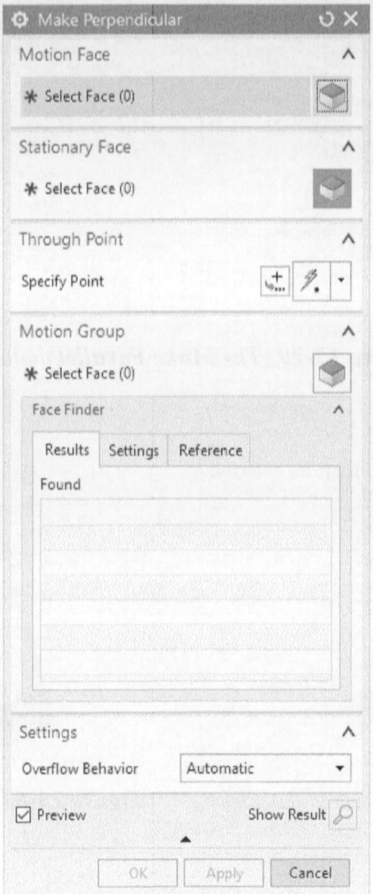

Figure 13-82 The ***Make Perpendicular*** *dialog box*

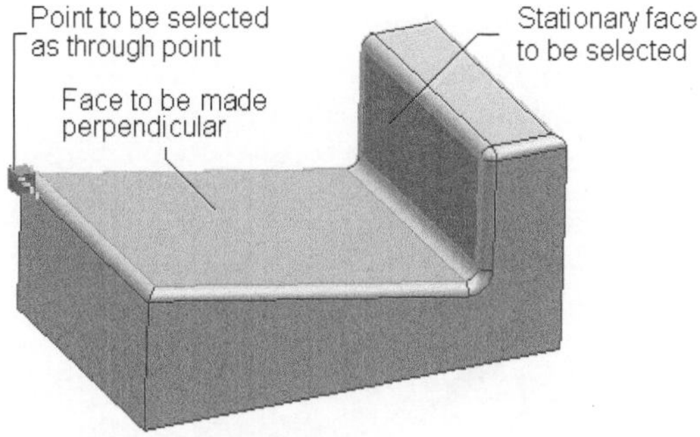

Figure 13-83 Faces selected to apply the ***Make Perpendicular*** *tool*

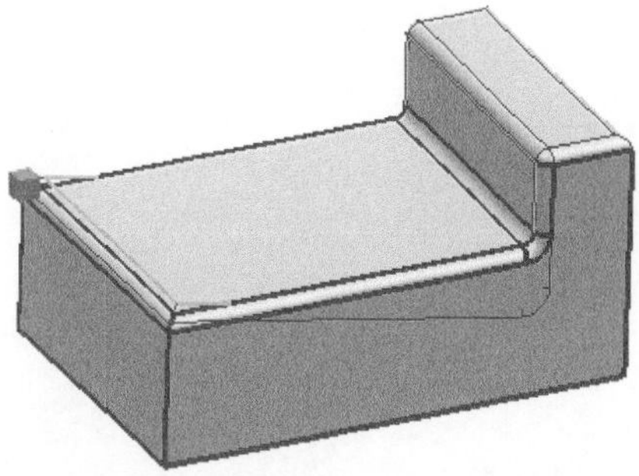

Figure 13-84 Preview of the resultant model

Make Offset

Ribbon:	Home > Synchronous Modeling > More Gallery > Relate > Make Offset *(Customize to add)*
Menu:	Insert > Synchronous Modeling > Relate > Make Offset

You can use the **Make Offset** tool to make a face offset to another face. To do so, invoke the **More** gallery of the **Synchronous Modeling** group and then choose the **Make Offset** tool from the **Relate** gallery; the **Make Offset** dialog box will be displayed, as shown in Figure 13-85, and you will be prompted to select the face to make offset. Select the face, refer to Figure 13-86; the **Face** button in the **Stationary Face** rollout will be chosen and you will be prompted to select the face that has to remain stationary. Select the face to be kept stationary, refer to Figure 13-86, and then enter the required offset distance value in the **Distance** edit box available in the **Offset** rollout; the preview of the resultant component will be displayed, as shown in Figure 13-87. You can also specify the offset distance by dragging the handle displayed on the model.

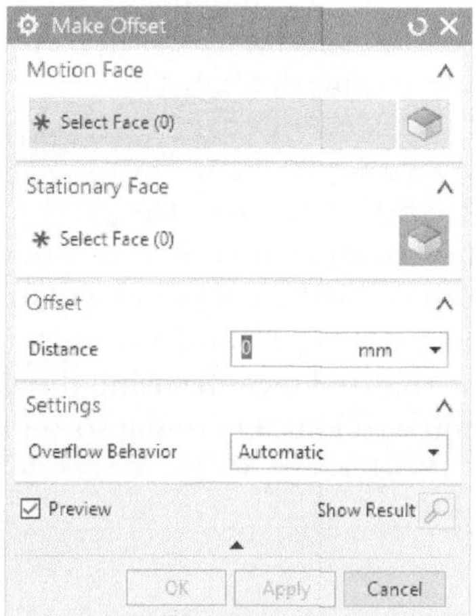

Figure 13-85 The ***Make Offset*** *dialog box*

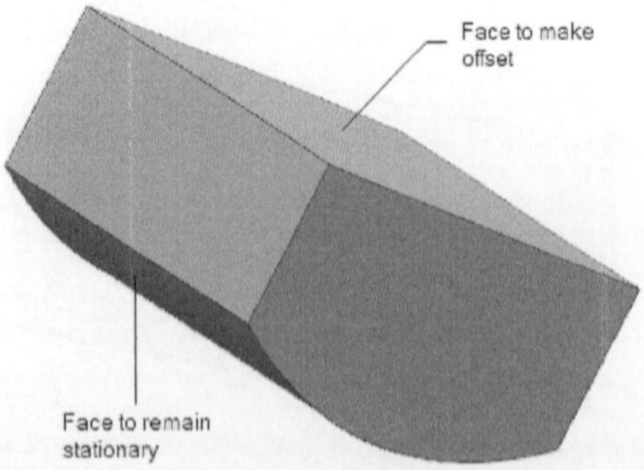

Figure 13-86 Faces selected to be made offset

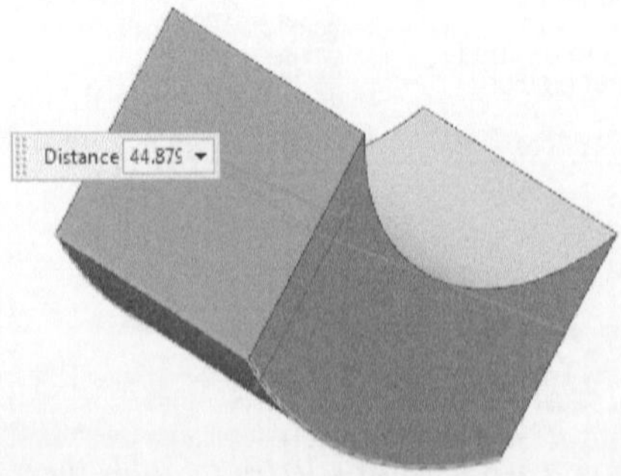

Figure 13-87 Preview of the resultant model

Linear Dimension

Ribbon:	Home > Synchronous Modeling > More Gallery > Relate > Linear Dimension *(Customize to add)*
Menu:	Insert > Synchronous Modeling > Dimension > Linear Dimension

The **Linear Dimension** tool is used to modify a model by modifying the linear dimension between two edges, axes, and faces. To modify a model, invoke the **More** gallery of the **Synchronous Modeling** group and then choose the **Linear Dimension** tool from the **Relate** gallery, refer to Figure 13-88; the **Linear Dimension** dialog box will be displayed, as shown in Figure 13-89, and you will be prompted to select the origin point or datum plane for dimensioning. Select an edge, datum plane, or axis as the stationary object so that further modifications can be made in the model with respect to it. Select the required edge; the distance between the origin and the selected edge will be displayed in the drawing window. Also, the OrientXpress tool is displayed. Choose the **Specify Location** button from the **Location** rollout, if it is not chosen automatically. Now, you can locate the dimension by clicking in the drawing window. On doing so, the face corresponding to the selected measurement object is selected and a dynamic edit box will be displayed, refer to Figure 13-90. You can move the selected faces by using the dynamic edit box or by specifying the required distance in the **Distance** rollout. On doing so, a preview of the resultant model will be displayed, as shown in Figure 13-91.

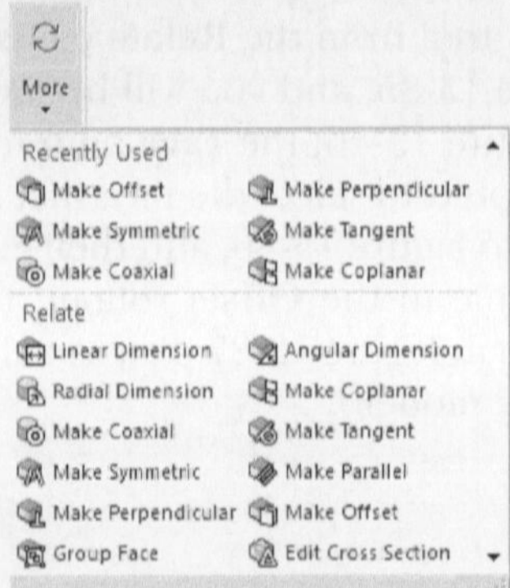

*Figure 13-88 The **Linear Dimension** tool of the **Relate** gallery*

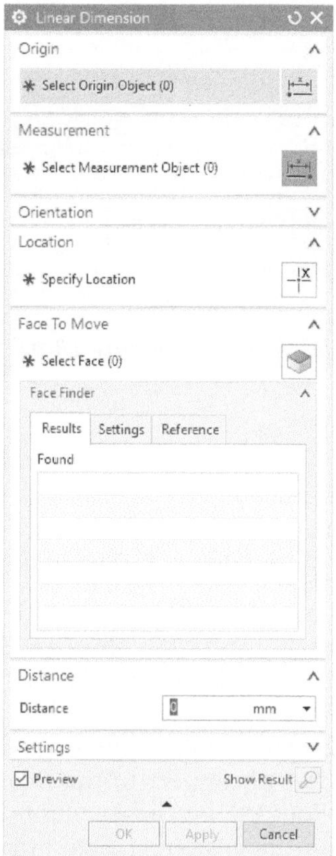

*Figure 13-89 The **Linear Dimension** dialog box*

In the **Orientation** rollout of the **Linear Dimension** dialog box, you can either specify the axis or plane, or both for dimensioning, so that the modification can be made in the model with respect to them. By default, the **OrientXpress** option is selected in the **Direction** drop-down list, so that you can specify the required axis, plane, and coordinate system using the **Direction**, **Plane** and **Reference** drop-down lists in the **OrientXpress** sub-rollout, respectively. If you select the **Vector** option in the **Direction** drop-down list, the **Orientation** rollout will be modified and you will be prompted to select the object infer vector. Specify the required vector; the linear dimension will be displayed along the specified vector and the plane to modify.

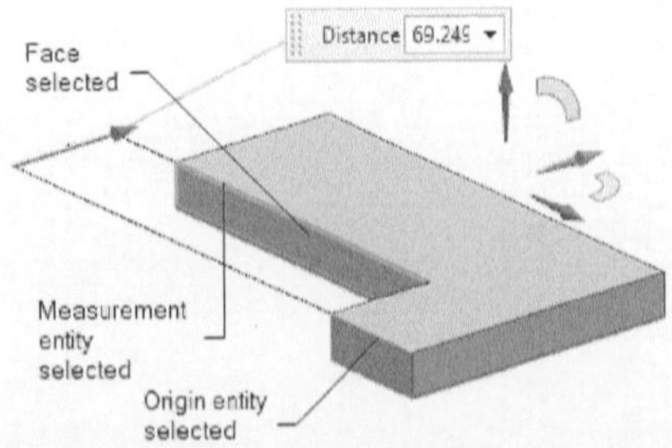

Figure 13-90 Edges selected for linear dimensioning

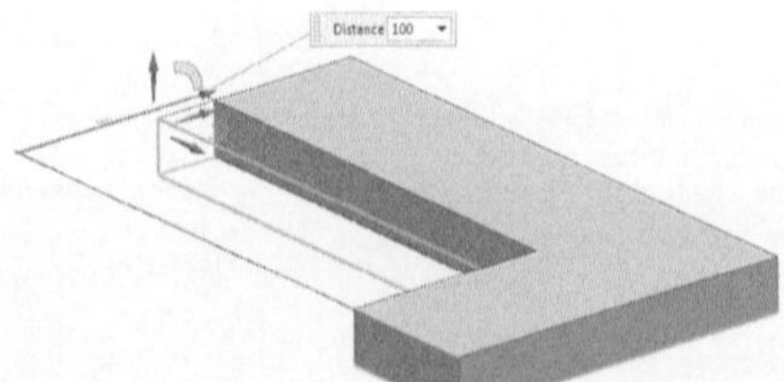

Figure 13-91 Preview of the resultant model

Angular Dimension

Ribbon:	Home > Synchronous Modeling > More Gallery > Relate > Angular Dimension *(Customize to add)*
Menu:	Insert > Synchronous Modeling > Dimension > Angular Dimension

The **Angular Dimension** tool is used to move surface angularly by modifying the angle between the two faces. To do so, invoke the **More** gallery of the **Synchronous Modeling** group and then choose the **Angular Dimension** tool from the **Relate** gallery; the **Angular Dimension** dialog box will be displayed, refer to Figure 13-92 and you will be prompted to select the origin object for dimensioning. Select a face as the origin object, refer to Figure 13-93. Now, further modifications can be made with respect to this face. Also, the **Measurement Object** button from the **Measurement** rollout will be chosen automatically and you will be prompted to select the measurement object for dimensioning. Select the required face; the angle between two objects will be displayed in the graphics window, attached with the cursor and the **Specify Location** button will be chosen automatically in the **Location** rollout. As a result, you can locate the dimension by clicking in the graphics window. Specify the location of the dimension. On doing so, the **Face** button from the **Face to Move** rollout will be chosen automatically and you will be prompted to select the faces to move. Select the faces that you want to move; an angular handle and a dynamic edit box will be displayed, refer to Figure 13-93. You can move the selected faces using the angular handle or the dynamic edit box. Alternatively, you can specify the required angle in the **Angle** edit box of the **Angle** rollout. A preview of the resultant model will be displayed, as shown in Figure 13-94. Note that in the **Angle** rollout, the **Alternate Angle** check box is clear. If you select this check box, the value of alternate angle will be displayed in the drawing window.

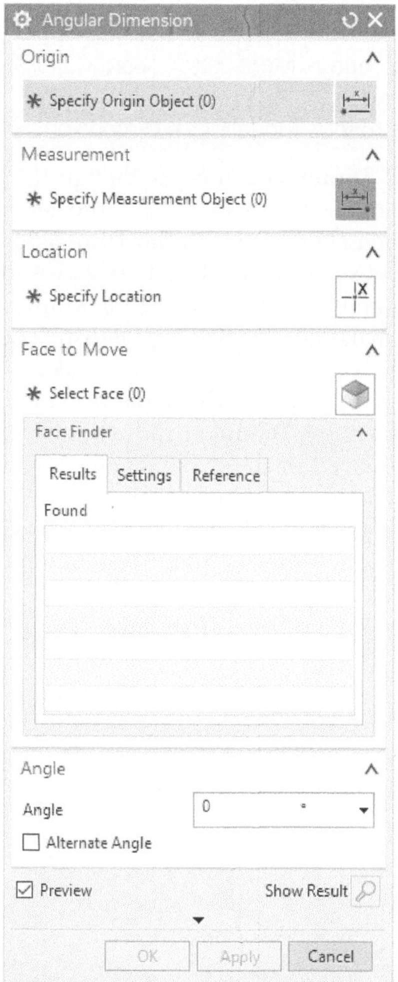

Figure 13-92 *The* ***Angular Dimension*** *dialog box*

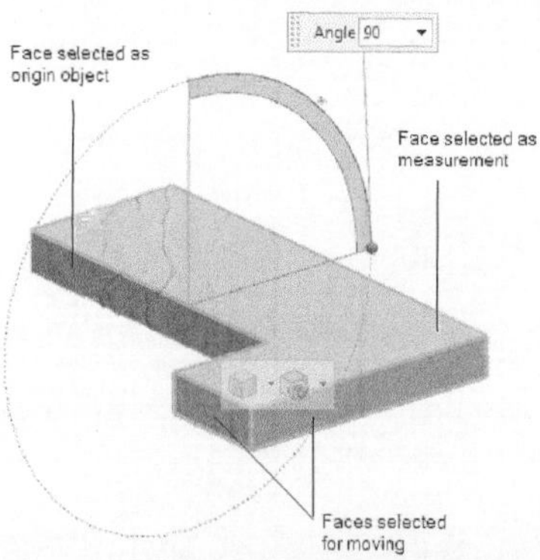

Figure 13-93 *Faces selected for angular dimensioning*

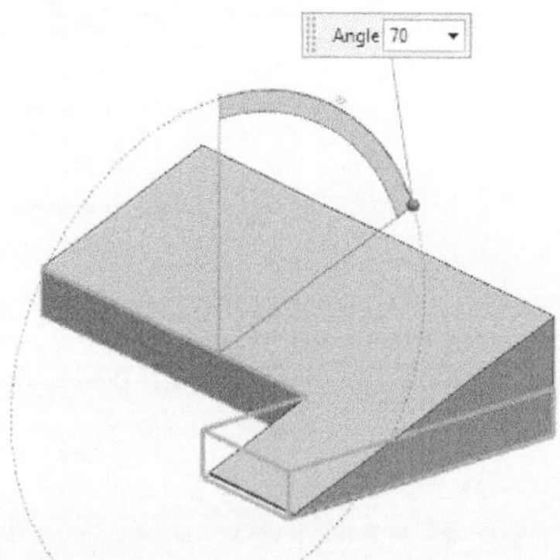

Figure 13-94 *Preview of the resultant model*

Radial Dimension

Ribbon:	Home > Synchronous Modeling > More Gallery > Relate > Radial Dimension *(Customize to add)*
Menu:	Insert > Synchronous Modeling > Dimension > Radial Dimension

You can use the **Radial Dimension** tool to change the dimension of a cylindrical or spherical face of the model. To do so, invoke the **More** gallery of the **Synchronous Modeling** group and then choose the **Radial Dimension** tool from the **Relate** gallery; the **Radial Dimension** dialog box will be displayed, as shown in Figure 13-95, and you will be prompted to select a face to dimension. You can select a cylindrical or spherical face. Select the face; a dynamic handle and a dynamic edit box will be displayed in the graphics window, refer to Figure 13-96. By default, the **Radius** radio button is selected in the **Size** rollout. As a result, the radius of the selected face is displayed in the dynamic edit box as well as in the **Radius** edit box of the dialog box. If you select the **Diameter** radio button in the **Size** rollout, the diameter of the selected face will be displayed in the dynamic edit box as well as in the **Diameter** edit box. After selecting the required radio button from the **Size** rollout, drag the handle to change the radial dimension of the selected face. Alternatively, you can enter the radius or the diameter values in their respective edit boxes. A preview of the resultant model will be displayed, as shown in Figure 13-97.

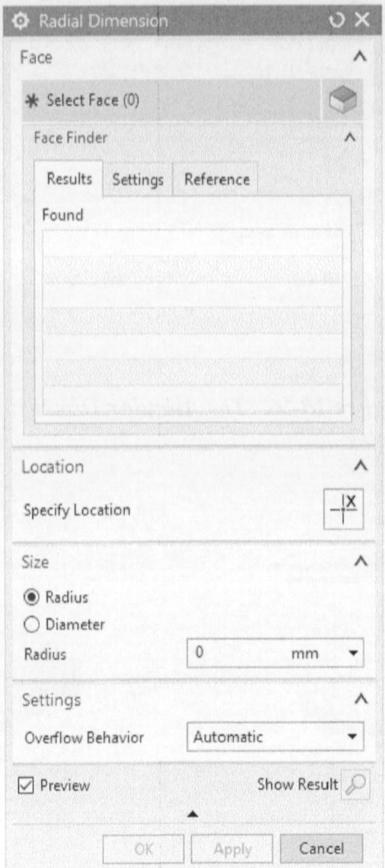

*Figure 13-95 The **Radial Dimension** dialog box*

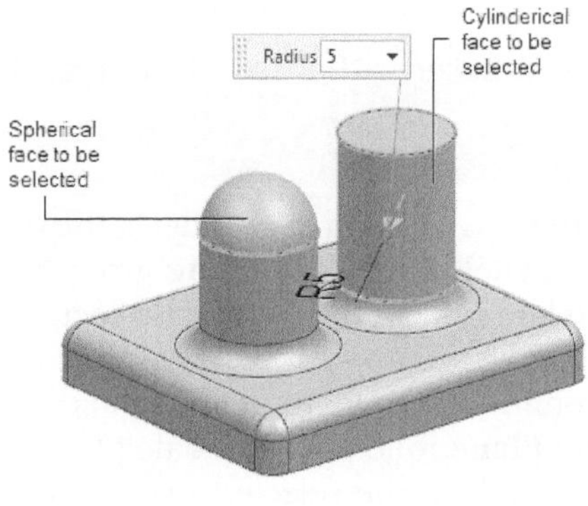

Figure 13-96 Faces selected for applying the radial dimension

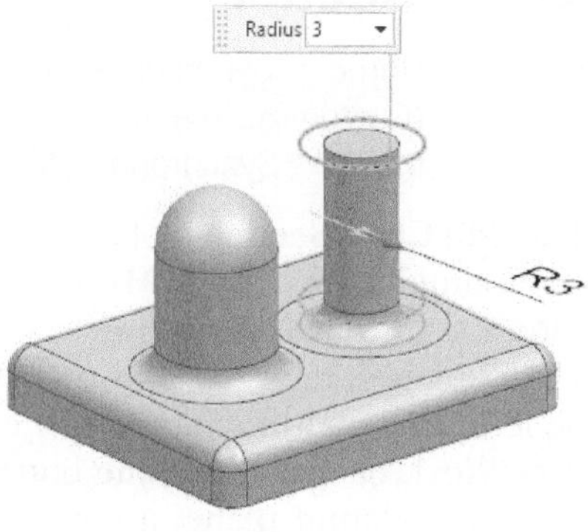

Figure 13-97 Preview of the resultant model

Group Face

Ribbon:	Home > Synchronous Modeling > More Gallery > Relate > Group Face *(Customize to add)*
Menu:	Insert > Synchronous Modeling > Group Face

The **Group Face** tool is used to create a group of selected faces of a model in such a way that if you select a single face, the remaining faces in the group are selected automatically.

Invoke the **More** gallery of the **Synchronous Modeling** group and then choose the **Group Face** tool from the **Relate** gallery; the **Group Face** dialog box will be displayed, refer to Figure 13-98, and you will be prompted to select the faces to add to the group. Select the required faces to create a group. Next, choose the **OK** button; a group of selected faces will be created.

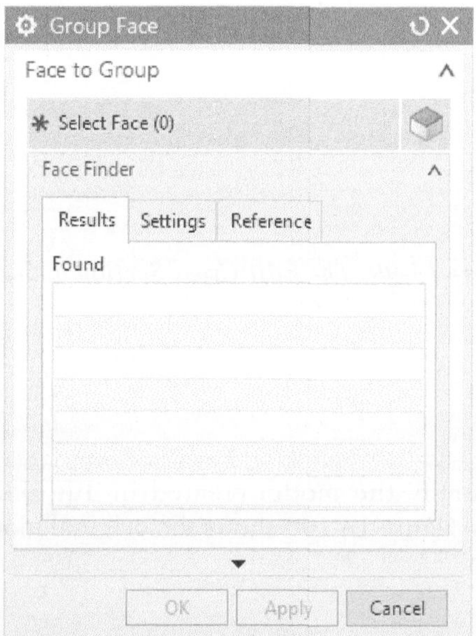

*Figure 13-98 The **Group Face** dialog box*

Edit Cross Section

Ribbon:	Home > Synchronous Modeling > More Gallery > Relate > Edit Cross Section *(Customize to add)*
Menu:	Insert > Synchronous Modeling > Edit Cross Section

The **Edit Cross Section** tool is used to modify the cross-section of a model in the sketching environment. Invoke the **More** gallery of the **Synchronous Modeling** group and then choose the **Edit Cross Section** tool from the **Relate** gallery; the **Edit Cross Section** dialog box will be displayed, refer to Figure 13-99, and you will be prompted to select faces to intersect. Hold the left mouse button and drag the cursor around the model to define a box and select all its faces. Next, choose the **Plane** button from the **Plane** rollout of the dialog box. Select a planar face or a datum plane; a cross-section is created on the selected plane. Choose the **Section** button from the **Section Curve** rollout; the Sketch in Task environment will be invoked. Now, change the cross-section of the model by dragging the entities or by dimensioning it. The way you change the cross-section, the model will be updated accordingly. After updating the sketch, exit the Sketch in Task environment. Choose the **OK** button from the **Edit Cross Section** dialog box; the cross-section will be saved in the **Part Navigator**.

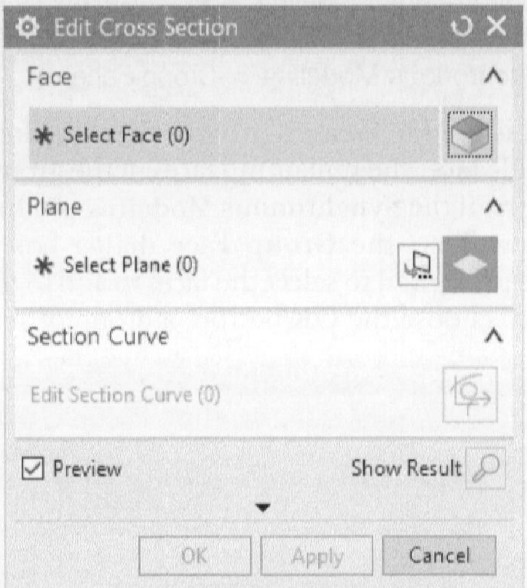

***Figure 13-99** The **Edit Cross Section** dialog box*

TUTORIALS

Tutorial 1

In this tutorial, you will modify the model created in Tutorial 3 of Chapter 5 using the Synchronous Modeling tools. Figure 13-100 shows the original model and Figure 13-101 shows the model after modification. **(Expected time: 30 min)**

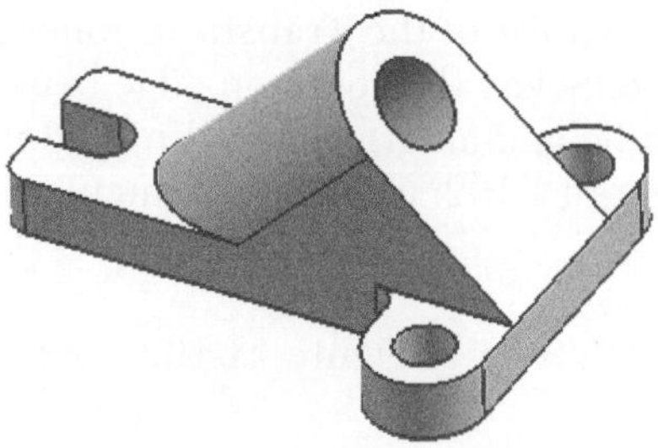

Figure 13-100 *Original model*

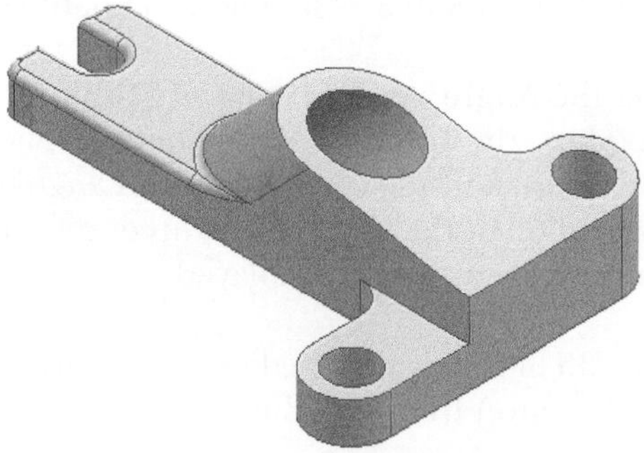

Figure 13-101 *Final model after modification*

Before modifying the model, using the Synchronous Modeling tools, you should determine the number of features in it by observing the feature tree in the **Part Navigator**. Then, you should decide the sequence in which the model should be modified to get quick results.

The following steps are required to complete this tutorial:

a. Copy the file from Tutorial 3 of Chapter 5 and then paste it at the location */NX/c13* and rename it as *c13tut1*.
b. Modify the angle between the inclined face and the vertical face using the **Move Face** or **Angular Dimension** tool, refer to Figure 13-102.
c. Increase the thickness of the base feature using the **Move Face** or **Pull Face** tool, refer to Figure 13-103.
d. Increase the length of the base feature using the **Move Face** tool, refer to Figure 13-104.
e. Align the inclined hole using the **Replace Face** tool, refer to Figure 13-105.
f. Decrease the thickness of the base feature using the **Move Face** tool, refer to Figure 13-106.
g. Align the horizontal face to the inclined face using the **Replace Face** tool, refer to Figure 13-108.
h. Change the radius of the fillet using the **Resize Blend** tool, refer to Figure 13-110.
i. Change the diameter of the vertical hole using the **Resize Face** or **Radial Dimension** tool.
j. Change the diameter of the inclined hole using the **Resize Face** or **Radial Dimension** tool.
k. Modify the distance between two vertical holes using the **Move Face** tool, refer to Figure 13-112.
l. Apply fillets to the base plate using the **Edge Blend** tool, refer to Figure 13-114.

Copying the File

1. Copy the part file created in Tutorial 3 of Chapter 5 and paste it at the location */NX/c13* and then rename it as *c13tut1*.

2. Open the *c13tut1* file.

Modifying the Angle

1. Choose the **Move Face** tool from the **Synchronous Modeling** group; the **Move Face** dialog box is displayed and you are prompted to select the face to be moved.

2. Select the inclined face; a dimension handle and a dynamic edit box are displayed.

3. Select the **Angle** option from the **Motion** drop-down list of the **Transform** rollout in the dialog box; the **Inferred Vector** button is activated. Select the common edge between the angular face and the vertical face; an angular handle and an arrow are displayed. Reverse the direction of the arrow, if required, refer to Figure 13-102. Click on the angular handle; the dynamic edit box is displayed.

4. Enter **-35** in the dynamic edit box and press ENTER, refer to Figure 13-102. Next, choose the **OK** button from the **Move Face** dialog box.

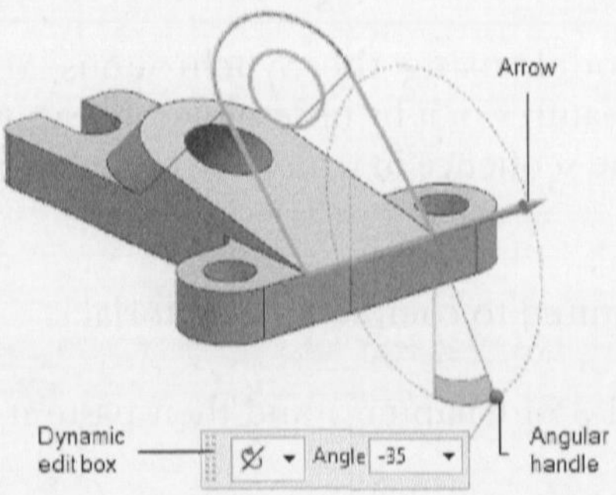

Figure 13-102 Common edge selected to move the inclined face

Modifying the Thickness of the Base Plate

1. Choose the **Pull Face** tool from **Menu > Insert > Synchronous Modeling** of the **Top Border Bar**; the **Pull Face** dialog box is displayed.

2. Select the **Point to Point** option from the **Motion** drop-down list of the **Transform** rollout; the **Specify From Point** area is highlighted in the **Transform** rollout. Note that if the **Point to Point** option is selected by default in the **Motion** drop-down list, then you need to click on the **Specify From Point** area of the **Transform** rollout to activate it. Select a point from the upper face of the base plate, refer to Figure 13-103; the **Specify To Point** area of the **Transform** rollout is activated. Select a point from the lower face of the base plate, refer to Figure 13-103; the **Face** button is activated in the **Face** rollout. Select the lower face of the base plate; the dynamic preview will be displayed, refer to Figure 13-103.

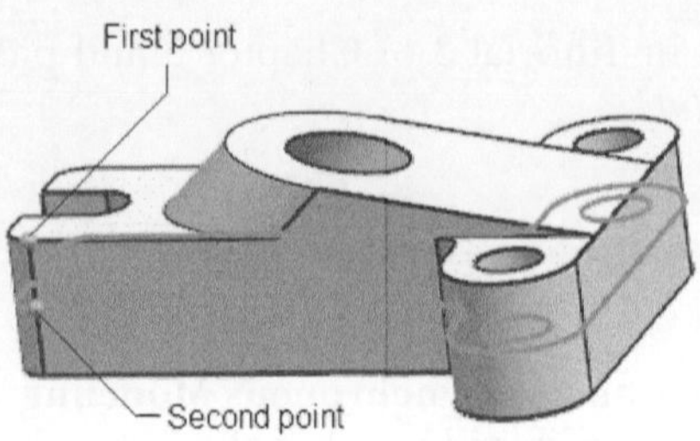

Figure 13-103 Entities selected to modify the thickness of the base feature

3. Choose the **OK** button from the dialog box to apply the changes and exit the dialog box.

Modifying the Length of the Base Plate

1. Choose the **Move Face** tool from the **Synchronous Modeling** group; the **Move Face** dialog box is displayed. 

2. Select the three faces of the base plate, refer to Figure 13-104.

3. Select the **Distance** option from the **Motion** drop-down list; the **Inferred Vector** button is activated.

4. Enter **15** in the **Distance** edit box of the **Transform** rollout and press ENTER, refer to Figure 13-104. Next, choose the **OK** button from the dialog box to apply the changes and exit the dialog box.

Aligning the Holes

Next, you need to align the hole in the base feature with the hole in the inclined face.

1. Choose the **Replace Face** tool from the **Synchronous Modeling** group; the **Replace Face** dialog box is displayed and you are prompted to select the faces to be replaced. 

2. Select the hole from the base plate, refer to Figure 13-105.

3. Choose the **Face** button from the **Replacement Face** rollout and select the face of the inclined hole, refer to Figure 13-105. Next, choose the **OK** button from the dialog box.

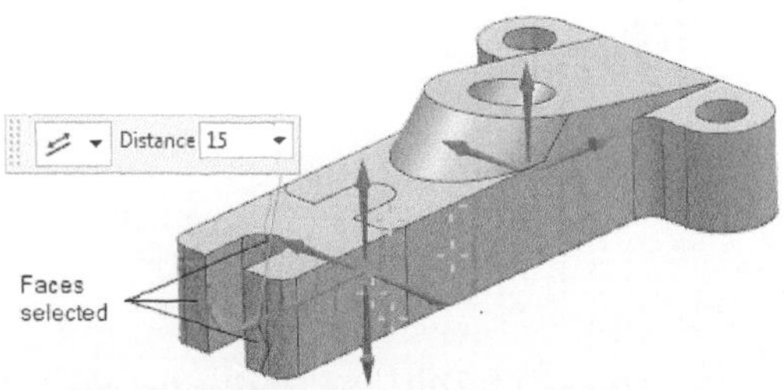

Figure 13-104 Entities selected to modify the length of the base feature

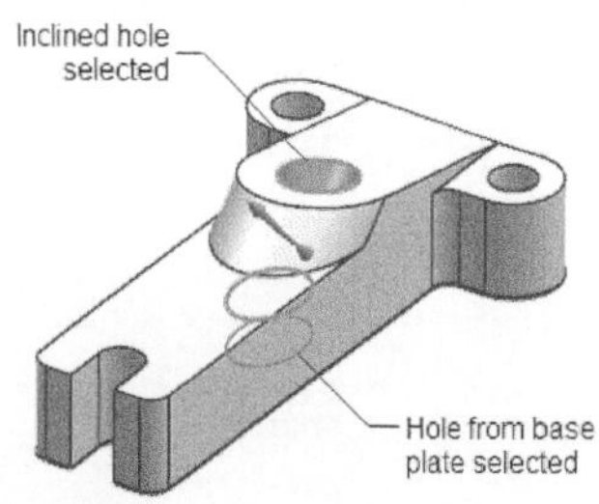

Figure 13-105 Entities selected to modify the inclined hole

Decreasing the Unwanted Thickness of the Base Plate

1. Choose the **Move Face** tool from the **Synchronous Modeling** group; the **Move Face** dialog box is displayed. 

2. Select the two faces of the base plate, refer to Figure 13-106, and then choose the **Reverse Direction** button from the **Transform** rollout.

3. Enter **5** in the **Distance** edit box of the **Transform** rollout and choose the **OK** button from the dialog box to apply the changes. Next, exit the dialog box. The resultant model is shown in Figure 13-107.

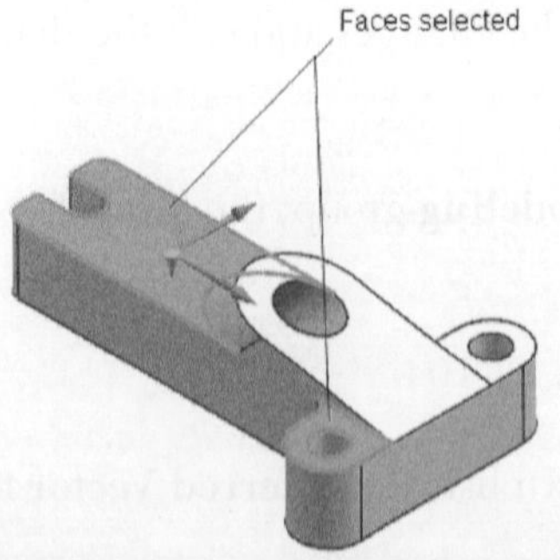

Figure 13-106 Entities selected to modify the thickness of the base plate

Figure 13-107 The resultant model

Aligning the Horizontal Face with the Inclined Face

1. Choose the **Replace Face** tool from the **Synchronous Modeling** group; the **Replace Face** dialog box is displayed. 

2. Select the horizontal face of the base plate, refer to Figure 13-108.

3. Choose the **Face** button from the **Replacement Face** rollout and then select the inclined face of the model, refer to Figure 13-108. Next, choose the **OK** button. The resultant model after aligning the selected faces is shown in Figure 13-109.

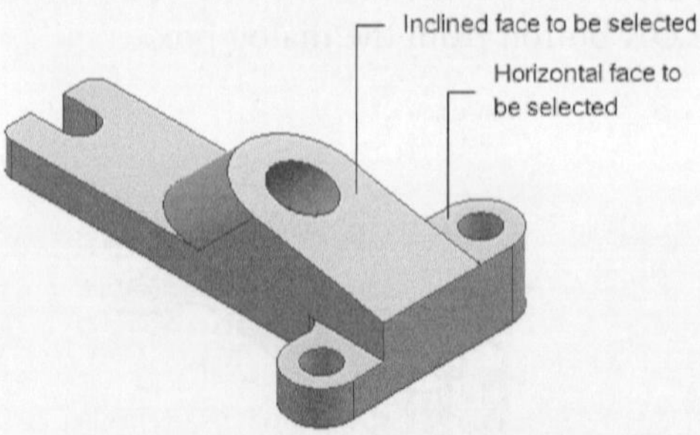

Figure 13-108 Faces to be selected

Figure 13-109 The resultant model

Changing the Radius of the Fillet

1. Choose the **Resize Blend** tool from the **Detail Feature** gallery of the **More** gallery; the **Resize Blend** dialog box is displayed. 

2. Select the two blends of the base plate, refer to Figure 13-110.

3. Enter **4** in the **Radius** edit box of the **Radius** rollout and choose the **OK** button from the dialog box. Figure 13-111 shows the rotated view of the resultant model.

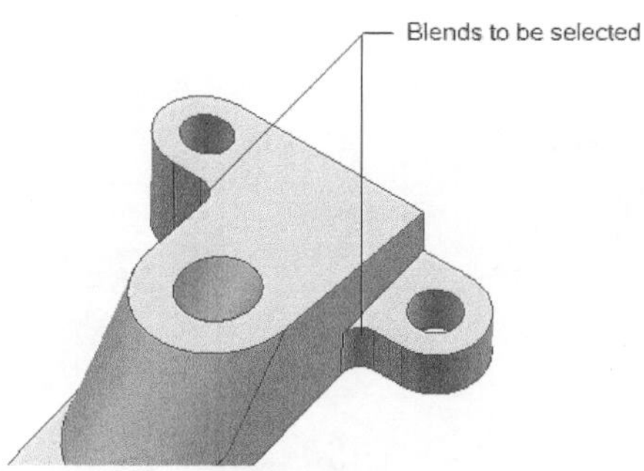

Figure 13-110 Blends to be selected

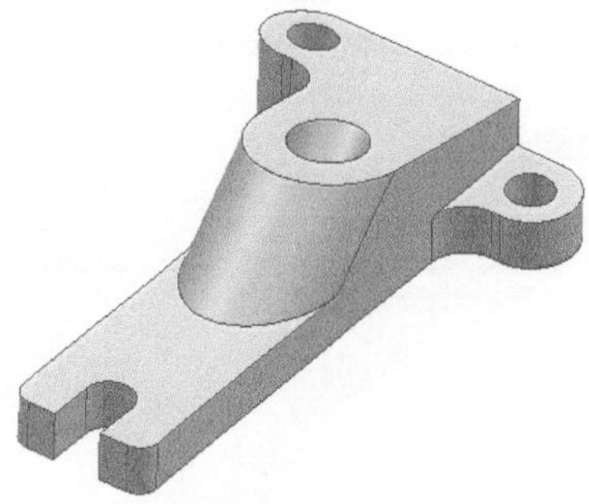

Figure 13-111 The resultant model

Changing the Diameter of Vertical Holes

1. Choose the **Resize Face** tool from **Menu > Insert > Synchronous Modeling** in the **Top Border Bar**; the **Resize Face** dialog box is displayed.

2. Select the vertical holes created on the base feature.

3. Enter **6** in the **Diameter** edit box of the **Size** rollout in the dialog box and choose the **OK** button; the diameter of the holes is updated.

Changing the Diameter of the Inclined Hole

1. Choose the **Radial Dimension** tool from **Menu > Insert > Synchronous Modeling > Dimension**; the **Radial Dimension** dialog box is displayed.

2. Select the inclined hole and then select the **Diameter** radio button from the **Size** rollout.

3. Enter **10** in the **Diameter** edit box of the **Size** rollout in the dialog box and choose the **OK** button; the diameter of the inclined hole is updated.

Modifying the Distance Between Two Vertical Holes

1. Choose the **Move Face** tool from the **Synchronous Modeling** group; the **Move Face** dialog box is displayed.

2. Select the **Distance** option from the **Motion** drop-down list of the **Transform** rollout; you are prompted to select the faces to be moved.

3. Select the circular face of the hole and the concentric semi-circular face of the base plate, refer to Figure 13-112.

Note

You need to unite all the components of the model before performing this operation.

4. Select the **-YC-axis** option from the **Infer Vector** drop-down list in the **Specify Vector** area of the **Transform** rollout of the dialog box.

5. Enter **5** in the **Distance** edit box of the **Transform** rollout and choose the **OK** button. Figure 13-113 shows the model after modifying the distance.

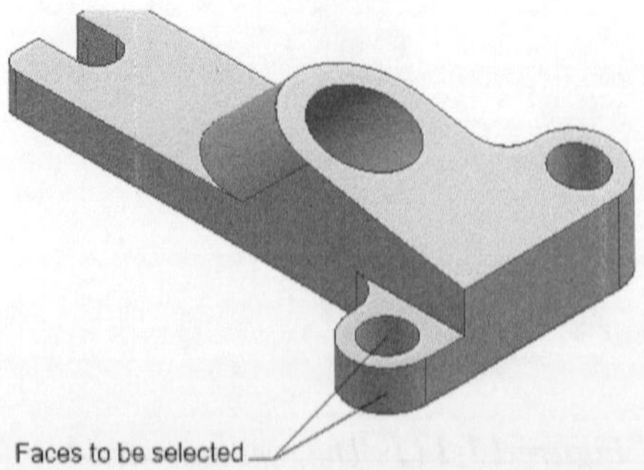

Figure 13-112 Faces to be selected

Figure 13-113 The resultant model

Applying Fillets to the Base Plate

1. Choose the **Edge Blend** tool from the **Feature** group; the **Edge Blend** dialog box is displayed.

2. Select the **Circular** option from the **Shape** drop-down list in the **Edge** rollout and then select the edges of the base plate, refer to Figure 13-114.

3. Enter **1** in the **Radius 1** edit box of the **Edge** rollout and choose the **OK** button; the final model is displayed, as shown in Figure 13-115.

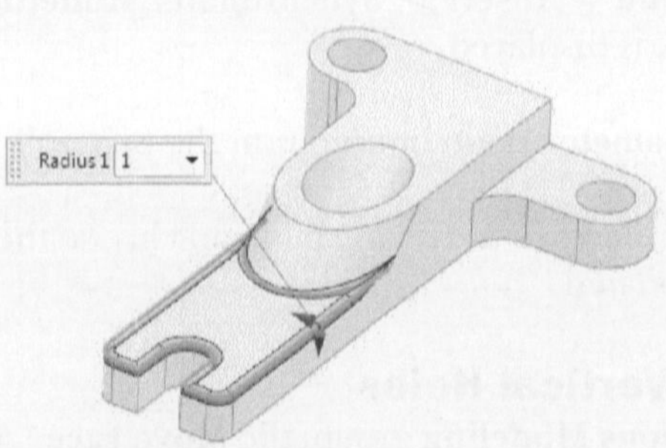

Figure 13-114 Edges selected to apply fillet

Figure 13-115 The final model

Saving and Closing the File

1. Choose **Menu > File > Close > Save and Close** from the **Top Border Bar** to save and close the file.

Tutorial 2

In this tutorial, you will modify the model created in Exercise 3 of Chapter 6 using the Synchronous Modeling tools. Figure 13-116 shows the original model and Figure 13-117 shows the model after modification. **(Expected time: 30 min)**

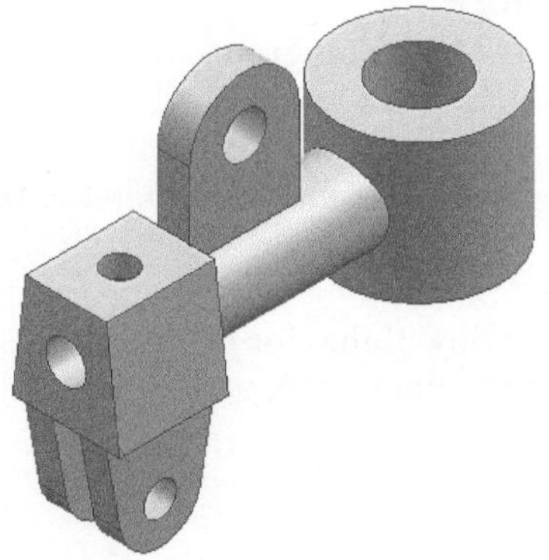

Figure 13-116 Original model

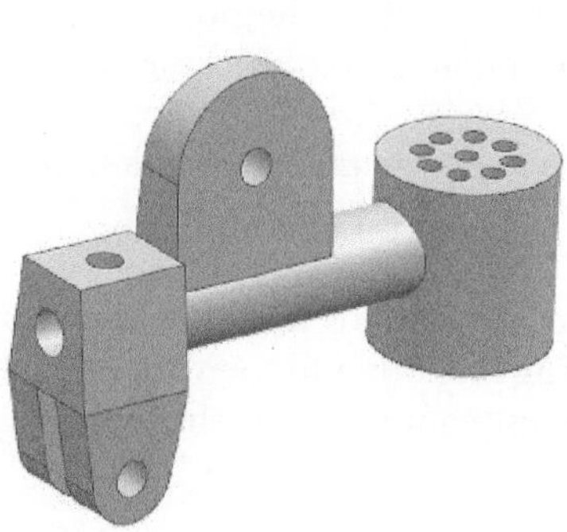

Figure 13-117 Final model after modification

Before modifying the model, you should determine the number of features in the model by observing the feature tree in the **Part Navigator** and then decide the sequence in which the model should be modified. This will help you in modifying the model quickly.

The following steps are required to complete this tutorial:

a. Copy the file from Exercise 3 of Chapter 6. Then, paste it at the location */NX/c13* and rename it as *c13tut2*.
b. Align the outer faces of the double flange using the **Offset Region** tool, refer to Figure 13-118.
c. Increase the length of the circular rod using the **Move Face** tool, refer to Figure 13-120.
d. Increase the length of the cylinder using the **Linear Dimension** tool, refer to Figure 13-122.
e. Align the face of the single flange using the **Angular Dimension** tool, refer to Figure 13-124.
f. Align the opposite face of the single flange using the **Make Symmetric** tool, refer to Figure 13-126.
g. Decrease the internal diameter of the cylinder using the **Radial Dimension** tool, refer to Figure 13-128.
h. Add two more holes to the cylinder using the **Copy Face** tool and then the **Paste Face** tool, refer to Figure 13-130.
i. Add six more holes to the cylinder using the **Pattern Face** tool, refer to Figure 13-132.
j. Increase the length of the single flange using the **Linear Dimension** tool, refer to Figure 13-133.
k. Make the hole coaxial to the curved face of the single flange using the **Make Coaxial** tool, refer to Figure 13-135.

Copying the File

1. Copy the part file created in Exercise 3 of Chapter 6. Paste it at the location */NX/c13* and then rename it as *c13tut2*.

2. Open the *c13tut2* file.

Aligning the Outer Faces of the Double Flange

1. Choose the **Offset Region** tool from the **Synchronous Modeling** group; the **Offset Region** dialog box is displayed.

2. Select the outer faces of the double flange, refer to Figure 13-118 and enter **5** in the **Distance** edit box of the **Offset** rollout.

3. Select the **Extend Incident Face** option from the **Overflow Behavior** drop-down list in the **Settings** rollout and then choose the **OK** button from the dialog box to accept the changes. The resultant model is shown in Figure 13-119.

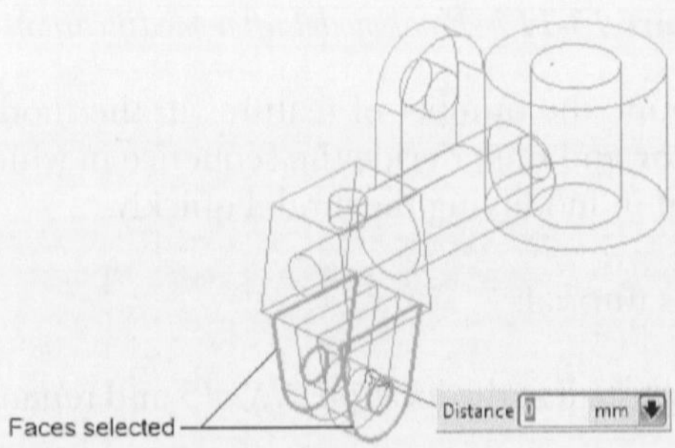

Figure 13-118 Faces selected

Figure 13-119 Resultant model

Increasing the Length of the Circular Rod

1. Choose the **Move Face** tool from the **Synchronous Modeling** group; the **Move Face** dialog box is displayed.

2. Select the **Distance** option from the **Motion** drop-down list in the **Transform** rollout of the dialog box; you are prompted to select the faces to move.

3. Select the outer face and the inner face of the cylinder, refer to Figure 13-120.

4. Select the **YC-axis** option from the **Infer Vector** drop-down list in the **Specify Vector** area of the **Transform** rollout. Next, enter **30** in the **Distance** edit box of the **Transform** rollout and choose the **OK** button from the dialog box. The resultant model is shown in Figure 13-121.

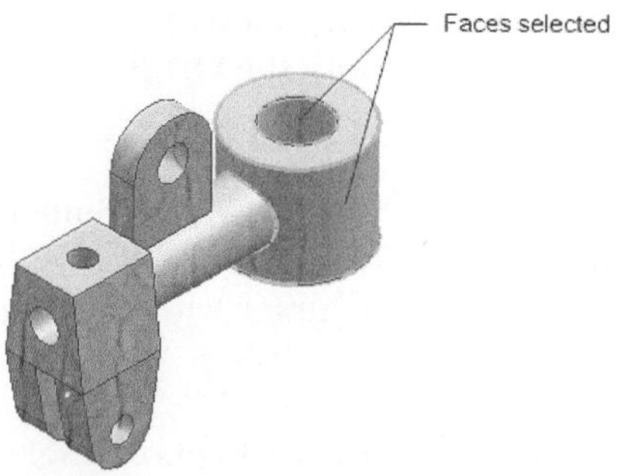

Figure 13-120 Faces selected

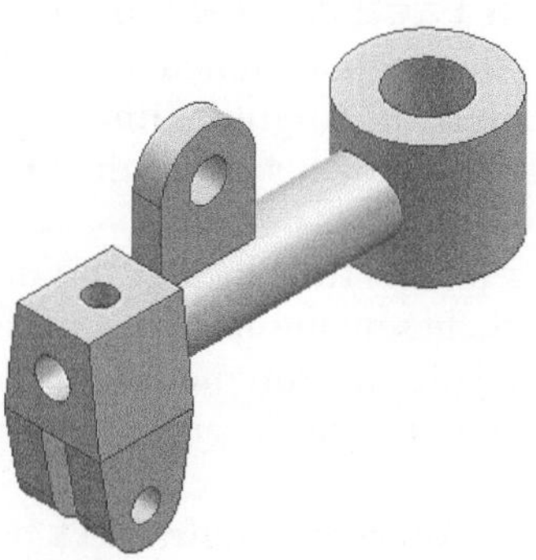

Figure 13-121 Resultant model

Increasing the Length of the Cylinder

1. Choose the **Linear Dimension** tool from **Menu > Insert > Synchronous Modeling > Dimension** of the **Top Border Bar**; the **Linear Dimension** dialog box is displayed with the **Origin Object** button chosen by default in the **Origin** rollout.

2. Select the outer edge of the upper horizontal face of the cylinder, refer to Figure 13-122; the **Measurement Object** button is chosen automatically in the **Measurement** rollout. Now, select the outer edge of the lower horizontal face of the cylinder, refer to Figure 13-122.

3. Once the edges are selected, a cursor with the distance value attached is displayed in the graphics window. Click in the drawing window to place the distance.

4. Enter **60** in the **Distance** edit box of the **Distance** rollout and press ENTER; a preview of the resultant model is displayed. Next, choose the **OK** button to accept the changes. The resultant model is shown in Figure 13-123.

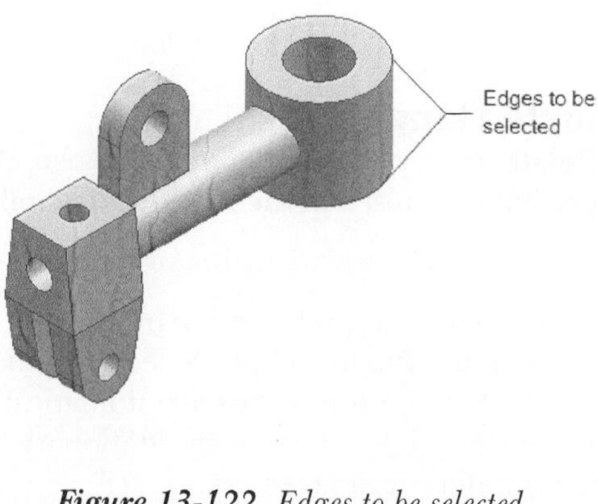

Figure 13-122 Edges to be selected

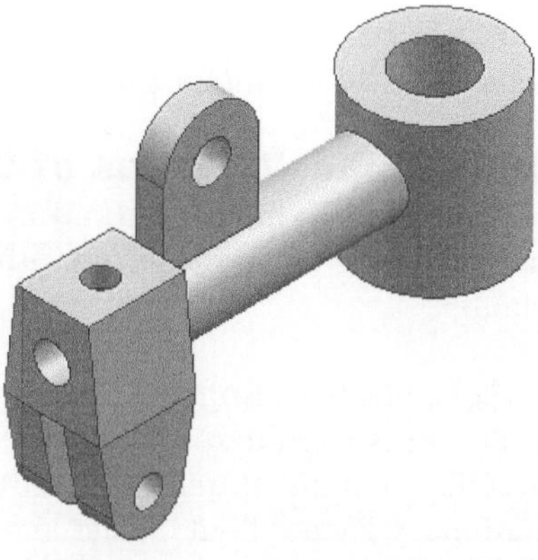

Figure 13-123 Resultant model

Aligning a Face of the Single Flange

1. Choose the **Angular Dimension** tool from **Menu > Insert > Synchronous Modeling > Dimension**; the **Angular Dimension** dialog box is displayed with the **Origin Object** button chosen by default in the **Origin** rollout.

2. Select a face of the block as the origin, refer to Figure 13-124; the **Measurement Object** button is chosen automatically in the **Measurement** rollout. Now, select a face of the single flange as the measurement object, refer to Figure 13-124; a cursor with the angle value attached to it is displayed in the graphics window.

3. Clear the **Alternate Angle** check box in the **Angle** rollout of the dialog box if selected.

4. Move the cursor at the bottom of the double flange and click to place the dimension.

5. Enter **177** in the **Angle** edit box of the **Angle** rollout and press ENTER; a preview of the resultant model is displayed. Next, choose **OK** to accept the changes. The resultant model is shown in Figure 13-125.

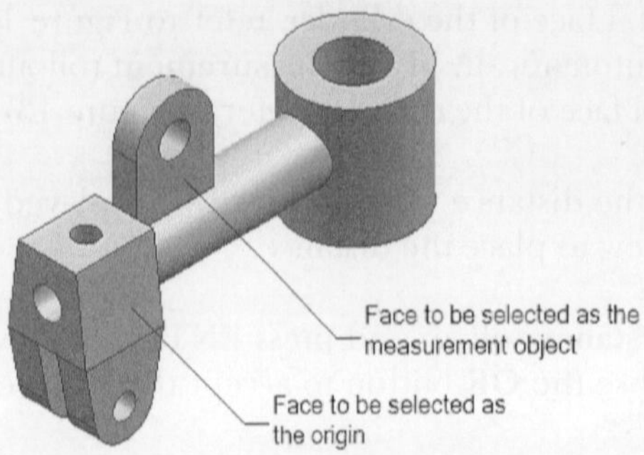

Figure 13-124 *Faces to be selected*

Figure 13-125 *Resultant model*

Aligning the Opposite Faces of the Single Flange

1. Choose the **Make Symmetric** tool from the **Relate** gallery of the **More** gallery; the **Make Symmetric** dialog box is displayed with the **Face** button chosen in the **Motion Face** rollout, by default.

2. Select the opposite face of the single flange as the motion face, refer to Figure 13-126. The **Plane** button is chosen automatically in the **Symmetry Plane** rollout. Select the middle plane of the component, refer to Figure 13-126; the **Face** button is chosen automatically in the **Stationary Face** rollout. Select another face of the single flange as the stationary face, refer to Figure 13-126; a preview of the resultant model is displayed.

3. Choose the **OK** button to accept the changes. The resultant model is displayed, as shown in Figure 13-127.

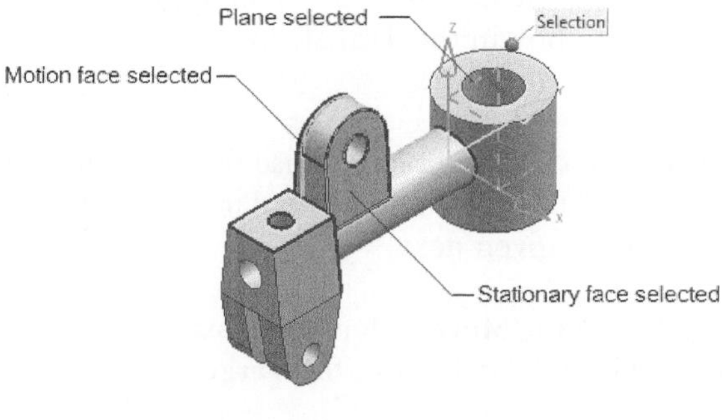

Figure 13-126 Entities selected to align the opposite faces of the single flange

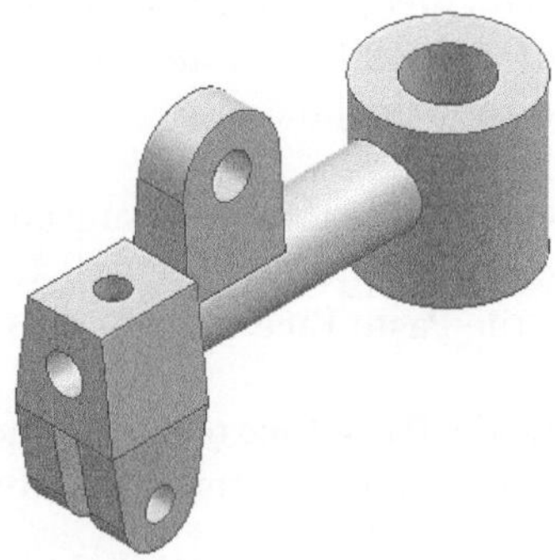

Figure 13-127 Resultant model

Decreasing the Internal Diameter of the Cylinder

1. Choose the **Radial Dimension** tool from **Menu > Insert > Synchronous Modeling > Dimension**; the **Radial Dimension** dialog box is displayed.

2. Select the inner face of the cylinder, refer to Figure 13-128. Next, select the **Diameter** radio button in the **Size** rollout and then enter **8** in the **Diameter** edit box of the **Size** rollout. Next, choose the **OK** button. The resultant model is displayed, as shown in Figure 13-129.

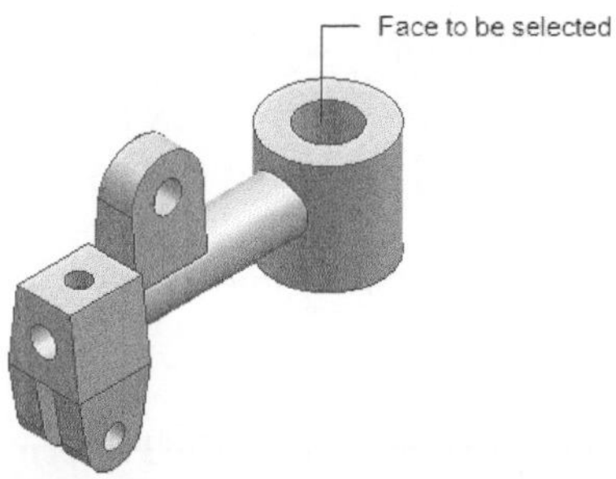

Figure 13-128 Inner face to be selected

Figure 13-129 Resultant model

Adding Two More Holes to the Cylinder

1. Choose the **Copy Face** tool from the **Reuse** gallery of the **More** gallery; the **Copy Face** dialog box is displayed.

2. Select the inner face of the cylinder, refer to Figure 13-130. The distance vector and the pivot point are selected by default. Enter **15** in the **Distance** edit box of the **Transform** rollout and then press ENTER; the model is updated and a preview of the hole is displayed in the graphics window.

3. Choose the **Apply** button to accept the changes.

4. Select the inner face of the cylinder once again to create another hole, refer to Figure 13-130.

Next, choose the **Reverse Direction** button to create the hole in a direction opposite to the already created hole. Enter **15** in the **Distance** edit box in the **Transform** rollout. Choose **OK** to copy the hole.

You will observe that the material is still inside the circular hole because only the circular surfaces are copied by this tool. To remove material from inside the circular face, you need to use the **Paste Face** tool. To do so, follow the steps given next.

5. Choose the **Paste Face** tool from the **Reuse** gallery of the **More** gallery; the **Paste Face** dialog box is displayed with the **Target Body** button chosen by default in the **Target** rollout.

6. Select the model as the target body; the **Tool Body** button is chosen automatically in the **Tool** rollout. Select the faces created by using the **Copy Face** tool on the cylinder as the tool bodies; the preview of the resultant model is displayed.

7. Choose the **OK** button to accept the changes. The resultant model after creating the two holes on the cylinder is shown in Figure 13-131.

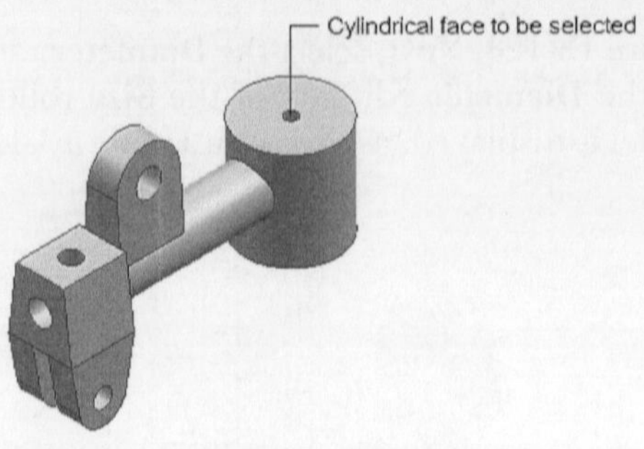

Figure 13-130 *Cylindrical face to be selected*

Figure 13-131 *Model after creating holes*

Adding Six More Holes to the Cylinder

1. Choose the **Pattern Face** tool from the **Reuse** gallery of the **More** gallery; the **Pattern Face** dialog box is displayed.

2. Select the **Circular** option from the **Layout** drop-down list; the **Face** button from the **Face** rollout is activated. Select the two outer holes created previously.

3. Click on the **Specify Vector** area in the **Rotation Axis** sub-rollout of the **Pattern Definition** rollout; a triad of vector is displayed. Select the vertical axis from the triad; the **Specify Point** area is highlighted in the **Rotation Axis** sub-rollout and you are prompted to select the object to infer point.

4. Select the center point of the center hole.

5. Enter **45** in the **Pitch Angle** edit box and **4** in the **Count** edit box of the **Angular Direction** sub-rollout in the **Pattern Definition** rollout. Press ENTER; the preview of the resultant model is displayed in the graphics window. Next, choose the **OK** button to accept the changes. The resultant model is shown in Figure 13-132.

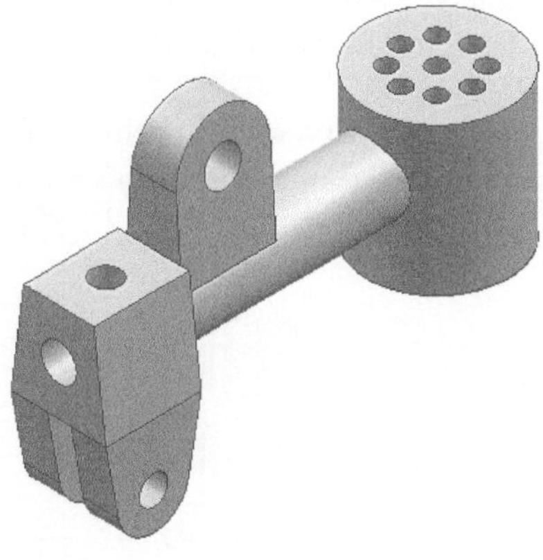

Figure 13-132 The resultant model

Extending face of the single flange

1. Choose the **Linear Dimension** tool from **Menu > Insert > Synchronous Modeling > Dimension** of the **Top Border Bar**; the **Linear Dimension** dialog box is displayed with the **Origin Object** button chosen by default in the **Origin** rollout.

2. Select the lowermost edge of the block, refer to Figure 13-133; the **Measurement Object** button is chosen automatically in the **Measurement** rollout. Now, select the lowermost edge of the face of the single flange, refer to Figure 13-133.

3. Once the edges are selected, a cursor with the distance value attached is displayed in the graphics window. Click in the drawing window to place the distance.

4. Enter **60** in the **Distance** edit box of the **Distance** rollout and press ENTER; a preview of the resultant model is displayed. Next, choose **OK** to accept the changes. The resultant model is shown in Figure 13-134.

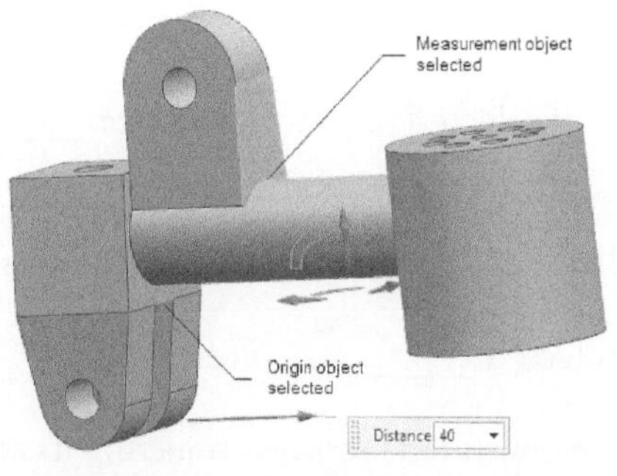

Figure 13-133 Edges to be selected

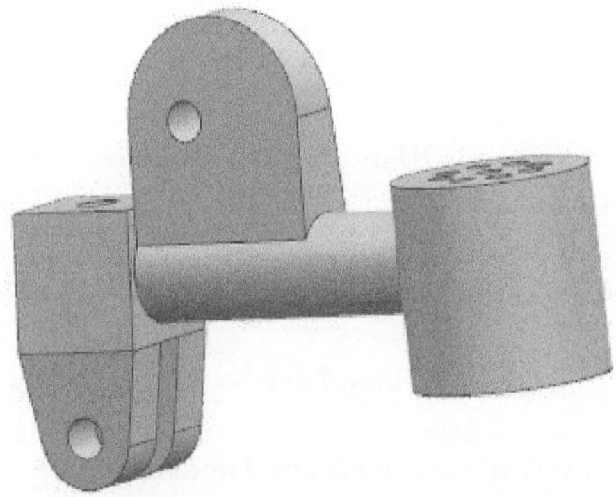

Figure 13-134 Resultant model

Making the hole coaxial to the curved face of the single flange

1. Choose the **Make Coaxial** tool from the **Relate** gallery of the **More** gallery; the **Make Coaxial** dialog box is displayed and you are prompted to select the object to be made coaxial. Also, the **Face** button is chosen by default in the **Motion Face** rollout.

2. Select the inner face of the hole, refer to Figure 13-135; the **Face** button in the **Stationary Face** rollout is activated and you are prompted to select the object to be kept stationary.

3. Select the curved face of the flange, refer to Figure 13-135; a preview of the resultant model is displayed in the graphics window. Next, choose **OK** to accept the changes. The resultant model is shown in Figure 13-136.

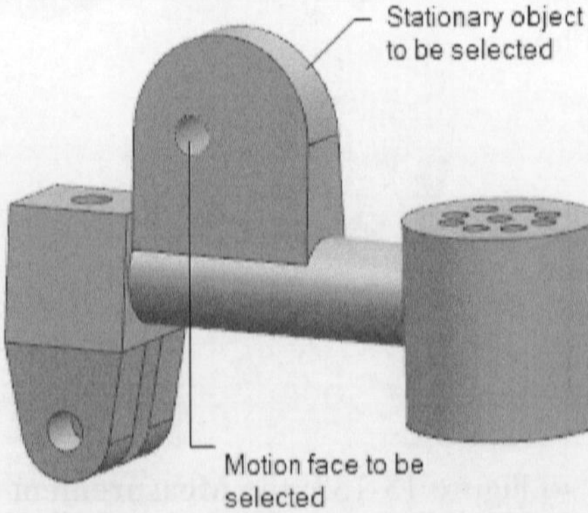

Figure 13-135 Objects to be selected

Figure 13-136 Resultant model

Saving and Closing the File

1. Choose **Menu > File > Close > Save and Close** from the **Top Border Bar** to save and close the file.

Self-Evaluation Test

Answer the following questions and then compare them to those given at the end of this chapter:

1. Using the **Offset Region** tool, you can offset a set of selected faces in a direction __________ to the selected faces.

2. Using the **Resize Blend** tool, you can change the __________ of the existing blends.

3. Using the **Resize Face** tool, you can resize the selected __________ faces.

4. You can use the **Delete Face** tool to __________ the unwanted faces by projecting its adjacent faces.

5. You can move the selected face in angular direction by modifying its value using the __________ tool.

6. The __________ tool is used to copy the selected faces and place them in the same body or in a different body.

7. You can create new designs using the Synchronous Modeling tools. (T/F)

8. You can reorient a selected face using the **Move Face** tool. (T/F)

9. The **Transform** rollout in the **Move Face** dialog box cannot be used for moving a face. (T/F)

10. The **Pull Face** tool is used to pull the selected face regardless of the adjacent geometry. (T/F)

Review Questions

Answer the following questions:

1. Which of the following tools is used to make two different cylindrical faces of a component coaxial?

   (a) **Make Coplanar** (b) **Make Tangent**
   (c) **Make Coaxial** (d) **Make Symmetric**

2. Which of the following tools is used to make one face of a component symmetric to another face?

   (a) **Make Symmetric** (b) **Make Coaxial**
   (c) **Make Tangent** (d) None of these

3. In which of the following environments, the cross-section of the model can be modified using the **Edit Section** tool?

   (a) Sketch in Task (b) Modeling
   (c) Assembly (d) Drafting

4. Which of the following tools is used to label the angular face as a chamfer?

   (a) **Label Notch Blend** (b) **Label Chamfer**
   (c) **Resize Face** (d) **Delete Face**

5. Which of the following tools is used to move a set of faces in angular direction by adding and then changing the dimension?

   (a) **Linear Dimension** (b) **Move Face**
   (c) **Cross Section Edit** (d) **Angular Dimension**

6. The ________ tool is used to make two different faces of a component coplanar.

7. You can change the diameter of a spherical face of the model using the **Radial Dimension** tool. (T/F)

8. The **Delete Face** tool is used to delete the unwanted faces of a model by projecting its adjacent faces. (T/F)

9. The **Copy Face** tool is used to copy and place the selected faces of a solid or surface body. (T/F)

10. The **Results** tab displays the list of all possible geometrical conditions of a selected face. (T/F)

EXERCISES

Exercise 1

In this exercise, you will modify the model created in Exercise 1 of Chapter 5 using the Synchronous Modeling tools. Figure 13-137 shows the original model and Figure 13-138 shows the model after modification. **(Expected time: 15 min)**

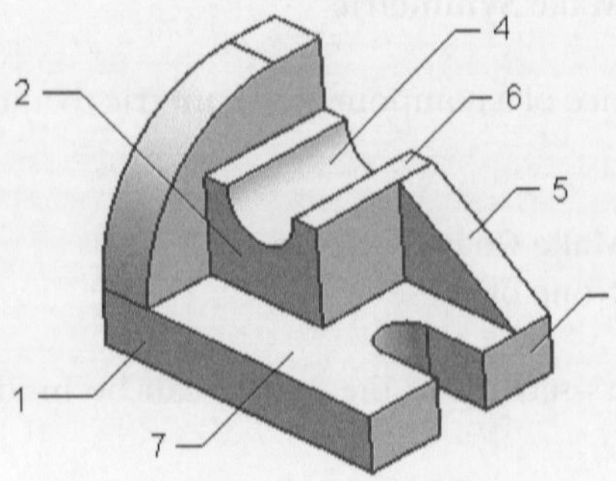

Figure 13-137 Model for Exercise 1

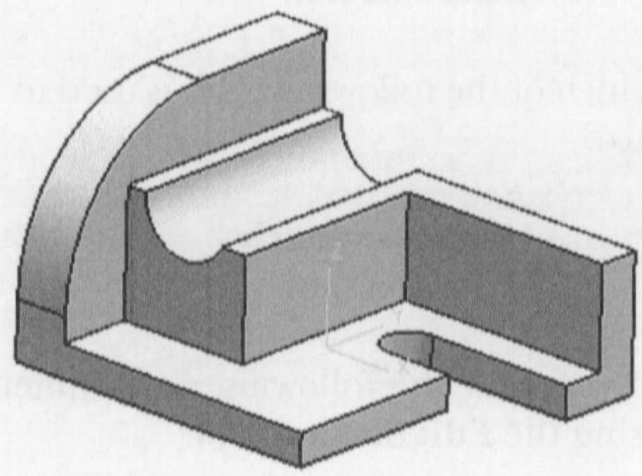

Figure 13-138 Final model after modification

Hint

1. Increase the length of faces 1 and 2 by a distance of 30mm.
2. Pull face 3 by a distance of 25mm.
3. Increase the diameter of face 4 to 28mm.
4. Replace face 5 with face 3.
5. Offset face 6 and 7 by a distance of -7mm.

Exercise 2

In this exercise, you will modify the model created in Tutorial 1 of Chapter 6 using the Synchronous Modeling tools. Figure 13-139 shows the original model and Figure 13-140 shows the model after modification. **(Expected time: 30 min)**

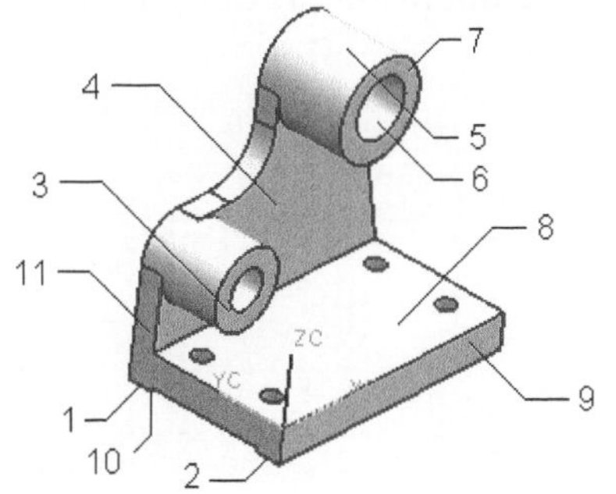

Figure 13-139 Model for Exercise 2

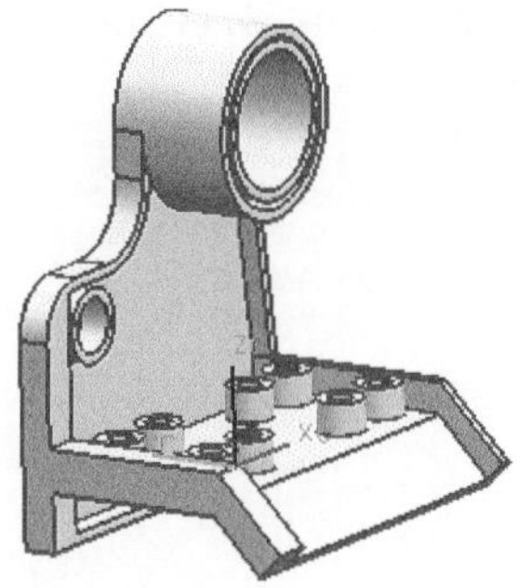

Figure 13-140 Final model after modification

Hint

1. Increase the length of faces 1 and 2 by a distance of 20mm.
2. Replace face 3 with face 4.
3. Increase the diameter of face 5 by 20mm.
4. Increase the diameter of face 6 to 50mm.
5. Add four more holes by an offset of 25mm.
6. Change the angle of face 2 to 45 degree.
7. Shell the component by piercing faces 7, 8, 9, and 10 (4 mm Shell thickness).
8. Increase the shell thickness of face 11.

Answers to Self-Evaluation Test

1. normal, **2.** radius, **3.** cylindrical, **4.** delete, **5. Angular Dimension**, **6. Copy Face**, **7.** F, **8.** T, **9.** F, **10.** T

Chapter 14

Sheet Metal Design

Learning Objectives

After completing this chapter, you will be able to:

- *Set the parameters for creating the sheet metal parts*
- *Create the base of the sheet metal part*
- *Add various types of flanges to the sheet metal part*
- *Add a jog to the sheet metal part*
- *Bend or unbend a sheet metal part*
- *Add corner bends to the sheet metal parts*
- *Create dimples, louvers, drawn cutouts, and beads in the sheet metal component*
- *Convert solid parts to sheet metal parts*
- *Create the flat pattern of the sheet metal parts*
- *Renew Features*

THE SHEET METAL MODULE

The components having a thickness greater than 0 and less than 12 mm are called sheet metal components. A sheet metal component is created by bending, cutting, or deforming an existing sheet of metal having uniform thickness, refer to Figure 14-1. As it is not possible to machine such a model, therefore, after creating the sheet metal component, you need to flatten it for manufacturing. Figure 14-2 shows the flattened view of the sheet metal component shown in Figure 14-1.

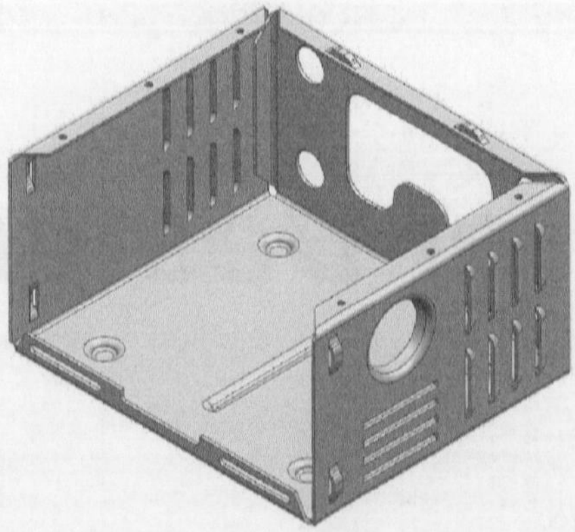

Figure 14-1 *Sheet metal component*

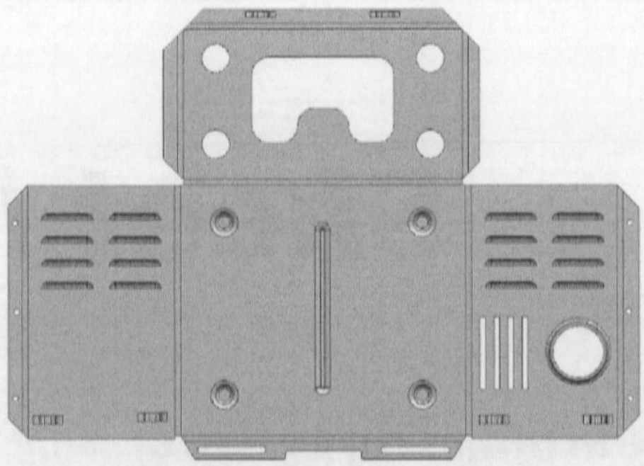

Figure 14-2 *Flattened view of the sheet metal component*

Note

All features of a sheet metal component cannot be flattened. For example, features such as louvers, dimples cannot be flattened because they are created using a punch and a die.

NX allows you to create the sheet metal components in a specific environment called the Sheet Metal environment. This environment provides all tools that are required for creating the sheet metal components.

To start a new document in the Sheet Metal environment, choose the **New** button from the **Standard** group of the **Home** tab in the **Ribbon**; the **New** dialog box will be displayed. Choose the **Sheet Metal** template from the **Templates** rollout in the **Model** tab, refer to Figure 14-3, and choose the **OK** button; a new document will open in the Sheet Metal environment, refer to Figure 14-4. In this environment, the different groups provide the tools that are required to create the sheet metal components.

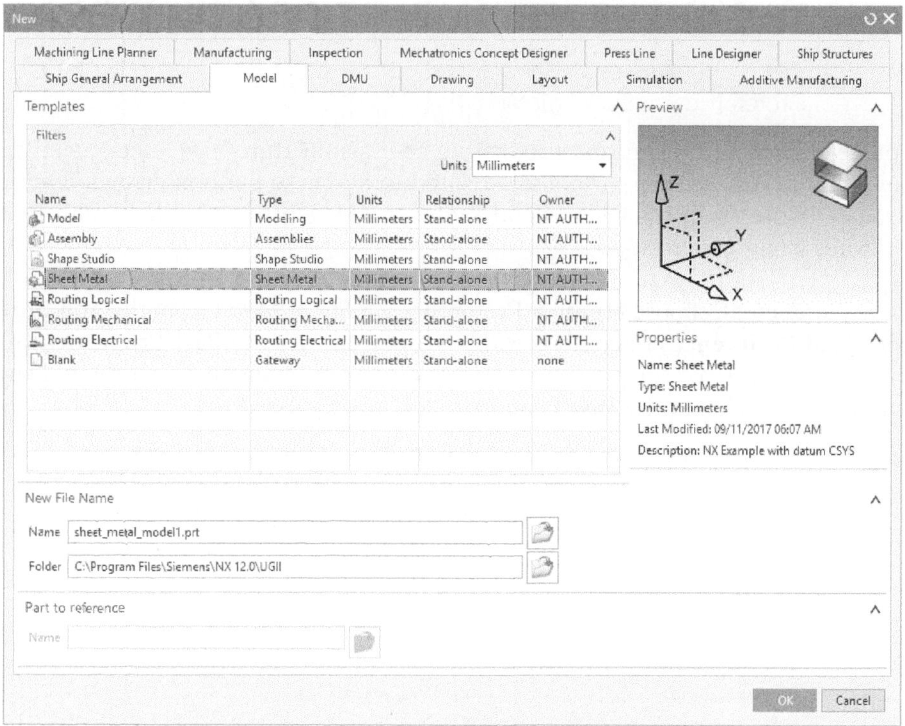

Figure 14-3 Starting a new sheet metal document

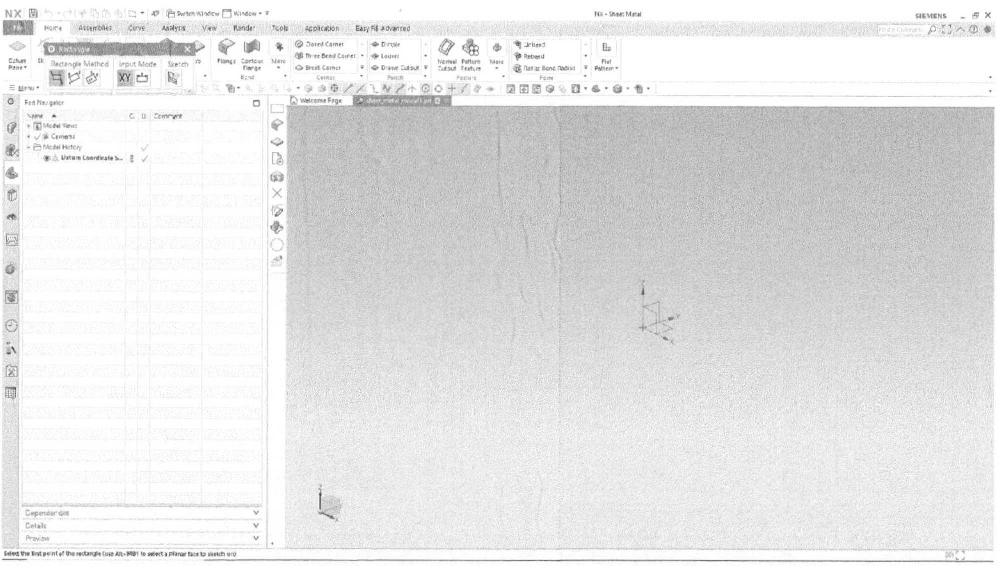

Figure 14-4 Default screen of the Sheet Metal environment

SETTING THE SHEET METAL PART PROPERTIES

Ribbon:	File > Preferences > Sheet Metal
Menu:	Preferences > Sheet Metal

Before proceeding with the process of creating the base feature of a sheet metal part, it is recommended that you set the parameters related to it. These parameters will determine the default values of the sheet thickness, bend radius, relief depth, and relief width that will be displayed while using various tools.

To set these parameters, choose **Menu > Preferences > Sheet Metal** from the **Top Border Bar**; the **Sheet Metal Preferences** dialog box will be displayed with the **Part Properties** tab chosen by default. This tab displays the parameters related to the sheet metal part, refer to Figure 14-5. The parameters available in the **Part Properties** tab are discussed next.

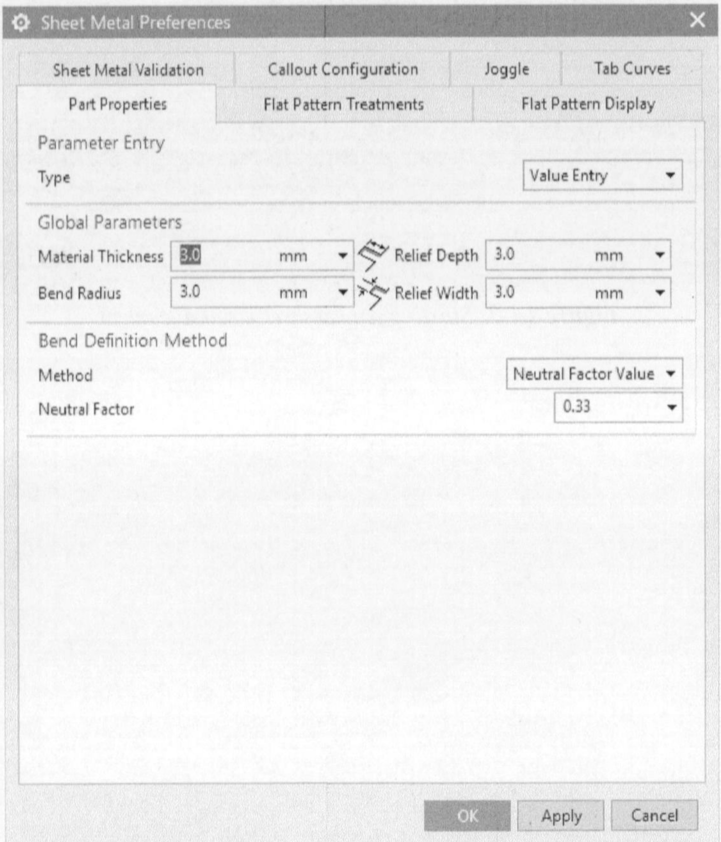

Figure 14-5 The ***Part Properties*** *tab of the* ***Sheet Metal Preferences*** *dialog box*

Parameter Entry Area

This area is used to specify the methods that will be used for defining the parameters of the sheet metal part. The options in the **Type** drop-down list of this area are discussed next.

Value Entry

On selecting this option, you can define the parameters related to sheet metal by using the options in the **Global Parameters** and **Bend Definition Method** areas. The options in these areas will be discussed later in this chapter.

Material Selection

Using this option, you can define the parameters of the sheet metal by selecting a predefined material available for the sheet metal part. On selecting this option, the **Select Material** button will be activated. Choose this button to invoke the **Select Material** dialog box, refer to Figure 14-6. Select a material from the **Available Materials** rollout at the bottom of the dialog box or you can select the desired parameters using the **Material Characteristics** rollout.

Tool ID Selection

Using this option, you can define the sheet metal parameters by specifying the predefined tool ID. When you select the **Tool ID Selection** option, the **Bend Definition Method** area will be modified and the **Punch** and **Die** drop-down lists will become available in it, refer to Figure 14-7. Using the options available in these drop-down lists, you can select the punch and die required for the operation.

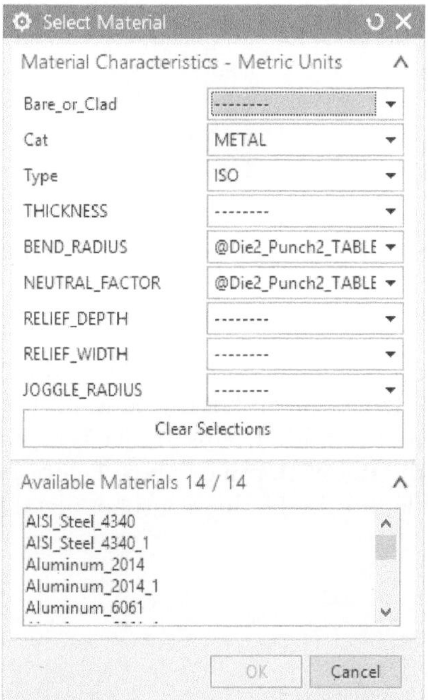

*Figure 14-6 The **Select Material** dialog box*

*Figure 14-7 The modified **Bend Definition Method** area*

Global Parameters Area

This area contains the options to specify the default values of the parameters for the sheet metal part. The options in this area are discussed next.

Material Thickness

This edit box is used to set the default thickness for the sheet metal part. The thickness specified in this edit box will be displayed as the default thickness whenever you invoke a tool to create the sheet metal part.

Note

While creating a sheet metal part, it is not necessary to accept the default sheet thickness. You can modify the default thickness as per your requirement.

Bend Radius

This edit box is used to set the default value for the bend radius. This value is used while adding flanges to the model or bending it. Figure 14-8 shows a sheet bend having a radius of 1 mm and Figure 14-9 shows a sheet bend having a radius of 5 mm.

Figure 14-8 *Sheet with 1 mm bend radius*

Figure 14-9 *Sheet with 5 mm bend radius*

Relief Depth

Whenever you bend a sheet metal component or create a flange such that the bend does not extend throughout the length of the edge, a groove is added at the end of the bend so that the walls of the sheet metal part do not intersect when folded or unfolded. This groove is known as relief. You can set a predefined depth for the relief using the **Relief Depth** edit box. Figure 14-10 shows a sheet metal part with relief depth of 2 mm and Figure 14-11 shows a sheet metal part with relief depth of 5 mm.

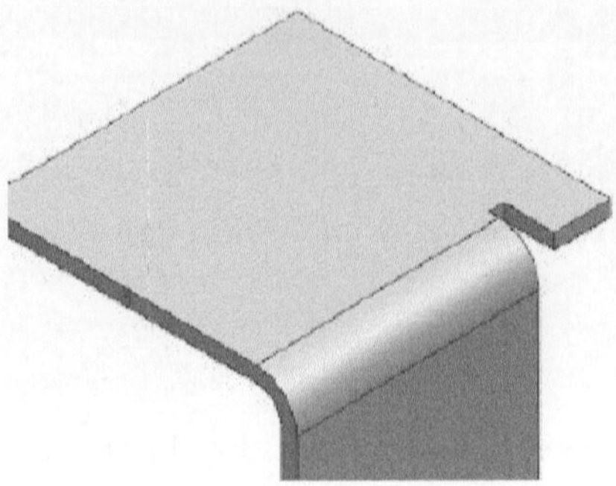

Figure 14-10 *Relief depth = 2 mm*

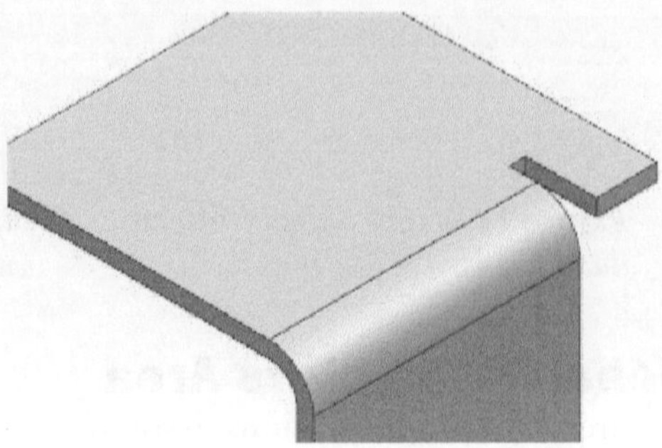

Figure 14-11 *Relief depth = 5 mm*

Relief Width

The **Relief Width** edit box is used to specify the value of width of the relief. The default value of the relief width is equal to the thickness of the sheet. Figure 14-12 shows a sheet metal component with a relief width of 1 mm and Figure 14-13 shows a sheet metal component with a relief width of 5 mm.

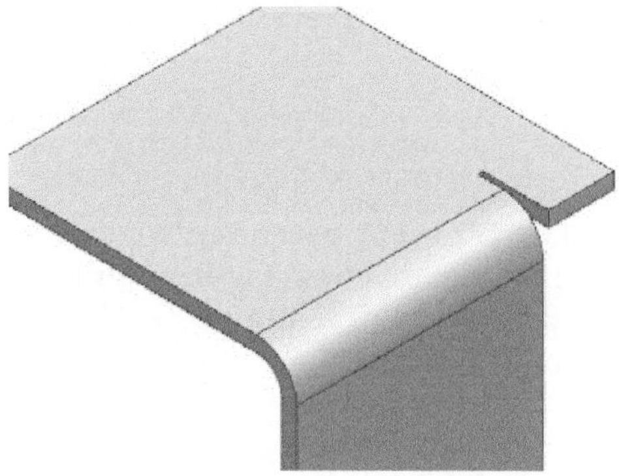

Figure 14-12 *Relief width = 1 mm*

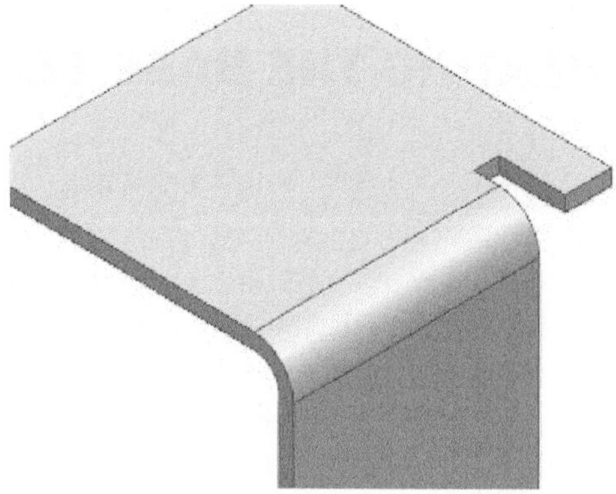

Figure 14-13 *Relief width = 5 mm*

Bend Definition Method Area

The options available in this area change depending upon the option selected from the **Type** drop-down list in the **Parameter Entry** area.

On selecting the **Value Entry** option from the **Type** drop-down list, the **Method** and **Neutral Factor** drop-down lists will be available in the **Bend Definition Method** area. The options in the **Method** drop-down list are discussed next.

Neutral Factor Value

On selecting this option, you can enter a value in the **Neutral Factor** edit box. The neutral factor depends on the properties of the material being bent. While bending, the outer surface of the bend is under tension and the inner surface is under compression. There is a layer in between them which is neither in compression nor in tension. The ratio of the distance of this surface from the inner bend to the thickness is the neutral factor. The default value is 0.33 and the value typically ranges from 0 to 1.

Bend Table

On selecting this option, the **Table** drop-down list will become available below the **Method** drop-down list. The options in this drop-down list are used to calculate the neutral factor. You can select the required option from this drop-down list.

Formula

This option is used to define a formula to calculate the bend allowance of the sheet metal part. On choosing this option, you can enter the bend allowance formula in the edit box available below the **Formula** drop-down list.

After performing the required settings, choose the **Apply** button to apply settings to the model and then choose the **OK** button to exit the dialog box.

Note

*You can change the values of parameters in the **Sheet Metal Preferences** dialog box any time during the designing processes.*

CREATING THE BASE FEATURE

Ribbon:	Home > Basic > Tab
Menu:	Insert > Tab

To create a sheet metal component, first you need to create a base feature. To create the base feature of the sheet metal component, choose the **Tab** tool from the **Basic** group of the **Home** tab; the **Tab** dialog box will be displayed, as shown in Figure 14-14. Also, you will be prompted to select the sketch plane to sketch or the section geometry to be extruded. If you select the sketch at this stage, the preview of the tab feature created using the default values will be displayed on the screen. Select the sketch plane, the sketching environment will be invoked.

Draw the sketch of the base feature of the sheet metal component and then exit the sketching environment; the preview of the tab feature will be displayed along with the Thickness handle, as shown in Figure 14-15(a). Note that no matter how long you drag the handle, the tab will be created based on the thickness specified in the **Sheet Metal Preferences** dialog box. You can choose the **Reverse Direction** button to reverse the direction of feature creation. After specifying all the settings, choose the **OK** button from the **Tab** dialog box; the base of the sheet metal is created.

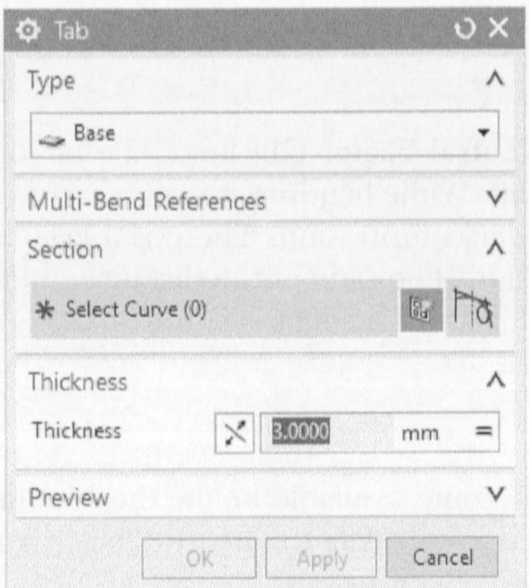

*Figure 14-14 The **Tab** dialog box*

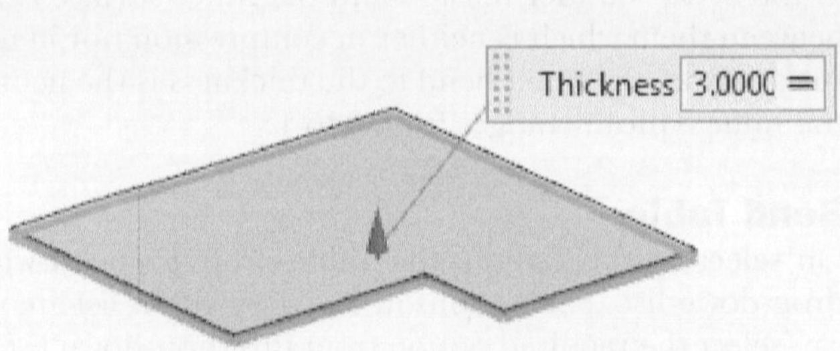

Figure 14-15(a) Preview of the tab feature

After creating the base feature, if you invoke the **Tab** dialog box again; the **Secondary** option will appear in the drop-down list in the **Type** rollout. Using the **Seondary** option, you can create a planar feature attached to the base feature. Note that this option will be available only if you have created a sheet metal feature earlier. Figure 14-15(b) shows a base feature and a sketch which will be used to create the secondary feature attached to the base feature. Figure 14-15(c) shows the secondary feature created and attached to the base feature.

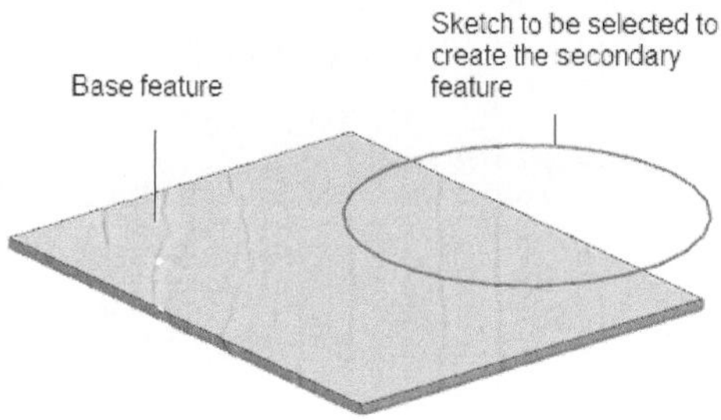

Figure 14-15(b) *Base feature and the sketch to be selected*

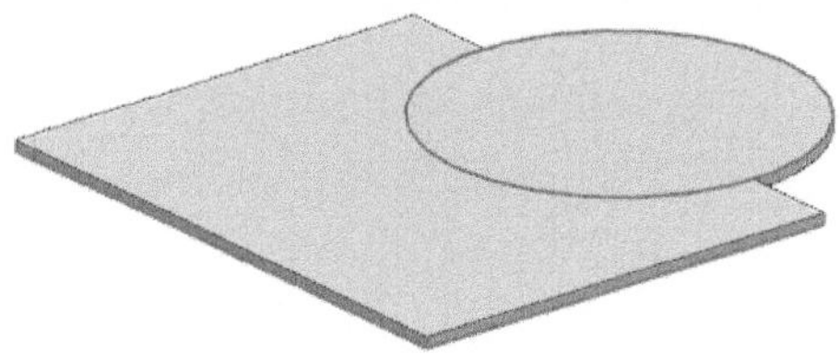

Figure 14-15(c) *The resultant feature*

Tip

*To enter a new thickness value of the sheet, click on the **Launch the formula editor** button which is located next to the **Thickness** edit box; a shortcut menu will be displayed. Choose the **Use Local Value** option from the shortcut menu and enter a new thickness value in the **Thickness** edit box.*

Note

*In NX, you can also create the base feature by using the **Contour Flange** and **Lofted Flange** tools. You will learn more about these tools later in this chapter.*

ADDING FLANGES TO A SHEET METAL PART

Enhanced

Ribbon:	Home > Bend > Flange
Menu:	Insert > Bend > Flange

Flange

Flange is the bend section of the sheet metal. NX allows you to directly add a folded face to the existing sheet metal part by using the **Flange** tool. To do so, choose the **Flange** tool from the **Bend** group of the **Home** tab, refer to Figure 14-16; the **Flange** dialog box will be displayed, as shown in Figure 14-17. The options in the **Flange** dialog box are discussed next.

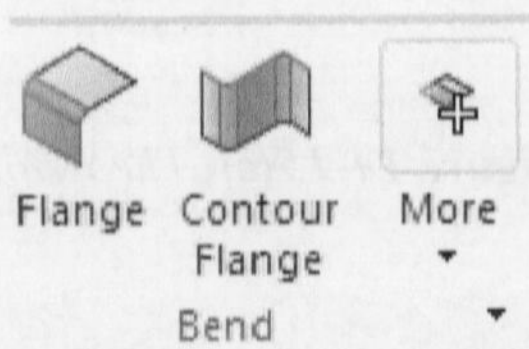

Figure 14-16 *The* **Bend** *group*

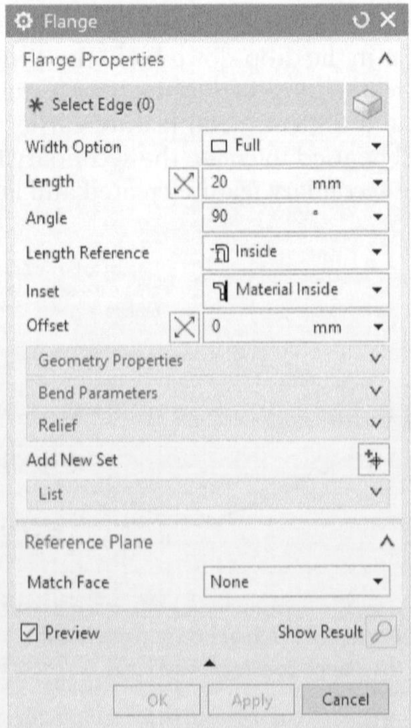

Figure 14-17 *The* **Flange** *dialog box*

Flange Properties Rollout

By default, the **Select Edge** area is highlighted in this rollout. As a result, you are prompted to select a linear edge. Select an edge from the base feature of the sheet metal part; preview of the flange will be displayed. The other options available in this rollout are discussed next.

Width Option

The options in this drop-down list are used to define width and position of the flange on the selected edge. These options are discussed next.

Full

This option is selected by default and is used to create the flange having width equal to the width of edge selected to create the flange.

At Center

This option is used to create the flange at an equal distance from the center of the selected edge. After selecting this option, the flange will be displayed at the center of the edge selected. To modify the width of the flange, specify the required value in the **Width** edit box.

At End

This option is used to create the flange at one of the ends of the selected edge. When you select this option, the **Specify Point** area will become available below the **Width Option** drop-down list. Next, click in the **Specify Point** area; you will be prompted to select the desired end of the edge. Select one of the endpoints of the edge; the preview of the flange will be displayed. Specify a value in the **Width** edit box to modify the width of the flange.

From End

This option is used to create the flange at a certain offset from one of the endpoints of the selected edge. When you select this option, the **Specify Point** area will be displayed below the **Width Option** drop-down list. Next, click in the **Specify Point** area; you will be prompted to select the desired end. After you select the desired end, the flange will be created with default values of its distance from the selected end and width. You can specify required values in the **Distance 1** and **Width** edit boxes to modify these values.

From Both Ends

This option is used to create the flange at a certain offset from both ends of the selected edge. After you select this option, the **Distance 1** and **Distance 2** edit boxes are displayed below the **Width Option** drop-down list. You can specify required values in these edit boxes to modify the distance from both the ends of the selected edge.

Length

This edit box is used to specify the length of the flange. This value is modified dynamically as you drag the Length handle displayed in the drawing window, refer to Figure 14-18.

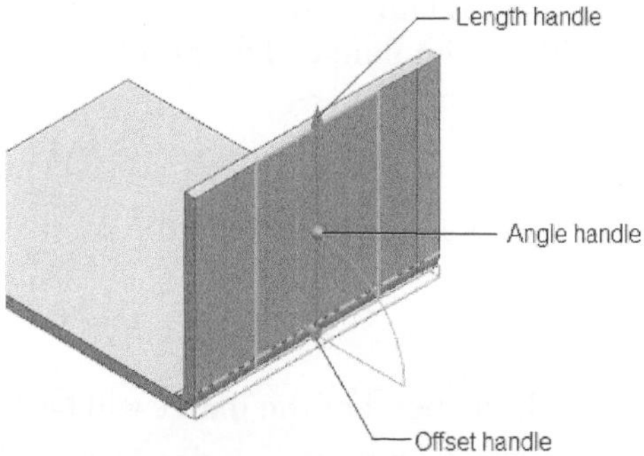

Figure 14-18 Handles displayed on the flange

Reverse Direction

This button is used to reverse the direction of the flange.

Angle

This edit box is used to specify the angle of the flange. The default value is 90-degree. You can enter the desired value in this edit box. You can also modify the angle dynamically by using the Angle handle, refer to Figure 14-18. Note that this edit box will be available only when you select the **None** option from the **Match Face** drop-down list in the **Reference Plane** rollout.

Length Reference

The options in this drop-down list are used to define the reference from which the length of the flange will be measured. These options are discussed next.

Inside

This option is selected by default and is used to specify the length of the flange from the virtual intersection of the tab faces that are adjacent to the inner bend face to the top of the flange.

Outside

This option is selected to specify the length of the flange from the virtual intersection of the tab faces that are adjacent to the outer bend face to the top of the flange.

Web

This option is used to specify the length of the flange from the starting point of the bend to the extreme edge of the flange created.

Tangent

This option is used to specify the length of the flange according to the DIN6935 standard.

Inset

The options in this drop-down list are used to specify material condition of the flange. These options are discussed next.

Material Inside

This option is selected by default and creates the flange such that the material is added inside the profile of the flange. The profile is automatically displayed when you place the flange.

Material Outside

Select this option to add the material outside the profile of the flange. You can also select this option after placing the flange.

Bend Outside

If this option is selected, the bend of the flange will be placed outside the profile of the flange.

Material Inside OML

If this option is selected, the bend of the flange sets into the base material so that outside face of the flange gets imaginary intersected with the opposite side of the selected edge.

Offset

This edit box is used to create a flange at an offset value from the selected edge. To do so, specify a value in the **Offset** edit box. You can reverse the offset direction by choosing the **Reverse Direction** button.

Geometry Properties

The options in this sub-rollout are used to replicate the geometry irrespective of the feature parameters. These options are discussed next.

Enable Geometry Mirror and Pattern

On selecting this check box, the geometry is replicated irrespective of the feature parameters. However, if you clear this check box, the geometry is replicated considering the feature parameters.

Miter

On selecting this check box, miter is applied to remove interferences between adjacent edges in a given set. However, if you clear this check box, the adjacent flanges are created with interfernce between them.

Bend Parameters

The options in this sub-rollout are used to specify the bend parameters of the flange. These options are discussed next.

Bend Radius

This edit box is used to specify the bend radius. By default, the value that was set using the **Part Properties** tab of the **Sheet Metal Preferences** dialog box will be used as the bend radius. If you want to modify this value, click on the **Launch the formula editor** button located next to this edit box and then choose the **Use Local Value** option from the shortcut menu displayed. Next, enter the required value in the **Bend Radius** edit box.

Neutral Factor

This edit box is used to specify the neutral factor value. By default, the value that was set using the **Part Properties** tab of the **Sheet Metal Preferences** dialog box will be used as the neutral factor.

Relief

Whenever you bend a sheet metal component or create a flange such that bend does not extend throughout the length of the edge, a groove is added at the end of the bend such that the walls of the sheet metal part do not intersect when folded or unfolded. This groove is known as relief. Expand the **Relief** sub-rollout to define the type of relief. The options in this sub-rollout are discussed next.

Bend Relief

This drop-down list is used to specify the type of relief to be added. You can add a square shape relief or a round shape relief by selecting the **Square** or **Round** option, respectively. If you choose the **None** option, no relief will be created. You can use the default value of the relief depth and width or enter a new value in the corresponding edit boxes. Figure 14-19 shows a sheet metal part with a square relief and Figure 14-20 shows a sheet metal part with a round relief.

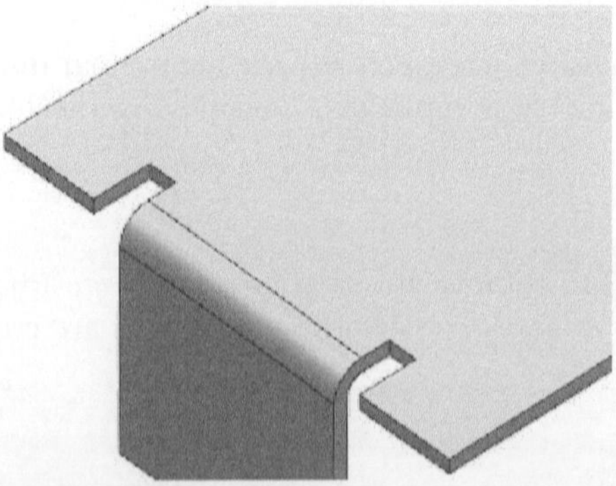

Figure 14-19 Part with square relief

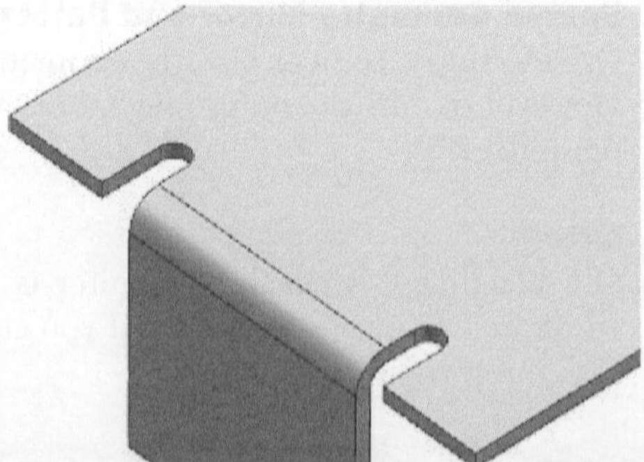

Figure 14-20 Part with round relief

Extend Relief

Select this check box to extend the relief to the edge selected to create the flange. If this check box is cleared, the relief will be applied only to the portion that is adjacent to the flange that you are creating. Figures 14-21 and 14-22 show flanges created with the **Extend Relief** check box selected and cleared, respectively.

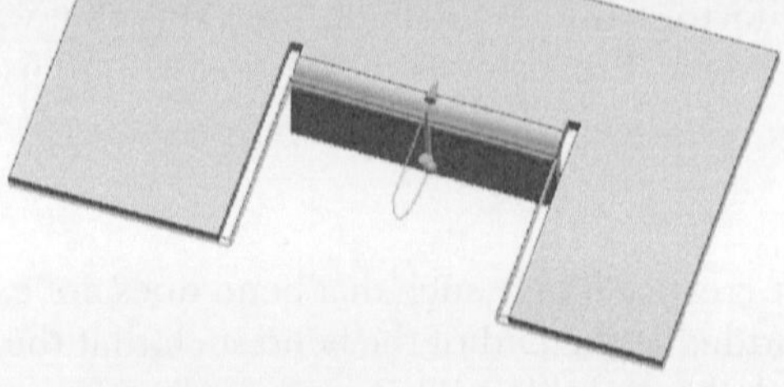

*Figure 14-21 Flange created with the **Extend Relief** check box selected*

*Figure 14-22 Flange created with the **Extend Relief** check box cleared*

Corner Relief

This drop-down list is used to add a corner relief to the flange. A corner relief is added when the flange termination forms a corner with another flange. If you select the **None** option from this drop-down list no corner relief will be added between two flanges, refer to Figure 14-23. You can add three different types of corner reliefs by selecting their corresponding options from this drop-down list. Figure 14-24 shows the **Bend Only** corner relief. Note that in this figure the corner relief is added to the existing flange and not to the one that you are creating.

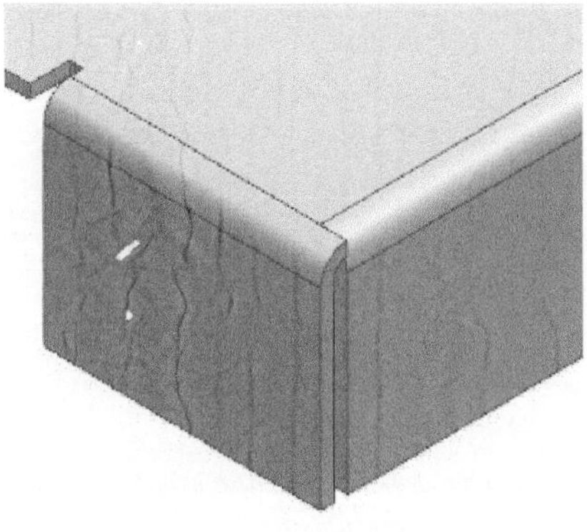

Figure 14-23 Flanges with no corner relief

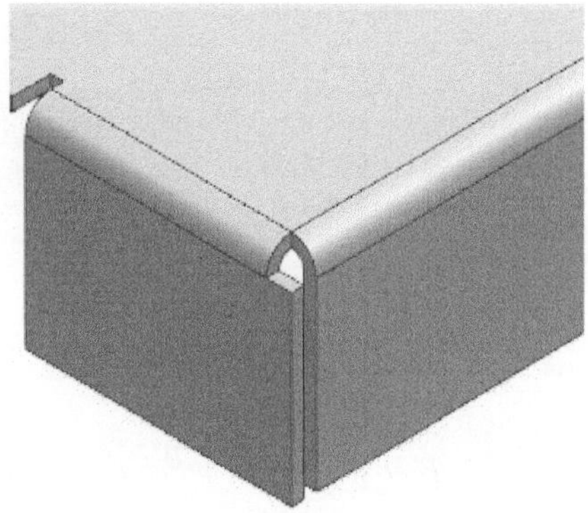

*Figure 14-24 Flanges with the **Bend Only** corner relief*

The third type of corner relief, **Bend/Face Chain**, is used when the first flange has a chain of faces. In this case, the corner relief is applied to the face chain. Figure 14-25 shows a sheet metal part in which the first flange forms a chain with another flange. In this figure, the **Bend/Face** corner relief has been added. Figure 14-26 shows the same model after adding the **Bend/Face Chain** corner relief.

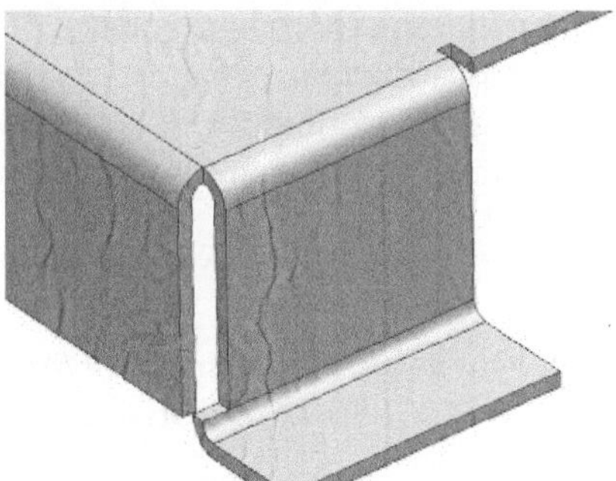

*Figure 14-25 Flanges with the **Bend/Face** corner relief*

*Figure 14-26 Flanges with the **Bend/Face Chain** corner relief*

Reference Plane Rollout

The **Match Face** drop-down list available in this rollout is used to specify a face or plane on which the outer face of the flange will coincide. To do so, select the **Until Selected** option from this drop-down list; you will be prompted to select a plane or face. Select a face or plane from the drawing window, refer to Figure 14-27; the flange will be created coinciding with the selected face, refer to Figure 14-28.

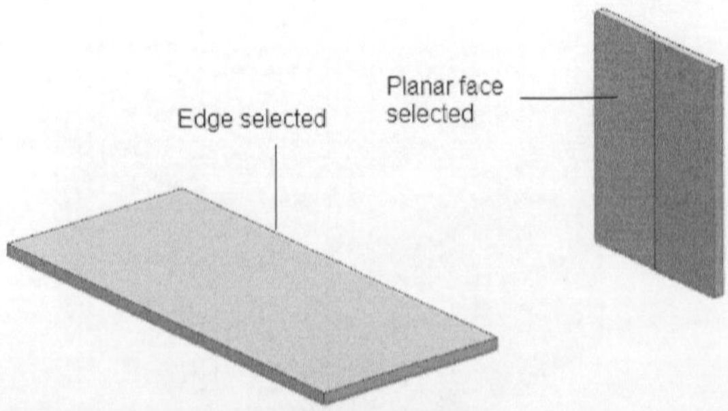

Figure 14-27 Face selected to match the outer face of the flange

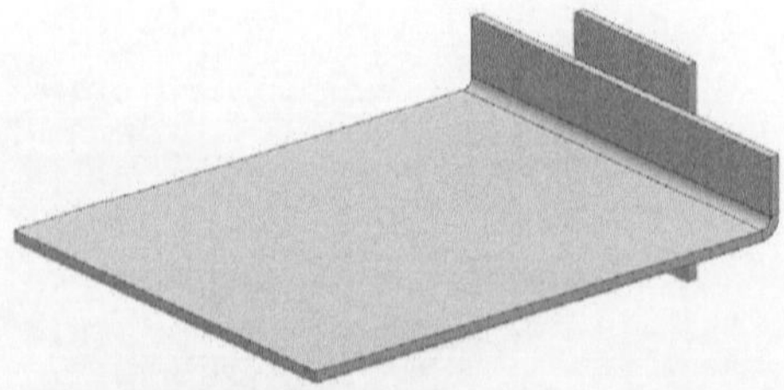

Figure 14-28 Flange created coinciding with the selected face

CREATING CONTOUR FLANGES

Ribbon:	Home > Bend > Contour Flange
Menu:	Insert > Bend > Contour Flange

Contour Flange

The flanges that are created by using an open sketched shape are called contour flanges. To create a contour flange, choose the **Contour Flange** tool from the **Bend** group; the **Contour Flange** dialog box will be displayed. Next, select the edge at which the normal plane will be placed to create the profile of the contour flange; the preview of the plane and the **Create Sketch** dialog box will be displayed. Specify the location of the plane and choose the **OK** button from the **Create Sketch** dialog box; the sketching environment will be invoked. Now, in this environment, you can draw the profile of the contour flange using lines and arcs. Note that you cannot use splines in the sketch.

Note

*If you are creating a contour flange as the base feature, you have to select the **Base** option from the Type drop-down list. Next, you need to select a sketch plane to invoke the Sketch in Task environment.*

After drawing the open sketch for the contour flange, exit the sketch environment; the preview of the contour flange will be displayed. Next, use the options in the **Width** rollout of the **Contour Flange** dialog box to define the flange width. The options in the **Width** rollout are discussed next.

Width Rollout

The options in the **Width Option** drop-down list of this rollout are used to specify the method for calculating the width of the flange. These options are discussed next.

Finite

This option is used to specify the width of the contour flange using a finite value. This option is selected by default. As a result, the **Width** edit box is displayed in which you can enter the value. Figure 14-29 shows the preview of a contour flange being created. This figure also shows the open profile for the contour flange.

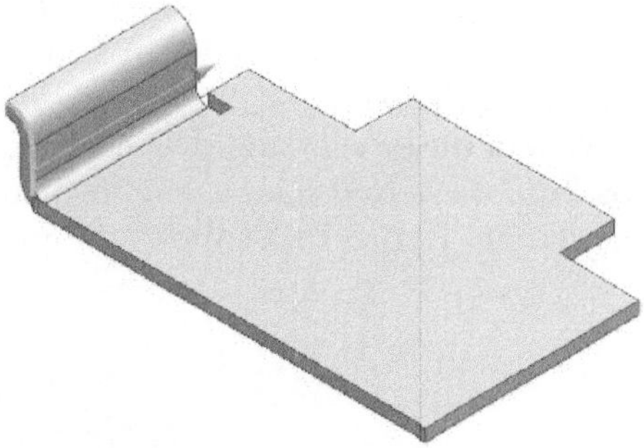

Figure 14-29 *Preview of a contour flange being created*

Symmetric

The **Symmetric** option is used to create a contour flange with the symmetric extent.

To End

This option is used to terminate the contour flange at the end of the selected edge.

Chain

This option is used to select a chain of edges on which the contour flange will be created. Figure 14-30 shows the base of the sheet metal component and the sketch to be used to create the contour flange. Figure 14-31 shows the contour flange created by selecting all four edges on the top face of the base.

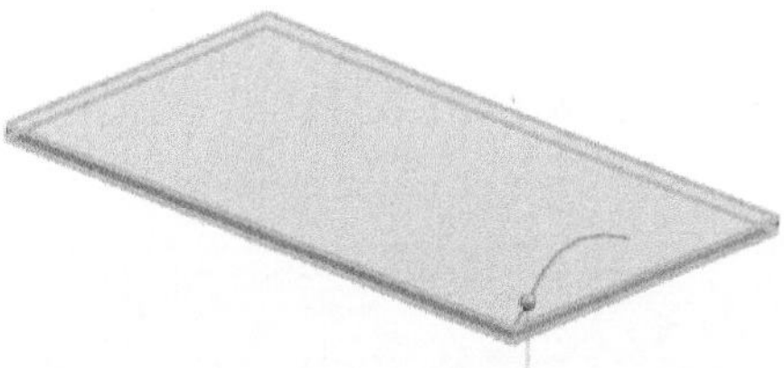

Figure 14-30 *Sketch for the contour flange*

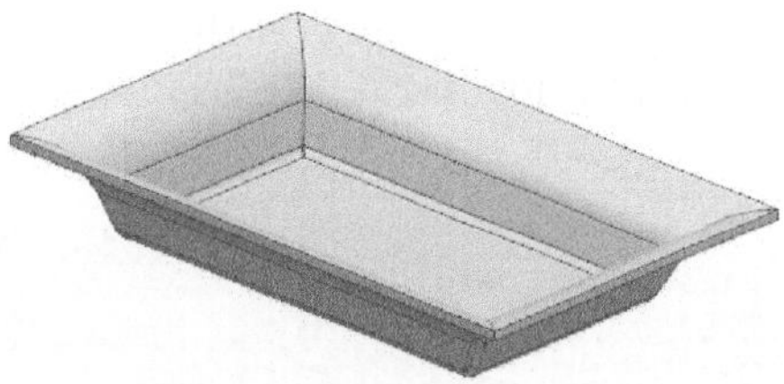

Figure 14-31 *The contour flange created by selecting all four edges on the top face*

CREATING LOFTED FLANGES

Ribbon:	Home > Bend > More Gallery > Bend > Lofted Flange
Menu:	Insert > Bend > Lofted Flange

You can create a sheet metal part between two selected profiles using the **Lofted Flange** tool. Note that the profiles being used should be open and they may or may not have the same number of elements. When you invoke this tool, the **Lofted Flange** dialog box will be displayed. Also, you will be prompted to select a plane to sketch or select a section. Select the sketching plane and then draw the first profile. Exit the sketch environment; the **Sketch End Section** button will be activated in the **End Section** rollout. Create a parallel plane and draw the second profile. After drawing the sketch of the second profile, as soon as you exit from the sketch environment, the preview of the lofted flange will be displayed. Choose the **OK** button from the **Lofted Flange** dialog box; the lofted flange will be created. Figure 14-32 shows the sketches for creating the lofted flange. Figure 14-33 shows the preview of the resulting lofted flange.

Figure 14-32 Sketches to be used to create the lofted flange

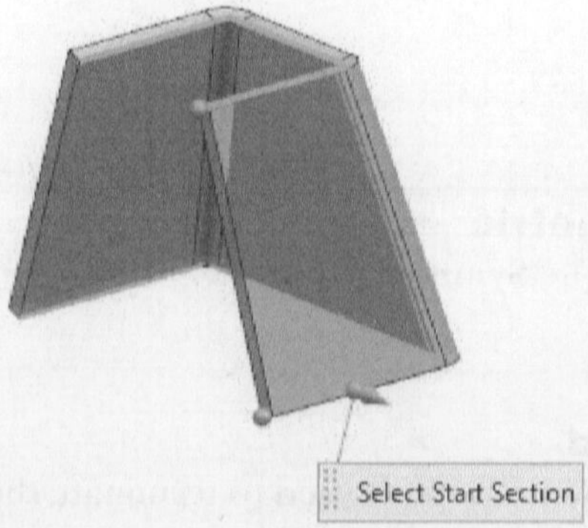

Figure 14-33 Preview of the resulting lofted flange

ADDING A JOG TO THE SHEET

Ribbon:	Home > Bend > More Gallery > Bend > Jog
Menu:	Insert > Bend > Jog

The **Jog** tool is used to add a jog to an existing sheet metal part using a sketched line segment. Figure 14-34 shows the base of a sheet metal part and the line to be used to add the jog. Figure 14-35 shows the sheet after adding the jog.

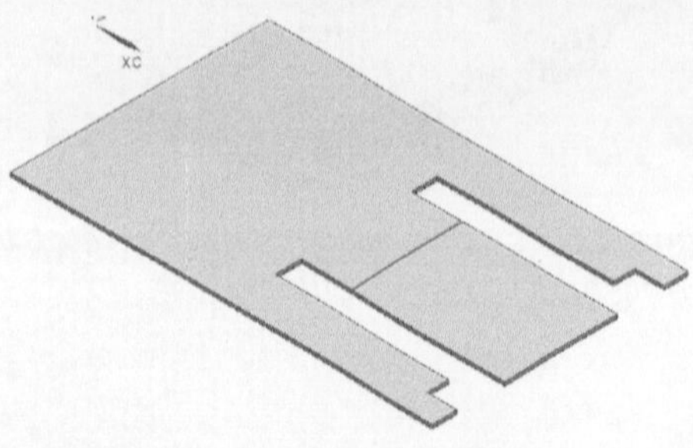

Figure 14-34 Base sheet and the line to add the jog

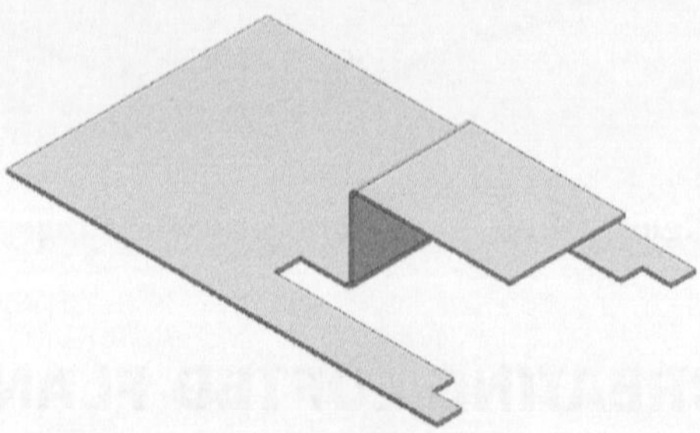

Figure 14-35 Sheet after adding the jog

To add a jog, invoke the **Jog** tool; the **Jog** dialog box will be displayed. Next, select the plane or the face of the base feature to draw the line segment for adding the jog. Draw a single line that will define the jog line on the base sheet and then exit the sketching environment; the default preview of the jog will be displayed. You can reverse the side and direction of the sheet on which the jog will be added by using the **Reverse Side** and **Reverse Direction** buttons. Next, you need to define the height of the jog by entering a value in the **Height** edit box of the **Jog Properties** rollout. Alternatively, you can drag the Height handle to specify the height of the jog. Next, set all the other options in the **Jog** dialog box. These options have been discussed earlier in the chapter. Choose the **OK** button from the **Jog** dialog box to create the jog.

BENDING THE SHEET METAL PART

Ribbon:	Home > Bend > More Gallery > Bend > Bend
Menu:	Insert > Bend > Bend

The **Bend** tool is used to bend an existing sheet metal part using a sketched line segment. To bend the sheet, invoke the **Bend** tool; the **Bend** dialog box will be displayed. Next, select the plane or the face of a feature to draw the line segment for adding a bend. Draw a single line that will define the bend line on the selected feature and then exit the sketching environment; the default preview of the bend will be displayed. You can use the **Reverse Side** button to reverse the side of the bend. The **Reverse Direction** button can be used to reverse the direction of the bend creation. Next, specify the angle of the bend by dragging the Angle handle or specifying a value in the **Angle** edit box of the **Bend Properties** rollout. You will notice that the **Outer Mold Line Profile** option is selected in the **Inset** drop-down list. Therefore, the sheet is bent outside the bend line. If you select the **Bend Center Line Profile** option, the sheet will be bent equally on both sides of the bend line. The **Inner Mold Line Profile** option is used to bend the sheet inside the bend line. The other options in the **Bend** dialog box are same as those discussed earlier. After setting all the parameters, choose the **OK** button from the **Bend** dialog box. Figure 14-36 shows a sheet metal part and the line to be used to bend it. Figure 14-37 shows the sheet after bending.

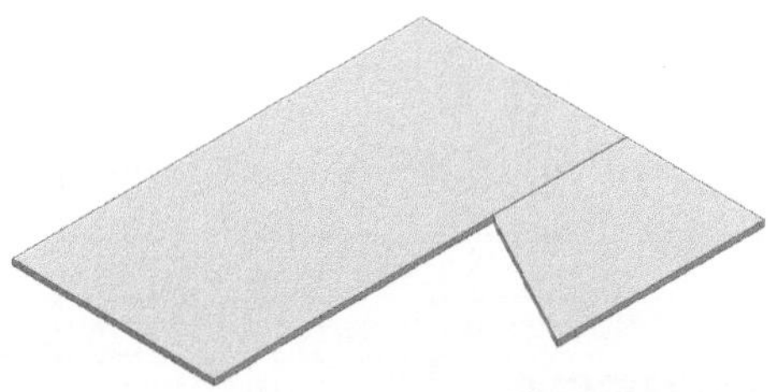

Figure 14-36 *Base sheet and the line to bend the sheet*

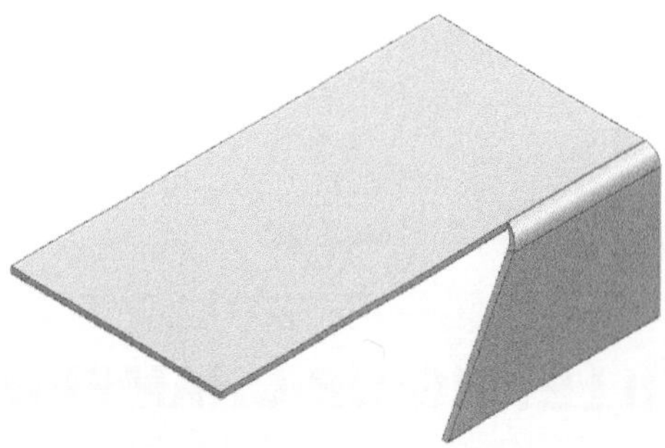

Figure 14-37 *Sheet after bending*

UNBENDING THE SHEET METAL PART

Ribbon:	Home > Form > Unbend
Menu:	Insert > Form > Unbend

The **Unbend** tool is used to unbend the portion of the sheet which has been bent using the **Bend** or **Flange** tool. This tool is highly useful when you want to create a feature on the bent portion of the sheet. On choosing this tool, the **Unbend** dialog box will be displayed and you will be prompted to select a planar face or a linear edge to remain fixed while the part is unbent. Select the face to be fixed; you will be prompted to select bends. Select the rounds of the bends or flanges. Next, choose the **OK** button to complete the unbending of sheet.

REBENDING THE SHEET METAL PART

Ribbon:	Home > Form > Rebend
Menu:	Insert > Form > Rebend

The **Rebend** tool is used to rebend the portion of the sheet that was unbent using the **Unbend** tool. When you invoke this tool, the **Rebend** dialog box will be displayed and you will be prompted to select the unbend faces. Move the cursor over the location where the bend was placed originally; the bend will be highlighted and then select it. Next, choose the **OK** button to exit the **Rebend** tool. You can also make the face stationary while rebending the sheet. To do so, choose the **Stationary Face or Edge** button from the **Stationary Face or Edge** rollout; you will be prompted to select the planar face or linear edge to remain fixed. Select the face to make it stationary.

Figure 14-38 shows an unbent sheet with the cut features created at the bends and Figure 14-39 shows the sheet after rebending.

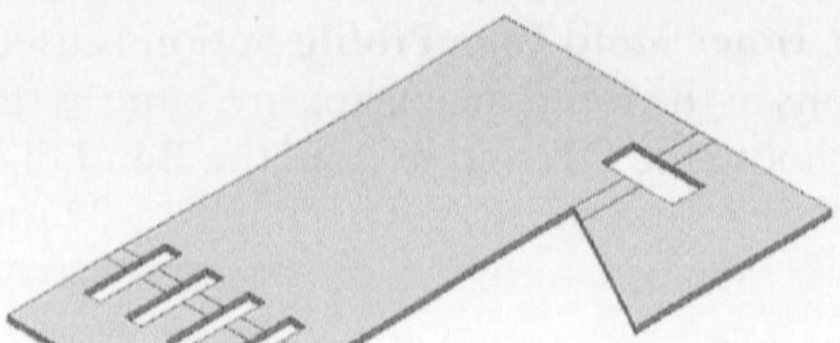

Figure 14-38 Cut features created on the unbent sheet metal part

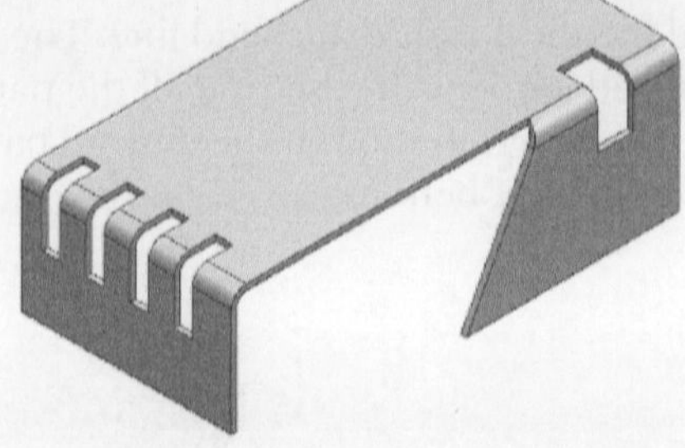

Figure 14-39 Model after creating the cuts and then rebending

FILLETING OR CHAMFERING CORNERS

Ribbon:	Home > Corner > Break Corner
Menu:	Insert > Corner > Break Corner

The **Break Corner** tool is used to add fillets or chamfers to the selected corners of the sheet metal part. When you invoke this tool, the **Break Corner** dialog box will be displayed and you will be prompted to select the edges to break or select a face to break all thickness edges. Select the edges that you want to fillet or chamfer. By default, the **Blend** option is selected in the **Method** drop-down list of the **Break Properties** rollout of the **Break Corner** dialog box. As a result, a fillet is added to the model. If you want to add a chamfer, select the **Chamfer** option from the **Method** drop-down list. It creates a 45-degree chamfer. You can enter the fillet or chamfer value in the **Radius** or **Distance** edit box, respectively.

CLOSING THE CORNERS OF A SHEET METAL PART

Ribbon: Home > Corner > Closed Corner
Menu: Insert > Corner > Closed Corner

The **Closed Corner** tool is used to close the corner created by two bends. When you invoke this tool, the **Closed Corner** dialog box will be displayed, as shown in Figure 14-40. Also, you will be prompted to click on the bends to be modified. Select the curved portion of the two bends to treat. The options of the **Closed Corner** dialog box are discussed next.

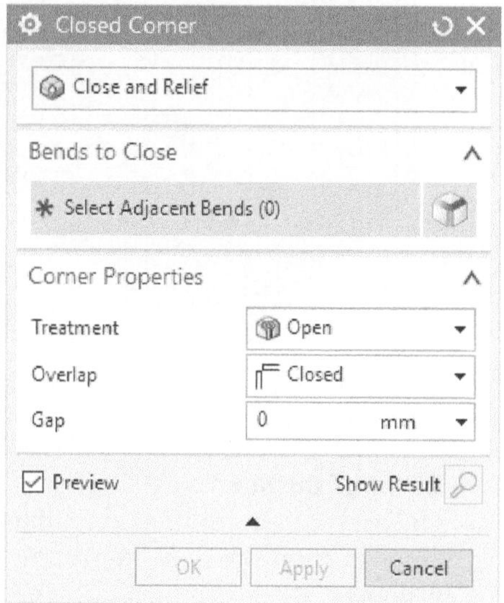

*Figure 14-40 The **Closed Corner** dialog box*

Type Drop-down List

Using the drop-down list, you can select whether to apply only relief to the corner or a relief with a closed treatment. Select the **Close and Relief** option, if not selected by default, to apply the closed treatment along with the relief. To apply only relief, select the **Relief** option.

Bends to Close Rollout

By default, the **Select Adjacent Bends** area is highlighted in this rollout. As a result, you are prompted to select the bend face adjacent to a corner.

Corner Properties Rollout

The options in this rollout are discussed next.

Treatment

The options in this drop-down list are used to specify the type of corner treatment and are discussed next.

Open

On selecting this option, the walls are closed but the corner remains open. Figure 14-41 shows the corner after the open corner treatment.

Closed

On selecting this option, the corners are also closed along with the walls, as shown in Figure 14-42.

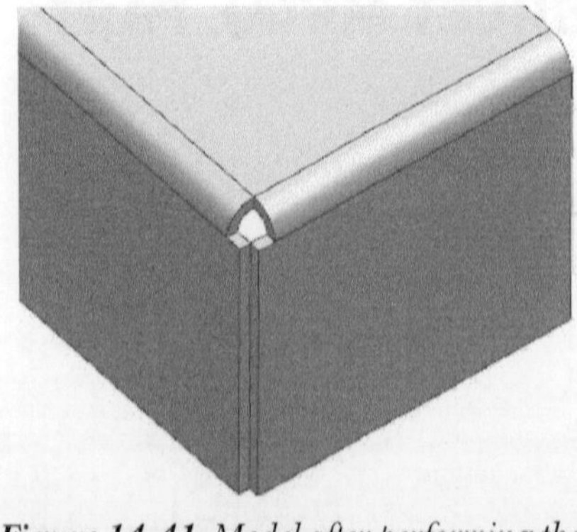

Figure 14-41 Model after performing the open corner treatment of two bends

Figure 14-42 Model after performing the closed corner treatment

Circular Cutout
On selecting this option, a circular cutout is created at the corner, as shown in Figure 14-43. You can enter the diameter of the circle in the **Diameter** edit box of the **Relief Properties** rollout.

U-Cutout
On selecting this option, a U-shaped cutout is created at the corner, as shown in Figure 14-44.

Figure 14-43 Model after performing the circular cutout corner treatment of the two bends

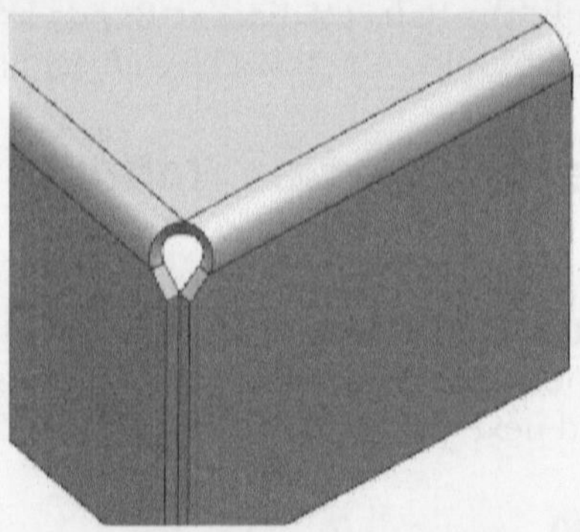

Figure 14-44 Model after performing the U-shaped cutout corner treatment of the two bends

V-Cutout
On selecting this option, a V-shaped cutout is created at the corner, as shown in Figure 14-45. You can specify the angles of the V-shape in the **Angle 1** and **Angle 2** edit boxes available in the **Relief Properties** rollout.

Rectangular Cutout
On selecting this option, a rectangular cutout is created at the corner, as shown in Figure 14-46. You can enter the length and width of the square in the respective edit boxes available in the **Relief Properties** rollout.

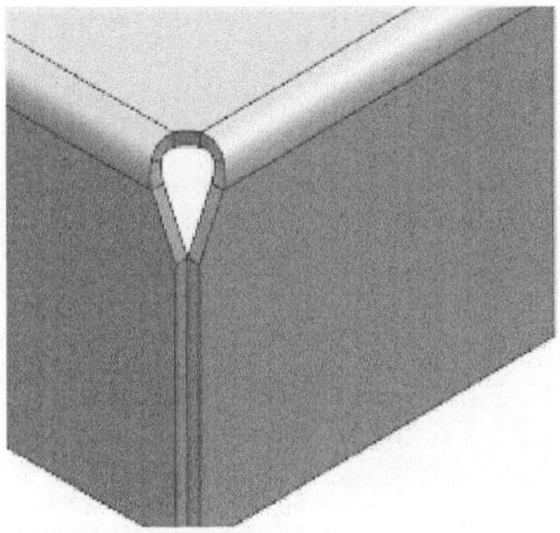

Figure 14-45 Model after performing the V-shaped cutout corner treatment

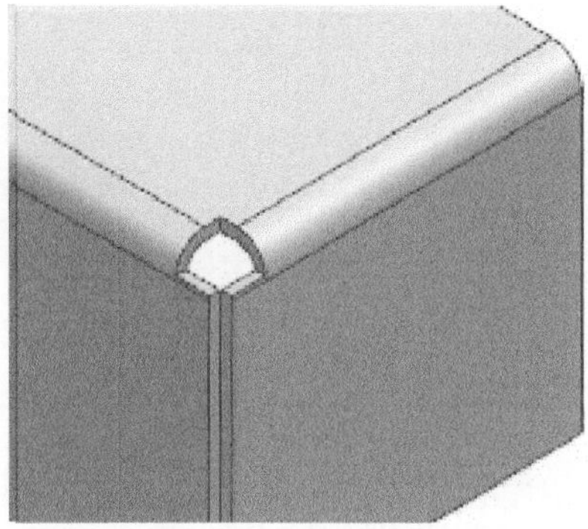

Figure 14-46 Model after performing the rectangular cutout corner treatment

Overlap

This drop-down list is used to specify the walls to be closed or overlapped. By default, the **Closed** option is selected. As a result, the walls are closed. You can overlap one wall on the other by selecting the **Overlapping** option from this drop-down list. Figure 14-47 shows the model with an overlap.

Gap

You can add a gap to the corner treatment by entering a value in this edit box. Figure 14-48 shows the model after performing the open corner treatment with a gap of 2 mm.

Figure 14-47 Overlapping of walls in the corner treatment

Figure 14-48 Model after performing the open corner treatment with a gap of 2 mm

Note

The gap value cannot be negative or greater than sheet thickness.

Miter Corner

On selecting this check box, a miter is created at the corner. Figures 14-49 and 14-50 show the model after performing the closed corner treatment with the **Miter Corner** check box selected and cleared.

Figure 14-49 The closed corner treatment with the ***Miter Corner*** *check box selected*

Figure 14-50 The closed corner treatment with the ***Miter Corner*** *check box cleared*

Relief Properties Rollout

The options in this rollout are used to specify the size and position of the corner treatment. These options are discussed next.

Origin

The options in this drop-down list are used to specify the origin point of the corner treatment. Select the **Bend Center** or **Corner Point** option to specify the origin of the corner treatment.

Offset

You can enter a value in this edit box to create the corner at an offset from the origin of the corner treatment.

The other options in this vary with the type of corner treatment selected. These options were discussed earlier. After specifying all the options in the **Closed Corner** dialog box, choose the **OK** button to create the corner treatment.

CREATING DIMPLES IN A SHEET METAL PART

Ribbon:	Home > Punch > Dimple
Menu:	Insert > Punch > Dimple

NX allows you to sketch a user-defined shapeand then use it to create a dimple in the sheet metal component. To create the dimple, invoke the **Dimple** tool; the **Dimple** dialog box will be displayed, as shown in Figure 14-51. The options in the **Dimple** dialog box are discussed next.

Section Rollout

The **Select Curve** area in this rollout is activated by default when you invoke the **Dimple** tool. As a result, you are prompted to select a planar face or section geometry. Select a face on which you want to sketch the profile of the dimple or an existing sketch.

Dimple Properties Rollout

The options in this rollout are discussed next.

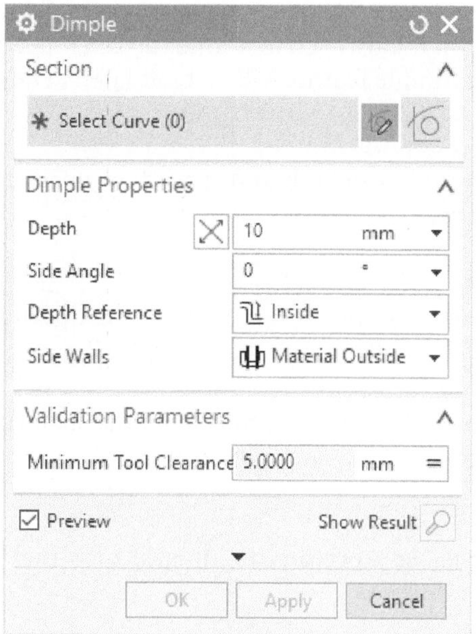

*Figure 14-51 The **Dimple** dialog box*

Depth

This edit box is used to specify the depth of the dimple. This value is modified dynamically as you drag the depth handle displayed in the drawing window.

Reverse Direction

This button is used to reverse the direction of the dimple.

Side Angle

This edit box is used to specify the taper angle for the dimple. Figure 14-52 shows a dimple with no taper angle and Figure 14-53 shows a dimple with a taper angle of 25 degrees.

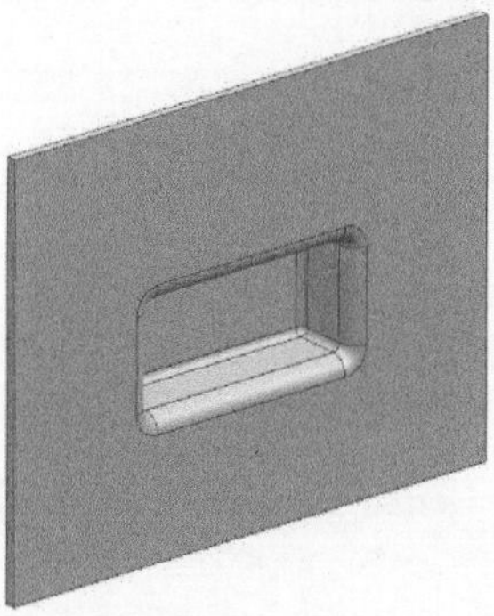

Figure 14-52 Dimple with no taper

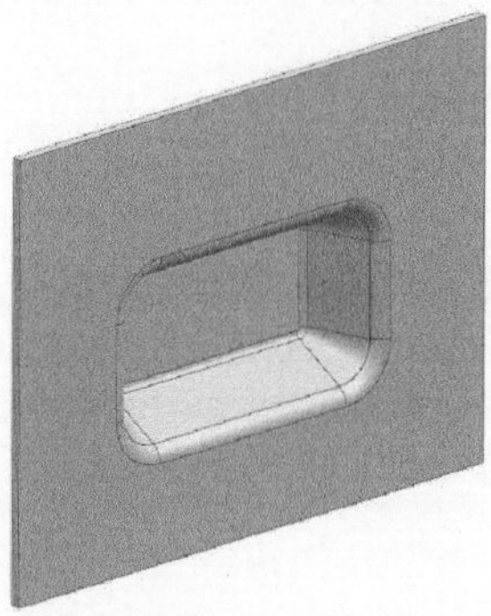

Figure 14-53 Dimple with a 25 degree taper

Depth Reference

The options in this drop-down list are used to define the reference point on the sheet metal part from which the depth of the dimple feature will be calculated. These options are discussed next.

Inside

This option is selected by default and is used to specify the depth of the dimple from inside the base sheet.

Outside

This option is selected to specify the depth of the dimple from outside the base sheet.

Side Walls

The options in this drop-down list are used to specify the material condition for side walls of the dimple.

Material Inside

This option is selected to create the dimple such that the material is added inside the profile of the dimple.

Material Outside

Select this option to add the material outside the profile of the dimple.

Settings Rollout

The options in this rollout are used to apply rounds to edges and corners of a dimple. These options are discussed next.

Blend Dimple Edges

This check box is selected to apply rounds to dimple edges. On selecting this check box, the **Punch Radius** and **Die Radius** edit boxes are displayed and they are discussed next.

Punch Radius

This edit box is used to specify the punch radius of a dimple feature, refer to Figure 14-54.

Die Radius

This edit box is used to specify the die radius of a dimple feature, refer to Figure 14-54.

Blend Section Corners

This check box is selected to apply rounds to the corners of a dimple section, refer to Figure 14-54. On selecting this check box, the **Corner Radius** edit box is displayed which is used to specify corner radius.

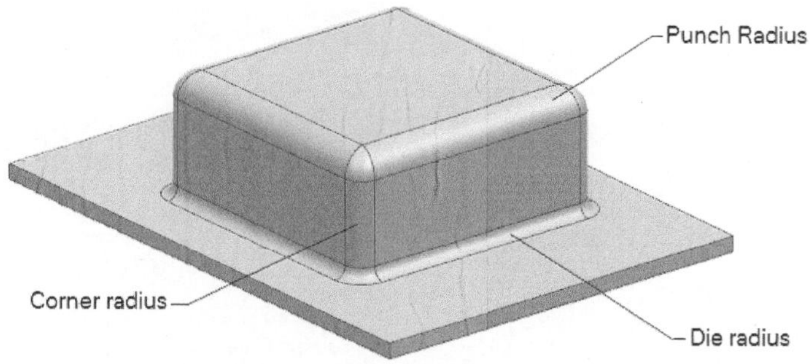

Figure 14-54 Dimple feature with rounds

NX also allows you to create open profiles for the dimple. Note that the open profile should be created such that when extended, the open entities intersect the edges of the model. Figure 14-55 shows the preview of a dimple created using an open profile. The open profile is also shown in the same figure. Note that in this profile, when the two inclined lines are extended, they intersect with the top edge of the sheet metal part.

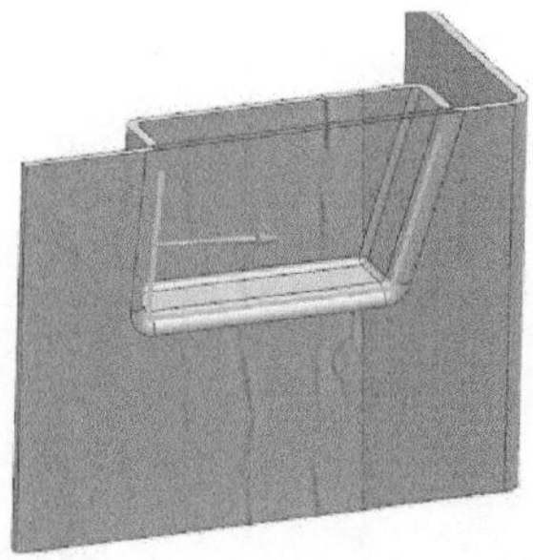

Figure 14-55 Dimple created using an open profile

CREATING LOUVERS IN A SHEET METAL PART

Ribbon: Home > Punch > Louver
Menu: Insert > Punch > Louver

Louvers are created in a sheet metal part to provide openings in it. Figure 14-56 shows a sheet metal part with a rectangular pattern of louvers on its top face.

In NX, louvers are created by sketching a single line segment defining the length of the louver. To create the louver, invoke the **Louver** tool; the **Louver** dialog box will be displayed, as shown in Figure 14-57. In this dialog box, select the shape of the louver from the **Louver Shape** drop-down list available in the **Louver Properties** rollout. There are two types of louvers available: Lanced and Formed. Figure 14-58 shows a pattern of the formed louver and Figure 14-59 shows a pattern of the lanced louvers.

Figure 14-56 Sheet metal part with a pattern of louvers on the top face

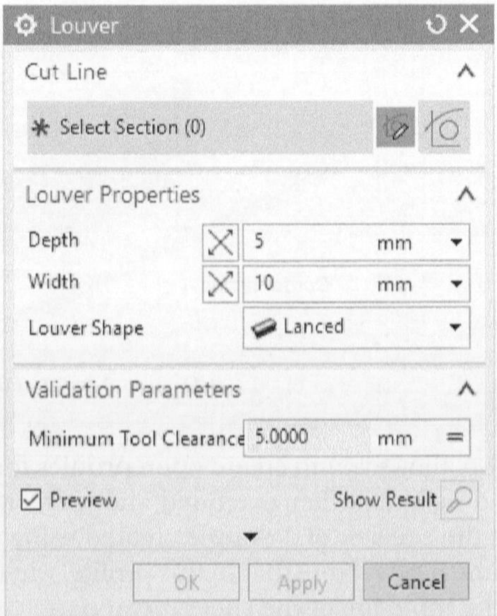

*Figure 14-57 The **Louver** dialog box*

Figure 14-58 Formed louvers

Figure 14-59 Lanced louvers

After selecting the type of louvers, select the face on which you want to sketch the profile of the louver; the sketching environment is invoked and you are prompted to draw the sketch. Draw the profile of the louver and then exit the sketching environment. Note that the profile has to be a single line segment. Next, you need to specify the width of the louver. You can enter the width in the **Width** edit box or specify it dynamically in the drawing window. Note that the width value is specified along the face on which the sketch is drawn and it should be less than half of the line length. You can use the **Reverse Direction** button located adjacent to the **Width** edit box to specify the side of the line on which the width of the louver will be added.

Next, you need to specify the depth of the louver. The depth is specified normal to the face on which the sketch is drawn. You can enter the depth in the **Depth** edit box or specify it dynamically in the drawing window. You can use the **Reverse Direction** button located adjacent to the **Depth** edit box to specify the side of the sheet on which the louver will be added. Note that the depth should be less than or equal to the difference of the width of the louver and the sheet thickness. Also, the depth should be more than the sheet thickness. For example, if the width of the louver is 10 mm and the sheet thickness is 2 mm, the height of the louver should be more than 2 and less than or equal to 8. Figure 14-60 shows the preview of a formed louver. The width of the louver is 10 mm and its depth is 5 mm.

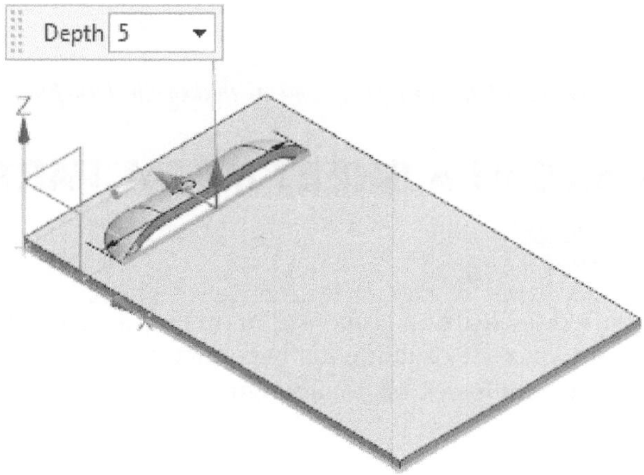

Figure 14-60 *Preview of the formed louver*

CREATING DRAWN CUTOUTS IN A SHEET METAL PART

Ribbon:	Home > Punch > Drawn Cutout
Menu:	Insert > Punch > Drawn Cutout

The drawn cutouts are exactly the same as the dimples with the only difference that in drawn cutouts the end face is open. Figure 14-61 shows a sheet metal part with two drawn cutouts of different shapes. In this figure, the rectangular cutout is created in the upward direction and the oblong cutout is created in the downward direction.

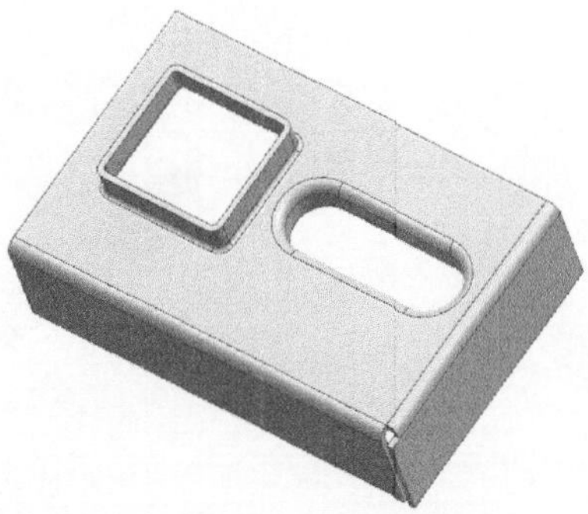

Figure 14-61 *Drawn cutouts of different shapes*

To create a drawn cutout, invoke the **Drawn Cutout** tool and select the face on which you want to sketch the profile of the drawn cutout; the sketching environment is invoked and you are prompted to draw the sketch. Draw the profile of the cutout and then exit the sketching environment. On doing so, the preview of the cutout will be displayed along with the Depth handle and an edit box showing the default depth of the cutout. Specify the depth of the cutout by entering the desired value in the edit box or by using the depth handle. You can change the direction in which the cutout is created by using the **Reverse Direction** button. You can also specify a taper to the cutout by entering the taper angle in the **Side Angle** edit box of the **Drawn Cutout** dialog box.

Note
*The working of the **Drawn Cutout** tool is same as that of the **Dimple** tool.*

CREATING BEADS IN A SHEET METAL PART

Ribbon:	Home > Punch > Bead
Menu:	Insert > Punch > Bead

The **Bead** tool is used to create an embossed or an engraved bead on a sheet metal part using a single entity or a set of tangentially connected entities, refer to Figure 14-62. Figure 14-63 shows an embossed bead and Figure 14-64 shows an engraved bead.

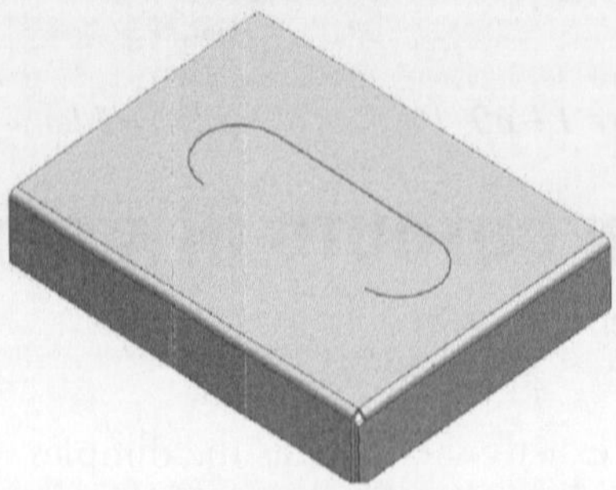

Figure 14-62 *A sketch to create the bead feature*

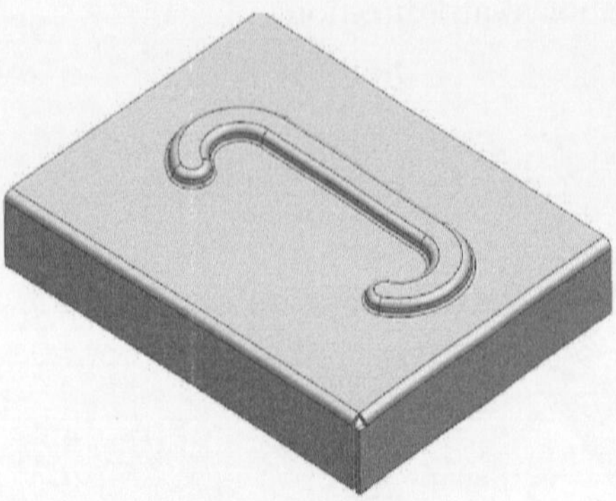

Figure 14-63 *Bead created in the upward direction, resulting in the embossed feature*

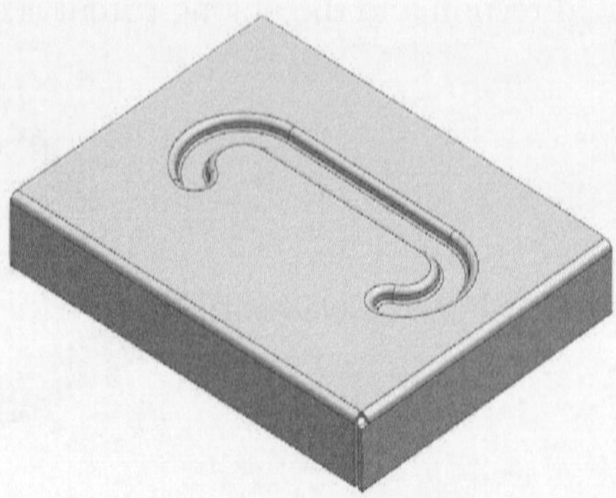

Figure 14-64 *Bead created in the downward direction, resulting in the engraved feature*

When you invoke this tool, the **Bead** dialog box is displayed, as shown in Figure 14-65.

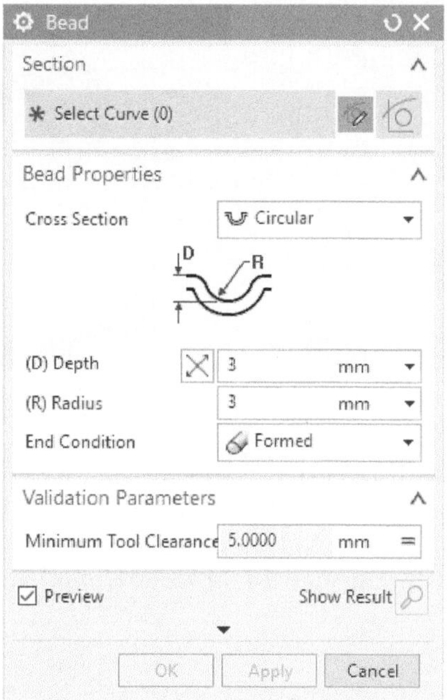

*Figure 14-65 The **Bead** dialog box*

Bead Dialog Box

The options available in this dialog box are discussed next.

Section Rollout

The **Select Curve** area in this rollout is activated by default. As a result, you are prompted to select a planar face. Select a face on which you want to sketch the profile of the bead; the sketching environment is invoked and you are prompted to draw the sketch. Draw the profile of the bead and then exit the sketching environment. Note that the profile has to be a single line segment or a set of tangentially connected open or closed entities.

Bead Properties Rollout

The options available in this rollout are used to specify the parameters of the bead. You can specify the cross-section of the bead using the options in the **Cross Section** drop-down list. You can specify the depth, radius, width, and the angle of the bead using the edit boxes available in this rollout. Figures 14-66 through 14-68 show beads created using different cross-sections.

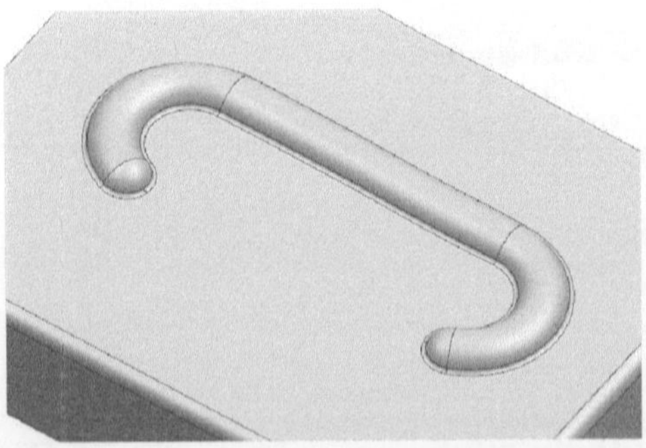

Figure 14-66 *Circular cross-section bead*

Figure 14-67 *U-shaped bead*

The **End Condition** drop-down list is used to specify the end conditions of the bead. You can specify the end condition as formed, lanced, punched, or tapered. The punch gap can be specified in the **Punched Width** edit box that will be available on selecting the **Punched** option from this drop-down list. Figures 14-69 through 14-71 show beads using different end conditions.

Figure 14-68 *V-shaped bead*

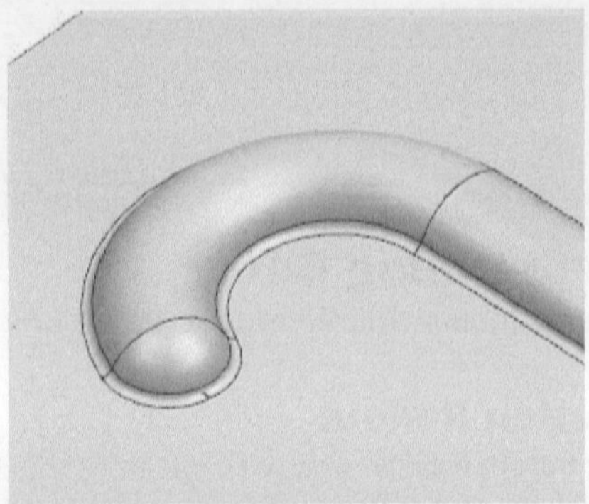

Figure 14-69 *Bead created using formed end condition*

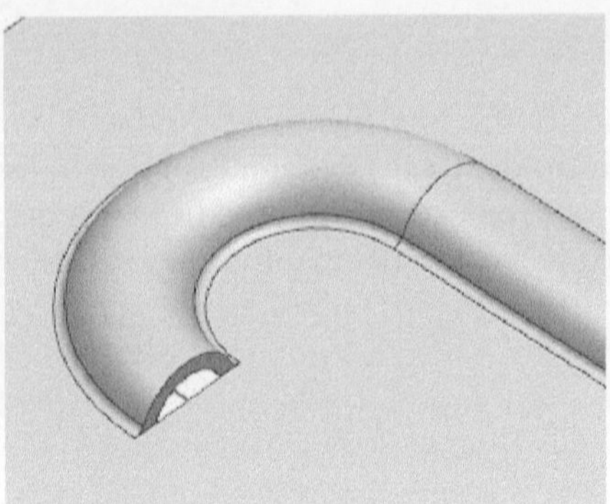

Figure 14-70 *Bead created using lanced end condition*

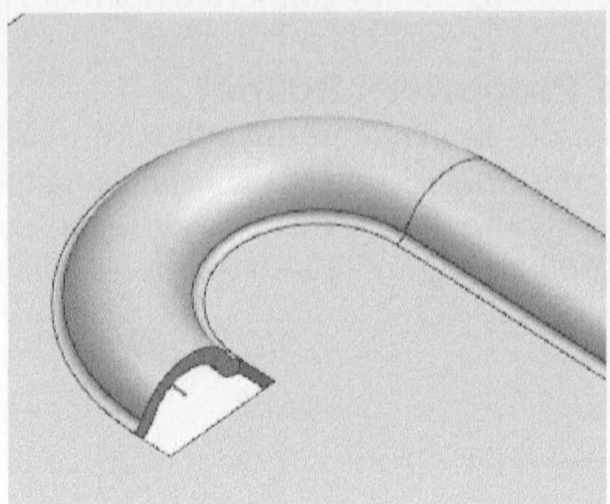

Figure 14-71 *Bead created using punched end condition with a gap of 2 mm*

Note

*The remaining options in the **Bead** dialog box have already been discussed.*

After specifying the bead options, choose the **OK** button from the **Bead** dialog box to create the bead.

ADDING GUSSETS TO A SHEET METAL PART

Ribbon: Home > Punch > Gusset
Menu: Insert > Punch > Gusset

Gussets are rib like stiffeners that are added to the sheet metal part to increase its strength. In NX, you can create an automatic gusset of round or square shape or a gusset with a user-defined profile. Figures 14-72 through 14-75 show various types of gussets that can be created in NX.

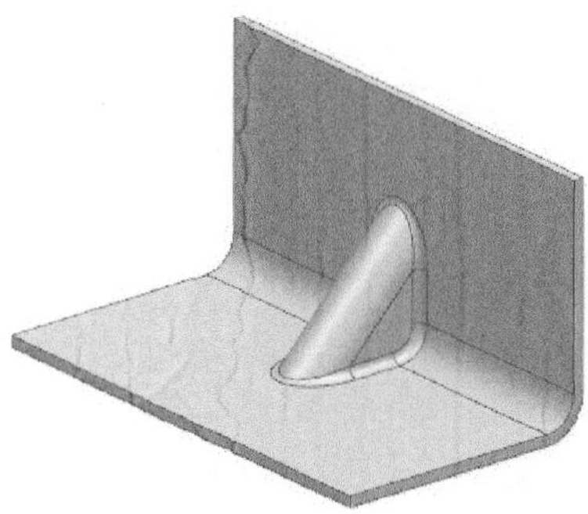

Figure 14-72 *Front view of a round gusset*

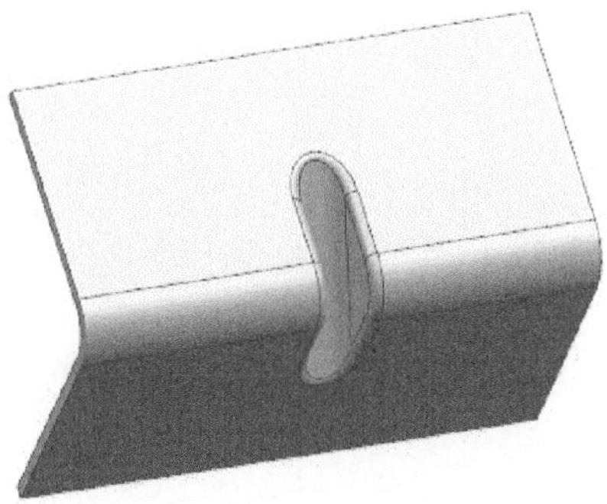

Figure 14-73 *Back view of the round gusset*

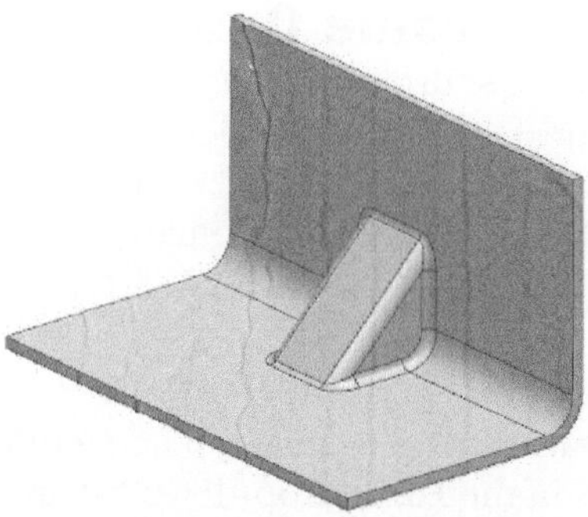

Figure 14-74 *A square gusset*

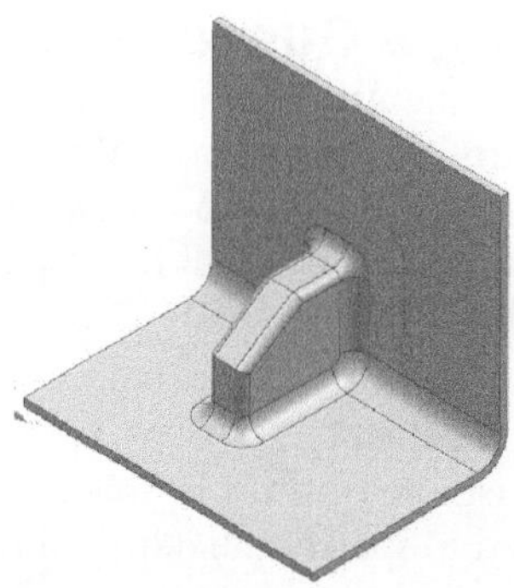

Figure 14-75 *A user-defined gusset*

To add a gusset to a sheet metal part, invoke the **Gusset** tool from the **Punch** gallery of the **Home** tab; the **Gusset** dialog box will be displayed, refer to Figure 14-76. In NX, you can create two types of gussets; Automatic and User-defined. These two types are discussed next.

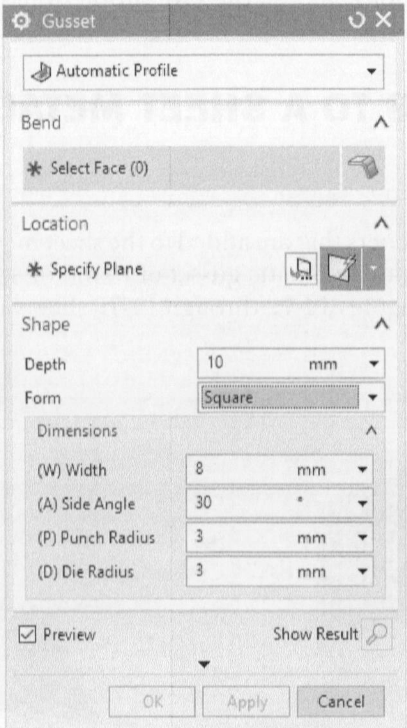

*Figure 14-76 The **Gusset** dialog box*

Creating a Gusset Using the Automatic Profile Option

By default, the **Automatic Profile** option is selected in the Type drop-down list and the **Select Face** area is activated in the **Bend** rollout. Select the bend face and then specify plane from the **Location** rollout to position the gusset; the preview of the gusset along with the handle and dynamic edit box will be displayed. The other options to create an automatic gusset are discussed next.

Shape Rollout

You can use the options in this rollout to control the parameters of a gusset. The **Depth** edit box is used to specify the depth of the gusset. The options in the **Form** drop-down list are used to define the shape of the gusset. You can create a gusset with a round shape by selecting the **Round** option, refer to Figure 14-77. The **Square** option is used to create a gusset with a square shape. You can also apply fillets to the sharp edges of a square gusset by entering the radius values in the **Punch Radius** and **Die Radius** edit boxes in the **Dimensions** sub-rollout.

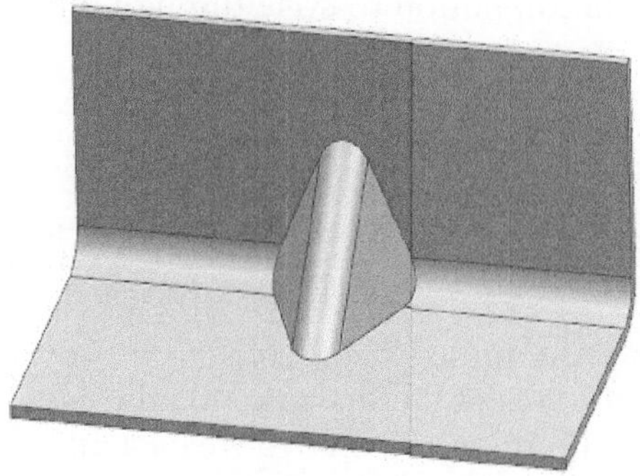

Figure 14-77 A gusset with a taper angle of 30 degrees

You can specify the width of the gusset in the **Width** edit box. The **Side Angle** edit box is used to enter the taper angle for the gusset. Figure 14-77 shows a gusset with a taper angle of 30 degrees.

Creating a Gusset Using the User Defined Profile Option

By selecting the **User Defined Profile** option from the Type drop-down list, you can create gusset with a user-defined profile. To create this type gusset, select the **User Defined Profile** option from the Type drop-down list and select an edge on the round on which the gusset is to be placed, refer to Figure 14-78; a plane normal to the selected edge will be displayed. Also, the **Create Sketch** dialog box will be displayed. Move the plane to the location at which you want to place the gusset and choose the **OK** button from the **Create Sketch** dialog box; the sketch environment will be invoked. Create the profile of the gusset and exit the sketch environment; the preview of the gusset will be displayed.

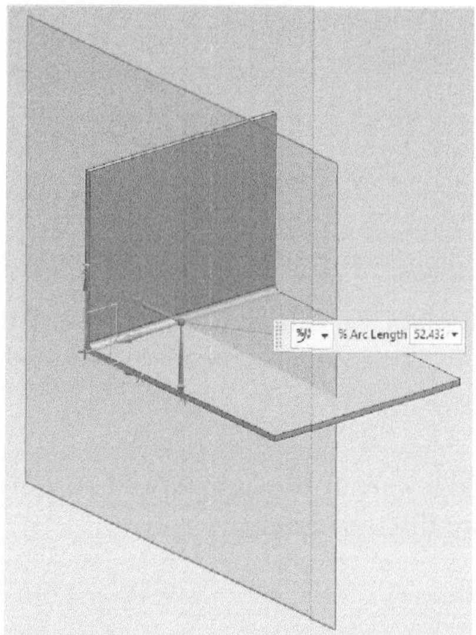

Figure 14-78 Edge selected on the round

You can use the options in the **Width Side** drop-down list to specify the side of the profile on which the gusset will be created. You can select the **Side 1**, **Side 2**, or **Symmetric** option from this drop-down list.

You can use the **Alternate Solution** button to cycle through the alternate possible solutions of the gusset.

ADDING HEMS

Ribbon:	Home > Bend > More Gallery > Bend > Hem Flange
Menu:	Insert > Bend > Hem Flange

Hems are defined as the rounded faces created on the sharp edges of a sheet metal component to reduce the area of the sharpness on the edges. This makes the sheet metal component easy to handle and assemble. To create a hem, invoke the **Hem Flange** tool; the **Hem** dialog box will be displayed, as shown in Figure 14-79. Also, you will be prompted to select an edge to hem. Select the edge and specify the hem parameters in the **Hem** dialog box.

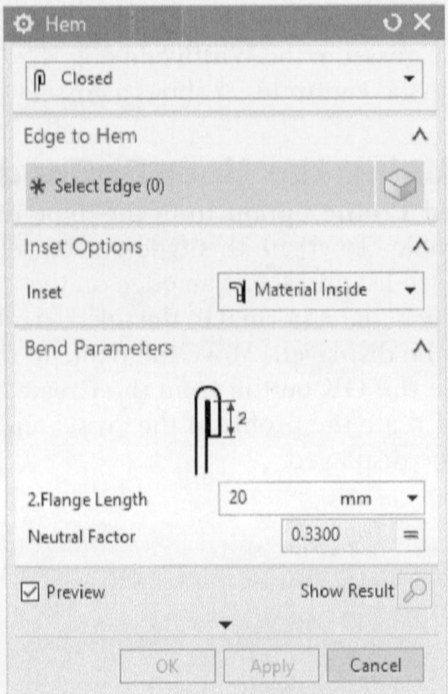

*Figure 14-79 The **Hem** dialog box*

The options in the **Hem** dialog box vary depending on the type of hem selected in the Type drop-down. Some of the options in this dialog box are discussed next.

Type Drop-down

The Type drop-down list is used to specify the hem type. There are seven types of hems available in this drop-down list which are discussed next.

Closed

This option is used to create a closed hem, as shown in Figure 14-80. The flange length can be specified in the **2.Flange Length** edit box available in the **Bend Parameters** rollout.

Open

This option is used to create an open hem, as shown in Figure 14-81. The bend radius and the flange length can be specified in the **1.Bend Radius** and **2.Flange Length** edit boxes of the **Bend Parameters** rollout, respectively.

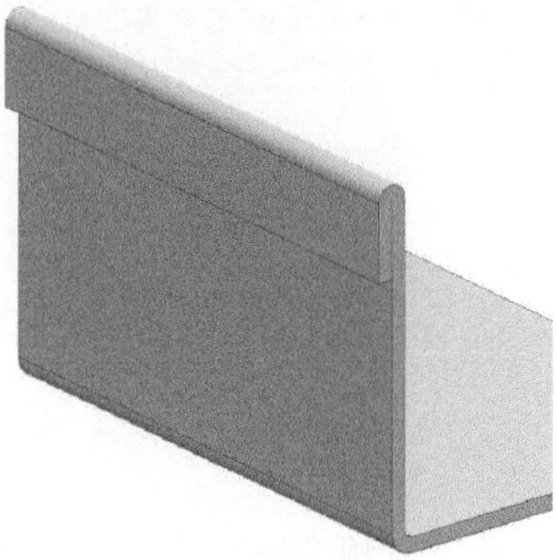

Figure 14-80 A closed hem

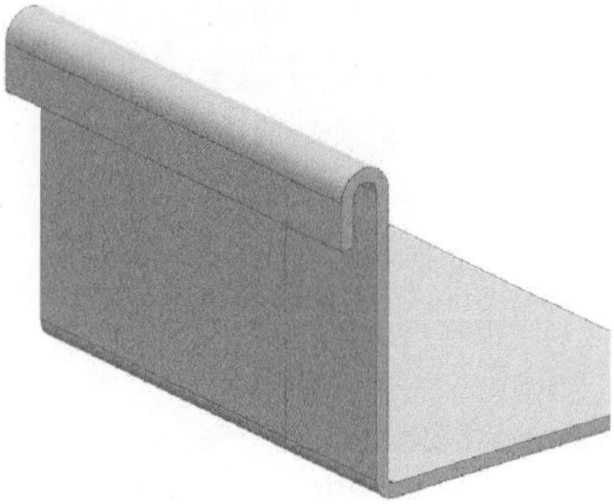

Figure 14-81 An open hem

S-Type

This option is used to create a hem with the S shape, as shown in Figure 14-82. The bend radius and the flange lengths can be specified in their respective edit boxes in the **Bend Parameters** rollout.

Curl

This option is used to create a curled hem, as shown in Figure 14-83. The bend radius and the flange lengths can be specified in their respective edit boxes in the **Bend Parameters** rollout.

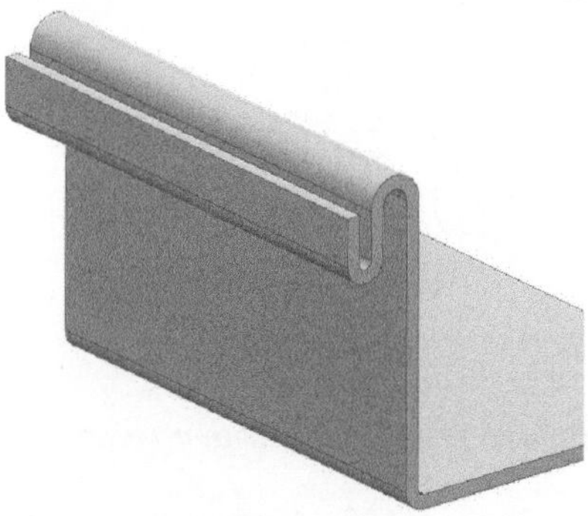

Figure 14-82 A S-shaped hem

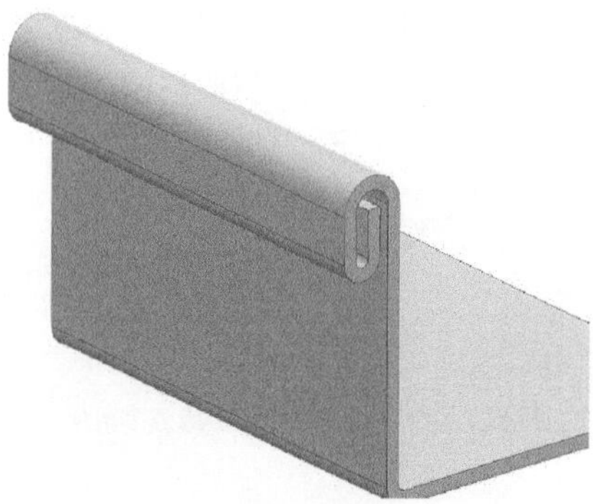

Figure 14-83 A curled hem

Open Loop

This option is used to create a hem that has an open loop, as shown in Figure 14-84. The bend radius and the included angle of the open loop can be specified in the **1.Bend Radius** and **5.Sweep Angle** edit boxes available in the **Bend Parameters** rollout, respectively.

Closed Loop

This option is used to create a hem that has a closed loop, as shown in Figure 14-85. The bend radius and the flange length can be specified in their respective edit boxes available in the **Bend Parameters** rollout.

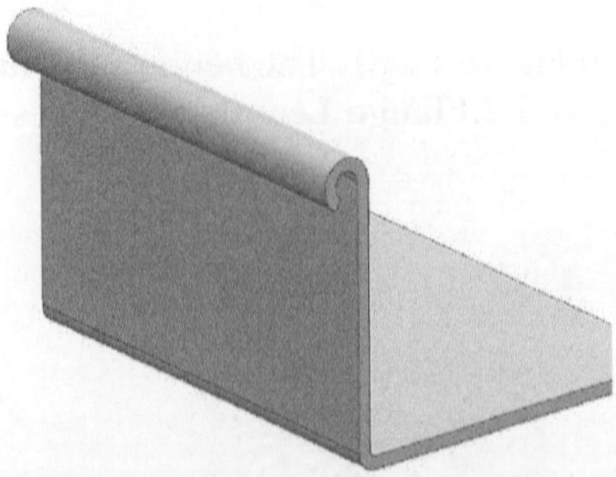

Figure 14-84 An open loop hem

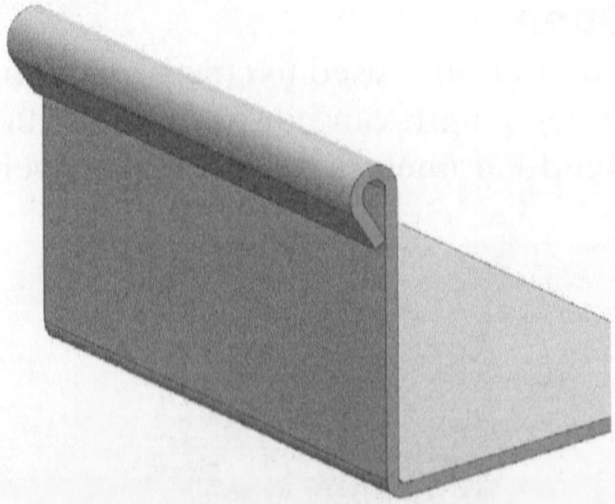

Figure 14-85 A closed loop hem

Centered Loop

This option is used to create a hem with a centered loop, as shown in Figure 14-86. The bend radius and the included angle can be specified in their respective edit boxes available in the **Bend Parameters** rollout.

Miter Rollout

The **Miter Hem** check box in this rollout is used to add a miter to the hem, as shown in Figure 14-87. To do so, select this check box and specify a value in the **Miter Angle** edit box.

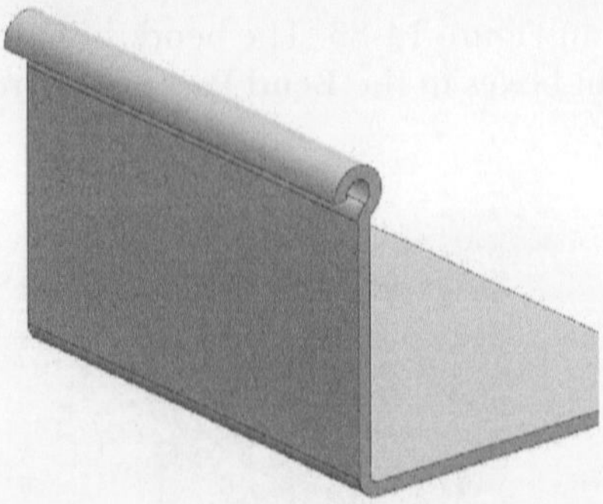

Figure 14-86 Hem with a centered loop

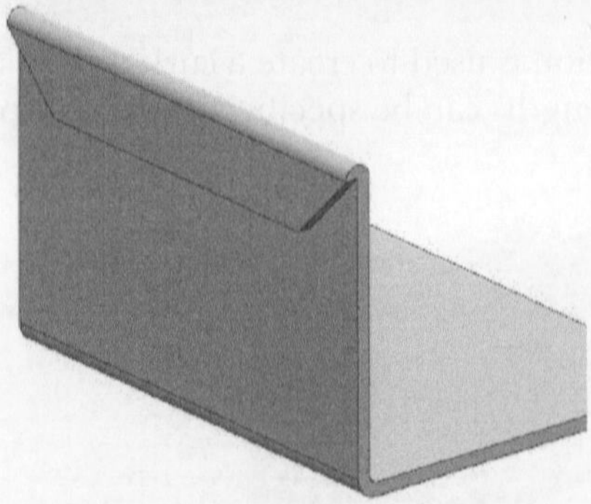

Figure 14-87 Hem with a miter

Note

The remaining options of this dialog box have already been discussed in this chapter.

CREATING A SHEET METAL PART USING SOLID BODY

Ribbon:	Home > Basic > Sheet Metal from Solid
Menu:	Insert > Bend > Sheet Metal from Solid

NX allows you to create a sheet metal part by using the shape of a solid part. To create a sheet metal by using a solid, invoke the **Sheet Metal from Solid** tool; the **Sheet Metal from Solid** dialog box will be displayed. Also, you will be prompted to select planar web faces. Select faces of the solid part. Note that you need to select a minimum of two faces from the solid. Also, if you select more than two faces, you need to select the bend edges manually. Next, choose the **OK** button from the **Sheet Metal from Solid** dialog box; the sheet metal part will be created on selected faces. Figure 14-88 shows the faces selected on a solid part and Figure 14-89 shows a sheet metal part created.

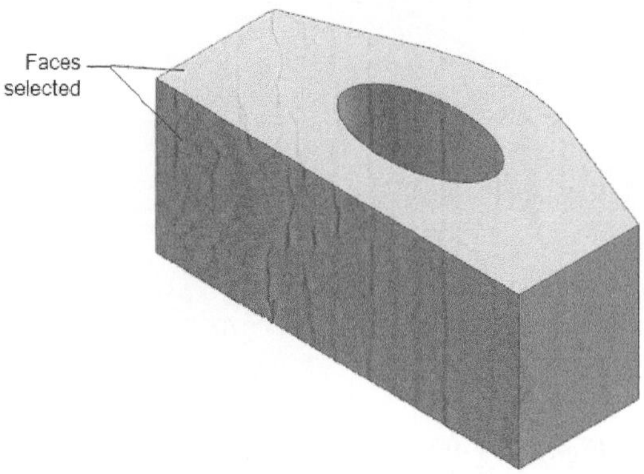

Figure 14-88 *Faces selected on the solid part*

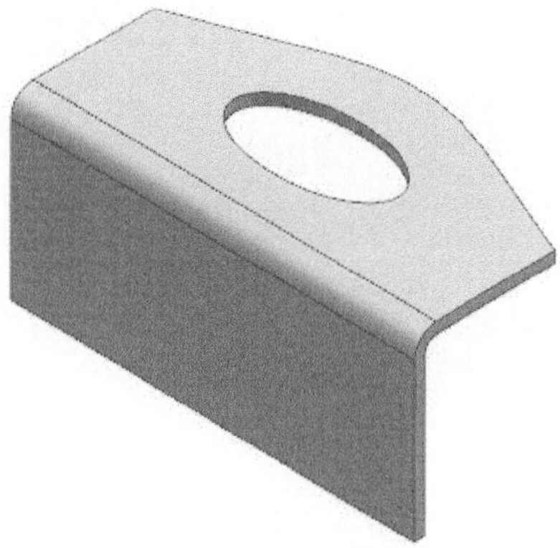

Figure 14-89 *Sheet Metal part created*

CONVERTING A SOLID PART INTO A SHEET METAL PART

Ribbon:	Home > Basic > Convert Gallery > Convert to Sheet Metal
Menu:	Insert > Convert > Convert to Sheet Metal

You can convert a solid part into a sheet metal part using the **Convert to Sheet Metal** tool. To do so, create a solid part in the Modeling environment and then invoke the Sheet Metal environment by choosing **Application > Design > Sheet Metal** from the **Ribbon**. Next, choose the **Convert to Sheet Metal** tool from the **Convert** gallery of the **Basic** group. Figure 14-90 shows a solid part created in the Modeling environment and Figure 14-91 shows the converted sheet metal part from the solid part. The procedure to convert a solid part into sheet metal part is discussed next.

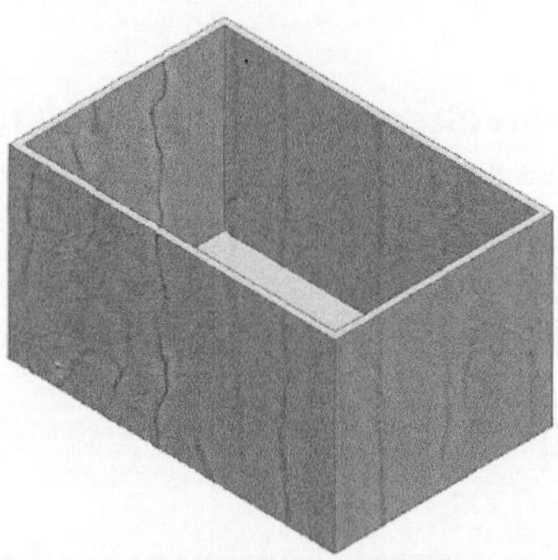

Figure 14-90 *The part created in the Modeling environment*

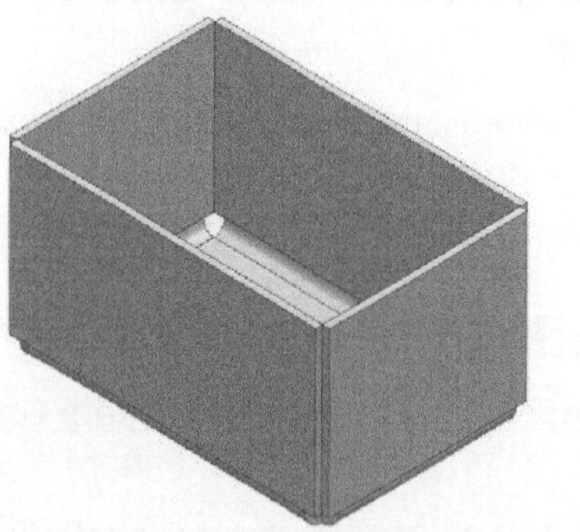

Figure 14-91 *Part converted to Sheet Metal component*

When you invoke the **Convert to Sheet Metal** dialog box, the **Select Base Face** area is activated by default in the **Global Conversion** rollout. As a result, you will be prompted to select the base face. Figure 14-92 shows the four vertical edges selected to be ripped. After selecting the edges to be ripped, choose the **OK** button from the dialog box; the solid model will be converted into a sheet metal part, as shown in Figure 14-93.

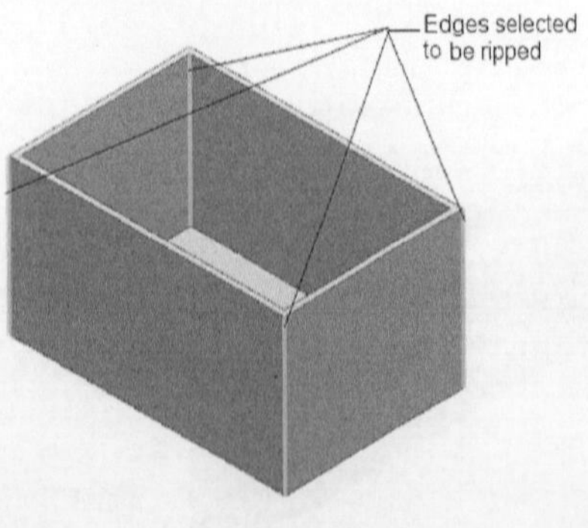

Figure 14-92 Edges selected to be ripped

Figure 14-93 Sheet Metal part after ripping the corners

RIPPING THE CORNERS OF A SOLID PART

Ribbon:	Home > Basic > Convert Gallery > Rip
Menu:	Insert > Convert > Rip

You can rip the corners of a solid part using the **Rip** tool. Note that when you use this tool, no corner relief is added to the model. To rip the corners, invoke this tool and select the edges whose corners you want to rip.

Note

*You can also use the other tools such as **Normal Cutout**, **Mirror**, and so on in the sheet metal environment. These tools are discussed in detail in the part modeling environment.*

CREATING THE FLAT PATTERN OF A SHEET METAL PART

As mentioned earlier, you need to flatten a sheet metal part after creating it in order to generate its flatten drawing views and manufacture it. NX provides a number of options to flatten a sheet metal part. Some of the options are discussed next.

Creating the Flat Pattern

Ribbon:	Home > Flat Pattern Gallery > Flat Pattern
Menu:	Insert > Flat Pattern > Flat Pattern

In NX, you need to create the flat pattern of a sheet metal component by using the **Flat Pattern** tool. On invoking this tool, the **Flat Pattern** dialog box will be displayed and you will be prompted to click on the face to be oriented upward in the flat pattern. Select the base face of the sheet metal part.

Figure 14-94 shows a sheet metal part and Figure 14-95 shows the flat pattern. Note that in the flat pattern, the lower horizontal edge close to the left endpoint was selected to define the X axis and the origin. To view the flat pattern, choose **Menu > View > Layout > Replace View** from the **Top Border Bar**; the **Replace View with** dialog box will be displayed. Select **FLAT-PATTERN** and then choose the **OK** button from this dialog box; the flat pattern will be displayed. To switch back to the model view, again invoke the **Replace View with** dialog box and select **Isometric** from the dialog box. Next, choose the **OK** button; the isometric view of the model will be displayed.

Note

1. In NX, you can control the orientation of the flat pattern view for the upward face having non-linear edges. To do so, specify a CSYS while defining the orientation.

2. You can represent the holes smaller than or equal to a specified diameter value as centermarks in the flat pattern view. This is useful when the hole creation needs a different manufacturing process.

3. You can create both associative and non-associative flat patterns with respect to the parent body.

Figure 14-94 The sheet metal part

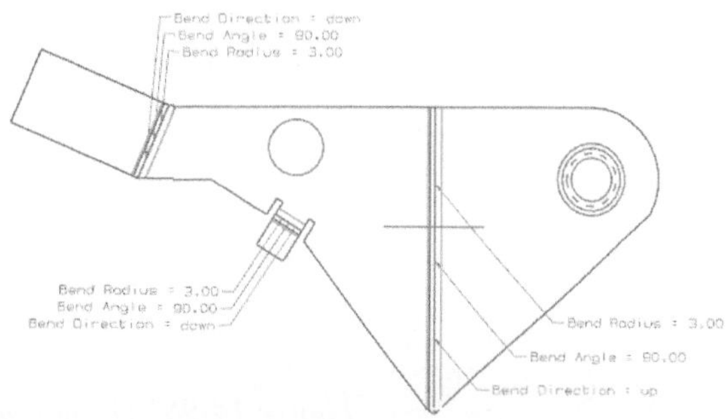

Figure 14-95 The flat pattern

Creating the Flat Solid

Ribbon:	Home > Flat Pattern Gallery > Flat Solid
Menu:	Insert > Flat Pattern > Flat Solid

In NX, you can create a flat solid of a sheet metal part. Further, you can use this flat solid to create drawing views. To create a flat solid of a sheet metal part, choose the **Flat Solid** tool from the **Flat Pattern** gallery; the **Flat Solid** dialog box will be displayed and you will be prompted to select a face that will remain stationary in the flat solid. Select a face from the drawing window and choose the **OK** button; the flat solid will be created, refer to Figure 14-96. If you select the **Select Edge** option from the **Orientation Method** drop-down list of the **Orientation** rollout, then after selecting the stationary face, you will be prompted to select an edge for X-axis orientation. Select an edge from the model, refer to Figure 14-97 and then choose the **OK** button; the flat solid will be created at the specified orientation, refer to Figure 14-98.

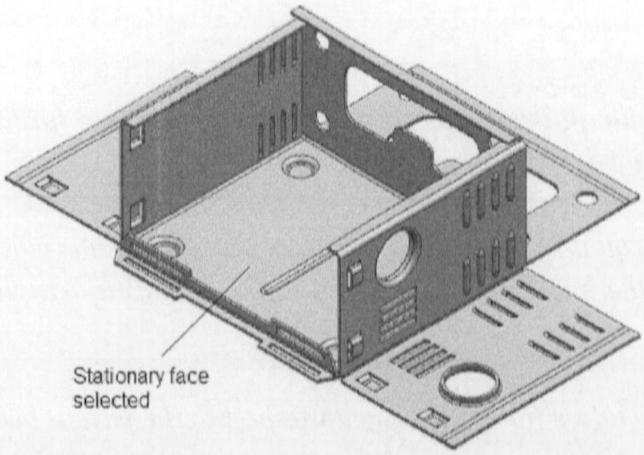

***Figure 14-96** The stationary face selected to create the flat solid*

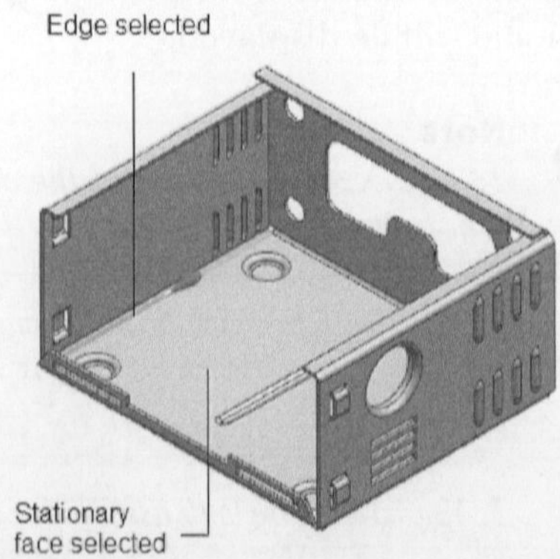

***Figure 14-97** The stationary face and edge selected to create the flat solid.*

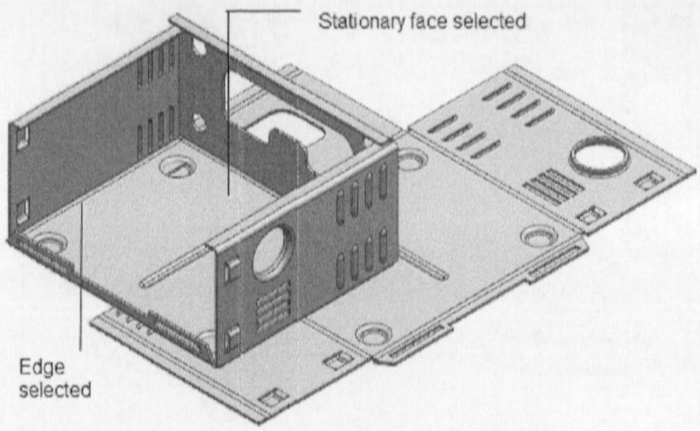

***Figure 14-98** The flat solid created at the specified orientation*

Exporting a Flat Pattern

Ribbon:	Home > Flat Pattern Gallery > Export Flat Pattern
Menu:	Insert > Flat Pattern > Export Flat Pattern

You can export a flat pattern to AutoCAD (*.dxf) or *.geo file. To export the flat pattern file, choose the **Export Flat Pattern** tool from the sheet metal environment; the **Export Flat Pattern** dialog box will be displayed. Select the file type from the Type drop-down list and then specify the name and location of the flat pattern file by choosing the **Browse** button from the **Output File** rollout.

RENEWING FEATURES

Ribbon: Home > Edit Feature > Renew Feature *(Customize to Add)*
Menu: Edit > Feature > Renew Feature

You can recompute the features created in earlier versions of NX to the current feature version by using the **Renew Feature** tool. This tool recreates a feature using code from the current NX version. Features are enhanced in each NX release to improve their performance and quality. To take advantage of these improvements, you can use the **Renew Feature** tool to recompute features up to the current feature version. To do so, choose the **Renew Feature** tool from the **Edit Feature** group of the **Home** tab; the **Renew Feature** dialog box will be displayed, refer to Figure 14-99.

Figure 14-99 *The* ***Renew Feature*** *dialog box*

Note
You cannot renew the features created in releases prior to NX 8.

Features Rollout

The **Sort** drop-down list in this rollout contains two options: **Time Stamp** and **Feature Type**. The **Time Stamp** option is selected by default in this drop-down list. As a result, the feature versions are shown in the listing window in the time stamp order. If you select the **Feature Type** option from this drop-down list, the feature versions will be shown in the listing window in a tree-like structure of expandable feature types.

Select the **Time Stamp** option from the **Sort** drop-down list, if not already selected and then select the feature that you want to renew from the **Feature List** column of the listing window; the **Apply** and **OK** buttons will be activated in the dialog box. Next, choose the **Apply** button; the **Renew Feature** message box will be displayed. Choose the **OK** button from it; the feature will be renewed to the current release of NX.

You can also select the **Feature Type** option from the **Sort** drop-down list. In this case, you need to expand the node of the feature to be renewed and then select it. Next, choose the **Apply** button; the feature will be renewed to the current version. Next, choose the **Cancel** button to exit the dialog box.

TUTORIALS

Tutorial 1

In this tutorial, you will create the sheet metal part of the Holder Clip shown in Figure 14-100. The flat pattern of the component is shown in Figure 14-101 and its dimensions are given in Figure 14-102. The material thickness, bend radius, relief depth, and relief width is 1 mm each. The specifications of the louver are given next.

Type: Formed-end louver
Length: 18mm
Width: 4mm
Height: 2.5 mm

After creating the sheet metal component, create its flat pattern. Save the component with the name *c14tut1.prt* at the location given next:
\NX\c14 **(Expected time: 45 min)**

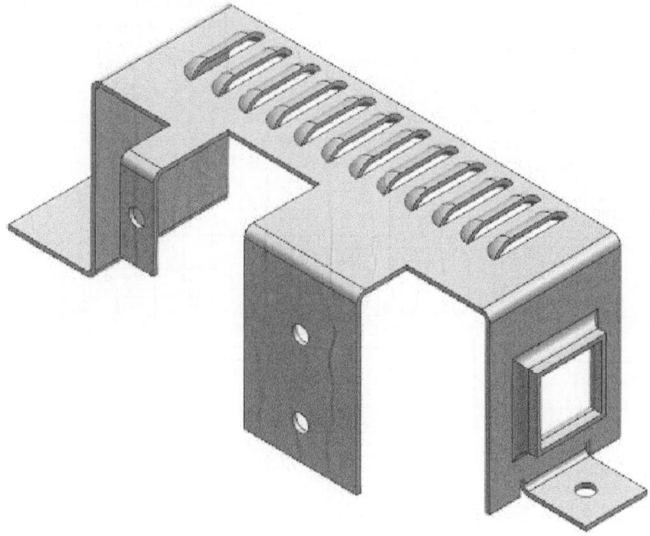

Figure 14-100 Sheet metal part for Tutorial 1

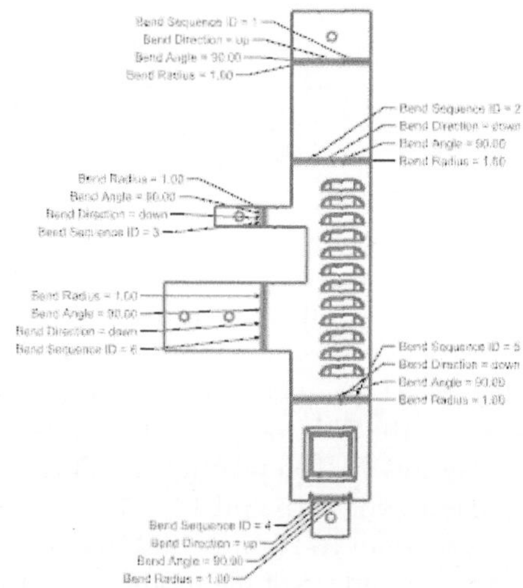

Figure 14-101 Flat pattern of the sheet metal part for Tutorial 1

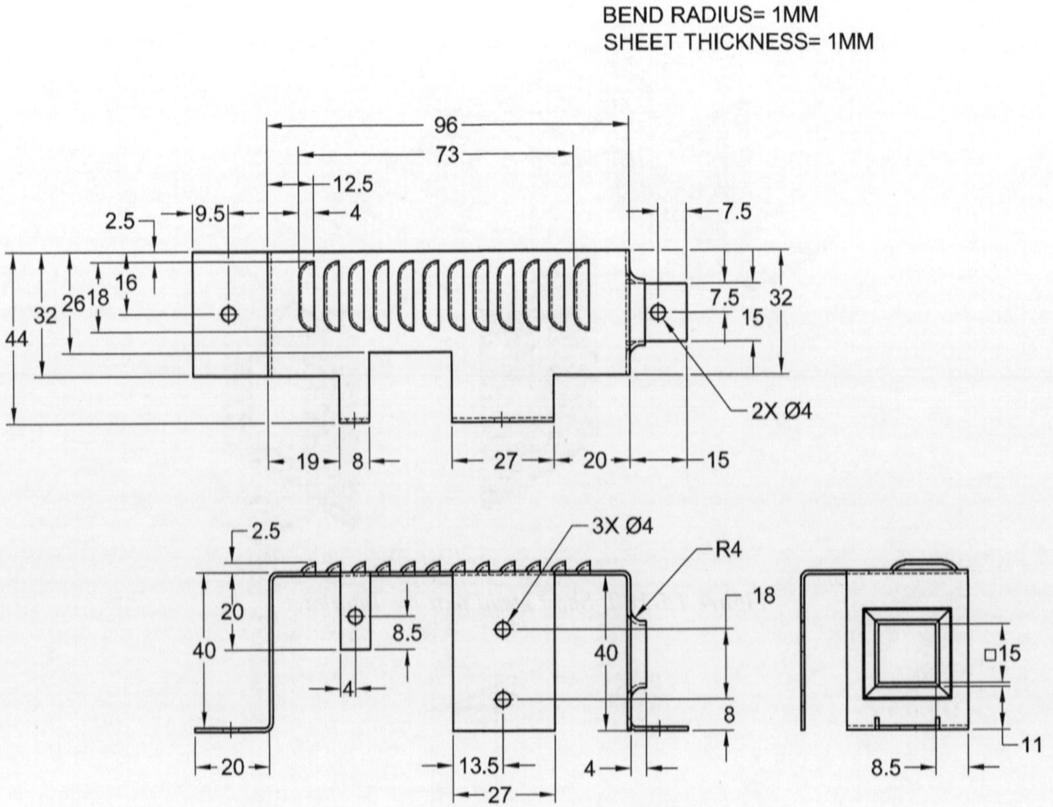

Figure 14-102 Dimensions of the sheet metal part

The following steps are required to complete this tutorial:

a. Start a new sheet metal file and set the sheet metal parameters.
b. Create the base feature by using the **Tab** tool, refer to Figures 14-103 and 14-104.
c. Create the flanges, refer to Figures 14-105 through 14-114.
d. Create the louvers, refer to Figures 14-115 and 14-118.
e. Create the holes on the flanges, refer to Figures 14-119 and 14-120.
f. Create the drawn cutout on the right face of the model, refer to Figures 14-121 and 14-122.
g. Generate the flat pattern of the model, refer to Figure 14-123.
h. Save the model.

Starting a New Sheet Metal File

1. Start NX by double-clicking on its shortcut icon on the desktop.

2. To start a new file, choose the **New** tool from the **Standard** group or choose **Menu > File > New** from the **Top Border Bar**; the **New** dialog box is displayed.

3. Select the **Sheet Metal** template from the **Templates** rollout of the dialog box.

4. Enter **c14tut1** as the name of the document in the **Name** text box of the dialog box.

5. Choose the button on the right side of the **Folder** text box; the **Choose Directory** dialog box is displayed.

6. In this dialog box, browse to *NX/c14* and then choose the **OK** button twice; the new file is started in the Sheet Metal environment.

7. Choose **Menu > Preferences > Sheet Metal** from the **Top Border Bar**; the **Sheet Metal Preferences** dialog box is displayed.

8. Choose the **Part Properties** tab and set the value of the material thickness, bend radius, relief depth, and relief width to 1mm each.

9. Specify neutral factor as **0.33** and choose the **OK** button to apply it to the model.

Creating the Tab Feature

1. Choose the **Tab** tool from the **Basic** group; the **Tab** dialog box is invoked and you are prompted to select a planar face to sketch or select the section geometry.

2. Select the **XC-YC** plane as the sketching plane and invoke the sketching environment.

3. Draw the sketch for the base feature of the part, as shown in Figure 14-103.

4. Exit the sketching environment and specify the thickness of the sheet metal part in the upward direction. Exit the **Tab** tool to create the base of the sheet metal part, as shown in Figure 14-104.

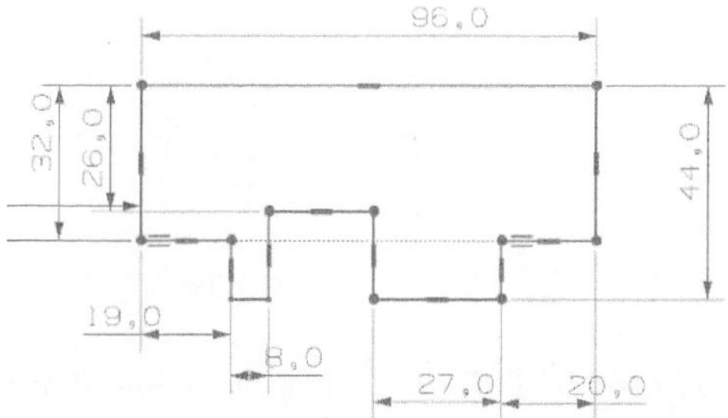

Figure 14-103 *Sketch for the top face of the part*

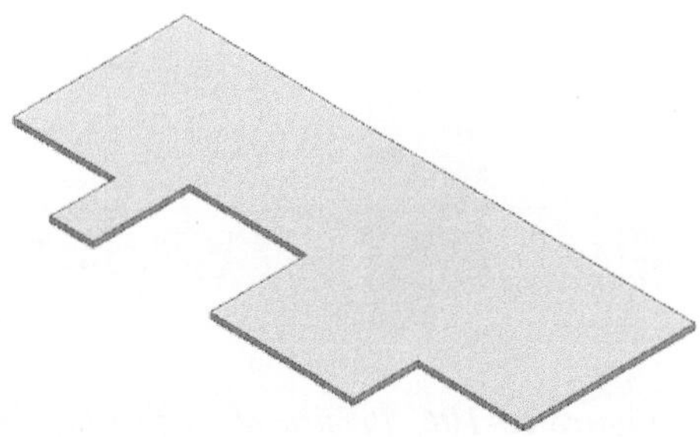

Figure 14-104 *The tab feature created*

Creating the Flanges

Next, you need to create various flanges on the top face of the sheet metal part. These flanges will be created using the **Flange** tool.

1. Choose the **Flange** tool from the **Bend** group of the **Home** tab; the **Flange** dialog box is invoked and you are prompted to select a linear edge.

Flange

2. Select the edge on tab to create the first flange, refer to Figure 14-105; the preview of the full-width flange along with an edit box is displayed.

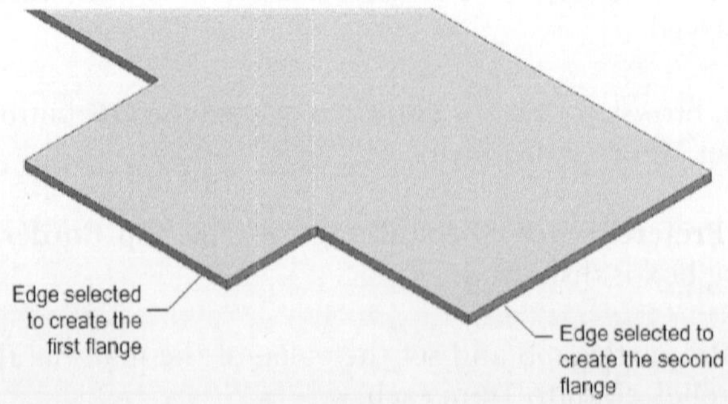

Figure 14-105 Edges to be selected to create flanges

3. Specify **40** mm as the distance of the flange in the **Length** edit box. Figure 14-106 shows the preview of the flange.

4. Similarly, create the second flange of 40 mm length by selecting the edge, refer to Figure 14-105. Figure 14-107 shows the preview of the flange created on the second edge selected. Next, choose the **Apply** button to create the flange.

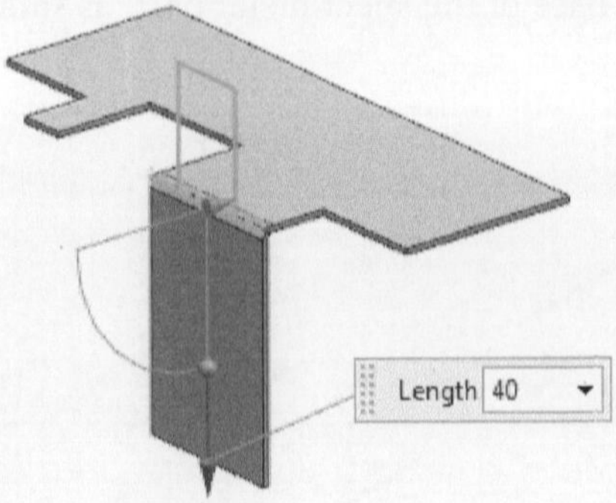

Figure 14-106 Preview of the first flange

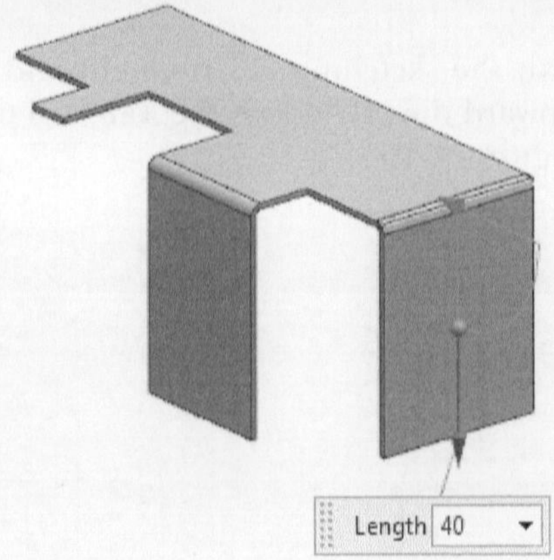

Figure 14-107 Preview of the second flange

Now, you need to create the centered flange.

5. Select the bottom edge of the second flange, refer to Figure 14-108.

6. Select the **At Center** option from the **Width Option** drop-down list in the **Flange** dialog box.

7. Enter **15** in both the **Width** and **Length** edit boxes of the **Flange** dialog box, and choose the **Apply** button; the centered flange is created, as shown in Figure 14-109.

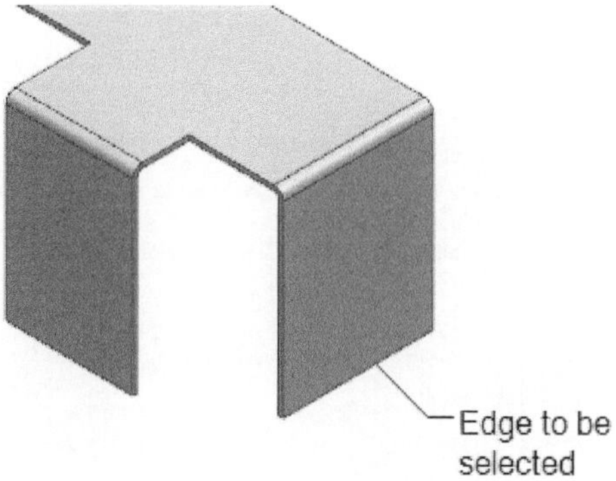

Figure 14-108 *Edge to be selected*

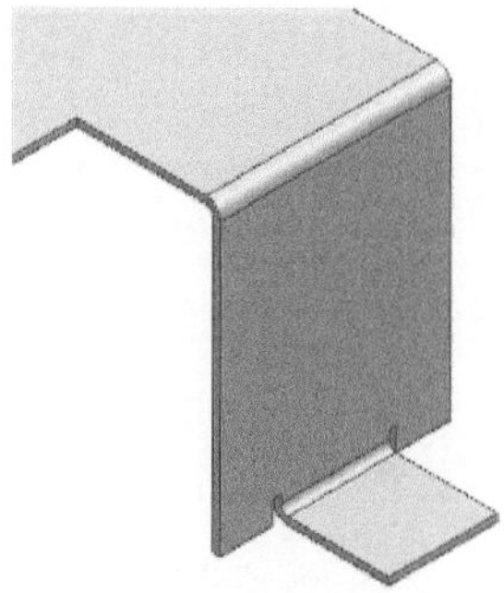

Figure 14-109 *The centered flange*

8. Select the edge, as shown in Figure 14-110.

9. Select the **Full** option from the **Width Option** drop-down list in the **Flange** dialog box.

10. Enter **20** mm in the **Length** edit box and choose the **Apply** button from the **Flange** dialog box; the fourth flange is created, as shown in Figure 14-111.

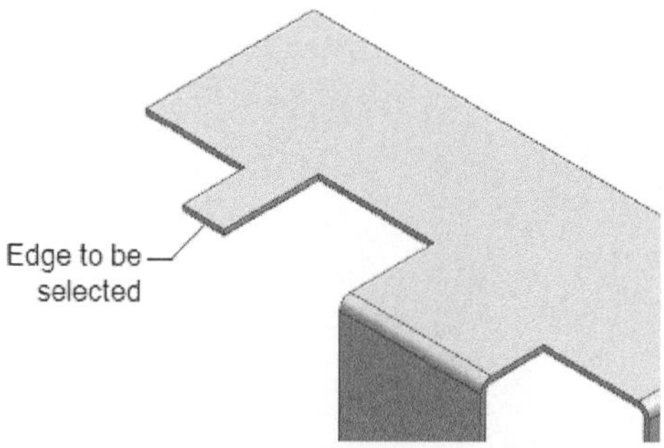

Figure 14-110 *Edge to be selected*

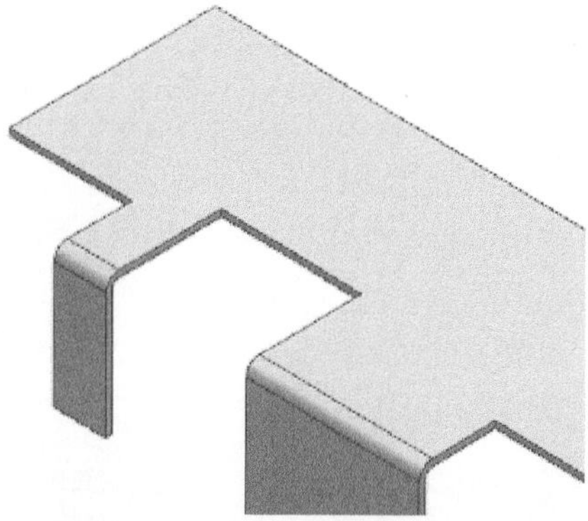

Figure 14-111 *The fourth flange*

11. Next, create the fifth flange of 40 mm length by selecting the edge, as shown in Figure 14-112. The preview of the flange is shown in Figure 14-113.

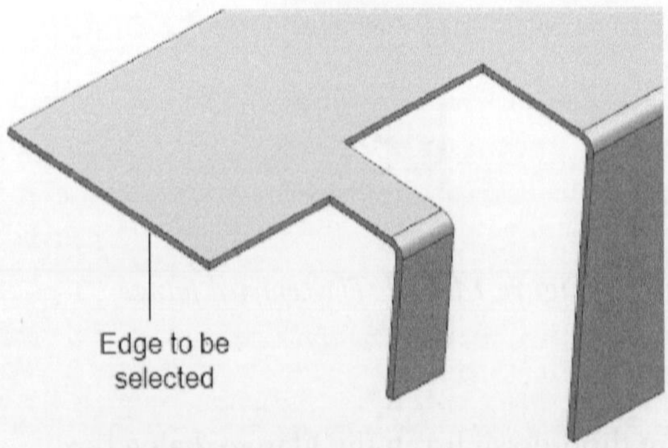

Figure 14-112 Edge to be selected

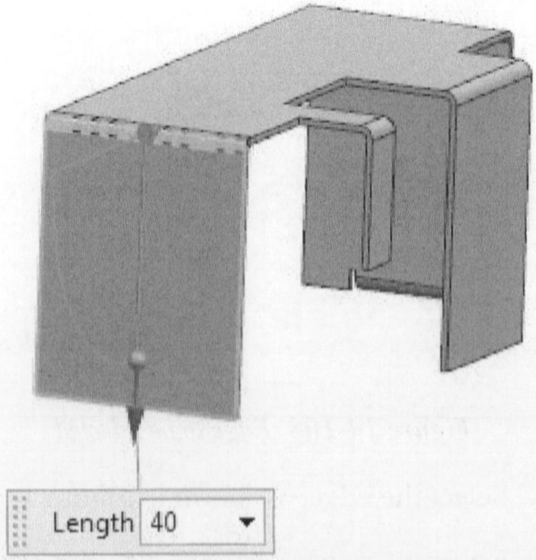

Figure 14-113 Preview of the fifth flange

12. Finally, create the sixth flange of 20 mm length on the bottom edge of the previous flange, refer to Figure 14-114 and then exit the **Flange** dialog box.

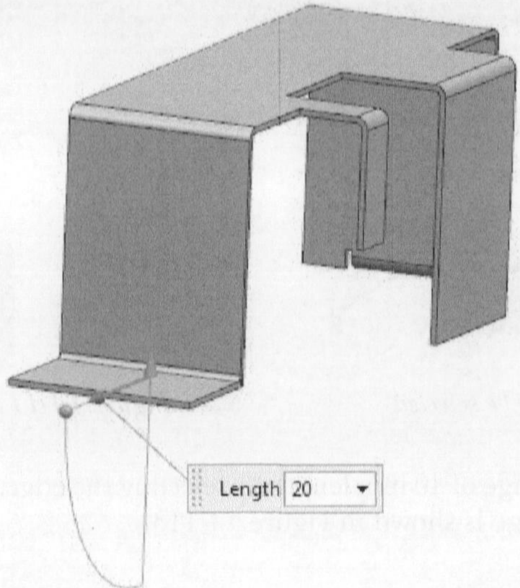

Figure 14-114 Preview of the sixth flange

Creating Louvers on the Top Face

Next, you need to create louvers on the top face. In this process, first you need to create one of the louvers using the **Louver** tool and then create its rectangular pattern.

1. Choose the **Louver** tool from the **Punch** gallery of the **Home** tab; the **Louver** dialog box is displayed; you are prompted to select a planar face or select a section geometry.

2. Select the top planar face of the sheet metal part; the Sketch in Task environment is invoked.

3. Draw the profile of the louver and add the required dimensions, as shown in Figure 14-115. Exit the sketching environment; the preview of the louver is displayed.

4. Specify the settings in the **Louver Properties** rollout, as shown in Figure 14-116, in the **Louver** dialog box for the louver to be created. Choose the **OK** button; the louver is created, as shown in Figure 14-117.

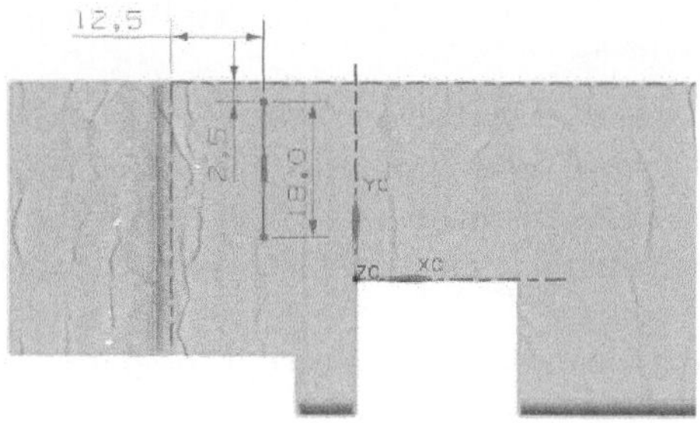

Figure 14-115 *Dimensions to position the louver*

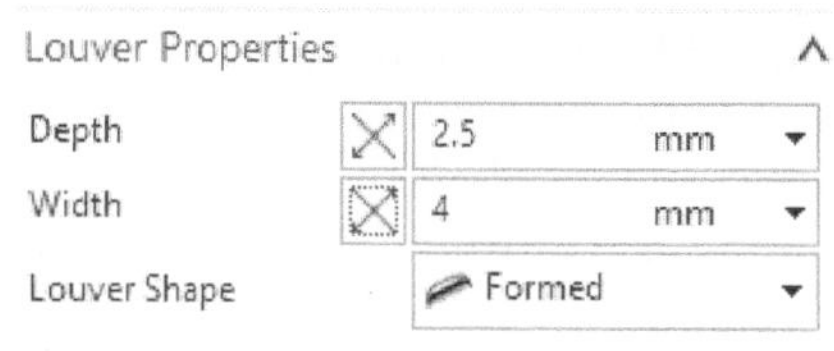

Figure 14-116 *The settings required for the louver to be created*

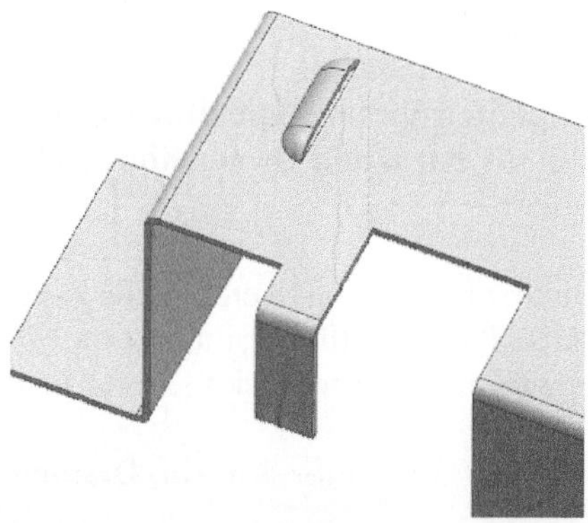

Figure 14-117 *Louver created on the top face*

Now, you need to create the pattern of the louvers.

5. Select the louver and choose **Menu > Insert > Associate Copy > Pattern Feature** from the **Top Border Bar**; the **Pattern Feature** dialog box is displayed.

6. In this dialog box, select the **Linear** option from the **Layout** drop-down list and click in the **Specify Vector** area of the **Direction 1** sub-rollout; a triad is displayed in the drawing window.

7. Select the axis of the triad, as shown in Figure 14-118 and then select the **Count and Span** option from the **Spacing** drop-down list.

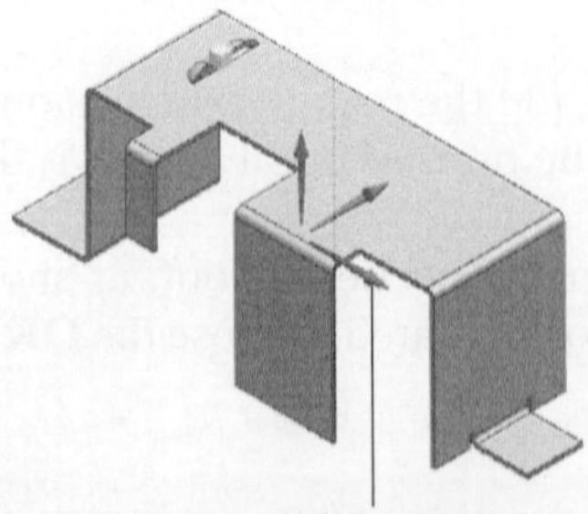

Figure 14-118 Axis to be selected from the triad

8. Enter **12** in the **Count** edit box and **73** in the **Span Distance** edit box to create a rectangular pattern of the louver with 12 instances along the selected direction.

9. Choose the **OK** button from the **Pattern Feature** dialog box to accept the pattern created.

Creating the Holes

1. Choose **Menu > Insert > Design Feature > Hole** from the **Top Border Bar**; the **Hole** dialog box is displayed and you are prompted to select the planar face to sketch or specify points.

2. Select the **General Hole** option from the Type drop-down list and the **Simple** option from the **Form** drop-down list in the **Form and Dimensions** rollout of the dialog box, if they are not selected by default.

3. Select the front face of the first flange; the Sketch in Task environment is invoked and point is placed on the selected face. Place another point and specify the position of both the points by adding dimensions. For positional dimensions, refer to Figure 14-102.

4. Exit the sketching environment and enter **4** in the **Diameter** edit box of the **Dimensions** sub-rollout.

5. Select the **Through Body** option from the **Depth Limit** drop-down list in the **Dimensions** sub-rollout. Next, select the **Subtract** option from the **Boolean** drop-down list.

6. Accept the other default settings and choose the **OK** button from the dialog box; two holes are created on the first flange, as shown in Figure 14-119.

7. Similarly, create the remaining holes on other faces of the sheet metal, refer to Figure 14-120. For dimensions of the holes, refer to Figure 14-102. The part after creating the holes is shown in Figure 14-120.

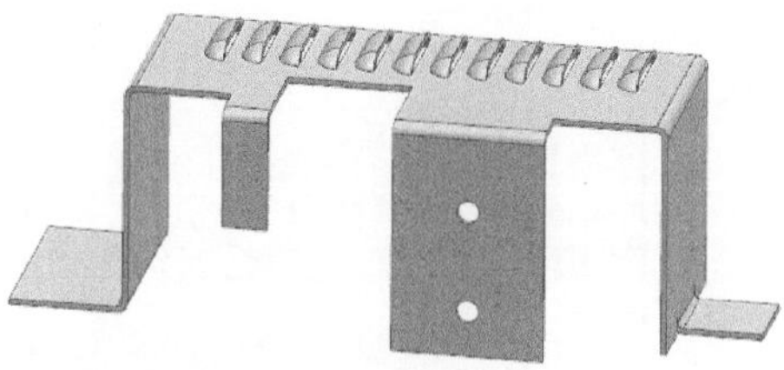

Figure 14-119 *Two holes created on the first flange*

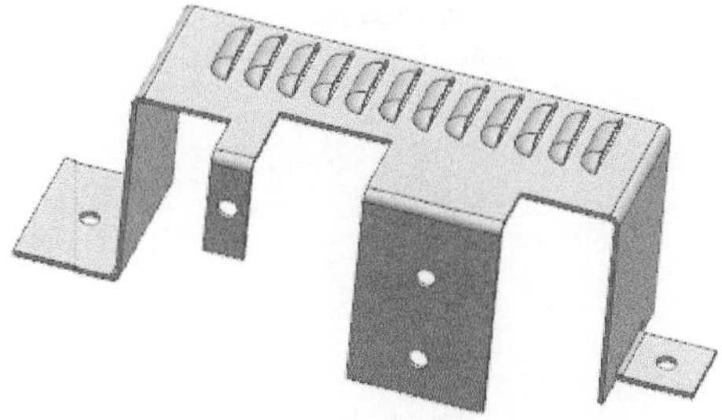

Figure 14-120 *Sheet metal part after creating the remaining holes*

Creating the Drawn Cutout on the Right Face of the Model

Next, you need to create the drawn cutout on the right face. The sketch for this cutout is a square that will be drawn in the Sketch in Task environment.

1. Choose the **Drawn Cutout** tool from the **Punch** gallery of the **Home** tab; the **Drawn Cutout** dialog box is displayed; you are prompted to select a planar face or select a section geometry.

2. Select the right face of the model and draw the profile of the drawn cutout, as shown in Figure 14-121.

3. Exit the Sketch in Task environment; the preview of the drawn cutout is displayed along with the **Depth** edit box.

4. Enter **4** in the **Depth** edit box and select the **Material Outside** option from the **Side Walls** drop-down list.

5. Expand the **Drawn Cutout** dialog box and enter **4** in the **Die Radius** edit box of the **Settings** rollout.

6. Clear the **Blend Section Corners** check box and choose the **OK** button from the dialog box; the drawn cutout is created.

The final sheet metal part is created, as shown in Figure 14-122.

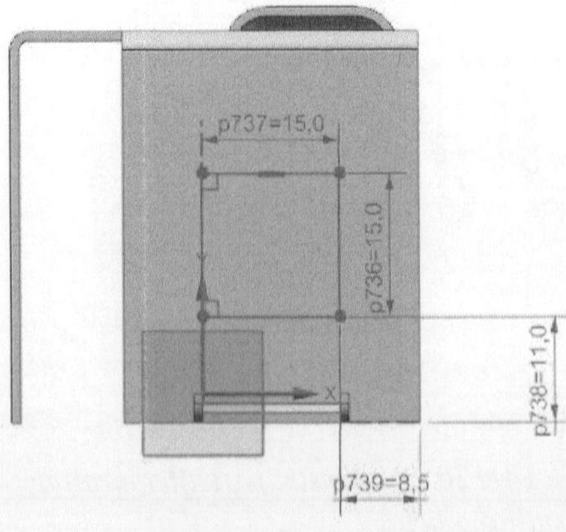

Figure 14-121 Profile of the drawn cutout

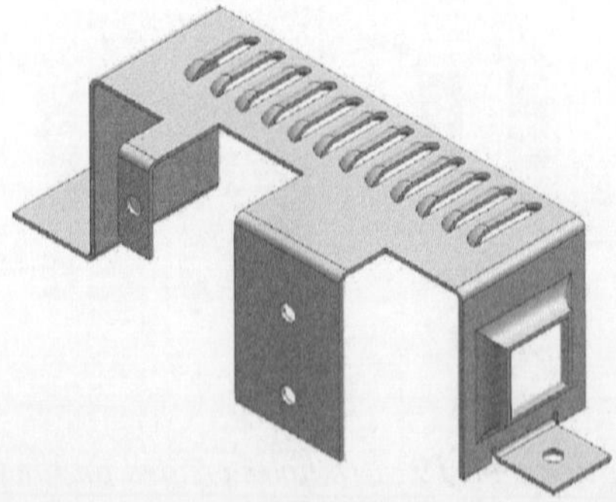

Figure 14-122 The final sheet metal part

Generating the Flat Pattern

Next, you need to generate the flat pattern of the sheet metal part created.

1. Select the **Flat Pattern** tool from the **Flat Pattern** gallery of the **Home** tab; the **Flat Pattern** dialog box is displayed. Also, you are prompted to click on the face to be oriented upward.

2. Select the top face of the sheet metal part.

3. Next, choose the **OK** button; the flat pattern is created. Note that the flat pattern is not displayed in the current view layout. You need to change the view layout to display the flat pattern.

4. Choose **Menu > View > Layout > Replace View** from the **Top Border Bar**; the **Replace View with** dialog box is displayed.

5. Select **FLAT-PATTERN#1** from the list box available in the **Replace View with** dialog box and then choose the **OK** button; the flat pattern is displayed, as shown in Figure 14-123.

Saving the Model

1. Save the model with the name *c14tut1.prt* at the location given next and then close the file.

   \NX\c14

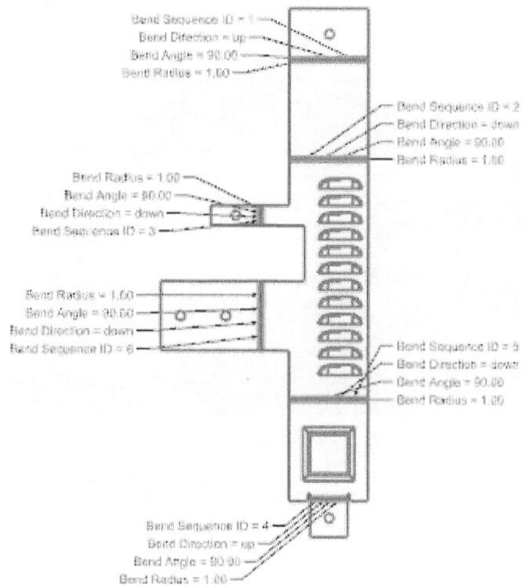

Figure 14-123 *Flat pattern of the sheet metal part*

Tutorial 2

In this tutorial, you will create the sheet metal component shown in Figure 14-124. The flat solid of the component is shown in Figure 14-125. The dimensions of the component are shown in Figure 14-126. The material thickness, bend radius, relief depth, and relief width is 1 mm each. Save the component with the name *c14tut2.prt* at the location given next:

\NX\c14 **(Expected time: 30 min)**

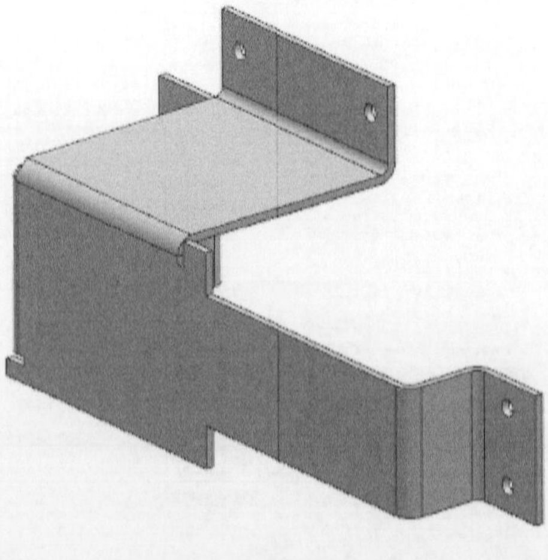

Figure 14-124 Sheet metal part for Tutorial 2

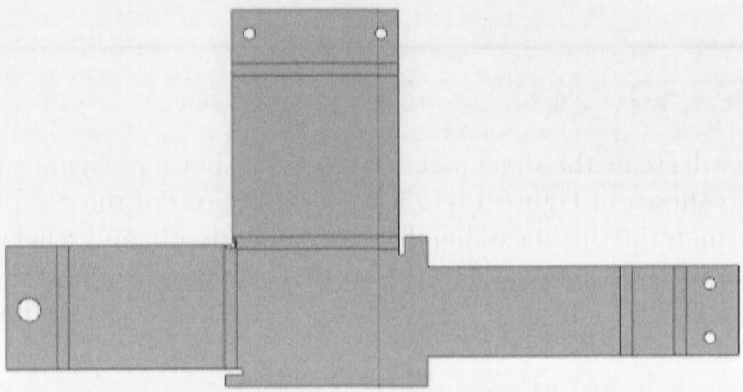

Figure 14-125 Flat solid of the part

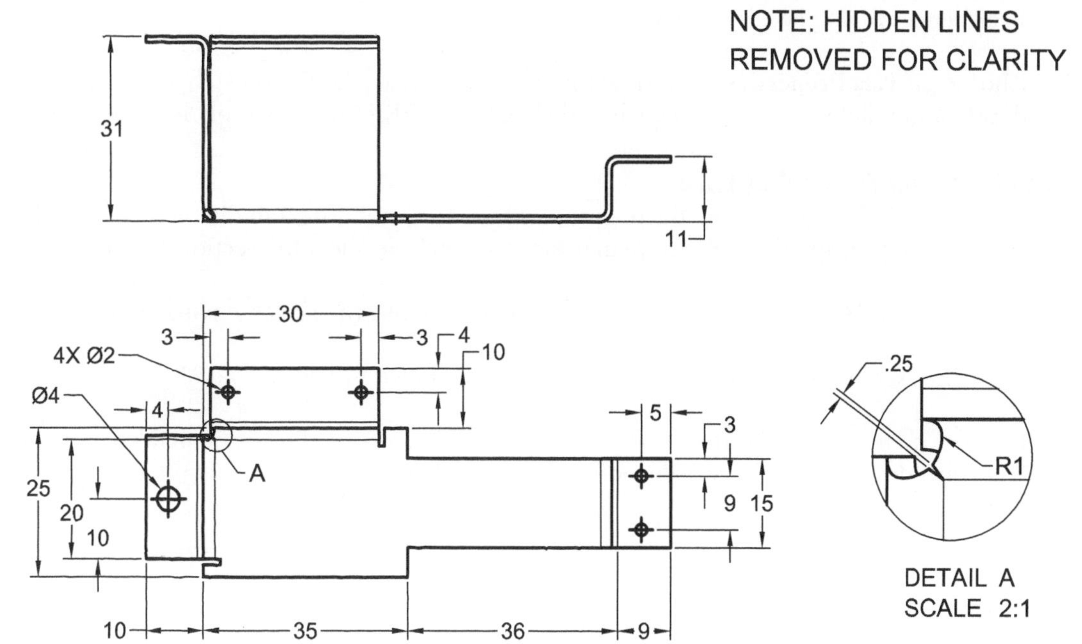

Figure 14-126 Dimensions of the sheet metal part

The following steps are required to complete this tutorial:

a. Start a new sheet metal file and set the sheet metal parameters.
b. Create the base feature of the model by using the **Tab** tool, refer to Figures 14-127 and 14-128.
c. Create the flanges on the front face base feature, refer to Figures 14-129 through 14-131.
d. Close the corners of the flanges, refer to Figure 14-132.
e. Create the holes, refer to Figure 14-133(a).
f. Generate the flat solid of the sheet metal part, refer to Figure 14-134.
g. Save the model.

Starting a New Sheet Metal File

1. Choose the **New** tool from the **Standard** group or choose **Menu > File > New** from the **Top Border Bar**; the **New** dialog box is displayed.
2. Select the **Sheet Metal** template from the **Templates** rollout.
3. Enter **c14tut2** as the name of the document in the **Name** text box of the dialog box.
4. Choose the button on the right side of the **Folder** text box; the **Choose Directory** dialog box is displayed. 
5. In this dialog box, browse to *NX/c14* and then choose the **OK** button twice; the new file is started in the Sheet Metal environment.

6. Choose **Menu > Preferences > Sheet Metal** from the **Top Border Bar**; the **Sheet Metal Preferences** dialog box is displayed.

7. Choose the **Part Properties** tab and set the value of the material thickness, bend radius, relief depth, and relief width to 1mm each and choose the **OK** button to apply it to the model.

Creating the Base Feature

1. Choose the **Tab** tool from the **Basic** group of the **Home** tab; the **Tab** dialog box is invoked and you are prompted to select a planar face to sketch or select the section geometry.

2. Select the **XC-ZC** plane as the sketching plane and invoke the sketch environment.

3. Draw the sketch for the base feature of the part, as shown in Figure 14-127.

4. Exit the sketching environment and specify the thickness of the sheet metal part in the backward direction. Exit the **Tab** tool to create the base of the sheet metal part, as shown in Figure 14-128.

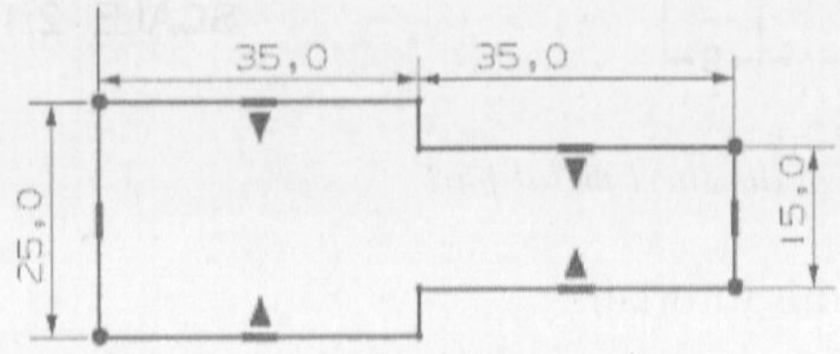

Figure 14-127 *Sketch for the base feature*

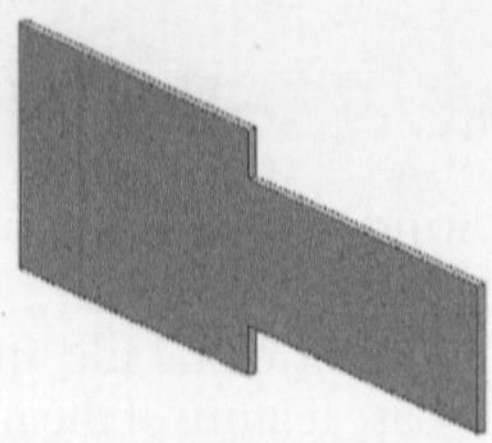

Figure 14-128 *Base of the part*

Creating the Flanges

Next, you need to create flanges on the front face of the sheet metal part. These flanges will be created using the **Flange** tool.

1. Choose the **Flange** tool from the **Bend** group; the **Flange** dialog box is displayed and you are prompted to select a linear edge.

2. Select the horizontal edge to create the flange, refer for Figure 14-129; the preview of the flange is displayed. Now, select the **At End** option from the **Width Option** drop-down list. Then, select the left endpoint of the top edge to locate the flange.

3. Specify the width of the flange as **30** mm in the **Width** edit box; the preview of the flange gets modified. Make sure that the flange is created in backward direction. Use the **Reverse Direction** button from the **Flange Properties** rollout, if the flange is displayed in the forward direction.

4. Enter **30** in the **Length** edit box of the **Flange Properties** rollout. Figure 14-129 shows the preview of the flange after modifying the width. Choose the **OK** button to create the flange.

   Now, you need to create a flange on the left face of the feature.

5. Select the left vertical edge and specify the length of the flange as **30 mm**.

6. Select the **At End** option from the **Width Option** drop-down list and select the top endpoint of the edge to position the flange. Next, click to define the side of flange and modify its width to **20** mm in the preview.

7. Select the **Bend/Face** option from the **Corner Relief** drop-down list in the **Relief** sub-rollout and choose the **OK** button to exit the dialog box; the second flange is created, as shown in Figure 14-130.

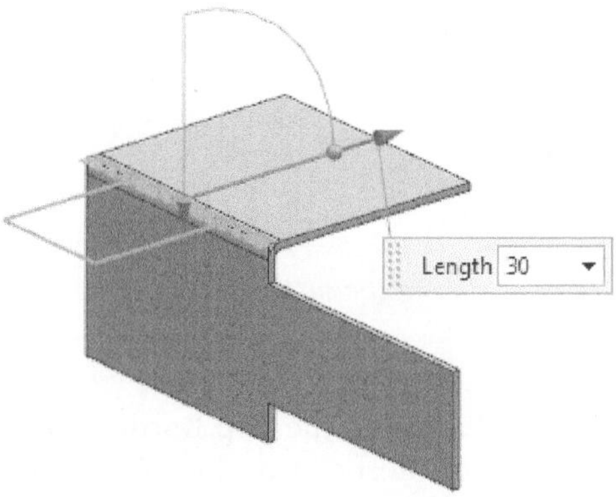

Figure 14-129 *Preview of the top flange*

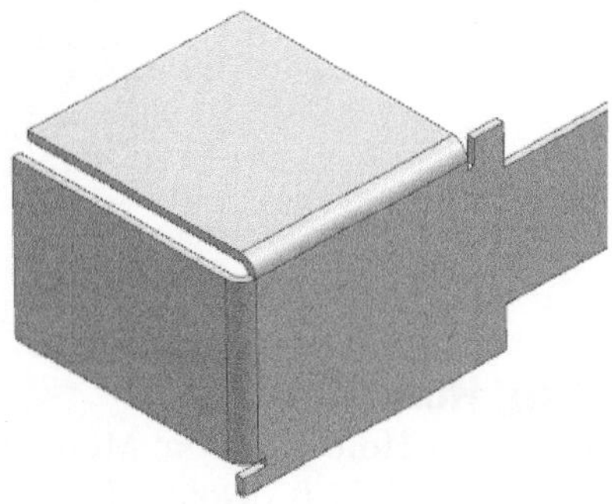

Figure 14-130 *Preview of the left flange*

8. Next, create the remaining flanges, as shown in Figure 14-131. For dimensions, refer to Figure 14-126.

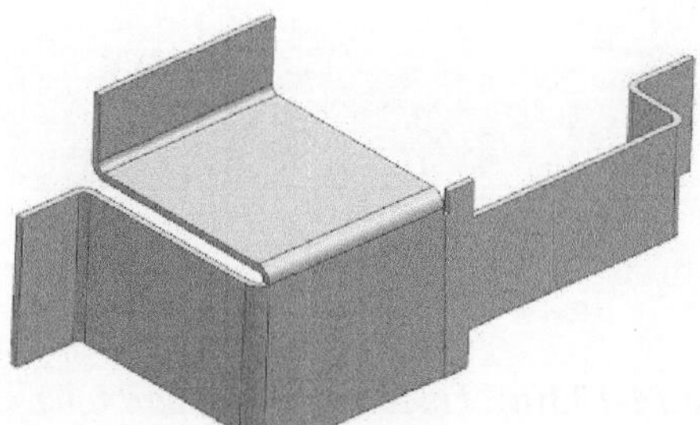

Figure 14-131 *Model after creating all flanges*

Closing the Corner between the First Two Flanges

The corner between the first two flanges needs to be closed. This is done using the **Closed Corner** tool.

1. Choose the **Closed Corner** tool from the **Corner** gallery of the **Home** tab; the **Closed Corner** dialog box is displayed and you are prompted to select the bend face adjacent to corner.

2. Select the bends of the first two flanges created to define the corner to be closed.

3. Select the **Circular Cutout** option from the **Treatment** drop-down list in the **Corner Properties** rollout. Specify the gap value as **0.25** mm and the diameter as **2** mm.

4. Choose the **OK** button to close the corner. The part after closing the corner is shown in Figure 14-132.

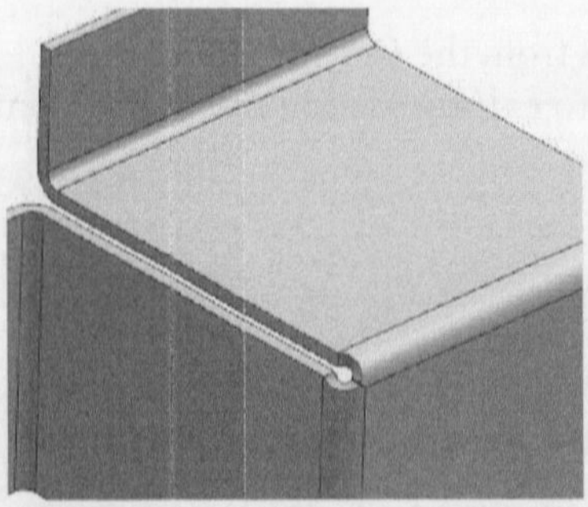

Figure 14-132 Partial view of the part after closing the corner

Creating Holes

1. Choose the **Hole** tool from **Menu > Insert > Design Feature** in the **Top Border Bar**; the **Hole** dialog box is displayed. Change the dimensions of the holes and create the holes on the left most flange. For dimensions of the holes, refer to Figure 14-126. Similarly, create the other holes. The final sheet metal part after creating the holes is shown in Figure 14-133(a). Figure 14-133(b) shows the final sheet metal part in trimetric view.

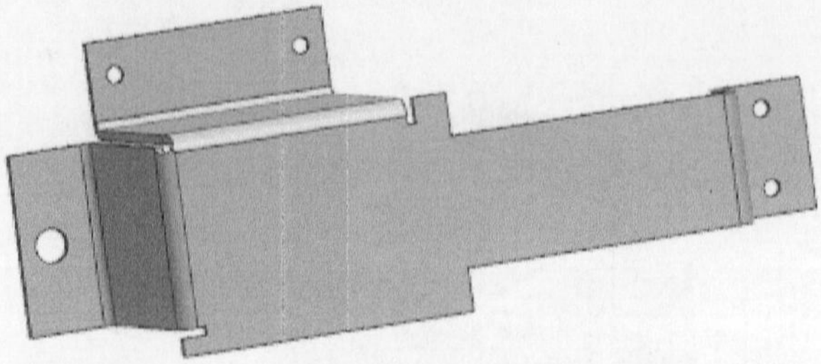

Figure 14-133(a) Final sheet metal part after creating the holes

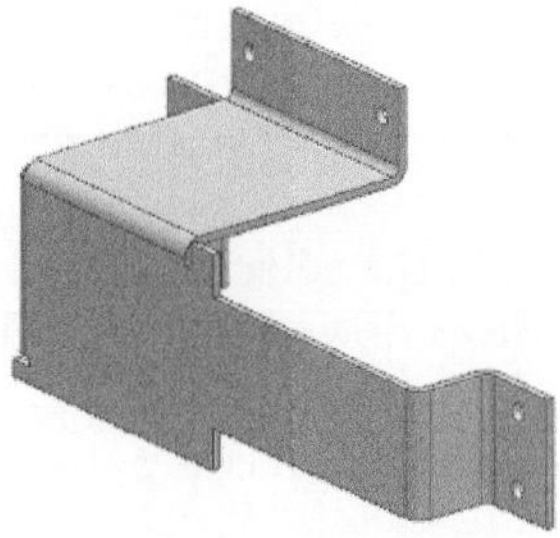

Figure 14-133(b) *Final sheet metal part displayed in trimetric view*

Generating the Flat Solid

Next, you need to generate the flat pattern of the sheet metal part.

1. Select the **Flat Solid** tool from the **Flat Pattern** gallery of the **Home** tab; the **Flat Solid** dialog box is displayed. Also, you are prompted to click on a face that you want to remain stationary in the flat solid.

2. Select the front face of the sheet metal part and then choose the **OK** button; the flat solid of the model is created, as shown in Figure 14-134. Next, hide the sheet metal part.

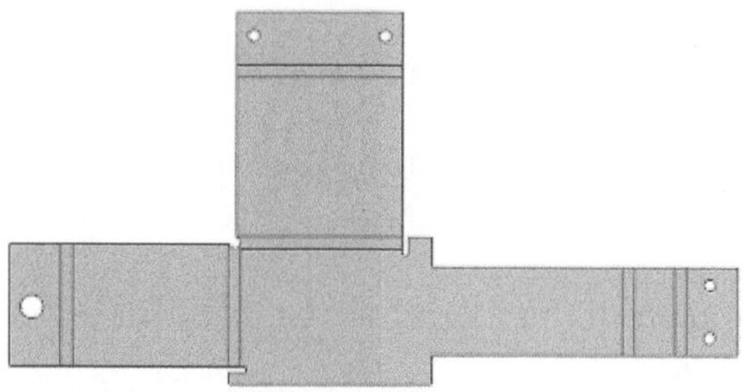

Figure 14-134 *Flat solid of the sheet metal part*

Saving the Model

1. Save the model with the name *c14tut2.prt* at the location given next and then close the file.
   \NX\c14

Self-Evaluation Test

Answer the following questions and then compare them to those given at the end of this chapter:

1. You can unbend a sheet metal part by using the __________ tool.

2. The unbent sheet metal parts can be bent again using the __________ tool.

3. In NX, the sheet metal parts are bent using a sketched ________.

4. NX allows you to close the corner between two flanges using the ________ tool.

5. To create the flange at the center of the selected edge, you need to choose the ________ option from the **Width Option** drop-down list in the **Flange** dialog box.

6. To convert a solid model into a sheet metal component, you first need to ________ it.

7. The sheet metal files are saved as the *\.prt* files. (T/F)

8. When you invoke a new sheet metal file, the sketching environment is invoked by default. (T/F)

9. NX allows you to sketch a user-defined shape and then use it to create a dimple in the sheet metal component. (T/F)

10. You can draw a closed or an open sketch for creating the dimple feature. (T/F)

Review Questions

Answer the following questions:

1. Which of the following is the shape of a louver?

   (a) Lanced (b) Formed
   (c) Both (a) and (b) (d) None

2. Which of the following types is not a type of treatment for a corner?

   (a) Open (b) Close
   (c) Circular cutout (d) Rectangular cutout

3. Which of the following tools is used to create a base of the sheet metal component?

   (a) **Flange** (b) **Contour Flange**
   (c) **Tab** (d) **Louver**

4. Which of the following tools can be used to fillet all corners of the base feature?

   (a) **Round** (b) **Break Corner**
   (c) **Chamfer** (d) **Closed Corner**

5. After creating a sheet metal part, you can modify its thickness using the **Part Properties** tab in the **Sheet Metal Preferences** dialog box. (T/F)

6. You need to change the view layout to view the flat pattern. (T/F)

7. You can set the material for the sheet metal part using the **Sheet Metal Preferences** dialog box. (T/F)

8. The height and the width of a louver are inter-related. (T/F)

9. The **Drawn Cutout** tool can be invoked from the **Punch** gallery. (T/F)

10. Beads can be created using the open or closed sketches. (T/F)

EXERCISES

Exercise 1

Create the sheet metal part shown in Figure 14-135. The flat solid of the part is shown in Figure 14-136. Its dimensions are shown in Figure 14-137. The value of material thickness, bend radius, relief depth, and relief width is 0.5 mm each. **(Expected time: 30 min)**

Figure 14-135 *Sheet metal part for Exercise 1*

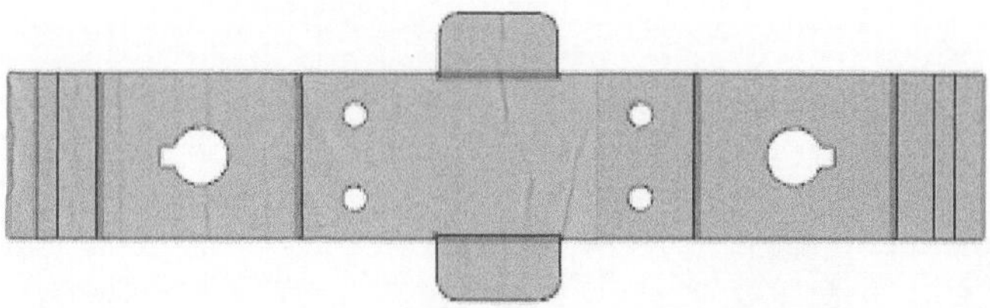

Figure 14-136 *Flat solid of the part*

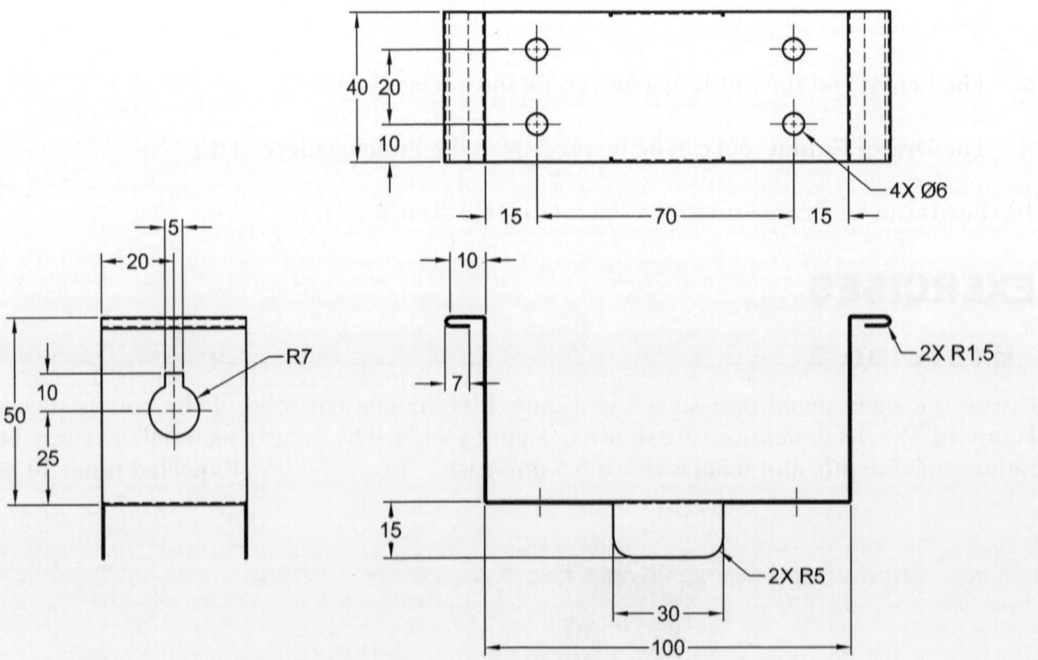

Figure 14-137 Dimensions of the sheet metal part

Exercise 2

Create the Holder Clip part shown in Figure 14-138. The flat solid of the part is shown in Figure 14-139. Its dimensions are shown in Figures 14-140. The value of material thickness, bend radius, relief depth, and relief width is 1 mm. Assume the missing dimensions.

(Expected time: 30 min)

Figure 14-138 *The Holder Clip part*

Figure 14-139 *The flat solid of the Holder Clip part*

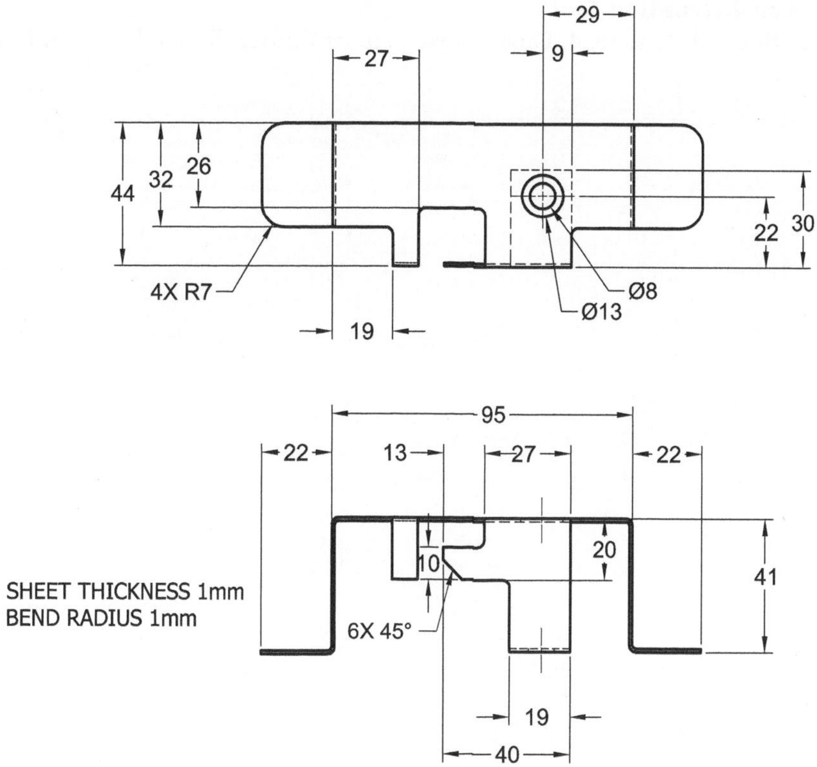

Figure 14-140 Dimensions of the Holder Clip

Answers to Self-Evaluation Test

1. Unbend, **2. Rebend**, **3.** Line, **4. Close Corner**, **5. At Center**, **6.** Shell, **7.** T, **8.** F, **9.** T, **10.** T

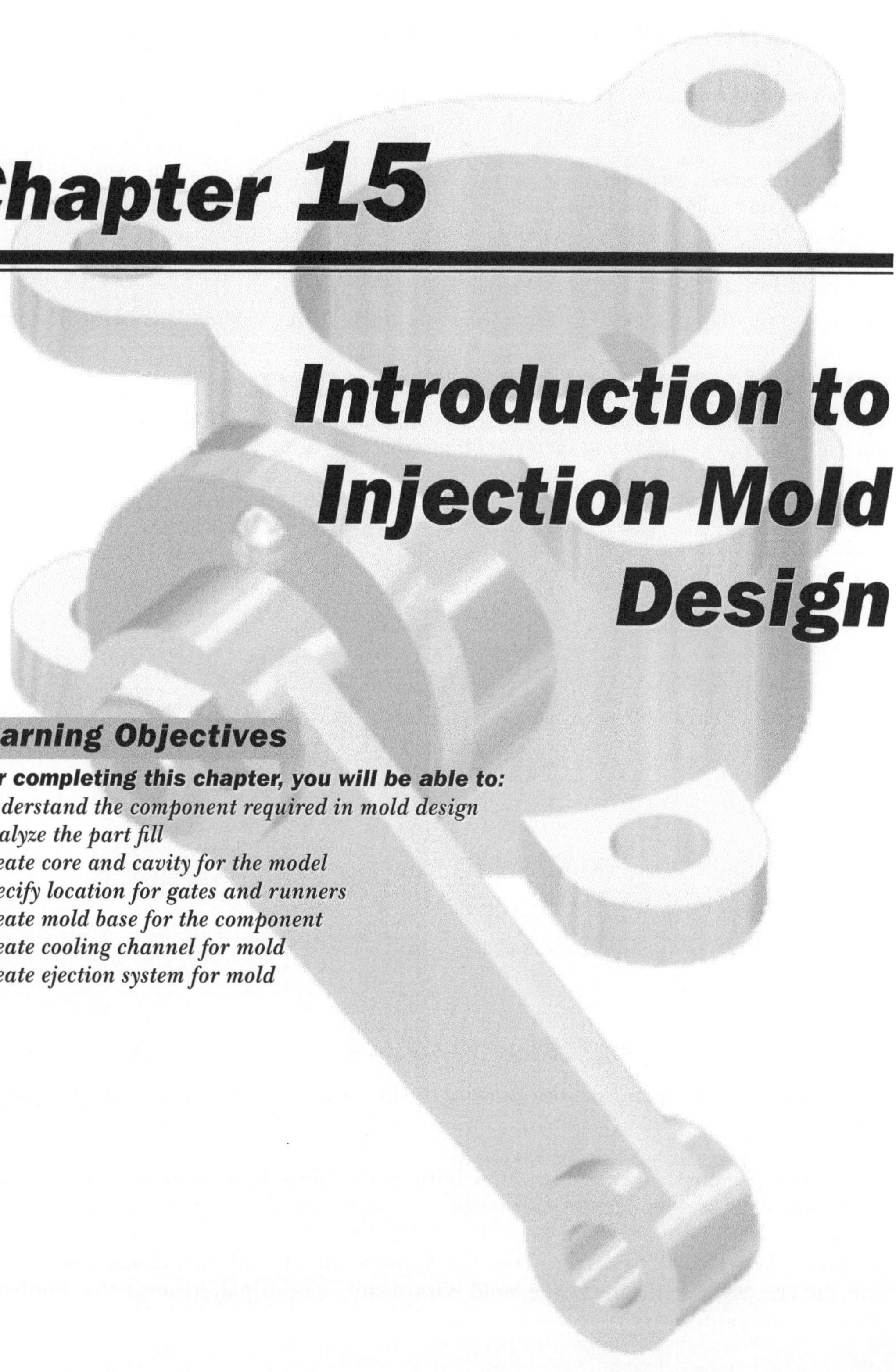

Chapter 15

Introduction to Injection Mold Design

Learning Objectives

After completing this chapter, you will be able to:

- *Understand the component required in mold design*
- *Analyze the part fill*
- *Create core and cavity for the model*
- *Specify location for gates and runners*
- *Create mold base for the component*
- *Create cooling channel for mold*
- *Create ejection system for mold*

INTRODUCTION TO INJECTION MOLD DESIGN

Injection molding is a process of manufacturing parts by injecting molten material into the mold. You can process thermoplastic as well as thermosetting polymers to create parts in injection molding machine.

An injection mold is an assembly of parts containing an impression into which plastic material is injected and cooled. This impression is formed by two parts of the mold:
(i) Cavity
(ii) Core

In NX, you can design a mold by using the tools available in the Mold Wizard environment.

INVOKING THE MOLD ENVIRONMENT

Before starting NX Mold Wizard, you need to add NX Mold Wizard library to NX. After that, you can use standard parts and material library to create a mold. Start NX by double-clicking on the shortcut icon of NX on the desktop of your computer. After the system gets loaded with all the files to start NX, the initial interface will be displayed, as shown in Figure 15-1.

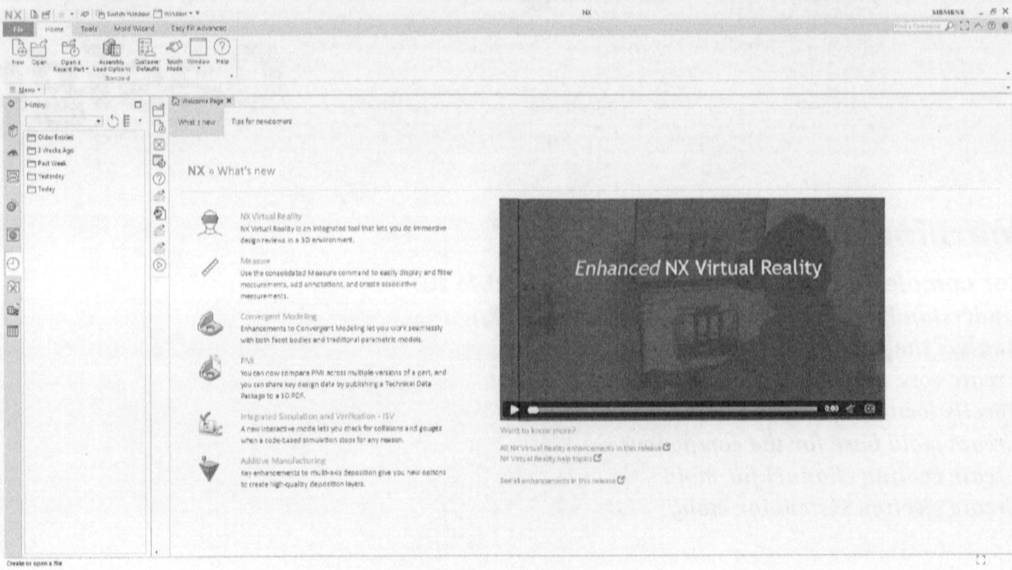

***Figure 15-1** The initial interface that appears after starting NX*

Next, choose **File > Open** from the **Ribbon**; the **Open** dialog box will be displayed, as shown in Figure 15-2.

Now, select the file and choose the **OK** button; the file will be opened in the Modeling Environment, as shown in Figure 15-3.

To invoke the NX Mold Wizard, choose the **Application** tab and then choose the **Mold** tool from the **Process Specific** group; the **Mold Wizard** tab will be displayed next to the **Application** tab, refer to Figure 15-4.

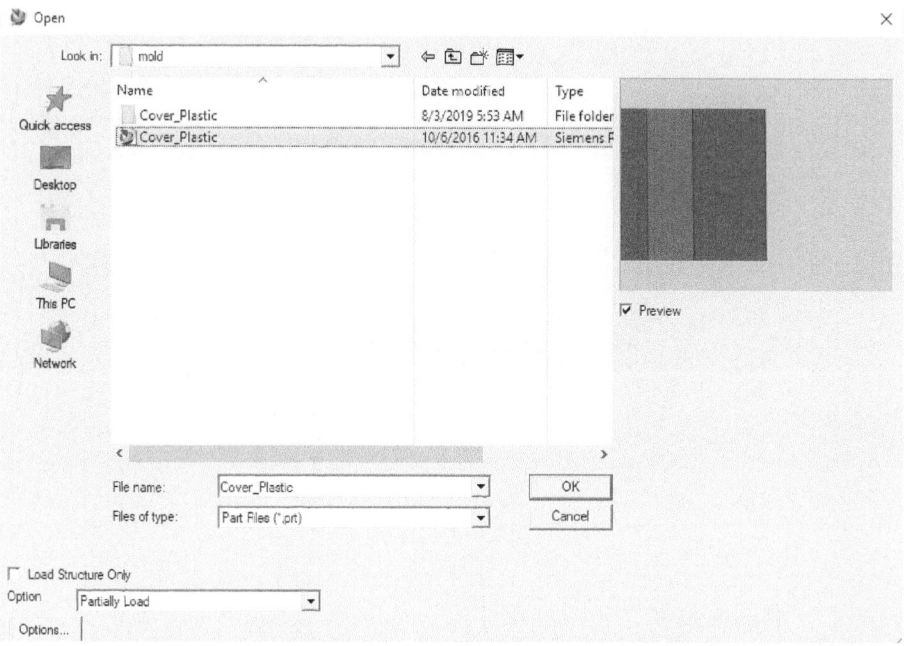

Figure 15-2 *The* ***Open*** *dialog box*

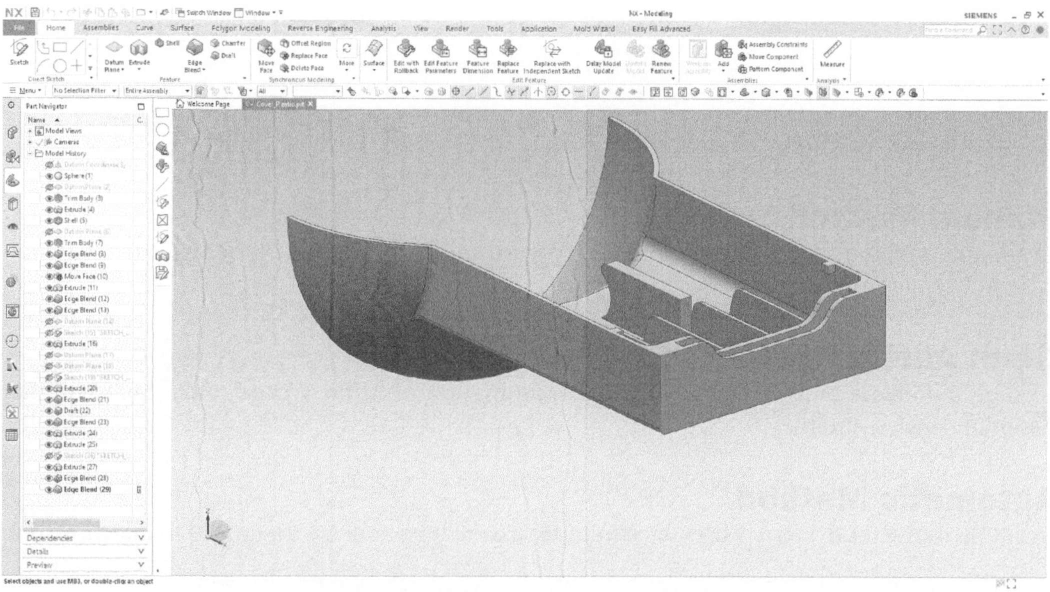

Figure 15-3 *The Modeling environment displayed on screen*

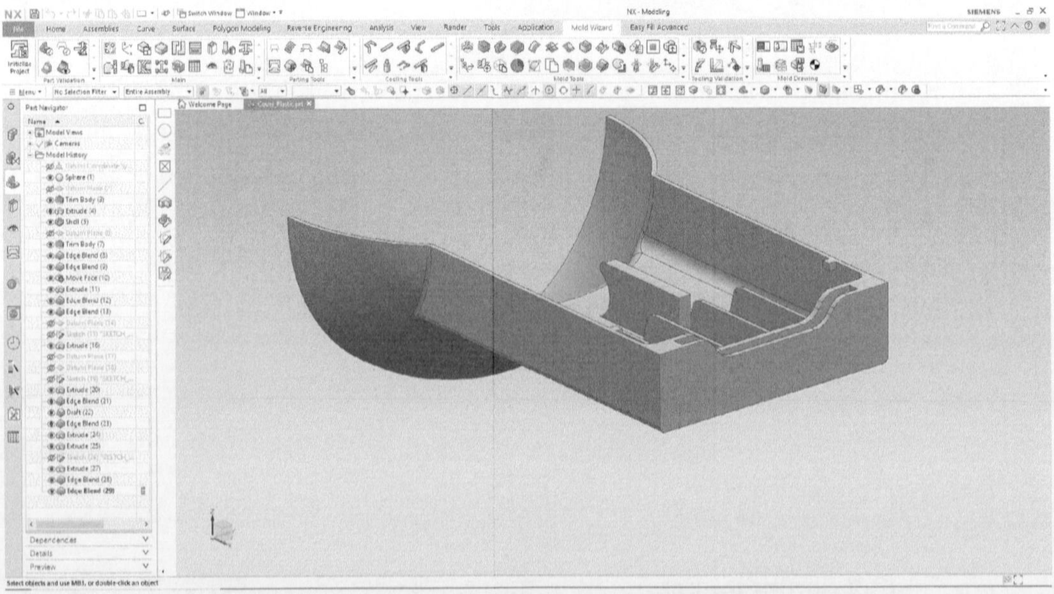

Figure 15-4 The Mold Wizard environment displayed on screen

VARIOUS METHODS FOR CREATING MOLD DESIGN

In NX, you can use the following methods for designing an Injection Mold:

(i) Manual
(ii) Semi Automatic
(iii) Automatic

These methods are discussed next.

Manual Method

In manual method, you will not use Mold Wizard but will use Part Modeling, Surfacing, and Assembly environments.

Semi Automatic Method

In semi automatic method, you will use a combination of Mold Wizard, Part, Surfacing, and Assembly environments.

Automatic Method

In automatic method, you will use only Mold Wizard environment for designing an injection mold.

ANALYSIS OF PART

For analyzing the part in NX, the Easy Fill Advanced plugin is being used in this book. You can also use Run Flow Analysis for analyzing the part but due to some constraints in the results the Easy Fill Advanced plugin is preferred for analysis.

As you install the Easy Fill Advanced plugin; the **Easy Fill Advanced** tab will becomes available in NX interface. Figure 15-5 shows the **Easy Fill Advanced** tab.

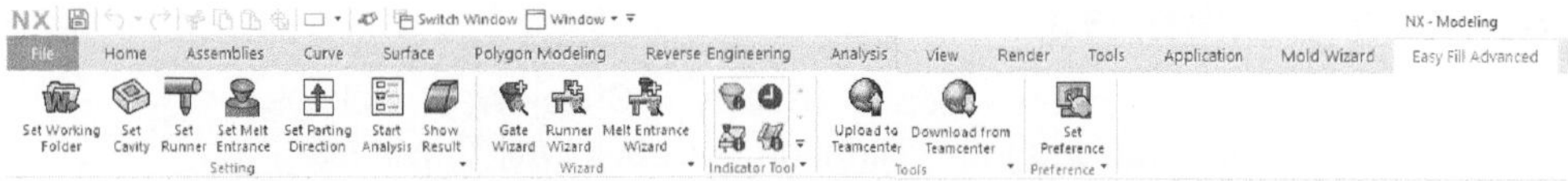

*Figure 15-5 The **Easy Fill Advanced** tab*

Before analyzing the part using the Easy Fill Advanced plugin, you should check the part undercut, draft angle, and wall thickness using the **Mold Design Validation** and **Check Wall Thickness** tools.

Mold Design Validation

Ribbon: Mold Wizard > Part Validation Gallery > Mold Design Validation

This tool helps to check the quality of the molded part. To check the undercut, draft angle, and mold part quality, invoke the **Mold Design Validation** tool from the **Part Validation** gallery of the **Mold Wizard** tab; the **Mold Design Validation** dialog box will be displayed, as shown in Figure 15-6. The options in this dialog box are discussed next.

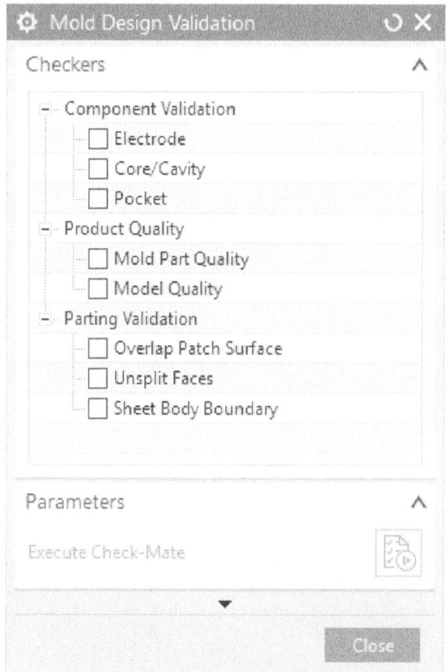

*Figure 15-6 The **Mold Design Validation** dialog box*

Component Validation

The check boxes available in this area helps to find out interference between the electrodes and the overlapping of core and cavity sheets.

Product Quality

The check boxes available in this area helps to find out the undercut and the draft angle of the molded part.

Parting Validation

The check boxes available in this area helps to find out the face required to split and checks overlap patch surface.

As you choose the **Execute Check-Mate** button from the **Parameters** rollout of the dialog box; the **HD3D Tools** window will be displayed, as shown in Figure 15-7. Depending upon the check box selected in the **Mold Design Validation** dialog box, the resulting parameter will be displayed in the **HD3D Tools** window. In this window, the status of the result is shown by symbols. Following are the symbols with their meanings:

 This symbol shows the result passed but with information.

 This symbol shows the result passed but with warning.

 This symbol shows the result passed.

Check Wall Thickness

Ribbon: Mold Wizard > Part Validation Gallery > Check Wall Thickness
Menu: Analysis > Molded Part Validation > Check Wall Thickness

Part with uniform thickness allows the mold cavity to fill more easily since the molten plastic does not have to be forced through varying restrictions as it fills. If the walls are not uniform then the thin section cools first as compared to thick section which leaves warpage or sink mark in part. You can analyze the thickness using the **Check Wall Thickness** tool. To analyze the thickness of part, invoke the **Check Wall Thickness** tool from the **Part Validation** gallery of the **Mold Wizard** tab; the **Check Wall Thickness** dialog box will be displayed, as shown in Figure 15-8, and solid body will be selected in the **Body** rollout. Choose the **Calculate Thickness** button from the **Process Results** rollout to analyze the solid body; the result will be displayed, as shown in Figure 15-9. Choose the **OK** button to close the dialog box.

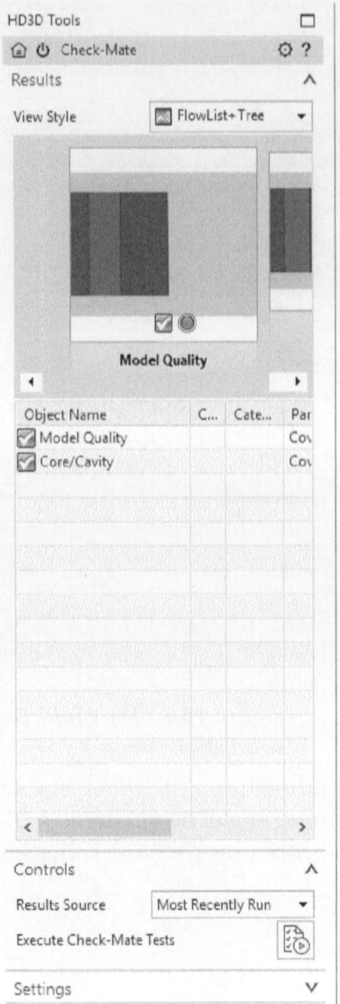

Figure 15-7 The ***HD3D Tools*** *window*

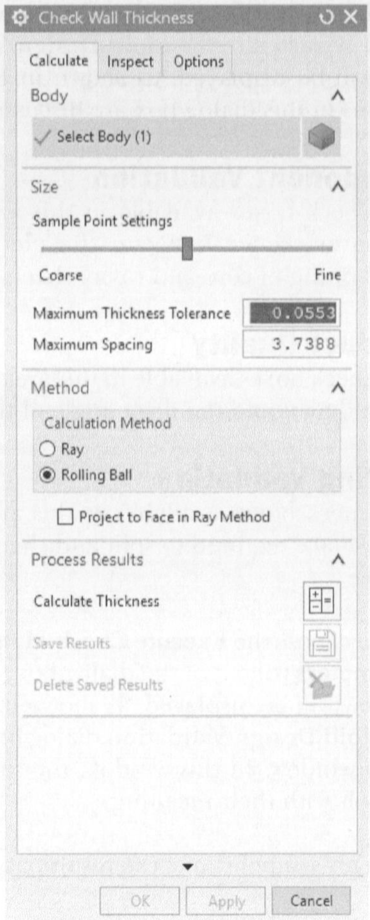

Figure 15-8 *The* ***Check Wall Thickness*** *dialog box*

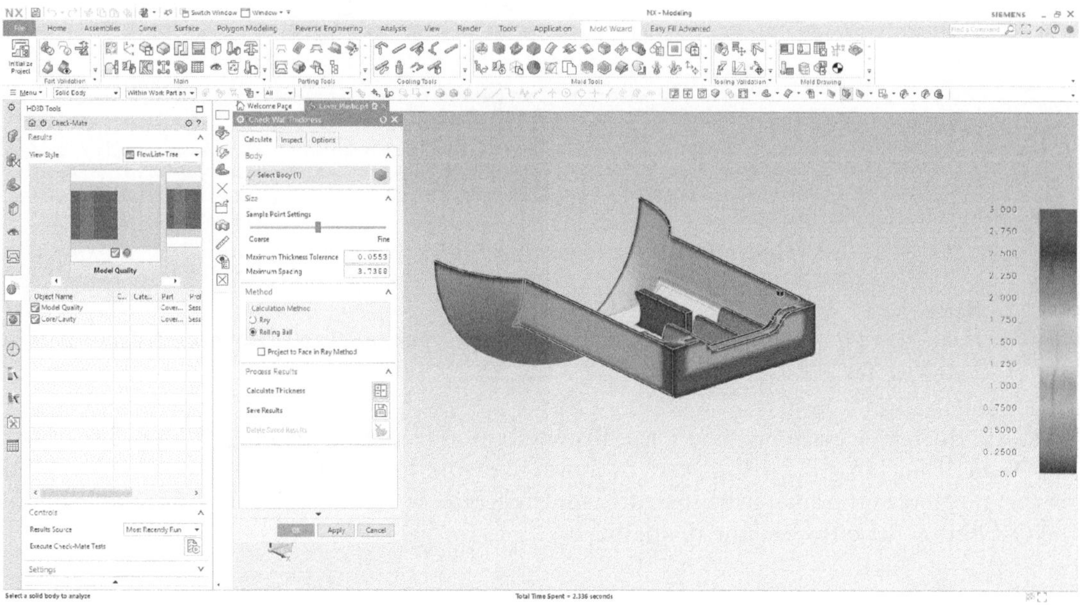

Figure 15-9 *The Part with thickness analysis*

Easy Fill Advanced

The tools in the Easy Fill Advanced plugin help you to simulate filling, packing and runner balancing of injection molding. Next, you need to understand why this plugin is preferred to use over NX run flow analysis.

Parameter	Easy Fill	Easy Fill Advanced
1) Simulation capabilities	Filling	Filling and Packing
2) Runner balance	N/A	YES
3) Gate Number	Multiple	Multiple
4) Results availability	10	36 (filling+packing)
5) Section Results	N/A	YES

This tab comprises of various tools which are discussed next.

Set Working Folder

Ribbon: Easy Fill Advanced > Setting > Set Working Folder
Menu: Analysis > Molded Part Validation > Easy Fill Advanced > Set Working Folder

Set Working Folder

This tool helps you to locate the analysis result in the specified folder. To set the working folder, choose the **Set Working Folder** tool from the **Setting** group of the **Easy Fill Advanced** tab; the **Working Folder** dialog box will be displayed, as shown in Figure 15-10.

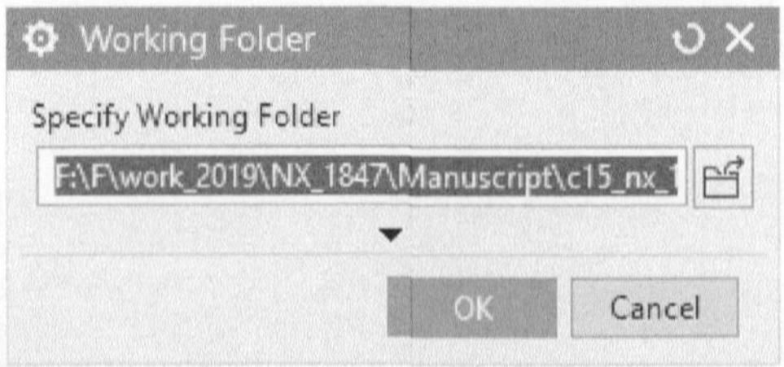

*Figure 15-10 The **Working Folder** dialog box*

Note

*If the **Easy Fill Advanced** message box appears after choosing the **Set Working Folder** tool then choose the **Yes** button to close this message box.*

To locate the folder location, choose the **Browse** button from the **Working Folder** dialog box; the **Open** dialog box will be displayed, as shown in Figure 15-11. From this dialog box, you can set the directory of the analysis result. After specifying the directory of the analysis result, choose the **OK** button twice to close the dialog boxes.

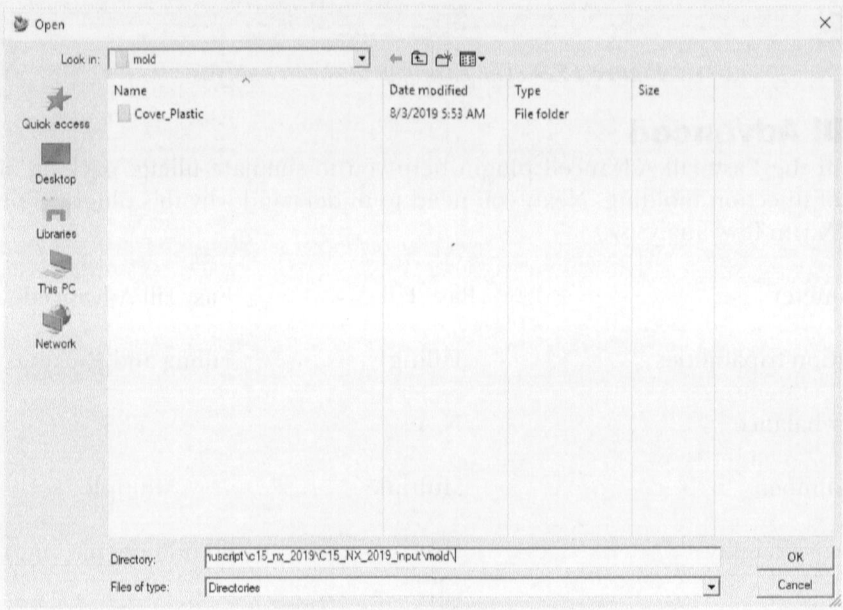

*Figure 15-11 The **Open** dialog box*

Set Cavity

Ribbon:	Easy Fill Advanced > Setting > Set Cavity
Menu:	Analysis > Molded Part Validation > Easy Fill Advanced > Set Cavity

Set Cavity

This tool helps you to specify the cavity of the component and assign material to the component. To specify the cavity, choose the **Set Cavity** tool from the **Setting** group in the **Easy Fill Advanced** tab; the **Select Cavity** dialog box will be displayed, as shown in Figure 15-12. Also, you will be prompted to specify solid body as cavity. Select the component from the drawing window. Next, choose the **Push button to select material** button from the **Material Setting** rollout; the **Moldex3D Material Wizard** dialog box will be displayed, refer to Figure 15-13. You can specify the name of material, producer name, and grade name in this dialog box. After specify the material, producer, and grade name; choose the **OK** button from the **Moldex3D Material Wizard** dialog box and next, choose the **OK** button from the **Select Cavity** dialog box.

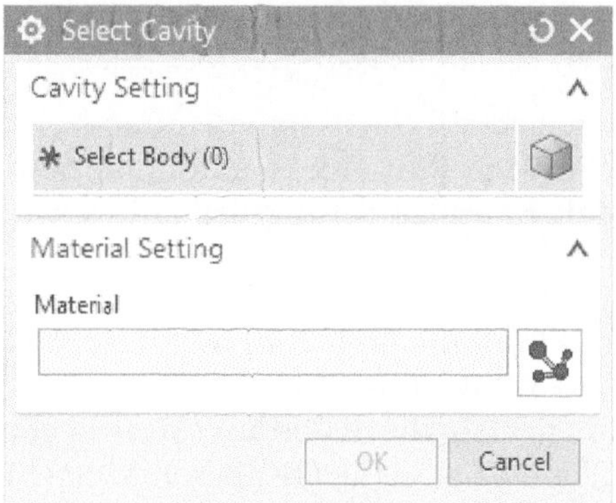

Figure 15-12 The ***Select Cavity*** *dialog box*

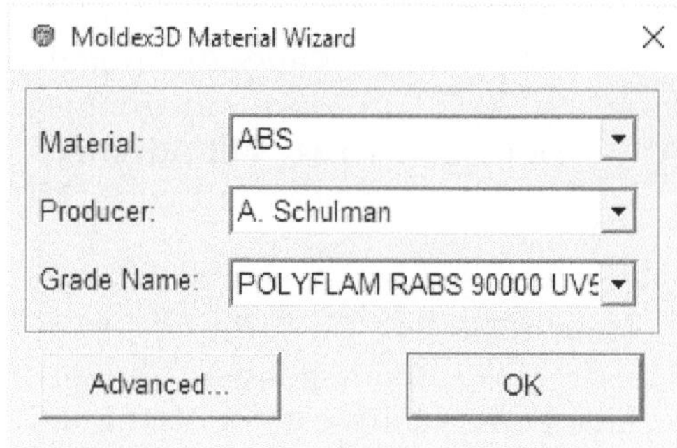

Figure 15-13 The ***Moldex3D Material Wizard*** *dialog box*

Set Runner

Ribbon:	Easy Fill Advanced > Setting > Set Runner
Menu:	Analysis > Molded Part Validation > Easy Fill Advanced > Set Runner

Set Runner

This tool helps you to define the runner system of the solid bodies. To set the runner system, choose the **Set Runner** tool from the **Setting** group in the **Easy Fill Advanced** tab; the **Select Runner** dialog box will be displayed, as shown in Figure 15-14. Choose the Specify Runner button from the **Runner List** rollout; the **Select Runner** dialog box will be displayed, refer to Figure 15-15. Also, you will be prompted to specify the curve or solid body to specify as Runner. Select the solid body or curve from the drawing window. Choose the **OK** button to close the dialog box; the **Settings** dialog box will be displayed. You can select type of runner from the **Type** drop-down list of the **Attribute** rollout. Choose the **OK** button to close the dialog box. You will notice that type of runner and name of runner will be displayed in the **Runner List** rollout. Choose the **OK** button to close the dialog box.

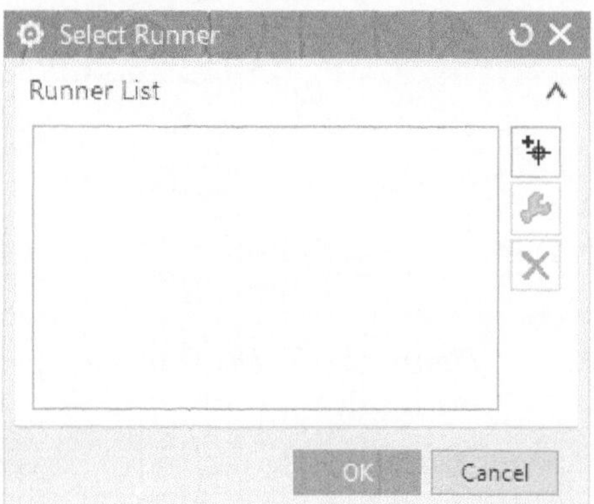

Figure 15-14 The ***Select Runner*** *dialog box*

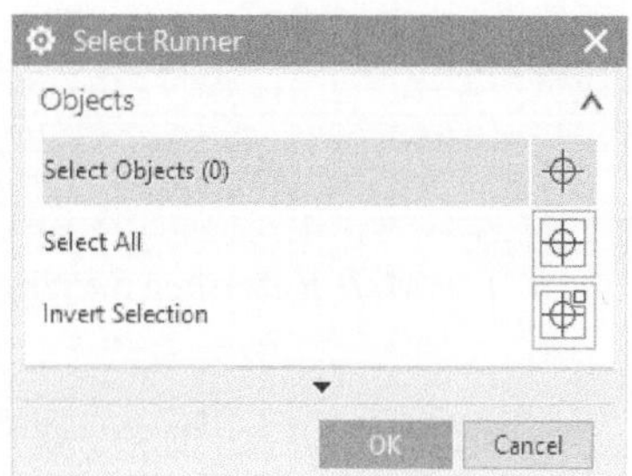

Figure 15-15 The ***Select Runner*** *dialog box*

Note

If you select a body for setting runner, then you can only define type of runner but if you select a curve, then you can define type of runner and its cross-section parameters.

Set Melt Entrance

Ribbon:	Easy Fill Advanced > Setting > Set Melt Entrance
Menu:	Analysis > Molded Part Validation > Easy Fill Advanced > Set Melt Entrance

Set Melt Entrance

Melt entrance is the path through which molten material comes into the runner. To set the Melt Entrance for the runner, choose the **Set Melt Entrance** tool from the **Setting** group of the **Easy Fill Advanced** tab; the **Melt Entrance Setting** dialog box will be displayed, as shown in Figure 15-16.

Next, choose the Specify Melt Entrance Position button from the **Melt Entrance List** rollout; the **Point** dialog box will be displayed, refer to Figure 15-17. By using this dialog box, you can place the Melt entrance position. Choose the **OK** button to close the dialog box. You will notice the Melt Entrance name in the **Melt Entrance List** rollout. Choose the **OK** button to close the dialog box.

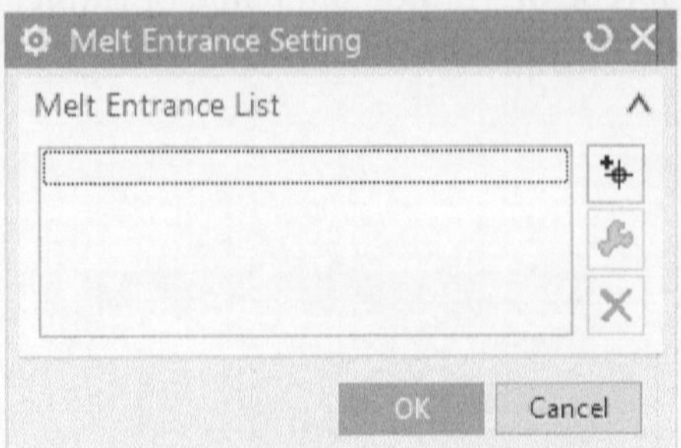

*Figure 15-16 The **Melt Entrance Setting** dialog box*

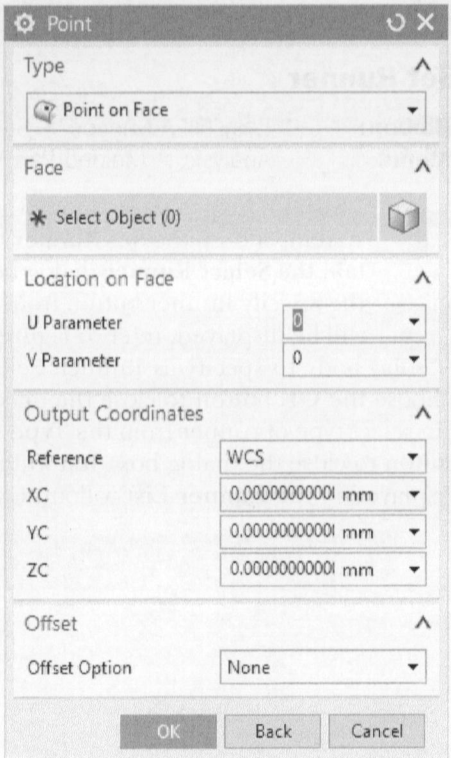

*Figure 15-17 The **Point** dialog box*

Set Parting Direction

Ribbon:	Easy Fill Advanced > Setting > Set Parting Direction
Menu:	Analysis > Molded Part Validation > Easy Fill Advanced > Set Parting Direction

Set Parting Direction

Parting direction of the component plays an important role in mold design procedure. So, you need to decide the parting direction carefully. To set the parting direction, choose the **Set Parting Direction** tool from the **Setting** group in the **Easy Fill Advanced** tab; the **Vector** dialog box will be displayed, refer to Figure 15-18. Select the direction of the partition by selecting the option from the **Type** drop-down list of the rollout. After specifying the correct orientation of the axis, choose the **OK** button to close the dialog box.

Gate Wizard

Ribbon:	Easy Fill Advanced > Wizard > Gate Wizard
Menu:	Analysis > Molded Part Validation > Easy Fill Advanced > Wizard > Gate Wizard

Gate Wizard

This tool helps you to create gate for analysis of flow. To create a gate, choose the **Gate Wizard** tool from the **Wizard** group in the **Easy Fill Advanced** tab; the **Create Gate** dialog box will be displayed, refer to Figure 15-19. Choose the **Point Dialog** button from the **Position of Gate** rollout; the **Point** dialog box will be displayed. Using this dialog box specify the location of the gate and then choose the **OK** button to close the dialog box. Select the type of gate from the **Type of gate** drop-down of the **Attribute** rollout. Specify the dimensions of the gate cross-section from the **Cross-Section Parameters** rollout.

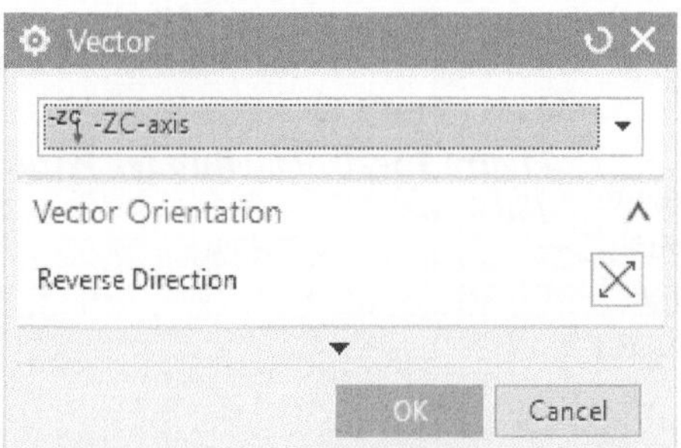

*Figure 15-18 The **Vector** dialog box*

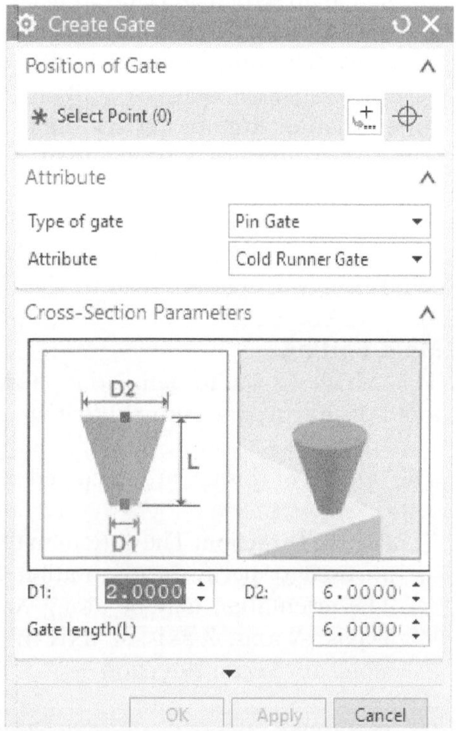

*Figure 15-19 The **Create Gate** dialog box*

In NX, the Easy Fill Advanced plug-in supports various types of gates :

i. Pin Gate
ii. Sprue Gate
iii. Edge Gate
iv. Fan Gate
v. Lapped Edge Gate
vi. Tunnel Gate
vii. Cashew Gate
viii. Tunnel Gate with ejector pin
ix. Cashew Gate with ejector pin

You can also set them as a Cold Runner or a Hot Runner gate. Depending upon the selection of gate, the dimension parameters of gate also gets changed. You can define the size of the gate by entering value in the edit boxes of these parameters. After entering the values, choose the **OK** button to close the dialog box.

Runner Wizard

Ribbon: Easy Fill Advanced > Wizard > Runner Wizard
Menu: Analysis > Molded Part Validation > Easy Fill Advanced > Wizard > Runner Wizard

Runner Wizard

This tool helps you to create runner system for flow analysis of material. You need to select only the gate location and it's size in the model, as a result, the runner wizard automatically calculates it's size, shape, and layout. This tool helps not only in creation of Runner but also helps in designing sprue and melt entrance. With the help of this tool, you can design runner system more efficiently. To create a Runner, choose the **Runner Wizard** tool from the **Wizard** group in the **Easy Fill Advanced** tab; the **Runner Wizard** dialog box will be displayed, refer to Figure 15-20.

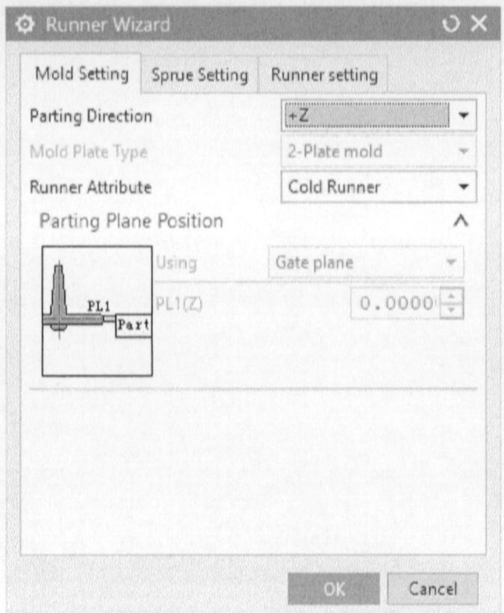

*Figure 15-20 The **Runner Wizard** dialog box*

Mold Setting

This tab allows you to define the parting direction, mold plate type, and runner attribute.

The options of this tab are discussed next.

Parting Direction: The options in this drop-down are used to specify the orientation of the runner. The orientation may be along X-axis, -X-axis, Y-axis, -Y-axis, Z-axis, -Z-axis or customize it along any vector direction.

Mold Plate Type: The options in this drop-down are used to specify the type of mold. According to the selection of the mold plate type the parameters of parting line or plane gets changed. The options in this drop-down list are:

(i) 2-Plate mold
(ii) 3-Plate mold

Runner Attribute: The options in this drop-down are used to define the type of runner. The options in this drop-down list are:
(i) Cold Runner
(ii) Hot Runner

Sprue Setting

This tab allows you to define the sprue position, sprue length, and sprue diameter. The options of this tab are discussed next.

Sprue Position Rollout: The options in this rollout are used to position the sprue.

Sprue Geometry Parameters Rollout: The options in this rollout are used to specify the size parameters of sprue.

Runner setting

This tab allows you to specify the cross-section and size parameters of runner.

After specifying the parameters of runner, choose the **OK** button to close the dialog box.

Melt Entrance Wizard

Ribbon:	Easy Fill Advanced > Wizard > Melt Entrance Wizard
Menu:	Analysis > Molded Part Validation > Easy Fill Advanced > Wizard > Melt Entrance Wizard

Melt Entrance Wizard

This tool helps you to specify from where molten material comes. To create melt entrance, choose the **Melt Entrance Wizard** tool from the **Wizard** group in the **Easy Fill Advanced** tab. As you choose this tool, the melt entrance automatically gets place in gate or runner location.

Start Analysis

Ribbon:	Easy Fill Advanced > Setting > Start Analysis
Menu:	Analysis > Molded Part Validation > Easy Fill Advanced > Start Analysis

Start Analysis

This tool helps you to apply the settings for the analysis of the component. To start the analysis of the component, choose the **Start Analysis** tool from the **Setting** group in the **Easy Fill Advanced** tab; the **Analysis Setup** dialog box will be displayed, refer to Figure 15-21. You can specify the process parameters, type of analysis, and the mesh level in this dialog box. Choose the **OK** button to start the analysis; the **Moldex3D SYNC Project Monitor** window will be displayed. This window shows the progress of analysis. After the analysis is complete, close this window by choosing the **Close** button; the **Moldex3D eDesignSYNC** message box will be displayed showing that all tasks have been completed. Choose the **OK** button to exit this message box.

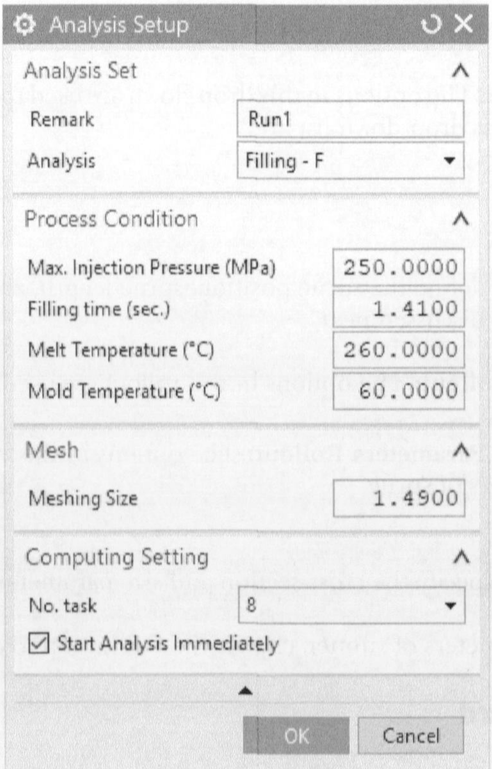

*Figure 15-21 The **Analysis Setup** dialog box*

Show Result

Ribbon:	Easy Fill Advanced > Setting > Show Result
Menu:	Analysis > Molded Part Validation > Easy Fill Advanced > Show Result

Show Result

This tool helps you to visualize and analyze the result. To invoke this tool, choose the **Show Result** tool from the **Setting** group of the **Easy Fill Advanced** tab; the **Show Result** dialog box will be displayed, as shown in Figure 15-22. Select result from the **Analysis Result** rollout; the dialog box gets modified, refer to Figure 15-22. You can select the **Filling** or **Packing** option from the **Analysis** drop-down list in the **Display Result** rollout. By default, the **Filling** option is selected. You can visualize the results by selecting appropriate option from the **Result Type** drop-down list. Choose the **Close** button to close the dialog box.

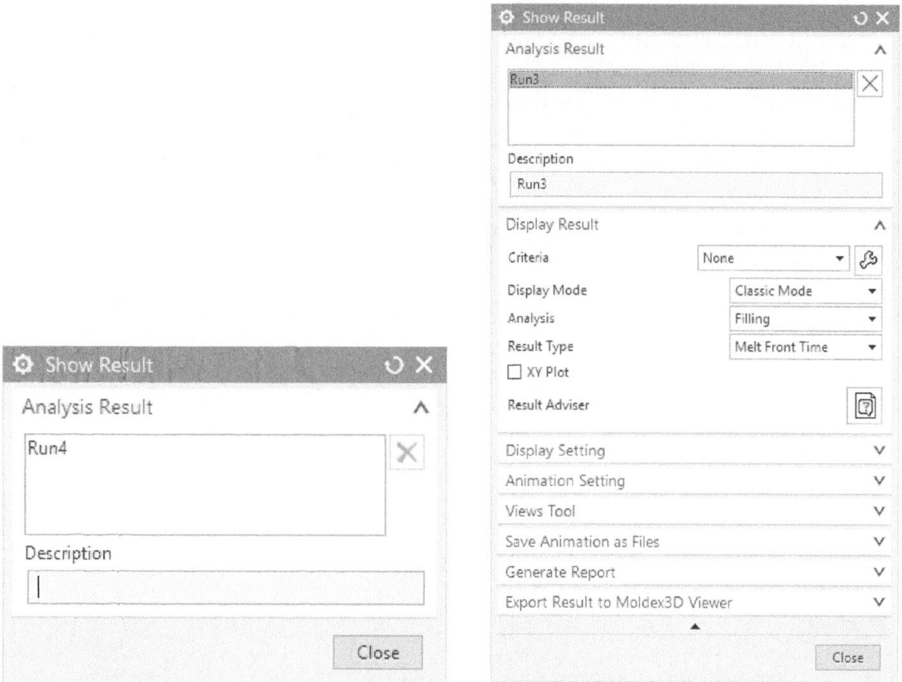

*Figure 15-22 The **Show Result** dialog box and its modified version*

MOLD WIZARD

The Mold Wizard tab contains tools that help you to design injection mold automatically. Before using this wizard you should ensure that the library related to the mold is installed. The tools in this wizard are discussed next.

Initialize Project

Ribbon: Mold Wizard > Initialize Project

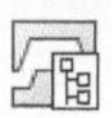

Initialize Project

The **Initialize Project** tool is used to create a new mold design project or to add new model to create a family mold. Choose the **Initialize Project** tool of the **Mold Wizard** tab, the **Initialize Project** dialog box will be displayed, as shown in Figure 15-23.

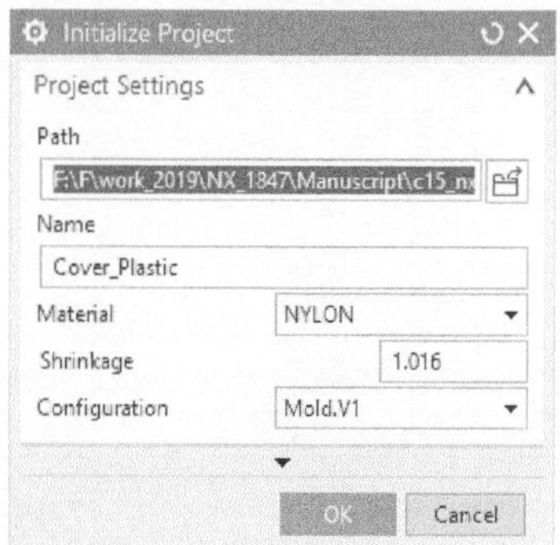

*Figure 15-23 The **Initialize Project** dialog box*

To specify the path of the project, choose the **Browse** button from the **Project Settings** rollout; the **Open** dialog box will be displayed, as shown in Figure 15-24.

Specify the path of the project and then choose the **OK** button to close the dialog box. Select the name of the material from the **Material** drop-down list of the **Initialize Project** dialog box. Next, choose the **OK** button to close the dialog box; the **New Iray+ Ray Traced Studio Rendering** window will be displayed. Choose the **OK** button to close the window.

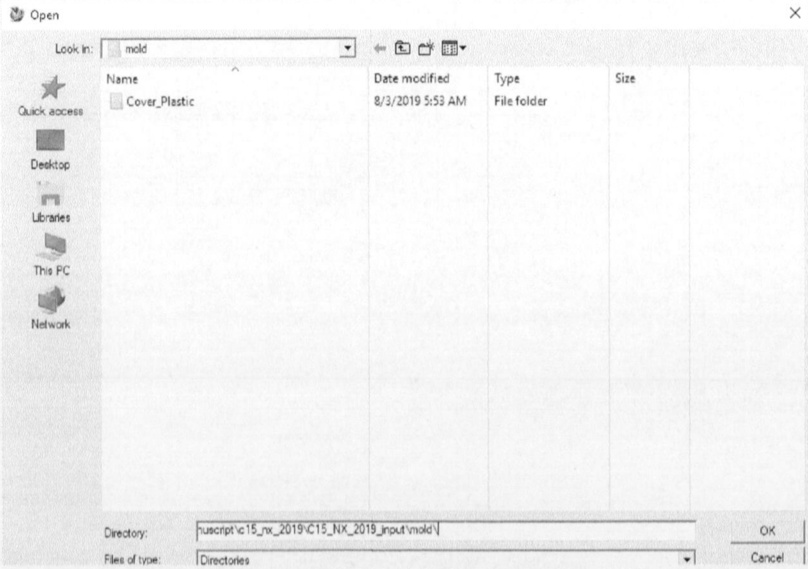

*Figure 15-24 The **Open** dialog box*

Mold CSYS

Ribbon: Mold Wizard > Main Gallery > Mold CSYS

The **Mold CSYS** tool is used to reposition the original component to the correct orientation according to the mold assembly or to the injection molding machine. While positioning the component, you should consider following points while placing the component in mold wizard:

- Orient the component so that ejection occurs in z-axis of the mold base.
- Position the component in such a way that parting plane lies on X-Y plane.

To orient the component, invoke the **Mold CSYS** tool from the **Main** gallery of the **Mold Wizard** tab; the **MOLD CSYS** dialog will be displayed, refer to Figure 15-25.

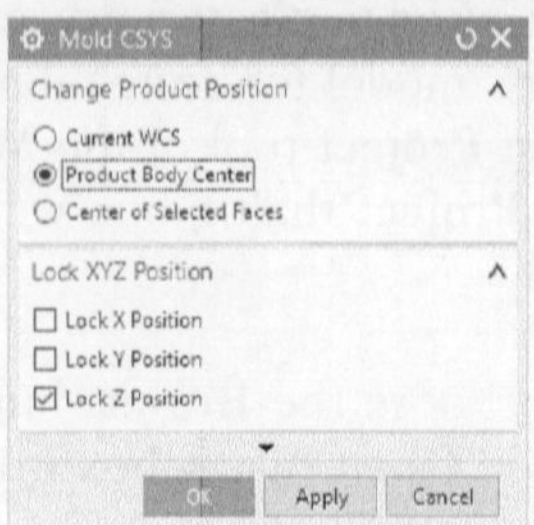

*Figure 15-25 The **Mold CSYS** dialog box*

In the **Change Product Position** rollout of this dialog box, there are three options to change the position of the component. These options are discussed next.

Current WCS

Select this radio button to reposition the component from the current WCS position and orientation to the position and orientation of the mold base.

Product Body Center

Select this radio button to reposition the WCS to the center of the component body. When you select this radio button, the **Lock XYZ Position** rollout will be displayed. The options in this rollout help you to lock the position of X,Y, and Z coordinates of the component.

Center of Selected Faces

Select this radio button to reposition the component from the center of one or more selected faces to the origin of the mold base. As you select this radio button, the **Lock XYZ Position** rollout gets available. The options in this rollout help you to lock the postion of X,Y, and Z coordinates of the component.

Shrinkage

Ribbon: Mold Wizard > Main Gallery > Shrinkage

When a molten plastic filled inside a mold is cooled, it solidifies and shrinks to some extent, this process is known as Shrinkage.

The **Shrinkage** tool helps you to apply the scale factor on the product model. While defining the scale factor, you should consider the following points:

- Type of molding material.
- Wall thickness of the molded part.
- Cavity surface temperature.
- Gate shape.
- Presence of additive material to the molding materials.

To apply shrinkage on the model, choose the **Shrinkage** tool from the **Main** gallery of the **Mold Wizard** tab; the **Scale Body** dialog box will be displayed.

Type Drop-down List

This drop-down list is used to specify the type of shrinkage that you need to apply to the component.

Uniform

This option is used to scale the body uniformly in all directions.

Axisymmetric

This option is used to scale the body symmetrically with a specified scale factor about specified axis.

General

This option is used to scale the body with different scale factors along the X,Y and Z directions.

After scaling the body, choose the **OK** button to close the dialog box.

Check Regions

Ribbon: Mold Wizard > Parting Tools Gallery > Check Regions

The **Check Regions** tool is used to analyze the draft angle of faces, set the color in the faces according to the draft values, and find undercut in the model. It also helps to find the core and cavity regions in the model. To analyze the core and cavity region of the model, invoke this tool from the **Parting Tools** gallery of the **Mold Wizard** tab; the **Check Regions** dialog box and the **Parting Navigator** window will be displayed, refer to Figures 15-26 and 15-27. Choose the **Calculate** button in the **Calculate** rollout and then choose the **Region** tab. In this tab, choose the **Set Regions Color** button from the **Define Regions** rollout; the color of the model gets changed. These colors represent core, cavity, and undefined region in the model.

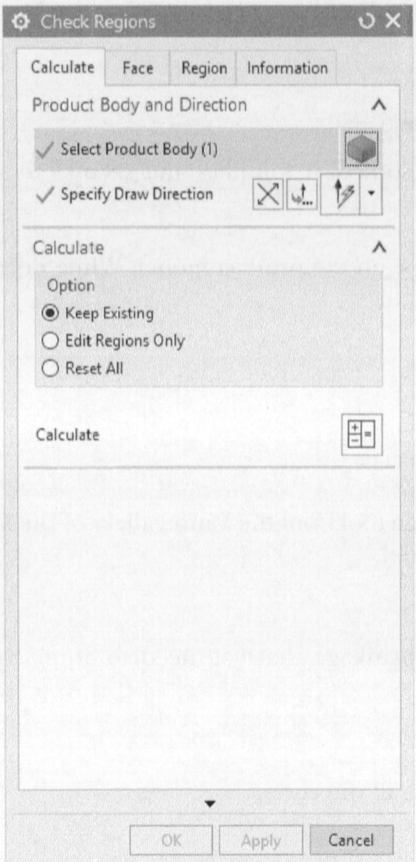

*Figure 15-26 The **Check Regions** dialog box*

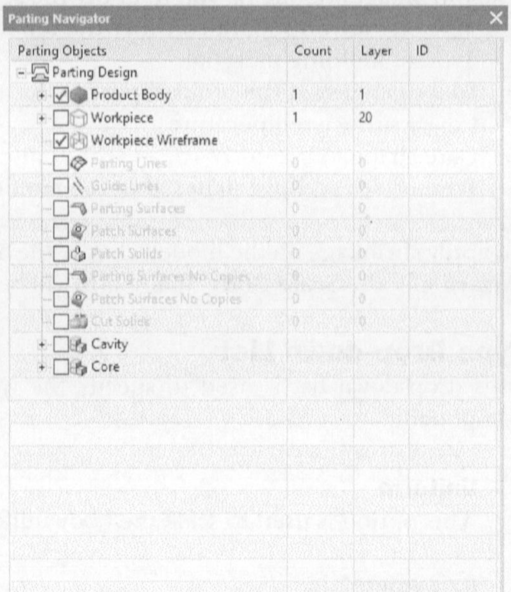

*Figure 15-27 The **Parting Navigator** window*

The **Cavity Region** radio button is selected by default in the **Assign To Region** rollout. Select the undefined region of the model and then choose the **Apply** button. The undefined region gets the color of the cavity region. Choose the **OK** button to close the dialog box.

Patch Surface

Ribbon:	Mold Wizard > Parting Tools Gallery > Patch Surface

This tool is used to create sheets to close openings in the model. To patch a surface, choose the **Patch Surface** tool from the **Parting Tools** gallery of the **Mold Wizard** tab; the **Edge Patch** dialog box will be displayed, refer to Figure 15-28. In NX Mold Wizard, you have three options in the **Type** drop-down list of the **Loop Selection** rollout: **Face**, **Body**, and **Traverse**.

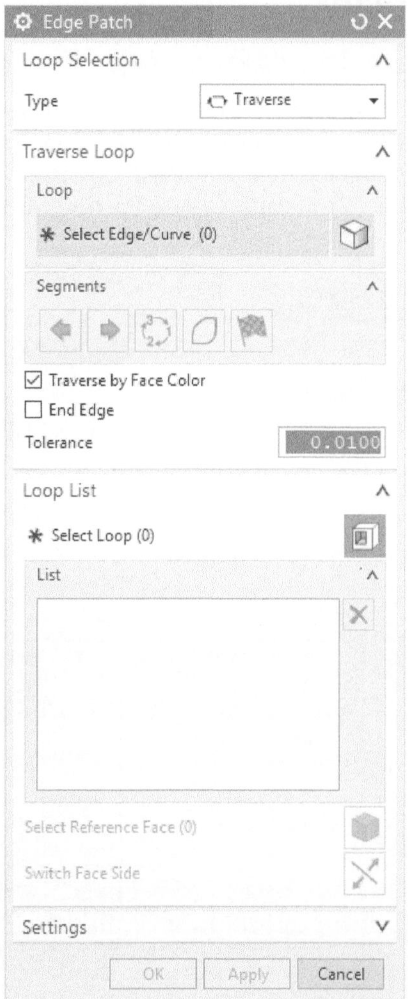

*Figure 15-28 The **Edge Patch** dialog box*

Define Regions

Ribbon: Mold Wizard > Parting Tools Gallery > Define Regions

This tool is used to create core and cavity region sheets, parting lines, and other region sheets (for sliders and lifters). To create core and cavity region sheets, choose the **Define Regions** tool from the **Parting Tools** gallery of the **Mold Wizard** tab; the **Define Regions** dialog box will be displayed, refer to Figure 15-29.

In the **Define Regions** rollout, you can examine the number of faces selected for cavity, core, and undefined faces which help you to identify the number of faces belonging to core and cavity. The procedure to create regions for core and cavity will be discussed in Tutorial 1.

Design Parting Surface

Ribbon: Mold Wizard > Parting Tools Gallery > Design Parting Surface

This tool is used to create a parting surface of the component. To create parting surface, invoke the **Design Parting Surface** tool from the **Parting Tools** gallery of the **Mold Wizard** tab; the **Design Parting Surface** dialog box will be displayed, refer to Figure 15-30. You can use the tools available in the **Auto Create Parting Surfaces** rollout to create parting surfaces.

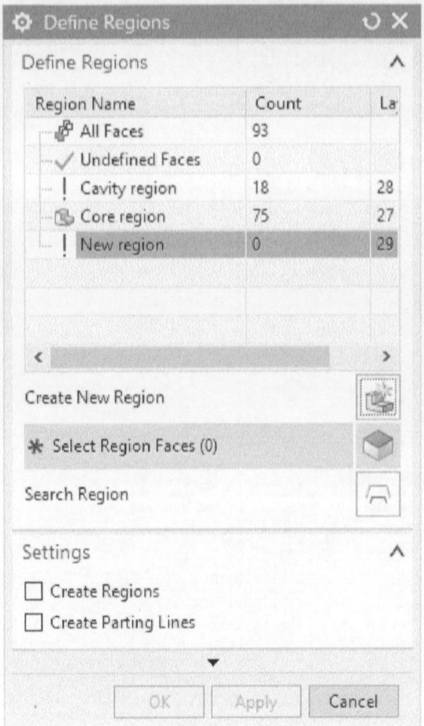

*Figure 15-29 The **Define Regions** dialog box*

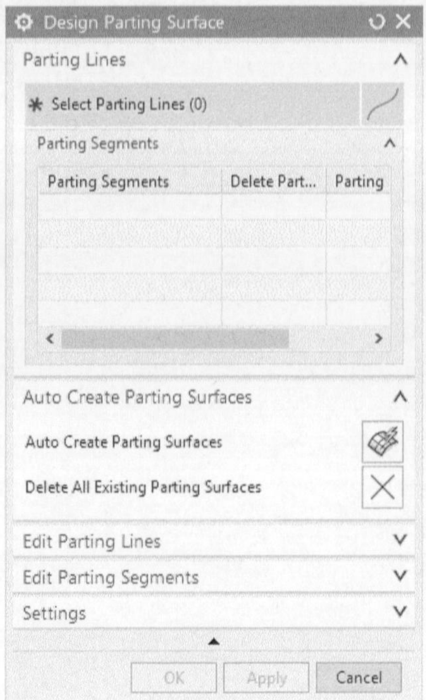

*Figure 15-30 The **Design Parting Surface** dialog box*

Edit Parting and Patch Surface

Ribbon: Mold Wizard > Parting Tools Gallery > Edit Parting and Patch Surface

This tool is used to delete parting and patch sheets. To edit parting and patch surface, choose the **Edit Parting and Patch Surface** tool from the **Parting Tools** gallery of the **Mold Wizard** tab; the **Edit Parting and Patch Surface** dialog box will be displayed, refer to Figure 15-31. You can select the type of surface to be edited from the Type drop-down list of the **Type** rollout.

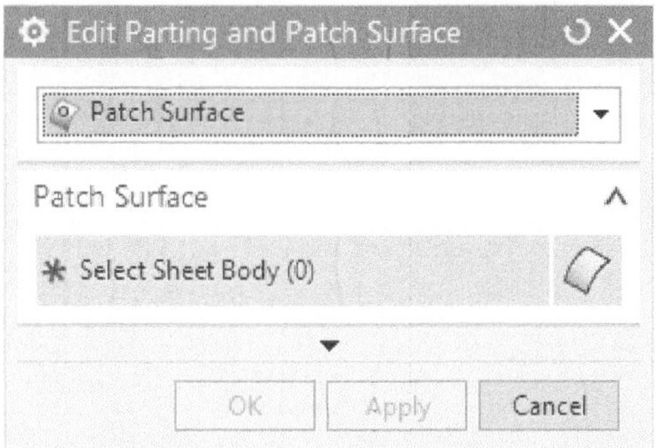

*Figure 15-31 The **Edit Parting and Patch Surface** dialog box*

Workpiece

Ribbon: Mold Wizard > Main Gallery > Workpiece

This tool helps you to define the size of core and cavity. To define the size, choose the **Workpiece** tool from the **Main** gallery of the **Mold Wizard** tab; the **New Iray+ Ray Traced Studio Rendering** window will be displayed. Choose the **OK** button from this window; the **Workpiece** dialog box will be displayed, refer to Figure 15-32. The options in this dialog box are discussed next.

Type Drop-down List

The options in the drop-down list are used to define whether you want to create core and cavity for single component or multiple components.

Product Workpiece

This option helps you to create the core and cavity for single component.

Combined Workpiece

This option helps you to create the core and cavity for multiple components.

Workpiece Method Rollout

The options in the drop-down list in this rollout are used to define the way you want to create the workpiece. The options available in the drop-down list are:

(i) User Defined Block
(ii) Cavity-Core

(iii) Cavity Only
(iv) Core Only

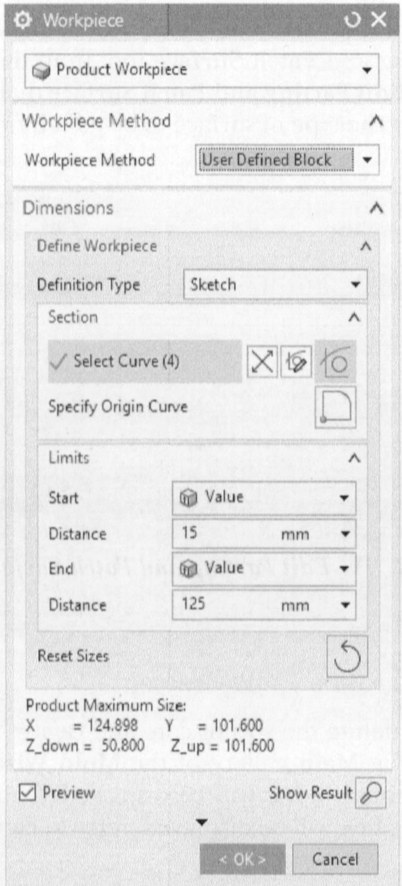

*Figure 15-32 The **Workpiece** dialog box*

Dimensions Rollout

The options in this rollout help you to define the size of the workpiece. After specifying the size of the workpiece, choose the **OK** button to close the dialog box.

Cavity Layout

Ribbon: Mold Wizard > Main Gallery > Cavity Layout

This tool helps you to create the layout of core and cavity workpiece. To do so, choose the **Cavity Layout** tool from the **Main** gallery of the **Mold Wizard** tab; the **Cavity Layout** dialog box will be displayed, refer to Figure 15-33. Also, the workpiece will be selected automatically, as shown in Figure 15-34. The options available in various rollouts of the **Cavity Layout** dialog box are discussed next.

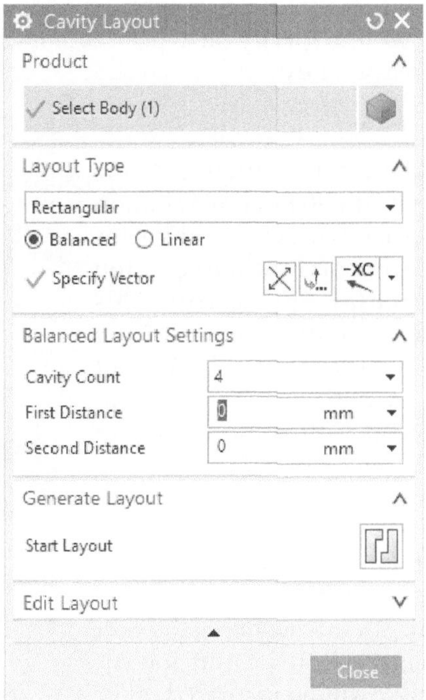

Figure 15-33 The ***Cavity Layout*** *dialog box*

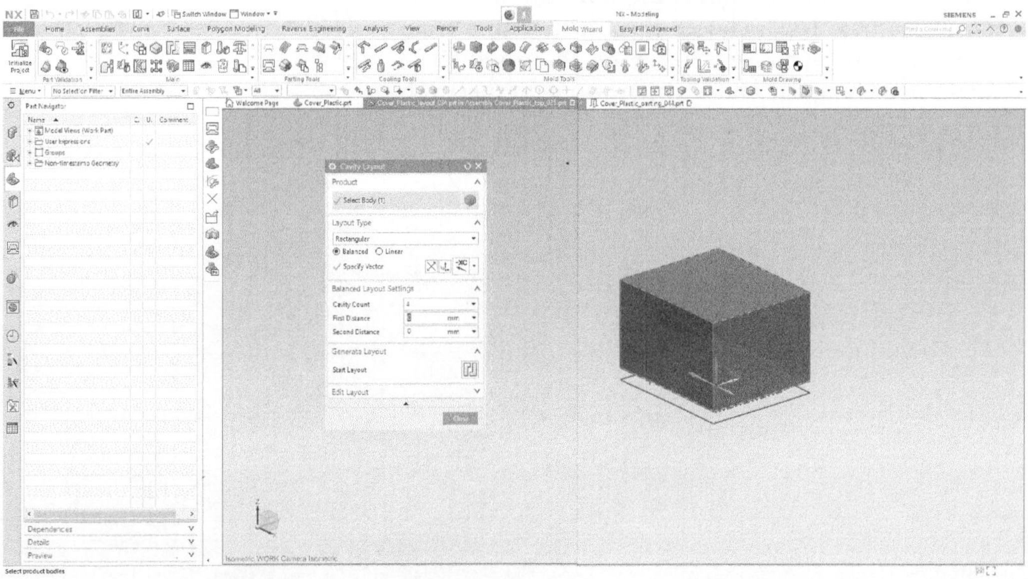

Figure 15-34 *The workpiece selected automatically*

Product Rollout

The option in this rollout is used to select the workpiece.

Layout Type Rollout

The options in this rollout are used to specify the type of orientation to be created. The options available in this rollout are discussed next.

Layout Type

The options in this drop-down list are used to define the layout type for the cavity. The **Rectangular** option in this drop-down list is selected by default and helps you to create rectangular layout of the workpiece. You can also choose the **Circular** option from this drop-down list to create a circular layout of the component. The **Specify Vector** area in the **Layout Type** rollout helps you to define the directional placement of the component with respect to other component. Specify the parameter of the layout in the **Balanced Layout Settings** or **Circular Layout Settings** rollout. To create the rectangular or circular layout, choose the **Start Layout** button from the **Generate Layout** rollout; the preview of the layout will be displayed in the window. After that, choose the **Edit Insert Pocket** button from the **Edit Layout** rollout; the **Insert Pocket** dialog box will be displayed, refer to Figure 15-35. Select the desired value from the **R** and **type** drop-down lists. Choose the **OK** button to close the dialog box. Next, choose the **Close** button from the **Cavity Layout** dialog box. Figures 15-36 and 15-37 show the rectangular and circular layouts respectively.

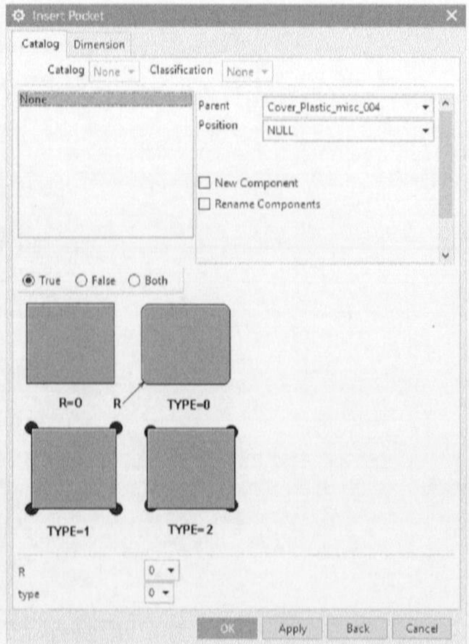

***Figure 15-35** The **Insert Pocket** dialog box*

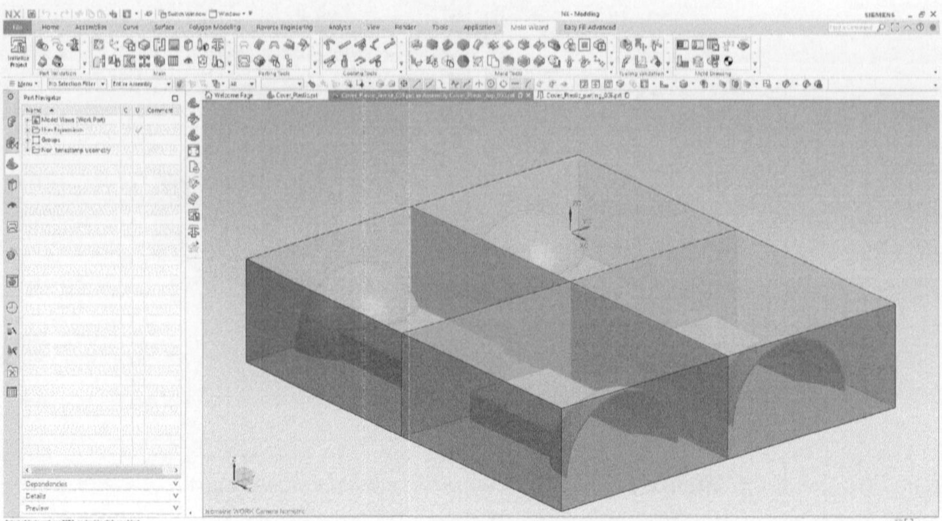

***Figure 15-36** The rectangular layout of workpiece*

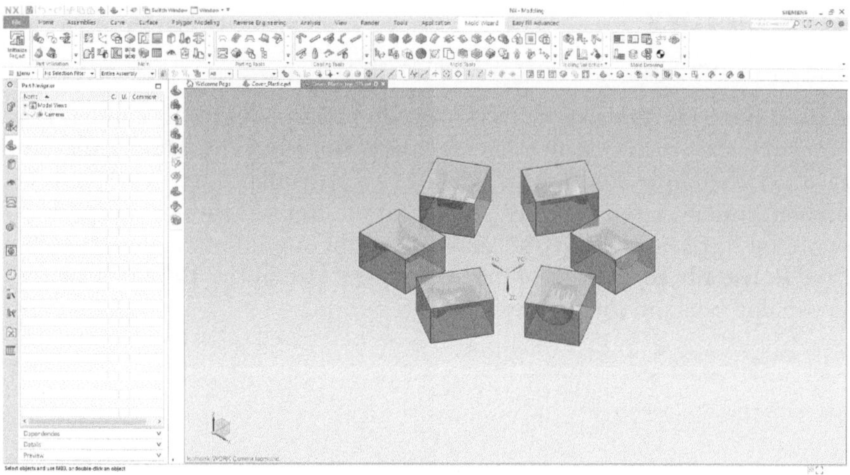

Figure 15-37 The circular layout of workpiece

Define Cavity and Core

Ribbon: Mold Wizard > Parting Tools Gallery > Define Cavity and Core

This tool helps you to create core and cavity of the component. To create core and cavity of the model, choose the **Define Cavity and Core** tool from the **Parting Tools** gallery of the **Mold Wizard** tab; the **Define Cavity and Core** dialog box will be displayed, refer to Figure 15-38. In the dialog box, the **Cavity region** area is selected by default in the **Select Sheets** rollout. Choose the **Apply** button; the **New Iray+ Ray Traced Studio Rendering** window will be displayed. Choose the **OK** button; the **View Parting Result** dialog box will be displayed. Check if the core or cavity is correct otherwise choose the **Reverse Normal** button. Choose the **OK** button; the **Define Cavity and Core** dialog box is displayed again. Select the **Core region** area from the **Select Sheets** rollout. Choose the **Apply** button; the **New Iray+ Ray Traced Studio Rendering** window will be displayed. As you choose the **OK** button to close the window; the **View Parting Result** dialog box will be displayed. Check the core or cavity is correct otherwise choose the **Reverse Normal** button. Choose the **OK** button to close the window; the **Define Cavity and Core** dialog box displayed again. Choose the **Cancel** button to close the dialog box. Click the left mouse button and then choose the **Switch Window** tool from the popup mini bar to check the core and cavity window.

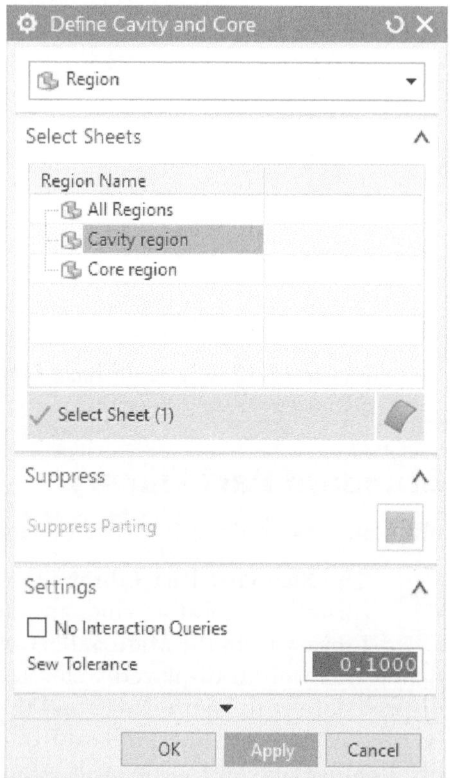

*Figure 15-38 The **Define Cavity and Core** dialog box*

Mold Base Library

Ribbon: Mold Wizard > Main Gallery > Mold Base Library

The **Mold Base Library** tool helps you to add mold plates to the core and cavity. To add mold plates, choose the **Mold Base Library** tool from the **Main** gallery of the **Mold Wizard** tab; the **Mold Base Library** dialog box is displayed, refer to Figures 15-39. Also, the **Information** window, refer to Figure 15-40 and the **Reuse Library** navigator on the left of the window will be displayed. Select the standard of the mold base from the **MW Mold Base Library** of the **Reuse library** navigator and specify the size in the **Details** rollout of the **Mold Base Library** dialog box and then choose the **OK** button.

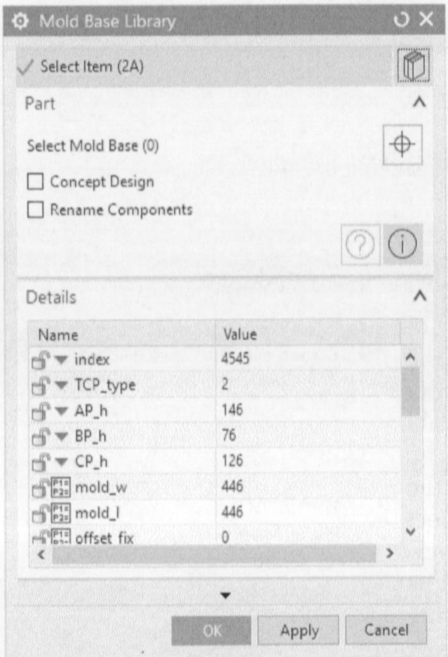

Figure 15-39 The ***Mold Base Library*** *dialog box*

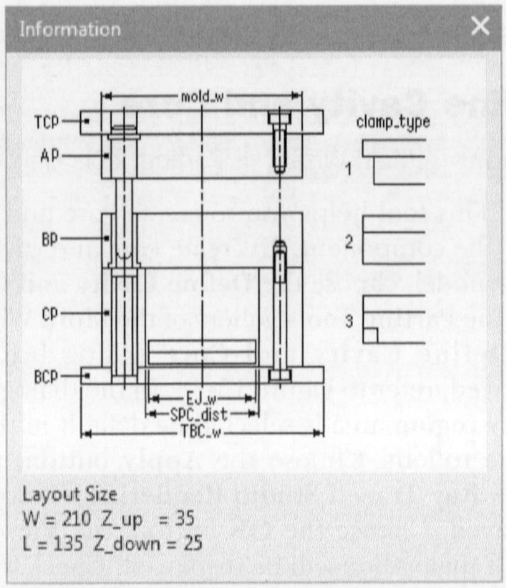

Figure 15-40 The ***Information*** *window*

Standard Part Library

Ribbon: Mold Wizard > Main Gallery > Standard Part Library

The **Standard Part Library** tool helps you to add the standard parts in the mold like sprue bush, locating ring, and so on. To add a standard part, choose the **Standard Part Library** from the **Main** gallery of the **Mold Wizard** tab; the **Standard Part Management** dialog box will be displayed, refer to Figures 15-41. Also, the **Information** window will be displayed, refer to Figure 15-42 and the **Reuse Library** navigator on the left in the window will be displayed. Select the standard from the **MW Standard Part Library** of the **Reuse Library** like locating ring and sprue bush. After specifying the parameters of the parts, choose the **OK** button to close the dialog box.

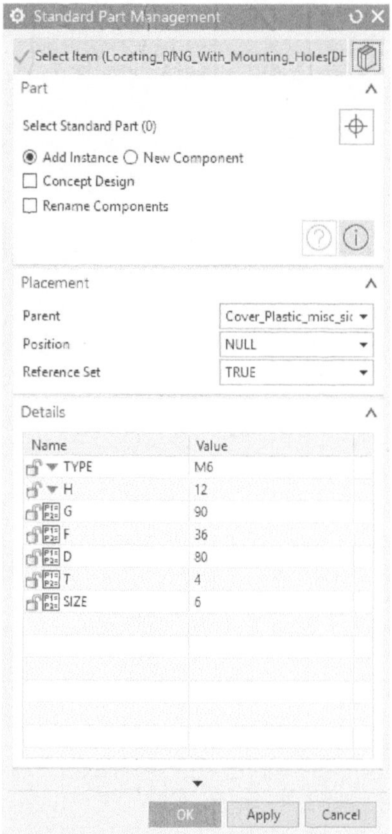

Figure 15-41 The ***Standard Part Management*** *dialog box*

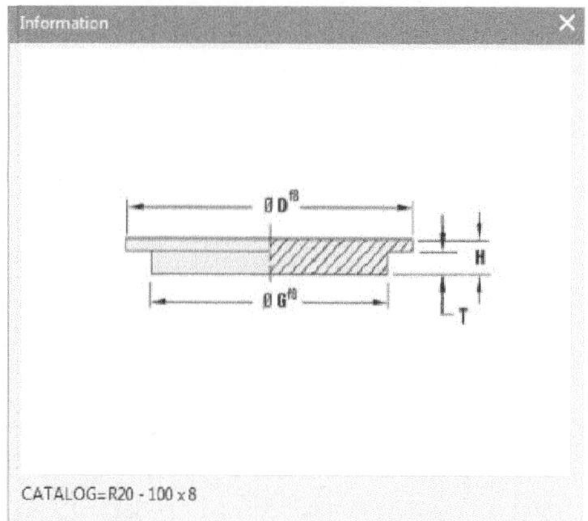

Figure 15-42 The ***Information*** *window*

Design Fill

Ribbon: Mold Wizard > Main Gallery > Design Fill

The **Design Fill** tool helps you to create a gate which connects with core or cavity. To create a gate, choose the **Design Fill** tool from the **Main** gallery of the **Mold Wizard** tab; the **Design Fill** dialog box will be displayed, refer to Figures 15-43. Also, the **Information** window, refer to Figure 15-44 and the **Reuse Library** will be displayed on the left in the drawing window. Select the required type of gate from the **MW Standard Part Library** of the **Reuse Library** and then specify the parameters in the **Details** rollout of the **Design Fill** dialog box and then choose the **OK** button to close the dialog box.

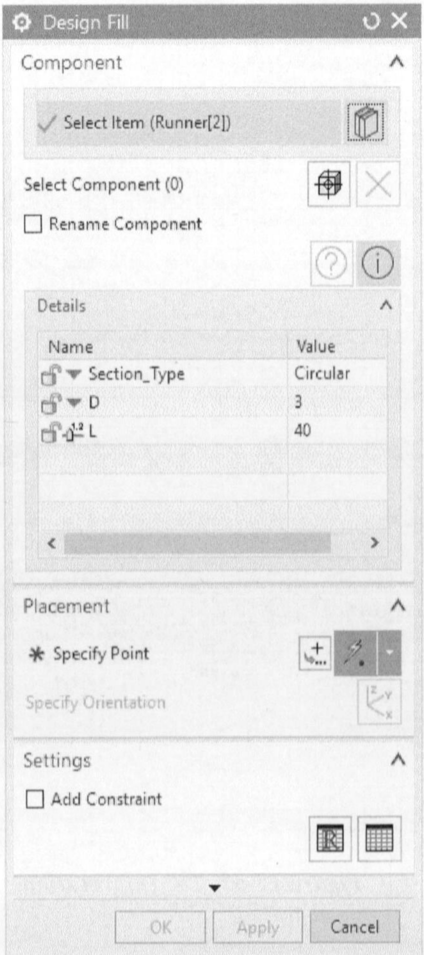

*Figure 15-43 The **Design Fill** dialog box*

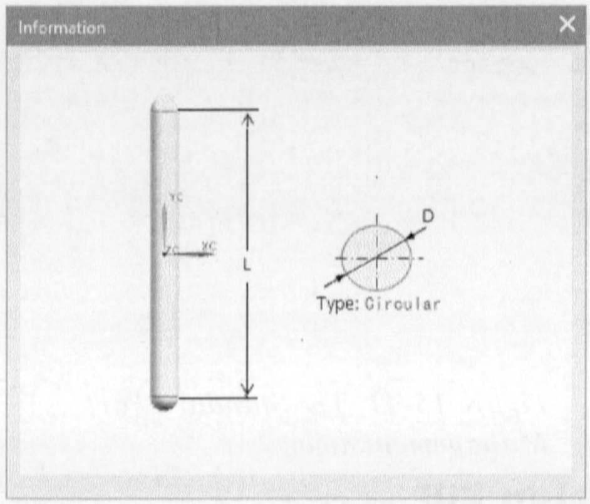

*Figure 15-44 The **Information** window*

Runner

Ribbon: Mold Wizard > Main Gallery > Runner

The **Runner** tool helps you to create the runner which connects with sprue bush and gate. To create a runner, choose the **Runner** tool from the **Main** gallery of the **Mold Wizard** tab; the **Runner** dialog box will be displayed, refer to Figures 15-45. Also, the **Information** window will be displayed, refer to Figure 15-46 and the **Reuse Library** will be displayed on the left in the drawing window. Create the sketch of the runner layout and select the type of runner cross-section. Specify the parameters of runner and then choose the **OK** button to close the dialog box.

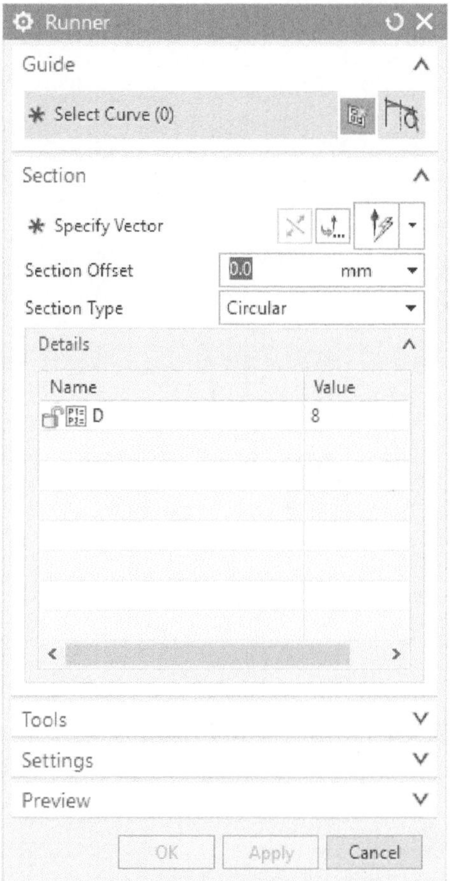

*Figure 15-45 The **Runner** dialog box*

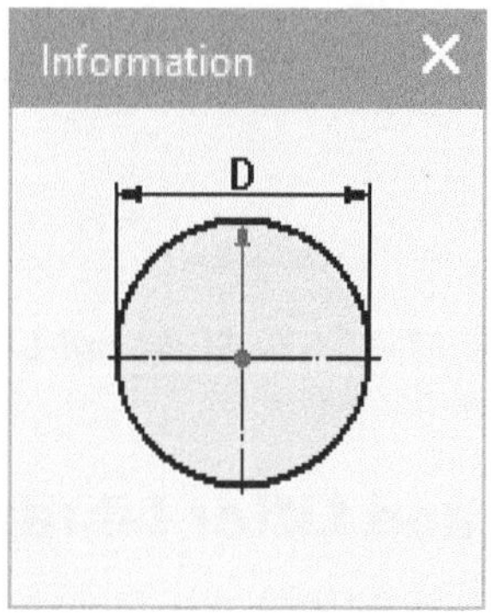

*Figure 15-46 The **Information** window*

Slider and Lifter Library

Ribbon: Mold Wizard > Main Gallery > Slide and Lifter Library

The **Slide and Lifter Library** tool helps you to create a slider in mold design. To create the slider, choose the **Slide and Lifter Library** tool from the **Main** gallery of the **Mold Wizard** tab; the **Slide and Lifter Design** dialog box will be displayed, refer to Figure 15-47. Also the **Information** window will be displayed, refer to Figure 15-48 and the **Reuse Library** navigator will be displayed on the left in the drawing window. Select the type of slider from the **Member Select** panel of the **Reuse Library** and specify the parameter in the **Details** rollout of the **Slide and Lifter Design** dialog box. Choose the **OK** button to close the dialog box.

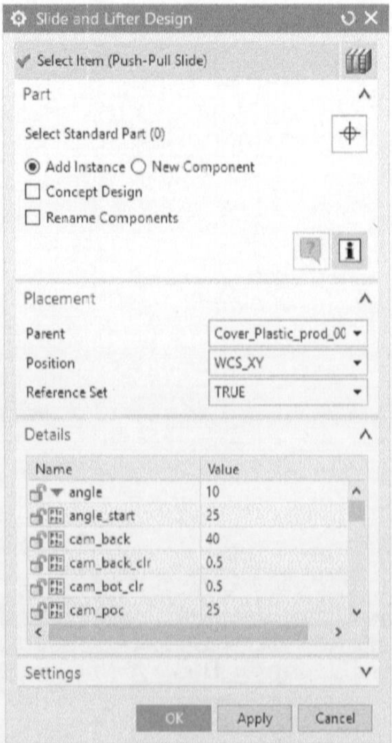

*Figure 15-47 The **Slide and Lifter Design** dialog box*

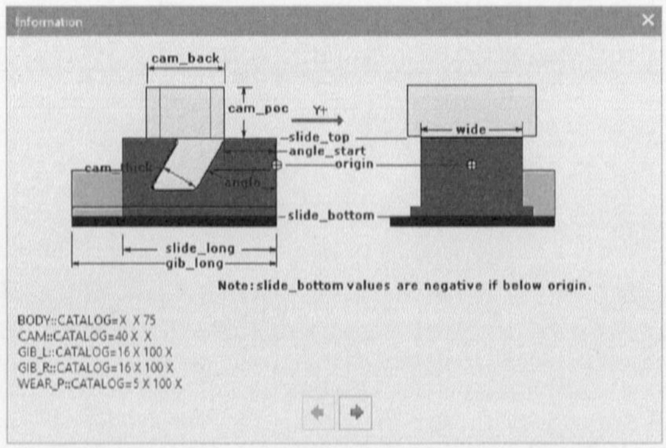

*Figure 15-48 The **Information** window*

Slider and Lifter Library

Ribbon: Mold Wizard > Main Gallery > Slider and Lifter Library

The **Slide and Lifter Library** tool helps you to create lifters in mold design. To create a lifter, choose the **Slide and Lifter Library** tool from the **Main** gallery of the **Mold Wizard** tab; the **Slide and Lifter Design** dialog box will be displayed, refer to Figures 15-49. Also, the **Information** window, refer to Figure 15-50, and the **Reuse Library** navigator will be displayed on the left in the drawing window. Select the **Lifter** from the **SLIDE_LIFT** sub-tree of the **MW Slide and Lifter Library** tree in the **Reuse Library**. Select the type of lifter from the **Reuse Library** and specify the parameters in the **Details** rollout of the **Slide and Lifter Design** dialog box. Choose the **OK** button to close the dialog box.

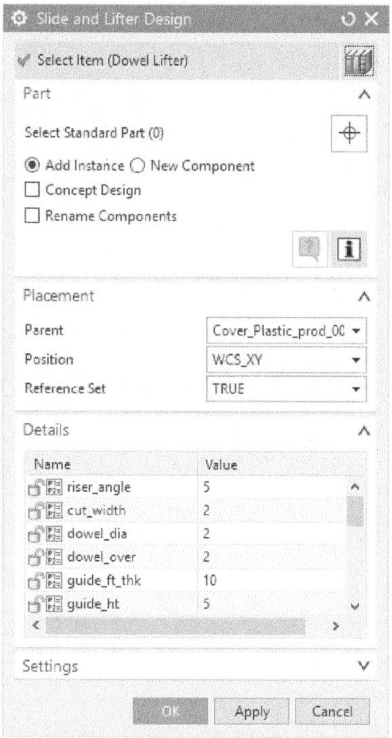

*Figure 15-49 The **Slide and Lifter Design** dialog box*

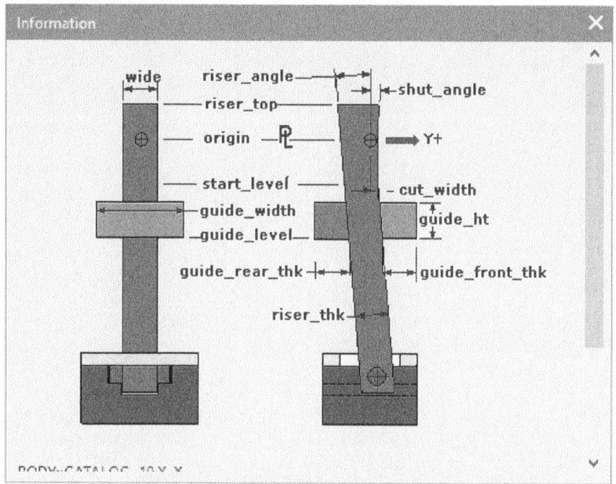

*Figure 15-50 The **Information** window*

Design Ejector Pin

Ribbon: Mold Wizard > Main Gallery > Design Ejector Pin

This tool helps you to create ejector pins that are used for ejection of the component. To create an ejector pin, choose the **Design Ejector Pin** tool from the **Main** gallery of the **Mold Wizard** tab; the **Design Ejector Pin** dialog box will be displayed, refer to Figure 15-51. Also, the **Information** Window, refer to Figure 15-52 and the **Reuse Library** navigator will be displayed on the left in the drawing window. Select the type of ejector pin from the **Member Select** panel of the **Reuse Library** and specify the parameters in the dialog box. Position the pin so that the ejection takes place and then choose the **OK** button to close the dialog box, refer to Figure 15-53.

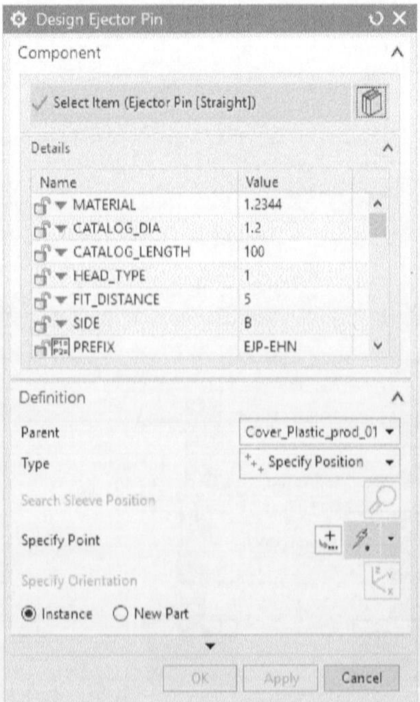

Figure 15-51 *The* ***Design Ejector Pin*** *dialog box*

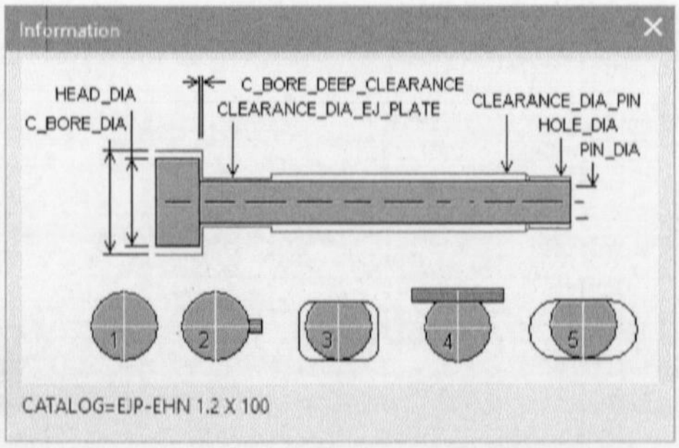

Figure 15-52 *The* ***Information*** *window*

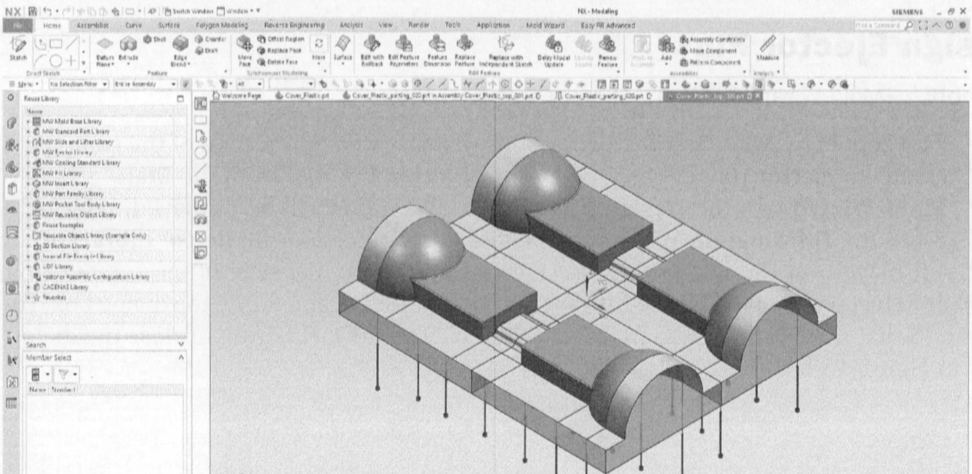

Figure 15-53 *The placement of ejector pin*

Ejector Pin Post Processing

Ribbon: Mold Wizard > Main Gallery > Ejector Pin Post Processing

This tool helps you to trim the ejector pin. To trim the ejector pin, choose the **Ejector Pin Post Processing** tool from the **Main** gallery of the **Mold Wizard** tab; the **Ejector Pin Post Processing** dialog box will be displayed, refer to Figure 15-54. Also, you prompted to select the target ejector pins. Select the ejector pins that you need to trim and then choose the **OK** button; the pins will be trimmed and the dialog box will be closed.

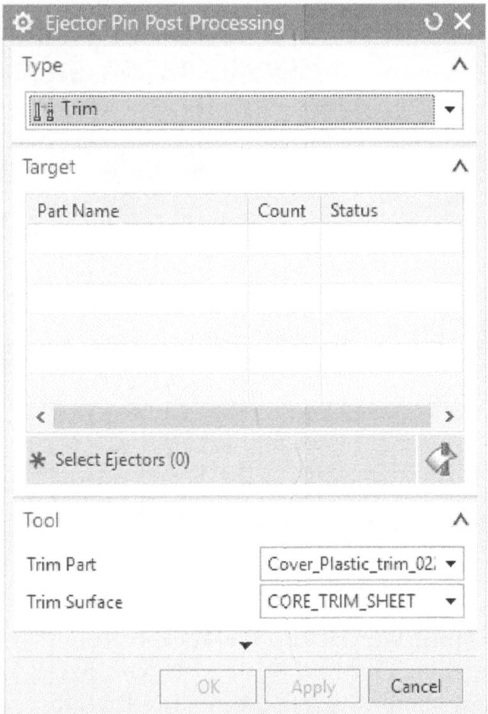

*Figure 15-54 The **Ejector Pin Post Processing** dialog box*

Sub-Insert Library

Ribbon: Mold Wizard > Main Gallery > Sub-Insert Library

This tool helps you to create and insert those components that go through wear and tear regularly or need regular replacement. Generally, the material of the insert is P20 or H13. To create the sub-insert in the core and cavity, choose the **Sub-insert Library** tool from the **Main** gallery of the **Mold Wizard** tab; the **Sub-insert Design** dialog box with the **Information** window will be displayed, refer to Figures 15-55 and 15-56. Specify whether you need **CORE SUB INSERT** or **CAVITY SUB INSERT** from the **Member Select** area of the **Reuse Library** navigator and then specify the parameters of the insert from the **Details** rollout of the dialog box. Choose the **OK** button to close the dialog box; the **Point** dialog box will be displayed. Specify the parameter in dialog box and then choose the **OK** button. Choose the **Cancel** button to close the dialog box.

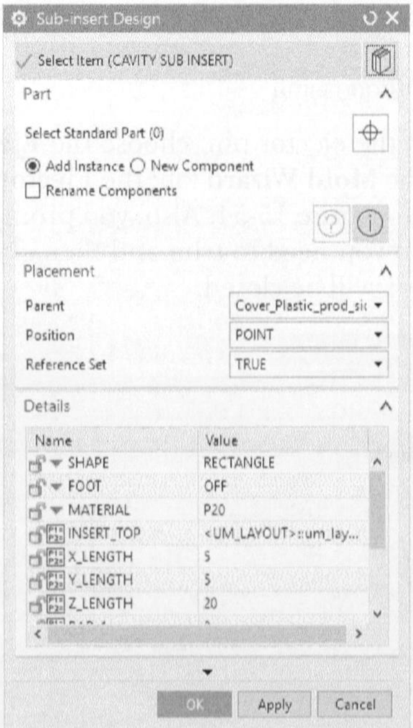

Figure 15-55 The **Sub-insert Design** *dialog box*

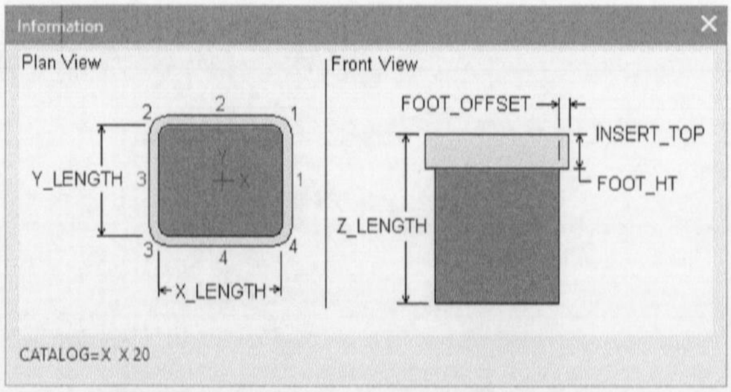

Figure 15-56 The **Information** *Window*

Pocket

Ribbon: Mold Wizard > Main Gallery > Pocket

This tool helps you to create pocket in the mold plates and inserts. To create a pocket, choose the **Pocket** tool from the **Main** gallery of the **Mold Wizard** tab; the **Pocket** dialog box will be displayed, refer to Figure 15-57. Also, you are prompted to select the target bodies, select the required mold plates or insert. By default, the **Subtract Material** option is selected in the **Mode** rollout of the dialog box. After selecting the body, click the **Select Object** area of the **Tool** rollout. Select the tool parts that are to be subtracted like ejector pin and then choose the **Apply** button from the dialog box. Repeat this step until the required subtraction has been done. Choose the **OK** button to close the dialog box.

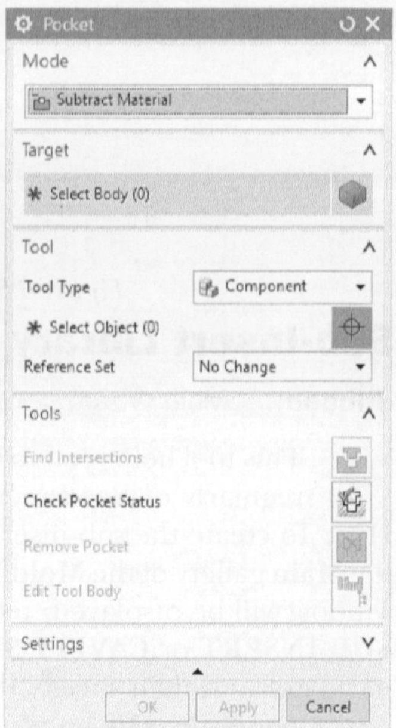

Figure 15-57 The **Pocket** *dialog box*

View Manager

Ribbon: Mold Wizard > Main Gallery > View Manager

This tool helps you to manage the display of the mold model components. As you choose this tool, the **View Manager** navigator will be displayed, refer to Figure 15-58. The functioning of this navigator is similar to assembly navigator.

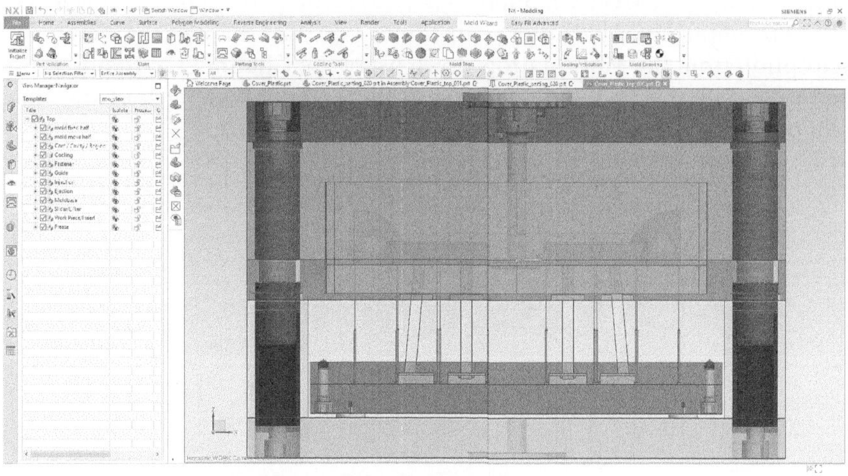

*Figure 15-58 The **View Manager** navigator*

Cooling

Cooling is a process required to cool the component. The cycle time of cooling plays an important role in mold costing. NX provides you the **Cooling Tools** gallery in which all the tools related to cooling are available. The procedure to create cooling channel are discussed next.

Pattern Channel

Ribbon: Mold Wizard > Cooling Tools Gallery > Pattern Channel

This tool is used to create the cooling channels using sketches or curves. To create a channel, choose the **Pattern Channel** tool from the **Cooling Tools** gallery of the **Mold Wizard** tab; the **Pattern Channel** dialog box will be displayed, refer to Figure 15-59. Also, you will be prompted to create the sketch or select the section geometry. After creating the sketch, specify the channel diameter in the **Setting** rollout and then choose the **OK** button from the dialog box.

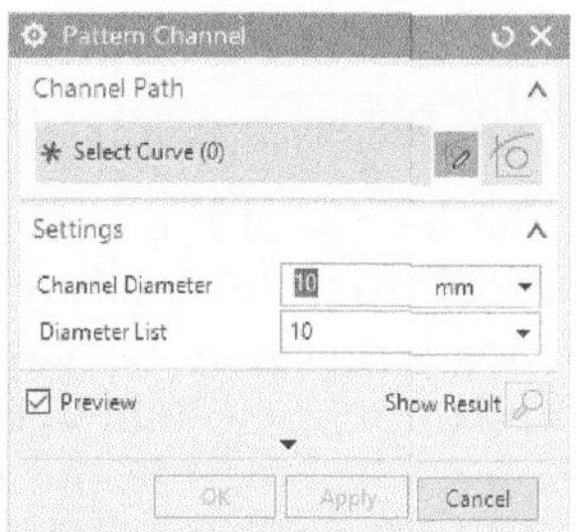

*Figure 15-59 The **Pattern Channel** dialog box*

Direct Channel

Ribbon: Mold Wizard > Cooling Tools Gallery > Direct Channel

This tool is used to create the cooling channel or baffle by specifying a specified point. To create a channel, choose the **Direct Channel** tool from the **Cooling Tools** gallery of

the **Mold Wizard** tab; the **Direct Channel** dialog box will be displayed, refer to Figure 15-60. Also, you will be prompted to select infer point. Select the start point of the channel. Next, select the **Distance** option from the **Motion** drop-down list of the **Channel Extrusion** rollout; you will be prompted to specify the vector direction and then enter the length of the channel in the **Distance** edit box. Choose the **OK** button to close the dialog box.

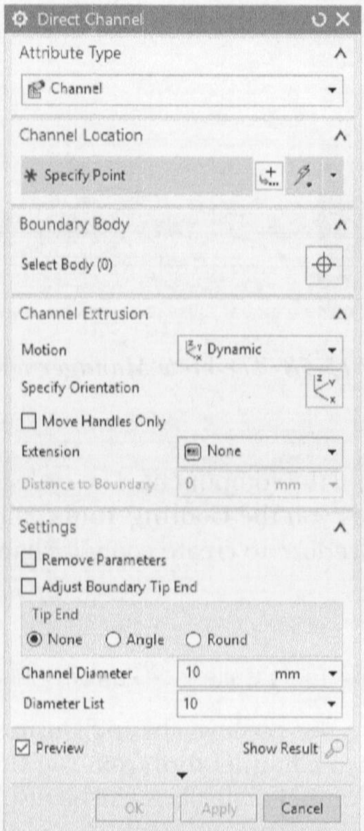

*Figure 15-60 The **Direct Channel** dialog box*

Extend Channel

Ribbon: Mold Wizard > Cooling Tools Gallery > Extend Channel

This tool is used to extend the length of the cooling channel. To extend the length, choose the **Extend Channel** tool from the **Cooling Tools** gallery of the **Mold Wizard** tab; the **Extend Channel** dialog box will be displayed, refer to Figure 15-61, and you will be prompted to select the cooling channel. Select the cooling channel and specify the length of the cooling channel in the **Distance** edit box. Choose the **OK** button; the length will be extended and the dialog box will be closed.

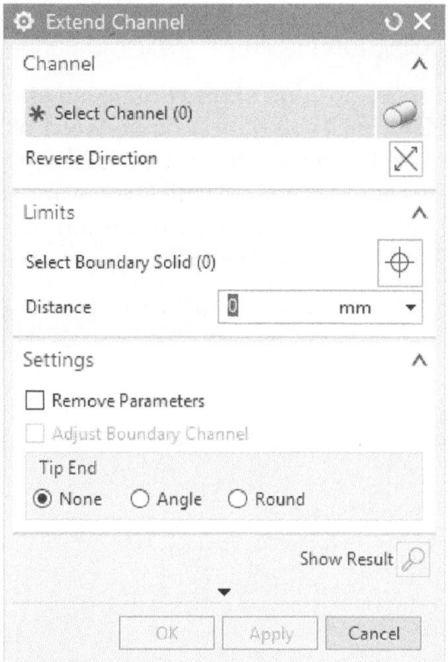

*Figure 15-61 The **Extend Channel** dialog box*

Connect Channels

Ribbon: Mold Wizard > Cooling Tools Gallery > Connect Channels

This tool is used to connect the cooling channel. To do so, choose the **Connect Channels** tool from the **Cooling Tools** gallery of the **Mold Wizard** tab; the **Connect Channels** dialog box will be displayed, refer to Figure 15-62. Also, you will be prompted to select the first cooling channel. Select the first cooling channel; you will be prompted to select the second cooling channel. Select the second cooling channel and then choose the **OK** button to close the dialog box.

*Figure 15-62 The **Connect Channels** dialog box*

Adjust Channel

Ribbon: Mold Wizard > Cooling Tools Gallery > Adjust Channel

This tool is used to adjust the position of the cooling channel. To do so, choose the **Adjust Channel** tool from the **Cooling Tools** gallery of the **Mold Wizard** tab; the **Adjust Channel** dialog box will be displayed, refer to Figure 15-63. Also, you will be prompted to select the cooling channel. Select the cooling channel which you want to adjust; a dynamic triad will be displayed on the channel. Move the channel by using handles and angular handles of the triad. After positioning the channel, choose the **OK** button to close the dialog box.

*Figure 15-63 The **Adjust Channel** dialog box*

Cooling Fittings

Ribbon: Mold Wizard > Cooling Tools Gallery > Cooling Fittings

This tool is used to add cooling fitting components to cooling channels. To add the components, choose the **Cooling Fittings** tool from the **Cooling Tools** gallery of the **Mold Wizard** tab; the **Cooling Fittings** dialog box will be displayed, refer to Figure 15-64, and you will be prompted to select the channel. Select the cooling channel and then choose the **OK** button; the dialog box will be closed and you will notice the o-rings in the mold cooling channel.

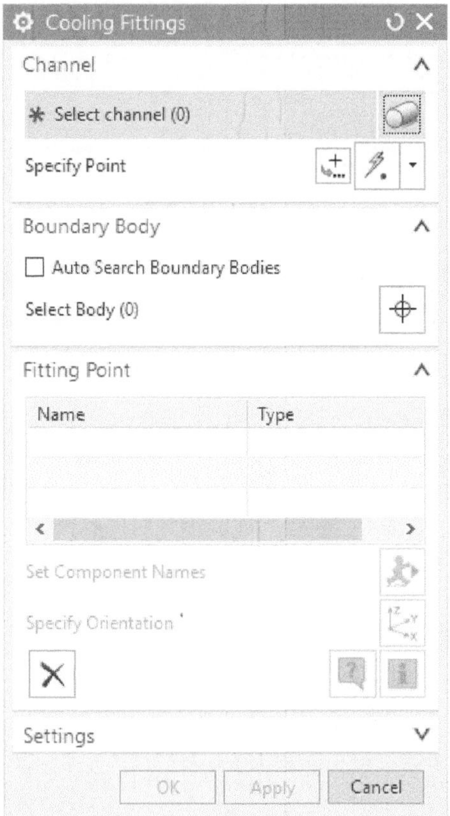

*Figure 15-64 The **Cooling Fittings** dialog box*

Assembly Drawings

Ribbon: Mold Wizard > Mold Drawing Gallery > Assembly Drawing

This tool helps you to create the drawing of the mold assembly. To create the drawing, choose the **Assembly Drawing** tool from the **Mold Drawing** gallery of the **Mold Wizard** tab; the **Assembly Drawing** dialog box will be displayed, refer to Figure 15-65. By default, the **Visibility** option is selected in the **Type** rollout. This option helps you to select the parts of the mold you want to show in the drawing. Select the component from the drawing area and then select the **Drawing** option from the drop-down list of the **Type** rollout. Select the **Self Contained** drawing type from the **Drawing Type** rollout and select the type of template from the **Templates** rollout. Choose the **Apply** button. Select the **View** option from the drop-down list of the **Type** rollout and then select the predefined views from the **View Control** rollout. Specify the scale value in the **Scale** edit box of the **View Control** rollout. Choose the **OK** button to close the dialog box.

***Figure 15-65** The **Assembly Drawing** dialog box*

Component Drawing

Ribbon: Mold Wizard > Mold Drawing Gallery > Component Drawing

This tool helps you to create and manage the drawing for components of the mold assembly. To create a drawing, choose the **Component Drawing** tool from the **Mold Drawing** gallery of the **Mold Wizard** tab; the **Component Drawing** dialog box will be displayed, refer to Figure 15-66. Select the component from the list in the **Drawing** rollout and then choose the **Create Drawing** button from the **Create Drawing** area of the **Drawing** rollout; the drawing will be generated.

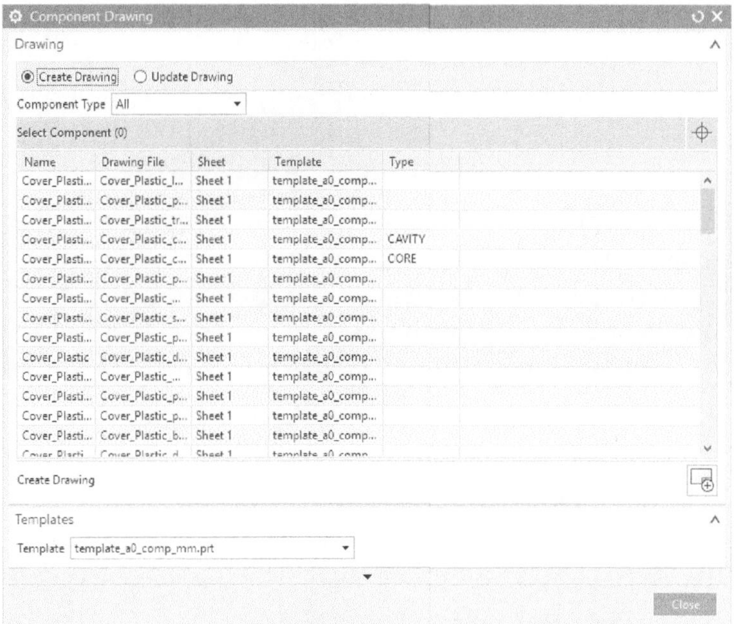

***Figure 15-66** The **Component Drawing** dialog box*

TUTORIAL

To perform the tutorial you need to download the zipped file named as *c15_NX_2019_input* from the Input Files section of the CADCIM website. The complete path for downloading the file is:

Textbooks > CAD/CAM > NX > Siemens NX 2019 for Designers > Input Files

After the file is downloaded, extract the folder to the location *C:\NX 2019* and rename it as *c15*.

Tutorial 1

In this tutorial, you will create mold design of the plastic cover part which is shown in Figure 15-67. Here, you will analyze the model and add mold base to it. Also you will create core and cavity, runner and gate, and add lifter, ejector pin, and cooling channels to the model.

After creating the mold design, save the mold design with the name *c15tut1.prt* at the location given below:

\NX\c15 **(Expected time: 3 hr)**

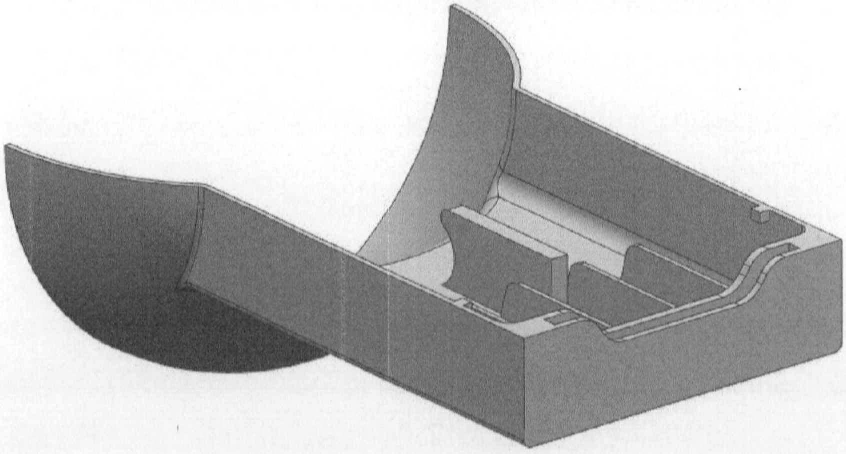

Figure 15-67 Plastic part for Tutorial 1

The following steps are required to complete this tutorial:

a. Start NX and open the model, refer to Figure 15-68.
b. Create gate for analyzing the model, refer to Figures 15-74 and 15-75.
c. Create runner and sprue for analyzing the model, refer to Figure 15-77.
d. Set Parting direction.
e. Start analysis and analyze the result, refer to Figures 15-85 through 15-90.
f. Initialize the project.
g. Orient the model, refer to Figures 15-94 and 15-95.
h. Create Parting surface, refer to Figures 15-99 through 15-103.
i. Create Core and Cavity, refer to Figures 15-110 and 15-111.
j. Add Mold Base, refer to Figure 15-113.
k. Add lifter for ejection and part shape, refer to Figure 15-116.
l. Add Register ring and sprue bush in mold, refer to Figures 15-118 through 15-120.
m. Add Ejector Pin for ejection of component, refer to Figure 15-124.
n. Create gate and runner, refer to Figures 15-129 and 15-130.
o. Create cooling channel for cooling the component, refer to Figure 15-133.

Starting NX and Opening a Model

First, you need to start NX and then open a new file.

1. Double-click on NX shortcut icon on the desktop of your computer to start NX.

Open

2. Choose the **Open** button from the **Standard** group of the **Home** tab or choose **Menu > File > Open** from the **Top Border Bar**; the **Open** dialog box is displayed.

3. Select **Cover_Plastic.prt** from the **Name** list; **Cover_Plastic.prt** is displayed in the **File name** drop-down list. Then choose the **OK** button; the model is displayed, refer to Figure 15-68.

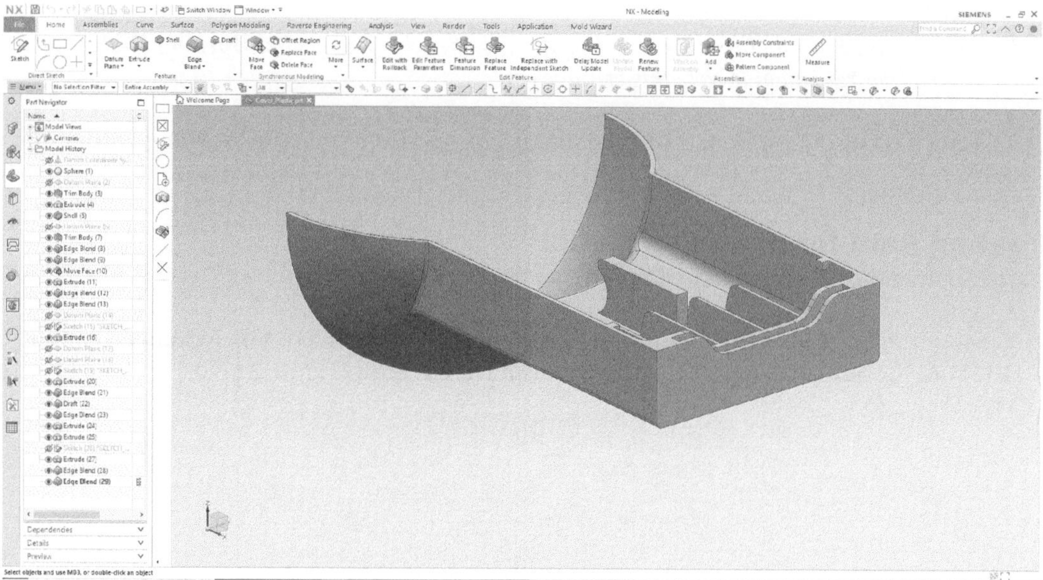

Figure 15-68 Plastic part in Modeling environment

Analyzing Model by Easy Fill Advanced

Now, use the tools in the **Easy Fill Advanced** tab for analyzing the model. It is a continuation process; if material does not fill properly then you need to do more and more iterations by changing gate, runner, coolant size, shape, or orientation.

1. Click on the **Easy Fill Advanced** tab and choose the **Set Working Folder** tool from the **Setting** group of the tab; the **Working Folder** dialog box is displayed.

2. Choose the **Browse** button; the **Open** dialog box is displayed where you can set the working folder, refer to Figure 15-69.

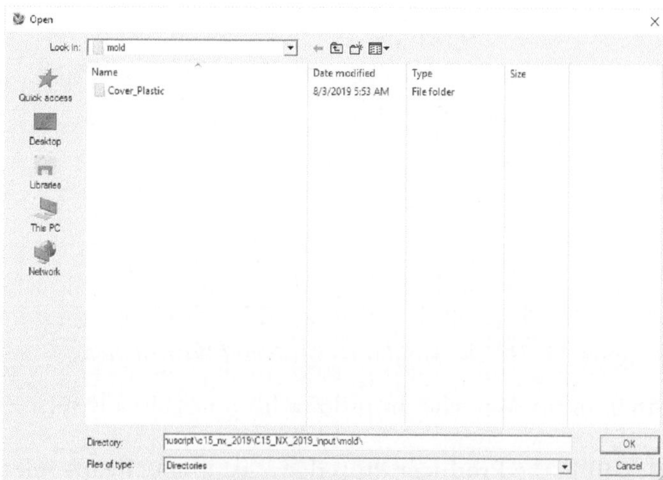

*Figure 15-69 The **Open** dialog box*

Note

*If the **Easy Fill Advanced** message box appears after choosing the **Set Working Folder** tool then choose the **Yes** button to close this message box.*

3. Choose the **OK** button from the **Open** dialog box and then from the **Working Folder** dialog box.

Creating Gate for Analyzing Model

To analyze the model you are going to create gate.

1. Choose the **Set Cavity** tool from the **Setting** group of the **Easy Fill Advanced** tab in the **Ribbon**; the **Select Cavity** dialog box is displayed, refer to Figure 15-70.

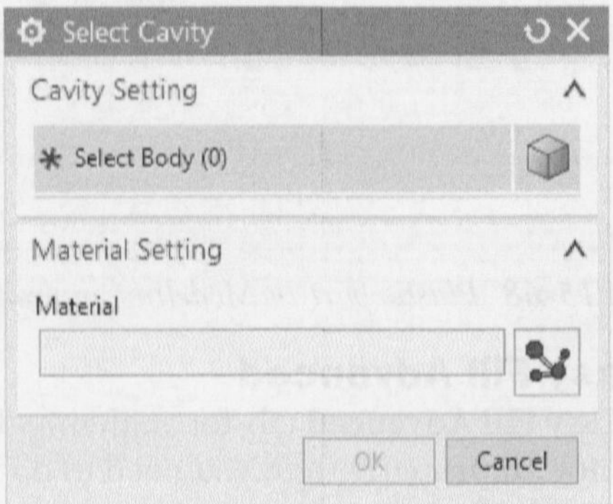

*Figure 15-70 The **Select Cavity** dialog box*

2. Select solid body from the **Select Body** area of the **Cavity Setting** rollout to specify solid body as cavity.

3. Choose the **Push button to select material** button in the **Material Setting** rollout; the **Moldex3D Material Wizard** dialog box is displayed, refer to Figure 15-71.

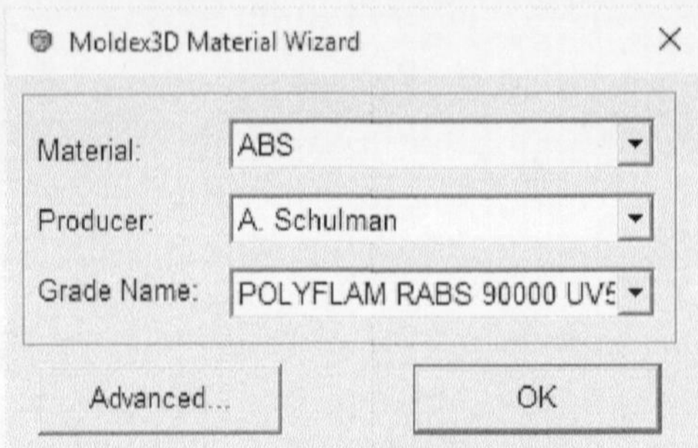

*Figure 15-71 The **Moldex3D Material Wizard** dialog box*

4. Select **ABS+PA6** from the **Material** drop-down list if not already selected.

5. Select **Styrolution** from the **Producer** drop-down list if not already selected.

6. Select **Terblend N NG-06** from the **Grade Name** drop-down list.

7. Choose the **OK** button from the **Moldex3D Material Wizard** and then choose the **OK** button from the **Select Cavity** dialog box.

8. Choose the **Gate Wizard** tool from the **Wizard** group; the **Create Gate** dialog box is displayed, refer to Figure 15-72.

9. Select **Edge Gate** from the **Type of gate** drop-down list to select the type of gate.

10. Select **Cold Runner Gate** from the **Attribute** drop-down list if not already selected.

11. Choose the **Point Dialog** button; the **Point** dialog box is displayed, refer to Figure 15-73.

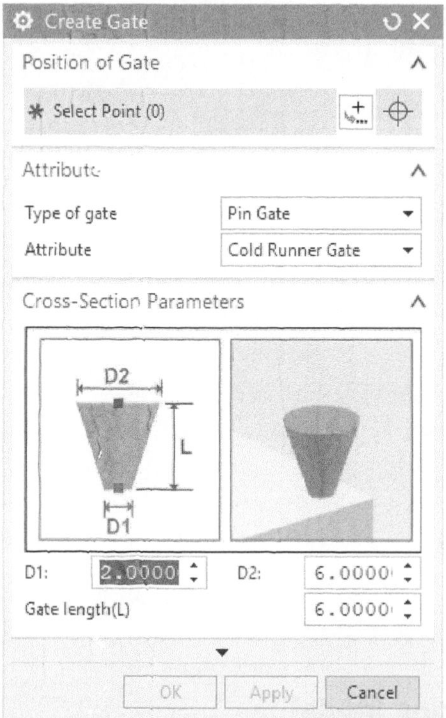

*Figure 15-72 The **Create Gate** dialog box*

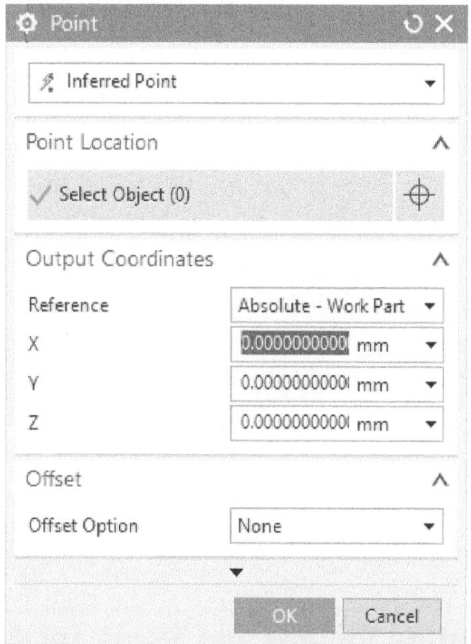

*Figure 15-73 The **Point** dialog box*

12. Select the **Point on Face** option from the Type drop-down list; you are prompted to select face at point location, refer to Figure 15-74, for face selection.

13. Enter **0.308** and **0.5** in the **U Parameter** and **V Parameter** edit boxes respectively, of the **Location on Face** rollout and choose the **OK** button from the **Point** dialog box to exit the dialog box.

14. Enter **90** and **5** in the **Angle** and **Gate length(L)** edit boxes respectively, of the **Cross-Section Parameters** rollout.

15. Choose the **OK** button to close the **Create Gate** dialog box. Refer to Figure 15-75 for model with gate.

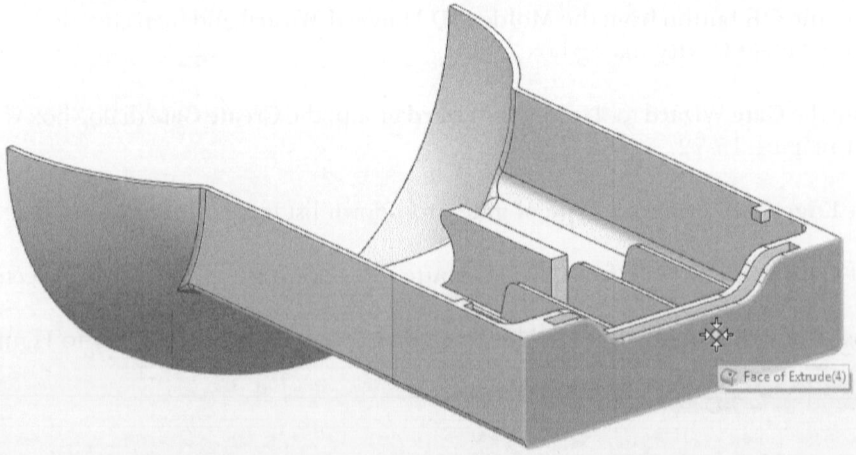

Figure 15-74 The face selected for gate placement

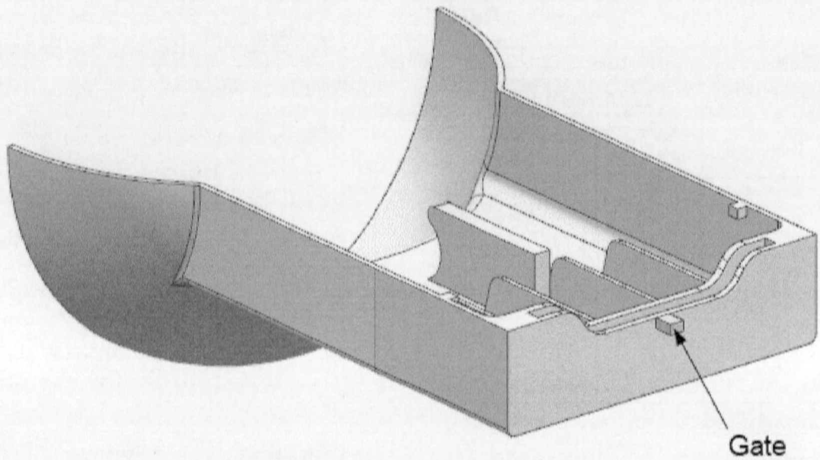

Figure 15-75 The model with Fan gate

Creating Runner and Sprue for Analyzing Model

To analyze the model, you are going to create runner and sprue.

1. Choose the **Runner Wizard** tool from the **Wizard** group; the **Runner Wizard** dialog box is displayed, refer to Figure 15-76.

By default, the **Mold Setting** tab is selected.

2. Select **- Z-Axis** from the **Parting Direction** drop-down list, **2-Plate mold** from the **Mold Plate Type** drop-down list, and **Cold Runner** from the **Runner Attribute** drop-down list.

3. Choose the **Sprue Setting** tab and enter **6**, **3**, and **45** in the **D1**, **D2,** and **SH** edit boxes respectively, of the **Sprue Geometry Parameters** rollout.

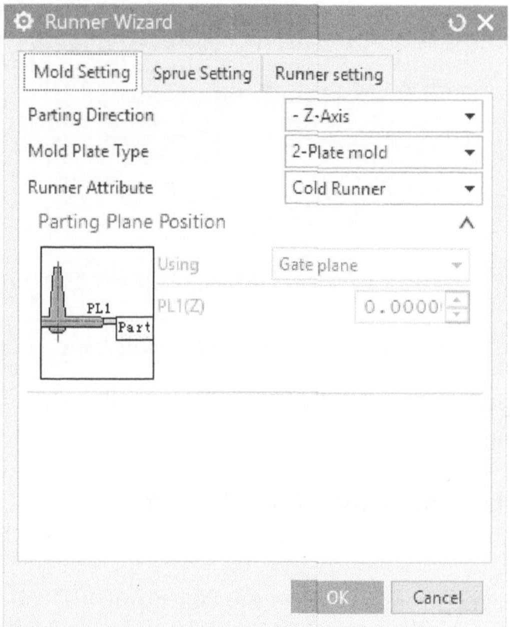

*Figure 15-76 The **Runner Wizard** dialog box*

4. Choose the **Runner setting** tab and then select the **Circular** type of cross section for runner from the **Type** drop-down list and enter **6** in the **D** edit box.

5. Choose the **OK** button to close this dialog box.

6. The gate, runner, and sprue are now attached to the model, refer to Figure 15-77.

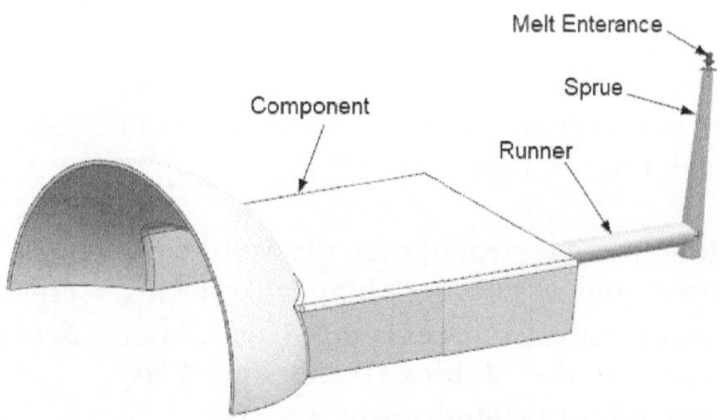

Figure 15-77 The Runner and Sprue with model

Setting the Parting Direction

To analyze the model, you are going to set the direction of ejection.

1. Choose the **Set Parting Direction** tool from the **Setting** group to set the parting direction of the model; the **vector** dialog box is displayed, refer to Figure 15-78.

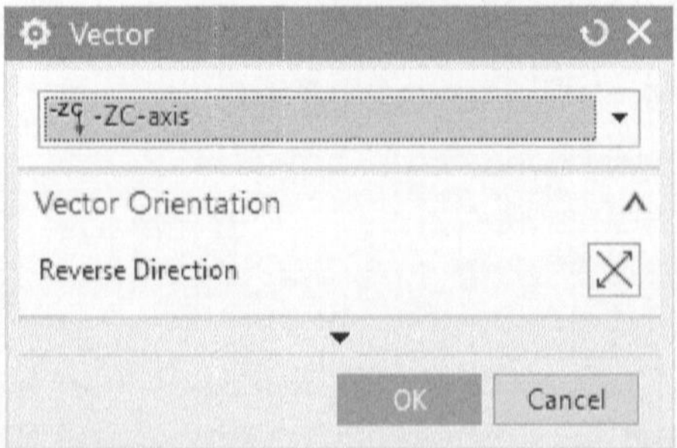

*Figure 15-78 The **Vector** dialog box*

2. Select the **ZC-Axis** option from the Type rollout if not already selected and choose the **OK** button to close the dialog box.

Starting Analysis and Analyzing the Result

The **Start Analysis** and **Show Result** tools help to analyze and show results.

1. Choose the **Start Analysis** tool from the **Setting** group to start the analysis of the model; the **Analysis Setup** dialog box is displayed, refer to Figure 15-79.

2. Select the **Filling & Packing - F P** option from the **Analysis** drop-down list of the **Analysis Set** rollout.

3. Enter **220, 0.25, 4.20, 250** and **60** in the **Maximum injection pressure, Filling time, Packing time, Melt Temperature,** and **Mold Temperature** edit boxes respectively, of the **Process Condition** rollout.

4. Choose the **OK** button; the dialog box closes and the **Moldex3D** window showing the solid mesh generation process gets displayed, refer to Figure 15-80.

   Note that after the solid mesh is created then the **Moldex3D SYNC Project Monitor** window showing filling and packing analysis progression is displayed, refer to Figure 15-81. After the completion of analysis, the **Moldex3D eDesignSYNC** window gets displayed, refer to Figure 15-82.

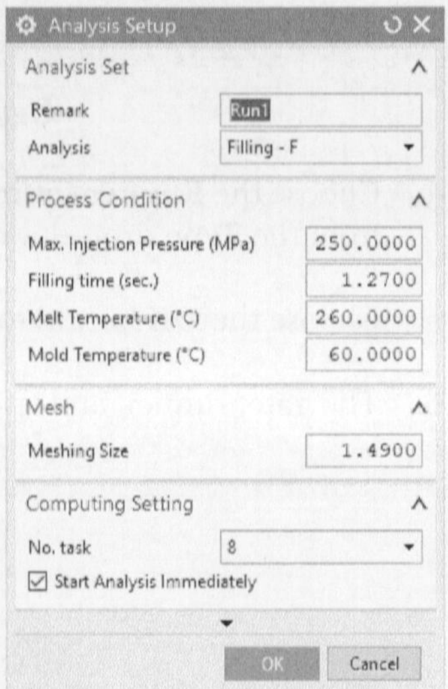

*Figure 15-79 The **Analysis Setup** dialog box*

5. Choose the **OK** button from the **Moldex3D eDesignSYNC** window and the **Close** button in the **Moldex3D Project Monitor** window.

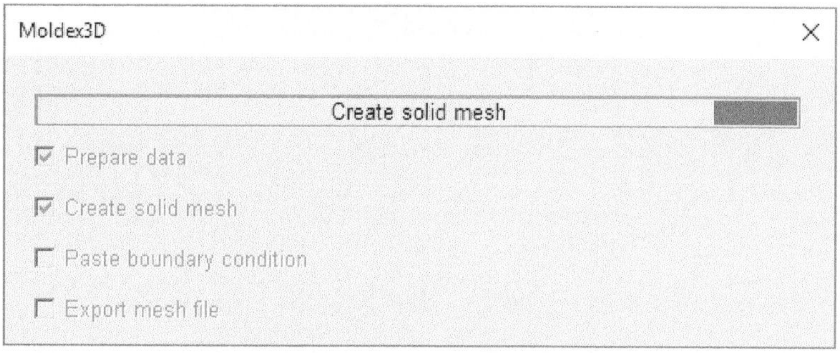

*Figure 15-80 The **Moldex3D** window*

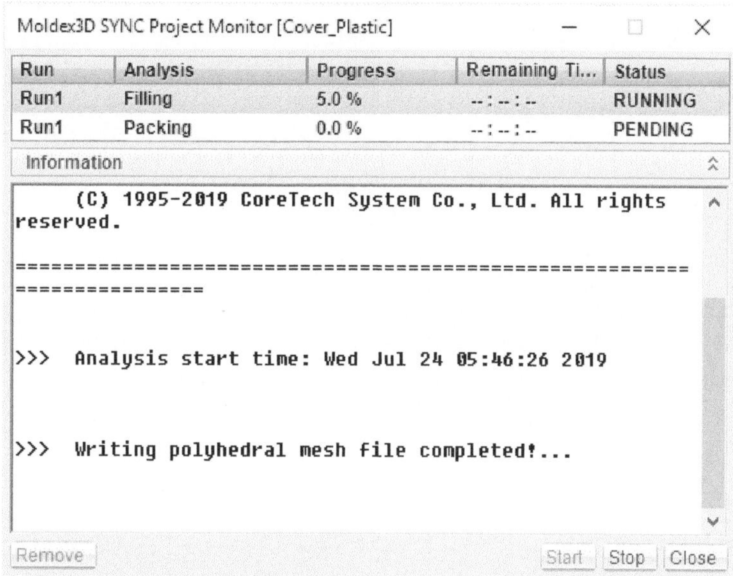

*Figure 15-81 The **Moldex3D SYNC Project Monitor** window*

*Figure 15-82 The **Moldex3D eDesignSYNC** Window*

6. Choose the **Show Result** tool from the **Setting** group; the **Show Result** dialog box gets displayed, refer to Figure 15-83.

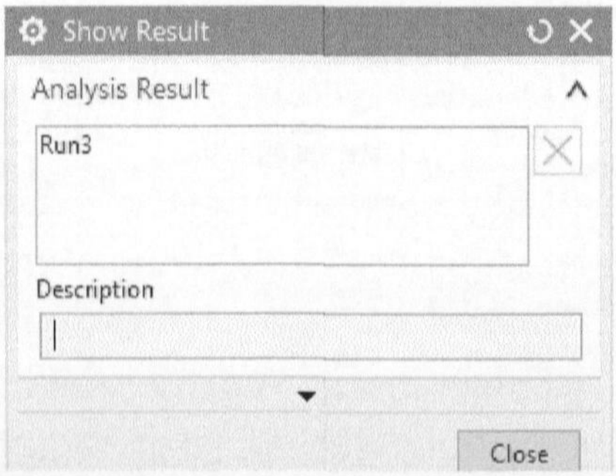

*Figure 15-83 The **Show Result** dialog box*

7. Select result from the **Analysis Result** rollout; the dialog box gets modified, refer to Figure 15-84.

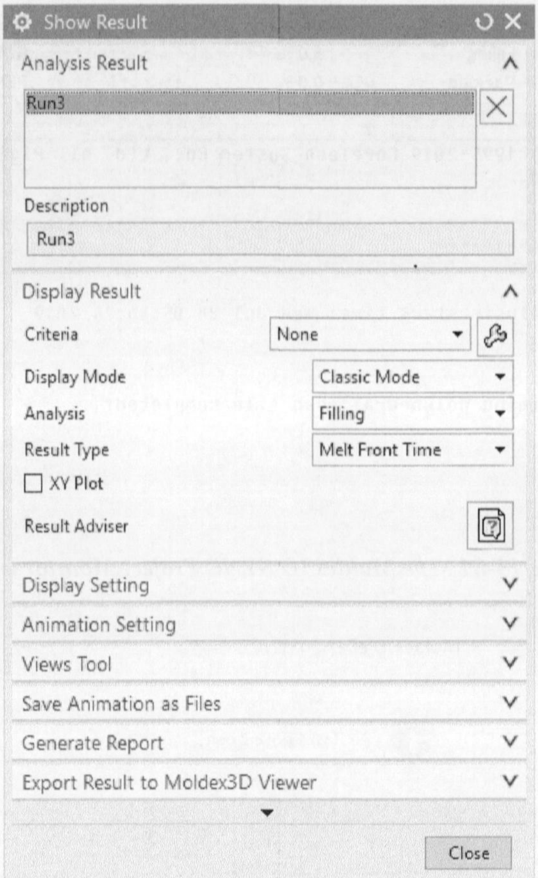

*Figure 15-84 The modified **Show Result** dialog box*

8. You can select the **Filling** or **Packing** option from the **Analysis** drop-down list in the **Display Result** rollout. By default, the **Filling** option is selected.

In this tutorial, you can visualize the results by selecting appropriate option from the **Result Type** drop-down list.

10. The options which can be selected for results are **Melt Front Time**, **Air Trap**, **Weld Line**, **Volumetric Shrinkage**, **Maximum Shear Stress**, and **Temperature**.

11. Select the **XY Plot** check box to activate the **XY Curve Type** drop-down list. Next, select the **Sprue Pressure** or **Clamping Force** option from this drop-down list; the resultant graphs are shown, refer to Figure 15-85 through Figure 15-90.

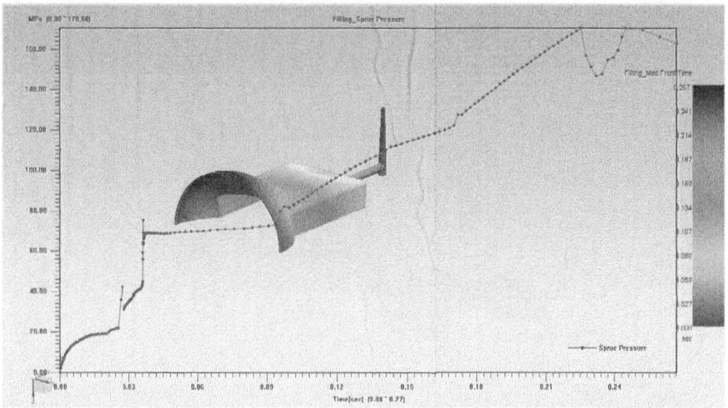

Figure 15-85 *The **Sprue Pressure** vs **Melt Front Time** graph*

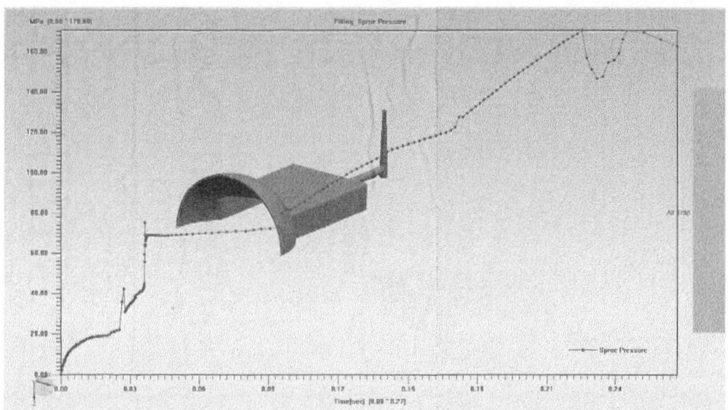

Figure 15-86 *The **Sprue Pressure** vs **Air Trap** graph*

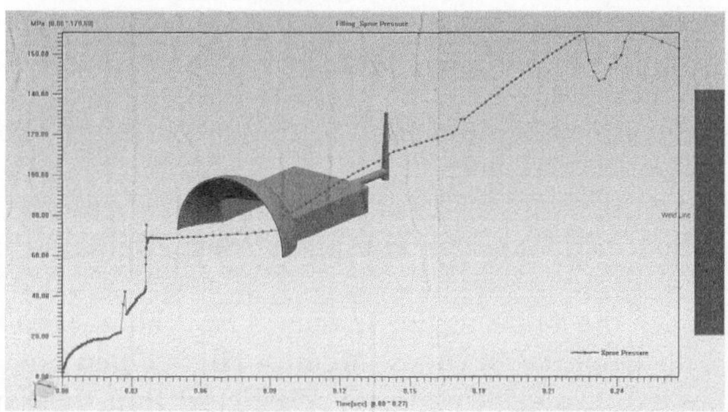

Figure 15-87 *The **Sprue Pressure** vs **Weld Line** graph*

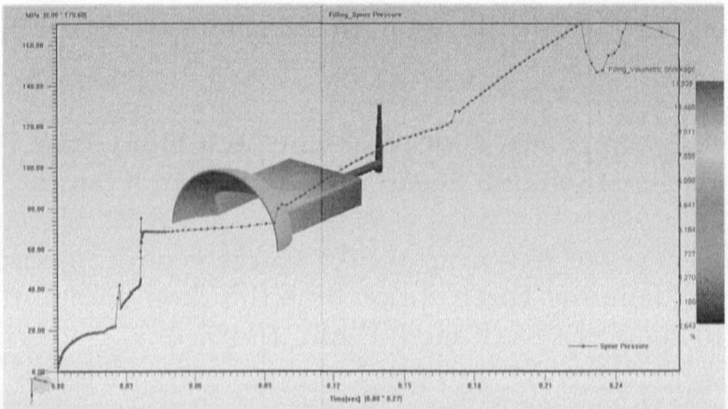

Figure 15-88 The ***Sprue Pressure*** *vs* ***Volumetric Shrinkage*** *graph*

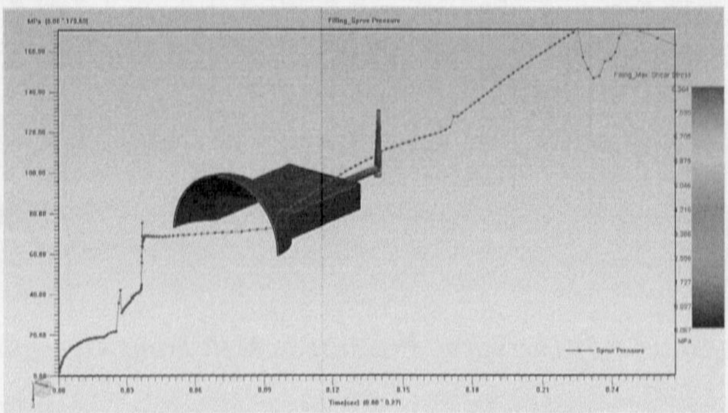

Figure 15-89 The ***Sprue Pressure*** *vs* ***Max. Shear Stress*** *graph*

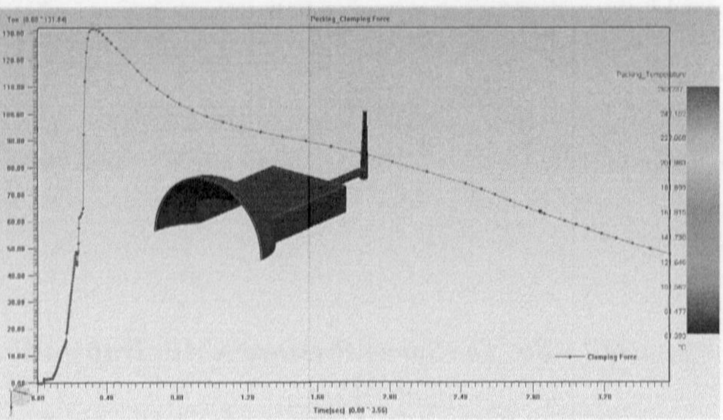

Figure 15-90 The ***Clamping Force*** *vs* ***Temperature*** *graph*

12. Choose the **Play** button from the **Animation Setting** rollout. Next, choose the **Close** button to close the dialog box.

13. Save the file to the specified folder by choosing the **Save All** button and closing NX.

    Next, you need to open the model again. To open a file, choose the **Open** button from the **Standard** group of the **Home** tab or choose **Menu > File > Open** from the **Top Border Bar**; the **Open** dialog box is displayed. Select **Cover_Plastic.prt** from the **Name** list; Cover_Plastic gets displayed in the **File name** drop-down list. Then choose the **OK** button; the model is displayed.

Initializing the Project from Mold Wizard Tab

Now use the **Initialize Project** tool to define the material and the path for saving the project.

1. Choose the **Mold Wizard** tab.

2. Choose the **Initialize Project** tool from the **Mold Wizard** tab; the **Initialize Project** dialog box is displayed, as shown in Figure 15-91.

3. Choose the **Browse** button from the **Path** area of the **Project Settings** rollout; the **Open** dialog box is displayed, as shown in Figure 15-92. After setting the path of the project, choose the **OK** button to close the dialog box.

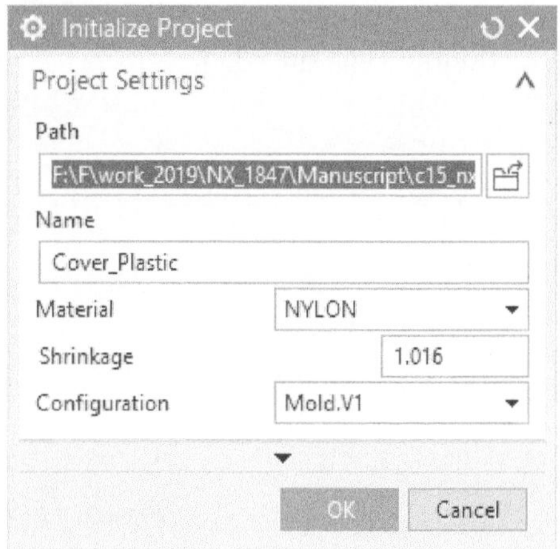

***Figure 15-91** The **Initialize Project** dialog box*

4. Select the **Nylon** material from the **Material** drop-down list; the **Shrinkage** edit box gets updated automatically depending upon the type of selection of material. Next, select the desired template from the **Configuration** drop-down list. By default, the **Mold.V1** template is selected. Choose the **OK** button to close the dialog box.

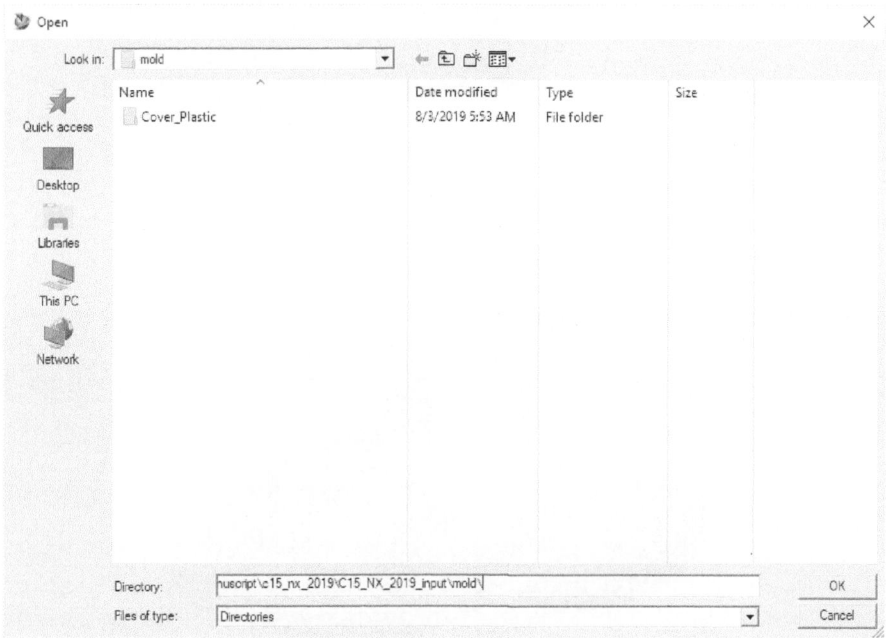

***Figure 15-92** The **Open** dialog box*

Reorienting the Model

Now use the **Mold CSYS** tool to reorient the model.

1. Choose the **Mold CSYS** tool from the **Main** group of the **Mold Wizard** tab; the **Mold CSYS** dialog box is displayed, as shown in Figure 15-93; you are prompted to double-click on WCS.

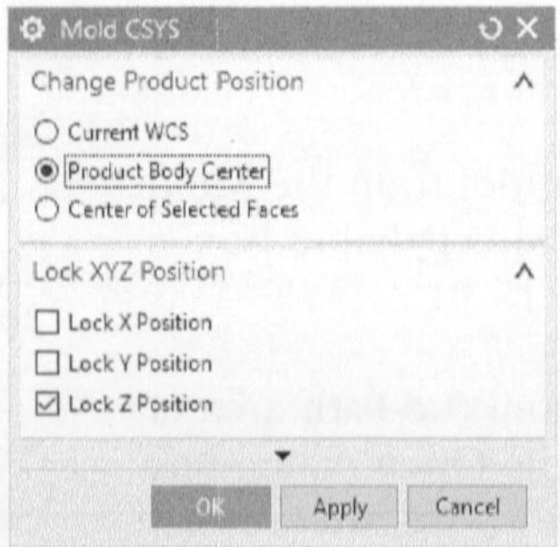

*Figure 15-93 The **Mold CSYS** dialog box*

2. Double-click the WCS, refer to Figure 15-94; you are prompted to drag a handle or select a handle. Select the handle of WCS; the **WCS Dynamics** dialog box is displayed.

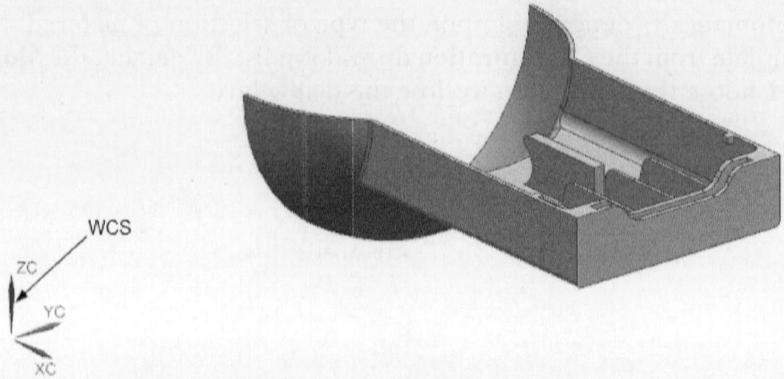

Figure 15-94 The WCS (work coordinate system)

3. Position the WCS as shown in Figure 15-95.

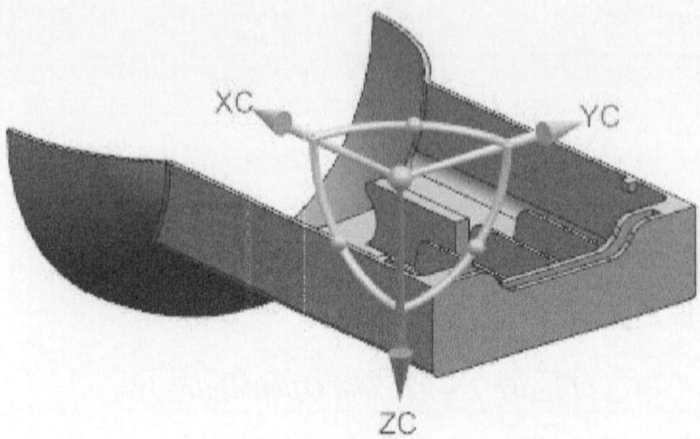

Figure 15-95 The WCS after positioning

4. Click the middle mouse button to close the **WCS Dynamics** dialog box.

5. Select the **Product Body Center** radio button from the **Change Product Position** rollout of the **Mold CSYS** dialog box. Next, choose the **OK** button from the **Mold CSYS** dialog box to close the dialog box.

Check Regions

You can use the **Check Regions** tool to check regions of core and cavity.

1. Invoke the **Check Regions** tool from the **Parting Tools** gallery; the **Check Regions** dialog box with the **Parting Navigator** window is displayed, refer to Figure 15-96. 

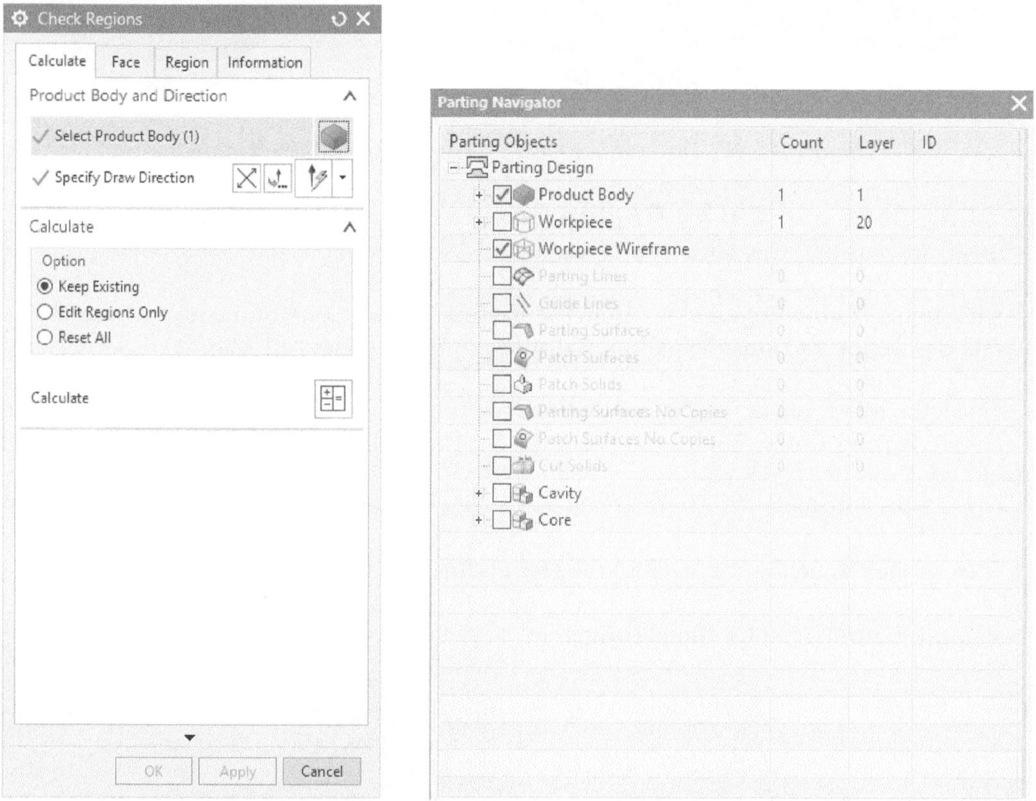

Figure 15-96 The ***Check Regions*** *dialog box with the* ***Parting Navigator*** *tree*

2. Choose the **Calculate** button from the **Calculate** rollout of the **Calculate** tab and then choose the **Region** tab. Choose the **Set Regions Color** button from the **Define Regions** rollout.

   Note, the color of the model gets changed. These color represent core, cavity, and undefined region in the model.

3. The **Cavity Region** radio button is selected by default in the **Assign to Region** rollout. Select the undefined region (back face) of the model and then choose the **Apply** button. Select the

Core Region radio button and select the undefined region (front face) of the model and then choose the **Apply** button; the undefined regions gets the color of the core and cavity region.

4. Choose the **OK** button to close the dialog box and close the **Parting Navigator** window. Modified model after using the **Check Region** tool, is shown in Figure 15-97.

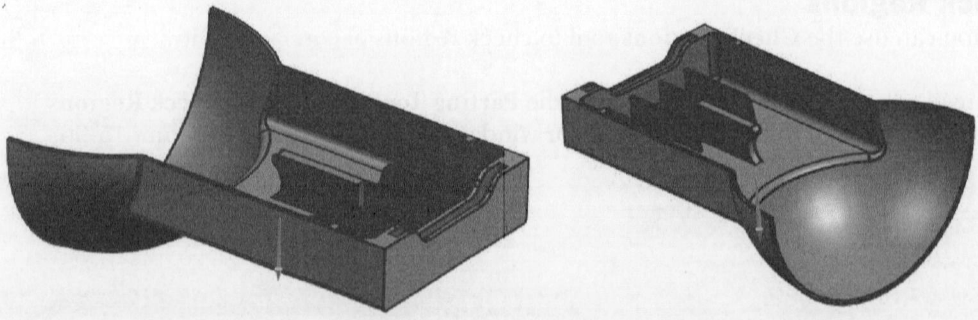

Figure 15-97 The modified model after using the ***Check Region*** *tool*

Creating Core and Cavity Region Sheets

To create parting lines, core, and cavity regions, you need to use the **Define Regions** tool.

1. Choose the **Define Regions** tool from the **Parting Tools** gallery of the **Mold Wizard** tab; the **Define Regions** dialog box is displayed, refer to Figure 15-98.

2. Select **Cavity region** in the **Define Regions** rollout and then select **Create Regions** and the **Create Parting Lines** check boxes from the **Settings** rollout.

3. Choose the **Apply** button; a green tick mark appears beside the cavity and core region.

4. Choose the **Cancel** button to close the **Define Regions** dialog box.

Refer to Figure 15-99 for the parting lines.

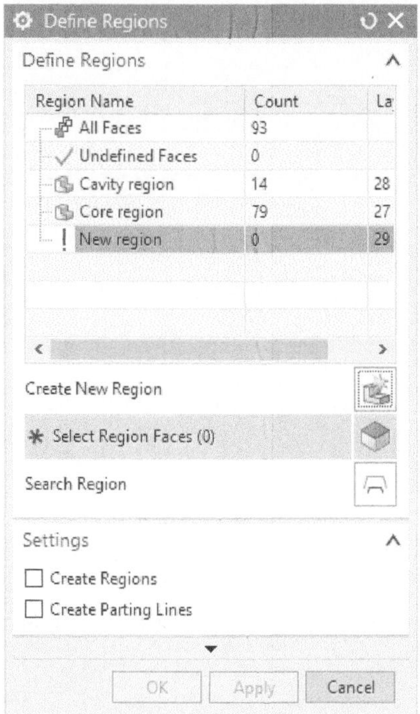

Figure 15-98 The **Define Regions** dialog box

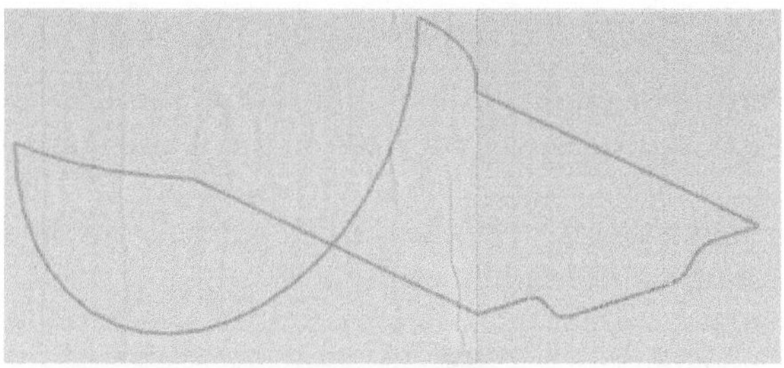

Figure 15-99 Parting lines of the component

Creating Parting Surface

To create parting surface, you need to use the **Design Parting Surface** tool.

1. Choose the **Design Parting Surface** tool from the **Parting Tools** gallery of the **Mold Wizard** tab; the **Design Parting Surface** dialog box is displayed, refer to Figure 15-100.

2. Choose the **Guided Extension** button from the **Method** area of the **Create Parting Surface** rollout.

*Figure 15-100 The **Design Parting Surface** dialog box*

3. Expand the **Edit Parting Segments** rollout and choose the **Edit Guide Lines** button; the **Guide Line** dialog box is displayed. Enter **200** in the **Guide Line Length** edit box. Next, select the parting line; guide line is created, refer to Figure 15-101. Similarly, create other guide lines, refer to Figure 15-102. Choose the **OK** button from the **Guide Line** dialog box; the **Design Parting Surface** dialog box is displayed.

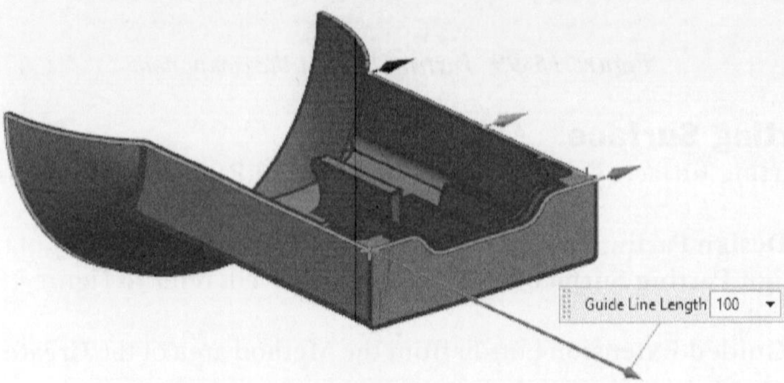

Figure 15-101 The guide line created

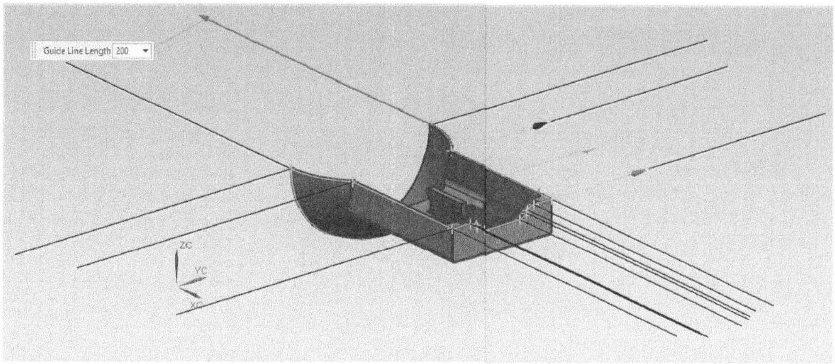

Figure 15-102 The guide lines created

4. Select **Segment 1** from the **Parting Segments** sub-rollout of the **Parting Lines** rollout. Next, choose the **Swept** button from the **Method** area of the **Create Parting Surface** rollout. Specify first and second direction. Enter **250** as the value in the **Extend Distance** dynamic edit box and choose the **Apply** button. Similarly, create parting surface for rest of the portion of the part, refer to Figure 15-103.

5. Choose the **Cancel** button to close the dialog box and the **Save All** button to save the file.

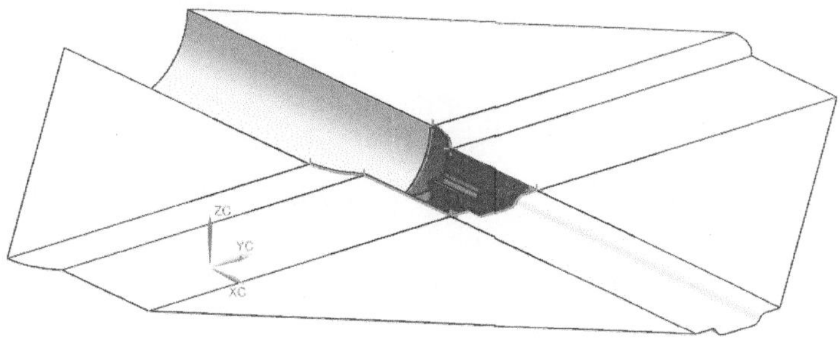

Figure 15-103 Parting surface of the component

Creating Workpiece

The **Workpiece** tool helps you to decide the size of the core and cavity insert.

1. Choose the **Workpiece** tool from the **Main** gallery of the **Mold Wizard** tab; the **New Iray+ Ray Traced Studio Rendering** window is displayed. Choose the **OK** button, the **Workpiece** dialog box is displayed, refer to Figure 15-104. By default, the **Product Workpiece** option is selected in the Type drop-down list and the **User Defined Block** option is selected in the **Workpiece Method** drop-down list. Refer to Figure 15-105 for core and cavity insert size.

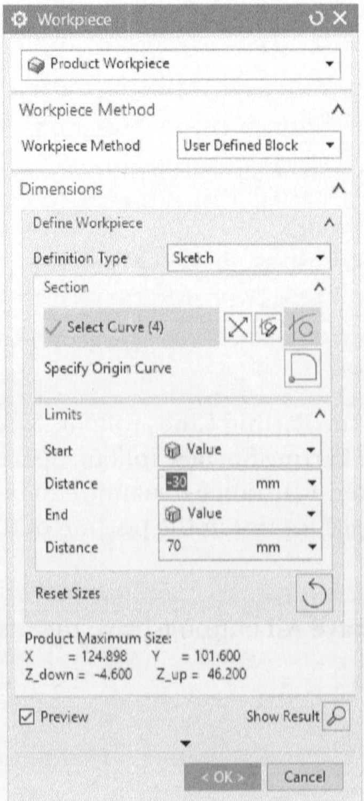

Figure 15-104 The ***Workpiece*** *dialog box*

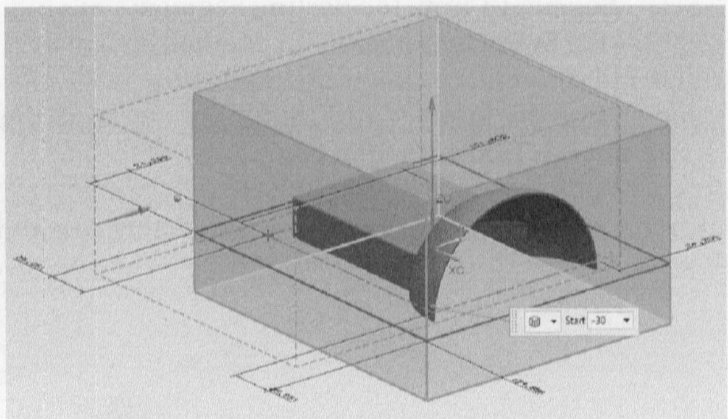

Figure 15-105 The Core and Cavity insert

Note, the size of insert is automatically defined. Choose the **OK** button to exit the **Workpiece** dialog box.

Creating Layouts of the Workpiece

Now, use **Cavity Layout** tool to create the layout of the core and cavity insert.

1. Choose the **Cavity Layout** tool from the **Main** gallery of the **Mold Wizard** tab; the **Cavity Layout** dialog box is displayed, refer to Figure 15-106. The body of the core and cavity is automatically selected and a green tick mark becomes visible in the **Select Body** area of the **Product** rollout.

2. Enter **4** in the **Cavity Count** edit box of the **Balanced Layout Settings** rollout.

3. Click in the **Specify Vector** area of the **Layout Type** rollout and select **-XC-axis** from the **Inferred Vector** drop-down list. Choose the **Start Layout** button from the **Generate Layout** rollout; the layout gets created, refer to Figure 15-107.

4. Choose the **Auto Center** button from the **Edit Layout** rollout to center the layout with mold base center.

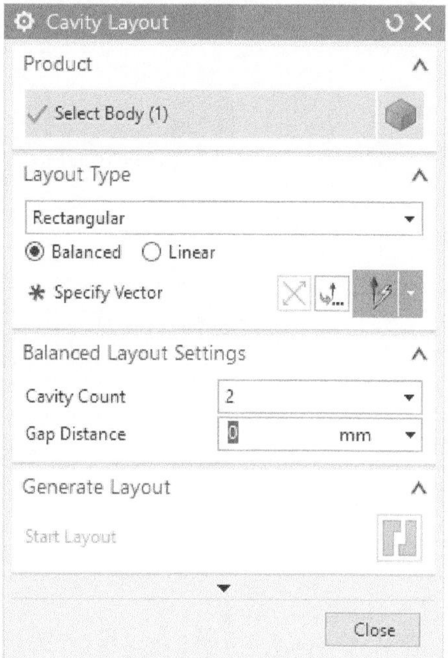

***Figure 15-106** The **Cavity Layout** dialog box*

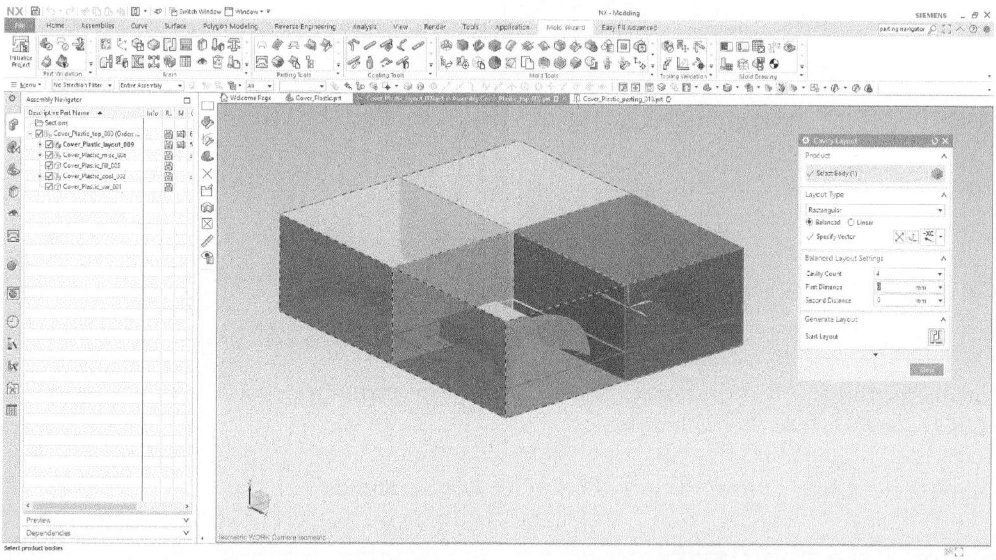

***Figure 15-107** The cavity layout of the workpiece*

5. Choose the **Edit Insert Pocket** button from the **Edit Layout** rollout; the **Insert Pocket** dialog box is displayed, refer to Figure 15-108.

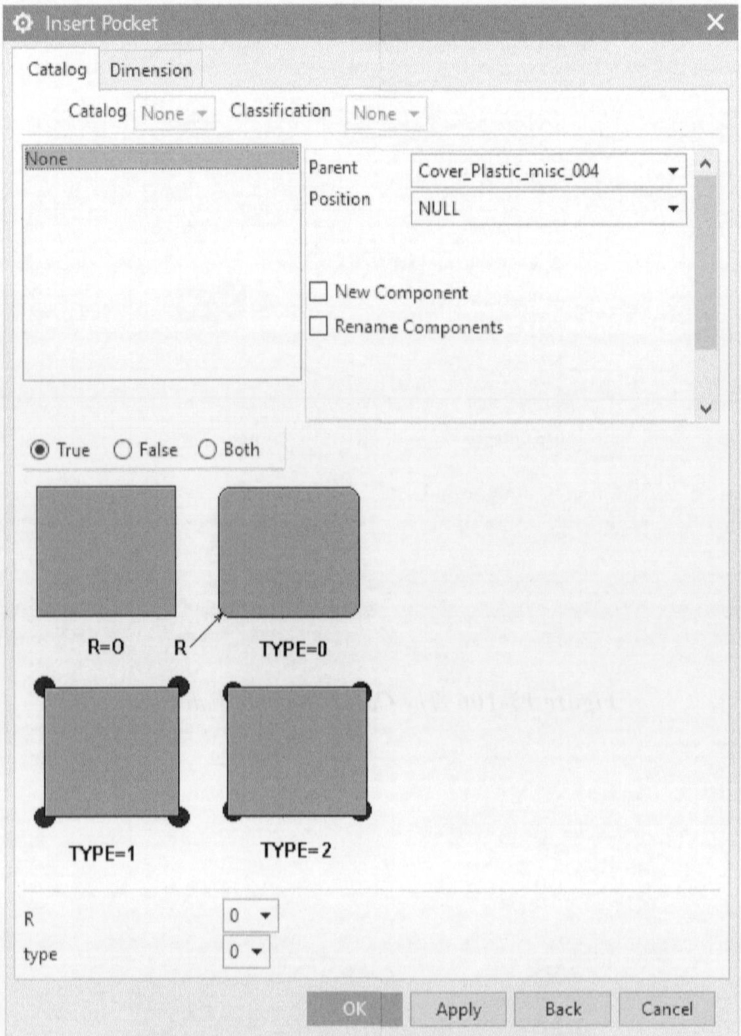

*Figure 15-108 The **Insert Pocket** dialog box*

6. Select **5** from the **R** drop-down list and **2** from the **type** drop-down list. Next, choose the **OK** button to close the dialog box.

7. Choose the **Close** button to close the **Cavity Layout** dialog box.

Creating Core and Cavity

Now, use the **Define Cavity and Core** tool to create the core and cavity.

1. Choose the **Define Cavity and Core** tool from the **Parting Tools** gallery of the **Mold Wizard** tab; the **Define Cavity and Core** dialog box is displayed, refer to Figure 15-109.

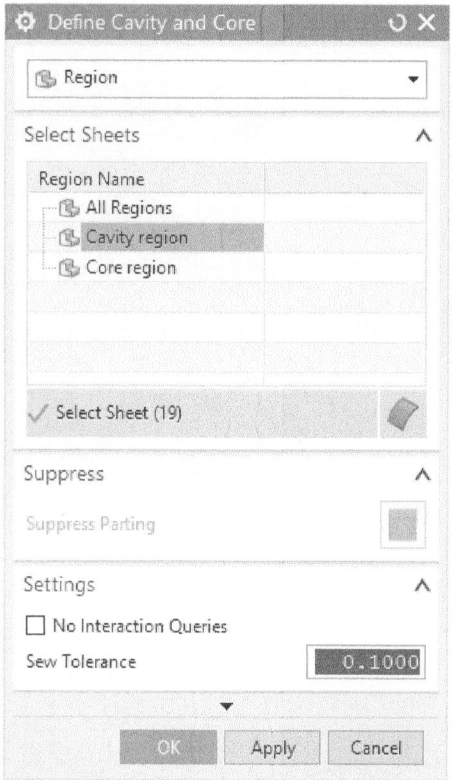

Figure 15-109 *The* ***Define Cavity and Core*** *dialog box*

By default, the **Region** option is selected in the Type drop-down list and the **Cavity region** is highlighted in the **Select Sheets** rollout.

2. Choose the **Apply** button, the **New Iray+ Ray Traced Studio Rendering** window is displayed. Choose the **OK** button; the **View Parting Result** dialog box and the cavity of the model get displayed, refer to Figure 15-110. Choose the **Reverse Direction** button to create other half of the cavity. Choose the **OK** button to close the dialog box; a green tick mark is displayed in front of **Cavity region** in the **Select Sheets** rollout of the dialog box. Now, select **Core region** in the **Select Sheets** rollout of the dialog box and repeat the same procedure as for the cavity; the core gets displayed, refer to Figure 15-111.

3. Choose the **Cancel** button to close the dialog box.

4. Select **Cover_Plastic_parting_xxx** in the assembly navigator and right-click on it; a shortcut menu is displayed. Choose **Cover_Plastic_top_xxx** from the **Open Parent in Window** drop-down list in the shortcut menu.

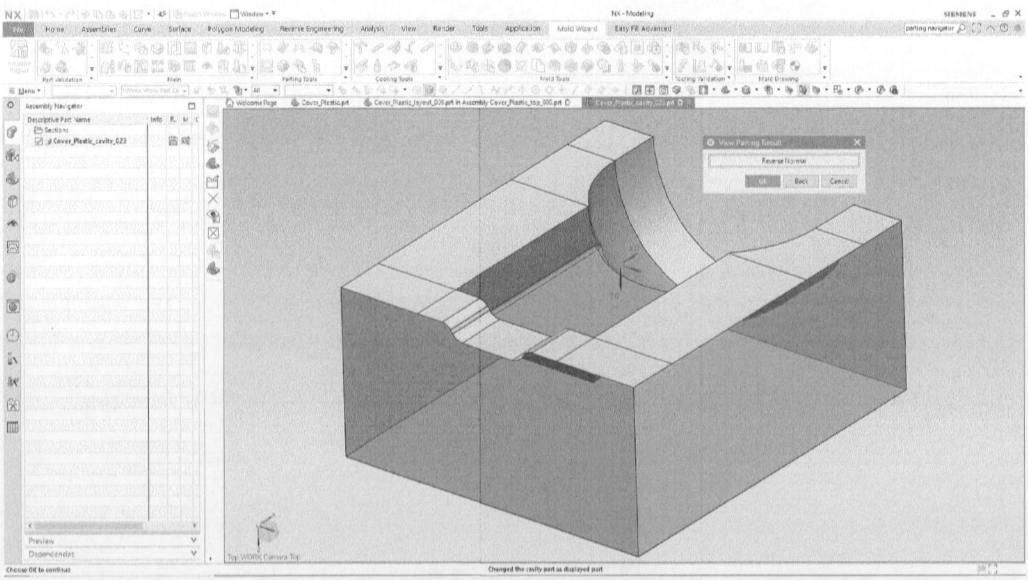

Figure 15-110 *The* ***View Parting Result*** *dialog box and cavity of the model on screen*

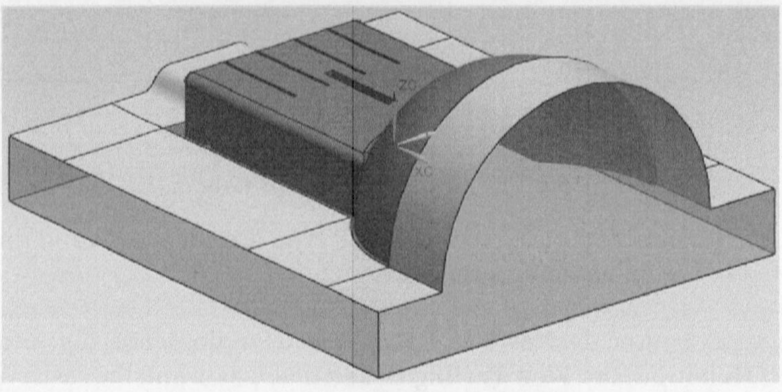

Figure 15-111 *The core of the model*

Adding Mold Assembly

Now, use the **Mold Base Library** tool to create the plates for the mold assembly.

1. Choose **Mold Base Library** tool from the **Main** gallery of the **Mold Wizard** tab; the **Mold Base Library** dialog box, refer to Figure 15-112 and the **Information** window is displayed.

2. Select **5050**, **2**, **106**, **36**, and **106** from the **index**, **TCP_type**, **AP_h**, **BP_h**, and **CP_h** drop-down lists respectively in the **Details** rollout. Next, choose the **OK** button to close the dialog box; the Mold plates are added to the assembly, refer to Figure 15-113.

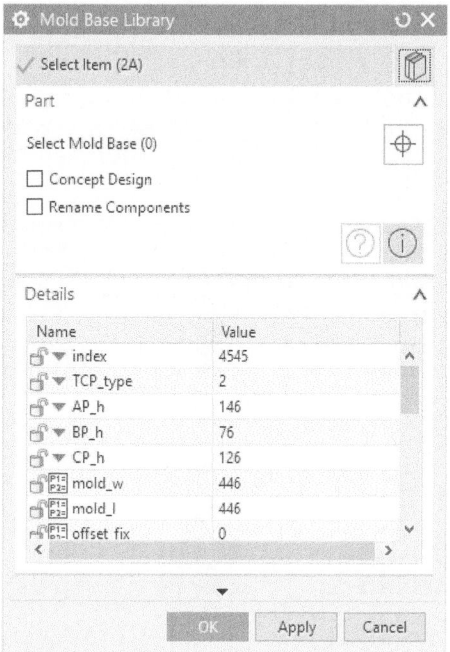

*Figure 15-112 The **Mold Base Library** dialog box*

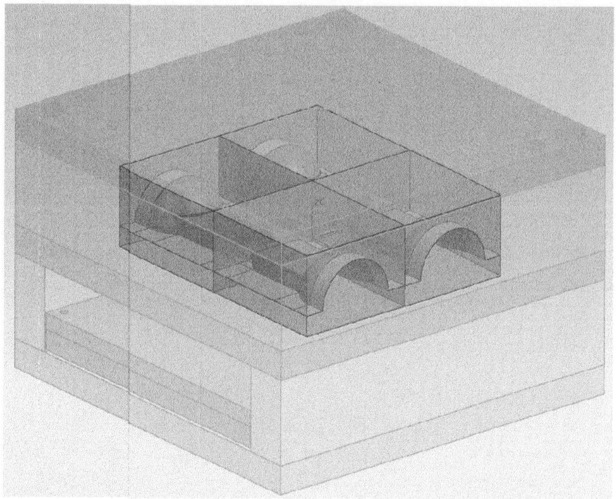

*Figure 15-113 The **Mold Plate** assembly*

3. Choose **File > Save > Save All** to save the file.

Adding Lifter in Mold Assembly

Now, use the **Slide and Lifter Library** tool to create the lifter for mold assembly.

1. Choose the **Slide and Lifter Library** tool from the **Main** gallery; the **Slide and Lifter Design** dialog box is displayed with the **Information** window.

2. Choose **Lifter** folder in Main Panel and **Dowel Lifter** in the **Member Select** panel of the **Reuse Library**; the **Slide and Lifter Design** dialog box gets modified with the **Information** window, refer to Figure 15-114.

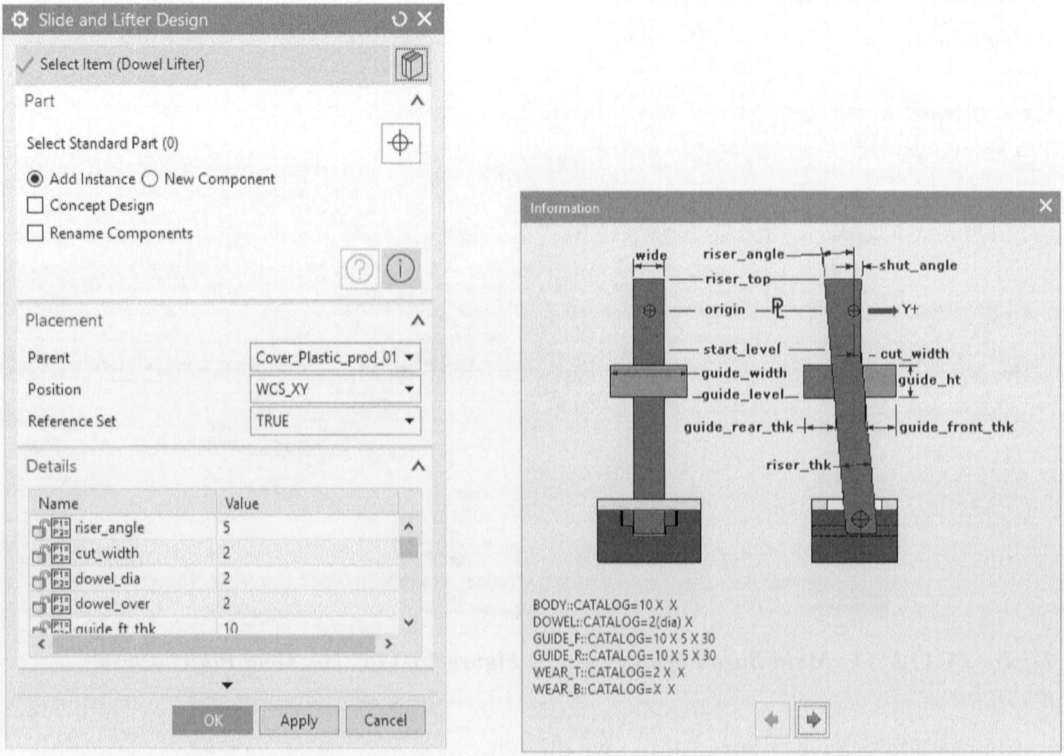

***Figure 15-114** The **Slide and Lifter Design** dialog box and the **Information** window*

3. Specify the parameter of the Lifter in the **Details** rollout and choose the **Apply** button.

4. You can position the lifter to place it in a correct way. Choose the **Select Standard Part** area of the **Part** rollout and then select the lifter which you want to place.

5. Choose the **Reposition** button in the **Part** rollout, the **Move Component** dialog box is displayed, refer to Figure 15-115.

6. You can place the lifter position using this dialog box, choose the **OK** button after placing the lifter to close the dialog box.

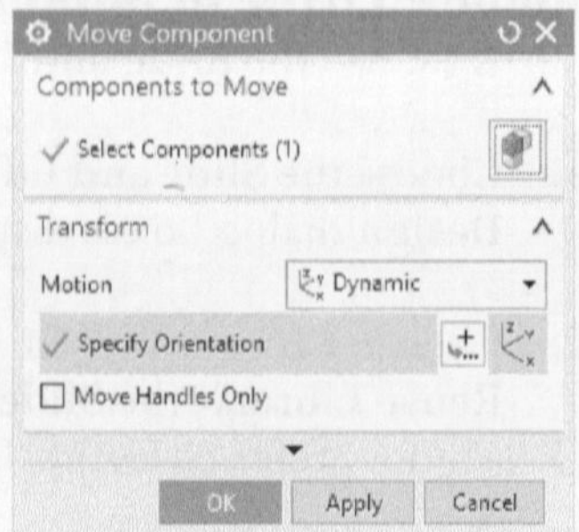

***Figure 15-115** The **Move Component** dialog box*

7. Choose the **OK** button to close the **Slide and Lifter Design** dialog box. Refer to Figure 15-116 for arrangement of lifter and repeat the same procedure for other lifters.

Note

If you create lifter for one component then other lifters automatically will be placed.

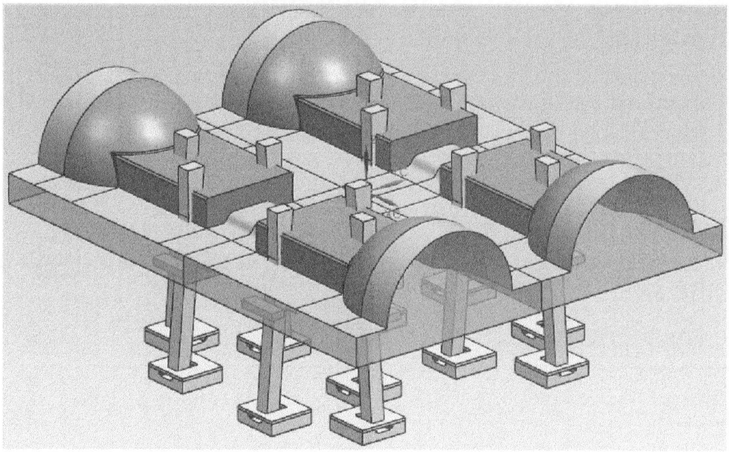

Figure 15-116 The arrangement of lifter

Trimming the Lifters

Now, trim extra part of the lifters.

1. Choose the **Trim Mold Components** tool from the **Mold Tools** gallery of the **Mold Wizard** tab; the **Trim Mold Components** dialog box will be displayed, as shown in Figure 15-117.
2. Select the lifters from the mold assembly and choose the **OK** button to trim the lifters. Refer to Figure 15-118 for the modified lifters.

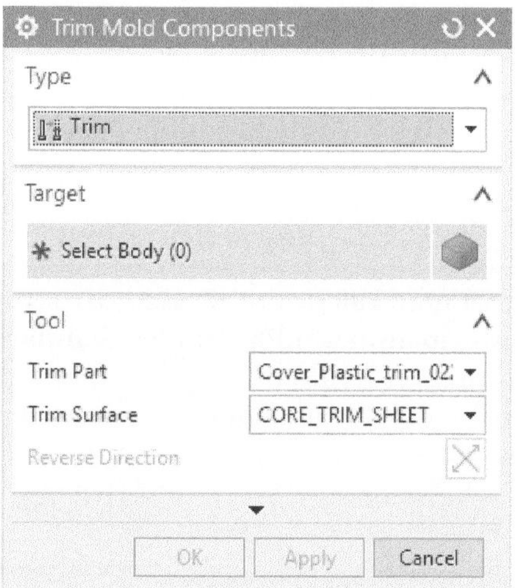

*Figure 15-117 The **Trim Mold Components** dialog box*

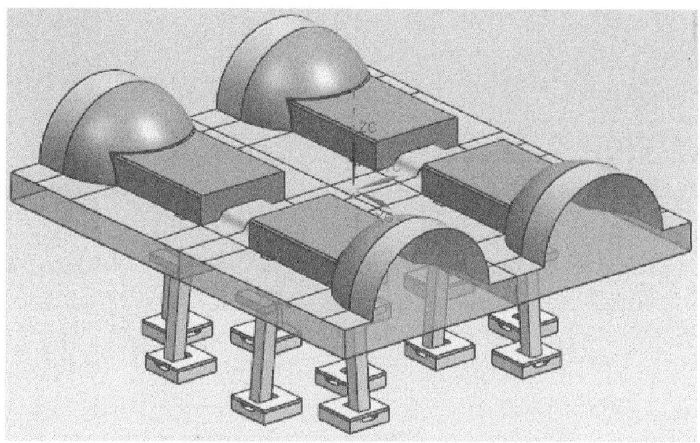

Figure 15-118 Modified lifters

Adding Register Ring to the Mold Assembly

Now, add Register ring in the mold assembly.

1. Choose **MW Standard Part Library** from the **Reuse Library**. Expand the **MW Standard Part Library** and then choose the type of locating ring from the **Injection** folder of **DME_MM** Standard.

2. Double-click on the **Locating_Ring_With_Mounting_Holes[DHR21]** from the **Member Select** panel, the **Standard Part Management** dialog box is displayed with the **Information** window, refer to Figure 15-119.

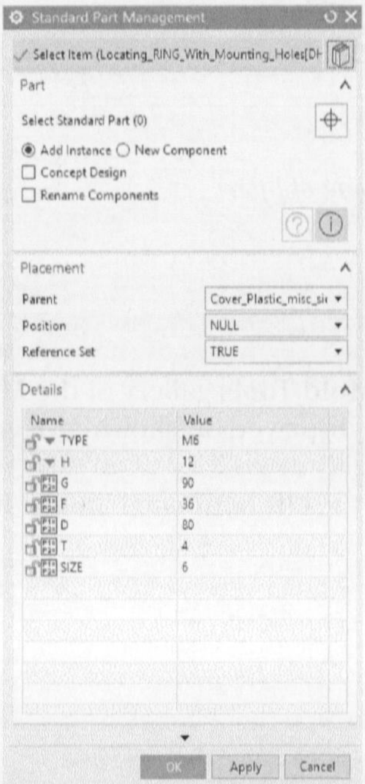

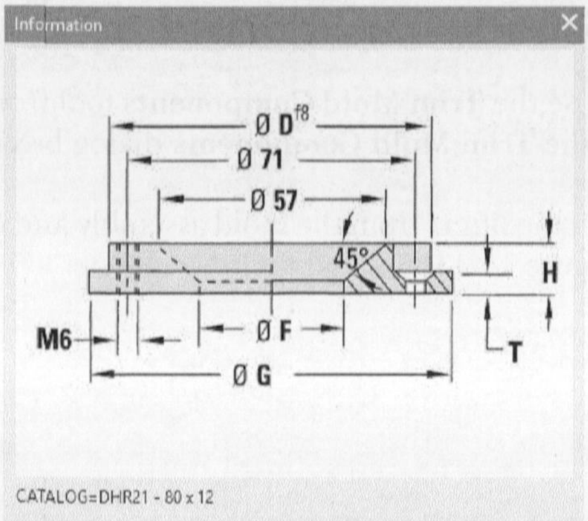

*Figure 15-119 The **Standard Part Management** dialog box and the **Information** window*

3. Select **M8** and **12** in the **Type** and **H** drop-down lists. Enter **100** in the **D** edit box of the **Details** rollout and then choose the **OK** button; the **Information** window and the **Standard Part Management** dialog box is closed. Another **Information** window is displayed; choose the **Close** button to close the window. Refer to Figure 15-120 for arrangement of Register ring.

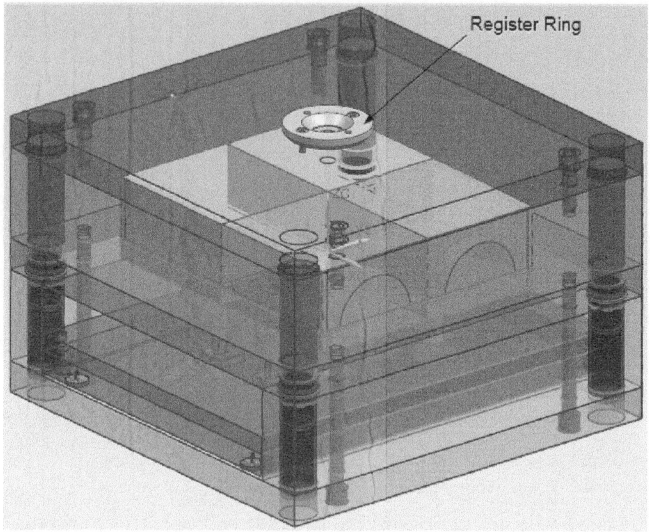

Figure 15-120 The arrangement of Register ring in the Mold assembly

Adding Sprue Bush in the Mold Assembly

This tool helps you to add the sprue bush to the mold assembly. Sprue bush helps to connect the molten flow channel between runner and Register ring.

1. Choose the **MW Standard Part Library** from the **Reuse Library**. Expand the **MW Standard Part Library** and then choose type of sprue bush from the **Injection** folder of **DME_MM** Standard.

2. Double-click on the **Sprue Bushing(DHR74)** from the **Member Select** panel; the **Standard Part Management** dialog box is displayed with the **Information** window, refer to Figure 15-121.

3. Enter **18**, **4**, **116**, **36**, and **24** in the **D**, **O**, **N**, **H**, and **K** edit boxes respectively, of the **Details** rollout.

   If the size of sprue bush is not appropriate then you can change it by double-clicking on the **Sprue Bushing(DHR74)** from the **Member Select** panel; the **Standard Part Management** dialog box is displayed. Select the **Select Standard Part** area in the **Part** rollout and then select the sprue bush in the mold assembly. Now, you can change the size parameters or reposition the sprue bush. Refer to Figure 15-122 for arrangement of sprue bush in the mold assembly.

4. Choose the **OK** button to close the dialog box.

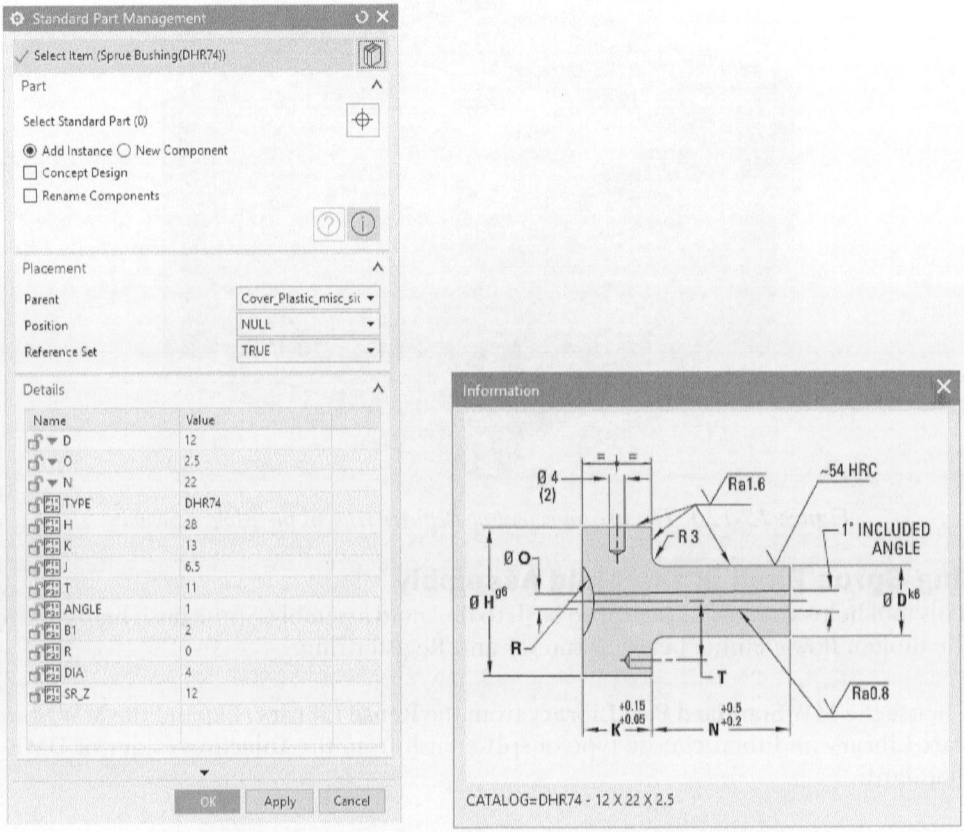

***Figure 15-121** The **Standard Part Management** dialog box and the **Information** window*

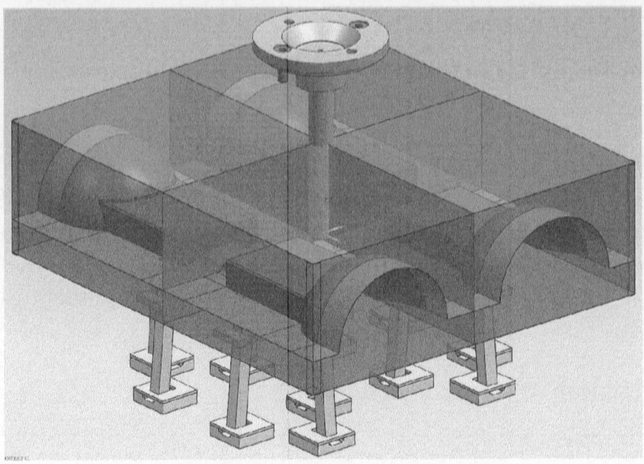

***Figure 15-122** The arrangement of sprue bush in the Mold assembly*

Adding Ejector Pin in the Mold Assembly

This tool helps you to add Ejector Pin to the mold assembly. Ejector Pin helps you to eject the component from the mold.

1. Choose **MW Standard Part Library** from the **Reuse Library**. Expand the **MW Standard Part Library** and then choose type of ejector pin from the **Ejection** folder of the **DME_MM** Standard.

2. Double-click on the **Ejector Pin [Shouldered]** from the **Member Select** panel, the **Standard Part Management** dialog box is displayed with the **Information** window, refer to Figure 15-123.

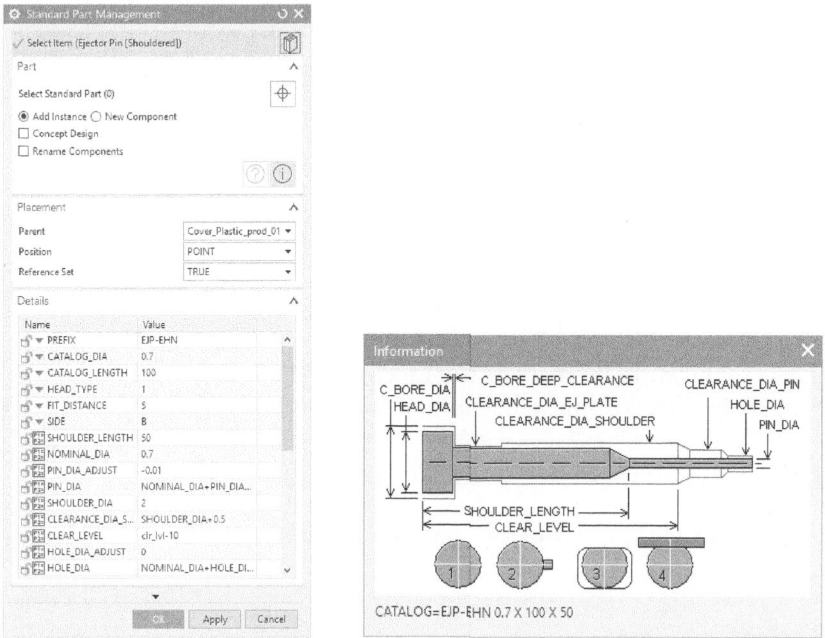

***Figure 15-123** The **Standard Part Management** dialog box and the **Information** window*

3. Select **1** and **160** from the **CATALOG_DIA** and **CATALOG_LENGTH** drop-down lists in the **Details** rollout. Choose the **Apply** button; the **Point** dialog box is displayed. Specify the position of the ejector pin by placing the point. Choose the **Cancel** button to close the dialog box. Next, choose the **OK** button to close the **Standard Part Management** dialog box and the **Information** window. Refer to Figure 15-124 for the arrangement of ejector pin.

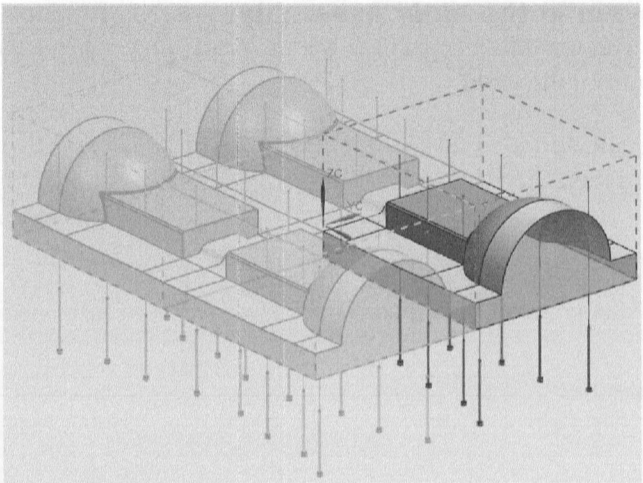

Figure 15-124 The arrangement of ejector pin in the mold assembly

Trimming the Ejector Pin

This tool helps you to trim the ejector pin which is larger in size.

1. Choose the **Ejector Pin Post Processing** tool from the **Main** gallery of the **Mold Wizard** tab; the **Ejector Pin Post Processing** dialog box is displayed, refer to Figure 15-125.

2. Select the ejector pins which need to be trimmed.

3. Choose the **Apply** button to trim the ejector pin. Choose the **Cancel** button to close the dialog box.

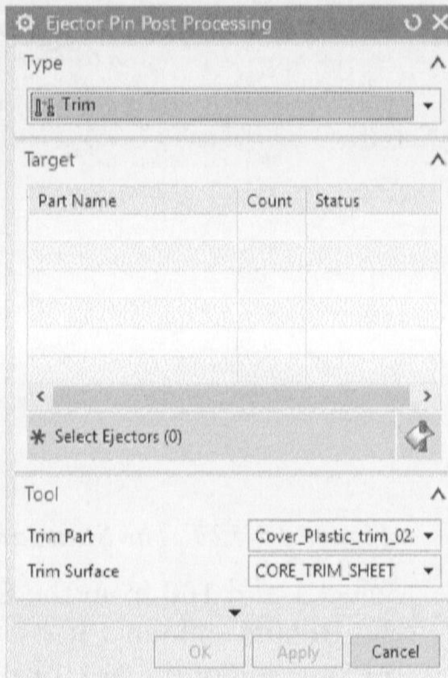

Figure 15-125 *The* ***Ejector Pin Post Processing*** *dialog box*

Create Pocket

This tool helps you to create pocket for components to be placed or moved.

1. Choose the **Pocket** tool from the **Main** gallery of the **Mold Wizard** tab; the **Pocket** dialog box is displayed, refer to Figure 15-126. You are prompted to select the target bodies. Select the target bodies from the mold assembly.

2. Select the **Select Object** area in the **Tool** rollout, choose the tool body for which you need to create pocket. Next, choose the **Apply** button to create pocket and the **Cancel** button to close the dialog box. Refer to Figure 15-127 for pocket in the core plate.

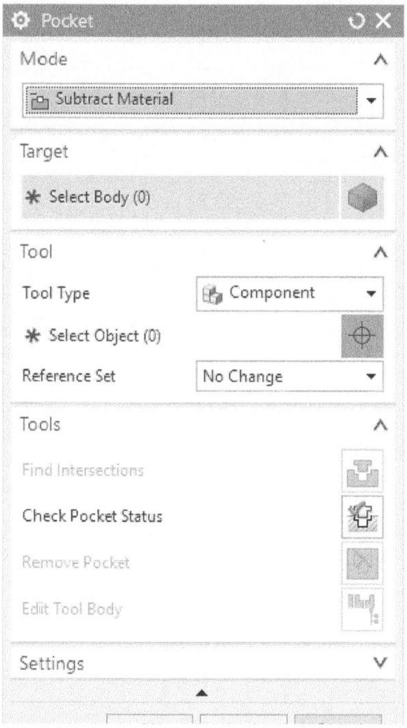

*Figure 15-126 The **Pocket** dialog box*

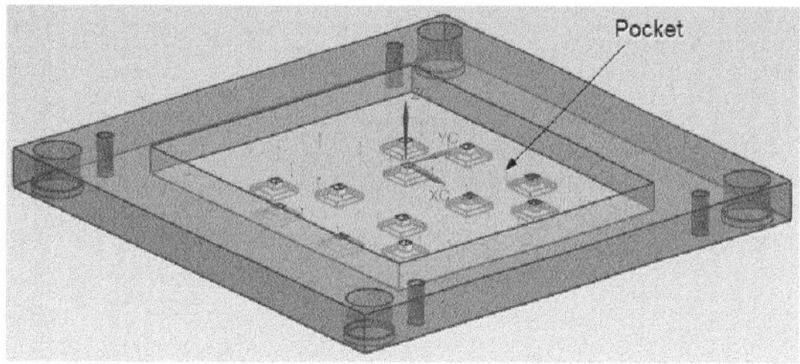

Figure 15-127 The pocket in the core plate

Creating Gate

This tool helps you to create gate. Gate is a channel which directly connects runner and part for molten flow of material.

1. Choose the **Design Fill** tool from the **Main** gallery of the **Mold Wizard** tab, the **Design Fill** dialog box is displayed with the **Information** window, refer to Figure 15-128. 

2. Select the type of gate from the **Member Select** panel in the **Reuse Library**. For this component use Fan gate.

3. Specify the parameters of the gate in the **Details** rollout of the dialog box. Select the **Select Object** area in the **Placement** rollout and specify gate position and orientation, refer to Figure 15-129.

4. After placing the gate, choose the **OK** button to close the dialog box.

*Figure 15-128 The **Design Fill** dialog box and the **Information** window*

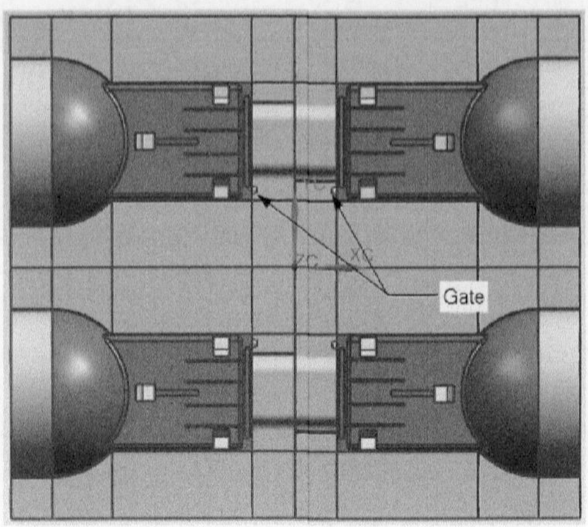

Figure 15-129 The gate position and orientation in the model

Creating Runner

This tool helps you to create runner. Runner is a channel which directly connects gate and sprue bush for molten flow of material.

1. Choose the **Design Fill** tool from the **Main** gallery of the **Mold Wizard** tab, the **Design Fill** dialog box is displayed. 

2. Select the type of Runner from the **Member Select** panel in the **Reuse Library**. For this component use **Runner[4]**.

3. Select **6.5** from the **D1** drop-down list and enter **92** and **50** in the **L1** and **L** edit boxes in the **Details** rollout of the dialog box. Select the **Specify Point** area in the **Placement** rollout and position the runner, refer to Figure 15-130.

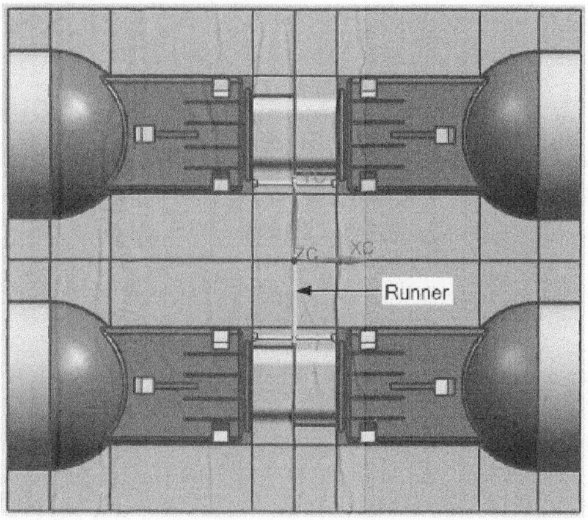

Figure 15-130 The runner position and orientation in the model

4. After placing the runner, choose the **OK** button to close the dialog box.

Adding Cooling Channel

This tool helps you to add cooling channel. Cooling channel helps to solidify the material. Effective cooling channel helps you to reduce cycle time.

1. Choose the **Pattern Channel** tool from the **Cooling Tools** gallery of the **Mold Wizard** tab, the **Pattern Channel** dialog box is displayed, refer to Figure 15-131. 

2. Select the **Sketch Section** button in the **Channel Path** rollout, the **Create Sketch** dialog box is displayed, refer to Figure 15-132.

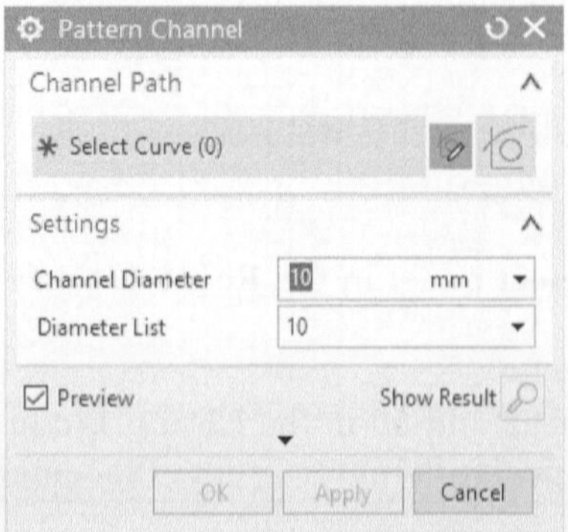

Figure 15-131 The ***Pattern Channel*** *dialog box*

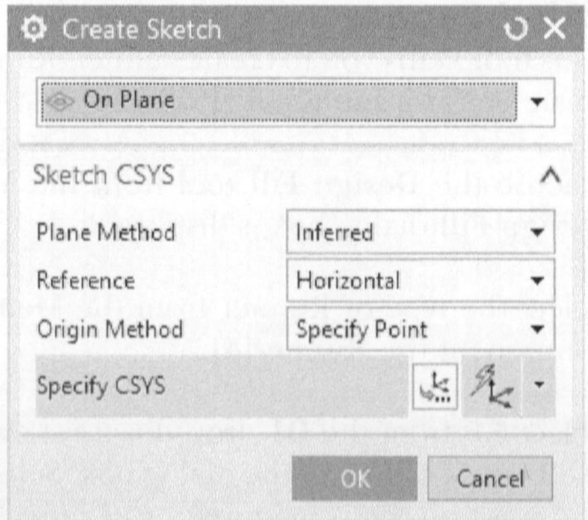

Figure 15-132 The ***Create Sketch*** *dialog box*

3. Create sketch for cooling channel on a plane and choose the **Finish** button to exit the sketch environment; the **Pattern Channel** dialog box is displayed. Specify the diameter of channel in the **Channel Diameter** edit box of the **Setting** rollout. Choose the **OK** button to close the dialog box. Refer to Figure 15-133 for cooling channel position and orientation.

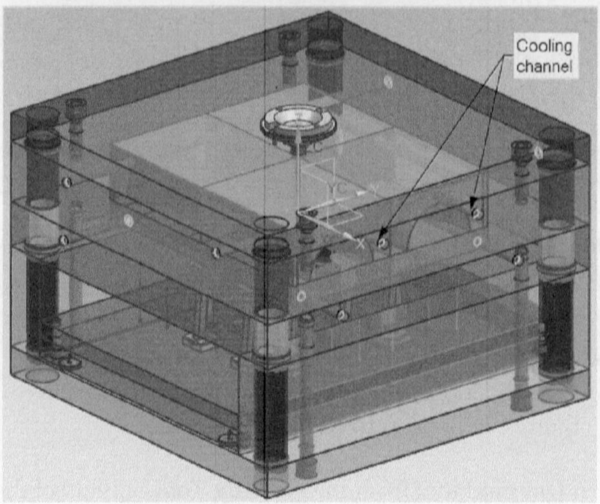

Figure 15-133 The orientation and position of cooling channel

Self-Evaluation Test

Answer the following questions and then compare them to those given at the end of this chapter:

1. The __________ tool is used to define the path of the mold project.

2. The __________ tool is used to assign the core and cavity regions in the model.

3. There are __________ types of **Configuration** in the **Initialize Project** dialog box.

4. You can change the orientaion of the model by the __________ tool.

5. The __________ tool is used to apply the material on model.

6. Gate is a channel which connects sprue bush to the component. (T/F)

7. Runner is a channel which connects sprue bush to the gate. (T/F)

8. Shrinkage is used to apply scale factor to the component. (T/F)

9. The **Patch Surface** tool is used to create the sheet to close the openings in the model. (T/F)

10. The **Design Fill** tool is not used to create gate. (T/F)

Review Questions

Answer the following questions:

1. Which of the following dialog boxes is displayed when you choose the **Patch Surface** tool from the **Parting Tools** gallery of the **Mold Wizard** tab?

   (a) **Patch Surface** (b) **Edge Patch**
   (c) **Patch** (d) **None**

2. Which of the following tools in NX Mold Wizard is used to create core and cavity regions?

   (a) **Check Regions** (b) **Define Regions**
   (c) **Patch Surface** (d) None

3. Which of the following dialog boxes is displayed when you choose the **Set Cavity** button from the **Easy Fill Advanced** tab to specify the cavity of the component?

   (a) **Set Cavity** (b) **Select Cavity**
   (c) **Cavity** (d) **Set**

4. The __________ tool is used to create parting surface of the model.

5. The __________ tool is used to add cooling fitting components to cooling channels.

6. The __________ tool is used to adjust the position of the cooling channel.

7. You can select the material from the **Select Cavity** dialog box. (T/F)

8. The **Design Gate** tool is used to create the runner. (T/F)

9. The **Assembly Drawing** tool helps you to create the drawing of the mold assembly.

10. The **Slider and Lifter Library** tool helps you to create slider in mold design.

EXERCISE

To perform the exercise you need to download the zipped file named as *c15_NX_2019_input* from the Input Files section of the CADCIM website. The complete path for downloading the file is:

Textbooks > CAD/CAM > NX > Siemens NX 2019 for Designers > Input Files

After the file is downloaded, extract the folder to the location *C:\NX 2019* and rename it as *c15*.

Exercise 1

Create the Mold Design of the model shown in Figure 15-134.

***Figure 15-134** The Trimetric view of the Phone Case cover*

Answers to Self-Evaluation Test

1. Initialize Project, **2. Check Regions**, **3.** three, **4. Mold CSYS**, **5. Initialize Project**, **6.** F, **7. T**, **8. T**, **9. T**, **10. F**

Chapter 16

Concepts of Geometric Dimensioning and Tolerancing

Learning Objectives

After completing this chapter, you will be able to:

- *Understand tolerances and allowances*
- *Understand tolerancing methods*
- *Understand datums, features, and material condition modifiers*
- *Understand geometric characteristics symbols*
- *Understand the form, orientation, position, profile, and runout tolerances*
- *Understand fits*

HISTORY OF TOLERANCES AND ALLOWANCES

The history of engineering drawing extends over a period of 6000 years but the practice of tolerancing and dimensioning was introduced for the first time only about 80 years ago. Gradually, engineers and designers realized that exact dimensions and shapes could not be attained in shaping physical objects. Therefore, a feasible scheme of interchangeable manufacturing that was crucial to mass production methods was established. During this era, skilled handicrafters, designers, and engineers took pride in the ability to work with exact dimensions. This meant that objects were dimensioned more accurately than they could be measured. However, the use of modern measuring instruments showed deviations from the sizes which were earlier believed to be exact.

At the start of industrial age, it was realized that variations in the sizes of parts had always been present and such variations could be restricted but not avoided. The slight variation in the size which a part was originally intended to have could be tolerated without impairment of its correct functioning. It became evident that interchangeable parts need not be identical parts, but rather it would be sufficient if the significant sizes that controlled their fits lay between definite limits. The problem of manufacturing interchangeable parts was resolved by holding the parts between two limiting sizes lying so closely that any intermediate size is acceptable.

The concept of limits essentially means that a precisely defined basic condition is replaced by two limiting conditions and any result lying on or between these two limits is acceptable.

In order to calculate limits and tolerances, following definitions must be clearly understood.

Basic Size (Basic Dimension)

Basic size or basic dimension is theoretically the exact value of dimension for which the limits are derived with the help of allowance and tolerance.

Limits of Dimension

The limits of dimension are the maximum and minimum values permitted for a specific dimension.

Allowance

The allowance is the intentional difference applied in the basic size of mating parts. Allowance can also be defined as the minimum clearance (positive allowance) or maximum interference (negative allowance) between the mating parts.

Tolerance

Tolerance is the total permissible variation in a given dimension. It is the difference between maximum and minimum limits.

METHODS OF TOLERANCING

Tolerances are expressed using one of the two methods: limit dimensioning or plus and minus tolerancing. These methods apply to both inch and metric drawings.

Limit Dimensioning

In the limit dimensioning method, only the maximum and minimum dimensions are specified. When dimensions require greater accuracy than a general note provides, individual tolerances or limits are shown for that dimension. During placement of dimensions, the larger dimension is placed above the lower dimension, refer to Figure 16-1. When limit dimensions are used for diameter or radial features and are placed above each other, only one diameter or radius symbol is used which is located at midheight, refer to Figure 16-1.

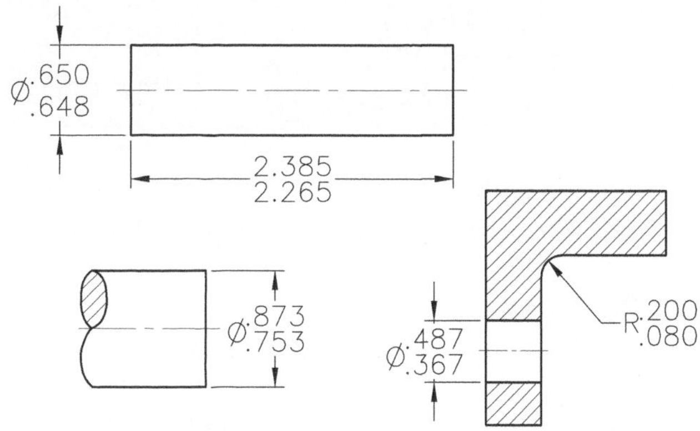

Figure 16-1 *Placement of limit dimensions*

If a maximum dimension has digits to the right of the decimal point, you need to add zeros to the minimum dimension after the decimal point and vice versa. This means that both the limits are expressed to the same number of decimal places, as shown in Figure 16-2.

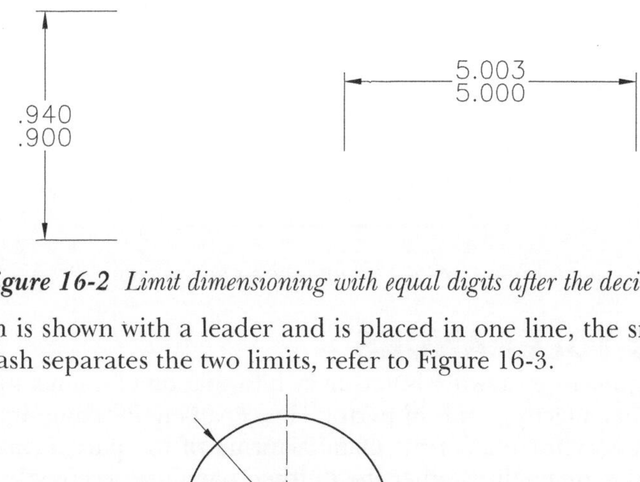

Figure 16-2 *Limit dimensioning with equal digits after the decimal*

When a dimension is shown with a leader and is placed in one line, the smaller size is shown first and a small dash separates the two limits, refer to Figure 16-3.

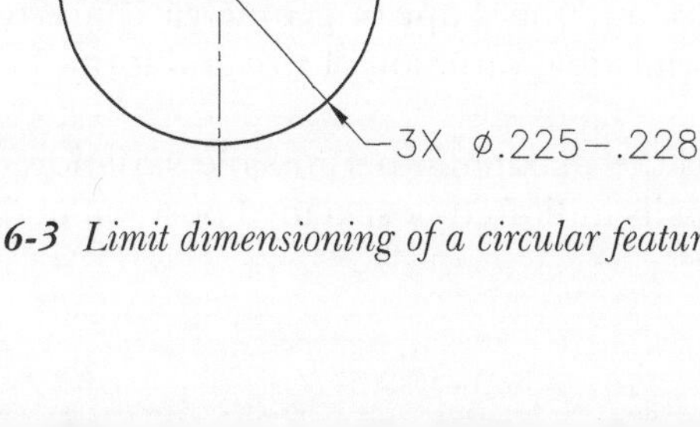

Figure 16-3 *Limit dimensioning of a circular feature*

For the case where only one limit is important and any variation from that limit in the other direction may be permitted, the MAX (maximum) or MIN (minimum) can be specified with the dimension value, as shown in Figure 16-4.

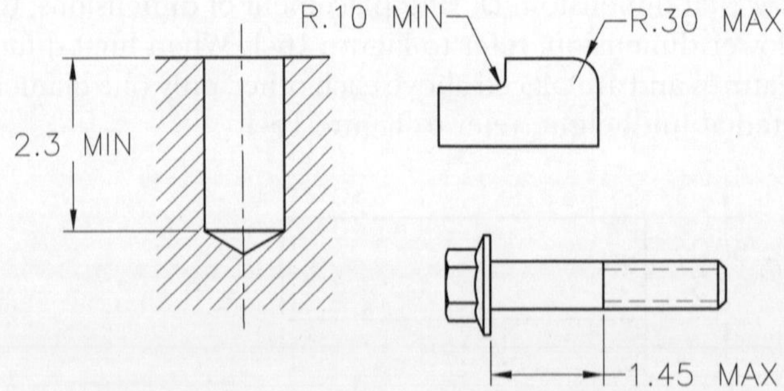

Figure 16-4 Limit dimensioning with single limit

Plus and Minus Tolerancing

In this method, the dimension is mentioned first and it is followed by a plus and minus tolerance expression. If the tolerance is expressed in plus and minus values then it is called bilateral tolerance, refer to Figure 16-5. The values of plus and minus limits need not be the same for bilateral tolerance.

If the tolerance is expressed with one value in plus or minus and the second one in zero then it is called as unilateral tolerance. A unilateral tolerance is the one that is applied in one direction such that the permissible variation in the other direction is zero, refer to Figure 16-5.

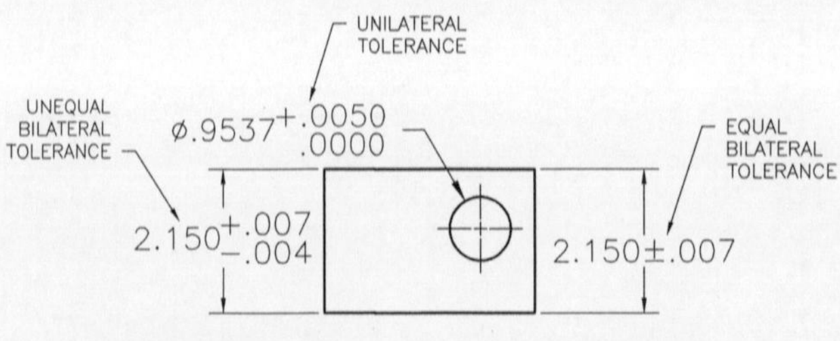

Figure 16-5 Plus and minus tolerancing

GEOMETRIC TOLERANCES

The intent of an engineering drawing is to convey information of the manufactured part from the designer to the manufacturer and inspector. Hence, an engineering drawing must contain all information necessary for the correct manufacturing of the part. It must also enable the inspector to determine precisely whether the finished parts are acceptable or not. Therefore, each drawing must convey three essential types of information: the material to be used, the size or dimensions of the part, and the shape or geometric characteristics of the part. The drawing must also specify the permissible variation of size and form.

A geometric tolerance is the maximum permissible variation of form, profile, orientation, or location of a feature from its indicated or specified position in the drawing. The tolerance value specifies that a feature would be allowed to have any variation of form or take up any position within the specified geometric tolerance zone. The tolerance value represents the width or diameter of the tolerance zone within which the point, line, or surface of the feature should lie. For example, a line controlled in a single plane by a straightness tolerance of .005 inch must lie within .005 inch wide zone, as shown in Figure 16-6.

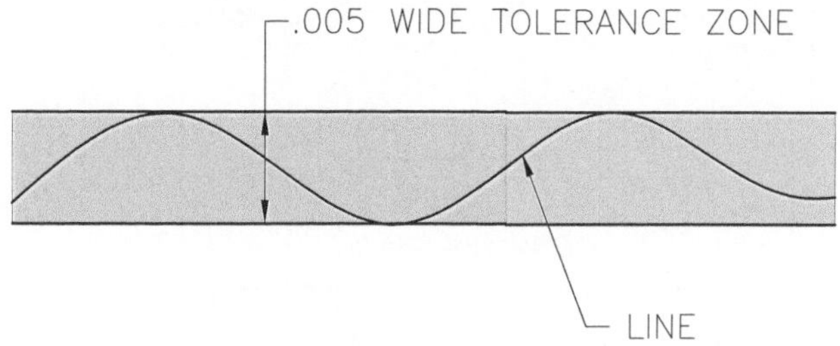

Figure 16-6 *Tolerance zone for straightness of a line*

The actual size of a feature must be within the size limits specified on the drawing. Each measurement made at any cross-section of the feature must not be greater than the maximum limit of size nor smaller than the minimum limit of size, refer to Figure 16-7(a) and Figure 16-7(b).

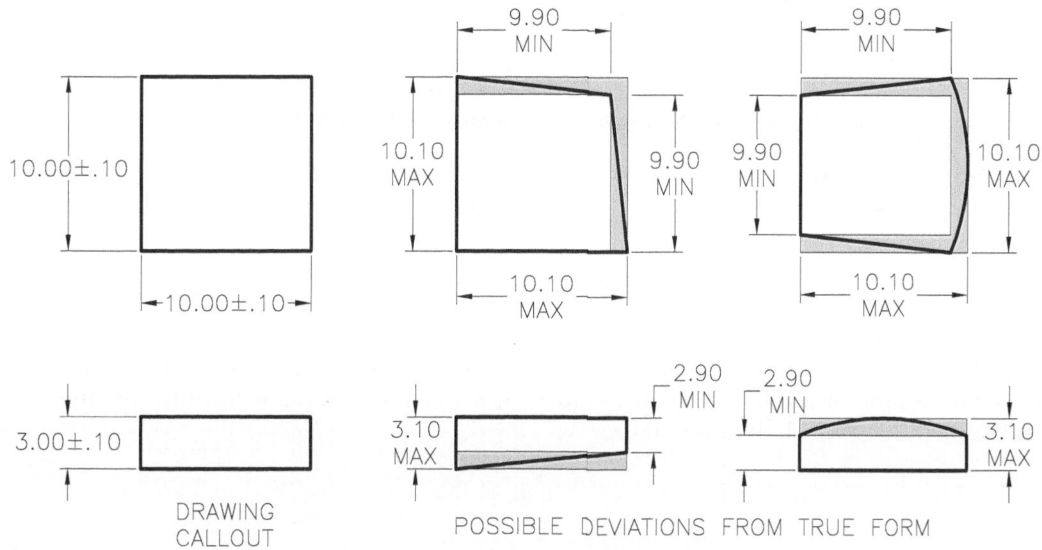

Figure 16-7(a) *Deviation of shape for flat features*

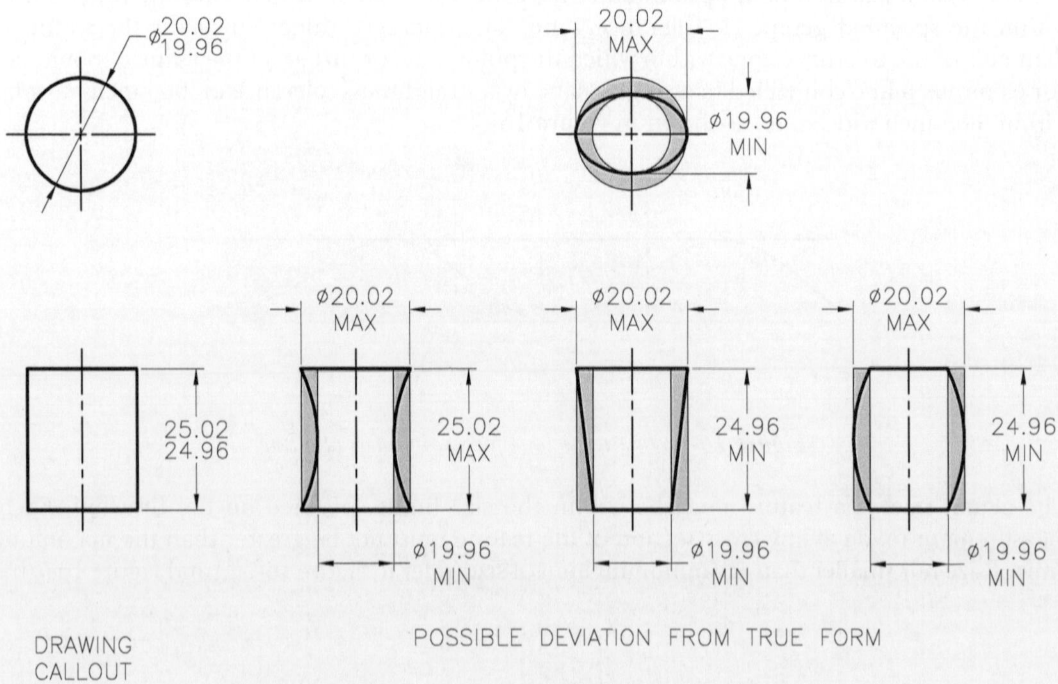

Figure 16-7(b) *Deviation of shape for cylindrical features*

Although each part is manufactured within the prescribed tolerance zones, the parts may not fit together because of deviation from their geometric form.

In order to meet functional requirements, it is often necessary to control the errors of form, including roundness and flatness as well as deviation from true size. To avoid any bending or deformation between mating parts, such as holes and shafts, it is usually necessary to ensure that they do not interfere the boundary of perfect form at their maximum material condition (the smallest hole or the largest shaft). Figure 16-8 shows deviation of form at the maximum material condition for shaft and holes.

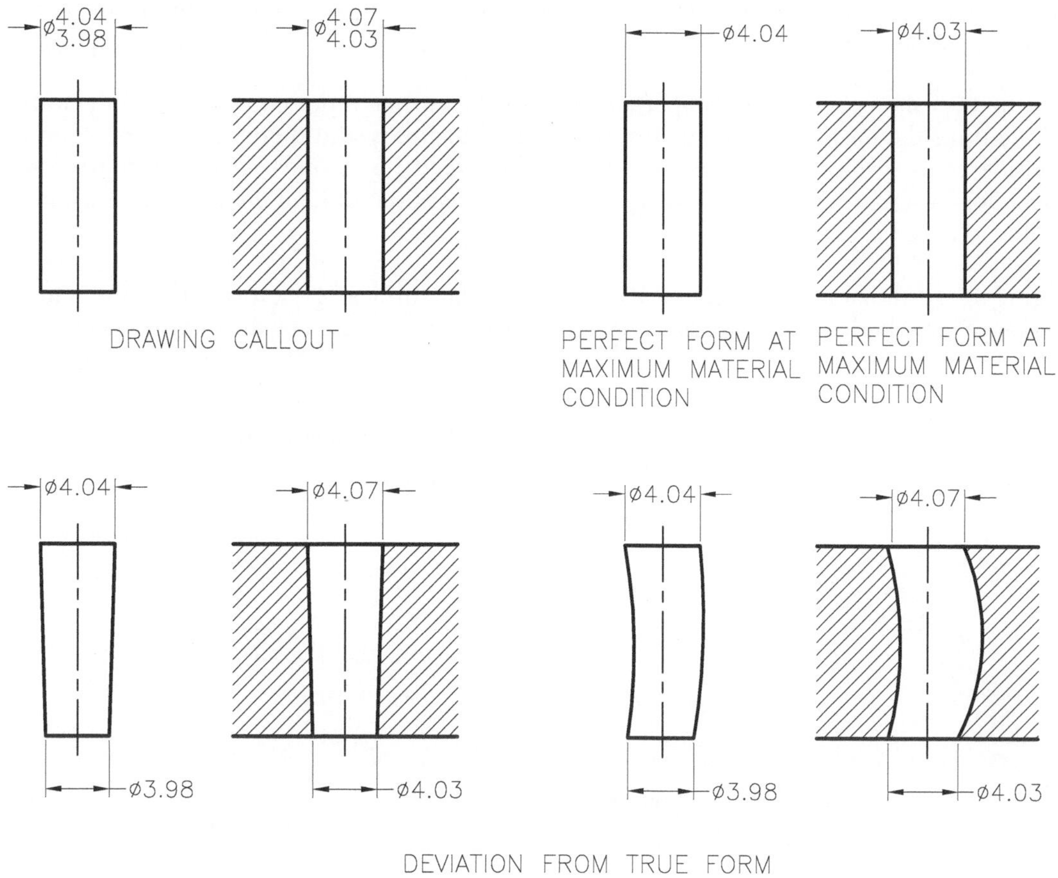

Figure 16-8 Deviation of form at the maximum material condition

Datums

Datums are imaginary references which are used to establish the location or geometric relationship between features of a part. The design of a part consists of many datums, each of which is a geometrically perfect form. A datum can be a straight line, a circle, a flat plane, a sphere, a cylinder, a cone, or a single point. As established from actual features, datums are assumed to be "exact" for the purpose of computation or reference.

Features

Features are real geometric shapes that make up the physical characteristics of a part. Features are specific component portions of a part which may include one or more surfaces such as holes, screw threads, profiles, faces, or slots.

Datum Reference Frame

Engineering, Manufacturing, and Inspection, all share a common three plane concept. These three planes are mutually perpendicular, perfect in dimension and orientation, and are exactly 90 degrees to each other. In geometric tolerancing, it is referred as Datum Reference Frame. The DRF consists of a system of features which are considered as the basis for dimensions for manufacturing and inspection. It provides complete orientation or a skeleton to which the part requirements are attached. The three main features of the datum reference frame are the planes, axes, and points.

Figure 16-9 shows a rectangular part fitted into the corner represented by the intersection of the three datum planes. The datum planes are imaginary and therefore perfect. They are considered as absolute reference base. There is a primary, a secondary, and a tertiary datum plane for each part. The part will vary from these planes even though the variation may not be visible to naked eyes.

Figure 16-10 shows a cylindrical part resting on a flat surface of the primary plane and the center of the cylinder is aligned with the vertical datum axis formed by the intersection of other two planes.

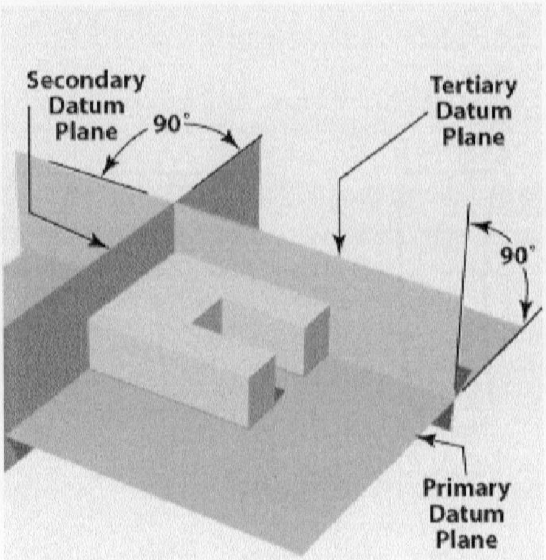

Figure 16-9 The datum reference frame with a rectangular plate

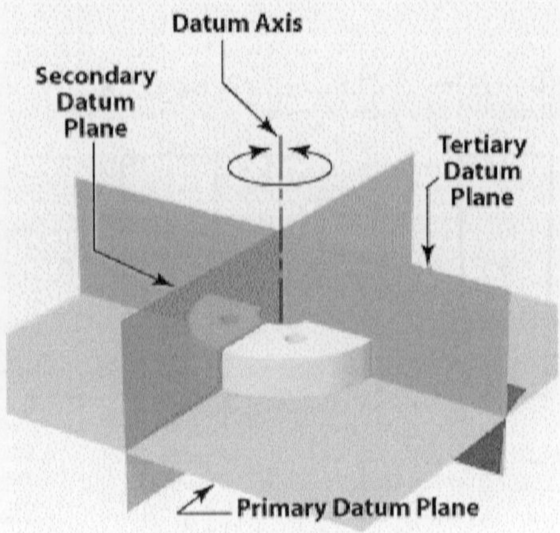

Figure 16-10 The datum reference frame with a circular plate

Material Condition Modifiers

Material condition modifiers tremendously impact the applied tolerance or datum reference. These modifiers can only be applied to features and datums that specify the size of the part. Examples of these features are holes, slots, pins, and tabs. If modifiers are applied to the features that are without size, they have no impact. However, if no modifier is specified in the feature control frame, the default modifier is regardless of feature size (RFS). The three types of material condition modifiers are explained next.

- **Maximum Material Condition (MMC)**
  This is a condition of a part feature where the part contains the maximum amount of material or the minimum hole-size and maximum shaft-size.

- **Least Material Condition (LMC)**
  This is the opposite of the MMC concept. This is a part feature which contains the least amount of material or the largest hole-size and smallest shaft-size.

- **Regardless of Feature Size (RFS)**
  When MMC or LMC is not specified with a geometric tolerance for a feature of size, no relationship is supposed to exist between the feature of size and the geometric tolerance. In other words, the tolerance is applied regardless of feature size.

  In this case, the geometric tolerance controls the form, orientation, location of the axis, or median plane of the feature.

Feature Control Frame

The current method uses feature control frame to specify geometric tolerances. A feature control frame consists of a rectangular box divided into two or more compartments containing the geometric characteristic symbol followed by the tolerance value or description, modifiers, and any applicable datum feature references, as shown in Figure 16-11. If the tolerance zone is cylindrical, then a diameter symbol has to be added before the tolerance value followed by a material condition symbol. Other compartments are added when there is a requirement of composite tolerancing for a geometric feature.

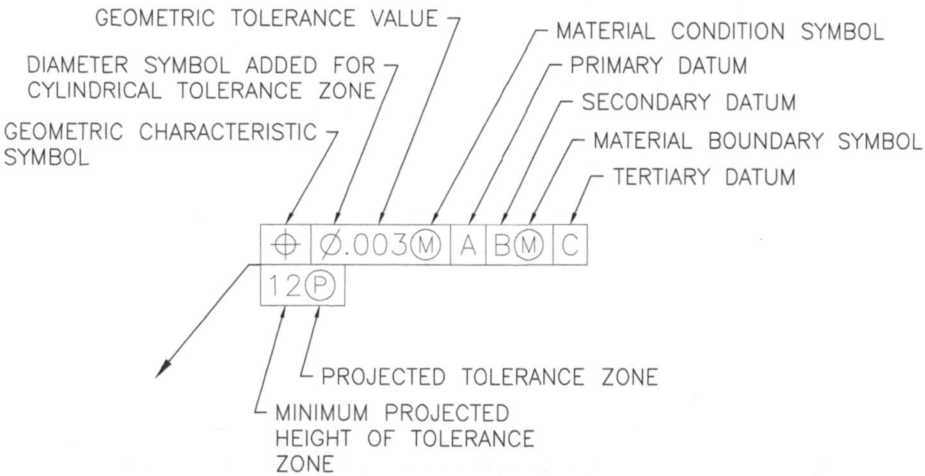

Figure 16-11 *The feature control frame*

Supplementary symbols, such as datum systems, datum targets, least and maximum material conditions, and projected tolerance zones are used in order to facilitate this precise interpretation of an engineering drawing. It is not always required to use geometric tolerances for every feature of a part.

Generally, if a feature meets all dimensional tolerances then the form variations will be adequately controlled by the accuracy of the manufacturing process and the equipment used. A geometric tolerance is also used to state functional or interchangeability requirements of the manufactured part.

System of Geometric Tolerancing

The system of geometric tolerancing offers precise interpretation of drawing requirements. The geometric characteristics of a part that are controlled by using geometric tolerancing are represented by a symbol. The following table shows different characteristics and their symbols:

FEATURES	TYPES OF TOLERANCE	CHARACTERSTICS	SYMBOL
INDIVIDUAL FEATURES	FORM	STRAIGHTNESS	—
		FLATNESS	▱
		CIRCULARITY(ROUNDNESS)	○
		CYLINDRICITY	⌭
INDIVIDUAL OR RELATED FEATURES	PROFILE	PROFILE OF A LINE	⌒
		PROFILE OF A SURFACE	⌓
RELATED FEATURES	ORIENTATION	ANGULARITY	∠
		PERPENDICULARITY	⊥
		PARALLELISM	//
	LOCATION	POSITION	⌖
		CONCENTRICITY	◎
		SYMMETRY	⌯
	RUNOUT	CIRCULAR RUNOUT	↗*
		TOTAL RUNOUT	⌰*

ARROWHEADS MAY BE FILLED OR NOT

FORM TOLERANCES

Form tolerances are used to control the form characteristics of the manufactured part. These characteristics include straightness, flatness, circularity, and cylindricity. Form tolerances are applicable to single feature or elements of single feature and, as such, do not require locating dimensions. The form tolerance must be less than the size tolerance. Form and orientation tolerances critical for the function and interchangeability of parts are specified where the tolerances of size and location do not provide sufficient control. A tolerance of form may be specified where no tolerance of size is given, for example, controlling the flatness of parts after assembly.

Straightness

Straightness is a condition in which the elements of a surface or the axes of a surface are in a straight line. The geometric characteristic symbol used for indicating straightness is a horizontal line. A straightness tolerance refers to a tolerance zone within which the considered element of the surface or center line must lie. The straightness tolerance is applied to the view where the elements to be controlled are represented by a straight line.

The straightness tolerance is specified on a drawing by means of a feature control frame, which is directed by a leader to the line requiring control. In Figure 16-12(A), the symbol of straightness states that the line shall be straight within .08 in. This means that the line shall be contained within a tolerance zone consisting of the area between two parallel straight lines in the same plane separated by the specified tolerance value, refer to Figure 16-12(B). Theoretically, straightness of a line can be measured by keeping a straightedge in contact with the line and then determining the space between the straightedge and the line. If the space does not exceed the specified tolerance then the edge is considered straight.

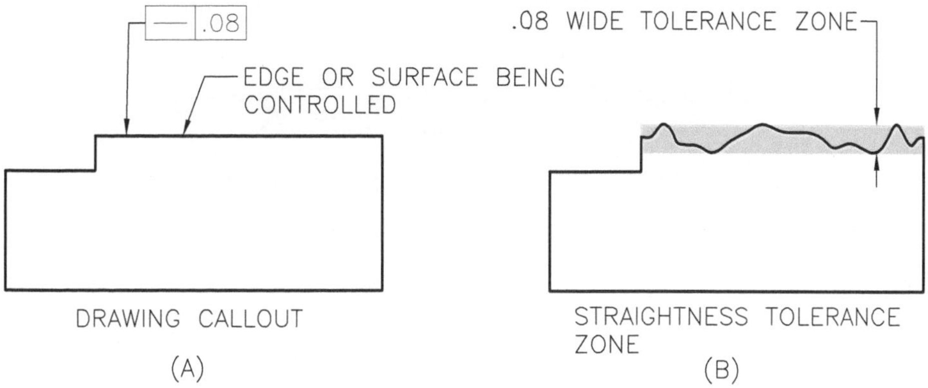

Figure 16-12 *Straightness tolerance applied to a flat surface*

For cylindrical parts or curved surfaces that are straight in one direction, the feature control frame should be directed to the side view where line elements appear as a straight line, as shown in Figure 16-13(A). Straightness of a cylindrical surface means that each line element of the surface shall be contained within a tolerance zone that consists of the space between two parallel lines, separated by the specified tolerance, when the part is rolled along one of the planes, refer to Figure 16-13(B). Theoretically, this could be measured by rolling the part on a flat plate and measuring the space between the part and the plate, refer to Figure 16-14.

The straightness tolerance applied to surface controls surface elements only. Therefore, it will only control the bending or a wavy condition of the surface, but it will not necessarily control the straightness of the axis or the conicity of the cylinder.

The straightness tolerance can be applied to a conical surface in the same manner as for a cylindrical surface, refer to Figure 16-15. In this way, it will ensure that the rate of taper is uniform. For controlling the actual rate of taper, or the taper angle, the tolerance must be applied separately.

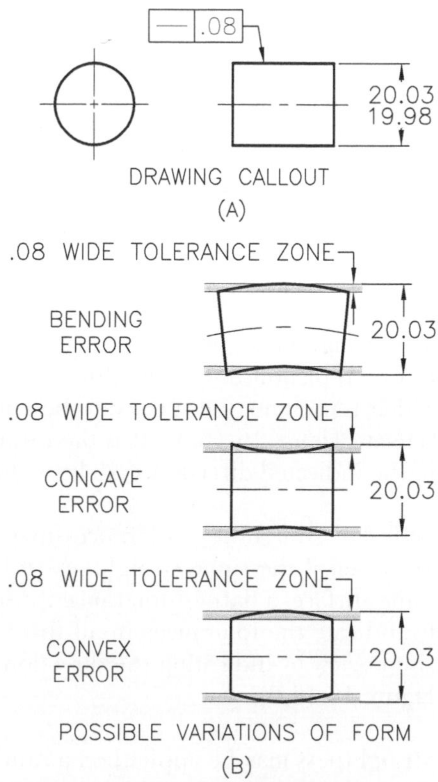

Figure 16-13 *Straightness tolerance applied to a cylindrical feature*

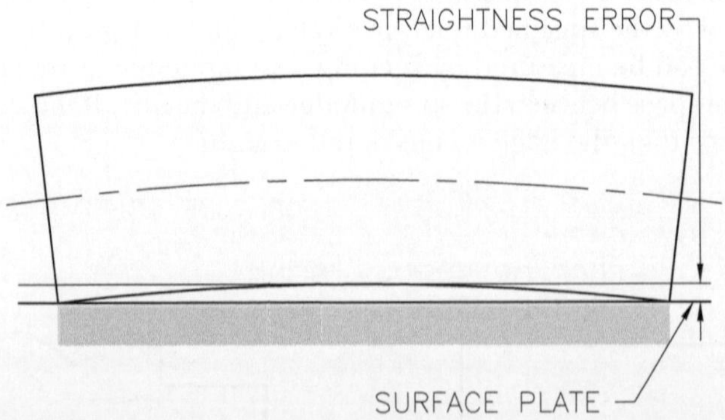

Figure 16-14 Measuring the straightness of a cylindrical surface

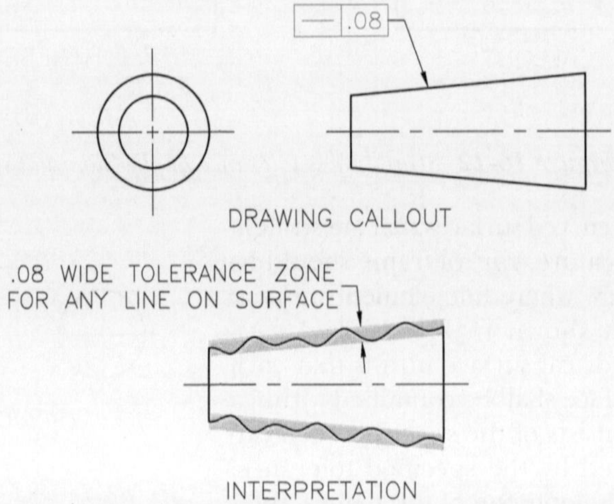

Figure 16-15 Straightness tolerance applied for a conical feature

The straightness tolerance applied to a flat surface indicates that the straightness is controlled in one direction only. Therefore, in this case, it must be directed to the line on the drawing which represents the surface to be controlled and the direction in which control is required, refer to Figure 16-16(A). It is then interpreted to mean that each line element on the surface in the indicated direction shall lie within the specified tolerance zone, refer to Figure 16-16(C).

Different straightness tolerances may be specified in two or more directions when required. However, if the same straightness tolerance is required in two coordinate directions on the same surface, a flatness tolerance is used instead of a straightness tolerance. It is not necessary to indicate the tolerances in all three views. The straightness tolerances may be shown on a single view by indicating the direction with short lines terminated by arrowheads, as shown in Figure 16-16(B).

Straightness may be applied on a unit basis for limiting unexpected surface variation within a relatively short length of the feature. While using a unit control on a feature of size, a maximum limit is typically specified to restrict the relatively large theoretical variations. If straightness is not particularly specified for the total length then it is obvious that straightness per unit length is given.

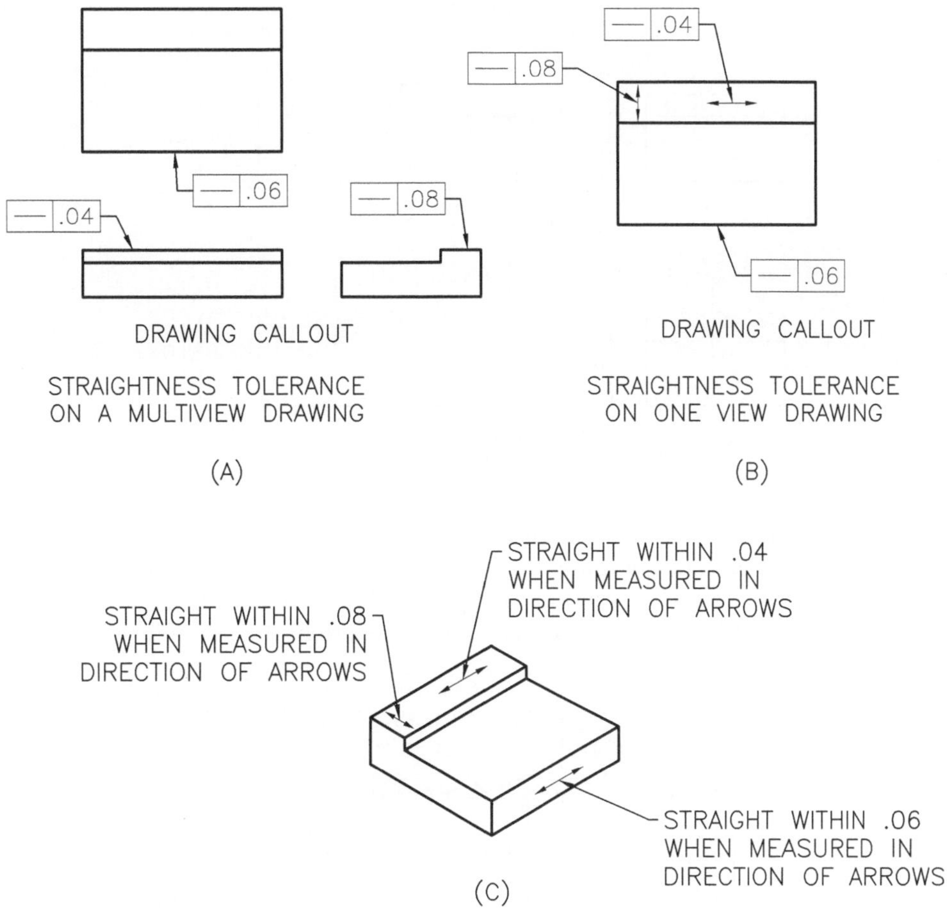

Figure 16-16 *Straightness tolerance in multiple directions*

Flatness

Flatness of a surface is a condition in which all surface elements lie in one plane. A flatness tolerance specifies a tolerance zone defined by two parallel planes within which all points on the surface must lie. These two parallel planes must lie within the limits of the size. These planes may be oriented in any manner to contain the surface but it is not necessary that they should be parallel to the base. The symbol for flatness is a parallelogram with angle of 60°.

When a flatness tolerance is specified on a surface, the feature control frame is attached to a leader and is directed to the surface or to an extension line of the surface. It is placed in a view where the surface elements to be controlled are represented by a line, refer to Figure 16-17.

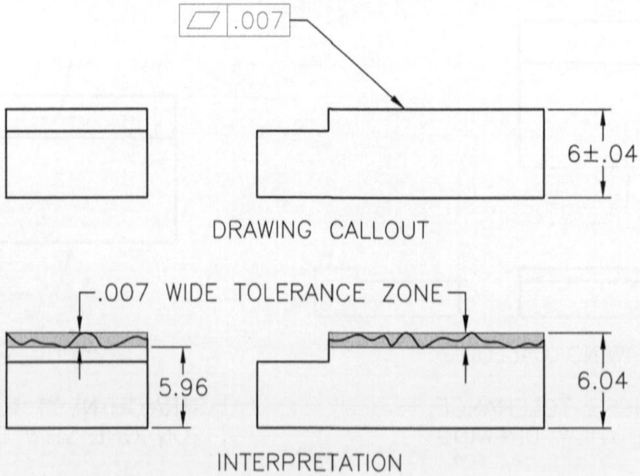

***Figure 16-17** Flatness tolerance applied to a surface*

If a surface is associated with a size tolerance then the flatness tolerance must be less than the size tolerance and it should be contained within the limits of the specified size. When flatness tolerances are applied to opposite surfaces of a part and the size tolerances are also shown, as shown in Figure 16-18, the flatness tolerance must be less than the size tolerance and it must lie within the limits of size.

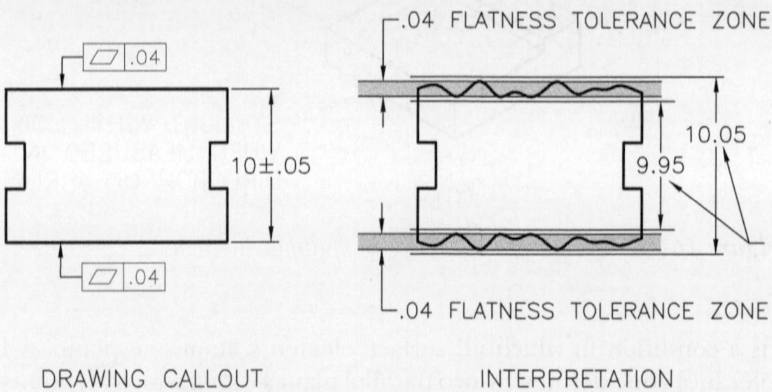

***Figure 16-18** Flatness tolerance within limits of size*

For limiting any unexpected surface variation within a relatively small area of the feature, flatness may be applied on unit basis. The unit variation is used either in combination with a specified total variation, or alone. It is expected to specify the maximum limit to restrict the relatively large theoretical variations. Since flatness involves surface area, the value of the tolerance is specified to the left of the area separated by a slash, refer to Figure 16-19.

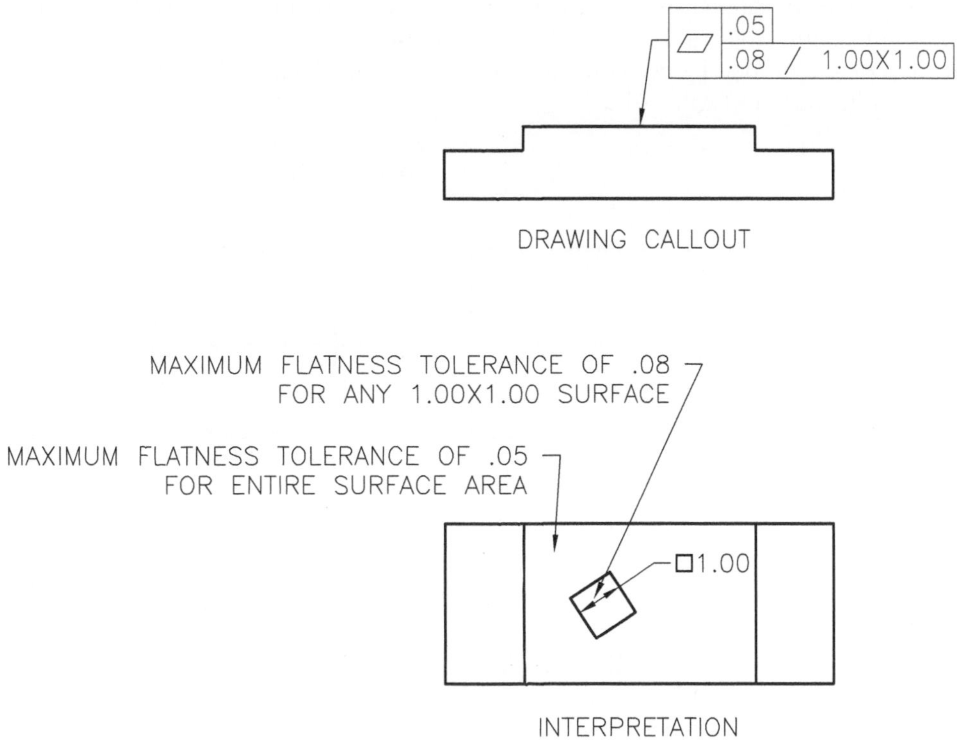

Figure 16-19 *Overall flatness tolerance combined with a flatness of unit area*

Circularity (Roundness)

Circularity is a condition on a surface of revolution (cylinder, cone, sphere) where all points of the surface are intersected by any plane perpendicular to a common axis (cylinder, cone) or by a plane passing through a common center (sphere) are equidistant from that axis or center. Circularity is similar to straightness with the only difference that in circularity, the line representing straightness is wrapped around a circular cross-section.

Common type of circularity errors of a circular line on the periphery of a cross-section of a circular feature may occur in the form of ovality, lobing, or as random irregularities. Possible deviations from a true circle are shown in Figure 16-20.

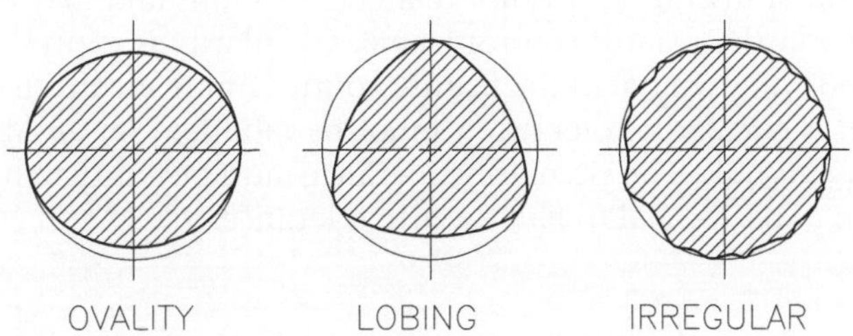

Figure 16-20 *Common types of circularity errors*

The symbol used for circularity is a circle. The circularity tolerance is specified by using this symbol in the feature control frame, as shown in Figure 16-21. A circularity tolerance specifies a tolerance zone bounded by two concentric circles within which each circular element of the surface must lie, refer to Figure 16-21.

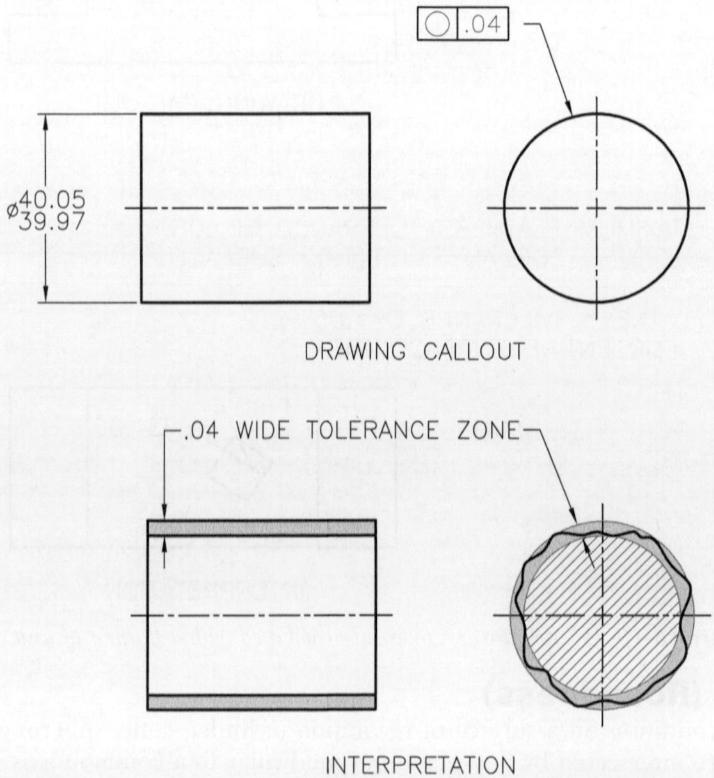

***Figure 16-21** Circularity tolerance applied to a cylindrical feature*

Circularity of non-cylindrical parts refers to conical parts and other features that are circular in cross-section but have variable diameters. As many sizes of circles may be involved in the end view, it is usually good practice to apply the circularity tolerance to the side views, as shown in Figure 16-22.

As circularity is a form of tolerance, it is not related to datums and may be specified by using the circularity symbol in the feature control frame. Circularity is expressed on an RFS basis. The absence of a modifying symbol in the feature control frame means that RFS applies to the circularity tolerance. A circularity tolerance cannot be modified on an MMC basis because it controls surface elements only. The circularity tolerance must be less than half the size tolerance because it must lie in a space equal to half the size tolerance.

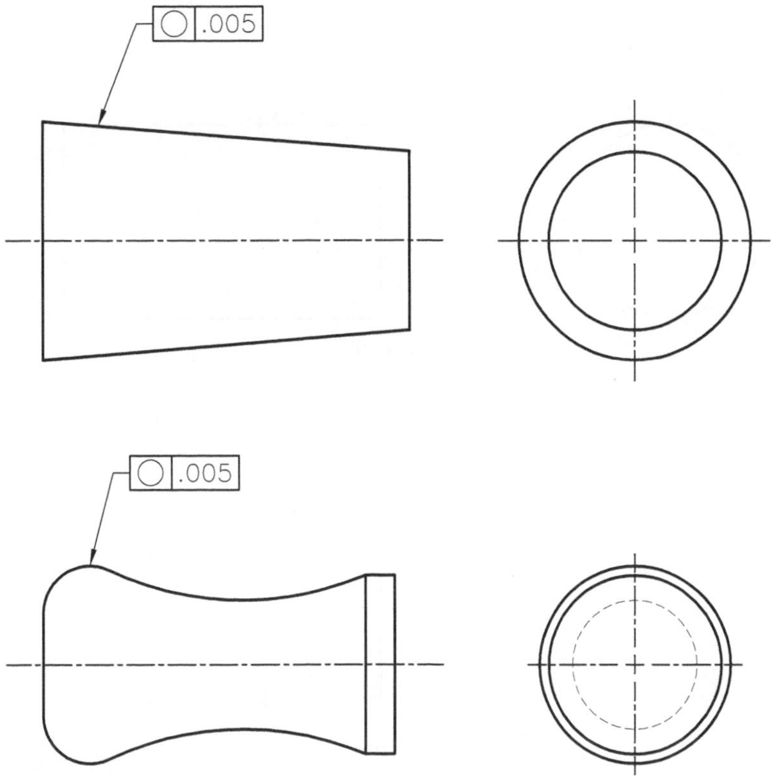

Figure 16-22 *Circularity tolerance applied to a non cylindrical feature*

Cylindricity

Cylindricity is a condition of a surface in which all points on the surface are at same distance from a common axis. It is like a flatness tolerance wrapped around a cylinder. The cylindricity tolerance is a composite control of form that includes circularity, straightness, and parallelism of the surface element of a cylindrical feature.

The geometric characteristic symbol for cylindricity consists of a circle with two tangent lines at 60°. A cylindricity tolerance that is measured radially specifies a tolerance zone bounded by two concentric cylinders within which the surface must lie. So the cylindricity tolerance must be within the specified limits of size. In an engineering drawing, cylindricity tolerance can be simultaneously applied for end view or side view, as shown in Figure 16-23.

The cylindricity tolerance must be less than half of the size tolerance. Since each part is measured for form deviation, it is obvious that the total range of the specified cylindricity tolerance will not always be available. The cylindricity tolerance zone is controlled by the measured size of the actual part. First the part size is determined and then the cylindricity tolerance is added as a refinement to the actual size of the part. Figure 16-24 shows some permissible form errors for the part shown in Figure 16-23.

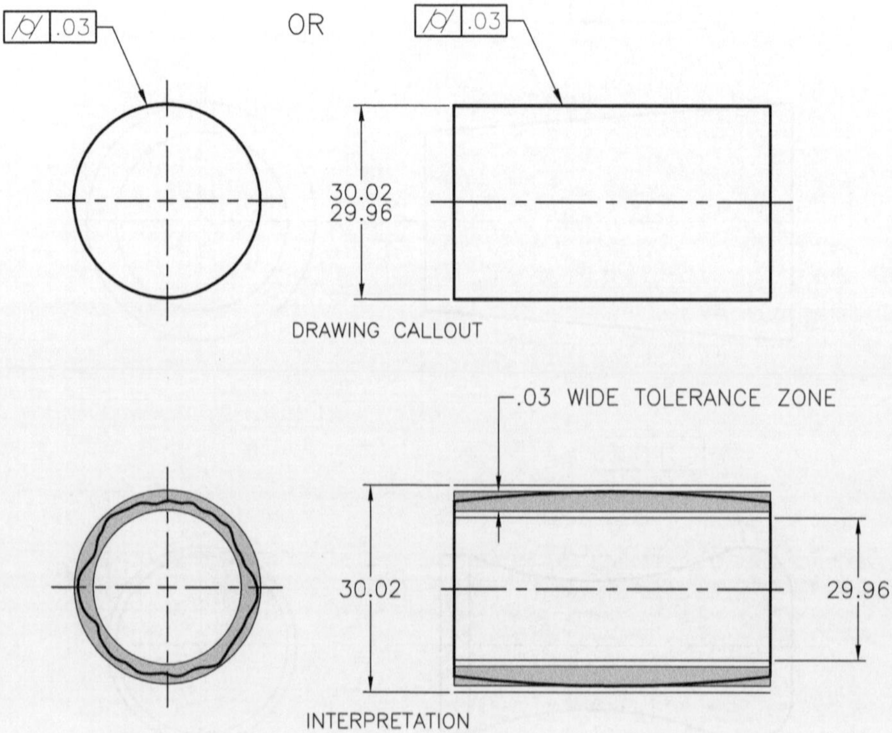

***Figure 16-23** Cylindricity tolerance applied to a cylindrical feature*

Cylindricity tolerances can be applied only to cylindrical surfaces, such as round holes and shafts. No specific geometric tolerances have been devised for other circular forms which require the use of several geometric tolerances. A conical surface, for example, must be controlled by a combination of tolerances for circularity, straightness, and angularity. Since cylindricity is a form tolerance much like the flatness tolerance, it controls surface elements only and cannot be modified on MMC basis. The absence of a modifying symbol in the feature control frame indicates that RFS applies is being applied on the part.

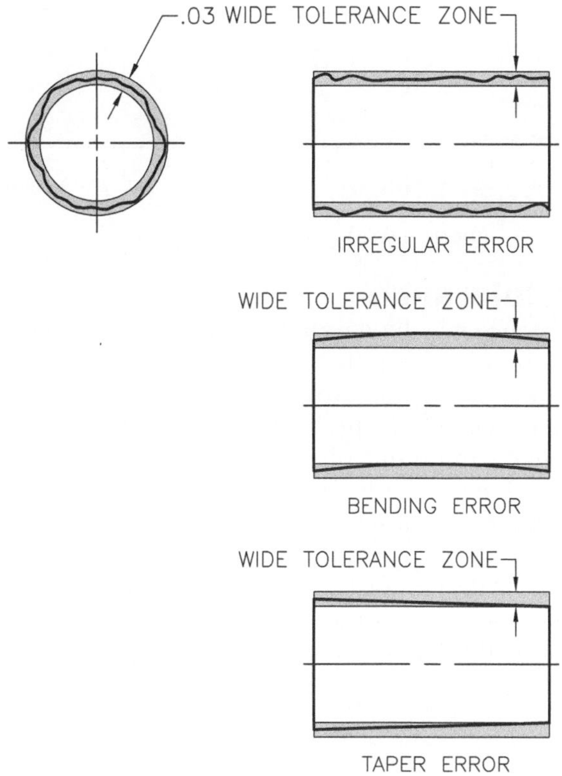

Figure 16-24 *Possible errors in a cylindrical feature*

PROFILE TOLERANCES

A profile is the outline form or shape of a line or surface. A line profile represents the edge of a part or it may refer to line elements of a surface in a single direction. A surface profile represents the form or shape of a complete surface in three dimensions.

Profile tolerances are used to control the position of lines and surfaces that are neither flat nor cylindrical. The elements of a line profile may be straight lines, arcs, or other curved lines. The elements of a surface profile may be flat surfaces, spherical surfaces, cylindrical surfaces, or surfaces composed of various line profiles in two or more directions. A profile tolerance specifies a uniform boundary along the true profile within which the elements of the surface must lie. MMC is not applicable to profile tolerances. The profile tolerance must be contained within the limits of size in the cases where it is used as a refinement of size.

There are two geometric characteristics symbols for profiles: one for line and other for surfaces. Separate symbols are needed because it is often necessary to differentiate between line elements of a surface and the complete surface itself. The symbol for the profile-of-a-line consists of a semicircle with a diameter equal to twice the size of the letters used in the whole drawing. The symbol for profile-of-a-surface is identical to profile-of-a-line except that the semicircle is closed by a straight line at the bottom, refer to Figure 16-25.

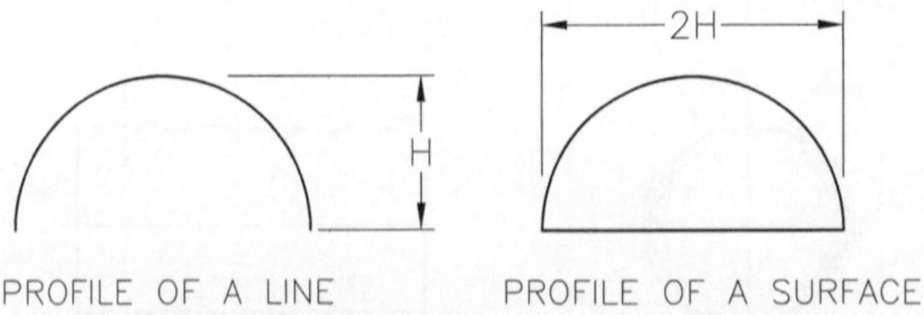

Figure 16-25 Symbols used for profile

Profile-of-a-line Tolerance

The profile-of-a-line tolerance may be directed to a line of any length or shape. In case the requirement is only the profile shape then the datums will not be used. Profile-of-a-line tolerancing is used where it is not desirable to control the entire surface of the feature as a single entity. The profile-of-a-line tolerance is specified in the usual manner by including the symbol and tolerance in a feature control frame directed to the line that is to be controlled, refer to Figure 16-26. The tolerance zone established by the profile-of-a-line tolerance is two dimensional, extending along the length of the considered feature. If the line on the drawing to which the tolerance is directed represents a surface, the tolerance is applied to all line elements of the surface parallel to the plane of the view on the drawing, unless otherwise specified. The tolerance indicates a tolerance zone consisting of the area between two parallel lines, separated by the specified tolerance which are themselves parallel to the basic form of the line being toleranced.

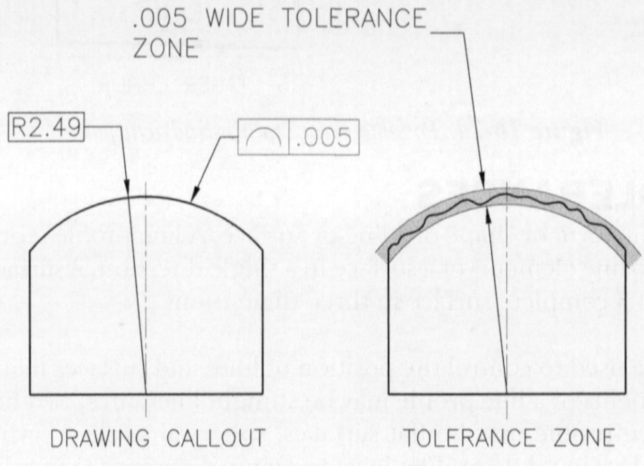

Figure 16-26 Profile-of-a-line tolerance

Profile-of-a-surface Tolerance

If the profile of line tolerance is applied to the whole surface then it is known as profile-of-a-surface tolerance. The tolerance zone established by the profile-of-a-surface tolerance is three dimensional, extending along the length and width or circumference of the considered feature or features. The profile-of-a-surface tolerance indicates a tolerance zone having the same form as the basic surface with a uniform width equal to the specified tolerance within which the entire surface must lie, refer to Figure 16-27.

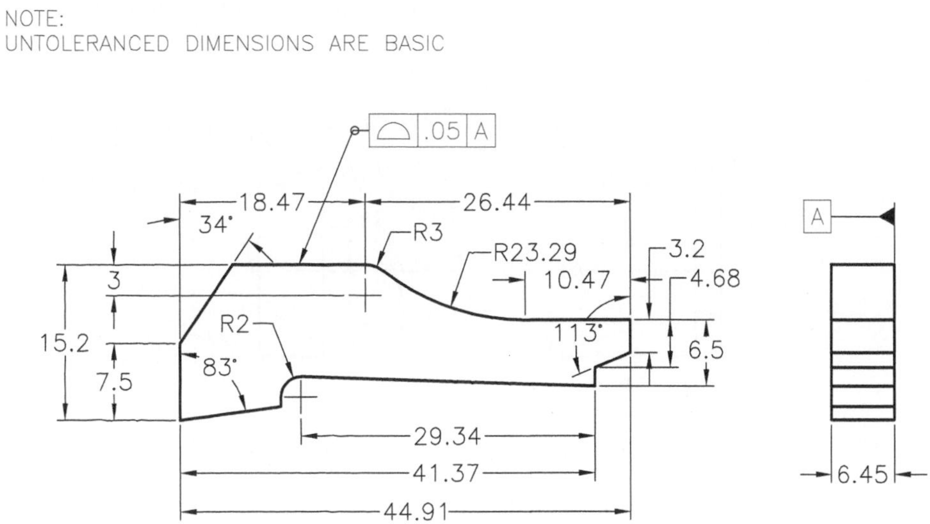

Figure 16-27 *Specifying the profile-of-a-surface tolerance*

Different profile tolerances may be applied on segments of a profile according to the requirement, as shown in Figure 16-28. Profile-of-a-surface tolerance is used to control form or combinations of size, form, and orientation. If it is used for the refinement of size, the profile tolerance must be contained within the size limits. Profile-of-a-surface tolerance may be applied to parts of any shape including parts having a constant cross-section, parts having a surface of revolution, or parts having a profile tolerance applied all over. Although the profile tolerance may be directed to the surface in either view, it is usually directed to the view showing the shape of the profile.

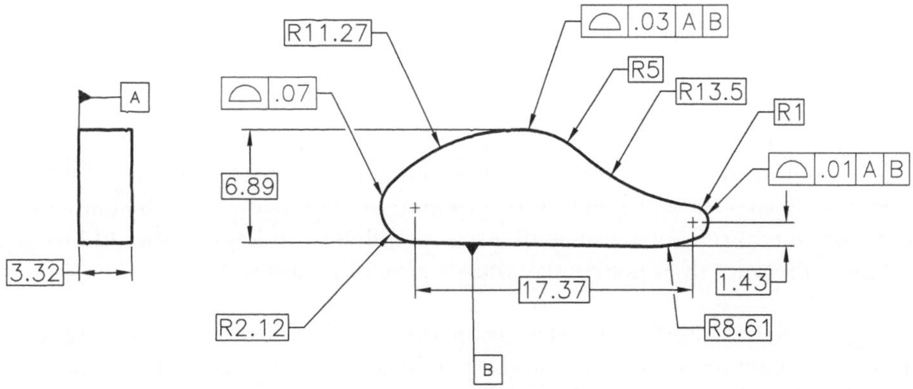

Figure 16-28 *Specifying different profile tolerances on a segment of a profile*

The basic rules for profile-of-a-line tolerancing apply to profile-of-a-surface tolerancing as well. However, in most cases, the profile-of-a-surface tolerance requires reference of datums in order to provide proper orientation of the profile. This is specified by indicating suitable datum with the feature. The profile is related to the datum by a basic or a toleranced dimension. It can be determined on the basis of certain criteria. This criteria distinguishes whether the profile tolerance is being applied to position or orientation.

Profile tolerancing may be used to control the form and orientation of plane surfaces. Profile-of-a-surface tolerance is used to control a plane surface inclined to a datum feature, as shown in Figure 16-29.

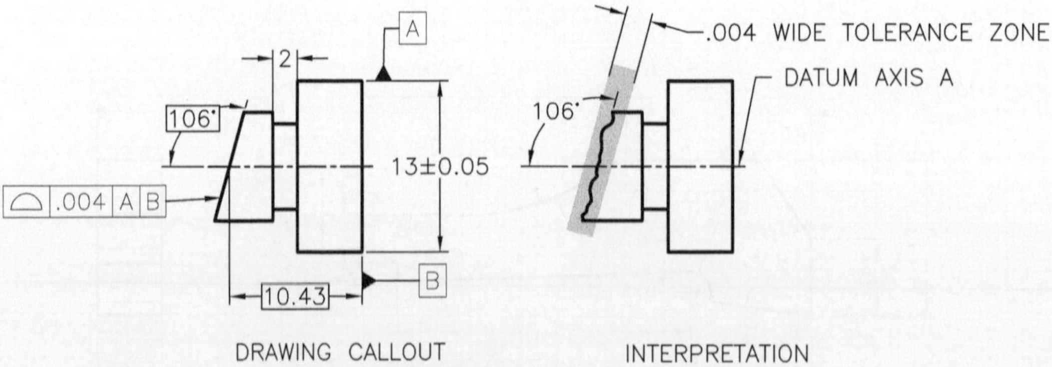

***Figure 16-29** Profile-of-a-surface tolerance zone*

ORIENTATION TOLERANCES

Orientation refers to the angular relationship that exists between two or more lines, surfaces, or other features. An orientation tolerance controls parallel, perpendicular, and all other angular relationships. As orientation refers to a certain degree, the limits of size control the form and parallelism, and the tolerances of location controls the orientation. The extent of this control should be considered before specifying the form or orientation tolerances. The general geometric characteristic for orientation is termed as angularity. This term may be used to describe angular relationships of any angle between straight lines or surfaces with straight line elements, such as flat or cylindrical surfaces. For two specific type of angularity, special terms are used. They are perpendicularity and parallelism. Perpendicularity (squareness) is used for features that are related to each other by a 90° angle, and parallelism for features related to one another by an angle of zero.

A tolerance of form or orientation may be specified where the tolerances of size and location do not provide sufficient control. Note that an orientation tolerance, when applied to a planar surface, controls flatness to the extent of the orientation tolerance. When the flatness control in the orientation tolerance is not sufficient, a separate flatness tolerance should be considered. An orientation tolerance does not control the location of features.

The three geometric symbols for orientation tolerances are shown in Figure 16-30. The proportions for the symbols are based on the height of the letters used in the drawing.

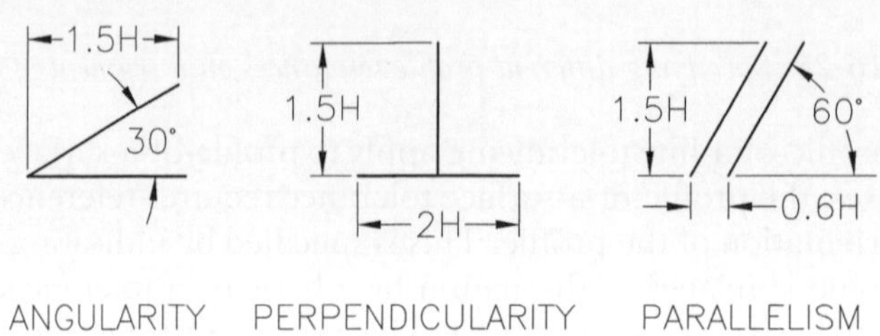

***Figure 16-30** Symbols used for Orientation tolerances*

Angularity Tolerance

Angularity refers to the angular relation of a surface or axis (at an angle other than 0° and 90°) with respect to a datum plane or datum axis. The angularity tolerance is a three-dimensional quantity and the shape of the tolerance zone depends on the shape of the feature. If applied to a flat surface, the tolerance zone is specified by two imaginary planes, parallel to the ideal angle and spaced apart at the prescribed distance, refer to Figure 16-31. If angularity is applied to a hole, it references to an imaginary cylinder around the ideal angle but the center axis of the hole must stay within that imaginary cylinder, refer to Figure 16-32.

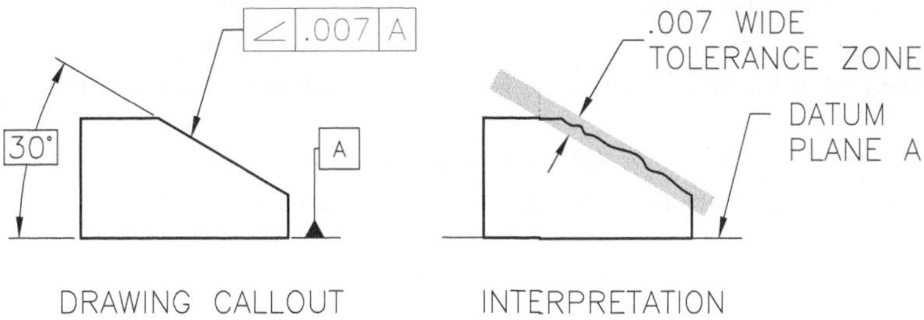

Figure 16-31 *Angularity tolerance applied to a surface*

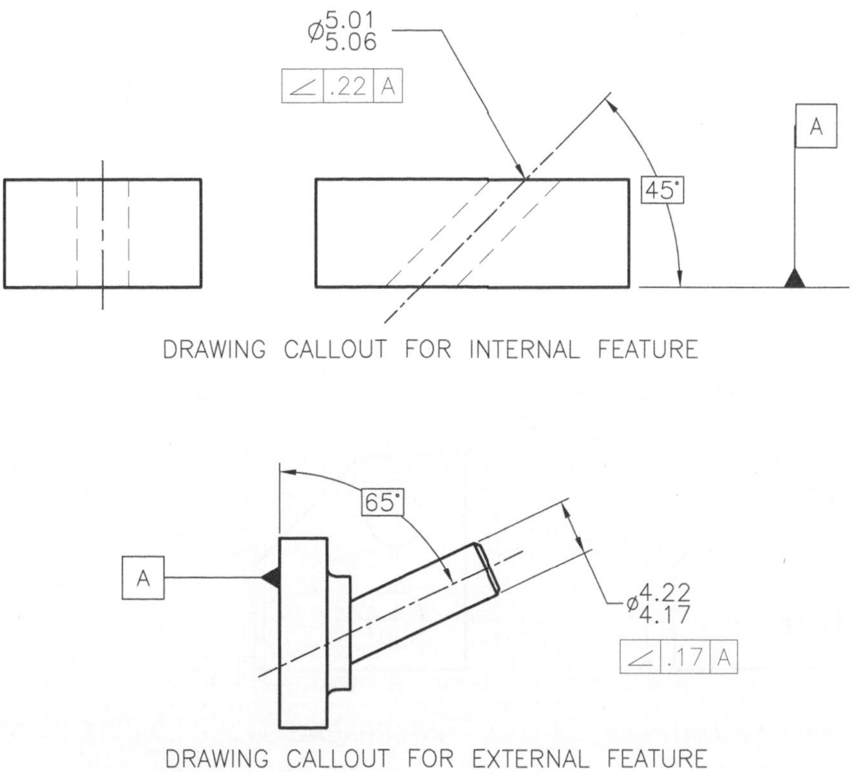

Figure 16-32 *Angularity tolerance applied to cylindrical features*

For geometric tolerancing of angularity, the angle between the datum and the controlled features should be stated as a basic angle. Therefore, it should be enclosed in a rectangular frame (basic dimension symbol) to indicate that the general tolerance note does not apply, refer to Figures 16-31 and 16-32. However, for perpendicularity (90°) or parallelism (0°), the angle need not be stated.

Perpendicularity Tolerance

Perpendicularity is the condition where a surface subtends 90° angle to a datum plane or axis. The perpendicularity tolerance for a feature specifies a tolerance zone defined by two parallel planes perpendicular to a datum plane or axis. The surface or axis of the considered feature must lie within this specified zone.

The perpendicularity tolerance specifies one of the following tolerance zones:

1. A cylindrical tolerance zone perpendicular to a datum plane or axis within which the center line of the considered feature must lie, refer to Figure 16-33.

2. A tolerance zone defined by two parallel planes perpendicular to a datum axis or plane within which the surface of the considered feature must lie, refer to Figure 16-34.

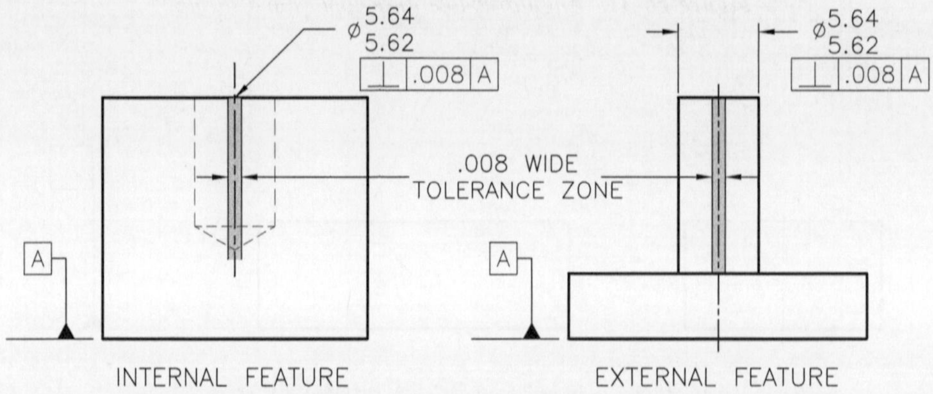

***Figure 16-33** Perpendicularity tolerance zone in cylindrical features*

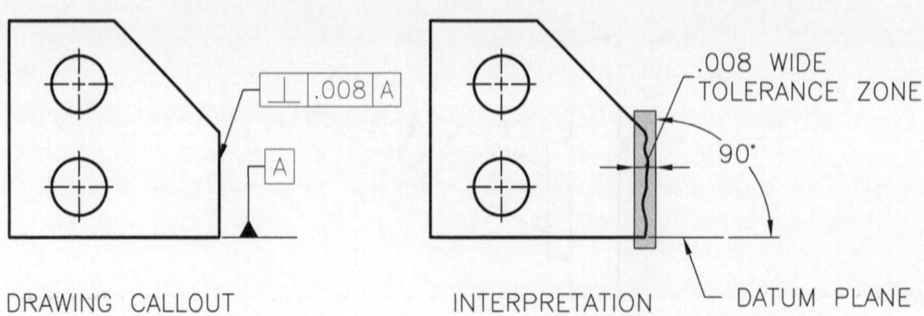

***Figure 16-34** Perpendicularity tolerance applied to a flat surface*

Parallelism Tolerance

Parallelism refers to condition where a feature is parallel to the reference datum plane. Parallelism can also be stated as the condition of a surface equidistant at all points from a datum plane. The parallelism tolerance for a flat surface or a cylindrical feature specifies a tolerance zone defined by two planes or lines parallel to a datum plane or axis. For a flat surface, line elements of the surface must lie within the specified tolerance zone, refer to Figure 16-35. For a cylindrical feature, the axis of the feature must lie within the specified cylindrical tolerance zone, refer to Figure 16-36.

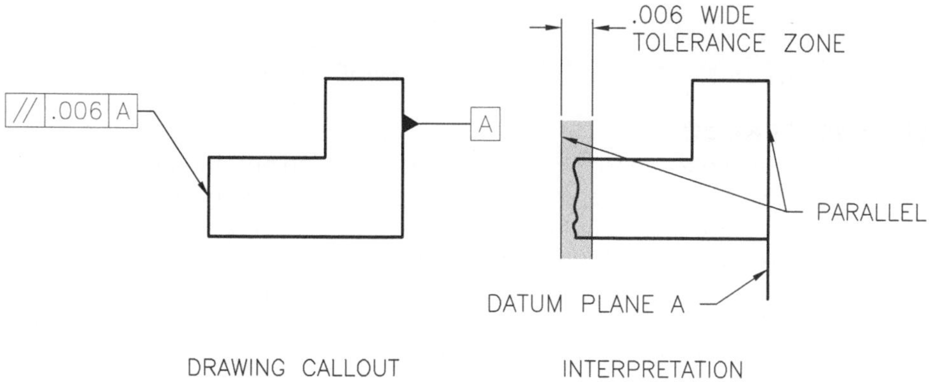

Figure 16-35 *Parallelism tolerance applied to flat surfaces*

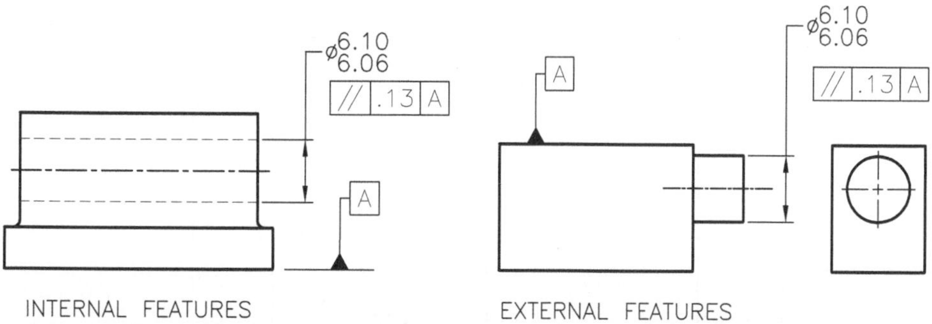

Figure 16-36 *Parallelism tolerance applied to cylindrical features*

Note

Flatness and parallelism are sometimes confused with each other. However, flatness is not related to another datum and it looks at the feature independently. Parallelism relates the inspected feature to another datum plane. Whenever an orientation tolerance is applied to a flat surface, it indirectly defines the flatness of the feature.

LOCATION TOLERANCES

Location tolerances include position, concentricity, and symmetry tolerances. Position tolerance is used to control coaxiality of features, the center distance between features, and the location of features as a group. Concentricity and symmetry tolerances are used to control the center distance of feature elements. The geometric characteristics symbols for the location tolerances are in the proportion of the text height used in the drawing, as shown in Figure 16-37.

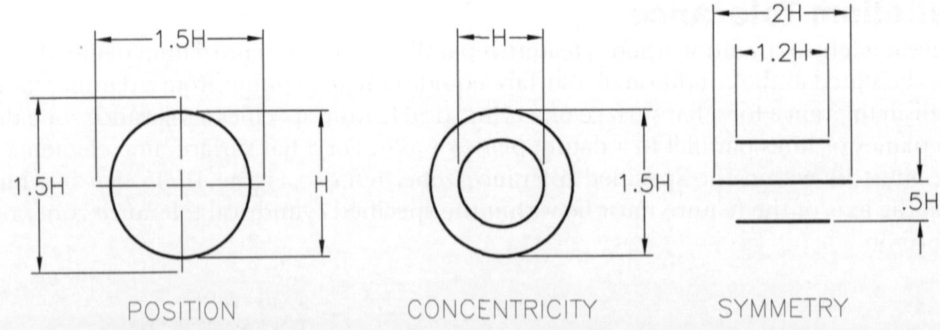

Figure 16-37 Geometric characteristics symbols for location tolerances

Position Tolerance

Position is the location of one or more features of size relative to one another or to one or more datum references. The position tolerance is one of the most common tolerances among the location tolerances and probably used more than any other geometric tolerance. The ideal or exact location of the feature is called true position. The actual location of the feature is compared to the true position and involves one or more datums to determine the true position. The exact location of a feature is defined by basic dimensions which is shown in a rectangular box and is established with reference to datum planes or axes, as shown in Figure 16-38.

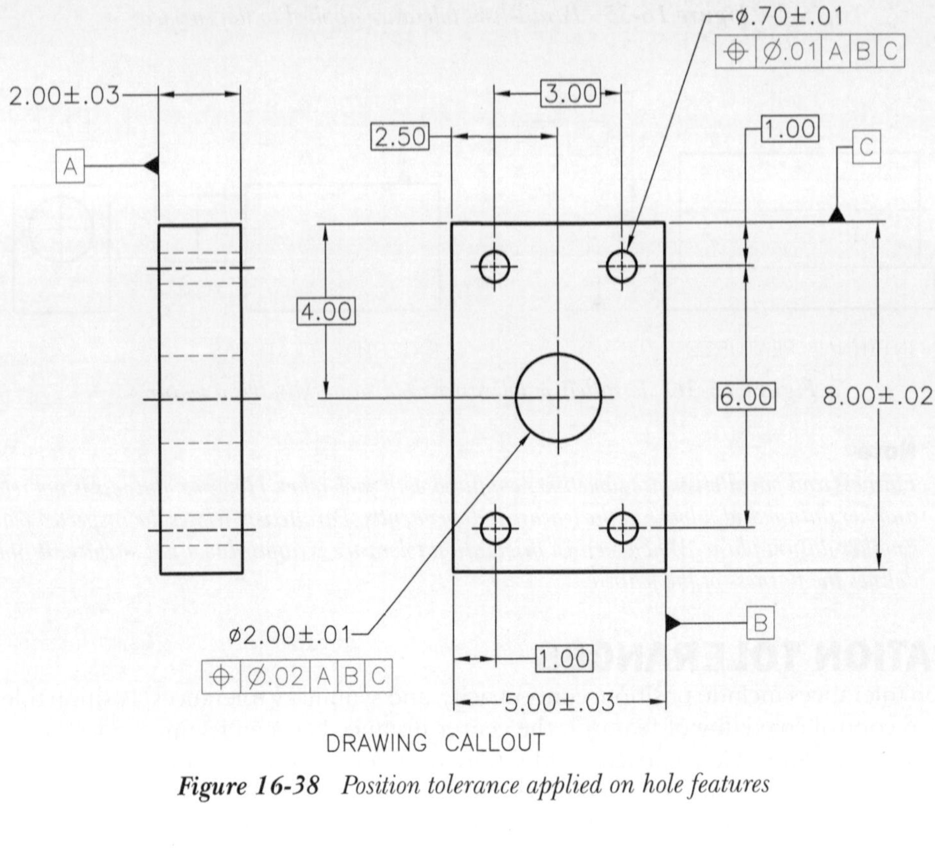

Figure 16-38 Position tolerance applied on hole features

A position tolerance locates center points, axes and median planes of the features. It has nothing to do with the size, shape, or angle of a feature. The position tolerance involves the location of center axis of the hole and the axis of the hole must be within the imaginary cylinder around the intended true position of the hole, as shown in Figure 16-39. If the toleranced feature is rectangular, the tolerance zone will be defined by two imaginary planes at a specified distance from the ideal true position.

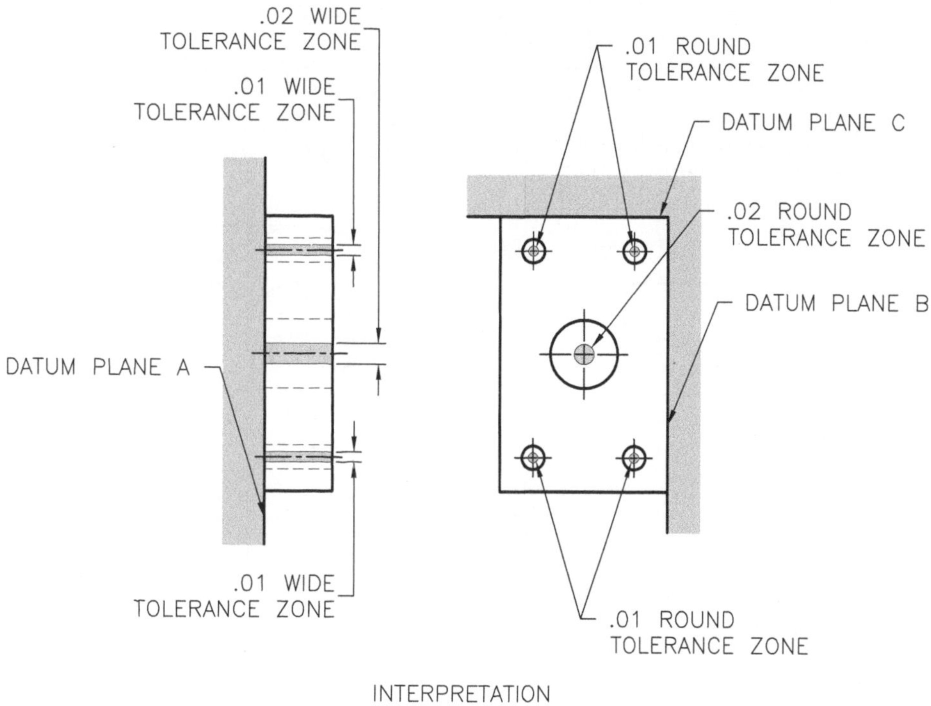

Figure 16-39 *Interpretation of true position*

Concentricity Tolerance

Concentricity is a condition where the median points of all diametrically opposed elements of a surface of revolution (or the median points of corresponding elements of two or more radially disposed features) are congruent with a datum axis or center point, refer to Figure 16-40. This tolerance is not used very often because median points are difficult to establish due to irregularities of form. The only reason to use this tolerance is to control the error of balance that can exist if the mass center is not close to the axis of rotation or center plane.

The concentricity tolerance is a cylindrical (or spherical) tolerance zone whose axis (or center point) coincides with the axis (or center point) of the datum feature(s), refer to Figure 16-40. Concentricity is measured using the median points of multiple diameters within the cylindrical tolerance zone. The median points of all corresponding elements of the feature(s) being controlled, regardless of feature size, must lie within the cylindrical (or spherical) tolerance zone.

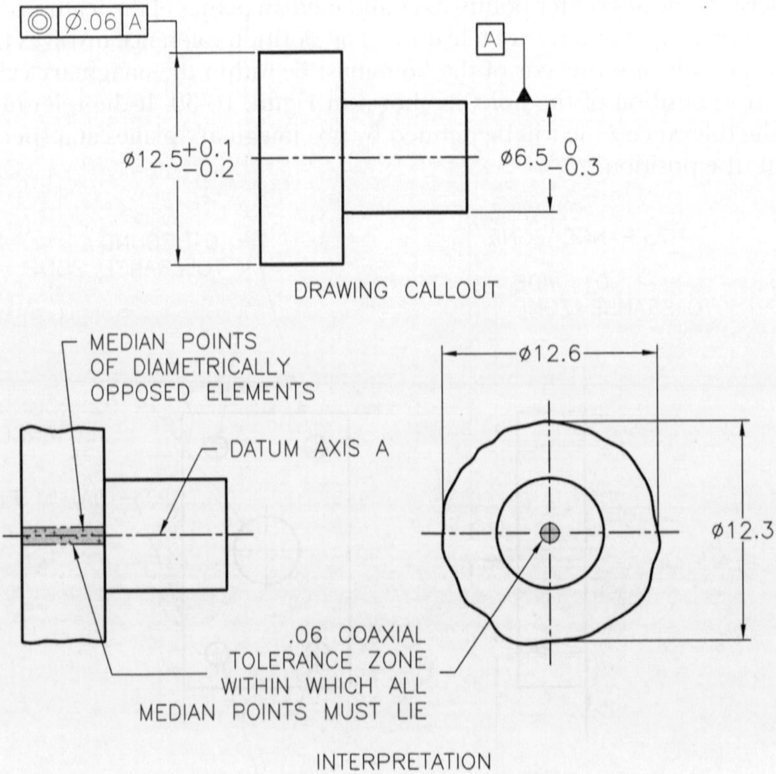

Figure 16-40 Concentricity tolerance applied to a cylindrical feature

Symmetrical Tolerance

Symmetry is a condition where the median points of all opposite or corresponding elements of two or more features (surfaces) are congruent with a datum axis or center plane, as shown in Figure 16-41.

Symmetry is much like concentricity except that it controls rectangular features and involves reference of two datum planes. Both of these control the median points of a feature of size. Concentricity is applied to circular features whereas symmetry is applied to non circular features. The tolerance zone is equally disposed about the datum plane. The median points of the toleranced feature, regardless of its feature size must lie within the tolerance zone which is defined by two parallel planes for symmetry, refer to Figure 16-41.

Note

Both symmetry and concentricity tolerances are difficult to measure and increase the cost of inspection. However, when a certain characteristic like balancing of a part is a primary concern, these tolerances are very effective.

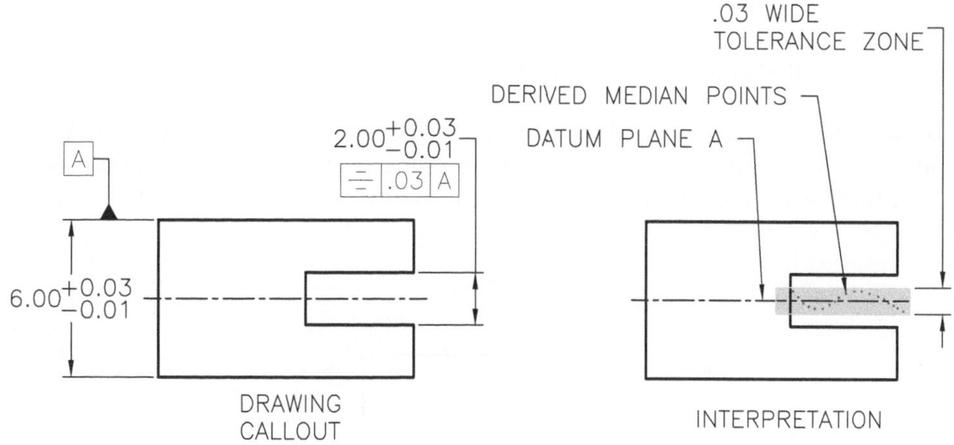

Figure 16-41 *Symmetry tolerance applied to a rectangular feature*

RUNOUT TOLERANCES

Runout tolerances are three-dimensional in nature and are only applied to cylindrical parts that rotate about an axis. Runout tolerances are used to control the relationship of a feature relative to a datum axis which is established between two diameters that are axially separated. Runout tolerances are composite tolerances and are used to control the relationship of one or more cylindrical features during a full 360⁰ rotation about the datum axis.

There are two types of runout tolerances used in the drawings: circular runout and total runout. Both circular and total runout reference a cylindrical feature to a center datum-axis and simultaneously control the location, form, and orientation of the feature. The type of runout tolerance used depends on design requirements and manufacturing considerations. Geometric characteristics symbols used for runout tolerancing are shown in Figure 16-42.

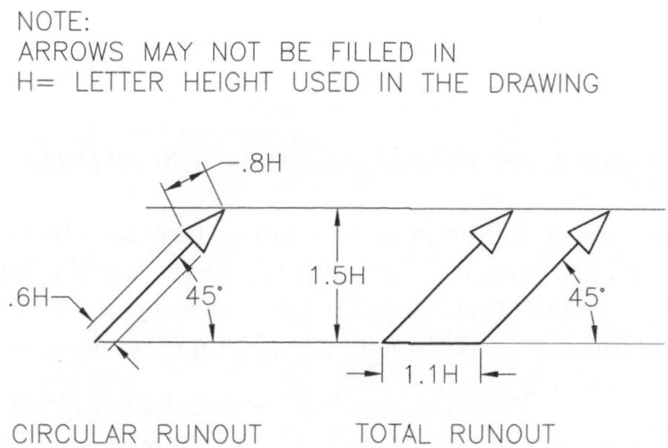

Figure 16-42 *Geometric characteristics symbols for runout tolerances*

Circular Runout

Circular runout provides control of circular elements of a surface. The tolerance is applied independently at any cross-section as the part is rotated 360°. If applied to surfaces that are constructed around a datum axis, circular runout controls variations such as circularity and coaxiality. When applied to surfaces constructed at right angles to the datum axis, circular runout controls wobble at all diametral positions.

For inspecting the circular runout, the part must be rotated about the datum axis. A calibrated instrument is placed against the surface of the rotating part to detect the highest and lowest points. The surface must remain within two imaginary circles having their centers located at the center axis, as shown in Figure 16-43.

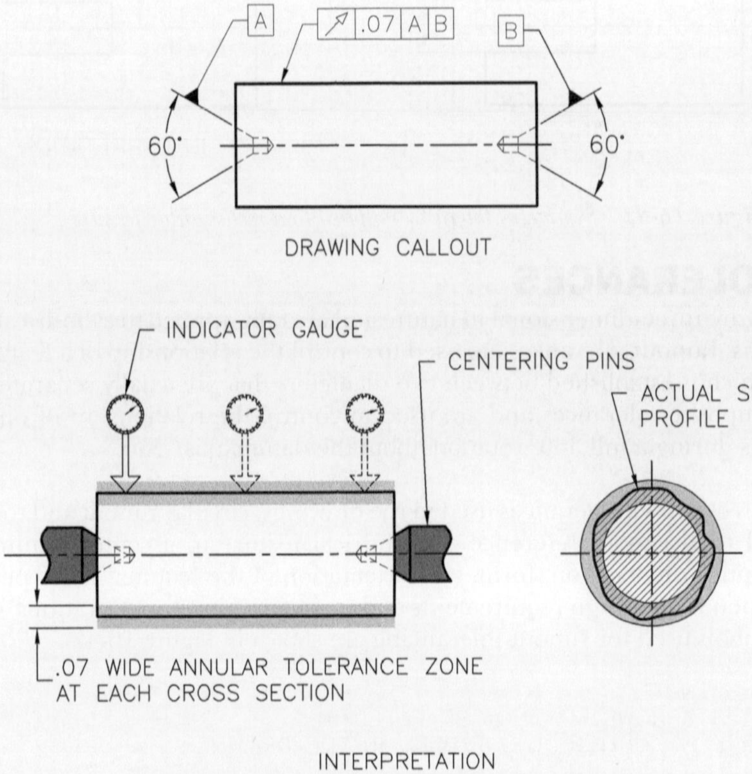

***Figure 16-43** Circular runout for cylindrical feature*

Figure 16-43 shows a surface measured at several points indicated by three different positions of the indicator gauge. At each position, the indicator movement during one revolution of the part must not exceed the specified tolerance. For a cylindrical feature, runout error is caused by eccentricity and errors of roundness. It is not affected by taper (conicity) or errors of straightness of the straight line elements such as barrel shaping.

A part where tolerance is applied to a surface at right angle to the datum axis is shown in Figure 16-44(A). In this case, an error generally termed as wobble will be shown when the surface is flat but not perpendicular to the axis, refer to Figure 16-44(B). Error will be shown if the surface is convex, concave, or perfect, as shown in Figure 16-44(C). Circular runout can also be applied to curved surfaces. Unless otherwise specified, measurement is always done normal to the surface.

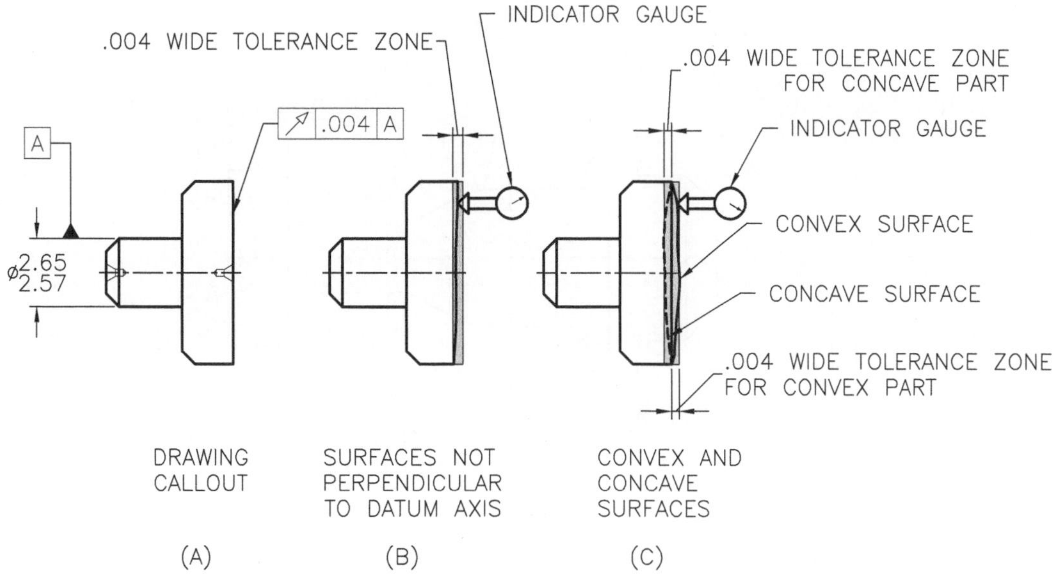

Figure 16-44 *Circular runout for flat surfaces perpendicular to datum axis feature*

If a runout tolerance is applied to a specific portion of a surface, a thick chain line is also drawn adjacent to the surface profile to show the desired length. Basic dimensions are used to define the extent of the portion as indicated in Figure 16-45.

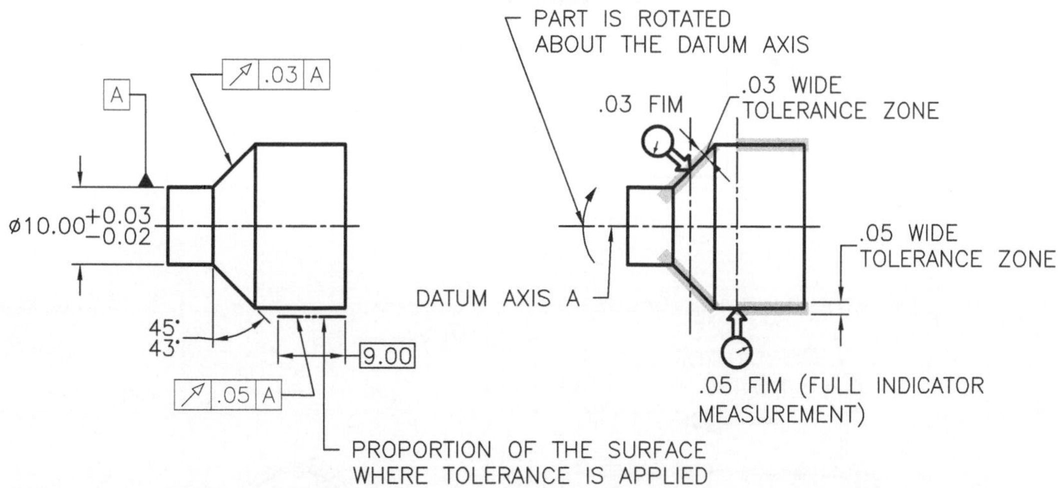

Figure 16-45 *Circular runout applied to a specific portion of a surface*

When runout tolerance is directed to a surface, it is applied to the full length of the surface until there is an abrupt change in the surface profile. If a control with the same tolerance is applied to more than one portion of a surface, additional leaders and arrowheads may be used. If different tolerance values are required, separate tolerances must be specified. If only part of a surface or several consecutive portions require the same tolerance, the length on which the tolerance needs to be applied can be indicated, as shown in Figure 16-46.

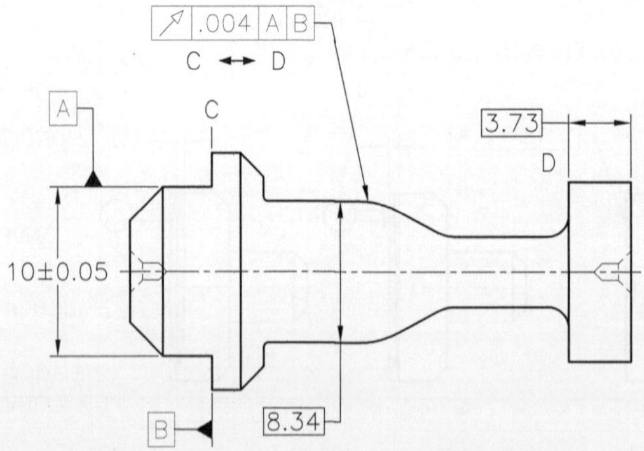

Figure 16-46 Circular runout applied to specified length of the part

Total Runout

Total runout is the runout of a complete surface and not merely of each circular element of the part. The tolerance zone is specified by two concentric cylinders separated by the specified tolerance value and coaxial with the datum axis, as shown in Figure 16-47. A total runout may be applied to surfaces at various angles, therefore it also controls the profile of the surface in addition to runout.

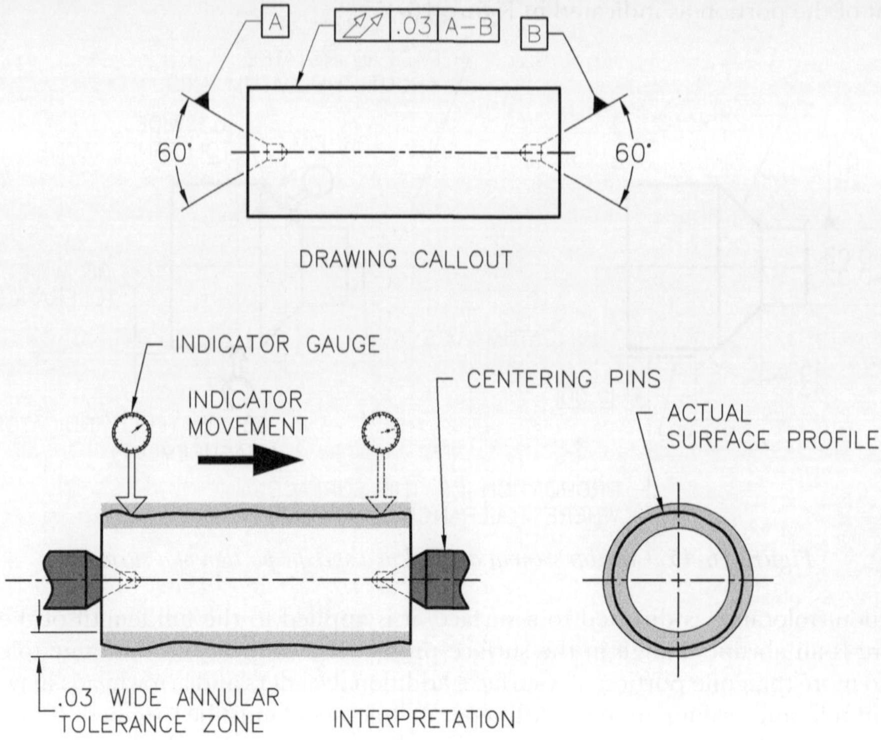

Figure 16-47 Measurement of tolerance zone for total runout

Unlike circular tolerance which is only affected by the errors of eccentricity and roundness, total runout is also affected by straightness and conicity of the surface.

For measuring total runout of a cylindrical surface, the indicator is traversed over the full surface while the part is revolved about its datum axis. Measurements are made over the whole surface without resetting the indicator. However, for measurement purposes, the indicator gauge must be capable of following the true profile direction of the surface.

The measuring process is comparatively simple for straight surfaces, such as cylindrical surfaces and flat faces. For conical surfaces, the datum axis can be tilted to the taper angle so that the measured surface becomes parallel to a surface plate. Total runout is the difference between the lowest indicator reading at any position and the highest reading at the same position or at any other position on the same surface.

FITS

Fit is a specific combination of tolerances and allowances in the design of mating parts. When two parts are assembled, the relation resulting from the difference between their sizes before assembly is called a fit. In a general term, fit is the degree of tightness or looseness between two mating parts.

A fit system is the system of standard allowance to suit specific range of basic size. Proper selection of these standard allowances ensures specific classes of fit in mating parts. Fits can be classified as per the two systems:

Hole Basis System

In the hole basis system, the size of the hole is kept constant and shaft sizes are varied to obtain various types of fits, refer to Figure 16-48. In this system, lower deviation of hole is kept zero, which means the minimum limit of the hole is same as the basic size. The maximum limit of the hole and the maximum and minimum limits for the shaft are then varied to give desired type of fit. The hole basis system is commonly used compared to shaft basis system. It is more convenient to make holes of fixed size as the tools like drills, taps and reamers have the standard size and are easily available for producing holes. On the other hand, size of the shaft produced by turning or grinding can be very easily varied.

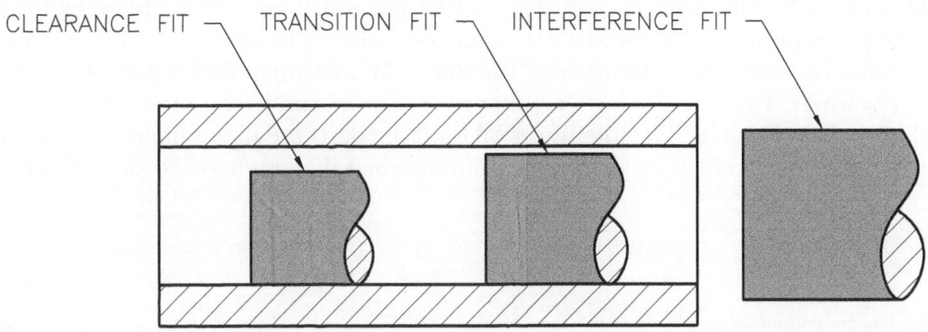

Figure 16-48 *Hole basis system of fits*

Shaft Basis System

In the shaft basis system, the size of the shaft is kept constant and fits are obtained by varying the size of the hole, refer to Figure 16-49. Shaft basis system is used when the ground bars or drawn bars are readily available. These bars do not require further machining and fits are obtained by varying the sizes of the hole. In this system, the upper deviation (fundamental deviation) of shaft is kept zero which means the maximum limit of the shaft is considered as the basic size and fits are obtained by varying the minimum limit of shaft or both the limits of the hole.

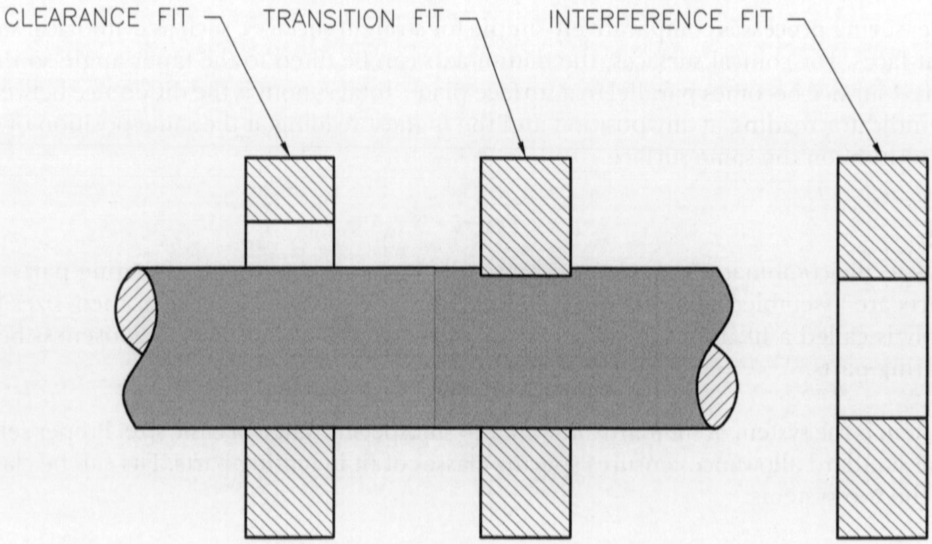

Figure 16-49 Shaft basis system of fits

Based on hole and shaft system, fits are categorized into the following three types

- Clearance fit
- Interference fit
- Transition fit

Clearance Fit

Clearance fit is the difference between the sizes of the hole and the shaft. Clearance fits have limits of size specified in such a manner that a clearance will always remain between the mating parts. When it is desirable for the shaft to rotate or slide freely within the hole, clearance fits are maintained between the mating parts. Clearance fits are intended for accurate assembly of parts and bearings. The parts having clearance fits can be assembled by hand because the hole is always larger than the shaft. The tolerances on both the parts are maintained in such a manner that the hole diameter will always be larger than the shaft diameter, as shown in Figure 16-50.

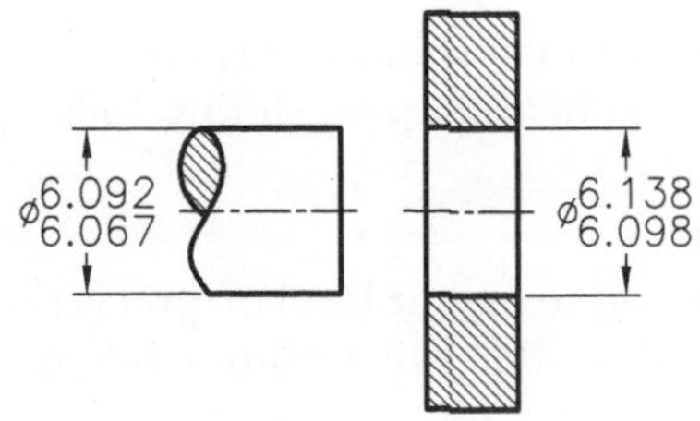

DRAWING CALLOUT

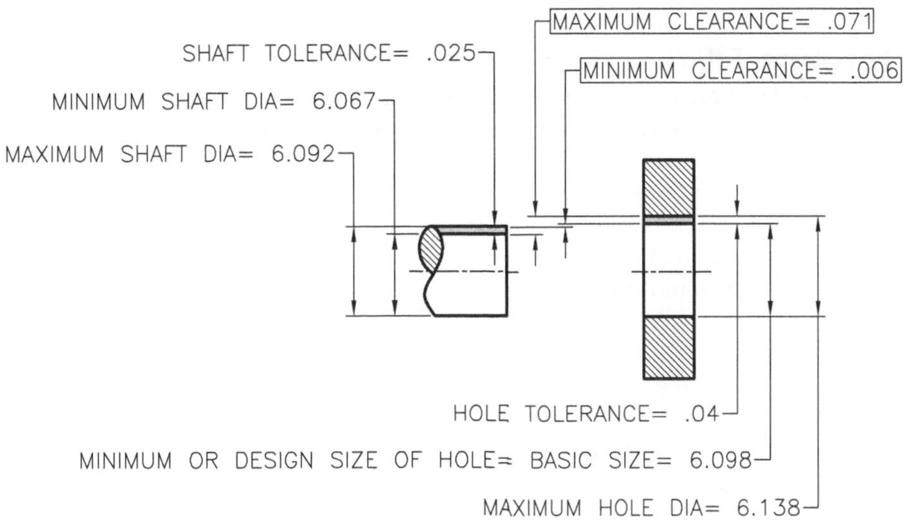

INTERPRETATION

Figure 16-50 *Calculation of clearance fit*

The clearance may be the maximum clearance or the minimum clearance. The minimum clearance fit is the difference between the minimum size of the hole and the maximum size of the shaft.

Minimum clearance = Minimum hole diameter - Maximum shaft diameter

The maximum clearance fit is the difference between the maximum size of the hole and the minimum size of the shaft.

Maximum clearance = Maximum hole diameter - Minimum shaft diameter

Clearance fit is classified into three categories.

Loose Fit

It is used between those mating parts where precision is not required. It provides minimum allowance and generally used on loose pulleys such as agricultural machineries.

Running Fit

For a running fit, the dimension of shaft should be smaller enough to maintain a film of oil for lubrication. Generally, it is used in bearing pair, sliding rods, spindles, and so on.

Slide Fit or Medium Fit

It is used on those mating parts where higher level of precision is required. It provides medium allowance and is used in tool slides, slide valve, automobile parts, and so on.

Note

Maximum clearance in a loose or sliding fit is always greater than zero. On the other hand, in a tight fit, both the maximum and minimum clearance are negative.

Interference Fit

Interference fits have limits of size specified in such a manner that the mating parts always have interference between them. In a general term, the hole will be always smaller than the shaft. In such a fit, the tolerance zone of the hole will always be lower than the tolerance zone of the shaft. Interference fits are used for permanent assemblies of parts which require rigidity and alignment, such as dowel pins and bearings in castings. Parts are usually assembled together by pressure or heat expansion. The tolerances on each part are maintained in a way that the shaft diameter will be larger than the hole diameter, as shown in Figure 16-51.

Maximum interference is an arithmetical difference between the minimum size of the hole and the maximum size of the shaft.

Maximum interference = Maximum shaft diameter - Minimum hole diameter

Minimum interference is the difference between the maximum size of the hole and the minimum size of the shaft.

Minimum interference = Minimum shaft diameter - Maximum hole diameter

Note

Interference fit has a negative allowance which means that interference exists between maximum limit of hole and minimum limit of the shaft.

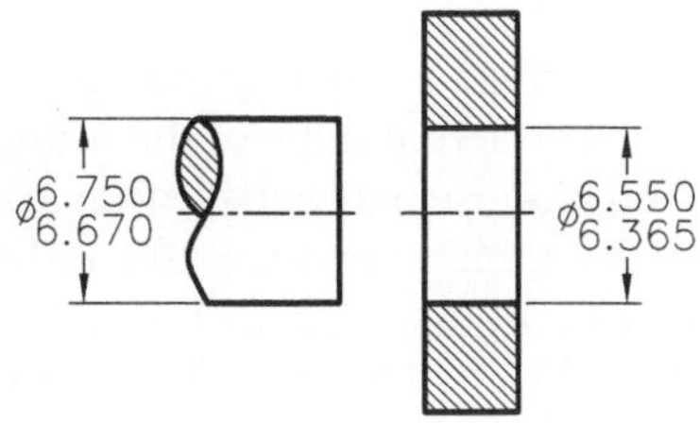

DRAWING CALLOUT

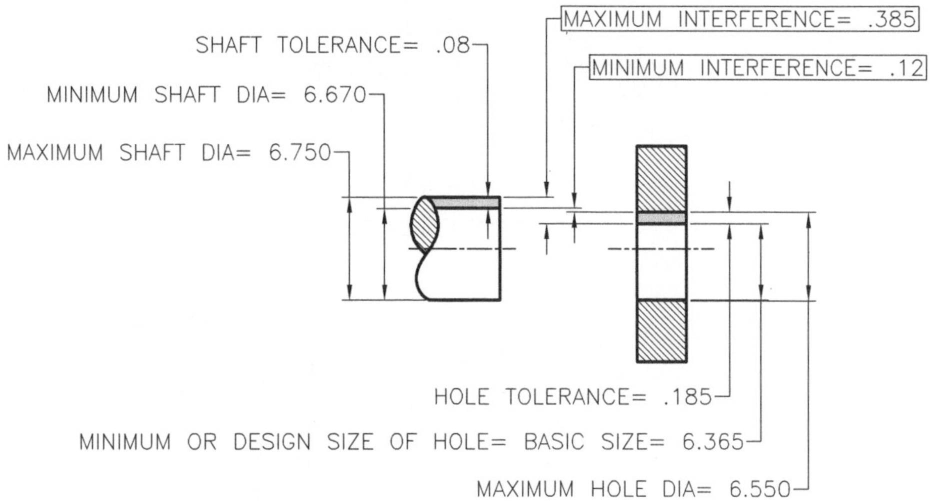

INTERPRETATION

Figure 16-51 *Calculation of interference fit*

Interference fit is classified into three categories.

Shrink Fit or Heavy Force Fit

Shrink Fit refers to maximum negative allowance. In an assembly of a hole and a shaft, the hole is expanded by heating and then rapidly cooled in its position. It is used in fitting of rims, seating rings, and so on.

Medium Force Fit

These fits have medium negative allowance. In this fit, considerable pressure is required to assemble a hole and shaft. Force fit is generally used in car wheels, armature of dynamos, and so on.

Tight Fit or Press Fit

One part can be assembled into the other with a hand hammer or by light pressure. A slight negative allowance exists between two mating parts. It gives a semi-permanent fit and is used on a keyed pulley and shaft, rocker arm, and so on.

Transition Fit

Transition fits have limits of size specified in such a manner that either a clearance or an interference may result depending on the actual value of the individual tolerances of the mating components. Transition fits are a compromise between clearance and interference fits. They are used for applications where accurate location is important but either a small amount of clearance or interference is permissible. When in an assembly of hole and shaft, hole is machined to its smallest size and the shaft is machined to its largest size, the result will be an interference fit, as shown in Figure 16-52. When the hole is at its maximum size and the shaft is at its smallest size, the result will be a clearance fit.

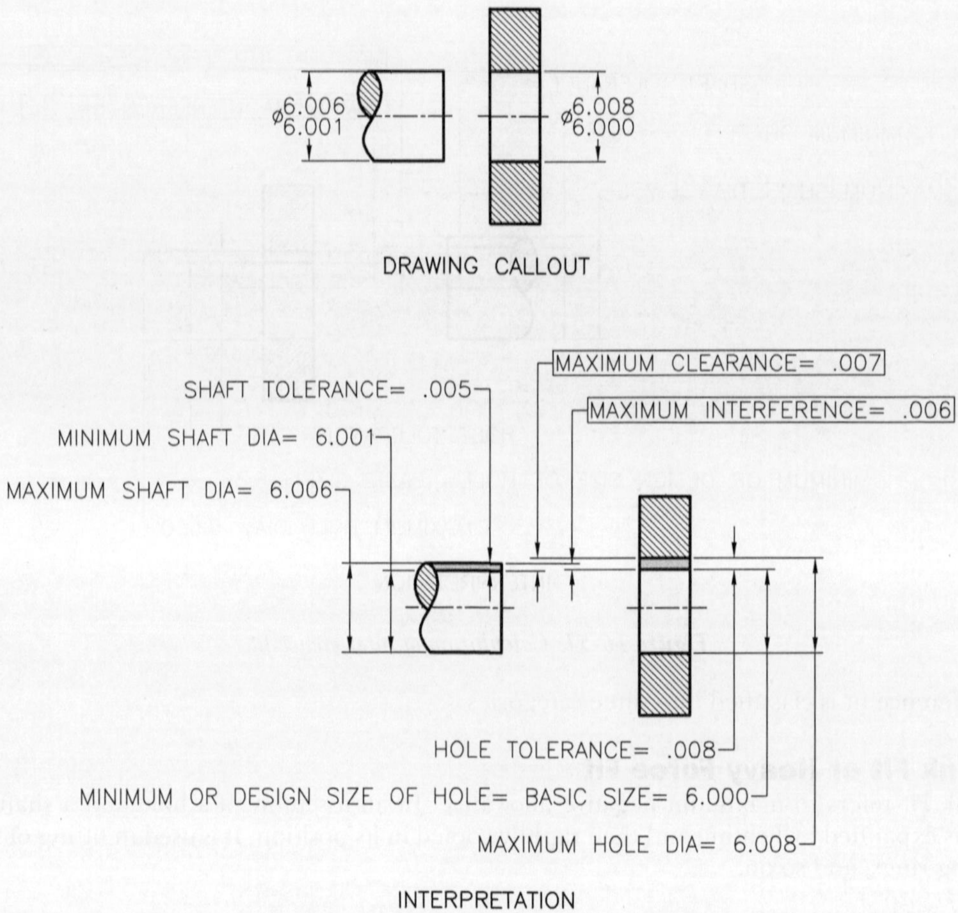

Figure 16-52 Calculation of transition fit

Transition fit is sub-classified into three categories.

Push Fit

In this type of fit, zero allowance and a light pressure is required in assembling the hole and the shaft. The moving parts show least vibration with this type of fit. It is also known as snug fit. This type of fit is used in automobiles and plastic components.

Force Fit or Shrink Fit

Force fit is used when two mating parts are to be rigidly fixed such that one cannot move without the other. For example, to assemble a hole and a shaft with a force fit between them, either high pressure is required to force the shaft into the hole or the hole needs to be expanded by heating. This type of fit is used in railway wheels, assembling a hardened gear onto a shaft, and so on.

Wringing Fit

A fit which allows less clearance than allowed in a running or sliding fit is termed as a wringing fit. In this type of fit, the shaft enters the hole by means of twisting and pushing by hand. It is used in fixing keys, pins, and so on.

STANDARD OF FITS

There are some standards designated for the fits that are used worldwide for designing purpose. The standard of fits provides preferred tolerances for limits and fits of non threaded cylindrical features and defines specific sizes, fits, tolerances, and allowances to use wherever they are applicable. Based on the standards, fits are categorized as inch fits and metric fits. These fits are discussed next.

Standard Inch Fits

The American National Standards Institute published the standard named "Preferred Limits and Fits for Cylindrical Parts" (ANSI B4.1-1967) to define terms and recommended standard allowances, tolerances, and fits for mating parts. The ANSI B4.1 tolerance charts are provided in thousandths (.001) of an inch. Standard fits are designated by the means of symbols and specifications as shown in Figure 16-53.

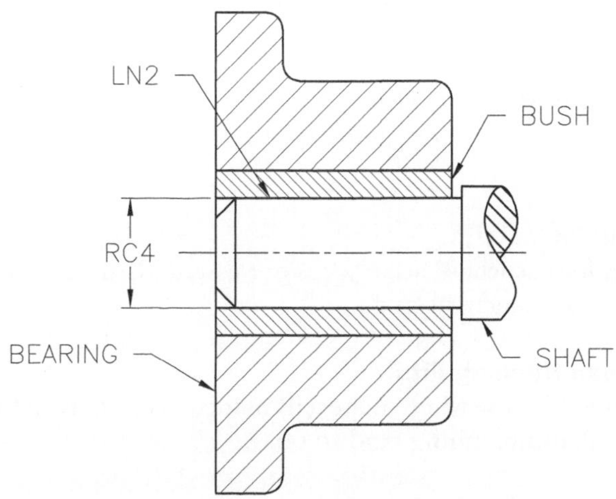

Figure 16-53 *Designation of standard inch fit*

The letter symbols used for standard inch fits are:

RC - Running and sliding fit
LC - Locational clearance fit
LT - Locational transition fit

LN - Locational interference fit
FN - Force or shrink fit

These letter symbols are used in conjunction with numbers representing the class of fit; for example, FN4 represents a class 4 force fit. Each of these symbols (two letters and a number) represents a complete fit for which the minimum and maximum clearance or interference and the limits of size for the mating parts are given directly in ANSI B4.1 chart.

Running and Sliding Fits

Running and sliding fits are intended to provide a smooth running performance with suitable lubrication allowance.

RC1 Precision Sliding Fit

This fit is intended for an accurate location of parts that must assemble without perceptible play for high precision work such as gauges.

RC2 Sliding Fit

This fit is intended for accurate location, but with greater maximum clearance than class RC1. In this type of fit, parts can move and turn easily but are not intended to run freely.

RC3 Precision Running Fit

This fit is the closest fit that can be expected to run freely and is intended for precision work at slow speeds and light journal pressures.

RC4 Close Running Fit

This fit is intended chiefly as a running fit for grease or oil-lubricated bearings on accurate machinery with moderate surface speeds and journal pressures where accurate location and minimum play are desired.

RC5 and RC6 Medium Running Fits

These fits are intended for higher running speeds and/or where temperature variations are likely to be encountered.

RC7 Free Running Fit

This fit is intended for use where accuracy is not essential and/or where large temperature variations are likely to be encountered.

RC8 and RC9 Loose Running Fits

These fits are intended for use where materials made to commercial tolerances are involved such as cold-rolled shafting, tubing, and so on.

Locational Clearance Fits

Locational clearance fits are intended for parts that are normally stationary but can be freely assembled or disassembled. These are classified as follows:

LC1 to LC4

These fits have zero clearance, but in practice the probability is that the fit will always have a clearance.

LC5 and LC6

These fits have a minimum clearance intended for close location fits in non-running parts.

LC7 to LC11

These fits have progressively larger clearances and tolerances and are useful for various loose clearances for assembly of bolts and similar parts.

Locational Transition Fits

Locational transition fits are a compromise between clearance and interference fits. These fits are applicable where accuracy of location is important and either a small amount of clearance or interference is permissible. These are classified as follows:

LT1 and LT2

These fits allow a slight clearance between parts. A light push is required to fit the parts.

LT3 and LT4

These fits allow no clearance between parts and are used where some interference can be tolerated.

These are sometimes referred to as an easy keying fit and are used for shaft keys and ball race fits. The assembling of these parts done by pressure or hammer blows.

LT5 and LT6

These fits allow a slight interference between parts, although appreciable assembly force is required to achieve this fit condition.

Locational Interference Fits

Locational interference fits are used where accuracy of location is of prime importance. These are classified as follows:

LN1 And LN2

These are light press fits with minimum interference suitable for parts, such as dowel pins, which are assembled with an arbor press of steel, cast iron, or brass. Parts can normally be dismantled and reassembled.

LN3

This is suitable as a heavy press fit in steel and brass, or a light press fit in more elastic materials and light alloys.

LN4 to LN6

While LN4 can be used for permanent assembly of steel parts, these fits are primarily intended as press fits for soft materials.

Force or Shrink Fits

Force or shrink fits constitute a special type of interference fit. In this kind of fit, the interference varies almost directly with diameter and the difference between its minimum and maximum limits is kept as small as possible to maintain the resulting pressures within reasonable limits. These fits are classified as follows:

FN1 Light Drive Fit
This fit requires light assembly pressure and produces more or less permanent assemblies. It is suitable for thin sections and for external members made of cast-iron.

FN2 Medium Drive Fit
This fit is suitable for heavier steel parts or as a shrink fit on light sections.

FN3 Heavy Drive Fit
This fit is suitable for heavier steel parts or as a shrink fit in medium sections.

FN4 And FN5 Force Fits
This fit is suitable for parts that can be highly stressed.

Standard Metric Fits

The system of preferred metric limits and fits was developed by the International Organization for Standardization (ISO) and is known as the ANSI B4.2 standard. It is approved and adopted for metric drawings. Metric system of fits designates symbols that are used to define specific dimensional limits on drawings. The system is specified for holes, cylinders, and shafts and is also applicable to fits between parallel surfaces such as keys and slots.

International Tolerance Grade or IT Grade

International Tolerance (IT) Grade establishes the magnitude of the tolerance zone or the amount of part size variation allowed for dimensions of internal and external features. The smaller the grade number, the smaller the tolerance zone, refer to Figure 16-54.

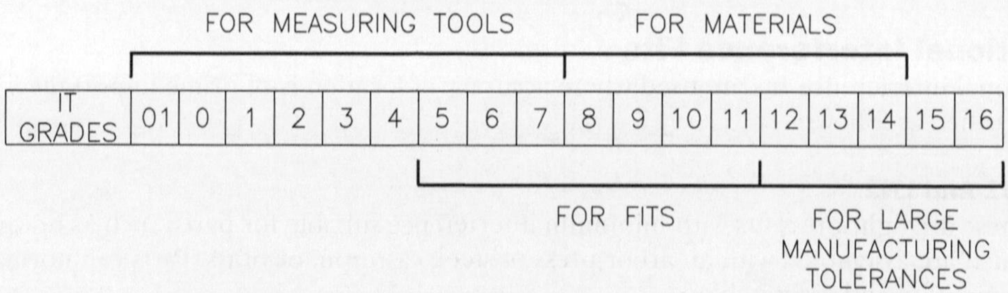

Figure 16-54 Application of International Tolerance (IT) grades

Grades 1 through 4 are very precise grades intended primarily for gauge making and similar precision work. Grade 4, however, can also be used in production work where higher accuracy is required. Grades 5 through 16 represent a progressive series suitable for cutting operations, such as turning, boring, grinding, milling, and sawing. Grade 5 is the most precise grade obtained by fine grinding and lapping while 16 is the coarsest grade for rough sawing and machining. Grades 12 through 16 are intended for large manufacturing operations such as cold heading, pressing, rolling, and other forming operations.

Symbols for Metric Fits

By combining the IT grade number and the tolerance position letter, the tolerance symbol is established that identifies the actual maximum and minimum limits of the part. The toleranced sizes are thus defined by the basic size of the part added up with the symbol comprising a letter and a number, refer to Figure 16-55.

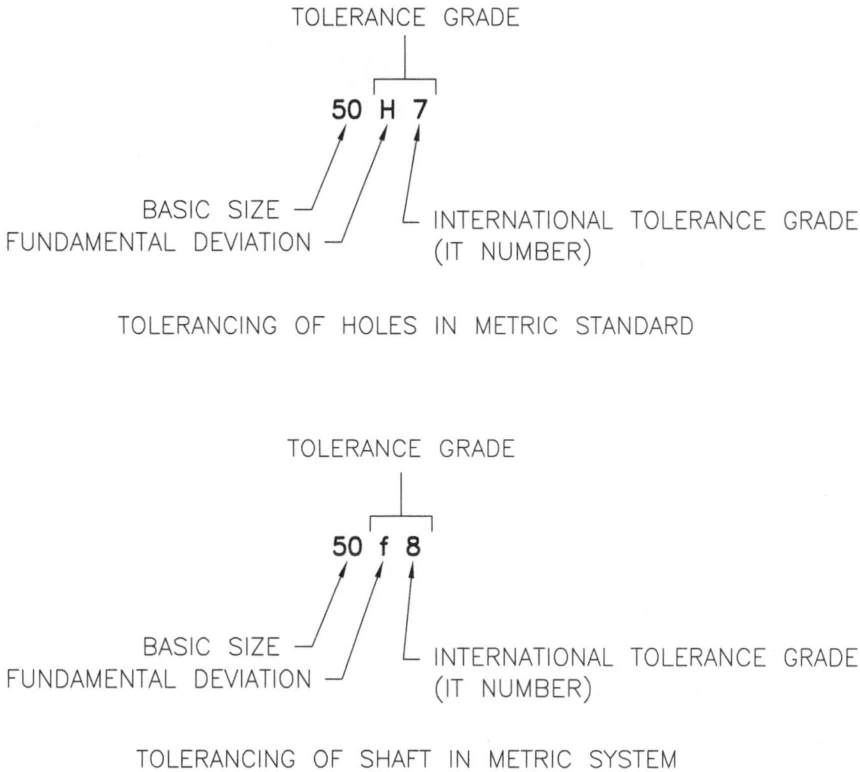

Figure 16-55 *Tolerancing of features in a Metric system*

Hole basis fits have a fundamental deviation of "H" on the hole, and shaft basis fits have a fundamental deviation of "h" on the shaft. Normally, the hole basis system is preferred over the shaft basis system because it is easier to produce holes of fixed size rather than producing shafts of fixed size.

A fit is specified by the basic size common for both hole and shaft followed by a symbol corresponding to each component with the internal part symbol preceding the external part symbol, refer to Figure 16-56.

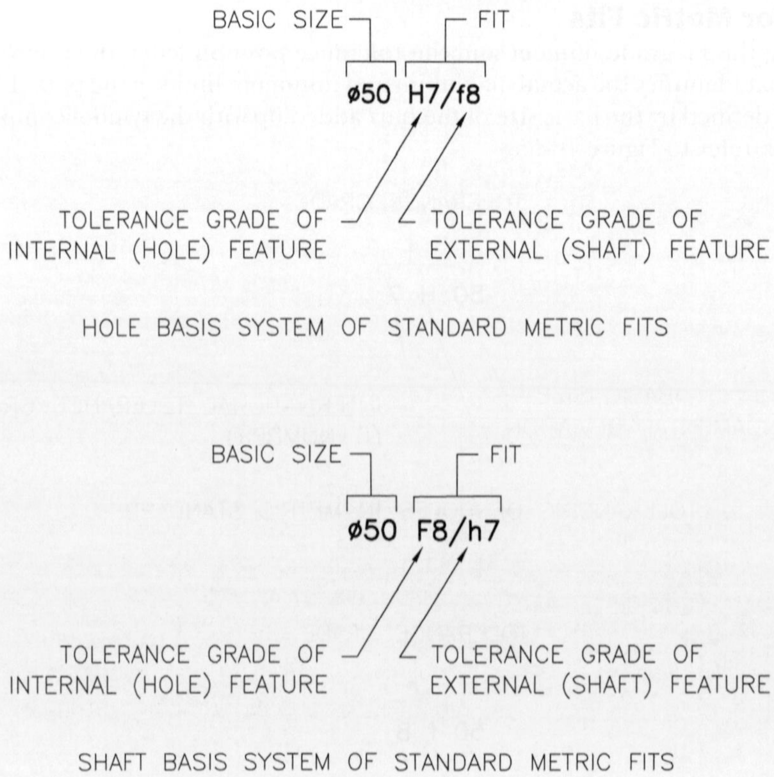

Figure 16-56 *Symbols used in standard metric fits*

Metric Standard Hole Basis Fits System

In the hole basis fits system, the minimum size of the hole is considered as the basic size.

For example, for a Ø16 H7/g6 fit, which is a Preferred Hole Basis Clearance Fit, refer to ANSI B4.2 (Preferred hole basis metric fits), the limits for the hole and shaft will be as follows:

Hole limits = Ø16.000 and Ø16.018
Shaft limits = Ø15.994 and Ø15.983

Minimum clearance = 0.006
Maximum clearance = 0.035

If a Ø40 H7/s6 Preferred Hole Basis Interference Fit is required, refer to ANSI B4.2 (Preferred hole basis metric fits), the limits for the hole and shaft will be as follows:

Hole limits = Ø40.000 and Ø40.025
Shaft limits = Ø39.957 and Ø40.059

Minimum interference = 0.018
Maximum interference = –0.059

Metric Standard Shaft Basis Fits System

The shaft basis fits system is recommended where more than two fits are required on the same shaft. Tolerances for holes and shafts are same as those for a basic hole system, however, the basic size becomes the maximum shaft size.

For example, for a Ø16 D9/h9 fit, which is a Preferred Shaft Basis Clearance Fit, refer to ANSI B4.2 (Preferred shaft basis metric fits), the limits for the hole and shaft will be as follows:

Hole limits = Ø16.050 and Ø16.093
Shaft limits = Ø15.957 and Ø16.000
Minimum clearance = 0.050
Maximum clearance = 0.136

According to metric standard hole and metric standard shaft basis system, the preferred hole and shaft fits are shown in Figure 16-57.

	ISO SYMBOL		DESCRIPTION	
	HOLE BASIS	SHAFT BASIS		
CLEARANCE FITS	H11/c11	C11/h11	LOOSE RUNNING FIT FOR WIDE COMMERCIAL TOLERANCES OR ALLOWANCES ON EXTERNAL MEMBERS.	MORE CLEARANCE
	H9/d9	D9/h9	FREE RUNNING FIT NOT FOR USE WHERE ACCURACY IS ESSENTIAL, BUT GOOD FOR LARGE TEMPERATURE VARIATIONS, HIGH RUNNING SPEEDS, OR HEAVY JOURNAL BEARINGS.	
	H8/f7	F8/h7	CLOSE RUNNING FIR FOR RUNNING ON ACCURATE MACHINES AND FOR ACCURATE LOCATION AT MODERATE SPEEDS AND JOURNAL PRESSURES.	
	H7/g6	G7/h6	SLIDING FIT NOT INTENDED TO RUN FREELY, BUT TO MOVE AND TURN FREELY AND LOCATE ACCURATELY.	
	H7/h6	H7/h6	LOCATIONAL CLEARANCE FIT PROVIDES SNUG FIT FOR LOCATING STATIONARY PARTS, BUT CAN BE FREELY ASSEMBLED AND DISASSEMBLED.	
TRANSITION FITS	H7/k6	K7/h6	LOCATIONAL TRANSITION FIT FOR ACCURATE LOCATION, A COMPROMISE BETWEEN CLEARANCE FIR AND INTERFERENCE FIT.	
	H7/n6	N7/h6	LOCATIONAL TRANSITION FIT FOR MORE ACCURATE LOCATION WHERE GREATER INTERFERENCE IS PERMISSIBLE.	MORE INTERFERENCE
INTERFERENCE FITS	H7/p6	P7/h6	LOCATIONAL INTERFERENCE FIT FOR PARTS REQUIRING RIGIDITY AND ALIGNMENT WITH PRIME ACCURACY OF LOCATION BUT WITHOUT SPECIAL BORE PRESSURE REQUIREMENTS.	
	H7/s6	S7/h6	MEDIUM DRIVE FIT FOR ORDINARY STEEL PARTS OR SHRINK FITS ON LIGHT SECTIONS, THE TIGHTEST FIT USABLE WITH CAST IRON.	
	H7/u6	U7/h6	FORCE FIT SUITABLE FOR PARTS SUITABLE FOR PARTS THAT CAN BE HIGHLY STRESSED OR FOR SHRINK FITS WHERE THE HEAVY PRESSING FORCES REQUIRED ARE IMPRACTICAL	

Figure 16-57 *Description of preferred metric fits*

TUTORIAL

TUTORIAL 1

In this tutorial, you will create the drawing views of the model shown in Figure 16-58. The views to be generated are shown in Figure 16-59. **(Expected time: 45 min)**

To perform this tutorial, you need to download the zipped file named as *c16_input* from the Input Files section of the CADCIM website. The complete path for downloading the file is:

Textbooks > CAD/CAM > NX > Siemens NX 2019 for Designers, 12th Edition > Input Files > C16_input

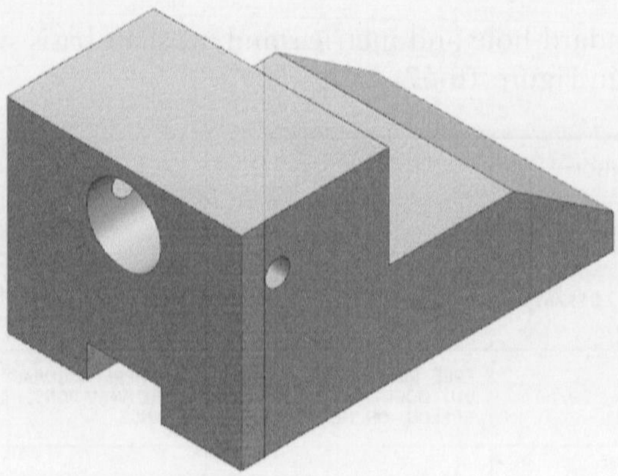

Figure 16-58 *Model for Tutorial 1*

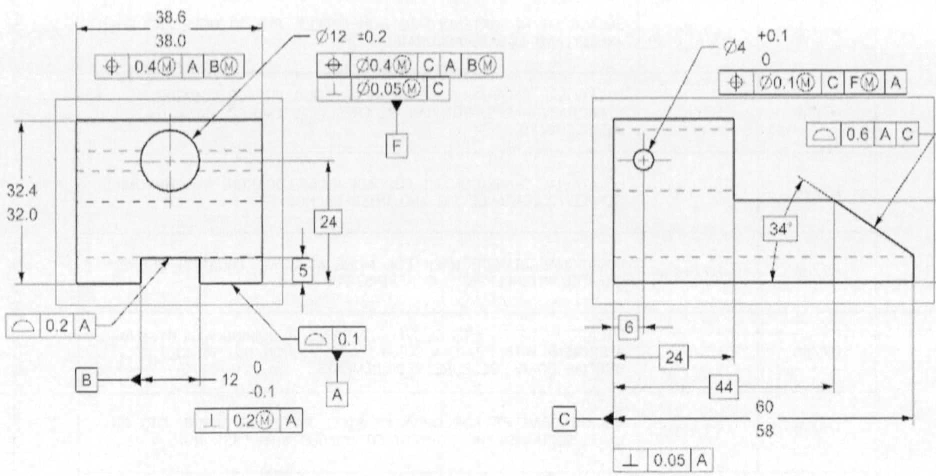

Figure 16-59 *Drawing views of Tutorial 1*

The following steps are required to complete this tutorial:

a. Open the model and invoke the Drafting environment.
b. Create the front and side views of the model, refer to Figure 16-60.
c. Dimension the drawing views, refer to Figure 16-61.
d. Add geometric tolerance to the required entities, refer to Figure 16-67.
e. Add datum reference frames to the drawing views, refer to Figure 16-70.

Opening the Model and Invoking the Drafting Environment

1. Open the downloaded model and choose **Application > Design > Drafting** from the **Ribbon**; the **Sheet** dialog box is displayed.

2. Select the **Standard Size** radio button from the **Size** rollout.

3. Select the sheet size **A3 - 297 x 420** from the **Size** drop-down list. By default, the **3rd Angle Projection** button is chosen and the **Millimeters** radio button is selected in the **Settings** rollout. Change the scale factor to **3:2** from the **Scale** drop-down list. Select the **Base View Command** radio button from the **Settings** rollout and choose the **OK** button.

Generating the Drawing Views of the Model

Once you choose the **OK** button from the **Sheet** dialog box, the **Base View** dialog box along with the floating top view of the model is displayed.

1. Generate the front and side views of the model, as shown in Figure 16-60.

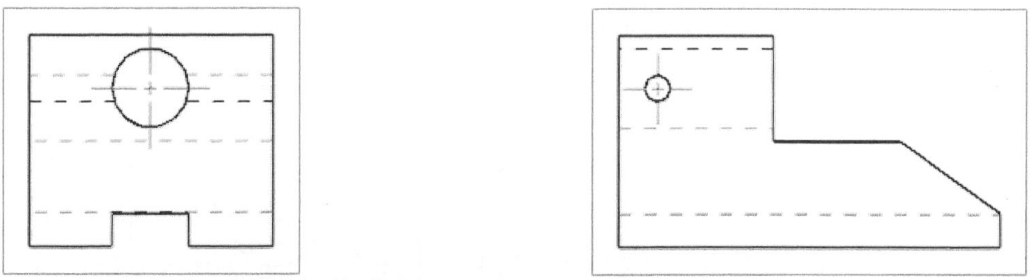

Figure 16-60 *Front and side views of the model*

Note

You will observe that in Figure 16-60, hidden lines are visible. You can change the visibility of hidden lines from the ***Settings*** *dialog box.*

Dimensioning the Drawing Views

1. Dimension the drawing views, as shown in Figure 16-61.

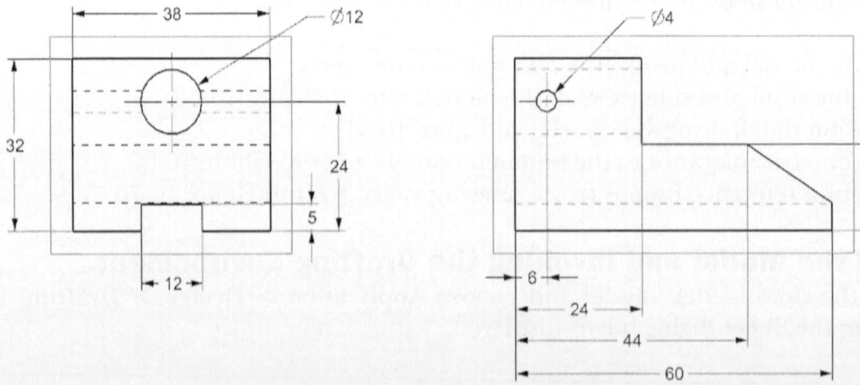

Figure 16-61 Drawing views with dimensions

Adding Geometric Dimensions and Tolerances

Now, you need to add tolerance to all the dimensions.

1. Double-click on the dimension of value 32 to add tolerance to this dimension; the **Linear Dimension** dialog box with the dynamic edit box is displayed.

2. Select the **+ Limit, 2 Lines** option from the **No Tolerance** drop-down list in the dynamic edit box; the dynamic edit box gets modified, as shown in Figure 16-62.

3. Replace the value from **0.1000000** to **0.4** and **-0.1000000** to **0** and press ESC. The selected dimension gets modified, as shown in Figure 16-63.

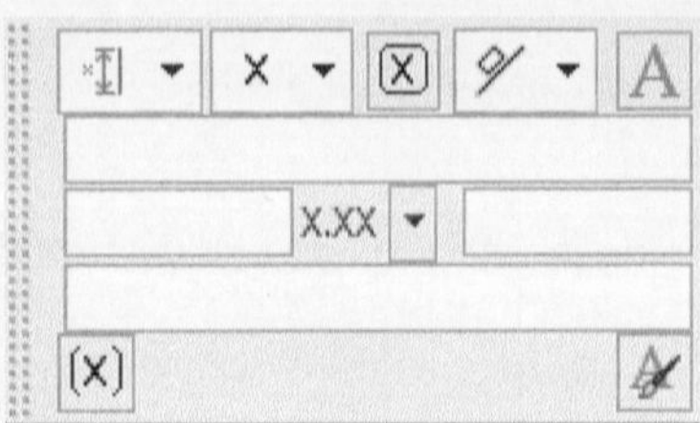

***Figure 16-62** The modified dynamic edit box*

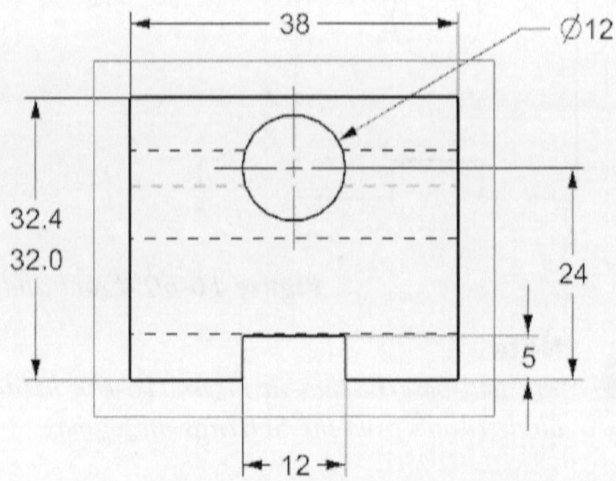

***Figure 16-63** Drawing view after modifying a dimension*

Note

*To display the trailing zeros, select the **Show Trailing Zeros** check box from the **Units** area in the **Text Settings** dialog box.*

4. Similarly, add tolerances to all the dimensions, as shown in Figure 16-64.

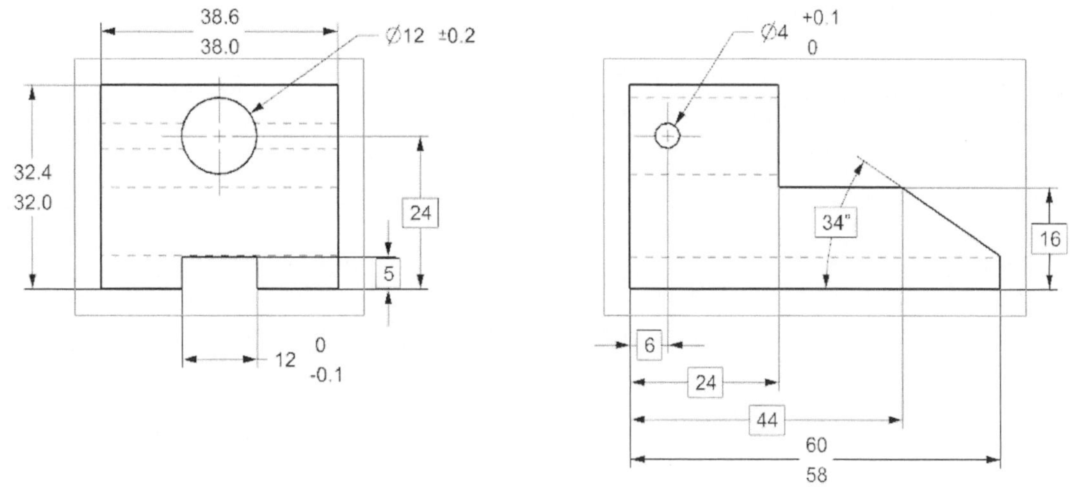

Figure 16-64 *Drawing views after adding tolerance to the remaining dimensions*

Next, you need to add feature control frames to define geometric tolerances of the model.

5. Choose the **Feature Control Frame** tool from the **Annotation** group of the **Home** tab; the **Feature Control Frame** dialog box is displayed, as shown in Figure 16-65 and a feature control frame gets attached to the cursor. 

   Now, create and place a feature control frame, as shown in Figure 16-66.

6. To add information in this feature control frame, you need to select the **Position** option from the **Characteristic** drop-down list in the **Frame** rollout. Next, select the **Diameter** option from the **None** drop-down list in the **Tolerance** sub-rollout.

7. Enter **0.4** in the edit box next to the **None** drop-down list. Next, select the **Maximum Material Condition** option from the drop-down list next to the edit box.

8. Select **C** from the drop-down list in the **Primary Datum Reference** sub-rollout. Similarly, choose **A** and **B** from the **Secondary Datum Reference** and **Tertiary Datum Reference** sub-rollouts, respectively. Next, select the **Maximum Material Condition** option from the **None** drop-down list of the **Tertiary Datum Reference** sub-rollout; the feature control frame is completed.

9. Place the feature control frame, as shown in Figure 16-66, and choose the **Close** button from the **Feature Control Frame** dialog box.

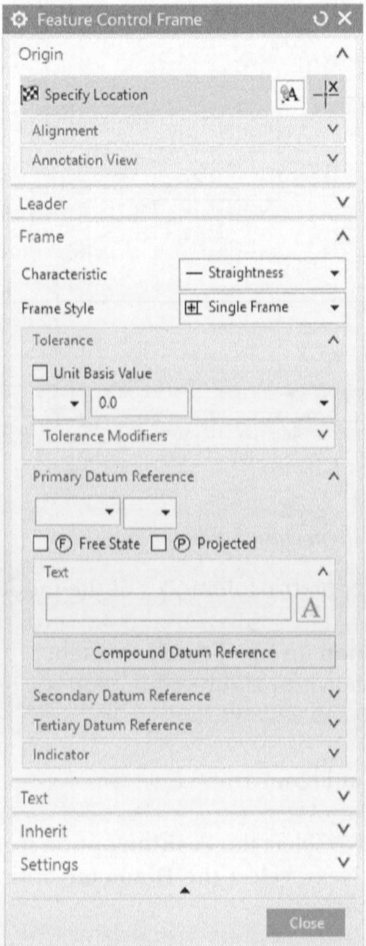

***Figure 16-65** The **Feature Control Frame** dialog box*

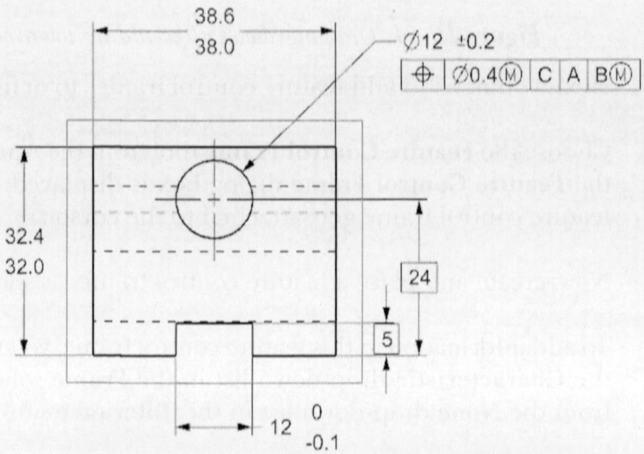

***Figure 16-66** Drawing view with feature control frame*

10. Similarly, create and place rest of the feature control frames, refer to Figure 16-67.

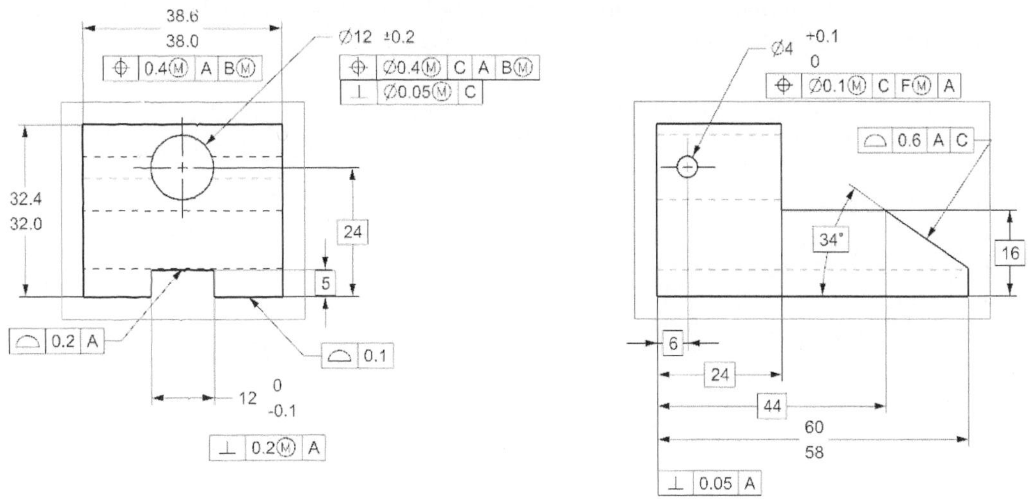

Figure 16-67 Drawing views after adding feature control frames

Adding Datum Feature Symbols

Next, you need to add datum feature symbols in the drawing views.

1. To add datum feature symbols, choose the **Datum Feature Symbol** tool from the **Annotation** group of the **Home** tab; the **Datum Feature Symbol** dialog box is displayed, as shown in Figure 16-68, and the datum feature symbol gets attached to the cursor. 

2. Choose the **Select Terminating Object** button from the **Leader** rollout of the **Datum Feature Symbol** dialog box and select the feature control frame which consists of the **0.1** tolerance with the **Profile of a Surface** symbol. Next, place the datum feature symbol, as shown in Figure 16-69.

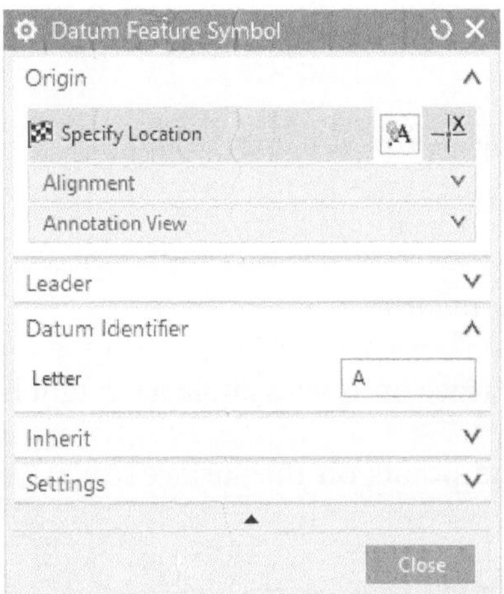

*Figure 16-68 The **Datum Feature Symbol** dialog box*

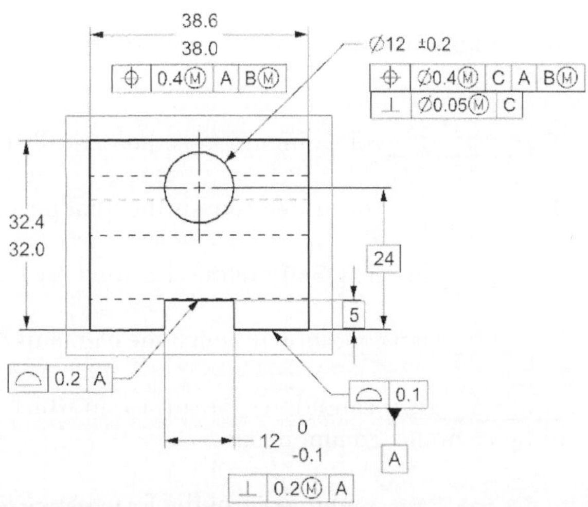

Figure 16-69 Drawing view with the datum feature symbol

3. Similarly, add the remaining datum feature symbols and choose the **Close** button from the **Datum Feature Symbol** dialog box, as shown in Figure 16-70.

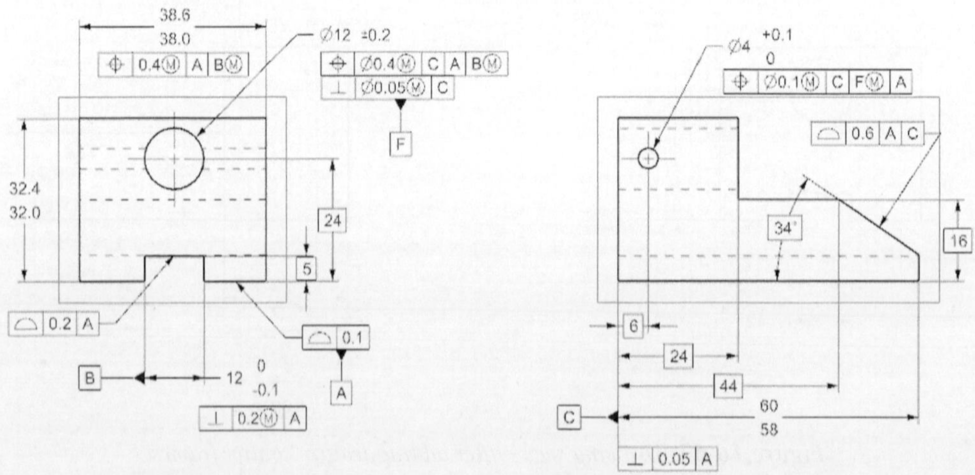

Figure 16-70 Drawing views after adding the datum feature symbols

Saving the Drawing Sheet

1. Choose **Menu > File > Save** from the **Top Border Bar**; the drawing sheet is saved. Next, close the file.

Self-Evaluation Test

Answer the following questions and then compare them to those given at the end of this chapter:

1. In the limit dimensioning method, only the __________ and __________ dimensions are specified.

2. The __________ of a dimension is theoretically the exact value of a dimension.

3. The __________ of a dimension is the total permissible variation in its size.

4. __________ are imaginary references used for locating features.

5. __________ is a condition in which the elements of a surface or its axes are in a straight line.

6. __________ is a condition of a surface in which all the points on the surface are at same distance from a common axis.

7. __________ are used to control the form characteristics of a manufactured part.

8. __________ of a surface is a condition in which all surface elements are in one plane.

9. The cylindricity tolerance must be greater than half of the size tolerance. (T/F)

10. Cylindricity tolerances can be applied only to cylindrical surfaces, such as round holes and shafts. (T/F)

Review Questions

Answer the following questions:

1. Which of the following is an interference fit?

   (a) **Push fit** (b) **Force fit**
   (c) **Wringing fit** (d) **Slide fit**

2. In which of the following components, the slide fit is applied?

   (a) **Keyed Pulleys** (b) **Seating Rings**
   (c) **Slide Valves** (d) **Bearings**

3. Location tolerances include the __________, __________, and __________ tolerances.

4. A force fit is used when the two mating parts are to be __________.

5. An orientation tolerance controls __________, __________, and all other angular relationships.

6. A condition of a part feature where the part contains the maximum amount of material is called as __________.

7. The maximum clearance fit is the difference between the __________ size of the hole and the __________ size of the shaft.

8. In the shaft basis system, the size of the shaft is kept constant. (T/F)

9. The maximum clearance in a loose or sliding fit is always greater than zero. (T/F)

10. The shaft basis fits system is recommended where more than two fits are required on the same shaft. (T/F)

EXERCISE

Exercise 1

Add GD&T to the drawing file created in Tutorial 3 of Chapter 12.

REFERENCES

ASME B4.1-1967 (R2009) Preferred Limits and Fits for Cylindrical Parts
ASME B4.2-1978 Preferred Metric Limits and Fits
ASME Y14.5-2009 Dimensioning and Tolerancing

Answers to Self-Evaluation Test

1. maximum, minimum, **2.** basic size, **3.** tolerance, **4.** Datums, **5.** Straightness, **6.** Cylindricity, **7.** Form tolerances, **8.** Flatness, **9.** F, **10.** T

Index

Symbols

A

B

C

D

E

F

G

H

I

J

L

M

N

O

P

Q

R

S

Other Titles of Interest - BPB/TICKOO SERIES

Publication by BPB/TICKOO SERIES

The following is the list of some of the publications by BPB/TICKOO series:

AutoCAD Textbook

- AutoCAD 2020 for Engineers and Designers - Basic and Intermediate
- AutoCAD 2020 Workbook

Autodesk Inventor Textbooks

- Autodesk Inventor Professional 2020 for Engineers and Designers
- Autodesk Inventor Professional 2019 for Designers, 19th Edition
- Inventor 2020 Workbook

AutoCAD MEP Textbooks

- AutoCAD MEP 2020 for Engineers and Designers
- AutoCAD MEP 2018 for Designers, 4th Edition

AutoCAD Plant 3D Textbook

- AutoCAD Plant 3D 2018 for Designers, 4th Edition

NX Textbooks

- Siemens NX 12.0 for Designers, 11th Edition
- Seimens NX 2019 Workbook

NX Mold Textbook

- Mold Design Using NX 11.0: A Tutorial Approach

AutoCAD LT Textbooks

- AutoCAD LT 2020 for Engineers and Designers
- AutoCAD LT 2017 for Designers, 12th Edition

Solid Edge Textbooks

- Solid Edge 2019 for Engineers and Designers
- Solid Edge ST 10 for Designers, 15th Edition

SolidWorks Textbooks

- SOLIDWORKS 2019 for Engineers and Designers
- SOLIDWORKS 2018 for Designers, 16th Edition

SolidWorks Simulation Textbooks

- SOLIDWORKS Simulation 2018: A Tutorial Approach
- SOLIDWORKS Simulation 2016: A Tutorial Approach

Creo Parametric Textbooks
- Creo Parametric 6.0 for Engineers and Designers
- Creo Parametric 5.0 for Designers, 5th Edition
- Creo Parametric 6.0 Workbook

CATIA Textbook
- CATIA V5-6R2018 for Engineers and Designers

AutoCAD Electrical Textbooks
- AutoCAD Electrical 2019 for Engineers and Designers
- AutoCAD Electrical 2018 for Electrical Control Designers, 9th Edition

Autodesk Revit Architecture Textbooks
- Autodesk Revit 2020 for Architects and Building Designers
- Exploring Autodesk Revit 2019 for Architecture, 15th Edition

Autodesk Revit Structure Textbooks
- Exploring Autodesk Revit 2019 for Structure, 9th Edition
- Exploring Autodesk Revit 2018 for Structure, 8th Edition

Autodesk Revit MEP Textbooks
- Exploring Autodesk Revit 2019 for MEP, 6th Edition
- Exploring Autodesk Revit 2018 for MEP, 5th Edition

RISA-3D Textbook
- Exploring RISA-3D 14.0

Bentley STAAD.Pro Textbooks
- Exploring Bentley STAAD.Pro (CONNECT Edition), 3rd Edition
- Exploring Bentley STAAD.Pro V8i (SELECT series 6)

AutoCAD Civil 3D Textbooks
- Exploring AutoCAD Civil 3D 2019 for Engineers and Designers
- Exploring AutoCAD Civil 3D 2018, 8th Edition

AutoCAD Map 3D Textbooks
- Exploring AutoCAD Map 3D 2018, 8th Edition
- Exploring AutoCAD Map 3D 2017, 7th Edition

Autodesk Navisworks Textbooks
- Exploring Autodesk Navisworks 2019 for BIM
- Exploring Autodesk Navisworks 2017, 4th Edition

Oracle Primavera Textbooks
- Exploring Oracle Primavera P6 Professional 18 for Planners and Engineers
- Exploring Oracle Primavera P6 R8.4

AutoCAD Raster Design Textbook
- Exploring AutoCAD Raster Design 2017

CINEMA 4D Textbooks
- MAXON CINEMA 4D Studio R20 Studio for Digital Artists
- MAXON CINEMA 4D Studio R19: A Tutorial Approach, 6th Edition
- MAXON CINEMA 4D Studio R18: A Tutorial Approach, 5th Edition

3ds Max Textbooks
- Autodesk 3ds Max 2019: A Comprehensive Guide, 19th Edition
- Autodesk 3ds Max 2018: A Comprehensive Guide, 18th Edition

Autodesk Maya Textbooks
- Autodesk Maya 2019 for 3D Artists
- Autodesk Maya 2018: A Comprehensive Guide, 10th Edition

ZBrush Textbooks
- Pixologic ZBrush 2018 for Digital Artists
- Pixologic ZBrush 4R8: A Comprehensive Guide, 4th Edition

Computer Programming Textbooks
- Introducing PHP/MySQL
- Introduction to C++ Programming, 2nd Edition
- Learning Oracle 12c: A PL/SQL Approach, 2nd Edition
- Introduction to Java Programming, 2nd Edition

CAD/CAM/CIM/ANIMATION/CIVIL BOOKS

by Prof. Sham Tickoo (Purdue University, USA and Autodesk Authorised Author)

Pixologic ZBrush 4R8
A Comprehensive Guide
ISBN: 9789387284128
Price: 899 /-

Pixologic ZBrush 2018
for **Digital Artists**
ISBN: 9789388511193
Price: 899 /-

AutoCAD 2018
A Problem Solving Approach
ISBN: 9789386551634
Price: 1299 /-

Advanced AutoCAD 2018
A Problem Solving Approach
ISBN: 9789386551603
Price: 899 /-

AutoCAD 2019
A Problem Solving Approach
ISBN: 9789388176286
Price: 1499 /-

AutoCAD 2020
for **Engineers and Designers**
ISBN: 9789389423099
Price: 1499 /-

Autocad 2020
Workbook
ISBN: 9789389423044
Price: 360/-

AutoCAD MEP 2018
for **Designers**
ISBN: 9789386551610
Price: 749 /-

AutoCAD MEP 2020
for **Engineers and Designers**
ISBN: 9789389423150
Price: 899 /-

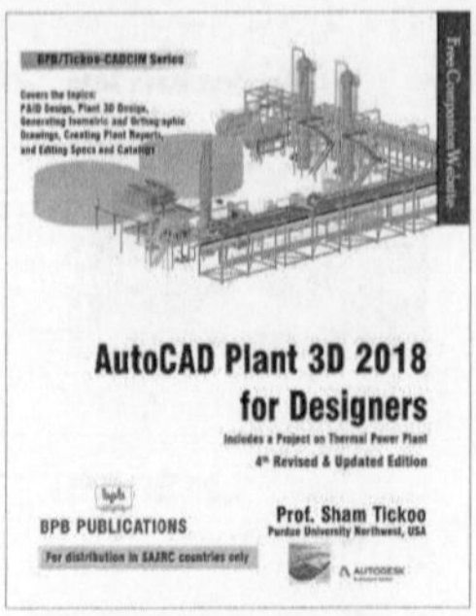

AutoCAD Plant 3D 2018
for **Designers**
ISBN: 9789386551719
Price: 799 /-

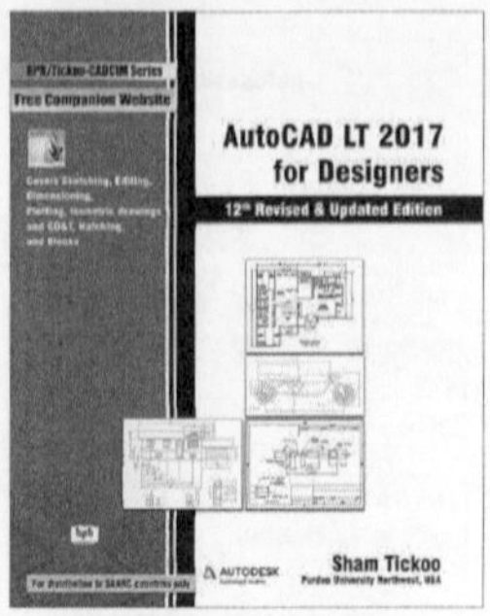

AutoCAD LT 2017
for **Designers**
ISBN: 9789386551252
Price: 1299 /-

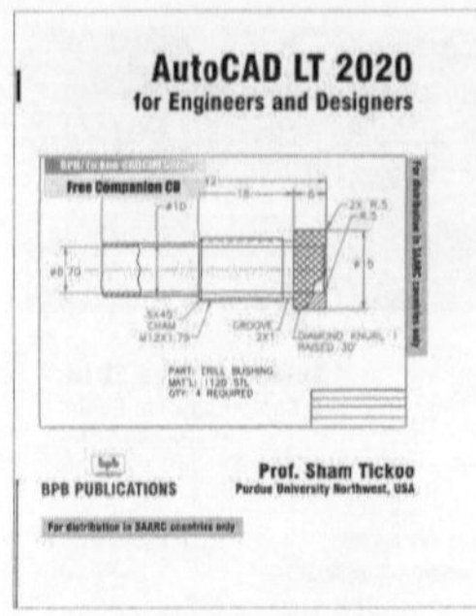

AutoCAD LT 2020
for **Engineers and Designers**
ISBN: 9789389423143
Price: 1399 /-

CAD/CAM/CIM/ANIMATION/CIVIL BOOKS

by Prof. Sham Tickoo (Purdue University, USA and Autodesk Authorised Author)

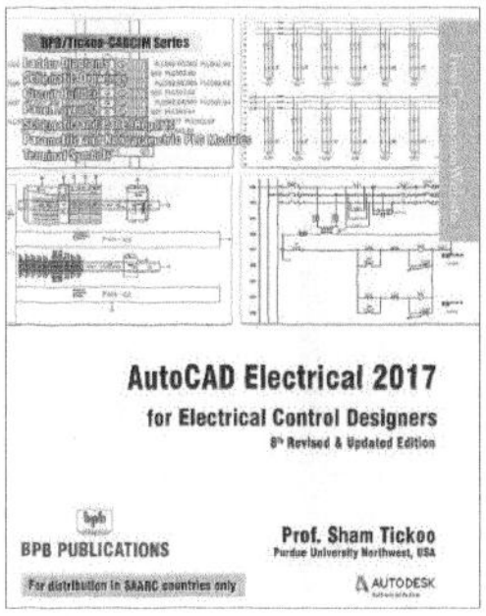

AutoCAD Electrical 2017
for **Electrical Control Designers**
ISBN: 9789386551238
Price: 1099 /-

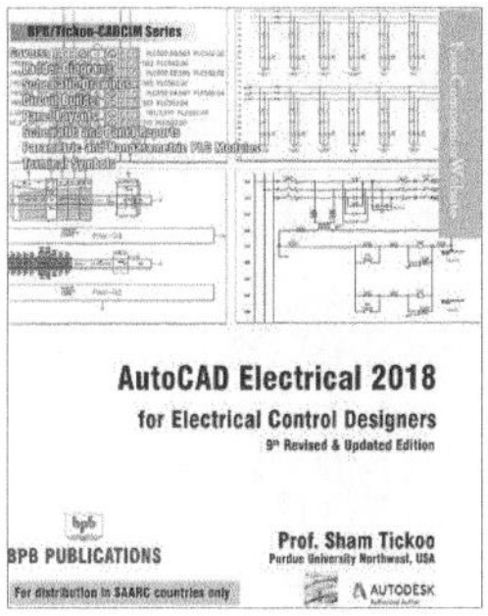

AutoCAD Electrical 2018
for **Electrical Control Designers**
ISBN: 9789386551627
Price: 1099 /-

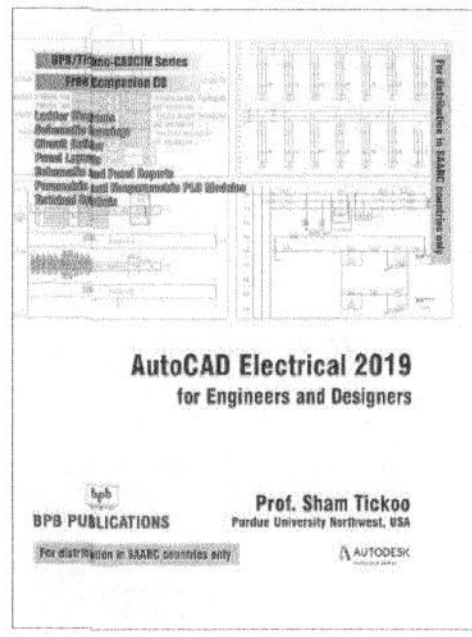

AutoCAD Electrical 2019
for **Engineers and Designers**
ISBN: 9789388511179
Price: 1299 /-

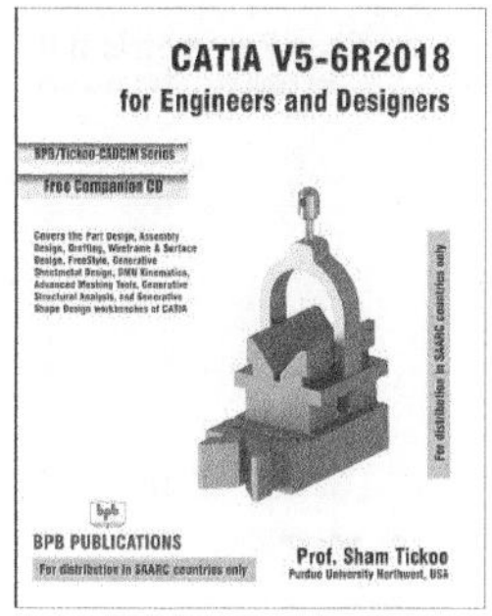

CATIA V5-6R2018
for **Engineers and Designers**
ISBN: 9789388511308
Price: 1399 /-

CATIA V5-6R2016
for **Designers**
ISBN: 9789386551191
Price: 1099 /-

CATIA V5-6R2017
for **Designers**
ISBN: 9789387284043
Price: 1099 /-

MAXON CINEMA 4D
R18 StudioA Tutorial Approach
ISBN: 9789386551115
Price: 799 /-

MAXON CINEMA 4D
R19 StudioA Tutorial Approach
ISBN: 9789387284050
Price: 799 /-

Maxon Cinema 4D R19 Studio
for **Digital Artists**
ISBN: 9789389423174
Price: 799 /-

Maxon Cinema 4D R20 Studio
Workbook
ISBN: 9789389423082
Price: 360/-

Creo Parametric 4.0
for **Designers**
ISBN: 9789386551658
Price: 1099 /-

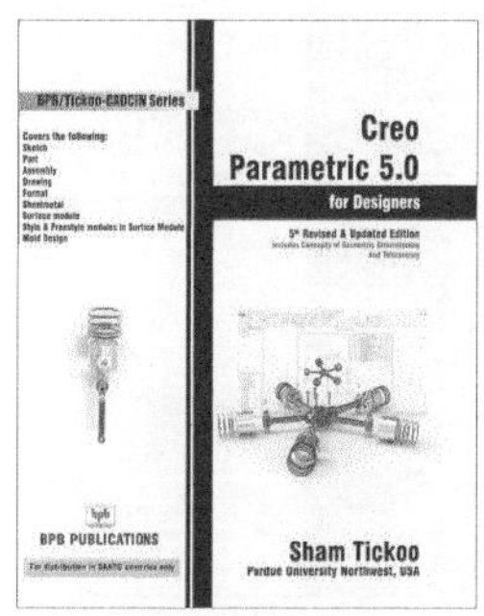

Creo Parametric 5.0
for **Designers**
ISBN: 9789388176309
Price: 1299 /-